Twentieth-Century Literary Criticism

Guide to Gale Literary Criticism Series

For criticism on	You need these Gale series
Authors now living or who died after December 31, 1959	*CONTEMPORARY LITERARY CRITICISM (CLC)*
Authors who died between 1900 and 1959	*TWENTIETH-CENTURY LITERARY CRITICISM (TCLC)*
Authors who died between 1800 and 1899	*NINETEENTH-CENTURY LITERATURE CRITICISM (NCLC)*
Authors who died between 1400 and 1799	*LITERATURE CRITICISM FROM 1400 TO 1800 (LC)* *SHAKESPEAREAN CRITICISM (SC)*
Authors who died before 1400	*CLASSICAL AND MEDIEVAL LITERATURE CRITICISM (CMLC)*
Authors of books for children and young adults	*CHILDREN'S LITERATURE REVIEW (CLR)*
Black writers of the past two hundred years	*BLACK LITERATURE CRITICISM (BLC)*
Short story writers	*SHORT STORY CRITICISM (SSC)*
Poets	*POETRY CRITICISM (PC)*
Dramatists	*DRAMA CRITICISM (DC)*
Major authors from the Renaissance to the present	*WORLD LITERATURE CRITICISM, 1500 TO THE PRESENT (WLC)*

For criticism on visual artists since 1850, see

MODERN ARTS CRITICISM (MAC)

ISSN 0276-8178

R

Volume 49

Twentieth-Century Literary Criticism

**Excerpts from Criticism of the
Works of Novelists, Poets, Playwrights,
Short Story Writers, and Other Creative Writers
Who Lived between 1900 and 1960,
from the First Published Critical
Appraisals to Current Evaluations**

Laurie Di Mauro
Editor

Christopher Giroux
Marie Lazzari
Thomas Ligotti
David Segal
Janet M. Witalec
Associate Editors

 Gale Research Inc. • DETROIT • WASHINGTON, D.C. • LONDON

STAFF

Laurie Di Mauro, *Editor*

Christopher Giroux, Marie Lazzari, Thomas Ligotti, David Segal, Janet M. Witalec, *Associate Editors*

Jennifer Brostrom, Jeffery Chapman, Jennifer Gariepy, Ian A. Goodhall, Margaret A. Haerens, Ted Mouw, Malabika Camellia Purkayastha, Lynn M. Spampinato, *Assistant Editors*

Jeanne A. Gough, *Permissions & Production Manager*
Linda M. Pugliese, *Production Supervisor*
Donna Craft, Paul Lewon, Maureen Puhl, Camille Robinson, Jennifer VanSickle, Sheila Walencewicz, *Editorial Associates*

Sandra C. Davis, *Permissions Supervisor (Text)*
Maria L. Franklin, Josephine M. Keene, Michele Lonoconus, Denise Singleton, Kimberly F. Smilay, *Permissions Associates*
Jennifer A. Arnold, Brandy C. Merritt, Shalice Shah, *Permissions Assistants*

Margaret A. Chamberlain, *Permissions Supervisor (Pictures)*
Pamela A. Hayes, Keith Reed, *Permissions Associates*
Arlene Johnson, Barbara Wallace, *Permissions Assistants*

Victoria B. Cariappa, *Research Manager*
Maureen Richards, *Research Supervisor*
Robert S. Lazich, Mary Beth McElmeel, Tamara C. Nott, *Editorial Associates*
Kelly Hill, Julie Leonard, Donna Melnychenko, *Editorial Assistants*

Mary Beth Trimper, *Production Manager*
Catherine Kemp, *Production Assistant*

Cynthia Baldwin, *Art Director*
Nicholas Jakubiak, C. J. Jonik, Yolanda Y. Latham, *Desktop Publishers/Typesetters*

Library of Congress Catalog Card Number 76-46132
ISBN 0-8103-7974-0
ISSN 0276-8178

Printed in the United States of America
Published simultaneously in the United Kingdom
by Gale Research International Limited
(An affiliated company of Gale Research Inc.)
10 9 8 7 6 5 4 3 2 1

I(T)P™

The trademark ITP is used under license.

Contents

Preface

Since its inception more than ten years ago, *Twentieth-Century Literary Criticism* has been purchased and used by nearly 10,000 school, public, and college or university libraries. *TCLC* has covered more than 500 authors, representing 58 nationalities, and over 25,000 titles. No other reference source has surveyed the critical response to twentieth-century authors and literature as thoroughly as *TCLC*. In the words of one reviewer, "there is nothing comparable available." *TCLC* "is a gold mine of information—dates, pseudonyms, biographical information, and criticism from books and periodicals—which many libraries would have difficulty assembling on their own."

Scope of the Series

TCLC is designed to serve as an introduction to authors who died between 1900 and 1960 and to the most significant interpretations of these author's works. The great poets, novelists, short story writers, playwrights, and philosophers of this period are frequently studied in high school and college literature courses. In organizing and excerpting the vast amount of critical material written on these authors, *TCLC* helps students develop valuable insight into literary history, promotes a better understanding of the texts, and sparks ideas for papers and assignments. Each entry in *TCLC* presents a comprehensive survey of an author's career or an individual work of literature and provides the user with a multiplicity of interpretations and assessments. Such variety allows students to pursue their own interests; furthermore, it fosters an awareness that literature is dynamic and responsive to many different opinions.

Every fourth volume of *TCLC* is devoted to literary topics that cannot be covered under the author approach used in the rest of the series. Such topics include literary movements, prominent themes in twentieth-century literature, literary reaction to political and historical events, significant eras in literary history, prominent literary anniversaries, and the literatures of cultures that are often overlooked by English-speaking readers.

TCLC is designed as a companion series to Gale's *Contemporary Literary Criticism,* which reprints commentary on authors now living or who have died since 1960. Because of the different periods under consideration, there is no duplication of material between *CLC* and *TCLC*. For additional information about *CLC* and Gale's other criticism titles, users should consult the Guide to Gale Literary Criticism Series preceding the title page in this volume.

Coverage

Each volume of *TCLC* is carefully compiled to present:

- criticism of authors, or literary topics, representing a variety of genres and nationalities

- both major and lesser-known writers and literary works of the period

- 10-15 authors or 4-6 topics per volume

- individual entries that survey critical response to each author's work or each topic in literary history, including early criticism to reflect initial reactions; later criticism to represent any rise or decline in reputation; and current retrospective analyses.

Organization of This Book

An author entry consists of the following elements: author heading, biographical and critical introduction, list of principal works, excerpts of criticism (each preceded by an annotation and followed by a bibliographic citation), and a bibliography of further reading.

- The **author heading** consists of the name under which the author most commonly wrote, followed by birth and death dates. If an author wrote consistently under a pseudonym, the pseudonym will be listed in the author heading and the real name given in parentheses on the first line of the biographical and critical introduction. Also located at the beginning of the introduction to the author entry are any name variations under which an author wrote, including transliterated forms for authors whose languages use nonroman alphabets.

- The **biographical and critical introduction** outlines the author's life and career, as well as the critical issues surrounding his or her work. References to past volumes of *TCLC* are provided at the beginning of the introduction. Additional sources of information in other biographical and critical reference series published by Gale, including *Short Story Criticism, Children's Literature Review, Contemporary Authors, Dictionary of Literary Biography,* and *Something about the Author,* are listed in a box at the end of the entry.

- Most *TCLC* entries include portraits of the author. Many entries also contain reproductions of materials pertinent to an author's career, including manuscript pages, title pages, dust jackets, letters, and drawings, as well as photographs of important people, places, and events in an author's life.

- The **list of principal works** is chronological by date of first book publication and identifies the genre of each work. In the case of foreign authors with both foreign-language publications and English translations, the title and date of the first English-language edition are given in brackets. Unless otherwise indicated, dramas are dated by first performance, not first publication.

- Critical excerpts are prefaced by **annotations** providing the reader with information about both the critic and the criticism that follows. Included are the critic's reputation, individual approach to literary criticism, and particular expertise in an author's works. Also noted are the relative importance of a work of criticism, the scope of the excerpt, and the growth of critical controversy or changes in critical trends regarding an author. In some cases, these annotations cross-reference excerpts by critics who discuss each other's commentary.

- **Criticism** is arranged chronologically in each author entry to provide a perspective on changes in critical evaluation over the years. All titles of works by the author featured in the entry are printed in boldface type to enable the user to easily locate discussion of particular works. Also for purposes of easier identification, the critic's name and the publication date of the essay are given at the beginning of each piece of criticism. Unsigned criticism is preceded by the title of the journal in which it appeared. Some of the excerpts in *TCLC* also contain translated material. Unless otherwise noted, translations in brackets are by the editors; translations in parentheses or continuous with the text are by the critic. Publication information (such as footnotes or page and line references to specific editions of works) have been deleted at the editor's discretion to provide smoother reading of the text.

- A complete **bibliographic citation** designed to facilitate location of the original essay or book follows each piece of criticism.

- An annotated list of **further reading** appearing at the end of each author entry suggests secondary sources on the author. In some cases it includes essays for which the editors could not obtain reprint rights.

Cumulative Indexes

- Each volume of *TCLC* contains a cumulative **author index** listing all authors who have appeared in Gale's Literary Criticism Series, along with cross references to such biographical series as *Contemporary Authors* and *Dictionary of Literary Biography*. For readers' convenience, a complete list of Gale titles included appears on the first page of the author index. Useful for locating authors within the various series, this index is particularly valuable for those authors who are identified by a certain period but who, because of their death dates, are placed in another, or for those authors whose careers span two periods. For example, F. Scott Fitzgerald is found in *TCLC,* yet a writer often associated with him, Ernest Hemingway, is found in *CLC.*

- Each *TCLC* volume includes a cumulative **nationality index** which lists all authors who have appeared in *TCLC* volumes, arranged alphabetically under their respective nationalities, as well as Topics volume entries devoted to particular national literatures.

- Each new volume in Gale's Literary Criticism Series includes a cumulative **topic index,** which lists all literary topics treated in *NCLC, TCLC, LC 1400-1800,* and the *CLC* yearbook.

- Each new volume of *TCLC,* with the exception of the Topics volumes, contains a **title index** listing the titles of all literary works discussed in the volume. In response to numerous suggestions from librarians, Gale has also produced a **special paperbound edition** of the *TCLC* title index. This annual cumulation lists all titles discussed in the series since its inception and is issued with the first volume of *TCLC* published each year. Additional copies of the index are available on request. Librarians and patrons will welcome this separate index; it saves shelf space, is easy to use, and is recyclable upon receipt of the following year's cumulation. Titles discussed in the Topics volume entries are not included *TCLC* cumulative index.

Citing *Twentieth-Century Literary Criticism*

When writing papers, students who quote directly from any volume in Gale's literary Criticism Series may use the following general forms to footnote reprinted criticism. The first example pertains to materials drawn from periodicals, the second to material reprinted from books.

[1]T. S. Eliot, "John Donne," *The Nation and the Athenaeum,* 33 (9 June 1923), 321-32; excerpted and reprinted in *Literature Criticism from 1400 to 1800,* Vol. 10, ed. James E. Person, Jr. (Detroit: Gale Research, 1989), pp. 28-9.

[2]Clara G. Stillman, *Samuel Butler: A Mid-Victorian Modern* (Viking Press, 1932); excerpted and reprinted in *Twentieth-Century Literary Criticism,* Vol. 33, ed. Paula Kepos (Detroit: Gale Research, 1989), pp. 43-5.

Suggestions are Welcome

In response to suggestions, several features have been added to *TCLC* since the series began, including annotations to excerpted criticism, a cumulative index to authors in all Gale literary criticism series, entries devoted to criticism on a single work by a major author, more extensive illustrations, and a title index listing all literary works discussed in the series since its inception.

Readers who wish to suggest authors or topics to appear in future volumes, or who have other suggestions, are cordially invited to write the editors.

Acknowledgments

The editors wish to thank the copyright holders of the excerpted criticism included in this volume, the permissions managers of many book and magazine publishing companies for assisting us in securing reprint rights, and Anthony Bogucki for assistance with copyright research. We are also grateful to the staffs of the Detroit Public Library Complex, and University of Michigan Libraries for making their resource available to us. Following is a list of copyright holders who have granted us permission to reprint material in this volume of *TCLC*. Every effort has been made to trace copyright, but if omissions have been made, please let us know.

COPYRIGHTED EXCERPTS IN *TCLC*, VOLUME 49, WERE REPRINTED FROM THE FOLLOWING PERIODICALS:

American Literature, v. 33, November, 1961. Copyright © 1961, renewed 1989 by Duke University Press, Durham, NC. Reprinted with permission of the publisher.—*The Antigonish Review,* v. 58, Summer, 1984 for "The Smile That Stings Herman Bosman of South Africa" by C. J. Fox. Copyright 1984 by the author. Reprinted by permission of the publisher and the author.—*Books in Canada,* v. 13, May, 1984 for "Witness to the Persecution" by Sherie Posesorski. Reprinted by permission of the author.—*Cahiers Ferdinand de Saussure,* v. 38, 1984. Reprinted by permission of the publisher.—*The Century,* v. 106, June, 1923. Copyright, 1923, renewed 1950 by The Century Co. Reprinted by permission of the publisher.—*Commonweal,* v. CXI, September 7, 1984. Copyright © 1984 Commonweal Publishing Co., Inc. Reprinted by permission of Commonweal Foundation.—*Critical Quarterly,* v. 30, Summer, 1988. © Manchester University Press 1988. Reprinted by permission of Basil Blackwell Limited.—*Drama Critique,* v. IX, Spring, 1966 for "Lorca: The Tragic Trilogy" by Manuel Blanco-Gonzalez. Reprinted by permission of the author.—*English Studies in Africa,* v. 20, September, 1977 for "Bosman's Marico Allegory: A Study in Topicality" by Stephen Gray. Reprinted by permission of the publisher and the author.—*The Eugene O'Neill Newsletter,* v. V, Summer-Fall, 1981; v. IX, Summer-Fall, 1985; v. X, Summer-Fall, 1986; v. XI, Summer-Fall, 1987. Copyright © 1981, 1985, 1986, 1987 by the Eugene O'Neill Newsletter. All reprinted by permission of the publisher.—*The Heritage of the Great Plains,* Spring, 1978. Reprinted by permission of the publisher.—*Hispania,* v. 69, December, 1986 for "The 'Prólogo' in the Theater of Federico García Lorca: Towards the Articulation of a Philosophy of Theater" by Francesca Colecchia. © 1986 The American Association of Teachers of Spanish and Portuguese, Inc. Reprinted by permission of the publisher and the author.—*Journal of Women's Studies in Literature,* v. 1, Spring, 1979 for "Edna St. Vincent Millay and the Tradition of Domestic Poetry" by Jeannine Dobbs. Copyright © 1979 Eden Press Women's Publications, Inc. Reprinted by permission of the author.—*The Library Chronicle of the University of Texas at Austin,* n. 4, February, 1972. Copyright © 1972 by the Humanities Research Center, University of Texas at Austin. Reprinted by permission of the publisher.—*The Markham Review,* v. 2, February, 1971. Reprinted by permission of the publisher.—*MLN,* v. 91, October, 1976; v. 94, December, 1979. © copyright 1976, 1979 by The Johns Hopkins University Press. All rights reserved. Both reprinted by permission of the publisher.—*Modern Drama,* v. 11, February, 1969. Copyright 1969 *Modern Drama,* University of Toronto. Reprinted by permission of the publisher.—*Neophilolgus,* v. LXXI, October, 1987 for "Control of the Wild in Andalusian Culture: Bull and Horse Imagery in Lorca from an Anthropological Perspective" by Catherine Davies and Garry Marvin. © 1987 by H. D. Tjeenk Willink. Reprinted by permission of the publisher and the authors.—*The New England Quarterly,* v. XLVIII, June, 1975 for "Millay's 'Ungrafted Tree': The Problem of the Artist as Woman" by Walter S. Minot. Copyright 1975 by *The New England Quarterly.* Reprinted by permission of the publisher and the author.—*The New Republic,* v. 120, March 26, 1984. © 1984 The New Republic, Inc. Reprinted by permission of *The New Republic.*—*The New York Review of Books,* v. XXXI, July 19, 1984. Copyright © 1984 Nyrev, Inc. Reprinted with permission from *The New York Review of Books.*—*The New York Times,* December 10, 1986. Copyright © 1990 by The New York Times Company. Reprinted by permission of the publisher.—*The New York Times Book Review,* January 29, 1984. Copyright © 1984 by The New York Times Company. Reprinted by permission of the publisher./ October 16, 1921. Copyright 1921, renewed 1949 by

Peer Gynt to the Present. Edited by John M. Weinstock and Robert T. Rovinsky. University of Texas Press, 1975. Copyright © 1975 by the University of Texas Press. All rights reserved. Reprinted by permission of the publisher and the author.—Peeples, Samuel A. From "Max Brand and the American Western Story," in *Max Brand: Western Giant, The Life and Times of Frederick Schiller Faust.* Edited by William F. Nolan. Bowling Green State University Popular Press, 1985. Copyright © 1985 by Samuel A. Peeples. Reprinted by permission of the publisher.—Ranald, Margaret Loftus. From *The Eugene O'Neill Companion.* Greenwood Press, 1984. Copyright © 1984 by Margaret Loftus Ranald. All rights reserved. Reprinted by permission of Greenwood Publishing Group, Inc., Westport, CT.—Sampson, Robert. From *Yesterday's Faces: A Study of Series Characters in the Early Pulp Magazines, Vol. I.* Bowling Green University Popular Press, 1983. Copyright © 1983 by Bowling Green State University Popular Press. Reprinted by permission of the publisher.—Saussure, Ferdinand de. From *Course in General Linguistics.* Charles Bally, Albert Sechehaye, Albert Riedlinger, eds., translated by Wade Baskin. McGraw-Hill Book Company, 1959. Copyright © 1959, by The Philosophical Library, Inc.—Schuleter, June, and Arthur Lewis. From "Cabot's Conflict: The Stones and Cows in o'Neill's 'Desire Under the Elms'," in *Critical Essays on Eugene O'Neill.* Edited by James J. Martine. Hall, 1984. Copyright 1984 by G. K. Hall & Co. Reprinted with the permission of the publisher.—Stanbrough, Jane. From "Edna St. Vincent Millay and the Language of Vulnerability," in *Shakespeare's Sisters: Feminist Essays on Women Poets.* Edited by Sandra M. Gilbert and Susan Gubar. Indiana University Press, 1979. Copyright © 1979 by Sandra M. Gilbert and Susan Gubar. All rights reserved. Reprinted by permission of the author.—Thiher, Allen. From *Words in Reflection: Modern Language Theory and Postmodern Fiction.* The University of Chicago Press, 1984. © 1984 by The University of Chicago. All rights reserved. Reprinted by permission of the publisher and the author.—Zeiss, Cecelia. From "Aspects of the Short Story: A Consideration of Selected Works of Frank O'Connor and Herman Charles Bosman," in *Literary Interrelations: Ireland, England and the World, Comparison and Impact, Vol. 2.* Edited by Wolfgang Zach and Heinz Kosok. Gunter Narr Verlag Tubingen, 1987. © 1987 Gunter Narr Verlag Tübingen. All rights reserved. Reprinted by permission of the publisher.

PHOTOGRAPHS AND ILLUSTRATIONS APPEARING IN *TCLC*, VOLULME 49, WERE RECEIVED FROM THE FOLLOWING SOURCES:

Culver Pictures, Inc.: **p. 54;** Courtesy of New Directions: **p. 62;** Reprinted by permission of the Estate of Federico García Lorca: **p. 84;** Photograph by Alfonso: **p. 118;** Courtesy of Vassar College Library: **p. 199, 209, 220;** Collection of American Literature, Beinecke Rare Book and Manuscript Library, Yale University: **p. 249;** House scene from *"Desire Under the Elms"*, showing Walter Huston, Charles Ellis and Mary Morris. Play by Eugene O'Neill. Greenwich Village Theatre, 1924. Reprinted by permission of Museum of the City of New York Theatre Collection: **p. 266;** Friedman-Abeles: **p. 282.**

Herman Charles Bosman

1905-1951

(Also wrote under the pseudonyms Ben Africa, P. de Beer, N. J. Gordon, and Herman Malan) South African short story writer, novelist, essayist, and poet.

INTRODUCTION

Bosman is best known for his short stories depicting rural Afrikaner life in the northwestern Transvaal. Despite his Afrikaner background, Bosman chose to write in English and, unlike most South African writers, published his books exclusively in South Africa. Praised for its wit, irony, and humor, Bosman's short fiction has been compared to that of Guy de Maupassant, O. Henry, and Saki.

Bosman was born near Cape Town but spent most of his youth in the Witwatersrand, where his father, a miner, was killed in an accident while Bosman was still a child. Although he spoke Afrikaans, which did not gain official recognition as a second language until 1925, Bosman was educated in English-language schools, where he excelled in the study of literature and showed particular interest in the work of Edgar Allan Poe, O. Henry, and the French Symbolist poets Charles Baudelaire and Arthur Rimbaud. After graduating from the University of Witwatersrand, he accepted a teaching position in the Groot Marico district of the northwestern Transvaal, a remote, sparsely populated area on the edge of the Kalahari desert. Bosman spent only one year there, but his experiences on the veld and the stories the old farmers told him provided material on which he drew for the rest of his life.

While visiting his family in Johannesburg in 1925, Bosman shot and killed his step-brother during an argument. Originally sentenced to death, Bosman spent a month on death row before his sentence was commuted to four years imprisonment. After his release, Bosman worked as a journalist, critic, and editor for various newspapers and literary magazines. Although Bosman's short fiction appeared in numerous South African journals during the 1930s and 1940s, he did not produce a book-length work until 1947, when he published a novel, *Jacaranda in the Night,* and *Mafeking Road,* a collection of short stories which became a best seller. *Cold Stone Jug,* a fictionalized recounting of his prison experience, followed two years later. Bosman died from a stroke in 1951.

Bosman's literary reputation rests principally on his short fiction, which critics have divided into two categories: the Oom Schalk Lourens stories and the "In die Voorkamer" stories. Like all of Bosman's fiction, the Oom Schalk Lourens stories are set in the northwestern Transvaal. The stories of the first group are narrated by Oom Schalk, an old Afrikaans farmer. Collected in *Mafeking Road* and *Unto Dust,* these stories are concerned with the hardships

of farming, the Anglo-Boer War, and human endurance in the face of adverse conditions. In "The Rooinek," for instance, Oom Schalk tells the tragic story of a Boer family who perishes while crossing the Kalahari Desert to escape drought and disease. Critics have praised Bosman's stories for their subtle irony and the incisive plot twists that reveal the weaknesses and prejudices of the farmers' view of life. For example, in "Unto Dust" Bosman satirizes an Afrikaans farmer's belief in the innate and obvious superiority of one race over another. During a fight on the veld, the protagonist's friend is killed by an African whom the farmer immediately shoots. Returning to the site months later, the farmer finds the bones of his friend and the native inextricably mixed and the native's dog watching over them. After separating the bones, he buries those of his friend in a cemetery. However, the dog arrives soon afterward and sits on the grave.

The "In die Voorkamer" stories, half of which have been collected in *A Bekkersdal Marathon* and *Jurie Steyn's Post Office,* were published weekly in a South African magazine. Featuring a group of characters who meet in Jurie Steyn's post office, these stories differ from the Oom Schalk stories in style and subject matter. In contrast to

Oom Schalk's highly structured reminiscences of turn-of-the-century South Africa, the "In die Voorkamer" stories are less formal in their narrative structure and focus on current events. "Go-Slow Strike," for example, deals indirectly with an actual work slowdown by telegraph operators in December 1950. Critics have praised Bosman's adept use of irony and humor to address such themes as society's propensity for myths in "Lost City" and "Monument to a Hero" and the futility of race classification in "Dying Race." In "Failing Sight," Bosman lamented worsening race relations in South Africa, a theme which received extended coverage in *Willemsdorp,* a novel concerning interracial sexual relationships. Although many of Bosman's stories address ethical concerns, his appreciation for understatement enabled him to avoid charges of didacticism. As C. J. Fox has observed, "the moral of a Bosman story . . . is always suggested in the mildest manner."

PRINCIPAL WORKS

The Blue Princess [as Herman Malan]   (poetry)   1932
Jacaranda in the Night   (novel)   1947
Mafeking Road   (short stories)   1947
Cold Stone Jug   (novel)   1949
A Cask of Jerepigo   (essays and sketches)   1957
Unto Dust   (short stories)   1963
Bosman at His Best   (short stories and sketches)   1965
A Bekkersdal Marathon   (short stories)   1971
Jurie Steyn's Post Office   (short stories)   1971
The Earth Is Waiting   (poetry)   1974
Willemsdorp   (novel)   1977
Almost Forgotten Stories   (short stories)   1979
Selected Stories   (short stories)   1980
The Collected Works of Herman Charles Bosman. 2 vols.
   (essays, short stories, and sketches)   1982

CRITICISM

F. E. Knight   (essay date 1948)

[*Knight is an English critic. In the following review of* Mafeking Road, *he commends Bosman for his objective portrait of Boer life and his insight into human nature.*]

The Transvaal Boer has appeared to the home-staying Briton in various guises. His existence virtually unknown before the last decade of the nineteenth century, he suddenly appeared as an arch fiend, obstinate, truculent, militant, a barrier to progress. At the commencement of the twentieth century, with the Boer War over and the Act of Union in the making, he was transmogrified under the influence of liberalism into a simple farmer, first cousin to the noble savage of a century ago, compounded of all

manly virtues, who had bravely defended his faith and his homeland against British imperialism. Misguided perhaps; but a valuable recruit now to the Empire and prepared to wave the Union Jack alongside the Indian prince, the Zulu, and the Red Indian.

This view of the Boer persisted until after the 1914-18 war, confirmed by the statesmanship of Louis Botha and Field-Marshal Smuts and the heroic contribution made by South Africa to the allied cause. Thus, the 1914 rebellion on the northern Transvaal frontier passed unnoticed, or at best ununderstood, in this country.

Later, as South African internal politics occasionally reached European headlines, and the growth of the Nationalist Party produced qualms in British breasts, the 'simple farmer' view became modified. We wondered if there was much to choose between the Afrikaner and the Irishman.

The truth, of course, lies between the two extremes, and Mr. Bosman reveals it in his [collection of] short stories [entitled *Mafeking Road*]. He reveals the character of the Boer from the inside; in passing he also reveals something of the character of the Briton as seen by the Boer, but that is by the way.

Mr. Bosman's Boer is a simple farmer; yet he can be cunning as any business man in scoring off his fellows. He is a poet, sincerely moved by the beauty of his beloved veld; yet he considers the killing of a black man rather less than the killing of a springbok. He reads the Bible daily; and he carouses on home-made brandy. In time of drought he will work all day in the burning sun pumping water for his cattle; but he most loves to sit on his stoep drinking coffee while his coloured boys work for him. He loves the peace of the veld, the companionship of solitude; yet he loves also politics, argument, debating societies, and, sometimes, war.

These sides of the Boer are shown in the stories, many of which are character studies rather than stories; or perhaps it would be fairer to say they are stories rather in the manner of Chekov than of de Maupassant. There is a delightful humour in most of them; bitter tragedy in some; a deep insight into human nature in all. One is left with a feeling of regret that they are stories of a vanishing race—a race that is at last succumbing to that same progress which it once so bitterly opposed. (pp. 168-69)

F. E. Knight, in a review of "Mafeking Road," in Life and Letters and the London Mercury, Vol. 57, No. 129, May, 1948, pp. 168-69.

David Wright   (essay date 1963)

[*Wright is a South African–born English poet and critic. In the following excerpt, he praises Bosman as a pioneer in South African literature and commends the short stories in* Mafeking Road *and* Unto Dust *for their blend of comedy, pathos, and irony.*]

When I last set foot in South Africa a dozen years ago the one man in it I really wanted to meet died (of a hangover, they said) the afternoon I stepped on the quay at Cape

Town. Weeks later somebody handed me a copy of a South African review called *Trek* which carried a memorial article about him. It had a photograph too: striking light-coloured eyes—personable—an Afrikaner face; elegant trilby hat—a smile part sardonic, part rueful—a precipitation of gaiety and intelligence. It was a good photograph.

I first heard of Herman Charles Bosman in 1949 via Roy Campbell, who had broadcast a few of his stories on the B.B.C. The book they came from—*Mafeking Road*—was (and still is) unobtainable in England; it had been published in Johannesburg. So I read the British Museum copy under the greasy dome of the Reading Room. Not the best place for the enjoyment of literature (though novelists in human form have been known to do their writing in it); even so I couldn't help being impressed by Bosman's veld intaglios, their craftsmanship and economy. It seemed extraordinary that stuff as good as this should be published in Johannesburg but not in London.

Eighty years ago Olive Schreiner placed *The Story of a South African Farm* in the hands of a London publisher and became the first colonial writer to win serious acceptance; and ever since, except for a few poets and novelists writing in Afrikaans, London has been the South African literary capital. It is not often realized that all but a handful of English-speaking South African writers have spent the best part of their lives abroad; while all, without exception, have made their reputations in Europe. The reasons are simple. There are still practically no South African publishing houses. English is a minority language. There is the political thing. Most South African writing, therefore, has been a literature of exiles and deracines. This is true even of the work of many who have stayed behind, members of a political and linguistic minority; they have been forced to become in a sense exiles in spirit if not in fact.

So it was a surprise, to say the least, to come across a South African writer of calibre who seemed to have reversed the established pattern. In his way, Bosman was a pioneer: the first really indigenous South African writer—indigenous in so far as it was wholly within the confines of his country that he published his work and won his reputation. As a corollary, to the rest of the world he has remained practically unknown. Now, twelve years after his death—he died in 1951 at the early age of 46—an English publisher has brought out a collection of his stories [*Unto Dust*], with a preface by William Plomer.

Those who knew or knew of Bosman—since his death he has been something of a cult among young intellectuals in Johannesburg—speak of his wildness, charm, and unexpectedness. His conversation exhilarated; he saw things from the unconventional, sometimes the uncomfortable, angle: 'a realist who wished to be romantic.' (pp. 78-9)

The Marico stories of *Mafeking Road* and the posthumous *Unto Dust* make a homogenous work; and they are Bosman's masterpiece. His poems are flawed; his one novel [*Jacaranda in the Night*] has its moments, but sprawls and wants authority; *Cold Stone Jug* is a readable, occasionally powerful, contribution to prison literature,

but not much more than a sort of South African preview of Jim Phelan and Frank Norman. It is in his Marico stories that Bosman, focusing upon a small pastoral community of farmers all but hermetically sealed off in their corner of the Transvaal backveld, succeeds in recording and creating an imaginatively valid world—local, remote, yet universal. Kipling did much the same with a now-vanished Anglo-Indian society. In these stories Bosman's mouthpiece, Oom Schalk Lourens, the teller of the tales, acts like a prism refracting light into its component colours. Oom Schalk is himself one of the Marico farmers, descendants of the Cape trekkers who inspanned their wagons and set off into the interior in 1836—not just to get away from the British but from Europe itself, from the liberal ideas established by the French Revolution. The old men remember the wars with the Natives and the English. Indeed, for them they are not over; here in the Marico time and history are suspended, till a half-mythic quality seems to enter Oom Schalk's wry anecdotes. Neither Olive Schreiner nor Pauline Smith manage to convey so immediately and unsentimentally the character of the backveld Afrikaner: its complicated mixture of wisdom, ignorance, 'slimness', fortitude, and stupidity, which yet has, for all the narrow Calvinism infecting it, a heroic magnitude. Meanwhile the naïveté, cunning, and prejudice of Oom Schalk throws into ironic relief the naïveté, cunning and prejudice of the people he talks about. One is constantly experiencing a double-take at passages of the blandest innocence.

All the tales are short—few take up more than a couple of thousand words. To invert a famous desideratum, Bosman's prose is as well-written as poetry ought to be. Every word is exactly sited and pulls its weight. The best of the stories walk a tightrope of comedy and pathos; a wrong step would spell a disastrous tumble into the facetious or mawkish. It's the kind of thing Chaplin brings off in *City Lights.* In **"Sold Down the River,"** one of the stories from *Unto Dust,* Bosman establishes, with great art, a moment of pure pathos at the end: an actress thrown over by her lover boards the train that is to take her away and unconsciously repeats the gesture that she uses on the stage at a similar moment of crisis. Yet the pathos is led up to and given weight by the broadest sort of comedy—Oom Schalk's deadpan account of the progressive modifications a travelling company of actors have to make to *Uncle Tom's Cabin* during their tour of the backveld, till in the end they 'so far adapted the play to South African conditions as to make Uncle Tom threaten to hit Topsy with a brandy-bottle. The result was that, by the time the company came to Zeerust, even the church elder, Theunis van Zyl, said that there was much in the story of Uncle Tom that could be considered instructive.' This is characteristic: other South African writers, in underlining the viciousness of colour prejudice and so on, range the gamut from moral indignation to sad reasonableness; Bosman laughs. Blandly he retails the reactionary attitude at its starkest. He makes no overt comment. The *reductio ad absurdum* is his game. And more than once he achieves—as in **"Makapan's Caves,"** a re-telling of an actual event, the extermination of a Native tribe in the Zoutspansberg—something of the bleak, poker-faced savagery of Swift's "A Modest Proposal." A similar double-edged detachment excoriates in the title story of *Unto Dust,* which hinges on the difficulty of telling the difference between a white man and a black from a heap of bones in the veld. Yet his irony remains a curious blend of affection, ferocity, and good humour. Now and then the twentieth century is his victim: Ortega y Gasset would have approved **"The Kafir Drum,"** a take-off of the bedevilment of civilized life by modern communications, which carry tidings of remote disasters to those whom they do not concern.

As he himself remarked, he was averse from 'any spirit of sociological crusading, which seems to demand of the individual a preconceived righteous indignation against the existing economic order—so that whatever is experienced and observed gets fitted into appropriate and ready-made emotions.' Bosman propounds no moral judgements. He sets down things as they are. And that is the job of the artist. No death could have been more inopportune than his, which took place on October 14, 1951, after a housewarming party for his new home in Johannesburg. His literary career was just beginning to gather momentum, while round him the nucleus of a group of young writers had already begun to form. The years to come, with their typical South African mélange of grand guignol and Alice in Wonderland—Sharpeville on one hand and the banning of *Black Beauty* on the other—might have profited from his bland and ironic eye and debonair barbed pen. Some things can resist moral indignation better than being laughed at: the most transfiguring criticism is oblique and comes from within. Bosman died ten years before the birth of the South African Republic; or he might have lived to be its Zoschenko. (pp. 80-2)

> *David Wright, "A South African Zoschenko,"* in London Magazine, *n.s. Vol. 3, No. 4, July, 1963, pp. 78-82.*

An excerpt from "The Rooinek"

Koos Steyn and his wife lay side by side in the sand; the woman's head rested on the man's shoulder; her long hair had become loosened, and blew softly in the wind. A great deal of fine sand had drifted over their bodies. Near them the Englishman lay, face downwards. We never found the baby Jemima. She must have died somewhere along the way and Koos Steyn must have buried her. But we agreed that the Englishman Webber must have passed through terrible things; he could not even have had any understanding left as to what the Steyns had done with their baby. He probably thought, up to the moment when he died, that he was carrying the child. For, when we lifted his body, we found, still clasped in his dead and rigid arms, a few old rags and a child's clothes.

It seemed to us that the wind that always stirs in the Kalahari blew very quietly and softly that morning.

Yes, the wind blew very gently.

> *Herman Charles Bosman, in his "The Rooinek," in* Mafeking Road, *Human and Rousseau, 1947.*

Geoffrey Haresnape   (essay date 1969)

[*In the following excerpt, Haresnape compares Bosman's fiction with that of Pauline Smith, focusing on their portrayals of an isolated community and human suffering.*]

At an early age [H. C. Bosman] killed his half-brother after a dispute, and was sentenced to death. This was later commuted to ten years' imprisonment. The horror of being under sentence and the rigours and crudities of prison life are startlingly revealed in his novel, *Cold Stone Jug.* His descriptions of his time in the death cell leave the reader with feelings of depression and emptiness. In the shadow of the gallows "a jest or a solemn speech meant just about the same thing." Finally the day arrives for his companion, Stoffels, to be hanged. Bosman describes the event with a kind of devastating sarcasm and mordant humor.

> No orders had to be given. Each man knew what was expected of him, even Stoffels,—who played his part tolerably well, considering the fact that he was not rehearsed in it and was getting no pay for it.

Stark realism follows; the sounds of scuffles and footfalls. From the cell to which he has been removed, Bosman hears Stoffels's voice, but he has difficulty in recognising it: "for only part of that noise seemed to come out of his throat. The rest of it seemed to have come out of his belly." Then the slam of the trap-door shakes the whole building, and, the dreadful event over, the prison starts the business of the day.

Bosman reveals a ready sympathy for the most hardened and hopeless of the convicts—those serving the indeterminate sentence, a system whereby they could be kept in jail indefinitely. In the prison they were called "blue-coats" on account of their distinctive dress. Their language was as colourful as their careers during the comparatively short spells that they were out of "boob." To Bosman they told the inside stories of burglaries which they had committed. He re-creates these with gusto, reproducing the "boob slang" in which they were originally related.

The other prisoners thought that he was mad to associate with these hardened types, and took it as an indication of his criminal tendencies. Actually his imagination enabled him to understand their problems, while his sensitivity and heart caused him to identify himself with them. Pauline Smith showed similar qualities when she interested herself in the *bywoner* class and the poor Whites in the Little Karoo. This interest was contrary to the general attitude of the Oudtshoorners amongst whom she moved. "I could never understand why Pauline Smith was interested in those people. They are stupid; they won't work; they're lazy," an acquaintance related. As with Bosman, the artistic imagination strips away the prejudice to see the characters for what, in reality, they are.

Cold Stone Jug also contains a frank discussion of sexual matters—the homosexuality which is widespread amongst the prisoners, the dreams of the prisoner, Huysmans, for Tossie, a twelve-year-old girl whom he had seduced in his class at school. Bosman confesses to his own longings and frustrations. This is a department of writing which is beyond Pauline Smith's experience and scope. She belongs to a more reticent and decorous school. But she never shies away from the reality and strength of sexual relationships. The hold of Jacoba Nooi upon Niklaas Dampers, and the violence of the young girl's passion for Jan Boetje in "The Schoolmaster" are well-portrayed. They are achieved, however, by implication and careful emotive writing rather than by presentation of (to quote a phrase of Bosman) "juicy details."

Bosman moves beyond the range of Pauline Smith in his analysis of frenzied states either bordering on or of outright madness. He describes how at one stage he had the nightmare notion of different kinds of animals propagating. "A pig and a rooster would have sexual intercourse: and the offspring they would produce would be half pig, half rooster. A snout and a comb, and a curly tail and feathers. And pigs' trotters with spurs."

Later he is taken to the prison doctor and is able to convince him that he is still sane. But on his return to his cell he is again swept by these moods of insanity. The urge takes him to crawl on all fours around the concrete floor. In his madness he retains a "strange cunning," and times the visits of the warders, ensuring that they will never surprise him in this compromising position. These descriptions remind the reader of descriptions of the deranged mind in the work of Edgar Allan Poe.

Cold Stone Jug is inclined to be repetitive. It conveys harsh and unpleasant experience with an incisive realism and caustic wit, which are far removed from the highly formal and carefully created effects of Pauline Smith.

Before Bosman was jailed, he had spent a short time schoolmastering in the Marico district of the Northwestern Transvaal. This region had a relatively sparse population of farmers; down-to-earth, rustic characters who spoke Afrikaans and remembered with emotion the days of the independent Boer Republic. Their sense of humour was broad and crude. They loved practical jokes. The everyday realities of running a farm and fighting against drought were uppermost in their minds, and persistently entered their conversations. Love, violence, and anecdotes from the Anglo-Boer War of 1899-1902 formed the subjects of their stories.

Bosman drew heavily on this material and created a unique character and atmosphere in the short stories first collected under the title *Mafeking Road.* Recently further stories in this series have been published in the book *Unto Dust.*

The principal character is Oom Schalk Lourens, a wily, good-natured farmer who acts as the storyteller for most of the tales. They range from highly lyrical love stories (e.g., **"The Veld Maiden"**) to accounts of grim reality, privation, and human endurance (**"The Rooinek"**).

Humour also plays an important part. Bosman frequently makes skilful use of incident to show the weaknesses and prejudices in the farmer's view of life. For instance, **"Unto Dust"** tells of the death of a burgher, Hans Welman. Hans was speared by a "Kafir" in a skirmish and his friend, Stoffel Oosthuizen, was so angered to see it happen that

he reined in his horse at great danger to himself and took a potshot at the murderer. His bullet found its mark. Later, he went back to collect Welman's remains for a Christian burial. To his chagrin he found that the disjointed skeletons of the "Kafir" and his friend were inextricably mixed. Stoffel shooed away a yellow dog which had belonged to the "Kafir" and was still keeping vigil over its master's remains, and sorted out the bones as best he could. He was intensely irritated. For him death was not the great leveller. Such an idea "sounded like out of a speech made by one of those liberal Cape politicians." When he had finished, he carted Hans Welman's bones to his farm and buried them in the graveyard. But some time later the faithful yellow dog was found squatting on the mound of the farmer's grave!

Bosman loves to tell a story which is carefully contrived, which will show up the stupidity of prejudice in a humorous and tolerant manner, and which contains an energetic and incisive twist at the conclusion. In his volume of essays, *A Cask of Jerepigo,* he expresses an admiration for O. Henry. He bears a resemblance to this writer in the taut manipulation of plot and in the use of the surprise ending.

Another humorous effect is gained when Bosman shows the reader that his (Bosman's) sympathy for the "Kafir" and understanding of the situation extend beyond that of the Marico farmers who are his characters. The Afrikaners acknowledge that Radipalong, a Bechuana woodcarver, is skilful in carving animals. [In **"Graven Image,"** he writes:]

> He could carve a hippopotamus, or a rhinoceros, or an elephant, or a yellow-bellied hyena—the more low sort of hyena—in such a way that you *knew* that animal exactly, through your having seen it grazing under a tree, or drinking at a water-hole, or just leaning against an anthill, without doing anything in particular.

But when he gets onto carving likenesses of the farmers, they will not admit that he has the same cunning. They buy these carvings "just for fun," and they laugh in embarrassment—both signs that they have recognised the skill of the work. Yet Radipalong remains "a lazy Bechuana, who would have been better employed in chopping up that wood and bringing a bundle of it into a farmer's kitchen." By means of the plot Bosman makes the reader understand that these carvings are very apt. It is only after she has seen Radipalong's carving of her fiancé, Karel Nienaber, that Louisa Wessels breaks off her engagement. Again this story has a sting in the tail. Most of it is written in a bantering and comic style. But at the end the reader is told that Nienaber left the Marico bushveld soon after the engagement was broken off, because he saw in Louisa's trousseau kist his own image with several rusty nails driven into the heart. With a sudden contrast Bosman moves from laughter to the grim world of witchcraft.

Other stories deal with heroism, fidelity, and endurance against unconquerable odds. **"The Rooinek"** [from *Mafeking Road*] tells of a trek into the Kalahari Desert which for one ox-wagon and its passengers ends in death. Gradually, Oom Schalk and his friends come to respect the Englishman, Webber, who had started to farm in the Marico district. He becomes friendly with Koos Steyn in particular, and when Koos alone decides to cross the Kalahari with his family, accompanies him. Koos has a daughter, Jemima, who was the Englishman's favourite. Later Webber's body is discovered. In his last, thirst-crazed moments he must have imagined that he was carrying the girl. Oom Schalk relates: "When we lifted his body, we found, still clasped in his dead and rigid arms, a few old rags and a child's clothes."

The pathos in **"The Rooinek"** is strong and genuine. On occasions Bosman is liable to grow sentimental; but these are to be found in his lighter love stories when he describes beautiful, young girls. Whenever he portrays death as a result of war (**"Makapan's Caves"**) or passion (**"The Gramophone"** and **"The Widow"**) his writing conveys an intense energy.

Clearly these stories invite comparison with Pauline Smith's *Little Karoo*. Both authors have been concerned in capturing the spirit of a relatively isolated community. Also, there are certain similarities in the temperaments of the men and women who provide their subject matter. The dwellers in the Marico and those in the Little Karoo share a brooding, intense spirit. They are liable to be violent. They are superstitious. God looms large in their thoughts. Mintje Lombard, wife of Andries in "The Miller," tramps sixteen miles down the Aangenaam Valley to fetch an eelskin which she believes will cure her husband of his cough. Oom Schalk Lourens's father pays a visit to a "Kafir" witch-doctor with his friend, Paul Kruger [in **"Yellow Moepels."**]

Both regions are subject to drought, when the spirit of endurance of the inhabitants is tested to the utmost. It is instructive to compare Pauline Smith's story of old Alie van Staden who trekked across the Verlatenheid with her grandson in search of the Hermansdorp of her memories, with Bosman's **"The Rooinek."** His description of the trek into the Kalahari Desert contains a compelling realism. He shows himself interested in the question of leadership. What makes the other trekkers follow Gerhardhus Grobbelaar, and why does he lose his authority in the end? Finally there is a portrayal of courage and the ultimate helplessness of men in the face of adverse elements. Pauline Smith presents the realities of drought as convincingly. But her treatment of Alie van Staden is more tender. She works her way into the depths of the decrepit *bywoner's* thoughts and feelings. She identifies herself with Alie up to the moment of her death. Bosman, on the other hand tends to present the deaths in the desert as a grim, real, and moving spectacle. He sees the characters from the outside—the reader watches them expiring. There is an element of cruelty in the way Bosman presents a tragic incident to the reader: "Look at it: face up to it," he seems to say. "See if you can take it like I can."

Generally, Bosman and Pauline Smith have a different emphasis. He presents humorous and absurd situations with a vision which is beyond her range. He has a strong satirical leaning which leads him to regard human failings as objects of amusement. She sees weaknesses with a tender sympathy. Although there is humour in her work, it is not accompanied by the satiric tang, which at times attains the dimensions of devastating cynicism in Bosman's work.

By the power of her imagination Pauline Smith transmutes the Little Karoo into a new and isolated world. The reader sees the characters moving against the backdrop of the mountains and in the fields as in a picture which bears many resemblances to, but is remote from the everyday. Bosman is much nearer to the Marico bushveld. It is not distanced (as the Karoo is for Pauline) by 6,000 miles of sea; neither is it a district associated with the cherished and luminous memories of childhood. (pp. 158-64)

> *Geoffrey Haresnape, "A Love for the Individual—H. C. Bosman, Uys Krige and Pauline Smith Compared," in his* Pauline Smith, *Twayne Publishers, Inc., 1969, pp. 158-69.*

Vivienne Dickson (essay date 1972)

[*In the following excerpt, Dickson remarks on Bosman's obscurity relative to other South African writers and his decision to write in English rather than Afrikaans.*]

In 1926 a twenty-one year old schoolteacher, Herman Charles Bosman, stood in the dock of the Supreme Court of South Africa to hear the judge condemn him to death for the shooting of his step-brother. The sentence was commuted to imprisonment with hard labor, and the prisoner lived to write what Roy Campbell has called "the best short stories that ever came out of South Africa." There were other writers who shared Campbell's enthusiasm: Alan Paton described Bosman as a "writer of international stature," and in 1962 William Plomer wrote: "South Africa has produced three outstanding writers of short stories—Pauline Smith, Nadine Gordimer, and Herman Charles Bosman." The South African public made his first book of stories a best-seller, and South African actors have toured the country with readings from his works.

And yet, twenty years after his death, Herman Charles Bosman is virtually unknown outside his own country, and in South Africa itself there has been no detailed assessment of his achievement. No collected edition of his writings has been published. His poems, translations, and first novel are out of print; many of his stories and essays are scattered, uncollected, through the pages of a dozen periodicals, magazines and newspapers. (p. 31)

The comparative neglect of Bosman, both inside and outside his own country, may be attributed to one cause: he was an outsider. An Afrikaans journalist who wrote little about politics and avoided literary circles and who published only in his own country (waiting fifteen years for **Mafeking Road** to come out in a poorly presented paperback) was an unusual figure in South African literature. Bosman's choice of local publishers, his subject matter and style (which is deliberately quite unlike the polished, sophisticated style of, say, Nadine Gordimer) have made him an outsider.

It is unusual for a South African writer of Bosman's stature not to publish his works abroad. Many South African writers, after an initial success in their own country—or after a brush with the government—have emigrated to Europe or America. The list is long: Roy Campbell, William Plomer, Pauline Smith, Peter Abrahams, Laurens van der Post, Doris Lessing, Ezekiel Mphahlele, Bloke Modisane . . . all are expatriates. Writers who have remained behind—Alan Paton, Nadine Gordimer, Jack Cope and Uys Krige among them—have usually followed the precedent set by older writers like Olive Schreiner and Sarah Gertrude Millin and published their works overseas. Although Bosman lived and worked in Europe for nine years, his books were produced only by South African publishers. The records of these publishers in the Humanities Research Center [at the University of Texas at Austin] and the account of the sale of his copyright, for which his widow, his third wife, paid £155, suggest that his motives were not economic. If Bosman did prostitute his talent—and there are signs he did so in his later stories and journalism—the wages of his sin were not high.

Possibly Bosman's motives were patriotic, but more probably he felt his most appreciative audience would be among the people who knew the country and who would recognize his characters and their milieu. Bosman's stories are "local color" stories, truly indigenous in their materials. But he is a "local" writer in the sense that Mark Twain, Bret Harte, Henry Lawson and R. K. Narayan are "local" writers: foreign readers may not appreciate every nuance or allusion, but they are not made aware of any such handicap, for the best local writers seem to confer upon their readers an honorary certificate of citizenship.

Bosman's stories are set in the Marico district of the Transvaal, about a hundred and fifty miles northwest of Johannesburg. The area was devastated by the end of the Anglo-Boer war in 1902. It was twenty years before the farmers came back into the area with their cattle and their "mielie" (maize) seeds. These men were, as Bosman said, "real Boers": as children they had trekked north with their families away from the detested "liberal" English; as men they had fought in the Kaffir Wars and gone out on commando in the Anglo-Boer wars. They were frontiersmen, living in sun-baked brick and thatch houses in dry thorntree country near the Bechuanaland border. Their language was a dialect of Dutch, their religion Calvinist. Drought, rinderpest, policemen, white ants, and tax-collectors were their enemies. Bosman wrote:

> There were occasional visits from the Dutch Reformed Church predikants. And a few meetings of the Dwarsberg Debatsvereniging. And there were several local feuds. For I was to find that while the bush was of infinite extent, and the farms very many miles apart, the paths through the thorn-trees were narrow. ["**Marico Revisited**," *A Cask of Jerepigo*]

In 1925 Bosman came to teach the children of these farmers and to chat with their parents on the stooeps, drinking coffee and peach brandy. "Some of those farmers had most interesting stories to tell. . . . And my mind absorbed whatever they had to relate provided that it was of a sufficiently inutilitarian order." ["**Reminiscences**," *A Cask of Jerepigo*]

Bosman, like the Boers, was Afrikaans speaking, but most of his stories are written in English. He created a character, Oom Schalk Lourens, as his mouthpiece, and created for him a deceptively simple, rhythmic style. The sentence structure echoes Afrikaans without precisely following it. The flavor of Afrikaans is preserved, but not through direct translation. Here is Oom Schalk:

> Now and again, from some traveller who had passed through Schweizer-Reineke, we who had trekked out of that stricken region would hear a few useless things about it. We learnt nothing that we did not already know. Ocker Gieljan was still on the Engelbrecht farm, we heard. And the only other living creature in the whole district was a solitary crow. A passing traveller had seen Ocker Gieljan at the borehole. He was pumping water into a trough for the crow, the traveller said. ["**Cometh Comet**," *Unto Dust*]

> In the meantime, the leopard had got up as far as my knees. He was studying my trousers very carefully, and I started getting embarrassed. My trousers were old and rather unfashionable. Also, at the knee, there was a torn place, from where I had climbed through a barbed-wire fence, into the thick bush, the time I saw the Government tax-collector coming over the bult before he saw me. The leopard stared at that rent in my trousers for quite a while, and my embarrassment grew. I felt I wanted to explain about the Government tax-collector and the barbed wire. I didn't want the leopard to get the impression that Schalk Lourens was the sort of man who didn't care about his personal appearance. ["**In the Withaak's Shade**," *Mafeking Road*]

> For this reason a kafir is not very happy when a wood-carver comes along to him with a piece of wood fashioned in the likeness of a human being, and informs him, "This is you." Even when the image hasn't got a piece of brass driven into its belly, the ordinary ignorant kafir, confronted with his own likeness cut out of wood, will bid the wood-carver tarry a little while in front of the hut—while he goes round to the back to look for his axe. ["**Graven Image**," *Unto Dust*]

> They say that after the girl has drunk the juba-juice she begins to forget all sorts of things. She forgets that your forehead is rather low, and that your ears stick out, and that your mouth is too big. She even forgets having told you, the week before last, that she wouldn't marry you if you were the only man in the Transvaal.

> All she knows is that the man she gazes at, over her empty coffee-cup, has grown remarkably handsome. You can see from this that the plant must be very potent in its effects. I mean, if you consider what some of the men in the Marico look like. ["**The Love Potion**," *Mafeking Road*]

Bosman naturally and unselfconsciously used Afrikaans words that have no adequate English equivalent, but he made no attempt to write the kind of "exotic" stories that found such a ready market overseas in the nineteenth and early twentieth centuries. Bosman eschewed melodrama, preferring understatement to overstatement, simplicity to complexity.

> One thing that certain thoughtless people some-
> times hint at about my stories is that nothing
> ever seems to happen in them. Then there is an-
> other kind of person who goes even further, and
> *he* says that the stories I tell are all stories that
> he has heard before, somewhere, long ago—he
> can't remember when exactly, but somewhere at
> the back of his mind he knows that it is not a new
> story. [**"The Selons-Rose,"** *Unto Dust*]

Old stories of lovers, jealousy, ghosts, commando sorties, cattle rustling, droughts, treks, loyalty, and anger: these are the stories of the Marico Boers.

Bosman's work does not belong to the older South African tradition of exotic adventure stories, but neither does it belong to a younger tradition whose themes are racial and political. His treatment of racial stress and conflict is oblique, for the people he writes about were living in pre-apartheid days in a rural community which was un-touched by the awakening racial consciousness of the towns. Africans were neither hated nor feared—such emo-tions were reserved for the "Rooineks," the British. Afri-cans were part of the landscape and only troublesome when schools and missionaries put "cheeky" ideas into their heads. In most of Bosman's stories the Africans are peripheral, but when they are central they are treated sim-ply as people, as characters, not racial stereotypes. No one was safe from Bosman's ironical glance. Bosman had no political tub to thump and was too great a writer to catego-rize people according to their shade of skin, language, or political views. One must turn to other novelists for direct examination of racial themes, but no other South African writer has drawn a better portrait of the Boers, the rural Afrikaner whose influence on the course of South African history has been so decisive. Joseph Sachs said of *Mafe-king Road,* "There is all of South Africa in that little book." (pp. 32-37)

> Vivienne Dickson, "Herman Charles Bos-
> man," in The Library Chronicle of the Uni-
> versity of Texas at Austin, *No. 4, February,*
> *1972, pp. 31-7.*

Stephen Gray   (essay date 1977)

[*In the following essay, Gray highlights the topicality of Bosman's "In die Voorkamer" stories and analyzes the stylistic and thematic differences between these stories and the Oom Schalk Lourens stories.*]

Between April 1950, and his death on 14 October 1951, Herman Charles Bosman produced a piece a week for *The Forum,* the liberal weekly magazine and newspaper, ed-ited by John Cope from Vanguard House, 176 Main Street, Johannesburg. *The Forum* was printed at *The Sun-day Express* where Bosman worked as a proof-reader. His weekly routine was to deliver a new incident in a sequence every Friday morning to appear under the rubric 'In die Voorkamer', usually about four pages from the end of each number, between the arts pages and sports. During this period he produced eighty pieces to deadline without

a break, thirty-nine of which reappear, edited by Lionel Abrahams, as *Jurie Steyn's Post Office* and *A Bekkersdal Marathon.*

As Abrahams explains in his compiler's foreword to *Jurie Steyn's Post Office,* he slightly rearranged these two vol-umes from their original chronology so as to link various obvious clusters (for example, the six pieces which deal with Pauline Gerber and which are scattered over the mid-dle of the series are gathered together in the *Jurie Steyn* volume). The pieces as now published do very approxi-mately run in the order of composition, and naturally fall into the two halves that Abrahams has titled, *Jurie Steyn's Post Office* containing the earlier half and *A Bek-kersdal Marathon* the later. His selection and regrouping seems entirely justified in view of the transference into book form; between covers the repetitions that a bread-and-butter journalist could get away with at intervals in the press would appear clumsy when available in a form that does not allow paced reading, and Abrahams has found patterns which the circumstances of composition did not call for and could not contain.

But the purpose of this article is to unravel these 'In die Voorkamer' stories, to some extent, in order to investigate what the two book collections have lost: the environment of events that spurred each individual story. It is generally apparent, as one reads through the book collections, that many of the stories have some kind of bearing on their times, yet it is only once they are read in the context of *The Forum* and datelined that what otherwise can only be guessed at becomes fully apparent.

In his current popularity, Bosman has come to be viewed as something of an "eternal artist" figure, breathing "mar-vellous home-truths for all men". But the truth about the later Bosman is that he became a writer who had a scrupu-lous, instant rapport with each passing day, and each yard of newsprint that underwent his professional scrutiny. His endlessly subtle in-references to the South Africa-in-progress of 1950-51 suggest that he meant himself to be taken as much as a commentator, a newspaper columnist if you like, whose medium happened to be fiction, as an artist plugging the eternal verities from above it all.

In the debate about politically engaged literature in South Africa, Bosman, always a writer of contrary spirit, tends to be overlooked, possibly because his methods of dealing with actuality are not generally obvious enough to classify him as committed to social change. Bosman never hit any-one *directly* over the head in his writing, although in the Voorkamer pieces he did tend to pull the carpet out from underneath the whole debate. And Bosman, we must re-member, died one hundred years after the first publication of *Uncle Tom's Cabin,* so that the debate itself is getting pretty stale by now.

In her obituary on Bosman in *The Forum* of 19 October 1951, Lily Rabkin, the paper's assistant editor, wrote: "Some months ago . . . a couple of [Bosman's] admirers told me that he was dissipating his energies on the Voorkamer and that he should be writing a novel. I dis-cussed what they had said with Herman, who dropped for once his usual flippant response to the subject of his writing. He said very firmly that he had no interest in the novel as an art form, that the short story was the contemporary lyric and the only thing worth doing. With equal firmness he told me that the Voorkamer stories were the best work he had ever done." (Yet Abrahams records that he left a novel incomplete, and the University of Texas catalogue of holdings of letters and manuscripts from Southern Africa lists more than one incomplete novel.)

I shall maintain that Bosman's own opinion of his last, scattered pieces is worth pursuing, that the sequence of pieces we have here was a very appropriate and pointed response to its time of composition, and relatedly that Bosman does in fact stand in a whole line of South African writers some of whose major work has been occasionally inspired. The line of South Africa's English journalist-writers commences with Pringle (*The South African Journal*, 1824), includes Sammons (*Sam Sly's African Journal*, 1840s), Blackburn and Gibbon, Plaatje and R. R. R. Dhlomo (numerous newspapers and magazines) and Black (*The Sjambok* in the early 1930s), and culminates in Bosman himself. For English writers in South Africa up to the 1950s, journalism shading into art was a means of earning an independent living with a pen. Each of these writers in turn owned at least a share in an independent printing press at one time or another and published his own newspaper and/or literary magazine or review. The private presses created a certain gleeful anti-establishment spirit, as this editorial comment shows: "How [do] the following people [feel]: grafting councillors, shady lawyers, tripe-talking parsons and professors, Salvation Army officers and pimps—how [do] these people feel about the fact that we have now acquired our own printing works?" (Blignaut and Bosman in *New Sjambok*, Vol. 1, No. 2, 25 July 1931.) In Bosman's life he passed from being a part-owner of a press into being a mere wage-earner, which all South African writers connected with news and magazines have been since.

With Bosman the commitment to topical commentary was always there. Vol. 1, No. 1 of *The Touleier* (December 1930), edited by Aegidius Jean Blignaut, with Herman Malan (as Bosman usually named himself then) as contributing editor, announced this policy: "*The Touleier* will burn like a storm-lamp through the darkness of the night, and if it must be extinguished, let it be extinguished with the dawn." This monthly journal of a new literary enlightenment launched early Bosman stories like 'The Rooinek', 'The Gramophone' and 'Makapan's Caves', which were to be collected together in *Mafeking Road*, first published in 1947, by which time their topicality was blunted. One of *The Touleier's* heralds was Hartman van Beek, of whom more later.

The Touleier gave rise in the succeeding two decades to a proliferation of Herman Malan fly-by-night scandalsheets that perfected a combination of literary artifice and current commentary in a fugitive, underground fashion: there was *New Sjambok* in 1931, *New L.S.D.* up to 1933, *Ringhals* (the first number of which was banned before publication) up to 1934 and *New Ringhals* in 1935 and 1939, *Sjambok* again in 1939, and *New L.S.D.* once more in 1946-7. This game of courting censorship and libel in the

interests of exposing scandalous truths is part of a venerable pressman's tradition in the Transvaal—in the 1890s of President Kruger's Z.A.R., Blackburn's *Sentinel* had to resurface as *Transvaal Sentinel* a week after closure, *The Critic* was apprehended and renamed *The Transvaal Critic*, and even *The Star* newspaper appeared as *The Comet* from 25 March to 14 April 1897, due to various suppressions that the independent journalist-writer could never take as anything more than encouragement to proceed.

But in the Oom Schalk Lourens stories, collected in *Mafeking Road*, and *Unto Dust*, there is a discernible process of turning away on Bosman's part from his earlier self. The two volumes contain forty-five collected stories, and over the two decades during which they were written Oom Schalk Lourens changed, and changed radically. We like to think of the early Oom Schalk as a lovable rogue and bumpkin, and we know by a process of double-take that he is a wily, deceptive ironist ("a simple Boer who is really the embodiment of sly ambiguity", as the blurb has it). [William] Plomer correctly remarks [in his Foreword to *Unto Dust*, 1963] that "Oom Schalk Lourens's generation had no direct contact with the beginnings in Africa of the industrial revolution or with the new political aspirations of black Africans that sprang up with it". And in the magazines mentioned Oom Schalk appears every so often not as marginal political commentator, but as pleasing relief from the hurly-burly of satirical journalism, a figure of calm and detached reassurance from an earlier and better time.

The early Oom Schalk derives from Bosman's brief spell as a teacher in the Marico district (three-quarters of a teacher's year in 1926). On his return to the Marico after the Second World War, Bosman recounted that, since cattle-smuggling across the Bechuanaland border was still on the go, he was "glad to find that the only part of my stories that could have dated had not done so. It is only things indirectly connected with economics that can change. Droughts and human nature don't" ('**Marico Revisited**', first published in *Trek*). Bosman's scanty acquaintance with the Marico corner of the Transvaal suggests then that his presentation of it was more a matter of intuitive recollection than careful reporting. Although he maintains above that the Marico did not change, it is significant in the essay '**Marico Revisited**' that he avoids describing more than the approach to the actual town. His return journey there was a renewal of contact with a Bosmanesque imaginative construct, not a real place. And his Marico was to change in many ways.

The early Oom Schalk is, of course, derived not only from the archetypal stoep-talker of the backveld of the twenties, but also from the journalist-writers whom Bosman emulated and adapted. Edgar Allan Poe is an obvious source, as Bosman frequently acknowledged. So is Mark Twain who, after personal experience of Oom Schalk's generation, wrote [in *More Tramps Abroad*] "They are fine marksmen, the Boers. From the cradle up, they live on horseback and hunt wild animals with the rifle. They have a passion for liberty and the Bible, and care for nothing else." Others are Ambrose Bierce, Josh Billings, Max Adler, Bret Harte, Artemus Ward and O. Henry, as he points out in his essays on Poe in *Trek* (July 1948) and on Stephen Leacock (included in **A Cask of Jerepigo**). In these two essays he seems not only to be paying tribute to, but also to be making farewell gestures to the inspirations behind Oom Schalk as he begins to scuttle his early mouthpiece.

Oom Schalk was a comparatively simple narrative device—you wound up Oom Schalk and let him talk his way through topics a, b, c. His predecessors in South African English fiction were Perceval Gibbon's Vrouw Grobbelaar of *Vrouw Grobbelaar's Leading Cases* (1905) and Sanni Metelerkamp's Outa Karel of *Outa Karel's Stories* (1914); his contemporary was C. R. Prance's Tante Rebella of *Tante Rebella's Saga* (1937). They were all examples of a loquacious, non-literate and virtually omniscient small-town narrator who could be relied upon to anthologize broad spectra of material, giving it focus and cohesion.

The basis of Oom Schalk's world-view was essentially no different from the one that [Olive] Schreiner attributes to her isolated Boer community in a story like 'Eighteen-Ninety-Nine' [in *Stories, Dreams and Allegories,* 1923]:

> . . . at last they settled on a spot where game was plentiful and the soil good, and there among the low undulating slopes, near the bank of a dry sloot, the young man built a house at last, with his own hands, a little house of two rooms.
>
> On the long slope across the sloot before the house, he ploughed a piece of land and enclosed it, and he built kraals for his stock and so struck root in the land and wandered no more. Those were brave, glad, free days for the young couple. They lived largely on the game which the gun brought down . . . Sometimes, too, traders came with their wagons and in exchange for skins and fine horns sold sugar and coffee and print and tar-cord, and such things as the little household had need of. The lands yielded richly to them, in maize, and pumpkins, and sweet-cane, and melons; and they had nothing to wish for.

Oom Schalk, like Schreiner's characters, once knew Eden as a reality. It was an Eden always subject to the threat of outside interference. Both Schreiner's and Bosman's use of Biblical cadence in their stories is a tonal reinforcement of the vision of paradise on earth that agrarian Boer communities appear to have made manifest. But post-1899 the physical props of that existence burned down—burning farmhouses are more than a symbol of the horrors of war; they are the appearance of hell on earth. And when the land itself "where game was plentiful and the soil good" has, by the 1930s of Oom Schalk, become denuded and unproductive, it is the sterile dust of that lost vision that Bosman can stir so ironically. It is "resonances of meaning" like these, as Geoffrey Hutchings calls them [in "A Master of Gossip: A Note on Herman Charles Bosman," *London Magazine* (1970)], that Bosman manipulates in the Oom Schalk stories, meanings that by the 1950s have become a mere gesture of regret over the loss of a world irretrievably gone. As L. M. D. Stopforth states [in "Herman Charles Bosman: An Evaluation," *Annals of the University College of the Western Cape* (1964)], without exploring

these implications, Oom Schalk was an "old Boer"; when he'd ridden on commando against Makapan, his father had told him: "when you shoot, always aim at the stomach" (**'Makapan's Caves'**), and during the Anglo-Boer War of 1899-1902 he had been taken prisoner and sent to St Helena, no less.

The last Oom Schalk stories (contained in **Unto Dust**) were being published within weeks of the Voorkamer series being under way. **'The Ferreira Millions'** (not collected) appeared not in *Trek* but in *The Forum* of 1 April 1950; and on 15 April **'The Budget'**, the first in the Voorkamer series, was in newsprint. Oom Schalk wavered and sank more or less with the health of *Trek,* a monthly that had merged with *The South African Opinion* in 1946, had run until becoming a purely literary review in March 1950, suspended publication in June-July 1951, and revived briefly in October 1951, repeating much earlier material and in time to handle the obituary of its chief literary contributor. Bosman, in phasing from Oom Schalk to the Voorkamer, from *Trek* to *The Forum,* became a different kind of writer.

As Lionel Abrahams has suggested, the move meant that the various channels through which Bosman could have his say in *Trek,* ranging from the 'pure' fiction of the Oom Schalk stories to the monthly social and political commentaries of various columns like 'Talk of the Town', 'Pavement Patter' and 'Indaba', and including his frequent extended literary articles and book reviews, had to merge into the one, new all-purpose Voorkamer form.

The general idea for the Voorkamer series derives from some of the details of the Oom Schalk stories, particularly one called, appropriately, **'Seed-time and Harvest'**, which features Jurie Steyn as a minor character who will move to centre stage of the action. Oom Schalk's Drogevlei Debating Society, a situational gag used in one story, becomes Steyn's post office at Drogevlei, in the voorkamer of which the new seminar group of previously background characters awaits the weekly mail delivery and perfects amongst its members the unconscious means of keeping an on-going debate in progress with more efficiency and acumen than anything Oom Schalk could handle.

> [Bosman's] priority audience was always South African, and he foresaw that "writing local" was more meaningful than aiming at some vague international audience that he knew well enough, and had found to be of no immediate relevance.
>
> —*Stephen Gray*

The coming to power of the National Party on 26 May 1948, marked the beginning of the turning point in this vast, sprawling continuum of Marico stories. Apparently Bosman threw his well-known trilby hat high at the news of the Nationalist victory at the polls, and declared the death of British colonial domination and the liberation of the South African writer. On that date the capital of South African English publishing moved from London to Johannesburg and Cape Town. Significantly, Bosman was the first major South African writer to publish in South Africa for South Africans, as it were. In 1948 Alan Paton was with Scribners, New York, and Doris Lessing two years later would head for Michael Joseph, London; Nadine Gordimer would take *Face to Face* (first published in Johannesburg in 1949) overseas, and Sarah Gertrude Millin was set on Constable's in London selling only a portion of each of her books to C.N.A. publishers. David Wright's remark in this connection is crucial: of the time when he first read *Mafeking Road* under the dome of the British Museum Reading Room he wrote: "it seemed extraordinary that stuff as good as this should be published in Johannesburg and not in London" ["A South African Zoschenko," *London Magazine* (1963)]. But Bosman was willing to forego international recognition in order to become more regionally potent. His priority audience was always South African, and he foresaw that "writing local" was more meaningful than aiming at some vague international audience that he knew well enough, and had found to be of no immediate relevance.

In *Trek* of October 1947, he observed: "I have always believed that we have stood in the way of the development of an English South African literature [by not fostering a] book trade in this country . . . to produce creative work essentially South African in content and spirit, rich in local colour and in those nuances of feeling and expression that constitute the sinew and life-blood of great art."

But, in another sense, that watershed date in the history of South African English publishing and of politics was the death of Bosman's affection for, and uses for, his comic mask, Oom Schalk Lourens. Before 1948 the relationship between the two was uncomplicated enough. Bosman's attitude to his art was in line with what Havelock Ellis deduced Huysmans's to have been in writing *A Rebours:*

> To abuse the mighty and exalt the humble seems to man the divinest of prerogatives, for it is that which he himself exercises in his moments of finest inspiration. To find a new vision of the world, a new path to truth, is the instinct of the artist . . . He changes the whole system of our perceptions. That is why he seems to us at first an incarnate paradox, a scoffer at our most sacred verities, making mountains of our molehills, and counting as mere mole-hills our everlasting mountains, always keeping time to a music that clashes with ours, at our hilarity *tristis, in tristitia hilaris* [Ellis in his Introduction to J. K. Huysman's *A Rebours,* 1930].

This definition of the artist as prophet and moralist keeping time to "another tune", is of course liable to abuse; many artists are not superior moralists. Although it explains a lot of Bosman in his precocious early works, as in the stories by Ben Eath, or as in his obscure early poems like those contained in *The Blue Princess,* which advocate the amoral aestheticism of ritualized dagga-smoking above all man-made law, one must observe that in the

Marico stories and in a work like *Cold Stone Jug* Bosman could combine this view of an artist's superior morality with a down-to-earth realism that debunks this very tendency to airy escapism at the same time that it is asserted. As early as 1931 he wrote in a story called '**Rita's Marriage**', published under the rubric '**Life as Revealed by Fiction**', that: "The real test as to whether a man is an artist or whether he is merely sponging on the Temple of Art is to find out how he faces up to a sanitary-cart" (*New Sjambok,* Vol. 1, no. 2, 25 July 1931).

After 1948, Oom Schalk Lourens was no longer a political underdog; he and his descendants were back in power for the first time since the Z.A.R. and 1899. Anyway, if Oom Schalk had fought in the Kaffir Wars, as he said he did, by 1948 he must have been getting on, and the last of the Takhaars was too senile to make a final stand. Oom Schalk represented a world of pastoral frontiersmen whom Bosman had idealized, romanticized and sentimentalized. By 1948 such attitudes to the past were mere nostalgia. Ross Bressler, a contributor to *The Forum,* responded to a Marico-like community (actually near Balmoral) as follows: "[Although] there is not enough land to keep all the children, so that they have to emigrate to the Rand to become teachers, business men, building contractors, [the older generation] have attained the secret of the good life, which so many of us have lost: in their primitive homes they enjoy standards of happiness infinitely superior to ours" (29 June 1951).

Oom Schalk sustained this myth of the happy innocence of the republican burghers. But the Voorkamer series is written specifically to deny it and discredit it. Bosman's piece, '**Sixes and Sevens**', published in the same issue of *The Forum* as Bressler's article, is a parable about that same older generation being a vulnerable prey to poverty and suffering, and to the opposite of bucolic contentment, which in Bosman's terms is greed.

The strain in Bosman's relationship with Oom Schalk after the National Party rise to power shows in a story like '**Unto Dust**'. It was first published in *Trek* in February 1949. That was the month that *Trek* remembered that Minister Ben Schoeman had declared on a Vrededorp street-corner that his government was determined to remove "Kaffers, Hottentots and Koelies" from the Common Voters' Roll. Park Station in Johannesburg was segregated. Jan Hofmeyr, chairman of *The Forum,* was about to die, followed by the "old saga of Irene", General Smuts. The Post offices of the easygoing Cape Peninsula were segregated, too. *The Glass Menagerie,* a play that, although about the American depression, most aptly expressed the economic conditions of South Africa at the time, was staged by the National Theatre and adjudged by one *Trek* critic as a "wallow in the slough of frustration". The South African Table Tennis Association was disaffiliated by the international body for upholding the Colour Bar. The Rev. Michael Scott was cleaning up "Torbruk", a camp outside Orlando Location.

Given this context, '**Unto Dust**' becomes quite a bleak comment from Oom Schalk on the times in which it first appeared (as '**Tot Stof**' in *On Parade* on 21 December 1948, and in its English version in *Trek* two months later).

Here Oom Schalk is not up to more than a nightmarish response to social movements of which he has little experience. Instead of ending his tale with the usual harmonious contentment, he lapses into uneasiness, dissatisfaction and despair. The story itself revalues all of the mythology that Oom Schalk has held dearest: heroics in a "bygone Transvaal Kafir War" that are not heroics (in fact, desertion), honour between comrades that is in fact not honourable (but betrayal), faithfulness which is in fact delusion, courage proved to be expediency. The pretext of the story is that you live by the myths you believe in, but when they begin to crack there is only "brooding".

What Oom Schalk broods on here is the theme of death as the great leveller (the equalizer—in death you are all dust). The imagery which Oom Schalk feverishly, and unconsciously, is obsessed with is that of "the whole world [as] a big burial-ground" and, ironically, he takes relief from the thought that "we Boers [have] properly marked-out places on our farms for white people to be laid to rest in, in a civilized, Christian way." The central symbol of the story is the underdog, in this case literally a "yellow kafir dog", who is more faithful, honourable, courageous and heroic than any of the human beings. There is one major moral point here: if you are not as humane as you purport to be, you are as low as you imagine a "yellow kafir dog" to be. Such is Bosman's contempt for the goings-on of the month in which he wrote **'Unto Dust'**, a contempt which Oom Schalk as narrator is not fully able to convey.

Edward Davis wrote of Bosman's technique in *Mafeking Road:*

> A less subtle artist, say a Schreiner or a Millin, would have dwelt very heavily on the lot of Bosman's bywoners, and pointed out with wearisome insistence, that if you prick these hairy creatures they bleed; that they have organs, dimensions, senses, affections, passions. This is as far as the unsubtle artist goes. Bosman doesn't point out anything. He proves, simply, that what happens to his hairy horrors is merely a back-veld variation on what happens to everybody; that comedy is comic even in the howling wilderness of the Marico; and tragedy tragic even though its hero or heroine does not wear boots (*Trek,* January 1948).

What Davis maintains about Bosman's technique holds for the earlier stories, but his point about comedy and tragedy does not later on. By the time of **'Unto Dust'** Oom Schalk is in a state of anxiety that neither comedy nor tragedy can contain and neatly pigeon-hole; he has gone into shock and finds no easy conclusions. Alongside the *Mafeking Road* stories that Davis can so easily handle, the complex stresses of **'Unto Dust'** are beyond definition, and they are more than Oom Schalk can express; he must go, outdated and humiliated.

Bosman's new narrator in the Voorkamer series is, as Gill Brownlee puts it [in "A More Sophisticated Bosman," *New Nation,* (1972)], "little more than a transparent minutes secretary of the eternal, inconclusive voorkamer debates; his freedom of approach to any topic is virtually unlimited, while the flexibility of the conversation form gives

his imagination full play." Brownlee also suggests that, in moving from *Trek* to *The Forum,* Bosman tried to play on the idea of *The Forum* itself: a blend of John Cope's editorials, Senator Edgar H. Brookes's notes from the diary of a liberal, Jordan K. Ngubane's Black point of view column, etc., all rambling round much the same theme of the week. If so, it is understandable that there were occasionally strained relationships between Bosman and *The Forum.*

But more interestingly one has to observe that, after twenty-five years of Maricoizing, Bosman still kept at it. Whereas the Marico was a quaint fancy before, and possibly a particularly pleasant reference point in Bosman's otherwise harrowing career, one must not suppose that Bosman himself was in any way a country bumpkin who could deal with no more than a Marico view of the world. He was born in Cape Town, lived for years in London, and spent the most productive part of his life in the city of Johannesburg. His one novel, *Jacaranda in the Night*—his "purple" novel—jacarandas are purple—does chart the drift of small-town Boers into city Afrikanerdom in the form of Herklaas Huysmans (a recurring play on his own name), but it does so from the city-dweller's point of view. So why, one wonders, this instant reflex to process new material through the Marico once more?

Firstly, as Brownlee states, the Voorkamer Marico exists almost a generation later, and it features farmers deracinated from the past, and detached from the present which they are ill-equipped to handle. And they are now imprisoned, impotently, within the four walls of the Drogevlei Post Office, cut off from the veld outside. Secondly, by now the Marico as a construct in Bosman's mind has become one huge allegorical setting for all of South Africa. And it is the immediate functionality of Bosman's allegorical intentions that makes the Voorkamer stories models of protest literature.

Here follows a selected list to demonstrate some of the implications of this approach to the Voorkamer pieces as part of an on-going allegorization of contemporary realities. Since the commentary in the Voorkamer stories is not schematic, these observations might at first sight appear somewhat haphazard.

The sixth Voorkamer piece, **'Local Colour'** (20 May 1950—not collected), establishes Bosman's view of the role of the South African writer-commentator by way of a caricature of a local colourist, who stands in for any number of colonial writers and has echoes of his old self too:

> We were talking about the book-writing man, Gabriel Penzhorn, who was in the Marico on a visit, wearing a white helmet above his spectacles and with a notebook and pen below his spectacles. He had come to the Marico to get local colour and atmosphere, he said, for his new South African novel. What was wrong with his last novel, it would seem, was that it did not have enough colour and atmosphere in it.

What was wrong with it was that it was too full of *meaningless* local colour and mere atmosphere.

In the thirteenth Voorkamer piece, 'White Ant' (8 July 1950), Bosman plays on racist colour phobias with Gysbert van Tonder's immortal *reductio ad absurdum: "he* wouldn't go into a polling booth alongside of an ant, to vote, even if the ant *was* white" (***Jurie Steyn's Post Office***). The conversation derives its political impact from the obvious play on the segregationist sloganeering of the day, gaining strength, but also, as is frequent in these pieces, from a source at first sight utterly incongruous to the political commentary—in this case, Eugene Marais's *Soul of the White Ant* (*Die Siel van die Mier,* 1934). In parodying Marais's veld romanticism, which can find an alternative world of a mystical order in termitaries that are object lessons to humanity, Bosman observes that one should not be deluded—white ants are actually destructive infiltrators and terrorists, absurd analogues of irrational fears of the Swart Gevaar. A year later one finds *The Forum* headline 'White Ants in Parliament', when Southern Rhodesia's legislative assembly took four days off while the floorboards were prised up and the white ants eating the struts exterminated (15 June 1951). That Marais's blend of escapism and the all-white voting issue can be imaginatively correlated is a subtle political observation.

Time references are actual in the Voorkamer series. 'New-Year Glad Rags' appeared on 22 December 1950, and "Dominee Welthagen had come over specially from Bekkersdal to hold an end-of-year service in that little bushveld schoolhouse" (***Jurie Steyn's Post Office***); and young Vermaak, the schoolmaster (his name means "entertainment") has quite realistically been on holiday for a few episodes. 'Black Magic', published on 5 January 1951, deals with a witchdoctor coming to the back door for a Christmas box. These pieces took place, not in the cloud-cuckoo land of eternal fiction, but *as one was reading them.*

'Go-Slow Strike' (29 December 1950) deals obliquely with an actual go-slow strike of telegraphists on that Christmas Eve 1950. "The newspapers say that it's not an official go-slow strike, but of course, you've joined it, haven't you, Jurie? We all know you started before the others. Years before, I should say. I mean, ever since this post office was opened here" is the remark of At Naudé, the Marico's media-man. Linked to the strike issue in this piece is *The Forum's* main concern of the week, South Africa's productivity: 5,5 bags of maize per morgen, compared with a world average of 12,8. That Bosman could relate maize-productivity and a post office blockage in one piece is a mark of his daring and of the flexibility of his new form. That the Christmas season and its significance is elided (which it is not in earlier stories) is in itself a comment.

In the week of 17 August 1951, *The Forum* made much of Mr. J. G. Strydom lamenting the passing of "the Free State of the old Boer tradition" as he proclaimed a second Witwatersrand on the new Orange Free State goldfields and issued stern warnings about his people not falling prey to "English capitalism". In the same number, in 'Five-pound Notes', Bosman allegorizes the theme of real versus counterfeit values and money, and responds to this threat of neo-republicanism with a bitter tale of the fall of the Stellaland Republic of old due to commercial exploitation.

In that same week *The Forum* carries a letter from Peter Abrahams, in exile in Paris:

> I wanted to show the rest of the world what a non-European could do if they gave him half a fair chance . . . My books are read in nearly all the countries of the world. And nearly all the countries of the world are against the colour bar in South Africa.
>
> And whenever any white South African comes to Europe and tells the people that the non-Europeans of South Africa are lazy and drunkards and thieves, the people here say: 'Well, what about Peter Abrahams?' And then the white South African has nothing more to say.

Two months before, Abrahams had published *Wild Conquest,* set in the same Zeerust area as Bosman's Marico. Like Plaatje's *Mhudi,* which it reaffirms, *Wild Conquest* deals with the Great Trek as a political event in anti-Nationalist terms and proposes that nature works against racial tyranny: Mzilikazi's watering place was the Marico River, Schweizer-Reneke was Mamuse, and Zeerust had seen Inzwinyani collapse before it. The Marico is indeed an area fraught with rich literary associations. But Bosman is more pessimistic than Abrahams about race relations: he had Oupa Bekker's ox-wagon undermined and blown to dust (in 'White Ant' again)—so much for the Ossewa Brandwag and its racist platform, recently merged with the N.P.

Bosman implicitly refutes the 'lazy, drunken thieves' attitude to Blacks in a story like 'Dying Race' (21 September 1951), the opening of which is not reproduced in *A Bekkersdal Marathon,* and is given here:

> We agreed with Gysbert van Tonder that, for ignorance, the T'hlakewa Bushman took a lot of beating. For real ignorance, that was, of course. And then it had to be a real T'hlakewa Bushman, also. It had to be the genuine article and no nonsense. We didn't want a Flat-Face Koranna that you could see by his toe-nails was half M'Chopi coming along and pretending to us that he was a Bushman.
>
> Nor did we mean the high society kind of Bushman, we said, that had lived a while at a mission station and had there learnt one or two civilized tricks. Like wearing a collar stud stuck through his ear lobe, we said. Or rubbing axle grease in his hair in place of the gemsbok fat that he had been used to. Or painting lines in washing-blue round his eyes and from there to his ears, to look like spectacles, we said. No, we certainly did not mean a Bushman like that, that had learnt city ways. When it came to proper ignorance, we said, it had to be a raw T'hlakewa Bushman just out of the desert: so raw that the soles of his feet were worn through, with his walking over hard ground after being used only to the sandier parts of the desert. That was what we meant by a raw Bushman, we said—one that had his feet raw. We didn't mean the kind of Bushman that, when he saw a petrol pump would go and get fuel for his lighter there.
>
> "It's funny that you should talk like that,"

Gysbert van Tonder said, "but I remember a Bushman in the Kalahari once mentioning to me about what he took to be a new kind of policeman in a red uniform that he had seen, shading his eyes with his hand, at a distance of about eleven miles—the Bushman having no wish to get any nearer to a policeman than that.

"I realised afterwards that it wasn't a policeman that the Bushman had seen there but a petrol pump painted red. But the Bushman took no notice of my explanation. 'How I know he was a policeman,' the Bushman said, 'is because he never moved more than he had to.' And so I still don't know if he was a real ignorant T'hlakewa Bushman or if he had learnt a thing or two."

The satire is, as ever, multilayered. Phrases like "real ignorant" recoil on the speaker. The vein of "laugh before the pathos hits you" is familiar Bosman. But the main theme here is the Bushman's slimness, and it was Oom Schalk Lourens, remember, who used to be the slim one.

Trying to untangle the layers of satire in an excerpt like this can be exceedingly frustrating, for they interpenetrate and interresonate, and Bosman's habit is to shadowbox in full view as a diversion while the bodyblows are delivered from where you least expect. On the face of it, these paragraphs are about the futility of classifying types of South African citizens: a Flat-Face Koranna M'Chopi halfbreed confuses the compartments, and a really raw T'hlakewa Bushman is more of a racial ideal than an actuality. There is a general strain of scorn on the Voorkamer characters' part for anyone trying to assume civilized airs (which is their own pretension), but Bosman views such attempts as sadly incongruous: the collar stud through the earlobe and the spectacles of washing-blue are telling details. The notion that primitive people trying to play civilized is comic at all, an attitude very prevalent in a lot of colonial fiction, is reversed here: collar studs and spectacles became the ludicrous vanities.

But with Gysbert van Tonder's entry into the debate, all these observations take on a fresh layer of meaning. Between the lines one gathers that Gysbert the cattle-smuggler, in his experience of a Bushman, had in fact relied on that eleven-mile vision while making an escape in the exercise of his old profession. That he was a criminal on the lam goes unsaid; that he was tricked by the same Bushman goes unsaid, too. The dying race, then, is the one that really suffers from vanity to the point of blindness. And the satirist's indulgence in allowing man his vanities seems particularly outweighed here with hatred for the Voorkamer characters' dishonesty; no Oom Schalk could have expressed such disillusionment.

By the end of October 1950, *The Forum* had changed format from a magazine into a tabloid newspaper—the regular articles of the magazine become embedded in copious news items that give it an air of greater currency and topical excitement. This transformation does not deflect Bosman's intentions with the Voorkamer series, but in-references to *The Forum's* own weekly contents become more obvious.

On 19 January 1951, when T. S. Eliot was making dire anti-television warnings, much as South Africa's parliament was inclined to do in similar terms, and his *The Cocktail Party* was about to tour South Africa with the National Theatre as an example of grand English culture, Bosman replies to Eliot with a story that shows "how slow news from the outside world was in reaching the Marico bushveld" (*Jurie Steyn's Post Office*). South Africa's isolation is exposed, so is its gullibility (as Jurie Steyn fancies the Jurassic period to have been named after him). Bosman does not try to stave off the media; he analyses what effect they can have on communities that are condemned, not to artificially recreated Greek tragedy, but to existence in an absurd predicament. Significantly *Trek's* and *The Forum's* editorial tastes in short stories were not for high art, but for social realism: early Gordimer, Lessing and Barney Simon; and in December 1949 *Trek* had carried Borges's cunningly mechanical piece of plotting, 'Emma Zunz'.

On 9 February 1951, amidst much nationalist rhetoric about the upholding of Western Civilization against the onslaught of the black hordes, Bosman responds with a piece entitled **'Divinity Student'** ('Student of Divinity' in *Jurie Steyn's Post Office*), which clinches on an image of a rickshaw-puller "apologising for all the boot-polish brown that was coming off his chin. He was working his way through college, he told me. He said it was steadier work than looking after babies or mowing lawns, the seashells rattling on him as he spoke." Economic pressures, Bosman maintains, are stronger than racial aversions.

The year 1951 in general sees the entrenchment of apartheid policy in its most noteworthy forms. Nineteen-fifty had been a year of racial unrest and increasing dispossession for the so-called non-white: January 29, native riots, Newclare; April 6, D.R.C. Congress adopts apartheid; May 1, native riot, Alexandra; July 7, Population Registration Act; July 17, Anti-Communist Act gazetted; November 27, Witzieshoek clash over removals. Educational and other trends were, as *The Forum* put it, towards the "kraaling" of the races.

Bosman's response to the Population Registration Act, and the subsequent Immorality Act, is a very specific one, and possibly his most moving gesture of protest in this series—the piece is **'Birth Certificate'**, first published on 12 August 1950 (*A Bekkersdal Marathon*). In this piece his new formula of theme and variation is most meticulously worked out. The opening sentence establishes the theme: "It was when At Naude told us what he had read in the newspaper about a man who had thought all his life that he was White, and had then discovered that he was Coloured, that the story of Flippus Biljon was called to mind."

A London publisher could certainly detect the overall impact of this statement: scorn at the absurdity of race classification in a multi-coloured country where an adoption of a doctrine of racial purity causes appalling individual human crises. But what one feels a London publisher might well not detect are the ironies in the tone, employed specifically to act upon a South African sensibility. "A man who had thought all his life that he was White" clearly had never thought twice about it in his entire lifetime.

Then "discovering" that he was Coloured is no casual "discovery": the word works two ways—first of all, it stresses the arbitrariness of the decision-makers, and secondly it suggests that a big thing is being made out of what is in fact piffling. That the story was "called to mind" suggests it had been long dormant, and would have stayed dormant without the intruding news from afar. Bosman alleges that such painful matters are being exploited for political ends. The tone reveals an underplayed attitude of amazed disbelief.

This theme is handled more gingerly than others by the Voorkamer debaters, for obvious reasons, and Bosman immediately has them defer the telling of the story of Flippus Biljon. The second sentence reads: "But because it was still early afternoon we did not immediately make mention of Flippus"—that is to say we postponed action, denying our immediate sense of outrage. And there is a secondary accusation: these deeds are nightwork. Bosman is commenting on the South African characteristic of avoiding an unpleasant subject, hoping it will go away, so that merely not believing the obvious becomes an excuse for never acting on it.

When the story of Flippus Biljon does come, willy-nilly, as a conclusion to this piece, the Marico observer remarks after Oupa Bekker has made a final twist of the theme: "it seemed to us like the end of the story. Consequently, we were disappointed when At Naude started making further mention of that piece of news he had read in the daily paper. So there was nothing else for it but that we talk about Flippus Biljon." While South Africans will do anything to avoid impending reality, the conclusion, the judgment will have to come. When it comes, perversely, the story of Flippus Biljon is an inversion of the opening statement. The punchline of the story, Flippus Biljon saying: "Thank you, *baas,* thank you, *my basie,*" on receiving his race classification, is a sour one that directly accuses baasskap ideology. That is the part, according to Davis, that a Schreiner or a Millin could have done; but what Bosman has done, apart from making an implicit protest against a particular new law of the day, is go behind the legislation and see how such legislation could come about in the first place.

The twists and turns that this theme takes between the opening statement of it and its inverted conclusion are an adroit manipulation of what one might call Swiftian tactics. Once again it is a Marais notion, apparently unrelated, which is pilloried—the notion that baboons and humans can be confused, that baboons can be "friends" (*My Friends the Baboons,* 1939) and pretty "human". In *The Forum* of 22 June 1951, for example, W. S. Chadwick "relates a strange incident to prove that baboons have a remarkably high degree of intelligence". This story-idea is a prevalent one in South African fiction, used many a time to wring a sigh or a laugh. In general, most English literature of the colonial period credits baboons with human intelligence, as above, so that the white Englishman retains his dignity, as with Tarzan. On the other hand, the downgrading of humans to baboon status is frequent—in Afrikaans cartooning Adonis the god is metamorphosed into Adoons, or in Campbell's satire on the same theme a sage

becomes Bongwi the Baboon. Swift uses the same incongruity in the incident of Glumdalclitch's monkey in *Gulliver's Travels*. But Bosman makes his own race classification here into apes that are apes, and humans that are human, and plays on the myth of man as a superior ape by letting his veld eclogue characters decide where they unconsciously categorize the so-called non-white population. Clearly his satirical method is aimed at inducing the decent sentiment that family bonds are more sacred than any classificatory system that is intent on severing them. Although they would never admit to such humanity, Bosman shows that his ignoramuses are not at heart inhumane, as when Oupa Bekker comes out with the story of Heilart Nortje and his wife whose child was kidnapped by baboons:

> And once . . . Heilart [had seen how] his son was then engaged in picking up a stone and laying hold of a scorpion that was underneath it. The speed with which his son pulled off the scorpion's sting, and proceeded to eat up the rest of the scorpion whole filled the father's heart of Heilart Nortje with a deep sense of pride . . . "And my wife and I held hands and we smiled at each other and we asked each other, where does he get it all from?"

Through the most ludicrous means, Bosman shows that family pride should rate above blatant prejudice in the South African psyche. One would love one's son, even if he were a baboon, even if he were—worse still—a Coloured. But the innuendo in "where does he get it all from?" suggests, most insultingly, that those who cannot see, and act upon, these home-truths, are the true baboons.

Bosman himself, meanwhile, happened when not using the idea satirically to be an admirer of baboons, as he states in his essay **'Simian Civilization'** (in *A Cask of Jerepigo*):

> I have never been able to view a monkey's drolleries in any spirit other than that of high seriousness—which I have not always, alas, been able to accord to the loftiest and most portentous products of the human mind.

> I have come to the conclusion, regrettably enough, that I have a great deal in common with the inferior class of monkey, the kind of monkey who, through an unhappy degeneracy of the spirit, is not able to approach the more solemn things of life with a proper sense of gravity.

In **'Birth Certificate'** the story-line is established, played by a process of procrastination through the necessary variations, and then resumed and brought to a definite conclusion, punchline included. And it has the finality of an Oom Schalk story, most of which were constructed on the same pattern. A neatly-contained story makes for a neatly-defined statement. **'Birth Certificate'** is an exception in the Voorkamer series for not many of the other stories are as cut and dried.

Oom Schalk's Marico was depopulated by the rinderpest of 1896 and its aftermath, the war. The Voorkamer series has as its apocalypse the soil erosion and the dustbowl conditions of the north-west Free State which are laying waste the old way of life. Oom Schalk's vision of Judgment Day is shown in a story like **'Cometh Comet'** (*Unto Dust*), which, ending as it does on an image of a new Jesus Christ, views redemption and recovery as part of the natural and spiritual properties of mankind. Yet in the new Marico allegory, apocalyptic morality is more prevalent, the end of the world is nearer at hand. "And when I see by my youngest son, Petrus's, quarterly report that he is good at sums, I think, yes, and I know what he's going to use all those sums for, one day, sitting on his front stoep with a pencil and a piece of paper, waiting for the rain. He'll need all the sums and more than they can teach him at school, I think to myself, then" (*A Bekkersdal Marathon*). The Voorkamer pieces are Bosman's version of Lessing's *The Grass is Singing*, about which *The Forum's* literary critic could find not much more to say than that it showed "a quite distinctive psychological insight." In the Voorkamer series there is no easy redemption in view.

Bosman's desertion of the closed, traditional short story form is symptomatic of a revision of his whole attitude to his writing and to his world. If he called his last pieces examples of the "contemporary lyric", it was because he felt them to be more personal and more topical than fiction is normally assumed to be, or at least because he felt the prose of these pieces could be read "poetically". That his own lyrics (in *The Earth is Waiting*, collected and first published by Human and Rousseau only in 1974) are rambling and romantically diffuse is not to the point here: his concepts of internal balance and symmetry within a somewhat loose piece of prose show a virtuoso sense of structure in short fictions (of around 1,500 words each). Since the very term short story presupposes a rigid view of the form, perhaps these short Voorkamer pieces should not be labelled short stories without due qualification. They are, both structurally and thematically, conversation pieces. Their frequent downbeat endings that force the reader to go back and re-assess, rather than offering ready deductions, make for a reading experience that is neither prejudged nor preconcluded. The open-endedness is part of the uneasiness that Bosman conveys through technique, as well as through theme.

By the middle of 1951 the new tensions that hit the Marico week by week are virtually uncontainable. The hard times of a recession meant fuel and food shortages. In May's austerity drive Mr Eric Louw, Minister of Economic Affairs, had banned cut-outs of swish models of motor cars on the backs of cereal packets. **'Failing Sight'** (22 June 1951) deals with these matters, as well as with how under the new regime the bonhomie between Black and White which in the past had existed, no matter how grudgingly, had now been socially and politically ruled out. In that same piece, Bosman deals with South Africa's failure to remember that it *could* ever have had good relations between the races, and the central image is of Chief Umsufu's new car being towed by a pack of trek-oxen, Oupa Bekker and the old chief seated in modern luxury within, both adamant in denying the benefits of progress—an ironic, common, fraternal bond. But what goes unsaid and what upsets the Voorkamer characters in **'Failing Sight'** is that a Black could own a car at all. This reaction of disbelief is akin to the national one over the rise to power of,

for example, Kwame Nkrumah and the preparatory news of the Gold Coast being about to change into Ghana; Sir Seretse Khama was returning to the neighbouring Bechuanaland then, which in turn would become Botswana (with Mafeking temporarily as its capital).

Although white South Africans could then join motor rallies from Algiers to the Cape, or take a month's holiday flying around Africa, the groundswells of the winds of change, and South Africa's increasing isolation from the rest of the continent and from Europe, were under way. On the day **'Failing Sight'** was published, Chief Albert Luthuli was elected head of the African National Congress. Paton, busy on the screenplay of *Cry, the Beloved Country*, was preparing to start work on his Hofmeyr biography. Gerard Sekoto was in exile, playing a piano in a Paris bar. Yet to the productivity of Sarah Gertrude Millin there was no end: her *The People of South Africa* was reviewed by Norman Bathurst as a "perpetuation of all the fallacies of South Africa and its history", although with an approved style of "dazzling garrulity or sparkling loquacity". Her sight, too, was failing.

By September 1951, the grand old men of European letters, Shaw and Gide, were dead. Frank Sinatra and Ava Gardner were giving rise to widespread matrimonial rumours. Bobby Locke was *the* golfer, and the bestseller of the year had been written by another Johannesburg resident—*The Cruel Sea* by Montsarrat. The Cold War was hotter and the Korean War colder; Eisenhower and Mao were in the ascendant, Churchill and Stalin on the wane. An issue of *Time* magazine containing an article by Alexander Campbell describing Johannesburg as "a city of padlocked doors, prayers for safety, watchdogs and revolvers—where Natives are driven to violence by oppression, injustice and wretched conditions" (*The Forum*, 14 September 1951) was banned for a while. The Sophiatown Renaissance group, articulating the needs of eight million 'non-whites', was getting under way via *Drum* magazine, to be banned to the last man. The leader of the opposition, Mr J. G. N. Strauss, was making no headway with the United Party's Bill of Rights.

The Forum continues with a John Creasey thriller called *Day of Disaster* in a few dozen parts, but it offers no disaster comparable with day-to-day political developments. In response, English South African culture can come up with only the usual commercial banality: Durban-born Noel Langley's *Little Lambs Eat Ivy* is produced in his hometown, and as *The Forum* comments (on 21 September 1951): "It seems that a Durban man must first have three plays on in London before Durban producers agree that he is a safe enough bet." André Huguenet is exported to the West End to play the lead in Flecker's *Hassan* for the Festival of Britain celebrations. Peter Brooke directs Gielgud at an early Edinburgh festival.

Bosman enjoys some feedback as, for once, his Voorkamer forum works in reverse. The week after he publishes the piece **'Weather Prophet'**, Dr H. O. Simon writes an article on the editorial page as follows: "The political weather is still uncertain. Every time it seems to be clearing up, a new cloud appears. Weather wizards have so often predicted thunderstorms and hurricanes that they have lost some of their credit" (3 August 1951).

In the week that 'Sailor' Malan and the (all-white) Torch Commando marched in protest against Dr Malan's National Party and Dr Dönges's Separate Representation of Voters Bill, by which the Coloureds were disenfranchized, Senator Brookes observed: "It is probable that South Africa has never been so divided in all the forty-one years of Union" (15 June 1951).

And on the book page of *The Forum* their reviewer over-enthusiastically welcomed *Wild Conquest* by the afore-mentioned Coloured writer, Peter Abrahams, as if in compensation for his being driven out, as the next in line in "the true South African tradition, the tradition that has given us Olive Schreiner's *Story of an African Farm,* Buchan's *Prester John,* Mrs. Millin's *God's Stepchildren,* Brett Young's *They Seek a Country,* and Alan Paton's *Cry, the Beloved Country*" (Norman Bathurst, 15 June 1951). The review is an early example of radical chic. *Mafeking Road,* although by then in its fourth impression of the second edition, is not included in the list, nor for that matter is Bosman's masterpiece, *Cold Stone Jug.* No one asks if a list of reasonably publicized but largely unread novels constitutes a "true tradition". (The tradition, if any, is more along the lines I have suggested—that of the writer-commentator in English, from Pringle through Plaatje to Bosman.)

The tradition of the suppression of civil liberties is, however, under way: the Group Areas and Immorality Acts are about to appear. Dr. Verwoerd, Minister of Native Affairs, abolishes the Natives Representative Council and puts the Bantu Authorities Bill through parliament, giving the term apartheid a flavour of its own. The cost of living, as it is in the habit of doing, rises. And R. K. (i.e. Jack) Cope had just written in regard to the prospects for English South African prose that "a moral or social purpose does not make literature, and it is a commonplace that the conscious aims of an author have sometimes been in contradiction to his creative achievement. The touchstone remains the truthfulness of spirit and material and the art of presentation. And these come only with immeasurable pains, devotion and honesty" ["The Prospects for South African English Prose," *Trek,* (March 1950)].

Bosman's honesty was there all right and so was his moral and social purpose, although he devoted a lifetime to smearing his spoor. In a parable about art and delusion, 'Lost City' of 3 August 1951, he plays on the power of misleading myths to dump one out in the desert. The same story considers Farini's myth of 1886 of the Lost City of the Kalahari, which in July 1950 had attracted yet another scientific expedition to scrutinize the wasteland for lost glories. Bosman's reluctance to formulate a statement of his own terms of quest in fiction is caused by his belief that such moral purposes as Jack Cope has doubts about are likely to prove mirages anyway, unless they are totally integral to artistic purpose.

On 4 May 1951, Bosman published '**Monument to a Hero'**. On the same page is a photo of Henry Moore next to one of his reclining figures; the dry caption is: "The figure . . . has no orthodox head, and much of the torso is hollowed out." It was the week of the Public Holiday Bill that would establish Kruger Day as a national holiday. A former M.P. for Bethlehem had this to say on a preliminary Kruger Day celebration in Bloemfontein: "General de Wet endured heat and cold for three years for his people; President Steyn lost his health in the struggle, and President Kruger went into exile. Today we cannot even go half a mile to pay homage to them." And *The Forum* quotes a leader in *Die Transvaler:* "Because some of the leaders of the past worshipped strange gods, they do not answer the requirements and are therefore not numbered among the heroic figures . . . The closer the Afrikaner volk comes to its destination, namely, the establishment of a republic, the greater is the stature of the heroes who strove for that ideal." One should note that the Havenga Press's monthly magazine that ran from August 1946 to the successful return of Dr Malan's party at the polls, edited by A. M. van Schoor, was named *Fleur* in honour of General de Wet's horse.

'**Monument to a Hero'** becomes a sharper parable against this background. It turns out that the monument, which is unveiled amidst much patriotic fervour in the middle of Marico life, is there to commemorate a figure no one dares admit they have never heard of. "I mean, who was [this hero]? . . . Was he a leader or a statesman? Was he a missionary or a great hunter or a great fighting man? Or did he save a lot of people's lives, like Wolraad Woltemade? Or was he maybe just even a writer? What *was* he?" (*Jurie Steyn's Post Office.*) The character trying to discover the actuality behind the function of the shaft of undressed rock in the centre of town is, naturally, the young Vermaak. (The monument is erected, by the way, to the memory of one Hartman van Beek.)

Bosman's last story in the series, published in the obituary issue of *The Forum* (19 October 1951) is called '**Homecoming'**, and is not included in the two collections of Voorkamer stories. It contains a picture of his younger self, the well-known Vermaak, dead. "One could readily picture that same schoolmaster in paradise, casually sauntering up to the nearest angel standing in a row and complimenting him on his outstanding talents as a harpist."

Doris Lessing wrote this about Marais and Bosman [in her *A Small Personal Voice*]:

> Marais was solitary, but one of a scattered band of South Africans bred out of the veld, self-hewn, in advance of their time—and paying heavily for it. Schreiner was one, always fighting, always ill. Bosman another, the journalist and shortstory writer who wrote the saddest of all prison books, *Cold Stone Jug.* His account of how hundreds of prisoners howled like dogs or hyenas through their bars at the full moon—everyone, warders too, pretending afterwards that it had never happened, has the same ring to it as Marais's description of the baboons screaming out their helplessness through the night after leopards had carried off one of their troop.

Lessing's tribute is, on the face of it, powerful and moving. Yet even she falls into the old cliché of viewing Marais, Schreiner and Bosman as "self-hewn" veld products, as if once conscious of the true dimensions of man's eternal dilemma they were spontaneously moved to some kind of automatic writing. She does not allow them the security of belonging to a long continuum that has interrelated them and fostered them. The pain, however, has always been real, even though the literature written in reaction to it has been derived from specific moments of history. (pp. 79-94)

Stephen Gray, "Bosman's Marico Allegory: A Study in Topicality," in English Studies in Africa, *Vol. 20, No. 2, September, 1977, pp. 79-94.*

Don MacLennan   (essay date 1980)

[*In the following excerpt, MacLennan examines the narrative technique of Bosman's short fiction and Bosman's ideas on the relationship between life and art.*]

'The Music Maker' (*Mafeking Road*) is the story of a Marico farmer who devotes himself totally to art. This conventional romantic gesture takes the very unconventional form of the neglect of a Marico farm for the farmer's genius as a concertina player. Manie Kruger, the farmer, wants to 'get into' history. His romantic revolt certainly does involve vanity, a lust for fame which the narrow world of the Groot Marico cannot satisfy. But the lust for fame in a wider world does not detract from the devotion to his art in which it is rooted; Manie practises all day. The narration of the story offers us an ironic view of the rather forced, even contrived, alienation involved in such a romantic rebellion. The conventional course is for the Promethean musician to die of consumption in the arms of a princess. 'Only it was hard to get consumption in the Marico, because the climate was so healthy.'

The nature of that 'history' that Manie Kruger wants to get into is significant. Oom Schalk Lourens sees history as 'the stuff children learn in school', that is, more or less useless information about 'a man called Vasco da Gama, who visited the Cape'. This stuff is contrasted to Dirk Snyman's experience of the Cape when he visited there and 'a kafir came and sat right next to him in a tram'. There seems to be a considerable gap between the views of the community, as represented by Oom Schalk and by Dirk, and the views offered in school. It is left to the reader to make the ironical connection, to see that the voyage of Vasco da Gama is part of a continuum of history in which attitudes to race and to segregation play a major part. Prefigured in this introduction to Manie Kruger's story is also the point that public history is inclined to be impersonal and indifferent to private life. Thus too, the ignorance of the Marico Boers is often more apparent than real.

Before his rebellion Manie Kruger occupies a recognised and important place in his community. Far from being unappreciated, he is valued as much for his musical gifts as for his farming. But the community cannot hold him once he chooses to devote himself exclusively to those gifts. The physical arrangements for his recitals are a superb parody of the *mores* of serious European music, and the Marico's reaction is one of hilarious incomprehension. But the recitals are packed out, and while the community is alarmed at the change in one of its members, it loves the music: 'And we all knew that it was the most wonderful concertina music we had ever listened to.'

The story parodies the entire notion of the artist as a Promethean figure struggling against the shackles of a heartless society. This myth has been fostered in our time and in Bosman's by a whole set of films and books purporting to offer intimate views of the lives of the great artists. (Ironically, Bosman's own life story, which certainly had its share of the melodramatic, has been assimilated into the myth, and it is surely only a matter of time before we get a film version!) Manie Kruger's rebellion is made more difficult by the fact that he is not unappreciated. That reality of some sort intrudes itself harshly upon the artist's life is part of the standard myth; in this story such 'reality' is made to intrude with a compelling irony. Thus Manie cannot fulfil his dream in the Marico partly because consumption does not flourish there; the stages of his musical progress are measured in the piecemeal selling of his farm and equipment; and the precarious formality of his first recital is interrupted when Manie rises 'to kick the kafir'. That this latter is a brutal intrusion is known to Bosman, and is a measure of the reality of the Marico community. Bosman, as his poetry shows very clearly, is deeply romantic, and, if he can poke fun at the myth of the romantic revolt, he also partly believes it. The woman in Manie Kruger's life is not a princess, but Lettie Steyn of the Groot Marico, and she too conforms to a romantic pattern as the girl who believed in him but was left behind, waiting, as Oom Schalk says in his worldly wisdom, 'for the lover who would come to her no more'.

Through the different levels of Bosman's humour the meanings of his stories layer themselves, and the process of understanding is like a peeling of skins from an onion.

—Don MacLennan

It is the conclusion that affirms Bosman's romanticism sheathed in a skin of irony. When Oom Schalk sees Manie once more playing in a Pretoria bar, Manie is 'playing as well as ever'. It is not the Marico farmers who stand convicted here as philistines, it is ourselves in the wider world.

Through the different levels of Bosman's humour the meanings of his stories layer themselves, and the process of understanding is like a peeling of skins from an onion. In this story we start off with history and Dirk Snyman and Manie Kruger, and a set of contrasts is established: public history against personal, fame against deserving. In the end, Manie Kruger gets into one sort of history through Oom Schalk, by being included in Oom Schalk's gossipy reminiscences. Oom Schalk is a device by which Bosman can have his cake and eat it. Bosman uses a first person narration through Oom Schalk, and yet, by the simple device of placing in parenthesis the phrase 'Oom Schalk Lourens said', Bosman frames that first person narrative in a third person authorial narrative. By this means Bosman can use a narrator who is himself a peripheral character in the stories; who frequently understands more than the main characters, and who can comment on the community as a part of the community. To take each of these points in turn: there are very few stories in which Oom Schalk plays a leading role—**'Willem Prinsloo's Peach Brandy'**, **'In the Withaak's Shade'**, **'Drieka and the Moon'**, for example—all fairly early stories (from *Mafeking Road*). Where Oom Schalk is peripheral he is often seen to understand a bit more than the central characters, witness his realisation in **'The Music Maker'** that the lover Lettie Steyn was waiting for would never come. A more subtle example is **'Unto Dust'**, a late story in which Oom Schalk's comments are extensively and skilfully contrasted with those of the central character, Stoffel Oosthuizen. The third advantage Bosman derives from his employment of this narrative technique is that Oom Schalk can comment on his community from within. Indeed, for all his irony, most of the community's values are those of Oom Schalk; his ideas on the value of school learning, for example, or his love of concertina music, or his notions of the qualities that make a good farmer: 'He knew just how much peach brandy to pour out for the tax-collector to make sure that he would nod dreamily at everything Manie said.'

Oom Schalk's sharing of the main values of the community becomes particularly important where either the logic of the story contradicts those values or Oom Schalk explicitly doubts them; there are good examples in **'Unto Dust'** and **'Funeral Earth'** (*Unto Dust*). Because there is an ambivalence in the stories' points of view, we frequently cannot be certain how much Oom Schalk understands, for his style is sometimes deadpan. It is important to recognise that Oom Schalk is not Bosman, and that there are some moments when we can recognise an irony that is clearly beyond Oom Schalk. For example, the reference in **'The Music-Maker'** to 'a musician who knew more about music than Napoleon did' and Bosman's sly glances at *The Picture of Dorian Gray* in **'The Picture of Gysbert Jonker'** (*Unto Dust*).

Through Oom Schalk, Bosman is able to reach a tradition almost as old as literature itself—that of the simple yarn. In a class-conscious literature like that of England this tradition has been largely suppressed. In American literature, however, with its more democratic impulses, the yarn, having flourished as a great oral tradition, penetrated written literature too, through such minor writers as Artemus Ward and Josh Billings, to writers of greater stature like Mark Twain, Herman Melville, Bret Harte, Ambrose Bierce and O. Henry, all of whom were known to Bosman. And in the great cultural cauldron of the United States, the tradition was no doubt strengthened through contact with such literatures as Russian, Yiddish and Celtic.

Yarn-spinning is a frontier activity, and a Bushveld tradition which persists down to this day. Not the least of the features which appealed to Bosman is its firm reliance on the unvarnished horse-sense of the teller. The audience is critical, and demands a very direct truth of character and situation of the teller. The features of a typical yarn are those characteristic of Bosman: a skilful use of suspense and an intimate sense of locality and gossip, so that much of the material seems very ordinary; but then this ordinariness is leavened by a love for the supernatural. And thus the humour, which is a necessary ingredient, can operate on a variety of different levels.

A typical Bosman story lies firmly within this tradition, though the framing device of Oom Schalk allows a complex irony of technique to lodge beneath a deceptive simplicity of narrative. Bosman's stories typically contain three elements. First there is a preface, often a web of generalisations about such things as history, story-telling, death, prophecy, school, the nature of other races. This preface is followed by the tale itself, which may be more or less obviously linked to the preface, and which may well be garnished with further sententious digressions of philosophical, theological or anthropological import. The third element is a terminal twist, which either defines the meanings of the tale, like the vision of Manie Kruger in the bar, (but see also the endings of **'Mafeking Road'**, **'Seed Time and Harvest'**, **'Makapan's Caves'**, **'The Affair at Ysterspruit'**), or else the twist surprises and sets up a new set of reverberations and dimensions of meaning (see **'Funeral Earth'** and **'The Prophet'**).

Bosman's use of the oral tradition, with much of his material clearly lifted from genuine folk literature, leaves us sometimes with an odd sense of conflation of life and art. The effect is reinforced by a reading of his essays in *A Cask of Jerepigo* and his brilliant account of his spell in prison, *Cold Stone Jug.* For Bosman, though sceptical, was a romantic for whom life was seen to imitate art. Art, after all, is ideally a living part of the community, as **'The Music Maker'** argues. There is in the Marico none of the 'mystification' of art upon which, *inter alia,* the Ph.D. industry in literature, music and fine art rests. Thus concertina playing, enamelled tobacco advertisements, voorkamer stories, ghost yarns and even prophecy all qualify as art.

In a well-known statement about technique (the opening of **'Mafeking Road'**), Bosman writes:

> When people ask me—as they often do, how it is that I can tell the best stories of anybody in the Transvaal (Oom Schalk Lourens said, modestly), then I explain to them that I just learn through observing the way that the world has with men and women. When I say this they nod their heads wisely, and say that they understand, and I nod my head wisely also, and that seems to satisfy them. But the thing I say to them is a lie, of course.
>
> For it is not the story that counts. What matters is the way you tell it. The important thing is to know just at what moment you must knock out your pipe on your veldskoen, and at what stage of the story you must start talking about the School Committee at Drogevlei. Another necessary thing is to know what part of the story to leave out.

And you can never learn these things.

Look at Floris, the last of the Van Barnevelts. There is no doubt that he had a good story, and he should have been able to get people to listen to it. And yet nobody took any notice of him or of the things he had to say. Just because he couldn't tell the story properly.

Accordingly, it made me sad whenever I listened to him talk. For I could tell just where he went wrong. He never knew the moment at which to knock the ash out of his pipe. He always mentioned his opinion of the Drogevlei School Committee in the wrong place. And, what was still worse, he didn't know what part of the story to leave out.

If Oom Schalk is serious—is he?—Bosman is being slyly disingenuous, for in the prefacing of this story and in its framing is a great deal of detailed craftsmanship and some fine observation. This story is not basically about the relationship of art to life, the point of the preface is rather to set up a sounding board on which the twist of the story's ending may reverberate.

The tale itself begins with the pathos of Floris van Barnevelt, the last of his line. It moves through the hopeful comedy of the setting forth to war, to the despairing comedy of the flight from Mafeking. And in the story of the flight we have, perfectly timed, a digression; the Englishman's account of the rejoicings in England at the relief of Mafeking. The brief digression throws into sharp relief the Boers' plight: 'broken columns blundering through the dark'. It establishes the depth of Oom Schalk's despair, and his knowledge, even then, that his cause was lost: 'The stars looked down on scenes that told sombrely of a nation's ruin; they looked on the muzzles of the Mausers that had failed the Transvaal for the first time.'

This in turn illuminates the stubborn character of the Boers' continued resistance, and thus establishes sympathy for the attitude of Stephanus van Barnevelt, who wished to surrender. There is also a nicely-observed piece of characterisation in the insecurity of the authority of the defeated veld-kornet, a clear observation of 'the way the world has with men and women'.

But then the tale twists to its conclusion, and the agonies of military defeat, about which Oom Schalk had still been able to joke, turn into the personal tragedy of the van Barnevelts. The point of the preface becomes clear as Floris van Barnevelt, after a long conversation with the schoolmaster, restores his dying family tree to his voorkamer wall with the words 'Obiit Mafeking' following the name of his son. And Floris begins to tell his story, a good story, in which 'he always insisted on telling that part of the story that he should have left out'. The framing is highly functional here, because by telling us about the defective narrative technique of Floris van Barnevelt, Oom Schalk does both tell the forbidden part of the story and not tell it. But behind Oom Schalk, Bosman tells it too, for the part Floris should have left out was the terrible point, and by telling us there was a point too terrible to tell, together with the logic of character, Bosman has told the whole story with a grim restraint. This conclusion con-

tains a further point about the sort of closed community in which everyone knows one another's secrets. Such a community creates self-protecting procedures for coping with the unthinkable. There is a further example in 'Unto Dust' where the members of the Boer burial party refuse to say what all are thinking. The schoolmaster in 'Mafeking Road' knew what he was doing in writing simply 'Obiit Mafeking' after Stephanus's name. The Marico farmers, who could be brutally truthful about hands-upping to the English, recognised some limits for the sake of sanity.

Two other stories in which art and life conflate are 'Ox Wagons on Trek' (*Mafeking Road*)and 'The Picture of Gysbert Jonker'. In the former, Bosman tells a story in which life is willed to imitate art. Minnie Brand, having seen the film about the young scapegrace whose sweetheart remains faithful even when he is tried and executed, has at the end of the story a 'slow look': 'It was a kind of satisfaction, almost, at the thought that all the things that came to the girl she saw in the picture had now come to her, too.'

It is fascinating how Bosman can take the suggestion of a film cliché to explore, yet again, romantic protest: the urge to defy the community. Surely Minnie Brand's look of satisfaction comes from having swum in deeper waters than usual.

But 'The Picture of Gysbert Jonker' is a much better, more subtle story. Here life appears to imitate art, but Bosman has, in fact, reversed the formula and art is made to follow the depredations of time. The self-conscious attempt, another romantic aspiration, of Gysbert Jonker to imitate art fails; or perhaps succeeds in ways beyond his imagining. Bosman starts again by taking Oom Schalk to the cinema, throwing in a sly joke outside Oom Schalk's frame of reference, about his use of an idea of Oscar Wilde. Bosman knew well that 'new ideas for my stories' may very well generate out of some very old ideas. The preface is about change and the fate of all new ideas—as is the story. Gysbert Jonker's romantic attempt to imitate art is also a vain attempt to arrest time and to acquire the ominous quietness of Keats's 'Ode on a Grecian Urn', but he is teased quite out of thought! Gysbert's vanity, so harmless-seeming at first, is eventually seen by the community as a desecration of the Sabbath, 'going about dressed as a tobacco advertisement on Sundays'. Ultimately it is a desecration and destruction of self, so that even when the vanity is finally thrust away by force of ironic circumstance, it has done its damage. In a marvellous *volte face* Bosman contrives the deterioration through rust and soiling of the enamelled portrait which Gysbert had attempted to imitate. Even the portrait's eyes seem at last to grow wistful like Gysbert's.

In Bosman's exploration of the themes of life and art the rich and charming 'Veld Maiden' (*Mafeking Road*) has an important position. He wrote a few better stories, like 'Funeral Earth' (*Unto Dust*), 'Mafeking Road', 'The Rooinek' (*Mafeking Road*) and 'The Prophet', and he found one or two symbols as powerful as the *femme fatale* of 'Veld Maiden', (for example the pot of earth in 'Funeral Earth'), but in 'Veld Maiden' we have a piece of quintessential Bosman that also offers us a powerful image out of the universal subconscious, rich in mythopoeic quality.

Here again we have a tension between Oom Schalk Lourens the earthy realist, the anti-romantic, and Bosman, the romantic poet of **The Blue Princess.** The story opens:

> I know what it is—Oom Schalk Lourens said—when you talk that way about the veld. I have known people who sit like you do and dream about the veld and talk strange things, and start believing in what they call the soul of the veld, until in the end the veld means a different thing to them from what it does to me. I only know that the veld can be used for growing mealies on, and it isn't very good for that, either.

This is necessarily an anti-romantic view, for the peasant whose livelihood depends on the veld cannot afford illusions about it. The passionate artist of the story, John de Swardt, ruined, in Oom Schalk's view, by 'the school in Johannesburg where they taught him all that nonsense about art', makes his affirmation: 'I want only the veld. Its loneliness. Its mystery.'

Oom Schalk complains that de Swardt picks only the useless bits of the farm to paint: 'a krantz and a few stones and some clumps of khaki-bos'. Yet Oom Schalk's scepticism is itself ambivalent, self-doubting, as if his narrative voice, so characteristically spare of imagery, were being perpetually restrained. For it is Oom Schalk who says of the veld,

> And it is not good to think too much about it. For then it can lead you in strange ways, and sometimes—sometimes when the veld has led you very far—there comes into your eyes a look that God did not put there.

This look Oom Schalk subsequently recognises in John de Swardt, and for all his sternness, for the sake of the look Oom Schalk grants de Swardt's ardent request for one more night on Oom Schalk's farm. Both men here understand the other's point of view. Oom Schalk's scepticism hides the wounds of experience. We can see both of these characters as self-dramatisations, projections of complementary facets of Bosman's personality.

John de Swardt has a vision of a beautiful Veld Maiden, a muse of tremendous seductive power. She is an African manifestation of La Belle Dame Sans Merci, or of the mermaid who drowns the sailors she takes with her to her watery bower. It is a romantic vision at odds with the values of society, as Oom Schalk points out when de Swardt shows him a painting: 'You mustn't let anybody here see this Veld Maiden unless you paint a few more clothes on her.'

Oom Schalk does not actually deny the strength or validity of the vision; he speaks perhaps from the perception that

> human kind
> cannot bear very much reality.
> [T. S. Eliot, "Burnt Norton,"
> in his *Four Quartets*]

Oom Schalk is well aware that the seductive power of the vision is also potentially destructive. He recognises in John de Swardt's romantic gesture a pride that we can recognise as that of Prometheus: ' . . . there comes into your eyes a look that God did not put there.' And Oom Schalk treats de Swardt with an affectionate tolerance, observing that he was 'only very young and innocent'.

The incarnation of de Swardt's vision is Sannie Welman, who is seduced by the vision, indeed seduced *into* the vision, so that de Swardt eventually has 'no need for' the picture. Even so, he begs Oom Schalk for that one last night in the tent on the farm before he and his Veld Maiden flee from the Marico community's orthodox anger. Again life and art are conflated.

For Bosman, the artistic vision is an experience of transcendent truth and beauty. But he who embraces that vision cannot stand outside life; art is not a paradisal garden into which the aesthete retreats. The vision comes out of life, and in turn sustains life. An art that devotes itself to escape from reality is ultimately of no value as art. The Welsh poet, R. S. Thomas, himself a backwoodsman by choice, like Bosman, has expressed the dilemma very beautifully [in "Now," in his *Laboratories of the Spirit*]:

> . . . Is it
> sufficient for us
> that we, like that minority
> of our fellows in the hurrying
> centuries, turning aside
> re-enter the garden? What
> is the serenity of art
> worth without the angels
> at the hot gates, whose sword
> is time and our uneasy conscience?

That Bosman was armed with the sword of time and our uneasy conscience, that he could not neglect the most insistent conflicts of life in South Africa, he magnificently demonstrated in the last three stories we propose to examine: **'The Rooinek'**, a very early masterpiece first published in 1931; **'The Prophet'**, first published in 1945; and **'Funeral Earth'** a beautiful late story published in 1950.

'Mafeking Road' is concerned with the great bitterness of Boer resistance to British Imperialism, and the effects of that bitterness in superseding even the most powerful of family ties. **'The Rooinek'** is also concerned with that bitterness, but this time there is a partial reconciliation even with the enemy.

What is frightening is that the outcome is not less tragic. The preface to this story makes two points. First, that 'Rooineks are queer'. Oom Schalk relates a story of curious gallantry, by both sides in the war, and yet again he makes a bluff, anti-romantic disclaimer to his nephew's gallantry: 'If he's a brave man and he's fighting on the wrong side, that's all the more reason to shoot him.'

But the occasional gallantry of war is powerfully contrasted against the second point of the preface, that war is very bitter; the forgiveness of God is more reliable than the forgiveness of man: 'Perhaps Hannes was right in saying that the Lord didn't mind about a little foolishness like dum-

dum bullets. But the mistake he made was in forgetting that the English did mind.'

More bitter still was the aftermath to the British policy of scorched earth and concentration camps. Oom Schalk says of his wife: 'and when I saw her again and noticed the way she had changed, I knew that I, who had been through all the fighting, had not seen the Boer War.'

The tale that follows begins with the Rooinek's arrival in the Marico, and the development of a friendship between him and Koos Steyn. Despite Koos's original misgivings about Englishmen, when Webber offers his hand, Koos takes it. The others do not, though Oom Schalk maintains an ambivalent impartiality, being swayed alternately by the arguments of Gerhardus Grobbelaar recalling the concentration camps and of Koos Steyn advocating conciliation. There is a curious echo in Koos Steyn's behaviour of the conduct of Oom Schalk's Neef Hannes who also responded very directly to an Englishman's human gesture.

Elsewhere Bosman shows us Marico farmers enjoying a sort of *luilekkerlewe,* spending all day lying on their backs under a withaak looking for cattle or countering ploughing sickness by sitting quietly on the stoep 'with one's legs raised slightly' drinking coffee. Here he shows us the other side of the same coin. Farming is here a matter of bitter experience—the phrase is no cliché as no book-learning can prepare one, and no foresight seems able to avert the disastrous effects of drought and disease. The Boers in their bitterness blame the English even for natural disasters, and decide to trek away from a land blighted by the shadow of the Englishman's flag.

Webber, the Rooinek, decides to accompany them simply out of loyalty to his friends the Steyns. The trek into the Kalahari is a disaster, and the narrative offers Oom Schalk the opportunity for a characteristic digression on leadership, one of his favourite topics. The digression has a delicate relevance however, for the austere patriarchal leadership of Gerhardus Grobbelaar is contrasted with the simple brotherhood which binds Webber to the Steyns. And when the party decides to retreat under the discredited leadership of Grobbelaar, Webber's loyalty holds to the Steyns as Koos Steyn makes his mad and fatal decision to go on. The conclusion is inevitable, and the twist at the end does not redefine any meanings, it merely reaffirms the point of departure, 'Rooineks are queer'. For though the subsequent search party does not find the Steyns' baby, they find the adults. 'When we lifted Webber's body, we found still clasped in his dead and rigid arms, a few old rags and a child's clothes.' Reconciliation is often tragic in Bosman.

'The Prophet' is a story about direct confrontation man to man, between a Boer and an African. It is a trial of strength between two seers, and significantly, it is the passive, earth-bound strength that wins, what Roy Campbell called [in "The Serf," in his *Collected Poems of Roy Campbell*]

> The timeless, surly patience of the serf
> That moves the nearest to the naked earth,
> And ploughs down palaces and thrones and towers.

The character Mosiko, the Witch-Doctor, is related in his unwavering and impenetrable consciousness of power to the farm-labourer Joseph in Dan Jacobson's *A Dance in the Sun.*

> Mosiko had hardly any clothes on. He sat up against a bush with his back bent and his head forward near his knees. He had many wrinkles. Hundreds of them. He looked to be the oldest man in the world. And yet there was a kind of strength about the curve of his back and I knew the meaning of it. It seemed to me that with his back curved in that way, and the sun shining on him and his head bent forward, Mosiko could be much greater and do more things just by sitting down than other men could do by working hard and using cunning. I felt that Mosiko could sit down and do nothing and yet be more powerful than the Commander-General.
>
> He seemed to have nothing but what the sun and the sand and the grass had given him, and yet that was more than what all the men in the world could give him.
>
> I was glad that I was there that day; at the meeting of the wizards.

Bosman is here labouring his point a little. Much more effective is the observation a little later when Stephanus Erasmus turns his terrible stare on Mosiko who turns away because ' . . . he didn't think that Stephanus was a man of enough importance for him to want to stare out of countenance.'

In the great bulk of South African literature in English, the African appears as a decorative figure in a landscape. We have observed how Manie Kruger interrupted his concertina recitals to 'kick the kafir' *en passant*. Here, on the other hand, the morality and effectiveness of 'kafir-kicking' comes under critical scrutiny. By all the logic of Bosman's narrative techniques, Mosiko is here seen through the eyes of the Marico Boers; it is an externalised portrait, with which Bosman had difficulty. But Mosiko is no longer just a figure in the landscape. In the course of the story he acquires a human stature and passes from a 'cheeky kafir' to the titled 'Witch-Doctor Mosiko' introduced with such formality by a puzzled Oom Schalk. This is a gradual process, beginning with Mosiko's great reputation as a diviner reaching the whites:

> . . . white people also started taking him presents. And they asked him questions about what was going to happen.

Then, when Stephanus Erasmus feels his own reputation threatened by Mosiko and marches boastfully to a showdown, Oom Schalk observes

> . . . he tried to pretend that we were determined to have Mosiko shown up. And this was not the truth. It was only Erasmus's quarrel. It was not our affair at all.

This is a very remarkable disclaimer of partiality, not just by Oom Schalk, but by the whole of his community, and it leads through to his statement that

I was glad that I was there that day; at the meeting of the wizards.

Oom Schalk then introduces Erasmus and Mosiko to one another on equal terms and the confrontation takes place, man to man. Erasmus takes the attitude of a white man whose dignity has been affronted by the black man's challenge; Mosiko in his strength takes his stand on his expertise as a seer.

The title of the story, **'The Prophet'**, is in the singular, for a real prophet, Oom Schalk says, can never lose his power as Stephanus Erasmus loses his. Thus, under pressure of dramatic events, Boer and African momentarily recognise one another's humanity. The point is made elsewhere in Bosman's work that Boer peasants and African peasants live off the same earth and inhabit the same moral world. In **'The Missionary'** (*Bosman at His Best*) we are shown the Reverend Keet's fascination with and aversion to 'Darkest Africa'. The expressive power of African craftwork he recognises as against the insipid and irrelevant prescriptions of the Education Department that children be taught to make paper serviettes with green tassels. And in the Reverend Keet's perceptions of evil threatening him, instinct and suspicion and superstition merge and become indistinguishable. Oom Schalk is sceptical, for he knows the Reverend Keet had been sick before he arrived in the Marico, but he discovers also the lock of the Reverend Keet's hair glued to his carved effigy and the nails that Elsiba Keet drove into the carved figure's heart.

The story in which these themes converge most powerfully is the magnificent **'Funeral Earth'**. The story takes off from some conventional ideas and attitudes, a sense of cruel and arrogant mission with what turns out to be, in the context of this story, a touch of self-deprecating irony:

> We had a difficult task, that time (Oom Schalk Lourens said), teaching Sijefu's tribe of Mtosas to become civilised. But they did not show any appreciation. Even after we had set fire to their huts in a long row round the slopes of Abjaterskop, so that you could see the smoke almost as far as Nietverdiend, the Mtosas remained just about as unenlightened as ever.

The story develops in a characterisation of young Fanie Louw, whose inexperience shows in the way he attacks the face-saving formulas of the commandos. The veld-kornets come to the conclusion that their enemy is hiding in the open turf lands where there are no trees and no long grass; Fanie Louw suggests that maybe they are hiding in the Volksraad itself: he is the little boy commenting on the emperor's nakedness.

The appearance of the Mtosas is a beautiful piece of writing:

> For we suddenly did see Mtosas. We saw them from a long way off. They came out of the bush and marched right out into the open. They made no attempt to hide. We saw in amazement that they were coming straight in our direction, advancing in single file. And we observed, even from that distance, that they were unarmed. Instead of assegaais and shields they carried burdens on their heads. And almost in that same

moment we realised, from the heavy look of those burdens, that the carriers must be women.

> For that reason we took our guns in our hands and stood waiting. Since it was women, we were naturally prepared for the lowest form of treachery.

> As the column drew nearer we saw that at the head of it was Ndambe, an old native whom we knew well. For years he had been Sijefu's chief counsellor. Ndambe held up his hand. The line of women halted. Ndambe spoke. He declared that we white men were kings among kings and elephants among elephants. He also said that we were ringhals snakes more poisonous and generally disgusting than any ringhals snake in the country.

> We knew, of course, that Ndambe was only paying us compliments in his ignorant Mtosa fashion.

Here the face-saving is institutionalised and ritualised as a political act so that both sides to the negotiations can conduct themselves in dignity. Of the gifts borne by the Mtosas the Boers prize most of all the 'witch-doctor medicines that protected you against goël spirits at night and the evil eye'. The Mtosas themselves prize most the pot of black earth, for it is time to sow crops and they are offering peace to the Boers. After the crops are sown they will continue the fight.

War is seen here as a game played periodically for exercise or boredom. The Boers see the war as an exercise to keep them in practice for the real enemy—the English. And the narrative then changes very suddenly and effectively from Jurie Bekker's recognition of his own brand-mark on the haunch of beef given them by the Mtosas to the war in earnest, the Second Anglo-Boer War. Fanie Louw has now grown up a bit, and his commando have grown very fond of him. As ever, Bosman counterpoints a story of bitterness and suffering against his humour, sometimes very suddenly:

> While we had got used to his jokes, and we knew there was no harm in them, we would have preferred it that he should stop making them.

> He did stop, and for ever, in a skirmish near a blockhouse. We buried him in the shade of a thorn tree.

The twist to this story is a revelation inwards, a discovery, that is, by the characters of themselves. As Commandant Joubert picks up a handful of earth to throw into the grave, he kneads it. 'We patterned after him', says Oom Schalk, choosing his verb with care, for it is in an intricate ceremony, a ritual of both life and death, that, for a moment, these Boers discover themselves. They remember it is the time for sowing, and they recognise the wisdom of the Mtosas: 'They who were also farmers'. (pp. 83-94)

Don MacLennan, "Herman Charles Bosman: Short Stories," in Perspectives on South African Fiction *by Sarah Christie, Geoffrey Hutchings and Don MacLennan, A. D. Donker, Publisher, 1980, pp. 83-95.*

Rose Moss   (essay date 1981)

[*Moss is a South African–born American writer, educator, and critic. In the following review, she comments favorably on* Jacaranda in the Night.]

Bosman's reputation rests largely on his short stories. Their wry, penetrating, compassionate humor flows from the characters "like blood from a wound." [*Jacaranda in the Night*], Bosman's first novel . . . , sounds a more spare and somber note.

Hannah Theron, a schoolteacher who leaves a dead love affair in Pretoria, comes to Kalwyn, a small town in the Northern Transvaal. She lacks "those intuitions that you develop through living in a dorp, so that . . . you pattern your life in accordance with what the community demands of you." Attracted by a masculine, graceful, confident building contractor, Hannah slides into a cohabitation that scandalizes the community. Bert Parsons, her "lover only in the most intricately technical sense of the term," abuses her with drunken lust and sadism. Like other men, he is blind to the loyalty that binds her to him and to the generosity that forbids her to deny him anything. Like others, he calls her a whore, and by the time he tires of her she feels a whore. He has smashed her heart "as black women use a block of wood for grinding dried mielies into very fine pieces in the mortar."

Hannah heals slowly. She recovers new integrity and loves with self-respect, but the story's promise of hope is tempered. Paradoxically, growth comes through episodes that include rape, manslaughter and a term in prison. Readers will recognize material that echoes Bosman's autobiographical account of the years he served time on a murder charge, but this novel avoids the convict jocularity of *Cold Stone Jug.* At times Bosman's analyses of the hidden surges and countercurrents of sexual attraction and animus, infatuation and sadism, inhibition and violence that move his characters resemble Lawrence. His plainspoken vision of Afrikaans village life and of manhood and womanhood recovered slowly and through adversity flows from his own life and in his own voice "like blood from a wound." (pp. 166-67)

Rose Moss, in a review of "Jacaranda in the Night," in World Literature Today, *Vol. 55, No. 1, Winter, 1981, pp. 166-67.*

A. M. Potter   (essay date 1981)

[*In the following excerpt, Potter investigates the theme of racial tension in Bosman's novel* Willemsdorp.]

On the final page of [H. C. Bosman's novel] *Willemsdorp,* Charlie Hendricks, fleeing to Johannesburg to escape a murder charge, points to the significance of Willemsdorp, the small Northern Transvaal town where most of the action of the book takes place:

> It suddenly struck him that, in the city of Johannesburg, that he had known all his life—the city of Johannesburg to which he was now returning along a road that went due south—in the city of Johannesburg life was a false thing that wore a double face. The backveld town of Willemsdorp was a place where Life was still spelt with an upper case L. It was Life with the mask off. It was Life lived with an intensity that city-dwellers had forgotten generations back.

Earlier, in the opening passages of the book, Bosman spends two-and-a-half pages placing Willemsdorp very carefully within a context that is nothing less than the entire history of South Africa. From these two passages it becomes clear that the action that takes place in Willemsdorp is designed by the author to be an extended metaphor for the South African experience, lived with an intensity that brings out strongly the hopes and fears, pressures and tensions that go to make up that experience.

The structure of society in Willemsdorp confirms this view, being a microcosm of South African society. The basic racial groups are present in the form of whites, coloureds, and blacks; the white group not only exhibits a typical cross-section of professions and social levels, but is also split along the classic South African lines of the En-

---

An excerpt from *Cold Stone Jug*

Disguise it how one will, the fact is that the Swartklei Great Prison is dominated, spiritually as well as architecturally, by the gallows chamber, whose doors rise up, massive and forbidding, at the end of the main wing in the building—the penal corridors.

The hangings are the worst part of life inside the prison. When a man has been condemned to death on the Rand or in any other Transvaal centre he is brought over to the Swartklei Great Prison, where he is lodged in the condemned cell adjacent to the gallows until such time as he is either reprieved or hanged. The period of waiting in that cell next to the gallows varies from about five weeks to two months. Then the case is settled one way or the other. Either the sheriff arrives with a printed document bearing the title "Greetings" in heavy black scroll and he notifies the condemned man that his execution has been set down for the morning after the next, or the Governor of the prison walks in, accompanied by the chief warder, and he informs the prisoner that the Governor-General has decided to commute his sentence to one of imprisonment, the term varying usually from ten years to life.

But during all this time the shadow of this hanging lies like a pall over the inmates of the prison, warders as well as convicts. During most of the months of the year the condemned cells are empty. There is nobody waiting up there at the end of the penal section with the death sentence suspended over him. But when the condemned cells are occupied, things in the prison are rotten all round. There is something inside the most hardened warder or anti-social convict that makes him shudder at the thought of death, of violent death, of the gruesome ceremony of doing a man to death above a dark hole, at a set time, with legal formality that does not extend beyond handcuffs and leg-irons and a sack drawn over the condemned man's head and a piece of coarse rope knotted behind his ear.

Herman Charles Bosman, in his Cold Stone Jug, *Human and Rousseau, 1969.*

glish and Afrikaans-speaking-cultural and political groupings.

Taken in isolation, some of the concerns of the book may be seen as universal rather than particularly South African: the eternal tragedy of the older man with the young wife who gives in to the passions of the flesh; the misfit who turns to some sort of narcotic as compensation for his social and personal failings; the irresponsible young man who wants all the fun of women, but none of the responsibilities; the woman with the unwanted pregnancy, and so on. However, these are interwoven with and subordinated to aspects of the book which can clearly be seen as uniquely South African. The story of the older man with the young wife, for example, is integrated into the sordid tale of sex-across-the-colour-line which constitutes the major concern of the book. This is achieved by the fact that the population of Willemsdorp immediately presumes that Erasmus commits suicide because he was the one who killed Marjorie, the coloured prostitute, so illustrating the South African obsession with racialism. Lena Cordier's story, too, is drawn into the racial arena (even though superficially it seems like a simple tale of a woman being made pregnant and getting an abortion in the big city) by the fact that her situation is played off against the discussions below her flat window of the black flatboy and watchman. The fact that it is an Indian doctor who performs the operation, and later attempts to establish a more intimate relationship with her, serves the same purpose. The introduction of race as an issue in every aspect of the highly complex plot, suggests that it is with the implications of the racial make-up of South African society, in particular the causes and effects of racial tension and interaction, that Bosman is primarily concerned in this book.

Sergeant Brits with his campaign to enforce the Immorality Act to the letter, is the ideal catalyst, ensuring full awareness of the racial issues provoked by the multi-racial nature of the country. His campaign brings out the problems of racial interaction at their most basic, intense, and problematic level. Equally, Charlie Hendricks, as a character, is carefully designed by Bosman to be particularly suited to bear the burden of the tensions and contradictions aroused by Sergeant Brits's campaign. He is an outsider, new to Willemsdorp life, having to confront it in all its intensity, without any of the habits and ready-made defences that a long-time inhabitant has developed to protect himself. His job as editor of a local newspaper enforces his active concern in the affairs of the town. At the same time he is made aware of the pressures of the cultural split in South African society, since he is an Afrikaner working for an English newspaper that professes Union Party politics. This split is not simply political, but involves different stances on basic issues, primarily the race issue.

Charlie Hendricks's involvement with the coloured prostitute, Marjorie, forces upon him the most vital head-on confrontation in the book. This confrontation with the basic racial attitudes and prejudices of South Africa is intensified by the fact that it is acted out in Willemsdorp, a place which by its nature allows no avoidance of moral issues whatsoever. This is conveyed by Lena Cordier's experience in Johannesburg, but may be applied to the book as a whole:

> But she was surprised to find that no school child in the lower standards pointed its finger at her and lisped, 'Whore'. It seemed that the world was like that—the world outside of Willemsdorp. All that the world outside of Willemsdorp seemed to be concerned about was that you should do your work all right. As long as you did your work all right, it seemed that the world—outside of Willemsdorp—didn't care what you did in your spare time. At least, no eleven-year-old child got up out of its seat and denounced Lena Cordier, proclaiming, 'Bitch! Harlot!'

The consequences of Charlie Hendricks's affair with Marjorie are extreme, and their implications are explored by Bosman to suggest that it is not merely the rights and wrongs of a controversial statute that are at issue, but a problem that lies at the very heart of the white man's presence in Africa.

Much of the book is, of course, concerned with questioning the moral issues raised by the Immorality Act, and this is functional to Bosman's ultimate purpose of examining the full ramifications of the existence of such a law. A major source of criticism of the law is the hypocrisy with which many of the white characters react to its provisions. A prime example is the newly-elected Provincial Councillor, Dap van Zyl. He is a legislative representative of a party whose ideology is based on the 'principle' of the separation of the races, yet he falls victim to the charms of Marjorie, and ruins his career. Robert E. Constable, van Zyl's opponent in the by-election, completes the picture of hypocrisy presented by both parties. Bosman here symbolically embraces the whole of South Africa in these two men.

In response to the Volksparty heckler's use of the derogatory term 'niggers', Constable finds himself instinctively taking up the term in his reply, despite the fact that *his* party platform ostensibly supports black advancement of a kind:

> 'Are youse Union Party going to give niggers the vote?' he asked.
> 'Only to civilised nigg-, that is to say, civilised Natives,' Robert E. Constable replied.
> The young men in the back row laughed derisively.
> 'There isn't no such thing,' Faded Blazer shouted.

Faded Blazer's response is significant not only because it defines the crudity of the average racial attitude of the white South African, but because it also indicates that the reason for the whites' rejection of non-whites is that they do not consider them civilised. The full significance of this will be brought out later.

Another source of criticism is the emphasis given to the terrible results of the Immorality Act for society. A prosecution under the Act leads invariably to disgrace for the white accused, even if he is acquitted, which is in itself a perversion of justice:

> I feel like arresting him just to teach him a lesson

not to be so low as to sleep with a kafir woman in a crafty way that we can't catch him at it. Because it will ruin him, all right. Even if he gets acquitted, it'll ruin him just as much as a conviction. Just to be mixed up in such a kind of a case will finish him off, all right. Even if, as I have said, he gets away with it.

Equally, the Act lays those who break it open to blackmail, and encourages others to use its perverted power to indulge in blackmail. Marjorie and Jossias make their living in this way. In other words, the Act simply encourages more crime. Ultimately it leads directly to murder, the final statement of the destructive effects it has on society.

More gently, Bosman presents a series of ironies which suggests that despite cultural differences and varying levels of sophistication, blacks and whites are almost identical in their basic attitudes and needs, and that a law which attempts to separate them artificially is a foolish one. A case in point is the placing of Lena Cordier and Marjorie, the white woman and the coloured prostitute, in almost identical situations—both are pregnant as the result of socially unacceptable sex. Similarly, the comment by Pieta, the flat-boy, that the dagga he is planning to get Mhlopi, the watchman, is 'of a sort that makes one forget great trouble—that makes one forget all trouble' is ironically juxtaposed with the predicament of Lena Cordier, who is up to her eyes in trouble. The following passage illustrates the point:

> Meanwhile Lena Cordier, awakened from sleep by a nightmare, remained standing at the window, drinking in the night, calmed by the sound of voices uttering words in a language she did not understand.
>
> 'It gives one dreams, my son,' the Zulu, Mhlopi, said then.
>
> 'Truly the *msangu* brings one great dreams. It is not for nothing that we say of it in Zululand that it brings one blue dreams. Is it not indeed good stuff, this *msangu*?'
>
> 'But it brings another kind of dream, too, my father,' Pieta responded, a touch of acerbity in his voice—for Mhlopi really was hanging on to the cigarette that time, 'especially if one smokes too much of it. Too much frightening dreams, my father.'

Both blacks and whites have bad dreams—nightmares—whatever the cause, while the fact that Lena feels comforted by the two voices under her window suggests that mankind can be bound together in bonds of sympathy transcending artificial barriers of colour. The evocation in the paragraph immediately preceding the passage quoted above of the two blacks having characteristics identical to any white man underlines the same point. In case we miss the inferences, Charlie Hendricks's feeling that in his relationship with Marjorie he 'could not detect that she was essentially different from a white girl that might have come to lie on the divan in his arms' makes the point explicit.

The most effective criticism of the Immorality Act, however, is the simple fact that it is contravened so frequently.

It has undeniable Canute-like qualities, standing foolishly as it does in front of the powerful tide of the most basic and urgent drive in human nature, and futilely urging it to stop its course.

So why does it still exist, if it seems in every conceivable way a statutory disaster? In answering this question we are approaching the heart of the problem Bosman is dealing with. The reason for its continuing existence, despite everything that cries out for its abolition, is indicated in a key passage, when Charlie Hendricks contemplates his inner state after his second sexual encounter with Marjorie:

> Charlie Hendricks remembered the contempt he had felt for his editorial predecessor, Esselen, when the suspicion had first entered his mind that Esselen had had illicit intercourse with Marjorie. There was a lot of hypocrisy about it, and all that, Charlie Hendricks realised. But all the same it was a real feeling. It was something you couldn't get away from. You just felt there was something low about a white man that went to bed with a woman that wasn't white.

Charlie Hendricks can see the hypocrisy of the white attitude to the Immorality Act with clear eyes—but he cannot deny, despite the clarity of his insight, the strength of the *feeling* within him that there is something basically low about a white man who sleeps with a black woman. The Act was created, stays on the statute books, and is enforced by people like Sergeant Brits, therefore, not because it is good in itself (Bosman has successfully shown that it has nothing intrinsically to recommend it whatsoever), but because it supports a basic attitude, a fundamental feeling within the law-making group—the white people—in South Africa.

The precise nature of this feeling can be identified. In the last four lines of the book, Charlie Hendricks, the man who has confronted the problems of the Immorality Act head-on, is not seen as running from the police, or from public opinion in Willemsdorp (he actually at one stage contemplates returning to Willemsdorp, despite everything); rather he is seen as running from himself:

> What was he running away from, anyway?
>
> But the moment he put the question, he knew the answer, too, of course. In the same way that he knew the answer right away when he had got the wind up, wandering into the bush above the cutting on the road to Kleinberg.
>
> But he knew the answer, this time, before he ran. Before he packed his suitcase. Before he sent Jones, the compositor, into the bank to cash his cheque for fifty pounds.
>
> All right, Charlie Hendricks knew that he was running away from himself.
>
> And it's when it's yourself you're running away from that you can never stop running.

Clearly, then, the murder, together with the accumulated guilt of his affair with Marjorie, has brought out an awareness of something within himself of which he is afraid. In the context of his function within the book as the main bearer of Bosman's concerns, this fear can be taken as the quintessential fear which all white men experience in South Africa.

The passage quoted above refers to the incident out in the middle of the bush between Willemsdorp and Kleinberg, when Charlie Hendricks first felt afraid, this time for no external reason, as events had not yet caught up with him. His fear is explained in the following terms:

> The name the wise old Boer applies to it is 'Ouma-bangheid'—fear of your grandmother—implying thereby that it is a terror not rooted in modernity, but that it is something going back pretty far. But if that same old Boer has taken to you, he will also try and put you right, winking as he delivers himself of his statement. Why you get frightened, he will tell you, is because in that narrow opening in the bush, cut off from all human companionship, you actually meet yourself. You encounter yourself face to face, the wise old Boer will say, and before God, is not that the most frightening and spine-chilling meeting that any man can have?

The use of the same explanation to account for both occasions of fear—that both are ultimately fear of himself—implies that what he felt in the bush and what he felt as a result of his affair with Marjorie are identical. The experience in the bush, therefore, lies at the heart of Bosman's examination of the South African experience.

The explanation for this fear is made explicit in a key passage:

> And suddenly Charlie Hendricks grew frightened. In the air he breathed there seemed to be the smell of blood. But what frightened him was not the veld's blood smell. It seemed like a very ancient fear, something he could not define. The leaves of the prickly pear seemed ancestral. The fragments of weathered cowdung were timeless. The anthill had always been there, and always it had been that same shade of grey. The weathered cowdung was more primeval than the Triassic rock that had been exposed by the cutting. About the anthill there was a vast antiquity that went beyond all geological reckonings. The prickly pear seemed alive in an awful, whilom sense, in that aeons ago it should have been extinct.

The bush awakens within Charlie Hendricks feelings which, like the prickly pear, should have been extinct 'aeons ago', primeval urges which he, as a civilised white man, should have shaken off forever. We are reminded of the comment Faded Blazer shouts at Robert E. Constable at the political meeting—the basic belief that there is no such thing as a civilised black man. Faced with an uncivilised continent that calls to him on a level he thinks he has forgotten, the white man in South Africa is afraid, basically, that any contact with the black man will drag him back, de-civilise him and return him to the ancient and barbaric ways which he thought he had left behind him—but which, as the book shows, still lie too perilously close to the surface for comfort. The fact that this is the white man's major fear is stressed when Charlie Hendricks discusses his fear of dagga with Cyril Stein:

> 'I'm not worrying that it might lead me to commit murder. What I am afraid of is that it will bring me down to wearing a blanket with a top-hat, and no shoes.'

Murder—the worst crime we can imagine—holds no fears for him; it is the reversion to barbarism that he fears most. This fear also explains why he is so fascinated by the type of life led by white people in the mining camps out in the veld:

> There was a monotony about these camps. Tents and galvanised iron huts. Fat, barefooted women and ragged children. Men in khaki shorts or disreputable-looking flannels making holes in the earth with pick and shovel. Their eldest sons helping them. And the same talk about bad roads and unfair prices. And the women carrying buckets to the *spruit* for water. And washing hanging on the line. And the women lying flat on their bellies to reach down to the water—their dresses pulling up and exposing their fat, white buttocks: for they had nothing on under their cotton frocks.

The image is reinforced and repeated deliberately by Bosman at the end of the chapter, showing how deep an impression it has made on Charlie Hendricks's mind:

> But meanwhile the picture of a whole series of corundum diggers' camps was passing through his mind. Men and women and greenish-black boulders and children. And yellow canvas and corrugated iron. And lines of washing hanging out to dry. And white women drawing water at spruits, exposing their bare backsides to the bushveld sun.

These people so fascinate Charlie Hendricks because they are whites who live in a way that is close to blacks; whites who to Charlie Hendricks have let the standards of civilisation slip, who have been dragged back by that mysterious call of the African veld into barbaric ways.

The fact that Charlie Hendricks flees to Johannesburg, is significant in the same context. Johannesburg is the largest city in South Africa, the most modern, the most obviously 'civilised' and 'Western' place in the country, where the primitive call of Africa is so muted as to be unrecognised and unacknowledged. Charlie Hendricks has seen how strong that call is, how easily he himself responded to its barbaric message, and he is afraid. Rather the life in Johannesburg, even if he knows it to be false and unreal, than the unbearable confrontation with crude, basic reality that he experienced in Willemsdorp, or in the middle of the African Bush, just off the road to Kleinberg.

Charlie Hendricks's flight from reality reflects a pattern that occurs throughout the book. There is scarcely a character who is prepared to confront his or her problems, who does not, when the going gets tough, escape in some way. Cyril Stein's escape into the daggasmoker's dream world, and Jack Brummer's 'business' trip after he hears of Lena Cordier's pregnancy are mild examples of the phenomenon, while Erasmus's suicide, and the murder of Marjorie reflect the desperate measures individuals will take in order to avoid confronting their problems—and themselves. Marjorie's murder brings us back to the theme of racial interaction in South Africa, and suggests the lengths to which people will go in order to avoid this particular problem. So does Charlie Hendricks's flight, and the dropping of the body down Wondergat, which is an attempt to 'bury' the truth. The fact that the murder is ultimately unsolved becomes in itself a paradigm for the insoluble nature of the racial problem in South Africa. As we have seen, Bosman believes this problem to have its roots in the white man's inability to define precisely how he sees his identity and role in the African context. So long as he refuses to confront this issue, so long as he, like Charlie Hendricks and many others, prefers to run away from rather than to confront his fears, so long will the problem, with all its tragic implications, continue to exist. (pp. 30-4)

A. M. Potter, "The Threat of the Wild: Sources of Racial Tension in H. C. Bosman's 'Willemsdorp',” in Unisa English Studies, Vol. XIX, No. 1, April, 1981, pp. 30-4.

C. J. Fox   (essay date 1984)

[*In the following excerpt, Fox notes the distinct imprint of Afrikaner culture on the style and themes of Bosman's fiction despite his decision to write in English rather than Afrikaans.*]

One Saturday night in the mid-1920s, a young Afrikaner schoolteacher, on holiday from his classes in a remote area of his Transvaal, returned to the house in Johannesburg occupied by his mother and her second husband, an Anglo-South African. The teacher, Herman Charles Bosman, found his brother Pierre struggling with their stepbrother David. Herman seized a rifle kept in the dining room and killed David.

The killing brought Bosman's turbulent youth to a catastrophic end and, his death sentence having been commuted, he served a grisly prison sentence which brought him to the brink of insanity. Since he eventually emerged to become one of South Africa's leading writers, the murder has been subjected to a host of interpretations—some Freudian, others construing it as the ruthless act of a swaggering Nietzschean or death-obsessed disciple of Edgar Allan Poe, still others portraying it as the outcome of family frictions aggravated by Afrikaner-English racial antagonisms.

There is no hint of anti-English bitterness on Bosman's part in the fiction and sketches he wrote about Boer life in the grasslands and near-desert of the northwestern Transvaal. Indeed most of his work was written in the English language and, born as he was in the Cape, he qualified as one of the "Cape Dutch"—that segment of Afrikaners who, in the words of one keen-eyed South African, did not descend from "the dyed-in-the-wool reactionary Calvinists who trekked north to get away from liberal British governments and missionaries with their blasphemous notion that blacks were human." Still, a writer-friend of Bosman's, Bernard Sachs, recalls that Herman Charles' step-father belonged to a circle which would apparently have resented the intrusion into its midst, by way of second marriage, of new, Afrikaner relatives. As for Bosman himself, he "suffered from no inferiority complex,

and when it came to haughtiness, racial or otherwise, he gave as good as he got," according to Sachs. And an Afrikaans writer, W. A. de Klerk, adds: "Make no mistake— Bosman was, in spite of his English education, unmistakably an Afrikaner" ["A View from Within," in *Herman Bosman* by Bernard Sachs].

Ostensibly, the linguistic circumstances of Bosman's literary career bear a certain resemblance to what used to be a classic French-Canadian dilemma. Here was an Afrikaner who could trace his ancestry back to the Dutch and Huguenot pioneers of South Africa. His spirit of racial identity was apparently strong—strong enough, possibly, to have helped rouse him to murder. Its strength is certainly manifest in the sheer incandescence of his stories about the Afrikaners of rural Transvaal. Yet he wrote in English, just as so many fervent French-Canadians of his generation and earlier were obliged to transact their affairs in that selfsame dominant tongue. In Bosman's case, if we are to believe de Klerk, it was no wonder his mother entered him in English-language schools since in "the drab characterless mining suburbs of the Rand" where the future writer and thousands of other recently urbanized Afrikaners were reared, schools teaching in Afrikaans were not yet even in the planning stage. Little wonder, too that later in life, when Bosman tried to use Afrikaans at some point in his writing career, "he felt less than entirely at ease in it for literary purposes and relied on editors to ensure that his style was idiomatic." The words are those of the leading Bosman authority, Lionel Abrahams, in a letter to the present writer. But Abrahams gives Bosman's preference for English a positive character rather than presenting it as a consequence of cultural *force majeure*. "I should say that the main factor in his choice of English was his profound response to English (including American) literature."

As for the general situation of the Afrikaners in the matter of language, it would be rash to take the comparison with the one-time plight of the French-Canadians very far. The positions of Canadian French and Afrikaans at the turn of the century differed, for one thing, in that language spoken by the French-Canadians could readily, in written form at least, be identified with classical French. Afrikaans, on the other hand, had strayed far from its official parent, Dutch. The contemporary novelist, André Brink, who writes in Afrikaans, calls it the product of "a wholly new environment, subject to all sorts of extraneous and international influences . . . a new language [which was] adapted to the needs of this new, African situation" [*Mapmakers: Writing in a State of Siege* 1983]. A. P. Grove and C. J. D. Harvey, in the introduction of their anthology of Afrikaans poetry, call Afrikaans "the youngest of the Germanic languages and one which—with, among other things, the loss of inflexions—displays an identity of its own quite distinct from Dutch" [*Afrikaans Poems, with English Translations*].

Moreover, at the time of Bosman's childhood, Afrikaans had barely evolved from the purely vernacular to the level of a written language. Unlike French in Canada, Afrikaans had a non-English rival for the position of alternative national language. This was High Dutch, whose Establishment supporters regarded Afrikaans as a merely "kitchen" variety of the parent tongue. The first important periodical in Afrikaans was founded only in 1876, the year after the creation of a group called the Association of True Afrikaners. Recognition as a school language, over and above Dutch, had to wait until 1914 and official status as a second national language, alongside English, until 1925, though Afrikaans-speakers outnumbered the Anglophone *parvenus*. It was the remarkable poet-naturalist Eugène Marais who, before his death in 1936, did most to establish Afrikaans as a formally acceptable language, editing the first newspaper in what had been considered—even by some, discreetly Anglophone, Boers—as the *taal* one spoke to the Black servants. (pp. 135-38)

If Bosman cannot be numbered among the writers who availed of the linguistic victories gained by the champions of Afrikaans, his stories nevertheless bear the imprint of the language. As André Brink has pointed out, "The syntactic patterns of Afrikaans are evident just below the surface" of these tales. But more pronounced still is Bosman's sense of identification with his native continent. Not for him any cultural subservience to Europe. "As a source of new cultural inspiration to the world Europe is finished," he asserted in one of his essays. "Europe has got a background of unrivalled magnificence. Almost every town and city of Western Europe is impregnated with ancient splendor. But . . . these are glories that have run to seed." And his Afrikanism is patent in his poetry as in his prose: "You chose me, Africa, laughing you chose / A lover's lips to share / Your wild things, Africa, oh, I am mad / With the swamp odors of your breath." Elsewhere, Bosman wrote that, in literature, "Africa has not spoken yet." But the continent does speak in his stories. Their chief stylistic characteristics are utter directness and simplicity, a total avoidance of affectation—qualities to be found as well in that epic of the Anglo-Boer War (also written in English by an Afrikaner), *Commando,* by Deneys Reitz. And their range encompasses all the races of South Africa.

Not that Bosman was in any way an avid campaigner for the rights of the Blacks. As William Plomer remarked in introducing the only selection of Bosman's stories to appear in Britain, the generation of his fictional narrator, Oom (Uncle) Schalk Lourens, had no direct contact with the beginnings in Africa of the industrial revolution or with the new political aspirations of Black Africans that sprang up with it. "And Bosman himself seems to have been too much involved with his personal life to show any of that obsession with racial conflicts which has been so marked in some of his contemporaries among South African writers." The collection of his journalistic essays and sketches, *A Cask of Jerepigo,* is bizarre for the absence of reference to what the outsider feels must have been, even forty years ago, the spectre haunting the city that dominates its pages. The question of the Black masses surging around and into Johannesburg is not broached. It is as if Bosman were writing about the placid home communities of O. Henry or Stephen Leacock or W. W. Jacobs, the talespinners he admired so much, and not about the bush metropolis which now, with its "shadow city" Soweto, is a byword for systematic racial suppression. Doubtless the color bar, long before its evolution into fullscale separa-

tion of the races under Apartheid, allowed the Whites of Johannesburg in Bosman's time the illusion of inhabiting an Elysium of effortless Caucasian predominance, *à la* Middle America.

Politically, Bosman as a young man dabbled in far-left campaigns. But this could have been out of sympathy with the poverty-stricken Afrikaners who, having migrated to the cities, formed a White proletariat roughly handled by the Smuts government in 1922, the year a general strike turned the Rand into a battlefield. For some at least of the militant White miners, the Blacks were deemed accomplices of the capitalists, since they formed a vast pool of cheap labor that could cost the Whites their jobs. The plight of the Black masses had not yet come into focus as the central concern of young White South African radicals in the Twenties, it seems, and they—including Bosman— continued to subscribe to, or at any rate acquiesce in, traditional attitudes toward the "natives." The vast absence of pro-Black posturings from Bosman's work may account for his current obscurity outside South Africa. It would detract further from his reputation if it were known that the only bookshop in London where his work can be found is that run by the notorious South African Embassy. The Pretoria regime thus seems to consider Bosman "safe"— but his stories in fact convey a different message, belying the weird official logic of acceptability.

In them, the Boers—the Afrikaner farmers of the sort Bosman consorted with in Groot Marico—are steadily satirized, with what Plomer called "that playful irony of Bosman's, that sly, mocking, humorous Afrikaner intelligence." If anything, the lack of didacticism on the subject of race gives the stories added force in their portrayal of Black humanity. As a poem by the South African David Wright so pithily puts it, Bosman was one of the "Masters of the ironic / Throwaway, the smile that stings / Where indignation wastes in weeping." The moral of a Bosman story, when there is one, is always suggested in the mildest manner. In **"Unto Dust,"** the title story of the sole Bosman collection published in England, Blacks and Whites are, by gentle implication, adjudged equal in the democracy of death. In **"The Prophet,"** which recounts the contest between White seer Stephanus Erasmus and the Black witch-doctor Mosiko, Stephanus "was beaten for always." Another story, **"Makapan's Caves,"** is a study in Black loyalty, actually narrated by the fictional Lourens in terms of White contempt, yet designed to negate this crassness. In **"The Kafir Drum"**—a tale which would have fascinated Marshall McLuhan—the wonders of White news communication are found wanting when compared with the mysteries and riches of the tom-tom.

One of Bosman's best stories is **"The Rooinek,"** which encapsulates, as only art can, the agonies of the Anglo-Boer War and its aftermath, in the same way Frank O'Connor's "Guest of the Nation" rendered the Irish anguish of the Twenties and what Yeats called—in an even greater work—"all that senseless tumult . . . the innumerable clanging wings that have put out the moon." This consummate story tells of a Rooinek, or "Redneck" Englishman, who, after the War, settles in a Boer farming community. Then come drought and cattle disease. "The blight of the English is over South Africa," cries the community's leader as the decision is taken to trek across the Kalahari Desert and into German West Africa. But the Englishman, Webber, by now a close friend of one of the Boer families, goes along, and the story thereafter recounts the perils of the trek and its final tragedy, which transcends all ethnic enmities. The tragic note is also struck early on, when the end of the War is recalled by the Boer narrator and with it the policies of scorched earth and concentration camp through which the British tried to subdue Boer civilians and commandos alike:

> I was in the veld until they made peace. Then we laid down our rifles and went home. What I knew my farm by, was the hole under the koppie where I quarried slate-stones for the threshing-floor. That was about all that remained as I left it. Everything else was gone. My home was burnt down. My lands were laid waste. My cattle and sheep were slaughtered. Even the stones I had piled for the kraals were pulled down. My wife came out of the concentration camp and we went together to look at our old farm. My wife had gone into the concentration camp with our two children, but she came out alone. And when I saw her again and noticed the way she had changed, I knew that I, who had been through all the fighting, had not seen the Boer War.

The stylistic danger Bosman faced in writing his stories was that of lapsing into the *faux-naïf* in his attempt to simulate the genuine folk voice. But this and its attendant flaw, sentimentalism, rarely occur, and the writing itself is impeccable. The performance is all the more remarkable since Bosman's work as a journalist is generally so pedestrian and *Cold Stone Jug,* though memorable for its brutally candid account of his prison ordeal and for its combination of gallows and rock-pile humor, is sometimes stylistically crude. The harrowing experience of incarceration lies behind a number of Bosman's better moments as a poet:

> I met in youth and in first love
> In streaming passion
> And gaudy power
> One soft as a dove . . .
> What gaoler is there who can fashion
> A chain as iron as the scent of a flower?

There is an echo of the prison years too in a novel *Jacaranda in the Night.* But this is a disastrous book which displays none of the artistry of the earlier short stories and indicates, as does the Forties journalism, a sad decline in Bosman's literary gift.

Thus Bosman's claim to distinction seems to lie with the stories he wrote in London in the Thirties, working quietly away in what he described as "the winter months of the Northern latitudes, when there is no sunshine to distract you, and each night is a dark tunnel of long, splendid hours, in which your imagination has free play." Now, in South Africa, the fruits of those nights are all, reverently, in print, as is anything else, good or bad, Bosman may have written, including the unfortunate *Jacaranda.* A Bosman industry has sprung up and scandal whirls posthumously about the writer's head, with one biographer—

as reported breathlessly by a Johannesburg newspaper— even suggesting that he may have been the product of an affair between his mother and her brother. But, whatever the prattle about his conception and sex life and however overblown the estimates of his worth by enthusiastic compatriots, he will live in his limpid evocations of the landscape and characters of Groot Marico, and of the little local rows from the likes of which, as Patrick Kavanagh observed, Homer made the Iliad. (pp. 139-43)

> *C. J. Fox, "The Smile That Stings: Herman Bosman of South Africa," in* The Antigonish Review, *Vol. 58, No. 0003-5661, Summer, 1984, pp. 135-43.*

Bosman's irony is delightful, and not merely on the surface. In story after story he brings into focus an ironical situation of a kind that throws into relief the common humanity of his characters.

—*William Plomer, "South African Writers and English Readers," in* Proceedings of a Conference of Writers, Publishers, Editors and University Teachers of English, *1957*.

Cecelia Zeiss   (essay date 1987)

[*In the following excerpt, Zeiss observes that the tone of Bosman's short stories is "comic-ironic" and maintains that the theme of alienation was one of his major concerns.*]

> Always in the short story there is this sense of outlawed figures wandering about the fringes of society.[. . .] As a result there is in the short story at its most characteristic something we do not often find in the novel—an intense awareness of human loneliness. [*The Lonely Voice*]

The loneliness that Frank O'Connor sees as the dominant mood of the short story is frequently objectified in the personal situation of the protagonists; O'Connor observes that the "short story has never had a hero", but instead a "submerged population group," and he offers a flexible interpretation of this phrase: "The submerged population is not submerged entirely by material considerations; it can also be submerged by the absence of spiritual ones." The submergence, then, may or may not be externally inflicted, but always it assumes an experience of otherness and separateness from a larger human community. Perhaps the creative dynamic of the short story is the isolation of individual experience, the relentless consciousness of endlessly "wandering about the fringes of society." The "lonely voice" speaks to us directly of his fringe-experience, and he does so in the dialogue and idiom of the group on whose fringe he hovers. To achieve this immediacy, O'Connor has drawn on Irish traditions of oral narration and has consciously projected, in his stories, "the tone of a man's voice, speaking" [Vivian Mercier, *Great Irish Short Stories*]. Outlawed and separated, the lonely voice also serves as a commentator on his particular social group.

The immediacy and directness of short story-telling often confronts the reader with a moral choice, and the effectiveness of this confrontation [O'Connor writes] "depends upon precisely how much information the writer feels he must give the reader to enable the moral imagination to function." Vivian Mercier, surveying aspects of Irish oral narrative techniques in the short story, notes that the dramatic centre of the modern story is a "psychological crisis, which may vary from slight and transitory to permanently traumatic." To spotlight this dramatic centre, a very "necessary thing is to know what part of the story to leave out", as Herman Charles Bosman has commented [in **"Mafeking Road"**]. The telescoping of incident to focus attention on a crisis of recognition, and the direct impact of the word as spoken, are characteristic elements in the drama: far more than the novel, the short story utilizes dramatic techniques for sustaining a dynamic interaction between narrator and reader. (pp. 121-22)

The alienation emphasized by O'Connor is central to much South African short story writing, which emanates from the multifarious 'submerged population groups' that make up South African society. Ironically, and independently of (indeed, in total ignorance of) Frank O'Connor's poetics, the term 'population group' has become South African officialese for the various cultural groups that inhabit the sub-continent. [In his introduction to *A Century of South African Short Stories*] Jean Marquard points out that: "Not only is the South African protagonist a nonentity within his own group, but he is likely to be a total stranger to the various other groups." Of the many lonely voices emanating from South Africa's submerged populations, Herman Charles Bosman, more than any other, invites comparison with modern Irish short story writers. . . . (p. 122)

Bosman himself embodied O'Connor's observations on the protagonist of the short story. Born in 1905, he died in 1951, and thus spent effectively all his life as a member of a then politically submerged group—the Afrikaners, or 'Boers'. He was considered unpatriotic by fellow-Afrikaners because he chose to write in English at a time when Afrikaans had just superseded Dutch as an official language. According to a friend, he made this choice

> not because he despised his mother tongue [. . .] but because he had an uncanny feeling for English. [. . .] for him to have quibbled at the medium in which the poetry in him chose to be born would have been like committing infanticide [Aegidius Jean Blignaut, *My Friend Herman Charles Bosman*].

At the age of twenty he shot and killed his stepbrother, and was condemned to death by hanging. Although this sentence was later commuted to hard labour, it placed him, psychologically, as an outlawed figure on the fringes of society. To borrow a phrase from Sean O'Faolain, the

circumstances of his life afforded him the "inside outside" perspective to reflect and comment on his world.

Bosman's most striking narrative device—like that of O'Connor—is his exploitation of the "tone of a man's voice, speaking". The tone is casually comic, and the voice is variously that of an omniscient author, an autobiographical persona, and a narrator called Oom Schalk Lourens. This last-mentioned is the story-teller of the Groot Marico farming district, and he bears a strong resemblance to the *seanchai* found in Irish country areas. He is a master-raconteur of anecdotes concerning local history and the characters who feature in it, and his remark, quoted above, on the necessity of knowing what to leave out, introduces the story **"Mafeking Road."** This is a personal experience of "Floris, the last of the Barneveldts", and a very good story it is, and a true one, but "nobody took any notice [. . .]. Just because he couldn't tell the story properly."

It occurred during the Second Boer War, when Floris and his son were members of a commando instructed to go to Mafeking and "shoot a man there called Baden-Powell." The veld-kornet leading the commando

> frequently got off his horse and engaged in conversation with passing kafirs [. . .]. Of course, it was right that our veld-kornet should explain to the kafirs that it was wartime now, and that the Republic expected every kafir to stop smoking so much dagga [=Marijuana].
>
> But we noticed that each time at the end of the conversation the kafir would point towards something, and that our veld-kornet would take much pains to follow the direction of the kafir's finger [. . .]. Somehow, after that, we did not have so much confidence in our veld-kornet.

The comic irony of the tone dissociates the author from his narrative, and invites us to question the assumptions of Oom Schalk's community: that the white man is *always* in a position to guide and enlighten the "kafir", and that it is the commando-fighter's duty *always* to follow, unquestioningly, the lead of his veld-kornet.

The inevitable happened. The commando arrived in Mafeking and "stayed there a long while, until the English troops came up and relieved the place [. . .]. We left quickly. [. . .] And this time our veld-kornet did not need kafirs, either, to point with their fingers where we had to go." The fastest rider on the return journey was young Van Barneveldt, who added insult to injury by deciding, en route to turn back and surrender to the English. His father Floris did not mention him again; he had dishonoured the name of Van Barneveldt, a family that had "fought bravely against Spain in a war that lasted eighty years." At last, peace was made at Vereeniging, and the farmers returned to their farms, "relieved that the war was over, but with heavy hearts that it had all been for nothing." The sense of indignity and futility is heightened by the narrator's interpolation of a conversation, held much later with an Englishman who said:

> There had been very great rejoicings in England when Mafeking was relieved, and it was strange to think of the other aspect of it—of a defeated

country and of broken columns blundering through the dark.

Eventually, Floris was persuaded to reinstate his son's name on the family tree, after an inspired schoolmaster suggested adding to it the parenthetical inscription *Obiit Mafeking*. (The community translated this freely to mean: "to ride up to the English, holding your Mauser in the air, with a white flag tied to it, near the muzzle"). Feeling the family honour thereby restored, Floris was prepared to tell his story:

> And then they took no notice of him [. . .] on the grounds that a man must be wrong in the head to talk in such an irresponsible fashion. But I knew that Floris had a good story, and that its only fault was that he told it badly. [. . .] And he always insisted on telling that part of the story he should have left out.
> (pp. 122-24)

An important quality of both [Bosman and O'Connor] . . . is the alternation of their characteristic comic-ironic and compassionate tones to highlight the experience of an individual isolated both by his suffering, and by the barriers erected by societies anxious to run smoothly along their ordained grooves. The psychological centre of this narrative technique is crystallized in Bosman's autobiographical story, **"Death Cell"** [an untitled chapter from **Cold Stone Jug** reprinted in **Bosman at His Best**]:

> Disguise it how one will, the fact is that the Swartklei Great Prison is dominated spiritually as well as architecturally, by the gallows chamber [. . .]. When the trap drops it is with a reverberation that shakes the whole prison building [. . .] and the fountain-head of life grows discoloured.

Bosman's persona has a companion in the death cell, and to dispel the ubiquitous shadow of the gallows the two men strenuously devote themselves to "trying to be funny." Their exertions reach a peak of raucousness during the nights when they understandably cannot sleep, and the night head-warder is moved to impose order:

> "You condemned men mustn't laugh so loud," he said. "The hard labour convicts got to sleep. They got to work all day. You two don't do nothing but smoke cigarettes all day long and crack jokes. You'll get yourselves in serious trouble if the Governor finds out you keep the whole prison awake night after night, romping about and laughing in the condemned cells."

In varying degrees of intensity, O'Connor and Bosman pass mocking judgement on the processes that frequently succeed in crushing those who stray from the approved route. At times, however, both writers demonstrate the eruption of an instinctive moral sense in unexpected triumphs of human compassion.

Bosman's story **"Dopper and Papist"** deals with the seemingly irreconcilable antagonism of the Dutch Reformed Afrikaner to the 'Papist'. Oom Schalk Lourens establishes his community's religious position through snatches of conversation between a *predikant* and an elder overheard by a transport-driver who takes them on their house-calls:

> The idolatrous form of the Papist Communion service [. . .]. A Catholic's vote was, naturally not as good as a Dopper's [*the predikant*] said, but the little cross that had to be made behind a candidate's name cast out the evil that was of course lurking in a Catholic's ballot-paper.

Inexplicably, the *predikant* insists on stopping at the house of a young woman, originally Dopper, who had married a Catholic called Piet Reilly and converted to her husband's faith. He finds the young woman in extreme distress; her child has been bitten, possibly fatally, by a snake, and she asks the *predikant* to administer the last sacraments 'the Catholic way': "The predikant's next words took us by complete surprise, "Have you got some kind of a prayer . . . that sets out the—the Catholic form for a. . . . " (pp. 126-27)

In his classic study of Irish comic and satiric literature [*The Irish Comic Tradition*], Vivian Mercier traces its remarkable continuity from archaic sources. He believes that the mythic and ritualistic foundation of other literatures can similarly be discovered in their comic forms, and thus implies that comedy is, ultimately, a deeply-rooted affirmation of the human spirit. Frank O'Connor reflects a tradition of Irish story-telling which expresses an intense spiritual vitality in a wide range of comic tones: "Even the gods are comic; if 'they kill us for their sport', we, like Homer, can win a sort of victory by laughing at them in our own turn." The lonely voice of Herman Charles Bosman would probably agree. (p. 127)

> *Cecelia Zeiss, "Aspects of the Short Story: A Consideration of Selected Works of Frank O'Connor and Herman Charles Bosman," in* Literary Interrelations: Ireland, England and the World, Comparison and Impact, Vol. 2, *edited by Wolfgang Zach and Heinz Kosok, Gunter Narr Verlag Tübingen, 1987, pp. 121-27.*

FURTHER READING

Bibliography

De Saxe, Shora Gertrude. *Herman Charles Bosman.* Johannesburg: University of the Witwatersrand, 1971, 42 p.
    Bibliography of works by and about Bosman.

Dickson, Vivienne. "A Bibliography of Herman Charles Bosman: The Published Prose and the Manuscripts at the Humanities Research Center," *Research in African Literature* 12, No. 3 (Fall 1981): 359-81.
    Catalog of Bosman's published and unpublished manuscripts available at the Humanities Research Center at the University of Texas at Austin.

Richter, Barbara, and Kotzé, Sandra. "Bosman, Herman Charles." In their *A Bibliography of Criticism of Southern Af-*

rican Literature in English, pp. 17-22. Bloemfontein, South Africa: University of the OFS, 1983.

   References to reviews, theses, and critical works on Bosman.

Criticism

Brownlee, Gill. "A More Sophisticated Bosman." *New Nation* 11 (June 1972): 23-5.

   Compares Bosman's Voorkamer stories with his Oom Schalk Lourens stories and concludes that the Voorkamer stories collected in *Jurie Steyn's Post Office* and *A Bekkersdal Marathon* "are more sophisticated in intention than any of Bosman's earlier writing."

Hutchings, Geoffrey. "A Master of Gossip: A Note on Herman Charles Bosman." *London Magazine* n.s. 10, No. 9 (December 1970): 44-51.

   Review of *Mafeking Road* in which Hutchings praises Bosman's irony, humor, and talent for finding the wider social and political relevance of life's trivialities.

Plomer, William. "South African Writers and English Readers." In *Proceedings of a Conference of Writers, Publishers, Editors and University Teachers of English,* pp. 54-72. Johannesburg: Witwatersrand University Press, 1957.

   Praises Bosman's use of irony which, Plomer contends, raises Bosman's fiction above the limitations of regional literature.

Roberts, Sheila. "South African Prison Literature." *Ariel* 16, No. 2 (April 1985): 61-73.

   Argues that the prison literatures of the West and South Africa exhibit a homogeneity of substance, tone, and mood. Roberts interprets the jaunty, humorous tone of *Cold Stone Jug* as Bosman's attempt to hide his shame and guilt.

Frederick Faust

1892-1944

(Full name Frederick Schiller Faust; also wrote under the pseudonyms Max Brand, Frank Austin, George Owen Baxter, Walter C. Butler, George Challis, Evan Evans, Frederick Frost, David Manning, and Peter Henry Morland) American novelist, poet, short story writer, journalist, and screenwriter.

INTRODUCTION

A prolific writer of fiction in various popular forms, Faust was best known for his westerns written under the pseudonym Max Brand. These works, most notably *The Untamed* and *Destry Rides Again,* are distinctive in the western genre for their emphasis on action rather than realistic characterization, romantic relationships or historical accuracy. In addition to his nearly 300 western novels, Faust published poetry, historical fiction, and spy and detective stories.

Born in Seattle and orphaned by the time he was thirteen, Faust endured a childhood of poverty and instability. During his teenage years he worked as a farmhand on a succession of ranches in California's San Joaquin Valley. In his spare time Faust read literary classics, including Thomas Malory's *Morte d'Arthur,* the works of William Shakespeare, and Greek and Roman mythology. According to biographers, Faust's early sense of financial insecurity and intellectual isolation led him to pursue success as a writer. With the guidance and financial help of a relative Faust was able to enter the University of California at Berkeley. There he held positions on both the school newspaper and literary magazine, in which he published satirical attacks on university policies. As a result of his conflict with the university administration, he was denied a degree in 1915. Faust settled in New York and became a writer for pulp magazines in 1917, writing westerns to support himself while trying to establish a reputation as a poet. In the early 1920s Faust became a regular contributor to *Western Story Magazine,* which often ran as many as three serials simultaneously in a single issue under three different pseudonyms. He moved to Italy in 1926 and continued his prolific output, which included not only westerns but spy and detective stories, historical fiction, and poetry collections. He settled in Hollywood in 1938, adapting his own work for motion pictures, most notably the Dr. Kildare series and his novel *Destry Rides Again.* In 1944 he was hired by *Harper's* to chronicle American military operations in Europe during World War II. That same year he was killed in the course of an Allied offensive in Italy.

Because of Faust's emphasis on heroes, adventure, and superhuman feats of strength, critics have called his novels adult fairy tales. Robert Sampson has commented that Faust's stories "exist at a singularly pure level, free of

time's limits, in a world more open, more dangerous, more intense than our familiar present." Indifferent to the verisimilitude commonly found in westerns, Faust did not offer detailed descriptions of frontier landscape or cowboy life. He typically did not attempt realistic characterization, instead investing his protagonists with mythical qualities: in *The Untamed,* Dan Barry is frequently described as an avatar, a primitive, animalistic man from another time and place, while Harry Destry, the protagonist of *Destry Rides Again,* is portrayed as a larger-than-life figure who displays the moral strength of the heroes of classical mythology. Rather than developing realistic characters and settings, Faust featured continuous and hard-hitting action, usually precipitated by conflict between two formidable adversaries. This conflict generally revolves around two basic themes: the warrior with an Achilles heel and the search for a father. *Destry Rides Again* incorporates both of these themes. Early in the story Destry is arrogant and mean-spirited, antagonizing the people around him until one of them frames him for a stagecoach robbery. After his release from jail, Destry becomes a father figure to the boy Willie Thornton and gains the humility and compassion essential for a real hero. In Faust's western novels such relationships are common between male characters, who critics observe often function in ways generally reserved for female characters in westerns, providing a supportive and settling influence on the hero. At the same time Faust is noted for underplaying the importance of women and romance in the lives of his protagonists. While Faust called his westerns "old melodramatic junk," critic William A. Bloodworth, Jr. praises these works as "a strangely American kind of proletarian writing, . . . which moved away from many genteel cultural assumptions and towards different models of psychological fulfillment."

PRINCIPAL WORKS

The Untamed (novel) 1919
The Night Horseman (novel) 1920
Trailin' (novel) 1920
The Seventh Man (novel) 1921
The Village Street, and Other Poems (poetry) 1922
Dan Barry's Daughter (novel) 1924
Beyond the Outpost (novel) 1925
Lost Wolf (novel) 1928
Pillar Mountain (novel) 1928
Mistral (novel) 1929
Destry Rides Again (novel) 1930
Dionysus in Hades (poetry) 1931
Smiling Charlie (novel) 1931
Montana Rides! (novel) 1933
Brother of the Cheyennes (novel) 1934; also published as *Frontier Feud*, 1934
Brothers on the Trail (novel) 1934
Call of the Blood (novel) 1934; also published as *War Party*, 1934
Montana Rides Again (novel) 1934
The Night Flower (novel) 1936
Secret Agent Number One (novel) 1936
The Song of the Whip (novel) 1936
South of Rio Grande (novel) 1936
Golden Knight (novel) 1937
Singing Guns (novel) 1938
Fightin' Fool (novel) 1939
Gunman's Gold (novel) 1939
Marbleface (novel) 1939
Calling Dr. Kildare (novel) 1940
Danger Trail (novel) 1940
The Secret of Dr. Kildare (novel) 1940
Wine on the Desert (short stories) 1940
The Border Kid (novel) 1941
Vengeance Trail (novel) 1941
Young Dr. Kildare (novel) 1941
Silvertip's Roundup (novel) 1943
The Border Bandit (novel) 1947
Hired Guns (novel) 1948
The Rescue of Broken Arrow (novel) 1948
Sawdust and Sixguns (novel) 1950
The Tenderfoot (novel) 1953
Speedy (novel) 1955
Blood on the Trail (novel) 1957
Lucky Larribee (novel) 1957

The Notebooks and Poems of Max Brand (poetry, letters, essays) 1957
The White Cheyenne (novel) 1960
Tamer of the Wild (novel) 1962
The Garden of Eden (novel) 1963
Larramee's Ranch (novel) 1966
Thunder Moon (novel) 1969
Cheyenne Gold (novel) 1972
The Phantom Spy (novel) 1973
Max Brand's Best Western Stories (short stories) 1981

CRITICISM

Robert Easton (essay date 1970)

[*Easton is an American novelist, biographer, and ecologist with a special interest in the American West. His biography of Faust, who was his father-in-law, has been called definitive. In the following excerpt, Easton chronicles Faust's prolific output in various genres and discusses the critical reception of some of his works.*]

Today it might take not one but two computer experts to total Faust's reading audience alone. His western novels regularly sell from 3,000 to 5,000 in hardcover, from 300,000 to 500,000 or more in soft. His historical romances continue to be popular, and his Dr. Kildare novels are frequently reprinted. A number of favorites, such as **The Untamed, Destry Rides Again, Singing Guns, Fightin' Fool,** and **The Border Kid,** have neared or passed the million mark, as have several Kildare titles. It is estimated that in the past twenty-five years, 20,000,000 of his books have been sold in the U.S. and many more millions abroad.

Perhaps the question of exactly how much Faust wrote will never be answered. Early records have been lost. Complicating the problem are known collaborations and ghost writing with John Schoolcraft, Kenneth Perkins, Robert Simpson, and perhaps others. It is certain that he was published under twenty names, but there may have been more. He himself said early in 1934 that he had written between twenty-four and twenty-five million words in the previous seventeen years, or the equivalent, at 70,000 words a book, of about 350 novels; but he wrote several million words after his 1934 statement. We have the assertion by Edward H. Dodd, Jr., in the March 26, 1938, *Publisher's Weekly,* that Faust had by that date published approximately twenty-five million words. Other authorities, including Carl Brandt, have put Faust's total printed output at between twenty-five and thirty million words. A recent reevaluation by William J. Clark, who says he has counted ninety-eight per cent of the words Faust published since college days, finds approximately twenty-two million words. This breaks down into 628 separate items, including 196 novels 50,000 or more words in length, 226 novelettes of from 20,000 to 50,000 words, 162 stories of less than 20,000 words, and 44 poems.

It seems safe to say Faust wrote between twenty-five and thirty million words and published about twenty-five million.

It seems probable that he published more varieties of prose fiction than anyone else on record. It seems certain that the bulk of this production took place in a remarkably short period of about seventeen years.

To evaluate Faust's work presents unusual difficulties. No critic has ever done so. No critic has known its full extent. It has been evaluated as Faust has been, by bits and pieces, under various aliases.

To begin with his prose, it is rather amusing to see how the reviewers responded to work published under various pseudonyms. *The New York Times,* for example, said this about **Brothers on the Trail** when it appeared in 1934, "For Western tales that are rough, swift, tense, and gripping, Max Brand is a top-notcher. He is prolific and uneven. Sometimes he grows careless about his plots and his writing. But this new yarn proves that he can take a fresh grip on himself and take pains with his work, for it is altogether the best written story of the last half dozen from his pen. It has conciseness, clarity, wit, punch, and hardly a superfluous word."

The *Times* said about Walter C. Butler's **The Night Flower,** when it appeared in 1936, "Action gets strongly under way on the first page of this exceptionally solid crime novel with the hold-up of an armored truck . . . The manifold intricacies of the plot are worked out with flawless skill and what is extremely rare in a tale of this genre, one can never positively foresee just what will happen next, or correctly conjecture what the conclusion will finally bring forth. The reviewer confidently chooses this book—he keeps an eye closely on the field—as the best written, most artfully constructed and thoroughly interesting crime-adventure novel published thus far within the year."

And about **Secret Agent Number One,** by Frederick Frost, also published in 1936, the *Times* reviewer said, "The story . . . stirs the pulse . . . and gives the reader a happy hour or two of vicarious excitement and that, no doubt, is what the author set out to do."

In 1937 the *Times* was saying about George Challis' **Golden Knight,** "If you like a rousing adventure story about one of the few great historical personages whose glamor has defied time . . . you will find 'the Golden Knight' wholly delightful."

In other newspapers as in the *Times,* the reviews of Faust's books were as a rule relatively extensive, well displayed, and favorable. The reviewers seem to have been as completely mystified as to the true identity of the author as were most of Faust's readers.

In later years when he was generally identified as Max Brand—and generally credited with having produced a wide variety of work under many pen names in addition to the well-known westerns and Kildares—critics tended to refer to him as one of the titans of popular literature. More recently, the publication of his collected best stories, which surprisingly included only one western, served to extend his reputation.

Still, no one was on solid ground when discussing Faust or his work. The subject was like an uncompleted picture puzzle. Quentin Reynolds, the official biographer of the Street and Smith publishing firm, said that *Western Story* once carried five Faust offerings in a single weekly issue. This is probably in error. There is no record of one issue of *Western Story* carrying more than three Faust contributions; however, this occurred approximately twenty times. *Argosy* once carried three contributions in the same week. In at least three consecutive monthly issues, *The American* carried two Faust offerings; the dates were November and December, 1937, and January, 1938.

As for Faust's poetry, the picture puzzle was relatively simple, since most of his verse was published under his own name. Such early verdicts as those of Benét and Le Gallienne—that the poetry contained promise and excellence but lacked mastery—applied at the end; when Bacon said of **Dionysus in Hades** in *The Saturday Review* for May 27, 1944, that it was "nobly planned, nobly felt, nobly written," while noting that it found little acceptance.

Now that the true dimensions of the subject are known, what can be said of Faust's work as a whole? The effort seems unparalleled in variety and extent. It covered practically every subject, genre, and locale that prose fiction can deal with: love, fantasy, westerns, mysteries, spy stories, adventure, the Arctic, the South Seas, big cities, the desert, the jungles, war, historical romance, aircraft, sailing ships, science fiction, animal stories, crime, high society, big business, and big medicine. For good measure there were the plays and the lyric and epic poetry on classical as well as contemporary themes, and some serious short stories. It represented a variety of influences from Homer to Kipling and a style that found acceptance at practically every level of readership.

There probably has been nothing else like it, nor will changing times permit it to occur again.

When his production of motion picture stories and screen plays is added, the range and versatility of Faust's talent become the more remarkable.

Among that notable cluster of American writers born in the decade between 1890 and 1900, which included some of the most capacious we have produced—MacLeish, Fitzgerald, Faulkner, Wilder, Hemingway, Benét, and Wolfe—Faust can reasonably be called the unknown giant. In various guises, he filled the empty spaces among his illustrious contemporaries and in a way embraced them all. He was serious and popular, poetry and prose, wine and corn, highbrow and lowbrow, American and cosmopolitan. None of them performed on a more gigantic scale and probably none reached a larger audience. (pp. 267-70)

Robert Easton, in his Max Brand: The Big "Westerner," *University of Oklahoma Press, 1970, 330 p.*

Faust's life-style:

He lives like a medieval prince in his Florentine villa. His swimming pool and tennis court are the envy of the petty aristocracy for miles around. He runs a pack of Newfoundlands and keeps the stars in sight with a telescope on his terrace. He has a weak heart which threatens momentarily to kill him; and against the advice of a battery of doctors he puts the heart in its place by drinking deep, smoking like Vesuvius, playing tennis like a champion, driving an Isotta Fraschini a hundred kilometers an hour through the Rhône valley, and keeping a work schedule that would murder a stevedore. He argues that the heart is a muscle and should be exercised. He loves his family and tyrannizes. He wants your happiness, wants to live and arrange it for you. He marries you, delivers you, buries you, thrashes a daughter, dries her tears, charms the women, and sees what the boys in the back room will have. And the novels are stacked like cordwood in the offices of Brandt & Brandt. He writes them faster than they can be printed. Faust is a one-man factory.

Martha Bacon, in the Atlantic Monthly, *July, 1955.*

Edgar L. Chapman   (essay date 1978)

[*In the following excerpt, Chapman addresses Faust's portrayal of Native Americans in his western fiction. The publication dates used by Chapman are those of magazine serialization not novel publication.*]

The first important Max Brand Western to deal with Indian life is *The White Cheyenne* (1925). This is a rather robust and at times rollicking saga of a gambler who befriends a white giant raised by the Cheyennes. The setting is the Great Plains in the 1870's. The novel is narrated in a serio-comic tone by the gambler, a scapegrace Southern gentleman who was run out of Charleston for killing a fellow "gentleman" in a duel. At first we expect Rivers to be the hero of the tale, although he makes it clear that he doesn't really believe in the Southern code of honor, and it was this, as well as his reputation as a black sheep, that provided the reason for his swift departure from Charleston. But Rivers's first person narration—and Brand practically invented this technique for the Western—functions with its sardonic humor to counterpoint the adventures of Lost Wolf, the White Cheyenne. Like many Brand heroes of the twenties, Lost Wolf is a kind of overwhelming natural force, at times comic and at times frightening, but governed by a different code from civilization, and being by his nature something of an affront to it.

Brand makes Lost Wolf admirable by several devices of characterization. Lost Wolf was supposedly raised by the Cheyennes, and then taken into white society by a plainsman, Danny Croydon. While with Croydon, Lost Wolf learned to read and write, and to speak flawless English. Both Lost Wolf and the Cheyennes talk in a highly poetic idiom, much like the translations of Plains Indian speech that we find in many books today. This is generally true for all of Brand's novels containing Indians; it is the whites who speak in a coarse slangy vocabulary; whereas Indian speech is invariably dignified, and admirable.

Moreover, Lost Wolf is a great warrior with six-guns and rifle, as well as with knife and bare hands. He is a good tactician, and among the Cheyennes, a rich man, owning many ponies and buffalo robes, thanks to his raids against the Pawnees and the Sioux. But since re-joining the Cheyennes, Lost Wolf has not taken part in any raids against whites; thereby, Brand assures the sympathy of his white readers.

Nevertheless, Lost Wolf does kill two white men, and he chases another out of the country. Since the man Lost Wolf frightens away is a bully and a gunfighter who has brutally beaten the narrator, the white reader will still approve of Lost Wolf's action. But Brand deals with white racism and challenges the reader to a sense of fairness toward the Indian in the sequence where Lost Wolf kills two white men. Here Lost Wolf is avenging an Indian friend who disappeared in the vicinity of a wagon train. The narrator becomes a spy for Lost Wolf, joins the wagon train, and learns that two brothers who hunt for meat for the train had shot Lost Wolf's Cheyenne friend as callously as they shoot buffalo. Rivers, the narrator, entices the two brothers away from the train, where Lost Wolf kills them (presumably in a duel) to avenge his Indian friend. The reader is thus led to condemn white racism, and to admire Lost Wolf as a man of honor who provides retribution for a red friend's murder. If the reader goes this far with Lost Wolf, he has accepted him as a hero, while also siding with the Indians for a change.

Lost Wolf's Cheyenne notions of honor and humor cause a good deal of trouble for the residents of the plains town of Zander City, and the citizens, already biased by white bigotry, rise up in arms when Lost Wolf kidnaps Peggy Gleason, their most celebrated beauty. But the novel has a happy ending, more or less according to pulp formula: Peggy Gleason is a spoiled young beauty used to intimidating young men, but Lost Wolf's dominance of her wins her love. Although he respects her chastity, he treats her pretty much as though she were a Cheyenne squaw when he brings her captive to the tribe. His rough handling causes her to love him; she is motivated apparently by the kind of feminine perversity so common in pulp fiction and the movies of the twenties (it was the age of *The Sheik* and Douglas Fairbanks's *Taming of the Shrew*). But the Cheyennes will not accept Lost Wolf's choice of a white wife. Lost Wolf and the girl are told to leave the Cheyenne tribe and to return to the whites (not presumably at Zander City, where he would be shot or hanged).

Rivers, the narrator, asks the inevitable question: "But do you think he will not be an outcast both from the reds and the whites?" However, the serious issues of the ending, Lost Wolf's marriage to a girl raised in white culture, and Lost Wolf's difficulties of adjustment to white ways, are both treated lightly. It is suggested that Peggy Gleason will soon dominate him, as he has "tamed" her. And a frontiersman named Danny Croydon dismisses the problem of accommodation to white society: "What he doesn't know by teaching, he knows by instinct. I think that lad will find a way to get on with the whites, when he bends his mind to it." Although Brand is capable of almost any kind of ending that sounds faintly plausible, since he viewed his writing as commercial hack work, he doesn't always follow the expected formulas. And a decade later, he was to treat assimilation to white culture more seriously.

In short, *The White Cheyenne* describes Cheyenne culture with sympathy, but it presents Lost Wolf as a curiosity, sometimes formidable, sometimes merely comic. Lost Wolf is a kind of Tarzan in the white world, and his Cheyenne attitudes are an excuse for Brand to draw the reader into a male chauvinist fantasy. (Interestingly enough, by the middle twenties, Brand was beginning to be a little disenchanted with his marriage, evidently because he thought his wife lacked intellectual seriousness and retreated too much into domesticity.)

Indians continue to show up as minor characters in some other Westerns of the next few years. In *The Border Bandit* (1926), the hero, raised as a milksop by a New England mother, comes to Texas to collect a legacy, but makes the mistake of giving a contemptuous push to a drunken Comanche. The Comanche chief, White Hawk, repays the insult by kidnapping Oliver Tay and selling him into slavery to a Mexican mine owner. Tay turns into a he-man, escapes, and becomes a border Robin Hood, wanted in the U.S. and Mexico, and also a deadly enemy of the Comanche chieftain. But the image of the Comanches is not entirely negative, for Tay becomes the brother of another Comanche warrior, Yellow Wolf. Here we find Brand moving into the tradition of Leatherstocking and Chingachgook. A similar relationship with an Indian is worked into *Sawdust and Sixguns* (1927-28) where another tenderfoot, Anthony Castracane, uses his training as a circus athlete to terrorize Dodge City. Outlawed by false accusations, Anthony finds blood brotherhood with Big Crow, an Osage warrior whom Anthony helps in a fight with the Pawnees. (Because the Pawnees were the perennial enemies of the Cheyenne, and because Brand relied heavily on Grinnell's books about the Cheyenne, the Pawnees seldom receive much sympathy in Brand's books.) In a much later novel, *Lucky Larribee* (1932), Larribee the hero, also establishes blood brotherhood with an Indian, this time a Cheyenne whom he fights to a standstill. The novel primarily deals with the pursuit of a wild horse, however, and Brand follows his sources in suggesting that Indians were rather rough in their treatment of their mounts.

Even the ferocious Apaches are treated kindly in *Tamer of the Wild* (1931), where the hero, a professional thief in the white world, wins some honor among the Apaches, and then gains the confidence to become a leader among whites. The novel is set in a remote part of Arizona (though Brand never names the territory, his setting is clearly the rough desert country we meet in novels about the Apache), where a lonely mine is menaced by Apaches. Rory Michel, the hero, feels some sympathy for the Apaches because of his profession of thief: as he says, Apache ethics make theft permissible in many situations. His success in healing a sick Apache child makes him a shaman to the Apaches, and helps him win the close friendship of one family in the tribe. However, he is unable to prevent a clash between Apaches and whites, and ultimately forced to side with the whites. This bitter battle between whites and Apaches erupts here because of two men: the chauvinistic and bigoted Colonel Ware, who owns the mine, and a scheming Apache medicine man who dislikes Rory and wants bloodshed. In the evil medicine man, Brand resorts to a cliche villain, and the novel ends somewhat unrealistically with the Apaches leaving the battle after Rory breaks the power of the wily shaman. Despite such flaws, *Tamer of the Wild* deserves some credit as an early attempt to treat Apache culture sympathetically (it was published in the same year as Will Levington Comfort's strong novel, *Apache,* dealing with the tragedy of Mangas Coloradas, a great Apache leader. And this is sixteen years before Elliott Arnold's *Blood Brother* was published in 1947; Arnold's novel is the basis for the taboo breaking Hollywood film, *Broken Arrow* (1950), treating Cochise sympathetically).

Brand was apparently fascinated by the theme of a white man leaving white civilization and finding honor and a sense of identity among Indians. He also seems intrigued by the challenge of portraying Indian culture "from the inside" in this kind of novel. One such plot deals with the white man who joins an Indian tribe, the basis for *The Rescue of Broken Arrow* (1929-30). This time, the hero is an Irish-American guttersnipe, Bandon Suir Cashel, from the slums of New York. Somehow Cashel has joined a wagon train to escape his past as a sneak thief, but the pioneers, led by a self-righteous egotist, Fitzroy Melville, expel Cashel and set him adrift on the prairie. Cashel befriends Broken Arrow, the greatest Cheyenne warrior, and again a great kinship develops. Broken Arrow is a man of unimpeachable honor, and the first person to treat Cashel decently. Cashel learns to have a conscience from Broken Arrow's example and hopes to become a member of the Cheyenne tribe in good standing. Yet he is not fully accepted until after Broken Arrow's capture by the Pawnees, when Cashel engineers one of the daring escapes that were Max Brand's stock in trade. (Northrop Frye calls this sort of thing the "Houdini motif.") After gaining hero status, Cashel is allowed to settle in the tribe and marry one of its most beautiful maidens. As frequently happens in a Brand romance, the hero finds better treatment from outcast, or minorities like Mexicans or Indians, than he does from the dominant whites. However, despite this sympathetic treatment of the Cheyenne, Indian life is obviously romanticized a good deal.

A variation on the theme of a white gaining honor among the Cheyennes shows up in *Vengeance Trail* (1931). When Brand tended to re-work a plot used earlier during his peak period in the thirties, he nearly always improved on it with better characterizations and more thoughtful treatment of theme. *Vengeance Trail* is a good example. In this story, a fourteen year old boy, Johnnie Tanner, is the main hero; joining the Cheyennes after a trek West, Johnnie becomes a tribal hero, although unlike Cashel, he eventually returns to the East. Like several Max Brand Westerns of the thirties, *Vengeance Trail* is cunningly conceived as both a "Western" and a "boy's book." I say "cunningly" because I do not think this is accidental: either Brand may have had some notion of marketing some of these stories in hardcover form as "books for boys," or, hungry for literary immortality, he may have written some Westerns in this way in the hope of at least gaining a kind of enduring fame as an author for adolescents.

However that may be, **Vengeance Trail** is an excellent narrative, both entertaining and fairly accurate historically, with a nice period feel to it. The time of the story is the late 1830's or early 1840's, when Cheyenne culture was at its height, before the Plains Indians were threatened by the Westward movement. (Brand almost never dates a novel by reference to historic events, but his narratives—at least from 1925 on—contain references that allow a careful reader to date them within a decade or so: thus, the presence of a movie house in Clayrock in **The Stranger** makes it a modern Western, some time in the period 1915-1929; on the other hand, **Sawdust and Sixguns** is clearly set in the 1870's in the heyday of Dodge City.) **Vengeance Trail** contains a revolver, invented by "Samuel Colt," at a time when these are a rarity, thus allowing us to date the book (presumably the gun is a Walker Colt).

Johnnie Tanner, at the "princely age" of fourteen, lives with his Aunt Maggie, who runs a boarding house in New York City. Johnnie's mysterious father is away as a sea captain in the South Seas, and Johnnie amuses himself with daydreams of pirates and Indians. Suddenly the father returns with a fortune and the announcement that his travels are over. As a special prize, the father exhibits the Colt, which almost seems to have a magic quality to it; and inside the Colt's handles are enormous pearls, the linchpins of Captain Tanner's fortune, it seems, which he had taken from a rival Yankee trader in a pitched battle at sea (not impossible in the early period of American trading in the South Pacific). After years of absence, the father wants the son's love, but feels he can't win it immediately; to speed up the process, he lends Johnnie the Colt to play with. The son in turn wants to love the father, but merely respects and fears him: he has an adolescent's feeling of inadequacy before a strong father figure. This sense of weakness is reinforced by guilt when Johnnie allows a stranger to steal the gun.

At any rate, the Colt proves to be a magic talisman for Johnnie Tanner, for it leads him into his adventure with the Cheyennes. The thief who steals the gun heads west with John in pursuit. Following the man to a ferry over the Hudson, John then pursues his quarry to Pittsburgh. Befriended there by some kindly folk, the boy follows the thief downriver on the Ohio. Finally John is taken under the protection of Hank Raney, a mountain man going back to the plains. Raney takes John on the Missouri River to Liberty and then to the Great Plains. The gun, it seems was stolen by "Pawnee Harry," a rascal who had lived with the Pawnees in the past, and was just starting back when the chance to steal arose. Raney and John join the Cheyennes, whom Raney knows of old, and Johnnie soon learns much about Cheyenne life. Since the Cheyennes are constantly at war with the Pawnees, John gets a chance to strike a blow for them; and in a daring raid on the Pawnee camp, he recovers his gun. The Cheyennes look on John as a warrior and "medicine man" or shaman, and at last he feels himself a hero. Regrettably, he and Hank must leave the tribe to return to white life; on their

trip back, they meet John's father, with whom the boy is reconciled.

Preposterous as this narrative sounds, in a bald summary, it is a delightful and nearly perfect boy's adventure story. (And what adventure story for boys does not sound absurd in a plot summary?) Life with the Cheyennes is presented as an idyllic world. Johnnie Tanner has the kind of hair-raising experiences that adolescent boys dream of; his adventure with the Cheyennes is a perfect Arcadian episode, despite its perils. The book in fact ends with a tone of regret, as though Johnnie were saying farewell to his boyhood, and the reader to Indians in the wild untroubled tribal life.

Thus, in these novels, the Cheyennes are depicted as fierce but noble warriors, living in an untroubled wild state; moreover, they are generally more honorable than whites, though Brand does provide them with one or two weak characters and a villain or two. The image of the Indians in these books is thus a highly positive one, even if somewhat romanticized. Generally, however, Brand has evaded or avoided portraying the darker side of Indian history, and he has tended to avoid the problem of white bigotry and racism, although he has touched on these in **The White Cheyenne** and **Tamer of the Wild.** In other books, he was to suggest something of the tragedy of Indian life.

A hint of the Indian's tragedy comes out in Brand's treatment of the reservation Indian. Although he generally evades presenting the harsh picture of the defeated Indian, there are two interesting incidents that deal with the Indian on the reservation.

The first of these is in **Smiling Charlie** (1927), one of Brand's worst novels. The book is largely a collection of twenties cliches of popular romance: the hero is a gentleman outlaw, actually the scion of an Eastern family out on a lark; there are two heroines, one a sentimental ninny and the other a clever and heartless flirt; there is a wealthy cattle baron, supposedly a benevolent despot, but actually a mean spirited manipulator of people; and there is finally a narrator, a brave deputy sheriff with some fighting ability but essentially a naive and stupid fellow. In addition to an inept plot, the novel has characters with whom no reader beyond the age of sixteen could sympathize.

One action sequence stands out from this mess, however. Billy, the deputy, describes the consternation through the mountain range of the "Sierra Blanca" when some reservation Indians escape and go on a tear. Billy himself is a racist, and describes the Indians as a "handful of copper scum," and he remarks, "They have educated Indians up into football teams and such civilized kinds of murder these days, but in the old times of the reservations there was no way that they was able to take out their meanness, except by gambling and throwing knives at a line," and so the "meanest" Indians went on a vendetta against whites. Billy's words are confirmed when the three renegade Indians shoot up a posse and later terrorize some mountain ranchers. In a bloody sequence, Billy kills the Indians in a showdown, after some racial slurs have been exchanged on both sides. However, Billy does acknowledge that he was frightened during the shootout, and he later speaks with some sarcasm about the white hysteria over the "red peril."

Since Brand makes it clear that Billy is not especially bright or morally perceptive, one tends to read most of what he says, other than pure description, as unintentional irony. The reader is therefore left to draw his own conclusions about this brutal incident. It is fairly clear from Billy's account that the Indians found reservation life to be a humiliating and boring existence, and that when they revolted violently against it, they were snuffed out contemptuously, like wild animals who had escaped from a zoo.

In a much better novel *Blood on the Trail* (1933), Brand introduces a reservation Indian as a spokesman, both for the Indian, and, surprisingly, on behalf of acceptance of life and the human condition. *Blood on the Trail* is an interesting novel, despite its hackneyed title, probably supplied by some harried editor. This Thoreauesque novel deals with Dave Regan, a young, slow talking, gentle giant, who leaves civilization in disgust and goes to live in the mountains with a wolf he has tamed. Regan has been a poor relation exploited by his uncle and cousins, shiftless ranchers who let Dave do much of the work while they fight and drink and condemn him as a "half-wit" behind his back. When he learns how little they care about him, Dave takes the only thing he loves, the wolf that he has tamed, and a knife, and goes into the mountains, where he lives a hermit-like existence, wholly dependent on his own resources. But one of the few people he meets is an elderly Indian who also dwells in the mountains: the Indian, a Cheyenne named Walking Thunder, had lived in the white world as a school teacher for a time; he speaks excellent English, thanks to the Carlisle school ("Not that I learned a great deal."). Walking Thunder counsels Dave that "you only get out of the world what you pay for . . .". The Indian lives in the mountains because his wife and children were killed in a fire, but he advises Dave that a young man should not live apart from human society until he has proved that he can live within it. Walking Thunder suggests that Dave return to the human world to find out what happened to a girl he was once attracted to. When Dave protests about the disadvantages he would face, Walking Thunder makes the simple comment: "I am a man with a red skin, and I live in a nation of white people," said the Indian simply. "What is your curse compared with mine?" Convinced, Dave returns to civilization, and eventual triumph over obstacles there.

Both Dave and Walking Thunder serve as comments on the necessity of struggle and acceptance of the human condition. The message could hardly have been lost on Brand's Depression readers, many of whom may have had little more than the Spartan fare that Dave and Walking Thunder lived on in the rimrock. Here, as in the last white Cheyenne novels, we see the Indian in Brand's fiction becoming a spokesman for hard won wisdom and enduring ideals.

In 1927, before he had reached the tough wisdom of the thirties novels, Brand had returned to the theme of the white Cheyenne. The second white Cheyenne novel, *Thunder Moon,* describes the childhood, youth, and young manhood of a white boy raised from infancy by the Cheyennes. Stolen by a childless brave named Big Hard Face, Thunder Moon grows up thinking himself to be a Cheyenne, until he realizes that his skin is too fair. To compensate for his lack of Cheyenne blood, Thunder Moon makes an effort to excel at sports and as a fledgling warrior. But he fails to endure the initiation ritual of the Cheyennes, which requires him to submit to a mutilation of the skin of his chest by a knife, and thus brings disgrace on his foster father. (Here Brand is engaging in a curious bit of genetic speculation: He seems to think that Thunder Moon's "white blood," or genes, would not allow him to submit stoically to the ritual knife. Obviously, this is highly suspect as biology; but the real point is that the ritual mutilation of the passage into manhood was revolting to Brand, and his implausible explanation of Thunder Moon's revulsion indicates his own inability to imagine the ritual in positive terms.)

Thunder Moon's disgrace, though felt strongly by the boy and his father, turns out to be only temporary. Thunder Moon becomes a hero by helping a Cheyenne warrior against the Pawnees, and he and Big Hard Face become rich in horses. Later Thunder Moon, famed as a horseman and hunter, goes to an American outpost, "Fort Humphrey Brown," and wins a horse race from a white competitor. Most of the whites want to cheat Thunder Moon of his prize, but an idealistic Army officer insists on fair play. Finally, Thunder Moon and another friend win an important battle against the Commanches of the Southern Plains.

Most of this episodic novel, it will have been noticed, takes place within Indian society and in clashes between the Cheyennes and other tribes. The setting is the timeless Great Plains before the Civil War; white society exists only in the fort, which is distant from the main centers of white civilization. There is no pressure on the Indian world to yield its land to whites, or to endure the presence of white settlers. While we are given a glimpse of white chicanery, bigotry, and greed at the fort, this is balanced out by some whites who believe in fair play. In short, Brand preserves the romantic and idyllic tone of the novel by setting it in the high tide of Plains Indian culture, and carefully evading the wars that were to come, and the tragic defeat of the Indians.

Within these limitations, *Thunder Moon* is a skillful recreation of Indian life. The Indians are portrayed as noble warriors who seldom go hungry, live a life of manly combat with other tribes, and live by religious ideals of honor. Brand shows himself to be fascinated by Cheyenne myths, and recreates something of their substance through Thunder Moon's reverence for the "Sky People," and the "Underwater People," that is, the gods and spirits that the Cheyennes created mythopoeically to identify with their environment. In his adult years, Thunder Moon becomes both a warrior and a shaman, a man singled out for special blessings by the "Sky People."

Although Brand avoided the problems of Thunder Moon's relationship to white society, and the coming clash of the whites with the Cheyennes, he apparently did arrange in a sequel for Thunder Moon to enter white society and to fall in love with a white woman. Unfortunately, this sequel is not readily available to scholars: it appears to exist only in the pulp magazine of fifty years ago, for unlike *Thunder Moon,* it has not yet been issued in an accessible book.

More impressive than the earlier novels about the Cheyenne is the Red Hawk trilogy. These novels, *War Party* (1934), *Frontier Feud,* (1934), and *Cheyenne Gold* (1935) were written near the end of Brand's career as a pulp Western author. Brand was at the peak of his powers in 1933-1936, and produced many of his best Westerns, including the Silvertip series and the Montana Kid trilogy in this time, while also shrewdly working at a conquest of the "slick" magazines. Just when his efforts to escape the pulps and to pay off chronic debts were being crowned with success, Brand accepted an offer to go to Hollywood and work on the Dr. Kildare movies, which grew out of a story he had written. Perhaps Brand was exhausted by the gigantic expense of energy required in these years; but after 1937, he wrote few Westerns or other kinds of adventure stories, devoting his energies mainly to films and to the Dr. Kildare novels which seem today to be only period pieces.

Composed in this great fecund period of the middle thirties, the Red Hawk trilogy represents Brand's definitive statement on the Indian and his clash with white culture. In the Red Hawk novels, Brand treats frontier life in a more tragic tone. War between Indians and whites is nearly always on the verge of eruption, with the uneasy peace threatened by bitter hatreds and bigotry, especially white racism. Moreover, Brand portrays Cheyenne life as much more than merely a warrior culture devoted to hunting and tribal wars. It has a highly ritualized and religious vision of the world, which Red Hawk responds to profoundly. Through Red Hawk's mysticism, Brand is able to describe the Cheyenne myths and their religious consciousness much more fully than before. Red Hawk is more a shaman than a warrior, and his visionary experiences play a large part in the trilogy. It is hard to read the books today as anything but a clearcut indictment of white society, and a defense of the Indian's poetic vision.

To be sure, the Indians are not presented as guiltless: the first chapter of *War Party* describes in harrowing style the Cheyenne raid on Kate Sabin's cabin, and the reaction of three year old Rusty, who will become Red Hawk, to his mother's death: "What instinct told the boy that she was going away beyond call—forever?" Thus the framework of a bitter and relentless hatred between Indians and whites is established, unlike the humorous and idyllic moods that dominate the earlier Cheyenne novels.

The themes of *War Party* are Rusty's initiation into young manhood and his discovery of his identity. As in most popular romances of this kind, a birthmark or an identifying piece of jewelry plays a role: Rusty carries his mother's green scarab necklace with him into his life as a white Cheyenne. In addition, Brand uses a romantic variation on the Sohrab and Rustem motif by building to a climactic battle between Red Hawk and his white father, the embittered Marshall Sabin, whose hatred for the Cheyennes has turned him into a white ally of the Pawnees. Unlike the usual Sohrab and Rustem tale, the novel concludes with a formula happy ending. Recognizing the scarab, Marshall Sabin is re-united with his son and Rusty becomes engaged to a white girl. This ending is really only a suspension of action, and is altered by the next novel. Despite the conventional framework of *War Party,* there are a number of memorable sequences.

Rusty's initiation into manhood begins with his failure to endure the ordeal of mutilation. After disgrace, he leaves the tribe to enter white society, but except for the kindness of Maisry Lester and her gentle and ineffectual father, he finds nothing but hatred and contempt in the frontier town of Whitherell (suggesting "wither all"). An agonizing year of labor in the blacksmith shop of the brutal Sam Calkins hardens Rusty Sabin physically and mentally. In vivid imagery, Brand portrays Rusty toiling secretly at night to forge a great knife as a weapon. After beating the hulking bully, Calkins, in a fist fight, to the joy of the coarse Mrs. Calkins, Rusty takes his leave of the white world by ritually washing off the grime of the blacksmith's trade: " . . . He was washing himself clean of all his days among the whites, of all the humiliation, the shame, the sorrow and the foulness that comes out a brooding mind . . ." Although he chooses to be an Indian once more, Rusty is still involved with the white world. Seeing Maisry Lester courted, unwillingly, by two crude and quarrelsome brothers, Rusty pledges himself to win her by tracking and capturing the legendary White Horse, or medicine horse.

Christianity has never made much of an impression on Rusty, for when younger, Rusty had received a sacred sign from the Cheyenne god, Sweet Medicine. He had undergone a purification ceremony at the entrance to the Sacred Valley in the Black Hills, the legendary holy ground where Sweet Medicine "dwells," and now in his pursuit of the wild stallion, Rusty, under his Cheyenne name of Red Hawk, returns to the worship of Sweet Medicine. His Indian mysticism gives Rusty the inner strength to pursue the famous horse on foot, and the quest becomes an epic one:

> Many people have heard of the hunting of the White Horse. The two names come ding-dong into the memory, like sound and echo: Red Hawk and the White Horse! It is generally known, also, that the hunt ran from the Canadian River on the South, to the Milk River on the north; up to the Yellowstone and the Powder Rivers, and up the forks of the Platte, both North and South. It is also known that the drama was concluded among the Blue Water Mountains.

By this time in his career, Brand has learned to make invented legend sound like authentic and credible folk tale and oral myth, as the quotation indicates with its use of phrases like "Many people have heard . . .". Brand also cleverly mixes actual place names with the invented one, the "Blue Water Mountains," the mythic branch of the Rockies where the Silvertip novels also have their setting in the post-Indian West. Such narrative skills make the Red Hawk novels take on the tone of an Indian legend retold.

After killing a vicious white hunter who proposes to kill the White Horse, Rusty tracks the stallion relentlessly on foot until he wears down the horse's resistance. He tames the horse for riding, in much the same way, using the mixture, of gentleness and strength in his personality. But after returning to the Cheyennes, Rusty feels that he must erase the memory of his failure at the initiation rite. With his horse, he rides into the Sacred Valley of Sweet Medicine, and passes through an ordeal of silence and hunger there for three days. On the third day, he receives a blessing in the form of an omen from Sweet Medicine: he also discovers gold, a fateful act, but he returns from the valley to great honor among the Cheyennes, who hail Red Hawk as a great shaman and prophet. It will not have escaped Christian readers that Rusty's passage through the holy valley parallels the three days of Christ's death and resurrection, when according to Christian tradition, Christ passed through the underworld and "harrowed" hell. Brand thus transforms Red Hawk into a kind of archetypal hero/redeemer figure.

From triumph among red men, Rusty returns to the white world, where his small cache of gold arouses greed in the Bailey brothers who have been courting Rusty's sweetheart. Rusty survives their greed when, after guiding the brutal Baileys to the Sacred Valley, he sees them kill each other in a quarrel. After his climactic fight with Marshall Sabin, the hero of the Pawnees, Rusty is recognized by his father and re-united with him. He also gains Maisry's love, and so appears to have triumphed over white bigotry and intolerance at the end of *War Party.*

In the second novel, *Frontier Feud,* (also known as *Brother of the Cheyennes*) Rusty's life among the whites is nearly turned to tragedy by the malicious Major Marston. In this book, the Sabins and the Lesters move to the Southern Plains and take up residence at Fort Marston, commanded by the ambitious major of that name (he has had his political friends in Washington name the fort for him.) Marston cannot bear to see so much apparent good fortune bestowed on a mere white Indian and blacksmith like Red Hawk, and his envy prompts Marston to plot a way to humiliate Rusty and to steal his fiancee.

A more villainous army officer than Marston would be hard to imagine; Brand comments sardonically:

> . . . The motto of Major Marston, when it came to Indian warfare, was "Be thorough." He believed the old adage that the only good Indians are the dead ones, and he lived up to his belief. Midnight attacks on Indian villages were his forte; and like the redskins themselves, he counted all scalps, no matter of what origin.

> If the hail of bullets which the major directed happened to strike down women or children, he expressed regret for the moment, but he was sure to include all the fallen in his list of "enemy killed."

> His troops hated him with all their hearts, but they respected him because he was always successful in whatever he set out to do.

Marston flogs Bill Tenney, a thief from Kentucky who had saved Red Hawk from drowning in the "Tulmac"

River, and then outlaws Red Hawk when Rusty and two Cheyenne friends help him escape. Using a forged letter and lies, Marston manages to destroy Rusty's engagement, and then he plots his biggest coup: to fall on the nearby Cheyenne village and ambush them, killing all the Indians as well as Rusty. Though there is no official war, Marston believes he can easily persuade Washington that his attack was justified because the Cheyenne had moved southward.

Marston is a melodramatic villain, but he is a very cool and plausible creation for all that, and his actions are uncomfortably close to the historical truth about such officers as Fetterman and Custer. Marston's plan to destroy a peaceful Cheyenne village is a precise parallel to Custer's actual destruction of Black Kettle's village on the Washita. Brand's villainous major is a harshly satirical caricature of the military mind, and at times seems to be modeled on an imaginative conception of Custer.

Marston's plot to burn the village is thwarted by Red Hawk; and under Rusty's leadership, the Cheyennes force a humiliating truce on the cavalry, depriving them of their horses and making them walk home. Believing that his career is ruined, Marston calls Red Hawk to a private duel in an isolated valley nearby. Although Marston hires the Laviers, three frontier toughs, to ambush Red Hawk at the showdown, the white Indian survives with the help of Bill Tenney, his friend and professional thief. Whereas Red Hawk's sense of honor and simplicity arouse malice in Marston, Red Hawk's nobility of character works to change the dog-eat-dog morals of Tenney into a more humane level of moral action. But even in death Marston does not change; mortally wounded by Rusty's huge knife, he cries in anguish, "A—a damned—a white—Indian . . .".

If in the first two books, Rusty faced white bigotry and the malice of the military mind, in the third book he has to deal both with white greed and red resentment. *Cheyenne Gold,* the conclusion of the trilogy, returns to the Black Hills, where Rusty goes after ending his engagement with Maisry, and then quarreling with the Cheyenne, thanks to the malice of an envious medicine man (a cliche villain who mars the book). Rusty is torn between his white and red loyalties here, and he is equally torn between two women, Maisry, the white girl, and Blue Bird, the half white and half Cheyenne girl he has known all his life. In his exile from both the white and the Indian worlds, Rusty returns to the Sacred Valley and lives for a time in lonely serenity: he may leave the Cheyennes, but nothing can shake his faith in Sweet Medicine. When Blue Bird joins him by accident, it appears that the two will settle down for a romantic idyl. But they are not allowed this private happiness: white greed spurs the people of Whitherell to seek the source of Rusty's gold in the Black Hills, and one ruthless scoundrel murders Maisry's father with an axe, hoping to find a map. Whites and reds are about to fight a pitched battle over gold and territory, when Rusty intervenes and brings about a temporary peace. But the peace is shaky, and Rusty cannot finally decide whether he is white or red. Nor can he choose whether to marry Maisry or Blue Bird; his confusion over the two women indicates his inability to choose between races. Either choice seems to be a tragic forfeiture of part of his being. Instead, he decides to ride away to the west to "tall, blue mountains, and blue is the color of heaven and of peace", as he says in his farewell note. He concludes that the conflict within him is too deep to allow easy solution:

> Farewell. My heart aches. My heart is colder than a winter morning. To die is not great sorrow; but it is not the will of the god that I should live among you. The red of my heart and the white of my skin have cursed me.
>
> Pray for me. Offer sacrifice. Love one another. Farewell.

Obviously, Brand had brought his character too close to the reality of white and Indian strife, and no conventional happy ending would satisfy him or convince any but the most naive of readers.

Although he worked within the limitations of popular romance, Brand's trilogy deals with the main causes of the Indian and white conflicts, and the books make a serious indictment of white treachery, malice, greed, and racism. In Red Hawk, or Rusty Sabin, Brand created a hero with touches of Christ and St. Francis of Assisi, a mythic figure whose visionary response to red culture made him far superior to any whites in the novels. Although the trilogy is flawed, it is strong enough as a literary work to make one wish that Brand had forgotten all commercial considerations and written for once with high art as his only aim. (pp. 23-38)

Max Brand was a romantic living in a time when serious art claimed to be "classicist" or "anti-romantic," and the only market for romantic fiction was a popular one. In addition, Brand needed the self-esteem of being tremendously prolific and of living in a princely life style. But perhaps under any circumstances, he could not have written a "great" book.

Yet Brand had a remarkable talent, and his treatment of the Indian in his Western fiction was strikingly fair and truthful, given the time when he wrote, and the sources he used. Of course, Brand was guilty of romanticizing the Cheyennes a good deal, but even more than Zane Grey, he attacked stereotypes of Indians in Western fiction. In the twenties and thirties, the cause was a good deal less popular than today, and he may have run some commercial risk in the process. This explains the necessity of the "white Indian motif"; readers could identify with an Indian hero more readily if they thought of him as "white" by birth. There was a spirit of reform in the thirties, and a willingness to look with favor on outsiders and defeated races in America. But it was many years before any of the Red Hawk novels except the second one found a hardcover publication; and only recently were the first and third Red Hawk novels given exposure to a large paperback audience.

Brand portrayed the American Indian as a great warrior, a man of honor and truthfulness, and through his device of the "white Indian" he was able to show the religious side of the Cheyenne culture in great depth. Brand was clearly ahead of his time as far as popular fiction goes any-

A cover of Western Story Magazine *featuring stories under the Faust pseudonyms Max Brand and George Owen Baxter.*

way. It was not until 1950 that Will Henry published a Western novel in which Crazy Horse was a hero and Custer a villain; and it was not until 1953 that Henry's *Yellow Hair* (published under the name of Clay Fisher) described Custer's treachery in massacring the Cheyenne on the Washita. By 1959, with Frederick Manfred's *Conquering Horse,* more serious novelists had taken up the cause of the Sioux. In 1964 Thomas Berger, probably using some of the same sources as Brand, gave a magnificent picture of the Cheyenne way of life in *Little Big Man.* In 1966, Richard Brooks' film *Hombre* based on a novel by Elmore Leonard, told a grimly tragic story of a white man raised by Apaches, who was forced to defend a stagecoach full of greedy and bigoted whites. That was three decades after the publication of the Red Hawk trilogy. Max Brand may have squandered a great literary gift on pulp writing, but he managed to tell Americans a good many unpleasant truths about the conflicts between white and Indian. (pp. 38-9)

Edgar L. Chapman, "The Image of the Indian in Max Brand's Pulp Western Novels," in The Heritage of the Great Plains, *Spring, 1978, pp. 16-45.*

William A. Bloodworth, Jr.   (essay date 1981)

[*In the following excerpt, Bloodworth distinguishes Faust's western novels from those of other popular western writers.*]

In the 1980s, at least on the paperback racks in drug stores and supermarkets, western novels by Max Brand seem almost as ubiquitous as they must have been as pulp stories in the twenties and early thirties. Certain segments of the public, it appears, continue to associate one of the most successful pseudonyms in the history of American publishing with the western story at its most traditional. According to book covers at the corner Stop and Go, Brand is still "King of the Action Western." But this common assumption that Max Brand represents standard western fare, that his stories are centrally located within the popular western tradition, is ironic and somewhat misleading. While the irony has much to do with Frederick Schiller Faust, the distinctly unwestern creator of Max Brand and at least eighteen other pseudonyms, what is misleading about Max Brand has to do with the actual content of his westerns. Max Brand represents a clever, sometimes graceful, frequently unpredictable exploitation of the genre. But neither during the years when Frederick Faust was turning out western adventures for the readers of pulp magazines nor at any time since can we claim a genuine sympathy between Max Brand and traditional mythic urgings of the popular western. In subtle but significant ways, Max Brand denies the affirmative and regenerative powers of the West that appear repeatedly in *The Virginian,* in Zane Grey, often in Ernest Haycox, in Luke Short, and in Louis L'Amour.

At stake here is the redaction of history in popular literature. Richard Etulain has pointed out that virtually all novelists of the American West have sought "a useful or useable past" in order to show "the continuities between past and present" ["Western Fiction and History: A Reconsideration," in *The American West: New Perspectives, New Dimensions,* ed. Jerome O. Steffan]. In the traditional popular western this quest for history has posed no great difficulty; by and large, westerns have mythologized the idea of the frontier that Frederick Jackson Turner phrased so convincingly in 1893 [in his *The Significance of the Frontier in American History*], especially the claim that the "continuous touch with the simplicity of primitive society" is the key determinant of American character. From the latter stages of such "touch," the popular western usually claims, comes not only national character but also virtue. "A strength born of this wilderness," Zane Grey would have it, "a heritage from fierce, ruthless, natural men" [*Code of the West*]. The mythic appeal of such simplified concepts is related to matters of formula and repetition, of course. Landscape, the setting from which strength and virtue derive, is of obvious importance. So, too, is romance—not just for the sake of sexual attraction but also for connotations of generation and history, sex being the most basic form of continuity between past and present.

Max Brand's West, however, constitutes another territory, one generally lacking the mythic refabrication of Turner, the frontier as a source of social or individual strength, and the interwoven themes of romance, generation, and history. Instead of such traditional elements, Max Brand offers a generous importation of European lore, a faith in action that reduces the significance of both characterization and setting, and a strangely complex treatment of men and women that shies away from serious romantic involvement. These three strategies do not mean that Frederick Faust actually wrote "anti-westerns," even though the threat of parody seems surprisingly near the surface of some of his later novels. But they do separate Max Brand from established mythic workings of the western and suggest that his stories have had an appeal quite different from that of many other popular western writers.

European lore, especially mythology and legend, is a Max Brand trademark. Robert Easton, Faust's biographer and son-in-law, points out that many western characters represent a reworking of figures from Greek, Norse, and Celtic myths. In *Hired Guns* (1923), Faust managed to put spurs even on Achilles and retell *The Iliad* in complete western garb. Easton also claims that Max Brand stories are linked to mythology "by means of simile, metaphor, and a poetic tone" in order to achieve "classical values of remoteness and timelessness" much in line with Faust's professed interest in traditional poetry. Easton is certainly correct in pointing out the frequency of Faust's reliance on European sources, but his suggestion that Max Brand's westerns involve an artful, even mythopoetic use of such material exaggerates the case. As several examples will show, even in early novels when Faust was repeatedly importing characters and plots, his mythological references are loose and even confusingly eclectic.

The mythological looseness of Max Brand may be seen best in the three novels telling the story of Whistlin' Dan Barry: *The Untamed* (1918), *The Night Horseman* (1920), and *The Seventh Man* (1921). In *The Untamed,* the very first Max Brand western, Dan Barry is several times described as "Pan of the Desert" in order to establish his fondness for nature and his early faun-like innocence. He is also compared with Achilles, whose anger his resembles after he is forced by the leader of an outlaw gang to taste his own blood. But in the next two novels, as Dan Barry's wildness becomes a threat to those who love him—especially the rancher's daughter whom he eventually marries—and he increasingly roams the forests and mountains with his two animal companions (a black horse named Satan and a wolf named Black Bart), Brand's mythological sources move northward from the Mediterranean into the darker territory of Germanic and Scandinavian folktales. In *The Night Horseman* Dan Barry is described explicitly as a werewolf, and in *The Seventh Man* the irrational revenge he seeks for the killing of a horse resembles a Berserker saga. No longer merely a centaur figure at one with his horse, the western hero here reveals qualities of totemism and evolutionary atavism. Moreover, the feminine qualities given the hero—his small size, his musical voice, his delicate wrists and fingers—not only accentuate his mysteriousness and his superhuman skill with guns and fists but even suggest that a primitive belief in the female power of transformation and magic may be associated with the character.

In *Singing Guns* (1928) the use of European lore is equally obvious; it is also consistent in its source, coming entirely from the Celtic *Mabinogi.* Rhiannon is the name of the outlaw hero; the sheriff who is first Rhiannon's adversary and then his closest friend is named Caradac. That these names have genuine mythopoetic significance, however, seems doubtful; Rhiannon, in fact, is a *female* figure in Celtic lore. Such mythological carelessness might suggest an unusual degree of intimacy between the outlaw and the sheriff—an intimacy corresponding, perhaps, to other sexual oddities in Max Brand. But the most obvious conclusion, here and in any number of possible other examples, is that mythology and legend are hardly programmatic in Brand's works. Understanding mythological sources seldom opens up new meanings; items of curiosity to the myth-seeking reader often turn out to be mere literary plunder, the results of Frederick Faust's ransacking of traditional sources for the raw materials necessary to sustain his incredible pulp productivity.

Yet while the European mythology and legend may not represent true mythopoetic achievement, it serves to remind us of a basic unwillingness, in Max Brand, to extend the mythic significance of the West as it has been conceived in much of American popular culture. Importing mythology from abroad implies that Frederick Faust found the American West to be an infertile landscape for his imagination. His reliance on Homer, Malory, and other sources from across the Atlantic goes hand in hand with the absence of landscape description in his stories, with his avoidance of historical characters, and with his reluctance to portray sexual relationships between men and women as fulfilling and fruitful. Here we can also find evidence of Faust's own private dislike of the West—"the disgusting West," he once called it—that he endured as a child and spent much of his adult life avoiding. In Max Brand mythology serves an almost antimythic role. Brand's untamed Pan of the Desert, Whistlin' Dan Barry, who behaves like a werewolf and shows up with the mark of the night on his face, is hardly a classic western hero committing necessary violence for the sake of civilization.

Similarly antimythic in Max Brand is an explicit faith in action, action of both literary and biographical importance. For Frederick Faust was obsessed with action. In his chief poetical work, *Dionysus in Hades* (1931), the figure of Dionysus emerges as a proponent of the value of action. While much in the poem is either fuzzy or forced, Dionysus' role as a champion of natural forces running counter to Apollonian contemplation is clear. In fact, at its climax Faust's poem presents no less authority than Zeus himself to make the Dionysian claim "that in deeds, however blind, / There is an end of doubt." This statement may be taken as the poetic correlative to Faust's life—from his unsettled years as an orphaned youth in California to his later distinction as a hard-drinking Hollywood writer and, finally, to his death as an overage correspondent on the front lines in World War II. "Ideals are the bunk. Only action matters," Faust as a student was reputed to have told the president of the University of California. "You worshippers of reason," he wrote in 1915, "I defy / To circumscribe my minutes with your laws." At the university he expressed such convictions so thoroughly in both words and action that they became an object of attack in the president's 1915 commencement address. Undaunted by this—and by the university's refusal to grant his degree—Faust transformed his creed of action into the exuberant and certainly Faustian dimensions of his later life. His drive to think, talk, travel, exercise, compose poetry, and spend money—all while burdened with heart trouble and pressed with the need to produce a complete pulp novel at least once every three weeks—was virtually compulsive.

In Max Brand, Faust's commitment to action became the basic story formula. "Action, action, action, is the thing," he said. Action dominates character in the westerns and rides rampant over setting. In the process it often becomes its own justification and a central theme. One of the reasons for the rightness of Dan Barry's bizarre, atavistic personality in the Untamed series is that it frees him from doubt into a realm of instinctual action. In *Brothers on the Trail* (1933) the most feared condition is the "prison shakes," the sheer inability to act after having been beaten into submission. In *The Garden of Eden* (1922) the chief advice given to the master of an isolated mountain paradise is to enter the world of action and chance. "I'll tell you what you are," an outsider tells David Eden, the master of the Garden. "You're a certain number of pounds of husky muscle and bone going to waste." Furthermore, in this peculiar western, the garden of David Eden, clearly a symbol of retreat and stasis (black slavery is a fact there, for instance), is described finally in terms of death. "It is black," Eden says as he leaves his garden. "It is full of death, and the world and our life is before us."

For the most part, though, Max Brand's commitment to action is a matter of plot, of stories never standing still even long enough for the landscape to be described, of lines of action always converging, of suspense that usually manages to work in spite of its dependence on predictable events. Pointing out these matters establishes no departure in kind from westerns by other writers, of course. But in Max Brand the action seems more intense than the demands of the genre; in its almost unconscious speed, which gives characters only rare moments of respite in which to reflect on what they are doing, it is an adjunct of the equally unconscious pace at which Frederick Faust wrote. In 1925, for instance, while touring in England with his family for pleasure, he turned out between twelve and fifty-two pages each day, weekends included. For Faust "a good, hard-slugging day" could mean fifty-five pages of prose.

One of the primary effects of action in his westerns is that it leaves history choking in its dust. Even recognizable place names are missing, making readers uncertain whether events take place in California or Texas. Neither does time impose any real restraint on what happens. Although Brand stories take note of the passage of time—and freely incorporate railroads, telephones, and automobiles into the action—history does not seem to change the quality of western life in really noticeable ways. In *Dan Barry's Daughter* (1924), for instance, which is set some twenty years after *The Untamed,* things are much the same in the vague "mountain-desert" country as they were when Dan Barry first roamed with Satan and Black Bart.

As with the use of European mythology, action in Max Brand diverts attention from the West as a place of historical or personal significance. On occasion, as in *Silvertip's Roundup* (1933), the plot of a story works to send an eastern character into the West for the sake of something resembling moral regeneration, thus drawing upon the pattern of *The Virginian* (where the narrator and the schoolmarm, both easterners, find their lives changed for the better) and of Zane Grey novels like *The Call of the Canyon* (1921) or *Code of the West* (1923), where young eastern women eventually discard their flapper lifestyles for the primitive but moral virtues of Arizona. More frequently, though, the West turns out to be a place of revelatory action having little to do with any deeply felt assumptions about the quality of life produced in the course of its history. In *Trailin'* (1919) the plot works mainly towards the hero's discovery of his real father; in *Vengeance Trail* (1931), the West is essentially a place of high costume where a boy pursues a stolen jewel that turns out not to have been the real item to begin with.

If mythology and action are so abundant in Brand that they tend to crowd the West itself out of the stories, sex is surprisingly sparse. Max Brand's West is not invested with strong romantic meanings, nor is love a part of the landscape to nearly the same degree that it is in Grey, Haycox, Short, L'Amour, and other writers. A large part of *The Virginian*'s original appeal was due no doubt to the seriousness of the love affair between Wister's cowboy hero and the eastern schoolmarm. In Max Brand plots sometimes end in marriage but sexual attraction is hardly ever a central concern. When a Brand hero falls in love he does so mainly as a friendly gesture towards convention; his heart is usually elsewhere.

Once again Dan Barry may serve as a primary illustration. His relationship with the rancher's daughter whom he eventually marries (Kate Cumberland) involves strong emotional conflict, a dispute over child custody, and the eventual death of the hero. At no point does it resemble the attraction between the Virginian and Molly Stark Wood whereby Wister's hero ultimately embarks upon a life of civilized success. In *The Untamed* Kate obviously loves Barry, even during his wild quest for revenge against Jim Silent, the outlaw leader. But at the end of the novel, after Silent is choked to death, when the reader expects Dan to settle down with Kate, the still untamed hero hears the call of wild geese flying and instinctively follows them instead of Kate, whistling his strange unearthly tune "sad with the beauty of the night" and "joyous with the exultation of the wind." In the next novel Barry returns to the ranch but still shows an inclination to roam with animals, especially at night, rather than enjoy the relationship that Kate offers him. Only at the end of *The Night Horseman* does Barry finally turn towards Kate; but he does so strictly on his own terms in a scene more suggestive of rape than love, with Kate drawn now against her will by Barry's mysterious personal power. As the hero and woman gallop off into a stormy night, another character wonders whether what has happened is "God's work or devil's

work." In the last novel in the series, after Barry and Kate have managed a few years of relatively peaceful existence in a mountain cabin with their young daughter Joan, Kate feels "that there was no danger of him ever slipping back into that terrible other self . . . that I'd never again have to dream of that whistling in the wind." Her tranquility proves shortlived, however, when Barry is driven to revenge the accidental shooting of a horse. Once again he becomes Whistlin' Dan, his eyes glowing yellow in anger and wildness. As he begins his departure from Kate and her hopes for a settled life, he takes their daughter to live with him in a cave. At the conclusion of *The Seventh Man,* after Barry has killed six men, Kate steals her daughter back and then proves to be the only person able to put an end to the untamed forces raging in her husband. In a moment of love and rather final understanding, she takes careful aim at the stitching on Dan Barry's shirt pocket and, with a pistol he had given her and taught her how to use, sends a bullet through his heart.

In view of the typical relationship between heroes and women in the western, the killing of Dan Barry is decidedly peculiar. It is a negative event, a narrative black hole that pulls into itself not only the life of the hero but also much of the intended significance of the romance as described by Northrop Frye—including the quest pattern in the hero's adventures, his role as a restorer of order, and his typical reward (a maiden saved from one kind of distress or another, useful for both sexual pleasure and proper lineage). While the scene does not negate love, since love motivates Kate's act and makes it merciful as well as deadly, it does deny the power of love as a stabilizing and generative agent in human affairs. In the context of the popular western, the bullet that Kate Barry fires announces Max Brand's refusal to participate in the formulaic synthesis of hero and woman in which the most virtuous qualities of wildness in the hero are successfully married to those qualities of rootedness, maternity, and generation symbolized by the heroine. Such an essentially Turnerian union, the symbolic and certainly mythic coming together of the best features of wilderness and civilization, is the exception rather than the rule in Max Brand.

Romantic passion is not really in question here. In fact, when Frederick Faust began writing about Dan Barry at the beginning of his pulp career, he had just completed over 20,000 lines of a poem (never published) on the Tristan-Iseult theme. Moreover, in isolated places in his pulp stories he pays tribute to the power of sexuality. But the nature of such power should be carefully noted. In *Trailin',* for instance, the second western Faust published, when the hero finds himself alone with a woman in a deserted cabin for the night, he is swept up by "blindingly intense" emotions; he realizes that "if . . . he looked into her eyes, the end would rush upon them, overwhelm them, carry them along like straws on the flooding river." This passage, along with Faust's interest in the Tristan-Iseult story and the strange end of Dan Barry, suggests that Faust easily—if unknowingly—connected sexual passion with death. Any probability of this kind of connection, for whatever reasons of biography or culture, means that the treatment of women in Max Brand would move away necessarily from procreation and, by implication, history.

Brand's depiction of women departs generally from the uses of sex in other westerns where women (or at least those women who qualify morally) are not only objects of heightened respect (even "pedestaled") but also serve as vital links to the landscape, to community, and to history. In Zane Grey's *Riders of the Purple Sage* (1912) Jane Withersteen recognizes Lassiter as a man capable of love, gives his love reason for expression, and transforms him from errant gunman to western hero; in *Nevada* (1926) Grey's title character burns with restlessness until he is united for good with Hettie Ide. In *The Call of the Canyon* Carley Burch, an ex-flapper experiencing culture shock in the Arizona wilderness, realizes "her female power to link life with the future. The power of the plant seed, the power of the earth, . . . almost the divinity of God—these were hers because she was a woman." In Ernest Haycox's *A Rider of the High Mesa* (1927) the hero not only heads towards marriage with the daughter of a settler but does so in a way that emphasizes his own ties to the specific landscape and society of the Snake River Valley; sexual attraction thus reinforces themes of community and history. In Louis L'Amour's *Hondo* (1953), as well as in most of L'Amour's westerns, the woman serves a clear traditional role: to give "a belief in stability, in the rightness of belonging somewhere." But in Max Brand the woman fires a small-bore slug into her husband's chest.

The lack of traditional western romance in Brand seems related to an abundance of Oedipal relationships in his stories. Faust himself was orphaned in early adolescence, and few of his pulp heroes have ordinary parental ties. Dan Barry, an orphan with no memory of father or mother, becomes the indirect cause of his foster father's death (in *The Night Horseman*). *Trailin'* not only follows the story of Oedipus in remarkable detail—with the hero raised by a foster father in a distant land and saved only in the nick of time from killing his real father—but was written at a time when Faust was reading Sophocles. A sequence of novels about a white Cheyenne named Red Hawk (*War Party, Frontier Feud,* and *Cheyenne Gold*—all published originally under other titles between 1933 and 1935) also sends a hero out to do battle against the man who is actually his father.

But we need not explore the implications of Oedipal fantasies to recognize Max Brand's unwillingness to assign women some of their traditional functions in the popular western. This unwillingness may help explain the feminine qualities associated with several of his heroes—Dan Barry again being a prime example—and the virtual usurpation of the woman's role by many of his male characters. In *Singing Guns* the outlaw Rhiannon yearns to settle down with a wife and does, in fact, fall in love with an appropriate woman by the time the novel ends; yet his desire for a woman remains entirely subordinate to his relationship with the sheriff Caradac. After wounding Caradac at the beginning of the novel, Rhiannon nurses him back to health with a solicitude equal to that of Molly's (for the Virginian) in *The Virginian*. In gratitude Caradac gives Rhiannon a small farm and helps him become a man of peaceful means. "Your way is my way," Caradac says quietly to Rhiannon at one point. "Your life is my life, and the trail you travel is the trail that I ride." The feelings between the two men, especially Caradac's Ruth-like constancy, appear genuine and deep. Rhiannon's yearning to settle down is, in fact, met by his male benefactor; the woman who appears later on in the plot is only a token, a half-hearted bow to the convention insisting that the hero be headed for the altar by the end of the story.

Destry Rides Again (1930) also denies the woman her usual role. Although the novel indicates that Harry Destry is in love with Charlene Dangerfield (nicknamed "Charlie") and devotes its last paragraph to announcing their wedding, it is not Charlie who converts Destry to an awareness of human compassion and equality. A boy, Willie Thornton, who risks his life to save Destry, is given this responsibility. When Destry holds the limp, nearly drowned body of the boy in his arms, he experiences a flush of self-consciousness entirely out of character for the typical western hero: "He felt all of paternity, all of motherhood, also, since both qualities lie mysteriously buried in the heart of man."

A similar androgynous quality appears occasionally in Jim Silver, the hero of thirteen "Silvertip" novels between 1932 and 1934. In *Silvertip's Roundup* (1933), for instance, which differs from most of Max Brand by assigning regenerative powers to the West, a safecracker from the East who has come west seeking revenge is possessed by a cynical, hardboiled view of human nature until he meets Jim Silver. Much as in *Destry Rides Again,* Taxi Ivors (the safecracker) is converted to a life of self-respect not by the western woman with whom he falls in love but by the example set by another male. Taxi loses his cynicism when he finally realizes that Silver is "capable of every good thing that he had dreamed of him, and incapable of the evil."

Examples of the denial of woman's formulaic rights in Max Brand might be endlessly expanded—as might the evidence of Brand's departure from the Roosevelt-Wister mode of "especially virile and aggressive heroes" described by Forrest Robinson [in "The Roosevelt-Wister Connection: Some Notes on the West and the Uses of History," *Western American Literature* (1979)]. In most cases, especially among the three hundred novels that Faust published under eleven pseudonyms in *Western Story Magazine,* with its promise of "Big, Clean Stories of Outdoor Life," the proper place for the heroine is simply on the sidelines of the action where neither her sexuality, her powers "of the earth," nor her ability to civilize the West can interfere in the games the men play. "There has to be a woman, but not much of a one," Faust felt. At the end of *The Song of the Whip* (1936), one of the last Max Brand westerns to be published in the pulps, the Montana Kid rides away from two women who love him and whose erotic appeal he has felt on occasion during two novels of adventures south of the Rio Grande. One of Montana's Mexican friends makes the obvious point: "There's nothing in the world that he cares about except a horse to carry him into trouble and a gun to fight his way out again." One short line in the notebooks of Frederick Faust, written in 1941, seems to have at least a cryptic significance in this regard: "To my son: Women, even daughters, still are strangers."

The clearest point is that Max Brand westerns show precious little interest in having women transform the lives of men. Yet this diminished role of women saves Max Brand from some of the enlarged and distorted views common in much of the literature of the West. There are no My Antonias in Brand whose maternal resources pour forth children upon the land and whose pastoral skills bring it to a fertility equal their own. Nor is it easy to find a Marion Starrett—from *Shane*—whose sexual presence tempts the gunfighter hero into a conflict where he must use his guns to help close an older, wilder West from which his own identity derives. Most obviously missing in Brand are the romantic extremes of Zane Grey, the "glorious and unutterable happiness" attendant upon a woman's awakening to herself, "to the woman within her," in the West.

Thematically, Max Brand westerns veer away from history and landscape, from a sense of rootedness in either the West or in human community. In more than one way they exemplify the culture of capitalism, not only because they functioned originally in the marketplace of pulp publishing (which Faust claimed was their sole purpose) but also because they emphasize individual action and show little real concern with the past. Even Clarence Mulford, who wrote novels about Hopalong Cassidy from the safety of his Brooklyn civil service job, made certain of his historical and topographical facts. Moreover, if we take all facts into account—including those of Faust's compulsive, intense life—we may recognize a recurring concern with death. This concern is clear in the strangely foreshortened life of Dan Barry, less clear but still evident in the frenetic movement and flight of many later stories. The resemblances to Jack London are obvious here. Faust's early life, the fact of his father's financial failures, the brutal agricultural labor he endured as a youth in the San Joaquin Valley, his dreams of literary success, his autodidact's sense of culture—all of these recall London. So, too, do the exaggerated heroes of Max Brand and the artistic suicide implied by Faust's mountainous production of pulp stories. Pushed along these lines, Max Brand may be seen, as Kevin Starr sees London, as "a modality of California madness."

Yet there is another view of Max Brand, one which deserves a particular emphasis in the history of popular western literature. Brand's deviations from the traditions of the western reveal a larger range to the "formula western" than we might otherwise see. The pulps allowed Frederick Faust to write in an almost Dionysian frenzy, his eye on the clock and the rising manuscript pages rather than literary quality. He pretended to know exactly what he was doing, referring to his stories as "brainless drip." Yet the truth is that he was far better as a pulpist than he ever could have been as a poet. The demands of western pulp writing unleashed something in Faust, produced not brainless drip but a unique spillage of material from various levels of a mind peculiarly imprinted with the marks of early twentieth-century American culture. The West he created consequently contains an amazing collection of plots and characters and cultural baggage of an obviously mixed kind: racist and sexist stereotyping combined with a curious affection for lower-class characters and readers,

violence and humor in close conjunction, masculinity and femininity occasionally confused.

Ultimately Max Brand shows that the western enjoyed different kinds of audiences in the years of its greatest popularity. The readers of *All-Story Weekly, Argosy,* and *Western Story* were not entirely the same people who read other writers who tended to publish elsewhere. Zane Grey, for instance, wrote nothing for *Western Story* (which published more of Max Brand than did any other magazine) and very little for any other pulp publication. His stories appeared instead in magazines like *Country Gentleman* (which published only three serials by Brand), *Ladies' Home Journal* (which published nothing under any Faust pseudonym), and other, mainly "slick" publications. Writing for the slicks held little interest for Frederick Faust. He wrote best when he wrote westerns at their broadest appeal: to the urban masses, to workers, to adults who had grown up reading dime novels. For such readers of the pulps he unconsciously pruned away historical nostalgia, descriptions of grand vistas and purple sage, and themes focusing on the regenerative powers of the West. His was a strangely American kind of proletarian writing, if we may use this term in reference to whom he wrote *for,* which moved away from many genteel cultural assumptions and towards different models of psychological fulfillment. (pp. 177-91)

William A. Bloodworth, Jr., "Max Brand's West," in Western American Literature, *Vol. XVI, No. 3, November, 1981, pp. 177-91.*

Robert Sampson   (essay date 1983)

[*In the following excerpt, Sampson discusses Faust's novels featuring Dan Barry.*]

Brand was a genius. He thought he was a poet, but he was something more. It is to this something more that our subsequent remarks are addressed.

The tension in a Brand novel frequently results from the conflict of qualified good with not-so-qualified evil. Many technical difficulties face writers who seek to convert symbols into living characters. Brand didn't always succeed, but he usually came close. He wrote tight, skin-crawling suspense stories about these opposing forces and he polished that story form until it glittered like a chrome icicle. His characters make sharp-edged decisions about the way they are going to behave (that constitutes the moral part). These decisions provide the emotional energy for the balance of the story. The action is determined—even predetermined—by a character's choice of behavior, simplified and contrasted for effect. The story traces out the consequences of that value judgment.

As early as 1918, Brand had developed many of the symbols and character types that would fill his later fiction. With these, he played increasingly complex variations, at first with the joy of a master improviser—later, more mechanically.

The best of the characters (both hero and villain) perform with really inhuman competence. Their abilities far exceed human physical limits. Their shadows stun. Their glances split rock. They are figures belonging more to myth than to narrative fiction.

Few of them begin larger than life. At first introduction, they appear as human beings. Only later do they begin to alter on the page. The process is rather creepy. As you read, their abilities grow almost diabolical. Gradually, the people of the story invest them with an aura of omnipotence once enjoyed only by Greek god-spirits. Without quite knowing what happened, you find yourself in the company of demi-gods, Beowulfs wearing pistols and rough shirts. They materialize in prose glittering with detail, heated by emotion raised to poetic intensity.

The prose tingles and snaps. Vigorous, fresh, it is as transparent as water. But not simple. Every action is motivated. Every character makes decisions and each must endure the consequences of his decisions. Each character is gnawed by the conflict between his wishes and the necessities of his experience. The story advances from the first interactions of the first characters. It continues, a fugue for full orchestra, ever more complex, modified by decisions of increasing desperation, to a climax whose savagery may involve no bloodshed at all. But there will be psychological tension screaming in harmonics almost beyond the ear's capacity.

The motivation is complex, detailed, emotional. The structure is that simplest of all narrative forms, the chase. But with differences. Mulford, a capable craftsman, fills his fiction with chases. But Brand is an artist. There is a difference in quality and in excellence.

Brand's first major series character was "Whistling Dan Barry," whose first appearance was in the six-part *Argosy All-Story Weekly* serial, *The Untamed* (December 7, 1918, through January 12, 1919). Two sequels followed: *The Night Horseman* (7 parts, September 18 through October 30, 1920), and *The Seventh Man* (6 parts, October 1 through November 5, 1921). Two years later, these were followed by the long serial, *Dan Barry's Daughter* (6 parts, June 30 through August 4, 1923), a sequel to the sequels.

Dan Barry is only outwardly human. Spiritually he is feral—a wild thing, part child, part nature demon. Consider him a nature elemental, if you will, a vital force risen from the high deserts that has briefly clothed itself in a human body. From time to time, Brand refers to him as an avatar—a throwback to a more primitive state of man—an idea often mentioned by Jack London. But Barry is hardly that human. His status is established immediately, in Chapter 1 of *The Untamed,* when he stalks and kills a rattlesnake with his bare hands. It is roughly the way he will deal with problems in the novels: directly facing into them, no discernible emotion, blinding physical agility, and death at the end.

He is no more concerned with human emotion than is the wind or sky. His closest friends are animal: Black Bart, part dog, mostly wolf, a ferocious killer, black, huge, powerful, recognizing only Barry's authority; and Satan, a satin-black horse taken from a wild herd by Barry—he walked out to the herd, holding a halter, and led the horse away. It was not a capture but an enlistment. Satan, too,

is entirely vicious, dangerous to all but his master. His master, it would seem, is dangerous to all.

These three are linked by tight cords of respect and understanding. Together, they are a single unit, communicating by gestures, more rarely sounds, hardly ever words, beings from some terrible Eden.

In person, Barry is slight, young, rather fragile, with slender hands. Almost womanish in appearance, he is diffident, meek-voiced. To those around him, accustomed to more burly forms, he is easily under-rated. For a time. Like any other wild thing, he will not tolerate himself to be touched. He moves with a soft padding step, a human cougar. And is as efficient, remorseless a killer as the cougar. He is one of the mostly deadly killers appearing in literature. More so, even, than Tarzan, for Barry operates purely at the instinctual level, with a few traces of those intellectual processes which humanized Tarzan.

Barry is as much a throw-back in muscular strength as in mind. His muscles (Brand remarks) reflect those primitive times when man's muscle fiber was three-four times more powerful per ounce. For all his slightness, Barry is far stronger than his contemporaries.

There is equal difference in his physical quickness and the power of his blow. Again the feral trace shows within his eyes. These are normally brown, until anger works in them. Then they go flickering to phosphorescent yellow, quite terrible.

What distinguishes him from all other men is his whistling.

It is his hallmark, a thin trilling fantasy, welling up spontaneously, a tissue of melodic fragments and improvisational runs:

> . . . a delicate thread of music. . . . It was a happy sound, without a recognizable tune . . . as if a violinist, drunk, was remembering snatches of masterpieces, throwing out lovely fragments here and there and filling the intervals out of his own excited fancy.

It was, as Brand elsewhere says, "the song and the summons of the untamed."

Nature elementals have no families. Barry is without history. Joe Cumberland, the rancher, found him as a boy walking across the desert, confident, whistling. He would admit to no parent. He was walking north, following the high track of the wild geese.

Cumberland brings the boy home and keeps him there—with difficulty—raising him in the company of his daughter, Kate. As *The Untamed* opens, Barry has entered his young manhood. So far Cumberland has been able to keep the boy from much contact with other men. Most particularly he has kept Barry from fighting, for he well knows the boy's latent nature. If once Barry fights, he will revert to those cougar-like traits barely concealed in his heart.

At this point in his development, Barry encounters a gang of outlaws. They are led by Jim Silent, an early version of the familiar Brand figure, The Large Man. That figure is characteristically huge of frame, immensely powerful, authoritarian, and deadly quick with weapons. (With minor modifications, Silent will later transform to Jim Silver, hero of a different novel series.)

Through a series of events partly accidental, partly psychological, Silent feels his authority endangered by Barry. Accordingly, he slaps Barry across the mouth and the taste of blood instantly undoes all Old Joe Cumberland's teaching. The yellow-lighted eyes flare:

> Dan was laughing. . . . Yet there was no mirth
> in it. It had that touch of maniacal in it which
> freezes the blood.

Attacking Silent bare-handed, Barry almost kills him before being felled with a chair. Silent rides away from the gang, his confidence severely shaken. Barry follows. Relentless, unyielding, he has shucked off all considerations other than revenge. Only Silent's death will take away the taste of blood in Barry's mouth.

Increasingly panicked as the chapters pass, Silent attempts to kill Barry by ambush, by complex trap, finally by maneuvering him into a false position where he will be outlawed. Earlier, Silent has captured Kate, planning to use her against Barry.

Finally a scheme is partly successful. Barry has trapped and jailed Lee Haines, a rider with Silent. Led to believe that Haines is Kate's lover, Barry rescues him from jail and a roaring mob. Gets himself shot in the process. He finds shelter with the family of Buck Daniels, a Silent man whose life was saved by Barry. Throughout Barry's illness, Buck conceals him from Silent. When it is evident that he wants Kate, Buck rides to Silent's camp and frees Kate, although he realizes that he is throwing away his life to do so.

At the moment Silent prepares to gun down both Buck and Haines, Barry comes whistling in through the night. In a vicious gun fight, most of the gang is killed. Silent escapes to town and issues a challenge to Barry.

It is a thoughtless gesture. Barry rides in the next day and strangles him.

After the bodies have cooled, it's time for the happy ending. Kate waits starry-eyed. But the wild geese fly. Dan's heart lifts on a cold thin wind and, as the book closes, he melts away, with wolf and horse, back to the desert.

> Across the white circle of the moon drove a fly-
> ing wedge of wild geese. . . . A faint honking
> was blown to them by the wind, now a distant
> jangling chorus, now a solitary sound repeated
> like a call.

It is Jack London's wolf call transposed to the upper air. The symbol repeats throughout the Dan Barry and the later Jim Silver books. The geese pass crying and the hero's heart answers that high cold music. The call of the untamed. The call of the wild. Name it what you wish. It's the wilderness speaking in its own language to ears that will hear.

The second Dan Barry novel, *The Night Horseman,* is one of those extraordinary books you read with a rising chill. It rings every nerve. To this commentator, it seems one of the great minor novels of American literature. In its pages, true enough, you find that "shock of recognition" (Edmund Wilson's glorious phrase) that strikes you when you are in the presence of literature. The book appears to be unknown to literary critics, as you may have anticipated. Those organizing seminars on American literature do not refer to it. But reader demand has kept it alive since its first appearance in print. Although neglected by those who should know better, *The Night Horseman* is superb. It was first published as a 7-part serial in *All-Story Weekly,* September 18–October 30, 1920. It is part horror story, part chase, part spiritual thriller, touched with parody, full of psychological penetration, emotionally exhausting.

It opens with humor. Dr. Randall Bryne, Ph.D. surgeon, genius, goes west for his health. In appearance, Bryne closely resembles those bulge-eyed men of *Amazing Stories* covers.

Dr. Bryne's function is multiple. He provides certain comic flashes to relieve the story's suffocating emotional tensions. He also provides an extreme contrast to the purely instinctual life of Dan Barry.

No sooner has the doctor arrived on the scene than Kate appears, takes him to the ranch where Joe Cumberland lies dying. He is, the doctor realizes, essentially dead, living only by force of will. He is waiting.

They all are waiting: Kate, Cumberland, Buck Daniels (now hopelessly in love with Kate). The entire ranch is gripped in brooding oppression. The doctor is baffled. Each person is waiting, his feelings intensely strong, each different. For what? The doctor cannot find out. Hints. Odd clues he cannot understand.

Skillfully the tension is built. Out there a doom figure approaches. Who knows when? Horror's yellow light glares across the prose. From out there will come something strange, which half paralyzes Buck with terror, sets Kate quaking with emotions too dark for analysis, keeps Cumberland alive, waiting.

Fearing that Cumberland will die, Buck rides out to find Barry. He leaves with bitter reluctance. He feels that Barry's presence can only destroy Kate.

In a distant town, he finds Barry idling away the days, waiting patiently to fight the massive killer, Mac Strann, whose brother Barry has shot. Regardless of Cumberland's need, Barry refuses to leave. That feral nature is in control. He has lost awareness of time. He has almost forgotten the people of the past. In desperation, Buck slaps Barry's face, flees across the plains toward the ranch, knowing that he has transformed Barry into a yellow-eyed killing machine who will follow.

At the ranch, Kate conceals Buck. When Barry enters, ready to kill, she diverts him to Cumberland. Barry administers to the sick man, gripping his hand, pouring out spiritual energy so intensely that a medium would have observed a crackling blue river flare between them. Dr. Bryne is nonplused.

While Barry is so occupied, Mac Strann, who has been trailing behind, fires Satan's stable, shoots Black Bart. He does this to lure Barry back to town where he will attack and Mac Strann can kill in self defense.

Doesn't work that way. Satan is saved. Barry remains to nurse Black Bart back to life. Kate is desperately seeking some way of reaching the human essence lost in Barry. She hopes to do so by gaining Black Bart's acceptance. It is a fearful problem. Black Bart has forgotten her utterly. He is too savage to approach.

Nevertheless, she approaches.

There follows a scene of extraordinary terror. Within reach of Black Bart's fangs, Kate kneels and dresses his wound. She is reeling with fear. The possibility that she will be torn to rags is immediate. The prose shocks, writing of force and technical virtuosity. It is like gripping a live wire. Later against this scene is played a similar one when Buck and Barry finally meet and Buck must find some way to reach Barry's buried humanity or be shot to death.

In a powerful scene, Kate and Buck do finally touch Barry's human elements. He begins to sense time. He even remembers old relationships again.

But he is not to be turned from chasing down Mac Strann. This unfortunate has finally yielded to the panic afflicting those Dan Barry hunts and he flees through a cloudburst. Barry saves him from drowning in a boiling creek in order to kill him personally. Mac Strann refuses to fight and turns away. Barry is amazed:

> Twice men had stood before him, armed, and twice he failed to kill. Wonder rose in him; wonder and great fear. . . . Were the chains of humanity falling about him to drag him down to a tamed and sordid life? . . . The strength of men could not conquer him; but how could their very weakness disarm him?

Returning to the ranch, he seizes Kate, rides off with her into the storm. She doesn't protest much. Buck, horror-stricken at her fate, grasps Joe Cumberland's hand as the old man dies. It is not Dan Barry's handclasp. But Cumberland thinks it is.

So the novel ends, dense with ambiguity. All characters have changed. Even the hero. As for Doctor Bryne—he returns to the East, his life deeply modified. The purely intellectual life, he finds, is not nearly enough.

The instant of his conversation gives the novel its title. The doctor, much disturbed for love of Kate, walks hotly into the night to cool his mind:

> ". . . looking back," he says, "I saw a horseman galloping with great swiftness along the line of the crest, very plainly outlined by the sky, and by something of the smoothness in the running of the horse, I knew that it was Barry and his black stallion. But the whistling—the music! Dear God, man have you read of the pipes of Pan? . . .

> "He was gone . . . but something had happened inside of me. . . . The ground no longer seemed so dark. There were earth smells—very friend-ly—I heard some little creature chirruping con-

tentedly to itself. . . . And then I looked up at the stars . . . and for the first time I was content-ed to look at them and wonder at their beauty without an attempt at analysis or labelling."

The symbol is powerful and, for Dr. Bryne, marks the moment of his rebirth. The symbol does not quite catch the central essence of the novel. Remember that Barry meant horror to some and death to others. Unity with Nature and nature's elementals does not mean a condition of perpetual sweetness.

This strong novel is followed by a six-part serial in *Argosy,* October 1 through November 5, 1921. Titled *The Seventh Man,* it does not rise to the emotional heights of *The Night Horseman.* Instead it proceeds as inexorably as classical tragedy. As in formal tragedy, each event occurs because of the personalities involved. Again, the action is determined by each character's choices.

In brief, a young miner, Vic Gregg, quarrels with his sweetheart and kills a supposed rival. Fleeing a posse, he takes refuge with Dan and Kate Barry (now five years married), and their young daughter, Joan. Barry decides to lead the posse on a false trail and rides out on Gregg's horse, Gray Molly. During the chase, a random bullet kills Gray Molly. Barry believes the killing to be deliberate, that the animal was slaughtered in spite. He determines to avenge the horse's death by killing every man in the posse. Which suggests that he does not well discriminate between human and animal life.

The vendetta proceeds. So successful is it that the posse is obliterated, but Barry is outlawed, in consequence. By this time, the methodical murdering has stripped from him the five years of civilized life with Kate. Reverting entirely to the feral, he carries off his little daughter, Joan, to a cave back in the hills.

Kate follows. She realizes that she has lost all influence with him. But she hopes to rescue Joan from a life lived at the instinctual level.

With some difficulty, she locates the cave and steals back her daughter. Barry comes close behind to reclaim the child. When he appears, Kate shoots him dead.

Now the mystic brotherhood of man-horse-wolf is broken. Black Bart and Satan return to the wild. The novel closes with the high, cold calling of geese.

A later novel, *Dan Barry's Daughter* (1923) traces Joan's later life. If loose ends bother you, be pleased to know that love eventually frees her from the lure of the wild goose call.

An exceptional series. Beside it, the other *Argosy* stories seem trivial and gray. You are not aware of reading a western novel. Only that it is a story full of passion and caring for people. The narrative force, glowing under pressure, numbs your judgment. If inconsistencies in Barry's character show from novel to novel, if the villains collapse into panic rather abruptly, if the wild geese cross overhead so very often, the tight, lyrical Brand writing overrides all flaws.

So far back, so long ago, Brand set standards of excellence

which, only infrequently, would be reached again in pulp magazine fiction, including his own.

Brand was a major event in the pulps. He demonstrated convincingly, over and over, how to present a realistically detailed story that presented perceptive and intelligent people interacting emotionally. He transformed the more leisurely Wister-type story to one seemingly in constant motion, using the chase and the impending retribution as suspense elements to maintain tension. He modified the Zane Grey style by removing the attitudinizing and most of the coincidences.

The Brand stories exist at a singularly pure level, free of time's limits, in a world more open, more dangerous, more intense than our familiar present. (pp. 216-25)

> Robert Sampson, "Fifty Miles South, Near the Pecos," in his Yesterday's Faces: A Study of Series Characters in the Early Pulp Magazines, Vol. I, *Bowling Green University Popular Press, 1983, pp. 190-247.*

Samuel A. Peeples   (essay date 1985)

[*Peeples is an American novelist, screenwriter, and historian, as well as an authority on Western fiction. In the following excerpt, he analyzes the defining qualities of Faust's westerns.*]

With the "Dan Barry" series, Max Brand joined a burgeoning group of writers who had elected to make the Western Story at least partly their own. When Faust made his debut in the field in 1918, it was already becoming crowded. And it must be remembered that Faust, while he made a respectable splash, by no means dominated the genre. Many of the Western writers who sold hardcover books, too, were better sellers, commanded larger advances, and held far higher literary reputations. Men like Peter B. Kyne, James Oliver Curwood, and many more, not only were far more popular in the field, it can probably be fairly stated that they wrote better stories. Not that they were better *writers,* mind you! We'll come back to this point a little later, for it is quite possible that the very weaknesses of Faust's Westerns proved in time to be their greatest strengths.

It is clear from Faust's own autobiographical jottings that he was driven to write more and more by financial need. The more money he made, the more he spent—an economical trap most of us have fallen into during our lifetimes. It is probably the basic reason he left the Munsey Magazine fold, and wrote almost exclusively for Street and Smith's fiction factory for the next thirteen years. Under a legion of names, he dominated the pages of *Western Story Magazine,* and Max Brand, George Owen Baxter, David Manning, John Frederick, and Peter Henry Morland each had a loyal fan following.

Basically, strength—physical and moral—was a major factor in most of Faust's fiction, and it was a theme totally acceptable in the 1920s and 1930s, a period when personal accomplishment was important to most Americans. It was a time for public heroes, both good and bad, and these larger-than-life figures were preeminently in the news.

Babe Ruth and Jack Dempsey became role models for under-privileged youths; Ruth had been an orphan, and Dempsey a common hobo riding the rails. They rose to become national heroes; my own boxing days were influenced by Dempsey's career, and I fought some 67 amateur bouts (and still have some scars to prove it!). These superhero legends somehow struck an answering chord within Frederick Faust, and he made them a part of his writing. While other genre writers tried their hand at this sort of hero occasionally, Faust seldom broke the mold; his heroes were strong, resourceful, and determined.

But there was much, much more to Frederick Faust's writing—even his most commercial, hurried output—then heroic legend-making. Even in his earliest stories can be found a beauty, a lyrical quality, that would always permeate his style. His handling of action sequences is not only melodramatic, it is a study in prose-poetry; he had the knack of making even the most banal scenes suddenly take on an almost operatic aura. His prose is always marked with crystal clarity, and so easily does it flow, that you are enchanted, and held spellfast. Many writers have been able to work magic with words; in Faust's case, it is an understatement. Even his wildest incidents, the dime novel escapades, the most hackneyed situations, are accepted by the reader because of the natural and sincere manner in which they are told. Once committed to Faust's word wizardry, your interest is so absorbed that you find yourself dwelling in the dream world he has created without questioning its reality.

Time and locale, and authenticity of event, were of paramount importance to Zane Grey. To Faust, these hardly counted at all. He would first establish the *potential*—physical, emotional, or mental—within his protagonist, and make certain that the reader was aware that this cardboard figure would be fleshed out, and the potential achieved, sometime during the course of the tale. Then he would begin to fashion a series of intensely melodramatic incidents, that, as they happened, would develop the legendary qualities of his heroes. In adversity there is strength and that knowledge was a theme that runs through most of his stories. These wildly improbable incidents and scenes often made up the whole tale, with little or no development of plot. A central problem, a hero who must find within himself new strength, these were the things that mattered. Setting, apart from establishment of cyclonic action, was never important; mountains were to be scaled, chasms to be leaped, deserts to be challenged; these were never more real in a Faust story than the stage-sets of a melodrama. They didn't have to be, for what always concerned Faust was his hero's innate potential for sheer magic with knife, gun, or fist. Sometimes this potential was being achieved when the story began; in others it served as a final climactic explosion.

As the years went by, Faust began to develop his own Never-Never Land to provide a locale for his stories. It lay somewhere in a "West" that never was. It was described as the "Hole-In-The-Wall Country" but bore absolutely no relationship to that very real outlaw territory. He created from whole cloth a mountain-desert, edged by his fictional "Blue Water Mountains" and when he wasn't laying a tale in an equally mythic Far North, or just as unreal Mexican Border, he placed his characters in this imaginary region, where they brawled and adventured their way through millions of words.

It was almost as if Faust felt his action had to be so swift, so all-absorbing, that realistic locales would only distract the readers' attention from the story. The same odd rule applied to the Time element in his yarns, and it is literally impossible to guess the approximate date of a Faust Western. He would casually mix in telephones when every other element of his story indicated that even the telegraph-line was unknown; he would start a Western in a modern city and promptly thrust his hero back in time to a Western Frontier that could only have any sense of actuality forty years before! He blithely gave his characters weapons, such as automatic pistols, that would not have been known before 1910 in the West, and these anachronisms even spilled over into his dialogue and plots.

There were exceptions. In 1924 Faust published a six-part serial in *Western Story, The Bronze Collar,* that could properly have been printed by any top slick-paper magazine. It isn't really a Western at all; it is an historical romance set in Spanish California and reflects Faust's obvious research into background and character. This *is* Spanish California, with every sentence ringing true, and not Faust's favored Never-Never Land. As a novel, it is simply superb.

The following year he published three more exceptionally fine Indian novels, *Beyond the Outpost, Lost Wolf* and *The White Cheyenne,* again establishing a realistic time and place, blending careful research on the American Indian with his imaginative approach to fiction.

Faust broke all the rules followed by other genre writers. The typical Faust Western is an extravaganza of melodrama, mingled with heart-touching dramatic moments, a perfect riot of color and movement. Sweeping tempestuously onstage is a horde of knights from the days of medieval romance, who have changed their shining armor for the garb of cowboy and Indian, tramp and gambler, gunfighter or desperado. They beguile us not with what *was,* but what might have been, if this were a different world, and with their brief moment upon the stage spent, they exit grandly—leaving the reader bemused, content, and wishing for more . . . .

Many old-time dime novel writers had latched onto the trick of making pace the most important element of a story, and it carried over into the pulpwood magazines. Faust took this trait, embellished it, and brought it to a level approaching perfection. He was well aware that in order for a story to hold a reader, it had to *move;* a dragging chapter can wipe out the sense of dramatic urgency so carefully built up through the rest of a story. In one sense, Faust was a forerunner of the hack Western writer who subjugated all else to action and still more action, most of it without motivation or even good sense. But, in the writings of Faust, there is a sense of exhilaration, of freedom from normal bonds and physical limitations. Unfortunately this cannot be said of the bulk of Western pulp fiction. This relentless pursuit of action for its own sake

reached the point where a more ambitious Western by an unknown writer stood little chance for publication. The blame, of course, is not Faust's; yet the very efforts of some of his rivals to achieve his speed of narrative was one underlying cause.

His women are, by and large, banal contrivances useful to evolve happy endings, and motivate the hero into acts of derring-do, but—like Zane Grey—he had a knack for bringing his animals to life. From the start (with *The Untamed*) his animals were as heroic and larger-than-life as his human characters; no man ever rode the hero's horse before, no man ever tamed the half-wild dog that he loved, and that loved him. . . .

Faust discovered that conflict between two super-strong men provided almost endless variations; and making weak men strong was another theme almost as useful as moral regeneration, which he also favored. While he toyed more than once with anti-heroes—even genuine losers—he either found them not to his personal liking, or else he was influenced against them by his vociferous readers.

I've written three hundred Western books and used only one plot—the good man becomes bad and the bad man becomes good—that way you have conflict. If the bad man stays bad and the good man stays good you have no conflict.

—*Frederick Faust*

Occasionally Faust would establish a Damon-Pythias arrangement that would make his characters seem real and vulnerable. He would bring moral opposites up against one another, and develop a love-hate angle seldom found in other pulp writers' output. His action was sometimes orchestrated at such a fast tempo it became almost kaleidoscopic in effect, indeed, there were occasions when he seemed to lose control over it, and it would take off and soar to new heights. In short, *all* the standard ingredients are present in Faust's work, but changed so drastically by Faust's innate ingenuity they are not always recognizeable for what they are.

Characterization, in a Western, must be tempered by the overall scheme of action. It was Faust's ability to blend characterization *with* action that makes his work unique.

He used brief lines of dialogue, broken phrases, physical contrasts, and significant pauses that continue the force of the story without slowing it. One of his favorite tricks was to build the character of a central figure without describing him, but by revealing him through the highly perceptive eyes of another character. It isn't the *author* telling you about this character, it is a third party, and somehow this conveys verisimilitude, a feeling that the character thus seen is *real,* and what he does, like the figures in a folk tale, seems possible. Adding to this was the underlying ca-

James Stewart and Marlene Dietrich in Destry Rides Again, *1939.*

pability of his heroes, their as yet untapped potentiality. In almost every Faust story the central protagonist is capable of handling *any* given situation. It doesn't matter if this inherent power is utilized during a story or not; its very presence is often enough. If a hero in a Faust tale is forced to back down you *know* it is for another reason than fear or inability to take charge and win.

This repeated theme is a credit to Faust's own enormous capacity for living, for doing; the endless hours of writing, the almost unbelievable wordage he ground out, the amount of reading, of feeling, absorbing background material from every possible source. The intense vibrancy of the man is evident in his fiction, stemming from an apparently limitless source of free energy he drew upon according to the seriousness of the work he was doing.

In 1926, in *Western Story,* he published three novelettes that became **The Border Bandit,** which is my favorite of all the millions of words of Westerns Frederick Faust wrote. Not my favorite Faust *story* as there are both mystery and historical pieces I like as well, but easily my favorite *Western* by Faust . . . and damned near, in my opinion, the best Western novel ever written, despite the fact it was patched together from separate novelettes to

make a complete novel. In it the entire panorama of Faust's created Mythic West is used.

For me, it was an inspiration. Two of my own books, *Broken Rainbow Ranch,* and my first published novel, *The Dream Ends In Fury,* were written because of it. Neither is in any sense in the style or pattern of Faust; *The Dream Ends In Fury* was the end result of three years' intense historical research, with every scene, every locale, exactly as it existed, even words in the principal characters' mouths are quoted from contemporary newspaper accounts. But the underlying spirit, the feeling of an American Saga, came from **The Border Bandit.**

What is there about Faust's writings, done for cheap pulp magazines, essentially, that has made them last a half-century, and will probably make them last as long as men care to read a rousingly good adventure story?

The answer, I believe, lies in the poet inside Frederick Faust, eternally struggling to be free; whenever that poetic soul of his could, it grabbed the ball—the story—and ran . . . Every Faust tale has lyric, singing passages, even the most artificial of them. His heroes face their dragons and slay them with a style the redoubtable St. George might envy. Poetry strikes an echoing chord inside us all, whether it is a popular song, a hard rock piece, or a love sonnet. Faust touched that chord, again and again. (pp. 66-71)

Samuel A. Peeples, "Max Brand and the American Western Story," in Max Brand: Western Giant, The Life and Times of Frederick Schiller Faust, *edited by William F. Nolan, Bowling Green State University Popular Press, 1985, pp. 63-71.*

Faust on plotting stories:

There is a certain *logic* in the working out of stories, a sort of mathematical necessity in the operation of order to get the right answers, and I think you can surrender yourself, in a way, to the nature and the kind of emotion with which you are dealing. It will lead you to the right denouements. I remember that when I started doing stories each one seemed to be the last I could find. I scraped the bottom of the basket to get each idea. But then by degrees the story-finding faculty increases. You spot stories in the air, flying out of conversations, out of books. Stories will rise also out of the inversions of things as you find them. When you read a story, pause when you are halfway through; finish the story in detail out of your imagination; write it down in brief notes. Then read the story through to the end. Often you will find that you have a totally new final half of a story. Fit in a new beginning and there you are. Also, you may take famous themes and simply alter the settings. Once I wrote the story of Troy, with Priam, Hector, Paris and Helen, Achilles and Patroclus, etc., and I merely established it in the West and it served pretty well—if only I had known enough West to make it real. You could chart the actions of a dozen characters. Then put all those lines down on one map—the map of your tale—and where the trails cross there is sure to be conflict—or love. But eventually the important thing is to offer your reader a glimpse into a world which you feel and know, and just how you open the door or lead his eye from figure to figure is not of the most vital importance.

Frederick Faust, in his The Notebooks and Poems of "Max Brand," *Dodd, Mead & Co., 1957.*

Cynthia S. Hamilton   (essay date 1987)

[*In the following excerpt, Hamilton focuses on prominent themes in Faust's westerns.*]

Faust's fiction has been condemned and praised as adult fairy-tales, and there is much in his works which is appropriate to such a categorisation, but Robert Easton hits closer to the mark when he comments that Faust saw the West in terms of 'the myth of the timeless man, reliving the age-old, cyclical stories of the son in search of an illustrious father or the warrior who had an Achilles heel.' Unfortunately, he does not recognise the true significance these myths had for Faust, nor does he develop a full argument for the mythic timbre of Faust's writings.

'Myth' is a slippery term, and a distinction must be drawn between the sense in which Faust is a mythic writer and the way Zane Grey uses myth. Grey assimilated the myths of his culture and used them to endow even the mundane aspects of his past with heroic import. In his fiction too, Grey explored the ideological myths which provided a ready-made value structure and sense of identity, and used them to supply the 'answers' he sought. This act of faith eliminated any need to generate personal myths.

Faust was influenced by the Greek myths he had absorbed in his extensive reading. He used the patterns furnished by these myths in a detached and self-conscious manner. He even claimed a Western modelled on the *Iliad*. But Faust could never use myth to give his experiences a heroic cast or view fiction as a substitute for life. His use of the classics does not explain the mythic resonance of his work.

Faust's most interesting work is mythic because it comes from the same wellspring as myth. Myth derives from the need to resolve a problem of overwhelming significance while disguising its presentation. Acknowledgement of the problem would precipitate overwhelming anxiety, so the distancing-process is important. There is a need to repeat this process over and over because the problem is at base unresolvable. The problems which generated Faust's intensely personal myths were the unresolved conflicts of his youth, centring on his acceptance or rejection of his father, with the implications this decision held for his own identity. Thus Grace Flandrau says of Faust's work,

'It had to pour out like automatic writing, like the material of a dream.' She said it had to be fiction, written out of some disassociated fragment of youthful personality, or else it had to be highly conscious verse, during the writing of which 'he probably thought too much, or rather, too exclusively. So that, distinguished as it was, it suffered from the absence of his daemon.'

Unlike Wister and Grey, Faust was not enamoured of the Western landscape and had little interest in proclaiming or exploring the essential Americanness of the West. Landscape plays only a minor role in his Westerns: 'His setting was a never-never land', Robert Easton has commented. 'He used a minimum of actual circumstance . . . chiefly because he was a natural tale teller and wanted to free his work from everyday reality.' It is a tribute to the strength and versatility of the Western formula that in Faust's work, where 'setting' does not matter, the key elements can be found in abundance.

The artificial distinction between East and West is maintained, with the West depicted as more open, physically and socially, and more lawless than the East. In *Trailin'*, Anthony Woodbury, seated in the library of a Long Island mansion, explains his feelings to the man he assumes is his father: 'I'd rather be out in the country where men still wear guns, where the sky isn't stained with filthy coal smoke, where there's an horizon wide enough to breathe in, where there's man-talk instead of this damned chatter over teacups—.' Needless to say, the young man soon heads west.

In *South of Rio Grande* we see the contrast of East and West from the Western point of view when, on seeing a greenhorn in trouble, the deputy comments, 'If I had my own way, I would have a special State fund for such cases as this; to put them on the train and ship them back East, where a man can be as small and as soft as you please so long as he knows how to walk and talk.' The contrast becomes much more ambivalent when the deputy describes the town's seamy lawlessness, however: 'It was a ragged, mean, low-down, crooked, dirty border town . . . and [I] wondered that the thin sides to its wooden shacks could hold in the murders, the stranglings, the knife fights, the gun plays, the robberies, treacheries, and thousand kinds of crime which they had known.' The sheriff even comes to see law as a positive good. None the less, contempt for the law as the refuge of the weak is the more common attitude. Chris Verner, a reformed bank-robber and successful farmer in *Larramee's Ranch,* strikes a keynote of the traditional attitude: 'Me and the law have got on tolerable well without leanin' none on each other for support.'

Such characters as Jerry Ash in *Marbleface* and Vincent Allen in *The Tenderfoot* head west to avoid real or imagined criminal prosecution in the East. Their flight supports the illusion of the West's openness. Jerry Ash is relieved when he arrives in Piegan, a small town four days hard riding from the railroad, and assumes his freedom is secure. Although a detective does come to arrest him, the lawman is ridiculed and sent packing. The town's attitude is summed up in the following exchange:

> 'You—behind me!' he snapped. 'I'm Detective Charles Richardson, of New York City. I have a warrant for this man's arrest.'
>
> Said Harry: 'I'm Harry Blossom, of Piegan, and you'll have to go to hell and back before you serve that warrant on Pokerface.'

Even the sheriff refuses to assist the New York policeman, committing a penitentiary offence in 'losing' the warrant. He justifies his action on the grounds of friendship. The contrast between the sheriff's loyalty and the detective's greed makes the sheriff's behaviour appear noble, but the value-set implicit in his behaviour remains problematic.

To place loyalty above law as Faust does quite explicitly in *Marbleface, Singing Guns, Brothers on the Trail* and *The Tenderfoot* exalts lawlessness of a very different kind from that which Wister and Grey portray with such enthusiasm. For Wister and Grey, the non-institutional law their heroes uphold is a necessary alternative to the non-existent, ineffective or corrupt legal institutions. The premium Faust places on loyalty strains the atavistic values at the base of the Western formula and introduces a conflicting ethical standard.

In *Singing Guns* (1928), the resultant conflict between individualism and self-denial can be seen very clearly. The two main characters are Owen Caradac, a sheriff, and Annan Rhiannon, a criminal. Caradac and the society he represents all profess social Darwinist values. Caradac defines himself as a hunter of men. When the sheriff tracks him down, however, it is Rhiannon who wins the shoot-out. Caradac's life is therefore forfeit 'by the law of the West, by the law of the wilderness, by the law of all beasts and the men who hunt for one another', but he does not die. Rhiannon, who has shot him in self-defence, nurses him back to health. Caradac's gratitude takes the form of

self-denial. He mixes his blood with that of his victor and pledges 'night or day, mountain or desert, *in the law or outside of it,* your blood is my blood, and my blood is your blood, so help me God!'

From this point on, Caradac leads a double life. On the one hand he maintains his position as sheriff and continues to pursue criminals; on the other he harbours a known criminal. When his duplicity is discovered, the populace is outraged. According to the code, he should either have defeated Rhiannon or have perished in the attempt; the code can not accommodate mercy and gratitude. Caradac responds by defending Rhiannon as the best man, thus placing the issue back within its familiar framework: 'How many men has Rhiannon killed?' enquires a representative of the Governor. 'From behind—from the side—sneaking by night, or ever taking an advantage—not one!' responds Caradac. The governor's representative goes on to observe that he has killed a good many, but Caradac has a ready retort: 'George Washington killed a lot more.'

Caradac is aided in his argument by the fact that Rhiannon has taken a rundown farm and transformed it into a thriving operation, a model of what hard work and ingenuity can accomplish. His case is also bolstered by the essential amorality of social Darwinism, which tempers the townsfolk's resentment and forces a local banker to admit, 'What harm did he ever do? Scratched the surface once in a while! Just scratched the surface. Good for our systems. He stirred us up when we got too settled!'

Rhiannon himself, the 'best man', operates within a different value system: he has a strong sense of social responsibility. Although he realises that the killing which drove him from society was justifiable as self-defence, he cannot excuse himself for what he sees as the misuse of his strength: 'But I seen that I wasn't fit to live around with people. Take when a man hits you; you got no right to get mad. Not when you're like me!' He has voluntarily removed himself from society to protect it from his anger. Admittedly, it is a rather warped sense of social responsibility which necessitates robbing society to supply his needs and killing pursuers on occasion. Still, Rhiannon sees his exile as self-denial. He wants to be a social being, and longs for a wife and family.

He challenges Caradac's 'hunter ethic', especially his practice of hunting men with a price on their heads. Rhiannon recognises that Caradac's 'reward' is 'blood money'. Here the two value systems clash unresolvably, and Caradac, caught between the two, feels confusion and guilt: 'Nobody else minds. The papers are full of what I done to him. Nobody grudges me what I get out of that sort of work', he protests. 'But *you* grudge me!'

In the overall scheme of the book, however, it is not Caradac who needs to defend his actions. It is Rhiannon's compassionate values which are inexplicable within the formula's framework, while his criminality and subsequent social rise are defensible. Rhiannon is pardoned by the governor, Caradac keeps his job, and Rhiannon earns the rewards appropriate to his new status as 'best man': a good woman and a comfortable fortune. Ironically, this happy ending is less forced than the traditional resolution of a

Grey or Wister Western. By introducing the value of loyalty and the notion of social responsibility, Faust allows for characters who are capable of long-term interpersonal involvement.

In *Destry Rides Again,* Faust gives extended, sympathetic treatment to the forbidden notion that the morally superior hero need not be the strongest or most skilful. The young Harry Destry boasts that he is the best fighter in Wham, and treats his victims with a sort of 'affectionate contempt.' One of his victims, Chester Bent, does not take his defeat gracefully; in revenge he frames Destry for the robbery of the express. While Destry spends six years in jail, Chet builds his fortune with the money from the robbery and develops his strength and shooting-skill for a second encounter. When they face each other for a second duel, Chet says,

> D'you think that I didn't start preparing for the day you'd get out of prison the day you went into it? Little things are fairly sure to float up to the surface, in time, and there was never a minute when I didn't half expect that I'd have to face you with a gun. The six years you've missed I've been working.

In their second encounter, Chet beats Destry to the draw, but the sheriff intervenes on Destry's behalf. Destry gives chase and is again beaten, this time in hand-to-hand combat. He must admit that he has met his master, an admission made more bitter because Chet has duped him. Chet is the best man in terms of the individualistic ethic: he is clever, strong, skilful and financially self-made. But he is also dishonest, vicious, cruel and a betrayer of his avowed friends. The good-hearted Destry is a failure, without occupation, duped and defeated, who wins in the end by luck alone, killing Chet and securing the traditional rewards: wealth and a good woman.

Only the letter of the formula is upheld, and, alarmingly, Destry discovers that every victor is a potential victim. As a result, he learns compassion and the importance of loyalty. Compare Wister's statement from *The Virginian,* 'All America is divided into two classes,—the quality and the equality', with Destry's mature outlook:

> Equal. For all men are equal. Not as he blindly had taken the word in the courtroom, with wrath and with contempt. Not equal in strength of hand, in talent, in craft, in speed of foot or in leap of mind, but equal in mystery, in the identity of the race which breathes, through all men out of the soil, and out of the heavens.

Faust has come a long way from the formula as articulated by Wister in *The Virginian.* The distance is not suprising. Faust did not view the world from the centres of power as Wister did; Faust's friends did not shape the events of their time as Wister's did; Faust did not come from a long distinguished lineage as did Wister. Faust's attempts to soften the brutality of social Darwinism can be seen as an attempt, perhaps an unconscious one, to defend his father. It can also be seen as a defence of the 'equality' from which he came against the 'quality' who held the centres of power. Or it can be seen as an attempt to compensate for the social poverty of his youth and the constant battles he

endured by emphasising non-competitive virtues. Whatever the preferred explanations, the fact remains that in Faust's Westerns there are relics of an ideology incompatible with the basic framework of the Western formula. Indeed, many of his works reveal the interweaving of two antagonistic ideologies. This conflict is evident in the treatment given to wealth as well.

For Faust as for Grey and Wister, the West is a land where the individual has great opportunity for personal enrichment. *Gunman's Gold* begins with these lines:

> The strategy of Lee Swain was simple. It consisted in being in the right place at the right time. He had managed to get there, through skilful planning, so often that he had stacked up what he considered a nest egg. He had done that in the Eastern States. When he wanted to make the nest egg grow into a whole brood of thriving birds, he decided to go West.

The potential of the land is shown by the rich mines in *Gunman's Gold, Marbleface, South of Rio Grande* and *Destry Rides Again,* and by the richness of the farmland in *Singing Guns* and *Larramee's Ranch.* In book after book, wealth and a girl are parcelled out at the end as a reward for the hero, but there are exceptions.

The tenuousness with which wealth is held is also manifest. In *Gunman's Gold* (1933), two prospectors are shot dead as they work. Bank-robberies or train heists occur in many books. More interesting are those books in which trickster figures use their wits to cheat others out of wealth. In *Montana Rides!* (1933), Montana successfully poses as the kidnapped heir of a wealthy rancher in order to siphon off some of the rancher's riches. He does not carry the plan through, however. In *Marbleface,* Colonel Riggs creates a short-lived speculative boom in Piegan by dishonestly besting a rival town both for the status of county seat and for the advantage of a railway connection.

The relationship between tenuousness, acquisitiveness and cleverness is given more positive and more explicit treatment in *Speedy.* Unlike the essential dishonesty of the ploys just discussed, Speedy's endeavours are seen as fair contests. The con-man hero even warns his intended victim 'We're all men, we all have a share of brains, we all want money, we all want an easy time. Well, your dollars are your treasure; your wits are the soldiers that guard it. If I can put your soldiers to sleep, I take your money. That's my game, and it's a good game. It beats chess all hollow.'

Whether it is gained by fair means or foul, Faust's attitude to wealth is ambivalent. Often one glimpses a distrust of riches and a dislike of those who possess them. One aspect of this already noted is Rhiannon's critique of 'blood money' in *Singing Guns.* In *Brothers on the Trail,* Rickie Willard defends his outlaw brother: 'There's a thousand gents up there in the mountains ready to die for him still, because he never did no harm. All he ever nicked was the big gents, the big operators that had so many millions they could afford to lose a few thousands here and there!' Rickie is careful to explain that the gang does not prey on poor folk even when resources are needed. This contempt for the wealthy is an inversion of the contempt for the underdog victim expressed by Wister in *The Virginian.*

Money is feared for its dangers as much as it is desired for its possibilities. It is recognised as a weapon as much as a status symbol. By paying Ralph Carr's debts in *Brothers on the Trail,* for example, Harry Loomis feels that his entitlement to Ralph's daughter is strengthened. In *Destry Rides Again,* Chet Bent uses money to frame Destry and later, when he pays his expenses, to purchase his gratitude and to blind and weaken him. Frances Jones, in *The Tenderfoot,* succinctly articulates the insidious power of money over the poor: 'Mother died before I could remember her. The rest of the time dad was fightin' wild hosses and a mortgage. He could beat the hosses, but he couldn't beat the mortgage. He used to say that a mortgage was like bad rheumatism: you couldn't get it out of your system.'

It is not surprising that wealthy men are often portrayed unsympathetically in Faust's Westerns. In *Speedy,* both well-to-do lawyers are made to look ridiculous when they fall victim to Speedy's schemes. There is a touch of villainy as well when Chalmers is described as 'dramatically pulling out his wallet, like a revolver, from his breast pocket.' Mr Julius Maybeck (*Larramee's Ranch*) stands as the archetypal capitalist who expects gratitude for minor philanthropy from those he exploits. He has built a bank 'in the guise of a Greek temple among the little bungalows of the village' and longs for a commemorative statue with the inscription, 'To Julius Overman Maybeck, philanthropist and financier, whose genius, whose generosity, and whose foresight created this city and all that is in it . . . .' In his hunger for public recognition, he has forgotten to acknowledge his primary motivation.

Not all wealthy men are villainous, of course, and it is not insignificant that wealthy transplanted Easterners tend to fare worse than their Western counterparts. Certainly this helps to fit the distrust of wealth into the value framework of the Western formula, as do such comments as Tom Holden's exclamation on learning of Larramee's fortune: 'Inherited money, eh? That's hardly fair!'

Faust's critique of wealth goes deeper than the social bias indicated so far, as can be seen in such books as *Speedy* and *Gunman's Gold,* two works which reject the traditional happy ending of the Western. In both the hero refuses to accept the reward held out to him at the end. Shannigan, in *Gunman's Gold,* accepts the girl, but refuses the money, twice. He will not touch a gold mine that has been the scene and motive of a murder. Later he declines his fee for the saving of Jack Reynolds: 'If Jack had been worth his salt, I would have taken your money—and a pile of it too. I would have sent in a bill that would have made your eyes pop. But as for this job with Reynolds—I charge that all on the wrong side of the ledger. I won't talk money with you.' The end which, in his own mind, justified his extra-legal efforts, has turned out to be unworthy. To accept money would be to disparage his work still further. Besides, money has become so corrupted by the greed, the dishonesty and the selfishness which surround it that Shannigan can not accept it as an honourable reward. The distrust of wealth on this level, together with the profes-

sional code, pinpoint an important transitional element in outlook from Western hero to private eye.

Speedy's objection to wealth is of a different tenor: he refuses both the girl and the fortune because they threaten to make him less free. With an echo of Dismuke's lament that his lifestyle has made him incapable of any other, Speedy says, 'I always thought that I was only killing time until a grand opportunity should come my way, but now that the opportunity has come, I see that the devil has been too careful a schoolteacher, for me, and I can't forget his lessons.'

Rejections in these terms go beyond Grey's uneasiness over the efficacy of a lasting reward or the ability of a man to enjoy his reward. Faust is questioning whether the 'best man', as he defines him, can feel morally justified in accepting a reward tainted by the lawlessness of the West. And he is asking whether the possibilities which wealth brings are worth their cost: the loss of freedom and the burden of defence.

In developing his heroes, Faust subverts key formulaic attributes, redefining such ideologically charged concepts as the protean nature of identity within American society, and the importance of strength and reputation in achieving high status. Once reworked, these key concepts offer Faust extensive possibilities for exploring his personal worries and preoccupations.

The issue of identity allows Faust to explore his anxiety over the relationship between parentage and identity. In *Montana Rides!,* the Montana Kid poses as the returning kidnapped son of a wealthy rancher. Although an imposter, he proves himself a worthy heir to Lavery, the owner, earning the respect and friendship of all who work with him and the love of his assumed family. The true son, whom Montana locates in an attempt to compensate for his deception, is a Mexican bandit; kidnapped and brought up by a Mexican outlaw, he has been taught to hate his real family.

What constitutes the essential characteristics of the father-son relationship, then? After Tonio Rubriz/Dick Lavery is told the true story of his parentage, he turns to the bandit and says, 'Padre, all these years have been a lie. . . . That man is my father!' The outlaw replies, 'You talk like a fool. You *are* a fool. Are you not my son? What is blood? The dogs and the cattle have blood. But my soul is breathed into you.' Tonio accepts the truth of this assertion. Although he changes sides when he learns that his adopted father plans to kill his blood relatives, the book suggests that no amount of time or love or change of culture will blot out his Mexican past. He crosses the border with his family, but at the end of the book he wears the ring the outlaw has left for him.

It is easier to make Montana, the pretender, into a true co-heir with Tonio, for he is without parentage, past or obligations: when asked his true name, he replies, blushing, 'Nicknames—that's all I've had, or synthetic names that people gave me when they took me in when I was a brat.' Although he is shamed by his namelessness, it leaves him free to become what he will. Both the sense of loss and the freedom of the orphan are thus recalled.

The freedom of anonymity is explored further in **Speedy.** The hero discusses his protean identity with a lawyer who thinks him a rogue: 'Sometimes . . . I'm a son who's been disinherited by a cruel father. . . . Sometimes . . . I'm about to go to work to earn enough money to finish my school course. Sometimes I'm recovering from an attack of the great white plague.' When asked his name he replies, 'I've been called a good many names . . . some of them long, and some of them short. I've been called more one-syllable names than almost anyone in the world, I suppose. But the one I prefer is Speedy.'

Speedy's identity as a con-man is a rather troubling offshoot of the self-made man, and the fact that he is a lovable rogue with a fairly strict professional code is only slightly reassuring. Such qualms are in the reader's mind, however. For Faust, the heart of the issue is a highly personal one: the fraudulence of an identity that results from the rejection or ignorance of one's parentage; from the denial of past.

Destry Rides Again explores the same ground from another viewpoint. Willie Thornton's parentage is never in question; the issue is whether the father is worthy of the son. One hears definite echoes of Faust's past when Willie confronts the truth of his father's character:

> It was for him the crashing of a world about his ears. He had not been able to avoid seeing the truth about many phases of his father's idleness and shiftlessness, but, no matter what else he might be, for these years he had loomed in the mind of Willie as a great man, because he was the companion of Destry, the famous. A hundred stories he had told Willie of adventures with that celebrated man, and now these stories had to be relegated to the sphere of the fairy-tale!

Willie's courage and devotion earn him a new and worthier father, Destry, who in turn feels the weight of responsibility as a chosen father: 'he felt a sudden scorn for the baser parts that were in him, the idler, the scoffer at others, the disdainful mocker at the labours of life. He wished to be simple, real, quiet, able to command the affection of his peers.' The notion that the father should be worthy of the son must have tugged heavily at Faust, only to be countered by guilt and an argument for the importance of loyalty.

Faust's treatment of strength, while less idiosyncratic, is also unusual in that his viewpoint is that of the underdog. In his work, strength is regarded with awe and envy; it is to be attained if possible, and countered by the wily tricks of the potential victim if not. Typically, he peoples his books with physical giants, and occasionally there are even good giants such as Rhiannon. More often, his giants are minor characters such as 'Gorilla' Jones in **Gunman's Gold,** employed to demonstrate the mettle of his heroes. Jones is a very effective jailer whose daily demonstrations of prowess keep the prisoners quiescent: 'his final exhibition was with the sandbag, which he smashed with either hand, dealing out terrible blows that seemed capable of driving straight through the body of an ordinary man.' As he does this, he wears an expression of 'animal intensity

of delight.' The performance holds the prisoners spellbound.

When the modest and unimposing Shannigan agrees to spar with 'Gorilla' in order to win the right to see a prisoner, the giant is filled with sadistic delight. For Shannigan the encounter is not a test of his courage so much as a test of his character, for Shannigan is confident that he can win; he possesses hidden resources of tremendous strength. Pictorially, the encounter appears as David against Goliath, with the expected victim magically transformed.

Speedy's confrontation with Big Alf has a similar flavour. When Mary asks how a small man such as Speedy could have beaten him Alf is exasperated: 'How do I know? When I reached for him, I just seemed to hit myself. That's all that I know about it. When I rushed him, I just tripped on the place where he'd been standing, and sailed right on and lit on my face.' Alf finally concludes by deciding 'Magician, that's what he is.' The bag of tricks Speedy brings to combat are considerable, and they form a veritable handbook for the survival of the weak: he knows how to use his opponent's strength to his own advantage, when to play dead, and when it is best to use every fibre of his being to fight for his life. He can judge whether he should run, or submit to temporary defeat. His tricks are hardly the usual array for a Western hero. As we have seen, they hark back to the clever folk hero, to the trickster.

The issue of reputation also engaged Faust's interest, most notably the problem of undeserved reputation, another taboo area for American ideology, but one of great interest to Faust, who was half ashamed of his own success. In **The Tenderfoot,** Allan's false notoriety as a bloodthirsty desperado destroys him, partly because the hero comes to believe what is said about him and is overcome with unwanted guilt. Even when those closest to Allan offer reassurance, he takes their assertions as misguided kindness.

More often, the undeserved reputation proves embarrassing because the man who possesses it feels unworthy. This is the case with Jerry Ash in **Marbleface.** When he downs a robber with a lucky snap shot, he knows how fortunate he has been, but everyone else thinks him extremely skilful. When Colonel Riggs tells him that there is something calm about his presence, Ash comments, 'I could have laughed in his face, when I remember[ed] that it was my practice in schooling my nerves for the sake of my rotten, crumbling, shattered heart that had given me this calm exterior.' Every time he tries to set the record straight, his attempt is seen as modesty, and his renown grows.

Ash's reputation is both liability and asset. While tempting to the ambitious who wish to enhance their own standing, it is also a powerful defence: 'I knew that there were fifty men in that one county who could shoot the eyes out of my head, who were far faster and surer in every way with a weapon of any kind. But the nerves of a good many of them would be upset by merely the reputation which was behind me . . . .' Ash is eventually bettered, but his honesty and fairness bolster him in defeat, and he remains high in the regard of the townspeople.

The way Faust subverts key terms does not negate the central thematic argument of the Western formula. After all, such champions of American-dream optimism as Grey are not immune to discontinuities. However, Faust does not use gender to apportion conflicting value-sets. This makes the incompatibility more obvious and more difficult to bridge. It also lessens the importance of his female characters, for it makes them seem superfluous to the central conflict, though more involved in the ways of the West. During their infrequent appearances, Faust's women are treated more as partners than as civilisers, but they still tend to be the minor partner, the little woman in the background.

The discontinuities revealed in Faust's work are also different in kind from those exposed in Grey's. Grey explores a rift which is characteristic of American society as a whole and reflects the standard remedy for channelling competing values. The discontinuities in Faust's work, on the other hand, are the product of different levels of ideology. Such values as self-reliance, independence and competence belong to the ideology built into the Western formula itself. Those of the underdog—loyalty, mercy, wily cleverness and endurance—are fragments of a working-class ideology which is never crystallised within the works. While the conflict of values with which Grey deals has wide relevance within American society, the conflict in Faust's work is only relevent to those on the bottom of the socio-economic heap: those who want to justify their own lack of success or the failure of someone close to them.

None the less, Faust's work asserts the fundamental primacy of the individual as social unit. In *Singing Guns,* the sheriff may develop a close bond with Rhiannon, but in the end Rhiannon must stand or fall on his own merits. That it is not admissable for a person to be a substitute in someone else's battles is the lesson of *Brothers on the Trail*: Rickie cannot fight in his brother's stead; the Chief must fulfil his own obligations and maintain his own position. Faust's heroes do succeed, and their rewards are often the familiar ones of material comfort and personal happiness.

Group action is given an unpleasant, often a villainous, representation. The angry mob that captures the sheriff in *Gunman's Gold* is fairly typical: 'Hands were laid on the sheriff. Leering, savage, rejoicing faces appeared before him, men who never had liked him, men who long had writhed under the heavy hand with which he occasionally bore down upon the rougher spirits in town. He could guess what mercy he would receive from them.' They are cowards emboldened by numbers; gullible enough to be easily manipulated by the villain or by the acting of a young girl, and sufficiently greedy to be quickly diverted by the prospect of personal gain. Mobs in *Marbleface* and in *South of Rio Grande* are given equally derisory treatment.

The continuity of values between East and West is also underscored. Anthony Woodbury (*Trailin'*, 1919) and Jerry Ash (*Marbleface*) are representative of the Easterners who successfully make the transition to the West. Similarly, there are many Westerners, Sheriff Caradac (*Singing Guns*) and Chris Verner (*Larramee's Ranch*), for example, who become successful ranchers or capitalists.

The complexity of the issues Faust explores in his Westerns brings into question his dismissal by critics. In Faust's case, as with Grey's, it is the crudities of his workmanship which account for the apparent superficiality of his work. His approach to his material is a strange amalgam of attitudes, and his style reflects this. A terse, hard-boiled style blends with elements of fantasy, sentimentality, folktale, and myth. He has little respect for his material, and treats it in an offhand, superficial manner. Too often the mechanical manoeuvrings of the writer are visible behind the prose.

In *Gunman's Gold,* for example, one can almost sense the line at which Faust decides he must shift the portrayal of a character to accommodate the developing story line. At the beginning of the story, Reynolds is generous and self-effacing. On p. 59, he has a small temper tantrum that throws slight doubts on his character, but by p. 65 these are put to rest when Shannigan offers what appears to be the final verdict on Reynolds: 'he's brave and pretty straight. He's not a saint, and he may not be a hero.' When questioned on p. 76, Reynolds exhibits intelligence. But on p. 111 his character takes a sudden turn for the worse, and from that point on he is foolish, selfish and greedy.

In *Singing Guns,* Faust seems to toy for about fifteen pages with the idea of turning Sheriff Caradac into a villain. If this is not the case, then these pages are a rather crude attempt to give the plot another twist. In either case, they jar, an obvious contrivance. Such sudden shifts indicate the shallowness of Faust's characterisation and the careless, hurried treatment he gives to his material generally.

Although Faust's style can be broadly labelled colloquial, it suffers from the same inconsistencies as his structure. He seems content to utilise whatever style or technique serves his purpose of the moment without worrying about unity of effect. *South of Rio Grande* is a good example. The book begins as a first person narration. The language is terse and understated, exhibiting a restraint that approaches the hard-boiled style: 'The chief had hit me hard. So hard that I had to look out the window, and looking out there into the street, I saw the kid in the middle of trouble.' But Faust does too much explaining to sustain this: 'The kid was all right; he meant no harm; but he was simply loaded with excess energy that couldn't take care of itself, and, of course, that meant trouble of the worst kind that far west of the Mississippi.' Worse still, the narrator turns frankly sentimental: 'I'm jealous of The MacMore for the first time. . . . I wouldn't mind having a kid like you in the family myself.' His young protégé replies by gripping his hand, saying, 'You are one of the family, Joe.'

By chapter 23, Faust has clumsily switched to third-person narration, explaining,

> For what immediately follows, I have not the narrative of Dennis MacMore, though it is about him and his strange adventures that I have to speak. I have not his version, for a reason that will soon appear; but all that I describe is substantiated by my knowledge . . . , by certain eyewitnesses, and by a mere use of sheer logic. . . .

By chapter 31, Faust is exploiting the romantic interest of the scene unabashedly: 'How far did she see the truth about him, and how clearly did he show that he was losing his mind about her? How much was she upset . . . ?' On p. 250 the first-person narration resumes, and it is the laconic style which has the last word.

Such a hodgepodge of techniques comes close to self-parody at times. Faust's rather backhanded reassurance that the third-person narration is 'no more a fiction than what has gone before' exhibits this self-mockery. Faust uses the term 'fairy-tale' as he uses it in *Destry Rides Again,* as a kind of epithet. It is used often, and, in books populated by giants, sorcerers, and heroes with magical ability, this too amounts to self-ridicule.

Faust's writing succeeds when it is stripped down to dialogue and a terse recounting of the ensuing action; when it uses a consistent colloquial style. In dialogue Faust seems to lose his bitterness, and demonstrates a good ear for conversation as this passage from *Singing Guns* demonstrates:

> 'G'wan away,' said the father to his son. 'I don't need you and I ain't asked for you. Gwynn, I'm glad to see you. I admire how you done up the old place, over there. I been by and admired to see it. I wanta buy that place. What you sell for?'
>
> 'It ain't mine,' replied Rhiannon. 'The sheriff, he owns it, Mr. Dee.'
>
> 'Ha?' exclaimed Oliver Dee. 'How old am I?'
>
> 'Fifty,' guessed Rhiannon, surrendering himself to the oddities of this conversation.
>
> 'Is that old enough to be mistered?' asked Mr. Dee.
>
> 'Maybe not,' said Rhiannon, and smiled. He rarely smiled!

The passage flows naturally, and builds a picture of Oliver Dee with a few easy strokes.

Faust is at his best when he puts the giants and sorcerers to one side and writes about humans on a human level. He does this in *Destry Rides Again,* where the only hidden potential is the ability to learn and to develop. Here his energy is funnelled into deepening his characters rather than enlarging them; the bitterness is contained and directed. *Destry Rides Again* is his best book, and a good one. (pp. 103-19)

Cynthia S. Hamilton, "Frederick Faust," in her Western and Hard-Boiled Detective Fiction in America: From High Noon to Midnight, *Macmillan Press, 1987, pp. 94-119.*

FURTHER READING

Atkins, John. "The Chancelleries of Europe." In his *The British Spy Novel: Styles in Treachery,* pp. 63-71. London: John Calder, 1984.
    Includes a critique of *The Phantom Spy.*

Bacon, Martha. "Destry and Dionysus." *The Atlantic Monthly* 196, No. 1 (July 1955): 72-4.
    Personal reminiscences by a family friend.

Bloodworth, William A., Jr. "Max Brand (Frederick Faust)." In *Fifty Western Writers: A Bio-Bibliographical Sourcebook,* edited by Fred Erisman and Richard W. Etulain, pp. 32-41. Westport, Conn.: Greenwood Press, 1982.
    Brief biography of Faust and critical survey of his westerns.

Etulain, Richard W. Introduction to *Destry Rides Again,* by Max Brand, pp. v-xi. Boston: Gregg Press, 1979.
    Critical introduction accompanied by photos from the 1939 movie.

Nachbar, Jack. Introduction to *The Untamed,* by Max Brand, pp. v-xii. Boston: Gregg Press, 1978.
    Provides a critical introduction to a special edition of Faust's first published novel.

Nye, Russell. "Sixshooter Country." In his *The Unembarrassed Muse: The Popular Arts in America,* pp. 280-304. New York: Dial Press, 1970.
    Asserts that in Faust's novels "the West furnishes little more than a backdrop for rubberstamped fiction."

Reynolds, Quentin. *The Fiction Factory: Or, From Pulp Row to Quality Street.* New York: Random House, 1955, pp. 180-92.
    Offers brief biographical sketch and chronicles Faust's contributions to pulp western magazines.

Additional coverage of Faust's life and career is contained in the following source published by Gale Research: *Contemporary Authors,* Vol. 108.

Federico García Lorca

1898-1936

Spanish poet, playwright, critic, and essayist.

For further information on García Lorca's career, see *TCLC*, Volumes 1 and 7.

INTRODUCTION

One of the most important figures in modern Spanish literature, García Lorca drew upon elements of Spanish life and culture to create works at once traditional and modern, personal and universal. In both his drama and his poetry, García Lorca's principal themes were death, frustrated sexuality, and the relationship between dream and reality. As a writer García Lorca was concerned that the lives of ordinary people remained central to his works: "No true man still believes in that rubbish about pure art, art for art's sake. At this dramatic moment in the course of world events, the artist must weep and laugh with his own people."

García Lorca was born and raised in rural Andalusia, the southernmost province of Spain and a region greatly influenced by Arabic and gypsy culture. He attended schools in the town of Almeria and studied law and literature at the University of Granada. After moving to Madrid in 1919 García Lorca continued his studies at the Residencia de Estudiantes, a center for writers, critics, and scholars. García Lorca's first volume of poetry, *Libro de poemas,* is a compilation of gypsy folklore García Lorca heard during his youth in Andalusia, and is recognized for its vivid, accessible language and imagery drawn from classical mythology. After the publication of this volume, García Lorca organized Spain's first *cante jondo* festival. *Cante jondo* ("deep song") is a traditional form of Andalusian music that, according to Felicia Hardison Londré, "combines intensely emotional yet stylistically spare poetry on themes of pain, suffering, love, and death with a primitive musical form." García Lorca's interest in the *cante jondo* is reflected in the collections *Canciones* and *Poema del cante jondo.* García Lorca's next collection, *Primer romancero gitano (The Gypsy Ballads),* is widely regarded as a masterpiece of Spanish poetry. In this volume, comprised of eighteen poems written between 1924 and 1927, García Lorca incorporated images of gypsy village life with traditional ballad forms to create verse both thematically accessible and lyrically complex. C. M. Bowra has observed: "[*The Gypsy Ballads*] is a book which has a special place in our time because it shows not only that the outlook of a highly civilized poet is in many ways that of the simplest men and women, but that the new devices which have been invented to express a modern sensibility are not restricted to urban and sophisticated subjects." While not as well known as *The Gypsy Ballads, Llanto por Ignacio Sánchez Mejías (Lament for the Death of a Bull-*

fighter, and Other Poems) is also highly regarded. The title poem of this collection is a four-part elegy occasioned by the mauling death of Spain's most celebrated matador, Ignacio Sánchez Mejías, who was one of García Lorca's closest friends. In this work García Lorca presents the matador as a vital individual who confronts death with playful indifference. In 1929, García Lorca traveled to New York City after suffering an emotional crisis. Deeply disturbed by the monotony of industrial life and America's reliance on mechanization, García Lorca began writing surrealistic poems that were later collected in the posthumous volume *Poeta en Nueva York (Poet in New York, and Other Poems),* a work that reflects a profound sense of chaos and alienation.

After returning to Spain in 1930, García Lorca composed the majority of his dramas, most prominently *Bodas de sangre (Blood Wedding), Yerma,* and *La casa de Bernarda Alba (The House of Bernarda Alba). Blood Wedding* is the story of a bride who runs off with another man on her wedding day. The bridegroom, understanding that his honor is at stake, follows the bride and her lover into a forest where the two men fight and eventually kill each other. Considered a violent and passionate account of peasant life, *Blood Wedding* addresses García Lorca's concerns with sexuality and death. In *Yerma*, García Lorca chronicles three years in the life of a young married woman, Yerma, who longs to have children despite being unsatisfied with her husband. After taking part in an annual pilgrimage of childless women, Yerma strangles her husband because he, unlike her, does not want children. *The House of Bernarda Alba* focuses on Bernarda, a tyrannical woman who virtually imprisons her five daughters in her home. When Pepe, the only eligible male in the village, becomes engaged to the eldest daughter, the others attempt to express their own sexuality through flirtatious behavior. The play ends tragically when the youngest daughter, who has been having an affair with Pepe, commits suicide after being led to believe that her mother has killed the young man. *The House of Bernarda Alba* has been interpreted as both a symbolic representation of totalitarian governments and as a realistic psychological study of women.

In 1936 political unrest in Spain forced García Lorca into hiding, despite the fact he had never aligned himself with any political party and referred to himself as "catholic, communist, anarchist, liberal, conservative, and monarchist." García Lorca was eventually discovered at the home of a friend and arrested by General Francisco Franco's nationalists. After being detained by the Civil Government in Granada for several days, García Lorca was executed by a firing squad in an olive grove outside the tiny village of Viznár and buried in an unmarked grave.

PRINCIPAL WORKS

Impresiones y paisajes (sketches) 1918
El maleficio de la mariposa (drama) 1920
  [*The Spell of the Butterfly*, 1957]
Libro de poemas (poetry) 1921
Canciones (poetry) 1927
*Mariana Pineda (drama) 1927
Primer romancero gitano (poetry) 1928
  [*The Gypsy Ballads*, 1953]
†La zapatera prodigiosa (drama) 1930
Poema del cante jondo (poetry) 1931
†Amor de Don Perlimplín con Belisa en su jardín (drama) 1933
Bodas de sangre (drama) 1933
  [*Blood Wedding*, 1939]
El público (drama) 1934
  [*The Audience*, 1958]
†Yerma (drama) 1934
†Doña Rosita la soltera (drama) 1935
Llanto por Ignacio Sánchez Mejías (poetry) 1935
  [*Lament for the Death of a Bullfighter, and Other Poems*, 1937]
†Así que pasen cinco años (drama) 1938
Retablillo de Don Cristóbal (drama) 1938
  [*In the Frame of Don Cristóbal*, 1944]
Obras Completas. 7 vols. (complete works) 1938-1946
Poeta en Nueva York (poetry) 1940

[*Poet in New York, and Other Poems*, 1940]
Selected Poems of Federico García Lorca (poetry) 1943
‡La casa de Bernarda Alba (drama) 1945
The Cricket Sings: Poems and Songs for Children (poetry) 1980
Deep Song, and Other Prose (lectures, poetry, and essays) 1980

*Translated as *Marian Pineda* and published in *Tulane Drama Review*, 1962.

†These works were translated and published in *Lorca's Theatre*, 1941.

‡Translated as *The House of Bernarda Alba* and published in *Three Tragedies*, 1947.

CRITICISM

Federico García Lorca (lecture date 1930)

[*In the following lecture first delivered in 1930 and later reprinted in 1955, García Lorca explains his concept of* duende, *or true artistic inspiration.*]

Whoever inhabits that bull's hide stretched between the Jucar, the Guadalete, the Sil, or the Pisuerga—no need to mention the streams joining those lion-colored waves churned up by the Plata—has heard it said with a certain frequency: "Now that has real *duende!*" It was in this spirit that Manuel Torres, that great artist of the Andalusian people, once remarked to a singer: "You have a voice, you know all the styles, but you will never bring it off because you have no *duende.*"

In all Andalusia, from the rock of Jaen to the shell of Cádiz, people constantly speak of the *duende* and find it in everything that springs out of energetic instinct. That marvelous singer, "El Librijano," originator of the *Debla*, observed, "Whenever I am singing with *duende*, no one can come up to me"; and one day the old gypsy dancer, "La Malena," exclaimed while listening to Brailowsky play a fragment of Bach: "Olé! That has *duende!*"—and remained bored by Gluck and Brahms and Darius Milhaud. And Manuel Torres, to my mind a man of exemplary blood culture, once uttered this splendid phrase while listening to Falla himself play his "Nocturno del Generalife": "Whatever has black sounds, has *duende.*" There is no greater truth.

These "black sounds" are the mystery, the roots that probe through the mire that we all know of, and do not understand, but which furnishes us with whatever is sustaining in art. Black sounds: so said the celebrated Spaniard, thereby concurring with Goethe, who, in effect, defined the *duende* when he said, speaking of Paganini: "A mysterious power that all may feel and no philosophy can explain."

The *duende*, then, is a power and not a construct, is a

struggle and not a concept. I have heard an old guitarist, a true virtuoso, remark, "The *duende* is not in the throat, the *duende* comes up from inside, up from the very soles of the feet." That is to say, it is not a question of aptitude, but of a true and viable style—of blood, in other words; of what is oldest in culture: of creation made act.

This "mysterious power that all may feel and no philosophy can explain," is, in sum, the earth-force, the same *duende* that fired the heart of Nietzsche, who sought it in its external forms on the Rialto Bridge, or in the music of Bizet, without ever finding it, or understanding that the *duende* he pursued had rebounded from the mystery-minded Greeks to the dancers of Cádiz or the gored, Dionysian cry of Silverio's *siguiriya.*

So much for the *duende;* but I would not have you confuse the *duende* with the theological demon of doubt at whom Luther, on a Bacchic impulse, hurled an inkwell in Nuremberg, or with the Catholic devil, destructive, but short on intelligence, who disguised himself as a bitch in order to enter the convents, or with the talking monkey that Cervantes' mountebank carried in the comedy about jealousy and the forests of Andalusia.

No. The *duende* I speak of, shadowy, palpitating, is a descendant of that benignest daemon of Socrates, he of marble and salt, who scratched the master angrily the day he drank the hemlock; and of that melancholy imp of Descartes, little as an unripe almond, who, glutted with circles and lines, went out on the canals to hear the drunken sailors singing.

Any man—any artist, as Nietzsche would say—climbs the stairway in the tower of his perfection at the cost of a struggle with a *duende*—not with an angel, as some have maintained, or with his muse. This fundamental distinction must be kept in mind if the root of a work of art is to be grasped.

The Angel guides and endows, like Saint Raphael, or prohibits and avoids like Saint Michael, or foretells, like Saint Gabriel.

The Angel dazzles; but he flies over men's heads and remains in mid-air, shedding his grace; and the man, without any effort whatever, realizes his work, or his fellow-feeling, or his dance. The angel on the road to Damascus, and he who entered the crevice of the little balcony of Assisi, or that other angel who followed in the footsteps of Heinrich Suso, *commanded*—and there was no resisting his radiance, for he waved wings of steel in an atmosphere of predestination.

The Muse dictates and, in certain cases, prompts. There is relatively little she can do, for she keeps aloof and is so full of lassitude (I have seen her twice) that I myself have had to put half a heart of marble in her. The Poets of the Muse hear voices and do not know where they come from; but surely they are from the Muse, who encourages and at times devours them entirely. Such, for example, was the case of Apollinaire, that great poet ravaged by the horrible Muse with whom the divinely angelic Rousseau painted him. The Muse arouses the intellect, bearing landscapes of columns and the false taste of laurel; but intellect is of-tentimes the foe of poetry because it imitates too much: it elevates the poet to a throne of acute angles and makes him forget that in time the ants can devour him, too, or that a great, arsenical locust can fall on his head, against which the Muses who live inside monocles or the luke-warm lacquer roses of insignificant salons, are helpless.

Angel and Muse approach from without; the Angel sheds light and the Muse gives form (Hesiod learned of them). Gold leaf or chiton-folds: the poet finds his models in his laurel coppice. But the *Duende,* on the other hand, must come to life in the nethermost recesses of the blood.

And repel the Angel, too—kick out the Muse and conquer his awe of the fragrance of the violets that breathe from the poetry of the eighteenth century, or of the great telescope in whose lenses the Muse dozes off, sick of limits.

The true struggle is with the *Duende.*

The paths leading to God are well known, from the barbaric way of the hermit, to the subtler modes of the mystic. With a tower, then, like Saint Theresa, or with three roads, like St. John of the Cross. And even if we must cry out in Isaiah's voice: "Truly, thou art the hidden God!" at the end and at last, God sends to each seeker his first fiery thorns.

To seek out the *Duende,* however, neither map nor discipline is required. Enough to know that he kindles the blood like an irritant, that he exhausts, that he repulses, all the bland, geometrical assurances, that he smashes the styles; that he makes of a Goya, master of the grays, the silvers, the roses of the great English painters, a man painting with his knees and his fists in bituminous blacks; that he bares a Mosen Cinto Verdaguer to the cold of the Pyrenees or induces a Jorge Manrique to sweat out his death on the crags of Ocaña, or invests the delicate body of Rimbaud in the green domino of the saltimbanque, or fixes dead fish-eyes on the Comte de Lautréamont in the early hours of the boulevard.

The great artists of southern Spain, both gypsies and flamenco, whether singing or dancing or playing on instruments, know that no emotion is possible without the mediation of the *Duende.* They may hoodwink the people, they may give the illusion of *duende* without really having it, just as writers and painters and literary fashion-mongers without *duende* cheat you daily; but it needs only a little care and the will to resist one's own indifference, to discover the imposture and put it and its crude artifice to flight.

Once the Andalusian singer, Pastora Pavon, "The Girl with the Combs," a sombre Hispanic genius whose capacity for fantasy equals Goya's or Raphael el Gallo's, was singing in a little tavern in Cádiz. She sparred with her voice—now shadowy, now like molten tin, now covered over with moss; she tangled her voice in her long hair or drenched it in sherry or lost it in the darkest and furthermost bramble bushes. But nothing happened—useless, all of it! The hearers remained silent.

There stood Ignacio Espeleta, handsome as a Roman turtle, who was asked once why he never worked, and replied with a smile worthy of Argantonio: "How am I to work if I come from Cádiz?"

There, too, stood Héloise, the fiery aristocrat, whore of Seville, direct descendant of Soledad Vargas, who in the thirties refused to marry a Rothschild because he was not of equal blood. There were the Floridas, whom some people call butchers, but who are really millennial priests sacrificing bulls constantly to Geryon; and in a corner stood that imposing breeder of bulls, Don Pablo Murabe, with the air of a Cretan mask. Pastora Pavon finished singing in the midst of total silence. There was only a little man, one of those dancing mannikins who leap suddenly out of brandy bottles, who observed sarcastically in a very low voice: "*Viva* Paris!" As if to say: We are not interested in aptitude or techniques or virtuosity here. We are interested in something else.

Then the "Girl with the Combs" got up like a woman possessed, her face blasted like a medieval weeper, tossed off a great glass of Cazalla at a single draught, like a potion of fire, and settled down to singing—without a voice, without breath, without nuance, throat aflame—but with *duende!* She had contrived to annihilate all that was nonessential in song and make way for an angry and incandescent *Duende,* friend of the sand-laden winds, so that everyone listening tore at his clothing almost in the same rhythm with which the West Indian negroes in their rites rend away their clothes, huddled in heaps before the image of Saint Barbara.

The "Girl with the Combs" had to *mangle* her voice because she knew there were discriminating folk about who asked not for form, but for the marrow of form—pure music spare enough to keep itself in air. She had to deny her faculties and her security; that is to say, to turn out her Muse and keep vulnerable, so that her *Duende* might come and vouchsafe the hand-to-hand struggle. And then how she sang! Her voice feinted no longer; it jetted up like blood, ennobled by sorrow and sincerity, it opened up like ten fingers of a hand around the nailed feet of a Christ by Juan de Juni—tempestuous!

The arrival of the *Duende* always presupposes a radical change in all the forms as they existed on the old plane. It gives a sense of refreshment unknown until then, together with that quality of the just-opening rose, of the miraculous, which comes and instils an almost religious transport.

In all Arabian music, in the dances, songs, elegies of Arabia, the coming of the *Duende* is greeted by fervent outcries of *Allah! Allah! God! God!,* so close to the *Olé! Olé!* of our bull rings that who is to say they are not actually the same; and in all the songs of southern Spain the appearance of the *Duende* is followed by heartfelt exclamations of *God alive!*—profound, human, tender, the cry of communion with God through the medium of the five senses and the grace of the *Duende* that stirs the voice and the body of the dancer—a flight from this world, both real and poetic, pure as Pedro Soto de Roja's over the seven gardens (that most curious poet of the seventeenth century), or Juan Calimacho's on the tremulous ladder of tears.

Naturally, when flight is achieved, all feel its effects: the initiate coming to see at last how style triumphs over inferior matter, and the unenlightened, through the I-don't-know-what of an authentic emotion. Some years ago, in a dancing contest at Jerez de la Frontera, an old lady of eighty, competing against beautiful women and young girls with waists supple as water, carried off the prize merely by the act of raising her arms, throwing back her head, and stamping the little platform with a blow of her feet; but in the conclave of muses and angels foregathered there—beauties of form and beauties of smile—the dying *Duende* triumphed as it had to, trailing the rusted knife blades of its wings along the ground.

All the arts are capable of *duende,* but it naturally achieves its widest play in the fields of music, dance, and the spoken poem, since these require a living presence to interpret them, because they are forms which grow and decline perpetually and raise their contours on the precise present.

Often the *Duende* of the musician passes over into the *Duende* of the interpreter, and at other times, when musician and poet are not matched, the *Duende* of the interpreter—this is interesting—creates a new marvel that retains the appearance—and the appearance only—of the originating form. Such was the case with the *duende*-ridden Duse who deliberately sought out failures in order to turn them into triumphs, thanks to her capacity for invention; or with Paganini who, as Goethe explained, could make one hear profoundest melody in out-and-out vulgarity; or with a delectable young lady from the port of Santa María whom I saw singing and dancing the horrendous Italian ditty, "O Marie!" with such rhythms, such pauses, and such conviction that she transformed an Italian gewgaw into a hard serpent of raised gold. What happened, in effect, was that each in his own way found something new, something never before encountered, which put lifeblood and art into bodies void of expression.

In every country, death comes as a finality. It comes, and the curtain comes down. But not in Spain! In Spain the curtain goes up. Many people live out their lives between walls till the day they die and are brought out into the sun. In Spain, the dead are more alive than the dead of any other country of the world: their profile wounds like the edge of a barber's razor. The quip about death and the silent contemplation of it are familiar to the Spanish. From the "Dream of the Skulls" of Quevedo, to the "Putrescent Bishop" of Valdés Leal; from La Marbella of the seventeenth century who, dying in childbirth on the highway, says:

> The blood of my entrails
> Covers the horse.
> And the horses' hooves
> Strike fire from the pitch.

to a recent young man from Salamanca, killed by a bull, who exclaimed:

> My friends, I am dying.
> My friends, it goes badly.
> I've three handkerchiefs inside me,
> And this I apply now makes four.

there is a balustrade of flowering nitre where hordes peer out, contemplating death, with verses from Jeremiah for the grimmer side or sweet-smelling cypress for the more

García Lorca's depiction of death, a major theme in his works.

Inside the garden
I shall surely die.
Inside the rosebush.
They will kill me.
Mother, Mother, I went out
Gathering roses,
But surely death will find me
In the garden.
Mother, Mother, I went out
Cutting roses;
But surely death will find me
In the rosebush.
Inside the garden
I shall surely die.
In the rosebush
They will kill me.

Those heads frozen by the moon that Zurbarán painted, the butter-yellows and the lightning-yellows of El Greco, the narrative of Father Sigüenza, all the work of Goya, the presbytery of the Church of the Escorial, all polychrome sculpture, the crypt of the ducal house of Osuna, the death with the guitar in the chapel of the Benavente in Medina de Río Seco—all equal, on the plane of cultivated art, the pilgrimages of San Andrés de Teixido where the dead have their place in the procession; they are one with the songs for the dead that the women of Asturias intone with flame-filled lamps in the November night, one with the song and dance of the Sibyl in the cathedrals of Mallorca and Toledo, with the obscure "In Recort" of Tortosa, and the innumerable rites of Good Friday that, with the arcane Fiesta of the Bulls, epitomize the popular triumph of Spanish death. In all the world, Mexico alone can go hand-in-hand with my country.

When the Muse sees death on the way, she closes the door, or raises a plinth, or promenades an urn and inscribes an epitaph with a waxen hand, but in time she tears down her laurels again in a silence that wavers between two breezes. Under the truncated arch of the Ode, she joins with funereal meaning the exact flowers that the Italians of the fifteenth century depicted, with the identical cock of Lucretius, to frighten off an unforeseen darkness.

When the Angel sees death on the way, he flies in slow circles and weaves with tears of narcissus and ice the elegy we see trembling in the hands of Keats and Villasandino and Herrera and Becquer and Juan Ramón Jiménez. But imagine the terror of the Angel, should it feel a spider—even the very tiniest—on its tender and roseate flesh!

The *Duende,* on the other hand, will not approach at all if he does not see the possibility of death, if he is not convinced he will circle death's house, if there is not every assurance he can rustle the branches borne aloft by us all, that neither have, nor may ever have, the power to console.

With idea, with sound, or with gesture, the *Duende* chooses the brim of the well for his open struggle with the creator. Angel and Muse escape in the violin or in musical measure, but the *Duende* draws blood, and in the healing of the wound that never quite closes, all that is unprecedented and invented in a man's work has its origin.

The magical virtue of poetry lies in the fact that it is al-

lyrical—but in any case, a country where all that is most important has its final metallic valuation in death.

The knife and the cart wheel and the razor and the stinging beard-points of the shepherds, the shorn moon and the fly, the damp lockers, the ruins and the lace-covered saints, the quicklime and the cutting line of eaves and balconies: in Spain, all bear little grass-blades of death, allusions and voices perceptible to the spiritually alert, that call to our memory with the corpse-cold air of our own passing. It is no accident that all Spanish art is bound to our soil, so full of thistles and definitive stone; the lamentations of Pleberio or the dances of the master Josef Maria de Valdivielso are not isolated instances, nor is it by chance that from all the balladry of Europe the Spanish inamorata disengages herself in this fashion:

"If you are my fine friend,
Tell me—why won't you look at me?"
"The eyes with which I look at you
I gave up to the shadow."
"If you are my fine friend
Tell me—why don't you kiss me?"
"The lips with which I kissed you
I gave up to the clay."
"If you are my fine friend
Tell me—why won't you embrace me?"
"The arms that embrace you
I have covered up with worms."

Nor is it strange to find that in the dawn of our lyricism, the following note is sounded:

ways empowered with *duende* to baptize in dark water all those who behold it, because with *duende,* loving and understanding are simpler, there is always the *certainty* of being loved and being understood; and this struggle for expression and for the communication of expression acquires at times, in poetry, finite characters.

Recall the case of that paragon of the flamenco and daemonic way, Saint Theresa—flamenca not for her prowess in stopping an angry bull with three magnificent passes—though she did so—nor for her presumption in esteeming herself beautiful in the presence of Fray Juan de la Miseria, nor for slapping the face of a papal nuncio; but rather for the simple circumstance that she was one of the rare ones whose *Duende* (not her Angel—the angels never attack) pierced her with an arrow, hoping thereby to destroy her for having deprived him of his ultimate secret: the subtle bridge that links the five senses with the very center, the living flesh, living cloud, living sea, of Love emancipated from Time.

Most redoubtable conqueress of the *Duende*—and how utterly unlike the case of Philip of Austria who, longing to discover the Muse and the Angel in theology, found himself imprisoned by the *Duende* of cold ardors in that masterwork of the Escorial, where geometry abuts with a dream and the *Duende* wears the mask of the Muse for the eternal chastisement of the great king.

We have said that the *Duende* loves ledges and wounds, that he enters only those areas where form dissolves in a passion transcending any of its visible expressions.

In Spain (as in all Oriental countries where dance is a form of religious expression) the *Duende* has unlimited play in the bodies of the dancers of Cádiz, eulogized by Martial, in the breasts of the singers, eulogized by Juvenal, and in all the liturgy of the bulls—that authentic religious drama where, in the manner of the Mass, adoration and sacrifice are rendered a God.

It would seem that all the *duende* of the classical world is crowded into this matchless festival, epitomizing the culture and the noble sensibility of a people who discover in man his greatest rages, his greatest melancholies, his greatest lamentations. No one, I think, is amused by the dances or the bulls of Spain; the *Duende* has taken it on himself to make them suffer through the medium of the drama, in living forms, and prepares the ladders for a flight from encompassing reality.

The *Duende* works on the body of the dancer like wind works on sand. With magical force, it converts a young girl into a lunar paralytic; or fills with adolescent blushes a ragged old man begging handouts in the wineshops; or suddenly discovers the smell of nocturnal ports in a head of hair, and moment for moment, works on the arms with an expressiveness which is the mother of the dance of all ages.

But it is impossible for him ever to repeat himself—this is interesting and must be underscored. The *Duende* never repeats himself, any more than the forms of the sea repeat themselves in a storm.

In the bullfight, the *Duende* achieves his most impressive

advantage, for he must fight then with death who can destroy him, on one hand, and with geometry, with measure, the fundamental basis of the bullfight, on the other.

The bull has his orbit, and the bullfighter has his, and between orbit and orbit is the point of risk where falls the vertex of the terrible byplay.

It is possible to hold a Muse with a *muleta* and an Angel with *banderillas,* and pass for a good bullfighter; but for the *faena de capa,* with the bull still unscarred by a wound, the help of the *Duende* is necessary at the moment of the kill, to drive home the blow of artistic truth.

The bullfighter who moves the public to terror in the plaza by his audacity does not *fight* the bull—that would be ludicrous in such a case—but, within the reach of each man, puts his life at stake; on the contrary, the fighter bitten by the *Duende* gives a lesson in Pythagorean music and induces all to forget how he constantly hurls his heart against the horns.

Lagartijo with his Roman *duende,* Joselito with his Jewish *duende,* Belmonte with his baroque *duende,* and Cagancho with his gypsy *duende,* from the twilight of the ring, teach poets, painters, and musicians four great ways of the Spanish tradition.

Spain is the only country where death is the national spectacle, where death blows long fanfares at the coming of each Spring, and its art is always governed by a shrewd *duende* that has given it its distinctive character and its quality of invention.

The *Duende* that, for the first time in sculpture, fills the cheeks of the saints of the master Mateo de Compostela with blood, is the same spirit that evokes the lamentations of St. John of the Cross or burns naked nymphs on the religious sonnets of Lope.

The *Duende* who raises the tower of Sahagun or tesselates hot brick in Calatayud or Teruel, is the same spirit that breaks open the clouds of El Greco and sends the constables of Quevedo and the chimaeras of Goya sprawling with a kick.

When it rains, he secretly brings out a *duende*-minded Velasquez, behind his monarchical grays; when it snows, he sends Herrera out naked to prove that cold need not kill; when it burns, he casts Berruguete into the flames and lets him invent a new space for sculpture.

The Muse of Góngora and the Angel of Garcilaso must yield up the laurel wreath when the *Duende* of St. John of the Cross passes by, when

> The wounded stag
> peers over the hill.

The Muse of Gonzalo de Berceo and the Angel of the Archpriest of Hita [Juan Ruiz] must give way to the approaching Jorge Manrique when he comes, wounded to death, to the gates of the Castle of Belmonte. The Muse of Gregorio Hernandez and the Angel of José de Mora must retire, so that the *Duende* weeping blood-tears of Mena, and the *Duende* of Martínez Montañes with a head like an Assyrian bull's, may pass over, just as the melancholy Muse of Cataluña and the humid Angel of Galicia must watch, with loving terror, the *Duende* of Castile, far from the hot bread and the cow grazing mildly among forms of swept sky and parched earth.

The *Duende* of Quevedo and the *Duende* of Cervantes, one bearing phosphorescent green anemones and the other the plaster flowers of Ruidera, crown the altar-piece of the *Duende* of Spain.

Each art has, by nature, its distinctive *Duende* of style and form, but all roots join at the point where the black sounds of Manuel Torres issue forth—the ultimate stuff and the common basis, uncontrollable and tremulous, of wood and sound and canvas and word.

Black sounds: behind which there abide, in tenderest intimacy, the volcanoes, the ants, the zephyrs, and the enormous night straining its waist against the Milky Way.

Ladies and gentlemen: I have raised three arches, and with clumsy hand I have placed in them the Muse, the Angel, and the *Duende*.

The Muse keeps silent; she may wear the tunic of little folds, or great cow-eyes gazing toward Pompeii, or the monstrous, four-featured nose with which her great painter, Picasso, has painted her. The Angel may be stirring the hair of Antonello da Messina, the tunic of Lippi, and the violin of Masolino or Rousseau.

But the *Duende*—where is the *Duende*? Through the empty arch enters a mental air blowing insistently over the heads of the dead, seeking new landscapes and unfamiliar accents; an air bearing the odor of child's spittle, crushed grass, and the veil of a Medusa announcing the unending baptism of all newly-created things. (pp. 154-66)

> *Federico García Lorca, in his* Poet in New York, *translated by Ben Belitt, Grove Press, Inc., 1955, 192 p.*

Arturo Barea (essay date 1944)

[*Barea was a Spanish novelist, biographer, journalist, and literary critic. In the following essay, he assesses the appeal of García Lorca's works to the Spanish public in the 1920s and 1930s.*]

Those of us who were born in Spain during the eighteen-nineties found ourselves thrown into a society in a state of permanent crisis. As children we came to feel the impact of all the shocks which racked our parents and their friends, many of whom defeat and poverty had made bitter and peevish. We grew up in a State battling against misery and inferiority just when other European nations seemed on the road to permanent prosperity and security.

By 1898 Spain had lost everything; she had lost her short-lived hope of a Republic which might have incorporated her in the democratic movement of Europe, and later she had lost the remnants of her Empire in the pitiful Cuban War. That crippled Spain lived on usurious foreign loans for which she paid by handing over her copper and iron, pawning her railways and selling her water power to foreign owners. Spain was without an industry when the big modern industries were growing in Europe and America. Her fertile but mismanaged lands were exhausted; the country was short of bread. But she was plagued by earthquakes, epidemics and floods which seemed to herald the Apocalypse in the eyes of the bewildered masses. The monarchy, ruled by blustering generals and flashy politicians, had become a germ-infested morgue.

The best writers and poets of that period strove to give shape to their haunting experience of defeat, to explain it and to overcome it. Valle-Inclán, Galdós, Unamuno, Azorín became the leaders of the movement of intellectual and social self-criticism, known as the Movement of '98. It has left deep traces in the spiritual life of Spain, which nothing has yet obliterated and hardly anything overlaid. They established contact with the world outside Spain, only to return to the problem which possessed them, the problem of their country's inner life.

When the generation born in the years of defeat had grown up, bitterness and unrest had deepened; the foundation of existence had shrunk further; the desperate criticism of the older rebels could not fill the void. There was a long period reaching from the last World War to the late 'twenties, when the young people of this generation—Lorca's and my own generation—tried hard to live their own life, bright against a dark background, without wrestling with the problem of Spain as those others had done.

The lonely poet Antonio Machado, who belonged to neither generation and to both, believed in our revolutionary mission. He thought that our generation would win for Spain that clean new life of which he only dreamed. In 1914, when Federico García Lorca was a boy on the verge of adolescence, he wrote the poem called 'A Young Spain'. (This is a prose translation which preserves the words and their meaning, but scarcely more than a reminiscence of their harsh and powerful rhythm.)

> It was a time of lies, of infamy. They put our
>   Spain,
> That sorely wounded Spain, in Carnival dress,
> And then they made her poor, squalid and
>   drunken,
> So that no hand should touch the open wound.
>
> It was yesterday; we were still adolescent;
> In evil hour, pregnant with sombre presages,
> We wished to ride unbridled a chimera,
> While the sea slept, glutted and tired with ship-
>   wreck.
>
> We left the sordid galley in the harbour
> And chose to navigate a golden vessel
> On the high open seas. We sought no shore
> But cast away our sails, our anchor and our rud-
>   der.
>
> Even then, the dark ground of our dreams—the
>   heirloom
> of a century that went, beaten and inglorious,—
> Was shot with dawn; light of divine ideas
> Was ever battling with our turbulence.
>
> Yet each one followed the set course of his mad-
>   ness,
> Waving his arms, advertising his prowess,
> Wearing his armour burnished like a mirror,

Each said: 'Today is evil, tomorrow—mine.'

Today is that yesterday's tomorrow. But this
   Spain
Is still decked out in Carnival's dirty tinsel,
Still poor and squalid and drunken, as she was,
But now with evil wine: blood from her wound.

You, younger youth, if from the heights beyond
The spirit comes to you, will seek your own ad-
   venture,
Awake and limpid in the divine fire,
Clear like the diamond, like the diamond pure.

The poet of that 'younger youth' was to be Federico García Lorca, in whose poetry the word Spain never occurs, who fought no social nor political fight, but who was so sensitive a recipient and transmitter of Spanish emotions that his work assumed a life of its own after he had been killed by unknown Fascists, at the beginning of the Civil War in which he had no conscious part.

There is no direct political meaning in Lorca's work; he emphasised often enough, and rightly, that he had no politics. Whenever his writings carry a social message it is, at least on the surface, a conservative one. The masses and what moved them as such did not interest him. And yet he belonged to the Spanish democratic movement for deeper reasons than that he happened to grow up to fame within and through the progressive intelligentsia of his country. Though he lived a privileged life in the charmed circle of Spain's aristocracy of letters, though he read his poems and plays to young people coming from his own social caste, and influenced the rising generation through them, though he played with the most esoteric forms of modern art, he became, not the poet of a 'high-brow' set, but a poet of the Spanish people.

For a great part of his work is 'popular' in the sense that it touched his people as though with the full charge of their own half-conscious feelings, intensified and transformed through his art. The emotional forces he released became part of the shapeless revolutionary movements of Spain whether he intended or not. Thus it was, I think, inevitable that he was killed by obscure fascist brutality and that his work became a banner to the Spanish masses.

It is of this Lorca that I want to speak first.

All Spanish intellectuals who have written about him can say: 'The Federico with whom I lived in the *Residencia de Estudiantes* . . . My friend Federico . . . When he read that poem to us . . . ' I myself never knew Federico García Lorca, though he was of my generation. I did not belong to his set. But I belonged to his public, the people, and it is the people's Lorca whom I know.

When the Civil War broke out in July 1936, and Lorca was shot in Granada, *milicianos* who could neither read nor write learnt his ballads by heart, and the tunes and rhymes of his simple little songs became war songs of the 'Reds'.

The famous slogan 'They shall not pass'—*No pasarán*—was used in meetings and in the press. But the soldiers in the trenches round Madrid preferred to sing the ditty:

'Through *Cuatro Caminos*

No one passes,
Oh my little mother,
No one passes.'

Cuatro Caminos is a workers' borough in Madrid; the name means 'Four Ways', and it was easily fitted to Lorca's tune of the *Cuatro Muleros*, 'The Four Muleteers'. The militia-men sang the gay lines in which Lorca had recast an old folksong as often as they sang the 'No one passes':

Of the four muleteers
Who go to the water,
He with the dappled mule
Has stolen my heart.

Of the four muleteers
Who go to the river,
He with the dappled mule
Has married me.

Why do you seek fire
There in the house,
If the live flame
Burns in your face?

I had a friend, almost illiterate, 46 years old, in the Republican militia from the first days of the struggle, who sometimes came to see me in Madrid when on leave from his post in Carabanchel, four miles away. He would produce a tattered copy of Lorca's **Romancero Gitano**, filthy with the grease of the trenches, and say: 'Explain this to me. I can feel what it means and I know it by heart, but I can't explain it.' And he would recite the opening lines of the **'Romance of the Spanish Civil Guard'**:

The horses are black,
Black are the horseshoes.
On their capes glint
Stains of ink and of wax.
Their skulls are of lead,
Therefore they have no tears.
With souls of varnished leather
They come down the road,
Hunchbacked, nocturnal.
Where they go they command
Silence of dark rubber
And fear of fine sand.
They pass if they wish to pass
And they hide in their heads
A vague astronomy
Of shapeless pistols.

I would try to tell him:

This is Spain—an enormous barracks of the Civil Guard. They are black, they, their horses, the horseshoes of their horses. Black means mourning. Everything in Spain is black. The Civil Guard are the keepers of this black soul of Spain. Their capes get stained with ink, the ink that runs out of the horn inkwell they use for filling in official reports which inundate Spain and stock her prisons. Their capes are stained with wax. Wax has dropped on them from all the candles in all the processions in which the Civil Guard went along to protect the precious jewels of famous saints. They are killers. It is their profession to raise their rifles and to kill Spaniards. The Civil Guard have never killed any but Spaniards. Therefore their brains, their minds, are full of the idea of killing with their rifles: their skulls are choked with lead. How could they shed tears at the death of a Spaniard whom they have killed with a bullet cast in the lead which fills their minds by day and night? Their souls are black, hard and glossy like leather covered with brilliant varnish. Two by two they ride along the roads and over the hills, their brains clogged with lead, their backs hunched with the load of their knapsacks. In those knapsacks they carry their horn inkwell so that they can write a report on the dead, and a candle-end so they can write it in the light of the moon and scan the face of the man they have just killed. For they ride by night. They hide in the darkness of the night with their ink and wax and rifle, and wait in silence. They aim at a man's shape in the moonlight and fire. Therefore, people walk on tiptoe wherever the Civil Guard go; they fall silent and walk as though on rubber tyres. And their teeth grate as when you walk on sand-strewn tiles.

'You know,' my friend Angel would say to me, 'while I was still a boy, I worked in Carabanchel, not far from the place where our trenches are now. In the winter, my brother and I walked back at night when the road was almost empty. Sometimes we heard the horses of the pair of Civil Guards, and then we threw ourselves down in the ditch until they had passed and we could no longer hear them, and then we ran home, half dead with fright, and told our father that we had met the Civil Guard. . . .

'But what I don't understand is why, after these verses, when you would expect this man to speak of the Civil Guard and the people, of the poor landworkers whom the Civil Guards have beaten and the workers whom they have shot, he suddenly starts saying: "Oh, City of the Gypsies!" and tells you a story about Jerez de la Frontera in a night of *fiesta*, when the Civil Guard make a raid. Haven't the Civil Guard beaten up others beside gypsies?'

Indeed, Lorca's ballad goes on to evoke the childlike and dreamlike Christmas festival in a gypsy quarter: harmless, gay people playing at miracle-making in an unreal city of their dreams, in a silvery, magic night, beyond the harsh laws of violence and want. Nothing could be more 'unpolitical' and 'unsocial' according to hackneyed rules. Nothing could seem farther away from the sordid reality of the clashes between Civil Guard and labourers, inevitably surging up in the memory of the common Spaniard hit by Lorca's merciless word-picture of the men with the 'skulls of lead'. Yet this very incongruity harassed the reader, who had waited in vain for the great social denunciation, until it stirred him to a feeling of human revolt.

Once I asked my friend Angel to read out the verses against which he protested. He stumbled along, muttering between the lines.

> When the night came,
> Night, oh what nightly night,
> The gypsies on their anvils
> Forged arrows and suns . . .

'Those *fiestas*, you know—good for children and maybe for gypsies. But we're grown up—'

> The Virgin and Saint Joseph
> Have lost their castanets

> And seek for the gypsies
> To see if they can find them.
> The Virgin is dressed
> In a mayoress's gown
> Of chocolate paper,
> With almonds for beads.
> Saint Joseph moves his arms
> Under the silken cloak . . .

'It's pretty, but what do I care about it?'

> Water and shadow, shadow and water
> At Jerez de la Frontera.

'Now I know what's coming. I know it well enough. The Civil Guard beat up the whole lot and kill some of them, just like that, without any reason. But what has it to do with us? There are other things they've done to hungry people—'

> Oh City of the Gypsies,
> Flags in all corners,
> Darken your green lights,
> The Civil Guard is coming . . .
> Two ranks deep, they advance
> Into the festive city,
> A rustle of immortelles
> In their cartridge cases.
> Two ranks deep, they advance,
> Double nocturne of dark cloth.
> They fancy the starred sky
> A glass-case studded with spurs.

> The city, free from fear,
> Opened countless doors.
> Forty Civil Guards
> Entered to loot.
> The clocks stopped
> And the brandy of the bottles
> Took the hue of November
> To escape suspicion.
> The weather-vanes spun
> In long screeches.
> Sabres cut rushing air
> Which the hooves crush.
> Through shadowy streets
> Flee old gypsy women,
> Dragging sleepy horses,
> Carrying crocks filled with coins . . .

'Can't you see the charge of the Civil Guard? I remember a strike—but then we knew after all what might happen to us—'

He went on, unbidden, caught by the verse he read so clumsily:

> Yet the Civil Guard
> Advance, scattering fires
> In which, young and naked,
> Imagination is seared.

> Rosa of the Camborios
> Sits groaning on the doorstep,
> Her two breasts, cut off,
> Lying on a platter . . .

> Oh City of the Gypsies,
> The Civil Guard move away
> Through a tunnel of silence
> While the flames circle you.

Oh City of the Gypsies,
Who that saw you does not remember?
Let them seek you on my brow,
Play of moonlight on sand.

'Only, don't you see,' said Angel after a pause, 'he can't mean it just about Jerez de la Frontera and the gypsies. He makes you see and smell the Civil Guard, curse them, but—'

I answered: 'But don't you recognize yourself and all Spaniards in those gypsies whom the Civil Guard assault and torture?'

He offered a timid suggestion: 'Do you remember the Sunday in July last year, the 18th it must have been, the day after Franco proclaimed the insurrection in Morocco? We all went out of town as if nothing had happened, because it was very hot and a beautiful day, and we fooled around like children. I went to the Jarama to bathe and you went to the Guadarrama and were nearly caught in San Rafael, only you didn't know it at the time. Just like those gypsies—though I don't think gypsies are at all like he says. But anyhow, he makes me think of how the soldiers shot at us from the *Cuartel de la Montaña.* And since then it has been as if we were fighting against the Civil Guard all the time, getting nearly as bad as they are, too—but I can't put it into words.'

This, I think, was the reason why this poem has made such a deep and lasting impression on the Spanish masses. Superficially, the **'Romance de la Guardia Civil Española'** describes nothing but a brutal clash between a group of Civil Guards and the gypsies celebrating their joyous Christmas Night Festival in the streets of Jerez de la Frontera—'Oh City of the Gypsies'. The common Spaniard, in his hatred and fear of the black horsemen who always hunted in pairs, would feel surprised and almost hurt that the poet, after his first verses with their load of sombre associations, turned away to the gypsy world. But after this jolt, he—the 'common reader'—would suddenly identify himself with those childlike, dreamlike gypsies at play, assaulted by the naked brutality of the State. The verses would make him feel the clash in his own body, even though he might consider the gypsies as a useless, inferior, good-for-nothing breed. And the unpolitical ballad with its novel use of old words and traditional rhythm would stir up rebellious emotions.

It must be difficult for the Non-Spaniard to understand why and to what degree the Civil Guard of Spain had become the symbol for the oppressive force of a hated State. And thus it must be difficult to understand how much Lorca spoke from the depth of popular feeling whenever the three-cornered hats of the *Benemérita*—the 'Meritorious Institute', as the official title put it—cast their shadows over his verse.

Founded as the arm of the civil administration, the Civil Guard was supposed to maintain law and order in remote villages and to keep lonely roads free from bandits. Its members were ex-servicemen and discharged N. C. O.s schooled in the wars and willing to live in rural barracks with their wives and children. The whole body was under the Minister of Home Affairs, in practice under the orders

and at the disposal of the Civil Governors of the provinces and their local henchmen. For generations, people in villages and small towns, who did not belong to the ruling caste, knew the Civil Guard solely as the powerful and ruthless instrument of the *caciques,* the political bosses, the landowners and the usurers. Under the Monarchy, it was taken for granted that at election time the commander of the Civil Guard in each village would arrest the men known for their opposition to the reigning clique; the secretary of the local administration would make out a polling list complete with the names of all inhabitants, including some already in the cemetery; and on the day after the poll the Civil Guard would release the arrested men. They hardly ever protested, for they knew the power behind the Corporal of the Civil Guard and had no wish to feel the end of his rifle-butt. But they came to hate the Civil Guard with that bitter personal hatred which it is difficult to feel for an impersonal system. To them, the Civil Guard *was* the system which made them work for 1.50 pesetas a day in the olive fields: it was the men of the Civil Guard who shot at them when they dared to protest and who beat them lame when they had the misfortune to be arrested during a strike. And they learnt ruthlessness from the Forces of Law and Order.

The 'pair'—the two local Civil Guards patrolling the roads—moved in this cloud of hatred and violence, and at their approach people shut their lips and averted their eyes. The Republic tried to build up its own police force, free from those associations, but the Civil Guard lived on, a sinister phantom, and became part of Franco's Spain.

True to his own way of expression, Lorca never showed the Civil Guard as a social and political machine; at least not consciously. Yet even apart from the **'Ballad of the Spanish Civil Guard',** all his many passing references to the *Benemérita* drew from the dark well of popular fear. He spoke of nothing but the traditional feud of police and smugglers, Public Order and vagrants; but every encounter between his gypsies, eternally childlike, reckless and gallant even in their small vanities, and Authority, embodied in the Civil Guard, turned into a clash between sombre organised violence and generous, gay, human freedom. And it was this underlying note which Lorca's simplest readers felt more clearly than his sophisticated public.

There is the **'Ballad of the Brawl'**:

The Judge, with the Civil Guard,
Comes through the olive groves.
Slippery blood groans
Its mute snake song.
'Gentlemen of the Civil Guard:
Here we have the same old story.
Here died four Romans
And five Carthaginians.'

Many Spaniards failed to understand the last lines, with their reference to the traditional masks in the religious processions of the South, Jews, Romans, Carthaginians, Phoenicians in fantastic costumes and belonging to rival Confraternities, who often came to blows in drunken brawls. But all recognized the Judge's hard accent: 'The same old story', and the chorus of the Civil Guard.

Then there is the **'Somnambulant Ballad'** of the mortally wounded smuggler pursued into his last refuge:

> The night became intimate
> Like a little square.
> Drunken Civil Guards
> Were beating on the door.

In the ***Poema del Cante Jondo,*** which Lorca wrote in 1921 and published in 1931, there is the **'Song of the Flogged Gypsy':**

> Twenty-four strokes,
> Twenty-five strokes.
> Later in the night my mother
> Will wrap me in silver paper.
> Civil Guard on your round,
> Give me a sip of water.
> Water with fishes and boats,
> Water, water, water, water.
> Oh you chief of the Guard,
> Up there in your room,
> There are not silk handkerchiefs enough
> To wipe my face clean!

To the Asturian miners who had escaped alive from police stations during the Black Years of 1934 and 1935, this cry of the thirst-tortured boy who dreams of drinking up the sea with its fishes and boats, who longs for the coolness of tinfoil and silk against his burning, lacerated skin, was stark realism and a call to action, not symbolist lyrics inspired by gypsy folklore.

During the first half of the Spanish War the ordinary men and women who lived and fought in Madrid were driven by a multitude of emotions like these, far more than by reasons of the head. Most of them felt no urge to hear about their own miseries and sufferings, their wrongs or rights, but they delighted in discovering themselves, in exploring their feelings, faculties and tastes. This made the trenches and factories of Madrid so rich in individual creative acts, so rich in absurd or heroic initiative. This made Lorca so beloved, for his verses had the power to make people feel and see familiar things in a new, clear light. (pp. 9-21)

It was not, as might be argued, Lorca's assassination in Granada which made him so widely and profoundly popular in Republican Spain. The same process which I tried to describe—this touching and awakening of emotions which are individual, yet so simple, ancient and common to all Spaniards that they assume the quality of mass emotions and provoke an awakening of the mind—turned a minor work of Lorca's into Republican propaganda at a much earlier stage.

Lorca's historical play ***Mariana Pineda*** had its first public performance in 1927. The military dictatorship was then nearing its end; the Throne was shaken; the public demanded more and more loudly a government account of the Moroccan disaster, until then adroitly glossed over. The movement for a democratic republic and against the dictatorial monarchy was gaining strength with every day. Censorship and repression were at work, with close control and with secret brutality in the police prisons and the barracks of the Civil Guard. The masses of the people searched for means of expression, and the simplest words

were given a double meaning. At that time the famous cartoonist Bagaría, prevented from publishing cartoons, published instead designs for needlework, whose esoteric meaning the public learnt to decipher like the secrets of crossword puzzles.

In this atmosphere, ***Mariana Pineda*** was staged. The performances of what Lorca called a 'popular ballad' were turned into public demonstrations. And yet, coldly analysed, this lyrical play has a reactionary rather than a revolutionary bias.

Its historical heroine was a woman of Granada who embroidered a Republican flag in preparation for the liberal insurrection against the reign of Ferdinand VII, in the thirties of the nineteenth century. The police learnt of the plot, the conspirators fled abroad, and the only evidence found was the flag embroidered by Mariana Pineda. She was arrested, and hanged because she refused to betray the names of her associates.

In Spanish history, Mariana figures as an active Republican; to Catholic and Monarchist Spain and its offspring, Falangist Spain, she is a dangerous revolutionary; to the Democrats a political heroine. To Lorca she is neither. This is his interpretation:

Mariana Pineda is blindly in love with Don Pedro de Sotomayor, a liberal conspirator whose political passion constantly clashes with her love. Because she loves him she, who pays no attention to politics but is a marvellous needlewoman, embroiders a flag for his Party—for him. When the conspiracy is discovered and the harmless woman arrested, Mariana expects that Don Pedro will come back as he has promised, to set her free or 'to die with her', and therefore resists not so much the demand of the Judge Pedrosa to name her accomplices, as his demand to give herself to him. She mounts the scaffold, deeply hurt by her lover's desertion and rising above her own disillusionment in a last effort to reach him:

> I embroidered the flag for him. I conspired
> To live and to love his very thought.
> More than myself and my children I loved him.
> Do you love Freedom more than your Mari-
>   anita?
> Then I will be that Freedom you adore.

That is to say: the heroine of political history becomes a woman in love, without any political ideas, a blindly enamoured woman very much in the Spanish tradition, who sacrifices herself for 'her man'. The revolutionaries become derisory cowards who abandon a woman and allow her to go to the gallows without even attempting a heroic gesture of rescue. Throughout the play there is no expression of popular feeling, nothing but the general cowardice in the face of the execution:

> There's a fear to make you afraid.
> The streets are deserted,
> Only the wind comes and goes,
> But the people lock their doors, . . .

says the gardener Alegrito, who tries to find the conspirators, so that they should save Mariana. And the Judge Pedrosa confirms it.

MARIANA.   . . . You forget
That ere I die all Granada must die,
That very noble gentlemen will come
To save me. For I'm noble, I'm the daughter
Of a ship's captain who himself was Knight
Of Calatrava. Leave me now in peace.

PEDROSA. No one in Granada will show himself
When you pass by with your last company.
The Andalusians talk, but afterwards . . .

A play which thus deviated from the idea of popular heroism and made the Republicans look ridiculous might easily have met with failure in the Madrid of 1927; or it might have been taken up by the Right and used for its purposes. But it came to be a play against the Right and for human rights. The great Spanish public, which would have rejected the idea of a woman sacrificing herself for political ideals (even for popular ones), easily understood the woman who sacrificed her life for the sake of love—and easily converted her into a political symbol. To quote Stephen Spender, though out of context: 'Poetry which is not written in order to advance any particular set of political opinions may yet be profoundly political.'

Señora Pilar, the concierge of Number 9, would be given a ticket to the play. She would look forward to hearing the story of 'that wicked woman who was hanged because she got entangled in politics', and tell everybody: 'Yes, sir, well hanged she was. Who told her to go and get all mixed up with those revolutionaries? Women belong to their homes anyway.'

But then in the theatre, when the soft music of the verses had reached her, she would begin to weep: 'Poor darling, they're going to hang her for that young scamp who deceived her! And he a grand gentleman! If it had been my Nicolas now, he's a Republican of the good old sort. Well yes, he's a bit simple. But if he knew they were going to hang me because I had embroidered a flag for him, he'd knock the judge's teeth in soon enough.' And she would rise from her seat and shout: *'Viva la República!'*

Scenes of this kind occurred almost daily in the *Teatro Español.* Through a drama with an anti-political argument and therefore a reactionary moral, Lorca had stirred popular sentimentality and sentiment, and set them in motion in a very different direction. (pp. 22-5)

The result was the same whether Lorca faced the people as poet, playwright or producer; it was always alien to his reasoned intention.

In 1931, the first year of the Republic, Lorca proposed to the Minister of Education, his friend Don Fernando de los Rios, the creation of a popular theatre to present classical plays and bring the Spanish drama to peasants and labourers. With official support, he organised a travelling company of University students which he called *La Barraca.* He licked them into shape and gave them something of his own vision and enthusiasm. *La Barraca* travelled the roads of Spain, pitching their stand in a village square, in a barn or a shed, and made bewildered landworkers listen to the sonorous verse of Lope de Vega and Calderón.

But *La Barraca* became a political weapon. Those spectators now moved for the first time in their lives by passion filtered through art were the same people who set their hopes on the new Republic, who listened in their village inn to the newly installed radio, who dreamed of a school for their children and believed that in future the soil would nourish instead of starve them. The words of the classical drama merged into their own present-day hopes. If the wicked nobleman in the play was punished because he offended a sixteenth-century point of honour, they identified him with one of the Señoritos, the sons of their own gentry, whom they had learnt to hate.

Of all the plays popularised by *La Barraca,* Lope's drama *Fuenteovejuna* held the greatest revolutionary appeal. It was written in 1619 and deals with an incident of the year 1476, the time of the 'Catholic Monarchs'. Its story is simple. Fernán Gomez de Guzmán, overlord of Fuenteovejuna and Knight-Commander of the Order of Calatrava, robs, kills and violates the simple people of the place—which still exists—until the whole village rises and slays him. The King and Queen, who knew him as a recalcitrant vassal, send a judge to the village. He subjects the whole population, even the children, to gaoling and torture; but the answer to his question 'Who killed him?' is always the same:

> *Fuenteovejuna,*
> *Todos a una.*
>
> Fuenteovejuna,
> All as one.

In despair the judge takes his findings to the Sovereigns. The villagers follow him to plead their cause, to ask for pardon, and to renew their oath of fealty to the King and Queen. These accept them as vassals and mete out justice to them.

Thus the play was originally superb Royalist propaganda, praising the supreme power of the King as the people's protection against the feudal lords. It is an interesting illustration of the class struggle at the beginning of the modern age in Spain. And at the time when *La Barraca* played it under Lorca's direction, it might have been excellent monarchist propaganda once again. But the Spanish monarchy had collapsed in 1931 precisely because it was incapable of meting out justice to *Fuenteovejuna,* to the common people of the whole of Spain. The labourers in the villages recognised themselves in the people of Fuenteovejuna, but they did not recognise their late King in the wise monarchs. The lesson which the play drove home to them was that a mass acting together and at the same time, *'todos a una',* becomes invincible.

I remember seeing an open-air performance of a 'Cape and Sword' play which *La Barraca* gave in one of the oldest squares of Madrid, with crooked little streets opening into it. The play came alive with torchlights, balconies and guitars, with cloaked gentlemen and astute servants, with a strict code of honour and complicated intrigues, with sudden passion and sudden violence. And it became a fascinating, repellent evocation of ghosts. There, in the homely streets, the public felt more deeply than it would ever have felt in a big, modern theatre that the world of the play was dead and ought to stay dead.

Thus the work of Lorca the producer, just as that of Lorca the poet, became part of the movement of the Spanish people. (pp. 27-9)

> *Arturo Barea, in his* Lorca: The Poet and His People, *translated by Ilsa Barea, Faber & Faber, 1944, pp. 9-29.*

Warren Carrier   (essay date 1963)

[*Carrier is an American educator, novelist, and critic. In the following essay, he maintains that García Lorca's dramas are poetic in their outlook and language.*]

Angel Ganivet made the startling observation in his *Idearium Español* that Spanish mysticism is "sanctified African sensuality." The Spaniard's sense of underlying reality informs his mysticism, his idealism, his poetry, his drama. Sancho Panza is ubiquitous; he bounces on his ass, eating cheese and onions, just below the level of the noble, if sway-back, Rocinante. If, in the end, Sancho has become quixified, and Quijote sanchified, the sharp dichotomies of the Spanish soul are inseparably part of a single whole.

The theatre of Federico García Lorca is poetic; there is no one in modern times who has brought such poetic beauty and insight to drama. His theatre is not drama in verse, it is poetry in the more profound meaning. In the mature plays, there is never a mere exercise of fancy; there are no pretty lines to embellish a scene, no flourishes to plump out a speech. This is a poetry rooted in reality, in the deepest sense of the dramatic. Life is made into poetry because poetry is the most immediate way into the heart of life; because life and poetry are inseparable.

Lorca's theatre might be called—modifying Ganivet's phrase—poeticized sanctified African sensuality, for it is at once erotic and cruel, rich and compellingly stark and direct. *Bodas de Sangre* (*Blood Wedding*) takes place in a landscape of black and white, a barren land where the code of peasant life is as simple and clear and absolute as the scene itself. The necessities of life—the bare land, which can only be made fruitful by irrigation, the lives, which can only be meaningful through work and children who will in turn work to produce—the necessities of existence reflect and are reflected in every aspect of life. There is no place for unproductive passion in the scheme of things; and yet it is passion which underlies and brings tragedy to their lives. This is a land of feuds, where a man's honor is in conflict with his need to produce and be fruitful. It is not enough that the land itself is difficult, it is that he has passion and pride, and that these inevitably lead to death; and, in conflict with the code, to sterility.

The Mother's first concern (for the characters are unnamed, except for Leonardo: They take their names from their roles in society. That is, the characters are interchangeable, and have their meaning only insofar as they fulfill their roles. Leonardo, the *individual,* fails to fulfill his role)—the Mother's first concern is for the knife that her son carries. Her husband has been killed with a knife; this instrument for pruning the vines is also an instrument of death. Things, like people, tend to fulfill themselves in their roles. A knife is made for killing; it will kill almost as though it had a will of its own. (See "**Reyerta**", of the ballads, for another image of the knife as an independent force.) The Mother is also concerned for the preservation of life and for production; she wants her son to be married. But she is fearful. Her fearfulness is, of course, a premonition of what is to come; it is her awareness, after a life of experience, of what life holds by its very nature. Thus in the first scene, not only the terms of the play, but the terms of Lorca's theatre may be found: the roots of life lie in productiveness, in the creative. When not in consonance with the necessities or the code of the society, the forces which nourish the creative—erotic passion and the passion of pride—bring inevitable tragedy and death.

Technically, the larger portion of the play is in prose. Poetry is used for the lullaby sung by the wife of Leonardo to her child, and then by various characters, such as the Moon, in the last act. The "vision" of the play, its very simplicity and directness, are poetic, and when the landscape of the play is moved from the bare scene and direct action of the first two acts to the abstracted level of the last, poetry becomes the natural mode of speech; for the whole play has become the metaphor by which it was informed in the beginning. That is, these people are caught up in a world which is severely structured and strictured; consequent upon each act is its result. Once the tragic action has been set in motion, there is almost the formality of a ritual or a dance in the manner of acting it out. If the knife almost has a life of its own at the beginning of the play, the Moon becomes animated, with speeches of its own at the end; and Death, a force, becomes an object as the knife, an object, becomes a force. The values are interchangeable, so that, by a poetic device, the objects and their meaning in life may be interchanged. Lorca's poetic technique fuses with his poetic vision; thus "life" is "poeticized." For Lorca, poetry is both a technique of writing and a technique for "seeing" his world.

It is clear, when one analyzes this play in conventional dramatic terms, that *Bodas de Sangre* depends upon its poetic vision for its claim to be successful tragedy. Conventionally, the play revolves about a triangle. The Bride was once engaged to Leonardo; Leonardo still has a passion for her, even though he is now married and has a child. After her marriage, and before its consummation, they run off together. They are pursued. Bridegroom and Leonardo kill each other. The women are left to lament. This rudimentary situation lacks intricacy of plot; it seems, indeed, to be the action of a ballad—as it surely is, for if Lorca's ballads are dramatic, his dramas have the quality and incisiveness of the ballad. Yet it is this very distillation of situation and action to ballad-like essence that makes Lorca's theatre so moving and so effective. The air of foreboding, the sense of inevitability of the ballad communicate themselves deeply through his poetic theatre. It was at the appointed hour—*en un día señalado*—between two and three, that these two men killed each other. This feeling for fate, genuine to the Spanish peasant with his fundamental stoicism, unites Lorca's drama with Greek tragedy.

The "problem" or situation of *Yerma* is as direct and essential as that of *Bodas de Sangre.* There is even a sort of triangle: Yerma, Juan and Victor-unborn-child. If Juan had been able, or willing, to have a child, there would have been no triangle, for Yerma would have loved the father for giving her the child. But here we encounter the difficulty; for Yerma does not love her husband as husband, and perhaps even had she had a child, the child might have been a very real and successful rival for Yerma's love and attention. Victor is also part of the third angle to this three-sided affair, for we understand by evidence which is always implicit that Victor, had she married him, might have given Yerma her child. And Victor might have been capable of arousing in her a true erotic passion—necessary for the fullest and most fruitful kind of life—for Yerma remembers how she trembled when Victor once lifted her over an aquaduct. She does not tremble when Juan touches her. It is, in fact, I think, a flaw in Yerma that she cannot feel erotic passion in conjunction with her desire for a son. She is compulsive not only because she is frustrated in her single-minded yearning for motherhood, but because she has neglected, or has never had an opportunity to know of, the love which is for the man alone. The image or dream of her son almost becomes the husband; this is a fixation comparable to narcissism. (The fault, of course, is not entirely hers, since it is Juan who is incapable of arousing her passion. Her passionate potential is thus turned inward.)

The theme of the play is again productivity, fruitfulness, fertility. And again passion and honor bring about sterility, death. Yerma could have her child, if she would accept the help of the Old Woman, for the Old Woman offers her a father for her child; or if she would discard her honor for Victor. But she is an honorable woman according to the *mores* of her society; and because she is honorable, she cannot fulfill her function as a woman.

However, the villain is not society and its morals, and there is never any suggestion that this is so; the villain is Juan. Yerma is caught between the code which she accepts and her husband's impotence (or incapability of will); the play offers her a way out which goes beyond her code, but she does not even consider it. Juan is aware that this is a possibility, for he is aware of his own lack of honor—i.e., the code requires him to be the father of children. He does not even want Yerma to be seen on the street—because of his honor; people will talk. He follows her to the pagan rite. He cannot trust her, even though he knows she is honorable, because he cannot fulfill his own "honorable" responsibilities. His "honor" receives its just reward; but, of course, he has succeeded in destroying Yerma.

The medieval split between erotic love and propagation of children underlies this play. These are the terms of Catholic Christian life. Erotic love is a necessary evil: it can become "sanctified" into motherhood, or into sainthood itself. But for Lorca the denial of any passion may bring tragedy, and it is here that he resembles Eruipides. Lorca's gallery of women may very well stand alongside Euripides'. Both Phaedra's compulsive passion for her husband's son and Yerma's passion for a son of her own are ineluctable, and both lead to tragedy.

Yerma is a play which finds its sources and its vitality in the realities of Spanish life. The desire for a son and the concept of honor that motivate Yerma would be understood by every Spanish woman—peasant or not. The sin of Juan in wanting Yerma for herself and not for her son would also be understood by every Spanish man. But this is not commonplace as drama; Lorca deals with the inner core of the reality of Spanish life in its physical and moral terms in a way that reminds one of the great Spanish dramatists of the Golden Age—Calderón de la Barca and Lope de Vega. Honor and "appearances" were very much of the essence in Golden Age drama; and so were the "problems" of lust and mysticism. But where Calderón would illustrate an "act of faith" in dramatic terms, Lorca, dealing largely with peasant life, accepts for his characters the stoic and realistic faith of the Spanish church in the country, and discovers the more fundamental attitudes and bases of life beneath it. For Spain, that most Catholic country of Europe, is also the most pagan. Stoicism, superstition, realism—all inform religion profoundly. If the Spanish peasant thinks of every loaf of bread and every glass of wine as the literal body and blood of Christ, it is because his is a realistic mysticism; life, in the face of existential survival, and all its meaning, is literally in the miracle of bread and wine. It is in this miracle that Lorca finds the vitality of his poetry and drama: literal mysticism, mystic realism. When Yerma kills her husband, she literally kills her son. And herself. This transference of qualities, of meanings, is as simple and direct and intelligible to the Spanish mind as the erotic-literal-mystical image that the Spanish St. Teresa used in describing the ultimate union with God as a spear piercing her entrails.

The "poetry" of *Yerma* is, again, of essential "seeing" of the bare heart of a life. Verse is used a good deal; Yerma sings of and to her unconceived child; women doing the washing in the river sing. The singing is natural; it is the heart, the blood singing, the mind working, desire finding voice, the continuum of dream; it is the natural world alive within the characters. The lullaby is again the center of the poetic form, as it was in *Bodas de Sangre.* The total form of the play reflects, again, the ballad form. There is more verse and less poetic abstraction; there is no scene which exactly corresponds to the final scene of *Bodas de Sangre* in its removal from the appearance of reality. The final scenes of the pagan rite, however, resemble, as do the scenes in the woods in *Bodas de Sangre,* the ritual nature of tragedy in its profoundest sense. In Greek tragedy the ritual often found its way into the play itself; in the final scenes of these two plays there are epiphanies in which the relation of man to his natural or supernatural world is confronted or celebrated.

In *Mariana Pineda* the love which Mariana feels for Don Pedro, the rebel patriot, is a natural and erotic love; it becomes identified with his patriotic cause, and when she refuses to divulge the names of the conspirators and Don Pedro abandons her to be caught and executed by the king's constable, her love becomes "sanctified" into a kind of patriotic sainthood. She maintains her illusion even when she learns that Don Pedro and his fellow-rebels have escaped to England. And by her belief in spite of the facts, she becomes a mystic and a symbol; she makes a "truth" out of the fact of her own faith where the facts failed. Mariana is herself a "poeticization of life." This play, less successful as drama, is more obviously poetry in the loosest sense. In his subtitle Lorca calls it a "Popular Ballad in Three Prints." An earlier play, the poetic vision is somewhat encumbered with poetic embellishment, and perhaps with the static "print"-like structure. This is life, but once removed; the story of Mariana Pineda, a Betsy Ross of Granada, is a popular legend, and Lorca, while he animates the legend, and "sees" it in terms of "sanctified Love"—a poetic image in the best sense—does not give it the full life of *Bodas de Sangre* or *Yerma.* This is a play on the way toward mature drama; it has its own merits, but they are the merits which were to come to full fruition in the later plays.

Perhaps the best way to regard the play, though it is a tragedy celebrating a local heroine, is to accept it as Lorca describes it: a ballad. In his ballads proper, Lorca tended precisely toward the alternation of dramatic dialogue with painterly scene that we find in *Mariana Pineda.* This is more clearly an extended ballad in dialogue. In many of his minor plays, particularly the comedies, Lorca "sees" his dramatic structure in terms of something else—some other form of art, usually. For example *The Love of Don Perlimplín and Doña Belisa in the Garden* is subtitled "An Erotic Lace Paper Valentine;" *Doña Rosita the Spinster* is subtitled "A Poem of Granada, Divided into Various Gardens;" and even *Yerma* is called "A Tragic Poem." Prints, valentines, gardens, poems—these are intended to be forms of art somewhere beyond drama. We should see *Mariana Pineda,* then, precisely in the fashion Lorca would have us, as a Ballad in Three Prints. Yet it is also drama, and because we have Lorca's mature drama to see it by, we can observe that the poetic and dramatic qualities have not here achieved the rich fusion they were to achieve in his later plays. Poetry in drama must be successful drama or it is not successful poetry.

This is the only play which deals with a theme of political implication. Perhaps poetry cannot be made of politics. Yet the political or historical frame is not of real importance in the play; the play is about another Lorca woman, Mariana herself, and her love, which is transformed and which in turn transforms her. If the real Mariana has been transformed into legend, the legendary Mariana has been made into Lorca's image of the essence of Spanish women, of erotic love transformed into saintliness.

It is a tragedy in which apotheosis receives the burden of emphasis. We watch Mariana move from her own situation—tragic enough—into the realm of spirit; rather we do not watch her move, we watch the prints, like a stopped movie, or—perhaps better—like the stations of the cross; and we understand the steps between and fix our attention upon the immediate, if static, scene.

La Casa de Bernarda Alba is mature drama; it is Lorca at his best. It is a play that can stand beside any great play. It is in prose; there is very little verse. It is so stark as prose, it is so essential in language and feeling, it stares so directly into the heart of the characters, that it may be said to be more poetic than many of the more patently poetic plays (*Mariana Pineda,* for example). Again, peasant life, women frustrated in their natural desires by a code of

honor; again sterility and death. If Lorca has been eminently successful in his portrayal of women, he surely reaches the height of his success in this play in which no man appears on the scene. This is a static society, but there is not a static moment; nothing happens on the stage, yet everything happens in the play. Woman in her Spanish essence is the character: the home which is at once a jail and a convent is the scene; the action is the meeting of the irresistible force of erotic love with the immovable object of maternal honor. The honor is not merely that of the cult of virginity—though that is ineradicably involved; it is the honor of class as well. Bernarda will not allow her daughters to marry beneath them. Since there is no one really worthy of her daughters, this condemns them to a saintly existence that is the opposite of life, and their natural desires come to explosion. The appearance of honor is even more important than honor itself—and again we perceive the echoes of Golden Age drama, of Lope and Alarcón; for when Adela dies, Bernarda insists she died a virgin. She should be dressed as a virgin, as though she died a virgin. Bernarda, incredibly strong character that she is, a tyrant of maternal honor, does not weep, and does not want any weeping from the others. They will do their ritual mourning later; she wants silence. And this imposition of her will to silence ends the play with incomparable power.

If in the other plays the force of passion erupting against a code of society has led to tragedy, the terms have been deepened and made more effective dramatically in *La Casa de Bernarda Alba* by personifying honor in the arbitrary tyrannical will of Bernarda. The bridegroom represents the acceptable *mores* of his society in *Blood Wedding;* he does not will them, he does not by his own expression of will make them effective; rather he naturally follows them to their inevitable conclusion, cost what it may. Yerma does not make her code of behavior, she fulfills it as it has been given her; it is part of her being. In *La Casa de Bernarda Alba* the nature of the code is seen not only in terms of the society, but in terms of the arbitrary will of Bernarda. If she would give a little, her daughters might marry beneath them; and, not having dowries, not be as respected by their men as they otherwise might. But the situation is not impossible. They could marry, fulfill themselves as women. While the plight of women in Spain is not like that of women elsewhere in this century, the basic situation is universal enough; erotic need is not a sufficient basis for marriage. There must be a basis for family, for status, for honor. This is the maternal interest. Beyond this, of course, is the cult of the virgin. A woman in Spain is either a mother or a prostitute; lust and family are at opposite ends of the spectrum, and the one is not to be allowed without the other. The other cannot exist unless there is a realistic base upon which it can be constructed. In short, Bernarda's arbitrary refusal to allow her daughters to marry beneath them, or without a dowry, is to protect them against the man who would not accept a wife with due honor unless she brought him her own honor (were a virgin and did not marry beneath her) and were well enough off to bring a dowry.

The natural instincts of a houseful of virgins must be protected then not only for the sake of morals, but for the sake of practicality; or rather it is, again, a union of the mystic with the real in a society where the basic code of behavior requires such double vision.

But Bernarda is, nevertheless, a terrible creature who leads her daughters into total frustration; she is, at the same time, a magnificent character. It is the paradox of her personality and situation which gives the play its ultimate strength. Bernarda is the image of Spain herself, cloistering herself into sterility and frustration for the sake of practical honor and religious mysticism. The terms of life are impossible.

Lorca's tragedies depend upon an acceptance of these terms. Life is fundamentally capable of fruitfulness, but the code of behavior which this society has arbitrarily imposed upon itself (and under which it has sunk into stasis) brings productiveness and honor into fateful conflict. These plays are not mere theatre, they are art in its most profound measure; they bring the heart of Spanish peasant life into the vision of an audience. The vision itself is poetry; the intensification, the stark capturing of that heart is poetry. Thus the poeticization of life is the truthful seeing of it through the form of a ritual art. (pp. 297-304)

> *Warren Carrier, "Poetry in the Drama of Lorca," in* Drama Survey, *Vol. 2, No. 3, February, 1963, pp. 297-304.*

García Lorca on the creation of poetic imagery:

[The] poet makes himself mentor of his five bodily senses—the bodily senses in the following order: sight, touch, hearing, smell, and taste. To command ideal images, he must open the doors of communication between the senses; and frequently he must superimpose his sensations at the expense of disguising his very nature. . . .

> *Federico García Lorca, in his "The Poetic Image in Don Luis de Góngora," 1927.*

Manuel Blanco-Gonzalez (essay date 1966)

[*Blanco-Gonzalez is a Spanish-born educator, critic, poet, and short story writer. In the following essay, he argues that García Lorca's* Blood Wedding, Yerma, *and* The House of Bernarda Alba *are closely related in content and theme.*]

Towards the end of his relatively short life, and after producing during the twenties work that included several short plays,—puppet plays and surrealistic fantasies, an historical drama and one comedy—García Lorca moved in the thirties to a more serious effort in dramatic poetry. The change coincided with his general poetic evolution after his short visit to the United States (1929-30), and paralleled the noticeable transformation of his lyric poetry in the collection **The Poet in New York.** One can see in all his previous plays the same elements, including imagery, which were to determine to a great extent the form and poetic characteristics of **Blood Wedding, Yerma** and **The House of Bernarda Alba,** the three dramas which

constitute his best known and best achieved works; but these elements underwent a development and a process of refinement, at the same time that they were used to pursue different effects in a new conception: the grotesque or comic was transformed into the tragic.

I have called Lorca's last three plays a tragic trilogy implying that they are in some respects so closely related as to warrant regarding them as a trilogy, despite the fact that their plots are unrelated to one another; and, further, that they illustrate Lorca's feelings about a modern poetic theatre that could achieve, in effect, what he came to see as modern tragedy. It is on this basis that I intend to discuss some traits common to the three plays and some of the implications, for modern tragedy, of their content.

It would be easy to trace the background and atmosphere of these last plays to the style and subjects of the **Romancero Gitano,** but they are also closely related as to their themes and the spirit that informs all three. They are Andalusian dramas, their action taking place in rural locales; the central problem of each revolves around marriage, love and sexual desire; the main feeling is anguish and despair, produced by frustration; and the resolution is always violent death. They are, as well, noticeably "feminine" plays, in that female roles predominate and command dramatic focus. Finally, the subject of each is clearly treated symbolically, as is evident not only from the symbolic names of the characters, but also from the appearance of allegorical figures, and poetic imagery charged with symbolic meaning.

Lorca's use of rural scenes allows him to deal with relatively primitive characters who, in close contact with nature and though not simple in their psychology, nevertheless exhibit strong, bare passion with clear, external manifestations. The depth of his characters is provided by the intensity of their feelings and the natural tension of the action; the "mystery" of the plays is increased by the subtlety of the poetry and its symbols. Thus he is free to proceed to complicated ends by manipulating simplified individuals, some of whom are very close to being motivated by the most elemental natural forces and instincts—most clearly, for example, in the case of Yerma, in whom the instinct of reproduction is practically the only will.

Simple, primitive characters who live close to the land provide Lorca with the first element of his approach to tragedy and to the universal forces and will which are to control it. He can, without sacrificing their individuality, plausibly transform them into symbolic figures that represent, besides an individual situation, a general problem and a prototype; for example, he uses the mother in **Blood Wedding** as really more than "a mother"—as, in fact, The Mother. Characters and setting have, moreover, an important relation to Lorca's singular type of poetry, which is always extremely rich in very direct sensuous imagery, in immediate contact with nature and folklore; they permit a spontaneous flow of deep and complex poetry that is without affectation, since these natural forces and folklore motifs are at one with the background. Also, this poetry constitutes the basis of intensity and universality in the plays, conferring on them the tragic "nobility" of style preached by the classicists.

There is an evident intention in the three plays to view the same problem from different angles, so that one could say they represent variations on a theme, with a progression towards a certain kind of thesis. In *Blood Wedding* the problem is an unconsummated marriage, with two females as protagonist and antagonist—mother and bride, and two principal male characters—bridegroom and lover. The bride escapes with the lover on the wedding day, the mother almost forces the revenge, the two men kill each other. In *Yerma,* the whole tragedy centers on the unhappy relations of husband and wife, because of his seeming infertility and Yerma's desire for motherhood. Finally, in *The House of Bernarda Alba,* the protagonist Bernarda, whose husband has just died at the beginning of the action, controls her household with an iron hand and impedes marriage and normal life for her daughters, to the point where the youngest, Adela, who has had a forbidden relation with a man, commits suicide.

There are curious variants in this use of unconsummated marriage in all three: in one because the bride escapes, in the second because there are no children, in the third because the mother's will and the rivalry of the sisters prevent it. In each, also, there is a curious insistence on the virginity of the three young women directly concerned, despite the fact that Yerma is married and the fact that Adela seems to have been Pepe's lover. As for parents, Lorca shows us in *Blood Wedding* only the mother of the bridegroom and the father of the bride; in *Yerma,* none (only the husband's three sisters represent family relationships); in *Bernarda Alba,* only Bernarda, the girls' mother. The number of male characters dwindles as the importance of their roles diminishes. In the first of the trilogy, father, bridegroom and Leonardo have a certain importance of function in the action; in the second, the husband Juan is almost a secondary character and the other man, Victor, hardly counts. In the third, no man appears on stage; the dead husband and Pepe are only referred to.

Along with this, though in another order of comparison, there is a gradual appearance of real names for the characters, and a gradual disappearance of special allegorical figures. The mother who dominates her son in *Blood Wedding* later becomes, so to speak, Bernarda, who controls her daughters absolutely; the daring and violent Leonardo is transformed into the rather mediocre, don-juanesque figure of Pepe el Romano. The death of the two men in *Blood Wedding* becomes in *Yerma* the death of Juan at the hands of a woman; and, finally, the suicide of a woman, Adela. Lastly, the sexual desire and passion that figure so importantly in *Blood Wedding* are transformed into the basic instinct of reproduction in *Yerma,* to be almost completely rejected and condemned as sinful in *The House of Bernarda Alba.*

All this, though it does not exhaust the list of variants, produces an impression of a thematic idea presented in evolution. To use an expression in vogue, the theme seems basically to be that of lack of communication between the sexes, a lack of agreement. It should be helpful to try to examine certain basic motivations found in this evolution.

In *Blood Wedding,* why does the bride escape with Leonardo? This is one of the most interesting questions of the play. The couple had been engaged, but had broken it off; the bride, without being very much in love with him, had accepted the bridegroom, and Leonardo had married another woman. Then, on the day of her wedding, with the ceremony already performed, Leonardo appears and the bride flees with him. We can readily accept a moment of passion as an explanation of their action; but when in the third act we again encounter the fugitives, the bride rejects Leonardo in what is treated as a conflict of passion and honor. Later, when both men are dead, the bride goes to the mother, who insults her at first but who, when the girl asserts her innocence on the grounds that she is still virgin and without sin, vaguely accepts her and ends by allowing the bride to pray and lament with her. We may accept this as believable only if we overlook what seems like inconsistency in the psychology and actions of the bride, and even of the mother. At a more subconscious and instinctive level, however, there seems to be a clearer explanation. We begin to notice—and will notice even more in the later two plays—that beneath this lack of communication between the sexes is a doubt as to the normal characteristics and behavior of male and female in their relations.

By means of typical lorquian symbols, the bridegroom and Leonardo are well defined as opposites: the "knife" and the "horse," not to mention the leonine suggestion of Leonardo's name. From the outset, the bridegroom is seen as a very respectful and obedient son; while Leonardo, though married, represents a bad husband and a bad son-in-law. The bridegroom's traits are made more obvious in the first scene, by the mother's wanting to take away his knife and, later, even more so by telling him she would have liked him to be a woman. That is to say, she tries to deprive him of his maleness. By contrast, when we meet Leonardo and his family, all the references are to horses; and the horse, for Lorca, is another symbol of masculinity, as can be seen in **"Romance Sonámbulo"** and **"Diálogo del Amargo"** in *Romancero Gitano.* Leonardo has a horse; therefore, Leonardo is a man.

On the day of her wedding, the bride cannot resist being attracted to the male or feeling disgust and revolt towards the "effeminate," mother-dominated bridegroom. She escapes with Leonardo, only to reject him because her concept of maleness is such that, in accepting her, Leonardo becomes in effect subjugated by the female. Although the ideal of honor may play a part in her attitude, it is a superimposed principle and hence less strong than her instinctive rejection of the man as effeminate because, in surrendering his freedom, he lets himself be dominated by a woman.

This reading of subconscious motivation applies as well to the bride's acceptance by the mother, and to their lament for the dead men, where the solution is one of fate. The knife reappears, to represent the destiny of the male: men are violent, they have to perish by the sword. The bride's assertion of innocence partly justifies her before the mother, because it proves that her flight was not caused by a guilty, sinful passion, but rather that she acted on her deep, fateful instinct as a female. The mutual killing of the two men proves that they were manly: they have followed their noble fate. Mother and bride are joined in their femininity.

In *Yerma,* because there are only two main characters, Lorca could simplify their motivation and his presentation of the relation of man and woman; but he complicates them, instead, because they are to have a more elaborate symbolic meaning. The wife Yerma wishes to be a mother, as would be normal. Because of this, her character grows through the play, taking on the noblest dimensions of a tragic heroine; but the figure of her husband becomes subdued and petty. Yet the misunderstanding that is the basis of their conflict is the same. Juan wants a wife and he does not find her in Yerma. By the end of the third act, when husband and wife speak openly to each other for the first time, he tells Yerma that he does not care for children and does not want to have them, and that there is no guilt in that. Yerma answers: "You search for me as when you want to eat a dove," and a moment later she kills him. Though there are allusions to Juan's impotence, it is nowhere definitively established. What we know for certain is that Yerma senses in her husband a lack of will to procreate when he lies with her; and that she, in her turn, experiences no passion in their embrace

Here we have again both the power of instinct at play and the lack of communication. Both characters are using, or trying to use, the other; but they have no real communion. Yerma, with a strong female instinct of reproduction, needs and desires the male for procreation. Juan, more egotistic than she, seeks only the fulfillment of his male sexual desire. What makes Yerma far superior to Juan, and justifies her reproach, is that sexual union has for her a more natural and a more noble meaning, since it is not merely for the satisfaction of her own selfish passion. Yet Yerma is, like any classical tragic heroine, guilty because she is denying to her husband the surrender of her personality, which he needs for his own complete fulfillment. As in *Blood Wedding,* though with a difference of emphasis and of terms, male and female cannot reach a complete communion; since for her union is mainly instinct of reproduction and need of maternity, and for him it answers the essential need of self-fulfillment.

As this theme evolves from play to play, there takes place an inversion of roles: the figure of the man grows weaker gradually and less important, while the women grow stronger and more domineering. This explains why Yerma can kill—even, in some way, *must* kill her husband; for, symbolically speaking, she will kill him simply by overpowering and destroying his personality. Her last words— "I have killed my son"—are the words of the female who, without the male, has destroyed her own fertility.

We enter a completely feminine world in *The House of Bernarda Alba:* men have been reduced to a condition similar to that of the drone in a beehive, a negligible quantity; it is significant that the play begins with the death of the husband and ends with the suicide of the youngest daughter. Bernarda is the masculine female, the woman who has grown so strong that she usurps man's functions and behavior. It is a curious detail that she has given birth only to five daughters, not a single male. Talking to La Poncia, she says there is no man in the village good enough for her daughters; by which she means, of course, that she will never consider *any* man good enough. Bernarda's old mother underlines this fact when, appearing toward the end of the first act, she says she wants to marry, since none of her granddaughters will ever marry.

Bernarda agrees contemptuously to a betrothal between her eldest daughter and Pepe el Romano, who will be marrying a woman far older than himself, and for money. Though he is repeatedly praised for being *handsome,* Bernarda cannot consider him as more than a puppet. Yet, when he later proves to be more dangerous than she had at first thought—thanks to his affair with Adela, Bernarda tries to kill him. Her action is believable from the point of view of honor, but even more so because of the particular nature of her character. When Adela commits suicide, Bernarda's immediate reaction is to exclaim that the girl has died a virgin, and then to impose this version of events on the rest of the household. Again, the point of family honor; but again also, Bernarda's distorted instinct.

If we recall the analysis of the two previous plays, this interpretation of the last one in the light of frustrated marriage and sexual relations, is self-evident: women, having become stronger than men, have finally won—have, in fact, replaced men; but then, ironically, they are lost in a world without men. That is probably why, in the last play, the main male character does not die but escapes, and why the one who dies is the woman, the youngest of them, the most passionate and rebellious.

In the development of his theatre, García Lorca followed the "feminine" line of tragedy—that of Euripides, Racine and Alfieri. This line has produced some of our most beautiful tragedies and tragic figures, moving in their humanity and psychological insight though necessarily less "heroic" in proportion than its "masculine" counterpart for reasons inherent in each sex—but also, for the same reasons, of a greater tenderness and with more appeal to our pity. Now the "feminine" line of tragedy is commonly related to a vision of decadence in society, for in it there is a pronounced diminution of man. And what Lorca presents in his tragic trilogy is very clearly a vision of decadence in Spanish contemporary society. It is his interpretation and explanation, among other possible ones, of certain traits and problems in Spanish society, and, by extension, in other societies as well.

Lorca's points of contact with Greek tragedy are many and obvious—most apparently, and perhaps least importantly, his use of a chorus. He seems to adjust his conception to the classical precepts of unity, with some concessions to time. And his use of rural characters for contemporary tragedy, in place of kings and princes that would have no immediate reality or importance, provides one of the best possible solutions to the problem of a modern, universal hero. If we agree that tragedy must have a supraindividual and national meaning, Lorca's "symbolic" peasants can best express the land and its people. As for the problem of style, Lorca seems consciously to adhere to the classical rule of separation of styles, maintaining a *noble* one that permits no intermingling of non-tragic elements. There is no comedy, no change of form, no relief from the tragic tension he seeks to create.

In these modern tragedies, the dionysiac spirit is ever-present in the obscure forces that lead the characters to their fate—a fate that is constantly present and, in my opinion, represented basically by the all-powerful strength of instinct. This need not, however, require us to accept a naturalistic thesis, because there are other human, natural, even religious and metaphysical factors that apply to these plays. I have not discussed them here, because my present purpose was to analyze the instinctive motivation; but in fairness one cannot disregard the human passions of love and hate, honor and sense of duty, that one encounters in the characters. They exist and play an important part in the action, although it is my contention that, taken by themselves, they cannot give a rational and completely satisfactory explanation of the plays; for that, the stronger, underlying power of natural forces and instinct is essential.

To answer the last and possibly most important characteristic of tragedy, implied in the ideas of cartharsis and fate, one must raise the question: what is Lorca's religious attitude, if any? This is a point which, though I can only indicate it here, could bear far more elaborate analysis. Lorca's presentation of the same problem in all three plays—the "tragedy" resulting from a lack of understanding between male and female, the consequent frustration of natural and social instincts, and the "tragic" fate of the guilty heroes—seems to me very closely related to a religious conception of sin and its consequences, individual and social. Lorca never depicts the natural and instinctive motivations as necessarily excluding more humane, conscious and religious feelings, but rather as a part of the individual's whole personality and of the meaning of his existence. His conception of love, sex and motherhood is particularly striking. Thus, for instance, the character of Yerma, probably Lorca's greatest creation, acquires a most painful and beautiful meaning as a symbol of sterility and uselessness. In her passion and revolt there is more than frustrated instinct only; there is, above all, a human being trying to find a *raison d'être,* a sense of her own existence. (pp. 91-7)

Manuel Blanco-Gonzalez, "Lorca: The Tragic Trilogy," in Drama Critique, *Vol. IX, No. 2, Spring, 1966, pp. 91-7.*

John Devlin   (essay date 1969)

[*Devlin is an American educator and critic who specializes in Spanish literature. In the following essay, he presents an overview of the structure and themes of García Lorca's* Poeta en Nueva York.]

Federico García Lorca's reputation is unquestionably secure as one of the truly great creative artists of modern times. In fact, his incredible gift for essential statement, combined with mastery of metaphor and poetic transmutation, may eventually place him among the handful of true immortals. Lorca's fame was gained through the enormous impetus of his unique style, which reached a certain climax of intensity in his *Gypsy Ballads.* The dramatic power of his poems is paralleled by the poetic fire of his dramas, especially the favorites *Blood Wedding,* *Yerma,* and *Bernarda Alba's Family.* Less well known and appreciated is the cycle entitled *Poet in New York.* Critics point to the obvious difficulties in understanding the poems, such as the poet's reliance on obscure aspects of baroque expression practiced by Góngora three centuries earlier. It is further asserted that the work is an expression of Lorca's frank dislike of North American civilization. Conrad Aiken claims that "he hated us, and rightly, for the right reasons." Roy Campbell and John A. Crow, along with many Spanish critics, felt that the work was an atypical excursion into areas not within the mainstream of Lorca's inspiration. Great emphasis has been placed on the "cultural shock" experienced by a representative of a more rural, traditional atmosphere upon being exposed to the mechanized complex of New York City. It has also been asserted that Lorca, a man who identified and empathized with the gypsies of his native Andalusia, found himself most at home in America among the Negroes of Harlem. Judgments are made linking the poems to such movements as surrealism, the ultra modern, and the contemporary preoccupations with chaos, the absurd, destruction, and centrifugal forces.

All of these statements contain much truth provided that they are not interpreted in a way that detracts from the essential greatness of the cycle or prevents the emergence of *Poet in New York* as one of the truly great affirmative statements of our epoch.

García Lorca opens the collection with a brief evocation of his feelings upon coming **"Back from a Walk"** during his stay at Columbia University in 1929. He is the "heaven-murdered one"; he struggles between symbols of destruction (the serpent) and of hope (crystal). He is "stumbling each day with my different face"—that is, he is losing his identity. The poems move rapidly into swirling images of decadence, destruction, sterility, and perversion. The poet resists but must descend among little animals with broken heads into the sociological inferno. The "tree-stump" is now "tuneless," his face the "egg-white face of a child." He moves in "the world of topless academies," of "the butterfly drowned in the inkwell," in "the world of the dead and castaway tabloids." At dusk at Coney Island he wanders in a **"Landscape of the Vomiting Multitudes"**; in a nocturn at Battery Park he creates the **"Landscape of the Urinating Multitudes . . . awaiting the death of a boy on a Japanese cutter."** He has eyes, but they are powerless to order the chaos of what they have seen and are seeing. He says in **"Interlude"**:

> Those eyes of Nineteen-Ten, my very eyes,
> saw only the blank wall, and the girls making water,
> the bull's snout, the poisonous mushroom,
> the unthinkable moon that lightened in corners
> dry lemon-rinds . . .
>
> . . . . .
>
> Little eyes, my very eyes: there.
>
> Question no further. All things, I have seen,
> that hold to their course find only their vacancy.

In **"Your Childhood in Menton"** Lorca personifies his identity through a supposed lost love, symbolized by a young girl. But the girl quickly becomes metamorphosed into a woman, thus eluding him. He now attempts to break through the mask of her maturity to find an anchor for his identity; yet the woman has as little meaning for him as do the places, hotels, and trains of New York. He is beset by forces that would wall him up or chain the ocean, that would kill beauty and hope or "unsex the created of heaven." But in all his anguish he still can perceive that Love exists, seen through its symbol, the sea, or "a running of deer / through an infinite bosom of whiteness." In **"Abandoned Church"** (subtitled "Ballad of the Great War") his lost eyes again seek identity in an imaginary son killed in World War I. He desperately fumbles amid the hollow arches and knocks on the coffin lids, as the son becomes transmuted into a daughter, a dead fish, the ocean, a giant, a bear. Had his son had the strength of a bear, he would not be lost nor would the poet have "feared for the crocodile's secret / nor gazed at a tree-tethered sea / to be ravished and bled by a rabble of troops."

Angel Del Río has pointed out that the cycle consists of five basic divisions or movements, each with various subdivisions. The first division consists of the "Poems of Solitude at Columbia University." This is followed by "The Negroes" and "Streets and Dreams"—basically a modern evocation of the medieval themes of a lost paradise and the dance of death. A section of poems follows based on the poet's stay in the country, fittingly first at Lake Eden in northern Vermont, later with friends in Newburgh, New York. It is a bucolic intermezzo. The imagery becomes clearer, the language less charged with violent emotion:

> It was another time's voice,
> unskilled in the flow of the thick and the bitter.
> I foresaw it, lapping my feet
> under dampened and delicate fern.

Later in this division Lorca turns to thoughts of death and develops this theme in a group entitled "Introduction to Death: Poems of Solitude in Vermont." The transmutation of imagery returns with greater intensity:

> Horse would be dog,
> dog would be swallow,
> swallow, a wasp.

In the fourth grouping, the poet finally recovers his equilibrium and identity, especially in the poem entitled **"New York: Office and Denunciation."** In the fifth and last group, joyful and confident, he "waltzes" back toward the Hispanic world, to Cuba.

The difficulty in understanding *Poet in New York* upon a first reading resides in the extremely rich but apparently confused metaphors and the constant interchange of symbols. The essential grammatical form—more than in any other work of Lorca—is the noun, which he handles with the spare intensity of St. John of the Cross. The nouns are rarely abstractions, however, and refer, as seen above, to every imaginable class of living and inorganic being: minerals, animals, natural phenomena, and objects made by man. There are few adjectives, and they are rarely found in normal associations. The majority of the verbs express motions: to change, grasp, stumble, seek, destroy, dissolve, agitate. That which is concrete dissolves while the

material takes on the motion associated with living beings. The diction is sinewy and yet heavily charged with strong emotion rather than ideological intent. Staccato impressions dot the pages with lines of four or five syllables. But frequently, as the emotion increases in crescendo, the lines become longer and undulate and breathe with intense passion:

> the madness of penguins and seagulls will come
>   down on the stone
> and give words to the sleepers and those who in-
>   tone on the streetcorners.

In general, the entire collection—like all of Lorca's work—is admirably suited to recitation aloud. A person familiar with the sonorities of the Spanish can try to imagine the original effect when sung in what John Brande Trend calls Lorca's *voz inefable*.

On first reading, the images and their transmutations can be confusing. Yet, if accepted at face value, the words frequently add up to precisely what they say. "A cat's paw smashed by a motorist" means exactly that. Of course, there are some symbols that even the persons closest to Lorca are unable to decipher. This transmutation of symbols—and of course Lorca was not the first to use the device—is marvelously apt for expressing his own disorder. He is "heaven-murdered" and each day has a "different face." The outlines of the ordinary landscape become twisted out of proportion. Confusion of symbols and the warping of reality's perspective are properties readily associated with psychic sickness—the poet's sickness or the city's sickness, or both.

Richard Saez in an illuminating essay has pointed out that a major source of Lorca's malaise and alienation is found in the fact that the city has lost contact with cosmic rhythm and expiatory ritual sacrifice. In the less industrialized civilizations of Europe, such as Spain, man is closer to the death and renewal of natural cycles: sunrise brings joy and hope; sunset suggests universal sadness. In the city the proposition is reversed: sunrise is often the bitter taste of renewed despair while joy or forgetfulness is enkindled as the lights go on in the bars and cafés. Spain is close in history and liturgy to the ritual sacrifice of blood in the ministrations of the Christian religion and the bullfight, as well as in the ritualistic bloodletting (supposedly in the name of renewal) of the medieval and Renaissance conquests and the Inquisition. Lorca feels there can be no renewal without the primordial and primitive expiatory sacrifice of blood. New York does not have it in this sense: "Blood has no doors in your night, lying face to the sky." The city is indeed bloodied: psychologically by the mistreatment of the poor and the Negroes; physically by the slaughter of countless animals, "four million ducks / five million hogs / two thousand doves, to a dying man's pleasure."

> The ducks and the doves,
> and the hogs and the lambs
> shed their blood drops
> under the multiplications;
> and the terrible babble of cattle stampeding,
> fills all the valley with weeping
> where the Hudson flows, drunk upon oil.

But the blood is spilled only to feed man's ego and his city, a monster whose materialism is symbolized by "those who drink down tears of dead girls in the bank-lobby."

One of the amazing aspects of *Poet in New York* is Lorca's prophetic role. A feeling of impending doom permeates the work and is rooted partially in World War I; it seems to stretch forward to the Spanish Civil War and World War II, both of which ended after enormous amounts of blood had been spilled. The work is also marvelously adapted to the mood of the stockmarket crash of 1929, contemporaneous with the poet's stay in New York, and the onslaught of the great depression. Strangely, too, the city of Lorca's nightmare, the city he could not bear to live in, seems as much like New York of the 1960s as of 1929. The current alienation from nature—population and ghetto explosions, slum conditions, air and water pollution—all these seem foreshadowed. Lorca's powerful evocative imagery is also most adequate for the latter-day experience of the danger of total nuclear destruction. In fact, Juan Larrea suggested that Lorca had allowed the collective unconscious to express itself in *Poet in New York* and accordingly became the voice of a suprahistorical dynamism that rules the hidden currents of history.

Most strange and gripping of all the prophetic aspects is the poet's prophecy of his own death. Already in the *Gypsy Ballads* he had foretold this event in a poem entitled **"The Death of Antoñito el Camborio"**:

> Ah, Antoñito of the Camborios
> worthy of an Empress!
> Remember the Virgin
> because you are to die.
> Ah, Federico García
> call the Guardia Civil
> Already my waist has snapped
> like a stalk of maize.

In *Poet in New York,* in **"Fable and Round of the Three Friends,"** he writes:

> They ransacked the cafés, the graveyards, the
>   churches
> they opened the wine-casks and clothes-presses,
> they ravaged three skeletons to gouge out the
>   gold of their teeth.
> But me, they never encountered.
> They never encountered me?
> No. Never encountered me.

There can be no doubt that Lorca's *Poet in New York* is in many ways similar to Eliot's *Wasteland.* In fact, Del Río states flatly that the Spaniard had read Angel Flores' Spanish translation, *Tierra Baldía.* Both poets evoke the sterility of modernity; both use such symbols as eyes that are unfulfilled; both use the device of transmutation. Furthermore, both poets, in their respective cycles as well as in their theater, stress the value of sacrifice—frequently bloody—as a rite of expiation.

Eliot's reliance on Dante has been the source of frequent comment. It is very evident that there are also parallels between *Poet in New York* and the *Divine Comedy,* although these may merely stem from Lorca's subconscious and the qualities that tend to be found in all superior products of the human spirit. In Dante's eleventh letter, addressed to

Can Grande della Scala, the great Florentine explicitly laid down the guidelines for the traditional fourfold interpretation of his masterpiece. They are well known—the literal, allegorical, tropological (or moral), and anagogical—although, as Dante says, the last three may all be said to be in a sense allegorical since "they differ from the literal or historic." The literal, thus, is the story itself; the allegorical, the extended meanings; the tropological turns toward man's moral attitudes—individual man or everyman; the anagogical refers to the effects of purgation and consequent regeneration, wholeness, and union with God.

In *Poet in New York,* therefore, the literal interpretation is just that—the poet's vision of the city in its inhuman aspect. The allegorical in the *Divine Comedy* refers to the life of Christ among men. A transference of Lorca's suffering to Christ (as exemplar) in no way vitiates the meaning of the cycle, although it should be applied cautiously and without rigidity. There are many other allegories, such as those suggested above in the context of the poet's prophetic sense. In this connection, it should be remembered that Lorca's reaction and denunciation refer not only to New York but—allegorically—to mechanized civilization in general. The tropological level is the record of Lorca's struggle with and eventual overcoming of his surroundings. Here is Lorca, the undoubtedly homesick man, Lorca suffering from cultural shock. Most probably, too, there is Lorca troubled by homosexual problems, and very likely on the verge of some psychic disorder triggered by his sense of alienation and his isolation from the rhythmic movements of the universe. Along with Lorca is everyman, brought there by the universality of the themes—everyman in New York, everyman caught up in mechanized society and alienated from nature, everyman sick with the diseases of modernity. One of the supreme moments of *Poet in New York* comes in **"New York: Office and Denunciation."** Suddenly Lorca (or everyman) seems to find his equilibrium. He denounces "all the living / . . . who pile up mountains of asphalt / where the hearts / of the little unmemoried creatures beat on." The transmutation of symbols ceases and he says, simply:

> This is not hell, but a street.
> Not death, but a fruit stand.

Then he offers himself as a sacrifice:

> I accuse!
>
> I accuse the conspiracy
> of untenable offices
>
>   . . . . .
>
> that efface the design of the forest;
> and I offer myself to be eaten by cattle, the rabble
> whose outcries have filled all the valley
> where the Hudson flows, drunk upon oil.

The tropological interpretation leads into the anagogical. The poet has made his moral commitment and is on his way to regeneration. Dante emerged from hell to look at the stars. Lorca, after having made his denunciation and offer of sacrifice, goes to the tower of the Chrysler Building and joyfully shouts his **"Cry to Rome."** Most probably this evocation of the Eternal City is not so much a headlong rush into the practices of the institutional Church as the summoning of a tangible symbol to affirm the inevitability of renewal, regeneration, and the permanence of love:

> But the old man, with light through his fingers
> will say: Love, love, love
> to the plaudits of perishing millions;
> will say: love, love, love,
> in the quivering tissue of tenderness;
> will say: peace, peace, peace,
> in the shudder of knives and the dynamite melons;
> will say: love, love, love,
> till his lips are sealed into silver

· · · · ·

> Meanwhile, and meanwhile, and meanwhile:
> the negro who sets out the cuspidors,
> the terrorized boy shaking under the livid director,

· · · · ·

> the mob of the hammer, the fiddle, the cloud—

· · · · ·

> let them cry
> cry like all darkness made one,
> cry with such ruinous voice
> that the cities will tremble like girls
> and break open the prisons of music and oil.
> Give us that daily bread, for we wish it,
> flower of the alder, threshed tenderness, world
>   without end;
> earth's will be done, for we wish it,
> who offers her harvest to all.

Thus **Poet in New York,** once again in the spirit of Dante is a "comedy." It must be realized that the word comedy is derived from the Greek *kōme* meaning village and *ōidē* meaning song. A village song traditionally begins in darkness and ends in light. Lorca saw the absurdity in life, but his basically buoyant and affirmative personality made it impossible to accept it as the final fabric of existence.

After the **"Cry to Rome"** comes a beautiful tribute to Walt Whitman. There follow the poems where the poet "waltzes" to Cuba and, by implication, back to Spain.

Some seven years after Federico García Lorca left New York, the Spanish Guardia Civil went to the house where he was living in Granada. They took him to a cemetery, where he was shot by a Fascist firing squad. And his body was never found. (pp. 131-40)

> John Devlin, "García Lorca's Basic Affirmation in 'Poet in New York'," in Studies in Honor of Samuel Montefiore Waxman, *edited by Herbert H. Golden, Boston University Press, 1969, pp. 131-40.*

Miguel González-Gerth   (essay date 1970)

[*González-Gerth is a Mexican-born American educator, poet, and critic. In the following essay, he considers the symbolism of blood and death in García Lorca's works.*]

In a very perceptive article entitled "Lorca and the Poetry of Death," the poet and critic Pedro Salinas, a contemporary of Federico García Lorca, states: "The vision of life and man that gleams and shines forth in Lorca's work is founded on death. Lorca understands, feels life through death." And he goes on: "Lorca was born in a country that for centuries has been living out a special kind of culture that I call the 'culture of death' . . . it should be no means be regarded as a . . . cult of death . . . [it] is a conception of man . . . in which the awareness of death functions with a positive force . . . within [which] a human being may affirm himself, not only in the acts of life, but in the very act of death. An existence in which the idea of death is hidden or suppressed . . . is lacking in the dimension of depth, in the dimension that gives life its tone of intensity and drama" [reprinted in *Lorca: A Collection of Critical Essays,* edited by Manuel Durán]. I have quoted at length from this essay because I believe that, obvious as all this may be to those of us who have read Lorca, it is a fundamental truth and the first of two premises upon which I have based this article.

In a public statement regarding the future of the Spanish theater, Lorca himself once said that he knew "the secret of keeping cool" because, as a true Andalusian, the blood that ran through his veins was ancient blood. And in a lecture entitled **"Theory and Game of the Goblin,"** he explained that the Andalusian *duende* (not a mere sprite but the ghost of a whole culture) is to be found in any human act which is the result of what Lorca called "effective instinct." "In other words," he went on, "it is not a question of ability, rather of a true life style, which is blood, which, in turn, is ancient culture. . . . " These two statements comprise my second premise.

"The secret of keeping cool" and the occasional presence of the goblin in one's behavior might seem contradictory elements. In reality they are the rare and quite compatible traits of a people's character which Lorca would exalt. They fuse into a coolness within emotionality which can look death in the face. And it must be borne in mind that Lorca employs the substantive "blood" and the adjective "ancient" to define this Andalusian heritage. Obviously, he was attempting to create or revitalize myths which would serve his artistic purpose. He was certainly not the first writer to do so, but it is important to take into account, because it is an integral part of his whole cultural background and attitude, and it helps to explain some of the symbols he used in his lyric poems and in his dramas. So when I speak of García Lorca's tragic symbolism, I will refer primarily to a recurrent image which I look upon as the climactic symbol of tragedy in Lorca's works, namely, the image of blood in all its symbolic variations. Furthermore, this symbol must be considered within a larger symbolic context, namely, that of human sacrifice, as I will try to point out later on.

As early as 1919 he wrote in his poem **"Balada de la placeta"** (**"Song of the Little Square"**) the following revealing lines: "What do you have there / in your hands like the springtime? / A rose of red blood and a lily white. / Wet them in the waters of the ancient song. / Clear stream, fountain so calm! / What do you feel there / in

The first page from the manuscript of García Lorca's "Ode to Walt Whitman," which was first published in 1933 and later included in Poeta en Nueva York.

your mouth red and thirsting? / The taste of the bones of my great big skull." Synthesized in lyrical and dramatic imagery we find a whole gamut of traditions and emotions that will later find a more elaborate reprise in Lorca's longer poems and in his dramatic pieces. As might have been expected, Lorca began by writing lyric poetry, but we are told by one who had known him since childhood, his brother Francisco, that Lorca was always interested in putting on plays. His first serious attempt was considered a failure: either the theme was not right or the talent had not matured. But in 1924 Lorca began writing the compositions which were to be published in 1928 under the title *Romancero gitano (Book of Gypsy Ballads).* Edwin Honig, among others, has pointed out that it was in the form of the traditional Spanish ballad, which partakes of the lyric and the dramatic-narrative, embellished as it may be in this case by surrealist elements, where the poet found the bridge that would enable him to cross successfully from the pure lyric to the larger and more complex work which Francis Ferguson has aptly called "Lorca's theater poetry" [Edwin Honig, *García Lorca;* Francis Ferguson, "*Don Perlimplín:* Lorca's Theater-Poetry," reprinted in *Lorca: A Collection of Critical Essays,* edited by Manuel Durán].

In both the *Book of Gypsy Ballads* and *Mariana Pineda,* a play produced in 1927, there are many instances in which the blood image is employed and the theme of sacrifice appears. Mariana Pineda was an historical character who was condemned to death in 1831 for having embroidered a flag meant to proclaim Andalusian independence, in the reign of Ferdinand VII. As Enrique Díez-Canedo has pointed out, the heroine, as conceived by Lorca, "embroiders her flag, not as a symbol of liberty, but as a lover's gift. And only when she understands that in the soul of her beloved the love for freedom is stronger than the love for herself, does she become transfigured . . . into a symbol of that very liberty." Her real tragedy is that she is sacrificed on the altar of love.

Another hero to be sacrificed upon that altar is the protagonist of the tragic farce entitled *The Love of Don Perlimplín for Belisa, in His Garden,* produced in 1933. The ridiculous title is, of course, intentional. It is modeled after one of those popular Spanish cartoons sold in the streets and called *aleluyas* since they were, originally, of a religious nature. The theme of this *aleluya* is the proverbial situation of an old man who marries a young girl. And in order to emphasize this conflict, Lorca gives the subtitle of "erotic *aleluya*" to his play. It develops as follows: Don Perlimplín, an old bachelor, marries his young neighbor, Belisa, who is interested only in her own physical charms and who proceeds immediately to be unfaithful to him. The scene following the wedding night, in which Perlimplín appears crowned with enormous horns and flowers, is both hilarious and pathetic.

When his own sexuality becomes aroused, Perlimplín realizes that the situation is impossible: since he is not the man both he and Belisa wish he were, his happiness cannot last. Yet neither is she as she should be, because she lacks a spiritual consciousness. And so, as a solution to this dual problem, Perlimplín decides to commit suicide, but not before he lets Belisa know that a certain young man who courts her is destined never to be hers, a young man whom Perlimplín invents and impersonates. Thus he shows Belisa how illusory physical attraction can be and, hence, endows her sensuous body with a true soul. At the end of the play Marcolfa, Perlimplín's servant, speaks these ritual words in the garden where her master died: "Belisa, you are now a new woman. You are now dressed in the most glorious blood of my master." Belisa recognizes her miraculous transformation when she replies: "Yes, yes, Marcolfa, I love him, I love him with all the strength of my flesh and of my soul." And finally, as if the one spoken about were still alive, Marcolfa whispers while the bells toll: "Don Perlimplín, sleep, sleep . . . Do you hear her?"

In this shorter work, the act of suicide is something transcendental, an act of self-immolation which aspires to Christian sacrifice. It stems from the conflict between flesh and spirit and is motivated by love. I submit that this little masterpiece is a daring parody of the Christ story. Who can doubt it after thinking about the word *aleluya,* which in Hebrew means "Praise ye the Lord," and the admonition Perlimplín makes to Belisa regarding his purpose? ". . . I wish to sacrifice myself for you . . . This which I do no one ever did before. But I am already out of this world and outside the ridiculous morality observed by people." My interpretation will not be too surprising if one considers that in *Poet in New York,* written about the same time as *The Love of Don Perlimplín for Belisa, in His Garden,* but published only in fragments during the poet's lifetime, there appear the themes of self-negation and self-immolation in the manner of the Christ story, with multiple uses of the blood image.

Any allusion to the supernatural presupposes a mythical context. Both the poem-sequence inspired by Lorca's anguished experience in America and Don Perlimplín's tragedy border on the Christian dominion, but they are respectively associated with pagan elements by the use of symbols such as nature-gods or totems in *Poet in New York* and the instrument of death in *Don Perlimplín:* an "emerald dagger . . . a fiery handful of precious stones." This pagan or, perhaps more properly, pantheistic element is also found in the play which I will now discuss as the touchstone for my aperçu. And I say this about it because, contrary opinion notwithstanding, I personally consider it to be Lorca's most accomplished work, the one in which he best integrates all the art forms and techniques at his command: the lyrical, the dramatic, the plastic, and the musical. I refer, of course, to *Blood Wedding,* whose title contains the germ of Lorca's most constant themes and symbols: the love-death theme, the sexual obsession, the blood image in all its symbolic possibilities, and the myth of sacrifice.

Blood Wedding, which also was put on stage in 1933, is a three-act rural play with a simple plot, presumably based on a newspaper account. The drama revolves around Leonardo, the only character who bears a proper name. The rest are country archetypes thus designated: the Wife, the Bride, the Groom, the Father, the Mother. There also appear several symbolic characters: the Moon, Death, and Three Woodcutters. Leonardo's relatives have killed the

Groom's father and older brother in a feud. The Groom's domineering mother is obsessed by the loss of her loved ones and places her last hope on the marriage of her younger son. "Knives, knives. Cursed be all knives and the scoundrel who invented them," she says at the very beginning, and the knife as a symbol of death reappears throughout the piece, even reflected by the Moon itself. Before marrying his wife, Leonardo had courted the Bride, the girl whom the Groom will marry. During the festivities immediately following the wedding, Leonardo and the Bride run away together, impelled by a passion never consummated. After a desperate chase, the Groom and Leonardo kill each other. The Mother's lamentations at the end reach a muffled climax: the knives have finished her whole family.

The title could not be more fitting. It is Leonardo as a man, more than the Bride as a woman, who insists on altering the normal course of events, which is none other than the course of their own blood. The blood image here has three, and later, four symbolic values. First, ancestral blood; second, nuptial blood; third, lethal blood. Of these, the first is the blood of a family or a race. The Groom's mother says: ". . . the way with men of good stock. Real blood. Your grandfather left a son on every corner. . . ." And the Bride's father comments on Leonardo's conduct: "That one is looking for trouble. He's not of good blood." The second is the blood that boils inside one's veins upon feeling sexual attraction, that is, erotic love. Three Woodcutters in the forest, almost like a Greek chorus, talk about the lovers:

> FIRST WOODCUTTER. They were deceiving themselves but at last blood was stronger.
>
> THIRD WOODCUTTER. Blood!
>
> FIRST WOODCUTTER. You have to follow the path of your blood.
>
> SECOND WOODCUTTER. But blood that sees the light of day is drunk up by the earth.
>
> FIRST WOODCUTTER. So what? Better dead with the blood drained away than alive with it rotting . . . they will have mingled their bloods and they will be like two empty jars. . . .

The third is the blood that is shed, the blood whose loss results in death. The servant sings: ". . . the bridegroom is a dove / with his breast turned into flame / and the fields wait for the sound / of the blood that is shed." Upon hearing of the flight of Leonardo and the Bride, the Groom's mother prophesies: "The hour of blood has come again." And the Moon (playing a very significant part in this drama) says, when the rivals are about to fight in the forest: ". . . this night there will be / red blood for my cheeks . . . O let me enter a breast / where I may find some warmth! / A heart for me! A warm / heart! that will spill / over the mountains of my chest. / Oh let me come in, oh let me!"

Of course, the above three symbolic aspects of human blood become one symbol when elevated to the level of a fourth, namely, sacrificial blood. But how does this notion enter into this drama? Blood, whether real or symbolic, is,

after all, liquid and must follow a course, a "path," as the Woodcutter says, or it must remain stagnant and "rotting." Such a course is the genealogical history of mankind. Normally the course is from the individual (personal blood) through the marriage bed where two individuals come together (nuptial blood) toward the founding of a family or race (ancestral blood, which is the accumulation of the first two and exerts influence on the future through heredity). But there are contradictory forces within and without the individual which sometimes tend to alter this normal function of the blood cycle. In *Blood Wedding,* it is at the second stage, that of nuptial blood, where the action turns toward tragedy. Leonardo is moved by an irresistible passion, and his influence on the Bride results in the closing of a valve which reverses the course of the blood. Instead of flowing from the personal to the ancestral, thus continuing the family, it runs from the ancestral to the personal, thus reviving the feud and bringing about the death of both men.

I believe it was August Winnig who said that blood and soil make up the destiny of a people. This is certainly true of the Andalusians as portrayed by Lorca in his tragedies. As a justification of his acts, Leonardo says to the Bride shortly before the catastrophe: "I am not the one to blame / the fault is of the earth / and this fragrance you exhale / from your bosom and your braids." And she answers with these lines worthy of Lope de Vega: "Oh how wrong of you to say! / from you I want neither bed nor food, / yet there's no minute in each day / when I don't want to be with you, / for you drag me, and I come, / then you tell me to go back / and I follow, follow you / like a wind-blown piece of chaff." Fatal love has had its effect, and the blood cycle has been altered: instead of the vital course, the lethal one; instead of procreation, disaster. Now, this end, brought about by the strongest of primitive passions, must be exalted by Lorca. And the death of the rivals is claimed as a sacrifice by the goddess of the dark, the Moon, so often an ambiguous symbol in Lorca's work. Here again is found the mixture of Christian and pagan or pantheistic elements.

Yerma, produced in 1934, is also a rural tragedy, but its central theme and characters possess greater psychological depth than those of *Blood Wedding.* Yerma is, of course, the heroine whose name Lorca derived from a word which means "desert." The drama develops around her burning desire to bear a child. Her husband, Juan, is apparently incapable of fulfilling this desire and does not even want to talk about it. The pregnancy of other women and the virility she imagines in Victor, another character, torture Yerma in her barrenness, but her sense of honor prevents her from seeking fulfillment of her desire with another man. She tries to solve the problem by indulging in the witchcraft practiced by the townswomen and by appealing to the miraculous power of a saint whose shrine is nearby. But neither the incantation nor the pilgrimage brings about the desired effect. Finally, when Juan tells her that he is happy without children, Yerma kills him.

This play is somewhat less "poetic" than *Blood Wedding* when considered from outside. Neither the moon nor Death appear as characters. But this is not to say that the structure of *Yerma* is not poetic. Francis Ferguson says that in *The Love of Don Perlimplín for Belisa, in His Garden* "the poetry is in the characters and their relationships, in the conception of each of the . . . scenes, and especially in the sharp but quickly resolved contrasts between scenes, and especially in the sharp but quickly resolved contrasts between them." Something like this could be said about *Blood Wedding* and even about *Yerma,* except that the latter is charged with a much denser atmosphere. In this play, too, Lorca has used the image of blood as a tragic symbol. The heroine's rebellion against her fate is expressed in terms of it. The reader can discern almost the same blood cycle: ancestral blood, nuptial blood, lethal blood, and ultimately sacrificial blood.

Yerma cries out: "Cursed be my father who left me his blood of a father of a hundred children. Cursed be my blood that searches for them, knocking against the walls." And the old woman who offers her a way out of her infecundity says: "My son is made of blood. Like me. If you come to my house, you can still smell the cradles." But ancestral blood can also be sterile. Revealing a biological notion of family stock, the old woman says: "Your husband is to blame . . . Neither his father, nor his grandfather, nor his great-grandfather behaved like men of good blood. For them to have a son heaven and earth had to meet." And Juan himself has to admit that "families have honor. And . . . honor is a burden that rests on all of us. But . . . it's both dark and weak in the very channels of the blood."

Then there are instances of nuptial blood. By the river the girls wash their clothes and sing this song:

> FOURTH LAUNDRESS. Through the air I sense my husband coming to bed. I, red gilliflowers; and he, a gilliflower red.
>
> FIRST LAUNDRESS. Flower to flower must be wed when the summer dries the reaper's red blood . . . And our body has the wild branches of a coral-tree . . .

And Yerma begs of Juan: "I'm looking for you; it's you I look for day and night without finding a shade where I can sigh. It's your blood and shade I want."

Toward the climax at the end of the play, Juan tries to comfort Yerma, saying "I'm looking for you. In the moonlight you're beautiful." Thus the influence of the moon is made known in this play also. After Juan says: "Kiss me . . . like this." And she answers: "That I'll never do," meaning with resignation to her fate. After she has strangled her husband, Yerma states: "Barren, barren, but certain. Now I really know it for sure. And alone. Now I'll sleep without startling myself awake, anxious to see if I feel in my blood another new blood . . . " The heroine has sacrificed her husband and her potential motherhood to the forces that inexplicably denied her what she wanted most.

Like *Poet in New York,* Lorca's *Lament for the Death of a Bullfighter* has a place in the development of his tragic symbolism. Perhaps the best known lines by Lorca which speak of the tragedy of human death in images of spilled blood are those from this elegy to his friend Ignacio Sánchez Mejías: "No, I don't want to see it! / Tell the moon to come, / for I don't want to see Ignacio's blood / spilled on the sand." In that peak of Lorca's lyrical accomplishment, one can find the tragic symbol of his whole vision of life and man. The bullfighter has been killed in the arena; he might have been killed in the fields, but fate would have it that his death is preceded by a long animated ritual. In any case, he has been sacrificed to the mysterious gods of nature.

The House of Bernarda Alba, Lorca's last published drama, is markedly different from *Blood Wedding* and *Yerma,* although usually they have been regarded as a trilogy. In it Lorca successfully attempted to move farther away from poetic drama, or theater-poetry, toward realistic drama. The integration and diction in *The House of Bernarda Alba* are not the same as those of the two preceding rural tragedies. However, it might be pointed out that there are some features which they have in common. And one of them, if I am not stretching reality too far, is precisely the possible echo of Lorca's tragic symbolism which leads to human death as sacrifice. After all, the death of Adela could be regarded as a sacrifice to the dark gods which live in the character and the atmosphere of Bernarda and her hapless house. The same human frustrations that one encounters in *Blood Wedding* and *Yerma* are essentially those of Bernada's daughters.

If indeed Lorca is the poet of death, why does his tragic symbolism tend toward a frequent consummation of human sacrifice and its ritual? My conclusion is that, apart from the aesthetic values that he may have seen in that ritual, Lorca wanted to dignify human death. He felt that human death was meaningful and he wanted to provide, in his art, a reason or a justification for it, whether it be one that promised a hereafter or not. It is one of the great ironies of modern literary history that this man, who tried to ennoble death by raising it to the level of sacrifice, should have been himself sacrificed, not to some mysterious and wonderful natural deity enhanced by myth, but to the base and obvious powers of injustice and brutality. (pp. 56-63)

Miguel González-Gerth, "The Tragic Symbolism of Federico García Lorca," in The Texas Quarterly, *Vol. XIII, No. 2, Summer, 1970, pp. 56-63.*

García Lorca on the nature of truth:

The truth is what's alive and now they try to fill us up with deaths and cork dust. The absurd, if it's alive, is true; the theorem, if it's dead, is a lie. Let the fresh air in! Aren't you bothered by the idea of a sea with all its fish tied by little chains to one place, unknowing? I'm not disputing dogma. But dread the thought of where "that dogma" leads.

Federico García Lorca, in a letter to his friend Sebastian Gasch, 1928.

Charles A. McBride   (essay date 1975)

[*In the following essay, McBride studies the portrayal of women in García Lorca's later dramas.*]

The case of the writer who suddenly finds himself in an unfamiliar place, radically different from his native milieu, gives rise to speculation concerning his peculiar way of experiencing the new surroundings, as well as their possible influence on his later works. For García Lorca's experience of New York in the years 1929-30, we have the poems of his *Poeta en Nueva York.* It is well known, furthermore, that after returning to Spain his literary efforts were devoted almost entirely to the theater, and that the most outstanding theatrical works of that final period in his life deal with the frustration and suffering of women. But in what way, if at all, is this concern related to the poet-playwright's sojourn in the American metropolis?

One critic speculates that Lorca, while in New York, perhaps began to think seriously about the social position of Spanish women because he was considering them from a new perspective, one that was provided by his first-hand knowledge of the comparatively independent position of the American woman [Manuel Durán, "García Lorca, poeta entre dos mundos," *Asomente* 18, No. 1 (1962)]. That he took notice of the women of New York seems evident: at least one person close to him at that time has reported the poet's admiration for their beauty. He apparently did not understand, however, their attitude of independence, which he saw largely as a cold exterior. Nevertheless, it does seem possible, even likely, that his consideration of their relative independence would lead him to think anew about the position of woman in the traditional Spanish family, and from there to produce his dramatic works which, by implication, attack customs and institutions that weigh heavily upon the feminine personality. In other words, it seems quite possible that the new perspective Lorca gained by his stay in New York influenced his later dramatic works in the direction of social criticism. Though this is indeed an attractive hypothesis, I nonetheless view it with some skepticism.

The questions we ought to ask here are: (1) To what extent can those later works legitimately be regarded as social criticism, and (2) do they represent a significant departure from the author's earlier works?

Of the theatrical works produced between 1930 and 1936, only two clearly portray tradition and customs relating to the family institution as acting oppressively upon the female characters. I am thinking of *Doña Rosita la soltera* and *La casa de Bernarda Alba.* Of the others, the one entitled *Así que pasen cinco años* is strongly surrealistic, dealing with a philosophic theme in such a way that esthetic and purely theatrical considerations predominate. Another play, the little known and never performed *El público,* also is of a surrealistic nature, nor does it deal with the position of women. *La zapatera prodigiosa,* which Lorca in fact began to write while in New York, centers attention upon the irrepressible vitality of the woman's character. The circumstances of her marriage belong to a tradition that is literary and have poetic, not realistic or social, significance in the work. *Yerma* places the tragic burden

upon one woman, whose instinctual desire for motherhood is frustrated by her husband's sterility, a fortuitous condition that can and does serve the purposes of tragedy, but which could hardly enter into a credible social criticism.

Turning to another of Lorca's rural tragedies, and probably the most frequently performed of his works, *Bodas de sangre* dramatizes a fundamental conflict between instinctual, irrational, chaotic impulses and, on the other hand, social forms that hold such impulses in check and channel them into socially acceptable behavior patterns. The "blood" of lust and revenge is an irresistible force sweeping the characters along to their grim destiny. This, of course, is the stuff that tragedy is made of. It is universal in its appeal and application. It applies to men and women alike, regardless of the particular customs or social institutions. Thus here, too, I fail to find the elements or the tone necessary to make up a work of social criticism.

This brings us back to *Doña Rosita la soltera* and *La casa de Bernarda Alba.* These, Lorca's last dramatic works, are in many ways at opposite poles: *Doña Rosita* has an urban setting, the other play, a rural one; in *Doña Rosita* the burden of frustration and suffering weighs almost entirely upon Rosita's shoulders, while in *Bernarda Alba* that burden is distributed among the five daughters; the story of Rosita unfolds within a thoroughly poetic conception (e.g., her life itself is conceived as the birth, maturity, and old age of a flower, the rose), and, by contrast, Lorca writes on the first page of *Bernarda Alba:* "El poeta advierte que estos tres actos tienen la intención de un documental fotográfico"—i.e., a realistic intention. Various aspects of *Doña Rosita* are similar to the literary form known as the comedy of manners; *Bernarda Alba* is unmitigated tragedy.

Underlying these differences, however, we find a basic similarity between the two plays in the themes of sexual frustration and the nonfulfillment of human personality and potentiality. As we finish reading, or viewing a performance of *Bernarda Alba,* we might well reflect on the fate of Bernarda's daughters and think, what a waste of human life! And the same thought occurs to us after Rosita's final scene, when we have seen her exit—pale and dressed in white, like the white rose of the evening—leaving the final impact to the eloquence of an empty stage and a curtain that flutters like a white rose losing its petals in the wind of time ("Y cuando llega la noche / se comienza a deshojar," says the poem).

But are the unfulfilled lives of those female characters evidence of the author's desire to write social criticism? In *Rosita* the playwright has shown us youth, vitality, a gay, exuberant impulse to live and love—which is ultimately frustrated largely by circumstances beyond her control, but also by her own pride and conventional sense of honor. The point I wish to make here, though, is that the particular social circumstances of Rosita's plight are absorbed into the esthetic experience. For example, besides structuring the work around the flower simile, Lorca recreates the three historical moments of the play in the form of general *poetic* evocations and impressions, i.e., society appears as poetry rather than harsh reality. Though we may indeed understand that the protagonist's personal situation derives fundamentally from society's relegation of woman to a circumscribed, subservient position, I believe that this social condition, in the author's tragic esthetic, remains in the background while he focuses upon the individual's frustrated need for self-fulfillment in the face of opposing forces, whatever their nature may be.

That same frustration is multiplied and intensified in *Bernarda Alba.* Five young women live virtually imprisoned in their house by the stern, implacable will of their mother, Bernarda, a woman obsessed with honor and propriety. Here Lorca has placed the characters in a Spanish rural setting, where tradition weighs more heavily than in an urban environment. His choice of setting was probably influenced to some extent by a first-hand familiarity with the small towns of Andalusia, but, more importantly, I believe that he, as a playwright, saw in that tradition-bound setting the conditions that he needed in order to represent artistically and dramatically his universal conception of tragedy. As I have suggested above, he conceives of human life as an eternal struggle between instinctual, natural forces, which are as spontaneous and vital as they are chaotic, and, on the other hand, the powers of order, authority, and tradition, which, in attempting to enforce norms and conformity, often become repressive for the individual personality.

Indeed, in the light of this tragic view, such diverse works as Lorca's plays, his gypsy ballads, and his New York poems may be seen as different parts of one unified whole—varying moments in an essentially consistent, deeply poetic, and deeply human conception of life. Thus, in my view, the works written by Lorca after 1930 represent not a deviation from his previous outlook but rather a dedication to continuing its expression now almost exclusively in dramatic form. (pp. 479-82)

> *Charles A. McBride, "The Metropolis and García Lorca's Tragic View of Woman," in* Romance Notes, *Vol. XVI, No. 2, Winter, 1975, pp. 479-82.*

Gustavo Correa   (essay date 1979)

[*Correa is a Colombian-born American educator, editor, and critic. In the following essay originally presented during the 1979 Winthrop Symposium on Major Modern Writers, Correa discusses the mystical dimension of the treatment of nature in García Lorca's poetry.*]

Federico García Lorca was a poet of nature. He was born in a small Andalusian town, near the city of Granada, and was surrounded by nature and steeped in it from his early childhood. His background was essentially a rural one. This means that the dawning of his consciousness as a poet took place in a constant and intimate communication with nature. His first vocabulary and mental outlook in the understanding of the world had to do with the people, the objects, the smells, colors and sounds of the rural landscape in the countryside of Granada. This first contact of the poet with nature will always be present through his poetry, whether he is exploring the mystery of his own self or of the universe, or delving into the dark forces of nature

and man, or trying to face the enigma of human destiny. The poet himself has dwelt on the importance that this early communication with nature had for him. In an interview published in his *Obras completas,* he has the following to say of his early childhood: "When I was a child I lived in an environment which was completely saturated with nature. As all children do, I used to give to every single thing, to every piece of furniture, to every object, tree, rock, their own personality. I used to converse with them and I loved them." And also: "I love the land. I feel that I am intimately tied to it, in all my emotions. My farthest recollections from my childhood have the taste of the land. The land, the countryside, have done great things in my life. The tiniest creatures of the earth, the animals, the country people, all of them have for me hints and suggestions that do not have for other people. I feel them now with the same spirit with which I felt them in my childhood years. Indeed, if it were not so, I would not have been able to write *Blood Wedding*." Nature, thus, acted for Lorca from the very beginning, as a kind of a primary code in the awakening of his poetic consciousness. It constituted a path for the structuring of his mental development and set the trajectory for the formulation of his emotional life. This absorption of nature by the poetic consciousness in its formative years is no doubt a key to the powerful appeal that the poetry of Lorca always has for us. He speaks to us with a vocabulary which is directly related to the soil, to mother earth, to a simple rural society and to the cosmic universe.

It will be important to notice, on the other hand, that the objects of nature with which the poet was able to converse when he was a child and that continued to give him hints and suggestions in his adult and creative life will actually become a repertory of symbols underlying the texture of his poetry. The sun, the moon, the wind, the water, trees, grass, mountains, rivers, brooks, horses, bulls, cows, fish, birds, different kinds of plants and fruits, oleander, jazmin, pomegranate, lemons, oranges, rocks, pebbles, all of these enter into his poetry with powerful calls pointing to concrete experiences and coherent structures of meaning. In *Deep Song (Cante jondo)*, one of Lorca's early books, the wind that blows through the olive trees carries all kinds of mysterious sounds, and is intermingled in a single experience with the green color of the groves, the neighing of the horses and the passionate shouts of people singing their songs of tormented love, out into the distant horizons of dark nights. In these poems, the sky is a continuation of the earth ("land of light / and sky of earth"), and black butterflies mix with white serpents to carry with them the dark-skinned girl of the gypsy song (**"Siguiriya gitana"**). The air vibrations at night and in the dawn are the same vibrations of the guitar strings, which, in turn, put in motion the foliage of the trees and the hair and skirts of the gypsy girls. The sound waves are reflected on the undulations of the dry earth, the "undulated desert." The long shades at dusk fuse with the burning grape vines and with the olive trees to form the labyrinthic maze within which man's destiny is being determined. Black and dreamy horses take men with inescapable fatality to a final labyrinth of crosses. Grief and dark premonitions permeate the landscape. Also, in his book of the *Gypsy Ballads (Romancero gitano)* the fate of man can be read in solidarity with the manifestations of nature. The death of a child and the drowning of a girl occur under the malignant influence of the moon light, at the moment when dawn is beginning to appear in the horizon. Men kill each other in a senseless fight (**"Reyerta"**) in the midst of ill auguring signs in the sky (clouds, lightning and rain). The gypsy outlaw, who has to appear before the authorities (**"El emplazado"**) can read his destiny in the hard and metal-like light of the nearby rocky hills. The black horses of the Civil Guard are, on the other hand, the carriers of bad omen for the city of the gypsies. Things and phenomena of nature acquire, thus, a symbolic significance in relation to human destiny and the realization of the self.

This compact solidarity of man and nature is expressed in a dramatic web of interrelations that gives rise to the texture of myth. If myth is fundamentally a fable, an archetypal story, in which the deep impulses of the subconscious and the representational world of primitive mentality are projected, then the whole spectacle of nature and man's actions and cognitions can be seen in the perspective of myth. We can observe three different levels in the presentation of myth in the poetry of Lorca. First, a spectacle of nature is seen in an anthropomorphic context of mutually interrelated movements. Second, a spectacle of nature is woven into an integrated story, in which man is an active participant. Third, a spectacle of nature is seen objectively as a mythical story, but it is one that has an avowed and direct relationship to the inner life of the poet. All of these levels of mythical representation come through the individual mind of the poet, since the poetic consciousness acts as the center of the interrelated movements, whether the mythical story is being played out in the external world, or whether there is an active participation between man and the universe. The mythical story conveys clarification to the content of the poetic consciousness.

It is of interest to notice that Lorca himself tried to shed light, on various occasions, on the process by which he came to grips with the problem of language and of the structuring of the poem. Although we can see changes of emphasis, in a very short span of five years, between a first stage in which he sees the faculty of the imagination as the instrument through which he gives expression to the content of his poetic vision, and a next stage in which he stresses the concepts of "evasion" and of "poetic logic," and finally one in which the mysterious impulses of the earth and the presence of death are his primary concern, we can, nevertheless, say that his various theories complement each other. On the one hand, he propounds for the clarity of vision. On the other hand, he incorporates in his formulations what could be called the darker aspects of the self and the earthy dimension of his inspiration. In one of his first lectures **"The Poetic Image of Don Luis de Góngora,"** these two traits are revealed in different proportions, with the first one, that of clarity of vision, prevailing over the second one. For Lorca, the important thing, in the case of Góngora, was his capacity to "tie down" his imagination, by imposing a measure of orderly limits in the material to be absorbed from the senses. Góngora, in effect, says Lorca, would not allow himself to be dragged by the dark forces of inertia or by the fleeting bril-

liancy in which so many unaware poets succumb. Lorca's vision of the hunting trip at night depicts this rigorous process of selection:

> The poet must press on to the hunt single-minded and serene; in virtual camouflage. He must stand firm in the presence of illusions and keep wary lookout for the quivering flesh of reality that accords with the shadowy map of the poem that he carries. At times, he will cry out loudly in the poem's solitude, to rout the evil spirits—facile ones who would betray us to popular adulation without order or beauty or esthetic understanding.

The resulting landscape will be one of order and clarity: "An ordered countryside, in which poetry itself sets the limits to its own feverish rapture." This formulation by Lorca is a far cry from the chaotic landscape alluded to by André Breton in his first declaration of surrealist doctrine. In another of his lectures, the one of **"Imagination, Inspiration and Evasion,"** Lorca defines the notions of "poetic truth," "poetic emotion," "poetic logic" and "poetic fact," and asserts that they are *sui generis,* that is, of an entirely different nature from the products of rational thinking. According to Lorca, the poetic fact is by definition a non-rational phenomenon, although it implies a coherent and significant design. Also, the notion of poetic logic does not exclude in any way the notion of complete freedom of the inspiration and of the absence of limits. In a letter Lorca addressed to his friend Sebastian Gasch in 1928, he says of the two new poems he is sending to him: "They reflect my new spiritualized manner, they contain a pure and bare emotion, completely devoid of all logical control, although ¡Beware! ¡Beware!, with a tremendous amount of poetic logic. Indeed, they have nothing to do with surrealism, ¡Beware!, the clearest consciousness illuminates them." Lorca finds, thus, that even at the moments of his greatest freedom and inspiration he is still guided by norms in his process of creation.

This personal will of the poet to an ordered created structure for the poem takes into account, on the other hand, the absorption into his poetry of the darker forces of nature and of his own subconscious. Lorca's poetry is characterized precisely by the presence of the mysterious in man and nature. In other of his theoretical pronouncements, he actually emphasizes these other aspects of the poetic process. In his lecture on **"Childhood Cradle Songs,"** for instance, he stresses how important it is for the poet to submerge himself into the deep river beds of traditional popular poetry. The poet's inspiration cannot but be enriched by his submersion. Nevertheless, even here, Lorca refers to that "abstract quality" which is projected in some of the landscapes that are suggested by these popular songs. This abstract dimension allows the mind of the child to enter into distant mysterious spaces. Also, in his two lectures on the *Cante jondo,* the first one of the year 1922 and the second one of the year 1931, the poet emphasizes the primitive quality of the inspiration in this kind of art, which fuses both the musical and the poetic. The primitive impulses of the *Cante* are manifested in thoughts of life and death and are charged with deep emotional content. Once more, nevertheless, the poet points to what constitutes the organizing and stylizing features in the poetry of the *Deep Song* couplets: "There is nothing, absolutely nothing in the whole of Spain, similar to it in the manner of stylization, or in the projected atmosphere, or in the precision of the emotional content." Finally, in his lecture on the **"Theory and Play of the *Duende*,"** Lorca thinks that the great moments of authentic and original poetic creation are related to the presence of the forces of the earth and to the powerful pulsations of one's own blood. For Lorca, the *Duende* (in its Andalusian meaning of creative originality) is "a power rather than an acting," and one that leads to a real confrontation with it in the moments of its appearance. The *Duende* excludes all exercise in thinking ("es un luchar y no un pensar"). It burns the blood and makes the poetic form explode, bringing with it the miraculous presence of newly created sensations, which prompt a religious enthusiasm. The *Duende* is bound to the roots of the earth, it is the spirit of the earth, and expresses itself in black sounds and black strokes of the brush: "These black sounds constitute the mystery, the roots that are nailed down to the very mud and which all of us recognize, even if we don't know much about it, but from which comes all that is essential in art." With the appearance of the *Duende* there is the persistent look of death, lying in ambush behind us. It is this condition of the *Duende* what gives the magic quality to the poem. Lorca points, at the same time, that it is on the arena of the bullfight, where the *Duende* reveals itself with overwhelming features, since it is here where it has to fight, on the one side with the abyss of death, and on the other with geometry. It is geometry and measure, says Lorca "that which constitutes the fundamental basis of the bullfight." Thus, once again, Lorca introduces the notion of order, when dealing with the presence of the darker impulses of poetic creation. The poet himself has given us clues for the interpretation of his poetry. The dark impulses coexist with the will to the clarity of vision. Myth and the mythification of nature will become one of the ordering paths in Lorca's poetic inspiration.

We shall now give concrete examples of the three levels of mythical patterns that appear in the poetry of Lorca. At the first level, the poem entitled **"Fable" ("Fábula")**, of his book **Canciones** (1921-1924), presents the well known mythological figures of the Cyclops and the Unicorns in deadly confrontation with one another, in a hurried stampeeding against the cliffs of the water's edge. There is no doubt that the cyclops, with their green eyes, are the projected figures of the green waves of sea water, while the unicorns appear as the embodiment of the reflections of light over the water:

> Unicornios y cíclopes.
>
> Una pupila
> y una potencia.
> ¿Quién duda de la eficacia
> terrible de esos cuernos?
> ¡Oculta tus blancos,
> Naturaleza!

The last words of the poem are a warning to Nature by the poet, in view of the efficacious power of the unicorns: "Nature, Hide your targets." The dramatic confrontation of the two sets of physical phenomena in the world of nature, that is, light and waves, which becomes a struggle of unicorns and cyclops at the level of myth, can certainly be symbolically referred to the creative forces of the artist. The unicorns, with their objective referent to light, point to the conscious and, therefore, ordering aspect of artistic creation. On the other hand, the bare forces of the cyclops, with their referent to the unrushing waves of the sea, represent the tumultous and chaotic forces of the subconscious and of poetic inspiration. In the end, the sea waves are hit by the horns of light.

The ballad **"Preciosa and the Wind" ("Preciosa y el aire")** exemplifies the second level of mythification of nature, that in which man is an active participant. The anthropomorphizing impulses start in the mind of the gypsy girl, who gives to a sudden gush of wind the attributes of an agressive lover ("viento hombrón"). The latter, in turn, threatens her with the loss of her virginity. The wind unleashes a real storm, which is then accompanied by lightning and rain and continues the persecution of the girl with its hot sword ("espada caliente") and its shining tongues. The frightened girl runs full of terror and takes refuge in a nearby house, while the masculine wind keeps on biting at the roof of the house. It is clear that in this story, the cosmic forces of the wind and storm act at the level of human configurations establishing, thereby, an interrupted continuum between man and nature. This makes possible the creation of a plot of lascivious pursuing the panicky fleeing. Such structure of meaning is magically enhanced by the presence of powerful images of light and fire, and by the cosmic orchestration of sounds, colors and the phenomena of temperature. The *Duende* makes here its appearance radiating its power into the projection of a well constructed and primitive story.

At the third level of mythical configuration, we find the enactment of a mythical story which is played out in a spectacle of nature, and which has a direct relationship to the inner life of the poet. Here, myth is an objectivization of subjective and unconscious states of mind, with a strong emotional content. Lorca builds up a trajectory of mythical representation that is related to human destiny, but also to his career as an artist, and to the broader context of the realization of the self. The poem **"Adam"** of his early book **Primeras canciones**, 1922, reveals the structure of a mythical plot concerning the birth of a new son out of the cosmic parents, the sun as the father and the moon as the mother of the newly-born day. The sun father, feverishly dreams of the new child that rushingly gallops over the pulsating beat of his two cheeks. This happens after the birth has taken place in a bloody spectacle ("Arbol de sangre moja la mañana"), and the bewailing mother, with no blood left in her veins, is forced to flee in emaciating paleness ("y un gráfico de hueso en la ventana"). Nevertheless, the poet contemplates this renewed story of the birth of the day and the presence of the energizing forces of nature, with a feeling of utter helplessness and frustration. He sees himself, in effect, as another "Adam," who only will be able to father a son that will burn out into nothingness, since he lacks the energizing power of the cosmic sun. The last tercet of the sonnet establishes the connection between the archetypal cosmic spectacle and the degraded personal story of a birth which is doomed to failure:

> Pero otro Adán oscuro está soñando
> neutra luna de piedra sin semilla
> donde el niño de luz se irá quemando.

The obscure Adam (the poet) can only dream of images of sterility ("a sexless stone moon without any seed"), which no doubt have to do with the feeling of lack of artistic potency.

The cosmic plot of the archetypal family and the birth of the day will soon expand in Lorca's poetry into a wide context of symbolization. In fact, the end of the day will constitute the continuation of the myth, since the red colorations of the sky at the moment of the sunset, is seen as another bloody spectacle that marks the death of the powerful mythical figure. The death of the sun makes possible, in turn, the appearance of the moon, whose full dominance in the horizon has a portentous influence on the life of man. If the sun implies vitality and the full realization of the self, the moon acts as an evil omen on man's trajectory. The two symbols are, thus, interrelated to one another, not only by their mutual position in the mythical story (man, wife and son), but also by the fact that their movements are determined by astronomical laws, including the succession of day and night. Their location in the sky, particularly at the moment of dawn and dusk and during the night, and also their coloration and shape, or even their full presence or absence, will reflect variations in their mythical representation, and, ultimately, in their manner of signification. The poetic structure will, thus, present definable signals, which will guide us in the process of decodifying its own meaning. The mythical story allows for the fusion of the obscure with the clear, of the shapeless with the schematic, of the undefinable with that which is plastically projected in figures, colors, and contrasts of light and darkness, all this within the texture of cosmic events.

It is to be noted, on the other hand, that the original plot of the birth and death of the day, marked by the appearance and disappearance of the sun and the counterpart movement of the disappearance and then the appearance of the moon in the horizon, is intertwined in the poetry of Lorca with the presence of the bull and the cow, in correlation with the figures of the cosmic father and mother. In Egyptian mythology, the solar god Osiris, the father, is the bull Apis, and the moon goddess Isis, the mother, is the cow. Out of the union of the two parents the child Horus is born. In fact, we can infer that Lorca found his correlation of the cosmic father, mother and son, from some knowledge of Egyptian mythology. On the other hand, the sunset will constitute for Lorca the enactment of the killing of the mythical figure, an event which will be associated with the killing of the bull on the arena of the bullfight. Moreover, the killing of the bull, that is, the sunset, will also be associated in Lorca with the myth of Saint John the Baptist, as it appears in Mallarmé's poem *Hérodiade.* The last part of Mallarmé's poem is entitled, in effect, "Canticle of Saint John" ("Cantique de Saint Jean"), and has as its theme the decapitation of Saint John, which, in the poem, is also the beheading of the sun,

although in reference to the summer's solstice, rather than to the sunset. This cosmic event coincides with the day of Saint John the Baptist, which takes place on the twenty fourth of June [Wallace Fowlie, *Mallarmé*]. All these correlations appear in Lorca's prose poem **"The Beheading of the Baptist" ("Degollación del Bautista"),** which was written around 1928, the same year in which he gave his lecture on "Imagination, Inspiration and Evasion." The poem presents masses of people, who are lined up as observers of a great spectacle, in which the actual participants in the confrontation are divided in two teams, the Reds and the Blacks, hence the reference to a large stadium, rather than specifically to the arena of the bullfight. The two colors imply, nevertheless, an allusion to the sun and shade areas in the disposition of the seats around the arena of the bullfight or of the stadium, according to which the various locations are termed "Sol y Sombra" or "Blanco y Negro," and in our poem "Rojos y Negros." The two colors appear here, nevertheless, as the actual name of the confronting teams. The division in Reds and Blacks alludes, on the other hand, to the colorations of red in the horizon and the approaching darkness of late afternoon. The spectacle of the **"Degollación del Bautista"** enacts, thus, the scene of the decapitation of Saint John, with implications of the killing of the bull in the sky and on the arena, in unison with the setting of the sun. The last part of the poem refers to the actual moment of the beheading of the mythical figure, in the midst of shouting crowds:

> El griterío del Estadium hizo que las vacas mugieran en todos los establos de Palestina. La cabeza del luchador celeste estaba en medio de la arena. Las jovencitas se teñían las mejillas de rojo y los jóvenes pintaban sus corbatas en el cañón estremecido de la yugular desgarrada.

La cabeza de Bautista:	¡Luz!
Los rojos:	Filo
La cabeza de Bautista:	¡Luz! ¡Luz!
Los rojos:	Filo filo
La cabeza de Bautista:	Luz luz luz
Los rojos:	Filo filo filo filo.

In addition to the figures of the bull and the cow, there is also in the poetry of Lorca, the figure of the horse, as one of the essential components of the mythical plot. The horse is of paramount importance in Andalusian culture and plays a constant role in the life of the gypsies. In the **Romancero gitano,** the horse allows man to move from one place to another and eventually leads him to meet his own destiny of death. In the context of the cosmic story, in Lorca's vision, the horse is identified with the rounded horizon, the celestial abode, which becomes the rump of the horse, and which keeps moving in order to let the protagonists appear in the sky and have their encounters. The image of the horizon as the rump of a shiny colt occurs in the ballad **"Prendimiento de Antoñito el Camborio,"** at the moment when Antoñito is taken to prison to be later executed:

> Y a las nueve de la noche
> le cierran el calabozo,
> mientras el cielo reluce
> como la grupa de un pobro.

Also, in the ballad **"Martirio de Santa Olalla,"** the dark night appears as a long tailed horse that runs and jumps among the streets of Mérida, while Roman soldiers await sleepingly the hour of the execution of Saint Eulalia:

> Por la calle brinca y corre
> caballo de larga cola,
> mientras juegan o dormitan
> viejos soldados de Roma.

We should remember now that in the poem **"Adam,"** the newly born creature appears galloping along a horse: "Adán sueña en la fiebre de la arcilla / un niño que se acerca galopando / por el doble latir de su mejilla." The horse is, thus, the dynamic impulse that sets in motion the other figures of the mythical story. Man's destiny is tied up to the inevitability of their movements and their encounters. As the sun, the primeval Adam, inexorably moves toward its own beheading, so is man's destiny, essentially a tragic one. The moon, in turn, radiates its own evil influence at night, from which there is no escaping. Man is a participant in this mythical story, together with the other figures that move on their own trajectory in the cosmic universe. The mythical plot helps to clarify man's destiny, and to give the mysterious and dark impulses of life a symbolic representation in an ordered pattern.

Although Lorca absorbed early into his poetry some of the components of his mythic vision, it is in the years 1927-1928, the period of composition of his prose poems, when he seems to have fully developed the mythic plot into a tight structure of mutual interrelations. This can be seen in the **"Beheading of the Baptist,"** but also in some of his other prose poems. In his letter to Sebastián Gasch, he alludes to the fact that he is sending him the two "degollaciones," out of three that he intends to write. We might surmise that the **"Degollación del Bautista"** was one of them. A second one could very well be the **"Degollación de los inocentes,"** whose very title alludes to the act of beheading. In this prose poem, the end of the massacre of the innocent children takes place at the end of the day, when blood is being splashed on all clocks at six in the afternoon:

> A las seis de la tarde ya no quedaban más que
> seis niños por degollar. Los relojes de arena
> seguían sangrando, pero ya estaban secas todas
> las heridas.

In another prose poem, **"Santa Lucía y San Lázaro,"** there appear images of physical violence, since Saint Lucía's martyrdom consisted of the gouging of her eyes. The other protagonist, Saint Lazarus, suffered death, was buried and then miraculously resurrected, according to the biblical story. The narrator in the poem travels to a town where he takes lodge and board at midnight in Saint Lucía's Inn (Posada de Santa Lucía). The next day, he goes around watching all activities, and in the afternoon he is able to observe that the show-cases in the stores are full of optical lens and prisms, and that monstrous eyes ("ojos terribles") are hanging in the horizon out of their pupils. There is here, no doubt, a reference to Saint Lucía's eyes, but also to the particular kind of light that now filters in the atmosphere. The moment finally approaches for the red coloration in the sky, which announces the beheading of the Baptist:

> Gafas y vidrios ahumados buscaban la inmensa
> mano cortada de la guantería, poema en el aire,
> que suena, sangra y borbotea como la cabeza del
> Bautista.

Concurrently, religious services are being conducted in the cathedral in honor of Saint Lucia. It is the moment in which horror prevails, on account of the impending bloodspout outside:

> El mundo de la hierba se oponía al mundo del
> mineral. La uña, contra el corazón. Dios de contorno, transparencia y superficie. Con el miedo
> al latido y el horror al chorro de sangre, se pedía
> la tranquilidad de las ágatas y la desnudez sin
> sombra de la medusa.

In the second part of the poem, the narrator walks toward the railroad station at night, which happens to be Saint Lazarus Railroad Station. On the way to his destination, he can still see Saint Lucia's eyes over the sea, by the side of the still bleeding bust: "Ojos de Santa Lucía en el mar, en la esfera del reloj, a los lados del yunque, en el gran tronco recién cortado." At two o'clock in the morning, he can see that another traveler is approaching with deathly eyes and dressed in a white suit. His intense paleness has the color of plaster and eggs: "Su mano derecha era de duro yeso y llevaba colgado del brazo un cesto de mimbre lleno de huevos de gallina." In addition, this is the night when Spain celebrates the great festivity (an apparent allusion to Saint John's night). Finally, a voice is heard calling Lázarus, and the strange traveler fades away among the last lights. By the imagery of the poem and the narrative thread, it seems clear that the situation of the story and its religious protagonists have to do with the phenomena of light in the horizon, particularly in the late afternoon and early dawn. The esoteric texture of the poem could very well correspond to what Lorca called the "poetic fact" in his lectures **"Imagination, Inspiration and Evasion."** The gouging of Saint Lucia's eyes is related to the beheading of the sun, through the images of blood. On the other hand, the appearance of the deathly Saint Lazarus, with his faint and whitish light, would be a forerunner of the resurrected sun.

It is with *Poet in New York,* nevertheless, that the full implications of the myth are revealed for Lorca's tragic vision, in the perspective of his own personal life. Lorca's trip to New York in the summer of 1929 brings him, in effect, to the alien atmosphere of a technologically advanced city culture, that is basically deprived of a direct communication with nature. In fact, there is no rural landscape in New York and whatever is left of nature is diminished by the presence of the tall skyscrapers along the narrow streets and the absence of daylight in the dark subway tunnels. Moreover, with the approach of Fall and Winter, with their cloudy skies, the sun and the moon rarely appear in the horizon. Also, the trees are without leaves and snow and slush cover the ground. Within this landscape, man's life is not fully integrated with the pulsations of nature, and so, his destiny is marked by the signs of sterility. The mythical figures have been mutilated and appear totally degraded. In the poem **"Cow"** (**"Vaca"**), for instance, one of the earliest of the collection, the feminine figure has been mortally wounded at dawn ("se tendió la vaca herida"), and its body has been cut into pieces, with its four hooves left trembling in the air ("Cuatro pezuñas tiemblan en el aire"). In a later poem, **"Dawn" ("La aurora")**, the dawn in New York collapses over its four pillars of mud, while a storm of black doves splash from the rotten waters. The early risers who come out of their homes know that they will drown in the mud of figures and norms. Others walk along, half asleep, as if coming from a bloody shipwreck. Also, in the poem **"The Birth of Christ" ("Nacimiento de Cristo")**, the bull can only dream of a bull full of holes and water, and the child weeps with the number three on his forhead. The birth of the Christ child is thus frustrated by the ominous signs of rain in the sky. On the other hand, the symbol of the dead child, or of the utterly fragile creature, who will die while being born, is one of the prevailing ones in the poems of *Poet in New York.* A dying child is bemoaned by the barking dogs in the poem **"Unsleeping City" ("Ciudad sin sueño")**: "y el niño que enterraron esta mañana lloraba tanto / que hubo necesidad de llamar a los perros para que callase." Similarly, the moon appears in the horizon without its fertilizing attributes, as if it were a stone without seeds, or is identified with the skull of a horse, as in the poem **"Ruin" ("Ruina")**: "Pronto se vio que la luna / era una calavera de caballo / y el aire una manzana oscura."

This degradation of the mythical figures in *Poet in New York* is, no doubt, a symbolic projection of the poet's lack of emotional and artistic self realization. Love here never reaches fulfillment, or it is strangled in the very initial process of its being manifested. On the other hand, the poet has to wrestle with the chaotic impulses of his creative power. Hence, the accumulation of negative signs and the ominous presence of the dead child. In the poem **"Nocturne of the Void" ("Nocturno del hueco")**, the powerful mythical figure has been beheaded at dawn over the empty arena: "En la gran plaza desierta / mugía la cabeza recién cortada." This event coincides with a love that has withered away and only offers empty gloves and hollow dresses. The gyrating voids are projected from the inner soul of the poet into the sky and on the face of the wounded moon:

> Ruedan los huecos puros, por mí, por ti, en el
>   alba
> conservando las huellas de las ramas de sangre
> y algún perfil de yeso tranquilo que dibuja
> instantáneo dolor de luna apuntillada.

In the second part of the **"Nocturne of the Void,"** the poet finds himself in complete solitude, inside empty spaces and only with the company of the very white void of a horse, which has ashes in its name. The horizon at dawn has thus been emptied of the mythical presence of the horse, and does not even show any imprints of blood:

> Yo.
>
> Con el hueco blanquísimo de un caballo.
> Rodeado de espectadores que tienen hormigas
>   en las palabras.
>
> En el circo del frío sin perfil mutilado.
> Por los capiteles rotos de la mejillas desangradas.

The poet's life has been anchored, with no feeling of movement: "Ecuestre por mi vida definitivamente anclada."

The poem **"Crucifixion"** fuses the cosmic impact of a dark and rainy day with the religious symbols of the crucifixion of Christ. The moon appears at dawn on the very white curve of a horse, although the child is already dead at the very moment of the circumcision. The weeping that can be heard coming from the south is due to the fact that the moon has been burning the phallus of horses in candle fire. A skull appears in the sky and is contemplated through the window by the three Holy Virgins. The galaxies are rusty and have been nailed down with thorns. Rain begins to fall drenching hearts and streets. At this point, the pharisees accurse the moon for the milk and bird-shots she is sending down to earth. In the afternoon, the sun has not yet appeared in the horizon, although the moment of redemption will be revealed, as soon as the moon has bathed with water drops the blistering horse-flesh. When night time comes, the pharisees withdraw to their houses in the midst of bloody taints in the sky. They accurse the moon for not letting them sleep. The poem ends with a parodic biblical allusion:

> Fue entonces
> y la tierra despertó arrojando temblorosos ríos
>   de polilla.

Man's destiny has, thus, lost all meaning in this vision of New York, where the mythical figures have been emasculated and degraded. There is no hope of salvation for man when deprived of a real participation with nature and the cosmic universe.

It is significant that after his New York experience, Lorca's poetic vision reaches the full strength of man's participation in the mythical plot. Man's destiny is indeed a tragic one, but his life is enhanced and made meaningful by his solidarity with the forces of nature. In *Blood Wedding* (1933), the passionate lovers, Leonardo and the Bride, flee from the scene of the wedding following the dictates of their most inner and dark impulses. In the end, the killing of the lover and the bridegroom takes place in the open spaces at night, under the ominous influence of the red moon light. In *Lament for Ignacio Sánchez Mejías* (1935), the death of the bullfighter occurs when he is facing the real bull on the arena, and at the moment when the other bull in the sky is close to its own beheading. The blood of the bullfighter's sacrifice is subsequently drunk by the thirsty ancient cow ("vaca del Viejo Mundo"), the cow of the Old World, the mythical figure which now appears in the sky with its unequivocal signs of an evil omen. The bullfighter's strength and vitality have been broken down by fate, but his life has been made significant by the full presence of the mythical figures. The bullfighter's blood drenches the arena and filters through the earth in a ritual sacrifice that fulfills the solidarity of man and cosmos. Lorca saw in nature man's way to self fulfillment, but also the inevitability of his own tragic destiny. (pp. 1-16)

Gustavo Correa, "The Mythification of Nature in the Poetry of Federico García Lorca," in The World of Nature in the Works of Federico García Lorca, *edited by Joseph W. Zdenek,*

Winthrop Studies on Major Modern Writers, 1980, pp. 1-17.

Carl W. Cobb (essay date 1983)

[*Cobb is an American educator and critic. In the following essay, he analyzes the tension between primitivism and civilization in García Lorca's* Romancero gitano.]

What kind of critical base should be set up for Federico García Lorca and the *Gypsy Ballad-book* that will be true to the poet's nature and purposes and that will properly place the book in Western culture? Since the book became extremely popular before and during the Spanish civil war and developed into a classic in succeeding years, it is clear that it touched a responsive chord not only in Spain but also in Europe and America. Thus the task is to seek out the book's message and present it through the poet's words and a critical presentation of his individual poems.

By the time of the publication of the *Ballad-book,* Lorca's poetic formation was essentially complete (he further developed the brotherhood theme in *Poet in New York*); and surely he would consider himself striving toward Ortega y Gasset's ideal of being a poet abreast of his times. No single characterization can totally embrace the poet, who of course fiercely resisted being categorized anyway. Lorca was genius enough to know what he was doing in the *Gypsy Ballad-book,* and thus a beginning here should perhaps be his statement of his intentions. As he was finishing the book, he confided to Guillén in a letter: "In this first part of the book I am trying to harmonize the *mythological gypsy materials* with the pure commonness of the present day, and the result is strange, but I believe of a new beauty." These words, while very general, set up a tension between the gypsy of myth (idealized, of course) and the conditions of European civilization in Lorca's day. As we shall see, even his gypsies have been contaminated by that civilization. For Lorca, civilization is the middle class, the Establishment, the System, which he characterized acidly as the *putrefactos,* the "rotten ones." Quite some time ago in a brilliant article, Juan López-Morillas ultimately reached this summation in regard to the *Ballad-book:* "Lorca's poetry dramatizes the conflict between primitive myth and modern ideas" ["Lyrical Primitivism: García Lorca's *Romancero Gitano,*" *Federico García Lorca: A Collection of Critical Essays,* edited by Manuel Durán]. Although the *Ballad-book* has been regarded as unique, the conflict between primitivism and civilization has in fact been a major theme in twentieth-century Western literature. And what of the second part of the book? Since in various statements Lorca stressed the Andalusian qualities of the work, I shall intrepidly declare that he attempted somewhat evasively to project himself as a "universal Andalusian" [Manuel Durán, "García Lorca, poeta entre dos mundos," *Federico García Lorca,* edited by Ildefonso-Manuel Gil].

On his traditional side, Lorca is a poet of myth, specifically, primitive myth, in its most general sense as "a recognition of natural conflicts, of human desire frustrated by nonhuman powers, hostile oppression, or contrary desires," with defeat by death as man's common fate [Suzanne Langer, quoted by López-Morillas]. In Andalusia, he grew up surrounded by popular or folk traditions, with their Christian, Moorish, and Jewish origins, and in early adulthood, stimulated by Manuel de Falla, he reached intense focus in his contact with the poetry, dance, and song of the cante jondo. Lorca's specific approach to the primitive is of course through the gypsy, a living "myth" in European culture, but a living reality in Andalusian Spain. His approach to the gypsy emphasizes the contrast between the traditional gypsy, who "roamed the mountains alone," and his Andalusian counterpart, who now lives an enforced sedentary existence. Lorca's creation of primitive gypsy characters takes advantage of the powerful "myth," the desperate yearning in Western culture for a return to a character free, vital, dominant, and whole. That Lorca exalts primitivism and attacks civilization is of course expected in modern Western culture. In Lorca's Spain, we now know that his fellow poet Vicente Aleixandre, recent winner of the Nobel Prize, has insisted upon exalting a primitive, paradisal figure over civilized man.

In his poetic way, Lorca characterized himself according to a number of rich traditions of Andalusia, of which he said the gypsy was the "aristocratic" representative. First of all, Lorca proudly establishes himself as a poet of the *duende,* a term related to "demon." In Andalusia, when functions considered essential, such as a song of the cante jondo, a folk dance, or a bullfighting pass, are performed to perfection, everyone says, "That has *duende.*" This duende is a power which takes over the life-force of the blood and heart. For Lorca, at one extreme, the duende can be satanic, in rebellion against the cosmic order itself; at the other, it can be a phallic symbol. And this duende is always closely associated with death. While Lorca finds duende in purest form in the gypsy singer of cante jondo or in the bullfighter (often a gypsy), he surprisingly joins in demonic brotherhood figures as disparate as Socrates, Descartes, Saint John of the Cross, and Quevedo. Lorca is also (in his enigmatic line) a *moreno de verde luna,* a dark figure under the sign of the green moon. This green is vitalistic and even chthonic, or fatally earthbound; the moon is the realm of ambivalent sexuality and death. The poet also designates himself as *el Amargo,* the "Bitter One"; bitter he means in the ontological sense of possessing consciousness of paradise and yet suffering alienation from it. Here Lorca's poetic expressions have their deepest origins in Andalusian popular traditions.

From the beginning, Lorca dwelt upon the point that the *Gypsy Ballad-book* was Andalusian rather than merely gypsy, once adding that Andalusia was not contaminated by anything English, the English representing for him commonsense morality. In 1931 he elaborated upon his initial idea: "In essence the *Gypsy Ballad-book* is an Andalusian tableau. . . . It is an Andalusian song in which the gypsies serve as a chorus." To be Andalusian, even in the philosophical analysis of Ortega y Gasset, is to be a creature of the body who delights in the elemental pleasures of an earthly paradise. Specifically, Lorca reduced Andalusia to his Granada, declaring that his book has a "single essential protagonist: Granada." And how did he view his Granada? "Granada is the persecuted, which instead of protesting becomes . . . a dance." Historically,

García Lorca with Salvador Dalí, 1927.

Lorca is saying that the Granadine in his "closed paradise" of the Vega has been "persecuted" by, in turn, the Romans, the Visigoths, the Moors, another wave of Moors, and finally the Christians from the north of Spain. Personally, he is saying that the persecuted one is the poet himself, whose "dance" is his poetry with its cry for freedom. In the final year of his life, in public recitations and discussions of the ballads, Lorca reiterated that the book was a "poem of Andalusia," not a picturesque Andalusia, but one of deep *feeling*. Finally he converted the theme of Granada-as-persecuted into an abstract one: "There is only a single real main character, which is the trouble [*pena*] that invades the book." Early in his work, *pena* is symbolized in a dark woman; she is recreated as Soledad Montoya in the **"Ballad of the Dark Trouble."** At times, speaking with either evasion, irony, or whimsy, Lorca insisted that even he could not fathom the mystery of his **"Sleepwalking Ballad."** Hence Lorca would read his *Ballad-book* as Andalusian, then as Granada under persecution, then as a character named Trouble—that is, in a direction toward himself.

While Lorca in general strives to bring the universe inward, we must endeavor critically to cast that universe outward and place the poet in the widest critical context in relation to Western civilization. As an avante-garde poet, Lorca himself adamantly resisted the limiting label of gypsy as simple primitive; in fact, even *before* the book appeared in print he was grumbling in a letter to Guillén: "I'm getting a bit tired of my myth of gypsydom." In the decade after the *Ballad-book* was created, Lorca watched the book become extremely popular, so commonly popular that he was infuriated at its being misunderstood. Apparently he felt that his ballads made an avant-garde, rebellious statement, while the public insisted upon finding the stereotype of the romantic gypsy. Although he never formulated it, he knew that the gypsy was free *only in his alienation from civilization.* (As [Kris Kristofferson] was to express it later, "Freedom's just another word for nothing left to lose.") Within his own culture the gypsy was shackled by custom. Moreover, as a primitive, the gypsy functioned from the unconscious in large part, without modern *consciousness* or awareness.

More than a decade ago, a perceptive Spanish critic, Francisco Umbral, convincingly discussed Lorca in the tradition of European poets who were demonic in their self-concerns and critical of the ethical and religious pretenses of Western culture. Umbral's book is entitled *Lorca, poeta maldito;* clearly he is utilizing the French phrase *poète maudit,* which has been applied to certain nineteenth-century figures such as Baudelaire, Verlaine, and Rimbaud. In English, perhaps the best translation of *maldito* ("accursed") is "satanic" or "demonic." (The French phrase poète maudit itself has a limited currency in English.) Thus Milton is satanic in some ways perhaps not intended, Blake and Byron in many; figures as different as Poe, Whitman, and Emily Dickinson are satanic in certain ways. Perhaps A. E. Housman is closest in English to being a satanic poet, albeit a soft-spoken one; behind his poetry is satanic anger, sexual heterodoxy, and early death (as poet inspired at least). For Umbral these are the three key conditions for the poeta maldito: "Aesthetic and personal rootedness in demonic forces, sexual heterodoxy, and tragic and premature death." As Umbral recognized, Lorca's insistence upon the Andalusian duende is local only in the specificity of the term there; the demonic in Western culture has deep and persistent roots. Recently, for example, Rollo May has defined and utilized the demonic (which he spells "daimonic") as "any natural function which has the power to take over the whole person" [Rollo May, *Love and Will*]. For May, biologically the demonic can be simply the male erection, but in the largest sense, harmony with the demon involves the integration of human potentialities, including both good and evil and life and death. The poète maudit, who cherishes ontological solitude as his lot, has especially aroused and infuriated the great middle class by flaunting the aesthetic at the expense of the ethical and the religious. I should hasten to clarify that no major poet remains outside his culture; in fact, in our confused and turbulent times, Lorca has become a major spokesman for the "people" and the beacon of that freedom which has so blinded us.

As a satanically tragic poet, Lorca fits Umbral's three qualifications admirably. In a poetic line Lorca states the demonic brutally: "And life is neither noble, nor good, nor sacred." Life just is: it is a "burning of the blood"; it is an outpouring of the life-force in the process of destruction. As for the aesthetic, Lorca chose as his tragic hero the bullfighter. And what value in the bullfighter's evanescent dramatic art does the poet choose to exalt? His "profile," that total visual profile which the bullfighter arrogantly projects as he performs his art in the critical moment of destruction. As a satanic poet, Lorca of course demanded personal freedom, especially sexual freedom. Even in his backward Spain, Lorca lived and expressed his homosexual orientation, yet in such a way that it could be hypocritically obscured. Lorca also demanded freedom of conscience, but in this he is only modern; the major modern poets (such as Yeats, Dickinson, Rilke, Jiménez) have generally placed their art above the traditional social, ethical, and religious values. Finally, Lorca's physical death was both tragic and untimely.

Therefore, while there is indeed a base of the primitive and the mythological in his *Ballad-book,* Lorca very early protested his "myth of gypsydom" and insisted upon a broader cultural interpretation. In another letter to Guillén he amplifies his earlier complaint: "The gypsy theme gives me a tone of lack of culture, of poor education and of *poet savage* that you well know I am not." Since there unquestionably *are* many "savage" notes in the *Ballad-book,* the civilized qualities which Lorca demands to be recognized must reside in effects not obvious. In fact, soon after the book appeared, Lorca declared: "Of course the 'rotten ones' have not understood my book, although they may say they have." Are the contents of the book therefore supercivilized, that is, decadent? A decadent may be merely a primitive with awareness, with conscience. Lorca was certainly aware that he was approaching heretofore "prohibited" themes in the *Ballad-book,* since after commenting upon the "barbarous" nature of one of them, he promised his conservative friend Guillén that he would "never, never" touch such a theme again.

Thus Lorca as a poet wanted to be received as one who had assimilated worthy past traditions, who was abreast of his times, and who was therefore prepared to break ground toward the future. If the primitive and the mythological came to him through the Andalusian popular element, the "civilized" elements came to him generally from Baudelaire all the way through the avant-garde movements gathering impetus during the 1920s. Through Valle-Inclán there is a connection with earlier decadent emphases. Through Rubén Darío and Jiménez there is a link with French aesthetic preoccupations, from Verlaine and Mallarmé, for example. From the Freudianism during his own time, Lorca in a general way received the emphasis upon the power of the libido (especially as it relates to undifferentiated sexuality), the unconscious, and the dream as wish fulfillment. While the primitive can be connected with many manifestations of sexuality, it remained for Freud rather to flaunt sexuality in all its varieties and power. (Freud himself, in the epigraph to *The Interpretation of Dreams,* said that if he could not storm heaven perhaps he could "shake up Hell" a bit.) Although surrealism proper developed a bit later, we can now see that Lorca had smelled out the major tenets of the movement. His gypsies are as totally *lawless* as the surrealists, although the special condition of the gypsies in Western culture makes their lawlessness seem less threatening. A few verbal thrusts in the *Ballad-book* suggest surrealism, and certain essential themes are expressed in the surrealist manner. It should be emphasized that the neoprimitive, the Freudian, the surrealistic, and the decadent tend to overlap, to blend together, and that Lorca is a product of these combined currents as they fit his nature. In his *Gypsy Ballad-book,* Lorca makes use of all these currents to project the conflict between primitivism and civilization, tragically assuming that the pure primitive will be destroyed by the effete civilized.

The predominant theme of the *Gypsy Ballad-book* concerns the presence, outpouring, and frustration of the life-force primarily in sexual ways. The expression of the sexual runs the gamut from the primitive through the Freudian and the decadent: Oedipal sexuality in the child, awakening sexuality in the virgin, sexuality as aggression in young men, sexuality in a nun, masculine sexuality in its brutality, incest, masturbation, and sadism. If this listing seems strained, in his last days Lorca himself, referring directly to his bristling drama *The Destruction of Sodom* (unfinished), apostrophized: "What a manifestation of the power of sex!" The expression of unbridled will (in regard to the primitive) or the all-demanding self (in the civilized sense) lends a special tone to erotic relations and hence the theme of love. Love becomes a form of aggression, a threat of engulfing or destroying the other. This expression of the self inevitably leads to violence; indeed, in the *Ballad-book* eroticism and violence are usually intertwined. For Lorca, blood is the essence of life: blood flows in the primal sex act; it is spilled in violent death. (Certainly he was prophetic; in our day "sex and violence" has become a stock phrase.) Violence leads to death, the threat of which hangs over the whole book. For Lorca, death is a vital act, in which his protagonist insists upon participating. The refusal to be "oppressed" by death is the final existential "freedom." Obviously, then, Lorca's gypsy protagonist is a creature intimate with sex, violence, and death; but let us remember that contemporary man has also been desperately bound up with exactly these three themes.

As a lyric poet of tragic vision, Lorca ultimately demands that the *Gypsy Ballad-book* express himself. In a book of traditional ballads each one conveys its own tragic note, as does each of Lorca's ballads. As a lyric poet, however, Lorca attempts to inject himself (or at least a protagonist who represents his perspective) into the book and to seize for himself the tragic impact of all the ballads. In fact, he utilizes the entire myth of the gypsy and the ballad as a giant metaphor to express his own tragic sense of life. This is not merely my interpretation. First, his protagonist speaks to Preciosa in **"Preciosa and the Air";** then he talks with Soledad in the **"Ballad of the Dark Trouble."** She is a transparent double of the poet himself. In the ballad of the death of Tony el Camborio, who is clearly equated with the poet in being a "Dark one inclined to green moon sign," Tony at the moment of death calls upon the poet by name for succor: "Ay, Federico García Lorca, / Call out the Guard for me!" But the strongest evidence is at the end of the powerful **"Ballad of the Spanish Civil Guard."** Despite the traditional reputation of the Civil Guard as Spain's Finest, for Lorca the guards become symbols of cruel oppression and destruction for the gypsies. With the gypsy "city" going up in flames at the end of the ballad, the poet focuses all this suffering upon his own face:

> Oh gypsy city, once truly seen,
> Who could forget you soon?

> Let them seek you upon my face,
> Interplay of sand and moon.

For this book of narrative and dramatic ballads to achieve its total lyric impact, perhaps it can best be visualized as a circle of characters from the ballads with the superimposed image of the poet's dark brooding face. Does the poet ever totally identify himself with the protagonist of a specific ballad? Does he succeed in usurping the power of his characters for his own lyric purposes? This remains one of the tantalizing problems concerning the *Balladbook.*

The glory of the poet is the creation of a poetic world whose life arises from tension between opposing worlds and which is thus replete with "ambiguities." Modern poetry is often suffused with irony in that the poet is torn between two or more sets of values. Certainly in Lorca's *Gypsy Ballad-book* the major tension results from the conflict between the mythological gypsy as primitive and what the poet sees as the commonness and lifelessness of civilization. This world of the gypsy (and of some other characters who are not gypsies) is telluric, with both man and the elements sexualized and made violent. These dynamic forces threaten the lifeless order of civilization, which responds collectively with counterviolence. The world of the gypsy ballads is also a metaphor of the poet himself, a creature of great vitality and promise, tragically thwarted by forces powerful unto death. (pp. 57-62)

> *Carl W. Cobb, in his* Lorca's "Romancero gitano": A Ballad Translation and Critical Study, *University Press of Mississippi, 1983, 116 p.*

García Lorca's attitude toward performance and publication of his poetry:

. . . Lorca was an archetypal exemplar of the strong musical and vocal tradition in Spanish poetry; performance was a necessary corollary to the text of his poems. His magnetic personality and his unforgettable voice—as well as the poems themselves, transmitted orally in widening circles by fellow students and their acquaintances—won Lorca a reputation as an important poet even before the publication of his first book of poems. . . .

Lorca's orientation to poetry as a performing art explains his lifelong habit of carelessness with his manuscripts; he often gave away his poems without keeping a copy. As late as 1933 he told an interviewer that he took no pleasure in publication: "Everything I've published has been wrested from me by editors or friends. I like to recite my verses, to read my work aloud. But then I have a great fear of publication. This fear comes when I copy down my things and I already begin to find flaws, and frankly they no longer please me."

Felicia Hardison Londré in her Federico García Lorca, *1984.*

Julianne Burton   **(essay date 1983)**

[*In the following essay, Burton explores García Lorca's portrayal of gender roles in Andalusian society in* Blood Wedding, Yerma, *and* La casa de Bernarda Alba.]

In the face of those who would interpret Lorca as above and beyond his social and historical context, I would like to propose an alternative view. His experiences abroad and the circumstances at home sensitized him to the social realities of the Spain of his day: an archaic, hypocritical, and crippling morality; a hierarchical, even tyrannical family structure; extreme social stratification and exploitation of the humbler sectors; and a social-sexual code which privileged men at the expense of women's autonomy, participation, and self-realization. His perception of these social ills, combined with other personal factors, such as his mother's repeated protests against the senseless waste of Spanish womanhood and his own perception of women as the transmitters of culture, led him to present female experience as the core of the three tragedies he wrote toward the end of his life. These plays present a vision of what some anthropologists now call the sex-gender system of southern Spanish society. The depth and scope of Lorca's social dimension suggest a concerted attempt to expose and denounce the social system which gives rise to such irreconcilable conflicts and untenable contradictions.

The seriousness of Lorca's commitment to exploring the complexities of sexual politics is apparent in the opening scenes of the first play, *Bodas de sangre (Blood Wedding)* (1933). All possibilities of marital status are present in act 1: a widow and her unmarried son in the first scene, a married couple in the second, an unmarried woman and her widowed father in the third. By using generic rather than proper names throughout the first play (Father, Wife, Mother-in-Law), Lorca suggests that the individuality of his characters is subordinated to their function as representatives of certain social roles or institutions. Lorca's female characters absorb more and more of his attention in succeeding plays: from his special focus on the mother and the bride (*novia*) in *Blood Wedding,* through his detailed exploration of the plight of a barren woman in *Yerma* (1934), to the sixteen female characters of *La casa de Bernarda Alba (The House of Bernarda Alba)* (1936), who, though they often feel the force of masculine presence, never once share the stage with a man. The main themes of the three plays make Lorca's interest in society as experienced by women even more explicit: *Blood Wedding* explores marriage, bereavement, and widowhood; *Yerma* is a study of married life and sterility; *The House of Bernarda Alba* offers an austere picture of matriarchy and spinsterhood.

The struggle between social prescription and individual impulse is at the core of Lorca's trilogy and of all of Lorca's work. The tragedies revolve around those characters who are unable or unwilling to resign themselves to their *sino* ("fate"). A grasp of the alternative interpretations of the *sino* is crucial to understanding the social dimension of Lorca's tragic vision. Whereas his characters most often perceive themselves as the hapless victims of mysterious forces beyond their control, Lorca weaves a counterview into the fabric of the plays, which suggests that definable social and material causes are responsible for the fate of individual characters. More specifically, four concrete factors account in the playwright's eyes for what the characters view as arbitrary destiny: environment, economic status, heredity, and the influence of *el qué dirán* ("community expectations") on the lives of individuals. His heroines' determination to transcend the social and moral confines of their sex in order to lay claim to the possibilities for self-determination traditionally reserved for men gives impetus both to their heroism and their tragedy.

"Hilo y aguja para las hembras. Látigo y mula para el varón" (For women, needle and thread. Mules and whiplashes for the men), decrees Bernarda Alba imposing society's rigid differentiation upon her five aging, yet still unmarried, daughters. Indeed, this distribution of tools is indicative of the sexual segregation of the whole society. The association of man with the whip, symbol of dominance over the brute beast, also suggests the man—weapon association, an especially prevalent theme throughout the poems of Lorca's famous *Romancero gitano* (*Gypsy Ballads*) and in *Blood Wedding,* where the mother laments, "Los varones . . . tienen por fuerza que manejar armas" (Men . . . are compelled to wield weapons). These associations are consistent with man's role as arbiter, avenger, and ruler. In the society which Lorca depicts, a needle is the nearest approximation to a tool or weapon accessible to women. [The critic adds in a footnote: "Bernarda, the most authoritarian of Lorca's characters, actually does use a rifle against Pepe, but she excuses her own inaccuracy: "No fue culpa mía. Una mujer no sabe apuntar" (It wasn't my fault. A woman doesn't know how to take aim).] When she is finally driven to violence, a woman has only her bare hands and the strength of her pent-up rage and long-repressed potential. The mother in *Blood Wedding* fears that one of the enemy family might be buried in the same plot as her slain husband and son. Infuriated at this idea, she threatens, "¡Y eso sí que no! ¡Ca! ¡Eso sí que no! Porque con las uñas los desentierro y yo sola los machaco contra la tapia" (And that will never happen! No! That will never happen! Because I'll dig them up with my fingernails and, all by myself, I'll crush them to pieces against the wall.) And when Yerma's repressed fury is turned against her husband, Juan, she strangles him to death.

With their needle and thread women painstakingly labor over trousseaus, fill hope chests, make baby clothes, and, in their leisure, fashion frilly, nonessential things. The lullaby Leonardo's wife and mother-in-law sing boasts of the child's steel cradle with its pillow and coverlet of fine linen. These—and her children—make up a woman's only wealth, a wealth, which, unlike the man's, has no exchange value and thus offers no economic independence. [The critic adds in a footnote: "Mourning the death of her last son, the bridegroom's mother laments, "Vendrán las vecinas y no quiero que me vean tan pobre. . . . Una mujer que no tiene un hijo siquiera que poderse llevar a los labios" (The neighborwomen will come, and I don't want them to see me so poor. . . . A woman without a single son to take to her lips). María avoids visiting Yerma

since Yerma always cries at the sight of María's son. "Me da tristeza que tengas envidia," María tells her. "No es envidia lo que tengo; es pobreza," Yerma replies ('It saddens me that you are envious.' 'What I feel is not envy, but poverty'). Children are the fulfillment and the legitimization of women, which is why Yerma so desperately seeks a child. They are also insurance for the legitimate wife. The social rights of Leonardo's wife are assured because she has borne him one child and awaits another. She can spurn him and dedicate herself to her children, preserving her own honor intact despite her husband's infidelity and disgrace."] Many references are made in the plays to other female occupations—cooking, cleaning, washing clothes, marketing, child rearing—all domestic and without market value. [The critic adds in a footnote: "The only exception is the reference made by Leonardo's wife to the women who gather capers, an occupation so humble and painstaking that it is relegated to women."] The mule and the whip are tools in the creation of male wealth, for man tills the fields and harvests the crops, shears the sheep, presses the oil and the wine, then exchanges his products for currency or for other goods necessary for his family's well-being.

In Lorca's plays, man's world radiates outward from the home; woman's activities confine her within it except for her occasional trips to the well for water, to the store for goods, or to bring lunch to her husband in the fields. She may leave the house to perform only the most essential duties, for most husbands share Juan's sentiments: "No me gusta que salgas. . . . La calle es para la gente desocupada" (I don't like you to go out. . . . The street is for people with nothing to do). [The critic adds in a footnote: "This injunction is particularly unjust and ironic in Yerma's case, for there is no one more unoccupied than she, or more reluctant to be so. When Juan tells her that a woman's place is in the home, she protests, "Cuando las casas no son tumbas. Cuando las sillas se rompen y las sábanas de hilo se gastan con el uso" (When the home is not a tomb. When chairs get broken and the linen sheets wear out from use)."] If she tarries along the way, she risks incurring the anger of her husband, as Yerma does when Juan comes upon her talking to his friend Victor: "¡Qué haces todavía aquí! . . . Debías estar en casa. . . . No comprendo en qué te has entretenido. . . . Así darás que hablar a los gentes" (What are you doing here still? . . . You should be at home. . . . I don't understand what has kept you. . . . Now you'll give people something to talk about). Man, however, can roam at will and even has horses to take him "al límite de los llanos" (to the edge of the plains), equivalent for Leonardo's wife and mother-in-law, confined as they are to their *mala choza,* to "el fin del mundo" (the end of the world).

Lorca underlines the fact that man is woman's master, and as father or brother or husband, governs her activities. He exercises this prerogative by virtue of his role as provider, as the case of Juan's two spinster sisters illustrates. Juan imports them to watch over Yerma, and they are obliged to accept their role as her wardens, for they have no other man to support them and no possibility of independent livelihood. On one occasion Juan scolds them for letting Yerma go out alone: "Una de vosotras debía salir con ella, porque para eso estáis aquí comiendo en mi mantel y bebiendo mi vino" (One of you should go out with her. After all, that's why you're here drinking my wine and dining at my table). Women's status is no more than that of a slave to the man; as Martirio, one of Bernarda's daughters, bitterly puts it, "una perra sumisa que les dé de comer" (a submissive she-dog to give them their food). As long as she is dependent upon a man, she must serve him, preserve his honor, and be subject to his will.

At certain points Lorca suggests that women in this society are viewed as mere extensions of the kinds of property controlled by men. For example, it is not until after a young man has acquired land that he can take a wife. With the children she then bears him his estate will be complete. The neighbor woman points out the almost causal relation between the two processes in the first scene of **Blood Wedding:** "¡[Tu hijo] al fin compró la viña! . . . ¡Ahora se casará!" ([Your son] has bought the vineyard at last! . . . Now he'll get married!). Because she is his personal property, Juan has the socially sanctioned right to chide Yerma for her wanderings, confine her to the house, and summon his sisters to keep watch over her. As he tells her during an argument, "No debía decirte: perdóname, sino obligarte, encerrarte, porque para eso soy el marido" (I shouldn't say 'forgive me,' but rather force you, lock you up because that's what I'm the husband for).

Woman's only autonomy comes when the dominant male figure in her life disappears. The bridegroom's widowed mother arranges his wedding, and since she tells him how many gifts he can buy, it is clear that the family finances are in her hands. In the absence of her husband it falls to her to maintain tradition and prepare her son for his new role. She is herself a victim of the desolation and incompleteness of a woman alone in that society. Yet when her widowhood gives her the opportunity to take a stand against male domination, even she works to perpetuate the most oppressive aspects of the patriarchy. This is dramatically illustrated in the advice she gives the bridegroom on his wedding day:

> Con tu mujer procura estar cariñosa, y si la notas infatuada o arisca, hazle una caricia que le produzca un poco de daño, un abrazo fuerte, un mordisco y luego un beso suave. Que ella no pueda disgustarse, pero que sienta que tú eres el macho, el amo, el que mandas. Así aprendí de tu padre. Y como no lo tienes, tengo que ser yo la que te enseñe estas fortalezas.

> Try to be affectionate with your wife, and if you notice her acting conceited or stubborn, caress her in a way that will cause her a bit of pain: a strong embrace, a bite followed by a soft kiss. Not enough to anger her, but enough to let her know that you are the *macho,* the one who gives the orders. This is what I learned from your father. Since you no longer have him, I have to be the one to teach you these manly defenses.
>
> (pp. 260-65)

In the man, strength, capability, beauty, honor, and purity are praised whereas the woman's praises center around her docility, industriousness, and practical skills. The discrepancy between Lorca's representation of society's standards and his personal ones is clear, for his heroines are women of moral and spiritual (not merely physical) strength and resilience, women who do not eschew the traits their society cultivates but exceed them.

The social environment discourages the full expression of the qualities and potential of Lorca's heroines. Barring open rebellion, they are left with only two responses to their restricted sphere of activity, and both serve only to exacerbate the problem. Women can turn their attention outward by casting themselves in the role of custodians of their neighbor's honor; and this is an alternative chosen by many. Gossip is a rewarding occupation, for it is one of the few paths to power open to women. Their guardianship of local morality through public commentary occasions an intense and hypocritical preoccupation with *el qué dirán* on the part of their fellow townspeople. This occupation also confers on the womenfolk the important role of oral "historians," shaping popular opinion and perpetuating local tradition. The injustice and the irony is that women, the most active repositories of such information, are also the main victims of the collective effort to maintain a rigid moral standard by means of verbal inference and censure. In this way, women become custodians of the evidence to be used in the domination and prosecution of their own sex.

Lorca's heroines, on the other hand, often remain aloof from this collective scandal mongering, choosing the second alternative. They turn their energies inward, developing an insight and sensitivity that the male views as foreign and often threatening. Yerma and Víctor agree that for a man, "Es todo lo mismo. . . . Vais a lo vuestro sin reparar en las delicadezas" (It's all the same . . . you go for what's yours without bothering about subtleties). Yerma typifies the woman who is more discriminating, more sensitive to the quality of life. In Yerma and Juan one sees the split between the man as realist, dealer in the concrete and immediate sensual perceptions; and the woman as dreamer, idealist, dweller in the abstract and potential. Juan says:

> Ha llegado el último minuto de resistir este continuo lamento por cosas oscuras, fuera de la vida, por cosas que están en el aire. . . . Por cosas que no han pasado y ni tú ni yo dirigimos. . . . Por cosas que a mí no me importan. . . . A mí me importa lo que tengo entre las manos. Lo que veo por mis ojos.

> This is the last time I'll stand for this continued lament for things which are outside of life, for things that are in the air. . . . For things that have not happened and are not under your control or mine. . . . For things that don't matter to me. What matters to me is what I can hold in my hands. What I can see with my own eyes.

The sensitivity of Lorca's heroines enables them to perceive painful ironies and injustices, but it only increases their sense of hopeless impotence. For women are constantly urged by men and women alike to endure patiently, suffer in silence, and resign themselves to their fate. As La Poncia, Bernarda's housekeeper, warns, "la que no se conforma se pudre llorando en un rincón" (the one who doesn't resign herself to her lot will rot crying in a corner). (pp. 265-66)

The male-dominated society which Lorca explores in these plays manifests the following paradox: by keeping women confined, ignorant, and passive, male-dominated society cultivates female weakness and leaves women virtually defenseless prey to stronger (that is, other male) forces. La Poncia realizes that Bernarda, headstrong and overconfident of her own power, "no sabe la fuerza que tiene un hombre entre mujeres solas" (doesn't know the power one man wields over solitary women). And the bride reproaches Leonardo: "Un hombre con su caballo sabe mucho y puede mucho para poder estrujar a una muchacha metida en un desierto" (A man with a horse has the knowledge and the power to put a lot of pressure on a girl stuck in a desert). As the bodies of her fiance and her lover are being brought back to the village, the bride presents herself before the mother, challenging the elder woman to avenge her son's honor by killing her, but not before the mother has seen for herself that the young woman—a virgin twice "widowed"—still retains her virtue intact. In one of the most powerful and moving speeches of the entire trilogy—one which transcends differences of age, position, and moral status—the bride appeals to the common condition of all women:

> ¡Porque yo me fui con el otro, me fui! Tú también te hubieras ido. Yo era una mujer quemada, llena de llagas por dentro y por fuera, y tu hijo era un poquito de agua de la que yo esperaba hijos, tierra, salud; pero el otro era un río oscuro, lleno de ramas, . . . Y yo corría con tu hijo que era como un niñito de agua fría, y el otro me mandaba cientos de pájaros que me impedían el andar y que dejaban escarcha sobre mis heridas de pobre mujer marchita, de muchacha acariciada por el fuego. Yo no quería, ¡óyelo bien!: yo no quería. Tu hijo era mi fin y yo no lo he engañado, pero el brazo del otro me arrastró como un golpe de mar, . . . y me hubiera arrastrado siempre, siempre, siempre, aunque hubiera sido vieja y todos los hijos de tu hijo me hubiesen agarrado de los cabellos!

> Because I ran off with the other one; I ran off! *You would have gone, too.* I was a woman burning with desire, full of wounds inside and out, and your son was a little bit of water from whom I hoped for children, land, health; but the other was a dark river, full of branches. . . . And I ran along with your son, who was like a little boy made of cold water while the other one sent hundreds of birds which blocked my way and left frost on my wounds—the wounds of a poor withered woman, of a girl caressed by fire. I didn't want to. Listen carefully to what I say! I didn't want to. Your son was my destiny and I have not deceived him, but the other's arm dragged me along like the pull of the sea . . . and would have kept me forever, forever, forever, even if I were an old woman and all your son's children were holding me by the hair! (my emphasis)

The passionately reckless response of Bernarda's youngest and most attractive daughter, Adela, to her oldest sister's

fiancé is a similar consuming passion fired by her rebellion against a similar confinement. In the bloom of her youth she is sentenced to eight years of mourning and forced to remain with her sisters within Bernarda's conventlike walls. She says to her sister Martirio, "Ya no aguanto el horror de estos techos después de haber probado el sabor de su boca" (I can no longer stand the horror of these walls after having savored the taste of his lips). She uses the same imagery as the bride in ***Blood Wedding***—"El me lleva a los juncos de la orilla" (He carries me off to the rushes along the shore)—to describe the sexual attraction Pepe holds for her. So great is her desperation that she is prepared to sacrifice honor, social position, family ties—everything—to assume the most despised place in society's eyes:

> Seré lo que él quiera que sea. Todo el pueblo contra mí, quemándome con sus dedos de lumbre, perseguida por los que dicen que son decentes, y me pondré la corona de espinas que tienen las que son queridas de algún hombre casado.

> I will be whatever he wants me to be. Let the whole town turn against me, burning me with their flaming fingers, let me be pursued by those who claim to be decent folk, and I will put on the crown of thorns worn by women who are the mistresses of some married man.

Both young women view their illicit lovers as saviors who will, by the warmth of their bodies and the strength of their passion, transform an unendurable existence. Throughout the trilogy, the overwhelming energy and determination of the female response loom disproportionately over the meager male stimulus. The growth of such desperate passion out of alienation, fear and stifling powerlessness renders its tremendous grip understandable. The ambivalence which other elements of the society feel toward this surrender to passion and the consequent rejection of public morality is relayed through the choruslike exchange between the woodcutters, who agree that Leonardo and the bride have done right to flee: one woodcutter says that a man must follow where his blood leads, but his companion reminds him that "blood which sees the light of day gets drunk up by the earth." They conclude that "Vale más ser muerto desangrado que vivo con ella podrida" (It's better to bleed to death than to live with your blood rotting inside you). [The critic adds in a footnote: "It is quite possible that these sympathetic judgments are not a factor of a relaxed moral standard employed by men but rather depend upon the woodcutters' inferior social status. Throughout the plays, servants, day laborers, and others of lowly social rank seem to enjoy a moral freedom, which society does not allow its more prominent groups. This point is of course difficult to decide conclusively because of the scarcity of evidence in the plays themselves as well as the lack of a detailed and independent description of Andalusian social hierarchy. At any rate, the relative moral tolerance demonstrated by the woodcutters is somewhat undercut by their fatalism: their conviction that the mortal price will inevitably be extracted for the surrender to passion precludes in their own minds the risk of ever having to act in accordance with their relatively liberal attitudes."]

101

It is clear that women are not the only victims of a confining moral and social code. Leonardo's fate is to a large extent also collectively determined; he has been discriminated against because of his family history and modest means. But the cumulative impact of the three tragedies indicates that, for Lorca, the structure of Andalusian society causes women to fall prey to its contradictions and impossible demands far more often than men do. As we have noted earlier, one of the ironies of this social system is that women, its most frequent victims, are the most uncompromising in their condemnation of one another and the most unrelenting in their demand for punishment and retribution. The chorus of washerwomen, for instance, soon overrules the only woman among them who shows sympathy for Yerma. The ruthlessness with which women pass judgment upon other members of their sex is necessary for the maintenance of a "shame culture." The possibilities for harsh judgments are multiplied by the fact that no proof is necessary since violation of the code does not require any *actual* transgression but merely the *possibility* of it. So generalized is the social distrust—particularly of women since they are clearly the victims of the social system's double bind—that whoever has the opportunity to violate existing codes of behavior is assumed to have done so.

Yerma (as well as Bernarda's daughters Amelia and Magdalena) directs mild criticism against *el qué dirán*. But only Adela, because she has herself transgressed the moral code and has therefore been compelled to look at the system as one outside it, protests its brutality. As her sisters run out to witness the mob's slaying of a young girl whose illegitimate child has been discovered by the townspeople, Adela screams, "¡Que le dejen escapar! ¡No salgáis vosotras!" (Let her escape! Don't go out!).

Of all the tragic heroines, Yerma sustains the longest battle with her fate. Over a period of some five years she hopes and struggles to conceive, desperately seeking her fulfillment as a woman through the only means society allows her. Aware of her unutilized physical and spiritual strength and frustrated by a society which blocks her every impulse, she rebels in isolated actions, such as spending the night at the threshold of her house and participating in the magic rites of Dolores the Sorceress; but she never once questions the justice or appropriateness of the role society has decreed for her. Her struggle is always to fulfill that role, never to escape, undermine, or destroy it although that is, of course, the indirect result of her final action. Given the ambivalence of Lorca's ending, we cannot predict what Yerma's future will be. Although the uncompromising nature of the society she lives in makes it look bleak, we know that after having murdered Juan and thus having eliminated all hope of a child—"¡Yo misma he matado a mi hijo!" (I myself have killed my son!)—she feels free and confident at last: "Marchita. Marchita, pero segura. Ahora sí que lo sé de cierto. Y sola. Voy a descansar sin despertarme sobresaltada, para ver si la sangre me anuncia otra sangre nueva. Con el cuerpo seco para siempre" (Withering. Withering, but steady. Now I know it for sure. And all alone. I'm going to rest without waking with a start, trying to detect whether my blood is proclaiming another's new blood. My body barren forever more). The relief she feels when at last she is totally alone echoes that

of the bridegroom's mother: "Aquí quiero estar. Y tranquila. Ya todos están muertos. A medianoche dormiré, dormiré sin que ya me aterren la escopeta o el cuchillo" (This is where I want to be. And at peace. Now they are all dead. At midnight I'll be sleeping—sound asleep and no longer terrified by shotguns or knives). Still, the destiny of a woman alone is a grim and lonely one, as Lorca stresses throughout the course of his plays. We remember the fate of Leonardo's widow: "Tú, a tu casa. / Valiente y sola en tu casa. / A envejecer y a llorar. / Pero la puerta cerrada. / . . . Clavaremos las ventanas. / Y vengan lluvias y noches / sobre las hierbas amargas" (Confined to your house, brave and alone. To age and to weep. But with the door shut. . . . We will nail down the windows. And let the rains and the nights pass over the bitter grasses).

Upon hearing the news that his daughter has run away with Leonardo, the bride's father is incredulous. He seems to wish for her another fate: "No será ella. Quizá se haya tirado al aljibe" (It must not be her. Perhaps she has thrown herself into the cistern). The bridegroom's mother counters him: "Al agua se tiran las honradas, las limpias; ¡ésa, no!" (Only pure, honorable women throw themselves into the water; not that one!). This is but one illustration of the fatal dilemma into which a ruthless social code forces nonconforming women. The mortal paradox is that only through dying can a woman prove her honor. Those women who endure their tragedy are soiled and shamed in society's eyes, although death would often appear an easy solution when contrasted to a life of ostracism, isolation, frustration, and remorse. We know this is what awaits the bride; the last exchange between her and the mother makes it quite clear: "Déjame llorar contigo." "Llora. Pero en la puerta." ('Let me weep with you,' the bride pleads. 'Go ahead and weep,' comes the sullen reply. 'But in the doorway'). Earlier, the bride had sought her own death repeatedly: she asked Leonardo to kill her "como víbora pequeña" (like a little viper), or to put the barrel of the gun into her "manos de novia" (bridal hands). Later she swears she will die with him because "Es justo que yo aquí muera / . . . mujer perdida y doncella" (It is just for me to die here, dishonored and still a virgin), but she returns alive to her mother-in-law's house, where for the third and last time she asks to be put to death. Adela, in contrast, disposed of herself as society demands, enabling Bernarda to preserve her precious façade by giving her daughter a virgin's funeral. Adela hanged herself in despair, believing her lover and savior had been slain by Bernarda. But her suicide was also an act of self-defense. She knew too well the revenge which an overly self-righteous society sees fit to take upon those women who have transgressed its codes and who no longer have a man to protect them.

Lorca sharply contrasts this savage severity, which castigates even minor infractions committed by women, to the liberal tolerance shown to men. The bride is admonished by her future mother-in-law: "¿Tú sabes lo que es casarse, criatura? . . . Un hombre, unos hijos y una pared de dos varas de ancho para todo lo demás" (Do you know what it means to get married, child? A man, some children, and a wall two rods wide for everything else). Men are allowed a freedom and self-indulgence women could never dream of. La Poncia informs Bernarda's daughters of the male's marital "obligations": "A vosotras que sois solteras os conviene saber de todos modos que el hombre a los quinces días de boda deja la cama por la mesa y luego la mesa por la tabernilla" (As unmarried women it behooves you to know anyway that two weeks after the wedding the man deserts the bed for the table and later the table for the tavern). Lorca incorporates Adelaida's bizarre family history in *The House of Bernarda Alba* to illustrate the society's unremitting tolerance of male infractions:

> MARTIRIO. Su padre mató en Cuba al marido de su primera mujer para casarse con ella. Luego aquí la abandonó y se fue con otra que tenía una hija y luego tuvo relaciones con esta muchacha, la madre de Adelaida, y se casó con ella después de haber muerto loca la segunda mujer.
>
> AMELIA. Y ese infame, ¿por qué no está en la cárcel?
>
> MARTIRIO. Porque los hombres se tapan unos a otros las cosas de esta índole y nadie es capaz de delatar.
>
> MARTIRIO. While in Cuba her father killed his first wife's husband in order to marry her. Then he deserted her here and ran off with another who had a daughter, then later had relations with that girl, who is Adelaida's mother. He married her after his second wife went mad and died.
>
> AMELIA. And why isn't that despicable character in jail?
>
> MARTIRIO. Because men cover each other's tracks in these matters, and no one has the nerve to denounce them.

The same double standard is apparent in the first scene of *Blood Wedding.* "Una mujer con un hombre, y ya está" (A woman has one man, and that's all there is to it), the mother decrees. A wife must never look at anyone else, and should she one day lose her husband, she must lock herself in her house and stare at the bare wall. Yet in the same scene she espouses a very indulgent standard for male behavior: "Tu padre sí que me llevaba. Eso es de buena casta. Sangre. Tu abuelo dejó a un hijo en cada esquina. Eso me gusta. Los hombres, hombres; el trigo, trigo." (Your father was the one who used to carry me away. That's what good stock is. Good blood. Your grandfather left a son on every corner. That's what I like—for men to be men, for wheat to be wheat). That she so openly condones flagrant promiscuity on the part of the male sex stands in ironic juxtaposition to her enraged denunciation of one woman's unconsummated infidelity, which causes her to incite her only surviving son to revenge and death.

This contrast points up the central contradiction in Andalusian society, both as portrayed by Lorca and as analyzed by anthropologists such as Julian Pitt-Rivers [in his *The People of the Sierra*]: a man's virility—upon which, in part, his honor depends—requires numerous sexual conquests whereas a woman's honor demands that she be above suspicion, that is, free even of the possibility of sexual contact with a man who is not her husband or a member of her immediate family. The female sex bears the brunt of pressure and punishment in this system of incompatible codes of behavior.

The most radical social criticism in the trilogy comes from a very minor character, a young girl whom Yerma meets one afternoon on the way back from the fields. Their conversation begins as she tells Yerma, "De todos modos, tú y yo con no tenerlos vivimos más tranquilas" (No matter what, you and I live more peaceful lives without children). Yerma wonders why she got married. The girl replies:

> Porque me han casado. Se casan todas. Si seguimos así no va a haber solteras más que las niñas. Bueno, y además, . . . una se casa en realidad mucho antes de ir a la iglesia. Pero las viejas se empeñan en todas estas cosas. Yo tengo diecinueve años y no me gusta guisar, ni lavar. Bueno, pues todo el día he de estar haciendo lo que no me gusta. ¿Y para qué? ¿Qué necesidad tiene mi marido de ser mi marido? Porque lo mismo hacíamos de novios que ahora. Tonterías de los viejos. . . . También tú me dirás loca, ¡la loca, la loca! Yo te puedo decir lo único que he aprendido en la vida: toda la gente está metida dentro de sus casas haciendo lo que no les gusta. Cuánto mejor se está en medio de la calle.
>
> Because they married me off. All the women get married. If things go on like this, the only unmarried women will be the schoolgirls. And besides, . . . the truth is that a girl gets married long before she goes to the altar. But the old women insist on all these things. I'm nineteen years old and I don't like to cook or to do laundry. So, I'm supposed to spend my days doing what I don't like to do. And for what? What need is there for my husband to be my husband? Because as sweethearts we did the same thing we do now. Old folks' foolishness. . . . You'll call me crazy, too. The crazy girl! The crazy girl! Well, I can tell you the one thing I've learned in my life: everybody is stuck inside their houses doing what they don't like. How much better you feel in the middle of the street.

This speech is perhaps the most problematic of any in the three tragedies. It sets in sharp relief the hypocrisy and coercive moral power of the old folks (particularly *las viejas*) and the unnaturalness of what the society considers to be the natural state of women. It advocates a refusal to conform to conventional social and moral obligations and the abandonment of house-bound confinement for the freedom of the street. One might argue against the relevance of this speech, for Lorca puts these words into the mouth of a secondary character who appears only twice in the play, a young girl who Yerma thinks is naïve and who the townspeople apparently think is crazy. She turns out to be the daughter of Dolores the Sorceress and thus a somewhat disreputable and marginal member of society. Yet for these very same reasons Lorca can have her lay claim to an objectivity and originality inaccessible to his other characters, confined as they are within the rigidly structured society which he expends so much effort to portray. In such a closed society, only with the marginal, the heretical, or the insane can opposing ideas or new perceptions originate. In her lunacy, María Josefa, Bernarda's mother, demonstrates a similar clairvoyance.

The distinguishing characteristic of Lorca's tragic heroines is their refusal to resign themselves to the fate society has decreed for them. Their rebellion takes various forms. One of the most significant is the attempt to bridge the separation between male and female roles. Adela wishes she could go out to the open fields and work like the men. The bride, only child of an aging father, is proud of her ability to do a man's work: "¡Ojalá lo fuera!" (I wish I were one!) she exclaims. And Yerma tells María, "Muchas veces bajo yo a echar la comida a los bueyes, que antes no lo hacía, porque ninguna mujer lo hace y cuando paso por lo oscuro del cobertizo mis pasos me suenan a pasos de hombre" (Many times I'm the one to go down and give the oxen their food—something I didn't do before because no woman does—and when I go through the dark part of the shed my footsteps sound to me like those of a man). Bernarda, the most authoritarian of all the characters, is known for her ability to "bregar como un hombre" (contend with difficulties like a man). La Poncia says that she is of the same school as Bernarda, and her accounts of how she used to keep her husband in line delight the daughters and cause them to exclaim, "¡Así deben ser todas las mujeres!" (That's the way all women should be!). All the heroines flout convention in minor ways long before they are actually compelled to break with it. Adela sheds her mourning clothes to parade in a party dress before the barnyard animals; the bride refuses to open her engagement presents, ominously throws her orange-blossom wreath to the ground and indecorously receives Leonardo in her petticoat; Yerma wanders seeking the texture of the earth on her bare feet and spends a night alone under the stars at the threshold of her house—all symbolic acts which foreshadow the coming crises.

In a society which prefers to silence truths it cannot accommodate, Lorca's heroines persist in verbalizing their frustrations. Yerma and the bridegroom's mother are unrivaled in their articulateness. The old neighborwoman has said to the mother, "A nosotras nos toca callar" (It's our turn to keep still), but that is the one thing the widow cannot do; her tongue is her only weapon. Yerma, initially open and frank, grows increasingly closed as her desperation mounts. She summarizes her frustrations in one symbolic passage: "Quiero beber agua y no hay vaso ni agua, quiero subir al monte y no tengo pies, quiero bordar mis enaguas y no encuentro los hilos" (I want to drink water but find neither the water nor the glass, I want to climb the mountain but have no feet, I want to embroider my petticoats but I can't find the threads). She thirsts after water, a symbol of male virility; she longs to climb the hill and make contact with the earth, a symbol of female fecundity; and the elusive embroidery thread symbolizes her incapacity to realize the female role she so ardently desires to fulfill. [The critic adds in a footnote: "A thorough study of the imagery in the three tragedies reveals that womanhood is associated with the earth, either barren or fertile, but always permanent and long-suffering. The male element is associated with more transitory and mutable symbols: wind and water, the latter especially associated with virility. See Julianne Burton, "Earth, Air, Fire, and Water: Imagery and Symbol in the Tragedies of Federico García Lorca," *García Lorca Review,* 3(2) (September 1975)."]

The fabric of Andalusian society, as Lorca depicts it, is rent in two along sexual lines. In no case do we witness the sustained fruition of a relationship between a man and a woman. [The critic adds in a footnote: "It might be argued that both the mother in **Blood Wedding** and Yerma's friend María enjoyed fulfilling relationships with their respective husbands. It must be remembered, however, that neither relationship was sustained. The bridegroom's mother is widowed after just three years of marriage, and María, a very secondary character, is a newlywed."] Lorca's heroines, trapped and beaten down by society's constraints, never reject the society itself but rebel only against certain isolated manifestations of its injustice. Yerma, for example, struggles desperately to uphold the most sacred precepts of her society: female marital fidelity, motherhood, and honor. The defiant Adela breaks Bernarda's hold upon her when she breaks her mother's cane, symbol of superior authority. Ironically, she sheds one tyrannical yoke for another, declaring, "En mí no manda nadie más que Pepe" (Pepe is the only one who can tell me what to do). (pp. 268-78)

In these three tragedies, Lorca explores the alternatives open to a woman who rejects enforced resignation to her lot: either she commits suicide like Adela (and symbolically Yerma); or she destroys her husband, as Yerma does with her own two hands, and as the bride does more indirectly. Widowhood, the most common fate of Lorca's women, serves as a metaphor for female destiny. Isolation, frustration, bereavement, and remorse constitute a bitter fate, yet they are preferable to the anguished coexistence with the male. This end is consistent with the thematic ascendancy and endurance of the female, a virtue which, like the other feminine virtues that Lorca portrays, goes unrewarded. Whether she plays the game or breaks the rules, woman is bound to lose, for, in Amelia's words, "Nacer mujer es el mayor castigo" (The greatest punishment is to be born a woman).

Is such categorical despair a reflection of Lorca's own views? These plays are in no sense programmatic. They do not posit solutions to the problems they raise. But the thoroughness and intricacy of their social vision is both an expression and a product of Lorca's commitment to a more egalitarian, humane, and personally fulfilling society. It is no accident that the fullest understanding of a particular social system should come at a time when conditions are ripe for its transformation. (p. 279)

> *Julianne Burton, "The Greatest Punishment: Female and Male in Lorca's Tragedies," in* Women in Hispanic Literature: Icons and Fallen Idols, *edited by Beth Miller, University of California Press, 1983, pp. 259-79.*

Francesca Colecchia   (essay date 1986)

[*Colecchia is an American editor, educator, translator, and critic. In the following essay, she demonstrates Gar-*

cía Lorca's use of the dramatic prologue as a forum for explaining his philosophy of theater.]

The prologue has existed for many years as a literary device. Hispanic authors as early as in the fourteenth-century work by Juan Manuel, *El conde Lucanor,* have felt constrained to preface an individual opus with a prologue, be that work a novel, a collection of poetry, or, as in the case of Lorca, a play. Setting aside the *Teatro breve,* seven of Lorca's thirteen known dramas have a prologue. Of the latter, five follow a traditional form, that is, someone enunciates them; two, the ones that precede *Mariana Pineda* and *El amor de don Perlimplí* are dramatized. Significantly, none of the Andalusian playwright's more popularly known works such as the trilogy, *Así que pasen cinco años* and *El público* possess such introductory comment.

A careful reading of letters written to his friends as well as their recollections of him suggest that the Andalusian poet/playwright did not write by impulse. Rather, he carefully thought a work through, frequently revising and polishing it until he achieved the form he wanted. In an interview given in 1935 Lorca describes his creative process as follows:

> En mi vida es distinto. Trabajo bastante.
>
> . . . . .
>
> En escribir tardo mucho. Me paso tres o cuatro años pensando en una obra y luego la escribo en quince dias. . . . Primero, notas, observaciones tomadas de la vida misma, del periódico a veces. . . . Luego, un pensar en torno al asunto. Un pensar largo, constante, enjundioso. Y, por último, el traslado definitivo de la mente a la escena.

Marie Laffranque corroborates this in her introduction to Lorca's *Comedia sin título* when she writes of the recently discovered manuscript of the play:

> Las dudas e imperfecciones subsistentes en nuestro texto demuestran que le faltaba, por lo menos, una revisión. Faltaría además, una vez terminada esa hipotética revisión, la prueba para él imprescindible: el reducido ensayo de otras lecturas completas de la pieza, y un tiempo indeterminado, corto acaso, pero también necesario, de último, meditativo silencioso madurar.

If one acknowledges such evidence, then one must also ask why the "prólogo" exists in better than half of Lorca's known theater. The answer lies in the prologues themselves.

Let us look at the two dramatized prologues first. The one with which *Mariana Pineda* opens consists of a brief sixteen-line popular ballad that recounts the story of the historical Mariana Pineda, a figure that had fascinated Lorca from his youth. Sung by a group of young girls, it coincides exactly with the primary dictionary definition of a prologue, " . . . an introductory speech, often in verse, calling attention to the theme of a play" [Clarence L. Barnhart, *The American College Dictionary*]. Without going beyond this point in the work, the reader already knows its plot. Mariana, irrespective of the consequences,

embroiders a flag for a forbidden political movement. The government, in the person of Pedrosa, discovers the flag. Mariana refuses to reveal her co-conspirators and is executed. Lorca concludes the play by having children repeat the four opening lines of his poem:

> ¡Oh, qué día triste en Granada,
> que a las piedras hacía llorar,
> al ver que Marianita se muere
> en cadalso por no declarar!

Though the prologue that prefaces *El amor de don Perlimplín* differs both in content and structure from the one found in *Mariana Pineda,* it also concurs with a dictionary definition, " . . . an introductory act of a dramatic performance" (Barnhart). The preface in this play introduces the public to the main characters and suggests the content of the acts which follow. However the prologue to this drama goes beyond a perfunctory introduction. In it the audience learns of Perlimplín's sheltered life and the hesitancy it has bred in him and of Belisa's sensuality which her studied air of innocence cannot belie. It also provides the opportunity to learn first hand of the concerns his servant, Marcolfa, and Belisa's mother have for those in their immediate charge. More significantly, the playgoer has the chance to observe how marriages were arranged in Spain, those marriages that rarely fostered anyone's happiness and frequently degenerated into endurance contests.

Both of the above-mentioned prologues fulfill a purpose, namely to introduce the public to the work it is about to see. Beyond this, they offer little information regarding the author's thinking about theater. Of the two, perhaps the latter might be considered more important because of the implied social criticism which will appear more strongly in other works by Lorca.

It is the non-dramatized prologues which offer insight into the author's concerns about theater. Although usually put into the mouth of "El autor," "El poeta," or someone not named, a careful reading between the lines of these preliminary observations suggests that it is Lorca himself who speaks. In fact, that such an identity between creator and creation does exist is substantiated in part by Lorca's own statement in an interview given in 1930 about *La zapatera prodigiosa:*

> El prólogo lo digo yo. . . . Esto es cosa mía. Debo compartir la zozobra del estreno como autor y como actor [Christopher Maurer, "Five Uncollected Interviews," *García Lorca Review* 7, No. 2 (Fall 1979)].

Additional corroboration of this circumstance is found in Lorca's own admission that when the *Zapatera* was presented during his visit to Buenos Aires, the playwright had to recite the prologue as the "Autor":

> Por cierto que el prólogo de *La zapatera* había de recitario yo todas las noches, con mi chistera verde, de la que salia una paloma.

A comparison of ideas expressed in the non-dramatized prologues with those made by Lorca in interviews and similar public statements lends support to the supposition that Lorca utilized the prologues as vehicles to articulate his own concerns about theater and its function.

El maleficio de la mariposa, the first of Lorca's plays to be produced commercially tells the bittersweet tale of Curianito's unrequited love for the beautiful Mariposa. Set in the insect world, this piece, which ascribed to insects the emotional complexities, dreams and frustrations more usually attributed to man, lasted for one catastrophic performance. Despite the failure of Lorca's initial venture into the theater, the prologue considered alone as well as a part of the whole play has particular significance.

Lorca does not name the person who delivers this prologue. From this one might conclude that it is the author himself who introduces his work. This is a poetic preface which prepares the audience for the unorthodox play which follows—the play which suggests that the lesser world of insects is structured in much the same manner as the world of humans. The opening line, "La comedia que vais a escuchar es humilde e inquietante comedia rota del que quiere arañar a la luna y se araña su corazón," defines the work. It is a humble and disturbing play, the story of one who wants to claw at the moon and ends by clawing at his own heart. In a few words Lorca tells his audience it is going to be challenged, made to feel uncomfortable about what will follow. He also suggests why, for this is the tale of one who has dared to go beyond his reach and having failed, has paid the ultimate price. Very skillfully, very poignantly, the author awakens in his public remembrances of dreams pursued and lost.

Hints of Lorca's early intuitions of inequities appear in this prologue. He asks, "¿Qué motivos tenéis para despreciar lo ínfimo de la Naturaleza?", and answers, "Mientras no améis profundamente a la piedra y al gusano no entraréis en el reino de Dios." Rather than a rewording of familiar religious teachings, Lorca presents a plea for tolerance of the most abject of God's creatures. Though he refers to the stone and the worm, these are really symbols for the humblest of men—people for whom Lorca had repeatedly expressed a deep concern. When he states later in the prologue, " . . . díle al hombre que sea humilde . . . " he reaffirms this concern. What one has here is Lorca, the critic and teacher, the playwright who stated in an interview with the late Mildred Adams that, "the theater is specially adapted to educational purposes here in Spain."

However one must read these opening observations closely to find the author's ideas, for Lorca has enveloped them in gentle poetic tones. He dares ask his audience to break free of mundane reality and believe that an aged sylph who slipped out of one of Shakespeare's books and hobbles about the woods on crutches told him the tale the audience is about to see performed. To add a note of authenticity to his story, he closes by advising the public that if it learns something from this play, on a tranquil night it should go out to the woods to seek out and thank the aged sylph who limps about on his crutches.

In an interview with Giménez Caballero in 1928, Lorca indicated he was at work on the puppet play known as **Los**

A scene from the premiere production of García Lorca's first play, El maleficio de la mariposa.

títeres de Cachiporra, subtitled *La tragicomedia de don Cristóbal y la seña Rosita.* Between this piece and the ill-fated *Maleficio, Mariana Pineda,* Lorca's first successful play, had been produced and the initial manuscript of *La zapatera,* completed. Continuing in the vein begun in *Maleficio,* Lorca also prefaces *Títeres* with a prologue put this time in the mouth of a nonhuman, Mosquito, described as ". . . mitad duende, mitad martinico, mitad insecto."

Though not quite as poetic as the prologue to *Maleficio,* this one is more forthright in its position, reflecting in part an increased breadth and maturity in the author. Mosquito also addresses the public directly, but instead of the more formal, "Señores" with which Lorca opens *Maleficio,* he calls forth, "¡Hombres y mujeres!", followed by reprimands to the audience. He criticizes the bourgeois theater where ". . . los hombres van a dormirse y las señoras . . . a dormirse también." Mosquito continues that he and his troupe had been locked up in the theater, that is, they had been symbolically deprived of poetic inspiration until he spied a star through the keyhole of the door. Whereupon he advised his friends to flee in search of the simple people and the simple things of this world. Compare this with Lorca's own admission:

> A mí me interesa más la gente que habita el paisaje que el paisaje mismo. Yo puedo estarme contemplando una sierra durante un cuarto de hora; pero en seguida corro a hablar con el pastor o el leñador de esa sierra. Luego al escribir recuerda uno esos diálogos y surge la expresión popular auténtica [Proel (Lázaro, Angel), "Galería: Frederico García Lorca, el poeta que no sequiere encadenar," *La Voz* (Madrid), 18 February 1935].

If we review the characters who people the Andalusian playwright's theater, we find that few of them are from the ranks of the noble, the royal, or the famous. They are just the "gente sencilla" of the world who held such great attraction for Lorca. Mosquito concludes his monologue and cries out, "¡A empezar!" He starts off stage only to hasten back to admonish the wind to fan the astonished faces of the audience and to wipe the tears away from the eyes of young girls without suitors. Here, as in the first play, the author closes his prologue on a poetic note, thus predisposing the audience for what is to come.

In the *Zapatera,* as in the remaining prologues discussed here, the introduction is interrupted by another of the characters, in this case, the protagonist. From backstage Lorca's Zapatera cries out twice during the preliminary comments that she wants to come out. Her impatience to get started with the play, i.e., the business at hand, alerts the audience to the impulsive nature of the heroine. In a move which differs from that in the previous prologues discussed, the Zapatera's interruption serves to bring the author's more serious reflections to a close. It also functions as a transition to the action itself. The final words directed by the "Autor" to his heroine are, "A empezar, tú llegas de la calle." The first act indeed opens as the Zapatera enters her home from the street.

In the prologue to this play Lorca reaffirms his preference for the simple folk expressed earlier in the prologue to *Títeres.* However, in the *Zapatera,* he goes one step further and explains his choice:

> El autor ha preferido poner el ejemplo dramático en el vivo ritmo de una zapaterita popular. En todos los sitios late y anima la criatura poética que el autor ha vestido de zapatera con aire de refrán o simple romancillo. . . .

The author has found a responsive chord in the humble Spaniard, a person whose lack of pretense makes him more sensitive to poetry and more accepting of the marvelous.

Lorca's thinking about the theater and its role has become more concise in this prologue. He does not hesitate to criticize the financial priorities and the public taste which determined much that happened in the Spanish theater of his times. He blames these two factors for the lamentable artistic state of the Spanish theater during the early decades of the twentieth century. At one point in his prologue to the *Zapatera* he notes that, ". . .por ser el teatro en muchas ocasiones una finanza, la poesía se retira de la escena en busca de otros ambientes. . . ."

The prologue to the Zapatera also closes with a touch of the marvelous. In taking leave of the public, the "Autor" removes his top hat which glows from within with a green light. As he tips his hat, a stream of water pours from it. The "Autor" shrugs his shoulders and with an "Vds. perdonen," departs. In this play one is not asked to go out in search of crippled sylphs, nor do creatures part goblin, part elf, part insect call out to the wind to brush away the tears of love-struck maidens. Significantly, in the *Zapatera* Lorca places the unreal, the marvelous in a human—the "Autor." This marks a coming of age for the Andalusian dramatist. He does not feel the need to resort to invented creatures and insects to justify his utilization of the poetic and the wondrous. For Lorca these qualities reside in that most remarkable of creatures, man.

In the ***Retablillo de don Cristóbal,*** Lorca turns again to the puppet theater. The "Prólogo hablado" which opens this work differs in two ways from previous prologues. First, the prologue appears to be divided into two sections, the first and more formal one addressed to "Señoras y señores," and the second more popular one which begins, "Hombres y mujeres, silencio; niño cállate." There are no stage directions to indicate whether one person delivers one half and another the second half, nor precisely where the prologue ends. From the simple, "Sale el poeta," which appears at the close of the first half of the prologue, one might presume that the same person presents both sections of the introduction. In the absence of other indications one might also assume that the first half is spoken with the poet off stage and the second half, on stage.

The content of the first half of the preface to this piece recalls the introduction to the *Maleficio* in that Lorca claims that the work did not originate with him. In this case, it came from the people. He states that, "El poeta . . . ha interpretado y recogido de labios populares esta farsa de guiñol . . .", calling it ". . . la expresión de la fantasía del pueblo."

In the second part, in a manner reminiscent of *Títeres,* Lorca addresses the people who actually occupy the seats in the theater. He admonishes them to be silent, so silent that one can hear whether a bird moves its wing or an ant moves its leg. The language suggests existences other than our own. Again, the author closes his introductory monologue on a poetic note. The Poet states he plans to eat a tiny bit of bread that birds have left him, and later iron the company's costumes. Then, looking about to see if anyone is watching, he announces, "Quiero deciros que yo sé como nacen las rosas y como se crían las estrellas del mar, pero. . . ."

The interrupted sentence brings us to the second difference between this prologue and the ones studied earlier, the substantial intervention in the prologue of another character, in this case, in the person of the "Director." However the dialogue between the Poet and the Director bears no relationship at all to the dramatized preface to *Perlimplín.* Nor do the two participants have any role in *Retablillo* as do those who appear in the prologue to the former play. Instead of an introduction to the characters in the play, or the play itself, the author provides the reader with a debate between the Director and the Poet concerning the role of the latter and his differences with the Director's understanding of the hero, don Cristóbal. A closer analysis suggests that this is more a confrontation than a discussion, one that the Poet loses. The exchange between the two restates in more vivid form Lorca's concern that creativity in the theater is stifled by those in control—directors, managers, impresarios. The Spanish dramatist underscores the power of money in the theater of his day when in the heat of their argument the Director asks the Poet, "¿No le pago su dinero?" The Poet, defeated, acknowledges the Director's upper hand. In response to the latter's question he says exactly what the Director orders him to say though it runs counter to his own beliefs. Lorca also closes this prologue on a poetic note. When the Director pays the Poet with five gold coins, he refuses them, asking instead for five silver ones for "las monedas de plata parece que están iluminadas por la luna."

The separation between the public and the poet is less clear in *Comedia sin título* than in Lorca's earlier works. Indeed much debate exists over whether or not this work has a prologue. No less a Lorcan authority than Marie Laffranque has reversed her position on the matter. In her study on this play published in 1976 in the *Bulletin Hispanique* she calls the monologue with which it opens a prologue. Two years later, in her introductory comments to the publication of *Comedia* she rejects this position stating that:

> Tal como aparece en este manuscrito, el "sermón" inicial del autor (en este caso productor o director de escena, distinto del Poeta según el clásico lenguaje del oficio teatral), ese "sermón," principio del primer acto en el "drama sin título," no pudo representar la primera redacción de un auténtico prólogo escrito como tal para otra comedia.

In a footnote to the statement cited above she adds that she discards the hypothesis originally promulgated in her earlier article in *Bulletin Hispanique.* Nonetheless, seven pages later, in discussing the genesis and chronology for this work Laffranque again refers to "El sermón o prólogo que encabeza la obra. . . ."

If we look chronologically at the prologues in Lorca's theater, we notice an increasing tendency to blur the line between the prologue and the corpus of the play. This is particularly pronounced in the *Retablillo* where the distinction between prologue and play is less clear than in earlier works with such preliminary observations. The only indication the reader has that Lorca's "Prólogo hablado" is over comes from the Director who, after paying the poet, declares, "¡Ja, ja, ja! Así salgo ganando. A empezar."

The opening pages of *Comedia* resemble those of *Retablillo.* Although the author does not indicate a specific prologue in *Comedia,* his initial monologue serves that purpose. In this prologue, as in all of the other nondramatized prologues, the person who delivers the monologue addresses the audience directly. The Author's first words, "¡Señoras y señores! No voy a levantar el telón para alegrar al público con un juego de palabras . . ." imply the preface to the main work rather than the beginning of the work itself. A careful reading of the content of this "sermón" lends support to this premise. Almost at the close of the monologue two things occur which suggest that in his first conception of the work Lorca may have intended this monologue to serve as prologue. The "Autor" refers to the author as though they were two separate persons:

> El autor sabe hacer versos, los ha hecho en mi juicio bastante buenos . . . pero ayer me dijo que en todo arte habia una mitad de artificio que por ahora le molestaba. . . .

He finishes his thought, claps his hands and orders a cup of coffee. A painted backdrop is lowered. The author sits down. Violin music is heard. He takes up his musings again only to be interrupted by the "Espectador primero." It would appear that at this point the play begins. In these initial pages *Comedia* parallels the *Retablillo* structurally with one major difference. In *Comedia* the person who enunciates the prologue continues as a character in the play itself.

More significant than the debate over the presence or absence of a prologue in *Comedia* are the ideas about theater expressed by the Author in these opening lines. In his insistence on showing the public reality rather than in merely amusing it, Lorca reaffirms the conviction expressed earlier in the interview with Mildred Adams to the effect that the theater serves an educational purpose in Spain. He criticizes the theater-going public which, because it pays for its tickets to the theater, assumes it has the right to decide the authors whose plays the theater will produce. "Venís al teatro con el afán único de divertiros y tenéis autores a los que pagáis. . . ." Later he adds, "Pagar la butaca no implica derecho de . . . juzgar la obra." Lorca chastises the urban public which seeks ways not to come to grips with reality. The playwright observes quite accurately that the spectator in the theater feels at ease precisely because the work on the stage does not focus on him. Lorca then observes, " . . . pero qué hermoso sería que de pronto lo llamaran de las tablas y le hicieran hablar . . . ," thus forecasting the work to follow. Lorca continues in this vein noting that " . . . el autor no quiere que os sintáis en el teatro sino en la mitad de la calle. . . ."

These last statements represent a radical departure from earlier ones by the author. Nonetheless they are consistent with Lorca's concern with reality. Note the comment made by him in an interview in 1935:

> Cada teatro seguirá siendo teatro andando al ritmo de la época, recogiendo las emociones, los dolores, las luchas, los dramas de esa época. El teatro ha de recoger el drama total de la vida actual. Un teatro pasado, nutrido sólo con la fantasía no es teatro.

This emphasis on reality does not signify the abandonment of the poetic on Lorca's part. In the last lines of the introduction to **Comedia,** the Author muses about the smell of the sea which emanates from the breasts of sirens, and wonders how one could bring the smell of the sea to the theater and inundate the orchestra seats with stars.

In reviewing the prologues that preface Lorca's dramas, one observes that with the exception of **Mariana Pineda** and **El amor de don Perlimplín,** they do not concern themselves exclusively with the content of the respective plays. The Andalusian playwright includes in them some of his own concerns about the theater as well as its relationship to society. Certain ideas appear as constants: the notion of the marvelous as an element of theater; the plea for love and understanding of our fellow man; the criticism of the financial considerations which place constraints on dramatic creativity of authors; criticism of the audience—its lack of imagination, the limitations of its preferences, its inattention; a partiality for the simple folk rather than the great for his characters. Other ideas, most notably the movement towards more realism while still retaining the poetic ambience, evolve gradually, culminating in the introduction to **Comedia.** Indeed much of Lorca's thinking about reality in the theater was expressed in 1936 when, in an interview with Felipe Morales, he indicated the need for both realism and poetry in the theater:

> Tengo un concepto del teatro en cierta forma personal y resistente. El teatro es la poesía que se levanta del teatro y se hace humana. Y al hacerse, habla y grita, llora y se desespera. El teatro necesita que los personajes que aparezcan en la escena lleven un traje de poesía y al mismo tiempo que se les vea los huesos, la sangre [Morales, "Conversaciones literarias: Al habla con Frederico García Lorca," *La Voz* (Madrid), 17 April 1936].

In an earlier interview in *El sol,* he talked about his plans and said:

> Quisiera terminar la trilogía de **Bodas de sangre, Yerma** y **El drama de las hijas de Loth.** Me falta esta última. Después quiero hacer otro tipo de cosas, incluso comedia corriente de los tiempos actuales y llevar al teatro temas y problemas que la gente tiene miedo de abordar. Aquí lo grave es que las gentes que van al teatro no quieren que se les haga pensar sobre ningún tema moral.

This last statement suggests very clearly that the author was thinking of changing direction and focus in his theater. More significantly, he appears to recognize a social obligation incumbent upon the theater to treat themes and issues of vital concern to man. In effect he still clings to the notion of theater as an educational medium.

A careful reading of both interviews by Lorca as well as the prologues to his plays makes it quite clear that the ideas expressed in the introductory lines of many of his dramatic works do not reflect isolated preoccupations of the Spanish playwright, but more fundamental, ongoing concerns about the nature of theater. One might presume that in much the same way that a drama matured for Lorca, so also did his philosophy of theater unfold. Interviews from his early years in the theater through the ones given the year he died offer evidence of this. In a sense, the prologues served as a sounding board for Lorca as he evolved his own philosophy about theater as well as an introduction to the respective plays. (pp. 791-96)

> *Francesca Colecchia, "The 'Prólogo' in the Theater of Federico García Lorca: Towards the Articulation of a Philosophy of Theater," in* Hispania, *Vol. 69, No. 4, December, 1986, pp. 791-96.*

Catherine Davies and Garry Marvin   (essay date 1987)

[*Marvin is an English anthropologist who has written several studies of cultural relationships between animals and humans. In the following essay, Davies and Marvin probe García Lorca's use of bull and horse imagery in his major works.*]

In his lecture **"Imaginación, inspiración, evasión",** Lorca discussed what he believed were the three stages of poetic creation. Imagination, the source of metaphor, is nonetheless "limitada por la realidad". It might well transform objects and reveal them as meaningful but, as a part of human logical thinking, "siempre opera sobre hechos de la realidad" and is controlled by reason and order. In contrast, the second stage of poetic creation, inspiration, breaks the norms of logic and evades reality, thus rendering poetry self referential. Throughout his writing on aesthetics, Lorca is seen to ride this tandem between imagination, restrained and dependent on the real world, and free, creative inspiration as described in **"Teoría y juego del duende".** His notion of "duende", spontaneous creativity subjected to the rigours of style, is illustrative of the tension which forms the basis of poetry: the *control* of creative flow without loss of free inspiration. His own creative work was rooted in a common human reality and the world of nature around him, hence its capacity for communication, yet Lorca was no naturalist. He believed mere image-making should be transcended and innovation given free rein to produce autonomous art. So Marie Laffranque concluded in her detailed study of Lorca's aesthetic ideas that his work was shaped by "le devoir de discipline" as well as "la règle de libre travail" [*Les Idées Esthétiques de Federico García Lorca*].

No doubt, these considerations led A. Pacheco Ransanz to see the horse in Lorca's work as a metapoetic symbol;

like imagination the horse needs to be limited and controlled ["Los caballos del *Romancero Gitano,*" *University of British Columbia Hispanic Studies,* Harold Livermore, ed.]. Continuing the analogy, this article argues that a complete understanding of Lorca's work may be furthered by recognizing and analysing his perception and interpretation of the natural world in the context of an Andalusian world-view wherein, according to anthropologists, control is a pre-eminent theme. Obviously, the world of Nature served Lorca as a prime source for poetic imagery. He himself confessed to suffer a "complejo agrario, que llamarian los psicoanalistas". But the very idea of a "natural world" needs to be questioned. The world of Nature becomes meaningful only when observed and reflected upon by human beings, whose perception is neither neutral nor totally idiosyncratic. An individual is significantly shaped by the cultural processes into which he is born and is socialized to the view of Nature which pertains to his society, a view constructed differently in diverse societies. Anthropologists, attempting to understand Andalusian society, have shown by prolonged inquiry into the opinions and forms of behaviour of the inhabitants of the region, that there are interrelated aspects of this culture which form and give meaning to the relations between people, on the one hand, and people, the natural and the supernatural worlds on the other.

One area of what can be termed an Andalusian cosmology is the relation between man and animal. Connotations of animal images and symbols are fully appreciated only if the animals of the images, *specifically selected for symbolic elaboration,* are examined within their socio-cultural context. Of the wide spectrum of animals chosen by Lorca, this article concentrates on just two, the horse and the bull, and the theme of control with which both are closely associated. They belong to an Andalusian culture to which the following applies: a fully developed, mature person is expected to exercise control not only over himself, but also over others and his environment although this might be difficult to achieve, despite his efforts, and it is expected more of men than women; two types of animal with which man has to deal are differentiated—the domesticated and the wild—inhabiting, respectively, the cultivated area of the countryside as the product of human endeavour, or the uncultivated "sierras" and "montes" where they cannot be restrained by man and often invade the zone of cultivation; the process of domestication is, therefore, vital for the transformation or reshaping of objects of the natural world to serve the needs of man, and involves the subjection of animal will to that of the human, usually in an unproblematic way which simply entails the penning or enclosing of animals; as in most systems of animal husbandry, in rural Andalusia such domesticating processes, involving the feeding, breeding and slaughter of animals, are applied uniformly to a collectivity of animals which are not individuated; the horse, however, is one domesticated animal that is strongly individuated as it is not herded but rather subjected to a complex domestication process by means of which a very close, ongoing relationship is established between itself and man.

Horses are reared, not for food, but to extend man's influence in the countryside and to be used they must be broken, tamed and trained. In Andalusia, specialist personnel, the "domador" and the "desbravador", take charge of this and there is an elaborate technical vocabulary to cover all aspects of the process and the range of equipment used to ensure that the will of the animal is sufficiently mastered so as to respond to human directions. The concept of mastery is particularly important because of the close, quasi-human relationship between man and animal. But the handling is continuous as the horse will attempt to re-assert its animal nature and revert to its unbroken state, especially stallions which are perceived to be extremely wilful, needing an exceptionally powerful person to control them. The horse obviously plays a key role in the Andalusian latifundia agricultural system, allowing man to operate effectively on large estates (note the *Feria de Abril* in Seville and the *Feria del Caballo* in Jerez, both focussing on horsemanship). Not surprisingly, a special term, "compenetrado", is applied to a good rider, in harmony with his mount and able to extend himself, exceeding the limits of his normal capacities, by travelling faster and further. Traditionally in Andalusia, the group of people most associated with horses, as dealers and breakers, are the gypsies who, appropiately, are seen to occupy an area which is intermediate between wild Nature and domesticated society, between the uncultivated and the inhabited. Lorca could hardly fail to have been acquainted with the intricate procedures of the mastery of horses in Andalusia and, more generally, these aspects of man's effort to bring the natural world within the purview of his will, a struggle which in many ways echoed his own as a poet.

The same Andalusian cultural themes concern man's relationship with the bull, not the unspecified animal reared for meat but more particularly the "toro bravo". It should be made perfectly clear that when Lorca writes of the bull, he does not refer to any sexually intact male of the bovine species but to the "toro de lidia", found nowhere outside the hispanic world. Anthropological study has shown that everyday usage of "toro" in Andalusia automatically implies "toro de lidia" and carries all the connotations of its place in the bullfight. This bull, originating in Spain, is raised on a ranch for the sole purpose of the "lidia", for the very undomesticated qualities of unmanagebility and "bravura" (translated as "wildness") which it embodies and against which a man must pit himself in the "plaza". On the ranch the bulls are named and, like the horse, are recognized as having individual characters and an individual development. In the arena such individuation is again epitomized by the close relationship structured on the response of one to the other. The popular image of the bull as a fierce, potent and aggressively assertive *male* is rooted in its central position in the bullfight, a key celebratory form in Andalusia.

In the bullfight, man's potential mastery, his control over himself, others and his environment, is put to be the crucial test. The event is set up as a dramatic, ritualized contest between two male representatives of different realms: the animal/natural and the human/cultural. The appropiate subjection of the former to the latter is made problematic as the central theme is the mastering of a wild animal by a man who, when faced with difficulties, remains in control, imposes his will and finally resolves the situation through a process of taming, domination (a kind of domestication) and death.

The "fiesta nacional" enjoyed a boom in popularity in Spain in the late twenties. As Eugenio Montale remembered, "En Madrid me sorprendió mucho la extraña veneración que muchos poetas tenian entonces por los toros. Era algo totalmente desproporcionado" [quoted in Eutemio Martín, "La actitud de Lorca ante el tema de los toros," *Insula* 322 (September 1973)]. Although, according to the García Lorca family, Lorca was not an "aficionado" (unlike his friends Rafael Alberti and Gerardo Diego), and although he only described the event in detail in the *Llanto* and the "Corrida de Toros en Ronda" (*Mariana Pineda*), he did, nevertheless, attend bullfights and he offered José María Cossío "todo el espacio preciso" for "temas taurinas" in his literary magazine *El Gallo del Defensor* (1927). His references to the bullfight in both prose and poetry suggest he understood all too well the complex layers of symbolic significance it involved. In an interview in 1936 Lorca said:

> el toro es probablemente la riqueza póetica y vital mayor de España, increíblemente desaprovechada por los escritores y artistas, debido principalmente a una falsa educación pedagógica que nos han dado y que hemos sido los hombres de mi generación los primeros en rechazar. Creo que los toros es la fiesta más culta que hay en el mundo: es el drama puro en el cual el español derrama sus mejores lágrimas y sus mejores bilis. Es el único sitio adonde se va con la seguridad de ver la muerte rodeada de la más deslumbrante belleza. . . .

To what extent, then, is the predominant theme of rural Andalusian cosmology relevent to Lorca's work? The control, taming and domestication of the wild, involving a marked separation between "cultural" and "natural" zones and a special relationship developing between man and an individuated animal wild undergoing domestication, is quite explicit in Lorca's "Andalusian" works (namely, the *Romancero gitano,* the *Llanto por Ignacio Sánchez Mejías* and the three rural dramas) and is implicit in many of his other works, yet critics have failed to acknowledge this presence. Of course, many diverse interpretations of Lorca's bull and horse imagery have been suggested by critics, without recourse to anthropological findings, and polysemic symbols such as the horse and bull unavoidably acquire multiple, often contradictory connotations, especially in Lorca's work where they gain meaning according to the narrative or dramatic flow. The horse, for example, in *Poeta en Nueva York* is as much a symbol of luxurious erotic vitality as a herald of death.

This is not surprising given the traditional literary attributes of horses; strength, usefulness, fertility and sensitivity, and their traditional association with fire, air, water and the phallus. Some critics have stressed the overtones of destiny and death in Lorca's horse imagery. For Ricardo Doménech the horse is "vehículo o instrumento ciego del destino" in *Bodas de sangre,* and it is included in Carlos Ramos Gil's list of animals which announce the presence of "lo oscuro", threats and portents of death [Domé-

nech, "Sobre la 'Nana del caballo grande,'" *Trece de Nieve* 1-2 (1976); Ramos Gil, *Claves Iíricas de García Lorca*]. Barry Weingarten believes the horse in *La casa de Bernarda Alba* represents "man's hurtling journey through life into death" [in *The World of Nature in the Works of F. García Lorca,* Joseph Zdének, ed.]. Another group of critics emphasize the erotic connotations; the horse is a symbol of libidinal power (Rupert C. Allen), of the "natural norm" or spontaneous, instinctual, sensual life (C. Michael Wells), or of "profunda e instintiva pasión" (J. M. Aguirre). Aguirre, borrowing from Jung, concludes that the horse is Lorca's representation of antisocial love in contention with the law [R. C. Allen, *The Symbolic World of F. García Lorca;* C. Michael Wells, "The Natural Norm in the Plays of F. García Lorca," *Hispanic Review* 38 (1970); J. M. Aguirre, "El sonambulismo de Federico García Lorca, *Federico García Lorca,* I. M. Gil, ed.]. Other critics concentrate on the close relationship between rider and mount. Francisco García Lorca sees the horse carrying the rider, against his will, to his death in the poem **"Córdoba"** and J. F. Cirre infers that the horse for Lorca is "vehículo de su dueño . . . jaca y caballista unifican su estado de ánimo" [Francisco García Lorca, "Córdoba, lejana y sola," *Federico García Lorca;* J. F. Cirre, "El caballo y el toro en la poesía de García Lorca," *Cuadernos Americanos* (November-December 1952)]. As Pedro Salinas writes, "este [tema] del caballo y el jinete se señalará como uno de los más persistentes" in Lorca's writings [*Literatura española del siglo XX*]. Furthermore, critics have identified riders as gypsies; "the vigorous activity and grace and speed" of the horse reflecting the noble qualities found in the gypsy [C. M. Bowra, *The Creative Experiment*]. All these varying interpretations are, of course, complementary and take into account Lorca's changing attitude to the natural world, from being hostile (*Romancero gitano*) to openly sympathetic (*Poeta en Nueva York*). Yet they can all be easily accommodated within the Andalusian world-view already described and are connected with the underlying theme of control.

Fewer critics have dealt with Lorca's bull imagery. Traditionally the mythical bull, very often synonymous with the ox and cow, is associated with fertility, sacrifice and brute force and is perceived primarily as a masculine solar animal (horns = sun's rays) containing feminine lunar elements (Horns = new moon). These mythical attributes are frequently ascribed to Lorca's bulls. For example, Gustavo Correa links the sunset to the killing of the mythical bull of the bullfight in the *Llanto* but he tends to confuse the bull symbol with that of the cow, mainly associated with the moon and the mother [Gustavo Correa, "The Mythification of Nature in the Poetry of F. García Lorca," *The World of Nature in the Works of F. García Lorca*]. Similarly, Carlos Ramos Gil, believing Lorca's bull represents primarily life and strength, connects it to the symbol of the ox which also accentuates "ímpetu, fuerza o coraje". Neither does Flys distinguish between "buey" and "toro" as images of largeness [J. M. Flys, *El lenguaje poético de Federico García Lorca*]. As previously stated, the "toro" in Lorca's work is, by antonomasia, the "toro de lidia", not to be confused with oxen or cows, and has special characteristics lacking in the traditional figure of myth. In a study of bull imagery in Spanish poetry of the sixteenth and seventeenth centuries, José María Cossío found the bull there was implicitly the "toro bravo", associated with anger, noise, pride, sexual potency and ardour, hardly qualities of the ox [*los toros*]. The same applies to Lorca. Few critics have recognized this particularity, although Nadine Lys in her analysis of the **"Casida del sueño al aire libre"** associated the bull of this poem not only with the powers of night, violence and blood, but, above all, with the male factor [Bréve interprètation d'un poème lorquien: La 'Casida del sueño al aire libre,' *Hommage* a Federico García Lorca]. J. F. Cirre also makes explicit the obvious connection between bull imagery and the "toro bravo" in his study of the ***Llanto:*** "Ni obediente, ni sumiso, el toro es potencia por sí mismo. Producto del suelo fecundo e indomable. Esta ahí como exponente de una muerte. Mas no de la pasiva, sino de la activa que hay que buscar con plena conciencia."

A more detailed study of a sample of Lorca's Andalusian work will highlight these points. The control or otherwise of a horse and the close tie between rider and mount is an essential theme in a group of poems of ***Romancero gitano.*** A contrast can be drawn between **"Romance del emplazado"** and **"Burla de D. Pedro a caballo"** accordingly. In the former, the rider is related in the correct manner to his horse which he directs with calm authority to serve his need, to carry him to his death. He is resigned to his foretold destiny and proceeds without rest or delay to the inevitable encounter. Such admirable tranquility, where the rider is in total control of himself and his mount, contrasts strongly to the struggling desperation of Don Pedro whose horse is uncontrolled, "sin freno", taking the rider to his death *against* his will. In this way Lorca chooses to express the noble dignity of fatalism, and ridicule the futile efforts of lesser men to avoid death. He creates the figure of a true horseman, the "emplazado", so well "compenetrado" with his mount that the latter becomes an extension of himself. Body, horse and self are fused into a singular entity, separate from any other ("mi soledad", "mi cuerpo", "mi caballo") which meets death with the solemnity of classical stoicism. But Don Pedro finally loses his horse and is therefore no longer a "caballero". Not having reached the standard expected of him in Andalusia, he is mocked and left "olvidado" in the water.

The poem **"Reyerta"** deals with the inexplicable "lucha sorda latente en Andalucía y en toda España de grupos que se atacan sin saber por qué" which Lorca censures through his use of horse and bull imagery. Lines 5-8 set the scene:

> Una dura luz de naipe
> recorta en el agrio verde,
> caballos enfurecidos
> y perfiles de jinetes.

The horses are mentioned first and share the adjective "enfurecidos" with the riders who only appear as silhouettes. This hierarchy, from light to knife ("recorta"), horses and men is a paradoxical and unnatural situation in Andalusia where riders should be conceded more importance than the mounts they control. In this poem, although riders and horse are closely identified, the riders are bestialized because they can neither restrain their animal passions nor

their horses which are "enfurecidos" and from which, therefore, they should be separated. The subversion of the natural order and the consequent bestiality of man is then zoomorphised in the violent image "El toro de la reyerta / se sube por las paredes". In this re-casting of a popular idiom, the bull denotes uncontrolled wildness and death, while the image is extended in "en los muslos / heridos de los jinetes" which suggests a goring. The fight is thus associated with a bullfight, but one in which only bestialized men are involved, a highly undesirable situation, anathema in an Andalusian world-view.

Similarly, the **"Martirio de Santa Olalla"** uses bull and horse imagery to provoke deep disturbance. The poem opens with a disquieting image; within an urban setting, a horse runs wild. Its long tail, unplaited by implication, stresses that it is not ridden. A free running horse in a street is quite inappropriate in Andalusian culture, hence the disturbed norms, the malfunction in society and the breakdown of natural order suggested by this brief but eloquent scene, which remains obscured if an Andalusian worldview is not taken into account. The distress is caused by the Roman centurions, related by Lorca to the Guardia Civil, who martyr the Saint sadistically, leaving her naked body hanging like a carcass of meat. The striking bull metaphor, "Brama el toro de los yunques", placed in the context of the preparations of the torture, the sharpening of the hooks and knives, indicates the releasing of violent, animal instincts in man and an impending, violent death. The forging of metal particularly implies the bullfight, perhaps even ritual sacrifice, as the "cuchillos" kill and the "garfios" are used to hang up the meat. Yet the ferocious killing is directed not at a bull but at a girl, hence the horror concentrated in these lines reflecting, once again, the brusque subversion of order and the perversity of the killers. In this "pasion de crines y espadas" the trophy is not cuttings from a bull, but the breasts of a girl.

In **"Prendimiento de Antoñito el Camborio"** Lorca uses bull imagery with analogous connotations in quite a different way; to describe a character. The protagonist is not only out to see a bullfight but he himself is subtly likened to a bull. His "stock" is a principal marker of his identity; he is "moreno" (black), "de verda luna" (moon / horns) and the description focuses on his "bucles", arrogantly displayed on the forehead between the eyes, and his swaggering gait, which suggests the image of a bull. Note Guillermo Díaz Plaja's terms when portraying Antoñito, significantly "la más completa figura del varón del ***Romancero gitano***". He refers to Antoñito's "aristocracia instintiva", "gesto de nobleza", "su marco natural y campero", all qualities which, together with the "trapio", or harmonious carriage of the head and body, are usually admired in a bull [Díaz Plaja, *Federico García Lorca*]. Bullfight connotations are reinforced when the day is likened to a "torero" with his cape (the evening) over one shoulder or swirled in a "larga torera", a "lance" in which the pink and yellow cape (never red) is trailed slowly in the sand as the "torero" runs the bull past him. Lorca, who knew this, (see his reference to "Lagartijo", famous for his "larga cordobesa") based the comparison between the cape and evening on pastel colours and slow movement. Antoñito, then, like a bull, is about to be accosted. However, he does not fight and after the encounter is led away "codo con codo", packed between the Guardia Civil just as an unfit bull is packed between oxen to calm it down when escorted out of the ring. A more common interpretation of this scene is to associate Antoñito not with the bull but with the "torero", about to face the beast-like "guardias" who wear "tricornios". Indeed, a "torero" who is afraid to perform is also led out by the Guardia Civil. Thus is the versatility of Lorca's complex imagery; Antoñito, a wild and natural being to be controlled, or Antoñito about to control the brutish Guardia. The former interpretation is, nevertheless, further substantiated with the reference to Antoñito's gipsy lineage as gypsies are seen in Andalusian culture as the human analogue of a wild animal that lives outside society. So Antoñito's "vara de mimbre", the instrument of the gipsy horsebreaker or "domador", is the emblem of his authority and, of course, of his masculinity. Whether seen as "toro" or "torero", Antoñito, despite being male, wild and of good stock, flees from conflict, fails to comply with what is expected of him, loses his "vara" and so dishonours his lineage. Having lost control of the situation, his energy and sense of power escapes like a horse, "una corta brisa, ecuestre, / salta los montes de plomo". Antoñito, no longer a "legítimo Camborio" looks from his cell at the sky, nostalgic for a horse as a means to freedom but also for his authority, the loss of which is signalled by the flight of the figurative "potro".

Bullfight connotations continue in **"Muerte de Antoñito el Camborio"**. The "voces de muerte" which open the poem are not only the voices of masculinity, "de clavel varonil", but refer also to the trumpets sounding for the final kill in the "plaza" of Sevilla, which actually stands on the Guadalquivir, thus indicating the precise time of the death of this male. The image of lines 13-16,

> Cuando las estrellas clavan
> rejones al agua gris
> cuando los erales sueñan
> verónicas de alhelí

refers to the art of "rejoneo", a form of elitist bullfighting carried out only by mounted "caballeros" using a decorated lance. It acts as a reminder of how Antoñito has lost his status of "caballero", while the presence of one-year bulls dreaming of their fate and the "verónica", a pass carried out with the pink and yellow cape, suggests the impending, violent death and the struggle of Antoñito himself. Finally, Antoñito, a ghost, is referred to as both "Camborio de dura crin" and "moreno de verde luna" which draws together the bull and horse imagery of the poem, evoking his truly masculine character (gypsy, horse, bull, "torero") before the fatal act of cowardice.

It will be clear by now the extent to which the bull necessitates the notions of masculinity in Lorca's work, thus differentiating it from the "buey". This can have important consequences for the interpretation of his poetry, as illustrated by the much discussed image "bueyes del agua" taken from **"Romance del emplazado"**. Not a common, popular expression, as Díaz Plaja sustains, it was specifically selected by Lorca, as most critics agree, to suggest the force of water. But José Carlos Lisboa, for example, believes that there is also suggested the actions of young

men fighting bulls, despite the fact that bulls are not mentioned [*Verde que te quiero*]. The use of "bueyes" implies rather that the water is not dangerous at all, but "tamed", restrained and posing no threat to the boys. The horns of the oxen, castrated animals, are "ondulados" and soft. If the presence of the moon in Lorca's work usually has fatal implications, here it points to the paradox that while the boys play with oxen, *mimicking* the risk of death, the rider makes his own way, relentlessly, to an unavoidable death, accompanied by the sound of hammers on anvils forging the shoes of his sleepless horse.

Other poems in **Romancero gitano** draw on the theme of the gypsy and the horse, related to that of control as previously described. **"Romance sonámbulo"** opens with a reference to "el caballo en la montaña". The fact that the horse is in the mountains and is not domesticated, in the village implies that its rider has been forced out of human society (cf. Leonardo in **Bodas de sangre**). Although this is appropriate for gypsies, the rider of this poem, usually seen as a smuggler, wants to assume a respectable domestic life and trade in his horse and knife for a mirror and blanket. He neither wants to die as a gypsy in the mountains, but in a bed within human habitation. Yet, like a wild animal, he has been wounded by his hunters, the Guardia Civil, who push him out further to the margins of society preferring to kill him rather than allow his return.

The gypsy spirit, as in **"Prendimiento de Antoñito el Camborio"**, is zoomorphised as a horse running wild and out of reach or control in the poem **"La monja gitana"**. She, like Antoñito, is submissive and imprisoned; yet she is aware of the possibilities of true gypsy energy which she has renounced. Hence, "Por los ojos de la monja / galopan dos caballistas". **"La casada infiel"** depicts a rider so "compenetrado" with his mount that he can ride "sin bridas y sin estribos". Although riding an unbroken horse, in this case feminine (a 'potra'), he is in total control, as becomes a good horseman and gypsy. The analogy, of course, is between the horse and the "casada" who is unbroken enough to be unfaithful to her husband. The rider mounts both woman and horse as wild creatures, without need to tie or domesticate either. The lines "Cobre amarillo, su carne / huele a caballo y a sombra" identify Soledad of the **"Romance de la pena negra"** with the gypsies in much the same way. The poem is also reminiscent of the **"Burla de D. Pedro"** as Soledad is warned to control her emotions through the image of a runaway horse; if not, her end will be fatal and undistinguished, "caballo que se desboca, / al fin encuentra la mar / y se lo tragan las olas".

In the **Llanto por Ignacio Sánchez Mejías** Lorca surpasses a literal description of a bullfighter's death by a symbolic, almost surrealistic use of bullfighting terms (contrast with the "romance" of the "Corrida de Ronda"). Part II, "La sangre derramada", describes the moon, the herald of death, appearing amidst the clouds, "de par en par" suggesting of course, the placing of "banderillas". The scene is set for the complex section beginning "La vaca del viejo mundo" which contains a wealth of bullfight connotations most easily explained by a commentary. Lorca refers to a mythical "vaca del viejo mundo" which has given birth to successive generations of bulls and is responsible for their deaths as well as for those of all bullfighters, including Ignacio. With her "triste lengua", she licks their wounds, "sangres" referring both to stocks and to blood. The "toros de Guisando" (almost stone, so almost alive) are the mythic representatives of all bulls and their bellowing, "como dos siglos", implies the two centuries of professional bullfighting, which began in the mid-eighteenth century. Overwhelmed with sorrow, the successive generations of bulls are now "hartos de pisar la tierra". Lines 25-33 describe Ignacio gradually attempting to fulfil himself as a man through the bullfight, "con toda su muerte a cuestas", alone, continually risking his life against the odds. At the moment of his death the whole bullfight world shudders on a cosmic scale, through time and space. Instinct (on earth through the "madres terribles", and beyond through the "toros celestes") causes the bull to kill. So, through use of myth, this single event acquires cosmic significance. Lorca passes from the particular to the generic and even from the bullfight to man's unequal struggle with fate, the "negro toro de pena". The masculine figure of Ignacio thus acquires mythical proportions and his blood returns "cantando" yet "sin alma" as a torrent to the "marismas y praderas" of the Guadalquivir—where the bulls have traditionally pastured—to the roots of the bullfight itself. There it will remain, apparent to all, a constant reminder of the immensity of this particular death. In this way, the bullfight worlds of myth and reality coalesce to eulogize Ignacio, a "true" man. In part III, "Cuerpo presente", Lorca uses horse imagery to suggest the atmosphere required before Ignacio's body lying in state, in recognition of the bullfighter's own character; "Yo quiero ver aquí los hombres de voz dura. / Los que doman caballos y dominan los ríos". So the analogy between "desboca" and "desemboca" of the **"Romance de la pena negra"**, recurs to stress that "true men are also those that control their passions and emotions. Similarly Ignacio's body with "las riendas quebradas", has lost control and direction because, obviously, he is "atado por la muerte".

The same key themes of Andalusian culture appear in the three rural dramas. In *Bodas de sangre* the Madre refers to "un hombre que es un toro" and this identification of a man with a fighting bull makes for a complex corpus of imagery throughout the play. It is implied that true men are powerful, aggressive and potent like bulls. Such was the Madre's husband, "de buena casta. Sangre". Leonardo is too; he cannot talk to the Novia about their past because "soy hombre de sangre". Likewise the Novio is "de buena simiente" according to his mother. On the other hand, the Felix family are referred to by the Madre as "los matadores" implying, by the use of this specific term and not "asesinos", the killing of bulls. The Mother despises them because they subvert accepted cultural norms and kill not bulls but men. The scene is set, therefore, for confrontation, encapsulated in the image "Como un toro la boda levantándose está"; the fiesta will end in death. Leonardo, identified with both bull and matador, will "kill" the wedding and the Novio, and will himself be killed. He will be hunted down like a wild animal for having infringed the accepted norms.

Leonardo is more obviously associated with the horse

which, as stated previously, should be controlled and tamed. The fact that he is not spells disaster. In the **"Nana del caballo grande"** Leonardo is associated with flowing water (with "large cola") and a free-running horse, both in need of restraint (cf. "desboca" / "desemboca"). The horse refuses water as Leonardo denies his passion for the Novia and the homely love of his wife. In his attempts to control his emotions, he is acting correctly within the parameters of Andalusian culture, but as a consequence is torn and tortured as an individual. His passion, which should be hot, is frozen and painful ("dolor de nieve"), yet he does not drink from the peaceful waters of his wife's love because "La sangre corría más fuerte que el agua". Either way his situation is insufferable. The horse that will not be tempted to drink makes off for "los montes duros" and in so doing it flees the social norms of human habitation, thus entering appropriately, an amoral zone of wild country. The Suegra commands it to remain there, in "los valles grises / donde está la jaca" with the Novia, who also lives far from the village and is similarly identified with natural, uncultured space. The tragic irony, of course, is that the Suegra wants Leonardo to return to his wife, yet she needs to separate the responsible man from the "caballo", that is, the wild uncontrolled passions which drive him.

Yet Lorca's complete fusion of rider and mount established throughout Act 1 Sc. 3 and Act 2 Sc. 1 makes the situation irremediable. As a lone horse (cf. Pepe el Romano), Leonardo instigates the drama; the Criada refers to Leonardo unleashing a fateful chain of events when she warns "Vas a matar al animal con tanta carrera". The Novia describes Leonardo as "un hombre con su caballo", a man with passion that should be controlled, who therefore "sabe mucho y puede mucho para poder estrujar a una muchacha metida en un desierto". Again, Leonardo refuses to ride in a carriage with his wife as a domesticated man, but insists on driving it in a frenzied way, as if riding an uncontrolled horse. Nevertheless, when Leonardo escapes with the Novia, she shares his mount and he finds himself for the first time tied and committed. He is limited, and consequently dies. In placing the "bridas nuevas" on the horse and the spurs on Leonardo, the Novia restricts him and controls the speed and direction both of his passion and his fate. Yet she, in turn, is governed by Leonardo ("Estas manos que son tuyas") and he by his passion; he could not hold the horse in check ("Pero montaba a caballo / y el caballo iba a tu puerta"). Ultimately, neither control the situation and Leonardo, the misplaced male, of "sangre" but not "buena sangre", breaks convention, refuses to fulfill his role in society and is finally controlled and punished by another male, the Novio.

In *Bodas de sangre,* the Mother instructs her son on how a man should behave to his wife, "tu eres el macho, el amo, el que mandas" and the theme is picked up again in *Yerma* in connection with fertility. It would seem that Juan is implicitly associated with the ox as he is "manso" and asexual. In Andalusian culture, a man who fails to produce offspring fails, in an essential sense, to fully realize his masculine identity and Juan's obvious indifference to the matter leads to tragedy. Ironically he fulfils his duty of maintaining his wife at home with honour and he is a good farmer but this is not sufficient. Yerma's situation is equally unnatural; she should not be involved with oxen as she herself admits, "Muchas noches bajo yo a echar comida a los bueyes, que antes no lo hacia, porque ninguna mujer lo hace, y . . . mis pasos me suenan a pasos de hombre". As the roles of the sexes are confused, so are their delimitations. Yerma finds that, during those moments when she is sure she will remain barren, "se me quedan vacías todas las cosas, y los hombres que andan por la calle y los toros y las piedras parecen como cosas de algodón". Strong, powerful, durable elements in the natural world (human, animal, mineral) seem to her pliant and ineffective. Her sense of masculinity depends on her becoming pregnant and her perceptions of the natural world are coloured by her lack of a "true" man. Hence, all strength seems weakness. Moreover, although she knows that men are out on the streets, she is expressly forbidden by Juan to leave the home for this very reason, as he says, "las calles están llenas de machos". Thus denying Yerma access to his own maleness, he denies her participation in the natural order.

The association of males, husbands and bulls is made explicit during the show of Act 3 Sc. 2 where a "macho" (holding a bull's horn and identified with both bull and bullfighter) and a "hembra" dance before the pilgrims in a fertility rite. The Vieja offers Yerma her son who, like a bull, is "de sangre" and will give her children, but Yerma refuses, "Yo soy como un campo seco donde caben arando mil pares de bueyes y lo que tú me das es un pequeño vaso de agua de pozo". She is inevitably associated with the "buey" which, although unassertive and impotent, does produce fertile land and represents domestic harmony. Yerma believes she has great domestic potential, but her fault is marrying only for this end, for children, *not* for passion of the male. In refusing the passion of a man, she denies herself fulfilment as a mother and a wife. Caught between passion and domesticity she needs, more than a sexual partner, her whole anomalous position in this culture resolved; the resolution is impossible, hence the tragedy.

At one point in the play, Yerma, referring to the pent up life force within her uses a horse image. She describes her breasts full of milk as "dos pulsos de caballo / que hacen latir la rama de mi angustia". Her energy is confined, "dolor de sangre prisionera", as she is confined to the house, and pushes to be free. Similar connotations are present in the horse imagery of *La casa de Bernarda Alba* where the main theme is the control of "natural" or animal sexual instincts. The story of Paca la Roseta sets the scene; the husband, a cuckold, is tied to the "pesebre", a place where domesticated animals, but never bulls, feed. The woman, meanwhile, is voluntarily carried off on the crop of a horse which has implicit sexual connotations. To prevent her daughters doing the same, Bernarda takes on the role of a man and becomes the "dominanta", or breaker of horses in order to control the passions and the sexual instincts within them. But Adela is accused by Matirio, who is afraid of men, of being a "mulilla sin desbravar", a young, wild animal, of domestic stock but as yet untrained, that will not be tamed ("desbravar" refers to an initial stage) by the "dominanta". The latent tensions, provoked by the enclosure of these women out of touch with

maleness accumulate throughout the play to culminate in the final act with the powerful symbol of the fretting stallion.

Bernarda instructs the white stud, which is hot and soon to be placed among the fillies at dawn, to be hobbled and let out into the corral, "Echadlo que se revuelque en los montones de paja. Pues, encerrad las potras en la cuadra, pero dejadlo libre". She decides how and when the stallion breeds, as is proper. She also discusses her herd of horses with Prudencia, stressing the financial problems involved. The stud, noted by Adela as a big, white, looming figure in the centre of the corral, in the position of domination, is a symbol of vigorous masculinity. It is also an allusion to Pepe, the male roaming loose outside the house where the daughters are enclosed, who also dominates the development of events at this stage of the play. Bernarda believes she must control the marriage and "breeding" of her daughters according to the conventions of her culture, in the same way as she controls the herd. She realizes that animals cannot govern their sex drive, "debe tener calor" but demands that her daughters control themselves. La Poncia implies that they, like the herd, are underpriced and wasted in that part of the country, so it is difficult to find them a suitable partner. Nevertheless Bernarda cannot stop Pepe from approaching her daughters at dawn, like the stallion and the fillies. At night, Adela visits the corral, an inappropriate place for a decent woman (following the analogy, she should be in the "cuadra" with the other 'potras'). It is she who establishes the direct connection between horse and man by referring to Pepe as "un caballo encabritado". He is obviously sexually excited and she, having rolled with him in the hay, believes she can dominate him as she offers the sexuality which appeases him. She breaks Bernarda's stick, the symbol of control, declaring that the true male will from then on rule, "El dominará toda esta casa". The widow's authority fails and Bernarda recognizes her limitations when the bullet she fires misses Pepe, "una mujer no sabe apuntar". While it is legitimate in Andalusian culture for a widow to take on the role of a man to exercise control, Bernarda, in her effort to succeed, exceeds her capacities. The tragedy stems not from her authoritarianism but from the unbearable position she and her daughters are placed in, as women without men, in a culture where control, domination and domestication are so important.

In conclusion, it is clear that the control, taming and domestication of the wild with its corresponding marked differentiation between "nature" and "culture", counterbalanced by a close bond established between individual men and certain individual animals, is a theme which is as essential to Lorca's Andalusian works as it is to an Andalusian cosmology. The continual confrontation between nature and man, or man and "the beast within" and the assertion of masculinity in the process of control, is usually expressed by Lorca through images relating to the bull and horse. These animals (whose role in human society he knew well) afforded him with both a powerful source of inspiration and a tool for the creation and expression of dramatical conflict and tragedy. Hopefully, an anthropological consideration of the Andalusian world-view in which Lorca was immersed and through which he interpreted the natural world, has helped highlight the importance of this theme and the subtle connotations of this imagery in his work. (pp. 543-56)

> Catherine Davies and Garry Marvin, "Control of the Wild in Andalusian Culture: Bull and Horse Imagery in Lorca from an Anthropological Perspective," in Neophilologus, Vol. LXXI, No. 4, October, 1987, pp. 543-58.

García Lorca commenting on his experiences in New York:

I'm living at Columbia University, in the heart of New York, in a splendid place near the Hudson River. I have five classes and spend the days greatly amused as if in a dream. I spent the summer in Canada with some friends and I'm now in New York, which is a city of unexpected happiness. I've written a lot. I have almost two books of poems and a theatrical piece. I'm relaxed and happy. That Federico of old, whom you didn't know but whom I hope you'll meet, has been reborn.

Federico García Lorca in a letter to Carlos Morla Lynch, November 1929.

Douglas Day   (essay date 1987)

[*Day is a Panamanian-born American educator, critic, and novelist. In the following essay, he outlines the major themes of García Lorca's poetry and plays.*]

A critic once wrote that "thematically, García Lorca's theater revolves on a single axis: *the preservation of Honor leads to the frustration of love, hence of life itself; this frustration, in turn, becomes a despair which leads to Death.* This is always the major theme. . . . " [Robert Lima, *The Theater of García Lorca*]. Is Lorca, Spain's greatest modern writer, to be circumscribed so easily? The answer, somewhat to our surprise, is yes, especially when we concentrate on his three splendid folk tragedies, **Bodas de Sangre** (1933), **Yerma** (1934), and **La Casa de Bernarda Alba** (1936). As a thinker, Lorca was swift and agile, but not deep. He didn't try to be, and he didn't need to be. During his years at the Residencia de Estudiantes in Madrid, he seldom attended lectures. Instead, he would ask friends like Salvador Dali and Luis Buñuel to tell him about the lectures. People told him what he might have gotten from books he hadn't read.

This is not to say that Lorca was a lazy, shallow man or that his great works, like the three tragedies, or **El Llanto por Ignacio Sánchez Mejías,** his long elegy to a dead matador, or his final, ferocious collection of poems, **El Diván del Tamarit,** lack depth: far from it. Their depths belong to things much harder than mere ideas for a critic to extract. To get to Lorca, one must be prepared to search for words that lie in that place where the tangible meets the intangible, that realm where air, song, love, earth, water, hatred all meet at once—and where death is both blossom

and root of the exotic Sephirotic Tree Lorca considered existence to be.

In fact, Lorca distrusted words, especially when set down to be read. He always considered himself a *juglar,* Andalusian antecedent to the Provençal jongleur or minstrel. He was happiest when he was singing his poems to his friends in his raspy but hypnotic voice (like that of an old flamenco *cantaor,* harsh from cognac and black-tobacco cigarettes) or chanting his plays to them in a manner either sprightly or doom-laden, as the dialogue required. He never read his work; he performed it, sometimes accompanying himself on guitar, sometimes swaying sinuously about on his imaginary stage.

For most of his career, his friends had almost to force him to publish his poems, to produce his plays. He was, unlike Yeats for example, indifferent to "correct" texts or definitive versions. He was after immediate and startling effects, not scholarship. Typically, he would sing a poem he had just composed, write it out casually on the back of an envelope, forget about it, then publish it years later as he best remembered it.

More important than his attitude toward his writing, though, was the emotional intensity Lorca wanted his work to possess. What he was after in these plays, as in his earlier poetry collections, **Romancero Gitano** (1928) and **Poema del Cante Jondo** (composed in 1921, but not published until 1931), was *cante jondo,* deep song, the darkest, most solemn form of what we loosely call flamenco, that ancient music that expressed for Lorca the soul of his Andalucía. When, late at night in a gathering of *cantaores* and *tocaores,* the wailing and lamenting reached their peak, a kind of frisson would run through the room where the performance was being given—so that the music produced that overdescribed and misunderstood thing called *duende.* In one of his infrequent lectures (**"Play and Theory of the Duende,"** 1931), Lorca cited his friend, the Gypsy *cantaor* Manuel Torre, as saying "All that has black sounds has *duende,*" and then went on to explain:

> These black sounds are the mystery, the roots fastened into the mire that we all know, that we all ignore, but where we reach what is deepest in art. . . . Thus, the *duende* is a power and not a work, a struggle and not a thought. I have heard an old maestro of the guitar say, "*Duende* is not in the throat; *duende* climbs up inside you, from the bottom of your feet." Meaning this: it is not a question of ability, but of true, living style, of blood, of the most ancient culture, of spontaneous creation.

This *duende* may arise not only in music, but also in the bullfight, when the matador is inspired to work his art with a genius he doesn't really possess, or when love and death and earth mix with such pain (the *pena negra,* the Gypsies call it) that the cry of *duende* is—as Lorca says in another essay—sharp enough to split the quicksilver from a mirror.

Now, for Lorca to write these three tragedies with the aim of conjuring up the black sounds, the *duende,* not only among the characters on stage but also within the audience itself, has little to do with what most of us today think of as "theater." We do have our avant-garde, which has its premise that we are all sophisticates, performing a sort of aesthetic gymnastics for the evening, and we allow a certain amount of fantasy and horror, but we must admit that most of our expectations for drama lie somewhere in the realm of the mimetic. Chthonic, shattering passion such as one finds in Lorca is too strong—even a little embarrassing. Overwrought, melodramatic, one might say. Or one might begin to realize that these plays are closer to opera than to "theater."

Lorca is sui generis. He has few antecedents, though attempts are made occasionally to link him with Maeterlinck, Yeats, or Synge. Of these, only Synge's plays connect with Lorca's tragedies. The first two playwrights may relate in various ways to Lorca's other, more surrealistic, more literarily "poetic" plays like *Asi que Pasen Cinco Anos* (1929-1930) or *El Público* (begun in 1930, and never completed or produced). Among his countrymen, only Ramón del Valle-Inclán comes close. And no one comes after him—except for a host of Anglo-American critics and reviewers, all of whom seem to begin their essays by writing, "The trouble with Lorca. . . ."

The trouble with Lorca, here, is that—for us Anglos, at least—his tragedies are overcharged with emotion. And with daring. He uses the conventional structure of drama (three acts, so many scenes, and so on), and he sets little traps for us to make us think that we are with him in a land that is foreign but recognizable. A note at the beginning of Lorca's original version of *La Casa de Bernarda Alba,* for instance, announces, "The writer states that these three acts are intended as a photographic document." So we believe that our expectations are going to be met: we are going to see a play about peasants in Andalucía and the harsh lives they lead.

In fact, each of the tragedies came to Lorca from the world we call "real." *Bodas de Sangre* derives from Lorca's fascination with a momentarily famous crime of passion that took place in the countryside near Níjar, in the southeastern province of Almería, in the summer of 1928. A bride had, on the day of her wedding, run off with her cousin. The bridegroom had followed them, and the two men had killed each other. After his fashion, Lorca thought about this for four years, then—without having made so much as an outline—wrote the play in one week.

For *Yerma,* Lorca thought of the annual spring pilgrimage to Moclín, a mountain village northwest of his Granada. Every year, barren wives and their shamefaced husbands made the climb to Moclín, where all manner of pious ritual and impious coupling went on. (*"Ay, que cachondeo!"* an old aunt of Lorca's exclaimed to me when I asked her about Moclín. *Cachondeo* doesn't translate well; but "What a horny time!" might do.)

And Lorca had ample opportunity to learn at first hand about the house of Bernarda Alba. She and her daughters lived next door to the Lorca family for several years in Fuentevaqueros, the town near Granada where Lorca was born, and (so the story goes) the adolescent Lorca would hide on the wall separating the patios of the two houses

and watch the goings-on of the vicious widow and her embittered daughters.

Partly because of this basis (however spurious or exaggerated) in a "real" world, the tragedies are indeed deceptive. Of course we expect Lorca to rearrange, modify, and select the facts of the Níjar case in composing *Bodas de Sangre,* and this he does do. And there is nothing very surprising about his introducing a very old, very famous *nana,* a lullaby, at the opening of Act I, Scene 2:

> Sleep, my child, and dream
> About the giant horse
> Who didn't want the water.

But when we read on and see how Lorca has modified the lullaby to include references to a silver dagger and to blood flowing faster than water and how he has allowed the mother-in-law to say to the horse:

> Go off to the mountain
> Through the grey valleys,
> Where the mare waits,

we realize that he is using his little lament to tell us in coded form what the plot of the play will become. Leonardo, the stallion, will ride over the mountains to the grey valley where the bride lives. She is a stream from which he cannot drink, and his life will end with a silver dagger. (Silver always connotes death in Lorca.) The single theme that [Robert Lima] defined so well on the first page of this introduction is working its way along, but throughout the play Lorca pays as much attention to color, music, and choreography (and flowers: think of the bridegroom's *waxen* orange blossoms, his wedding gift to the bride) as he does to methodically working out the plot.

But there is still nothing too unusual or startling about this sort of poetic symbolism. It is not until we come to the beginning of Act III in the improbably tropical (and phallic) forest where Leonardo and the bride have hidden, and we encounter the three woodcutters who speak to the accompaniment of two violins, that we realize Lorca has been leading us up to the wild cries of deep song. The Moon (a young woodcutter with a silver face) comes in to foretell the couple's doom. Then Death itself, in the person of an old Beggar Woman, enters to lead the bridegroom to the place where his betrayers are hidden. From now until the end of this stunning scene, when we hear the twin shrieks of the young men as they die, Lorca is pulling us as far as he can into "the mire that we all know, that we all ignore, but where we reach what is deepest in art." And with the final, contrapuntal dialogue between the bridegroom's mother and his virgin widow, we come as close to real *duende* as anything that is not true *cante jondo* can come:

> With a knife, with a little knife
> That . . . penetrates precisely
> Through the astonished flesh
> To stop exactly at the place
> Where, trembling and entangled,
> Lies the dark root of the stream.

This is poetry, all right, but it is not "poetic drama"—not, that is, if by poetic drama we mean T. S. Eliot or Christopher Fry. It is more like the poetry of an old flamenco *letra* that goes:

When they put my mother
In her grave
I covered her face with a handkerchief
So the earth would not fall in her mouth.

In *Yerma,* too, there is a fatal triangle: Yerma, the barren woman, strangles her feckless husband, Juan, while Victor, the shepherd whom nature intended as her mate, stands forlornly out in the fields with his sheep. By classical definitions and by its theme (the same theme always), *Yerma* is indeed a tragedy; but there is a strange tenderness throughout the play to remind us that Lorca could write not only with and about frustration and violence, but also about such things as the way a pregnant woman feels: "Haven't you ever had a live bird held tight in your hand?" Or about the anguish of a barren woman in a peasant culture: "Why am I barren? Am I going to spend my best years feeding birds and hanging starched curtains in my window? No! You must tell me what I have to do, and I'll do whatever it is, even if you make me stick needles in the most sensitive parts of my eyes!"

But the poignancy and lyricism gradually yield to true bitterness and despair as the years pass, and Yerma turns savage in her frenzied attempts to find a way to become pregnant by Juan (it must be Juan, her husband, because Yerma is an honorable woman). At the pilgrimage to Moclín that I mentioned earlier, Lorca gives us two of his most brilliant pageants: one is a pious procession of women who go in penitence to pray for fecundity; the other is a scene of what Lorca himself calls "great beauty and earthiness." This is a ceremonial pagan fertility dance, involving archetypal male and female figures (Lorca calls them *Macho* and *Hembra*), and the author leaves little room to doubt that he prefers the latter ceremony to the former. But it is all too late for Yerma; it has been too late since the day she married Juan. She ends by standing over Juan's body, screaming at the crowd that is gathering:

> What do you want to know? Don't come near
> me, for I have killed my son! I myself have killed
> my son!

In *Yerma,* as throughout most of Lorca's work, it is the woman who gets his sympathy; his men are generally there either to torment his women or to stand vapidly by as the brutal action unfolds against the woman. Woman suffers; man inflicts suffering. Man, or his institutions, like the Church. Or his ideas, like Honor, and Respectability.

So it should come as no surprise that in the last of his plays, *La Casa de Bernarda Alba,* the women are imprisoned, practically speaking forever, by a woman who, all feminity driven from her by a lifetime spent in a world that men and the Church and an inverted sense of honor have built, rages at her five daughters. The walls of the house are white. The women wear black. There is only one other color in the play: the green dress that Adela, the youngest daughter, wears as her way of defying the awful mother. Except for the mad, pathetic songs of Bernarda's ancient mother, there is no music in this play, no poetry. As Wilfred Owen said, "The poetry is in the pity." If there is pity in this play, it must be that which the audience feels for the characters, for they feel almost none for themselves. It is almost as if Lorca had said to himself: "Write about

hatred. Write about what makes women hate." And hate they do, more than any characters since the Revenge Tragedies of the sixteenth century; so much so that by the time we reach the last scene, we are not even too appalled at hearing Martirio, one of the sisters, say of Adela: "I'd like to pour a river of blood over her head!" Adela finally hangs herself, and we end with the spectacle of an old woman in black demanding silence in a room in which there is no sound at all (and where there will never be a sound) and crying out in defiance to the world that her daughter died a virgin.

There is no starker drama than this. This is what *cante jondo* can come to, if it is true enough, felt strongly enough: the dancer and the guitarist cease, and there is left only the hopeless wail of the bereft singer. Lorca succeeded: a superior performance (or a careful reading) will arouse the spirit of *duende.* A few months after completing *La Casa de Bernarda Alba* he was dead, assassinated in the hills above Granada. He left fragments of new plays, but we have no way of knowing whether or not he could have surpassed his last one. I think not. (pp. ix-xvi)

> *Douglas Day, in an introduction to* The Rural Trilogy: Blood Wedding, Yerma, and the House of Bernarda Alba *by Federico García Lorca, translated by Michael Dewell and Carmen Zapata, Bantam Books, 1987, pp. ix-xvi.*

Nigel Dennis   (essay date 1988)

[*Dennis is an English novelist, dramatist, and critic. In the following essay, he examines the motif of the mirror in García Lorca's poetry.*]

Despite the range and variety of Lorca's work and the inevitable pitfalls of any generalization concerning it, there

García Lorca in April 1936.

does seem to be a clearly discernible overall theme to his poetry. This theme centers on the human predicament which the poetry outlines with some degree of insistence, especially in its early and late stages. The predicament begins with the acknowledgement that everything contained in the past has been definitively surrendered, an idea bluntly condensed in the lines from the opening poem of *Libro de poemas:* "las cosas que se van no vuelven nunca, / todo el mundo lo sabe." It then develops into an exploration of the sense of estrangement and separation from a past self, dwelling on the malaise that stems from nostalgia and disorientation and describing it in progressively more jarring and anguished terms. Finally, though not always clearly, it broaches the possibility of a future recovery of the wholeness and articulacy that have been lost. This broad thematic concern is articulated in a number of different ways in Lorca's poetry, one of the most intriguing of which is by means of what might be termed "strategies of perception," or, more precisely, "strategies of self-perception." This is to say that one of the emphases that Lorca gives to his poetry, as he voices the different aspects of this central human predicament, is on the visual: on the principles of seeing and not seeing, and on the ways in which the subject sees and sees itself.

These "strategies of perception" open up several different paths of enquiry. They underline, for example, the primacy of the visual in Lorca's writing in general and how in particular works, such as *Impresiones y paisajes,* a markedly pictorial sensibility is in evidence. They also raise the whole issue of the status that eyes themselves enjoy in Lorca's poetry, especially the emblem of blindness and its relationship with death, expressed in such phrases [in *Poeta en Nueva York*] as "la escarcha de los ojos apagados" and "los ojos de cristal definitivo." Equally significantly, they draw attention to those agents that cloud or distort vision, such as the cancer of "El niño Stanton" which "abrió su quebrada rosa de vidrios secos y manos blandas / para salpicar de lodo las pupilas de los que navegan," or the "inocente dolor de pólvora en mis ojos" evoked in another poem from *Poeta en Nueva York.* These may be viewed as component parts of an overall interpretative scheme, but, in order to give this discussion a clear focus, I want to examine one particularly suggestive part of this scheme that revolves around the importance Lorca attaches to reflecting surfaces, above all to mirrors. There is a curious tendency in Lorca's writing to avoid direct vision and to prefer to describe things as they are seen indirectly in their reflected forms. It is a tendency enshrined in the famous lines from **"La monja gitana"**— "Por los ojos de la monja / galopan dos caballistas"—but is by no means an isolated instance. On a number of occasions Lorca adopts the same unusual angle of perception, apparently turning away from what the subjects of his poems are actually seeing and describing it instead in terms of its diminutive reflected representation in their own eyes. This is clearly the case in the following lines from *Canciones*—"Vi en tus ojos / dos arbolitos locos"— and in another poem from *Romancero gitano*—**"Muerto de amor"**—where, strangely, it is the subject rather than the narrator of the poem who states "En mis ojos, sin querer, / relumbran cuatro faroles." This principle is coherently extended in a variety of ways by Lorca. He some-

times rivets attention, for example, not on the actual form or substance of the people who appear in his poems but on their reflected representation:

> Mi sombra va silenciosa
> por el agua de la acequia . . .
>
> . . . . .
>
> Una luz nace en mi pecho,
> reflejado, de la acequia.
>
> *[Canciones]*

This inevitably leads to an emphatic use of mirrors since they lend themselves ideally to this mode of perception, as can be seen in a poem like **"Romance de la guardia civil española,"** where Lorca describes how "Por los espejos sollozan / bailarinas sin čaderas."

Mirrors, however, threw out a special challenge to Lorca's visual sensibility and allowed him to formulate a whole series of ideas central to his understanding and interpretation of the human condition in general and, perhaps, of his own condition in particular. The frequency with which mirrors appear in Lorca's work is evident in the long inventory of *espejos lorquianos* compiled by Concha Zardoya ["Los espejos de Federico García Lorca," *Asomante* 18 (January-March 1962)]. The importance that Lorca clearly attached to them can be gauged by the multiple functions they perform, many of which were identified by Zardoya. By narrowing the focus and pursuing at some length a number of suggestions made by Zardoya, it is possible to explore more fully the relationship between the use Lorca makes of mirrors and the expression of the general human predicament outlined at the beginning of this discussion.

There is a poem in the early series **"Suite de los espejos"** that provides an ideal point of departure. It is entitled aptly, if rather solemnly, **"Initium"** and reads as follows:

> Adán y Eva.
> La serpiente
> partió el espejo
> en mil pedazos,
> y la manzana
> fue la piedra.
>
> *[Poemas sueltos]*

In a sense this poem neatly summarizes the dominant theme of *Libro de poemas:* the loss of innocence and the harrowing initiation into adulthood. Here, however, the idea is relieved of the specifically personal associations it has in that collection and is elevated, by means of the biblical terms in which it is couched, to the status of categoric judgement on the human condition in general. It is significant that the agent of destruction in **"Initium"** is *la manzana,* used on a number of occasions in *Libro de poemas* as a conventional emblem of knowledge, of sexual experience, of sin and corruption. What is most noteworthy, however, in the poem from **"Suite de los espejos"** is that the consequences of knowledge and corruption—the irredeemable loss of the edenic wholeness that man once enjoyed—are formulated in terms of the shattered mirror. Man's fall from grace, in other words, is conveyed by means of the destruction of the instrument that enabled him to see himself in his entirety, as an inviolate whole. Man's essential condition—and one might say the essential condition of Lorca's poetry too—is initially determined not only by his expulsion from the Garden of Eden but also by his fragmentation. His subsequent destiny, in figurative terms at least, is to search among the splinters of that shattered mirror for his own lost innocence and identity.

This generic condition is alluded to in *Libro de poemas* itself, once more in biblical terms, where Lorca writes:

> Y el hombre miserable
> es un ángel caído.
> La tierra es el probable
> paraíso perdido.

As they make their way uncertainly through that earthly "lost paradise," the subjects of Lorca's poems continually encounter reminders of disarticulation, of things that have been broken and soiled. In *Libro de poemas,* for example, Lorca harps mournfully on the way "se deshojan las rosas en el lodo" and evokes the desolate scene in which the *veleta,* "lírica flor de torre,"

> dispersa sus pétalos,
> para caer sobre las losas frías
> comida por la oruga
> de los ecos.

In *Poeta en Nueva York* too there is a lucidly anguished realization that "todo está roto por la noche," an idea taken up in the poem **"New York. Oficina y denuncia,"** in which Lorca describes how all the slaughtered animals of the city "dejan los cielos hechos añicos." The fact that these examples are taken from collections separated by almost twenty years stresses how this vision of breakdown, of a fragmented condition, spans practically all Lorca's poetry.

The analogies between the disintegration of the world and the sensations of inner dissolution are frequent and largely predictable, and tend to be characterized by the kind of vague melancholy evident in the following lines from *Libro de poemas:*

> Mi alma está madura
> hace mucho tiempo,
> y se desmorona
> turbia de misterio.

The most suggestive instances, however, are those that describe how the subject's voice, and more pertinently his sight, are fractured. In *Libro de poemas,* for example, there are subjects that inhabit "un campo / de miradas rotas," or that complain how "en la dulce tristeza / del paisaje que muere / mis voces se quebraron." Similarly, in **"Poema doble del lago Eden,"** the speaker describes how / "mis ojos se quiebran en el viento / con el aluminio y las voces de los borrachos." It is entirely apposite that in an eloquent poem from *Canciones* the representation of the critical state of the poet's critical activities should rest on an image of broken perception. Contrasting the wholeness or distinctness of past selves with a current indeterminate identity ("Yo era . . . you fui . . . pero no soy"), the poem in question concludes with the parenthetical admission: "(Ante una vidriera rota / coso mi lírica ropa)." The

entire notion of falling, dissolving, decaying, enacted in the outside world in order to represent a parallel inner breakdown, is condensed in a poem in *Libro de poemas* in which the speaker openly acknowledges the analogy between the *chopo viejo* that keels over and dies and his own fallen condition:

> Has caído
> en el espejo
> del remanso dormido.
> Yo te vi descender
> en el atardecer
> y escribo tu elegía
> que es la mía.

Significantly, the *chopo/poeta* breaks its own image as it falls and dies, clouding or splintering "el espejo / del remanso dormido."

The mirror does not necessarily have to be shattered in order to draw attention to this breakdown in identity. The same problem can be effectively posed by making use of an intact mirror and exploiting the uncertainty created by the subject contemplating its double. The idea is conveyed in another poem from **"Suite de los los espejos,"** aptly entitled **"Confusión,"** in which the speaker confronts the uncannily exact but plainly misleading representation of itself:

> Mi corazón
> ¿es tu corazón?
> ¿Quién me refleja pensamientos?
> ¿Quién me presta
> esta pasión sin raíces?
> ¿Por qué cambia mi traje
> de colores?
> ¡Todo es encrucijada!
> ¿Por qué ves en el cielo
> tanta estrella?
> ¿Hermano, eres tú
> o soy yo?
> ¿Y estas manos tan frías
> son de aquel?
> Me veo por los ocasos
> y un hormiguero de gente
> anda por mi corazón.

Alarmed and disorientated by the image, the subject attempts to engage in dialogue with itself, questioning insistently the nature of the relationship between itself and its visual representation. Instead of a single, fixed, unchanging identity, the speaker perceives only multiple, shifting, surrogate forms.

The exclamation in this poem "¡Todo es encrucijada!" is a particularly arresting one. The mirror, or indeed any reflecting surface, can be understood to be the point at which the self confronts its image or separates into its representation. Consequently, it is both a meeting place and a place of departure. This is emblematic, in a sense, of an essential principle of perception which Lorca's poetry proposes: the eyes are the surface at which the inner world branches out into the outer world, functioning as crossroads at which sense, understanding, direction, and navigation all become critical. There is another poem from **"Suite de los espejos,"** entitled simply **"Los ojos,"** which brings this idea sharply into focus:

En los ojos se abren
infinitos senderos.
Son dos encrucijadas
de la sombra.
La muerte llega siempre
de esos campos ocultos . . .

. . . . .

Las pupilas no tienen
horizontes.
Nos perdemos en ellas
como en la selva virgen.

The task of maintaining or salvaging identity, of coming to terms with the enigmas it creates, is sometimes undertaken precisely at those two "encrucijadas / dc la sombra" at which inner meets outer, sharpening the sense of mystery and estrangement:

Yo, en mis ojos, paseo por las ramas.
Las ramas se pasean por el río.

Llegan mis cosas esenciales.
Son estribillos de estribillos.
Entre los juncos y la baja tarde
¡qué raro que me llame Federico!.

[*Canciones*]

Part of the problem—as the poem **"Confusión"** implies, with its reference to that "hormiguero de gente"—is clearly that mirrors not only reflect and confuse the subject by confronting it with its double, but also multiply. Multiplication diffuses identity, corroding the specificity of the self until it may eventually disappear altogether:

Siete corazones
tengo.
En el alto monte, madre,
tropezábamos yo y el viento.
Siete niñas de largas manos
me llevaron en sus espejos . . .

. . . . .

Siete corazones
tengo,
¡Pero el mío no lo encuentro!

The search for identity, the insistent and often painful process of self-examination, is renewed at practically every encounter with the reflected image. Each polished, reflecting surface graphically represents the enigma that the speaker seeks to resolve, providing a stimulus for meditation and self-questioning:

¿Qué leo en el espejo
de plata conmovida
que la aurora me ofrece
sobre el agua del rio?

The desire for oneness, for a coherently articulated whole, is firmly spoken:

En la mañana viva,
yo quería ser yo.
Corazón.
Y en la tarde caída,
quería ser mi voz.
Ruiseñor.

[*Canciones*]

However, as has already been suggested, the difficulty lies in the fact that this desire is continually frustrated. The subjects of Lorca's poems seem to be hounded by a sense of estrangement from their own representations, by their realization that from the moment at which that original edenic wholeness was ruptured, they have become somehow distinct and separate, disfigured, emptied, or sinisterly absent. The idea is voiced on a number of occasions in *Poeta en Nueva York,* in **"Fabula y rueda de los tres amigos":**

Cuando se hundieron las formas puras
bajo el cri cri de las margaritas,
comprendí que me habían asesinado . . .

. . . . .

Ya no me encontraron.

¿No me encontraron?
No. No me encontraron.

And we hear it equally emphatically, though in more explicitly visual terms, in the following lines from **"Paisaje de la multitud que vomita":**

¡Ay de mí! ¡Ay de mí! ¡Ay de mí!
Esta mirada fue mía, pero ya mo es mía.

In the **"Canción del naranjo seco"** the tree asks the plaintive question: "¿Por qué nací entre espejos?" The source of the discomfort and suffering expressed in this context is essentially the same as the one that can be identified in other more personalized poems: the contemplation of the self is an unpleasant reminder of imperfection, of the flaws that sully and scar identity. The orange tree sees its own extinction as a welcome release and pleads with the woodcutter: "Córtame la sombra. / Líbrame del suplicio / de verme sin toronjas." The analogy between the tree and the poet, used frequently by Lorca in his early poetry, is not made explicit here, but the critical condition of each is basically the same. If the orange tree cannot endure being confronted, through its own reflection, with the fact of its sterility, so the poet tends to voice his own unease and pain at seeing the enigma, the falsification or dissolution of his own self in its various reflected representations. This is the kind of idea expressed in *Poeta en Nueva York* in a poem like **"Vuelta de paseo,"** where in the line "tropezando con mi rostro distinto de cada día," Lorca chooses to emphazise the perplexing effect of encountering a succession of seemingly unrelated, discontinuous reflected selves.

The orange tree and the poet appear to be bound by the same mournful desire formulated succinctly in the words of the tree: "Quiero vivir sin ver." Since the tree is inevitably passive, it is unable to realize this desire. Only the active intervention of the woodcutter with his axe could put an end to the tree's suffering by banishing those painful images from its surroundings. The human subjects of Lorca's poems, however, are in a position to take the initiative: they themselves can act as agents of their own obliteration, personally assuming the responsibility of eliminating the pain that self-contemplation can cause by breaking their own images. But by shattering the mirror that holds their image they also destroy, figuratively at least, themselves, a consequence Lorca seemed perfectly aware of in one of the most haunting poems of *Canciones,* appropriately entitled **"Suicidio":**

> (Quizá fue por no saberte
> la Geometría)
>
> El jovencito se olvidaba.
> Eran las diez de la mañana.
>
> Su corazón se iba llenando
> de alas rotas y flores de trapo.
>
> Notó que ya no le quedaba
> en la boca más que una palabra.
>
> Y al quitarse los guantes, caía,
> de sus manos, suave ceniza.
>
> Por el balcón se veía una torre.
> El se sintió balcón y torre.
>
> Vio, sin duda, cómo le miraba
> El reloj detenido en su caja.
>
> Vio su sombra tendida y quieta
> en el blanco diván de seda.
>
> Y el joven rígido, geométrico,
> con un hacha rompió el espejo.
>
> Al romperlo, un gran chorro de sombra
> inundó la quimérica alcoba.

This is a deeply disturbing poem that poses nagging problems of interpretation. The narrative voice is curiously detached from the scenes and sensations it describes, and charts in an abrupt, matter-of-fact, coldly methodical way the sinisterly ritualistic act, speaking the extraordinary as if it were the obvious. The narrator's attitude to the incident is condensed in the laconic, parenthetical epigraph/explanation with which the poem opens; but the problems of understanding begin precisely with that ambivalent, speculative commentary: is the reader to understand that some failure at the school subject of geometry is the motive for this "suicide"? Has some calamity in the classroom inspired this decision to end it all? Or is the "Geometría"—and the capital with which the word is written may be significant in this connection—tied in some way to the visual representation of the young boy "rígido, geométrico"? Would the word "geométrico" not refer, perhaps, to the reflected image: to the two-dimensional representation, the principles of which the boy cannot understand? Is he rigid with fear at the unsettling effect of self-contemplation, unable to formulate the question voiced in a poem quoted earlier: "¿Hermano, eres tú / o soy yo?" Is he paralysed in the same way that time itself is in the "reloj detenido"? Why is he wearing gloves at ten o'clock in the morning, anyway, and what is that single, unspoken word that he still possesses?

Despite these elusive and puzzling details, there is much that is immediately recognizable in the poem: the sensation of dissolution and breakdown in the "alas rotas;" the notion of disfigurement and soiling in the "flores de trapo;" the sense of the bankruptcy of language, the failure of articulacy, the decay and decomposition of the self. The principle of disorientation is invoked once more: the subject is displaced, *becomes* the things it sees ("El se sintió balcón y la torre"), relinquishing the fixed specificity—the

locus—of his own identity. This concept of self-separation is emphasized in the way the subject is represented by its least substantial attribute, namely its own shadow, the serenity of which bears no resemblance to the inner turbulence that the subject evidently feels. There is a characteristic visual realignment too that complements this suggestion in the lines: "Vio, sin duda, cómo le miraba / el reloj detenido en su caja." The more active seeing agent is an inanimate object in the room, a detail that usually prefigures or underlines the death of the human subject in Lorca's poems.

Some of the poem's difficulty may lie in the fact that the entire scene could be understood as taking place *within* the mirror. This is to say—and this is more of a suggestion than an assertion—that the objects named ("balcón," "torre," "reloj," "sombra" . . .) are seen *inside* the mirror, imprisoned like the subject's own geometrical image within the confines of the mirror's frame, all being part of the "quimérica alcoba." Yet the fact that the poem is not exclusively visual—it includes sensations that are felt and interpreted as well as things that are seen—serves as a reminder that the mirror is more figurative than real. When all is said and done, **"Suicidio"** is more a poem about self-examination and introspection than about literal self-contemplation. This is unsurprising since, at their most suggestive, Lorca's mirrors are usually instruments that provide access to the abstract inner recesses of being and not just to its surface manifestations. This accounts for the fact that the suicide mentioned in the title of the poem is a purely figurative one: in the terms posited by the writer, the destruction of the image is tantamount to the destruction of the self. The shattering of the mirror should be understood as a metaphor for death: with no image or reflection, there is no being.

The ending of the poem **"Suicidio"** can be linked to the act described in the poem **"Initium"** with which this discussion began. The broken mirror in the latter signals Man's point of departure following his fall and expulsion from paradise, while in the former it could be viewed as a symbolic gesture that wipes the slate clean, establishing the need or at least the opportunity of beginning again, of reassembling the scattered parts of identity. It would seem that for the poet the destruction of the mirror sets in motion an ongoing process of unease, uncertainty, and questioning, thereby determining the subsequent desire for restoration and the recovery of lost wholeness. I mentioned at the beginning of this discussion that there is a suggestion in Lorca's poetry that this wholeness may indeed eventually be recovered. Part of the prophecy of *Poeta en Nueva York* is concerned with the prospect of reintegration. The primeval world inhabited or at least recollected by the negroes is depicted as being impervious to those agents of destruction that haunt the poet's own world, and is characterised by, among other things, its intactness. In **"Norma y paraíso de los negros,"** for example, Lorca conjures up an

> azul sin un gusano ni una huella dormida,
> donde los huevos de avestruz quedan eternos
> y deambulan intactas las lluvias bailarinas . . .

When he assumes this prophetic posture, Lorca evokes a

future time when what he—and perhaps Man too—has lost will be regained, his powers of articulation, for example, regenerated in **"Cuidad sin sueño":**

> Otro día
> veremos la resurrección de las mariposas diseca-
>   das
> y aun andando por un paisaje de esponjas
>   grises y barcos mudos
> veremos brillar nuestro anillo y manar rosas
>   de nuestra lengua . . .

However, this postulated future recovery may also be understood in the same visual terms used, as this discussion has suggested, to outline the human predicament evident in much of his poetry. This is to say that some of those same "strategies of perception" are invoked when pointing to a future retrieval of an integrated self. Lorca implies, in fact, that the resolution of some of the central conflicts he presents in his poetry depends on an overcoming of the malaise and disorientation generated by self-contemplation. He makes use of the same basic concepts—the vocabulary of the visual, the language of mirrors—to argue that permanent peace can only be found beyond the reflection, beyond the image, on the other side of the mirror:

> Detrás de cada espejo
> hay una calma eterna
> y un nido de silencios
> que no han volado.

[Poemas sueltos]

However, as is customary in Lorca, that ultimate tranquility is possible only in death, when the vigilant image ceases forever to hound the subject:

> Yo sé que mi perfil será tranquilo
> en el musgo de un norte sin reflejo.
> Mercurio de vigilia, casto espejo
> donde se quiebre el pulso de mi estilo . . .

(pp. 41-53)

Nigel Dennis, "Lorca in the Looking-Glass: On Mirrors and Self-Contemplation," in "Cuando yo me muera . . .": Essays in Memory of Federico Garcia Lorca, edited by C. Brian Morris, University Press of America, 1988, pp. 41-55.

FURTHER READING

Biography

García Lorca, Francisco. *In the Green Morning: Memories of Federico.* Translated by Christopher Maurer. New York: New Directions, 1986, 258 p.
    Memoir of García Lorca by his brother.

Gibson, Ian. *The Death of Lorca.* Chicago: J. Philip O'Hara, 1973, 217 p.
    Comprehensive study detailing the circumstances surrounding García Lorca's execution in 1936.

————. *Federico García Lorca: A Life.* London: Faber and Faber, 1989, 551 p.
    The standard English-language biography of García Lorca.

Criticism

Allen, Rupert C. *The Symbolic World of Federico García Lorca.* Albuquerque: University of New Mexico Press, 1972, 205 p.
    Uses García Lorca's works as examples to illustrate the relationship between poetry and the psychological theory of symbols.

Duran, Manuel, ed. *Lorca: A Collection of Critical Essays.* Englewood Cliffs, N.J.: Prentice-Hall, 1962, 181 p.
    Essays by various critics about Lorca's major works and principal themes.

Klibbe, Lawrence H. *Lorca's Impresiones y paisajes: The Young Artist.* Madrid: Studia Humanitatis—José Porrúa Turanzas, 1983, 171 p.
    Analyzes García Lorca's little-known first publication to form a picture of his early development as a writer.

Londré, Felicia Hardison. *Federico García Lorca.* New York: Frederick Ungar, 1984, 208 p.
    Views García Lorca's career as a progression toward a synthesis of the visual, poetic, musical, and dramatic arts.

Martínez Nadal, Rafael. *Lorca's The Public: A Study of His Unfinished Play (El Público) and of Love and Death in the Work of Federico García Lorca.* London: Calder & Boyars, 1974, 247 p.
    Study of García Lorca's "most difficult play" and of major symbols of love and death in his works.

Ramsden, H. *Lorca's Romancero Gitano: Eighteen Commentaries.* Manchester, England: Manchester University Press, 1988, 126 p.
    Provides close readings of each of García Lorca's gypsy ballads.

Sinclair, Alison. "Lorca: Poet in New York." In *Unreal City: Urban Experience in Modern European Literature and Art,* edited by Edward Timms and David Kelley, pp. 230-46. New York: St. Martin's Press, 1985.
    Chapter on García Lorca probes the image of city life and urban landscapes presented in *Poeta en Nueva York.*

Trend, J. B. "García Lorca." In his *Lorca and the Spanish Poetic Tradition,* pp. 1-23. Oxford: Basil Blackwell, 1956.
    Traces García Lorca's major themes and notes their sources in Andalusian and Spanish culture and poetic forms.

Walsh, John K. "The Woman in Lorca's Theater." *Gestos* 2, No. 3 (April 1987): 53-65.
    Examines the role of women in the Spanish theatrical establishment of García Lorca's day, arguing that his emphasis on strong female protagonists derives in part from that system.

Additional coverage of García Lorca's life and career is contained in the following sources published by Gale Research: *Contemporary Authors,* Vols. 104, 131; *Dictionary of Literary Biography,* Vol. 108; *Drama Criticism,* Vol. 2; *Hispanic Writers; Major 20th-Century Writers; Poetry Criticism,* Vol. 3; *Twentieth-Century Literary Criticism,* Vols. 1, 7; and *World Literature Criticism.*

Knut Hamsun

1859-1952

(Pseudonym of Knut Pedersen; also wrote under pseudonym of Knut Pedersen Hamsund) Norwegian novelist, essayist, playwright, memoirist, and short story writer.

For further information on Hamsun's career, see *TCLC*, Volumes 2 and 14.

INTRODUCTION

Hamsun is widely considered the greatest novelist in Norwegian literature. Highly praised during his lifetime by such eminent contemporaries as Thomas Mann and André Gide, he received the 1920 Nobel Prize for literature on the merits of *Markens grøde* (*Growth of the Soil*). In this novel, as in his others, Hamsun depicted the daily activities of simple, hardworking farmers and small-town folk, showing his admiration for the strong, spiritually independent individual as well as his deep affection for the beauty of the Norwegian countryside.

Hamsun was raised in Nordland, a scenic region above the Arctic Circle where his parents owned a small farm called Hamsund. Deciding at an early age to become a writer, Hamsun published three books by the time he was nineteen. Disappointed in his attempts to have his work accepted by a major publisher and frustrated in his efforts to raise money for a university education, he emigrated to the United States during the 1880s, supporting himself by working at various times as a journalist, farmhand, streetcar conductor, and lecturer on world literature. In 1889 he returned to Norway and published the essay collection *Fra det moderne Amerikas aandsliv* (*The Cultural Life of Modern America*), in which he attacked what he considered the shallowness of American thought and the materialism of American society; *The Cultural Life of Modern America* was followed a year later by *Sult* (*Hunger*), the novel many critics consider Hamsun's masterpiece. Following the success of *Hunger,* Hamsun published an article "Fra det ubevisste Sjeleliv" ("From the Unconscious Life of the Mind"), which outlined the literary ideas expanded upon in the lectures on Norwegian literature he gave throughout 1891. Following his plan to create a new psychological literature, Hamsun's most famous novels were written in the 1890s; after the turn of the century, however, Hamsun started writing realistic novels that focused upon social issues. Hamsun wrote little during the 1930s, although by that time he was renowned throughout Europe as a literary master. His reputation plunged in 1940 when he welcomed the invading Nazis into Norway, writing: "Norwegians! Throw away your rifles and return home. The Germans are fighting for us and all neutrals." Hamsun was arrested in 1945 after the fall of Vidkun Quisling's collaborationist government and charged with treason, but, because of his age and allegedly unbalanced mental state, he was not held responsible for his actions. His memoir of the wartime and postwar eras, *Paa gjengrodde stier* (*On Overgrown Paths*), is considered a convincing rebuttal to the charges made against his mental stability. Hamsun died in 1952.

Hamsun's works written from 1890 until the end of his career are often divided into two overlapping periods. During the first, which lasted until approximately 1913, Hamsun wrote what many critics believe to be his finest works: the novels *Hunger, Mysterier* (*Mysteries*), *Pan,* and *Victoria.* Autobiographical in many respects, *Hunger* describes the thoughts of a starving writer who is driven to practice his profession despite the poverty it entails. Unlike much Norwegian literature of the time, *Hunger* is devoid of any overt social message, reflecting Hamsun's desire for a fiction devoted to the psychology of the individual. Believing that individuals are motivated by psychological processes too intricate to be conveyed through traditional literary techniques, he developed an impressionistic method in

Hunger similar to the stream-of-consciousness style later developed by James Joyce. Like *Hunger*, the other novels of Hamsun's early career are concerned with outsiders who live according to nonconformist values. In *Mysteries*, life in a quiet Norwegian coastal town is disrupted when an eccentric stranger suddenly appears in the village and then, a few weeks later, disappears just as abruptly. Through this character, Hamsun revealed his admiration for Friedrich Nietzsche's amoral *Übermensch* ("superman") as well as his contempt for politicians and the infirm elderly. In *Pan* the protagonist is a hunter who lives alone in the forest, while *Victoria* describes a writer's love for an aristocratic woman.

In many of his novels, Hamsun expressed his deep contempt for urban society, which he regarded as a social sickness leading to the conditions he had come to loathe in American cities: low cultural standards, unthinking social conformity, and gullible subservience to an essentially corrupt intellectual and political elite. Owning a farm in southern Norway, Hamsun came to consider himself as much a farmer as a writer, seeing the land and its husbandry as a source of physical, psychological, and spiritual nourishment. This attitude is reflected in the most important of Hamsun's later novels, *Growth of the Soil*, which depicts the life of a rugged, uncomplaining farmer for whom working on the land and enjoying its yield offer a fulfilling purpose in life. Written in a grand, lyrical style reminiscent of the Old Testament, *Growth of the Soil* has received praise for its descriptions of natural beauty as well as unfavorable criticism for its brutal naturalistic elements, such as its frank, impassive account of a mother's strangling of her deformed newborn daughter. Other notable works of Hamsun's later career include *Landstrykere* (*Vagabonds*), *August*, and *Men livet liver* (*The Road Leads On*), a trilogy of sardonically humorous novels concerning the life of a wandering musician and inventor.

From 1940 until the mid 1960s, much of the criticism on Hamsun's work tended to focus on the author's controversial social and political beliefs. Some critics, notably Leo Lowenthal, have traced a totalitarian bent throughout Hamsun's work, citing as evidence his anti-intellectualism, his contempt for democracy, his primitivism, and his glorification of youth and power. Critics have traced many of the controversial aspects of Hamsun's thought to the influence of Arthur Schopenhauer, August Strindberg, and Nietzsche, whose philosophies are reflected in Hamsun's pessimism and exaltation of the amoral individual as well as his disdain for women. In recent years, English and American critics have focused on more traditional thematic and technical aspects of Hamsun's works, particularly his skillful characterization, vivid description of his settings, and the experimental techniques of his early novels. Cited by the German critic Paul Fechter as "the first of the great twentieth-century modernists," Hamsun has been called Norway's greatest literary figure after Henrik Ibsen and acknowledged as a major influence on the work of many of the most prominent writers of the twentieth century.

PRINCIPAL WORKS

Den Gaadefulde (novella) 1877
Fra det moderne Amerikas aandsliv (essays) 1889
[*The Cultural Life of Modern America*, 1969]
Sult (novel) 1890
[*Hunger*, 1899]
Mysterier (novel) 1892
[*Mysteries*, 1927]
Ny Jord (novel) 1893
[*Shallow Soil*, 1914]
Redaktør Lynge (novel) 1893
[*Editor Lynge*, 1901]
Pan (novel) 1894
[*Pan*, 1920]
Ved rigets port (drama) 1895
Livets spil (drama) 1896
Siesta (short stories) 1897
Aftenrøde (drama) 1898
Victoria (novel) 1898
[*Victoria*, 1923]
Munken Vendt (drama) 1902
I æventyrland (novel) 1903
Dronning Tamara (drama) 1904
Svaermere (novel) 1904
[*Dreamers*, 1921; also published as *Mothwise*, 1921]
Under høstsjernen (novel) 1906
[*Under the Autumn Star*, published in *Wanderers*, 1922; also published in *The Wanderer*, 1975]
Benoni (novel) 1908
[*Benoni*, 1925]
Rosa (novel) 1908
[*Rosa*, 1926]
En vandrer spiller med sordin (novel) 1909
[*A Wanderer Plays on Muted Strings*, published in *Wanderers*, 1922; also published in *The Wanderer*, 1975]
Livet ivold (drama) 1910
[*In the Grip of Life*, 1924]
Den sidste glæde (novel) 1912
[*Look Back on Happiness*, 1940]
Børn av tiden (novel) 1913
[*Children of the Age*, 1924]
Segelfoss by (novel) 1915
[*Segelfoss Town*, 1925]
Markens grøde (novel) 1917
[*Growth of the Soil*, 1920]
Konerne ved vandposten (novel) 1920
[*The Women at the Pump*, 1928]
Siste kapitel (novel) 1923
[*Chapter the Last*, 1929]
Landstrykere (novel) 1927
[*Vagabonds*, 1930; also published as *Wayfarers*, 1980]
August (novel) 1930
[*August*, 1931]
Men livet lever (novel) 1933
[*The Road Leads On*, 1934]
Ringen sluttet (novel) 1936
[*The Ring Is Closed*, 1937]
Paa gjengrodde stier (memoirs) 1949
[*On Overgrown Paths*, 1967]

CRITICISM

Brian W. Downs   (essay date 1966)

[*In the following excerpt, Downs outlines the character-istic elements of Hamsun's drama and fiction.*]

In the succession of great Norwegian authors Knut Hamsun ran true to type in one respect at least. He was a publicist, fertile and wide-ranging, as well as a writer of fiction, drama and poetry. Faithful as he remained to the ideal of 'art for art's sake', accepted by almost all who came to the front at the same time as he, he kept, however, the two sides of his activity in watertight compartments. Although his total personality invites a study of profound interest, literary history can ignore many aspects of it.

With *Hunger* (*Sult,* 1890), in which he first made his assumed name famous, he produced at once a perfect specimen of the literature he was pleading for in the denunciation of his 'utilitarian' seniors, a piece of pure impressionism. Everything in it is just as it seems to the narrator, a man near to extinction from starvation, wandering homeless and friendless through Christiania town. He is never seen from outside, rarely forms part of a composition in which he is one of the figures. One hears occasionally of the pains in his body, but even his speculations on what is going on there take an insignificant place compared with the sights seen through his eyes and the welter of other thoughts that race or mull in his mind. The alternations induced by his condition between mental haze, sudden spurts of revolt or joy and the preternatural sharpening of the senses, projected in isolated scenes of extreme concrete vividness, provide for a variety and sense of completeness that make *Hunger* a *tour de force* unsurpassed in its kind by any of the French psychologists whose example he wished followed.

Hamsun never wrote nor tried to write another completely egocentric work like *Hunger.* The impressionistic manner, there carried to the extreme, came, however, to characterize all his most distinguished writing. It took on a new perspective through the impressions received by invented characters—a good deal of his superb natural descriptions comes in that way—and through the impressions of an uninvolved, neutral spectator of their doings.

Two long steps towards his perfected technique were made very quickly after *Hunger*: *Mysteries* (*Mysterier,* 1892) and *Pan* (1894).

Between *Mysteries* and *Pan,* in 1893, Hamsun published two novels very different in kind from them: *Editor Lynge* (*Redaktør Lynge* and *New Ground* (*Ny Jord*). They have a Christiania setting, are told in a middle-of-the-road realistic manner and have nothing of mystery, fantasy, poetry or 'soul' about them. Such interest as they possess lies in the view Hamsun takes of society around him. It is a low one. The savagery with which he pillories the agents of publicity in their mere opportunist commercialism is only equalled by his contempt for their weak-kneed, debauched clients, the artists and writers, who puff themselves out with the claim that they are breaking new ground—and what ground, a putrid swamp! By contrast with them

stand some solid, hard-working entrepreneurs, who really produce something. Linked with these two novels by similar *milieu* and the reintroduction of a character from them—a recurring phenomenon in Hamsun's *œuvre,* as with so many Norwegian authors—is his first play, *At the Gates of the Kingdom* (*Ved Rigets Port,* 1895). It deals with the pressure put upon a research student of philosophy to modify his unconventional tenets with a view to the advancement in his career so urgently demanded by his poverty. In Kareno's racking struggle with his conscience and his manuscript he neglects his loving, but quite uncomprehending little wife; and in the end he is left deserted by her for a more assiduous lover and desperately working at the emasculation of his dissertation so that it may gain the approval of the academic Establishment and the loaves and fishes in its gift.

At the Gates of the Kingdom moves on a high level of intellectual and 'human' interest. It is good 'theatre' too. The domestic crisis through which Kareno passes has some almost unbearably poignant moments, curiously heightened by his very imperfect awareness of it. But, in view of the strictures which Hamsun passed on the drama that was generally acclaimed, it is curious also in being somewhat conventional, and that in more than its outward guise. In moments of exceptional inspiration Gunnar Heiberg might have written it, and—of all things—it suggests at once a comparison with *Hedda Gabler,* Ibsen's own nearest approach to the fashionable drama of the time. The cards may be shuffled, but we are presented with another brilliant and original, defeated scholar, and again we have man of learning at the heart of a grave matrimonial crisis which almost passes over his head. And it is much to be doubted whether, gauged by *Hedda Gabler,* Hamsun succeeded in imparting to his play the psychological subtlety and authenticity in which, he held, drama had been so lamentably deficient.

Hamsun presumably recognized this: that the coarsening and simplifying which he stigmatized in a Shakespeare, a Holberg and an Ibsen are inevitable in the conditions of dramatic presentation. Certainly, after *The Gates of the Kingdom,* he avowed that he wrote plays only for the royalties they might bring in, and they never came near such artistic success as his first venture had attained. The two sequels to it, *The Play of Life* (*Livets Spil,* 1896) and *Evening Glow* (*Aftenrøde,* 1898), which show Kareno's progressive degeneration, and *In the Grip of Life* (*Livet Ivold,* 1910) are a muddle of intentions and of talk, punctuated by high explosives.

The hope of gain, however, can hardly have lured Hamsun to his two remaining dramatic ventures, the prose tragedy *Queen Tamara* (*Dronning Tamara,* 1903), which the enemy of historicism wrote about a virtually unknown Caucasian princess of the thirteenth century, and *Monk Vendt* (*Munken Vendt,* 1902), likewise laid in the past and 'romantic' in its allures; he must have anticipated that theatre-audiences of every kind would assign them at once to the *genre ennuyeux.* Some of Hamsun's distinguishing qualities, certainly, are allowed to appear—ecstatic outbursts, the insistence on human incalculability, for instance—but for dramatic effectiveness such are handicaps rather than advantages. *Monk Vendt* (a nickname, attributable to a bald pate and a little knowledge of Latin) possesses, however, two points of adventitious interest: written in rhymed verse, sufficiently 'correct', but wooden in its rhythms and very long-winded (there are eight acts of it), it marks Hamsun's public début as a poet; and in the hero, something of a Peer Gynt, as Kinck's Horse-Coper was to be, he presented in full length the character of the vagabond, who in a variety of guises was to reappear in all his later books.

During the eight years following on *Pan* Hamsun had written little that gave scope to his finest qualities. His best of this time was the novel *Victoria* (1898), a tragic little story, told with a tenderness that avoids all sentimentality, of the poor village boy—a poet to boot—who loves the squire's daughter. In 1903 and 1904, however, two volumes came out which gave a new relief to his personality and his art. *In Fairy-Tale Land* (*I Æventyrland*), called forth by the long journey he made right through Russia to the Caucasus and the fringe of Persia, is one of the most brilliant of travel-books. It is, as one might expect, an entirely personal record—no history, no archaeology, no statistics, no politics, a minimum of 'social' speculation, let alone political prophecy. It rests content with conveying in a superb unforced style, shot with the irony that from now on becomes steadily pervasive in Hamsun's manner, the magnificences, squalors and personal predicaments that crowded in on his senses from nature, strange races and fellow-travellers, and the wonder, the joy rising to ecstasy with which they filled him.

The second book was his collection of verse, *The Wild Choir* (*Det vilde Kor*, 1904). Hamsun's approach to poetry sounds unusual; it is, he declared, 'the only form of literature which is not at the same time pretentious and meaningless, but is simply meaningless [*intetsigende*, nothing-saying]'. A less brusque way of putting it would be to say that it is, or should be, purely lyrical. So interpreted, Hamsun's practice conformed to his theory; the contents of *The Wild Choir* are all what an earlier generation would have called effusions. Some are short reproductions of a fleeting sight of sentiment, in which the personal is usually brought out at once by the use of the first person present:

> *Jeg* vanker indover det brune Fjeld . . . ;
>
> *Jeg* blaser med Tuten *min egen* Basun . . . ;
>
> Det synger i *mig* en Tone . . . ;

and, simple and regular though their structure may be, from time to time a unique, elegiac beauty rises out of it. . . .

As the irony approaches satire, Hamsun's poetry, despite his disclaimer, *does* occasionally 'say something'. His dislikes enter in: his antipathy to the proletariat and the Christian religion, to Arctic explorers and champions of 'welfare', to feminism and the ideal of universal peace. More unexpected is the positive factor, the admiration he expresses for Byron, for the Swiss painter Böcklin, for Drachmann ('the last singer in the land') and, in two magnificent poems, for Bjørnson.

Three heterogeneous elements characterize Hamsun's greatest fiction. They are the figure of the wanderer; the evocation of the remote, vast Nordland; and the indissoluble mixture of sympathy and ironic detachment with which those who live their lives in its wastes, homesteads and little towns is presented. One or other of these elements often predominates (or may be absent), but, usually, in varying proportions, they form his unique amalgam.

There is a faint flavor of the fairy tale about Hamsun's novels. What quickly strikes the reader is the somewhat capricious way in which his characters respond to common circumstances and the apparent gratuitousness of their behavior. All this inevitably causes one to cock an ear for the clash of symbols.

—*D. J. Enright, in his* Man Is an Onion: Reviews and Essays, *1972.*

The figure of the wanderer fascinated Hamsun all his life through, all the more strongly perhaps when the experience of the long, grim years when he was but a sojourner in two hemispheres were well behind him. *In Fairy-Tale Land* had shown him a zestful and adventurous traveller, but his middle and later years very rarely took him far afield, divided as they were between the cares of his estate and the strict, long office-hours he kept over his manuscripts.

The wanderer takes on many guises, from the lay-about of *Hunger* to the old man who called his last book *On Overgrown Paths.* He may be little more than an unuprooted piece of seaweed floating backwards and forwards at the mercy of the tide or he may be a mighty hunter before the Lord, like Lieutenant Glahn. After the heroes of *Hunger, Mysteries, Pan* and *Monk Vendt,* an odd variant appears in the titular hero of *Benoni* and its sequel *Rosa* (both of 1908). A postman to begin with and then, when he has been sacked from the public service, a prosperous fish-dealer, he certainly leads a fairly peripatetic life in both capacities. Primarily, however, he is a *parvenu* adventurer, recklessly pursuing the main chance in business, towards which Hamsun's attitude was typically ambivalent. The sedentary shop-keeper was his pet aversion, but from risk-taking enterprise of all sorts, especially if it proved successful, he could not withhold all admiration.

Benoni and *Rosa,* where the telling of a moderately complicated story with a good deal of bustle and superficial intrigue seems to be the author's chief concern, formed an undistinguished interlude in the composition of three linked novels with which Hamsun's second great period of creation may be said to begin: *Under the Autumn Star* (*Under Høstsjernen,* 1906), *A Wanderer plays on muted Strings* (*En Vandrer spiller med Sordin,* 1909) and *The Last Joy* (*Den sidste Glæde,* 1912). The wanderer here is not in the least an adventurer; in character, and what his mind makes of his experiences he is much more like what Hamsun himself would have been had he taken to the road, and that point is, in fact, doubly driven home by the use of the first person singular throughout and by giving the fictitious narrator Hamsun's proper name, Knut Pedersen. An honest, hard-working labourer, not in his first youth, he comes from a spell of road-making into the service of Captain Falkenberg, a country gentleman, and the first two parts of the trilogy (which in all covers some thirty years) centre on his life there. It is fairly colourful. His appearance and good manners recommend him to the ladies, and three of them are amorously attracted to him; in one case, that of his master's wife, the attraction is reciprocated, but nothing tangible comes of these affairs, and the wanderer leaves his job. Colour there may be, but it is matt. The air and light of autumn are over all. Intelligent and fine-feeling, Knut observes and speculates on the little world around him and, not least, on himself. More accurately, perhaps, he reflects on them: the opening of *Under the Autumn Star* makes clear that what he is recounting took place many years ago, indeed that his viewpoint is that reached at the end of the trilogy.

The minor key which is maintained throughout and gives the whole its distinctive soft beauty is announced by the title of the second part, *A Wanderer plays on muted Strings;* Knut returns after six years to his old employer, and his old love for Fru Falkenberg, now a desperately unhappy woman, revives—with the same negative outcome. In *Under the Autumn Star* he had learned to master his passion, now he is resigned to its futility. A fatal accident to Fru Falkenberg sets the full stop to it, and Knut goes off on his wanderings once more. *The Last Joy* is supposed to take place when Knut, become an elderly (and, against expectation, a well-to-do) man, all passion spent, has settled down in solitude as a 'universal uncle', unobtrusively watching over and helping those for whom he feels affection. The tints throughout have been those of the amazing Norwegian autumn, and now they are merging into winter. His last joy is not even beneficence or the sight of a new generation growing up, but the great peace of immersing himself in the impassive vastness of the earth about him and the stars above.

In the linked novels *Children of the Age (Børn av Tiden,* 1913) and *Segelfoss Town (Segelfoss By,* 1915) Hamsun covered his widest canvas to produce two indubitable masterpieces. The background is twofold: the immense expanse of Nordland land, water and sky, usually in their benign aspect, and, on the other hand, the lonely little community that becomes Segelfoss Town, with its comings and goings, troubles, aspirations and successes. Nowhere is the time of action precisely stated, but, somewhat foreshortened, it is the span of fifty years in which Hamsun had known Hamarøy; the *Children of the Age* and *Segelfoss Town* make up a chapter of social history as surely as does Zola's Rougon-Macquart series. But the means employed are as different as the ambience; there are no elaborately detailed inventories, no melodramatic abysses or sublimities, no 'close-ups' of passion or brawling, neither Machiavellian intrigues nor the stirrings of mass-emotion. Steadily, but with kindly irony, an Olympian

looks down on the ant-hill below, fully aware of all that goes on in the homes and hearts of his creatures, even if he does not always see fit to tell of everything he knows.

In the forefront of his panorama, but still small to the Olympian eye, are three figures—a fourth is advancing to join them—who, successively dethroning one another, have, it may be said, the fortunes of the neighbourhood in their hands. The first is the hereditary 'lord of the manor' Lieutenant Willatz Holmsen, the stoic who unobtrusively holds patriarchal sway over his crofters and fishermen, helping their families in distress, paying their debts and having their promising children educated, even when he detests them, as a plain matter of inherited duty. He is succeeded by Holmengraa, the 'wanderer' of the story, the energetic adventurer who suddenly appears from the Cordilleras, bit by bit buys up Willatz Holmsen's bankrupt estate, uses it for building saw-mills, granaries, wharves, new houses for the work-people and the like, and then disappears again, leaving the field to Theodor paa Bua, the shopkeeper of the now sizeable settlement, which runs to a hotel (victualled by thefts from Holmengraa's stores), with café, dance-hall and theatre, and a regular service by mail-steamer.

Olympian though Hamsun's viewpoint may be, his detachment—the 'I' has disappeared from his narratives—is not complete. Jove, while sincerely if uneffusively loving his creatures, even the sinners and wastrels among them, also judges them. In his tacit summing-up, he notes a degradation. The entrepreneur Holmengraa, much cleverer, much better versed in the ways of the Age that has caught up with Lieutenant Willatz Holmsen, has none of his innate sense of values, no sense of the dignity due to himself and all men. Yet he creates something, brings work and prosperity to a poor stagnant village. His supplanter, Theodor paa Bua, merely buys and sells what others have made, a monopolist battening on a community that has gone awhoring after the idols of the market-place. This steady undertow of deep pessimism stirs the web and woof of Hamsun's irony and empathy, to give them, as it were, a third dimension.

Growth of the Soil (Markens Grøde, 1917) is 'O, Pioneers' in the guise of a saga; commerce and speculation come into it, only to vanish like the smoke of an autumn bonfire. Isak, a 'great barge of a man', comes to Sellanraa, an uninhabited tract of land verging on moor, half a day's journey from the nearest settlement, sets to, all by himself, to clear and break it up, erects his cabin and (after all this has been done) obtains a legal title to the holding. He takes to wife his hare-lipped servant girl Inger, who labours by his side as valiantly as he. For long unaided, they fell, plough, sow, reap and raise stock; they raise also a small family and, bit by bit, the buildings and appurtenances of a complete, self-supporting, perpetually working homestead. Their example spreads. By the time the story ends, twenty-five years or so from the beginning, ten family farms have struggled up in the unpeopled waste. This pioneers' saga, which in itself has all the charms of a Robinson Crusoe story, with the realistic but almost laconically presented details that Hamsun knew from his own experiences, is diversified by incidents, both in the domestic and in a slightly wider sphere—but they are incidents, almost brushed off as irrelevancies, and always leading back to the steady plodding of the main theme. Inger, seeing that her third baby has a hare-lip too, at once wrings its neck and buries it, but a little act of piety betrays the deed, and she is away from Sellanraa for six years expiating it in prison. Isak—who suspected what had happened, but steadfastly adhered to his principle of 'least said, soonest mended'—utters no word of reproach or lamentation, and when, as naturally as a homing-pigeon, Inger returns to Sellanraa, they just go on as before—plus a sewing-machine. Copper is found on their holding, attracts speculators and is worked for a time, but turns out unprofitable. Isak gets a certain amount of cash for his mineral rights, but it all drips away through the pocket of his 'refined' elder boy, who sets up as a shopkeeper for the new community and has to decamp to the United States. But there are left his younger brother, a hefty chip of the old block, and the girl who will probably marry an enterprising neighbour. Soon Isak and Inger will retire to the small 'dower-house' with which he has rounded off his building programme, and the growth of the soil, laboured for and contemplated in peace and contentment, will go its unbroken way around them.

The horizon of Isak's saga is as far as he can see; it is broad enough, but not as wide as that conjured up in the Segelfoss books, and the distance from which it is seen is not so great. There is still some irony, however, to give perspective, very quiet, indeed affectionate: in the presentation of Inger, for instance, the devoted helpmeet, who goes off the rails from time to time, to pietism and adultery and her tragic crime, and who eventually acquires a great local reputation as an arbiter of fashion for which the sewing-room of Trondheim gaol has given her the necessary qualification. The author's detachment, however, is not so complete as when he surveyed Segelfoss. Jove, one may say, has been replaced by the Jehovah of *Genesis,* who 'saw everything that he had made, and, behold, it was very good'.

The Growth of the Soil betrays even a curious little piece of self-involvement on Hamsun's part. It escapes from the 'wanderer' of the tale, Geissler—like Benoni, a dismissed civil servant—who pops up from nowhere, kindly, understanding and helpful, whenever a crisis is upon Isak and then vanishes again, on no one knows what errand. Suddenly the man recalls a bridge and smells again the smell from it he knew as a child, and that bridge is firmly designated as that at Garmo, where Hamsun himself was born. Is Geissler, the man whom nothing can hold and who plays Providence whenever he appears, another variant of the wanderer that Hamsun would have liked to have been?

Most of those who have dealings with Geissler distrust him, now shabby and penniless, at other times, it seems, bursting with cash, always lavish with what he has. How warmly, if at all, do his ceaseless comings and goings, his plans and stamped papers, feather his own nest? How much of a fox is he? And, by extension, how much of a fox was Hamsun?

If Hamsun was a fox, he never played his game better than when he qualified for the Nobel Prize with *Growth of the Soil.* It not only exhibited his art at its most superb—in the world of 1920 the Swedish Academy could have found none with a stronger claim on that count. But it was also, one might say, custom-built to the conditions of the award, and in that measure, most famous of his books though it may be, it is untypical. The 'idealistic tendency' stipulated by the founder, scarcely discernible elsewhere, here is both pervasive and stated in words of naked appeal to all who, like the Swedes and Norwegians, had just faced economic isolation in the World War: 'Behold, a tiller of the ground, body and soul; a worker on the land without respite. A ghost risen out of the past to point to the future, a man from the earliest days of cultivation, a settler in the wilds, and withal a man of the day'.

For another twenty years Hamsun's productivity continued unabated; but it is more than doubtful whether any of his later novels would have met that exacting condition for a Nobel Prize award which in its day had non-suited Ibsen. He concentrated again on the rootless man, sometimes in an openly humorous vein—the trilogy *Tramps* (*Landstrykere,* 1927), *August* (1930), *But Life is Alive* (*Men Livet Lever,* 1933)—sometimes with kindly resignation, as in the last, *The Ring Closed* (*Ringen sluttet,* 1936), sometimes with a biting, if restrained, irony; nothing that looks at all like a model of edification is provided.

The Women at the Pump (*Konerne ved Vandposten,* 1920), the next book to follow on *Growth of the Soil,* displays Hamsun's more characteristic art in its perfection. Such story as it may be said to have revolves round the most degenerate type of humanity that Hamsun was to exhibit in full, a hypocritical wittol and eunuch. (Nevertheless, the Olympian who once more holds the pen cannot disguise some admiration for the tenacity with which he wriggles his way along through the slime.) His environment, effectually quelling any who in any way try to rise above it, is as rotten as he—a Segelfoss at one step lower in degeneration. The originality, even attraction of what is, over all, a disgusting and depressing chronicle of moral squalor—not deficient, however, in opportunities for much sardonic humour—lies in the manner of its telling. Substantially all is conveyed through the tattle of the town's housewives as they draw their water at the pump. Literary impressionism carried to the extreme, it has the effect of listening in to a tangle of conversations in a telephone exchange, with its abrupt switches from one line to another, its unanswered questions and answers to questions which can only be guessed at, its tantalizing gaps, the occasional exclamations of someone—is it the God in the machine?—breaking into the dialogues or monologues. But mosaic bit by mosaic bit, the day's gossip builds up a full picture of the gossipers' community and the lives of those of their neighbours which most intrigue them. The sardonic upshot, quite literally, speaks for itself. Even if the Women at the Pump are little more than gabbling automata, through them Hamsun created the supreme example of his special 'psychology', a stream-of-consciousness novel transposed from the reactions of the individual to those of a community. It exemplifies too the break-up, in a master's hands, of the century-old European novel-form, and for that reason may fitly be placed side by side with the *Ulysses* that James Joyce was writing just at the same time. (pp. 174-88)

Brian W. Downs, "Kinck and Hamsun," in his Modern Norwegian Literature, 1860-1918, *Cambridge at the University Press, 1966, pp. 165-88.*

Harald Naess   (essay date 1975)

[*In the following excerpt, Naess discusses Hamsun's concept of the hero by examining the protagonists of his novels.*]

Knut Hamsun called his last novel *The Ring is Closed,* and, though he is not known to have said in particular what he meant by the title, most readers will feel that it conveys some sense of finality, like a return to the original point of departure. But it is not easy to decide whether it applies only to the action of the novel in question, or to Hamsun's whole opus, symbolizing somehow the breaking of his magic wand. However that may be, I shall use the title metaphorically in an attempt to come up with a formula for the Hamsun hero. The ring will be taken to mean not the hero's return to the point of departure, but rather a ramification of his road, with two major avenues parting and converging as the ring is closed. Already Hamsun's first novelette, *The Enigmatic One,* which was referred to by its publisher as scribbled nonsense, has the beginnings of this dichotomy. The weft of Hamsun's rich texture—what Georg Brandes called "the infinitely small"—is almost totally lacking, but in return the warp—what Brandes referred to as "the infinitely great"—is almost entirely exposed, giving the book its special interest for students of literature. It is a very rudimentary tale of a poor country boy, Rolf Andersen, who wins the rich man's daughter—actually a variation of the myth of the disguised prince, since the boy, as it later turns out, is really Knut Sonnenfield, the son of a wealthy city merchant. Hamsun, however, is less interested in the dramatic effect when the enigmatic character finally throws off his guise, than he is in the way this character taxes the townspeople's curiosity. Hence Hamsun's first book is a romantic work, not only because of its fantastic course of events, but also because the author has chosen as protagonist an outsider who fools the whole parish.

The Enigmatic One appeared in the heyday of Norwegian realism, whose heroes, like Torbjørn Granlien (of Bjørnson's *Sunny Hill*), conquered themselves and then went on to become pillars of the community. This realism is not without sentimental moments, as when Torbjørn plants Solveig's flowers during the night, but it is still different from the kind of romanticism Hamsun displayed when he provided his budding businessman with the following burst of *Weltschmerz:*

> Today—or rather this evening—Rolf had a different suit on. This time it was gray worsted. It consisted of: a coat, or jacket, pants, leather shoes with brass buckles, and a double-breasted vest, and finally a velvet cap with a visor, all of the latest cut. In these clothes, which suited him so well, Rolf looked like a gentleman, and he also walked on the road like one. When he had come to the top of the hill near Aabakken, he sat down on a place covered with red flowers and

> gathered some of the most beautiful into a bouquet. It was as nice a bouquet as anyone could wish for. Its center was a carnation. When the bouquet was done, he placed it in a rubber strap on the left side of his cap. It now suited him much better. He looked like a verituoso [*en Verituos*], on whose head a lady had placed a wreath. He then sat down supporting his head in his hand, looked straight ahead, and thought of the last time he was here and with whom. As he sat there, the bouquet fell from his hat. He looked at it. He said to himself: Dust. From dust we have come and unto dust we shall return. It will happen to us what has happened to these flowers, one moment flourish and bloom but then wither and fall into the grave. Oh "if we were only then prepared."

> [*The Enigmatic One*]

The quote is meant to be as deadly serious as the rest of this curious first work, which Hamsun never wanted to see reprinted till after his ninetieth year. By that time he had created many practical country boys who tried to win princesses. And, if he temporarily repressed the "verituoso passage" like some dark shed where his hero first bared himself to innocent readers, after long years of failure in Europe and America, where he learned to laugh at himself, he turned that shed into a theatrical dressing room from which he fitted out a series of tragicomic protagonists in striking garments. Even if *The Enigmatic One* is scribbled nonsense, it contains the beginnings of the romantic irony that characterizes all Hamsun's art and that is already fully developed in his great novels of the nineties.

For all their differences—the humor of *Hunger,* the mystery of *Mysteries,* the poetry of *Pan,* the sweetness of *Victoria*—these novels do form some sort of unity, and in their roughest shape the protagonists have all come from the same mold. In them Hamsun has realized his own expressed ambition to arrive in a small town completely unannounced, live there incognito for some time, and then disappear as mysteriously as he came. The protagonists are all visitors trying to make a living in a foreign milieu and, finding that the experiment does not work, in the end taking their leave. In *Hunger* a young writer from the country spends the fall season in Kristiania; in *Mysteries* another young man, presumably with some big-city background, spends a summer in a small coastal town; in *Pan* a lieutenant from Kristiania stays from spring to fall in a small fishing village up north. The case is somewhat different in *Victoria,* in that Johannes, a poet, is socially rather than geographically displaced; his temporary visit does not so much concern a different locality as a different class: he is the miller's son among the landed gentry.

Furthermore, the protagonists are androgynous in much the same manner as Strindberg in Hamsun's early description of him; Strindberg, he said, was partly coarse and tough as a butcher, partly delicate as a woman. "Tangen" in *Hunger* is strong enough to push a streetcar, yet his poor eyesight makes him unfit for service in the fire brigade. Nagel is known for his broad shoulders, but he is of small stature and has the delicate mouth of a woman. Glahn is a commanding officer, yet in company with people he is not only unimposing, but also awkward and timid. Johannes again is somewhat different, actually quite a healthy farm boy, but he tortures Camilla by saying he has thrown away her gifts to him, and, on the other hand, the tone of his stories shows him as possessing the soft sensitivity of women. He, like the rest of these heroes, falls into a category usually referred to by psychologists as sadomasochist.

It is significant that all these protagonists are artists or at least artistically gifted. Johannes and "Tangen" are writers, Glahn is a very literary kind of diarist, and Nagel, the teller of fantastic stories, impresses the townspeople as being a rather unusual agronomist. The popular image of artists as unconventional people suits these characters; they are outsiders of a special kind looking for a lost paradise, even though their search has so far led them nowhere near the goal. Yet the fact that they are still at the scene, rather than dead by their own hands, shows that they wish to make one last attempt to find the lost paradise, even at the cost of having to adapt themselves painfully to the norms of modern society. This is their experiment, and its various stages are presented on many levels, realistic and symbolic, sometimes humorous, sometimes tragic or pathetic. More particularly the experiment is presented symbolically in the love story that each book contains. The protagonist finds that a woman is able to give new or different meaning to his existence. She appears at first like an exotic princess or a refreshing child of nature—Ylajali reclining on a bed of yellow roses, or Iselin, or simply Dagny; but this dream does not last. The original paradise gives way to its fake imitation: Ylajali is just an average Kristiania girl, Edvarda is an unkempt, ignorant child, and Dagny, whom the hero now refers to as Dangny, is nothing more than the perfect wife for her naval officer. Victoria is different, but, for all her admired aristocratic qualities, her allegiance is to society: she does the so-called right thing in order to save her family's reputation.

The attempt to approach society through a woman's love, then, is no more likely to bring success than is marriage to one of these women. These men are not made for happiness, and deep down they must know that their lovers are as fake as the society they represent. They are all romantic protagonists; their world is the dream world of Goethe's Werther.

At this point it might be useful to ask what Hamsun had hoped to achieve as a writer after his last return from America. In the articles entitled **"Kristofer Janson"** and **"From the Unconscious Life of the Mind,"** and particularly in his three lectures on literature in 1890 and 1891, Hamsun had presented a fragmentary theory of a new fictional hero. First and foremost, this hero would be more complex than the heroes of the Norwegian naturalist movement, who were made according to Taine's formula of the *faculté maîtresse.* In their stead Hamsun would place a personality that was split and multiplied, feverish, with bleeding nerves. The novelist's task was to investigate the roots of this hero's instincts, or, in his favorite anatomic terminology, the intestines of his soul. Hamsun, though he did not say anything about this hero's *Weltanschauung,* was very explicit about his own; he was against positivism,

materialism, democracy, science, and Christianity, and his heroes naturally reflect these sentiments. Hamsun's novels, then, after a generation of realistic Norwegian *Bildungs-romane* from *Sunny Hill* to *St. John's Festival,* reinstate the romantic protagonist. This protagonist shares the antisocial stand, if not the revolutionary spirit, of the early Byronic hero; he also shares the crippling ambivalence of the later romantic nonhero, as in the works of Stendhal and, particularly, the great Russians Lermontov and Dostoevsky. He is new mostly because of a self-consciously humorous approach to his own excessively nervous temperament, what Hamsun calls his neurasthenia, and what other people have called decadence. The morbid disposition of Hamsun's hero, however, applies only to his mind; physically he is of extraordinary health, and for this reason alone the word *decadent* in its conventional sense may seem out of place. In the light of his later development, it would probably be correct to say that, under his neurasthenic surface, Hamsun's hero from the nineties possesses qualities that correspond to the following unusual definition. The decadent, says Anatole Baju, a literary critic of the period, "is a man of progress. He is clean, economic, hard working and regular in all his habits. A man of simple attitudes and correct in his morals, his ideal is to find the beautiful in the good and he strives to bring his act into harmony with his theories. He is a master of his mind, which he has learned to control, he has the quiet placidity of a sage, and the virtues of a stoic."

This definition is a good starting point for a discussion of the concept of the double in Hamsun's novels, what Hamsun himself in one of his literary lectures referred to as double consciousness. In **Hunger** there are several scenes in which the protagonist hears and sees himself as a strange person; parts of his body are alienated, then assume personality, becoming himself looking at himself. One further step is the actual creation of a kind of double, in **Hunger** an old cripple who waddles in front of the protagonist, stopping when he stops, walking when he walks, and destroying his happy morning mood with his ugly looks and gait. In Hamsun's next novel, **Mysteries,** the old cripple is easily recognizable as the person called the Midget, with the difference that in the latter novel he has a much more central position; he is an important minor character and endowed with independent action: just as Nagel observes and plots against the Midget, so the Midget observes and plots against Nagel. More than any other single feature, the presence of characters like the Midget in Hamsun's work shows him as the new romantic writer. His mode is ironic; everything beautiful must call forth its counterpart.

The master of romantic caricature in Norwegian literature is Henrik Ibsen, but, with the exception of *Peer Gynt,* Hamsun had little understanding of the dramatist's work, as one would expect. The characters Rosmer and Brendel are a romantic pair of the kind Hamsun used in **Mysteries,** but with the important difference that Rosmer's aristocracy, unlike Nagel's, is of a Christian kind: to be noble is to forgive. Hamsun, to whom aristocracy was synonymous with pride, strength, and an inborn sense of security, had nothing but contempt for Ibsen's ideal. "Rosmer is soft and tender," he writes; "he is so helplessly noble that he is happy when Ulrik Brendel fools him again and again to get money for drink." Hamsun's romantic pair is differently arranged. The Midget, as clown, provides a caricature of Nagel's exhibitionism, but he is at the same time a carrier of Rosmer's Christian ideals, while Nagel is a man of Nietzschean views. Since *Mysteries* is a detective story, the difference between appearance and reality is particularly important. Nagel's task as private investigator is to search for immoral motives behind the Midget's meek countenance of Christian love. In later works the cripple from *Hunger* will undergo many changes; the Christian elements will be fused with qualities found in the clown-artist—such as inconstancy, drunkenness, impotence—but always they will be defined by their opposite, which is a morality based on noblesse oblige. Nagel, for all his clownishness, has a side to his personality that refuses to be degraded by life; and the protagonist of *Hunger,* in the midst of all his suffering, is always concerned about keeping up his moral standards. A striking reversal of this dichotomy, whereby society is upheld against the outsider, is seen in one novel from the 1890's, *Shallow Soil.* Here the protagonist is a hard-working businessman surrounded by artistic parasites. His temperament is in most respects the opposite of Nagel's, but he shares with him a deep sense of moral propriety, which makes it impossible for him to go on living after his sweetheart's loss of innocence.

In addition to presenting protagonists who gradually fall more and more distinctly into categories that could be referred to as either moralistic or artistic, Hamsun in the 1890's began to develop a technical differentiation that gradually assumed great importance. For all its advantages of immediacy, the first-person novel lacks the multiple perspectives of the third-person narrative, and authors have naturally looked for ways in which to expand its single-tracked viewpoint. In *Hunger* the protagonist is sometimes able to view himself from the outside; in *Mysteries*—a third-person novel with a single viewpoint—Nagel sees in the Midget a symbol of certain negative qualities in himself, so that when Nagel and the Midget discuss a third person, for instance Dagny Kielland, one view serves as a corrective of the other. In *Pan* Hamsun provides two entirely different viewpoints: Glahn's diary is followed by an epilogue in which one of his hunting companions tells the story of Glahn's death in India. Hamsun, however, did not use this technique again. Rather than using two narrators, he construes the plot in such a way that the characters, regardless of temperament, serve mainly one of two functions, being either participants or observers. The observer is usually an artist-protagonist rather than a moralist-protagonist, and in most cases he is also personally involved in the action. He is usually, but need not be, a central character.

Now, after these preliminary notes, I would like to approach some of the major protagonists in Hamsun's work in the twentieth century. In its first decade Hamsun wrote ten books that form an intermezzo in his production, pointing backward to the great individualistic works of the nineties as well as forward to the monumental epics of the World War I period. They are at once humorous, poetic,

and polemic, and they illustrate not only his problems of marriage and age, but also a growing need to leave the fin de siècle camp and orient himself in the new century. Like his contemporary, the Norwegian painter Edvard Munch, who shifted his interest from the violent love and death scenes of the so-called *Life Frieze* over lyrical landscapes to the monumental Aula decorations, so Knut Hamsun moves from the city to the country, and, while he still worships the young, it is not now so much for their neurasthenia, as for their greater physical strength. Norway during these years gained independence from Sweden and emancipated itself economically, and Hamsun's attitude to such a show of energy can be seen in his praise of enterprise in the two great poems honoring Bjørnstjerne Bjørnson. However, his attitude is again one of ambivalence: he is of two minds about the industrialization of Norway, and he also recognizes that, at fifty, he cannot be part of the new order except as a spectator and commentator. This recognition colors the six novels he wrote between 1903 and 1912. They fall into two categories, one more humorous and purely entertaining—*Mothwise, Benoni,* and *Rosa*—and one more poetic and polemic—the trilogy about the wanderer.

The *Wanderers* novels do not possess the kind of unity one expects from a trilogy. The first two books, with their petty landed gentry, have a quasi-feudal atmosphere reminiscent of *Victoria,* while the third, with different characters and the setting of a modern mountain hotel, points forward to Hamsun's later social satires. What holds the works together, besides a general poetic tone, is the extraordinary protagonist Knut Pedersen. He shares with Hamsun's older heroes a sudden and mysterious arrival on the scene, but his flight is less dramatic, as are his actions. His pains and pleasures derive from vicarious living; he is a masochist more than a sadist, less participant, more observer and voyeur. There is no mistaking his excitement as he watches the seduction of his beloved and much admired Lovise Falkenberg by a young, unsympathetic engineer; yet he identifies with her stoical husband and would do anything to help improve the relationship between this lord and his lady. In the last volume, Ingeborg Thorsen's adventures with a young actor strike him again with the painful pleasures of jealousy, but he is also instrumental in getting her married to healthy, uncomplicated Nikolai Palm. Just as these books, judged by their quality, could be referred to as an intermezzo in Hamsun's production, so the protagonist is caught, as it were, between the battles. Rather than concentrating on his own hopeless social experiment, he is helping others succeed with theirs: like Bjørnson's King Sverre (*Between the Battles*), Knut Pedersen is a disguised God. The author is actually describing his own problems of jealousy and age: Ingeborg Thorsen with her college degree and actor friends is easily recognizable as Hamsun's second wife, Marie Andersen, and this almost complete lack of distance has shaped the style of these books, which resemble nothing so much as Hamsun's autobiography (published in 1949). The exuberance of his earlier works is gone, and, though the humor of *Hunger* has been revived after several serious books, this humor is low-keyed; the irony, when it is turned against the protagonist himself, has a bitter quality not evident before. The protagonist of the *Wanderers* trilogy is closer than ever to Knut Hamsun, and, as narrator, he is closer than ever to the actual author. Indeed there are certain sections of volume three in which he addresses his readers directly; they read like letters to the editor or, rather, like reprimanding letters to his wife. This form, in which the distance between the implied and the actual author occasionally disappears altogether, was taken up with great force by younger Norwegian writers twenty years later, but in Hamsun's own production it marks a climax in the development of his narrator. Not only is the last part of the trilogy the last of his novels to be written in the first person, but also, in the half-dozen novels following, the implied author disappears steadily until, in *Vagabonds*, he is completely hidden within the work. The observer also disappears, giving way to new protagonists—artists, men of action, and, in one single case, the moral man.

After Hamsun had temporarily settled his own personal problems by taking up farming and producing children, he must have felt a need to create a fictional character whom readers could look to for inspiration. Life in the new Norway was characterized by enterprise and energy, but during this time new ways of thinking replaced time-honored values, and Hamsun, for all his modernism in form and style, was politically conservative. As a young man he had sympathized with the Haymarket anarchists because they represented the rights of the young individualists against old oppressors, and, along the same line, as a middle-aged man he had supported the liberals in their fight for Norwegian independence from Sweden. But, being at heart a disciple of Nietzsche, he had fought all along against Christian slave morality and the demands of women and workers. He had attacked Rosmer's humanism, and he, like his protagonists from the nineties, Nagel, Høibro, and Kareno, had dreamed up the ideal leader, variously referred to as a Napoleon, a Byron, a man who strikes, a great terrorist. This person would have to be a man of high moral principles and great personal fortitude, a man unbending in adversity. Hamsun conceived such a character during his years in the United States, where he had first come because Europe could not help a young farmer who wanted to change his caste. After only a few years in America, however, Hamsun was cured of his belief in democracy as a means of avoiding social conflict. He had never visited the South, but he now imagined that the master-servant relationship there was on the whole a happy one, one that could serve as a model for a harmoniously stratified society. The most striking example of Hamsun's curious preoccupation with aristocracy is probably the novel *Victoria*. Such names as "the castle" and "the castle master" are particularly anomalous in a Norwegian situation and help give the novel some of its fairy-tale quality. However, the "castle master," who ruins his estate because he cannot adapt to modern industrial society and who then burns himself to death by setting fire to the manor, is a type that then interested Hamsun considerably. In the first two *Wanderers* novels he returns as Captain Falkenberg, this time a much more central character, with serious marital problems, but it is not until *Children of the Age* that the protagonist is fully developed as Lieutenant Holmsen. The ideological content of the novel is not new—social satire is part of *Mysteries* and the central issue already in *Shallow Soil*—but the style is different, as

can be seen in the novel's composition. The short lyrical chapters of the *Wanderers* trilogy have given way to long descriptive chapters in which more than thirty characters and much colorful detail serve as a broad background for the Holmsen portrait. And this background is caricature of a new kind, not the crude exaggerated satire of *Shallow Soil*, but more realistic, more subtly ironic. By placing his small town in his own Nordland—as he had done before in *Mothwise, Rosa,* and *Benoni*—Hamsun was able to give his little crooks an almost endearing touch of humanity. The least sympathetic characters are as always the arrogant civil servants from Kristiania; even the self-made Nordland magnate, Holmengraa, who brings industry and corruption to the place, is shown more respect. Above them all is Willatz Holmsen, a third-generation local landowner, who is defeated in his attempt to bend a woman to his will and ruined by coming industrialization, yet who remains upright till the end. Compared to Nagel, he is an uninteresting character, but Hamsun, because he admired him more than his other protagonists, has been able to give him stature. He is unique in Hamsun's production, unique also in his ridiculous pride and stubbornness, but the author has reserved for him some of his finest characterization; for example, he says of his lonely wandering in the night: " . . . he passes like a figure in a ghostly landscape—tall, upright—tenacity embodied." Lieutenant Holmsen must be mentioned in a consideration of Hamsun's hero, not only because he is the middle-aged Hamsun's answer to Ibsen's *Rosmersholm,* but also because certain character traits—which he represents in their purest form—are recurring features in the Hamsun hero. Still, it cannot be denied that many readers of this novel will take more interest in what Hamsun calls the landscape than in its lonely figure, probably because they find Hamsun's Holmsen about as abstract as Hamsun found Ibsen's Brand.

Similarly abstract, despite his many human touches, is Isak Sellanraa in *Growth of the Soil.* While he has become Hamsun's best-known protagonist, this popularity is due to the fact that his attractive ideals are shared by city dwellers all over the world: Robinson Crusoe will always be more popular than Timon of Athens. *Growth of the Soil* has rightly been called the least typical of Hamsun's major works, but this does not mean that Isak is a stranger among Hamsun's people: even though *Growth of the Soil* is the only novel in which the active man is the central character, he has both precursors and successors in Hamsun's production, and, as is true of Holmsen, his personality is part of the Hamsun hero. In Hamsun's protagonists of the nineties, work in the sense of regular bodily activity does not exist. These people act only in extraordinary, usually heroic, circumstances, as when called upon to save people from drowning. *Shallow Soil,* with its hardworking businessmen, was therefore a surprising breach of the pattern when it appeared in 1893, though, as is evident now, it was also a sign of new things to come. Twelve years later, in the *Wanderers,* Knut Pedersen does not consider it beneath his dignity to cut lumber and dig ditches, and the farm hand Nils is a first step in the direction of Isak; finally, in the last *Wanderers* volume, Nikolai Palm is a direct forerunner of the great farmer-hero. Hamsun's negative attitude toward the farmer can be seen in all his writings from the nineties, for example, in the name of his chief villain from that time, Endre Bondesen, which means "son of a farmer." As late as 1908, when commenting upon Johannes V. Jensen's apotheosis of farmers, Hamsun still had no belief in them, and it was not until he married an actress whom he insisted on turning into a peasant girl that Hamsun changed his view and went on to create his giants in the earth, Isak and later Ezra.

Other novelists, such as Laxness, have felt a need to correct Hamsun's picture of the farm worker's social situation. *Growth of the Soil* has also failed to interest most of the younger Hamsun scholars, and the reason is not difficult to see. It is not so much the novel's idyllic qualities, its clear message and happy ending, but rather the atypicality of the purely active man as Hamsun hero. One dimension is lacking here, the tension and ambivalence that are key criteria of the authentic Hamsun protagonist. For this reason, and in spite of the broad sweep of his biography, with its many humorous and moving details, this active-man protagonist is less intriguing as a character than is his guardian spirit, the bailiff Geissler. The bailiff, like Knut Pedersen, belongs to the observer category; he is a disguised God; and, from the evidence of one line in which he recalls his childhood at Garmo in Lom, he is clearly a self-portrait of the author: a somewhat shady character, quarreling with his family and, though a man of sound judgment and occasional enterprise, mostly lazy and given to dreams of grandeur. Not a very flattering picture, but, while it is a long way down from Nagel, it is also a long way up from Oliver in *Women at the Pump,* the novel with which, in 1920, Hamsun shocked all new admirers of the recent Nobel Prize winner. Oliver, the new nonhero, fits into none of the categories mentioned above; he is not a reflective observer, not a moral person; neither is he a man of action. He is not artistic in the sense that he creates works of art; therefore, a few words of clarification will be needed to explain why he should be called the artist-dreamer.

Hamsun's first fully developed artist, the protagonist of *Hunger,* combined strict moral standards with a lively imagination, which made him see his miserable existence reflected symbolically in the invalid beggar who always seemed to follow him. The situation is further developed in Nagel, a man of high principles and a teller of beautiful tales, who sees himself as a clownish entertainer in the character known as the Midget. Hamsun's apotheosis of the powers of nature is accompanied throughout his production by a corresponding downgrading of the artist. However, in his early work he did not present the artist-dreamer in pure form, or at least not as a main character. Either he was given added moral qualities—as in the early protagonists "Tangen," Nagel, and Johannes and the later observer types like Knut Pedersen, Baardsen, or Geissler—or he was presented as a minor character like the artist-scroungers in *Shallow Soil,* or the Midget, or Lars Manuelsen and Brede Olsen in the Segelfoss novels and *Growth of the Soil.* That Hamsun now introduces him in his ugliest form, and as a central character in a major novel, must have something to do with his deep disillusionment after World War I. Oliver is amoral, inactive, unreflective. He is misshapen and impotent, he has no dig-

nity, even his jealousy is faked. He offers his creditors the sexual services of his wife and causes the death of his tormentor Olaus. Still, here as always, Hamsun reserves his worst sarcasm for the civil-servant class, the doctor representing science, and the lawyer and schoolmaster representing politics and useless learning. Oliver, however repulsive, is drawn without hatred and actually with some compassion. The reader is made to understand how, because of his misfortune, he has become an outcast, how he is forced to defend himself through lies and delusions. The suicidal thoughts of early Hamsun protagonists never occur to Oliver. On the contrary, life has rewarded him considerably; miracles, when they happen, happen to him: not only does he salvage a whole ship singlehanded and find banknotes in the eiders' nests, but he, who can produce no offspring of his own, is a devoted father of his wife's children, who become a source of pride and joy to him as they grow up. Oliver may well be the ugliest of Norwegian antiheroes—Hjalmar Ekdal and Jakob Engstrand in one—yet he is very human and very important for the development of a character known as August, the greatest of Hamsun's protagonists in the new century.

German scholars have referred to Hamsun's hero as a Northeastern hero, that is, a Scandinavian hero with Russian ancestry, and Hamsun's neurasthenic temperament as well as his expressed admiration of the great Russian masters of the novel would support such a label. On the other hand, the American qualities of the Hamsun hero have not received much attention, even though it is common knowledge that Hamsun spent his formative years in the United States and early developed a taste for the special humor of Mark Twain. Arne Garborg felt that in his first literary attempts Hamsun had learned too much from the Russians, but he later referred to him as a Yankee, as did many other Norwegian critics after *Mysteries* had appeared, and Johannes V. Jensen, in 1907, claimed that Hamsun's happy style was a product of his years in America. Furthermore, the emphasis on physical health and activity that gradually emerges in Hamsun's writing is more typical of the West than of the East; particularly Western is that spirit of restless enterprise that colors the trilogy about August, Hamsun's most "American" protagonist, and his most elaborate symbol of modern times, city life, business, and industry.

August differs from Oliver mainly in his greater activity and his ability to tell tall tales. While Oliver's enterprise is limited to a little fishing, August is busy in a hundred ways, draining a marsh, setting up a bank and a shooting range, as well as a tobacco plantation and a herring-meal factory. Like Oliver, August does not have much prestige in his little society and needs to produce fantastic stories about himself. August, however, tells them with special flair—there are art and humor in his stories, and, not surprisingly, after his death he himself becomes literature, when a street ballad about his colorful life begins circulating among the common people. Like Oliver, too, August has little success as a lover; not only does the novel describe his defeat in the wooing of Cornelia, but also readers are made to understand that throughout his long life he has mostly had to buy his love, and the girl with the lion mane even left him with a "reminder," a "disease of two and a half years' duration." August's disease is symbolic. "This single individual," says the author, "had it in his power to corrupt both town and countryside." However, as in the case of Oliver, that judgment is tempered with many positive traits—August is said to be unselfish, conscientious as an ant, innocent of malice. "Here he stands in his old age, and, in the language of Gordon's accountancy, his assets exceed his liabilities."

Nagel had shaken his head and smiled at Ibsen's little verse about the poet sitting in judgment over his self, but in the case of the August trilogy that seems to be exactly what the poet is doing, and with much the same result as in *Peer Gynt* : the final sentence is indefinitely suspended, but it is implied that, if the defendant were to be saved, it would have to be on the grounds of his artistic contributions. August is Hamsun's Peer Gynt, and, just as Norwegian folklore gave Ibsen's identity play its special texture, so in the August trilogy there is a youthful spirit, drawn, perhaps, from literary impressions of life on the seven seas and from Hamsun's reminiscences of his own vagabond days in North Dakota. The tone is that of the popular ballad, not only in its mock heroism, but also in its anonymity: in no other work of Hamsun's does the story tell itself so spontaneously as here, where Hamsun takes one last good look, more distant, and more objective than ever before, at the artist-dreamer as good-humored clown.

In the novel August is defined through a variety of lesser characters, such as the farmers Ezra and Joachim, both firmly rooted in the microcosm of their home grounds, but particularly through Edevart, who becomes a victim of August's nomadic habits but differs from him in that he preserves a tragic sense of displacement. The pale cast of thought with which Hamsun tinted his early hero and the high ethical sense of Lieutenant Holmsen are recognizable in Edevart; he is a good late example of the moral-reflective type and a steppingstone to Hamsun's last great protagonist, Abel Brodersen, whose life style is oriental, though he lives in the West, more particularly in Green Ridge, Kentucky. At seventy Hamsun had taken up his old interest in the States, not now the bustling North, but the decadent South, which he knew from modern American fiction.

Like the books of the August trilogy, *The Ring Is Closed* was probably meant to be a novel of good companionship, with Lawrence, who is only referred to, resembling August, at least in generosity and poetic imagination. As it is, there is only one protagonist, and, though he is more like Edevart than like August, he has in him some of both characters. In him that ring is closed which opened up in Nagel forty years earlier. He is called Abel, like the best of Oliver's stepchildren, and his name ought to be significant. It is confusing, however, that Abel's situation is that of Cain: he causes the death of his friend Lawrence and is uprooted from his home. He further resembles Cain's offspring in being technically and artistically gifted, and he uses these gifts for criminal ends: when Hamsun therefore calls him Abel, the reason may be not only Abel's extreme docility, but also a realization, later emphasized in Aksel Sandemose's work, that society is to be blamed for the character murder that finally kills all ambition in this

protagonist. The son of an old, niggardly sea captain and his second, alcoholic wife, Abel was not socially acceptable to the novel's antiheroine, Olga. The early Hamsun hero could hope to win his princess only through his artistic powers, but Abel's weapon is a perverted art: Olga incites him to rob the church on two occasions; also on two occasions, the excitement of sleeping with a real murderer makes her spend the night in bed with him. The text says that, during the scene in which Abel mistakenly tells Olga how he shot Angèle and her child, he bared his teeth like an animal—a good starting point for critics who wish to place Abel at the definite low point in the development of the Hamsun protagonist. It is true that, in addition to the ramification of the protagonist's road, there has been a steady downhill trend in his path, changing the colorful Byronic hero of the nineties into the pitiful non-hero of the twentieth century. This is a natural result of the author's growing age and general disillusionment, but it does not mean that he denies Abel stature. Indeed, a little listening to the novel's inner voice should convince the reader that Abel is intended to occupy a very prominent place in Hamsun's pantheon. The problem of Abel is an old and a difficult one: how to combine Rosmer and Brendel, or, as Hamsun says, gentleman and vagabond, in one character. Even Abel's vagabond years are not without style—his life among the Negroes in Green Ridge, Kentucky, and later in a shed in his home town, is not colorfully heroic, but it is based upon an Eastern philosophy that Abel is capable of defending with as much conviction and less rhetoric than Hamsun himself in his articles from Turkey. As for his qualities as a gentleman, it is significant that, on leaving the scene after his "experiment in living," Abel, like only the great protagonists—"Tangen," Glahn, Nagel, Holmsen—takes great care to set his house in order. It is also significant that Abel, so different from the many miserable cuckolds that people Hamsun's novels, will not tolerate his wife's adultery: his crime passionnel even appears to have the author's approval.

In *The Ring Is Closed,* as in all of Hamsun's work after *The Enigmatic One,* clothing is a very central symbol. But unlike Victoria's father, who even in death had the presence of mind to flick away a grain of dust on the sleeve of his evening dress, Abel sullies everything, both his uniform and his many new suits. In this way he is able to demonstrate a final and decisive unlearning of social ambition; dress has finally come to symbolize a perversion of art, as a means of achieving social disapproval. In Hamsun's early work, the protagonist, despite his romantic whims, wished to work his way back into society. Abel wants to get out of society. Also in this respect *The Ring Is Closed* resembles an end game, something like a blown-up denouement of an early Hamsun novel. In other ways, however, the ring is not closed: not only is the work incomplete, but also, like most of Hamsun's books, it is an open novel, a novel that leaves the reader asking at the end where the protagonist now stands, and also where he as reader stands in relationship to the kind of hero this protagonist typifies.

To sum up, I think it is important, if one attempts—as I have, perhaps unsuccessfully, attempted—to find a general formula for the Hamsun hero, not to concentrate only on the great works from the nineties. Holmsen and August are probably the most archetypal of Hamsun's protagonists and should not be left out of any full-size picture of his hero. It might also be useful to mention some of Hamsun's house gods, particularly the great ones, like Dostoevsky and Bjørnson, or even Strindberg and Mark Twain, but here it is important to draw a line between Hamsun's strictly creative writing and his political journalism. On hearing of Hitler's death in May of 1945, Hamsun published a curious eulogy of the *Führer,* which harmed his reputation and left the impression among readers all over the world that Hamsun approved of the authoritarian state. Whatever views Hamsun expressed as a politically interested private person, his fictional hero can best be described as an anarchist in the sense of extreme individualist and social outsider. Such labeling is supported by his many conflicts with the central state authority, the police, who play an important part in *Hunger,* as they do sixty years later in the autobiography, when the old man is caught smuggling a letter out of the detention home. Otto Weininger's characterization of Hamsun as a *Verbrecher*—a criminal type—is interesting in this connection, as is Johannes V. Jensen's observation that Hamsun never learned to see the importance of governmental rules and regulations.

Hamsun's question—how to avoid the corrupting influence of social institutions—is also Ibsen's, but Ibsen's answer—by changing the institutions—is not Hamsun's. Ibsen, with his persistent dreams of a third empire, could be called a romantic with regard to the future, just as in his earliest writings he was a romantic with regard to the past. Hamsun is a romantic only in his relationship to the present; his works are free from the trappings of history as well as from social programs of any kind. But Hamsun's hero exists in a social situation, and therefore he has to develop a set of simple rules to live by. Thus he is willing to sacrifice his life for his fellowmen; in most cases Hamsun has his hero save another person from drowning. Furthermore, the hero's generosity knows no bounds: the destitute protagonist of *Hunger* takes great pride in giving away his last pennies, and Abel insists on helping even when it means that he himself must do without. Finally, the hero keeps his promises. Not surprisingly, when asked in an *enquête* what human quality he held in highest esteem, Hamsun answered *redelighet*—honesty. In other respects Hamsun's hero is outside society, or rather he is a society all his own. Indeed, the word Hamsun uses repeatedly to sum up Abel's existence is *sovereignty.* One might interpret this word to mean "sufficient unto oneself" and see this as another contrast to Ibsen's ideal of being in the sense of "becoming oneself." Hamsun is not concerned with improving the self ethically, but he is concerned with authentic living, and by his example his hero shows the reader how such authenticity can be achieved. Turning away from society, this hero communicates with nature in a manner not seen before in Norwegian literature. And it is not only Lieutenant Glahn, but also Isak and even Abel, seeing his soul reflected in the stunted cactus plants, who find fulfillment in such harmony with nature. Another, equally typical, way of transcending is through the experience of love, which Hamsun has described as no other Norwegian prose writer has, whether it be the delightful promiscuity of Ylajali, or Edvarda's more typical love-hate, or Eva's selfless passion, all terminating in tragedy. Another kind of love is everlasting and ideal love, often represented allegorically and summed up in the autobiography's story of Alvilde, whose memory Martin Enevoldsen hides deep in his humble heart. Finally, readers of Hamsun cannot fail to recognize the kind of transcendence offered by artistic experience, whether it be the passionate tales of Johannes, or Willatz Holmsen's opera, or the many technical inventions that color the more prosaic lives of the later Hamsun heroes, from Knut Pedersen's mechanical wood saw to Abel's lockless casket. Knut Hamsun, the greatest ecologist in Norwegian literature, had started out as an interpreter of what he called, somewhat mysteriously, "the whisper of the blood and the entreaty of the bone." What he meant was, more prosaically, the power of nature, love, and art to produce joy in our daily lives. Through Hamsun's protagonists these powers speak to the readers, sometimes in the tone of Don Quixote, sometimes in that of Sancho Panza, but in the final view of the Hamsun hero, those tones are harmoniously blended into one unique yet familiar voice. This is how Henry Miller describes it: "It was from your Knut Hamsun that I derived much of my love of life, love of nature, love of man. All I have done, or hope I have, in relating the distressing story of my life, is to increase that love of life, nature and all of God's creatures in those who read me. 'Praise God from whom all blessings flow!' " (pp. 65-83)

Harald Naess, "Who Was Hamsun's Hero?" in The Hero in Scandinavian Literature: From Peer Gynt to the Present, *edited by John M. Weinstock and Robert T. Rovinsky, University of Texas Press, 1975, pp. 63-86.*

Alfred Turco, Jr.   (essay date 1980)

[*In the following essay, Turco argues that the narrator of* Pan *and of its epilogue, "Glahn's Death," are both the same character.*]

> But within the speech that is spoken, another lies concealed, like the veins under the skin, like a story within a story.
>
> Hamsun: *The Last Joy*

This essay is an exploratory attempt to account for the strange postscript to Hamsun's *Pan* (1894). Written first and published as a short story in 1893, **'Glahn's Death'** was later used by Hamsun as the conclusion to his most finely wrought novel. One wonders why: is not the book manifestly complete without this anticlimactic appendage? In *Pan* proper, the sights and sounds of northern Norway were rendered with a sureness of touch that is notably absent from the epilogue's flat monochrome of the hero's later adventures in India. We can readily believe that ex-lieutenant Thomas Glahn, first-person narrator of the main story, really lived in the forests of Nordland, hunted and fished for his livelihood there, and told time by the sun and tides as he says he did. In comparison, the exotic setting of **'Glahn's Death'**—with its 'thick-lipped' natives, tea plantations, rubber plants, and paddy fields— reads like a compilation put together from a guidebook.

It is true that the narrator of the epilogue, since he is legally guilty of murdering Glahn, has a motive for calculated imprecision in respect to details of place. It is nonetheless a loss that the lyrical mood, so sensitively rendered in the body of the book, is snapped. Juxtaposing *Pan* and its postscript almost tempts one to ask: how could the same man have written both?

The shift in tone results largely from the different voice of the anonymous chronicler of **'Glahn's Death'**. At times he sounds so blatantly villainous as to strain credibility. 'Thomas Glahn' he tells us near the start, 'had his faults, and I am not disposed to conceal them, since I hate him'. At first this may seem like charming candor, but the effect palls rapidly. Throughout the epilogue, the invective of the narrator (let us call him Mr X for now) grows more unrelievedly shrill. If Glahn never missed when shooting, it was because 'his gun was better than mine'. When Glahn rushes to the rescue of a child attacked by a tiger, Mr X is unimpressed: 'Why did he take his rifle instead of his shotgun if he really was so brave?' Yet interspersed with these fulminations are traces of the narrator's almost feminine sensitivity to Glahn's handsome features and physique. The resulting persona is so disconcerting that the authentic historical basis of the events he narrates is felt far less than in Glahn's own portion of the book. Does Hamsun's apparent lapse into melodrama serve some special function?

It will not do to maintain that the afterpiece is necessary to show us what finally happens to Glahn—specifically, the strange 'suicide' he commits in India by taunting a jealous friend into discharging a loaded rifle into his face. Glahn's eventual self-destruction is already a foregone conclusion by the end of *Pan* proper, when it becomes clear that his romance with Edvarda Mack is over. No one (least of all Glahn himself) takes seriously his terminal disclaimers: he doesn't care about the girl anymore, he has written these chapters only 'to while away the time', and so forth. It was evident from the start that Glahn's act of recording his experiences was a desperate attempt to recover the past by recreating it fictionally. At moments he succeeds and seems almost to live *in* the past; hence those lurchings into an ecstatic present tense ('Happiness is intoxicating [*Glaede beruser*]'. But on the whole, the effort fails—for reasons that will soon become clear. By the end of his own narration, we already sense that Glahn is finished: **'Glahn's Death'** does not make—but rather coarsens—the point. No wonder Rolf Nyboe Nettum feels that 'the epilogue does not play an essential role for our understanding of *Pan*' [*Konflikt og Visjon: Hovedtemaer i Knut Hamsuns forfatterskap 1890-1912*]. For Rolf Vige, the piece is 'diluted fruit juice after champagne' [*Knut Hamsuns Pan*]. The temptation to extricate the novel from its conclusion becomes very real.

Yet I have always suspected that there was something not so much wrong, as *uncanny,* about the relation of **'Glahn's Death'** to the rest of *Pan*. Could it be that the apparent anticlimax of the conclusion is a kind of dare to the reader—a code Hamsun is challenging us to crack in order to grasp the full significance of his book? This hypothesis will not seem implausible if we recall Hamsun's recognized

slyness as a writer, his fondness for the casual hint which only later falls into its proper place in the puzzle. Sometimes this almost sinister dexterity even operates *across* books. It is a slight shock to discover that the name of the hero of *Mysteries* is nearly an anagram of the name of the hero of *Pan:* Nagel in 1892 becomes Glahn in 1894. We may never have noticed this; yet once the correspondence has been pointed out, who will believe it to be an accident? Since readers of Hamsun's early books will have come to expect mysteries of all kinds, might we try the experiment of reading *Pan* as a detective story? To the extent this approach works, one can expect to find that surface appearances both disguise and disclose a deeper truth.

As a first step, let us see if the main objection already raised against **'Glahn's Death'** can be turned instead into a clue to the piece's meaning. What if Hamsun's replacing the suggestive atmosphere of the first part by the brittleness of the second is not an accident, but a deliberate effect? The snapping of the mood might then be seen as an achievement rather than a blemish. Glahn in India becomes like a jewel out of its setting: he does not belong among the grassy plains and naked children as he did among the hills and lakes of Nordland. At home, he lived in a hut and felt at home in the forest; abroad, he lives in an attic and uses the forest as a game park. The very drabness of the account serves to heighten the poignancy of the contrast: India relates to Norway as a negative to a print. What matters is not the convincingness of particular details of physical setting per se, but the ability of this whole alien geography to suggest the new rootlessness of the hero's existence. The shift in tone is not a lapse, but a jolt.

A further gain arises unexpectedly from the fact that the epilogue is the one part of *Pan* not written from Glahn's own point of view. We might have supposed that Glahn's stature would be whittled down as a result of his now being evaluated from a hostile perspective, yet Hamsun paradoxically contrives for the opposite to happen. Mr X's hatred is so extreme that it works to promote our empathy with Glahn. A careful reading of Glahn's own narrative cannot help but betray that this darkly vital figure has his blind spots: his own view of his relation to both love and nature never quite squares with the reality we sense between the lines. But when the epilogue finally gives us a chance to see Glahn from an external point of view, our respect for him is—surprisingly—increased rather than diminished. The new narrator's invective backfires: anyone whom Mr X hates that much can't be *all* bad. Glahn in India stands in splendid isolation both from his native terrain and from such tawdry envy as his antagonist displays. Hamsun expertly plies the dynamics of increasing his hero's stature by viewing him through the eyes of an enemy. The manifest condemnation conceals a subtle martyrology.

Appearances are equally deceptive for understanding the relationship between Glahn and Edvarda Mack. It is of course tempting to respond to *Pan* as a mythic mood piece, excelling in the sense conveyed of a romance slowly going sour without anyone being able to say why. But there is no need to blame the outcome on a 'mysterious God of the heart' who works his inscrutable will in matters such as these. The problem is rather that each person is drawn to something in the other that is not genuine. Glahn is touched by Edvarda's frailty. At first sight she seems 'a mere child, a schoolgirl' who has 'no figure'. Later the 'forlorn expression in her eyes' moves him deeply: Edvarda has now graduated to a 'whole thin figure' which the narrator finds irresistible. Glahn values the girl's helplessness as an implied compliment to his own strength. She is the perfect foil to his grandiose sense of pathos, a human analogue to the poor twig the mere sight of which causes his eyes to water. Yet we learn from the doctor, a former disappointed suitor turned acerbic critic of the girl's foibles, that Edvarda's girlishness is itself a pose. She is no pubescent waif, but a woman of twenty.

Edvarda is in turn drawn to Glahn's equally unreal projection of himself as a 'son of the forest'. He can indeed speak evocatively of nature—the descriptions of the reef in a storm, the caterpillar 'like a bit of green thread', or the shooting star in autumn come readily into mind. Yet Glahn's relation to nature is by no means one of pure elemental repose. Some of his other effusions are pickled in pre-Raphaelite formaldehyde: 'I feel myself lifted out of my context, pressed to an invisible breast, tears spring to my eyes, I tremble'. Is this love of nature or love of self? In either case, the insistence upon union with the All virtually dooms Glahn to a self-conscious gaucheness in society: it seems purposeful that he scratches the floor with his boots, overturns glasses, and inevitably says the wrong thing. For a 'wild man of the woods', such *faux pas* are truly *de rigueur*. Glahn derives a perverse enjoyment from allowing himself to be placed in situations where he will be indisposed. Suspecting that the doctor still has designs on Edvarda, he vows to 'give this man every advantage I could since he was my rival'. Shortly after, he obligingly shoots himself through the foot to implement Edvarda's advice that he emulate the lame physician. Surely, this is being chivalrous to a fault!

As McFarlane notes [in his *Ibsen and the Temper of Norwegian Literature*], each character projects his or her ideal on the other—with disastrous results, since both pursue the relationship primarily for *self*-gratification. Glahn's meetings with Edvarda are something for him to savour when he returns to the forest; romance adds piquancy to solitude: that is all. Edvarda in turn is eager to enliven her bourgeois surroundings by the presence of this token noble savage; but to satisfy her, Glahn would have to be both a child of nature *and* someone presentable in her intimate circles. Since this dual function is impossible for Glahn, she needs to keep him at a psychological distance even while encouraging his physical nearness. Edvarda may seem merely petty when she tells Glahn of her preference for the desiccated Baron: 'He knows how to behave in company . . . I feel ashamed of you'. But what is at issue here is not merely a distaste for Glahn's country manners, but a fear of her own potential rebellion against her family's values. Edvarda is not really fickle; she is only a coward.

Understanding the involuted psychology of **Pan** is made more difficult because the love relationship, which originally involved two people, is told by only one of them. Ev-

erything *except* the epilogue is presented from Glahn's perspective, and at least once we catch him giving different versions of the same incident for purposes of his own. On first meeting Glahn and his dog Aesop, Edvarda asks the doctor: 'Who was Aesop? All I remember is that he wrote fables'. When Glahn later recounts this moment to Eva (his more readily forthcoming mistress), he alters the quote slightly and adds: 'And as far as I remember, she also talked about Aesop having Xanthus as a teacher . . . what the devil is the point of telling the company that Aesop had Xanthus as a teacher?' This may seem like a trivial misrecollection, but it does have the effect of making Edvarda look more pretentious than she did in the first version. Other choices of emphasis and omission in Glahn's reporting—for instance, his callous dismissal of Edvarda's moving appeal at the end of Chapter 23—point to a similar submerged design. The retrospective narration underscores the hero's insensitivity; the passage of two years between the events themselves and his writing them down has not inclined Glahn to reflect on what he reports. Since the narrator's slanting is calculatedly unobtrusive, it is all the more important that we read his book in a suspicious frame of mind.

Once we do, the indispensable clue to the epilogue's meaning is not long in coming. The first page of **'Glahn's Death'** contains the following passage.

> When he looked at you with his animal eyes, you could not help feeling his power; even I felt it. A woman is supposed to have said: 'When he looks at me I am lost; I feel as though he were touching me.'

Mr X seems as susceptible to Glahn's attractions as the lady in question: his words uncannily parallel a passage in Glahn's own narrative, where Edvarda disingenuously tells what a purported friend of hers has said about him.

> 'She says you have an animal look, and when you look at her it makes her mad. It is as though you touched her, she says.'

What McFarlane renders both as 'animal look' and 'animal eyes' is in Norwegian the same word: *dyreblik*. First used in the passage just quoted, the term recurs four more times in the next few chapters of Glahn's report—always in conjunction with a recollection of this particular exchange with Edvarda. So by now *dyreblik* is an old friend; its reappearance is remarkable only because someone *other* than Glahn uses the term. That two persons separately hit upon the same word to describe Glahn may not seem particularly odd, but then in both cases the next sentence goes on to quote the woman who complained of being fingered by his glance. More than coincidence could be at work here. While there are other passages from the novel that are also strikingly similar, what gives this particular pairing its importance is that these parallels occur in sections of the book narrated by different persons—Glahn and Mr X.

Such close correspondences might suggest that one text was derived from the other: did Glahn perhaps show his novella to his irascible companion, who then imperfectly recollected certain details in writing his own account? Unfortunately for this suggestion, the narrator's remarks about the affair in Nordland seem based on general 'report [*beretning*]' and fall far short of the degree of specificity one might expect had he actually read Glahn's paper. To be sure, Mr X does offer one interesting comment on Glahn's subsequent conduct: 'He ran wild, behaved like mad, he drank, created scandal after scandal, and resigned his commission. That was a queer way of taking revenge for a jilting!' But the very fact that this information is new to us means that the first part of *Pan* could not have been its source. There are simply no grounds on which to suppose that the narrator of '**Glahn's Death**' even knows of the existence of Glahn's manuscript, much less that he wrote his own paper with the latter open at his elbow. The only person in *Pan* who did see Glahn's pages for certain is Glahn himself, but *he* can hardly be the author of an account of his own death. Yet juxtaposing the parallel passages involving *dyreblik* almost tempts one to ask: how could the same man *not* have written both?

And in fact the same man did: '**Glahn's Death**' is a literary hoax perpetrated by Glahn. The passages already quoted are not the only ones which suggest the possibility that the hero is not dead, but has gone underground. Early in his first chapter, Mr X tells of the following incident:

> Another time, after we had come to live in the same house together, he showed his silliness in a most obvious way; my landlady came in one morning and asked what I wanted for breakfast, and in my hurry I happened to answer: 'A bread and a slice of egg.' Thomas Glahn was sitting in my room at the time . . . and he began to laugh as any child might at this little slip of the tongue, delighted with it. 'A bread and a slice of egg,' he kept on saying over and over again, until I looked at him in astonishment and caused him to be silent.

This interaction recalls the doctor's annoying habit of twitting Edvarda by correcting her errors in grammar and wording. To quote but one instance from *Pan* proper:

> Her cheeks flushed at the thought and she made a slip in what she was saying: 'Nobody would be more happier than I the day . . .'
>
> 'More happier . . . ?' said the doctor.
>
> 'What?' she asked.
>
> 'More happier!'
>
> 'I don't understand.'
>
> 'You said more happier, that's all.'

Edvarda's cheeks flushed in the first line because she had been speaking about 'the joy of travelling to distant places'. This reverie annoyed Glahn, who would have preferred to be the focus of her thoughts. At last having transported himself (by literary means) to a place suitably distant, Glahn now assumes the doctor's role of bland scourge. Edvarda's latest rejected suitor has resourcefully borrowed a leaf from the book of his predecessor! Significantly, Glahn does this as a means of teasing a new friend whose strange ambivalence toward him recalls Edvarda's own erotically tinged hostility.

The preceding passages are not the sole instance of a dominance tactic being carried over from one part of the work to the other. In the third chapter of the epilogue, Glahn and his mysterious companion go off on a shooting trip. Embarrassed to have killed a leopard inelegantly, Glahn shoots the dead animal again through the head, giving as his reason that 'I can't have people saying I hit a leopard in the flank'. On their return to the village, they are greeted by Maggie, a young girl whose obvious interest in Glahn Mr X is quick to resent:

> 'Who shot it?' she asked.
>
> And Glahn answered: 'You can see for yourself, two bullet holes; we shot it this morning when we went out.' And he turned the beast over and showed her the two bullet holes, one in the flank and one in the head. 'That's where my bullet went,' he said, pointing to the one in the flank; in his frivolous way he wanted to let me take the credit for having shot it in the head. I could not be bothered to correct him, so I said nothing. . . .
>
> 'You both shot it,' said Maggie to herself, but she looked all the time at Glahn.

Glahn's idea for this scene comes from an analogous episode in the main text when, feeling neglected by Edvarda during a boating trip, he seized her shoe and flung it into the water to be retrieved by the oarsman. At a ball shortly thereafter, Edvarda made Glahn uncomfortable by her standard trick (already used on the doctor) of paying undeserved compliments:

> 'And listen,' she continued, her eyes sparkling, 'you gave our boatman five *daler* for saving my shoe from drowning. That was too high a price.' And she laughed heartily and looked around at all the others.
>
> I stood open-mouthed, confused, and helpless. 'It pleases you to jest,' I said. 'I have never given any boatman five *daler*.'
>
> 'Oh, haven't you indeed?' She opened the door to the kitchen and called the boatman in. 'Jacob, you remember our trip out to Korholmerne, when you saved my shoe that had fallen into the water?'
>
> 'Yes,' answered Jacob.
>
> 'And you received five *daler* for saving the shoe?'
>
> 'Yes, you gave me . . .'
>
> 'All right! You can go!'

Once again we see Glahn contriving a second fiction out of the materials of his first. This initial encounter has been reworked to make it more emotionally gratifying to the author, who has written himself out of the role of dupe. In the epilogue Glahn mimics Edvarda's device by exploiting it to annoy Mr X, who substitutes for Glahn's former distraught self.

Even the innocent Maggie becomes part of Glahn's design. In her simple sensuousness she reminds one of Eva, whose love for Glahn in *Pan* proper had so annoyed the jealous Herr Mack that he revealed the affair to Edvarda as a means of turning her heart against Glahn. This strategem worked; now in the epilogue Glahn counters with his own. At one point he had remarked to Eva, 'In the end you will come with me when I leave this place'; and in a figurative sense this turns out to be true. For when Glahn 'leaves' Norway he tauntingly 'takes' Eva with him by transforming her into Maggie—a creature who arouses Mr X's jealousy as Eva aroused Edvarda's. It is already plain that Mr X is not to be identified neatly with any one character from the first part of the book; he is a polyvalent projection of Glahn's shifting obsessions, antagonisms, and fears. In the scenes with Maggie, the romantic rivalry between Glahn and Mr X recreates in parodistic terms the earlier rivalry between Glahn and the Baron—subjecting the latter to ridicule by depicting his surrogate's unflattering inferiority to Glahn as a lady-killer. And the cowardice that led Edvarda to prefer the Baron is rebuked in turn by Maggie's refusal to be coaxed away from Glahn. Once we realise that Glahn himself is writing the epilogue for Edvarda as his intended audience, such seemingly contrived parallels converge to a clear punitive point.

There is nothing sudden about Glahn's assumption of the mantle of authorship—**'Glahn's Death'** continues, with a new twist, exactly what Glahn has been doing from the first sentence of *Pan* proper. There are many ways to recover from disappointment in romance; Glahn chooses to do so by writing a book about it. Moreover, his book is no unadorned diary, but a highly sophisticated structure. From the start the surface of the prose ripples with hints: Glahn has just received two green feathers in the mail, he has a touch of arthritis in his foot, he once had a dog which he shot, he has noticed blocks of rock toppling down from the mountain. The reader is supposed to be asking: who sent those green feathers? How did Glahn get arthritis in his foot? Why on earth did he shoot his dog? Will someone be killed in an avalanche?—all questions which are answered as the plot unfolds. It is all rather neat, of course—even Herr Mack's white shirt front reappears later to identify him as the man sneaking from Eva's house at night. The air of these introductory chapters is heavy with calculated casualness—but not because Hamsun was a secret emulator of Eugène Scribe. We must proceed carefully here. No one would think of criticizing *Hunger* for its chaotic and fragmented organization: the book's lack of form clearly mirrors the mind of its deranged narrator. Precisely because the shape of *Pan* seems so much nearer to that of a traditional novel, the book's organization as an aesthetic equivalent of the hero's consciousness is harder to detect. Yet the novel's well-made techniques are just as much a means of indirectly characterizing the hero who exploits them. The narrator who goes about presenting his reminiscences in this portentous way is recognizably the same fellow who later shoots himself in the foot for effect, spits in the Baron's ear, tries to 'plot' his rival's death in a landslide in the first part of the work, and engineers an equally theatrical demise for himself in the sequel.

Even among the select subgroup of rejected lovers who might choose to write about their misadventures, there would be few who would go as far as Glahn does in indulging a penchant for rococo aesthetics. Recall in particular

the poetic cameos concerning the old blind Lapp, the maid locked in the tower, and the several episodes involving Iselin. These vignettes enrich the text considerably. The old Lapp endures adversity by a heroic passivity the lack of which grinds Glahn down. For the betrayed maid who can still affirm her love, 'time passes' as it no longer will for Glahn. And Iselin is his fantastic translation of the squeamish Edvarda into a mythic female who unites fey charm with erotic clout. Sometimes directly, sometimes through contrast, these three figures underscore the despair, rigidity, and destructive idealization which are masked by Glahn's posture of indifference to his fate. That Glahn may himself be quite unaware of their thematic significance makes such vignettes all the more ironic, but they would hardly have been included at all in a story narrated by someone without his specifically literary bent. Moreover, these interludes appear not to be derived from existing Scandinavian folklore; they are invented by Glahn as subfictions within the main fiction. In this respect, **'Glahn's Death'**—in psychological if not literary terms—is Glahn's supreme fiction. The epilogue is his 'answer' to Edvarda's latest letter, his attempt to exorcise the gloom into which it plunged him, and a final punishment meted out to her—just how devastatingly well-calculated we have yet to see—for his own failure to recreate the past in writing *Pan* proper.

I do not mean to suggest that Glahn actually went and posted his squib to the baroness. One cannot say for sure, but a victory in an imaginary agon was probably all he ever sought. No guesswork is needed, however, to show that Knut Hamsun remained interested in the subject of Glahn's death long after he finished writing *Pan.* Upon visiting Edvarda at Sirilund, the narrator of *Rosa* (1908) discovers that Glahn is still very much in this unhappy woman's thoughts: 'He was an animal; I was so wonderfully fond of him, he was big and kind. Sometimes he must have eaten reindeer moss, for his breath smelt like a reindeer's. There was a sort of gamy taste in his breath'. Not surprisingly, she has not succeeded in finding a replacement for this aromatic soulmate. 'He's dead, they say' is her qualified conclusion. When the narrator suggests that 'perhaps Glahn is not dead?', Edvarda at first replies 'I don't know,' but then adds: 'Yes, he must be [dead]'. Her afterthought seems defensive, as if she were trying to put the possibility of Glahn's being alive out of her mind in order to mask a deeper fear that she has died to *him*. In *Rosa's* final chapter, Edvarda reveals information for which **'Glahn's Death'** must be the indirect source: 'Now he is dead . . . in India. It's in the paper. His family announced it'. The narrator suggests that the report may be 'a mistake of identity' resulting from the distance the news has travelled. 'Oh no!' Edvarda responds curtly, but then hedges: 'Do you think that [the report could be a mistake]? . . . Perhaps'. Edvarda has apparently not seen **'Glahn's Death'**, but the thought that Glahn may still breathe has at least occurred to her. The possibility must necessarily have occurred to Hamsun as well, since he alludes to it twice in a novel where there is no need to bring the subject up. For its real-life author, *Pan* was not quite a closed book.

I noted earlier that a major problem with **'Glahn's Death'** is that the voice of its narrator is so shrilly villainous as to seem unreal. The new supposition of the epilogue's authorship suggests a solution to this difficulty. Mr X need not seem real, since he does not exist. Of course he is not convincing viewed as a real person, for this is precisely what he is not. But he can be all the more convincing as the voice of Glahn attempting to write from the point of view of someone who detests him. By extension, Mr X serves as an objectification of Glahn's sense of how 'others' view him in general. We must not forget that Glahn is a man whose sensitivity borders on the pathological. He fancies he can read people's minds, and what he sees in them usually places their motives toward him in a negative light. There is a telling scene where Glahn behaves outrageously to the doctor, who nonetheless holds out his hand and responds compassionately: 'There is something wrong with you. If you will tell me what it is, perhaps . . . '. Momentarily shamed, Glahn later repents his vulnerability for fear that the doctor 'would gloat over it, I thought'. If one senses that Glahn's own insecurity makes him need to believe that people dislike him, revel in his psychic pain, and are out to trick him, it seems entirely credible that he would concoct a black presence like the epilogue's narrator to embody the forces which menace him from without and within.

Mr X is Glahn himself to a greater extent than Glahn realizes. For all the dislike of his adversary, Mr X's personality may easily recall unsavoury elements in Glahn's own—both are intense, inflexible egotists who solve problems with a gun. Though Glahn characteristically exaggerates such tendencies to the point of parody, this self-inflicted cruelty has its compensations: for beneath the superficial scorn for his rival, Mr X stands in obvious awe of Glahn for reasons the latter would surely applaud. The image Mr X has of Glahn is quite close to the romantic image Glahn has of himself elsewhere—sexually glamorous, the great hunter, and somehow strangely different from the rest of the world! What more could Glahn ask than that the rest of the world see him in exactly this way? At moments Mr X's attraction for his enemy becomes unmistakably sexual; even the murder—with Glahn dressed as a bridegroom intoning a wedding hymn—mocks a marriage rite. Given Glahn's own mixture of masochism and megalomania, one can hardly overestimate the appeal to him of a literary prose which thus enables him to take his knocks and get his kicks at the same time.

The hero of *Pan* seems to have borrowed a weapon from his predecessor in *Mysteries:* Johan Nagel also knew how to revile himself to his own greater glory. Nagel arrives in town with a violin case, receives telegrams mentioning large sums of money, and owns a medal given him for saving a man who tried to throw himself overboard. Later he lets Dagny Kielland learn that the violin case contains dirty laundry, that he sent the telegrams to himself, and that he bought the medal. Yet Nagel's fraud consists primarily in proclaiming himself to be one; for in time we discover that he does play the violin, must have plenty of money to sustain his way of living, and has come by the medal legitimately in the world's—if not his own—eyes. Early in the book Nagel prevents a bully named Reinert from humiliating the Midget in a cafe, but then gives

Dagny a typically self-demeaning account of what took place: '[Reinert] jostled me going through a door. . . . like an idiot I jumped up, called him names, shook a beer mug under his nose, and bashed in his hat—whereupon he walked out'. Dagny, who knows what really happened from eye-witnesses, is aghast: 'Why do you talk yourself down like that?' Nagel obligingly explains:

> 'You will see that when I gave you my version of the incident with Reinert, perhaps distorting the facts slightly, perhaps even talking myself down a bit, it was purely for my own benefit; I want to get all I can out of this. I'm being honest with you because I assume that one day somebody will tell you the true story, and since I have already demeaned myself as much as I possibly can in front of you, I stand only to gain by it—to be richly rewarded. I would rise in stature, acquire a reputation for magnanimity and nobility of spirit which I could not easily earn otherwise. Am I not right? But I can only attain this by being so lowly and so crude that I thoroughly disgust you. I have to confess all this to you, because you deserve complete honesty. . . . '

> She kept looking at him, completely baffled by this man and what he had just said . . . 'Imagine, going around saying all those ghastly things about yourself with a straight face—it's so self-destructive! What can you possibly hope to achieve by it?'

Dagny may be baffled, but Glahn would have understood. 'Telling all these terrible things' about himself, Nagel assures the girl later, is 'part of the scheme—I'm doing it deliberately. I'm hoping . . . that my complete frankness will make some impression on you . . . But perhaps you feel that I'm trying to achieve by guileful and devious means something that others gain by being bold and straightforward? . . . All right, I don't deny it. I am a phony'. By the still more guileful means of penning a false attack on himself in *Pan*'s epilogue, Glahn aims to produce on his audience a favourable impression analogous to that Nagel hoped to make on Dagny. To be sure, the device of two distinct narrators now replaces the earlier protagonist's shifting from active agent to detached observer of himself. But the underlying syndrome is the same: he that humbleth himself shall be exalted. That is precisely what both these self-humblers intend.

Earlier I suggested a possible defense of the epilogue as the one place in *Pan* where we catch Glahn from a point of view other than his own. The truth turns out to be much trickier, since we are now in a position to see that this apparent benefit to the reader is in fact a rhetorical tactic Glahn adapts for self-serving purposes. In the simplest sense, his strategy is transparent: he merely wishes to throw his officious pursuers off the track in order to protect the solitude he said he wanted at the end of *Pan* proper. But he also has the mischievous design of erecting a monument to his own magnificence: if the narrator's hatred backfires and increases our sympathy for Glahn, might this not be just the effect Glahn aimed to produce? On first reading 'Glahn's Death' one may think: what a paragon Glahn must be if even *this* churl stands in awe of him! Such a response must now be re-interpreted as the result not of Hamsun's attempt to raise our opinion of his hero, but of Glahn's oblique exercise in self-glorification. *He* is the subtle martyrologue, inflating his own stature by pretending to view himself through an enemy's eyes! Glahn need not have consciously plotted out every detail of this scheme. In dim purposefulness he oddly resembles Edvarda, whom the doctor once described to him as 'irrational and calculating at the same time'. Whatever validity these words may have as a description of the book's heroine, they admirably fit its hero. In Nietzsche's words, 'one is much more of an artist than one knows' [*Beyond Good and Evil*].

The strongest argument in favour of Glahn's authorship of the epilogue is that so much apparently bad writing in **'Glahn's Death'** by dint of irony now acquires a truly scabrous sheen. Here is Mr X again on his associate: 'He looked magnificent, was full of youthful vigour and had an irresistible way with him'. Spoken by a true authority on the subject. Or his telling Glahn's family to desist from seeking their prodigal son: 'It irritates me constantly to come across their ludicrous advertisements'. No doubt it does. What a heady swirl of contradiction arises from the ambivalence of **Pan**'s central character towards himself! 'Thomas Glahn was in many ways an unusual and likeable man', Mr X begins. Almost immediately, he continues: 'I still feel hostility towards Glahn and the memory of him rouses my hatred'. Near the end of this chapter, Mr X announces: 'I hate Thomas Glahn and I am ready to believe the worst of him'. Yet he adds: 'I thought his smile was very attractive'. Is the narrator Glahn's prosecuting attorney or publicity agent, his foe or sweetheart? Doubtless a person may harbour contradictory feelings about someone else, but this would seem an almost comically extreme instance—especially in the absence of a context that would explain such attitudes in terms more interesting than those of soap-operatic sexual rivalry. However bizarre these clashing quotes may seem if viewed as one man's comment on another, they readily make sense if we view them as reflecting a split within a single self. Perhaps we are being nudged to think along these lines by Mr X's seemingly innocuous observation that he and Glahn 'were about the same age'. Previous critical attempts to see the narrator as a 'double' or 'shadow' of Glahn (along the lines of Nagel and the Midget in *Mysteries*) become much more convincingly grounded if we understand Mr X as a fictional persona created by Glahn himself. It seems more natural for the hero's new literary mask to be an alter ego, than for a stranger he meets abroad to turn out to be a Jungian category. Greek wisdom held that friends are one soul abiding in two bodies; Glahn and Mr X are enemies because they are two souls abiding in the same body. The hero's expertly stage-managed death is a murder, suicide, marriage, and *Liebestod* rolled into one. An impressive economy of contradictions is effected.

Yet beneath the surface of the epilogue's bloody denouement runs a more lurid figurative violence; for while Mr X is apparently stalking Glahn, Glahn is really stalking Edvarda—implementing the doctor's 'discipline' of her by a more refined and gratifying cruelty. Ever the resourceful author, Glahn rings a masochistic change on the theme of sexual rivalry—his earlier plan to kill the Baron is now in-

verted to become a plan to be killed *by* Mr X. At the second remove from real life, Glahn finally does it right: whereas his scheme to blast his actual rival aborted ludicrously, his attempt to get blasted by his fictional one succeeds brilliantly—if only on paper. In contriving to portray himself as victim of a false friend's scorn, Glahn is in effect saying to Edvarda: this is what *you* have done to me. And he tries to say it in a way that will cause her the most intense pain possible. Earlier, the doctor had said: 'She is waiting for her prince, but he has not yet come . . . she thought that you were the prince, especially since you had an animal look [*dyreblik*] . . . But he must come from outside, appear suddenly one day as a being apart'. Apparently Norway was too close to home: 'India' will provide a more exotic stage on which this splendid creature may embrace his doom. As the climax nears, Mr X sounds duly impressed:

> Yet even at that moment his smile was beautiful; it was as if he were weeping inwardly; and indeed his lips trembled although he pretended to be able to smile at such a solemn moment.

For us this may seem only a reversion to Iselin's droopy raptures, but it is clear that here or nowhere is Edvarda's 'prince'. Shrewdly sensing the girl's emphatic response to his ultimate peril, Glahn shoves her back cruelly—'I was no woman,' chides the narrator—and fires. His subsequent deadpan assurance that 'Thomas Glahn died in an accident [*ulykkestilfaelde*]' will have a special resonance too for Edvarda, who will not have forgotten Glahn's mock-serious account of how he happened to shoot himself in the foot:

> 'It happened like this,' I stammered. 'I wanted to put the gun away in the corner, but I was holding it wrongly, pointing down, like this; then suddenly I heard a shot. It was an accident [*uheld*].'
>
> 'An accident [*uheld*],' she said thoughtfully, and nodded. 'Let me see, it is the left foot—but why the left particularly? Yes, of course, an accident [*tilfœlde*] . . . '
>
> 'Yes, an accident [*tilfœlde*],' I interrupted her. . . .
>
> She looked at me reflectively.

For all the epilogue's reiterated messages to the 'Glahn family' this frigidly intimate document is aimed at an audience of one. It is not the life of drunken dissipation in India, but the act of writing **'Glahn's Death'** itself, which constitutes Glahn's real 'revenge for a jilting.'

While Glahn's strategy may successfully accomplish its punitive purpose, what still needs stressing is the destructive cost of this vindictive victory to Glahn himself. It will already be clear that the first part of **Pan** is no mere neutral narrative of events, but an act of historical interpretation on the part of its hero. Careful reading shows that self-justification is the hidden agenda behind Glahn's literary exercise; and in the process of attempting to justify himself, he records a great deal that works to his detriment. While our insight into the hero is enriched through reading his account, there is nothing to suggest that his own insight was deepened through writing it. No wonder he feels no better after finishing: on the last page, time still drags for him as slowly as it did on the first. Yet it is not inevitable that Glahn remain frozen into his own reified design. As Peter Berger has noted, 'common sense is quite wrong in thinking that the past is fixed, immutable, invariable, as against the everchanging flux of the present. On the contrary, at least within our own consciousness, the past is malleable and flexible, constantly changing as our recollection reinterprets and re-explains what has happened' [*Invitation to Sociology: A Humanistic Perspective*]. If Edvarda's return of the two green feathers is the goad which sets Glahn to work on his first narrative, the 'roundabout' receipt of her subsequent imploring letter now offers him the opportunity to shape his biography into a less self-serving fiction. This is precisely what Glahn's pride makes him unable or unwilling to do. The epilogue only becomes his means of extending the battle to dominate the 'other'—if sending Aesop's corpse to Edvarda apparently didn't do the trick, perhaps *this* will! Glahn reacts in this way not because he is an inhuman monster, but because he has an all-too-human resistance to acknowledging the fact of loss. Given a chance to rethink the past, he only rehashes it. Seen as an eerie exercise in self-realization, his last literary testament is not without a certain perverse distinction. Glahn the narcissist splits himself in two and makes one part love the other. Glahn the masochist splits himself in two and makes one part kill the other. In the very instant that his self-hatred is brought to fulfillment, his self-love ceases to be an unrequited passion. No mean trick, surely. But seen instead in terms of Glahn's own potential for more authentic self-awareness, the epilogue makes him fully deserve the very criticism he once made of the doctor for chiding Edvarda: 'He had made a plan and was following it to the bitter end. And what if in spite of all he lost? . . . He would never show it'.

The 'bitter end' is bitter most of all for Glahn, who is too sensitive a character not to infer the self-destructive cost of his own triumph. The very style of the epilogue—for all its straining after a tone of demonic panache—betrays polemical fatigue. Even Mr X's use of the historical present acquires a frightening new urgency: '*I hate Thomas Glahn*' [my italics]. This is no longer a survivor's rancour toward a dead man, but that man's expression of his own *self*-contempt. Glahn is destroyed not because he loses Edvarda, but because he cannot bring himself to admit that he needs her. The hero's fake physical death functions validly as a symbol of his real spiritual death. Mr X's opening reference to Glahn—'He will never come back again. He is dead'—is truer than Glahn knows. For in the end it does not matter whether Glahn is writing *Pan*'s epilogue from an attic in India or holed up in Hammerfest with a Baedeker. In either case, '**Glahn's Death'** turns out to be an unexpectedly appropriate title for this piece of postludic pretension.

Readers familiar with the history of *Pan*'s composition may feel that I have put the cart before the horse. Since '**Glahn's Death'** was published before the main body of the text had been written, parallels between the parts may be accounted for by a more prosaic explanation than the one

here offered. Perhaps the 'same man' who allegedly wrote both is not Hamsun's hero but Hamsun himself, who mined his own earlier story in working up his novel. In that case echoes between the two might result not, as previously held, because the narrator based his second fiction (the epilogue) on his first (*Pan* proper), but rather because the *author* based what was chronologically his second fiction (*Pan* proper) on the pre-existing epilogue. Thus the parallels upon which my own argument depends may have arisen gratuitously from the unusual circumstance that '**Glahn's Death'** served as both source and conclusion for the same book.

To know these peculiarities of *Pan*'s genesis is doubtless interesting—like knowing that Wagner composed the operas of his *Ring* in reverse order. But it is only by sheer luck that we do know such things; finally a work of art must stand or fall by the finished product—which in *Pan*'s case includes '**Glahn's Death'**. Perhaps Hamsun from the start conceived the novel as an entity even though he wrote the conclusion first, or perhaps the first and longer part of the book was an inspired afterthought to what originally had been an independent short story. In either case, I find it hard to believe that an author so attuned to the significance of trifles and the deceptiveness of surfaces could have been—or expected his readers to be—unaware of the function of a section so essential to his book's full impact. That the correspondences noted have arisen by accident seems especially unlikely in view of the author's own claim, in a letter to his publisher, that he never worked so slowly as in writing *Pan*: 'every chapter is a poem, every line worked hard on.' Hamsun was not more of an artist than he knew. Far from being a dispensable addendum to an idyll, "**Glahn's Death'** completes *Pan* by bringing to harrowing perfection the hero's drive to nurture his own self-destructive tendencies. These were hinted at much earlier in the book: 'Was Pan sitting in a tree watching to see how I would act? And was his belly open; and was he crouching so that he seemed to sit and drink from his own belly?' Here Glahn comes closer than ever again to the truth about himself; the epilogue sadly reveals him as fully vindicated in his own eyes.

I would like to conclude by bringing Glahn's motives for writing the epilogue into clearer alignment with Hamsun's own: might the author have wished to keep Glahn alive under some other identity in order to return to him at a later point? I do not mean that he wanted to bring back Glahn as an actual character into his fictional world, as he did Mack and Edvarda in *Rosa*. Glahn is more important than them precisely because he is not *just* a character, but a type of hero with whose ramifications Hamsun remains preoccupied throughout his career. [In his essay 'Who was Hamsun's Hero?' in *The Hero in Modern Scandinavian Literature*, eds. John M. Weinstock and Robert T. Næss has shown that figures such as Nagel and Glahn in the early novels, the middle-aged Knut Pedersen in the '**Wanderer'** set, and August in the trilogy inaugurated by *Wayfarers* make it as appropriate to speak of a 'Hamsun hero' as of a Hemingway hero. These leading figures are usually surrogates for their author (Knut Pedersen was Hamsun's given name). Typically, they are wanderers who never quite succeed in breaking free from a social context that alienates them. Each is a mixture of humourist and brooder, shady dealer and artist, entrepreneur and dreamer. Their degrees of ambivalence, affirmation, and self-dramatization vary; but all seek harmony between an inner identity and what lies outside them. While there are many heroes, there is only one quest; each new name is a pseudonym signalling another stage in the developing authorial alter ego.

Nothing suggests that the Hamsun hero is a divine being in disguise, for his great gifts go hand in hand with all-too-human failings and mortality. Yet it is striking how few of these key figures (in contrast to secondary characters in the same books) actually die. Even late, attenuated variants of the type—Oliver in *The Women at the Pump* (1920) or Abel in *The Ring is Closed* (1936)—remain above ground on the last page. Of those mentioned here, August is the one indisputable casualty: he is swept over a cliff by a stampede of sheep after enough adventures to glut several lifetimes. Nagel in *Mysteries* appears to have committed suicide at the end of the penultimate chapter: bubbles rise to the surface of the water after he leaps off a dock. But we have already watched Nagel die by inches on one previously suicidal occasion, only to discover later a natural explanation of why he has landed on his feet. Given the extent of narrative sleight of hand throughout *Mysteries,* can one help wondering if amidst those bubbles the hero may arise yet again, shake himself off, and head North? The strange fate of his successor, Thomas Glahn, strengthens the case for Hamsun's use of mystification as a strategy for avoiding closure. In a letter from 1890, Hamsun maintained that 'it has always been my ambition to be able to appear incognito, unexpected . . . time and again, in each book with sudden effect, and then disappear again—till the next time.' Perhaps Hamsun felt that killing off one of his exemplary protagonists would not just mean the end of a particular person, but a foreclosure of the possibility of returning to the basic heroic type. By holding open the slim chance that the paradigmatic figure is still alive, Hamsun remains free to whisk him back—'incognito . . . with sudden effect'—when it is time to resume the central quest. While the point cannot be proved, it seems plausible that Hamsun had a vested psychological interest in preserving Glahn as a *living* link in the chain that leads from *Hunger's* nameless hero to Knut Pedersen and beyond. One advantage of my own hypothesis of the authorship of **'Glahn's Death'** is that it enables us to see *Pan* as an instance of—rather than an exception to—the pattern of submergence and re-emergence so typical of Hamsun's quite mortal—yet strangely unkillable—heroes. (pp. 13-27)

Alfred Turco, Jr., "Knut Hamsun's 'Pan' and the Riddle of 'Glahn's Death'," in Scandinavica, *Vol. 19, No. 1, May, 1980, pp. 13-29.*

Peter Lewis   (essay date 1980)

[*In the following essay, Lewis reflects on the political character of literary criticism as it is revealed by the response to Hamsun's associations with Nazi Germany.*]

The Scandinavian literatures have not been major benefi-

ciaries of the modern translation boom, and writers from the various countries still remain largely unknown in England. We can all make the connection between Kierkegaard and Denmark, Ibsen and Norway, Strindberg and Sweden, Laxness and Iceland, but then the headscratching tends to begin. Oh yes, Björnson, now he was . . . um . . . Norwegian? And Martinson, of course, he's a . . . um . . . um . . . Swedish? Perhaps some of the energy that has gone into the Englishing of Ibsen and Strindberg over and over again could more profitably have been expended on making other good, if lesser, writers available.

Knut Hamsun, however, is one of the favoured few Scandinavians to have been translated fairly comprehensively. Following the award to him of the Nobel Prize for Literature in 1920, he achieved widespread international recognition as the most outstanding Norwegian writer since Ibsen, and during the 1920s much of his output became accessible in English, with his new books of the inter-war years being translated not long after their publication in Norway.

With the Second World War, and for various political reasons, Hamsun's reputation suffered and has taken some time to recover, but in recent years Souvenir Press have been gradually reissuing his most important novels in new and very readable translations. Although less ambitious than the monumental Oxford edition of Ibsen, and without its scholarly purpose, this Hamsun project is no less welcome and praiseworthy. Hamsun is, in artistic stature, the nearest Norwegian equivalent in the first half of this century to Ibsen in the second half of the nineteenth century, despite the great differences between them.

The controversy over Hamsun is not only about politics. *Growth of the Soil* is usually claimed as his masterpiece, but it has also been condemned as a weak novel, not nearly in the same class as *Hunger* and *Mysteries.* Yet although critics sometimes disagree strongly about the merit of individual books, and even find something ideologically unpleasant in them, there is a genuine if sometimes 'grudging' consensus that Hamsun belongs to the élite of major twentieth-century writers. And, like a significant proportion of that exclusive band, Hamsun was a man of the Right, indeed the Radical Right.

For someone with his artistic and philosophical roots in German and Nordic Romanticism, and for a disciple of both Nietzsche and Strindberg (though with his own brand of passionate revolutionary individualism), this is not surprising, but it eventually led to his espousal of Fascism, his approval of the Nazi occupation of Norway in 1940, and his famous meeting with Hitler in 1943. Hamsun's position in Norway after 1945 was even more embarrassing for the authorities than Pound's in America, since he was a major writer, a leading national figure, a very old man, and also a "traitor"—not a label he accepted, as his refusal to recant and his defence of his war-time position indicate. Hamsun's Nazi phase has been put down to senility, which gets him off the hook, but this argument plays down the fact that some aspects of Fascism were perfectly consistent with his own earlier thinking.

Closely related to this issue is the problem Hamsun presents to literary criticism. Modern Anglo-American criticism, with its underlying liberal and humanistic ideology, has found a way of admiring the writings of major authors with objectionable political and philosophical views by divorcing their creative work from their ideas and convictions. Yet this position, advocated by the New Critics, is neither satisfactory nor honest. As contemporary Marxist critics readily concede, however disconcerting it may be for liberals, the extraordinary achievement of the great modernists with anti-bourgeois, anti-liberal and reactionary opinions (including Yeats, Pound, Eliot, Lawrence, Wyndham Lewis, Faulkner) is actually inseparable from their theoretical stance.

Indeed the inner contradictions of that stance, as a response to the breakdown of nineteenth-century liberalism and humanism and the crisis of so-called late capitalism, proved to be the source of their creative power. And in Hamsun's case too, you cannot have the baby without the bathwater, however dirty you may find it. If he had not believed what he did believe, he simply would not have been the major writer he is. His primitivism, irrationalism, and antiegalitarian individualism, all of which bring Lawrence to mind, are the springs of his art and also led him, however misguidedly, straight into the arms of the Führer.

The latest title to be issued in the Souvenir Hamsun is **Wayfarers**, James McFarlane's translation of **Landstrykere** (1927). This was the first of three related novels Hamsun wrote in the late 1920s and early 1930s, when he was about seventy and generally thought to be well past his creative peak. But "decline" is a relative term, and although **Wayfarers** does not compare with the novels of his prime, it is anything but the stale, tired work of a writer in his dotage. It is characterized by the freshness, energy, inventiveness, and compelling readability that are among his literary virtues; and although any novel of this amplitude (well over 150,000 words) is almost bound to flag in places, Hamsun sustains the narrative momentum and imaginative pressure for most of the distance.

The narrative voice itself, with its gentle irony and wry humour, is immediately recognizable as Hamsun's highly personal idiom and is one of the most attractive and enjoyable features of the novel. He has an engaging way of involving the reader by generating a sense of almost conversational intimacy, in the way that excellent speakers do, while nevertheless maintaining a monologue. One sometimes has the impression that one is listening to Hamsun rather than reading him. In this respect, his narrative mode has its roots in an old, oral tradition of storytelling, and the cultivated naivety he exploits for such excellent comic and ironic effect has affinities with the _faux-naif_ techniques of the early Romantic poets, even though the ends they pursued were different. Typical of this technique are the interjections, exclamation, and colloquial repetitions with which he peppers the text: "What was Edevart to do now? Answer! Answer at once!" or "Oh, August! What a damned remarkable man! Clever, unreliable, wild—but clever." Such literary use of speech mannerisms epitomizes the sophisticated primitivism of Hamsun's style, an entirely appropriate one for the world he creates.

It is important to emphasize the racy fluency and exhilara-

tion of Hamsun's writing at its best, since those who have not read him often have a false picture of him as worthy but heavy and humourless, full of Scandinavian gloom and foreboding. Hamsun's fictional world may seem remote, but all human life is there, just as it is in Sherwood Anderson's _Winesburg, Ohio,_ which sounds equally unpromising. An inability to place the Lofotens on a map is no obstacle to an appreciation of the human richness Hamsun creates in his fictional Norway.

In this novel, the principal wayfarers of the title, Edevart and August, are two young men from the Nordland village of Polden, who are close friends but also very different, despite the restlessness they both feel and their consequent inability to settle anywhere for long. August is a would-be sophisticate and adventurous man-of-the-world, a charming but unscrupulous rogue also capable of devotion and loyalty, a self-deluder and a deluder of others. The more central figure of Edevart, on the other hand, is closer to the semi-disillusioned Romantic idealist and therefore to the typical Hamsun hero, such as Johan Nagel in **Mysteries.** Among the characteristics of such figures are their impulsiveness, their irrationality, their dislike of urban life and bourgeois society, their sense of deracination combined with a yearning for lost roots, and their quest for individual values in a corrupt world. Hamsun's concept of _en tilvaerelsens udlending_ is a familiar figure in Western culture from early Romanticism to contemporary Existentialism—the outsider. Initially Edevart is a figure of innocence who, when exposed to the corruption of the world, oscillates between maintaining his integrity and compromising himself with institutionalized deceits and double-dealings. Innocence and experience are crucial polarities in the novel, just as money and trade are important themes.

Edevart's personal situation symbolizes that of the peasant, preindustrial and self-sufficient society he comes from at a time when it is being contaminated and eroded by "progress" (cf Lawrence's depiction of the Brangwyns in _The Rainbow_). It is indicative that when the village of Polden suddenly achieves prosperity as the result of a huge herring catch the effect is spiritually debilitating.

Hamsun follows the itinerant lives of both Edevart and August over a period of years, as they repeatedly return to Polden only to leave again, no longer feeling at home there. The novel is full of arrivals and departures; of people emigrating to America, returning to Norway, then emigrating again (like Hamsun himself); of wanderers like the old Jewish watchseller Papst and the Armenian minstrels. Yet although the novel's undertones are pessimistic, Hamsun's ironic detachment from his characters, which prevents this from being a psychological novel and recalls some of the English eighteenth-century comic novelists, notably Fielding, produces a work that has been described as picaresque and that does not accord in the least with the stereotype of the slow, interminable earnestness of Scandinavian literature.

Peter Lewis, "Dispelling the Nordic Gloom," _in_ The Times Literary Supplement, _No. 4034, July 18, 1980, p. 798._

David J. Mickelsen   (essay date 1985)

[*In the following essay, Mickelsen considers the nature of the psychological portrait presented in* Pan.]

As the revolutions of the early part of this century recede from us, we perhaps forget that giants like Proust, Joyce, and Kafka did not spring, full-grown, from the forehead of Joseph Conrad. They had a number of precursors, especially in the last two decades of the nineteenth century, and not just in France, England, and Austria-Hungary. One of these early leaders in the break from the prevailing realistic mode of fiction was the Norwegian Knut Hamsun. He was one of the first Scandinavian novelists to direct primary attention to what he called, in an 1890 article, "the unconscious life of the mind" ("det ubevidste Sjæleliv"). Hamsun is certainly not a complete unknown, but most non-specialists are probably not fully cognizant of his innovative attention to the consciousness of his protagonists.

In 1891 Hamsun delivered a series of polemical lectures throughout Norway, attacking the established writers and touting his own species of novel. He complained that "Zola's manner of writing is like a traffic-director's, and his mood analyses are extremely primitive." . . . "Ibsen's characters have too often been mere apparati, standing forth to represent concepts and ideas." . . .

Hamsun on the poet's use of language:

The poet must always, in every instance, have the vibrant word . . . that by its trenchancy can so wound my soul that it whimpers. . . . One must know and recognize not merely the direct but the secret power of the word; one must be able to give one's writing unexpected effects. It must have a hectic, anguished vehemence, so that it rushes past like a gust of air, and it must have a latent, roistering tenderness so that it creeps and steals into one's mind; it must be able to ring out like a sea-shanty in a tremendous hour, in the time of the tempest, and it must be able to sigh like one who, in tearful mood, sobs in his inmost heart. There are overtones and undertones in words, and there are lateral tones.

Knut Hamsun, in his "Kristofer Janson,"
1888.

Ibsen offers, for Hamsun, no psychological depth or subtlety. As James McFarlane puts it, "To the early Hamsun, the issues were simple and unambiguous. The world of literature fell into two parts: the literature of external event and that of inner motive. Here was the social or 'problematical,' there was the psychological; here the worthless, there the valuable." As Hamsun argues in **"Psykologisk Literatur,"** "there are emergent, bizarre mental stories, distorted feelings, quite strange disturbances in the life of the will, for example, remarkable nervous activities of which science can only posit the existence." . . . This whole area of experience, Hamsun asserts, deserves fictional attention.

At the very least, Hamsun sought equal status for internal events. He asks whimsically, "is a fantasy which actually occurred less real than an actually existing overcoat or a pair of fire tongs?" . . . In short, novels focussing narrowly on an individual's psychology were as important as complex social intrigues. The twentieth century novel, we know, has agreed with Hamsun's preferences by often confining itself to portrayals of an individual's consciousness—frequently through the limited perspective of the individual in question.

Hamsun's early novel **Hunger (Sult)** attends centrally and unambiguously to the crazed state of mind of its starving central character. But **Pan,** written just four years later, at first glance seems to avoid this aspect. This novel, however, which like **Hunger** features a first-person narrator, actually goes even further into the consciousness of its protagonist, to the point of broaching the problem of how an individual conveys a sense of his own subconscious.

Rolf Vige locates the action of **Pan** in "a borderland between dream and reality." . . . If we conceive of "reality" being first of all social and interpersonal, as did many of Hamsun's contemporaries, then **Pan** constitutes a significant retreat from it. The retreat is perhaps not as radical as that begun by novelists in other countries (Huysmans' *A Rebours* [1884], Dujardin's *Les Lauriers sont coupées* [1887], or Maurice Barrès' *Le Culte du Moi* [1887-91], to mention only French innovators), but Hamsun is clearly deflecting attention from society to self to an extent attempted by few other Scandinavians. He does it, moreover, in a way which anticipates by some twenty years the innovations of modernist writers. He both suggests the unconscious and records it as manifest in dreams.

Pan is a retrospective account by the protagonist, Lt. Thomas Glahn, of a summer he spent two years earlier in Sirilund, a small town in the north of Norway, and of his short-lived romance there. His recollections are short, spare, and often unconnected, though presented in chronological order. They recount not only his quickly deteriorating relationship with Edvarda, a local girl, but also his carefree days alone in the hills and woods beyond the town. An epilogue, written by an unidentified person, relates Glahn's eccentric behavior and "accidental" murder (by the narrator of this section) on a hunting expedition in India four years after his stay in the North. This brief summary, however, scarcely begins to convey the freshness and the psychological subtlety of the novel's deceptively simple surface.

In **Pan** Hamsun's shift toward the psychological begins with a simple physical distancing of his protagonist from society. The frequency of dialogue in the novel, evidence that social interaction remains important, does not contravene Glahn's constitutional estrangement from society. Glahn's failure to relate to Edvarda, a girl very much a part of the town, is merely the centerpiece of a more far-reaching disability. Glahn is inept and awkward in the presence of others, and he is more at home in the forest, where he takes refuge from the pain of "civilized" contacts. Indeed, Glahn has an ecstatic, almost orgiastic, sexually-charged relation with nature. This feeling surfaces most visibly in his paean to the "large, white flowers" open to receive hawkmoths: "they are sexually aroused flowers and I see how they are aroused." . . . Glahn is happiest when alone, free to indulge in meditative, lyric responses to nature:

> Quiet and hushed everywhere. I lie the whole evening and look out the window. An enchanted light hung over field and forest at that hour, the sun had set and coloured the horizon with a fatty, red light, motionless like oil. Everywhere the sky was open and pure, I gazed into that clear sea and it was as if I lay face to face with the depths of the earth and as if my heart beat fervently toward that pure earth and was at home there. . . .

Having isolated his meditative protagonist, Hamsun can explore/expose his mind. However, his choice of narrative mode has effectively eliminated direct access to the subconscious. Omniscient narrators, virtually by definition, can easily record the subconscious life of their characters through the technique of what Dorrit Cohn, in a study of representation of consciousness, calls "psycho-narration." Interior monologue is another solution, first used on an extended basis by Dujardin five years before *Pan*. Narrated monologue offers yet another alternative for representing consciousness—common in Flaubert and, later, in Joyce, Kafka, and Mann. But Hamsun has complicated his goal of making accessible the mind of his character, for none of the techniques just mentioned is available in the first-person mode (even interior monologue is "overheard" rather than narrated; it is not true "self-narration." And since an individual cannot present his *own* unconscious life—cannot be conscious of what is unconscious—Hamsun seems obliged to restrict himself to the conscious sector of his protagonist's mind.

But Hamsun largely bars us even from the conscious inner life of his protagonist. Glahn is hardly a loquacious narrator (the novel runs barely ninety pages in the collected edition). The narrative is essentially a series of abrupt sketches, brief but suggestive tableaux. An extreme example is this depiction of a picnic: "Light dresses, blue eyes, the ring of glasses, the sea, the white sails. We all sang a little. Cheeks grew flushed." . . . Less pictorial but equally elliptical is the opening of chapter 34: "A man said: 'Have you given up shooting now? Aesop has scented something in the woods, he is chasing a hare.' I said: 'Go and shoot it for me.' Some days passed. . . ." . . . And Glahn goes on to another scene.

More surprisingly, given Hamsun's polemical stance, the general terseness of this spare account dwindles to virtual silence when approaching the protagonist's thoughts. Hamsun rejected Zola's slice-of-life Naturalism as focussing too exclusively on externals. But *Pan* is not even a very full slice of Glahn's internal life, for most of Glahn's thoughts are omitted—despite Hamsun's proclaimed interest in the mental life of his characters. Typical is the bare report, "my thoughts are full of joy." . . . That is all—this from the avowed proponent of the life of the mind. The tale generally recounts actions and situations rather than reactions to them, thus the workings of Glahn's mind must generally be deduced rather than observed. "When she had gone," Glahn says of Edvarda, "I sat down again to think about it all. I wrote a letter and asked for my uniform to be sent." . . . We assume the decision about the uniform stems from his meeting with Edvarda, but we are not told so, or why. At times, to be sure, the narrative does recount the thoughts as well as the actions of Glahn, . . . but more typically they are vaguely summarized or elided. When Glahn leaves Sirilund, with Edvarda standing on the quay, our only indication of his state of mind is the shorthand "A wave of sadness passed through my heart." . . . Whether unwilling or unable to examine himself closely, Glahn furnishes little description of his personal feelings and motives.

Beyond this characteristic terseness, Glahn also provides very little explanation. His account is "undigested." For instance, the questions raised by several pointed references to Edvarda's poor clothing are never answered. Fortunately, unexplained situations are usually transparent enough that no narrative commentary is needed. Edvarda returns to Glahn a memento he had given her: "An icy terror runs through me, I grow cold. Two green feathers! I say to myself. Well, what is to be done about it? But why should I grow cold? See, there's a damned draft now from those windows." . . . The real origin of Glahn's chill is of course obvious, but this example shows how deduction is vital to penetrating the situation's subtext.

The absence of interpretation and commentary can be traced to Hamsun's choice of narrative situation. Although this novel is a retrospective first-person narrative, it exemplifies what Cohn calls "the consonant type of self-narration": that is, novels in which the temporal disjunction between narrating self and experiencing self does not result in a corresponding disjunction of point of view. The two "selves"—then and now—are "consonant," they largely agree. As a result, the reader does not benefit from the narrator's hindsight.

In *Pan* consonance is achieved by simple suppression of the narrating self, which intrudes only briefly and occasionally, and then often unreliably (as when Glahn claims to be writing for "amusement"). The experiencing self dominates. Much of the work is pure report, and the narrative by and large follows in almost diary-like fashion a straight chronological course, as if related at the time of the events. Act, emotion, and verbalization closely follow one another in this passage: "I upset my glass; I rose unhappily. 'Oh dear, I have upset my glass!' I said." . . . Or: "A fir cone falls with a dull thud to the ground. I think: A fir cone fell!" . . . Glahn's narrative bears little stylistic evidence of narrative control. Lack of sentence subordination (and indeed lack of subordination on all levels) betrays the moment-to-moment quality of the narrative. Phrases are linked by "and" (eight in the first four sentences alone) or by no conjunction at all, as in this single sentence: "I came out of the wood and saw two people ahead of me, two people wandering along, I overtook them, it was Miss Edvarda, I recognized her and greeted her; the Doctor was with her." . . . This kind of blunt juxtaposition suggests that experiences are being relived, without any kind of interposed interpretive framework—even the minimal grammatical one. And as other critics have noted, the constant shifting back and forth between present and past tenses implies that the narrative's retrospective quality is not very firmly anchored. This pressure toward the now, this immediacy, forecloses yet another dimension of the protagonist's consciousness: that contributed by the narrating self.

More often than not, if comments are forthcoming, they are unreliable—whether deriving from the narrating or the experiencing self. Distortion, to be sure, is the logical and even necessary consequence of non-omniscient narration, which by definition cannot be complete and correct. And Glahn is, in fact, often unreliable. Vige observes that "Edvarda stands directly before us as if illuminated by the midnight sun's unreal glare." . . . He neglects to emphasize, however, that the "unreal glare" derives directly from the nature of the narrating consciousness, and that it extends throughout the whole novel. To Glahn things in the north are "distorted" ("fordreiede"); even the seasons are different and the people, he claims, are peculiar. Later they are bewitching ("bedårende").

The novel's first paragraph already arouses suspicions of unreliability, and the third paragraph contains patent inaccuracies: "I no longer always think of her, not now, no I have completely forgotten her." . . . The unwary critic, perhaps reserving unreliability for the twentieth century, may take everything that Glahn says at face value (as Sehmsdorf apparently does when he assumes, for example, that Glahn is unaware of the consequences of blowing up the mountain). Perhaps Glahn is indeed naively candid, and his "unplanned" arrival at Edvarda's party, for example, was actually caused by his gun deflecting the compass, or "perhaps it was fate." . . . More likely he represses, deliberately or not, the painful awareness of that period of his life. For readers of *Pan, l'ère du soupçon* must arrive early and stay late.

Indirectly, however, it is precisely these unexplained and incorrectly explained events which entice the reader toward the "unconscious life of the mind." Gaps invite filling, distortions invite correcting. In effect, the reader must recognize distortions and provide missing data (this is true in the epilogue as well). Hamsun's novel is, in fact, a remarkable early example of a gambit common in the twentieth-century novel: getting the *reader* to provide interpretation and even detail—though not, as in later novels, organization as well (cf., for example, the novels of Robbe-Grillet). An obvious example of such a gap occurs when Glahn asks Henriette about how she has been embraced. " 'Did he do it like this?' 'Yes,' she whispered trembling." A new paragraph begins, "It was four o'clock." . . . It is not difficult to supply the omitted time and event, but the point is that Hamsun's narrative choice forces that kind of reader involvement. This involvement moves toward Glahn's mind in his conversation with Herr Mack. Mack says playing solitaire " 'comes out all right with a little bungling.' . . . 'The solitaire comes out with a little bungling?' I asked. 'Yes.' It came to me that I could read in his eyes . . ." . . . But *what* is "read" is carefully omitted—another open invitation for the reader to fill in the gap.

Every novel, of course, requires this kind of activity to some extent, though few nineteenth-century novels do to the same degree as *Pan.* Nor do omissions and distortions really suffice to show "det ubeviste Sjæleliv"—they only

hint at it, encourage guesses about it. So Hamsun resorts to yet another means to lead his readers to the "inner life" of his protagonist: dreams. Like Dostoevsky in *Crime and Punishment,* for example, or Strindberg in *Miss Julie,* Hamsun used dreams as a powerful means of unveiling his characters. And in *Pan* they are necessary means. The terseness and unreliability of its narrator require some direct glimpse into his unconscious, some firm ground for grasping his character. In short, dreams provide the hints, the interpretive keys that orient the reader among the confusing distortions and omissions of the "conscious" narrator.

Hamsun clearly recognized that dreams can be an important means of revelation. In one of his lectures, he asserted that modern writers must look *behind* external facts to inconspicuous but revelatory causes and influences—and even to dreams and flights of fantasy. Like later writers, Hamsun focuses on conjecture, recollection, and dream instead of concrete current choice and present action. Interiorization reflects a change in values: a person is no longer one who *does,* but one who *thinks.* In the case of Glahn, although there is little direct record of his thoughts, Hamsun manages to insinuate us into his mind by indirection and, especially, by dreams.

Dreams are moments of intensity which, simply by contrast with "real" events, provide emphasis. From the very first page the narrative's status is equivocal: "something happened to me, or else I dreamed it." . . . Referring to Edvarda, Glahn admits he has loved a dream. . . . And as he concludes his tale, he refers to a letter: "I understand it at once or perhaps I dreamt it one sleepless night." . . . These statements appear in structurally important positions, the beginning and end of Glahn's section. If not actually calling the reality of these events in doubt, they at least suggest a continuity between Glahn's dream life and his social life, and, in a broader sense, underline the narrative's thorough-going subjectivity.

Dream life is represented by two major dreams. Hamsun draws attention to these dreams by devoting considerable narrative time to them and by investing them with an aura of what we might call the "mythical." Thus emphasized, dreams are, in effect, *moments privilégiés,* special nodes of attention for the protagonist and for the reader. For Glahn, they are especially important since they function as a refuge from interactions (and inevitable embarrassments and anxieties) with others. His dreaming is at once a symptom of his isolation from the "real" world of Sirilund and an outlet for the frustrations generated there. And for the reader, these dreams offer what is conventionally assumed to be a more reliable picture of the character, one unfettered by the constraints of propriety and reason.

Glahn's love for Edvarda is the generative force of the entire narrative; hence the appropriateness of Hamsun's original title, *Edvarda.* The changes in his way of life begin soon after her appearance, and he is never able to return to his original state. In effect, rather than his "social self " being disrupted by exposure to the Dionysian (as Sehmsdorf would have it), we should reverse the formula to say that his self is disrupted by exposure to the social; his troubles begin when he comes down from the hills to town.

The major figure in Glahn's dreams is Iselin. She was a forest dweller, a sort of itinerant spirit devoted to hunters. She lived in a quasi-legendary era four generations before, yet she is still seen—at least by Glahn. There is a primitive quality both in her desires and her freedom from sophisticated restraints. The passages associated with her, even more than the novel in general, are striking for their natural imagery and their elemental, lyrical simplicity. Ultimately, of course, these qualities derive from Glahn himself, the originator of the dreams. In addition to the legendary overtones she carries, Iselin embodies what the title (and indeed Glahn himself, by his goatish appearance) only suggest: man's inclination to submerge in an unrestrained reign of physical desire. But since she appears only in dream, she also embodies man's turning inward for satisfaction (note the vision of Pan who "seemed to . . . drink from his own belly." . . . Simply described, Iselin is the dream fulfillment of Glahn's sexual impulses. The major component of both dreams is sexual, and both are followed by actual sexual encounters. Henriette and Eva appear as if "brought forth from the erotic mood in nature and in Glahn's mind. Dream and reality combine: the real love story seems as unreal as the daydream." . . . Iselin only appears after Glahn has been frustrated with Edvarda. Rather transparently, Iselin is a dream-surrogate for Edvarda (not a competitor, as Sehmsdorf argues, and she is followed in her turn by other, real-life surrogates: Henriette and Eva. After Edvarda's departure, Glahn says "Iselin, Eva," thereby listing the women who compensate for his lost "dream of love." Glahn had admitted to Eva, "I love three things . . . I love a dream of love I once had, I love you, and I love this patch of earth." Eva asks, "And which do you love best?" "The dream," he replies. . . . He is left with only dream.

The function of dream for Glahn can be seen more clearly if we go beyond the binary oppositions favored by most Hamsun critics. Three areas of experience govern Glahn's life. The first revolves around the pantheistic enjoyment of nature mentioned earlier. Glahn's summer in the north begins when this "son of the forest" has come from a social situation and has chosen to seek refuge in the solitude of the wilds. "In the forest did all within me find peace, my soul became tranquil and full of might." . . . He says at the conclusion, now more wistful than true, "I belong to the forests and solitude." . . . He is at home there, even though staying just for the summer. He loves everything and enjoys the changing seasons, changing weather, the smallest parts of nature. More often than not, the descriptions of nature are iterative, covering extended states rather than reactions to specific episodes—an appropriate mode for describing the cyclical events of nature.

The second area of experience involves Edvarda. With her, Glahn is thrust fully back into a social situation. Solitude is now gone forever—soon after he says "I had never tried to be more alone." . . . Soon, however, he is intoxicated with happiness because of Edvarda. "What am I happy about? . . . I think of her, I close my eyes and stand still on the path and think of her; I count the minutes." . . . Here the descriptions are typically durative, rather than iterative—appropriate for situations which are not cyclical, but singular and irreversible, irrecoverable.

The act of narration itself suggests a desire to return to or reclaim these experiences, hence the focus on the experiencing self, but the project is doomed. Despite Glahn's disclaimers, Edvarda's image still dogs him everywhere, even in India, but he can't go back to his original solitude and peace. He cannot forget, he cannot erase Edvarda's memory.

Hence the third area of experience, the third source of satisfaction. Even while still in the Nordland, Glahn can slow the irresistible flow of events only in sleep, and dream. That is why he loves the dream best. As Olaf Øyslebø notes, the stories, dreams, and legends in *Pan*—fictions within a fiction—are in effect atemporal and aspatial ("stedløs"), thus effectively isolating Glahn from the pressures of his relationship with Edvarda. But more lasting measures are required. Near the end he says, "I am weary of my sorrow, I want to forget it, drown it." . . . On the third "Iron Night," expectantly awaiting a great change, he closes his eyes and is lulled until he feels himself "lifted out of my context." . . . God or a spirit seems nearby; dead tired, he sleeps. At several other important junctures sleep is the catalyst or the result, especially of the second Iselin dream. But losing oneself in this way is again only temporary. Sleep must be followed, eventually, by the Big Sleep: Glahn embarks on a course of alienation and self-mortification (including the act of narration, which probes his wound even while denying it), and his self-destructiveness finally culminates in his being shot. Death, the static durative, the eternal iterative, is the ultimate cure. Dream has simply offered a pale anticipation of it.

The narrator of *Pan* provides little direct (explicit) information about his thoughts, and what we read is probably distorted. Yet Hamsun has taken measures to ensure that we come in contact with his protagonist's state of mind. The consciousness of limits encourages us to look beneath the surface, and dreams offer specific information from that region. Dream and wish, unconfined by external contingencies, are thus crucial in discerning the character's internal configuration. Hamsun uses dream and the dream-like to provide a qualitatively different perspective on personality—a perspective far removed from the usual, incomplete opinion gained by deducing a person's motives and attitudes from his behavior. If his use of dream is not always subtle, this is because his readers had not been to the school of Freud, Joyce, and Proust.

Hamsun's distinction lies not in his special use of dreams, but that he used them at all. Few of his contemporaries in the 1890s even suspected, much less exploited, the potential for character portrayal offered by this area of experience. Putting *Pan* in this broad generic context—the move toward the modern novel's attention to consciousness—simply provides another indication of Hamsun's stature as Norway's foremost novelist. (pp. 195-205)

David J. Mickelsen, "Representation of Consciousness in 'Pan': Knut Hamsun as Modernist," in Symposium, *Vol. XXXIX, No. 3, Fall, 1985, pp. 195-206.*

Harald Naess (essay date 1985)

[*In the following excerpt, which was taken from a lecture originally delivered at the University of Cambridge on 4 December 1985, Naess sketches the circumstances surrounding the composition of* Growth of the Soil *and discusses some of the critical responses this novel has provoked.*]

In the summer of 1916 Knut Hamsun began writing a novel about a pioneer, one Isak, who makes his way into the wilderness of Northern Norway, where the Lapps live. After building himself his first sod hut, he is joined by Inger, who, because of her harelip, apparently had no chance of finding herself a husband down in the parish. Together they begin to till the soil, raise cattle, bring up children, and in all of this they are aided miraculously by the local bailiff, Geissler, seemingly a shady character who soon loses his job, though he remains faithful to his settlers in the wilderness. After two boys, a girl is born to Isak and Inger; she is afflicted with a harelip like her mother, and Inger, thinking of what she has had to suffer because of the blemish, kills the baby, and, when the murder is discovered, goes to prison for six years. Geissler, the former bailiff, brings industry, mining workers and money to the area, and Isak's Inger, now returned from prison, where she learned the ways of the city, has periods of flightiness followed by dark religion. Of the two sons, Sivert is a trusty farmer like his father; the oldest, Eyeseus, however, inherits his mother's restlessness and disappears to America, from where he never returns. The mining industry, too, disappears, and at the end the people are left in the wilderness as peacefully and content as when they came, except for the fact that in the meantime they have been joined by nine other families, one of them Aksel and his pregnant live-in Barbro. Their life story repeats that of Isak and Inger, though in a minor key as it were, adding depth to the theme.

Hamsun in the summer of 1916, then, set out to give his countrymen a Norwegian family Robinson or, rather, an agricultural success story of the kind he had seen thirty years earlier among the Norwegian settlers in the American Midwest. On its appearance in December of 1917, as *Markens grøde—Growth of the Soil*—the novel became immediately popular and three years later earned for its author the Nobel Prize in literature. The reaction of H. G. Wells was typical: 'I do not know how to express the admiration I feel for this wonderful book without seeming to be extravagant. I am not usually lavish with my praise, but indeed the book impresses me as among the very greatest novels I have ever read. It is wholly beautiful; it is saturated with wisdom and honour and tenderness.' These generous words should probably be seen in their context of World War I pessimism. In the year 1920 thinking people everywhere were concerned with what Wells called 'the salvaging of civilization.' As a social critic, Hamsun had been a voice in the wilderness for ten years; now, for the first and only time, people listened to him as a prophet, and not only because of the art of Hamsun the poet but because of the persuasiveness of the message of a real-life farmer.'

Knut Hamsun was of farming stock and spent his child-

Caricature drawing of Knut Hamsun, by David Levine. Reprinted by permission from The New York Review of Books. *Copyright © 1971 Nyrev, Inc.*

hood on farms in South and North Norway. At the age of fourteen he had had enough of farming to know he did not want to make it his living. Even so, he had to work on farms in the American Midwest before finally choosing the big city—Oslo, Copenhagen, Helsinki, Moscow, Paris—as the natural locus for developing his talents. In his early novels, even though they have pastoral scenes, the farmer is looked down upon as 'nothing but lice, peasant cheese, and Luther's catechism.' But in 1908 Hamsun's younger Danish friend and colleague, Johannes V. Jensen, published an article entitled 'Farmer Civilization,' in which he gave his concept of the farmer a new definition. Frank Norris and Theodore Roosevelt even had something of the farmer in them. Bjørnstjerne Bjørnson *was* a farmer, and Knut Hamsun was 'the farmer in excelcis.' Unfortunately, said Jensen, Hamsun was caught by the false enticements of city culture, for he wanted above all to become a gentleman. In order to attract attention he decked himself with eccentricity; in order to prove his genius he pretended to be insane. This was so because Hamsun did not understand the farmer. Jensen wrote: 'The most highly valued literary treasures have come to us from anonymous commoners. Modern civilization from Newton and George Stephenson to Darwin and Edison derives in its entirety from the nature-bound imagination of the farmer.'

Hamsun replied in an article similarly entitled '**Farmer Civilization,**' in which he described the development of the artist as a movement away from nature, from the primitive origins of popular culture. If, by farm culture, Jensen had meant the practical achievements of everyday life, Hamsun preferred to call it by its right name, materialism; and he did not consider such materialism a suitable subject for modern literature. As for himself, only by going to the city, where he had eliminated the farmer in him, had Hamsun been able to produce art. Even so, Hamsun must have had second thoughts. In 1909, after years of restless wandering, he entered into a new marriage, which was not without its problems, for, as he told his bride-to-be: I who despise the theatre, love an actress. In 1911 he travelled with his actress-wife 600 miles north to the farm Skogheim on Hamarøy. He continued to write, often living in hotels away from home because of bad nerves and crying children, while his wife, the former actress, looked after the crops and the cattle. Still, Hamsun, when he was not writing, was a proud farmer, working hard to improve his land.

In December of 1915 Hamsun's novel **Segelfoss Town** had appeared and in July of the following year we can see from his letters that he has something new under way. Six months later, though, he complains of having made no headway; he knew exactly what each chapter was to contain, but he had written no more than forty pages. Not until the summer of 1917 does he seem to be progressing with the manuscript and he speaks for the first time of what he calls his 'agricultural novel.' At the same time he wants to get rid of Skogheim, since there is nothing more to cultivate: 'I want to get another homestead,' he writes, 'it would have to be tillable land, working the soil is the most enjoyable thing I know.' But not long after that Skogheim is taking all his time. 'I need to be lifted away from this place,' he moans, and he now hopes to find a house without land. In July of 1917 he moved again south, living in the city of Larvik until November of 1918, when he bought another, much bigger farm, Nørholm. It is during this landless year, then, that Hamsun composes his novel about the pleasures of cultivating the soil. 'What we need,' he told an acquaintance, 'is getting more of the proletariat out of the towns and back to the country.' Even so, another topic was equally pressing and probably inspired the writing of the novel in the first place. In Hamsun's letter from the war years there are few references to the battle field, but many to children suffering because of the war. 'It is worst for the children,' he writes again and again, though he may not be thinking of the war casualties as much as of newborn children in Norway being killed by their unwed mothers who tried to conceal their pregnancy and, as Hamsun thought, were encouraged in their crime by the new and too liberal legislation. Already in January of 1915 he had published an article about these so-called child murders with the following incredible lines: 'Such a mother and such a father are hopeless. Hang them, hang both parents, do away with them. Hang the first hundred of them, that will give respect, then perhaps these terrible conditions will improve.' During the following

months, after being attacked in the press by writers and psychologists, Hamsun wrote several other articles, but he must have found that this was not the most effective way of expressing his ideas. Already in April of 1916 he wrote to his younger colleague Johan Bojer, who had recently had his first play produced at the National Theatre: 'What if you were to take up for dramatic treatment these terrible child murders every winter and spring, which are being defended by sterile mothers and so-called humane judges. You can do it, I can't.' Later Hamsun may have felt the subject was too serious for the theatre, or that Bojer was too young too handle it. This is when he begins writing *Growth of the Soil.*

Unfortunately for Knut Hamsun, his view of man and the world has sometimes been construed on the basis of his intemperate outpourings in the daily press rather than on his creative writings. The difference between Hamsun's journalism and his art is nowhere more striking than in *Growth of the Soil,* where the murder of newborn children by unwed mothers is treated with considerable understanding, where the sterile mothers are not sterile after all, and where the humane judges are drawn without malice. Mrs Heyerdahl's defence of Barbro seems to be made up of arguments taken from Hamsun's antagonists in the press, and so cleverly and realistically that some readers overlook the irony, probably because this irony is critical and affirmative at the same time throughout the book. Aksel is pinned to the ground for seven hours by a falling tree, yet we are told, and made to believe, that Nature is a healer of all wounds. These people have the health and the manners of animals; Isak has a rasping voice, rough looks, and tremendous strength; Inger, we are told, 'always tried to comfort and speak hopefully through her harelip. It was not pretty to hear when she spoke, for a sort of hissing, like steam from a leaky valve, but a comfort all the same out in the wilds.' This generous optimism explains the sustained popularity of the novel, though among critical readers, H. G. Wells' praise of its wisdom, humour and tenderness has been replaced by a sense that there is something sinister and inferior about the novel.

In 1937, Leo Lowenthal—partly inspired by Georgij Plekhanov's criticism of forty years before—found fascist streaks in *Growth of the Soil* and other novels by Hamsun; and post-war Marxist critics in Norway and Germany have been busy attacking what they consider to be its *Blut und Boden* mysticism. Lowenthal speaks correctly of Hamsun's lifelong suspicion of urban society, and of his emphasis on women as mothers. Hamsun's admiration of the farmer was also unmistakable by 1917, though Lowenthal could have pointed out that it was a very recent development. Furthermore his emphasis on the importance of rhythm in Hamsun's fiction is interesting, even if it seems unfair in Norway's greatest novelist to criticise the musicality of his prose. Of another kind of rhythm Lowenthal writes:

> The endless reproduction of natural phenomena, the cyclic order of nature, as opposed to the apparent disorder and happenstance of all individual and historical facts, testifies to the powerlessness of man. It is the extreme opposite of human self-assurance before nature. In this new ideolo-

gy, which seeks to transfigure helplessness and subjection, the individual in seemingly free volition lays down his arms before a mythical power. [*Literature and the Image of Man*]

These interesting observations are not surprising coming from a sociologist of the Frankfurter School. What is surprising is that Lowenthal should have found many willing followers among Danish and Norwegian critics. After all, in Scandinavia, it is possible not only to be a progressive social engineer and yet be drawn to the solitude of the woods or to appreciate a sense of personal insignificance vis-à-vis all-powerful nature. A native of these countries might accept the term 'paganism,' but hardly 'fascism' for this attitude.

Other critics, to the degree they were drawn to Hamsun's modernism of the 1890s—*Hunger, Mysteries, Pan*— tended to condemn *Growth of the Soil* as an anomaly, and some of them, like Ronald Popperwell's teacher, Brian Downs, indicated Hamsun had written the novel with a view to winning the Nobel Prize. Of the novel's mining speculator, Geissler, Professor Downs writes:

> How much of a fox is he? If Hamsun was a fox, he never played his game better than when he qualified for the Nobel Prize with *Growth of the Soil.* It was custom-built to the conditions of the award, and in that measure, most famous of his books though it may be, it is untypical. [*Modern Norwegian Literature 1860-1918*]

If, when calling it untypical, we are thinking of the monumental conception and positive tone of *Growth of the Soil,* we do well to compare with Edvard Munch's Oslo University Aula decorations from the same period, also regarded as untypical by all who think of Munch as the painter of decadence. But there are healthy people, farmers, and happy children in Munch's works immediately before the Aula decorations, and even if we go back to the early nineties, there are canvasses by Munch filled with sunshine. Similarly, in such Hamsun novels as *Dreamers, Benoni, Rosa, Children of the Age* and *Segelfoss Town* there are many examples of happy enterprise, and, sandwiched in between such tragic works as *Mysteries* and *Pan,* there is a novel praising practical business men at the expense of parasitic artists. This novel from 1893 admittedly has no farmers, but it is called *Shallow Soil,* and, at Hamsun's own recommendation, it was the first of his works to be translated for the American market.

There are certainly many ways in which *Growth of the Soil* is untypical of Hamsun's work. There are no suicides, no one spits into the ear of an eager listener, no one sends his sweetheart a dead dog, no rich businessman spends his Christmas Eves on a waterbed with his parlour maid, though more than such excesses, its seeming lack of irony is what made readers think of *Growth of the Soil* as an atypical and, sometimes, inferior novel. During the last half dozen years, however, such Hamsun scholars as Allen Simpson and Øystein Rottem have pointed vigorously to the presence of the ironic mode throughout the text of *Growth of the Soil,* thereby repudiating both the notion of fascist ideology and artistic superficiality. Much recent criticism is inspired by a hermeneutics of suspicion, in the

novel the critic no longer trusts the narrator, he may accept what is being told, but he does not believe the teller. The early readers of *Growth of the Soil,* including perhaps those who gave Hamsun the Nobel Prize for the novel, believed the narrator when, usually through the character of Geissler, he assured them that farmers were needful on earth, that they maintain life, generation after generation, and that this is the meaning of eternal life. More recent readers, recalling that Geissler is a sentimental drunk and worse, the person who brings mining industry to the district, will have difficulties accepting the novel's narrator as a representative of the author Knut Hamsun.

This is the line taken by Professor Allen Simpson, who taking his cue from the work of Herbert Schneidau, sees agriculture as culture, so that, like other forms of civilization—what Schneidau refers to as history—farming produces alienation from nature. In the biblical story of Cain and Abel, Abel the shepherd was killed by Cain the agrarian murderer, who later became a city builder and whose descendants became vagabonds. This means that, in the last resort, the yeoman Isak is only an early stage of the vagabond Geissler, who, according to Simpson, 'ends up . . . singing . . . a sentimental hymn to the beauties of nature . . . , even after he has assisted in its destruction' [in *Scandinavian Studies* 56 (1984)]. Nature by Schneidau is seen as feminine, a matriarchal universe, subjugated and eventually destroyed by history, by a patriarchal intelligence. Inger, and her darker counterpart Barbro, as well as the Lapps, represent Nature, hence it could be said that, when Inger goes to prison, Isak loses nature to gain a farm, and when Inger returns from prison without her harelip after cosmetic surgery, this is nature with history added, etc. Even though these are interesting ideas, supported by modern ecology, a careful reading of *Growth of the Soil* hardly warrants this siding with the nomadic Lapps against the agrarian settler Isak. In his eagerness to add irony to Hamsun's paradise, Professor Simpson seems to me to have filled it with more snakes than belong there.

Much earlier, in an article comparing Halldor Laxness's novel *Independent People* and Knut Hamsun's *Growth of the Soil,* Ronald Popperwell wrote as follows about Knut Hamsun's *Weltbild:*

> There is never any catastrophic disparity between the individual and environment in *Growth of the Soil,* since the individual always seeks out and is able to find the environment which best suits his particular organism. And as each is also a human organism, it has specifically human characteristics even when it is a "weed", like Brede Olsen or Oline, and this has consequences for Hamsun's characterization. Although determinism is implicit in this way of depicting people, it involves no streak of pessimism but rather the reverse since it embodies a belief that each individual is the subject of purposive development; it would be difficult to imagine any character in *Markens grøde* committing suicide. That this view of man has an amoral and anti-intellectual aspect will at once be obvious, for although the individual is not necessarily engaged in an entirely brainless activity in fulfilling his bi-

ological purposes, he is placed in the position of being the subject of impulses over which he has no control. The possibility of choice in human affairs is discounted, and everything that happens wears an inconsequent air; snakes or good fairies may suddenly appear, and human existence has an absurd aspect. It is this absurd aspect Hamsun acknowledges in his ironic attitude to his characters, and in the puppet-like quality he gives them. It is also here we find the intellectual kernel in Hamsun's work, since it involves an evaluation of the human situation. But this evaluation of the human situation is unambivalent, for although Hamsun finds that human existence has its absurd aspect and although irony includes disdain and thus a certain contempt for life, there goes with it a strong feeling for life and a belief in its intuitive ways. [*Studie Centenalia in Honorem Memoriae Benedikt S. Porarinsson*]

I find this to be both sensible and perceptive, based on the reasoning and the literary instinct of a person well acquainted with Hamsun's work, and I shall merely add some ideas about the character of Geissler, whom Popperwell does not include in his treatment, even though he is, with the exception of Eleseus, the only psychologically interesting character in the novel. Of all Hamsun's symbolic pictures of an artist, Geissler is probably the one who comes closest to a self-portrait. He is Lieutenant Holmsen and Tobias Holmengraa of the novel *Children of the Age* in one person. Actually, *Growth of the Soil* for all its stated untypicality, is a variation of this earlier novel about the conflict of the landed estate and the industry brought to the district by the vagabond. What is new is the way the vagabond of *Growth of the Soil* is responsible for both farming *and* industry. The confusion, as we can see from letter, is Hamsun's own. He told a Danish woman: 'You and I should not live on poetry and emptiness, we should be active as human beings, marry and have children, establish homes and cultivate the soil. Think of it. I am old and know it. I have written perhaps 30 books, I don't remember exactly, but I have five children, they are my great blessing. What should people do with those books. Without my children I wouldn't even have a right to my grave.' On the other hand, he spoke more seriously of writing as being his real vocation, and misspellings of his name, or the addition of a title such as 'Herr Novelist Knut Hamsun' infuriated him, since, as he told his well-meaning addressors 'there is one single person in Norway called Hamsun, that's me, and I don't think there is anyone else in the world by that name.'

There are several ways in which *Growth of the Soil* is not romantic in the sense of being idealized. Hamsun's utopia is not Virgil's Arcadia, not a city's person's dream of happy days in the country, but neither is it the primitivist's dream of unspoilt nature—the Lapps are treated as an inferior race and modern machinery is welcomed with open arms. Rather what we have is an experienced town-and-country planner's blueprint for a farming community, with careful add-on plans and built-in contingencies—accidents of weather and human passion, or the temporary invasion of debilitating city manners—but all of this is overcome by a life force which is perhaps more mythical than realistic. Certainly the size of Isak's acreage and the

speed with which he proceeds from settler to margrave in the course of twenty-five years is American rather than North Norwegian. And the mechanized farming equipment would not have come as early to the settlers had it not been for the curious character Geissler, who is also of mythical dimensions. Still, the myth is tempered throughout by the irony of which Dr. Popperwell speaks. Isak is a barge of a man, but, for a hero, rather simple of mind; Inger is referred to as a vestal, a curious term when we consider her frequent sexual escapades with young Gustav; and tight-fisted Aksel, saved from death by Oline and Brede, contrives to get his two rescuers into a fight so as to avoid paying either of them. It is a loving irony, and we are reminded of Ibsen's words about *The Wild Duck*, that daily association with the characters in this play had endeared them to him in spite of their manifold failings. And, once *The Wild Duck* is brought in, it is useful to reflect that, as in Ibsen's play, the happy wilderness area is the creation of an outsider, himself viewed ironically. Dr. Relling and Geissler are both drunks, perhaps the authors' way of indicating that each of them has difficulty roughing it in his borderland of dream and reality.

Geissler is being described as unreliable and superficial, though the readers will feel that the narrator here, where he represents the villagers, is not himself reliable. More trustworthy is his characterization of Geissler as an impatient person who can't bear to listen or to be thanked, who wants nothing free of charge, an adventurer, extravagant, though well-studied and of remarkable judgment. The description suits other Hamsun characters and, indeed, Hamsun himself. As is well known, Hamsun has identified with Geissler to the extent of giving him his own birthplace of Garmo in Gudbrandsdal. But for readers who know Hamsun's biography, the portrait of Geissler shows a number of other details taken from Hamsun's life. For instance, Hamsun was extravagant and philanthropic, gambling away his wife's fortune like Geissler. That Geissler, like also Hamsun late in life, was ostracized by his countrymen does not need to be explained as prophecy, but rather as the natural result of an unusual arrogance shared by both characters. Geissler, being a bailiff, does not technically belong among Hamsun's few artist heroes, but if we think of Hamsun's perhaps most typical depiction of artist inspiration, that of the composer Willatz Holmsen in *Segelfoss Town,* it is paralleled in the account of Geissler's irrigation project—the planning, the intense activity, followed by exhaustion and seeming lack of interest but also by his conviction that, though the result may not be immediate, in time the fields of Sellanraa will flourish in the wake of this bright idea. Actually, Sellanraa is Geissler's bright idea, he gave the farm this unusual name, to that extent he is also technically a creator. One, I think legitimate, step further is seeing him as a portrait of the artist as a middle-aged man, and in that capacity he reminds us of the somewhat younger cello-playing telegraphist Baardsen of *Segelfoss Town* and through him of the still younger violin-playing agronomist Nagel of *Mysteries.* Nagel, like Hamsun himself in one of his lectures, spoke out against the over-estimation of poets, probably from the conviction that a poet's remarkable facility with words is often accompanied by an unusual need for erotic and social recognition, which Nagel finds highly objectionable. In *Mysteries* this humbug and mountebank aspect of the poet is symbolised in Nagel's curious double, Johannes Grøgaard, referred to as the Midget, who earns a penny by gnashing his teeth and dancing in the market square, and Nagel attempts to save him from these indignities by supporting him economically and teaching him pride. Toward the end of the novel, however, Nagel watches the Midget dancing once more in the market square: he has gone back to his old profession. Whether or not Nagel's suicide is the result of his broken hopes vis à vis the Midget is not clear, but there seems to have been some project of the will inspired by a deep distrust of art and artists. As was mentioned earlier, Hamsun made this distrust the dominant idea in a novel from the following year, *Shallow Soil,* the distrust is also part of the argument in his novel *Victoria,* and, as Hamsun approached his own middle age, this problem became central once more: how to make poetry respectable, not only in society's but in the poet's own eyes.

'It has always been my ambition,' Hamsun wrote in a letter from 1890, 'to turn up anonymously, unexpectedly, with sudden effect, time after time, with each book with sudden effect, and then dive under again—till the next time.' Hamsun is referring to his novel *Hunger,* which had originally appeared anonymously, but he could have used the same language of himself as a mysterious visitor, in real life and, through his characters, in his novels. Hamsun's first story from 1877 has the title *The Enigmatic Man,* and its action is repeated with variations in many of his later works. This mysterious visitor, during his stay in a small town, gets involved in a love story, which is essential to the plot in Hamsun's early novels, though when Hamsun, with his own growing years, changed his mysterious visitor from a youthful lover to a middle-aged voyeur and commentator, another motif, that of philanthrophy, is emphasized. But then giving, like loving, can be a way of gaining power, indeed, as benefactor, the middle-aged mysterious visitor becomes a kind of God in disguise, wandering across the earth and bestowing his blessings on the just. In none of Hamsun's novels is this theme more clearly evident than in *Growth of the Soil,* where the old love story is deconstructed, minimized, and parodied in one single chapter about Eleseus. Franz Kafka, who knew his Hamsun well, has the following diary entry: 'Eleseus hätte auch der Held des Buches werden können, wäre es sogar wahrscheinlich in Hamsuns Jugend geworden.' Kafka may well be right, in Hamsun's youth love would have been central to the story, and Eleseus its hero. The new emphasis, on good deeds rather than love, is first evident in the trilogy about the wanderer Knut Pedersen, a well-known writer disguised as a farm worker in East Norway, who watches with sadness the gradual estrangement of a military captain and his young wife, though Pedersen loves this woman secretly and sentimentally. As we can see more clearly in volume three of the trilogy—where the scene of action has changed to Northern Norway—creating happiness for others is now more important for the wanderer. He deplores the wasted energies of a city girl, Ingeborg Torsen, in her relationships with various men, but in the end manages to get her married off to a carpenter and farmer, Nikolai, big, burly, ugly, taciturn, and persistent. The title of the novel—*The Last Joy*

(translated as *Look Back on Happiness*)—is variously interpreted in the text, the final joy at first is 'sitting alone in the dark', later it is 'having children', and in the end Miss Torsen agrees that our children are indeed our last joy. She is already grey, she has lost one of her front teeth, but she is happy and enterprising. The novel about Ingeborg Torsen is also a novel about Hamsun's second wife, Marie, formerly an actress, who like Ingeborg Torsen lost a front tooth and with it her happy smile for several bleak winter months, which seemed not to worry her writing husband. Yet, she too learned to accept her life as a mother and farmer at Skogheim. For Hamsun the motif apparently was important, he took it up again with few changes in his novel *Chapter the Last,* but first and foremost in *Growth of the Soil,* where the love story is repeated in the account of Aksel and Barbro, while the benefactor Pedersen is revived as Geissler. (pp. 6-13)

> *Harald Naess, "Knut Hamsun and 'Growth of the Soil',"* in Scandinavica, *Vol. 25, No. 1, May, 1986, pp. 5-17.*

Atle Kittang   (essay date 1985)

[*In the following essay, Kittang offers a psychoanalytic reading of Hamsun's novel* Hunger, *suggesting that the novel dramatizes absence as the condition of artistic creativity.*]

It is generally agreed upon today that *Sult* belongs to those literary works from the end of the nineteenth century which mark a turning point in the history of the European novel. Knut Hamsun himself may have been well aware of this. In a letter to Georg Brandes, written shortly after the publication of *Sult,* he repeatedly insists that he has not wanted to write a conventional novel with "marriages and picnics and parties". This antagonistic attitude towards the prevailing norms of narrative art is also a constant theme in those famous lectures from 1891, by means of which Hamsun confirmed his position as the *enfant terrible* of the Norwegian literary institution.

But to describe *Sult* negatively as an early specimen of the "anti-novel" does not bring about any clearer understanding of the book's positive characteristics. What kind of literary work is *Sult?* What makes it such an original and astonishingly *modern* novel?

One answer, which has the advantage of being close to Hamsun's own general ideas of the novel during the early 1890s, is that *Sult* belongs to the tradition of psychological Naturalism. In his letter to Georg Brandes Hamsun compares his book not only with Dostojevsky's *Crime and Punishment,* but also with the *Germinie Lacerteux* of the Goncourt brothers, that is, with a kind of literature where conventional novelistic plots and characters have been replaced by documentary investigations into the peculiarities of physio-psychological cases. If we add to this all the years of starvation and misery which characterize Hamsun's own biography during the difficult years of the 1880s, we get the model from which so many interpretations of *Sult* have taken their general idea: *Sult* is a documentary study, based upon personal experience, of how starvation affects a sensible mind.

Such a reading may explain some of the links between the novel and its author, and thus shed some light upon that ambiguous space between fiction and autobiography from which so many of Hamsun's works seem to emerge. But it does not explain the structural aspects of the book, nor its deeper thematic purport. And consequently, the interpretation it offers of the main motif, of the novel's hero, and of its plot, is too narrow and even superficial.

Let me substantiate this claim by a couple of preliminary remarks touching upon some selected aspects of the novel.

First of all, there is no simple relationship between the hero's hunger and his peculiar destiny. Starvation is of course—as in "real life"—the sympton of a real physiological lack. But on the other hand, not all the strange behaviour and reactions of the hero can be explained as consequences of his hunger. Hamsun himself has emphasized this, in a letter from 1888, when the first fragment of what was to become the novel of *Sult* was published in the Danish review *NyJord*. On the other hand, the motif of starvation goes far beyond the mere "Naturalistic" or physiological level of meaning. In Hamsun's book hunger is also a metaphor, signifying a more fundamental lack or emptiness, which is a central aspect of the psychological deep structures investigated by the writer.

Secondly, *Sult* is not only a meticulous *report* on the psychology and social situation of a starving young man. It is also a very complex *story* which takes us from early autumn to winter, from a situation of misery where (to a certain extent, at least) the starving hero nevertheless is able to write creatively, and into a deep crisis where he destroys his manuscripts and abandons his artistic vocation. But paradoxically enough, this disastrous course of events also brings our hero from a state of total *isolation,* living in a narrow shed of a room which is compared to a coffin (the meaning of this simile will be discussed later on), and to a kind of social *integration* within the grotesque family in the lodging house in Vaterland. On his way from isolation to integration, the hero has to pass through the tragicomic love affair with Ylajali. The profound irony of the whole thing is, however, that our hero meets his Waterloo as an artist in a situation where starvation has ceased to be any problem, since food is regularly provided by the landlady. Thus, *Sult* appears as a kind of negative novel of education, or better: its plot is that of a true novel of disillusionment.

My third preliminary remark concerns the narrative form of the novel. *Sult* is in fact a first person novel of a rather peculiar kind. It starts in retrospect: . . . "All of this happened while I was walking around starving in Christiania—that strange city no one escapes from until it has left its marks on him . . .". But this narrative distance between the first person narrator and the "narrated I" is gradually abolished. Throughout the rest of the novel the narrative movement, that is, the totality of the text, is inseparable from the gradual development of a consciousness. This consciousness, without name and biographical antecedents, is nothing but a string of perceptions and fantasies, ambitions, desires and strange kinds of behaviour, kept together as a textual unity by two permanent traits

only: its inner lack (symbolized by the hunger, but also specified as erotic desire) and its artistic drives.

This peculiar and productive connection between the textual movement of the novel and its all-dominating consciousness is seen very clearly in the opening sequence of the book, where the hero is presented in a state of awakening: . . .

> I was lying awake in my attic room; a clock struck six somewhere below; it was fairly light already and people were beginning to move up and down the stairs. Over near the door, where my wall was papered with old issues of the *Morning Times,* I could make out a message from the Chief of Lighthouses, and just to the left of that an advertisement for fresh bread, showing a big, fat loaf: Fabian Olsen's bakery. . . .
>
> It was getting lighter, and I concentrated on the advertisements by the door; I could even read the slim, mocking typeface declaring: "Shrouds available, Miss Andersen, Main Entrance, to the right". That satisfied me for a long time. . . .

The sequence describes a transitional situation where light gradually replaces darkness. Out of this transition the text's own consciousness is born, a psychological being is created, so to speak, from the nothingness of the night, from the nothingness which marks the limits of the text's own life. Gradually we learn about his social situation as an unemployed writer with no money and with nothing to eat. But here, at the starting point, what is worth noticing is that when this mind comes to life, it is as a consciousness of symbols, and more precisely of linguistic symbols, of texts. What is grasped as the light gets clearer, are fragments of the *Morning Times:* letters, messages, information.

These textual fragments papering the walls of his coffin-like attic are certainly not chosen at random. They refer in fact to central themes and motifs in the novel. The baker's advertisement prefigures the dialectics of starvation and nourishment; later, when the hero wishes to mark his difference from the rest of humanity, he will envisage himself as a shining lighthouse, standing erect in the middle of an ocean of human misery. And the grim, mocking letters announcing "Shrouds available" are in fact the first signals of the death motif, pointing to one of the secret thematic centres of the novel. But what strikes us most strongly here in this opening sequence, is not so much the motifs as the textual character of their introduction. Let me put it this way: just as the reader's mind constitutes itself as a consciousness of the text called *Sult,* so the text's own consciousness is born as a consciousness-of-text. The passage from nothingness to being, symbolically expressed through the awakening of the hero, is in both cases mediated through the mode of textuality.

This interpretation may appear like pure sophistry, like a splitting of the hairs of Hamsun's text. However, my reason for insisting upon the initial scene of awakening the way I have done, is not only to exemplify how narration and story are closely interrelated right from the beginning of the novel. The awakening scene also offers the first indication of the basic psychological structures which form the main field of investigation in Hamsun's text. The story of a starving writer and his tribulations in the city of Christiania is, on a more profound level, a novelistic analysis of what a philosopher would have described as a phenomenology of consciousness. Instead of presenting us with a fully-fledged character, the text shows how a human subjectivity is beginning to take shape, in a dialectic interplay between the nothingness of pure consciousness and some exterior fragments of symbols, that is, of meaning. It is not a process where the outer world is firmly grasped by a mind already formed as an identity, nor is it a process where the mind seeks to identify with the outer world. It is rather a process where the mind's access to the world is mediated through an order of symbols which makes recognition possible and, simultaneously, separates consciousness from reality itself. Rephrased in the terms of Lacanian psychoanalysis (which has contributed essentially to my subsequent interpretation), what is at stake in the opening sequence of *Sult* is the constitution of the subject through the mediation of The Other—locus and carrier of the Symbolic Order.

Let us leave for a while the philosophical subtleties and take a brief look at some of the episodes following immediately after the awakening scene, describing the first of those aimless walks through the streets of Christiania which form the main substance of the book.

This first walk is characterized by a series of *meetings* which all make a strong impression on the hero. He meets an old woman in front of a butcher's shop; then he begins to follow an old cripple; the third meeting is with two women, one of whom will reappear later as Ylajali; and finally, on a bench in a park, he experiences a rather strange "meeting with himself".

There are considerable differences between these four meetings. The early glimpse of Ylajali introduces the thematics of desire in *Sult* and triggers off what eventually will develop into a veritable "novel within the novel". The hero's meeting with himself is the first indication of a particular existential experience—a state of harmonious narcissism, sometimes with pantheistic shades—which never ceases to appear in Hamsun's work. Against the apparently positive characteristics of these episodes (—apparently, because all states of harmony in Hamsun are more or less brutally undercut by some hidden conflict), the two other meetings strike us as unambiguously negative.

However, the four meetings have at least two important traits in common. In some way or other, they all express what I would call "mirror experiences", and they all involve a curious tension between identification and aggression. It is as if the recognition implied in every specular experience is hampered by an irresistible impulse to split and separate.

Actually, both the old woman and the cripple embody in a rather grotesque way the hero's own existential condition. In the eyes of the old woman, "still full of sausage", he finds a reflection of his own hunger. And the cripple, who by the way is compared with a "huge limping insect",

is not only as penniless and hungry and miserable as the hero himself. He also appears as a curious prefiguration of the hero's physical defect during the tragi-comic love game with Ylajali towards the end of the novel. Suffering from an injury in his leg after an accident in the street, the hero will in turn appear like a limping insect in his erotic pursuit of Ylajali around the family table in her apartment. Hamsun critics like Aasmund Brynildsen have recognized in such episodes the motif of the Double, so important in several of Hamsun's early novels. (Another example would be the couple Nagel/Minutten in *Mysterier*). However, an adequate interpretation of this motif will have to consider its other face also, that is, the role played by aggression. The meeting with the old woman and her look "still full of sausage" fill the hero with disgust and nausea; and his reaction towards the cripple is aggressiveness pure and simple. In fact, if the two figures can be interpreted as grotesque mirror images of the hero's own condition, it is as if he needs to maintain a distance towards these exterior images of himself: as if the irresistible fascination has to be controlled by an act of mental separation.

This is even more striking in the park episode, where the hero "meets himself": . . .

> Lying in this position, letting my eyes float down over my chest and legs, I noticed the tiny leaping movement my feet made every time my heart beat. I sat up partway and gazed down at my feet. At that moment a strange and fantastic mood came over me which I had never felt before—a delicate and wonderful shock ran through all of my nerves as though a stream of light had flowed through them. As I stared at my shoes, I felt as if I had met an old friend, or got back some part of me that had been torn off: a feeling of recognition went through me, tears came to my eyes, and I experienced my shoes as a soft whispering sound coming up towards me. "Getting weak!" I said fiercely to myself and I closed my fists and said, "Getting weak." I was furious with myself for these ridiculous sensations which had overpowered me even though I was fully conscious of them. I spoke harsh and sensible phrases, and I closed my eyes tightly to get rid of the tears.

What is described here is a profound experience of existential integrity: a unification in the Ego of something that hitherto only existed as "some part of me that had been torn off", a harmonious identity between mind and body which enables the hero to mirror himself in the separate parts of his body. But the feeling of integrity is triggered by an experience of alienation (the feet lead so to speak their own "leaping" life), and this initial splitting or separation is repeated at the peak of ecstasy, when the "I" turns aggressively against his own existential harmony, scolding himself as a father would scold an irresponsible child, driving as it were a wedge of language into the whispering and speechless communication between mind and body.

The meeting with the unknown ladies follows the same pattern. The moment of physical contact with Ylajali's arm, comparable to the hero's awareness of his own feet in the park, creates immediately a kind of erotic communication which is repeated as a specular communication between the two of them, across St Olaf's Place, when Ylajali has reached her apartment and looks down at her pursuer in the street: . . . "We stood looking into each other's eyes without moving; this lasted a minute; thoughts shot between the window and the street, and not a word was said". But between those moments of erotic contact and specular identification a moment of aggression has already interfered: the hero's strange . . . "desire to frighten this woman, to follow her and hurt her in some way", and to address her by means of meaningless phrases which strengthen her anxiety and unease.

In all these meetings, then, identification and separation, contact and aggressiveness, are woven into a complicated psychological pattern. The feeling of identity and wholeness which is created in the hero's mind, nevertheless originates outside him, in some other figure (be it his own feet) functioning as a mirror image. Into this specular experience some kind of separation is then invariably introduced, mostly in the shape of an aggressive impulse, splitting as it were the I away from a self-absorbing communication with his mirror image.

In this process, language and discourse act as a force of separation and aggression, as in the park episode and during the meeting with Ylajali. But language can also be a vehicle of the desire for harmonious wholeness and unity. This aspect is also most clearly seen in the meeting with Ylajali. In fact, the hero's fantasy name "Ylajali", with its . . . "smooth, nervous sound", emerges in order to fill and sustain the distance created between them by the hero's mocking aggression. The name is not only a symbolic substitute for the desired woman. It is also a symbol of desire itself—considered in the Lacanian sense of a drive sustained by lack, sliding from element to element in the chain of symbolic substitutes, and which can never be fulfilled without losing its character of being desire: Y-la-ja-li. . . .

Before I continue my interpretative investigations into the text of *Sult,* I will present some more theoretical remarks on the psychological structure that I have analysed so far. My starting point will be the psychoanalytical theory of narcissism, and my aim is to establish a set of thematic categories which are sufficiently general to convert Hamsun's literary discourse into cognitive terms, and sufficiently flexible to secure this hermeneutical transformation without betraying the real complexities of Hamsun's text.

In the Freudian tradition, the theory of narcissism refers originally to the phenomenon of self-love or auto-eroticism, interpreted both as the first decisive step in the psychosexual development of the child, and as a structure of the Unconscious. Primal narcissism precedes any awareness of sexual difference; it is a kind of infantile (that means also prelinguistic) mirror experience where the child is able to organize the chaos of scattered sensual feelings into a unifying perception of its own body. Thus primary narcissism is the main condition of the foundation of an Ego. But as the French psychoanalyst Jacques Lacan has argued in his theory of the mirror stage, this crucial process presupposes an external image which the child

may interiorize, and on which it can organize its growing self-awareness. Following Lacan, who builds his theory on clinical observations made by specialists like H. Wallon and M. Klein, the *infans,* still without language and bodily co-ordination, enters the mirror stage between the sixth and the eighteenth month of its life. By means of identifying with an equally formed body (in "pure" form its own mirror image), the child grasps the image of a total, unified form upon which the future Ego will be organized. Central in such a theory is the role played by The Other in the development from *infans* to *individuum:* The Other being this "place" outside of me where both my Self Image, "my" language and "my" desire originate.

This means, however, that narcissistic identification is not only the interiorization of an image. It is also the interiorization of a relation, that is, of the primary relation between Mother and Child. Since this relationship is essentially a sexualized relationship, narcissism means that an erotic structure is being implanted, originating, as Lacan puts it, in the desire of The Other (that is, of the Mother).

In *Sult* the hero's "meeting with himself " in the park and the specular communication between Ylajali and himself illustrate these two basic aspects of narcissistic relationship. In the park episode, fragmentary sensual perceptions are unified into an experience of identity and wholeness, by way of which the hero is able to grasp himself as an Ego, and even finds confirmation of this Ego-identity in his surroundings. The mirror contact with Ylajali adds to this confirmation a promise of erotic communication which prefigures the hero's desire for reunification with a Mother figure, as I will try to show later.

However, these two episodes, together with the two other meetings in the first part of the novel, also indicate the other main aspect of the psychoanalytical theory of narcissism. In fact, the process of identification upon which my Ego is founded is already undermined by some splitting or separation. Birth itself, when I am physically separated from the symbiosis with the maternal body, is the first moment of splitting out of which, eventually, something like a human individual being develops. This complex process attains its most dramatic stage during the oedipal period, where the desire of a reunification with the Mother and the corresponding dream of an invulnerable and all-powerful Ego are shattered against socio-psychological laws and interdictions. Unconsciously, this crisis of narcissism is overcome by means of a castration fantasy, which eventually puts an end to the dangerous regressive wishes and sustains my further development into psychological independence and maturity. The unconscious message of castration teaches us that separation and lack are essential aspects of our psychological make-up, and that our existence as individual beings depends upon such an inner void or split in our existence. This profound message is, however, in permanent conflict with our infantile dreams of unity and reintegration, and also with our deepest convictions of being an autonomous Ego, a self-contained psychological entity.

The role played by language and symbols in the life of human beings is explained by psychoanalytical theory as a function of this primordial splitting. As Freud argued in

Beyond the Pleasure Principle, and as Melanie Klein and Jacques Lacan have repeated in various ways, the acquisition and mastery of language and of symbolization in general are closely linked with our early experiences of absence and lack. Language and symbols represent both the absence of something (in Freud's famous "Fort! Da!" example: the absence of the Mother), and the desire to substitute something for this lack. They sustain the distance that separates me from the order of reality. They prevent me from any self-destroying fusion with the world surrounding me, as when the hero in *Sult* employs language as a means not only of aggression but also of self-defence. And they fill the inner and outer void with substitute representations, as when the hero invents the name of "Ylajali".

Not only the opening sequences, but in fact the whole text of *Sult* with its various plot elements, can be interpreted as a modulation upon this tension between narcissistic desire and splitting (or castration). This does not mean, of course, that Hamsun's novel is some kind of unconscious allegory about children's desire for their Mother, or about castration anxiety, etc. It is my contention, however, that in *Sult* Hamsun is approaching the same fundamental level of consciousness and the same psychological deep structures as Freud did some years later, along the paths of clinical experience and self-analysis. Here, in this astonishing correspondence between the novelist's investigations into the deep conflicts of subjective and intersubjective existence, and the future revolutions in psychology, lies perhaps the real modernity of Hamsun's early (and even later) works.

It can easily be shown how the tragi-comic love affair between Ylajali and the *Sult* hero reflects this pattern of conflict. The desire which eventually brings the hero into the bourgeois apartment of Ylajali is both a regressive oral desire for her breasts and lips (this is very neatly emphasized in the text), and a desire for recognition as an Ego. But all along the various scenes of seduction the hero is in multiple ways marked by the stigma of castration. During their second meeting, the hero is suffering from a sore finger—a self-inflicted wound which saved him from the dangerous lethargy of self-pity. His sore foot makes him limp like the old cripple when he is pursuing Ylajali around the family table. And the erotic spell is brutally broken when Ylajali notices, at the moment of sexual fulfillment, that he is even losing his hair—the third mark of castration on the hero's miserable body. Consequently, the love scene ends in frustration. The hero is ruthlessly expelled just as he is enjoying the prospect of being reunified with a maternal body.

It would be a simplification though, if this expulsion from the Paradise of the maternal body (which also happens to be a Paradise of the bourgeois Family) were construed as a negative experience only. It must also be interpreted as a salvation. From such a viewpoint, the signs of castration on the hero's body correspond to his moments of aggressiveness in those other narcissistic experiences that I have already analysed. Castration is so to speak his talisman which prevents him from being absorbed and dissolved in the erotic fusion with the (M)other.

This interpretation is sustained by the rather striking par-

allels between the erotic plot in *Sult* and the grotesque social integration within the family in the lodging house, which forms the hero's main temptation in the last part of the novel. What is described here is the fascinating effects upon the hero of a demonic family life to which he clings desperately, although it threatens both his pride, his self-respect, and his sense of individuality. In fact he is on the point of losing himself in a terrifying "family romance", and the magic centre of this romance, the landlady in the lodging house, is definitely a Mother figure (more so than Ylajali). Not only is she the one who feeds the hero, thus partly compensating for this inner lack of which the hunger is the main symbol. She is also pregnant with a child, and consequently a true symbol of maternity—of the biological symbiosis between Mother and Child which precedes any moment of splitting. The hero's experiences in the lodging house end, as does the Ylajali plot, with an act of expulsion. But this time its positive signification is unmistakable: it rescues the hero from the dangers of total regression.

The two secondary plots of *Sult* which I have mentioned briefly here, indicate two of the central thematic fields in the total novelistic universe of Hamsun: the conflicts and psychological mechanisms of love (e.g. *Mysterier, Pan, Victoria,* and the vagabond novels from the beginning of the twentieth century), and the inner and outer conflicts of social life (e.g. *Benoni, Rosa,* and *Konerne ved vandposten*). But *Sult* is above all a novel about the illusions and disillusions of an artist. For that reason I shall concentrate the following part of my interpretation upon the metapoetic plot of the book, trying to give some idea of how this principal theme is related to the structures that I have analysed so far.

To begin with, it is important to notice that what Hamsun offers in *Sult* is in fact a double portrait of an artist. On the one hand, he describes his hero as a *writer,* who has chosen this risky profession not only in order to earn a living, but also in order to gain recognition and fulfil some socially sanctioned ambitions. However, the hero's career as a writer brings him very little success and ends in total failure. On the other hand, the hero is furthermore presented through his powerful *force of imagination,* appearing as a breeding place of myriads of fantasies: erotic and sensual daydreams, exotic flights from reality, hallucinations of food, love, and music, visions of colours and forms, strange adventures and identities.

The innermost dream of the *writer* is to gain access to the Literary Establishment—to the Holy Family of Letters where the Almighty Editor (the Chief, as he is called in the novel) reigns as some sort of quasi-divine Father figure. To reach this aim the hero is willing to sacrifice his own individual talent on the altar of conformity and taste. He tries to write about the subjects and ideas that are most popular at the time, and at the Editor's request he attempts to remove from his articles and sketches all the traces of fever and intensity which come from his restless imagination. Behind this ambition it is easy to find a dream of social recognition and a narcissistic wish for self-realisation and integration which correspond to the erotic dreams and wishes that I have commented upon already.

The dream of the writer is once more a mirror dream: a desire to recognize his own genius, his artistic Ego, in those signs of public recognition which arrive from The Other. Therefore, he has to conform to the images of success that Society keeps putting before him, like a mirror.

Why is this ambition never crowned with success? The hero himself seems to have a simple and straightforward answer to this question. It is because he always lacks the necessary material resources, such as paper and pencil when inspiration comes over him, or a place to work, or most importantly: enough food to eat. But underneath this simple answer the text hints at a more complex one, which puts the emphasis on the ironic aspects of the hero's situation as an artist. This complex answer focuses on the curious separation between the hero as a writer and his capacity of imagination—between the hero's ambitions and his creativity. In fact, on one occasion only do imagination, inspiration, and writing intermingle as productive forces in a successful creative process. This privileged moment is situated in the first part of the novel, and it marks at the same time its point of bifurcation: from now on, inspiration and writing, imagination and ambition will be definitively separated and will remain so throughout the rest of the novel.

As will be noticed from the following quotation, it is difficult to distinguish between Hamsun's description of poetic inspiration and those countless descriptions which can be found everywhere in the platonic-romantic tradition of aesthetics. Metaphors and motifs are in fact strikingly conventional: . . .

> I wrote as if possessed, and filled one page after the other without a moment's pause. Thoughts poured in so abruptly, and kept on coming in such a stream, that I lost a number of them from not being able to write them down fast enough, even though I worked with all my energy. They continued to press themselves on me; I was deep into the subject, and every word I set down came from somewhere else.

Of far greater importance is the setting of the scene. As in the opening sequence it is a scene of awakening, situated on the borderline between nothingness and being, in a room already presented by the text as . . . "this empty room whose floor gave a little with every step was like a badly put-together coffin". In this room, associated not only with death, but also with the image of the sea (the association is evident in the original, but almost imperceptible in the English translation),—in this no man's land the hero experiences poetic inspiration as an irresistible force, emerging from "somewhere else": from Otherness.

One of the consequences of this privileged moment will appear to be devastating: I am thinking of the hero's *hubris,* his self-deceptive arrogance which makes him leave the coffin-like attic room, although it appears later on to have been the only place where inspiration was found! Hamsun describes this arrogance with profound irony. But what is so special about such a miserable shed of a room? The answer can only be given by looking closer at its symbolic significance. As an image of death and nothingness it expresses exactly this fundamental lack or void which is the necessary condition of every act of imagination and symbolization; as an image of the sea it indicates this dynamic restlessness which characterises the forces of imagination. By treating such a symbolically loaded room with contempt, the hero is in fact alienating himself from the precondition of creativity. The rest of the novel is there to prove the disastrous nature of his decision.

This link between imagination and nothingness, enigmatic as it may seem, forms one of the central thematic points of the novel, which can be easily shown from the following two examples.

First of all, it is not accidental that the hero's most powerful fantasies are born not in the park or elsewhere in the city, but near the harbour, where the soft movements of the sea and the ships will act like a trigger on his imagination. However, the harbour is not only sea and ships and promises of exotic voyages. It is also, like the attic room, the image of a terrifying darkness inhabited by black monsters raising their bristles and waiting to pull him into the mortal void beneath the "heavy drowsiness" of its surface: . . .

> In front of me, the sea rocked in its heavy drowsiness; ships and fat, broad-nosed barges dug up graves in the lead-coloured plain, shiny waves darted out to the right and left and kept going, and all the time the smoke poured like feathery quilts out of the smokestacks and the sound of pistons penetrated faintly through the heavy moist air.
>
> . . . . .
>
> The darkness was thicker now, a light breeze furrowed the pearl-grey sea. The ships whose masts I could see outlined against the sky looked, with their black bodies, like silent monsters who had raised their bristles and were lying in wait for me.

But paradoxically, from this feeling of dissolution and submergence imagination begins its work, developing around the name of Ylajali a glittering erotic fairy-tale: . . .

> Not a sound came to disturb me—the soft dark had hidden the whole world from me, and buried me in a wonderful peace—only the desolate voice of stillness sounded monotonously in my ear. And the dark monsters out there wanted to pull me to themselves as soon as night came, and they wanted to take me far over seas and through strange lands where no human being lives. And they wanted to bring me to Princess Ylajali's castle, where an undreamed-of happiness was waiting for me, greater than any person's! And she herself would be sitting in a blazing room all of whose walls were amethyst, on a throne of yellow roses, and she would reach her hands out to me when I entered, greet me, and cry "Welcome, O knight, to me and to my land!"

And the fantasy continues until it reaches the climax of an oral, erotic fusion: Ylajali's kiss.

My second example refers to a totally different episode,

the hero's terrifying experience of darkness and anxiety at the police station. What this nightmare prefigures is the experience of individual death and dissolution: . . . "What if I myself become dissolved into the dark, turned into it?" To begin with, the hero tries to defend himself by an imaginary act of regression: humming lullabies to himself like a Mother to her frightened Baby. Then another kind of salvation is introduced, so to speak, in the shape of symbolism itself: the invention of a new "word", *kuboå* saves him from a complete breakdown. But this new combination of letters is not like the words of ordinary language. It has no meaning of its own, it can only be defined as a pure *difference,* and is in fact so described in the text; . . . "I had formulated my opinion on what the word did not mean, but I had not yet come to a decision on what it did mean". Such a decision will never be reached. As a hole—or gap—in language, the word *kuboå* signifies nothing more and nothing less than the void of emptiness which is the necessary condition for symbolism and meaning in general.

There are several connections between this nightmare episode and the hero's moments of inspiration and fantasy. On the one hand, we have some evident resemblances between the police cell and the coffin-like room of divine inspiration; these resemblances are also connected with the hero's experiences in the harbour. On the other hand, it is important to notice that the meditation upon the word *kuboå* leads directly on to a fantasy which is nothing less than a version in negative of the Ylajali fantasy from the harbour: . . .

> God in heaven, how black it was! And I started again to think about the harbour, the shops, the dark monsters who lay waiting for me. They wanted to pull me to themselves and hold me fast and sail with me over land and sea, through dark kingdoms no man had ever seen. I felt myself on board ship, drawn on through waters, floating in clouds, going down, down. . . .

In this way the nightmare episode becomes a central clue to the understanding of the metapoetic theme in *Sult.* It expresses in a negative mode what the other episodes express more positively: namely, that fantasy, imagination, creativity and true writing are necessarily preconditioned by nothingness itself. Hunger, lack, emptiness and the principle of separation, by virtue of which individual consciousness, or Ego, is always already divided from the image of totality and fullness that constitutes the object of narcissistic desire:—those are the gaps and splits in human existence from which symbols, fictions, poetry and art emerge. This view of the nature of imagination is never absent from Hamsun's work, although it is often contradicted by more "positive", ideological conceptions of the artist and his functions. It is most clearly (and brutally) developed in the rather monstrous novel from 1920, *Konerne ved vandposten,* where the hero, Oliver Andersen, is not only an eunuch, but also a master of fiction, and thus a grotesque symbol of the Hamsunian artist: restless imagination drawing its force from a fundamental lack, and converting a self-sufficient world of fiction into an equally self-sufficient mode of existence. There can be no doubt about the sharpness of Hamsun's irony in *Konerne ved*

vandposten. But irony, in Hamsun, is very seldom a rhetorical means of persuasion. On the contrary, it is the textual expression of deep insights into the existential truth of illusion: its central, and necessary, place in human life.

From this point of view, the failure of the *Sult* hero as a writer has to be interpreted as a consequence of his own arrogant blindness as to the real truth of his creative power. When he leaves his coffin-like attic room in order to seek public acceptance and social integration in the city of Christiania, he walks straight into the traps of narcissistic desire. However, he avoids being definitively trapped. Lack is so to speak his faithful talisman, it inhabits his being in different ways: as hunger, as signs of castration and incompleteness, and as a profound force of separation and division. In the final scene of the novel, when the hero is leaving Christiania and his scattered ambitions, all these forces of nothingness and separation are concentrated into an image not of defeat, but of victory: . . .

> When we were out on the fjord, I straightened up, wet from fever and exertion, looked in toward land and said goodbye for now to the city, to Christiania, where the windows of the homes all shone with such brightness.

Pushed by the disastrous course of events, the hero separates himself not only from the city of disillusionment and misery, but first and foremost from his own erotic and social dreams and wishes. Logically, this final act of separation is imagined as a sea voyage—as a flight into the realm of death, emptiness and movement, the field of imagination itself. What is left behind is the symbolic image of narcissistic desire: the homes, shining with brightness, idyllic but treacherous promises of integration and "family romance".

However, this image of liberating separation is ambiguously permeated with nostalgia. And the goodbye is not a definitive one. Later in Hamsun's work there will always be a hero who returns from the sea, seeking the illusions of comfort and identity in some little town. We meet him again in Hamsun's next novel, where Johan Nilsen Nagel, passing by on the coastal steamer, is so fascinated by the sight of the small town that he spontaneously decides to go ashore. In *Mysterier* this proves to be a disastrous decision: trapped in the labyrinths of love and social life Nagel seeks his death by returning to the sea. But the ending of *Mysterier* is rather exceptional in Hamsun's work. As a rule, the typical Hamsun hero resists the temptations of narcissistic desire, clinging to his inner emptiness, his "hunger", as to his life. This is perhaps most clearly demonstrated in Hamsun's last novel, the enigmatic *Ringen sluttet,* whose main character, Abel Brodersen, bears such a strong resemblance to the *Sult* hero. The novel about Abel Brodersen is, fundamentally speaking, nothing but a repeated pattern of arrivals and departures, elaborated around an inner void: a human being devoid of any "character" or "identity". The *Sult* hero has no name; the hero of *Ringen sluttet* has a name filled with mythological connotations. But its etymological core reflects precisely the existential emptiness and restless movement around which Hamsun closes his ring of fiction: "air, wind, nothingness". (pp. 295-307)

Atle Kittang, "Knut Hamsun's 'Sult': Psychological Deep Structures and Metapoetic Plot," in Facets of European Modernism: Essays in Honour of James McFarlane Presented to Him on His 65th Birthday, 12 December 1985, edited by Janet Garton, University of East Anglia, 1985, pp. 295-308.

Ronald Popperwell (essay date 1986)

[*In the following essay, Popperwell discusses similarities between* Pan *and Hamsun's later works, examining the novel's narrator, Glahn.*]

Pan, subtitled 'Af Løjtnant Thomas Glahns Papirer' ('From Lieutenant Thomas Glahn's Papers') appeared in December 1894. The idea of the novel had probably been in Hamsun's mind from the time of the composition of the short story **'Glahn's Død'** (**'Glahn's Death'**) which had appeared in *Samtiden* in May 1893. In a letter from Paris to Philipsen, dated 17 April 1893, he wrote: 'Tomorrow I am beginning on a strange story from Nordland in Norway', but it was not until 7 January [1894] that he reported to the German publisher Albert Langen that the work had begun. In June he left Paris for Christianssand in southern Norway, apologising in a letter to Langen (who was supporting him financially) for his abrupt disappearance, and explaining that he could not work in Paris and would finish the book by September.

In further letters to Langen (written in imperfect English), he gave indications as to the content of the book: 'Think of Nordland in Norway, the regions of the Lapper [sic], the mysteries, the grand superstitions, the midnight-sun think of J. J. Rousseau in this [sic] regions, making acquaintance with a Nordlands girl,—that is my book. I will try to clear [sic] [express] some of the nature-worshipping, sensitivity, overnervousness in a Rousseauian soul' (letter of 22 July). He was also uncertain about the title: 'The girl in my book will be a new one, her name is Edvarda, but I don't like her name for the title of the book . . .' (letter of 19 August). However, on 2 September he wrote that 'Edvarda' was 'a good title in Norwegian too'. Finally (1 October) he concluded that " 'Edvarda" was unlikely to be the Norwegian title of the book because it was less about Edvarda than about the hero', and on 6 October he informed the Larsens that he had decided to call the book **Pan.** A curiosity of the concluding stages of its composition seems to be that it was only at the last moment that he resolved to make **'Glahns Død'** (in a slightly revised form) the conclusion of the book. In a letter to Philipsen dated 15 October [1894] he wrote: 'It is a question as to whether I ought to include [trykke] **"Glahn's Death"** as the conclusion of this book . . . In this way the whole book would get a sort of historical character, based on documents'.

Contrary to his belief that, because of the hostility of the critics, it should be published under a pseudonym—'otherwise it too will be slaughtered' (letter to Larsens of 23 November [1893], **Pan** had on its appearance a generally favourable reception. Hjalmar Christensen who had previously been very critical of Hamsun wrote enthusiastically of it and since then most critics have seen **Pan** as one of Hamsun's most important books, an exception being D. H. Lawrence who, in spite of Hamsun's affinities with himself, referred to it as a 'wearisome sickening little personal novel' (*The Novel*). Given its title and its Neo-Romantic character it was to be expected that **Pan** would be popular, the Pan motif was of course a central one in European literature of the time. Hamsun's novel, it has been suggested, contributed to the fashion by being the inspiration for the founding of the German periodical *Pan* in 1895.

In **Pan** Hamsun returned, for the first time since **Sult,** to first-person narrative; he also discarded the polemical element which had been a feature of the intervening books—writing to the Larsens on 30 October 1893 he said: 'There will be no polemics in it, just people living under a strange heaven'. Another feature of **Pan** is that the love motif, which in the earlier novels had been on a secondary plane, now becomes the principal theme, whilst the motifs of the 'new man' and 'the family in decline' (which were prominent in **Redaktør Lynge**) are little more than suggested. The overt critique of the artist has also disappeared.

The first-person narrator in **Pan,** Lieutenant Thomas Glahn, tells us that he is 30 years old and that the events he is describing took place two years earlier in 1855. Like the hero of **Sult** and Nagel in **Mysterier,** he is the exception to the normal run of the society in which he finds himself. He is a temporary visitor living in a turf hut in the forests on the coast of Nordland in north Norway, spending his time fishing and hunting, and alone but for his dog Aesop. But he is not entirely deprived of human society, which is at hand in the near-by trading centre of Sirilund. His account begins with the coming of spring and ends with autumn and his departure.

Glahn's experiences during his Nordland summer are of two main kinds: on the one hand of the mountains, forests and coasts of Nordland with its plant, animal and insect life, an experience which he recounts with the fervour of pantheistic belief, compounded with wonder, compassion and an awareness of unseen presences; and on the other, of his passion for Edvarda, the daughter and only child of the widowed Ferdinand Mack, the merchant at Sirilund and the chief magnate of the place. In addition, he has minor affairs with Eva, the wife of the smith (to begin with he thinks she is the smith's daughter), and a brief encounter with Henriette, a goat-girl. Thus Glahn also has a *Pan-theistic* aspect.

Whilst **Sult, Redaktør Lynge** and **Ny Jord** were located in Christiania, and **Mysterier** in a small coastal town, **Pan,** by contrast, is set in the Nordland of Hamsun's childhood and youth. In a sense this change of setting follows naturally from tendencies in the works which preceded it. In them the town was shown as inimical to the 'outsider', thus Glahn's retirement to the forests of Nordland may be construed as an attempt by the 'outsider' to withdraw completely from society; when Coldevin in **Ny Jord** left Christiania he was on his way to a post in Nordland.

As an 'outsider' Glahn does not aspire like the hero of **Sult** to be a respectable member of society, or (like Nagel) to shock it out of its assumptions, or (like Coldevin and Højbro) to reprove it. Because he does not easily fit into the routines of society, he is clumsy and has a preference for solitude—'I belong to the forests and loneliness' are his concluding words. But there is no conflict between him and society as an institution; indeed much of his behaviour has a social orientation. However, in his quick response to things and persons and his deep concern with his own feelings, Glahn shows the characteristics of the 'outsider'. He reacts to experience rather than reflects on it, and is content to be borne along by his thoughts and feelings rather than take any action involving the will or conscious decision. In the flux which characterises much of his life, Glahn is very much of a piece with the processes of nature. In fact in his relationship to nature he achieves a more complete self-identification with it than any previous Hamsun character (the hero of *Sult* resisted it as a threat to his identity; Nagel in *Mysterier* sought self-obliteration in nature rather than self-identification); this endows him with a kind of elemental power, an irresistible *attrativa,* especially in his relations with women. Thus Edvarda comments on the bewitching 'animal look' in his eyes as does the author of the postscript **'Glahns Død';** in fact, the latter's hostility to him is largely aroused by the effortless spell-binding force of Glahn's whole appearance and manner.

When Glahn first meets Edvarda, his impression of her is of 'a child, a schoolgirl, tall, shapeless, between fifteen and sixteen'. Later he notices that her face could look 'vacant and not very attractive', that her lower lip sagged, that her breasts were flat, and her hands not clean. He observes that her jacket has been re-dyed, that her party frock is a converted confirmation dress and far too short, and that her shoes are down-at-heel. He is shocked at her occasional disregard of social propriety as for example when she suddenly kisses him several times at a party. Thus, objectively, he judges her on the basis of conventional criteria. However, subjectively, he sees her in a quite different way: 'I could not resist the forsaken look in her eyes and the whole of her thin body'; 'the chaste expression in her thumb affected me tenderly and the wrinkles over the knuckle were full of friendliness'. Even her lack of grammar touches him. He speaks of 'her mysterious forehead' and 'the mysteriously tender expression in her hands' and he admires the curve of her arched eyebrows. Tiemroth suggests that she can be seen as a moon-goddess and that this enters into the way she affects Glahn. Be that as it may, Glahn does express a feeling of attachment to the moon on more than one occasion.

The Doctor, who when he first came to Sirilund was regarded as a candidate for Edvarda's hand, analyses her for Glahn. She is 'a child who has been spared the rod, a woman with many caprices'. 'She is not a little romantic [eventyrlig], she has a powerful imagination, she is waiting for a Prince'. She is twenty but wants to pass for seventeen. She is looking for someone who will 'rule over her body and soul'. 'She is not a happy soul'. The Doctor also speaks of her charm: 'People respond to her, nobody shows her indifference'. Whilst this evaluation of Edvarda is a valid one, it is not the whole story. If, like Glahn, she possesses charisma, it is not just involuntary. She is active,

not passively reactive to circumstances, and seeks to impress her own will on her surroundings, less in order to to exercise power directly than to create the conditions in which she can play the role she has assigned to herself. She wants to be submissive but on her own terms. Thus she is only in one sense the maiden, unwilling to grow up and shut within the confines of Sirilund, waiting for her prince to arrive. In her relationship with Glahn it is she who takes the initiative; unlike his 'dream of love', her prince does not represent an unrealisable ideal. She is looking for a real lover and her love can find expression in definite practical acts, like offering him accommodation when his hut is burnt down. Although subject to the dictates of convention and passion, she can rise above them by acts of will of which Glahn seems incapable. In her activity and independence Edvarda represents, as Hamsun had promised, a new kind of heroine.

Edvarda's father, Ferdinand Mack, is the great man of Sirilund, exercising a kind of *droit de seigneur* over Eva the smith's wife. It is he who pulls the strings at Sirilund, and to his own advantage; he is a man concerned with making the externals of life come right by ignoring difficulties or by sheer ruthlessness. Thus, as he readily admits, when he plays patience in the evening, he usually ends by cheating, or after Glahn's hut has burnt down he blandly commiserates with him although he himself was responsible for it and knows that Glahn knows this. At this Glahn reflects: 'It was suddenly as if the world's wisest man stood before me'. But although Mack has the inherited authority of the seigneur, there are indications of cultural decline from the days when, as Mack invariably relates, his grandfather received the diamond clasp he is wearing from the hands of King Carl Johan himself; the fine collection of books which look inherited are housed in a side room while pride of place is taken by the new ornate oil lamps. It looks, too, as if the family name will die out with him and at the age of 46 he feels himself physically in decline. His bedraggled shirt front is perhaps an emblem of this.

The Doctor is a rationalist; to him things are explicable. He operates within the social structure as it is and appears to have come to terms with his own situation—he is lame and has, evidently, been rejected by Edvarda as a suitor. He uses the conventions of language usage to exercise an influence over her (he is always correcting her) in order, as he explains to Glahn, to make her a more reasonable person. Even when he is grossly insulted by Glahn, he responds by offering him his hand, a social gesture which maintains the fabric of society as he understands it. His social orientation is crystallised in the hope he expresses that when he dies his place in eternity will be near London or Paris where he can hear the roar of the 'can-can of humanity the whole time'; his physical lameness is perhaps symbolical of his restricted view of life. As one who has worked his way up from nothing he represents a social mobility which, although only faintly adumbrated, makes him something of a 'new man' in the context of Hamsun's work.

Eva, the smith's wife, provides a contrast to Edvarda. In one sense they represent, as their names suggest, the dichotomy feminine/masculine woman. Whilst Edvarda is active, has social and intellectual pretensions, and engages in a battle of the sexes with Glahn, Eva is passive, even motherly, an 'ignorant woman', as she says. She has the aspect of the eternal Eve, receiving the attentions of three men: her husband, Mack, and Glahn. To Glahn she shows a Solveig (or Gretchen)-like devotion. Seen in the context of the acculturation of the erotic impulse, she occupies a midway stage between the primitive, purely sensuous Henriette (or the seductive Iselin of Glahn's dreams) and the modern Edvarda hemmed about by culturally generated circumstances. Eva's devotion to Glahn has the status of a simple piety not dissimilar to the deeply reverent nature of his own (pantheistic) experiences in the forest, involving submission to a natural force but also a kind of worship implying the possibility of collaboration between the human and the natural sphere. But in *Pan* there is interference not collaboration with nature (at least as far as the principal characters are concerned). Eva dies because of such interference and it is perhaps symbolical of this situation that when she is killed by falling boulders it was not due to a natural occurrence (boulders fall elsewhere in the book as part of the processes of nature) but to Glahn's mining the rock to fire a salute to the departing Baron. It is noteworthy that the three men with whom Eva has had relations (two of whom had certainly maltreated her) are in different ways connected with her death: her husband, who forges the rods which Glahn uses to make the bore holes in which he inserts the explosive; Mack who sends her to tar a boat underneath the place where Glahn is mining; and Glahn who is apparently unbelievably obtuse in not seeing that what he is doing will lead to her death.

Like Mack and the Doctor who both in their different ways maintain the existing social structure, the visiting Baron who eventually marries Edvarda is a clear-cut social type. He is the aristocrat, but as his physical degeneration—thin beard, poor eyesight, yellow nails—suggest, is in decline; in him society is formalised to the nth degree; he is also a man of science and represents both in his social aspect and in his relationship to nature the opposite polarity to Glahn. For him, the hidden resources of nature are something to be brought up from the bottom of the sea to be catalogued and placed in museums. His piercing eyes matched by the five-pointed crest of his baronetcy, the colourless clammy clay, the cold wet seaweed and rocks of his researches, are all suggestive of the opposite of life as represented and experienced by Glahn. It is noteworthy that his departure with nature packed in crates coincides with the death of Eva, 'the wild child of life', as Glahn calls her.

Within the social and cultural pattern at Sirilund and the different levels at which it can be seen, Glahn has a multiple role. He is a migratory bird occupying a turf hut during the summer, leaving when it is at an end (later, in the postscript, he has migrated to India). As a Pan-like figure hunting in the forest and sporting with the maidens, he has links with the animal world but also with the divine: he possesses a marked capacity for metaphysical experience and mythmaking; Edvarda even sees him as a god. He is a member of one of the conventional professions, the army, and has a distinct social awareness, is observant of the minutiae of dress, embarrassed by social lapses, and

concerned at what people think of him. He is predisposed to bourgeois comfort: besides being a lair his hut is a 'home' and his dog Aesop his 'family', waiting for him at the window to greet him when he comes home, and together, so he says, they cosily prepare the evening meal. He is also an educated man with literary interests and talents: *Pan* is said to be taken from Lieutenant Glahn's papers, while the name of his dog Aesop and the figure of Pan on his powder horn bear witness to his classical interests. It is as if Glahn encompasses within himself a whole range of cultural stages.

This multiplicity of cultural stages is also paralleled in the society of Sirilund. Seen under this aspect the uninhibited Henriette (significantly a goat-girl) suggests the instinctive life of the pastoral age; the smith, the age of metals; Mack, feudal society (with Edvarda as chatelaine, Eva as the commonalty subject to the will of the seigneur, and the Doctor as a sort of court retainer and tutor). On another level Eva as the embodiment of the 'eternal feminine' is Romantic woman; the Doctor a humanist; and Edvarda modern woman.

However, although it has these implications, society at Sirilund is on the surface a trading post in Nordland in the middle of the nineteenth century, with certain pretensions to modernity and social sophistication. Mack has the first paraffin lamps to come so far north, but the telegraph has not yet reached them; Edvarda's jacket is dyed, presumably for fashionable rather than economic reasons, and her pinafore is tied low to give the impression of a long bodice which was in fashion then; Mack wears a white shirt front but it is crumpled and unstarched; the tails of the Baron's morning coat, which has come straight from his suitcase, are similarly crumpled. Sirilund has its 'ball', to which Glahn comes in his fishing gear, and there are two boat excursions. It is as if Sirilund is aping the fashions of the big centres of social sophistication without mastering them. In this account of Sirilund we can see a reflection of Glahn's conventionality (that he notices such discrepancies), and possibly also a general critique of influences from the town—it is noteworthy that the two most urbanised characters are the physically decadent Baron and the lame, pedantic, but humanist Doctor.

Basic to the cultural situation in *Pan* is nature, depicted in its deterministic aspect, in the cycle of seasons, in the activity of the birds and insects as dictated by that cycle, nature without intrusions from the hand of man, reproductive rather than productive. Related to this activity and, in differing degrees reflecting it, are the working of the unconscious life of the individual, particularly as expressed by the erotic drive. It is perhaps in this connection that Hamsun's remark in a letter to the Larsens (12 April [1894]) that *Pan* was 'not a novel, thank God, but a "little natural history"' is best understood. *Pan* is, in fact, in one sense the account of the birth and death of passion coinciding with the birth and death of the brief, hectic Nordland summer.

Of the generality of people at Sirilund Glahn says that they were 'strange and of a different kind from the people I had known earlier; sometimes one night was enough to make them blossom out in all their glory, mature and fully grown'; it is as if they follow the dictates of nature and show little conscious awareness. Thus Henriette, the goat-girl, comes to Glahn and gives herself to him in the summer night but as winter approaches she passes him by, 'the autumn, the winter has seized her, her senses were already asleep'. Eva, too, belongs, at least in part, to the forest (Glahn meets her when she is gathering wood) and her coming together with him is likewise presented as having the same instinctive quality, but she nevertheless achieves a conscious awareness and constancy in her relationship with him. Edvarda can also act instinctively but she has imagination, a capacity for reflection, social sense, and her devotion to Glahn outlives the summer season, even though it appears to fade and die.

The underlay of nature against which reflection, discrimination, social patterns, in short civilisation moves and does battle seems to be suggested in two places in the book by the symbol of the ship struggling in a stormy sea. It is an underlay which also shows through in characters who otherwise are well adjusted to the social aspects of life. The urbane Mack had the hairy neck of a satyr and does not shrink from what amounts to murder when his instincts are thwarted—Glahn forms a subjective impression of him as a bird of prey: 'He [Mack] came towards me in his long pointed shoes, stuck both thumbs in his waistcoat pockets and flapped his arms like wings'; the pedantries of the doctor vis-à-vis Edvarda are a fairly transparent substitute for the sex battle, designed to keep Edvarda on a schoolgirl level and thus disabled as he himself is; and there is a suggestion that even the devitalised Baron is prepared to see his research, which includes 'interesting stone deposits' trodden underfoot when he tells Edvarda to stamp on the diamond brooch he has given her—in the novel *Rosa* (1908), after he has married Edvarda, we learn that he has committed suicide.

However, it is in Glahn that the disparities between nature and civilisation have their most powerful embodiment; he is in fact, physically poised between the two, his being situated on the edge of the forest with a view over Sirilund and its warehouses and quays. As has already been pointed out he appears to be at one with nature in his tendency to react rather than act; he corresponds, too, to the Pan of the myth in being possessed of a natural force which makes him strongly attractive to the opposite sex, although, we should note that when, because of his involvement with Edvarda, he shoots himself through the foot he becomes in effect a maimed Pan. His response to nature is also characterised by primitive attitudes: by an implicit animism in the way he projects his subjective feelings on to trees and stones or interprets a gust of wind as the presence of a deity in the forest, and by a piety devoid of moral or ethical considerations, involving a thankfulness for life as it is in his toast [Skaaltale] to the forest in chapter XXXVI in which the wild cat that springs on a sparrow in the darkness deserves, if anything, a more rousing toast than the rest. But Glahn is not part of the natural world as the blue-eyed, plant-like, local inhabitants are, or even as Eva is. He is conscious of what happens in nature, observes its forces and interprets them, and has considerable botanical and entomological knowledge. He also consciously identifies himself with happenings in nature, gets

up early to participate in the 'joyful noise which birds and animals made when the sun rose'; he is aware that spring has come to him too. He introduces ballad-like elements into nature, stories of Diderik and Iselin, young Dundas, Svend Herlufsen, and implicates himself in their doings; at times he sees nature in the light of romance: the horizon is clad in lilac and gold; festivities are in progress up there in the heavens with music from the stars, and boating parties gliding down the rivers.

Indeed Glahn's experience of Nordland is to a marked degree the experience of something exotic—here we may compare what Hamsun said to Langen about Nordland in his letter dated 22 July 1893. His descriptions of nature reflect this and at times when he speaks of the great white flowers, the great leaves of the deciduous trees, the strange growths and lilac-coloured flowers he wades through on the island where 'people perhaps had not been', it sounds more like the exoticism of southern climes, a construct of Glahn's own fantasy rather than a description of the reality of Nordland.

Glahn's response to nature provides many examples of his orientation towards society; for him nature is seldom sufficient in itself. He styles himself 'the son of the forest' and declares 'my only friend was the forest and the great loneliness'; but a few moments later he is rattling two coins together to break that loneliness. Though he may apprehend that nature is self-sufficient (he imagines he sees Pan in a tree drinking from his own stomach), he does not act as if it were. As already observed he projects on to it his own subjective images, endowing it with those attributes which fit in with his own situation at the time. He makes nature minister to his needs for companionship, for God, and the fulfilment of his visions. For Glahn, nature is never autonomous; it never operates on its own account. This gives him the satisfaction of being in complete control (unlike his relationship with Edvarda), since he sees what he wants in nature, namely a reflection of himself.

Whilst Glahn is in the forest his response to nature is a matter private to him, but there are fateful consequences when Edvarda is involved. When he looks at her subjectively, he projects on her his attitudes to nature. Just as nature has an exotic aspect for him, so has Edvarda—unlike the blue-eyed natives of the place she is dark-complexioned with dark eyes and high-arched eyebrows; he describes them as 'strange' and finds something mysterious [selsom] about her forehead, her hands. At other times she appears to him as an uncared product of nature which moves him to pity in the same way as a decaying twig in the forest moves him; or he sees her as unsullied nature with her thumbs expressive of maidenly chastity. What he fails to do is to take a straight look at her, a failure which prevents him from seeing that, although she has her capricious moments, Edvarda's behaviour is by and large that of a normally constituted young woman. For example, in chapter XIII he contemplates the activity of the insects in the summer night and sees how 'The great white flowers open in the forest, their stigmas are open, they breathe. And hairy hawk-moths sink into their leaves and make the whole plant tremble. I go from flower to flower, they are intoxicated, they are [sexually (1909 ed.)] intoxicated flowers, and I see how they are intoxicated'. Edvarda appears and it is clear that the hawk moths and the flowers prefigure their own situation. She throws her arms around Glahn's neck, breathing heavily and with her pupils dilated, but he jumps up suddenly and when she asks him why, he replies: 'because it is so late. . . . Now the white flowers have closed up again, the sun is rising, the day begins'. From this point Edvarda's attitude to Glahn changes, their relationship has not followed the instinctive pattern prefigured for it by nature, but one deriving from Glahn's own reading of nature.

The role the mind plays in Glahn's experience of nature is well illustrated in chapter XXVI. It is 22 August, the first of the so-called Iron Nights, when traditionally frost may occur in those latitudes and put the crops in jeopardy. It is night and Glahn is in the forest with his gun and dog. He begins to soliloquize, proposing an eloquent toast and a vote of thanks for the life of the forest and its creatures, for silence and sound, for God's presence and his own being. But this toast [Skaaltale] (actually something taken from social life) is prompted by the *idea* of the Iron Nights rather than the actual facts of the situation. There is no frost, nor is there on the two succeeding Iron Nights, something which Glahn actually complains about: 'Instead of frost there was a stagnant warmth after the sun of the day, the night was like a tepid morass.' The whole chapter has, in fact, very much the character of something imagined. Eva appears and Glahn confesses that he loves three things: 'I love a dream of love I once had, I love you, and I love this patch of earth', but when Eva asks him what he loves most, he replies: 'The dream'. Thus it is fantasy which sustains Glahn. In spite of there being no frost, his experience of the Iron Nights is so intense that it becomes the climacteric of his experience of nature. The power of the imagined over reality is reinforced by the story he tells Eva of the Lapp who has been blind for 58 years yet believes that he sees better every day.

Besides giving wider, even universal, significance to Glahn's twofold nature and situation the use of the title *Pan* prefigures the general regressiveness we find in the work. This regressiveness is also reflected in the time structure of the novel. *Pan* appeared in 1894, but Glahn is supposed to be writing in in 1857, two years after the events he describes; the period is, however, more likely to be in the 1870s, the time of Hamsun's youth in Nordland, so that both he and Glahn are looking back in this book. The time perspectives within the novel are also in certain respects receding, in the intimations we receive of earlier cultural stages, the use of quasi-legendary figures, and the overall prefiguration of the Pan myth.

In recalling his experiences Glahn affects a nonchalance, saying that he is only writing them down to make time pass. Nevertheless, it is clear that those events are more important to him than the present, and it is an aspect of his regressiveness that he not infrequently does his best to make recalled past time stand still by using the repetition of a words or phrase to suggest duration—he wants to return to the past. Then time moved quickly or slowly according to the intensity of his relationship with Edvarda; now in the city where he is writing, time drags. Although

he says that he can tell the time from nature, Glahn's time does not always follow the inevitability of nature's time but is a largely personal one, its passing dictated by the mind, mood and emotion. However, I think one can detect in Glahn's experience of time stages analogous to the multiple role he has within the social and cultural pattern at Sirilund: nature's time (inevitable and cyclic); time past (static and becoming myth); and personal time (fragmented but containing beginnings and ends). Indeed, taken together, Glahn's experience of time forms the basis of the novel's *Gestalt.*

Considered in his migratory aspect, Glahn participates in the inexorable rhythms of nature; structurally this is underpinned by the spring to autumn time span of the novel, and by the arrival of the green feathers which trigger off the beginning and also provide the conclusion and the occasion for a new beginning or cycle—his trip to India. In his experience of time past he presents it with the immediacy of the present, not only in respect of his experiences of two years earlier but also in his presentation of intimations of earlier cultural stages; his whole tendency is in fact towards myth-making. But in the town, removed from absorption in the rhythms of nature and myth-making, Glahn finds the tick-tock of clock time impersonal and empty of meaning; this drives him to personalise it, give beginnings and ends by writing his book or calling in his drinking companions. There is a lack of a continuum of time and this is reflected in the nonexplicit, episodic development of the plot and the general lyrical nature of the novel with its prefigurations and recurring motifs. Hamsun said that every chapter of *Pan* was conceived as a poem.

The regressive nature of Glahn's whole way of thinking can also be seen in his propensity to proceed from observation to metaphor, to intimations of anthropomorphic relationships, to myth. In chapter III he watches the storm-tossed sea; the shapes it forms become first men, horses, and torn banners (a feudal image); then its activity transforms itself into the workings of the earth's brain [Jordens Hjærne], into which he is looking. These intimations (of the processes of creation?) seem to be shared by his dog Aesop who becomes uneasy, sniffs the air and stands with his legs quivering. In chapter IV Glahn looks out of the window. The evening landscape is enveloped in fairy light. The setting sun colours the horizon with a thick red light leaving the sky clear and open. He feels that he is face to face with the bed rock of the world [Verdens Bund] against which his heart beats, absorbed and at rest there.

What is involved here are intimations from the 'unconscious life of the mind', expressed by the use of images which project a mental picture of things not actually present. However, on other occasions the welling up of the unconscious life fails to find any adequate form of verbal expression: Glahn is reduced to weeping to express his feelings towards nature; enraged he can use words as a bludgeon from which verbal meaning is absent; sensations are given an autonomous status ('a feeling of compassion wanders through my heart'), as if his actual feeling of compassion could not be expressed. By contrast the Doctor whose concern is with the surface of life *uses* words to gain control over Edvarda.

The workings of the unconscious life also receive symbolical expression in artifacts. The pieces that Edvarda collects from the glass that Glahn broke achieve communicative importance; when Edvarda's shoe falls off it is symbolically a provocation and Glahn's action in throwing it overboard a rejection of that provocation—later Edvarda praises the Doctor (her tame attendant) for leaving her shoes in peace; the shoe also occurs in Glahn's fantasies about Iselin; a white scarf is a recurring symbol (Eva has a woollen one; Edvarda a silk one)—Glahn tells Edvarda the story of a young lady who has lent him her white scarf which she tied round his neck, three years later he discovers that she has kept the scarf wrapped in paper, unwashed, just as he had used it: thus the scarf has become a kind of fetish, something of herself which had become impregnated by Glahn—later in the novel Edvarda, in an attempt at reconciliation, offers Glahn her scarf, the symbolical offering of herself.

The propensity of the 'unconscious life of the mind', of the Hamsun hero to express itself in socially unacceptable ways, is particularly marked in Glahn. It generates in him an 'antic disposition' which leads him to a number of assaults: apart from throwing Edvarda's shoe overboard, he spits in the ear of the Baron (after making as if to whisper something to him, thus abusing a gesture of intimacy); he holds out his rifle and invites the Doctor to jump over (thus reducing the Doctor to the status of a dog); he shoots himself through the foot, and shoots his dog Aesop (in both cases misusing his rifle, a tool of his avocation as a soldier and huntsman).

Thus we see that the workings of the unconscious life of the mind find expression on different levels, and frequently in non-verbal terms, as if language were inadequate; by irrational conduct (in this respect we may compare Glahn with the young man in **'Fra det ubevidste Sjæleliv'** who shot a horse because it looked at him from the side); by the use of unsophisticated symbols (like the shoe) and of fetishes; and by the employment of images and language of great poetic potentiality. As with other aspects of *Pan* the expression of the unconscious life of the mind carries with it the suggestion of a multiplicity of cultural levels. Nevertheless, its status remains dubious, for while it can achieve grandeur in its regression from the everyday when given artistic expression, its encounters with the actual world tend to find it incapable of verbal communication. It reminds us once again that Hamsun's literary manifesto **'Fra det ubevidste Sjæleliv'** referred to the *artistic* use of 'the unconscious life of the mind'.

Although *Pan* lacks the third-person narrator of *Mysterier, Redaktør Lynge,* and *Ny Jord,* whose mobile position provided further perspectives on the events in those books, it does have a postscript written by another hand which sees Glahn from the outside. In it the facts surrounding Glahn's death are told anonymously by the person responsible for it—a man Glahn meets on a hunting trip to India. In one sense **'Glahns Død'** may be regarded as the public chapter of a story of which *Pan* was later to provide the explanatory inside account ('Glahns Død' was published before *Pan*); technically it is a device for giving an account of how Glahn met his death, of telling us what happened afterwards, and providing that documentary evidence, which Hamsun referred to in a letter to Philipsen; **'Glahns Død'** is subtitled 'Et Papir fra 1861' ('A Document from 1861').

The narrator gives no reasons for his writing of **'Glahns Død'**, although implicitly it would seem that he is trying to justify his shooting of Glahn. Officially his death was recorded as an accident; thus, like *Pan* itself, 'Glahns Død' is the inside story of what actually happened as opposed to what is publicly believed. In his account the narrator regards Glahn with a mixture of hatred and reluctantly expressed admiration. He is prepared to believe the worst of him and the tone of his narration is of a biassed, small-minded petit-bourgeois, whose cliché-like judgments show no understanding of the nature of the man he is describing. However, in spite of this the charisma, vitality, and exceptional character of Glahn emerge, and not least, paradoxically, because of the author's repeated insistence that he is dead.

In relation to *Pan* the most important event in the Post-script is the arrival of a letter for Glahn which the narrator believes is from the young woman in Nordland, about whose relationship with Glahn he has heard. Glahn's remarks about a married woman who proposes to a man and his cry: 'Never, never, I'd sooner be quartered' leave little doubt that the letter is from Edvarda; subsequently, Glahn conducts himself in such a way that his hunting companion is goaded into shooting him. However, the letter is only the instrument in hastening a process which has already begun. In the last chapter of *Pan* we learn that Glahn has resigned his commission and taken to drink, something which the narrator of 'Glahns Død' confirms. It is clear too, that Edvarda is the catalyst which has continued its subterranean operations and that he is neither able to forget her nor, when the letter arrives, willing to return to her. He has reached a dead point between the dream of love and the possibility of reentry into life and is incapable of moving from it. The 'antic disposition' which characterised Glahn's behaviour in *Pan* when the course of his relations with Edvarda eluded his control has in **'Glahns Død'** been succeeded by a general attitude of destructiveness. Though we have only the narrator's account, it seems clear that nature is now nothing more than a plaything for him: he shoots animals for the fun of it and to demonstrate his prowess as a marksman—in *Pan* he only shot in order to live; there is no feeling that Glahn is part of nature. Although his relationship with Maggie might seem like his relationships with Henriette and Eva, it is actually merely a part of his campaign to antagonise his hunting companion into killing him.

The Postscript looks back in some ways to *Mysterier.* The dead point which Glahn reaches is reminiscent of Nagel and the relationship between Glahn and the narrator with its mixture of hate, admiration and provocation seems to be another example of the duality of relationship found between Nagel and Minutten. There is a characteristic ambivalence on which the fact that the hotel at which Glahn and his companion stay is run by a *half*breed and Maggie being a *half*-Tamil is perhaps a wry comment from the author (Hamsun). In another respect the Postscript marks a culmination of a trend in Hamsun's work. It is the last occasion on which because of the idealisation of the feminine the relation of the hero to reality is catastrophically weakened and when sexual jealousy actually leads to murder.

The lack of polemics in *Pan* removes a link which in the novels Hamsun wrote after *Sult* made it easy to establish a relationship between him and his principal characters. There are, nevertheless, indications in *Pan* as to where he stands in relation to Glahn. It is for example clear that the intensity with which Glahn recounts his subjective and metaphysical experiences has the ring of authorial identification and consent; it gives him stature in relation to other characters in the book. There is also present an authorial stance, similar in kind to the generally ambivalent role of the narrator in Hamsun's novels written in the third person. On occasions Glahn is put in situations which make him appear absurd, even gratuitously so. These generally involve actions by him which are grotesquely out of context, like his pausing in the midst of his toast to the forest (chapter XXVI) to make sure that no one is listening to him, or his running into the woods to be alone with his happiness and then coming back to see if anyone has noticed he had gone there (chapter XII); this self-proclaimed son of the forest is also not averse to having a charwoman visit him. Here the authorial stance is implicitly that of the ironical observer. But in the 'white flowers' episode, authorial management achieves a much more subtle and ambivalent effect: Edvarda appears and, quite unmotivated, Glahn tells her a story of a girl at a ball whom no one asks to dance—although her mother was a perfect beauty and her father had won her by storm, she herself was born lame; the story prefigures the situation of Glahn and Edvarda immediately afterwards for, here too, the circumstances for their coming together were propitious but the outcome was a crippled one. The episode ends when the door of the smith's cottage opens and Mack appears, after a visit to Eva. On the one hand Glahn appears in an absurd light in his failure to respond to Edvarda's obvious willingness to consummate their relationship, and the appearance of Mack (who presumably has not let the appropriate moment escape him!) may be construed as a somewhat coarse comment on this, but, on the other hand, there is a sadness in the story of the lame girl which reflects Glahn's feeling for the vagaries of nature, and in the appearance of Mack a reminder of crude sensuality compared with the chaste, if idealised, restraint of Glahn's response to Edvarda.

Glahn's absurdity has a deeper existential aspect in which we can also see the hand of the author. It is implicit in the structure of the book that Glahn is poised between nature and society; as Tiemroth says: 'He stands in reality outside both the world of nature and the world of man' [*Illusionens vej: Om Knut Hamsun's forfatterskah*]. Thus it is not surprising that in many ways his mind is fragmented, that he lacks decision, and knows nothing with certainty, for he belongs nowhere. The story of Eva's death in chapter XXXII is illustrative of his whole situation. He had earlier noticed how boulders tumbled down into the sea from the mountain as part of the processes of nature, but when he himself explodes a charge in the mountain a loosened boulder falls on Eva and kills her. The implication is that the processes of nature are by definition natural and that Glahn's mind-directed intervention in them leads (as it also does in his relationship with Edvarda) to disaster. But intervention in nature is a basic activity of man, however looked at existentially, Glahn is playing both at human activity (blasting the cliff) and at nature (making the boulder fall); this is the reason for his obtuseness in not seeing that what he is doing will lead to Eva's death, an obtuseness which becomes comprehensible when we realise that it is the expression of his non-relatedness both to the human and to the natural sphere. Glahn's existential situation is one of general significance, which was to recur in Hamsun's work. In his own case Glahn eventually finds a solution to his situation when, prompted by the Doctor, he sends for his uniform and gives himself, notionally at least, a role in society though too late to have any effect. It is characteristic of the Hamsun 'outsider' that he has no role in society; conversely, the successfully functioning individual in Hamsun is one who is secure in his role and who can manipulate the surface of life, like Mack, whom Glahn in a moment of insight characterises as 'the wisest man in the world'.

Seen in the context of Hamsun's work of the period, *Pan* brings to the forefront the love motif in the earlier novels and looks forward to *Victoria* (1898). In doing so the characteristic inability of the Hamsun hero to act in relation to his beloved and to see her in the round is writ large. In Glahn's projections on to Edvarda the critique of the imagination degenerated into fantasy—found in *Redaktør Lynge* and *Ny Jord*—continues; and there is indirect criticism of the artist in Glahn's self-indulgence as a writer. The novel also adds a further query as to the status of the workings of the unconscious life: at the end of it not only are Eva and Aesop its victims, but so too is Edvarda. Though there is truth in the Doctor's analysis of her, its truth is more in the ballad-like substratum of the book than in the realities; likewise the suggestion that some critics have made that Glahn and Edvarda are parallel in projecting their ideals on to each other is only true in a limited sense. The fact is that although she may be capricious it is Edvarda who takes all the initiatives in the relationship with Glahn; it is she who, despite her romantic notions, lives in the real world of social relationships and duties, and it is she (in the Postscript) who makes a last effort to salvage their relationship. Perhaps Hamsun's original idea to call the book 'Edvarda' showed a correct instinct; she is the most positive character in the book but her virtues had to wait until the title figure in Hamsun's next novel *Victoria* to be fully realised. (pp. 19-31)

Ronald Popperwell, "Knut Hamsun and 'Pan'," in Scandinavica, *Vol. 25, No. 1, May, 1986, pp. 19-31.*

FURTHER READING

Biography

Ferguson, Robert. *Enigma: The Life of Knut Hamsun.* London: Hutchinson, 1987, 453 p.

Comprehensive account of Hamsun's life and work that attempts to take into account his relation to Nazi Germany.

Naess, Harald [S]. *Knut Hamsun.* Boston: Twayne Publishers, 1984, 194 p.

Study of Hamsun's works supported by relevant biographical material.

Criticism

Bach, Giovanni, and Blankner, Frederika. "Neo-Romanticism and Neo-Realism." In *The History of the Scandinavian Literatures,* edited and translated by Frederika Blankner, pp. 54-68. New York: Dial Press, 1938.

Assesses Hamsun's place in Norwegian literature.

Buttry, Dolores. "Knut Hamsun's Supposed Anti-Semitism: A Refutation." *EDDA* 2 (1986): 123-33.

Questions the evidence on which the allegations concerning Hamsun's associations with Nazi Germany and his tendency towards anti-Semitism are based.

————. "A Thirst for Intimacy: Knut Hamsun's Pyromania." *Scandinavica* 26, No. 2 (November 1987): 129-39.

Offers a psychoanalytic reading of Hamsun's fiction in accordance with his repeated reference to images of fire and light.

————. "Down and Out in Paris, London, and Oslo: Pounding the Pavement with Knut Hamsun and George Orwell." *Comparative Literature Studies* 25, No. 3 (1988): 225-41.

Contrasts the depiction of poverty found in Orwell's *Down and Out in Paris* and *The Road to Wigan Pier* with Hamsun's *Hunger,* arguing that Orwell examines the social aspects of poverty while Hamsun provides a psychological perspective.

————. "Earth Mother or Femme Fatale?: Femininity as Envisioned by Jean-Jacques Rousseau and Knut Hamsun." *Neophilologus* 72, No. 4 (October 1988): 481-98.

Examines the ways in which the concept of the ideal woman is reflected in relationships in the writings of Jean-Jacques Rousseau and Knut Hamsun.

Jacobs, Barry. "A Start and End in Controversy." *The New York Times Book Review* (16 July 1967): 5, 16.

Reviews *On Overgrown Paths,* attributing the importance of the novel to the insight it gives into Hamsun's relationship to nazism.

Lovett, Robert Morss. *"Growth of the Soil."* In his *Preface to Fiction: A Discussion of Great Modern Novels,* pp. 41-52. Chicago: Thomas S. Rockwell Co., 1931.

Analyzes *Growth of the Soil* as part of an epic tradition in literature.

Mazor, Yair. "The Epilogue in Knut Hamsun's *Pan:* The Questionable Combination, the Analagous Connection and the Rhetorical Compensation." *EDDA* 6 (1984): 313-28.

Assesses "Glahn's End," the epilogue to *Pan,* pointing to its narrative incongruities in relation to the rest of the novel.

Naess, Harald S. "A Strange Meeting and Hamsun's *Mysterier.*" *Scandinavian Studies* 36, No. 1 (February 1964): 48-58.

Describes Hamsun's source for Kamma, a character in his *Mysteries.*

Popperwell, Ronald G. "Critical Attitudes to Knut Hamsun 1890-1969." *Scandinavica* 9, No. 1 (May 1970): 1-23.

Overview of the critical reception of Hamsun's works.

Riechel, Donald C. "Knut Hamsun's 'Imp of the Perverse': Calculation and Contradiction in *Sult* and *Mysterier.*" *Scandinavica* 28, No. 1 (May 1989): 29-53.

Discusses the psychology of the narrators in *Hunger* and *Mysteries.*

Slochower, Harry. "The Antaean Tradition." In his *No Voice Is Wholly Lost. . . . : Writers and Thinkers in War and Peace,* pp. 130-46. New York: Creative Age Press, 1945.

Considers the different ways in which the settings of Hamsun's novels advocate a return to nature.

Vernon, John. "Labor and Leisure: *Hunger.*" In his *Money and Fiction: Literary Realism in the Nineteenth and Early Twentieth Centuries,* pp. 142-71. Ithaca and London: Cornell University Press, 1984.

Describes the relationships between money, literary creativity, and narrative structure in *Hunger.*

Etty Hillesum

1914-1943

(Full name Esther Hillesum) Dutch diarist.

INTRODUCTION

In her diaries and letters Hillesum chronicled her experiences as a Jewish woman living in Nazi-occupied Amsterdam and as a prisoner at a Nazi transit camp. Critics have especially praised Hillesum's rendering of her spiritual development under extremely oppressive and dehumanizing conditions as well as her expression of steadfast faith in humankind's inherent goodness. As Terrence Des Pres has commented: "The diaries of Etty Hillesum . . . offer a story of spiritual growth such as I have seldom seen anywhere, least of all in accounts of the shut-down world of the Holocaust."

Hillesum was born in Middelburg, Netherlands, where her father was an educator and scholar and her mother had settled after escaping religious persecution in Russia. By the age of twenty-five Hillesum had earned a law degree, studied the works of Sigmund Freud and Carl Jung, and was learning several Slavic languages at the University of Amsterdam. Shortly before the beginning of World War II, Hillesum moved to Amsterdam. A voracious reader, she greatly admired the spiritual quality she found in the works of Fedor Dostoevski, Rainer Maria Rilke, Leo Tolstoy, and Saint Augustine, and she strove to emulate these authors in her own search for meaning. Hillesum spent much of her time contemplating what Jan G. Gaarlandt called "the sources of her existence," preferring to keep World War II and the Holocaust at the periphery of her consciousness.

In March 1941 Hillesum began keeping the diaries that were later published as *Het verstoorde leven: Dagboek van Etty Hillesum, 1941-1943* (*An Interrupted Life: The Diaries of Etty Hillesum, 1941-1943*). Her earliest entries largely reflect her relationship with Julius Spier, a palmist trained in psychoanalysis by Jung, who prompted what Gaarlandt described as Hillesum's "constant search for the essential, the truly human, in dramatic opposition to the inhumanity around her." In the early sections of her diary Hillesum rarely mentioned the events of World War II or anything that occurred outside of her circle of friends and family. Most of her observations focus on her sexuality, her relationships with men, and her thoughts on God. However, as persecution and mass deportations became more prevalent in Amsterdam, Hillesum began to react directly to external events. In July 1942 she was hired as a typist by the Jewish Council, an organization designed by Nazis to mediate between themselves and Jews, and learned of the thousands of Jews who were sent to Westerbork, a Dutch transit camp from which most were sent to Auschwitz, Poland. Hillesum volunteered to accompany

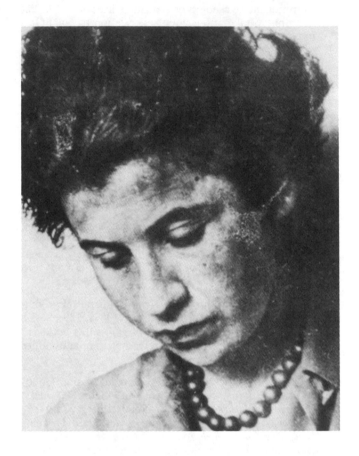

a group of Jews to Westerbork, where from August 1942 to September 1943 she worked in the local hospital.

The majority of Hillesum's observations while at Westerbork appear in her numerous letters to friends and are collected in *Denkende hart van de barak* (*Letters from Westerbork*). Her diary entries record her thoughts during her travels to Amsterdam and to her parents' home in Deventer. Hillesum's writings of this period demonstrate a passionate faith in the value of life; in the midst of imprisonment, illness, despair, and death she affirmed, "Despite everything, life is full of beauty and meaning." Hillesum strove to be what she called "the thinking heart of the barracks" and refused all offers from friends to take her to a safe location while she was still permitted to travel.

After June 1943 Hillesum was imprisoned in Westerbork along with her parents and brother. She looked after her own family's needs and eased the sadness and despair of her friends through letters in which she spoke of her return after the war, though she recorded in her diary that she knew she would not survive. In September 1943 Hillesum and her family were transported to Auschwitz, where they all perished in the gas chambers. Although Hillesum kept no written record of her last days, she was described by a friend as having a cheerful disposition and concern for the welfare of others.

Hillesum's writings have been praised by critics both as evidence of her considerable spiritual growth and her masterful prose style. Many critics have suggested that Hillesum's works stand apart from other Holocaust memoirs because they transcend the horrors of the Holocaust and distinguish Hillesum as a writer possessed of profound insights into the human condition. Speculation continues on whether Hillesum maintained her optimism and belief in the essential goodness of humankind while imprisoned at Auschwitz; her views on the nature of God and religion are the subject of much discussion. Irving Halperin has observed: "Through her writing and her humanity, [Hillesum] praised the sanctity of life. Looking outward, beyond the self, looking squarely and clearly at the historic moment, she had come of age in an age of genocide."

PRINCIPAL WORKS

Het verstoorde leven: Dagboek van Etty Hillesum, 1941-1943 (diaries) 1981
[*Etty: A Diary, 1941-1943*, 1983; also published as *An Interrupted Life: The Diaries of Etty Hillesum, 1941-1943*, 1984]

Denkende hart van de barak (letters) 1982
[*Letters from Westerbork*, 1986]

CRITICISM

Terrence Des Pres   (essay date 1984)

[*Des Pres was an American educator and critic whose works include* The Survivor: An Anatomy of Life in the Death Camps *(1976). In the following review of* An Interrupted Life, *he gives high praise to Hillesum's "literary flair" and to her capacity for spiritual growth amid adversity.*]

By now we are familiar with a kind of autobiographical writing called "survivor testimony," that bears personal witness to the unimaginable suffering of some 11 million victims, the majority of them Jews, who perished during the years 1939-45 when war and the Nazis dominated Europe. These are stories that can never be told completely or often enough. There is, however, a problem. The testimony in many languages is already extensive, and although each person's narrative is unique, there is a terrible sameness in accounts of Hitler's genocide. The more we learn about it, the more we find individual destinies meeting within an increasingly predictable story of ghettos, of trains and camps and the final seep of ash into mud.

No doubt, I overstate the case, but from these narratives

we hardly expect refined portraits of spirit in adversity. We are amazed to see spirit existing at all under such brutal and inhuman conditions. To ask for more—some growth or deepening of the soul in that time and those places—would be unseemly, even cruel.

But what we have no right to expect might still be given—and in *An Interrupted Life* it comes like a marvelous gift. The diaries of Etty Hillesum, written in Holland between 1941 and 1943, offer a story of spiritual growth such as I have seldom seen anywhere, least of all in accounts of the shut-down world of the Holocaust. The book is in all ways unique, not least in the way it disturbs our notions of political resistance and physical survival. Etty Hillesum did not fight and she did not survive, but she deserves to be counted among the heroes.

Etty breaks every rule I thought I knew, starting with the first words of her first entry: "Here goes, then." That hints at literary flair and, in matters so grim, seems out of place. Holocaust documents are supposed to be artless and wounded, but the diaries of this young Dutch Jew are written with the interior richness and woven design of a Jamesian novel. At 27, nine months after Adolf Hitler occupied the Netherlands, this bright young woman sat down at her desk in Amsterdam and began writing—not about war and Nazi terror but about Eros and the soul. She had decided to examine her life by starting a diary, a task that felt faintly shameful to her but also emancipating. And to have begun, as she says immediately, is "like the final, liberating scream that always sticks bashfully in your throat when you make love."

We are in the presence of something very different, unexpected, perhaps also a little shocking. For as Etty goes on in that very first entry:

> I am accomplished in bed, just about seasoned enough I should think to be counted among the better lovers, and love does indeed suit me to perfection, and yet it remains a mere trifle, set apart from what is truly essential, and deep inside me something is still locked away.

But if these lines were to evoke D. M. Thomas's novel *The White Hotel*, it would be misleading; because fantasy is not part of Etty's life, and although she died, she approached her fate deliberately and was not, like Lisa Erdman in *The White Hotel*, haphazardly crushed.

Anne Frank also comes to mind, not merely because she, too, kept diaries but because both Anne and Etty shared a faith in human decency that seems, in the light of history, more than their situation justified. But what a difference between the girl in the attic and the woman listing things (sturdy shoes, a Russian edition of *The Idiot*) she wants to carry with her into the camps. It is as if Etty's diaries complete Anne's; except that in Etty's example there is no room for pathos. Her true counterparts are to be found among women of exceptional mind and strength, Hannah Arendt or Nadezhda Mandelstam or, most strikingly, Simone Weil. What Etty seeks is first confronted as Eros, then affirmed as a mystical condition called "Life," and at last entered into as a state of the soul she calls "God." She moved from self-absorption to a remarkable sense of historical destiny and participation in the common fate of European Jews.

Etty came from a family of highly educated, highly assimilated Jews, who all died in the camps. By the time the war began she had taken a law degree, knew the works of Freud and Jung, was proficient in philosophy and at work on Russian literature. She had what was once called "a European mind." She also lived in a sort of commune, had many lovers (two at once in the diaries), and enjoyed the Bohemian freedom of graduate study at the University of Amsterdam. Still, she was unsatisfied and yearned for spiritual focus; she wanted to write a novel about "the girl who could not kneel."

She believed that writing was her "real talent," and surely it was. But there were other talents of which she was only dimly aware. She had an instinct for becoming her own woman, and when first we meet her she has embarked on something very like the archetypal feminist struggle. She writes: "You are always thrown back onto your own resources. There is nothing else. The rest is make-believe. But that fact has to be recognized over and over again. Especially since you are a woman. For a woman always longs to lose herself in another. But that too is a fiction." Early on she says that "for all I know I shall always continue to be in search of my one man. And I wonder to what extent that is a handicap, a woman's handicap." Later she says of her relation to her lover: "My salvation must be wrought with my own strength, not his." This, remember, in the middle of a war.

Etty, it turns out, is a woman who wants to learn to kneel, as she herself says many times, but not to another human being. Only to God will she bow down, and to that which proves, upon testing, to be inescapably real. She is possessed by a spiritual lust to reside at the heart of the actual, and in this we rightly detect a religious, and finally a mystical, bent. She gradually becomes that rarest of beings, the hardheaded realist for spiritual reasons. She loves books and reads constantly—Dostoyevsky, St. Augustine, Rilke especially—but reading, she knows, is not the thing itself. Her problem is anyone's, and she knows exactly what it entails. She writes that

> one must keep in touch with the real world and know one's place in it; it is wrong to live only with the eternal truths, for then one is apt to end up behaving like an ostrich. To live fully, outwardly and inwardly, not to ignore external reality for the sake of the inner life, or the reverse—that's quite a task.

Yes, quite a task, especially for a European Jew in 1941.

As her diaries proceed and the surrounding darkness deepens, Etty comes to see her work as an act of bearing witness to her time and her people. But at first she is absorbed in herself and for many pages the catastrophe in progress is mentioned only in passing. In the beginning Etty sees the Germans as mainly a problem in hatred—how not to be angry with the German girl in her house who does the cooking. Only after Amsterdam's Jews are forced to wear the yellow star (April 29, 1942) does the horror begin to close in. Then she writes: "Only a few

months ago I still believed that politics did not touch me and wondered if that was 'unwordliness,' a lack of real understanding. Now I don't ask such questions anymore."

Holocaust documents are supposed to be artless and wounded, but the diaries of [Etty Hillesum] are written with the interior richness and woven design of a Jamesian novel.

—*Terrence Des Pres*

Much of Etty's story is taken up with an extraordinary love affair, but if her diaries were about only the affair they would still be worth reading. The man was Julius Spier whom Etty refers to as S. He was older, a German Jew, one of Carl Jung's students specializing in "psychochirology"—the reading of palm prints. In Amsterdam Spier had a clinical practice, and Etty went to him for help in sorting out her life. Most of his patients were women, and his methods of treatment were odd. He insisted that "body and soul are one" and that sessions between analyst and patient must therefore begin with a wrestling match. Etty's pride is that her first time with Spier *she* floored *him*.

Theirs is one of the most bizarre but endearing love stories I have found, in fiction or in fact. It is infinitely nuanced, on its own terms quite convincing, and the war, of course, contributes to its power. No doubt Spier was a womanizer and a charlatan, but Etty never doubted his worth. She was certainly in love, but she could still see him for the "dear spoiled man" he was. He died before the transports to the camps began. At one point Etty writes: "We have had wild and unfettered lives in many strange beds and we are nevertheless shy all over again, each time. I find this very beautiful and delight in it. Now I shall put on my brightly-colored dressing gown and go downstairs to read the Bible with him." More than lovers merely, they were companions in spirit.

Being privileged and relatively well off (she kept her own rooms, there was always something to eat), Etty had the distance, and above all the time, to watch and ponder events around her. In a clear-eyed, almost matter-of-fact way, she saw that the Jews of Europe were doomed. At this point she begins to speak increasingly of a "common destiny" and of "our common fate." It was, I think, her apartness that allowed Etty her growing sense of oneness with the historical moment. Briefly, in the summer of 1942, she worked for the Cultural Affairs Department of the Jewish Council, and what she saw there further cemented her sense of destiny. The sort of political dealing that went on at the council appalled Etty: "The mental horizon of all the people I work with is so narrow. . . . They intrigue, they are still ambitious to get on, it is all a great big, dirty mess." And the worst of it was, in Etty's eyes, "that one section of the Jewish population is helping to transport the majority out of the country."

To remain "exempted," as she then was, became intolerable. What she therefore decided to do might shock us, as indeed it shocked her friends. Etty volunteered to accompany a group of condemned Jews to the transit camp at Westerbork—the place from which trains departed for Auschwitz. Whether or not she could have escaped is a question that cannot be answered. The point is that she did not try. She could have gone into hiding, as some Jews did in Holland. For a time she even had a special pass that allowed her to go back and forth between Amsterdam and the camp at Westerbork. Etty reminds me of Ernie Levy in *The Last of the Just,* and maybe that is what she was— one of those who feel compelled to carry within themselves the suffering of the world. She reminds me even more of Simone Weil, not so much in rigor of intellect as in discipline of spirit—the desire to be with those who suffer, the attentive waiting upon God's will, the strange, self-aware combination of Jewish and Christian attitudes.

From a secular point of view, Etty's decision does not make sense. What are we to make of a person who prays to God in the following way:

> I want to be sent to every one of the camps that lie scattered all over Europe, I want to be at every front, I don't ever want to be what they call 'safe,' I want to be there, I want to fraternize with all my so-called enemies, I want to understand what is happening and share my knowledge with as many as I can possibly reach.

For *those* reasons she implores the Lord to "let me get healthy." And of course, Etty's fierce religiosity is the crux of the matter. Her mystical acceptance of reality was the "thing still locked away" when, two years earlier, she began her first diary.

This acceptance is, I expect, the hardest thing to credit about Etty's behavior. We might well be skeptical when she writes, for example, that "the blisters on my feet and the jasmine behind the house, the persecution, the unspeakable horrors—it is all as one in me and I accept it all." All? But mystics do express themselves that way, and what makes this convincing is that Etty's religious acceptance stays rooted in immediate circumstances recorded daily, as if the diaries had become a kind of prayer. One day in the overcrowded corridors of the Jewish Council, amid the desperate faces, Etty "suddenly felt the urge to kneel down right there, on the stone floor, among all those people. The only adequate gesture left to us in these times: 'kneeling down before You.' " She is speaking to God, or in fact, talking with Him, and this is, I think, the authentic language of sainthood. Of St. Augustine she writes: "He is so austere and so fervent. And so full of simple devotion in his love letters to God." The same can be said of Etty and her diaries.

We can see, from letters written in Westerbork and appended to the diaries, that Etty was keenly aware of horrors present and horrors to come. She knew. But if her train left Westerbork for Auschwitz on Sept. 9, 1943, and the record of her death is given as Nov. 30 of that year,

then she existed in the worst of the death camps for almost three months. During that time anything, absolutely anything, might have happened to her. I must wonder if her power of spirit sustained her to the end. I cannot know, and therefore I choose to believe that it did. I also wonder, since the diaries were edited and cut, if the portrait in *An Interrupted Life* is wholly accurate. If it is, then we have before us the testimony of a very special person. Despite the book's misleading title, Etty Hillesum's life was not interrupted. It was, as few lives are, whole, complete, given. (pp. 1, 32-3)

> Terrence Des Pres, "Eros, God and Auschwitz," in The New York Times Book Review, *January 29, 1984, pp. 1, 32-3.*

Marie Syrkin   (essay date 1984)

[*A Swiss-born American political activist, educator, translator, and critic, Syrkin was the founder and editor of the monthly* Jewish Frontier *for fifteen years. In the following essay, she examines* An Interrupted Life, *highlighting Hillesum's simple yet steadfast religious beliefs.*]

She has already been likened to Simone Weil, this young Dutch Jewess whose recently published diary [*An Interrupted Life*] spans the fateful years 1941-1943, and stops abruptly with her death in Auschwitz at the age of 29. The comparison highlights the differences. No fierce ascetic bent on self-immolation, Etty Hillesum is an exuberant celebrant of life. In her first entry she describes herself as an accomplished bedfellow with a varied erotic past. She has other impressive accomplishments. A lawyer, a gifted linguist, obviously talented, determined to be a writer yet unsure of her direction, she could be a contemporary liberated woman beset by traditional and untraditional perplexities about marriage, career, sex, love. Much of the diary could be dated 1984 without loss of credibility, though current feminists would resent such heresies as her worry that a woman may be handicapped because she "longs for a man not mankind." And her funny, poignant description of sessions with her therapist, a remarkable German Jewish refugee twice her age who becomes her moral guide and lover, almost brings to mind the techniques of later encounter groups in Southern California: wrestling matches in which both are physically aroused, then spiritually fulfilled by reading Thomas à Kempis.

Yet, the significance of the diary lies not in its honest self-portrait of a remarkable young woman or in her fascinating relationship to her curious mentor. It lies in the time in which the love story is cast. How does this young woman react to the events of which she is a part? Though probing into the psyche of the Jewish victims has become a literary industry often pursued with more obtuseness than imaginative understanding, the question is inevitable.

Critics have hailed this diary for being no run-of-the-mill catalogue of horrors, for sparing the reader the danger of being tormented by still another recital of intolerable suffering. This dubious compliment is only partly merited. To the usual questions, Etty provides unusual, baffling answers. In contradistinction to the memoirs of survivors, unrevised Holocaust diaries have the tension of dramatic irony; the actors are ignorant, the readers, knowing. In the case of Etty, the prescient reader, who notes the dates on the successive pages, cannot help wondering at which point her joyous affirmation of the beauty and goodness of life will falter.

By 1941 the anti-Jewish measures of the Nazi occupiers of Holland are in full swing, but Etty, sheltered in a household of warm Christian friends, is as yet spared the direct impact of the terror. At this stage, in an early entry, she can write:

> I am sometimes so distracted by all the appalling happenings round me that it's far from easy to find the way back to myself. And yet that's what I must do. I mustn't let myself be ground down by the misery outside.

The rose on her desk or a poem by Rilke (her great literary passion) are as "real and important" as any outer circumstance. Even on the day that she must report to the Gestapo she records first her pleasure in a cup of genuine Van Houten's cocoa and some bread and honey she has just eaten "with what you may call abandon." Then she adds,

> I opened the Bible this morning at random but it gave me no answers this morning. Just as well because there were no questions, just enormous faith and gratitude that life should be so beautiful, and that makes it a historic moment, *that* and not the fact that S. [her lover] and I are on the way to the Gestapo.

Willful bravado or a consistent philosophy? It will become the latter.

At the Gestapo office she feels compassion for the brutal German officer who harasses helpless Jews, and she fights the temptation to hate the Germans. "Every atom of hate we add to this inhospitable world makes it more inhospitable." Whenever she wavers, she returns more firmly to her insistence on life's beauty. On the day that Jews are compelled to wear yellow stars, she notes one man's defiant gesture: "He was wearing a huge golden star, wearing it triumphantly on his chest. . . . All that yellow—I suddenly had a poetic vision of the sun rising above him, so radiant and smiling did he look." Fortunately she has the good sense to add an earthy corrective: "Come now, Etty, my girl, things aren't as congenial as you make out, and you really seem to gloss things over with your flights of poetry."

Does she blaspheme by prettifying the monstrous, by declaring that a sprig of jasmine, a walk along the canal, a Rilke poem, are experiences as intense as her awareness of the concentration camps across the border? On the last night of 1941 she takes stock of the evening's satisfactions: a gas fire, red and yellow tulips, a piece of chocolate, her lover, and her books. Nineteen forty-one has been the richest, most fruitful, and the "happiest" of all. Heroism, or an aesthete's egoism?

As restrictions against Jews multiply, she continues to recite her self-centered idyll; whatever the space there is room enough for music and love. She wants to counsel a bereaved friend:

> Yes, life is beautiful and I value it anew each day even though I know that the sons of mothers, and you are such a mother, are being murdered in concentration camps. . . . Do not relieve your feelings through hatred, do not seek to be avenged on all German mothers, for they too sorrow at this moment for their slain sons.

Yet just when the ordinary reader loses patience with her high-minded detachment, she becomes sufficiently self-critical to wonder whether she is so philosophical because so far she is little affected personally.

At the same time it would be unjust to minimize her emotional involvement. As information of the carnage in Poland reaches Amsterdam, she reasserts her credo:

> I am with the hungry, with the ill-treated and the dying every day, but I am also with the jasmine and the piece of sky beyond my window; there is room for everything in a single life. For belief in God and for a miserable end.

To prepare for the miserable end she prudently visits a dentist and packs a small bag leaving room for Rilke and the Bible, but she still does not believe, despite the rumors, that the Germans are engaged in a calculated extermination program. She expects to be shipped to a "labor camp" whose cruelties may result in death. She naively begins to train for coming hardships by drinking buttermilk instead of cocoa for breakfast. The one reality her imagination cannot encompass is that of the gas chamber.

As her mood darkens, she cries out, "And if God does not help me to go on, then I shall have to help God!" Her dialogue with God, her religious transcendence, account for the great impression this diary made in Holland when it appeared in 1981. Affiliated neither with synagogue nor church, and not a mystic in the strict sense, Etty escapes categories. A revealing sentence betrays her unconventional religiosity: "I hold a silly, naive, or deadly serious dialogue with what is deepest inside me which for the sake of convenience I call God." Yet despite this ambiguous definition, her prayers use the terms of the simple believer:

> Oh, God, times are too hard for frail people like myself. I know that a new and kinder day will come. I would so much like to live on, if only to express all the love I carry within me. And there is only one way of preparing for the new age. By living it in our hearts.

Her spiritual evolution has setbacks. Despite her contempt for the Jewish Council whose role in the deportations she excoriates, she briefly accepts a job with the Council in the hope of a respite. Though she dreamed of being "a center of peace in that madhouse," she finds intolerable the actual contact with desperate human beings pleading for delay in their transfer to supposed labor camps. After a few weeks she joins, of her own accord, a transport of Jews to Westerbork, a Dutch transit camp that is the final stop before Auschwitz. "I want to be sent to every one of the camps that lie scattered all over Europe. . . . I don't ever want to be safe. . . . I want to fraternize with my so-called enemies."

In Westerbork she meditates on how she will live "out

there," the unknown destination, and she comforts herself with the reflection that Dostoyevsky spent four years in a Siberian prison with inadequate sanitary arrangements and only the Bible for reading matter. Alternating between visions of destruction and plans for the new world she will help remake, she searches for a "great redeeming formula" and speculates that there will be "enough space to fold two hands in prayer." If in one mood she sounds irritatingly like Pippa Passes, "God's in his heaven, all's right with the world," in another she has the insight to pray, "Oh, God, give me the strength to bear the suffering you have imposed on me and not just the suffering I have chosen for myself."

Her final communication is a long letter to her Christian friends in Amsterdam. In Amsterdam she had proudly declared that she would be no chronicler of horrors. She cannot keep the promise. Her overwhelming, detailed description of wailing babies and children dragged away in the deportation of a thousand Jews from Westerbork is, except for its literary power, a characteristic Holocaust document. "So that's what hell is like." No assertion that life is beautiful, or expressions of compassion for the Nazis who conduct the operation, appear in this long account. And the only reference to God is impious, "God Almighty, what are you doing to us?" Yet the letter concludes with a bewildering assurance, "I am firmly resolved to return to you after my wanderings." She was herself soon deported to Auschwitz with her parents and her younger brother, a musical prodigy. All perished, Etty in three months.

In Westerbork, in a phrase reminiscent of Donne's "naked, thinking heart," she had prayed to be the "thinking heart of the barracks." Did God die for her in Auschwitz or did she continue to be sustained by what was "deepest" inside her? There is no escaping the reflection that her generosity of spirit and religious exaltation had not been tested to the utmost before Auschwitz. Critics heartened by the comforting difference between this diary and other Holocaust memoirs ignore the fact that the life of a Dutch Jew situated like Etty bore no resemblance to existence in the ghettos of Eastern Europe. No rivers of blood flowed in Amsterdam and the streets were not littered with corpses. Roundups of Jews took place openly in the West, but the ultimate exhibitions of savagery were saved for Poland. The death camps operated behind a barricade of secrecy; the Nazis had a discreet regard for the squeamish West. Yet Etty was not unique in her struggle against dehumanization. (pp. 33-5)

Children wrote poems for the *Gazeta Zydowska*. One such by "Martha" read:

> I must be saving these days
> I have no money to save . . .
> I must save my nerves
> And my thoughts, and my mind,
> and the fire of my spirit
> I must be saving of tears that flow . . .
> There is so much I need in my life
> Warmth of feeling and a kind heart . . .
> All these, the gifts of God, I wish to keep.

These were the words of an anonymous girl who probably shared Etty's fate. . . .

The diaries of the marvelous young deepen the sense of loss and tease the mind with possibilities. Had Etty survived Auschwitz would she have become an avenging spirit like Beate Klarsfeld, or perhaps a sorrowing figure transcending hate like Nelly Sachs, now honored in Germany as the poet of reconciliation? No systematic religious thinker, she would not likely have developed into a minor Simone Weil. In any case the comparison does Etty an injustice in a crucial respect: Weil's saintly compassion for human suffering did not extend to the Jews. . . . Etty, on the other hand, with no doctrinaire commitments, from an equally assimilated background, studied St. Matthew and drew closer to her people the more they suffered. (p. 36)

> *Marie Syrkin, "Do Not Go Gently," in* The New Republic, *Vol. 190, No. 12, March 26, 1984, pp. 33-6.*

Sherie Posesorski (essay date 1984)

[*In the following review of* An Interrupted Life, *Posesorski discusses Hillesum's strong bond with Jewish people tortured in death camps and her decision to volunteer to go to a camp herself.*]

Two diaries by two dark-eyed, dark-haired, young Jewish women record their daily lives during the Nazi occupation of Holland in 1941. As the Dutch Jews were marked by yellow Stars of David, quartered in ghettoes, and shipped off to Auschwitz, Anne Frank noted the domestic disputes of the Frank family, hidden away in an attic. The Franks waited, enchanted by the evil spells of the Nazis, for a fairy-tale rescue and resolution.

Etty Hillesum, 27 years old, sat at her desk on the other side of Amsterdam, writing in her small, hard-to-decipher handwriting: "What is at stake is our impending destruction and annihilation. We can have no more illusions about life. . . . My personal fate is not the issue. . . . If I have one duty in these times, it is to bear witness." She refused offers from friends to help her into hiding. Instead, she volunteered to accompany the Jews sent to Westerbork, a transit camp, and spent a year travelling freely between Amsterdam and the camp hospital. In September, 1943, Etty, her father Dr. L. Hillesum, her mother Rebecca, and her brother Mischa were all transported to Auschwitz, where they were to die.

Surviving through hiding or seeking has become a critical question for scholars re-examining the nature of survival in the Second World War. At one pole, Terrence Des Pres (in *The Survivor: An Anatomy of Life in the Death Camps*) espouses surviving at any cost, in any form. In opposition to him, Bruno Bettelheim contends in his essay, "The Ignored Lesson of Anne Frank," that "those who faced up to the announced intentions of the Nazis prepared for the worst as a real and imminent possibility. It meant risking one's life for a self-chosen purpose, but, in doing so, creating, at least, a small chance for saving one's life, or those of others." The fate of the Franks demonstrates, according

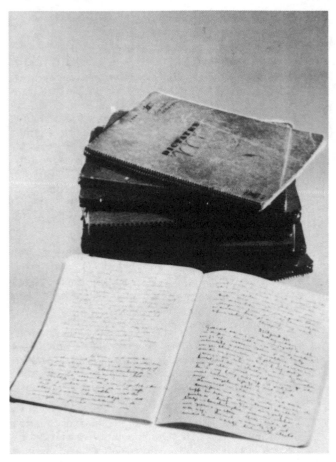

The notebooks in which Hillesum kept her diaries.

to Bettelheim, the danger of retreating deep into a private world, passive, frozen, and inactive on one's own behalf.

The selections [in *An Interrupted Life*] from the eight notebook diaries of Etty Hillesum, written from 1941 to 1943, are a remarkably moving account of the other form of survival. Hillesum believed that "it is wrong to live only with external truths, for then one is apt to end up behaving like an ostrich. To live fully outwardly and inwardly, one can not ignore external reality."

Hillesum was born in 1914 into a family of educated, assimilated Jews. By 1939 she had taken a degree in law, studied the works of Freud and Jung, and was learning several Slavic languages (her father was a professor of Slavic languages at the University of Amsterdam). Her lifestyle was bohemian. She lived in a commune with two men—a father and son who were her lovers, at different times—and three other women. On the first page of her diary, she notes with self satisfaction that she considers herself an accomplished lover. A considerable amount of her diary, initially, is occupied with erotic fantasies about Julius Spier (S. in the diaries), a portly, eccentric, 54-year-old psychochirologist (palm reader) who began his sessions with a wrestling match between himself and the patient.

As the diaries progress, however, we witness the evolution

of Hillesum from a woman locked in the plastic bubble of her own consciousness, to one who breaks free of her autistic existence as she comes to identify with the common fate of her people, the Jews. Her consciousness becomes a blend of Dostoevsky's underground man and Henry James's John Marcher (in the short story "The Beast in the Jungle"). Like the underground man, she records the barometric readings of her body's aches and pains, and her own moods and depressions, all of which is rendered with the fine gradations of a Jamesian consciousness. Like Marcher, she lives in a state of perpetual anticipation: "I had the feeling that nothing I did was the real thing," she writes, "that it was all a preparation for something else, something greater, more genuine."

Her private life circles around two obsessions: her writing and her sessions with S. Although she feverishly declares that writing is her "real talent," she oscillates between moments of exalted faith in her ability and her sense of herself as a miserable, deluded creature. Her writing is intense, saturated with breathless rushes of acute ideas and perceptions.

The tension that exists in her relationship to her writing carries over into her sexual tension toward S. Their first session ends in a wrestling match in which she floors him. Initially, he refuses to consummate the relationship, being rather preoccupied with the activities of his wife and mistress. The affair develops into a caring, intellectual, and sexual companionship, however, that ends only with his death.

Both her writing and her sessions aid her in her search for meaning. Kneeling on a coconut mat in her bathroom, she addresses the God in herself. In these litanies her thoughts are grasped, counted like rosary beads, giving her strength. She finally breaks out of her isolated, private concerns on the night of the decree of the yellow star, when she feels strong enough to accept the fate of being a Jew.

Hillesum's work for the Jewish Council exempted her from deportation, but the situation disgusted her, and eventually she volunteered to work in Westerbork. "Nothing can atone for one section of the Jewish population helping transport the majority out of the country," she writes. "We go too far in fearing for our unhappy bodies while our forgotten spirit shrivels up in some corner." The horror of the camp is documented in her letters to friends. But her faith grows stronger. "I want to be there," she writes, "right in the thick of what people call horror, and still say life is beautiful." The last image of her is recounted in a letter by her friend Jpoie, who watched Hillesum board the train for Auschwitz, grasping a Bible in one hand and Tolstoy in the other. (pp. 14-15)

Sherie Posesorski, "Witness to the Persecution," in Books in Canada, *Vol. 13, No. 5, May, 1984, pp. 14-15.*

Neal Ascherson   (essay date 1984)

[*Ascherson is a Scottish journalist and critic. In the following excerpted review of* An Interrupted Life, *he out-*

lines Hillesum's progression through the diaries to her discovery of "a religion of action."]

Etty Hillesum [author of *An Interrupted Life: The Diaries of Etty Hillesum, 1941-1943*] was a young woman, a Dutch Jew, who lived in Amsterdam. She was twenty-six when the Nazi occupation of the Netherlands took place. In the spring of 1942, the mass deportations of the Jews began, at first to the huge transit camp of Westerbork in eastern Holland. From there, that summer, the sealed trains began to leave for an unknown destination in Poland, which in fact was Auschwitz. Etty Hillesum went to Westerbork in July 1942 of her own free will, to work in the camp hospital. Her turn for the transports came on September 7, 1943. She died at Auschwitz on November 30 that year, although it seems to be unknown whether she was sent to the gas chambers or perished of disease and hunger. Her entire family died there too, with the exception of one brother who survived Auschwitz but died on the way back to Holland.

By turns earthy, lyrical, and relentlessly honest in their pursuit of self-understanding, these journals [in *An Interrupted Life*] are the record of an extraordinary process of spiritual maturation and development. Indeed, this book might have been better named "A Completed Life," for it witnesses to the possibility of a wholeness and integrity that can be achieved in the midst of great suffering even at an early age.

—*John McDargh, in a review of* An Interrupted Life *and* Letters from Westerbork, *in* Commonweal, *1987.*

This is only a frame of a portrait. Etty Hillesum was an intellectual who wanted to be a writer. She kept a diary from 1941 onward, but the diary is at first hardly at all and later only indirectly the story of the destruction of the Jews in Holland. It is about herself and her relationships, initially about friends and lovers and then, increasingly, about her own very individual vision of a God. Etty came from a gifted, scholarly family in Deventer, studied law and Slavonic languages at the University of Amsterdam and then applied herself to psychology. By the time the journal begins, Etty had almost completed one major subjective struggle; she had become an independent and sexually liberated young woman, with only residual doubts about her own rather startling style of life, only spasmodic anxieties about the position of men and women. The diaries themselves record a second struggle, as Etty Hillesum in a sense abandons herself to find herself. The notes and entries are at first concerned with expanding her own sensibility, with rhapsodic accounts of emotions and sensations, with injunctions to herself to put more effort into her own self-realization as a writer.

Gradually, the tone changes, as the Nazi noose is drawn steadily tighter around her and her friends and as it becomes apparent that some sinister fate—its true nature unknown to her, although there are horrifying flashes of intuition—is being prepared for them all. Etty's interest in her own fulfillment becomes a search for the right attitude to adopt in the face of doom, an expedition to find selflessness. The inner strength which, in the end, she finds is not just passive acceptance. Certainly, she rejects resistance, as she rejects all invitations to escape or hide. It would be impossible, for instance, to learn from her diary that Amsterdam was the only German-occupied city in Western Europe in which Jews organized themselves to fight physically on the streets against their persecutors.

> My acceptance is not indifference or helplessness. I feel deep moral indignation at a regime that treats human beings in such a way. But events have become too overwhelming and too demonic to be stemmed with personal resentment and bitterness. These responses strike me as being utterly childish and unequal to the fateful course of events. . . . It is not as if I want to fall into the hands of destruction with a resigned smile—far from it. I am only bowing to the inevitable and even as I do so I am sustained by the certain knowledge that they cannot rob us of anything that matters.

She does not exactly "find God," but rather constructs one for herself. The theme of the diaries becomes increasingly religious, and many of the entries are prayers. Her God is someone to whom she makes promises, but of whom she expects and asks nothing.

> I shall try to help You, God, to stop my strength ebbing away, though I cannot vouch for it in advance. But one thing is becoming increasingly clear to me: that You cannot help us, that we must help You to help ourselves. . . . Alas, there does not seem to be much You Yourself can do about our circumstances, about our lives. Neither do I hold You responsible. You cannot help us, but we must help You and defend Your dwelling place inside us to the last.

Etty describes her lovers with candor. On the first page of the diary, she reflects:

> I am accomplished in bed, just about seasoned enough I should think to be counted among the better lovers, and love does indeed suit me to perfection, and yet it remains a mere trifle, set apart from what is truly essential, and deep inside me something is still locked away.

At the time she was living with, or at least sharing the bed of, her landlord, a man in his sixties. But she was on the brink of a new affair with another man much older than herself, and her portrait of this extraordinary person, enriched in entry after entry as she came to love him more deeply, is an unforgettable literary feat. Julius Spier, who was fifty-four when Etty encountered him, was a German-Jewish refugee. He had been a banker and a publisher before becoming, after training analysis under Jung in Zurich, the founder of "psychochirology." Spier read palms, using palmistry as the foundation for his own strange and liberating brand of analysis. He also practiced therapy by wrestling with his patients, grappling with them, and forcing them to the ground (or sometimes, as with Etty, being floored himself), a technique whose strongly sexual connotations he in no way rejected.

In Amsterdam, as elsewhere, Spier had assembled around him an ashram of adoring disciples. For Etty, he radiated wisdom and compassion, and yet her own moods about him continually change. The wrestling seems at first exhilarating and sexless, then—as he deliberately arouses her while insisting that she must not fall in love with him—as a bewildering outrage. When she finally wins him as a lover, she is satisfied but realizes that it is the man's mind and soul, rather than his body, that she needs. At moments, Spier is described as an entrancing, experienced sensualist; at others, as a rather fat elderly man with false teeth. But he remained for her a liberator. It was not merely that the "magical personality" for which he is remembered steadied and calmed her. Etty learned the self-abnegation that became her creed in the last months in part by overcoming her own possessiveness about Spier, and by recognizing that this was a man she must share with others. As the months passed, as the movements of Jews were steadily restricted and the Yellow Star introduced, and the deportations to Westerbork began, Etty and Spier watched the black cloud of catastrophe moving inexorably across the disappearing landscape toward them, and sought to prepare themselves for whatever might lie within it.

Julius Spier escaped the gas chambers. He died suddenly in September 1942. But his work with Etty was already over; she had already volunteered to go with the first transport of Jews to Westerbork, and from now on her courage and resolution never failed her. The diary soon ends, but is supplemented by a group of long and brilliant letters from Westerbork to friends. They are almost unbearable to read; Etty had to help sick women and children pack and dress warmly when the summons came for the next transport to the destination in the east. The trains were loaded and sealed on a siding in the camp itself.

At times, Etty grasped at the illusion that this was something that she might survive, that with Rilke, the Bible, and Tolstoy in her rucksack and "the pure lambswool sweater knitted by a friend" on her back, she would somehow come through. But there were also terrible moments. One day she looked at the faces of the guards on the latest train to arrive at the siding—

> I looked at them, each in turn, from behind the safety of a window, and I have never been so frightened of anything in my life as I was of those faces. I sank to my knees with the words that preside over human life: And God made man after His likeness. That passage spent a difficult morning with me.

As the weeks passed, Etty understood calmly that she was in Hell. And she recorded every cry, every tumult as the hospital huts were emptied once more in the middle of the night. "The wailing of the babies grows louder still, filling every nook and cranny of the barracks, now bathed in ghostly light. It is almost too much to bear. A name occurs to me: Herod."

It was a religion of action that Etty discovered. As she had put it, she tried to help her God by helping those around her; so important did her strength become that the Jewish camp leaders tried desperately, but vainly, to have her exempted when her name finally came up for the next train. A friend watched her go.

> And there she stepped on to the platform . . . talking gaily, smiling, a kind word for everyone she met on the way, full of sparkling humour, perhaps just a touch of sadness but every inch the Etty you all know so well.

The Bible and Tolstoy were safely in her rucksack when they closed the doors on her. Later, farmers near the German border found a postcard she had thrown out of the train. It read: "We have left the camp singing."

> *Neal Ascherson, "In Hell," in* The New York Review of Books, *Vol. XXXI, No. 12, July 19, 1984, p. 9.*

Renee Neu Watkins   (essay date 1984)

[*In the following laudatory review of* An Interrupted Life, *Watkins highlights Hillesum's resolve to "[push] what she had learned as a daughter and a woman as far as it would go" in order to cope with the Holocaust.*]

[In *An Interrupted Life: The Diaries of Etty Hillesum* a] Dutch Jewish woman in her late twenties looks at herself. She is a student of literature and of psychoanalysis. She is social, sexual, and solitary. Her main tone and concern is self-exhortation—she wants to live up to the best that is in her. For the first 130 pages, her diaries run along, a little rambling and overenthusiastic, but always interesting and suggestive of more than they say; after that point, without losing any value as a spontaneous document, they also rise to poetic power.

The diaries begin in 1941. From the start, Etty feels the impact of the German occupation on her world, which is that of the Dutch intelligentsia. In time persecutory decrees press with special force on Jews—they can't walk in parks, they can't ride trams, they can't ride bikes, and, most serious in this time of severe shortages, are forbidden to shop in more and more stores. When the harassment changes to round-ups and deportations to "an unknown destination" in Poland, she understands the immensity of it, and comes to realize the murderous intent. She recognizes that she, too, will be swept away. The horrors rivet her attention, but it is a deliberately subjective attention. While she comes face to face with evil, she is determined—and able to the end—to bear witness that, even under these circumstances, life is "beautiful" and "meaningful" and "worth living."

Etty Hillesum is able to show that some—herself included—could surface from waves of fear or hate to feel the beauty of life and to love others. Since the recent belated publication of these diaries, some readers have seen her as a kind of Jewish saint or heroine. Others, emphatically not. Certainly the complex novelistic content of the journals as well as the weight of Etty's moral and psychological reflections pushes the reader into a process of judgment that is worthwhile just because it is hard.

A distinct plot emerges from these diaries. At the beginning the writer declares her intention to put aside inhibition and to write. She wishes to set her inner life in order. She believes that Jul Spier, the newly met Jungian guru she has begun to consult, will help her do it. What is this relationship? she asks herself. Spier, who begins his therapeutic sessions by literally wrestling with his patients, teaches her to recognize the union of mind (emotions) and body. But he takes advantage of the situation, he shows desire, and she feels seduced and angry. Seeing through him as a seducer, and also seeing through the simplistic content of his discourses, she nonetheless feels his power, and believes in his wisdom. She views Spier and herself as engaged in a similar struggle of mind (moral thought, will, wisdom) against body. In fact, she falls in love.

A rationalist in upbringing and a student in life style, Etty wants to free herself from dependence on men, from trying to live through them rather than through her own experience of the world. Emancipated enough to take responsibility for herself and to live in a humble kind of semi-independence, she has thought of liberation. Yet, she admits, she will suppress her own impulse to write if Spier wants to dictate "something about a case."

She sees Spier through critical images, a teddy bear, a decadent sensualist, a weary old man. But she remains generous with him. The love affair, not fully consummated for a long time, becomes the great experience of her life. For Spier, belief in God complements a psychological wisdom that revolves around acceptance of both suffering and joy. As time goes by, Etty feels that he has led her to God.

Meanwhile she gives just enough information to let us follow the drama of other aspects of her life. The half-hidden story of her communal household in Amsterdam and that of her parents in the little town of Deventer gives a context to the overt story of Etty's psychological and spiritual growth. Her household is a mixed but loyal group, Dutch Jew and Dutch non-Jew and even German non-Jew; young and old, they are headed by Etty's long-time friend and lover, Han. Under the conditions of war and occupation, life becomes hard. They eat the "rabbit food" they can get, barter for turnips, stand in line for potatoes and don't always get them. They remain through it all cooperative, intensely companionable, informal.

In the Deventer home of her parents, by contrast, Etty finds the atmosphere stagnant and suffocating. Her father is gentle and humorous, but through his philosophical vagueness she sees his deep personal despair. Her mother expresses loud and limitless misery. Her younger brother has suffered one nervous breakdown in the past and is barely sane. Her older brother leaves home—a scene. Perhaps he wants the family, who are waiting passively for arrest, to attempt to hide or resist.

Through hints and bits of description, we enter Etty's life and share her feelings. She can be skillfully self-analytical, drawing us into an understanding of her inner dilemmas. She looks into her attitude toward her father, which turns out to be a key to her character—the basis for her "feminine" submissive attitudes, and a kind of psychological tunnel or rut for her energy. As she works on herself with will and imagination, the painful attitude towards her father will turn into a conscious choice, in the midst of danger, to forget herself and to devote herself to service to others.

In the spring of 1942, "something has crystallised." She accepts the fact that Jews are one and all threatened with death. "Even if we are consigned to hell," she says, "let us go there as gracefully as we can." And adds, "I did not really want to put it so blandly." By June she writes, "the English radio has reported that 700,000 Jews perished last year alone . . . " and "I have already died a thousand deaths in a thousand concentration camps. I know about everything . . . " Later, "I often see visions of poisonous green smoke . . . " Etty systematically prepares herself for exile and hardship. She reduces her need for her friends, her room, her privacy. She concentrates on the books that give her strength: Dostoevsky's *The Idiot*, Rilke's poems and letters, St. Augustine. Whether taking care of her sickly body or neglecting it, she moves toward more and more dualism of mind (observation, judgment, will) and body. From this point on, in life and in writing, she focuses on the adventure of her own spirit, and blossoms in her relation to the God, personal and impersonal, to whom she speaks.

Etty's older brother and friends got her a job as typist at the Jewish Council, a liaison agency between the Nazi government and Jewish citizens. She accepted the job because, repellent though it was, it would save her life. After two weeks of typing the pleas of Jews for exemption from internment, she went to Westerbork, the deportation camp. She worked there for more than a year, an official observer or social worker rather than an inmate, until in September of 1943 the Nazis changed her status and sent her on the next shipment to Auschwitz. At Westerbork she did not keep her journal, but she put her artist's energy into letters which, appended to the journal, show us her writing at its best: vivid, empathic, and objective.

Resting at home, in her old room, in July of 1943, on a two-week pass from the camp, she reflects back on her earlier, despairing thought—"It is inside this little skull that this world must be rethought." Then she talks about present feelings:

> I felt once more in the flesh, last night, what human beings have to suffer these days. It is good to be reminded of that from time to time, if only to learn how to fight it. And then to continue undisturbed through the wide and open landscape that is one's own heart.

She has not given up the internal reworking of the world, but she has moved the arena from head to heart, given up what she once called her "greed" to put things into the right words. At Westerbork, she writes:

> How is it that this stretch of heathland surrounded by barbed wire, through which so much human misery has flooded, nevertheless remains inscribed in my memory as something almost lovely? How is it that my spirit, far from being

oppressed, seemed to grow lighter and brighter there? It is because I read the signs of the times and they did not seem meaningless to me. Surrounded by my writers and poets and the flowers on my desk I loved life. And there among the barracks, full of hunted and persecuted people, I found confirmation of my love of life. Life in those draughty barracks was no other than life in this protected peaceful room. Not for one moment was I cut off from the life I was said to have left behind. There was simply one great meaningful whole. Will I be able to describe all that one day? So that others can feel too how lovely and worth living and just—yes, just—life really is?

She has arrived at a non-dogmatic religion which she herself thinks of as Christianity: God has provided everything, we share somehow in a depravity which some human beings, devil-like, embody. God cannot help us in this situation, but we can help God. She stands among the miserable crowds in the camp and walks from one place to another, sometimes full of pity, but often weeping in ecstatic gratitude to God. She is living intensely and preparing for death.

After the mass arrests begin in April 1942 Etty resists the idea of flight: for any one who does not go, someone else must go instead. In a letter from the camp in 1943 she tells how even the slightest attempt to run away leads to additional suffering for others—one boy's momentary escape leads the Germans to jam twenty more prisoners onto the cars.

What Etty Hillesum could never do, it seems, was to put any faith in action. Like her professors and friends, she always believed that eventually the war would end and the Germans would lose; she had hopes for engaging then in a struggle for a better postwar world—specifically through a large-scale psychological therapeutic movement—but, unlike many, she put no present hope in revolution or an invasion by England or even in bombs that could have stopped the deportations. According to the introduction, Etty was in touch with the resistance, and it is easy to see why she would not have written about it in her journals— an omission which could lead us to think her more passive than she was. The overall impression one gains from the diary, however, is that she really had no great faith in the power of subversion.

But she condemns collaboration. Without exempting herself at all, she says in no uncertain terms, "Nothing can ever atone for the fact, of course, that one section of the Jewish population is helping to transport the majority out of the country. History will pass judgment in due course." She discusses the horrible fact that in the camp she is "helping" (her quotation marks) to dress babies and to calm mothers who will get on trains that lead to further horrors and eventual destruction. What is going on? she asks. "The answer cannot simply be that we are all cowards. We're not that bad. We stand before a much deeper question . . . " In a letter she describes her choice of a kind of passivity: "I have never been able to 'do' anything; I can only let things take their course and if need be suffer.

This is where my strength lies and it is great strength indeed." And she adds, "But for myself, not for others."

It disturbed me to read these diaries: I too was once a middle-class Jewish girl in Holland, and if I had not escaped, would have shared Etty's fate. I did to a great extent share her upbringing and culture. My father, too, was a highly educated and Europeanized Jew, while my mother, too, was more narrowly passionate, more "difficult." As a young adult in the 50s, I kept my European literary loyalties. Like Etty, I thought of woman's role as a trap and struggled against it with intellectual ambition and a similarly idealistic style of sexual adventurism. I recognize in her a certain vanity and excessive humility that in myself covered up something like a recurrent paralysis of the will to live. For me the tendency to agonize over being myself and to find relief in mysticism and in empathy—especially empathy for psychological crisis—goes back to the holocaust itself. Unlike Etty, I was saved by my parents, but their bitterness suggested to me that I had not deserved my life. My father occasionally spoke of his feeling that it had been a mistake to leave, "to act from fear." My

---

An excerpt from *An Interrupted Life: The Diaries of Etty Hillesum, 1941-1943*

In this tempestuous, havoc-ridden world of ours, all real communication comes from the heart. Outwardly we are being torn apart and the paths to each other lie buried under so much debris that we often fail to find the person we seek. We can only continue to live together in our hearts, and hope that one day we may walk hand in hand again.

I cannot tell, of course, how I shall react when I really do have to leave him. His voice over the telephone this morning still rings in my ear; tonight we shall have a meal together; tomorrow morning we shall work together and then lunch at Liesl and Werner's, and in the afternoon we shall play music together. He is still here. And perhaps in my heart of hearts I do not really accept that all of us are about to be separated. A human being, after all, is only human.

Many accuse me of indifference and passivity when I refuse to go into hiding; they say that I have given up. They say everyone who can must try to stay out of their clutches, it's our bounden duty to try. But that argument is specious. For while everyone tries to save himself, vast numbers are nevertheless disappearing. And the funny thing is I don't feel I'm in their clutches anyway, whether I stay or am sent away. I find all that talk so cliché-ridden and naive and can't go along with it any more. I don't feel in anybody's clutches; I feel safe in God's arms, to put it rhetorically, and no matter whether I am sitting at this beloved old desk now, or in a bare room in the Jewish district or perhaps in a labour camp under SS guards in a month's time—I shall always feel safe in God's arms. They may well succeed in breaking me physically, but no more than that. I may face cruelty and deprivation the likes of which I cannot imagine in even my wildest fantasies. Yet all this is as nothing to the immeasurable expanse of my faith in God and my inner receptiveness.

Etty Hillesum, in her An Interrupted Life: The Diaries of Etty Hillesum, 1941-1943, *Pantheon Books, 1983.*

mother, filled with rage at her own lack of health, spoke of her wish to die. I found, as my twenties wore on, that I could not, like "everybody," resolutely pursue my own well-being. I see a similar emotional limitation shaping Etty's religious "quixotism," as her father called it.

Yet let me stress the unique achievement of Etty Hillesum. At the very time that her family was falling to pieces, she resolved: "I will have to dare to live life with all the seriousness it demands and without thinking that I'm being pompous, sentimental or affected." In the crisis, she pushed what she had learned as a daughter and a woman as far as it would go. A kind of Dostoevskian Christianity, like that of Myshkin in *The Idiot,* came out of it. This—as Etty certainly recognized—was a highly individualistic solution, if it was a solution at all. Her kind of goodness may make victims happier, but despite what Buddhists and Friends have taught, it does little or nothing to reduce violence in the world. And while during that year amidst that unimaginable mass persecution it was a heroic stance to take, I wonder if it is a model for living one's life in the ordinary disorder of our world. What *is* still to be viewed as exemplary is Etty's decision not to think herself pompous, sentimental, or affected, which freed her as Hillesum, the author, to reveal with clarity and honesty where she stood. If such clarity of mind is indeed a mental force against violence in the world, it presents us with the problem of integrating and modifying, not abandoning, her ambiguous legacy of feminine spirituality.

> Renee Neu Watkins, "A Season in Hell," in The Women's Review of Books, *Vol. I, No. 11, August, 1984, p. 5.*

Frederick Franck   (essay date 1984)

[*Franck is a Dutch-born American artist and critic. In the following review, he praises* An Interrupted Life, *calling it "an intimate travelogue of the human inner journey against the backdrop of subhuman barbarity."*]

Etty Hillesum's dearest wish was to become a "real writer." It took forty years after the Nazis cremated her to achieve such status. The English title, *An Interrupted Life,* is as misleading as the one of the Dutch original "A Life Disturbed," but it is not Etty Hillesum who chose either: she just scribbled down her heartrending, yet liberating story. Eight almost undecipherable exercise books evoke a life not so much interrupted or disturbed as converted into a pilgrimage to the Other Shore, completed in two short years, so that in her last, her twenty-ninth year, she attained what most of us fail to achieve in three score and ten.

Her book is not another Holocaust book. It is an intimate travelogue of the human inner journey against the backdrop of subhuman barbarity.

She is no Simone Weil this Etty Hillesum, nor is she an older Anne Frank or an Edith Stein. She is her own woman, a woman of more than ordinary intelligence, who at twenty-six had earned degrees in Law and Slavonic languages, and had just started to study psychology. Far from being a blue-stocking, however, she was a full-blooded,

sensual young woman of a type which forty years later still strikes one as being as emancipated as anyone her age today.

When in March 1941 Etty started to record her odyssey, she was still living in a sunny and comfortable room overlooking Amsterdam's largest square, notwithstanding the gloom that was enveloping Nazi-occupied Holland. She felt "full of fear of letting go, of allowing things to pour out of me." Still "this is what I must do if I am ever to give my life a reasonable and satisfactory purpose. . . ." On this first page she also avows being "accomplished in bed, just about seasoned enough to be counted among the better lovers. Love indeed suits me perfectly." But she adds, "yet it remains a mere trifle set apart from what is really essential, deep inside me there is still something locked away." What was locked away would be set free between these first entries and that final one of August 24, 1943, at the end of her pilgrimage: "We should be willing to act as a balm on all wounds."

Eight almost undecipherable exercise books [excerpted in An Interrupted Life] evoke a life not so much interrupted or disturbed as converted into a pilgrimage to the Other Shore, completed in two short years, so that in her last, her twenty-ninth year, she attained what most of us fail to achieve in three score and ten.

—Frederick Franck

Her involvement with Julius Spier, the man she refers to as S. had just started. In it she found her capacity for a love that would not remain "set apart from the really essential" in her, that would grow into that greater love which lays down life for friend.

S. has been characterized in one review I read, as a charlatan. He was nothing of the kind, this gifted man who after a career as a banker and then as a publisher had studied with Carl Jung, and was encouraged by Jung to use professionally his extraordinary capacity of reading character in palms. From Etty's description he was on as urgent a search for the specifically, centrally human in himself as she was, an urgency no doubt intensified by the impending doom of which both were fully aware. S. was the man who "taught me to speak of God without embarrassment." The relationship between these two was as erotic as it was prayerful and contemplative: it was complete. They were not merely lovers, but fellow pilgrims on the ultimate pilgrimage. They could share Etty's "addressing God in that silly, naive and deadly serious dialogue with what is deepest inside me and which for convenience sake I call God," and S.'s dream of being baptized by the Christ in person.

What sets this book so apart from usual autobiography, and even from any other log book of the inner journey, is the total absence of all posturing, all embellishments.

Etty's journey simply had to include all the experimentation she ascribes to her "erotic adventuresomeness," until she came to the painful realization "all the adventures and transient relationships I have had, have made me utterly miserable, torn me apart . . . what I really want is a man for life." If this vital girl is to be called a mystic, which I do without hesitation, her way was of the Tantric kind.

In the first period of her diary, she is still confident that she is "a match for most of life's problems, yet at times nothing more or less than a miserable, frightened creature, despite the clarity with which I express myself." At this early stage she sees S. as "a charming man . . . charming smile despite his false teeth," and soon after as "a fifty-four-year old in whom the struggle between the spirit and the flesh is still in full cry." He fascinated her, but she cannot yet imagine "ever being in love with him." She discovers, however, how naturally they complement one another, understand one another: "we have had wild and unfettered lives in many strange beds, and nevertheless we are shy all over again . . . Now I go down to read the Bible with him."

She was at the time still living with another man, even older than S., for whom she had both a high regard and warm tenderness. If both relationships only clashed in her on rare occasions, it was not through some perversion, but because both involvements existed on different levels of this complex personality who in "near ecstatic moments feels herself capable of God-knows-what," only to sink back in the deepest pit of uncertainty: "I fail to work each day at what I believe to be my only real talent, writing. . . ."

It was S. who from the beginning impressed on her that what "he had in the head must get down into the heart" and who tried to help her in letting this happen. She at first doubted how his efforts could bring it about, but soon admitted: "They did! He assigned to their proper place all that went on inside me, like a jigsaw puzzle with all the pieces mixed up, he put them together properly."

Although she still tells herself that she is not "really in love with him," she concedes that in this relationship she has gone through a process of maturation she had never thought possible. She was well on her way to becoming the woman she was born to be. "In men like S. a woman's soul is given welcome and shelter."

Meanwhile the setting of this love story in which the bifurcation between the erotic and the spiritual had fallen away was getting more ghoulish by the day: ever increasing harassment and terror, Stars of David to be worn, arrests, "the arbitrary dragging off of fathers, sons, brothers and sisters to concentration camps," prohibitions for Jews to ride street cars and bicycles, to sit on park benches, to buy food at greengrocers. . . .

What is happening to this sophisticated girl growing to her full womanhood against this backdrop is unbearably moving. "There is a really deep well inside me, and in it God dwells . . . There are people who pray with their eyes turned to heaven, they seek God outside themselves. And there are those who bow their heads and bury their faces in their hands. I think they seek God inside." She is clearly

one of the latter, is driven "to be true to that in me that seeks to fulfill its promise. I know that I must see You amongst people in the world . . . Oh, let me feel at one with myself. . . . " At times she believes that the

> foolish and passionate desire to "lose myself in S." has vanished. All that is left of it is the will to yield myself up to God . . . a desire to kneel down sometimes pulses through my body or rather, my body seems made and meant for the act of kneeling.

And "I love him a bit more every day . . . it is the first time I really kissed a man, it is the sharing of the breath that counts. . . . " And then again: "At his side I ripen into a genuine and adult human being."

As all of us, she is full of contradictions, but then she is neither a logician nor a moralist. She is simply true to herself and to her way. The narcissism of the overture, the double relationship with two older men, the awakening to God in the deep well of the Self are as unconventional as they are true to her nature.

Etty's book has been called both typically Jewish and typically Christian. It is, typically, hurtingly human. One would have to apply strictly racist criteria to categorize the man who feels baptized by Christ, the girl who sees herself as made for kneeling down, as Jewish; one would have to be fanatically Jewish to excommunicate them, narrowly Christian sectarian to exclude them from the Mystical Body.

She was given a job with the Jewish Council, a liaison body set up by the Nazis for their convenience, and is forced to play an inevitably sinister role in assisting "the cold-blooded fanatics who clamor for our destruction" but of whom she was less afraid than of her "own demons I have to battle inside."

"Ours," S. says to her "is real Hell. Dante's Inferno is comic opera by comparison." But Julius Spier was to be spared the deepest pit of this hell, he became ill and died. By then, everything that happened seemed to strengthen Etty's "crystal clear mysticism."

"I love people so terribly, because in every human being I love something of You. . . . " Did she say it to the fellow pilgrim she lost? To God? To both? But it is surely to S. that she cries out: "You were the mediator between God and me, you taught me to speak His Name. Now that you have gone, my path leads straight to God, and I shall be the mediator for any soul I can reach. . . . "

A friend, who survived, saw her at the train to Auschwitz "talking gaily, a kind word for everyone she met . . . perhaps a touch of sadness. Then the shrill whistle when the train with a thousand 'transport cases' was moving out." She still threw a postcard out of the train, which a farmer found and mailed: "We left the camp singing," it said.

On November 30, 1943, the drop of water that had been Etty Hillesum fell into the ocean of infinity, ready for it. (pp. 471-72, 474-75)

Frederick Franck, "True to Herself, True to

Her Way," in Commonweal, *Vol. CXI, No. 15, September 7, 1984, pp. 471-72, 474-75.*

Michiko Kakutani (essay date 1986)

[*In the following review, Kakutani applauds* Letters from Westerbork *as one of the most memorable works of Holocaust literature in recent years.*]

The diaries of Etty Hillesum, published several years ago under the title *An Interrupted Life,* revealed a remarkable woman—ardent, strong-willed and possessed of enormous spiritual resources and a quick, fierce ability to love. Begun in 1941, some nine months after the Netherlands fell to Hitler, these journals traced the growing shadows cast by the Nazi occupation of Europe, but they also chronicled the moral awakening experienced by this young Dutch Jew.

The daughter of a well-to-do professor, Miss Hillesum had studied philosophy, as well as Freud and Jung, and she moved freely in bohemian circles: she lived in a sort of commune, took several older lovers and committed herself to a search for identity—as an intellectual and as a woman. Yet in the space of two years, as the reality of the war increasingly impinged on Amsterdam's daily life, Miss Hillesum's self-involvement slowly gave way to an awareness of the common fate shared by European Jews— and with this realization came both a mystical embracing of God and a determination to come to terms with the beauty and horror of life.

While these letters [in *Letters from Westerbork*] lack the clear-eyed introspection of the diaries that gave us such a lucid window into Miss Hillesum's heart, they attest to the same virtues of sympathy and faith evinced by those earlier writings, and they give us one of the most indelible portraits of life inside a Nazi camp to emerge from Holocaust literature in recent years. The Westerbork camp—where Miss Hillesum worked as a social volunteer and later became a prisoner—was not, strictly speaking, a death camp. Rather, it was a transit camp near Assen in the northeastern Netherlands—the last stop before Auschwitz, where many Dutch Jews awaited their grim future. Although Miss Hillesum had plenty of opportunities to escape—as a member of the Jewish Council, she was given certain travel privileges—she was determined to share the fate of her fellow Jews, and on Sept. 7, 1943, she joined her parents and her brother Mischa on a transport bound for Auschwitz. The Red Cross reported her death on Nov. 30 of that year.

As Miss Hillesum notes, Westerbork was both "a stable community in the making"—complete with an orphanage, a synagogue, a small mortuary, a shoe-repair factory and a jail ("a prison within a prison")—and

> a camp for a people in transit, great waves of human beings constantly washed in from the cities and provinces, from rest homes, prisons and other prison camps, from all the nooks and crannies of the Netherlands.

It is a community in which old rivalries persist ("The Jews from Haarlem said somewhat loftily and acidly: 'those Amsterdammers have a grim sense of humor' "), a community in which "you can find every attitude," "every class, ism, conflict and current of society." And yet it is also a community under sentence of death; and that condition, Miss Hillesum observes, makes one suddenly realize "that it is not enough to be an able politician or a talented artist." She continues: "In the most extreme distress, life demands quite other things. Yes, it is true, our ultimate human values are being put to the test."

Miss Hillesum describes the barracks where hundreds of people sleep on metal springs without mattresses or blankets. She describes the rhythm of fear and exhaustion created by the weekly rounding-up of prisoners to be shipped off to Auschwitz. And she describes the modicum of satisfaction created by tiny things—the arrival of a package from home, the discovery of a piece of paper on which to pen a note, the news that the orphanage has been allowed to have a flower show.

In fact, one of the most devastating things about these epistles is their casual juxtaposition of the ordinary and the horrific, the lovely and the awful. In one letter, Miss Hillesum is chattering on about her dental problems; in the next, writing about the railroad cars that will carry them off to Poland. While waiting to learn whether their names appear on the next transport list, old friends discuss philosophy and poetry, as they might have done years before in Amsterdam; and mothers are overheard saying to their children, "If you don't eat your pudding up straightaway, then Mummy won't be with you on the transport!"

"The sky is full of birds," Miss Hillesum writes,

> the purple lupins stand up so regally and peacefully, two little old women have sat down on the box for a chat, the sun is shining on my face— and right before our eyes, mass murder. The whole thing is simply beyond comprehension.

Even though Miss Hillesum occasionally gives in to the overwhelming despair of her situation—"everything here is quicksand," she exclaims at one point—her optimism continually manages to reassert itself. "I have so much love in me, you know, for Germans and Dutchmen, Jews and non-Jews, for the whole of mankind—there is more than enough to go around," she writes a friend. And to another correspondent: "And yet life in its unfathomable depths is so wonderfully good, Maria—I have to come back to that time and again. And if we just care enough, God is in safe hands with us despite everything."

All Holocaust writings, of course, must deal with the inadequacy of words in the face of events that defy the imagination, but while Miss Hillesum frequently speaks of her inability to convey the awful magnitude of events around her, she proves herself a most eloquent witness to history—a witness whose grave yet shining testimony attests to the resilience of the human spirit in the face of incalculable odds.

"One always has the feeling here of being the ears and eyes of a piece of Jewish history," she writes,

> but there is also the need sometimes to be a still, small voice. We must keep one another in touch

with everything that happens in the various out-posts of this world, each contributing his own little piece of stone to the great mosaic that will take shape once the war is over.

Michiko Kakutani, in a review of "Letters From Westerbork," in The New York Times, *December 10, 1986, p. 28.*

[Etty Hillesum's] is a soul open to mystery in the midst of abysmal misery, whose writings give courage forty-five years later.

—*Ann Belford Ulanov, in a review of* **Letters from Westerbork,** *in* **Commonweal, 1988.**

Irving Halperin   (essay date 1990)

[*Halperin is an American educator and critic whose works include* Messengers from the Dead: Literature from the Holocaust *(1970). In the following essay, he traces Hillesum's spiritual development as evidenced in* An Interrupted Life *and* Letters from Westerbork.]

> The jasmine behind my house has been com-pletely ruined by the rains and storms of the last few days, its white blossoms are floating about in muddy black pools on the low garage roof. But somewhere inside me the jasmine continues to blossom undisturbed, just as profusely and delicately as ever it did. And it spreads its scent round the House in which You dwell, oh God. You can see, I look after You, I bring You not only tears and my forebodings on this stormy, grey Sunday morning, I even bring you scented jasmine. And I shall bring You all the flowers I shall meet on my way and truly there are many of these.

This prayer to God was written by Etty Hillesum in the summer of 1942. The writer of extraordinary diaries and letters, she has been described as the adult counterpart of Anne Frank. Like Anne, Etty believed in the existence of a just and loving God, the meaningfulness and beauty of human life, the benificence of Nature, the importance of keeping a diary. Like Anne, she loved Holland and the Dutch people. And like her younger counterpart, she achieved an unusually large measure of spiritual growth in a brief span of time and despite the pressures of dehu-manizing circumstances. (p.1)

Etty Hillesum's diaries and letters are today being read by an international audience. What sets them apart from many eyewitness accounts and personal narratives written by those who survived the Holocaust and by others who did not is that a highly intelligent, sensitive, and talented writer intensely ponders issues concerned with religion, morality, faith, love, community. Her writings are a stun-

ning achievement of the human spirit in the darkest days of the twentieth century.

My purpose here is to examine Etty's spiritual develop-ment from the first diary entries in 1941 when she is fre-quently depressed, confused, and not a little self-absorbed to both the last entries of 1943 and the letters from Westerbork when she appears steadily calmer, clearer, un-shaken in her belief that life is meaningful, and increasing-ly attentive to the tragic plight of the doomed Jewish com-munity.

As the first diary entries of March 1941 reveal, Etty is be-coming emotionally involved with a charismatic psycholo-gist in his fifties, Julius Spier, a refugee from Nazi Germa-ny who had trained under Carl Jung and who had a repu-tation for reading hands and palms with insight. She had sought professional help from him for what she called her "spiritual constipation." Part of her therapy consisted of wild wrestling matches with Julius, a practice employed in that era by some West European psychotherapists. However one may question certain aspects of his profes-sional work, the fact is that he did encourage Etty to keep writing, and he guided her efforts to cope with frequent spells of depression, headaches, stomach ailments and nausea (some of these symptoms were, as eventually she herself would recognize, psychosomatic in origin). She possessed enough self-awareness to recognize that she had an "unholy father-complex" about older men and that Ju-lius, as guru and man, was flawed ("My dear spoilt man" she refers to him in the diaries). While acknowledging her dependence on Spier, she resents the compulsion to find her identity through him; she would like to be free of the need to seek Absolute Love from a man. Not without much conflict on both their parts (he tries to stay faithful to his fiancée in London, and she fears sex will undermine their teacher-disciple relationship), they became lovers. Still, determined not to remain a passive partner, Etty comes to draw on her own strength, and they eventually relate to each other as equals.

As late as the spring of 1942, at a time of increasing re-strictions on the populace by the Occupation, Etty, by her own admission, finds life fairly pleasant. "I don't think there's another person in all Holland who has it as easy, at least that's how it seems to me." She confesses to feeling guilty about the masses who must stand in long queues for food, while she is economically free (she earns some money by tutoring students, and her expenditures for food, rent and entertainment are modest) to enjoy bicy-cling, concerts, reading and writing at leisure, strolling along the city's canals, and observing the visual beauty of Amsterdam, especially its world of flowers, which she de-scribes with a sensuous verbal imagination reminiscent of Colette's artistry: "I should like to write about yellow marsh-marigolds, my chestnut twigs, that have stopped blooming now, their small hands stretched out as graceful-ly as a dancer's and at at the same time raised so defensive-ly towards the sky."

In the early entries there is ample expression of Etty's be-lief in a universal love. She declares that one should not hate the Germans, not only because man is made in the image of God, but also because "hatred of Germans poi-

Hillesum at work on her diaries.

sons everyone's mind." Hearing someone curse, "let the bastards drown, the lot of them," she impulsively throws her arms around that person, as though to stifle this outburst of hatred. If there is but one decent German somewhere, she argues, it is unjust to malign an entire people; rather than hate the Germans for their brutality, one ought to hate only the evil that is within one's self. As late as September 1942, in a letter to a friend, she professed to have "much love . . . for Germans and Dutchmen, Jews and non-Jews, for the whole of mankind—there is more than enough to go around."

Etty expressed these sentiments some two years before she and her family were transported to a death camp and well before she realized that the Nazis were bent on not just enslaving but in fact systematically destroying European Jewry.

Meanwhile, apart from her involvement with Spier and her scholastic activities, she focuses on the act of reading. When she can lose herself in the works of her favorite writers, she feels calm and centered. Are not their writings as real, a higher reality, she speculates, than the present realities of the Occupation? For her a poem by Rilke is "as real and important as a young man falling out an aeroplane." So it is that we see her reading at her desk, which she calls "the most beautiful place on earth." On it, beside a vase full of ox-eye daisies, faded tea roses, a geranium and pine

cones, are books by some of her favorite writers: Rilke, Dostoyevsky, Tolstoy, Pushkin, St. Augustine, Jung. Their writings strike Etty as a confirmation of her view that life is meaningful and beautiful.

She realizes that her intense attraction to the insights of certain writers stems from her uncertainties and confusions. She searches their writings for some "great redeeming formula" to bring order and clarity to her inner turmoil. At the same time, she grasps what an antidote might be for this dependency: "what does it matter whether I study one page more or less of a book? If only I listened to my own rhythm and tried to live in accordance with it." Moreover, she senses that something in her unconscious is protesting at such woolly abstractions in her lexicon as "purpose," "mankind," "solution of problems." "I find them pretentious," she writes, and adds with a touch of disarming self-deprecation: "But then I'm such an ingenuous and dull young woman still so lacking in courage." In this context, she is quick to acknowledge that her views about the beauty of life may be so much sophomoric theorizing. In short, she knew that she had not yet been tested. All too soon, she would be.

Torn by self-doubt, troubled by her complicated relationship with Spier, Etty increasingly turns to prayer while kneeling on the floor of her room. In one improvised prayer, which is representative of the tone of her religious fervor, she pledges to accept whatever struggles and difficulties are before her:

> God, take me by Your hand, I shall follow you dutifully, and not resist too much. I shall evade none of the tempests life has in store for me, I shall try to face it all as best I can. But now and then grant me a short respite. . . . I don't want to be anything special, I only want to try to be true to that in me which seeks to fulfill its promise. . . . And if I cannot be, because it is not in my nature, then I must face that as well. In any case I must not try to fool myself. And I must keep within my own limitations. And remember that I alone can set these.

If she is a long way from attaining clarity and inner peace, her spiritual development nevertheless moves slowly forward through a process of organic growth—the gradual, unhurried, cumulative unfolding that her beloved Rilke advocated in his *Letters to a Young Poet* as necessary for living a creative life. She finds herself complaining much less often about being unhappy and confused. What has been disparate and fragmented within, she has faith, will eventually come together.

The diary entries of early 1942 also reveal Etty's closer attention to the darkening circumstances of the Jewish community. More and more "No Jews" signs are posted in shops. Jews are prohibited from sitting in cafes, traveling by tram, walking in the open country, being in the streets past the curfew hour of eight, using swimming pools, hockey fields, tennis courts. On observing how eight people occupy one small room in the Jewish district, she is honest enough to question whether she could still cling to her belief that life is beautiful if she were forced to live in similar conditions.

Days of oppression, humiliation, extreme danger—and yet on certain evenings it seems hard to believe that it is wartime when she looks out through the open window of her bedroom and inhales the jasmine-scented air and feels "as if life with all its mysteries was close to me, as if I could touch it. I had the feeling that I was resting naked against the breast of life, and could feel her gentle and regular heartbeat. I felt safe and protected." Of one such evening she writes: "The sky within me is as wide as the one stretching above my head. I believe in God and I believe in man and I say so without embarrassment."

The wheels of Hitler's genocidal machine are turning swiftly. Rumors are widespread: British radio reports that 700,000 Jews may have perished in Germany and in the occupied countries. Reflecting on this report, Etty predicts—and this, tragically, would come to pass for many Holocaust survivors—that "even if we stay alive we shall carry the wounds with us throughout our lives." Then she adds, in what obviously is intended as a symbolic statement, "I have already died a thousand deaths in a thousand concentration camps. I know about everything and am no longer appalled by the latest reports. In one way or another I know it all. And yet I find life beautiful and meaningful. From minute to minute."

Well, she could not possibly know "everything"; not about Westerbork, not about Auschwitz. Even with her gift of prescience, she could not have pictured the kinds of trials that were before her. And Etty herself must have realized that such statements were not based on experiential reality. After writing that "Suffering has always been with us, does it really matter what form it comes? All that matters is how we bear it and how we fit it into our lives," in the next breath she challenges the validity of her own declaration: "Am I merely an armchair theorist safely ensconced behind my desk, with my familiar books around me and the jasmine outside? Is it all theory, never tested in practice?"

Whether her notion here about the meaning of suffering is merely "theory" or not, what does ring clear is that now she no longer has any illusions about the fate of Dutch Jewry. "They are out to destroy us completely, we must accept that and go on from there," she writes. "Today I am filled with terrible despair, and I shall have to come to terms with that as well. Even if we are consigned to hell, let us go there as gracefully as we can. I did not really want to put it so blandly."

Largely because of what is happening in the streets, the widening Nazi plague, something inside her, she feels, has crystallized: she resolves to look beyond her desk at the disquieting facts of daily life in the Occupation. Describing this stage of her inner development, Etty avers: "I have come to terms with life. . . . By 'coming to terms with life' I mean: the reality of death has become a definite part of my life; my life has, so to speak, been extended by death, by my looking death in the eye and accepting it, by accepting destruction as part of life and no longer wasting my energies on fear of death or the refusal to acknowledge its inevitability." In expressing these sentiments about death, Etty had not yet seen a dead person. In her own words, she has a "virginal" sense of death. "Just imagine: a world

sown with a million corpses, and in twenty-seven years I have never seen a single one." In Westerbork, she would not be spared the sight of corpses.

> [Etty's] writing was both a defense against despair, the death of the spirit, and a form of spiritual resistance against the oppressors. Through her writing and her humanity, she praised the sanctity of life. Looking outward, beyond the self, looking squarely and clearly at the historic moment, she had come of age in an age of genocide.
>
> —*Irving Halperin*

More and more Dutch Jews are being called up for "labor camps" in, presumably, Germany. Etty expects to receive her call-up papers soon. She is certain, given her medical history of susceptibility to anemia, colds, fatigue, and stomach ailments, that in a camp she would break down within three days. And if she should die there? In two of the most resonant sentences in the diaries, she states:

> It doesn't matter whether my untrained body will be able to carry on, that is really of secondary importance; the main thing is that even as we die a terrible death we are able to feel right up to the very last moment that life has meaning and beauty, that we have realized our potential and lived a good life. I can't really put it into words.

Now she begins making practical and what she calls "inner preparations" for a call-up. What would she do on receiving papers with orders to leave in, say, a week's time? First, she would try to see her parents and reassure them. Then she would have a dentist fill her cavities ("For that really would be awful; suffering from a toothache out there.") She would have her hair cut short, discard her lipstick and have a pair of trousers and a jacket made from leftover winter coat material. How would she pack all her underwear, blankets and food into the one allowable suitcase for the three days' journey to a camp? And what about her books? Certainly she would have to find room for the Bible, the "rugged and tender, simple and wise" Bible which gave her much pleasure and instruction and which could help her through difficult days, as it had for a writer with whom she identified, Dostoyevsky, when he was incarcerated in a Siberian prison. Yes, and there would have to be room in the suitcase for Rilke's *Letters to a Young Poet*, two small dictionaries, Tolstoy's folk tales, Dostoyevsky's *The Idiot*.

That is what she would do by way of practical preparations. But what about others who would be called up with her—how to help them? Would she be able to reassure the parents whose children would be going without them to "unknown destinations" (Why speak of unknown destinations? Etty writes, "Wherever I go, won't there be the same earth under my roving feet and the same sky with now the moon and now the sun, not to mention all the stars, above my grateful head?") by promising, "Don't worry, I'll look after your children"? Directly after posing this question, she pulls herself up sharply, "But I am still talking in much too philosophical, much too bookish a way, as if I had thought it all up to make life more pleasant for myself."

Etty's inner preparations for call-up include a vow to bear witness, to become a chronicler of what is happening in Holland and elsewhere. Here her tone is, uncharacteristically, almost militant: "And I shall wield this slender fountain pen as if it were a hammer and my words will have to be so many hammer-strokes with which to beat out the story of our fate and of a piece of history as it is and never was before." And if in a camp she is not able to write? Then she would carry her observations within. In any event, she counsels herself, there is no cause for despair; even from behind barbed wire one would be able to exercise inner freedom ("there will always be a small patch of sky above, and there will always be enough space to fold two hands in prayer").

At this point, July 1942, Etty's friends urge her to go into hiding instead of waiting to be called up. (On one occasion, according to Jan G. Gaarlandt, who wrote the introduction to *Letters from Westerbork,* she resisted an attempt by friends to take her by force to a safe address.) When she refuses to do so, they accuse her of passivity and unworldly naïveté. To this charge her response is that she does not want to be "saved" when so many thousands have to go to labor camps, " . . . it is sheer arrogance to think oneself too good to share the fate of the masses." Besides, she is certain that the enemy cannot harm her as long as she feels safe in God's arms. "They may well succeed in breaking me physically, but no more than that. I may face cruelty and deprivation the likes of which I cannot imagine in even my wildest fantasies. Yet all this is as nothing to the immeasurable expanse of my faith in God and my inner receptiveness." To those who would call her an incorrigible dreamer or mystic, she would reply that though her realities might be different from what many people would call reality, still they *are* realities.

We come now to a phase of Etty's life which would push her away from, as she wrote, "her peaceful desk into the midst of the cares and sufferings of this age." Prodded by a close friend, she reluctantly applies to the Jewish Council office in Amsterdam (reluctantly because she realizes that the Wehrmacht-controlled Council has been coerced into transporting Jews to Westerbork) and given a typist's job. In undertaking this assignment, she hopes to keep her family and friends off the transport lists. Working there is unpleasant: a hundred people are crowded into a small, noisy room; her typing chores are monotonous; her fellow workers are preoccupied with intrigues and petty grievances. There are times when she doesn't think she can endure another day in this atmosphere. But then she would tell herself that she has no right to complain when she is well off compared with some of her friends who are forced to work in factories for 60 hours a week. So she resolves to hold on there.

Reviewing her inner progress over a year's time, Etty affirms that she possesses a new calmness, and this enables her to endure the dispiriting work at the Jewish Council. "Had all of this happened to me only a year ago, I should certainly have collapsed within three days, committed suicide or pretended to a false kind of cheerfulness."

In the late summer of 1942, Etty volunteered to accompany the first group of Dutch Jews to Westerbork transit camp, which was located on a heath in northeastern Netherlands near the German border. Her status as an employee of the Jewish Council permitted her to come and leave there at will. Within a half square kilometer of huts and wooden barracks, dust, mud and human misery, fields of regal purple lupines grew beside the barbed wire of this camp. Westerbork had been built in 1939 to accommodate no more than 1500 displaced German Jews, but after 1942 it bulged with as many as 10,000 inmates at any one time. From July 1942 to September 1944, 93 transports, on the average of a thousand men, women, children and invalids in each one, left the camp for "unknown destinations." A transport consisted of sealed freight cars with some 70 people to a car. The "passengers" slept, when they could sleep, on hard floors. Paper mattresses were provided for invalids. A single bucket for bodily needs was placed in the middle of a car. The journey usually took three days.

At her writing desk in Amsterdam, Etty had felt safe and peaceful. In Westerbork, before going there, she wondered whether she would continue to believe that life is beautiful and meaningful? And would she have the will and stamina to describe what she observed there? She would not find answers to these questions during her brief initial encounter with Westerbork, although later, back in Amsterdam, Etty would speak of this experience as having been "the two richest and most intense months" of her life. There would be further "rich" (if this is an apt word for describing life in Westerbork!) and "intense" months on her subsequent returns to the camps, and through these experiences her ability as a writer would be exercised and validated.

At the end of August 1942, she arrived in Amsterdam in time to be at the side of her dying lover. Julius Spier's health had been steadily deteriorating. His death affected Etty profoundly. Not that she had deluded herself into supposing that they had a future together; he had a fiancée in London, and there was the great difference in their ages. More important, even before his illness, she had recognized that the ultimate importance of Julius in her life was not that of a lover or therapist but rather that of a "mediator" between herself and God. It was from him that she had first learned "to speak the name of God without embarrassment."

Kneeling beside Julius's death bed, she admonishes herself to be grateful both for the great happiness she had known in their relationship and also for his having been spared the additional suffering that the Occupation most certainly would have inflicted upon him. She addresses his spirit in these words: "You could be impatient about small things, but about the important things you were so patient, so infinitely patient. . . . All the bad and the good that can be found in a man were in you—all the demons, all the passions, all the goodness, all the love."

Looking at the first dead person that she has ever seen, Etty vows to "live on with that part of the dead that lives forever, and I shall rekindle into life that of the living which is now dead, until there is nothing but life, one great life, oh God."

In the aftermath of Julius Spier's death and during her recuperation from an illness that she had contracted at Westerbork, Etty would look back at her brief stay in the transit camp with, astonishingly, almost a feeling of homesickness, as witness the September 23, 1942 diary entry which contains this memorable passage: "At night the barracks sometimes lay in the moonlight, made out of silver and eternity: like a plaything that had slipped from God's preoccupied hand." This stunning trope clearly attests to her rich sensibility. Here it is as though she has dreamed that Westerbork is merely a temporary aberration within God's universe. This recollection also suggests that Etty sensed it was morally imperative for her to be back in Westerbork, sharing the fate of her people.

In November 1942, bearing a special permit from the Jewish Council, she returned to the transit camp in the role of a social worker. Much of her activity consisted of looking after patients in the hospital barracks. Although her permit from the Council allowed her to journey to Amsterdam to pick up medical supplies and to deliver messages from the camp's inmates, in Westerbork she did not receive preferential privileges. Like the other inmates, she slept on the same plank beds in barracks insufferably hot and stifling in summer and bitterly cold in winter and ate the same miserable scraps of food. At night she lay awake on a triple-deck bed amid women and girls who were dreaming aloud, tossing and turning, sobbing. Perhaps there were times when she would look around at such nightmarish scenes and wonder whether they were the handiwork of a feverish imagination. She had traveled a considerable distance from her peaceful desk in Amsterdam to the plank beds of Westerbork.

Before coming to the transit camp, she had vowed to be a chronicler, "the eyes and ears of a piece of Jewish history." Now, in Westerbork, among Jews from all over the Netherlands, she wants to be "the thinking heart of the barracks." But how to describe the indescribable? To depict the miserable and grotesque conditions here—so grotesque that they border on the unreal—she writes to a friend, one would have to be able to write fairy tales.

She has come a long way from a privileged life in Amsterdam, and yet Etty is sometimes severely critical of her attitude in Westerbork. Astonishingly, for such a serious and responsible person, she speaks of herself as frivolous and easy-going and too much the mere spectator of the misery in the camp, as though she were an outsider on a brief visit. "I have fallen short in all ways, my real work has not even begun," she berates herself.

But the fact is that her "real work" had begun: she was a scrupulous chronicler of the Westerbork hell. In her diaries and letters, powerfully and painstakingly recorded, are some of the most horrifying and tragic sights and

scenes in the literature of the Holocaust. In a letter dated August 24, 1943, we read of mothers sitting helplessly beside the cots of their sick children; "the piercing screams of babies dragged from their cots in the middle of the night"; the distress of abandoned children who are ignored by women who have enough worries looking after their own families; a partly paralyzed young girl who has just learned that she has been selected for a transport ("We look at each other for a long moment. It is as if her face has disappeared, she is all eyes. Then she says in a level, grey little voice, 'Such a pity isn't it? That everything you have learned in life goes for nothing. . . . How hard it is to die' "; a deranged looking woman who cries out to Etty: "That isn't right, how can that be right, I've got to go and I won't even be able to get my washing dry by tomorrow. And my child is sick, he's feverish, can't you fix things so that I don't have to go? . . . Can't you hide my child for me? Go on, please, won't you hide him, he's got a high fever, how can I possibly take him along?"; a young mother selected for transport warns her screaming baby, "If you don't behave yourself, mummy won't take you along with her!"; a colleague of Etty's squatting beside the bed of her dying mother, who has swallowed poison.)

Scenes from an inferno, and in its midst an elderly woman asks Etty, "Could you tell me, please, could you tell me, why we Jews have to suffer so much?" Etty cannot bring herself to reply, but later she cries out, silently, "God Almighty, what are You doing to us?" And there were the times when the screaming of sick and terrified children would especially get to her, and she would despair, seeing "nothing but blackness and nothing makes any sense at all."

In Westerbork Etty wasn't merely an observer and chronicler; she wanted to help others, to be, in her words, "a balm on many wounds." So we see her going from barracks to barracks, squeezing tomato juice for babies, calming distraught mothers, doling out coffee among hundreds of inmates, comforting a hundred-year-old woman by listening to her life story. Such selfless acts probably account for why some survivors of Westerbork still speak with awe of her "shining personality."

How did Etty view the camp's persecutors? In a departure from the times in Amsterdam when, in an all-embracing profession of love for humanity, she would admonish her friends not to hate the Occupation's oppressors because they too were made in the image of God, she is revulsed and frightened by the faces of a squad of guards who go about their grisly business on the night before a transport. "Oafish, jeering faces in which one seeks in vain for even the slightest trace of human warmth," she writes. "At what fronts did they learn their business? In what punishment camps were they trained?" She simply cannot reconcile her notion of humanity in the image of God with those brutal faces.

The intensity of her life in Westerbork takes its toll. Etty becomes anemic, has to lie on her bunk for hours at a time, and finally is brought to an Amsterdam hospital for the treatment of gallstones. "You have too cerebral a life, it's bad for your health, your constitution isn't up to it," a Dutch doctor scolds her. While admitting to her "demonic" intensity, Etty feels that the doctor doesn't grasp that she calms herself by reading. She is especially moved by St. Augustine, viewing him as "full of simple devotion in his love letters to God."

Etty was to administer more "balm on wounds" with the arrival of her parents and brother Mischa in Westerbork on June 21, 1943. Given their genteel background, she fears that they will not survive the camp's hardships. But they soon cope admirably. For example: her father gives lessons in Greek and Latin and reads Homer and Ovid to two young patients in the hospital barracks. All the while, Etty futilely considers ways by which her family might be kept off the transport lists, but, realistically, she knows that the trains leave the camp every week and that the quotas must be filled. In the meantime, she does whatever she can to lighten their burdens. With misgivings, because she hesitates to impose upon her Amsterdam friends who are not finding it easy to get by in a wartime economy of strict rationing, Etty makes what she calls mundane requests. "I feel awful, but there's no help for it," she writes in a letter. "What we need urgently for Father is rusks and things like that. He hasn't eaten for days and must be helped back to his usual form slowly; the camp bread is terrible." In another letter to this same friend, after apologizing for "causing a lot of trouble," she asks, "Could you get some little Antifones at a chemist's? They're the things you put in your ears to block out noise. In Mother's barracks it is very noisy at night, with a lot of small children who are sick—really there's nowhere here that isn't noisy—and now she wants to try sleeping with the earplugs."

For her family everything, for herself very little. And when she does ask something for herself the tone of the request is that of a self-denying person. "Do you know what I would still love to have here?" she writes to a friend. The "what" are a woolen dressing gown, a felt hat and a knitted dress, all of which are stored in her former residence. "It's fairly cold here sometimes," she explains, "and in case I should suddenly be put on a transport—you never know what will happen." Here Etty breaks off the request, as though regretting having made it. She was never to receive these garments. Five days after this letter was posted, Etty was placed on a transport to Auschwitz.

As late as four months before her death, she continues to maintain that life is good. Making light of her "little bit of physical discomfort" behind barbed wire, she writes that Westerbork cannot deprive her of her freedom. From a bunk she would look up at the sky over the camp to see some gulls in flight and think, "They are like free thoughts in an open mind." She intuits that she will not survive, but no matter. What is important is to reflect on *how* one meets death. "What tens and tens of thousands before us have borne, we can also bear. For us, I think, it is no longer a question of living, but of how one is equipped for one's extinction."

Then it was the turn of the Hillesums. On September 7, 1943, Etty, her parents and Mischa—her older brother was brought to Westerbork later, and he too did not survive—were placed on a crowded transport to "somewhere" in Poland. Long before, she had steeled herself for this moment ("Even if we are consigned to hell, let us go there as gracefully as we can.")

And that is how she went, according to Jopie Vleeschouwer, a friend of hers and also an inmate of Westerbork, wrote of Etty's departure in a letter:

> Talking gaily, smiling, a kind word for everyone she met on the way, full of sparkling humor, perhaps just a touch of sadness, but every inch the Etty you knew so well. 'I have my diaries, my little Bible, my Russian grammar and Tolstoy with me and God knows what else'. . . . I only wish I could describe for you exactly how it happened and with what grace she and her family left!

From a window in a wagon goods train, Etty threw a postcard which was recovered later; it read:

> Opening the Bible at random I find this: "The Lord is my high tower." I am sitting on my rucksack in the middle of a full freight car. Father, Mother, and Mischa are a few cars away. In the end, the departure came without warning. On sudden special orders from The Hague. We left the camp singing. . . .

She died in Auschwitz on November 30, 1943.

In what state of mind she perished we cannot know, though one can imagine that she went with her kind of grace. What we do know is that the trajectory of her spiritual journey was from that of a self-absorbed, private person to one who willingly and heroically assumed large communal responsibilities. The diaries and letters written in Westerbork indicate that Etty no longer was romantically theorizing on the meaning of suffering or thirsting after spiritual adventures; rather she seemed to have attained a genuine inner peace. In the camp she made meaningful connections with other Jews and linked herself with their destiny. Her writing was both a defense against despair, the death of the spirit, and a form of spiritual resistance against the oppressors. Through her writing and her humanity, she praised the sanctity of life. Looking outward, beyond the self, looking squarely and clearly at the historic moment, she had come of age in an age of genocide.

In Amsterdam, at her desk, Etty asserted that life is full of beauty and meaning. In Westerbork, behind barbed wire, she apparently found confirmation for this belief.

> Surrounded by my writers and poets and the flowers on my desk I loved life. And there among the barracks, full of hunted and persecuted people, I found confirmation of my love of life. . . . Not for one moment was I cut off from the life I was said to have left behind. There was simply one great meaningful whole. Will I be able to describe all that one day?

(pp. 2-14)

Irving Halperin, "Etty Hillesum: A Story of Spiritual Growth," in Reflections of the Holocaust in Art and Literature, *edited by Randolph L. Braham, Social Science Monographs, 1990, pp. 1-15.*

FURTHER READING

Biography

Gaarlandt, J[an] G. Introduction to *An Interrupted Life: The Diaries of Etty Hillesum, 1941-1943,* by Etty Hillesum, translated by Arno[ld J.] Pomerans, pp. vii-xiv. New York: Pantheon Books, 1983.

>   Provides biographical information about Hillesum and discusses the means by which her diaries came to publication.

————. Introduction to *Letters from Westerbork,* by Etty Hillesum, translated by Arnold J. Pomerans, pp. xi-xviii. London: Jonathan Cape, 1987.

>   Gives biographical information on Hillesum and a brief history of Westerbork and the Jewish Council.

Criticism

Ergas, Yasmine. "Growing Up Banished: A Reading of Anne Frank and Etty Hillesum." In *Behind the Lines: Gender and the Two World Wars,* edited by Margaret Randolph Higonnet, Jane Jenson, et. al., pp. 84-95. New Haven, Conn.: Yale University Press, 1987.

>   Compares the diaries of Hillesum and Anne Frank to determine "what they say about developing identities in the context of genocide."

Additional coverage of Hillesum's life and career is contained in the following source published by Gale Research: *Contemporary Authors,* Vol. 137.

Maurice Leblanc

1864-1941

(Full name Maurice Marie Emile Leblanc) French short story writer, novelist, playwright, and journalist.

INTRODUCTION

Leblanc is chiefly remembered for his popular detective fiction featuring Arsène Lupin. A "gentleman burglar," Lupin is distinguished by the ingenuity of his thefts and avoidance of violence. In later works featuring this character, Lupin acts as a detective who helps the police catch violent criminals.

Leblanc was born in Rouen. After earning a law degree, he worked in his family's business and as a journalist. His first published works of fiction were psychological novels focusing on bourgeois life. In 1905 Leblanc was asked to contribute a crime story to a new journal, *Je sais tout,* and responded with "L'arrestation d'Arsène Lupin" ("The Arrest of Arsène Lupin"). Encouraged by the popular success of this effort, Leblanc continued to write short stories focusing on Lupin during the next two years. The first collection of Lupin stories, *Arsène Lupin, gentleman-cambrioleur (The Exploits of Arsène Lupin)*, was published in 1907. During the next three decades Leblanc published more than twenty short story collections and novels focusing on Lupin, as well as numerous other volumes of detective and psychological fiction. Leblanc died in 1941.

Critics have noted that as the Lupin series developed the emphasis gradually changed from delineation of Lupin's own outrageous criminal exploits to his activities as an amateur detective who solves particularly heinous crimes. For example, in an early short story, "Arsène in Prison," Lupin informs a wealthy baron that he intends to steal several valuables from his art collection. Lupin is promptly thrown in jail and the police are called in to guard the baron's treasures. The "police," however, turn out to be Lupin's disguised associates, who carry out the robbery as planned. Lupin later returns the valuables after the baron agrees to pay a large sum of money and drop all charges against him. In a later work, *Les dents du tigre (The Teeth of the Tiger)*, Lupin is both a suspect in a series of mysterious deaths and the detective who discovers the murderer. Throughout the series Lupin displays considerable skill in manipulating both his victims and the police with disguises and ingenious deceptions. Leblanc is thought to have reformed Lupin in response to demands from his readers, yet the early tales of Lupin's criminal exploits are more often valued by modern commentators. While the Lupin stories have been widely translated and attract considerable attention from French critics, commentary on Leblanc's works has been fairly limited in English-speaking countries. A *New York Times Book Review* critic observed: "The Arsène Lupin stories are too well known

to call for serious criticism in the name of a public that either likes them very much or not at all."

PRINCIPAL WORKS

Des couples (novel) 1890
Une femme (novel) 1893
Les heures du mystère (short stories) 1896
L'œuvre de mort (novel) 1896
Armelle et Claude (novel) 1897
L'enthousiasme (novel) 1901
Arsène Lupin, gentleman-cambrioleur (short stories) 1907
   [*The Exploits of Arsène Lupin,* 1907; also published as *The Seven of Hearts,* 1908; and *The Extraordinary Adventures of Arsène Lupin, Gentleman-Burglar,* 1910]
Arsène Lupin [with Francis de Croisset] (drama) [first publication] 1908

Arsène Lupin contre Herlock Sholmès (short stories) 1908
   [*The Fair-Haired Lady,* 1908; also published as *Arsène Lupin versus Holmlock Shears,* 1909; *Arsène Lupin versus Herlock Sholmes,* 1910; *The Blonde Lady,* 1910; and *The Arrest of Arsène Lupin,* 1911]
L'aiguille creuse (novel) 1909
   [*The Hollow Needle,* 1910]
813 (novel) 1910
   [*813,* 1910]
Une aventure d'Arsène Lupin [with Francis de Croisset] (drama) [first publication] 1911; also published as *Le retour d'Arsène Lupin,* 1911
La frontière (novel) 1911
   [*The Frontier,* 1912]
Le bouchon de cristal (novel) 1912
   [*The Crystal Stopper,* 1913]
La robe d'écailles roses (short stories) 1912
Les confidences d'Arsène Lupin (novel) 1913
   [*The Confessions of Arsène Lupin,* 1913]
L'éclat d'obus (novel) 1916
   [*The Bomb-Shell,* 1916; also published as *The Woman of Mystery,* 1916]
Un vilain couple (novel) 1916
Le triangle d'or (novel) 1918
   [*The Golden Triangle,* 1917]
L'île aux trente cercueils (novel) 1920
   [*Coffin Island,* 1920; also published as *The Secret of Sarek,* 1920]
Les trois yeux (novel) 1920
   [*The Three Eyes,* 1921]
* *Les dents du tigre* (novel) 1921
   [*The Teeth of the Tiger,* 1914]
Le formidable événement (novel) 1921
   [*The Tremendous Event,* 1922]
Les huit coups de l'horloge (short stories) 1922
   [*Eight Strokes of the Clock,* 1922]
Dorothée, danseuse de corde (novel) 1923
   [*Dorothy the Rope-Dancer,* 1923]
La Comtesse de Cagliostro (novel) 1924
   [*The Candlestick with Seven Branches,* 1925; also published as *Memoirs of Arsène Lupin,* 1925]
La vie extravagante de Balthazar (novel) 1925
La demoiselle aux yeux verts (novel) 1927
   [*The Girl with the Green Eyes,* 1927; also published as *Arsène Lupin, Super-Sleuth,* 1927]
L'agence Barnett et cie (short stories) 1928
   [*Jim Barnett Intervenes,* 1928; also published as *Arsène Lupin Intervenes,* 1929]
La demeure mystérieuse (novel) 1929
   [*The Melamare Mystery,* 1930]
De minuit à sept heures (novel) 1932
   [*From Midnight to Morning,* 1933]
La femme aux deux sourires (novel) 1933
   [*The Double Smile,* 1933; also published as *The Woman with Two Smiles,* 1933]
Victor, de la brigade mondaine (novel) 1933
   [*The Return of Arsène Lupin,* 1934]
Le chapelet rouge (novel) 1934
L'image de la femme nue (novel) 1934
   [*Wanton Venus,* 1935]

La Cagliostro se venge (novel) 1935
Le scandale du gazon bleu (novel) 1935
Les milliards d'Arsène Lupin (novel) 1941

*This work first appeared in English translation.

CRITICISM

The Nation, New York   (essay date 1907)

[*In the following review, the critic discusses Leblanc's deviations from crime and mystery conventions in the stories collected as* The Exploits of Arsène Lupin.]

Arsène Lupin is a French counterpart of Mr. Hornung's "Raffles," the hero of short stories of criminal mystery treated from the criminal side. Yet if Gallic traits are displayed by Lupin himself, they are displayed quite as much by his creator. For every trick which the criminal plays on his victims, the author is playing one on his readers. All those rules of fair play which have been formulated for the benefit of the reader of fiction of this type are here thrown to the winds. For example, a number of stories in [*The Exploits of Arsène Lupin*] are told in the first person. In all these curiosity is aroused as to where Arsène Lupin is, and what he is doing. But sometimes the narrator turns out to be a victim, sometimes a bystander, sometimes Arsène Lupin himself. This is gross betrayal of a trusting reader. Or, in certain stories, Lupin is introduced under other names, and after going half or two-thirds through a story under an alias which the reader accepts without question, he unmasks between sentences. Even Sherlock Holmes comes into these stories under the thin disguise of Holmlock Shears. All this is not melodrama but Christmas pantomime.

Yet the character which M. Leblanc has created, an arch criminal who controls a newspaper of his own for the recording of his strange exploits, whose selfish criminality is relieved constantly by acts which are generous or patriotic or merely spectacular, is one to afford a good deal of entertainment. The stories, aside from the unaccountable manner of their unfolding, are of uneven merit, but some are capital.

   A review of "The Exploits of Arsène Lupin," in The Nation, *New York, Vol. LXXXV, No. 2215, December 12, 1907, p. 545.*

Charles Henry Meltzer   (essay date 1913)

[*In the following essay, Meltzer reports on an interview during which Leblanc discussed the origins of the Arsène Lupin character and his views on the morality of creating a criminal protagonist.*]

Crime has at all times charmed the loftiest minds. It prompted Shakespeare to produce *Macbeth.* It caused Shelley to create his play, *The Cenci.* Balzac and countless other men of genius found inspiration in the depths of crime. Some authors, like the Russian Dostoievsky, have treated it as a tragedy, while many have preferred to view it lightly. Before Edgar Allan Poe wrote his weird tales, the criminal had had his place in literature. Bismarck, the man of iron, and Gladstone, the idealist, used to relax, they say, by reading Gaboriau. And if the greatest have been spell-bound by the romance which seems attached even to burglary, how can we wonder at the rapture with which tens of thousands, perhaps even millions, have devoured the works of writers who invented such heroes as Sherlock Holmes, or such rogues as Raffles and the brilliant Arsène Lupin?

In "Arsène Lupin," a distinguished Frenchman, Maurice Leblanc, has created a scoundrel who, to the skill of Sherlock Holmes and the resourcefulness of Raffles, adds the refinement of a casuist, the epigrammatic nimbleness of a La Rochefoucauld, and the gallantry of a Du Guesclin. This Arsène Lupin is no common thief. He is in some respects the most attractive type of rascal as yet known in modern letters. He robs with method, and he picks his victims carefully. At moments he is capable of deeds which win him public sympathy. The ablest and most earnest of his enemies have admired him. Repeatedly his wit has outmatched their own. And even Sherlock Holmes, who had moved heaven and earth (in books) to rid society of its new foe, was beaten by the amazing tricks of Lupin, as set forth by M. Leblanc. France soon took Arsène to her heart; America imitated her; so did England. And soon, from the story and the novel, the new "hero" made his way on to the boards!

Maurice Leblanc, the accomplished gentleman to whom we owe what enjoyment we have got from watching Lupin in his bad and mad career, is a brother of Mme. Georgette Leblanc, the actress-singer, and a brother-in-law of no less a personage than Maurice Maeterlinck. Whatever we may think of the effect his works may have, none can deny his art. His novels and short tales are more than clever. They have the merit of being almost literature. And what deep knowledge of the mysteries of crime his books reveal! You feel, as you devour his entrancing narratives, that he has lived and talked with the arch-rogue whom he portrays. But this was theory—and I was bent on facts when, with a burning wish to see him face to face, I asked permission of M. Leblanc to call on him.

For nine months in the year he lives at Passy. In summer he retires to Normandy, where, at the Château de Tancarville, near Honfleur, he plays and works beside the river Seine. To Tancarville I went, one August day, by devious ways, in trains and motor-cars. The trains, as usual in the west of France, were late. It rained in torrents when I reached the château, where, at the end of a wide, shady drive, M. Leblanc stood waiting. Above me rose the majestic remnants of what, in the Conqueror's time, had been the stronghold of the powerful Lords of Tancarville. Beyond them was a vast, three-storied mansion, the modern château, flanked by stone ramparts, which confined broad lawns. A hundred feet below spread marshy wastes. The river, broad and calm, wound through the plain; skirting high, wooded hills and little towns till it was lost in space.

The ruins of the ancient feudal fortress were green with ivy and eglantine. The chapel walls and arches were but shells.

M. Leblanc was not at all what I had pictured him. Instead of the disconcerting, cynical person I had seen in my mind's eye, I found a quiet, friendly man, of middle height. His face—a large and rather cheerful face—was lit up by his bright and kindly eyes. His mustache, which overhung a humorous mouth, strayed here and there. His wide and receding forehead spoke of thought. His scanty hair was of an iron gray. The impression that he made on one was pleasant. That was my first surprise. The author led me through the château grounds to a small, open shed, furnished with chairs, a table, and a writer's tools.

"This little shelter serves me as my study," said M. Leblanc. "I work outdoors. In Paris, which I make my winter home, I have had another shed like this built in my garden. Winter and summer, in all kinds of weather, I write in the open air. But every afternoon, at five or so, I shut myself up in my room and draw the curtains, while I map out what I intend to do next morning. No one is allowed to interrupt me in this corner of the grounds. The view, the air, the quiet—all are helpful. I mix but little in the château life."

I asked him how he happened to know so much of criminals. "But I am blankly ignorant!" he assured me. "I never met or talked with thieves and rogues. Once only in my life have I met a detective. As for the criminals of whom I write, they do not interest me. I never had the faintest wish to know them. Of course my stories are pure romance—the fictions of my brain—the merest fancies. There *is* no person like my Arsène Lupin. It was by accident that I created him. For years I had been writing novels of real life, which had had some success. One day, M. Lafitte, now director of *Excelsior* and a close friend of mine, asked me to send him a short story of adventure for *Je Sais Tout,* then a new magazine. On reflection, an idea occurred to me which I developed into what I named **'The Arrest of Arsène Lupin.'** As you perhaps recall, it dealt incidentally with wireless telegraphy. That scientific touch amused me. The story, which was quite short, made a hit.

" 'Keep it up,' said the editor. 'Give us more tales about Arsène Lupin, and you may have as much success as Conan Doyle has had with those Sherlock Holmes stories.'

" 'But I can't keep it up,' said I; 'Lupin has been arrested.'

" 'Bah! Think it over. Lupin is worth saving.'

" 'I rescued him. I grew to like the fellow. More stories followed. I collected them, and they appeared in book form, as **Arsène Lupin, Gentleman Burglar.** That was the first of the four Arsène Lupin volumes I have published. The second in the series was called **Arsène Lupin versus Homelock Shares.** The third I named **L'Aiguille Creuse,** and the fourth **813.** I have another volume in the press—**Le Bouchon de Cristal** (or **The Crystal Stopper**). And that, in turn, may have at least two sequels. I have imagined them, Monsieur, like all the rest. I know nothing of crime and criminals."

When I recovered from this second, greater shock, I asked the author if he had made a study of criminology.

"I have read Edgar Allan Poe and studied Balzac," he replied. "All the romance of crime was suggested in Poe's works. I don't remember anything besides Poe and Balzac that could have helped me to work out my plots—unless my fondness for the game of chess was useful. Chess helps one to make plays. And why not novels?"

Leading me to an isolated building at the far end of the grounds, he continued: "Here is the 'Tour de l'Aigle,' which I make my headquarters. It was constructed, I believe, about a hundred years ago, with stones that came from that old castle over there. In this bedroom I do my thinking, in pitch darkness. And now, suppose we have some tea? Talking fatigues me."

We touched on Sherlock Holmes.

"I have been accused of pilfering Conan Doyle," said M. Leblanc. "That is hardly fair. I have read Conan Doyle, and I admire his works. I have not pilfered him. It was a friend of mine who suggested my introducing Sherlock Holmes into my stories, and the idea seemed natural. But I admit that I have not been wholly fair in my descriptions of that character. Whenever Lupin meets him, Lupin conquers. And though, of course, Conan Doyle owed much to Gaboriau, I confess that I regret some things I have written of his hero. Not only because I may have been unjust. But—well, because I may have offended English sentiment."

The green hills and marshes by the Seine grew faint. A veil of rain obscured the noble stream. M. Leblanc paused and looked out on the broad landscape. "I love that picture," he observed. "It sets me thinking of the victories of my ancestors, those Normans who, in other days, sailed down the Seine and ravaged St. Wandrille. I have some Italian blood, too, in my veins. But here at Tancarville I am Norman—only Norman."

So, after all, there *was* a lawless taint in the inventor of those Arsène Lupin tales. Why should I spare him?

"I have to charge you with a grave offense. Do you not think you have done some harm by making a hero of a man like Arsène Lupin?" And I quoted instances.

"No," said the author, in an earnest tone. "I think my conscience is at least as nice as most. And if I thought that I had harmed my fellows—but I do not. I don't believe that any novels influence morals. Nothing we put into our books is like real life. To those who read them, my Arsène Lupin tales are romances of adventure. They could not change one single honest man into a criminal. To charge me with promoting crime is unreasonable. Would you accuse Paul Bourget of promoting infidelity?" Why not, indeed?

"My Lupin really is, in his own way, a hero. He is brave and chivalrous. Who are his victims? People inferior to himself, not worthy of sympathy. And Lupin only robs. He does not kill. Take him for all in all there is more good in him than in some rich lords and barons. The good in him outweighs the evil. Just now Lupin stands between

Law and the *Canaille*. He laughs at one, and he destroys the other. Meanwhile, he takes the goods of the *Canaille*—their gold and treasures. He also, I admit, took the 'Joconde' and hid it in the 'hollow needle' at Etretat. Queer, was it not, that I should have hit on that? That is not all," M. Leblanc went on, forgetting for the nonce that books were impotent. "I will go further. Not only do I not believe that Lupin is harmful, I believe he is useful: although a mere creation of my brain, he has helped society, by teaching it that it needs self-protection. If robberies are committed with such ease, it is because we are careless and forget to shield ourselves. But for the interest aroused by Lupin, would the prefect of police, M. Lepine, have dreamed of founding a school for his agents? Between ourselves, I doubt if it will do much good. Still—it will be founded. You take the Anglo-Saxon view of things. I take a French view. Moreover, though at present he seems lawless, a change is coming over Arsène Lupin. By slow degrees he is becoming virtuous. The first signs of this moral transformation may be perceived in my next novel. Before long, Arsène Lupin may be aiding justice. Perhaps—But I must not give up all my secrets. There was a time, I won't deny, when I was vexed, as you seem to be, by the idea that Arsène Lupin might do harm. I did not like to let my boy Claude read my books. Since then, however, I have changed my mind. Here comes my son. You may question him."

I took the lad aside and talked with him. He was frank and intelligent: "Do you like Lupin, my young friend?" "Oh, yes, Monsieur!" "Why do you like him?" "First, because he is brave. And then, you know, because he is so droll." "Do you approve of him?" "Monsieur, he amuses me." "You have never wished nor hoped to be a Lupin?" "Oh, no, Monsieur. If he came here to-night, I'd send him away."

That surely should have silenced all my doubts. But somehow they would not down. As for the father of the lad, he seemed at ease. Perhaps, as he suggests, we Anglo-Saxons do take things too seriously. If "Arsène Lupin" can prompt men to burglary, may not "Macbeth" have caused others to do murder? The ready wit of Lupin charms your Frenchman. The cunning of "Macbeth" may affect your Englishman. Yet which of us would call the play immoral? And if a child, like little Claude Leblanc, is amused, without being harmed, by "Arsène Lupin," why need his elders not be just as wise? Quite true, you say. But Macduff kills Macbeth. So right, in that case, gets the upper hand, and wrong is punished. Suppose, though, Arsène Lupin should reform? Would you refuse to let him have your saving grace? He is a rascal, if you will, and not a saint. And, as M. Leblanc again proclaimed, before I turned my back on Tancarville, there never was a Lupin in real life. He is an airy, fairy creature, born of dreams; the imagination of a gifted writer. When he has thrilled or shocked you with his daring crimes, he is still a dream. It may be best to keep your anger for real rogues—to keep your virtuous indignation for real crimes. Lupin and Raffles and the rest—are mere bubbles. (pp. 770-73)

Charles Henry Meltzer, "Arsène Lupin at Home," in Cosmopolitan, *Vol. 54, No. 6, May, 1913, pp. 770-73.*

The New York Times Book Review (essay date 1914)

[*In the following review, the critic faults the length and overly complicated plot of* The Teeth of the Tiger *but praises the novel overall as an excellent detective story.*]

To all appearance, certainly, Arsène Lupin was dead. Was not his body found—along with the charred remains of the adventuress whom he had killed—in the ruins of a burned chalet in Luxemburg? Was it not true beyond the shadow of a doubt—that the Prefecture of Police in Paris had nothing further to fear or to hope from this master-mind among thieves?

And yet, here is Arsène Lupin. In *The Teeth of the Tiger* he appears not as a thief, but as a detective and benefactor. If his return and his change of front are mysterious things, his goodwill is none the less sincere. He is final heir to a fortune of one hundred million francs, only in case of the death or disappearance of the will-maker's relatives. Some one is systematically finding and murdering the heirs of the rich man; Arsène Lupin hunts down the criminal, puts an end to the crimes, defeats all possibility of winning the fortune for himself, and flings a triumphant challenge in the "tiger's" teeth. But, robber or philanthropist or detective, he is just the same Arsène Lupin he always was; there isn't any doubt about that.

At the story's beginning two persons have been murdered and two more know that they are about to be killed. A rich man's death is proved to be not accidental, but planned; and the Police Inspector, who is on the track of the plot, is himself mysteriously poisoned. The next night the second two—a father and his son—are found dead. The only clue—"the teeth of the tiger"—points to a woman who had herself, in the matter of the legacy, good reason to commit all four murders if she had felt so inclined. But there is another strange woman whose actions may well arouse suspicion. And there is a mysterious man who shoots a Police Inspector under the detectives' eyes. This is the problem that Arsène Lupin must solve; but from the beginning of the story until its end Arsène Lupin knows—and the reader knows with him—that he himself is under perhaps the gravest suspicion of all.

The Arsène Lupin stories are too well known to call for serious criticism in the name of a public that, either likes them very much or not at all. [*The Teeth of the Tiger*] is, on the whole, an excellent detective story. Its plot, in piling up mystery upon mystery, becomes somewhat too complicated: and the story is open to the usual censure that its "villains" are sometimes too stupid, and its "heroes" too lucky, to be quite true. *The Teeth of the Tiger,* too, is quite too long. But it is not impossible, for all that, that it may be "read at a sitting." (pp. 411-12)

> "Arsene Lupin," in The New York Times Book Review, *October 4, 1914, pp. 411-12.*

F. M. Holly (essay date 1916)

[*In the following review, Holly assesses* A Woman of Mystery *as implausible but entertaining.*]

The Woman of Mystery is a war novel, and it seems a bit artificial when compared with the big human stories we read every day in the newspapers, but perhaps when we have a different perspective fiction and fact will each retain its true value.

Monsieur Le Blanc uses the first months of the war for his setting. The story opens in the summer of 1914, just after the marriage of Paul Delroze and Elizabeth. Their happiness is short lived, for a few days after their marriage the husband makes a startling discovery. In the photograph of Elizabeth's mother, he recognizes the murderer of his father. The wife has unbounded faith in her mother's purity and innocence, while the husband is equally confident that she is no other than the wicked woman whose face has been indelibly impressed on his mind.

Then come the days of mobilization and the invasion of Belgium. Elizabeth is held prisoner by no other than the Crown Prince of Germany, while Paul is fighting not only for his country, but to find his wife and rescue her from her peril. He is also on the trail of the Mysterious Woman. When cornered the Spy confesses that she is the Countess von Hohenzollern. "The actions which you in your simple way, call murder, yes, I committed them—all. It was my duty to my Emperor, to the greater Germany. A Spy, not at all. Simply a German woman—and what a German woman does for her country is rightly done." This is how the woman of mystery justifies herself.

The author paints his picture of the Emperor with a free hand.

> It was difficult to recognize in him the figure represented by his photographs and illustrations in the newspapers, for the face had aged into a worn and wasted mask, furrowed with wrinkles and disfigured with yellow blotches.

There are many thrilling scenes in the life of the French officers, and a most improbable one when Paul has an interview with the Kaiser, and persuades him to release twenty French prisoners in return for information that he can give as to the whereabouts of the Crown Prince. M. Le Blanc pictures Paul as quivering with hatred in the presence of the Emperor, "not so much a personal hatred aroused by the recollection of his own sufferings as a hatred made up of horror and contempt for the greatest criminal imaginable."

We must be willing to grant any or all impossible situations if we are to enjoy this particular brand of mystery story, for after all the mystery is interesting and well sustained and Paul and Elizabeth emerge unscathed from their harrowing experiences. (pp. 842-43)

> *F. M. Holly, in a review of "The Woman of Mystery," in* Publishers Weekly, *Vol. XC, No. 12, September 16, 1916, pp. 842-43.*

H. Douglas Thomson (essay date 1931)

[*In the following excerpt from his* Masters of Mystery: A Study of the Detective Story, *Thomson discusses the Arsène Lupin series, analyzing the conception of the character of Lupin and pronouncing Leblanc most successful when he writes in a humorous vein.*]

According to *Le Matin* M. Leblanc works very slowly and conscientiously, and "he is considered to have done for French literature exactly what Sir Arthur Conan Doyle has done for English." Arsène Lupin, "gentleman cambrioleur," is the most familiar figure of French detective fiction. He has a far greater public than Rouletabille or even Lecoq. He captured the popular fancy as early as 1907, and he is still going strong. Lupin is the apache of romance, but he is credited with a little more intelligence and a little less of the animal than this absurd figure is usually made to have. Lupin's pose is an old one—that of a street urchin with his fingers to his nose. He attacks the conventions, because law in the shape of the policeman is a pompous ass.

Lupin is completely a-moral. He is not a legendary Robin Hood or Dick Turpin robbing the nasty rich to relieve the honest poor. Nor is he a Raffles stealing from horrid plutocrats to support charity. He burgles because he finds it amusing, because he loves the sport of it just, and for the same reason, as the detectives love to whip out their magnifying glasses. In part Lupin is a parody of the conventional detective; and the fact that he was on the other side of the fence *makes* the parody. It is true that Lupin runs with the hare and hunts with the hounds, that it is impossible at times to know in what camp he is serving—whether he is teaching the stupid but zealous Prefecture its business, or is merely being a "smiling, damned villain." (For four years Lupin—as Lenormand, the head of the Paris detective force—"directed operations against himself!") Yet Lupin's pose is unsatisfactory. He stops short of murder. Why? If he appears to blackmail we later see it was a piece of bluff. Why? When he loses his heart, which is not seldom, he has moments of remorse. Why? Because Lupin was within an ace of becoming a low criminal. Battery and assault are, of course, not actionable in a detective story. Lupin's wit, his virility, his impudence, his self-confidence are all right up to a point. . . . E. M. Wrong hit the nail on the head when he drew this conclusion:

> To make a hero of the criminal is to reverse the moral law, which is after all based on common sense, for crime is not in fact generous and open, but mean . . . not even success can make robbery appeal to us as a truly noble career. Is the criminal then to try other crimes than theft? Blackmail hardly provides a fitting career for a hero, and we are driven back on murder. Now it is possible for murderers to show courage and resource, to be less mean than the pickpocket or forger. But murder to be successful must be selfish. . . .

Analysed in the cold light of reason, Lupin is not so supremely clever as he himself (or possibly M. Leblanc) imagined. His bag of tricks consists of an infinite capacity for masquerade and impersonation; an acrobatic agility, and an "iron nerve."

M. Leblanc has two moods—the sensational and the humorous. The nature of the Arsène Lupin joke once considered, it is easy to deduce that he is more successful when he is in lighter vein. In fact, his sensational novels, such as *The Teeth of the Tiger, The Hollow Needle* and *The*

Eight Strokes of the Clock, are second-rate. Lupin is really out of place in the sensational thriller. Bent on amusement, he stumbles unwittingly upon murder. It is almost as distasteful to Lupin himself as it is to us, for M. Leblanc loves lurid pigments, and his blood-and-thunder is of a crude, almost brutal description.

But it is in the collections of short stories—*The Exploits of Arsène Lupin, The Arrest of Arsène Lupin, The Seven of Hearts,* etc.—that M. Leblanc scores. Not the least interesting feature of these tales is the burlesque on Sherlock Holmes and Dr. Watson, or Holmlock Shears and Wilson, as he sometimes calls them. The burlesque is all the more interesting as it comes from France. M. Leblanc, it is worth mentioning, had a tremendous admiration for Conan Doyle, and on the latter's death wrote one of the most striking tributes. Holmes and Watson are called in to join issue with Lupin, since the police have proved their incompetence. Naturally Holmes gets the worst of it, but only just. Lupin recognises that he has a redoubtable opponent: so does Holmes, but Dr. Watson is sanguine in his confidence. It is a great joke, and both parties treat it as such and entertain a studied politeness to each other. It is perhaps worth mentioning just those traits in Holmes which appealed to M. Leblanc. Holmes is always caught lighting his pipe. (It was a shocking mistake to make him roll a cigarette on one occasion.) He has lost his epigrammatic skill and adopted the brazen attitude of a supersalesman. In appearance he now resembles a city clerk. He relies on intuitions and cigarette ash.

> He was a sort of miracle of intuition, of insight, of perspicacity, of shrewdness. It is as though Nature had amused herself by taking the two most extraordinary types of detective that fiction had invented, Poe's Dupin and Gaboriau's Lecoq, in order to build up one in her own fashion, more extraordinary yet and more unreal.

Dr. Watson is drawn in a much coarser caricature, and has even to submit to some knock-about. He gets his arm broken for his pains on one lamentable occasion. But the best scene of all is where Holmes and Dr. Watson encounter Lupin and his biographer. After an exchange of greetings Sherlock magnanimously calls for four whiskies and sodas. That is in the grand manner! (pp. 118-21)

> *H. Douglas Thomson, "The French Detective Story," in his* Masters of Mystery: A Study of the Detective Story, *1931. Reprint by Richard West, 1978, pp. 92-121.*

A. E. Murch   (essay date 1958)

[*In the following excerpt, Murch discusses the literary predecessors and development of the Arsène Lupin character and examines some principal features of the Lupin series.*]

Maurice Leblanc (1864–1941), a journalist and the author of half a dozen light romances, was, in 1906, asked by the editor of *Je Sais Tout* to write a crime story for that periodical. He produced *Arsène Lupin, gentleman-cambrioleur,* which was published in volume form in 1907, and in English translation as *The Seven of Hearts*

(1908). In addition to his descriptive title, Leblanc's hero may owe something to [English novelist and short-story writer E. W. Hornung's character] Raffles, whose success certainly indicated that the public still liked reading of an attractive rogue. But Lupin is essentially French, a re-incarnation, not of Raffles, but of Rocambole—the Paris *gamin* who loves flouting the conventions and the police, the gay, adventurous leader of a gang of thieves. Like Rocambole, Lupin has a fancy for masquerading as a prince, a duke, or a Spanish Grandee, and both rascals are young, handsome, supremely self-confident, incredibly daring and quick-witted. Rocambole once captured an English detective, Simouns, and impersonated him at Scotland Yard. Lupin caps these achievements by kidnapping an important government official, Daubrecq, and having him secretly conveyed from Switzerland to Paris in a trunk on the roof of a cab. For four years, Lupin, posing as Lenormand, *chef de la Sûreté*, takes charge of the police investigations into his own activities!

Leblanc makes frequent use of neo-gothic features that had been popular in *feuilletons* from the time of the *roman noir*, ruined castles, subterranean passages, secret trap-doors and other outmoded contrivances, and his plots are, for the most part, borrowed from Ponson du Terrail, or from Gaboriau and his imitators. 'Scientific' methods of detection play little if any part, and, even when attempted, are inaccurate. The detectives who challenge Lupin—Guerchard, or Isadore Beautrelet, even the Prefect of Police himself, Louis Prasville, cannot be compared with the 'scientific' detectives who were popular in English fiction of the same period.

Leblanc certainly had English detectives in mind in his second story in the series, *Arsène Lupin contre Herlock Sholmès* (1908), a heavily sarcastic parody in which Lupin outwits 'the great detective.' Herlock Sholmès, slow and ponderous, with red hair and a moustache, is totally unlike Doyle's hero, while his friend and biographer, Wilson, prone to over-indulge in whisky and fond of a brawl, bears no resemblance to Watson. Leblanc borrowed both figures from the 'comic' Englishmen of French vaudeville, fifty years earlier. After this regrettable lapse, the saga of Lupin was resumed in *L'Aiguille Creuse* (1909), *813* (1910), *Le Bouchon de Cristal* (1912), *Les Confidences d'Arsène Lupin* (1914), *Les Trois Crimes d'Arsène Lupin* (1917), other volumes appearing at short intervals until the 1930's.

Throughout his long career, Lupin is, first and foremost, the 'master-brain' behind a succession of burglaries which completely baffle the police. In *Le Bouton de Cristal* his rôle begins to undergo the inevitable change, and he agrees to assist the police, though for his own reasons. Other adventures follow, most of them short stories or episodic novels, with Lupin either correcting the blunders of the police without their knowledge, or putting them on the right track when it suits him to do so. His later exploits, *Les Dents du Tigre* (1920), and especially *Les Huit Coups de l'Horloge* (1922), show him openly engaged in detective investigations, but shorn of most of his earlier glamour. He is far better at evolving brilliant schemes of his own than in fathoming the plans of others. His explanations are not always sound, and minor problems are left unsolved. His daring and his quick perceptions stand him in good stead, but his inability to resist a joke or a love affair, his fondness for the melodramatic, and his sympathy with the criminals among whom he once reigned supreme—all these handicap his efforts as a detective, and he is most convincing as originally created, the resourceful, irresistible gentleman-burglar. (pp. 195-97)

> *A. E. Murch, "The Early Twentieth Century,"*
> *in her* The Development of the Detective
> Novel, *Philosophical Library, Inc., 1958, pp.*
> *192-217.*

Oliver Edwards (essay date 1965)

[*In the following essay, Edwards reminisces about the appeal of Leblanc's Arsène Lupin stories for youthful readers.*]

Arsène Lupin. The name caught my eye in a letter to *The Times* two or three weeks ago. On the instant I felt an irrational pleasure.

It was irrational because if I had liked Maurice Leblanc's hero all that much I would surely have gone back to him occasionally in the past 40 years. I still, from time to time, pick up Raffles or Holmes. Lupin is not in their class. He is not really of their kind.

And yet there was something about him. His exploits stirred the heart when one was a boy. What would now annoy as ridiculous extravagance or sheer impossibility then helped to create a world of fantasy. Arsène Lupin's spell was that he existed on a plane where the impossible *could* happen. One knew it was all nonsense—the fantastic disguises, the incessant discomfiting of all adversaries, the world within a world in which Lupin was king—and yet one was always ready for more. Whereas both Hornung and Conan Doyle knew their strength depended on keeping at least one foot on the ground, Leblanc cavorted in a world of complete make-believe. It did not matter; the reader's belief was eagerly suspended. Some of the magic, I now think, lay in the name itself. Arsène Lupin. The slow, sardonic sound of the first word, followed by the nimbleness of the second. The effect reminds me now of nothing so much as of Strauss's motto theme for Euloenspiegel. Lupin was in fact another Tyll. Even when he should have been most thoroughly dead he just would not lie down. Turn the page and he is scampering off again.

As I have said, one had to take a good many of these escapes, and other exploits as well, on trust. Leblanc was something of a boy's magician. He was sure that he had only to say "Hey presto" and the trick would come off. How right he was.

Leblanc was not a particularly good contriver of plots. Even his most famous novel, *L'Aiguille Creuse,* is a hotchpotch. He was anything but subtle with his characters. Not for him the psychological insight of a Simenon. Lupin himself is such a palimpsest of different characters that it is hard to say which is the real, original man.

What Leblanc did have was an inexhaustible gusto and a gift for suspense. The adventures of Arsène Lupin were more or less contemporary with the exploits of Elaine. Both hero and heroine were perpetually confronted with final disaster, which of course never happened. Yet the trick never palled. The magician's twentieth flourish had all the panache of the previous nineteen. Whether Lupin is duke or detective, patriot or gentleman-cambrioleur, always he is larger than life, a Chestertonian superman who was all other six days of the week as well as Thursday.

And always he entertained. Leblanc truly wrote "Le nom seul d'Arsène Lupin était un gage d'imprévu, une promesse de divertissement pour la galerie. Et la galerie, c'était le monde entier". The gallery were never let down.

If they were English, however, they could accuse Leblanc of some rigging. Arsène Lupin had, of course, to cross swords more than once with Sherlock Holmes. The confrontation could not be escaped. But what Leblanc calls "la lutte de ces deux grands artistes" is unequal combat. Herlock Sholmès (I don't know why the accent is there; Leblanc also wrote of Sherlock Holmès) is a blundering dunderhead of an impostor. He may be accompanied by his faithful Wilson, and live at 219 Parker Street, but there all resemblance ends. He deduces nothing; he achieves nothing except to shoot dead Lupin's beloved wife, Raymonde. Nor is it merely a question of his being outmatched because he is abroad. He allows Lupin to kidnap him in London and ship him off on a slow boat round Africa. As Lupin promises, Trafalgar is avenged, but only by pitting a destroyer against a coracle.

Inspector Ganimard is no better. His henchman is appropriately named Folenfant. The only detective worthy of Lupin's esteem is Isidore Beautrelet. It is not without significance, that he is a schoolboy. He does at least try some deduction. (Naturally Lupin outwits him.) He does decipher the mysterious message that was handed down from a king of France. He is human enough to get scared; and vain enough to be as ready as Lupin to flourish himself in the newspapers. A schoolboy hero for schoolboy readers. Leblanc took a dash of Doyle, a handful of Haggard, and a heap of Hornung (shades of Raffles; at the end of one of the novels Lupin contemplates going off to die for France in the Foreign Legion) and allowed none of it to mature. Even Lupin's love affair is boyishly unsexual. He added such gaiety and verve as only a Frenchman could. He did not mean to be taken seriously. Arsène Lupin was an engaging puppet. His adventures could excite, his wrath could momentarily chill, his chivalry could win him sympathy. When the reader finally grew away from childish things and put the puppet in its box, if it were taken out years later the joints showed, and they creaked.

Yet neither Arsène Lupin nor Maurice Leblanc can be totally written off on that account. To hold enthralled the boy in all of us is no mean service. Today it can be done only in space.

> Oliver Edwards, "Boys' Own Caper," in The Times, *London, November 4, 1965, p. 14.*

FURTHER READING

Haycraft, Howard, ed. *The Art of the Mystery Story: A Collection of Critical Essays,* pp. 62ff. New York: Simon and Schuster, 1946.
　　Numerous brief references to Leblanc throughout various essays on detective fiction collected in the book.

Hopkins, Mary Alden. Review of *The Teeth of the Tiger,* by Maurice Leblanc. *Publisher's Weekly* LXXXVI, No. 16 (17 October 1914): 1291.
　　Comments on the transformation of Arsène Lupin from criminal to detective.

Law, Graham. " 'Il s'agissait peut-être d'un roman policier': Leblanc, Macdonald, and Robbe-Grillet." *Comparative Literature* 40, No. 4 (Fall 1988): 335-57.
　　Examines the relationship between detective stories and postmodernist fiction, focusing on Maurice Leblanc's *Les dents du tigre,* Ross Macdonald's *The Three Roads,* and Alain Robbe-Grillet's *Les gommes.*

Review of *The Frontier,* by Maurice Leblanc. *The New York Times* (9 June 1912): 355.
　　Compares *The Frontier* favorably with Leblanc's Arsène Lupin stories.

Review of *The Frontier,* by Maurice Leblanc. *The Spectator* No. 4,365 (24 February 1912): 315.
　　Comments favorably on the psychological aspects of Leblanc's characterizations but questions the political wisdom of portraying a fictional conflict between France and Germany.

Additional coverage of Leblanc's life and career is contained in the following source published by Gale Research: *Contemporary Authors,* **Vol. 110.**

Edna St. Vincent Millay

1892-1950

(Also wrote under the pseudonym Nancy Boyd) American poet, playwright, short story writer, essayist, librettist, and translator.

For further information on Millay's career, see *TCLC,* Volume 4.

INTRODUCTION

Millay was a popular American poet whose best-known poems reflect the exuberant mood of social change that characterized the Jazz Age of the 1920s. Her verse is also notable for extending the boundaries of traditional subject matter for women writers and for portraying the feminine character with vastly expanded range and depth. Much of Millay's poetry is private and introspective in tone, exploring emotions associated with childhood, nature, love, and death. She has been deemed one of the most accomplished sonneteers of the twentieth century and praised for her use of classic sonnet structure to present modern themes.

Millay was born in Rockland, Maine. When she was eight years old, her parents divorced, and Millay lived with her two sisters and her mother. Encouraged by her mother, Millay began composing verse during her childhood. Several of her poems appeared in the children's magazine *St. Nicholas,* and she was first acclaimed as a poet at age twenty when her poem "Renascence" was published in 1912 in the anthology *The Lyric Year.* With a scholarship obtained partly through the notoriety she gained from the publication of "Renascence," Millay attended Vassar College, where she studied literature and theater. In 1917, following her graduation, she published her first collection, *Renascence, and Other Poems,* which received positive reviews and established her in the literary world. During the early 1920s Millay lived in Greenwich Village, where she continued writing and worked as an actress. During this time she was widely perceived as a free-spirited and rebellious social figure whose celebration of love and life is reflected in such works as *A Few Figs from Thistles* and *Second April.*

In 1923, following a nervous breakdown and a two-year sojourn in Europe, Millay published *The Ballad of the Harp-Weaver,* for which she was awarded the Pulitzer Prize in poetry. Her libretto for Deems Taylor's *The King's Henchman* was produced in 1926 and is considered an important contribution to American opera. Influenced by the escalation of global tensions in the years leading up to World War II, Millay began to address political and philosophical issues in such works as *The Buck in the Snow, and Other Poems* and the sonnet sequence "Epitaph for the Race of Man," included in *Wine from These Grapes.* Millay's works became increasingly political dur-

ing the 1930s, but her efforts at propaganda in such volumes as *Make Bright the Arrows: 1940 Notebook* and *The Murder at Lidice* were generally criticized as overly sentimental and less successful than her writing on personal subjects. During the final decade of her life, Millay was plagued by isolation, illness, and artistic stagnation. In 1944 she suffered a nervous breakdown that prevented her from writing for several years. Her final volume, *Mine the Harvest,* was completed shortly before her death from a heart attack in 1950 and published posthumously.

Much of Millay's verse, particularly that written during the early 1920s, has been characterized as an effective representation of the unconventional and exciting atmosphere of the Jazz Age. Her public image of independence and rebellion during this time was strengthened by the flippant tone of her volume *A Few Figs from Thistles.* This image was particularly evident in such poems as "Thursday," in which she playfully denigrated social conventions by depicting women who remain casual and unattached in love relationships—attitudes traditionally associated with men.

Despite the common perception of Millay's verse as lighthearted and brash, many of her poems are deeply introspective. "Renascence," for example, expresses the poet's spiritual awakening and is noted for its vivid nature imagery and childlike tone. Critics have also praised the exuberance and insight of such poems as "Journey," which celebrates nature, and "The Bean-Stalk," which portrays feelings of fear and euphoria associated with artistic expression. Recent critics have suggested that aspects of Millay's poetry evince an affinity with the dark themes and subject matter and anguished feminine perspectives in the works of such modern American poets as Anne Sexton and Sylvia Plath, noting that many of Millay's poems present images of vulnerability, suffering, and victimization. In "Moriturus," Millay portrayed a struggle between herself and the personification of death: "With his hand on my mouth / He shall drag me forth, / Shrieking to the south / And clutching at the north." Although early reviewers emphasized the poem's tone of defiance, later critics have asserted that Millay's language in this and other poems suggests an experience of violation and exploitation. "The Fitting," for example, depicts a woman's experience of rigid social conditioning and depersonalization through the metaphor of an uncomfortable dress alteration, and "Sonnets from an Ungrafted Tree" describes feelings of emptiness and disillusionment within an unsatisfying marriage.

In several works Millay addressed philosophical, social, and political themes. In her sonnet "Euclid Alone Has Looked on Beauty Bare," she associated the abstract concept of beauty in nature with the logical concepts of symmetry and perfection in mathematics. Her poem "Justice Denied in Massachusetts" bitterly decries the executions of Nicola Sacco and Bartolomeo Vanzetti, political radicals whose convictions on charges of murder and theft were widely protested. In the sonnet sequence "Epitaph for the Race of Man," Millay considered the dichotomy between humanity's penchant for self-destruction and its capacity for integrity and virtue. These and her other political works were considered an indication of her declining talents. Nevertheless, critics have assessed her best poems as significant reflections of an exciting and unconventional age in American culture and as authentic expressions of what William Lyon Phelps called the "mysterious flashes of inspiration which reveal truth apart from any conscious process of reasoning. . . . "

PRINCIPAL WORKS

"Renascence" (poetry) 1912; published in *The Lyric Year.*
Renascence, and Other Poems (poetry) 1917
A Few Figs from Thistles (poetry) 1920; [enlarged edition], 1922
*Aria da Capo (drama) 1921
*The Lamp and the Bell (drama) 1921
Second April (poetry) 1921
*Two Slatterns and a King (drama) 1921
The Ballad of the Harp-Weaver (poetry) 1922
The Harp-Weaver, and Other Poems (poetry) 1923

Distressing Dialogues [as Nancy Boyd] (essays) 1924
The King's Henchman (libretto) 1927
The Buck in the Snow, and Other Poems (poetry) 1928
Fatal Interview (poetry) 1931
Wine from These Grapes (poetry) 1934
Conversation at Midnight (poetry) 1937
Huntsman, What Quarry? (poetry) 1939
Make Bright the Arrows: 1940 Notebook (poetry) 1940
Collected Sonnets (poetry) 1941
Collected Lyrics (poetry) 1943
Letters of Edna St. Vincent Millay (letters) 1952
Mine the Harvest (poetry) 1954
Collected Poems (poetry) 1956
Edna St. Vincent Millay: Selected Poems (poetry) 1991

*These works were published as *Three Plays* in 1926.

CRITICISM

Harriet Monroe (essay date 1918)

[*As the founder and editor of* Poetry *magazine, Monroe was a key figure in the American "poetry renaissance" of the early twentieth century.* Poetry *was the first periodical devoted primarily to the works of new poets and to poetry criticism, and from 1912 until her death Monroe maintained an editorial policy of printing "the best English verse which is being written today, regardless of where, by whom, or under what theory of art it is written." In the following review, she praises several poems included in* Renascence, and Other Poems, *focusing on the title work.*]

Renascence and Other Poems is a very exceptional first book, a book which is achievement rather than promise. One would have to go back a long way in literary history to find a young lyric poet singing so freely and musically in such a big world. Almost we hear a thrush at dawn, discovering the ever-renewing splendor of the morning.

"Renascence" gave me the only thrill I received from Mr. Kennerley's 1912 anthology, *The Lyric Year.* It was so much the best poem in that collection that probably it's no wonder it didn't receive any one of the three prizes. Reading it once more, after six years' discipline in modern poetry, I am thrilled again. The surprise of youth over the universe, the emotion of youth at encountering inexplicable infinities—that is expressed in this poem, and it is a big thing to express. Moreover, it is expressed with a certain triumphant joy, the very mood of exultant youth; and the poet gets a certain freshness and variety into a measure often stilted. The poem is too compact for quotation—it should be read entire. Possibly its spiritual motive is summed up in the couplet:

> God, I can push the grass apart
> And lay my finger on Thy heart!

This poem is much the biggest thing in the book; indeed,

one almost sighs with fear lest life, closing in on this poet as on so many others, may narrow her scope and vision. It requires a rare spiritual integrity to keep one's sense of infinity against the persistent daily intrusions of the world, the flesh and the devil; but only the poet who keeps it through the years can sing his grandest song.

But even without **"Renascence"** the book would be exceptional. Not so much for **"Interim,"** though its emotion is poignantly sincere and expressed without affectation, as for some of the briefer lyrics. Such songs as **"Kin to Sorrow," "Tavern," "The Shroud,"** are perfect of their very simple and delicate kind; and one or two of the sonnets are admirable—**"Time does not Bring Relief"** and **"Bluebeard."** (pp. 167-68)

> *Harriet Monroe, in a review of "Renascence, and Other Poems," in* Poetry, *Vol. XIII, No. III, December, 1918, pp. 167-68.*

William Lyon Phelps   (essay date 1921)

[*An American critic and educator, Phelps was the author of influential critical studies and a prominent literary journalist whose criticism was noted for its enthusiastic tone. In the following review of* Renascence, and Other Poems *and* Second April, *he praises the high quality and restraint of Millay's writing and asserts that her apparent interest in death is typical of a young poet.*]

No one can read **Renascence** without believing in the author's lyrical gifts. The only indubitable sign of youth in her work is the writer's pre-occupation with the theme of death. Nothing is more normal than for a young poet to write about death—the contrast is romantic and sharply dramatic; it is the idea of death that appeals to youth.

The eighth sonnet in the volume, **"Second April,"** is thoroughly typical of Youth standing in contemplation before Death:

> And you as well must die, beloved
> And all your beauty stand you in no stead;
> This flawless, vital hand, this perfect head,
> This body of flame and steel, before the gust
> Of Death, or under his autumnal frost,
> Shall be as any leaf, be no less dead
> Than the first leaf that fell—this wonder fled,
> Altered, estranged, disintegrated, lost.
> Nor shall my love avail you in your hour.
> In spite of all my love, you will arise
> Upon that day and wander down the air
> Obscurely as the unattended flower,
> It mattering not how beautiful you were,
> Or how beloved above all else that dies.

In Tennyson's first volume, the details of dissolution appear again and again, and the thought of death shadows nearly every page. When a poet is old, he does not write about death so much or in his early manner. Death is too close; it has become a fact rather than an idea. To youth death is an astounding, amazing, romantic tragedy, and yet somehow remote from the writer; it may not cost as much worry as a dentist appointment or an ill-fitting gown; but when one is old, death seems more natural. In St. Paul's early letters, he talks about the second coming

of his Lord: in the last ones, about his own imminent departure.

The manner of approaching the grim subject changes with advancing years. In Tennyson's first volume, we find:

> The jaw is falling,
> The red cheek paling,
> The strong limbs failing;
> Ice with the warm blood mixing;
> The eyeballs fixing.

When he was 80, he wrote

> Sunset and evening star,
> And one clear call for me,
> And may there be no moaning of the bar
> When I put out to sea.

Thus to find the constantly recurring idea of death in the first two volumes by Miss Millay is quite the opposite of anything abnormal; I imagine, apart from her poetic gift, that she must be a natural, healthy-minded young girl. It is only fair to add that, in addition to the romantic idea of death as material for poetry, there are in the second volume beautiful tributes to the memory of a college friend, sincere expression of profound grief.

No matter how long we live, or how rich and varied our experience, Beauty always comes to us as a surprise; thus the reader will be happily struck more than a few times in these pages. But it is not surprising that they should be the work of youth; for all poets of quality achieve some perfection in early years. If one has reached the age of 22 without writing some admirable poetry, one might as well resign ambition to become distinguished as a poet. Undergraduate verse is probably on a higher level at this moment in America than it has ever been before; but the wonder is that so little of permanent value is produced.

The mysterious flashes of inspiration which reveal truth apart from any conscious process of reasoning—and which are the glory of poetry and music—appear more than once in the poems of Miss Millay. In **"Interim,"** for example:

> Not Truth, but Faith, it is
> That keeps the world alive. If all at once
> Faith were to slacken—that unconscious Faith
> Which must, I know, yet be the cornerstone
> Of all believing—birds now flying fearless
> Across would drop in terror to the earth;
> Fishes would drown; and the all-governing reins
> Would tangle in the frantic hands of God
> And the worlds gallop headlong to destruction!

The rhetorical flourish in the last line quoted is not common in these volumes; there is usually a restraint in expression rather remarkable, by which, of course, feeling gains in intensity. Extravagance of language, the prevailing fault in this nervous and excitable age, where everybody either swears or talks in italics, is not characteristic of the work of Miss Millay. It is pleasant also to see that the greedy attitude toward life, so frequently seen just now in novels and poems, is here absent; she loves life as an artist loves beauty, without wanting to eat it. There can be no true love of beauty if it be mingled with desire. One often falls into the fallacy of thinking one loves beauty when all one really loves is one's self. Consider the appalling picture presented in May Sinclair's "Waddington."

Remembering that the following poem appears in the earliest volume, we can have no doubt of our author's originality:

> If I should learn, in some quite casual way,
> That you, were gone, not to return again—
> Read from the back page of a paper, say,
> Held by a neighbor in a subway train,
> How at the corner of this avenue
> And such a street (so are the papers filled)
> A hurrying man—who happened to be you—
> At noon today had happened to be killed.
> I should not cry aloud—I could not cry
> Aloud, or wring my hands in such a place—
> I should but watch the station lights rush by
> With a more careful interest on my face,
> Or raise my eyes and read with greater care
> Where to store furs and how to treat the hair.

She has the poet's sight and the poet's hearing, which are more to be envied by us outsiders than any renown. She sees visions in nature beyond our range, and hears sounds to us inaudible. These extra powers give to many of her verses a delicate charm.

City Trees

> The trees along the city street,
> Save for the traffic and the rains,
> Would make a sound as thin and sweet
> As trees in country lanes.
>
> And people standing in their shade
> Out of a shower, undoubtedly
> Would hear such music as is made
> Upon a country tree.
>
> Oh, little leaves that are so dumb
> Against the shrieking city air,
> I watch you when the wind has come—
> I know what sound is there.

Miss Millay would not be a child of the twentieth century if she did not occasionally attempt to write in the vein of light cynicism and disillusion, in a manner recalling the less valuable work of Rupert Brooke. The little volume published this year, *A Few Figs from Thistles,* is exceedingly well named, and the result is one more proof of the truth of what you find in the Bible. These whimsies are graceful and amusing enough, but of no importance—not even to their author. A fig for such poetry!

William Lyon Phelps, "Edna St. Vincent Millay, Poet and Dramatist," in The New York Times Book Review, *October 16, 1921, p. 10.*

Carl Van Doren   (essay date 1923)

[*Van Doren is considered one of the most perceptive critics of the first half of the twentieth century. He worked for many years as a professor of English at Columbia University and served as literary editor and critic of the* Nation *and the* Century *during the 1920s. A founder of the Literary Guild and author or editor of several American literary histories, Van Doren was also a critically* acclaimed historian and biographer. In the excerpt below, he discusses Millay's poetry in relation to the renaissance of lyric poetry that took place in the United States during the early twentieth century, praising her verse for its lucid style, its representation of the mood of youthful rebellion against social conventions that characterized the 1920s, and its unique presentation of a woman's perspective on love and life.]

The little renaissance of poetry which there has been a hundred historians to scent and chronicle in the United States during the last decade flushed to a dawn in 1912. In that year was founded [*Poetry*], a magazine for the sole purpose of helping poems into the world; in that year was published an anthology which meant to become an annual, though, as it happened, another annual by another editor took its place the year following. The real poetical event of 1912, however, was the appearance in *The Lyric Year,* tentative anthology, of the first outstanding poem by Edna St. Vincent Millay. Who that then had any taste of which he can now be proud but remembers the discovery, among the numerous failures and very innumerous successes which made up the volume, of **"Renascence,"** by a girl of twenty whose name none but her friends and a lucky critic or two had heard? After wading through tens and dozens of rhetorical strophes and moral stanzas, it was like suddenly finding wings to come upon these lines:

> All I could see from where I stood
> Was three long mountains and a wood;
> I turned and looked another way,
> And saw three islands in a bay.
> So with my eyes I traced the line
> Of the horizon, thin and fine,
> Straight around till I was come
> Back to where I'd started from;
> And all I saw from where I stood
> Was three long mountains and a wood.

The diction was so plain, the arrangement so obvious, that the magic of the opening seemed a mystery; and yet the lift and turn of these verses were magical, as if a lark had taken to the air out of a dreary patch of stubble.

Nor did the poem falter as it went on. If it had the movement of a bird's flight, so had it the ease of a bird's song. The poet of this lucid voice had gone through a radiant experience. She had, she said with mystical directness, felt that she could touch the horizon, and found that she could touch the sky. Then infinity had settled down upon her till she could hear

> The ticking of Eternity.

The universe pressed close and crushed her, oppressing her with omniscience and omnisentience; all sin, all remorse, all suffering, all punishment, all pity poured into her, torturing her. The weight drove her into the cool earth, where she lay buried, but happy, under the falling rain.

> The rain, I said, is kind to come
> And speak to me in my new home.
> I would I were alive again
> To kiss the fingers of the rain,
> To drink into my eyes the shine
> Of every slanting silver line.

Suddenly came over her the terrible memory of the "multi-colored, multi-form, beloved" beauty she had lost by this comfortable death. She burst into a prayer so potent that the responding rain, gathering in a black wave, opened the earth above her and set her free.

> Ah! Up then from the ground sprang I
> And hailed the earth with such a cry
> As is not heard save from a man
> Who has been dead, and lives again.
> About the trees my arms I wound;
> Like one gone mad I hugged the ground;
> I raised my quivering arms on high;
> I laughed and laughed into the sky.

Whereupon, somewhat quaintly, she moralized her experience with the pride of youth finally arrived at full stature in the world.

> The heart can push the sea and land
> Farther away on either hand;
> The soul can split the sky in two,
> And let the face of God shine through.
> But East and West will pinch the heart
> That cannot keep them pushed apart;
> And he whose soul is flat—the sky
> Will cave in on him by and by.

"**Renascence,**" one of the loveliest of American poems, was an adventure, not an allegory, but it sounds almost allegorical because of the way it interpreted and distilled the temper which, after a long drought, was coming into American verse. Youth was discovering a new world, or thought it was. It had taken upon itself burdens of speculation, of responsibility, and had sunk under the weight. Now, on fire with beauty, it returned to joy and song.

Other things than joy and song, however, cut across the track of this little renaissance. There was a war. Youth—at least that part of it which makes poems—went out to fight, first with passion for the cause and then with contempt for the dotards who had botched and bungled. Gray Tyrtæuses might drone that here was a good war designed to end war, but youth meantime saw that it was dying in hordes and tried to snatch what ecstasy it could before the time should come when there would be no more ecstasy. Boys and girls who would otherwise have followed the smooth paths of their elders now questioned them and turned aside into different paths of life. Young men and maidens who would otherwise have expected little of love for years to come now demanded all that love offers, and demanded it immediately for fear it might come too late. The planet was reeling, or looked to be; all the settled orders were straining and breaking. Amid the hurly-burly of argument and challenge and recrimination a lyric had a good chance to be unheard; yet it was a lyrical hour, as it always is when the poet sees himself surrounded by swift moments hurrying to an end. Some sense of this in the air, even amid the hurly-burly, gave to the youth of the time that rash, impatient, wild ardor and insolence and cynicism which followed in such fleet succession, growing sharper as the war which was to have been good turned into the peace which was bound to be bad. (pp. 311-13)

The decade since the little renaissance began has created a kind of symbol for this irresponsible mood in the more

or less mythical Greenwich Village, where, according to the popular legend, art and mirth flourish without a care, far from the stupid duties of human life. No one so well as Miss Millay has spoken with the accents credited to the village.

> My candle burns at both ends;
> It will not last the night;
> But ah, my foes, and oh, my friends—
> It gives a lovely light!

Thus she commences in **"A Few Figs from Thistles."** And she continues with impish songs and rakish ballads and sonnets which laugh at the love which throbs through them. Suckling was not more insouciant than she is in **"Thursday":**

> And if I loved you Wednesday,
> Well, what is that to you?
> I do not love you Thursday—
> So much is true.
>
> And why you come complaining
> Is more than I can see.
> I loved you Wednesday—yes—but what
> Is that to me?

With what a friendliness for wild souls she tells the story of the singing woman "Whose mother was a leprechaun, whose father was a friar."

> In through the bushes, on any foggy day,
> My Da would come a-swishing of the drops away,
> With a prayer for my death and a groan for my birth,
> A-mumbling of his beads for all that he was worth.
>
> And there sit my Ma, her knees beneath her chin,
> A-looking in his face and a-drinking of it in,
> And a-marking in the moss some funny little saying
> That would mean just the opposite of all that he was praying!
>
> He taught me the holy-talk of Vesper and of Matin,
> He heard me my Greek and he heard me my Latin,
> He blessed me and crossed me to keep my soul from evil,
> And we watched him out of sight, and we conjured up the devil!
>
> Oh, the things I have n't seen and the things I have n't known,
> What with hedges and ditches till after I was grown,
> And yanked both ways by my mother and my father,
> With a 'Which would you better?' and a 'Which would you rather?'
>
> With him for a sire and her for a dam,
> What should I be but just what I am?

Speaking in this manner, Greenwich Village seems a long way from the village of Concord, heart of the old tradition, even though Hawthorne loved a faun when he met one, and Thoreau was something of a faun himself. In the classic village any such mixture as this of leprechaun and friar would have been kept as close a secret as possible, and conscience would have been set to the work of driving the leprechaun taint out. In Greenwich Village the friar is made to look a little comical, especially to the mother and daughter who conspire to have their fling behind his back.

This tincture of diablerie appears again and again in Miss Millay's verse, perhaps most of all in the candor with which she talks of love. She has put by the mask under which other poets who were women, apparently afraid for the reputation of their sex, have spoken as if they were men. She has put by the posture of fidelity which women in poetry have been expected to assume. She speaks with the voice of women who, like men, are thrilled, by the beauty of their lovers and are stung by desire; who know, however, that love does not always vibrate at its first high pitch, and so, too faithful to love to insist upon clinging to what has become half-love merely, let go without desperation. A woman may be fickle for fun, Miss Millay suggests in various poems wherein this or that girl teases her lover with the threat to leave him or the claim that she has forgotten him; but so may a woman show wisdom by admitting the variability and transience of love, as in this crystal sonnet:

> I know I am but summer to your heart,
> And not the full four seasons of the year;
> And you must welcome from another part
> Such noble moods as are not mine, my dear.
> No gracious weight of golden fruits to sell
> Have I, nor any wise and wintry thing;
> And I have loved you all too long and well
> To carry still the high sweet breast of spring.
> Wherefore I say: O love, as summer goes,
> I must be gone, steal forth with silent drums,
> That you may hail anew the bird and rose
> When I come back to you, as summer comes.
> Else will you seek, at some not distant time,
> Even your summer in another clime.

What sets Miss Millay's love-poems apart from almost all those written in English by women is the full pulse which, in spite of their gay impudence, beats through them. She does not speak in the name of forlorn maidens or of wives bereft, but in the name of women who dare to take love at the flood, if it offers, and who later, if it has passed, remember with exultation that they had what no coward could have had. Conscience does not trouble them, nor any serious division in their natures. No one of them weeps because she has been a wanton, no one of them because she has been betrayed. Rarely since Sappho has a woman voiced such delight in a lover's beauty as this:

> What's this of death, from you who never will
>   die?
> Think you the wrist that fashioned you in clay,
> The thumb that set the hollow just that way
> In your full throat and lidded the long eye
> So roundly from the forehead, will let lie
> Broken, forgotten, under foot some day
> Your unimpeachable body, and so slay
> The work he had been most remembered by?

Rarely since Sappho has a woman written as bravely as this.

> What lips my lips have kissed, and where, and
>   why,
> I have forgotten, and what arms have lain
> Under my head till morning; but the rain
> Is full of ghosts to-night, that tap and sigh
> Upon the glass and listen for reply;
> And in my heart there stirs a quiet pain
> For unremembered lads that not again
> Will turn to me at midnight with a cry.

In passages like these Miss Millay has given body and vesture to a sense of equality in love; to the demand by women that they be allowed to enter the world of adventure and experiment in love which men have long inhabited. But Miss Millay does not, like any feminist, argue for that equality. She takes it for granted, exhibits it in action, and turns it into beauty.

Beauty, not argument, is, after all, Miss Millay's concern and goal. She can be somewhat metaphysical about it, as in her contention that

> Euclid alone has looked on Beauty bare.
> Let all who prate of Beauty hold their peace,
> And lay them prone upon the earth and cease
> To ponder on themselves, the while they stare
> At nothing, intricately drawn nowhere
> In shapes of shifting lineage.

For the most part, however, she stands with those who love life and persons too wholly to spend much passion upon anything abstract. She loves the special countenance of every season, the hot light of the sun, gardens of flowers with old, fragrant names, the salt smell of the sea along her native Maine coast, the sound of sheep-bells and dripping eves and the unheard sound of city trees, the homely facts of houses in which men and women live, tales of quick deeds and eager heroisms, the cool, kind love of young girls for one another, the color of words, the beat of rhythm. The shining clarity of her style does not permit her to work the things she finds beautiful into tapestried verse; she will not ask a song to carry more than it can carry on the easiest wings; but in all her graver songs and sonnets she serves beauty in one way or another. Now she affirms her absolute loyalty to beauty; now she hunts it out in unexpected places; most frequently of all she buries it with some of the most exquisite dirges of her time.

These returning dirges and elegies and epitaphs are as much the natural speech of Miss Millay as is her insolence of joy in the visible and tangible world. Like all those who most love life and beauty, she understands that both are brief and mortal. They take her round and round in a passionate circle: because she loves them so ardently she knows they cannot last, and because she knows they cannot last she loves them the more ardently while they do. Dispositions such as hers give themselves to joy when their vitality is at its peaks; in their lower hours they weep over the graves of loveliness which are bound to crown their courses. Having a high heart and a proud creed, Miss Millay leaves unwept some graves which other poets and most people water abundantly but she is stabbed by the essential tragedy and pity of death. Thus she expresses the tragic powerlessness of those who live to hold those who die.

> Nor shall my love avail you in your hour.
> In spite of all my love, you will arise
> Upon that day and wander down the air
> Obscurely as the unattended flower,
> It mattering not how beautiful you were,
> Or how belovèd above all else that dies.

Thus she expresses the pitiful knowledge which the living have that they cannot help the dead:

> Be to her, Persephone,
> All the things I might not be;
> Take her head upon your knee.
> She that was so proud and wild,
> Flippant, arrogant and free,
> She that had no need of me,
> Is a little lonely child
> Lost in Hell,—Persephone,
> Take her head upon your knee;
> Say to her, "My dear, my dear,
> It is not so dreadful here."

Are these only the accents of a minor poet, crying over withered roses and melted snows? Very rarely do minor poets strike such moving chords upon such universal strings. Still more rarely do merely minor poets have so much power over tragedy and pity, and yet in other hours have equal power over fire and laughter. (pp. 313-16)

> *Carl Van Doren, "Youth and Wings," in* The Century, *Vol. 106, No. 2, June, 1923, pp. 311-16.*

Allen Tate   (essay date 1931)

[*An American critic closely associated with the Agrarians and the New Critics, Tate attacked the tradition of Western philosophy which he felt had alienated persons from themselves, one another, and nature, while he considered literature the principal form of knowledge and revelation. In the following review of* Fatal Interview, *Tate praises Millay's skillful use of Shakespearean form, sharply defined imagery, and classical symbols. He considers Millay the spokesperson for a generation but suggests that her poetic achievement is limited by her failure to present a "comprehensive philosophy."*]

More than any other living American poet, with the exception possibly of T. S. Eliot, Miss Millay has puzzled her critics. Contrary to the received opinion, her poetry is understood even less than Eliot's, in spite of its greater simplicity, its more conventional meters and its closer fulfilment of the popular notion of what the language of poetry should be. Of contemporary poets whose excellence is beyond much dispute, she is the most difficult to appraise. She is the most written about, but her critics are partisans: they like her too well or not enough. There is something like worship here, patronage or worse there; both views are unjust; and what is worse, they are misleading. Less interested readers of her verse are tired of violent opinion; the more skeptical, perhaps, are put off by her popularity in an age of famously indifferent taste.

This, too, is misleading. Apart from her merit as a poet,

Miss Millay is, not at all to her discredit, the spokesman of a generation. It does not behoove us to enquire how she came to express the feelings of the literary generation that seized the popular imagination from about 1917 to 1925. It is a fact that she did, and in such a way as to remain as its most typical poet. Her talent, with its diverting mixture of solemnity and levity, won the enthusiasm of a time bewildered intellectually and moving unsteadily towards an emotional attitude of its own. It was the age of The Seven Arts, of the old Masses, of the Provincetown Theatre, of the figure and disciples of Randolph Bourne. It has been called the age of experiment and liberation; there is still experiment, but no one is liberated; and that age is now dead.

Miss Millay helped to form that generation, and was formed by it. But she has survived her own time. Her statement about those times, in *A Few Figs from Thistles* and *Second April,* was not, taken philosophically, very profound; morally, it has been said, it did perceptible damage to our young American womanhood, whose virgin impatience competed noisily with the Armistice and the industrial boom. There were suicides after *Werther* and seductions after *Don Juan.* Neither Byron nor Miss Millay is of the first order of poets. They are distinguished examples of the second order, without which literature could not bear the weight of Dante and Shakespeare, and without which poetry would dry up of insensibility.

Being this kind of poet, Miss Millay was not prepared to give to her generation a philosophy in comprehensive terms; her poetry does not define the break with the nineteenth century. This task was left to the school of Eliot, and it was predictable that this school should be—except by young men who had the experience to share Eliot's problem—ignored and misunderstood. Eliot penetrated to the fundamental structure of the nineteenth-century mind and showed its breakdown. Miss Millay assumed no such profound alteration of the intelligence because, I suppose, not being an intellect but a sensibility, she was not aware of it. She foreshadowed an age without bringing it to terms. Taking the vocabulary of nineteenth-century poetry as pure as you will find it in Christina Rossetti, and drawing upon the stock of conventional symbolism accumulated from Drayton to Patmore, she has created, out of shopworn materials, a distinguished personal idiom: she has been able to use the language of the preceding generation to convey an emotion peculiar to her own.

The generation of decadence—Moody, Woodberry and Louise Imogene Guiney—had more than Miss Millay has; but she has all that they had which was not dead. By making their language personal she has brought it back to life. This is her distinction. It is also her limitation. As a limitation it is not peculiar to her, her age or any age, but common to all; it is the quality that defines Collins and Gray, and, in the next century, poets like the Rossettis and Tennyson. Poets of this second order lack the power of creation in the proper sense in which something like a complete world is achieved, either in the vast, systematic vision of Milton, or in the allusive power of Webster and Shakespeare where, backed only by a piece of common action, an entire world is set up in a line or even in a single phrase. In these poets the imaginative focus is less on the personal emotion than on its substructure, an order of intellectual life, and thus their very symbolism acquires not only a heightened significance but an independent existence of its own. Not so with Miss Millay; we feel that she never penetrates to the depth of her symbols, but uses them chiefly as a frame of reference, an adornment to the tale. It has been frequently and quite justly remarked that Miss Millay uses her classical symbols perhaps better than any other living poet; we should add, I believe, that she uses them conventionally better. She takes them literally, subtracting from them always only what serves her metaphor; whereas even a modern like Yeats is capable, in his sonnet "Leda," of that violent addition to the content of the symbol as he finds it which is the mark of great poetry.

Miss Millay's success with stock symbolism is precariously won. I have said that she is not an intellect but a sensibility: if she were capable of a profound analysis of her imagery she might not use it: such an analysis might disaffect her with the style that she so easily assumed, without necessarily leading her, as Yeats was led in mid-career, to create a new style of her own. The beautiful final sonnet of the sequence [in *Fatal Interview*] is a perfect specimen of her talent, and it is probably the finest poem she has written:

> Oh, sleep forever in the Latmian cave,
> Mortal Endymion, darling of the moon!
> Her silver garments by the senseless wave
> Shouldered and dropped and on the shingle
>   strewn,
> Her fluttering hand against her forehead
>   pressed,
> Her scattered looks that trouble all the sky,
> Her rapid footsteps running down the west—
> Of all her altered state, oblivious lie!
> Whom earthen you, by deathless lips adored,
> Wild-eyed and stammering to the grasses thrust,
> And deep into her crystal body poured
> The hot and sorrowful sweetness of the dust:
> Whereof she wanders mad, being all unfit
> For mortal love, that might not die of it.

We have only to compare this, magnificent as it is, with Mr. Yeat's "Leda" to see the difference between the two kinds of symbol that I have described. The difference is first of all one of concentration and intensity; and finally a difference between an accurate picture of an emotion and an act of the imagination:

> A sudden blow: the great wings beating still
> Above the staggering girl, her thighs caressed
> By the dark webs, her nape caught in his bill,
> He holds her helpless breast upon his breast.
>
> How can those terrified vague fingers push
> The feathered glory from her loosening thighs?
> And how can body, laid in that white rush
> But feel the strange heart beating where it lies?
> A shudder in the loins engenders there
> The broken wall, the burning roof and tower
> And Agamemnon dead.
>
>   Being so caught up,
> So mastered by the brute blood of the air,
> Did she put on his knowledge with his power

Before the indifferent beak could let her drop?

In an age which, in Mr. Pound's phrase, has "demanded an image"; an age which has searched for a new construction of the mind, and has, in effect, asked every poet for a chart of salvation, it has been forgotten that one of the most valuable kinds of poetry may be deficient in imagination, and yet be valuable for the manner in which it meets its own defect. Miss Millay not only has given the personality of her age, but has preserved it in the purest traditional style. There are those who will have no minor poets; these Miss Millay does not move. The others, her not too enthusiastic but perhaps misguided partisans, have seen too much of their own personalities in her verse to care whether it is great poetry or not; so they call it great.

It is doubtful if all of Miss Millay's previous work put together is worth the thin volume of these fifty-two sonnets. At no previous time has she given us so sustained a performance. Half of the sonnets, perhaps all but about fifteen, lack distinction of emotional quality. None is deficient in an almost final technique. From first to last every sonnet has its special rhythm and sharply defined imagery; they move like a smooth machine, but not machine-like, under the hand of a masterly technician. The best sonnets would adorn any of the great English sequences. There is some interesting analysis to be made of Miss Millay's skillful use of the Shakespearean form, whose difficult final couplet she has mastered, and perhaps is alone in having mastered since Shakespeare.

The serious, austere tone of her later work must not deceive us: she is the poet of ten years ago. She has been from the beginning the one poet of our time who has successfully stood athwart two ages; she has put the personality of her age into the intellect and style of the preceding one, without altering either. Of her it may be said, as of the late Elinor Wylie, that properly speaking she has no style, but has subtly transformed to her use the indefinable average of poetic English. We have seen the limitations of this order of talent. When the personal impulse lags in a mind that cannot create a symbol and invent a style, we get the

---

pastiche of *The Buck in the Snow:* the defects of such a talent are defects of taste, while the defects of Blake are blunders. Let us say no more of it. Miss Millay is one of our most distinguished poets, and one that we should do well to misunderstand as little as possible. (pp. 335-36)

Allen Tate, "Miss Millay's Sonnets," in The New Republic, Vol. LXVI, No. 857, May 6, 1931, pp. 335-36.

James McBride Dabbs   (essay date 1938)

[*Dabbs was an American critic who wrote primarily about the fiction and culture of the American South. In the following essay, he discusses the major conflicts Millay explored in her poetry, and asserts that her verse is weakened by its personal and rhetorical tone.*]

"We make out of the quarrel with others, rhetoric, but of the quarrel with ourselves, poetry." Though Edna St. Vincent Millay has with the passing years achieved a weightier accent, she has written an increasingly large proportion of rhetoric. If Yeats is correct, she is more and more inclined to quarrel with others.

She was never inclined to quarrel with herself, though from the first she had sufficient reason. **"Renascence,"** which made her famous at twenty, was, and is, a remarkable poem, both in its lyricism and in its mysticism. But, for an understanding of her later development, her tendency toward rhetoric, its significance lies in the duality of its mystic vision. The two pictures do not fuse. Suddenly conscious of the misery of man, the poet is crushed beneath the weight, and dies. From this death she is revived by a vision of natural beauty, so convincing that at last she cries out:

> God, I can push the grass apart
> And lay my finger on Thy heart!

But how does this conclusion follow? Only, it seems to me, by an evasion of the problem the poet herself set. The sufferings of man are not resolved in the beauty of nature; they are forgotten. The poet's renewed life springs up without root, and is therefore destined to wither soon. "What we live by we die by," says Robert Frost. And what we die by we live by. But here the poet finds renewed life in something unrelated to her death. If anyone urges that the poem represents merely the development of a mood, a development to be judged only by itself, I reply that the development of one mood may be sentimental, the development of another honest, and that certainly, in the light of Miss Millay's career, the development here is, as we shall see, symptomatic. There is revealed here a fissure that cuts straight through the spiritual life: on one side tortured man, on the other a peaceful God. The poet flees from man to God. This is to flee from oneself. A greater poet would have remained to quarrel with himself until he should have made one picture out of the two. Avoiding for some reason this quarrel, Miss Millay has been forced inevitably into a quarrel with the world.

She kept this quarrel hidden for a while by her enthusiasm for even the shining fragments of life. She closes **"Renascence"** in an unjustifiably happy mood. In many of her later poems, she recounts with such force the struggle of her will with the world, and laments with such poignancy its frustration, that we are apt to overlook the incompleteness of her vision. By the time that she reaches *The Buck in the Snow,* however, her native enthusiasm is waning, and the inevitable somberness of her confused quarrel with the world is coming to the surface.

But the false optimism of **"Renascence"** is revealed here and there much earlier than this. The introductory poem to *Second April* contains these lines:

> To what purpose, April, do you return again?
> Beauty is not enough. . . .
>
> Life in itself
> Is nothing.

In so short a time she who had fled from the pain of human life to sing of the beauty of April has been disillusioned.

For that matter, the concluding vision of **"Renascence"** is denied in the same volume, in **"Interim."** Here, in the breathlessness of sudden insight, the poet sees even the natural universe unrolled before her in chaos and doom, and in the blackness of that vision cries out:

> Not Truth, but Faith, it is
> That keeps the world alive.

Truth has become black and faith is false. This is the inevitable reaction from the unjustified optimism of **"Renascence,"** and is itself as unjustifiable, as incomplete, as romantic as that. Allen Tate, though he does not mention Miss Millay, describes very well her development in a discussion of what he calls romantic poetry: "There is the assumption that Truth is indifferent or hostile to the desires of men . . . that, Truth being known at last in the form of experimental science, it is intellectually impossible to maintain illusion any longer, at the same time that it is morally impossible to assimilate Truth.

"The poet revolts from Truth; that is, he defies the cruel and naturalistic world to break him if it can; and he is broken." "The whole thing," says Ludwig Lewisohn, speaking of Miss Millay's career, "in its totality is like a medieval morality."

This spiritual fissure, which divides the supposedly single world of **"Renascence,"** into two worlds, and which, if it could have been recognized by the poet and made the cause of a quarrel with herself, might have kept her more of a poet and less of a rhetorician, appears in Miss Millay's poetry in the form of several unresolved conflicts. First and basic is the one already suggested: man *versus* nature, with God on the side of nature. In such a conflict man is bound to fail. Wordsworth was conscious of no such dichotomy. He felt in nature

> A sense sublime
> Of something far more deeply interfused,
> Whose dwelling is the light of setting suns,
> . . . and in the mind of man.

And he heard oftentimes "The still, sad music of humanity." There is, indeed, in one of Miss Millay's poems, **"The Little Hill,"** an attempt to bridge this chasm between the calm of nature and the passion of man, but it is a rather sentimental attempt, in which the poet attributes to the "little hill" feelings that seem to be hers alone. There are two other poems that represent nature as a refuge, however poor, for the man who has failed: in Sonnet X, of the unnamed series in *The Harp-Weaver,* the poet is shown as returning from inconstant love to the sullen but changeless rocks and skies (they were not sullen in **"Renascence"**); and in the opening poem of *Wine from These Grapes* she represents man as returning, after the failure of wife and friend, to the warm but uncomprehending woods. For a moment in this volume she touches a quiet wisdom, when, in the lines **"From a Train Window,"** she sees even the rickety graveyard on the hill in a neighborly light: "As if after all, the earth might know what it is about." But on the next page, in **"The Fawn,"** she reveals herself as poignantly conscious of her rejection by nature: she does not belong. A poem to set beside this is Robert Frost's "Two Look at Two," in which the lovers, though separated from the buck and doe, are accepted by them, and are made happy in the certainty that earth returns their love. In general, in her last volume, Miss Millay represents the universe as indifferent to man. This is essentially what she said at first, in **"Renascence."**

A second conflict foreshadowed by **"Renascence"** and revealed throughout her work is that between human love and beauty. In the human love—the sense of humanity—that revealed to the young poet the pain of life there was hidden a tragic beauty. Unable, however, for some reason, to realize this, she turned from the pain to the "multicolored, multiform, Beloved beauty" of nature. In **"The Concert"** (*The Harp-Weaver*) she turns away from love, which, she says, is of the body, to live awhile in the abstract beauty of music. This conflict between love and beauty appears from time to time in *Fatal Interview.* The poet is ashamed she has brought beauty—her lover—to terms, and more ashamed that she cannot let him go. Again, she says beauty has never heard of love. But in Sonnet XLV, though she insists that beauty continues to exist despite the passing of love, she seems to admit that beauty came because of love. Unfortunately, however, this cause-and-effect relation between love and beauty is not generally perceived. Love is to her too much a function of the practical will, an endeavor in which the will either succeeds or fails; too much a quarrel with others, an occasion for rhetoric. She needs more of that imaginative insight that teaches the poet "to discover immortal moods in mortal desires, an undecaying hope in our trivial ambitions, a divine love in sexual passion."

In her last volume, she has turned clean away from untrustworthy man (whom, as we shall see, she has never trusted) to impersonal, uncomprehending Beauty. Though the poetry is good, the attitude is desperate, and leads nowhere; indeed, she revealed it for what it was years before in the introductory poem to *Second April:* "Beauty is not enough."

We may admit the excellence of her famous sonnet on Euclid and yet point out that it too suggests the division that cuts through her life. Beauty is mathematical; beauty is inhuman. This, as in **"The Concert,"** is a flight from human

life instead of the discovery of immortal moods in mortal desires.

There is a third conflict apparent in **"Renascence,"** which, though not very important in that poem, assumes importance in Miss Millay's work as a whole. It is the implied conflict between the poet's fear of life in general and her intense delight in the sensory aspect of life, in sensation. It is probably this delight in sensation that has caused many to admire her for her love of life. If we consider what this phrase means as applied to Miss Millay, we shall understand better the conflict implied in **"Renascence"** between the fear and the love of life.

Miss Millay's love of life is largely practical. On the imaginative or spiritual level it is extremely weak. She has a desperate will for life (Harriet Monroe called **"Renascence"** a poem of desperate faith); it is this that has made her the spokesman of such a large audience, most of whom have, in greater or less degree, this same practical will. She is not noted, however, for that love which is understanding and that understanding which is love; for that detached love which is the mark of the artist, and of every man in so far as he is an artist. Nor, indeed, has she a quality that belongs to all love at its best—trust. She could never say with Job, "Though he slay me, yet will I trust in him." Even in her love of nature she is at times possessive. In the oft-quoted poem **"God's World,"** she expresses the desire, not to behold the world, but to establish herself among and in things.

> That gaunt crag
> To crush!   To lift the lean of that black bluff!

"A poetry of the will," says Allen Tate, "is a poetry of sensation, for the poet surrenders to his sensations of the object in his effort to identify himself with it, and to own it."

As to that aspect of the love of life which is revealed in the love of persons, this, in Miss Millay, is shot through with distrust. There is rarely, if ever, relaxation and peace. "Even in the moment of our earliest kiss," she says, I knew our love was doomed. (Why? Because, being country-bred, she knew that the frost would blacken the leaves. This identification of spiritual and physical life is common in Miss Millay.) Neither Emerson nor Hawthorne were great lovers surely, but both were far nearer wisdom than this, when they discerned immortal moods in mortal desires; Dante found in his love for Beatrice the love that moves the sun and all the stars. Again, love has not come to her, like a gracious fate prepared from the beginning; she has sought for it, striven for it, been ready at any moment to desert one lover for another.

> Oh, think not I am faithful to a vow!
> Faithless am I save to love's self alone.

But what is love's self alone? One suspects that it is no more than the poet's will to be loved. She takes love, and holds it, by main force, in her hands. This is the dominant tone of *Fatal Interview;* and this desperate will to have her way is called the love of life. It would appear that Miss Millay has never learned to let go with the hands. She does not trust love: it will fly away. Of course it will—from anyone who does not trust it. Or it will die. Of course—unless we give it life.

There is too constantly in her love poems a fear of being trapped by love, of losing her freedom in love. She wishes to remain free of love, while having love as something to use, to make free with. Apparently she wishes to be loved without loving in return. If she were willing to accept absolute freedom—but she is not. A late poem, **"On the Wide Heath,"** tells of the traveler who returns to his loveless, unlovely home because it is "Too lonely, to be free." She does not understand freedom in love, being too concerned for the wreaking of her individual will upon the world.

Distrustful of human relationships, she is also distrustful of time as "a bringer of new things." "We'll to the woods no more," she cries, "The laurels all are cut." As for the cause of her distrust,

> It is that a wind too strong
> Bent my back when I was young,
> It is that I fear the rain
> Lest it blister me again.

She has a sulky mind, she says, slow to forget the tempest in the new morning light. In **"Pueblo Pot,"** she hears the voice of wisdom telling her that broken beauty cannot be consoled, it must be made whole. ("The ruins of time," said Blake, "build mansions in eternity.") But she fears wisdom, and turns, but now in vain, to consider the shards. "I was ever a ten-o'clock scholar at the school of experience," she says. And it is true. She has been so busy telling life what she wanted that she has only rarely heard life telling her what it can give.

Though it is partly her scorn of those conventional people who sacrifice the full-bodied present to an abstract future, it is more largely her distrust of the future that makes Miss Millay emphasize the moment. For if she trusted time, and life, and let herself go, she would find in the moment both future and past: the moment would take on something of the quality of timelessness. Instead of this, she grasps at the moment as she does at life; and of course the moment slips away—which is what she expected. In her attempt to seize life, she has merely succeeded in breaking it to pieces. But, for that matter, the very attempt to seize it indicates that it is already broken to pieces, or at least divided into spiritual and physical and so destroyed. The physical quality of a moment can be known sensuously, can be grasped, which means it will escape the grasp; the complete moment, physical and spiritual, can be known only imaginatively, and thus known it remains. Trying to grasp time, Miss Millay becomes time's slave. If I loved you Wednesday, then I do not love you Thursday, for now on Thursday Wednesday is gone. And, indeed, I could not be sure even on Wednesday that I loved you, for thousands of days, each with its possible love, still lay before me, and, about these,

> How shall I know, unless I go
> To Cairo or Cathay . . . ?

This is to break time up into an infinite series of moments and out of these to construct, if possible, life. It is not possible, for life is not a mathematical sum but a poetic experience, the moments of which are not fractions but symbols of the whole. Life is not quantitative, but qualitative. Oc-

Millay on August 29, 1912, the day Caroline B. Dow heard her read "Renascence" and subsequently helped her to secure a scholarship to Vassar College.

casionally Miss Millay realizes this, as in such a poem as **"Recuerdo."** Usually, however, she falls into the same error against which she revolted, and reduces life to an abstraction.

Distrusting life, grasping at time, feeling the moments slip like sand between her fingers, Miss Millay lives continually in the presence of death, fears it, and struggles, though she knows futilely, against it. Occasionally she is so weary that she longs for death. Generally, however, her attitude is one of rebellion. It is in this attitude that she becomes most rhetorical. Her practical will, continually thwarted by death, turns inward and laments its thwarting. "Rhetoric," says W. B. Yeats, "is the will trying to do the work of the imagination." Miss Millay seems to some very brave in her refusal to be resigned to death, but not very wise. For in the actual world death occurs regardless of our will. Rhetoric is useless against it. Only poetry, only the imagination, illumining the subject from within, understanding it, can avail anything. Mankind generally has understood this and has written its dirges with music.

In spite of all her talk about death, Miss Millay understands, for a poet, far too little of what she is talking about.

She attempts to make up for this lack of knowledge by intensity of will. She senses death too much, sees it too little.

This emphasis upon sensation, upon the material side of life, has fooled many of her admirers into the belief that she is intensely alive. But intensity of sensation is a quality of decadence as well as of health. Miss Millay has been called a belated Elizabethan: the phrase refers, at least in part, to the concrete, earthy quality of her writing. In one of her happier, early elegies she wrote:

> She is happy where she lies
> With the dust upon her eyes.

But the Elizabethan, from our point of view truly young, wrote this:

> Upon my buried body lie
> Lightly, gentle earth.

The earth itself is imagined as sentient and sympathetic. A child is not disturbed that its mother's body lies in the grave; its mother is in heaven. There is little childlikeness in either Miss Millay's experience or memory of life, or in her thought of death. Take the poem **"Spring in the Garden"**: the lupine and monkshood pierce the earth, but the dead lies numb and stupid from his first winter underground. Anyone who has lived must admit that the body is important, but this is to make the person the body alone, and surely we do not think of persons like that. Miss Millay is not imagining death; not giving it spiritual form. She is breaking her will against death—and that is merely suicide.

Indeed, for Miss Millay, the physical world is more of a trap for the spirit than a means of spiritual life. (When the rhetorician writes, says Yeats, it is "The struggle of the fly in marmalade"—or on flypaper.) This appears most in her love poems, especially in the sonnet sequence *Fatal Interview.* Though there is evidence of passion here—"desire touched with imagination"—there is more evidence of simple desire. When we consider other subjects than sexual love, we find that, though earth—the physical, the felt—is important, it is well balanced by something more than earth. Now, in so far as we find life physical, we shall find death physical; in so far as we find life more than physical, we shall find death more than physical. It is the fact that Miss Millay finds life so much more than physical that makes unwarranted her black picture of death. Angered by the thwarting of her will—and death is surely a thwarting of the will—she attacks the disorder of death rhetorically instead of attempting to reduce it to order imaginatively. If only she would ponder her own experience, she would find that something is saved from the wreck. I shall mention a few of the poems that suggest this. She still has something of Pao-Chin, though Pao-Chin himself may be dead. "Immortal page after page" of the poet remains. Love is something more than the physical. Love will outwit time, its greatest foe. Or, if time does take love away, it will change it into "a jewel cold and pure." Death, though he conquers at last, is shaken by love. Finally, the two great lines:

> How far from home in a world of mortal burdens
> Is Love, that may not die, and is forever young!

But if this is so, where is the home of love? Miss Millay knows too much not to know more. Important answers lie in her own experience, but instead of asking herself questions she denounces and laments, instead of quarreling with herself she quarrels with the world. She demands of life why it thwarts her, instead of asking herself how it thwarts her.

Yet, though Miss Millay has worried life, and herself, with the wrong questions, she has come slowly, by means of her sensibility, to at least a deeper sympathy with men. Her self-pity is more and more a pity for mankind. In *Wine from These Grapes,* says Louis Untermeyer, "the poet turns from prettiness and the pangs of romantic love, concerning herself with the unhappy, bewildered, self-torturing human spirit." More and more she sees herself as symbolic, her troubles as "the troubles of our proud and angry dust." This is the road that opened to her at the very beginning, in **"Renascence"**; unfortunately she has followed it hesitatingly and unwillingly. In the human pity that at least in part motivated that poem, even in the self-pity of lesser poems, she had found an attitude which, if it could have been boldly adhered to, would have brought an inspiring sense of the oneness of men. "For sudden the worst turns the best to the brave." But she was not able boldly to adhere to it; indeed, as we have already seen, in **"Renascence"** she fled from it. In Sonnet IV, in the same volume, oppressed by earth's pain, she longs to gather up her little gods and go. In the poem **"To the Wife of a Sick Friend,"** she expresses pity, but a separate and ineffective pity. A modern sensibility, she feels the grief of life beating upon her, but her life is too separate, too uncertain of any place in the world (too modern), for her to move outward toward others on this tide of grief. The same attitude appears in **"The Anguish,"** and, slightly modified, in **"Hangman's Oak,"** both of which relate to the Sacco-Vanzetti case. The latter poem expresses the sense of the oneness of life, but it is a oneness, not in life, but in apathetic peace, in death. In another poem she is filled with pity for that "blithe spirit," the skylark, so lost in this hard world. Here are the tears that one must feel for life, but where is the strength that should follow the identification with life that the tears suggest?

Once or twice Miss Millay touches this strength. Winter brings into view, she says, the summer-hidden hill. Again, distress makes men neighborly. In Sonnet XI, of **"Epitaph for the Race of Man,"** she tells of how a man, ruined by disaster,

> . . . saw as in a not unhappy dream
> The kindly heads against the horrid sky,
> And scowled, and cleared his throat and spat,
> and wept—

moved to tears both by his own disaster and by the suddenly recognized goodness of man. In the poem **"To a Young Girl"** Miss Millay speaks of the wisdom of weeping, but it is all idyllic and picturesque, and she doesn't believe deeply what she says. As for herself, she wants to weep but cannot. Why not? She does not say. But I should guess it is because of our modern pride, our desire to be self-sufficient and free.

The strength of Miss Millay's poetry becomes plainly evident through her reading voice. It is, paradoxically, a powerful pathos. It is also a plangent pathos. She is evidently "making an endless battle without hope." But her voice also reveals the weakness of her poetry. It is a personal poetry. Unfortunately in such a poetry one can disagree personally with the poet. This is only another way of saying that Miss Millay's poetry leans toward rhetoric, and one is tempted to agree or disagree with the view she expresses as that view confirms or refutes one's own opinion. We agree with an argument; we do not agree with poetry. Now, we tend to take Miss Millay personally, not only, as I have been saying throughout this paper, because of her inclination to quarrel, like a rhetorician, with the world, but also because of her individual manner of speech. She has attained, I said, a weightier accent; but on which level, the rhetorical or the poetical?

Because of the general similarity of their views, it may be illuminating to compare for a moment Miss Millay and A. E. Housman. In spite of the apparently personal quality of his poems, Housman is far more dramatic: his own voice is veiled and transmuted by a complex screen, and comes to us, not as his own, but somewhat as the voice of life. J. B. Priestley points out several dramatic elements in Housman's poems: they are moods presented "in a more or less definite atmosphere, on a more or less consistent plan"; a Roman soldier, a sort of shadow against the sky of the Shropshire Lad, stands vaguely in the background; in their natural speech we seem to hear the voice of the people ("It is this that makes his mournful folk seem to cry from the heart, as few others do in the poetry of our time"); and their many references to death are in a definite tradition (the classic instead of the romantic).

Miss Millay's voice is not transmuted by any such complex screen, partly because this screen is not available to her (Housman was a thorough classical scholar), partly because she does not wish to use it. What screen has she had for modifying her personal voice? From the first she has had the very definite music of song, the formal quality of which served as a screen, but it is significant that with the passage of time she has begun to use also the more indefinite music of the speaking voice. She has, like Housman, a command of the language of the people ("What's out to-night is lost") but she relies more heavily upon her own personal language. Why does she not use more extensively these modes of speech that at least would modify her own personal voice? Because it is her own personal voice—her will—that she wishes to express: her poetry is largely the expression of her rebellious or frustrated will. There is in Housman's poetry an acceptance of life foreign to Miss Millay's. His poetry consequently describes, as Charles Williams says, "a single hard curve down to death." Since he does not quarrel with life, he does not arouse in his readers the desire to quarrel with him.

But even had Miss Millay been willing (or able) to transfer her quarrel from the world to herself, and so hide her personal voice behind an imaginative screen, she would not have had available the screen that Housman had. It is probably safe to say that for both Housman and Miss Millay the Christian tradition had generally broken down. Housman had available, however, in the Stoic philosophy

and the classical tradition, with which as a scholar he was acquainted, a scheme of reference in which he could lose, and find, himself. Miss Millay was a neo-pagan, set adrift from the modern wreck of Christianity, but unaware of any other tradition, and tossing rudderless on the open sea. There was little left for her but to be personal.

Her imagery of death is an illustration. After discussing Housman's classical imagery of death, Mr. Priestley adds: "But most of our poets, and indeed rhetoricians, have very naturally taken the medieval or romantic, as opposed to the classical, the Christian as opposed to the pagan, view of the matter." The medieval emphasis upon the material body of death was by way of contrast to man's immortal spirit. But Miss Millay has lost the central faith, the belief in the spirit's value, and retains merely a bit of the machinery by means of which the medieval mind intensified the value of the spirit. It is a striking fragment, but being a fragment it is senseless.

Perhaps, more than anything else, it is the poverty of her tradition that has so often forced Miss Millay, in spite of her splendid technical equipment, on to the rhetorical plane. "We make out of the quarrel with ourselves, poetry." But what is this quarrel with ourselves? May it not be, at least in part, the attempt to strike a balance between the personal and the traditional? between life as it is personally apprehended, and life as it is traditionally ordered? When the tradition is unquestioned, there is no inner struggle; after it has ceased to exist, there is none. Given a poetic talent, says Allen Tate, poetry results when "the intellectual and religious background of an age no longer contains the whole spirit, and the poet proceeds to examine that background in terms of immediate experience. . . . The poet in the true sense 'criticizes' his tradition . . . *discerns* its real elements and thus establishes its value. . . . The poet finds himself balanced upon the moment when such a world is about to fall. . . . This world order is assimilated . . . to the poetic vision; it is brought down from abstraction to personal feeling."

The scene upon which Miss Millay appeared no longer expressed a world order. Unable to quarrel, therefore, except spasmodically, with herself, she has quarreled splendidly with the world. (pp. 54-66)

James McBride Dabbs, "Edna St. Vincent Millay: Not Resigned," in South Atlantic Quarterly, *Vol. XXXVII, No. 1, January, 1938, pp. 54-66.*

Mary M. Colum　(essay date 1951)

[*Colum, who contributed criticism regularly to such publications as the* New Republic *and the* Saturday Review of Literature, *was called "the best woman critic in America" by William Rose Benét in 1933, although others have argued that her critical judgment was sometimes colored by personal prejudice. In the following essay, she discusses Millay's status as a popular poet in relation to her expression of unconventional ideas and personal emotion, and her use of traditional forms.*]

In the nineteen twenties Edna St. Vincent Millay was America's sweetheart. It was one of the rare periods when poetry, and especially lyrical poetry, was considered important. Now the fact is that this country has seldom been enthusiastic about lyrical poetry, and this largely explains the attitude to Edgar Allan Poe and to that troubadour, Vachel Lindsay. In a favored poet—Robert Frost—what gives him authority is not his lyrical but his narrative and meditative poetry. But Edna Millay struck a mood in American life when lyricism was being welcomed as something strange and moving. Then, what was called her philosophy roused to excitement not only the young men and women but their elders, too. Said philosophy was simply an attitude to life made familiar throughout the ages by the men poets—Herrick's "Gather ye rosebuds while ye may," Horace's "Carpe Diem," Catullus' "Vivamus mea Lesbia. . . . Give me a thousand kisses, then another thousand. . . . For when our brief life ends there is a never ending night and a never ending sleep." Edna Millay was probably the first woman in literature to back such ideas wholeheartedly, for women have been notoriously diffident in their support of hedonism. Her reputation for unconventionality caused her to be discussed by people for whom her poetic expression was not of first interest. It also caused W. B. Yeats, who was not overly impressed by her poetry, and Thomas Hardy, who was, to be excitedly interested in her personality.

When Edna Millay first began to be noticed, American women still could not smoke in restaurants or swim in such garb as the European *maillot* or without stockings to cover their legs; it was a time when people confused the regulations of *The Book of Etiquette* with the highest principles of ethics. She seemed to be the standard-bearer for the breakdown of futile conventions and of taboos. She advertised her love affairs and her sex affairs, and in her work she really made a differentiation between the two with a nicety that male poets seldom matched. Of her sex affairs:

> I find this frenzy insufficient reason
> For conversation when we meet again.

or:

> What lips my lips have kissed, and where and
>   why
> I have forgotten, and what arms have lain
> Under my head till morning.
>
>   . . . . .
>
> I only know that summer sang in me
> A little while that in me sings no more.

Then of her love:

> Women have loved before as I love now;
> At least in lively chronicles of the past,
> Of Irish waters by a Cornish prow,
> Or Trojan waters by a Spartan mast.

These unconventional emotions and ideas she expressed in that most conventional form of verse, the sonnet, which has such an attraction for American women poets. The form enticed her to go on and on, expressing the same emotions and ideas in an unceasing flow of sonnetry. Even people expert in knowing poetry by heart after a couple of readings find it difficult to distinguish one sonnet from another, though this can readily be done in the case of Eli-

nor Wylie's love sonnets, where each reveals a distinct emotion and thought. But Elinor Wylie was a trained and disciplined artist in a sense that Edna Millay never was. She had the faculty to become an artist and a scholar, too; she never let her mind and emotions ramble as did Edna Millay.

The sort of mental and professional training that teaches poets how to say effectively what they have to say was not to be found in the New York of Millay's time. No one was there to show her, not so much the technique of writing verse, which she could learn for herself, but that higher technique of getting beyond one's private world, which would have prevented her repetitiousness. A woman admirer of hers, confusing artistic with conventional education, sent her to college after the publication of her first poems. In no country do people learn the essentials of the art of literature in colleges, but they learn even less of them in America than elsewhere. Edna Millay probably had a good time in college, but she learned little if anything of what might be useful to her as an artist. She could have learned more by staying at home and reading poetry with a few fellow writers, for as Yeats says, "There is no singing school but studying Monuments of its own magnificence." And, to put it in prose, there is this sentence of T. S. Eliot's: "It is important that the artist should be highly educated in his own art, but his education is one that is hindered rather than helped by the ordinary processes of society which constitute education for the ordinary man."

Most of the delighted readers of [Millay's] poetry never noticed her concern in nearly every poem with death—her own personal death and her artistic death, the fear that her work might be forgotten.

—Mary M. Colum

In this sense, Edna Millay, in her art, had not sufficient education to allow her to use effectively her poetic endowment, though occasionally, and especially in her earlier poems, she did so use it. This inadequacy of artistic education also injured her self-criticism: in spite of her interest in ideas, she could not cope with them in writing, and this is seen explicitly in her symposium, *Conversation at Midnight*, and her later work, [*The Murder at Lidice*]. She plunged into translating Baudelaire, for which she was not only linguistically but temperamentally unfitted. She could talk French fluently, but she was no French scholar and got confused by genders and difficult constructions. Then she was too feminine a poet to be able to deal with such a masculine, revolutionary, powerful mentality as that of Baudelaire, who could make an ugliness of nature—decrepit old men and women, a corpse rotting in a ditch—into a high beauty of art. Edna Millay could only deal with the acceptedly beautiful. Death, however, did fascinate her, though in a romantic style. Most of the delighted readers of her poetry never noticed her concern in nearly every poem with death—her own personal death and her artistic death, the fear that her work might be forgotten. In **"The Poet and His Book,"** one of her best poems, she wrote:

> Down, you mongrel Death,
> Back into your kennel . . .
> You shall scratch and you shall whine,
> Many a night, and you shall worry
> Many a bone before you bury
> One sweet bone of mine.
> Boys and girls that lie
> Whispering in the hedges,
> Do not let me die. . . .

This was really the burthen of many of her poems, "Do not let me die." What aided her popularity in her heyday was her warmth of heart, her generosity, her compassion for the beaten, the downtrodden, and this not in the current way of an impersonal, generalized humanitarianism, but with a rich feeling that made her adherence a strong personal emotion. Few of her admirers realized her fundamental loneliness, her shyness, her sadness, which made her gladly leave the turmoil of New York for an isolated country house where she seldom saw anybody and where she died alone and lonely. As she has written:

> Lovers and thinkers, into the earth with you.
> Be one with the dull, the indiscriminate dust.
> A fragment of what you felt, of what you knew,
> A formula, a phrase remains—but the best is
> lost.

(pp. 17-18)

Mary M. Colum, "Edna Millay and Her Time," in The New Republic, *Vol. 124, No. 11, March 12, 1951, pp. 17-18.*

Walter S. Minot (essay date 1975)

[*In the following essay, Minot presents a biographical interpretation of Millay's "Sonnets from an Ungrafted Tree" and suggests that Millay's overall artistic achievement was impeded by her unresolved psychological conflicts, which, he asserts, reflects the problematic nature of the woman as artist in America.*]

The reputation of Edna St. Vincent Millay as an American poet is small, and despite recent attempts to show that critical reaction against her work has been too harsh, her position in our letters is unlikely to change much, even with a sympathetic reassessment. She is, and probably will be considered, a minor poet. Nevertheless, her work and life are worth examining; perhaps they may help explain why a talented artist, who wrote as promising a poem as **"Renascence"** in her late adolescence, never achieved poetic greatness. Millay's career may be especially useful in explaining why so many talented American women have failed to attain the stature of major poets.

This essay will consider the biographical implications of Millay's neglected sequence, **"Sonnets from an Ungrafted Tree,"** especially in relation to the *Harp-Weaver* volume in which it appears. Its thesis is that the sonnets are a symbolic attempt, perhaps subconscious, at murdering her fa-

ther. From there, I shall suggest how her unresolved psychological conflicts led to her later severe neurosis and perhaps disabled her as a poet and as a person. Then I hope to suggest how Millay's situation reflects the problem of the woman as artist in America.

The **"Sonnets from an Ungrafted Tree"** are unlike most of Millay's other sonnets in several respects. Their subject is not passionate love, but love turned cold and bitter. The *persona* is not her usual first-person lover, but a third-person narrator who describes her protagonist coldly and objectively. Indeed, critics have commented on Millay's use of objective details, and Jean Morris Petitt compares Millay's realism to that of Frost and Masters. Moreover, this sequence is notable for its consistently grim tone. There are very few tonal shifts or emotional peaks and valleys such as one finds in most of Millay's sonnets, and especially in *Fatal Interview* (1931). Finally, the sonnets do not follow the Shakespearean rhyme scheme strictly, and each closing couplet contains seven feet per line. In technique and form, **"Sonnets from an Ungrafted Tree"** is different from most of Millay's other work, especially her work up to this time.

"Sonnets from an Ungrafted Tree," as a whole, traces the actions and thoughts of a woman who returns to care for her estranged, dying husband. As the first sonnet indicates, she returns out of a sense of duty rather than love; she is described as "Loving him not at all."

The basis for this sonnet sequence is the visit which Millay made to Kingman, Maine, in 1912, when her father, Henry Tolman Millay, was seriously ill. Thus, the dying husband would be Henry Millay, and the wife a combination of Cora Millay, who had divorced her husband, and Edna, who went to visit him in March, 1912. I hope to establish the basis for this interpretation with details from the poems that can be confirmed biographically, and then to discuss the significance of these details.

The very title, **"Sonnets from an Ungrafted Tree,"** suggests the metaphor of a family tree in which the fruits, or children, are left untended and uncared for. The children, like fruit from an ungrafted tree, grow up bitterly resentful of their father who abandoned them. This may describe Millay's feelings, perhaps unconscious, toward her father.

That the woman in the sequence is partially Cora Millay is borne out in several ways. First of all, she was divorced from her husband. Second, she made her living as a private nurse, often living-in with others to tend the sick, just as the woman in the poems is doing for her estranged husband. Third, as sonnet ix of this sequence indicates—"[he] had come into her life when anybody / Would have been welcome . . . "—their marriage was not based on any great mutual sympathy, but was basically one of incompatible spirits. Fourth, like the woman in the sonnets, Mrs. Millay loved to plant flowers, especially nasturtiums, which are mentioned in the second sonnet. While some of this evidence may seem slight, the basic situation and details seem to refer to Cora Millay, the estranged wife and professional nurse.

That the woman in the sonnets is also partially Edna Millay is shown in several ways. First, she actually did visit her father when he was seriously ill. Second, the time of year was late winter or early spring, as indicated in sonnet xi, though that poem mentions April rather than March. Third, the character of the woman bears some strong resemblances to the poet. Sonnet v, describes how "whirred / Her heart like a frightened partridge" and how the woman hid from the grocer's man. The motive seems to be an irrational fear, much like that of the aberration Vincent Sheean attributes to her: "At times she was so afflicted by self-consciousness and dislike for the external world that she could hardly utter a word; I have seen her cringe . . . actually physically cringe, when she felt herself being observed." Perhaps, too, the fear has a more reasonable basis in the inability of the Millays to pay their bills. Several sources suggest that they may have spent money on books and music when they hadn't paid the bills for the necessities. In the next sonnet, the grocer's man is described as "he forced the trade-slip on the nail"—certainly a reminder of unpaid bills. Moreover, the woman's refusal to go to the door and meet women who brought jellies for her husband is another reminder of Millay's fear of strangers. Grace Shaw Tolman remembers that on her visit to Kingman, Edna Millay seemed distant and hard to get to know.

There are other details in the poems that may also have biographical significance. For instance, in the final sonnet of the sequence, there is one outstanding simile in which the woman goes into the bedroom to view her husband's body and compares herself to "one who enters, sly, and proud, / To where her husband speaks before a crowd, / And sees a man she never saw before—". Henry Millay, the Superintendent of Schools and First Selectman of Kingman, was considered a fine speaker. Edna marvels in her letter from Kingman that her father is so important a personage in Kingman, and her tone is similar to that of the simile in the last sonnet.

Now whether this biographical analysis of **"Sonnets from an Ungrafted Tree"** seems justifiable and worth pursuing might be open to question if this sonnet sequence were not considered in relation to both the volume in which it appears and the larger pattern of Millay's life. Such consideration should justify a close analysis.

The Harp-Weaver and Other Poems was dedicated by Millay "To My Mother," and the title poem, **"The Ballad of the Harp-Weaver"** tells how a destitute widow magically weaves a beautiful suit of clothes for her son on her harp. The action takes place on Christmas Eve, an extremely cold night, and next morning the widow is frozen to death, but her son has "the clothes of a king's son" and is saved by his mother's heroic love and sacrifice. Despite the substitution of a son for a daughter and a widow for a divorced woman, critics and biographers agree that the poem is Millay's idealization of her relationship with her mother. Moreover, as Floyd Dell points out, Cora Millay told him that she "brought her [Edna] up . . . like a son—to be self-reliant, fearless and ambitious. She was called 'Vincent' rather oftener than 'Edna.'"

In a volume dedicated to her mother and with a title poem that idealized her mother, whom Millay deeply loved, the placing of **"Sonnets from an Ungrafted Tree"** is quite sig-

nificant, especially since these sonnets appear as the last section of the book. These sonnets are Millay's symbolic repudiation of her father, while she glorifies and embraces her mother. The sonnet sequence is Millay's punishment of her father for abandoning her, and it may be a symbolic murder, probably unconscious, by the Edna-Cora woman, who is Edna's psychic projection of herself and her mother, who have suffered greatly and now triumph over this male figure. Perhaps, too, this symbolic murder was necessary in that it somehow set Millay free to marry Eugen Boissevain in 1923, the same year in which these sonnets were published.

The significance of Millay's relationship with her father has probably been greatly underestimated, though Jean Gould's recent biography and Joan Dash's recent study have gone a long way toward correcting the picture of Millay's relationship with her parents. Dash sums up effectively the formative forces on Millay's character: "Edna . . . adored her mother and saw life . . . through her mother's eyes; accordingly she called herself by the boy's name and became . . . the boy of the family. It was a tendency only strengthened by there being, in Henry Millay's absence, no other male in it. There was . . . no one to act out for her the differences between male and female, neither was there a model of womanliness . . . who took pride and pleasure in being female. . . . " The lack of fatherly affection and the general dominance and aggressiveness of her mother produced in Millay an uncertainty about sexual roles and a distrust of men that may have crippled her as a person, and could be the cause of her failure to achieve the poetic greatness that many predicted for her.

If we accept Dash's interpretation of Millay's personality, at least as a working hypothesis, some significant patterns emerge. Vincent Millay, grew up in a fatherless home with an aggressive and ambitious mother whom she adored. She went to Vassar, a woman's college, and was graduated in 1917, the year that *Renascence,* her first volume of poetry, was published. She was already in love with Arthur Davison Ficke, a fellow poet who was married. She moved to Greenwich Village, and there had love affairs, either actual or hoped for by her suitors, with various literary men, including Floyd Dell, Witter Bynner, Edmund Wilson, and John Peale Bishop. But whenever it appeared that one of these affairs was moving toward the permanency of marriage, it was Millay who seemed to want to avoid marriage. For example, when Witter Bynner proposed to her by mail, she hedged so much that marriage would have been demeaning for Bynner. Indeed Millay, half-jokingly but perhaps half-seriously, talked of having her mother join her in Europe for a honeymoon and of publishing the *Love Letters of Edna St. Vincent Millay and Her Mother.* Another indication that she saw men as rivals to her mother is evident in this comment from a letter to her mother: "I have a curious feeling that someday I shall marry, and have a son; and that my husband will die; and that you and I and my little boy will all live together on a farm." This attempt to create a husband for herself out of her mother seems a serious distortion of rôles, but it reveals Millay's intense distrust of men.

Millay's poetry was concerned with such themes as the inconstancy and brevity of love, the frailty of love and beauty, and the need of women to be as sexually free as men. Although Millay's dwelling on these themes seemed daring when her work was first published, it now seems almost compulsive. Such lyrics as **"The Spring and the Fall"** and **"Keen"** and such famous sonnets as **"What Lips My Lips Have Kissed," "I Know I Am but Summer,"** and **"Pity Me Not"** (all taken, for emphasis, from *The Harp-Weaver*) reveal Millay's fears of committing herself to love or of trusting men.

When Edna St. Vincent Millay finally did marry, it was to Eugen Jan Boissevain, who was an unusual husband for an unusual marriage. Eugen, a Dutchman by birth, had previously been married to Inez Milholland, a suffragette leader and graduate of Vassar. In this marriage, Eugen and Inez had, according to Max Eastman, taken vows of unpossessive love, which meant complete freedom for both partners, and had maintained their love without possessiveness until Inez's untimely death. This same freedom apparently also characterized the marriage of Eugen and Edna.

The marriage was indeed an unusual one. According to Max Eastman, who shared an apartment with him for several years, Eugen was a rare and lovable character: "He is handsome and muscular and bold, boisterous in conversation, noisy in laughter, yet redeemed by a strain of something feminine that most men except the creative geniuses lack." Eugen Boissevain's feminine instincts were revealed in his management of the housework and his wife's business affairs, along with the duties of managing the farm they bought in Austerlitz, New York. Eugen did everything he could to free Millay from the tasks of normal living in order that she could devote herself to writing poetry. He was not only a husband to her, but a kind of father, mother and nursemaid—an arrangement that both of them seemed to accept. They accepted, too, childless marriage at Steepletop, their farm in Austerlitz, perhaps because, as Janet Gassman suggests, she considered poetry more important and enduring than any human relationships.

Despite their mutual acceptance of this unconventional marriage and despite their mutual devotion to Millay's poetic achievements, the couple's retreat to pastoral bliss did not remain happy. After the early 1930's, Millay's poetry declined sharply in quality as she began to write about social and political issues unsuited to her lyric gifts. Her health, both physical and emotional, led her to a kind of perpetual nervous exhaustion, probably intensified by excessive drinking. The degeneration of her personality is evident in Edmund Wilson's description of her in 1948: "She was terribly nervous; her hands shook . . . Eugen brought us martinis. Very quietly he watched her and managed her. At moments he would baby her in a way . . . that had evidently become habitual, when she showed signs of bursting into tears over not being able to find a poem. . . . My wife said afterwards that Gene gave the impression of shaking me at her as if I had been a new toy. . . . " Although she did manage to write some good poetry again, which is to be found in the posthumous *Mine the Harvest*,

she lived only a bit more than a year after Eugen's death in 1949.

Joan Dash has questioned Eugen's excessive protectiveness of Edna Millay, suggesting that this protectiveness was partly selfish and possessive and that Millay's decline as poet and her disintegration as a person may have been a result of her failure to have to face the realities of daily life. Whether Eugen is to be praised or blamed is a matter of conjecture, though Nancy Milford's projected biography, with the help of Norma Millay Ellis, may do much to confirm or deny some of these speculations.

Nevertheless, Millay's life and poetic career do tell us a good deal about the situation of the woman writer in America. That her great promise was never fulfilled may have many causes, but it seems clear that her inner conflicts, unresolved and so basic to life, were formidable obstacles to personal and poetic maturity. Millay's struggle to be independent and sexually free was probably too great a strain on a girl who grew up in a small town in Maine. The psychic price that she, as a woman, had to pay to achieve the independence and artistry that her mother desired for her was too high a penalty for her spirit to pay. And, unfortunately, that very high price seems to be one that women have had to pay if they wanted to be poets in our society. The suicide of Sylvia Plath and the breakdowns of Millay and Anne Sexton bear witness to the pressures that being a poet places on a woman in American society. The eschewing of a more conventional style of living brings conflicts that may be too great, especially for women who also desire marriage and children.

In an even larger social perspective, we can see that any woman who goes against accepted customs and mores creates conflicts and problems for those around her. When Cora Millay divorced Henry Millay, she followed a brave and independent course, especially when one considers the prim morality of small towns at the turn of the century. Not only did she have to pay a heavy price to be independent, but part of the debt devolved upon her children, especially Vincent. The results can be seen in Millay's life and work.

Whether, in the long run, the heavy price is worth paying is impossible to determine. But Edna St. Vincent Millay's life and work illustrate both the glory and the misery of a woman who is determined to be an artist and independent person in our society. (pp. 260-69)

Walter S. Minot, "Millay's 'Ungrafted Tree': The Problem of the Artist as Woman," in The New England Quarterly, *Vol. XLVIII, No. 2, June, 1975, pp. 260-69.*

Frederick Eckman   (essay date 1976)

[*Eckman is an American poet and critic. In the following essay, he disputes the validity of Millay's "Roaring Twenties" public image in light of her frequent focus on death and desolation in her poetry, and concludes that Millay has more in common with such contemporary poets as Sylvia Plath and Anne Sexton than with poets of the Jazz Age.*]

The year 1912 is well enough remembered in modern literary history as that *annus mirabilis* which marked the founding of the Imagist Movement and the first appearance of *Poetry: A Magazine of Verse.* At the time, however, neither of these events seemed so auspicious to the American literary world as the publication of Edna St. Vincent Millay's precocious visionary poem, **"Renascence"** in a widely-publicized anthology, *The Lyric Year.* Though the poem had received only fourth place, and no prize, in the anthology's national competition, the book's readers, its editors (after agonizing post-publication reappraisal), and even its prize winners, all agreed that **"Renascence"** deserved much better than a runner-up position.

For the next twenty-five years or more, Edna Millay, the tiny auburn-haired woman from Maine, enjoyed a combination of popularity, public notice, and high esteem unmatched by any other American poet in this century. Even though Millay's critical reputation has languished since her death in 1950, at least a few of her poems hold a sacred place in the hearts of the American reading public hitherto occupied only by the most familiar verses of Poe, Longfellow, Whittier, and Dickinson. In Hayden Carruth's *The Voice That Is Great Within Us,* a 1970 anthology of American poetry since Frost, only two of the twenty-four women poets represented (H. D. and Denise Levertov) have more poems than Millay. Even in the trend-conscious 1973 *Norton Anthology of Modern Poetry,* she is represented by ten poems, one more than Stevens, H. D., and Wilfred Owen; only one less than Marianne Moore, and a mere two less than either Whitman or Auden. Her poems continue to appear in high school and college textbooks, as well as specialized anthologies: poetry by women, poetry for children, social-protest verse, and love poetry. Cloth-bound editions of her *Collected Sonnets* (1941), *Collected Lyrics* (1943), and *Collected Poems* (1956) have remained constantly in print since their publication.

It should not, however, surprise anyone familiar with patterns of American popular taste to find that the public, the beloved, the prestigious poet is not the *essential* poet. In literature, as in music and art, Americans exercise their democratic rights: rather predictably they choose the sunny, the funny, the sentimental and nostalgic, the pleasantly instructive, and the mildly scandalous. Even grim works, when not truly terrifying but merely scary, can delight American readers. Partisan considerations of "high culture" and "developed taste" aside, the general reading public is quite as selective, according to its lights, as the most discriminating connoisseur. Interestingly enough, the legends it forms about its favorite writers are almost identical to those formed by the high-brow reading public.

What appealed to readers in **"Renascence,"** I suspect, was the image of none other than Howells' ideal reader of a generation before, the saintly "girl of sixteen," given a voice and a habitation. Even the young woman who emerged immediately thereafter in the most widely quoted and reprinted of her "Jazz Age" poems was a logical 20th-century transformation: the clever, vivacious, slightly wicked (but still sensitive and intelligent) Greenwich Village soul-sister of Daisy Buchanan, Lady Brett Ashley,

and Lorelei Lee. Probably no other poet in recorded history has acquired a more enduring public image from six lines than Millay did from these two epigrams in her second volume, *A Few Figs From Thistles* (1920):

First Fig

My candle burns at both ends;
It will not last the night;
But ah, my foes, and oh, my friends—
It gives a lovely light.

Second Fig

Safe upon the solid rock the ugly houses stand;
Come and see my shining palace built upon the
    sand!

These two "figs," along with certain other poems in the volume, not only revived a moribund tradition of light verse in America, through the work of such disciples and contemporaries as Dorothy Parker, Samuel Hoffenstein, Richard Armour, Phyllis McGinley, and Ogden Nash; they fixed in the American mind a simulacrum of the modern woman poet that has only recently begun to change into the troubled likeness of a Sylvia Plath. Yet, as later portions of this essay will imply, the poetic imaginations of these two poets—questions of relative excellence aside—are a good deal more alike than their public images.

The first impression that comes from reading Millay's *Collected Poems* from beginning to end (as I have done three times in as many months) is that she is so totally a *literary* poet. One expects the early work of any writer to reflect various admirations and influences. Most poets at any age are bookish, if not always imitative or allusive. But Millay's poems simply never stop drawing from the imagery, language, rhythms, forms, and allusions of other poets. If there is truth in Eliot's mock-solemn dictum that major poets commit grand larceny while minor poets are guilty only of shoplifting, then Millay is indisputably major. In another, more serious context, Eliot discusses this matter:

> Immature poets imitate; mature poets steal; bad poets deface what they take, and good poets make it into something better, or at least something different. The good poet welds his theft into a whole of feeling which is unique, utterly different from that from which it was torn; the bad poet throws it into something which has no cohesion.

At best, certainly, Millay makes her thefts from Shakespeare, Shelley, Keats, Tennyson, E. B. Browning, the Pre-Raphaelites, Housman, the Georgian Poets (especially de la Mare), Yeats, Frost, Sandburg, MacLeish, Jeffers, and such women contemporaries as Anna Hempstead Branch, Elinor Wylie, and Sara Teasdale into "something different." She is a true and good mockingbird. Allen Tate's conclusions on this aspect of Millay's poetry are more perceptive than anything I could hope to write:

> Taking the vocabulary of nineteenth-century poetry as pure as you will find it in Christina Rossetti, and drawing upon the stock of conventional imagery accumulated from Drayton to Housman, she has created out of shopworn materials an interesting personal attitude: she has been

able to use the language of the preceding genera-tion to convey an emotion peculiar to her own. . . . She has been from the beginning the one poet of our time who has successfully stood athwart two ages: she has put the personality of her age into the style of the preceding age, with-out altering either.

There can be little doubt that Millay's constant echoing of the familiar has done much to increase her popularity. By Pound's much harsher standards of excellence, she is the sort of "diluter" who is often preferred by a casual reader of poetry to the genuine article. But both Eliot and Tate make a distinction about derivative work that Pound—himself a compulsive borrower—failed to make: the difference between imitation and transformation. And though Millay's poems cannot always stand up to this test, she is quite often able to employ another's style in the best interests of her own poem.

The next, and deepest, impression that comes to me from reading Millay's poetry *in toto,* and the central topic of this essay, . . .: its overwhelming, obsessive concern with death and desolation. Frequently it is human death, in the most literal, naturalistic sense: graves, tombstones, decay-ing corpses, drowned bodies, shrouds, skulls, and skeletal bones. Even her ubiquitous nature imagery—which arises from the precise, loving observation of a person totally at home in the natural world—is strongly impelled toward falling leaves, bare fields and hills, stagnant pools, with-ered flowers, slain or hunted wild creatures, snow, frost, cold winds, floods, blighted grain, weeds, maggots, vora-cious dogs and wolves, venomous snakes and gnawing ro-dents. Likewise, her domestic imagery always seems to be moving away from the warm, comfortable, and secure, to-ward burnt-out fires, empty cupboards, blank and hostile windows, gaping doors, shabby furnishings, rancid and sour household odors, decayed food scraps, irritating day-time and ominous night noises, funerals, sickrooms, dim or extinguished lamps, cobwebs, broken or unwashed crockery, leaking roofs, and mortgages. Since Millay is seldom a poet of verbal paradox or irony, we can usually accept this accumulation of images at face value. And more important than their conventional sign-values is their totality of impact from poem to poem, over the entire canon.

At this point I would like to brush away all temptation to indulge in amateur psychoanalytic criticism, especially that of the Freudian persuasion, which seems always to end with patronizing moral-esthetic judgments that re-duce both poet and poem to mere curious objects of pa-thology. Death is, after all, one of the givens of the natural world; in the human realm, coming to terms with it is such an agonizing central struggle that, existentially speaking, we are better served by suspecting as abnormal the person who boasts of not being disturbed about it. As a critic I am not at all interested in determining whether the woman Edna St. Vincent Millay had a death wish, an immature horror of death, or even a creepy fascination with decay. I *am* interested in trying to demonstrate that themes of death and desolation in her poetry are evidence that her work needs reassessment, deliverance from the stock opin-ion (largely unchanged from her earliest reviews) that she

is primarily a poet of praise, affirmation, and celebration. It is possible, of course, to select from such a large body of work enough images, or even complete poems, to prove almost anything. And I am well aware that death, dying, desolation, loss, and grief can, routinely employed, be no more than empty literary postures.

More convincing to my argument than any of the numer-ous poems *about* death are those in which such imagery works to another purpose. A simple instance is the lyric, **"Passer Mortuus Est"** from Millay's first volume:

> Death devours all lovely things;
> Lesbia with her sparrow
> Shares the darkness,—presently
> Every bed is narrow.
>
> Unremembered as old rain
> Dries the sheer libation;
> And the little petulant hand
> Is an annotation,
>
> After all, my erstwhile dear,
> My no longer cherished,
> Need we say it was not love,
> Just because it perished?

In this elegantly clever little poem, the "turn" of the third stanza serves to remind us that *carpe diem* is, after all, grounded in a darker view of existence than its surface fri-volity would indicate. We note also that the oft-borrowed Catullan tag in the title and first stanza is put to an alto-gether original use.

Another poem from the early 1920's employs a personified Death, to purposes beyond mere mortality:

Siege

> This I do, being mad;
> Gather baubles about me,
> Sit in a circle of toys, and all the time
> Death beating the door in.
>
> *White jade and an orange pitcher,*
> Hindu idol, Chinese god,—
> Maybe next year, when I'm richer
> Carved beads and a lotus pod . . .
>
> And all this time
> Death beating the door in.

From the traditional form of the "mad song," a splendidly compact and original poem emerges. On a first level, it is a personal parable of the poet, collecting at great cost a small hoard of rare and beautiful artifacts against, or in defiance of, the ravages of mortality. At another level, the poem can be read as a statement about the human necessi-ty to create order—any order—against the chaos of exis-tence. Read as a woman's poem, it would seem to refute Thoreau's sneer at "the ladies of the land, weaving toilet cushions against the Last Judgment." Whatever the read-ing, Death cannot be dismissed as a stock poetic device: he is hammering down the door like a storm-trooper or a National Guardsman; whether the speaker's lack of re-sponse to him comes from indifference, preoccupation, or defiance might be arguable, but one is not obliged to make a choice.

> **[Millay's] domestic imagery always seems to be moving away from the warm, comfortable, and secure, toward burnt-out fires, empty cupboards, blank and hostile windows, gaping doors, shabby furnishings, rancid and sour household odors, decayed food scraps, irritating daytime and ominous night noises, funerals, sickrooms. . . .**
>
> —*Frederick Eckman*

In Millay's fourth volume, *The Harp-Weaver and Other Poems* (1923), there appears a remarkable seventeen-poem sequence entitled **"Sonnets From an Ungrafted Tree."** Only one critic, [Walter S. Minot], to my knowledge, has paid it more than cursory attention; and I am in total agreement with Sister Mary Madeleva's 1925 opinion that it is a really outstanding work. In its language, rhythms, and imagery, the sequence is heavily indebted to Frost; yet somehow Millay managed to repay her debt by making Frost's familiar idiom sound as if it were her own. The plot of the narrative is about dying and death, but the central concern is with the altering consciousness of a survivor. A woman has come back to her estranged and dying husband, after an indefinite absence, to care for him in his last weeks. For most of the sequence, the dying man is only an object in another room; the real focus is on the woman and the house, with glimpses of the New England village where the story takes place.

> So she came back into his house again
> And watched beside his bed until he died,
> Loving him not at all. The winter rain
> Splashed in the painted butter-tub outside,
> Where once her red geraniums had stood,
> Where still their rotted stalks were to be seen;

The details are lovingly rendered, perhaps from memory: early in 1912 Millay had gone to care for her seriously-ill father, who had been divorced from her mother for a dozen years. Although the father recovered, her memories of the event—especially her own ambivalent emotions—must have remained fresh and poignant over the ensuing decade. The woman in the sequence hears the grocer's delivery man outside; in panic she flees to the cellar until he has left:

> Sour and damp from that dark vault
> Arose to her the well-remembered chill;
> She saw the narrow wooden stairway still
> Plunging into the earth, and the thin salt
> Crusting the crocks; until she knew him far,
> So stood, with listening eyes upon the empty
> doughnut jar.

The theme of a marriage gone sour, along with Millay's uncharacteristic bending of the sonnet form, suggests another debt: George Meredith's *Modern Love;* but again, the borrowing becomes a transformation. An entire tract on the randomness of choice in marriage could not cover more ground than this quatrain:

> Not over-kind nor over-quick in study
> Nor skilled in sports nor beautiful was he,
> Who had come into her life when anybody
> Would have been welcome, so in need was she.

The boy has attracted her attention by flashing a mirror in her eyes at school. Soon there is an episode of swimming and seduction at the lake:

> So loud, so loud the million crickets' choir . . .
> So sweet the night, so long-drawn-out and
> late . . .
> And if the man were not her spirit's mate,
> Why was her body sluggish with desire?

Thus they marry, and the sequence moves back into the grim present:

> Tenderly, in those times, as though she fed
> An ailing child—with sturdy propping up
>
> Of its small feverish body in the bed,
> And steadying of its hands about the cup—
> She gave her husband of her body's strength,
> Thinking of men, what helpless things they
> were,
> Until he turned and fell asleep at length,
> And stealthily stirred the night and spoke to her.

Her days become dream-like and hallucinatory. Fact and fantasy, in her deathbed attendant's routine, become confused:

> Upstairs, down other stairs, fearful to rouse,
> Regarding him, the wide and empty scream
> Of a strange sleeper on a malignant bed,
> And all the time not certain if it were
> Herself so doing or some one like to her,
> From this wan dream that was her daily bread.

I hesitate to summon again the august shade of Mr. Eliot, but passages like these inevitably suggest his concept of the "objective correlative": "a set of objects, a situation, a chain of events which shall be the formula of that *particular* emotion. . . ."

The heroine of this sequence is not unusually perceptive or even, beyond her household and nursing chores, able; what makes her heroic is her honesty. When the doctor asks her about preparations for the inevitable funeral,

> She said at length, feeling the doctor's eyes,
> "I don't know what you do exactly when a person dies."

Finally, viewing her husband's dead body from the bedroom door,

> She was as one who enters, sly, and proud,
> To where her husband speaks before a crowd,
> And sees a man she never saw before—
> The man who eats his victuals at her side,
> Small, and absurd, and hers: for once, not hers,
> unclassified.

So the sequence ends. I have not been able to give more than fragmentary glimpses of a suite of poems where emotion is skillfully controlled—dammed up, as it were, by precisely-rendered and composed details; and where dramatic power is released smoothly in the flat, lucid flow of the narration, like Williams' "river below the falls." Throughout the poems, images of death and loss are in the employ of answering that ultimate question posed by Frost's oven bird: "what to make of a diminished thing." That is to say, of existence itself. If the answer here seems to be no more than the stoic formula, "See things through," then we must be reminded that extracting messages and "paraphrasable content" from poems is only another intellectual game: the poem *is* the message, and ever so much more than the message.

Any reassessment of Edna Millay's poetry, then, should come from the poetry itself—the body of work. All but a few of her critics are useless, except perhaps as bad examples. John Crowe Ransom, the most eminent critic of that moment, chose in ["The Poet As Woman" in *The Southern Review,* Spring 1937] to set her record straight through a review of Elizabeth Atkins' critical study, [*Edna St. Vincent Millay and her Times*], published a year earlier. The essay, surely the silliest, most pretentious and patronizing thing Ransom ever wrote, attacks the poet—through her perhaps equally silly champion—for (a) being a woman in the first place, (b) her "lack of intellectual interest," and (c) not being John Donne or a modern facsimile thereof. His method is the usual New-Critical strategy of attack: to pick apart, word by word, a few chosen poems, then set bleeding and mutilated passages beside those of poets he admires. About Ransom's first objection, a writer in our time can only shake his head sadly; about the second and third, he may reflect nostalgically on fashions in critical taste, wondering if perhaps the New Critics are by now at least as shopworn as Millay's Jazz Age flippancies. But from Ransom's method one can surely draw a lesson: that no poet (with the necessary exception of Chidiock Tichbourne) ought to, or need to, have a lifetime of accomplishment balancing on the point of one poem—or two, or even three.

My discussion of **"Sonnets From an Ungrafted Tree,"** then, is intended only to point a direction. If a poet can be read first of all in terms of the large patterns in the work, then a critic may well proceed, depth by depth, to what is at once the most important and the most elusive of critical goals: a true understanding of the individual poetic imagination in all its range and complexity. Such a study as I have outlined might well show us that Millay's imagery of death and desolation gives her more in common with the contemporary poets we now most prize—Roethke and Berryman, Plath and Sexton—than with the Roaring Twenties bohemians, the Depression radicals, and the quivering sensibilities of small-town poetry societies, where she is usually found nowadays. (pp. 193-203)

Frederick Eckman, "Edna St. Vincent Millay: Notes toward a Reappraisal," in A Question of Quality: Popularity and Value in Modern Creative Writing, *edited by Louis Filler, Bowling Green University Popular Press, 1976, pp. 193-203.*

Jeannine Dobbs   (essay date 1979)

[*In the following excerpt, Dobbs asserts that Millay's domestic poems, which have suffered critical neglect, are among her best works.*]

Despite the quality and quantity of Millay's domestic poetry, her reputation was built on poems expressing disillusionment with people and on those celebrating sexual freedoms for women. Two of her sonnet sequences, **"Epitaph for the Race of Man"** and *Fatal Interview* typify these concerns. The former is abstract philosophizing on the folly of humankind; the latter a proficient but somewhat academic exercise in the tradition of the courtly love sonnet sequence.

Many of Millay's New Women type poems are successful and interesting; but the speakers usually are not portrayed as real, individualized women. They are witty and clever and sexually emancipated, but as women they are a stereotyped abstraction. The speaker of the following sonnet, for example, is a disembodied voice:

> I, being born a woman and distressed
> By all the needs and notions of my kind,
> Am urged by your propinquity to find
> Your person fair, and feel a certain zest
> To bear your body's weight upon my breast:
> So subtly is the fume of life designed,
> To clarify the pulse and cloud the mind,
> And leave me once again undone, possessed.
> Think not for this, however, the poor treason
> Of my stout blood against my staggering brain,
> I shall remember you with love, or season
> My scorn with pity,—let me make it plain:
> I find this frenzy insufficient reason
> For conversation when we meet again.
>   **The Harp-Weaver,** 1923

The impersonal speaker works here because she represents all women: "I, being born a women. . . ." There is no personality here. There is no environment, no dramatic interplay. There is no real man involved, only a "person fair," a "body." There is not even any particularized emotion, just generalities: a "certain zest," a "frenzy." When the speaker is stereotyped and the situation generalized in this way, identification with the speaker must be made totally on an intellectual level. Many of Millay's burning-the-candle-at-both-ends type poems portray only a voice, and all portray the same voice.

In more successful poems, Millay places the speakers in a setting or in a situation with which women can identify. **"The Fitting"** (*Huntsman, What Quarry?* 1939) is such a poem. Here the speaker's body is portrayed as being impersonally, even roughly handled by dressmakers, "doing what they were paid to do." As this activity proceeds, the woman thinks of her lover. The brief mention of the lover invites comparisons between the present touch of the dressmakers and the anticipated evening with the lover, when his touch, as [Norman A. Brittin in his *Edna St. Vincent Millay*] notes, will not have to be paid for.

It was these kinds of love poems—love poems declaring or illustrating women's independence in the face of social conventions—which most interested Millay's public. Many of these poems appear to be autobiographical, con-

Millay correcting proofs for The Murder of Lidice.

fessional. Therefore, as much attention was paid to guessing the identity of the lover(s) as to the poems themselves. With the appearance of this type of heroine and this kind of love poem (especially in *A Few Figs from Thistles*), Millay began to be encouraged to write for all the wrong reasons: shock, titillation, idle speculation. "Gossip and scandal . . . enhanced her sales," Dorothy Thompson reports [in "The Woman Poet" in *Ladies Home Journal,* January 1951]. The fact that *Fatal Interview* describes an illicit affair may help to explain the popularity of that sonnet sequence. Also, it was undomestic, academic, and abstract. It was, therefore, pronounced "intellectual" and "masculine," a superior work according to Millay's critics. Thus, Millay's public, her editors and critics have emphasized and praised some of her less successful and actually less important work and have neglected or ignored work that best reveals her talent, her domestic poetry.

Millay was one of the number of bright, young women who converged on New York and the capitals of Europe in the early 1920s to pursue the new liberated life women felt they had won along with suffrage. By this time, Millay was a published and recognized poet; and, for a while, she undertook a simultaneous career as an actress. During this time, she half-heartedly agreed to marry two or three of her numerous suitors; meanwhile she practiced her belief in free love. She feared marriage because she thought it might kill her creative voice. Floyd Dell, one of the rejected lovers, recalls "that she was probably afraid that by becoming a wife and mother, she might be less the poet. She wanted to devote herself exclusively to her poetry and did not want to 'belong' to any one except herself. She did not want to spend her energies on domestic affairs." In spite

of her fears, Millay married Eugene Boissevain in 1923. She was thirty-one; he was forty-three. He gave up his career in order to take up the household duties and free Millay for her writing. When Allan Ross MacDougall interviewed Boissevain for an article in the *Delineator* some years after the marriage, Boissevain recalled: "When we got married I gave up my business. It seemed advisable to arrange our lives to suit Vincent. It is so obvious to anyone that Vincent is more important than I am. Anyone can buy and sell coffee—which is what I did . . . But anyone cannot write poetry."

In the same year as her marriage, Millay published a sonnet that warns a husband what may happen if he scorns his wife's intellect and insists instead on subjugating her to stereotyped wifely roles—to being submissive, nonintellectual and vain:

> Oh, oh, you will be sorry for that word!
> Give back my book and take my kiss instead.
> Was it my enemy or my friend I heard,
> "What a big book for such a little head!"
> Come, I will show you now my newest hat,
> And you may watch me purse my mouth and prink!
> Oh, I shall love you still, and all of that.
> I never again shall tell you what I think.
> I shall be sweet and crafty, soft and sly;
> You will not catch me reading any more:
> I shall be called a wife to pattern by;
> And some day when you knock and push the door,
> Some sane day, not too bright and not too stormy
> I shall be gone, and you may whistle for me.
> *The Harp-Weaver,* 1923

Perhaps because Millay was so aware of the potential threat to her career posed by her marriage and certainly because of Boissevain's willingness to accept an untraditional domestic situation, the marriage endured until his death twenty-six years later.

Although some of Millay's domestic poems seem clearly autobiographical, it is difficult to discern any over-all correlation between the events of her life and the periods when she wrote on domestic subjects. She alternates between writing some domestic poems and writing none at all, but for no apparent reasons. She wrote about marriage before she became a wife, culminating with **"Sonnets from an Ungrafted Tree."** After her marriage, domesticity virtually disappeared from her work until the 1939 volume *Huntsman, What Quarry?,* a rather strange mixture of war and domestic concerns. During the war years, propaganda held her captive; but the poems collected posthumously in 1954 in *Mine the Harvest* reveal that she ultimately returned to her more basic subjects: nostalgia for childhood, nature, and domesticity. Hence, it is more useful and enlightening to see her domestic poetry not in terms of chronological progression, but in terms of certain recurrent themes.

The same domestic themes run through all three of the the periods of Millay's career in which she wrote about her own or other women's experiences. The **"Sonnets from an Ungrafted Tree"** sequence deals with one of the most common: the relationship between husband and wife. This sequence appeared in the May 1923 issue of *Harpers* before it was collected in *The Harp-Weaver* volume. Millay did not marry until August 30th of that year. Thus, the poems were written before she herself could have had any actual experience as a wife. This fact makes the sequence all the more remarkable since it is one of the most striking portraits of a wife's situation in twentieth-century American poetry.

These sonnets tell the story of a wife who returns to the deathbed of her estranged husband. The wife Millay creates or describes here is a woman whose body has trapped her into marriage with a man she knows to be her intellectual and spiritual inferior. The woman was aware that her husband was "not over-kind nor over-quick in study / Nor skilled in sports nor beautiful" when she met him in school, but she married him anyway. Apparently even his physical passion did not prove to be a match for hers. In Sonnet IV, the woman's "desolate wish for comfort" and her intense efforts at starting a fire among "the sleeping ashes" seem a metaphorical experience suggesting the woman's frustrated efforts to kindle a physical passion in her past marital relationship. The woman is "mindful of like passion hurled in vain / Upon a similar task in other days." She brings her whole body to bear upon the "hilt" of the coals.

The woman's story is told primarily through such small domestic actions, rather than through explicit statements. We are told that the man does not measure up to the woman's dreams, that she married him because she was "so in need." But we are not told explicitly how their previous life together progressed or why they separated. What we are given are subtle insights into the woman's character and flashes of what her life in the house once was. Thus, we see her in Sonnet I in the past, presumably a new wife, "big-aproned, blithe, with stiff blue sleeves . . . plant[ing] seeds, musing ahead to their far blossoming." There is something promising and maternal in this picture of the woman planning ahead to a distant crop. In contrast are the geraniums, the "rotted stalks" of the present. She has not provided the necessary care to ensure that her plants survive the winter season. She abandoned them when she left her husband.

Sonnet I provides a further contrast with the woman's actions later in the sequence. Her figure, "big-aproned" and "blithe" in a past spring is contrasted to her discovery in Sonnet XI of an apron which she had lost in a long ago snowstorm. Finding the apron, she is struck "that here was spring, and the whole year to be lived through once more." It is as if the resurrection of the apron represents not a new year at all, but only the same year to be lived again. In fact, none of the promise of the image of the woman from her past is fulfilled. She comes back only to mother her dying husband and to muse, in the end, upon his corpse.

These poems do not reveal what has motivated the woman to return to care for her dying husband. Perhaps it is a sense of guilt or perhaps a sense of duty—certainly it is not love that has brought her. Her behavior, her desire to remain invisible to the eyes of the neighbors, suggests guilt.

Her instinct is always to flee. She leaves only the fanning of a rocker to the eyes of the grocer, just as the small bird she thinks she may have seen has left only its flash among the dwarf nasturtiums (shades of Emily Dickinson!). And the train's whistle at night brings her magic visions of cities that call to her as the whistle must have done when she first lived with the man as his wife.

The woman immerses herself in housekeeping as a distraction from her dying husband's "ever-clamorous care." She discovers that there is a "rapture of a decent kind, / In making mean and ugly objects fair." (It is to this kind of rapture that her desires have come.) She polishes the kitchen utensils, changes shelf paper, and replaces the table's oilcloth; but she is now only a visitor to the kitchen that once was hers. She has not been the one to position the soda and sugar; thus, they seem strange to her.

It is unclear whether or not the woman views domestic chores as a part of the trap of marriage. Perhaps it is only her disillusionment with the man and not her functions in the house which have caused the estrangement. The clean kitchen seems to give her pleasure; on the other hand, she finds saving the string and paper from the groceries a routine that is "treacherously dear" and "dull." And this is a woman who needs magic in her life, a woman for whom the common and everyday must be transformed.

As a girl she was blinded by a reflected light in a mirror held by the boyfriend, not by the vision of the boy himself. When it occurs to her that his dazzling her with a mirror is unmiraculous, she persists in viewing him by moonlight rather than by the clear and truthful light of day. The unsuccessful outcome of her marriage has not disillusioned the woman in general; she is still affected by the magic of the train's whistle. Only in matters concerning her husband has she given up hope of magic or surprise. She anticipates that in death he will be "only dead." But there is irony here. In Sonnet XVII, the last and perhaps the finest of the sequence, the woman is surprised by her dead husband. Considering him as "familiar as the bedroom door," she is surprised to discover in him a new dimension. In death he has a mystery about him that, in life, he had long since lost, or that she had only pretended was his.

These sonnets are serious, quiet, delicate pieces of work. Except for the epiphany in the final poem, the grand emotions of these characters are over. But the work is not slight or trivial. Much of Millay's work is uneven; however, except for the somewhat weak concluding couplet to Sonnet IX, this sequence is extremely well-written. Also, the sequence reveals a remarkable degree of imagination and insight into the female condition. Even though the essence of the story is said to be true [according to Jean Gould in her *The Poet and Her Book*], and even though Millay had done some housekeeping as the eldest daughter of a divorced and working mother, her understanding of the woman's emotional responses toward her husband—especially the epiphany in the concluding sonnet—is unaccounted for by what we know of her actual experience.

Whenever Millay writes about marriage, it is usually in the sad tone of **"Sonnets from an Ungrafted Tree,"** or in a disillusioned or cynical voice. A person is trapped, biologically, into marriage, or, like the husband in **"On the Wide Heath"** (*Wine from These Grapes,* 1934), trapped out of loneliness. This husband goes home "to a kitchen of a loud shrew" and

> Home to a worn reproach, the disagreeing,
> The shelter, the stale air, content to be
> Pecked at, confined, encroached upon,—it being
>   too lonely, to be free.

Also, the married person is one who resists being totally possessed. The speaker of **"Truck-Garden-Market Day"** (*Mine the Harvest*) for example, is happy to remain at home while her husband takes the produce to town because solitude gives her relief from his "noises." The time she is left alone represents to her the small part of herself she keeps from giving to him. She has already given him so much: "More than my heart to him I gave," she says, "who now am the timid, laughed-at slave." But she must not allow him to see how she feels, because:

> He would be troubled; he could not learn
> How small a part of myself I keep
> To smell the meadows, or sun the churn,
> When he's at market, or while he's asleep.

The woman is portrayed as preferring even a small housekeeping chore to the man's company. The woman's experience is different from her husband's, but by choice; and it is not necessarily inferior.

Perhaps Millay's most successful poem about marriage is one titled, **"An Ancient Gesture"** [from *Mine the Harvest*]:

> I thought, as I wiped my eyes on the corner of
>   my apron:
> Penelope did this too.
> And more than once; you can't keep weaving all
>   day
> And undoing it all through the night;
> Your arms get tired, and the back of your neck
>   gets tight;
> And along towards morning, when you think it
>   will never be light,
> And your husband has been gone, and you don't
>   know where, for years,
> Suddenly you burst into tears;
> There is simply nothing else to do
>
> And I thought, as I wiped my eyes on the corner
>   of my apron:
> This is an ancient gesture, authentic, antique,
> In the very best tradition, classic, Greek;
> Ulyssess did this too.
> But only as a gesture,—a gesture which implied
> To the assembled throng that he was much too
>   moved to speak.
> He learned it from Penelope . . .
> Penelope, who really cried.

This combining of the classic and the homely is surprising but perfectly appropriate. The poem expresses the universality of domestic experience for women as well as the differences in the nature of experience between women and men: Penelope, the stay-at-home, the weaver, contrasted with Ulysses, the venturer, adventurer, orator. Penelope's weaving, which according to myth never gets done, is a perfect symbol for woman's condition. Ulysses learns

something from his wife but then uses it superficially—to further his own ends. The sincerity and suffering of the woman are contrasted effectively with the political expediency of the man.

"Menses" (*Huntsman, What Quarry?*) is another poem that deals with marriage and with the differences between the sexes. The speaker is a man who humors the woman in a patronizing way. When the woman attacks him brutally, however, he forgives her, thinking to himself merely that she is "unwell." (She says at one point: "Lord, the shame, / The crying shame of seeing a man no wiser than the beasts he feeds—/ His skull as empty as a shell!") The poem ends with the woman's denunciation of her own weakness: "Just heaven consign and damn / To tedious Hell this body with its muddy feet in my mind!" Thus, it seems that the woman is as much or more concerned with the effect psychologically of her menstrual period on her intellect as with the effect on her relationship with the man.

The relationships between women and men and the differences between the sexes are thematically important to Millay's work. Maternity as subject or theme concerns her much less, although **"The Ballad of the Harp-Weaver,"** the poem for which she won the Pulitzer, tells the story of a mother's sacrifice for her child. In other poems, Millay oddly enough envisions herself (or her speakers) in strangely intense, maternal relationships with nature. Sometimes these visions are bizarre. In the apocalyptic poem **"The Blue-Flag in the Bog"** (*Second April,* 1921) she adopts a maternal posture toward the last flower left on earth. In **"The Little Hill"** (also *Second April*), she pictures herself as the mother of the hill where Christ died. But these conceits are mere oddities. Millay, although she had no children, could and did write successful poems about them. One example is an untitled poem [included in *Mine the Harvest*] in which she identifies with a child rather than with its mother. This poem deals with an adult's perception of birth as a betrayal. The second half reads:

> If you wish to witness a human countenance
>   contorted
> And convulsed and crumpled by helpless grief
>   and despair,
> Then stand beside the slatted crib and say There,
>   there, and take the toy away.
>
> Pink and pale-blue look well
> In a nursery. And for the most part Baby is
>   really good:
> He gurgles, he whimpers, he tries to get his toe
>   in his mouth; he slobbers his food
> Dreamily—cereals and vegetable juices—onto
>   his bib:
> He behaves as he should.
>
> But do not for a moment believe he has forgotten
>   Blackness; not the deep
> Easy swell; nor his thwarted
> Design to remain for ever there;
> Nor the crimson betrayal of his birth into a yel-
>   low glare.
> The pictures painted on the inner eyelids of in-
>   fants just before they sleep
> Are not pastel.

The sentiment almost inherent in this subject—baby in its pretty crib—is played off effectively against the strong ending of the poem. Removing the child's toy, which to the child is incomprehensible loss, signifies the incomprehensible losses and terrors life holds. The child still recalls the "betrayal" of its birth; and thus its dreams are not, as we might sentimentally like to believe, "pastel."

Another major theme, although not a familial one, is the preference for nature to housekeeping. One early (1920) and possibly autobiographical poem entitled **"Portrait by a Neighbor"** describes this preference. The poem begins:

> Before she has her floor swept
> Or her dishes done
> Any day you'll find her
> A-sunning in the sun!
>
>   *A Few Figs from Thistles*

And the same subject is more effectively treated in a late (1954), untitled poem in which the speaker recalls the discovery of nature's beauty and wonders how as mere child she could have withstood "the shock / Of beauty seen, noticed, for the first time." The speaker, now adult, still is staggered by the experience of encountering natural beauty—to the extent that she finds it impossible to turn from it to mundane, domestic chores:

> How did I bear it?—Now—grown up and encased
> In the armour of custom, after years
> Of looking at loveliness, forewarned
> And face to face, and no time
> And too prudent,
> At six in the morning to accept the unendurable embrace,
>
> I come back from the garden into the kitchen,
> And take off my rubbers—the dew
> Is heavy and high, wetting the sock above
> The shoe—but I cannot do
> The housework yet.
>
>   *Mine the Harvest*

"Cave Canem" (*Mine the Harvest*), another seemingly autobiographical poem (probably written after Boissevain's death), also reveals her preference for nature as well as continued concern over the encroachment of domesticity on her writing. In this lyric, the speaker complains that she must "throw bright time to chickens in an untidy yard"; and that she is "forced to sit while the potted roses wilt in the case or the / sonnet cools."

In **"The Plaid Dress"** (*Huntsman, What Quarry?*), Millay uses something feminine in much the same way that Edward Taylor used the homely and commonplace as an emblem through which to treat larger concerns:

> Strong sun, that bleach [sic]
> The curtains of my room, can you not render
> Colourless this dress I wear?—
> This violent plaid
> Of purple angers and red shames; the yellow stripe
> Of thin but valid treacheries; the flashy green of kind deeds done

> Through indolence, high judgments given in haste;
> The recurring checker of the serious breach of taste?
>
> No more uncoloured than unmade,
> I fear, can be this garment that I may not doff;
> Confession does not strip it off,
> To send me homeward eased and bare;
>
> All through the formal, unoffending evening, under the clean
> Bright hair,
> Lining the subtle gown . . . it is not seen,
> But it is there.

The speaker's violently-coloured dress is used as a metaphor to represent her emotions—her "purple angers and red shames." She can suppress these, but she cannot purge them from her personality.

Millay's letters to her editors reveal her own opinions about some of her work. They indicate that she preferred poems such as **"The Plaid Dress"** to what she called her more "modern" poems, poems of "the revolutionary element" concerning "the world outside myself today." It is revealing that she felt it necessary to defend her more personal, feminine poems, almost to apologize for them. The reason for her attitude undoubtedly lies in the critical reception to her work: when she wrote in the male tradition—that is, "abstract" and "intellectual" poetry—or when she wrote "shocking" verse, she was praised; when she wrote outside that tradition—the domestic poems—she was usually ignored or downgraded.

Of course Millay's "feminist" verse is important. It was flippant, fresh, and fun. It was popular with the public and helped gain her fame, and it was widely imitated by Dorothy Parker and other women poets of the period. But a reassessment of Millay suggests that her greater contribution and achievement have been in the poems she wrote of a more personal, more immediate nature, poems out of her own experience as a woman and out of her understanding of that experience on the part of other women. (pp. 94-105)

> *Jeannine Dobbs, "Edna St. Vincent Millay and the Tradition of Domestic Poetry," in* Journal of Women's Studies in Literature, *Vol. 1, No. 2, Spring, 1979, pp. 89-106.*

Jane Stanbrough (essay date 1979)

[*In the essay below, Stanbrough argues that despite Millay's public image of liberation and self-assurance, the language and structural patterns of her poetry suggest an inner world of vulnerability, submission, confinement, and frustration.*]

In 1917, when Edna St. Vincent Millay moved to Greenwich Village, her image as a woman of spirit and independence was already legendary. Previously, at Vassar, Millay had become a notorious public figure. She was a publishing poet, an impressive actress, and a dramatist of growing reputation. She had all along flaunted her independence impudently, smoking against the rules, cutting classes that were boring, earning a severe faculty reprimand which nearly deprived her of participation in her graduation ceremonies. This image of defiance was enhanced by her move to Greenwich Village, known as a hotbed of free-thinking radicals, and by her publication of five poems under the heading **"Figs from Thistles"** in *Poetry* in 1918, poems which vivified her inclination toward bohemianism and promiscuity. The famous first fig—"My candle burns at both ends; / It will not last the night; / But ah, my foes, and oh, my friends— / It gives a lovely light!"—immortalized her public image of daring and unconventional behavior. It came as no real shock, then, when in 1920 she published an entire volume of poetry (including the first five figs) entitled *A Few Figs from Thistles,* dominated by a narrative voice that irreverently mocked public opinion and public morality, that scorned imposed values and prescribed behavior.

This image of liberation and self-assurance is the public image Millay deliberately cultivated, the self-projection that stole the show, demanded applause and attention, suited a loud and raucous jazz-age temper. For half a century it has captivated readers and critics and minimized or veiled entirely a private anxiety-ridden image of profound self-doubt and personal anguish with which Millay contended all her life. The braggadocio of the public image is, in fact, contradictory to experience as Millay inwardly felt it and is belied by both the language and the form through which she reflected her deepest sense of that experience. Although the poetry in *Figs* solidified that public image of defiance and independence, it did so in language and structural patterns that divulge a private image of submission and constriction. The dominant tone of the body of her work—the tone of heart-rending anguish—is apparent when she works at flippancy. Millay is unquestionably a woman who suffers, and the greatest source of her suffering seems to lie in an overwhelming sense of personal vulnerability—and ultimately of woman's vulnerability—to victimization by uncontrollable conditions in her environment.

This sense of vulnerability provides one of the richest linguistic patterns in her poetry, for in spite of her efforts to repress and protect a part of her emotional life, Millay is exposed and betrayed through a language pattern which calls attention to the emotional conflicts and tensions, the psychic realities of her existence. This pattern of self-revelation appears consistently throughout her work, though sometimes disguised by attitudes associated with the public image. **"Grown-up,"** for example (from *Figs*), seems to be merely a cute, little versified cliché about the disillusioning process of growing up.

> Was it for this I uttered prayers,
> And sobbed and cursed and kicked the stairs,
> That now, domestic as a plate,
> I should retire at half-past eight?

Notice the violence in the verbs; aptly, they do evoke an image of an unruly child, but they also suggest the strength of the frustration of the narrator for something absent from her life. The contrasting image, domestic as a plate, is perfectly appropriate to imply the flatness and brittleness and coldness that condition her existence.

Growing into adult domesticity for this woman has been a process of subduing the will and shrinking the soul. The last line carries the shrinking image to its ultimate conclusion: oblivion, implied by the verb "retire." The woman is painfully aware of the disparity between her childhood hopes and the realities of her adult experience, a theme Millay treats at length in **"Sonnets from an Ungrafted Tree."** Here, the emptiness of the woman's life is made explicit by the fact that she retires at half-past eight, when for many the evening's activities have barely begun. This poem is a strong statement of protest against the processes that mitigate fulfilling and satisfying experience. Certainly, the poem might be read simply as a statement of the inadequacy of experience to measure up to the imaginative conception of it. But it is more. It is a specific statement about woman's experience. "Domestic as a plate" is an image that fits woman into her conventional place at rest on a shelf and out of the way. The poem reflects Millay's fears of her own fate and aids our understanding of the poet's excessive urge to proclaim herself a free and unconfined spirit.

Other poems in the *Figs* volume seem just as adolescently superficial as **"Grown-up"** but under closer analysis corroborate this deep sense of confinement and frustration. Both **"The Unexplorer"** and **"To the Not Impossible Him"** employ a central metaphor of limited travel to suggest the nature of the oppression and restriction felt by the narrators. In **"The Unexplorer,"** the child-narrator is inspired to "explore" the road beyond the house, but on the basis of information provided by her mother—"It brought you to the milk-man's door"—she has resigned herself to confinement. She rather wistfully explains, "That's why I have not travelled more." The implications of familial repression in the socialization process of the female are rather grim. In **"To the Not Impossible Him,"** while the tone is light and the pose coyly provocative, the issue again is serious. The last stanza concludes:

> The fabric of my faithful love
> No power shall dim or ravel
> Whilst I stay here,—but oh, my dear,
> If I should ever travel!

Confining the female, denying her experience, the narrator suggests, is the only sure way of forcing her into the social mold. Millay says a great deal more about this process in *Fatal Interview,* a collection of fifty-one sonnets published in 1931.

The structural simplicity and childlike narrative voice are techniques Millay used frequently in her early work. **"Afternoon on a Hill,"** published in 1917, appears to be too simple a poem to give a serious reading. In imitation of childhood speech and thus childhood experience, its regular meter and rhymed quatrains, its childlike diction and sentence structure effectively convey the notion of woman as child. The stanzas, significantly without metrical variation, measure out their syllables as repetitiously as the child's days:

> I will be the gladdest thing
> Under the sun!
> I will touch a hundred flowers
> And not pick one.

I will look at cliffs and clouds
With quiet eyes,
Watch the wind bow down the grass,
And the grass rise.

And when lights begin to show
Up from the town,
I will mark which must be mine,
And then start down!

Though appearing to lack subtlety and complexity, the poem does create a tension through an ironic disparity between the directness in tone and structure and the implications of the experience. The speaker seems to symbolize childhood's innocence and freedom. But the freedom, in fact, is artificial, for the child is regulated and restrained. She reaches out; she withdraws. "I will touch a hundred flowers," she decides, but then promises obediently: "And not pick one." The passivity outlined in this poem—looking, watching, obeying—again ends with the narrator's total retreat. It is, on the surface, an innocent-looking action. But it is a form of surrender. Throughout the poem one hears the promises of the "good little girl." She will do what is expected of her; she will watch quietly and disturb nothing.

Psychological experiences merely hinted at in this poem are verified directly and harshly in later poems. In **"Above These Cares"** Millay's narrator nearly screams out her recognition of her state:

Painfully, under the pressure that obtains
At the sea's bottom, crushing my lungs and my
   brains
(For the body makes shift to breathe and after
   a fashion flourish
Ten fathoms deep in care,
Ten fathoms down in an element denser than air
Wherein the soul must perish)
I trap and harvest, stilling my stomach's needs:
I crawl forever, hoping never to see
Above my head the limbs of my spirit no longer
   free
Kicking in frenzy, a swimmer enmeshed in
   weeds.

The woman's vulnerability is absolute because she is so helplessly ensnared. Her feelings of oppression and spiritual suffocation are excruciatingly described, and she craves a numbing of her consciousness to dull the pain of her awareness. The psychological disintegration resulting from thwarted experience shown in this poem is further displayed in **"Scrub,"** where the disillusioned narrator reflects bitterly on the meaning of her oppression and recognizes its origins in childhood:

If I grow bitterly,
Like a gnarled and stunted tree,
Bearing harshly of my youth
Puckered fruit that sears the mouth;
If I make of my drawn boughs
An inhospitable house,
Out of which I never pry
Towards the water and the sky,
Under which I stand and hide
And hear the day go by outside;
It is that a wind too strong
Bent my back when I was young,

It is that I fear the rain
Lest it blister me again.

Made vulnerable by its natural inclination to stretch and grow, the tree is thus subjected to attack and mutilation by forces in its environment; it is bent and blistered into submission. Terrorized and intimidated in the process, the woman—like the child who reaches to touch the flowers—makes a complete withdrawal inside "An inhospitable house, / Out of which I never pry / Towards the water and the sky, / Under which I stand and hide. . . ." Imagining herself like the tree to be deformed and grotesque, the mutilated narrator bemoans the psychological crippling of denied opportunities and punitive restrictions.

Millay found the child-narrator device very suggestive of woman's susceptibility to intimidation. In her vulnerability to victimization, the child in **"Afternoon on a Hill"** is psychologically parallel to the terrorized woman of **"Assault,"** a poem first published in 1920 in *The New Republic.*

I had forgotten how the frogs must sound
After a year of silence, else I think
I should not so have ventured forth alone
At dusk upon this unfrequented road.

I am waylaid by Beauty. Who will walk
Between me and the crying of the frogs?
Oh, savage Beauty, suffer me to pass,
That am a timid woman, on her way
From one house to another!

Here, ostensibly, is the narrator's expression of her sensitivity to and appreciation for the beauties of nature. But the word choice and the ideas evoked call into question so superficial a reading. The speaker describes the experience as an ambush where she is assaulted, "waylaid," forced by a savage attacker into terrified submission, an image obviously suggestive of rape. The woman is confused as well as terrified, and her bewilderment is apparent in the ambiguity of her perceptions. She calls her assailant Beauty, suggesting a benign, even attractive attacker. Yet, she describes the attack as savage and further qualifies its nature by defining Beauty in the shape of frogs. She thinks she hears them crying, and in a spontaneous outburst of identification with their pain, she too cries, "Oh, savage Beauty, suffer me to pass." The choice of "suffer" is brilliantly placed to capsulize the poem's theme, which is a vivid description of the author's sense of vulnerability and the suffering that accompanies it. The speaker feels isolated, unprotected, intimidated. In this poem Millay has cleverly succeeded in defining woman's sense of her true condition by capitalizing on a common assumption about the excessive emotional nature of women. At the same time, she has implied that woman's oppressor is a deceptively disguised external force.

Millay's insistent use of verbs of assault and bombardment is an index to her concept of reality. She may title a poem **"Spring,"** but she really sees the brains of men eaten by maggots; she may claim that she sorrows over the **"Death of Autumn,"** but she portrays a malign force controlling the world, for the autumn rushes are "flattened"; the creek is "stripped"; beauty, "stiffened"; the narrator, crushed.

> Millay's victims are all alike: innocent, helpless, unsuspecting, unarmed, in every way vulnerable. And they are all embodiments of Millay, the anguished, writhing, defenseless, and finally defeated victim.
>
> —*Jane Stanbrough*

All around her in the systematic operation of the elements Millay perceives the processes of barbaric intrusion and fatal attack. Millay's use of nature, which seems to depict typical romantic disillusionment with the transcience of beauty, is in fact loaded with psychological and social implications. In **"Low-Tide,"** the tide's movements, like the conditions of her existence, are inexorable. There are beautiful surfaces, but treacherous realities: "No place to dream, but a place to die." Here, again, the figure of a child qualifies the state of vulnerability. The narrator lacks knowledge and experience. Trusting and unsuspicious, she is susceptible to betrayal. This childlike susceptibility is consciously rendered in **"Being Young and Green"**:

> Being young and green, I said in love's despite:
> Never in the world will I to living wight
> Give over, air my mind
> To anyone,
> Hang out its ancient secrets in the strong wind
> To be shredded and faded. . . .
> Oh, me, invaded
> And sacked by the wind and the sun!

Millay's use of "ancient secrets" is highly suggestive of the private self she wishes to protect, but neither consciousness nor will is a strong enough defense against attack and exposure. The words "invaded and sacked," like "way-laid" in **"Assault,"** indicate both the treacherousness of the assailant and the devastation of the attack. Fearing ridicule as well as exposure, the narrator tries to forearm herself, but she is helpless against the assaulting invisible powers, which she names here as wind and sun. The intrusion is forced and, in a social context, implies the act of rape. The intensity of Millay's sense of personal violation is felt in the imagery of **"Moriturus"**:

> I shall bolt my door
> With a bolt and cable;
> I shall block my door
> With a bureau and a table;
>
> With all my might
> My door shall be barred.
> I shall put up a fight,
> I shall take it hard.
>
> With his hand on my mouth
> He shall drag me forth,
> Shrieking to the south
> And clutching at the north.

The attacker in this poem is identified as death, but for Millay the horror of the experience is not in the idea of dying, but in the vision of the brutalizing attack by which she is forced to a complete surrender. Millay's narrator is vulnerable to attack and to exploitation because of some basic inferiority, and, as the rape image implies, it lies in her sexuality.

When Millay left Vassar in 1917 to do whatever she liked with the world, as President McCracken had assured her she could, she must soon have been stunned and distressed at the world's reception of her. She tells her family:

> Mrs. Thompson, a lovely woman who helped put me through college wants me to come & be her secretary for a while— . . . but I just don' wanna! . . . Of course, I feel like the underneath of a toad not to do what she wants me to do—but I can't make up my mind to address envelopes and make out card catalogues all fall . . . be called on to answer the telephone and make appointments & reject invites. I might have been governess to the Aults, except for a similar feeling about my independence.

Professionally, at graduation, she wanted more than anything to be an actress. She hoped also to continue to write plays and poetry. She believed in her own genius, and **"The Bean-Stalk,"** published in 1920 in *Poetry,* seems to reflect the *Figs'* public image of self-confidence:

> Ho, Giant! This is I!
> I have built me a bean-stalk into your sky!
> La,—but it's lovely, up so high!
>
> This is how I came,—I put
> Here my knee, there my foot,
> Up and up, from shoot to shoot—

The possibilities are exhilarating:

> What a wind! What a morning!—

But imagery in a middle section of the poem counteracts that sense of exhilaration and faith with a description of the real effects of the climb and the wind upon the climber. Even the first line's intention to emphasize the speaker's identity is undercut by the notion of "giant." The climber becomes suddenly insecure and uncertain in her position; she realizes that she is open to the wind, vulnerable to attack. She may even doubt her talent:

> . . . bean-stalks is my trade,
> I couldn't make a shelf,
> Don't know how they're made,

The wind, first viewed as an exhilarating force, is soon felt as an assailant which nearly dislodges her, an assailant which she can neither see nor combat:

> And the wind was like a whip
> Cracking past my icy ears,
> And my hair stood out behind,
> And my eyes were full of tears,
> Wide-open and cold,
> More tears than they could hold,
> The wind was blowing so,
> And my teeth were in a row,
> Dry and grinning,
> And I felt my foot slip
> And I scratched the wind and whined,
> And I clutched the stalk and jabbered,

With my eyes shut blind,—
What a wind! What a wind!

The blowing, whipping, cracking force of the wind strips her to a skeleton. Though the experience is terrifying and the climber confounded by the violence of the attack and the wind's capriciousness, the climber holds her position, struggling to resist the devastating power of her adversary. It is a tentative position, however, for the wind is a treacherous force, invisible, deceptive—an excellent symbol for the undefined powers which seem to impede Millay's efforts and cause her such suffering, powers she ultimately associates with social oppression and political tyranny.

Millay did not become an actress. She wrote few plays. She spent her life struggling for survival as a poet. This may be difficult for readers to understand who know that Millay was a Pulitzer Prize winner, a popular lecturer, a well-known and sought-after personality whose poems were published, reviewed, and read. But we are not dealing with external data merely; we are examining the poetry for insights into the truth of Millay's inner sense of herself and her achievements. The language pattern of vulnerability suggests strongly that Millay saw herself as a misfit and a failure and that she believed that some external forces in her life impeded her development and inflicted permanent injury. An untitled poem in her posthumous collection, *Mine the Harvest,* conveys an understanding of the power and insidiousness of the enemy and a resignation to her fate. Again the verb pattern defines the sense of vulnerability and impending disaster felt by the narrator; the image of the overpowering force of the wave summarizes a lifetime of futile effort to transcend and resist a society which she feels has conspired to destroy her.

> Establishment is shocked. Stir no adventure
> Upon this splitted granite.
>
> I will no longer connive
> At my own destruction:—I will not again climb,
> Breaking my finger nails, out of reach of the
>   reaching wave,
> To save
> What I hope will still be me
> When I have slid on slime and clutched at slip-
>   pery rock-weed, and had my face towed under
> In scrubbing pebbles, under the weight of the
>   wave and its thunder.
> I decline to scratch at this cliff. *If* is not a word.
> I will connive no more
> With that which hopes and plans that I shall not
>   survive:
> Let the tide keep its distance;
> Or advance, and be split for a moment by a thing
>   very small but all resistance;
> Then do its own chore.

Here Millay identifies the malignant force assailing her as the establishment, and the causes for her deep sense of victimization are less opaque. She feels outside the establishment, in opposition to social tradition and authority. She had sensed as a young woman that the world was "no fit place for a child to play." She had discovered that for women, as for children, the beautiful things were out of reach. For Millay, the realities of her life were found in the rigidly structured patterns of social behavior: you must

not smoke at Vassar; you must not be an actress if you want Lady Caroline's financial assistance; you must consider being a social secretary if you really seek employment; you must marry; you must have children; you must not offend conventional morality if you want recognition; you must be male if you want serious criticism of your poetry.

Millay concedes in this untitled poem that society does not tolerate its individualists; especially does it not tolerate its independent women. To be a nonconformist is to be exposed and intimidated, like the woman in **"Assault"**; it is to feel like the lone traveler in **"How Naked, How Without a Wall,"** chilled by the night air, struck by sharp sleet, buffeted by wind, vulnerable to the wolf's attack. The social ramifications are explicit in this poem. For this traveler, since he chooses to venture "forth alone / When other men are snug within," the world is a terrifying place of loneliness, alienation, inevitable catastrophe. Most people, Millay feels, are vulnerable to social pressures; some will compromise. Some will suffer self-betrayal rather than isolation, as another of Millay's travelers does in **"On the Wide Heath,"** surrendering himself to a loud shrew, a poaching son, a daughter with a disdainful smile:

> Home to the worn reproach, the disagreeing,
> The shelter, the stale air; content to be
> Pecked at, confined, encroached upon,—it being
> Too lonely, to be free.

The imagery of confinement and attack offer an unbearable alternative to the individual who is forced to acknowledge, as this narrator does in that haunting statement of vulnerability: "it being / Too lonely, to be free."

For Millay, reality is oppression and victimization, and she feels attacked by forces that tyrannize, whether she names them sun and wind, as she does in her early poetry, or hangmen and huntsmen, as she does later. The shift in focus is significant, for it marks a deliberate attempt by Millay to explain her sense of victimization in a larger context of social injustices. She sees that justice is denied in Massachusetts and that the huntsman gains on the quarry.

Victimization by totalitarian powers is subtly suggested in **"The Buck in the Snow,"** where we see death, as in slow motion, "bringing to his knees, bringing to his antlers / The buck in the snow." Horrified, with the narrator, we witness the capitulation, the ultimate defeat of beauty and freedom and life. The buck, vulnerable, defenseless, goes down before an invisible, armed, socially sanctioned slaughterer. In **"The Rabbit,"** the speaker, suffering excruciatingly for her greater awareness of reality than the rabbit has, screams a warning to the rabbit.

> 'O indiscreet!
> And the hawk and all my friends are out to kill!
> Get under cover!' But the rabbit never stirred;
>   she never will.
> And I shall see again and again the large eye
>   blaze
> With death, and gently glaze;
> The leap into the air I shall see again and again,
>   and the kicking feet;
> And the sudden quiet everlasting, and the blade

of grass green in the strange mouth of the interrupted grazer.

The real significance of the whole range of verbs of assault
is crystalized here in the verb "kill." Millay's victims are
all alike: innocent, helpless, unsuspecting, unarmed, in
every way vulnerable. And they are all embodiments of
Millay, the anguished, writhing, defenseless, and finally
defeated victim. Millay's profound suffering and her constant rendering of personal vulnerability become increasingly comprehensible in the context of her imagery of
woman as victim.

Virginia Woolf understood the agonies and stresses of gifted women struggling against conditions of oppression.
"For it needs little skill in psychology," she wrote in *A
Room of One's Own,* "to be sure that a highly gifted girl
who had tried to use her gift for poetry would have been
so thwarted and hindered by other people, so tortured and
pulled asunder by her own contrary instincts, that she
must have lost her health to a certainty." Millay's personal feelings of oppression and the realities of social restrictions imposed on her own professional ambitions and desires are poignantly stated in Section V of **"Not So Far as
the Forest,"** where the figure of the wounded and confined
bird suggests an authentic self-projection:

> Poor passionate thing,
> Even with this clipped wing how well you
> flew!—though not so far as the forest.

The bird initially presents an appearance of freedom and
capability, striking for the top branches in the distant forest. But the bird's weakness, his vulnerability to defeat, invisible at first in his attempted flight, is ultimately disclosed. It is his ambition, described in the poem as "the
eye's bright trouble," that has made him vulnerable. He
has been victimized by "the unequal wind," that seductive
environmental force with its seeming beneficence but real
destructive power; and he has been chained by a human
hand:

> Rebellious bird, . . .
> Has no one told you?—Hopeless is your flight
> Toward the high branches. . . .
>
> Though Time refeather the wing,
> Ankle slip the ring,
> The once-confined thing
> Is never again free.

Millay responded passionately and deeply to visions of
suffering victims, from the starving man in Capri to the
war victims of Lidice. These visions correspond closely to
her view of herself as victim, and her use of language patterns of vulnerability take on greater significance as she
develops her understanding of herself as a woman in a
world where women's values and feelings are either predetermined or discarded. Millay's frequent use of the childlike narrator is increasingly understandable in the context
of her vulnerability to the world's view and treatment of
her as a woman. The nature of her existence, like the nature of her vulnerability, is thus qualified by the fact that
she experiences the world as a woman.

"The Fitting" is well titled to suggest Millay's sense of
woman's social conditioning to fit the narrow role prescribed for her. Through verbs that attempt to mask the
degree of harm inflicted in the process, the narrator bitterly expresses her sense of personal violation. She submits
to the fitting in a state of mannikin-like paralysis.

> The fitter said, *'Madame, vous avez maigri,'*
> And pinched together a handful of skirt at my
>   hip.
> *'Tant mieux,'* I said, and looked away slowly,
>   and took my under-lip
> Softly between my teeth.
>
> Rip—rip!
> Out came the seam, and was pinned together in
>   another place.
> She knelt before me, a hardworking woman with
>   a familiar and unknown face,
> Dressed in linty black, very tight in the arm's-
>   eye and smelling of sweat.
> She rose, lifting my arm, and set her cold shears
>   against me,—snip-snip;
> Her knuckles gouged my breast. My drooped
>   eyes lifted to my guarded eyes in the glass, and
>   glanced away as from someone they had never
>   met.
>
> *'Ah, que madame a maigri!'* cried the *vendeuse,*
>   coming in with dresses over her arm.
> *'C'est la chaleur,'* I said, looking out into the
>   sunny tops of the horse-chestnuts—and in-
>   deed it was very warm.
>
> I stood for a long time so, looking out into the
>   afternoon, thinking of the evening and
>   you. . . .
> While they murmured busily in the distance,
>   turning me, touching my secret body, doing
>   what they were paid to do.

The narrator suffers both indignity and depersonalization
in the fitting process. For one moment only—in a single
line in the poem—does Millay allow the imaginative escape to seem a possibility. This emphasis is quite different
from that of **"The Bean-Stalk,"** where fantasized possibility is the poem's overriding effect.

Two of Millay's best and longest sonnet sequences, *Fatal
Interview* and **"Sonnets from an Ungrafted Tree,"** dramatize further through metaphors of love and marriage the
fatality of woman's vulnerability to social conditioning.
Fatal Interview is an extended metaphorical illustration
of the consequences to women of their limited range of experience and their susceptibility to emotional exploitation.
"Women's ways are witless ways," Millay states in a *Figs*
poem, and *Fatal Interview* dramatically narrates how
woman is trained to react emotionally to her environment
and how devastating the results of such training are. The
title suggests the nature of the results. Sonnet xvii of the
sequence portrays woman's naiveté and lack of preparation for such an "interview" as she encounters:

> Sweet love, sweet thorn, when lightly to my
>   heart
> I took your thrust, whereby I since am slain,
> And lie disheveled in the grass apart,
> A sodden thing bedrenched by tears and rain,
>
>   . . . . .

Had I bethought me then, sweet love, sweet
    thorn,
How sharp an anguish even at the best,
When all's requited and the future sworn,
The happy hour can leave within the breast,
I had not so come running at the call
Of one who loves me little, if at all.

An innocent believer in the value of her feelings, the woman opens herself to her lover's thrust. The sexual implications of "thrust" give emphasis to the irony of the woman's willing surrender to rape and murder. Through the image of happy submission to her slayer, Millay sharply renders the utter pathos of woman's susceptibility. Too late she discovers the insignificance of her self, her life. The sequence dramatizes the spiritual disintegration that must occur through the social conditioning that explains woman's nature as essentially emotional and her greatest need as love. The entire sequence is relentless in its presentation of love's ravaging and immobilizing effects upon women whose lives are so isolated and confined. Sonnet lxxi epitomizes the victim's scarred state:

This beast that rends me in the sight of all,

   . . . . .

Will glut, will sicken, will be gone by spring.

   . . . . .

I shall forget before the flickers mate
Your look that is today my east and west.
Unscathed, however, from a claw so deep
Though I should love again I shall not go. . . .

Throughout the sonnets, the narrator exposes her emotional vulnerability to assault, humiliation, abuse, abandonment, annihilation.

How drowned in love and weedily washed
    ashore,
There to be fretted by the drag and shove
At the tide's edge, I lie— . . .

   . . . . .

Small chance, however, in a storm so black,
A man will leave his friendly fire and snug
For a drowned woman's sake, and bring her
    back
To drip and scatter shells upon the rug. . . .

Brutalization and victimization characterize woman's existence.

In **"Sonnets from an Ungrafted Tree"** the New England woman narrator poignantly and unforgettably reveals how she has been trapped by her illusions of romance and by her dreams of beauty into a relationship which strangles her emotionally and spiritually. One of Millay's most brilliant images of woman's spiritual suffocation is found in Sonnet xi of this sequence:

It came into her mind, seeing how the snow
Was gone, and the brown grass exposed again,
And clothes-pins, and an apron—long ago,
In some white storm that sifted through the pane
And sent her forth reluctantly at last
To gather in, before the line gave way,

Garments, board-stiff, that galloped on the blast
Clashing like angel armies in a fray,
An apron long ago in such a night
Blown down and buried in the deepening drift,
To lie till April thawed it back to sight,
Forgotten, quaint and novel as a gift—
It struck her, as she pulled and pried and tore,
That here was spring, and the whole year to be
    lived through once more.

Representing woman's condition, the apron, confined to the clothesline, is contrasted to the figure of clashing armies, suggestive of her imagined dreams of adventure and romance—dreams fulfilled only in a masculine world. The apron, obviously an article of domestic servitude, is a symbol for the woman's relinquished self, "Board-stiff," "blown down and buried" years before. Even then, this woman had half perceived the futility of her dreams and had gone out reluctantly to pull and pry and tear at the apron to try to resurrect it. Ultimately, the woman surrenders

   . . . her mind's vision plain
The magic World, where cities stood on end . . .
Remote from where she lay—and yet—between,
Save for something asleep beside her, only the
    window screen.

The restrictive realities of her life—something asleep beside her and the window screen—are stark contrasts to the waning dreams of her imagined self.

It is understandable why Millay's two extended narratives of woman's psychological disintegration are presented in sonnet sequences. Millay persistently resorts to the constraints of traditional verse forms. Given her time and place in the history of American poetry and given the external evidence of her unconventional childhood and youthful radicalism, one would expect to find her in the company of the avant-garde of American poetry. But Millay is no true Imagist. She eschews the freedoms of form which Ezra Pound had defined as essential to the new poetry. The sonnet, her best form, is a fit vehicle to convey her deepest feelings of woman's victimization. Through it, Millay imaginatively reenacts her constant struggle against boundaries. The wish for freedom is always qualified by the sense of restriction; couplets and quatrains suit her sensibility.

In Millay's poetry, women, in their quiet lives of fatal desires and futile gestures, are tragic and heroic. She identifies herself with suffering women, women whose dreams are denied, whose bodies are assaulted, whose minds and spirits are extinguished. She states her consciousness of the universality of women's vulnerability and anguish in **"An Ancient Gesture,"** contrasting Penelope's tears with those of Ulysses:

I thought, as I wiped my eyes on the corner of
    my apron:
Penelope did this too.
And more than once: you can't keep weaving all
    day
And undoing it all through the night;
Your arms get tired, and the back of your neck
    gets tight;

And along towards morning, when you think it
    will never be light,
And your husband has been gone, and you don't
    know where, for years,
Suddenly you burst into tears;
There is simply nothing else to do.

And I thought, as I wiped my eyes on the corner
    of my apron:
This is an ancient gesture, authentic, antique,
In the very best tradition, classic, Greek:
Ulysses did this too.
But only as a gesture,—a gesture which implied
To the assembled throng that he was much too
    moved to speak.
He learned it from Penelope . . .
Penelope, who really cried.

From the earliest volume, **Renascence,** where even her youthful awakening is accompanied by its grief-laden songs of shattering, through her posthumous harvest of mature experience, Millay records, unrelentingly, her life of pain and frustration. If she too loudly insisted on the public self's claims for freedom to love and think and feel and work as she pleased, she nevertheless quietly throughout her work continued to send out her linguistic distress signals. It is her profound insight into her self's inevitable capitulation that makes Millay ultimately so vulnerable and her poetry so meaningful. (pp. 183-99)

> *Jane Stanbrough, "Edna St. Vincent Millay and the Language of Vulnerability," in* Shakespeare's Sisters: Feminist Essays on Women Poets, *edited by Sandra M. Gilbert and Susan Gubar, Indiana University Press, 1979, pp. 183-99.*

Debra Fried   (essay date 1986)

[*In the following essay, Fried discusses the significance of Millay's use of traditional sonnet form in relation to the influence of modernism on her poetry, her repudiation of social conventions, and her status as a woman poet.*]

In a critical climate in which we are rediscovering the powerful experiments of American women poets in the modernist era, the tidy verses of Edna St. Vincent Millay have remained something of an embarrassment. Tough-minded as they can be about sex, betrayal, and the price of being a woman who can write candidly about such matters, Millay's poems, particularly her sonnets, can often seem like retrograde schoolgirl exercises amidst the vanguard verbal dazzle of H. D., Mina Loy, Gertrude Stein, and Marianne Moore. In revising the history of modernism to make more central the achievements of these innovative poets, it has been convenient to dismiss Millay's work as copybook bohemianism. Millay may rightly be judged as a minor star in this constellation, but this is not, I think, why there have been so few serious investigations of Millay of late. Our silence attests rather to a failure to ask the right questions about how traditional poetic forms such as the sonnet may serve the needs of women poets. Why does a woman poet in this century elect to write sonnets? What sort of gender associations can a poetic form

such as the sonnet accumulate, and how may such associations, and consequent exclusions, make that genre an especially lively arena for the revisionary acts of women's poetry? What model of the relation between generic restraints and expressive freedom is suggested by the sonnet? How does genre shape the meanings of allusion within a sonnet, particularly allusions to other sonnets? And, most centrally for thinking about Millay, how has the sonnet historically implied connections between formal (generic, metrical, rhetorical) constraints and sexual ones?

Instead of asking such questions, we have tended to assume that we know just how and why a poet like Millay must use circumscribed, traditional poetic forms: to rein in her strong, unruly feelings. This idea is a commonplace in earlier writing on the poet, as in Jean Gould's observation in her popular biography [*The Poet and Her Book*] that Millay "found security in classical form: the sonnet was the golden scepter with which she ruled her poetic passions." We can find similar claims in two recent essays on Millay's poetry. Jane Stanbrough caps a persuasive analysis of the deep sense of submission and constriction that lies behind Millay's seemingly defiant, unharnessed poetry [in her "Edna St. Vincent Millay and the Language of Vulnerability" in *Shakespeare's Sisters: Feminist Essays on Women Poets,* edited by Sandra Gilbert and Susan Gubar] with the observation that Millay's sonnets and sonnet sequences illustrate her tendency to "resort to the constraints of traditional verse form":

> The sonnet, her best form, is a fit vehicle to convey her deepest feelings of woman's victimization. Through it, Millay imaginatively reenacts her constant struggle against boundaries. The wish for freedom is always qualified by the sense of restriction; couplets and quatrains suit her sensibility.

This claim, sensible as it sounds, calls for considerable scrutiny. What poetic "sensibility," we may ask, is not in some degree suited to the strictures of poetic form? (Isn't that what it would mean to have a poetic sensibility?) The identification of sonnets with a creative temperament that both needs boundaries and needs to strain against them is by no means applicable exclusively to Millay or to women poets. Too many assumptions go untested in Stanbrough's implication that in Millay's dependence on poetic constraints to embody the drama of vulnerability and resistance we witness a particularly female response to lyric form. A full declaration of those assumptions would require an inquiry into the ways a potentially stifling poetic form may amplify—give pitch, density, and strength to—a poet's voice. If we are to isolate the particular resources, if any, with which a woman poet may rebel against formal constraints, we must begin with an examination of the tropes for the sonnet that are part of the history of that genre. Only then can we determine the particular uses a woman poet can make of the liberating fetters of the sonnet form. The power of Millay's sonnets, and their usefulness for the study of the relations between gender and genre in twentieth-century poetry, derives from the readiness with which, while working within formal boundaries, they challenge the figurations for which the sonnet has been traditionally a receptive home. Through her revisions of those tropes and related devices—particularly as found in sonnets of Wordsworth and Keats—Millay's allusive sonnets, I will contend, reclaim that genre as her plot of ground, not chiefly by planting it with "woman's" themes or using it as mouthpiece for the woman's voice (though she does both these things), but by rethinking the form's historical capacity for silencing her voice.

It is this kind of reflectiveness about what it means to work within traditional forms that another recent essay would seem to deny to Millay. In a study of the Elizabethan sonnets of Millay and Elinor Wylie, [in *Poetic Traditions of the English Renaissance* edited by Maynard Mack and George de Forest Lord], Judith Farr argues that Millay's particular temperaments, attitudes, and skills sometimes led her to

> marshall against the lively but serene mathematics of contained forms like the sonnet, quatrain, or couplet a battery of dissheveled impulses expressed in terms calculated to shock. . . . Millay's best work exhibits a tutored sensibility that enabled her to compose effectively within literary traditions she respected. The Petrarchan conventions to which she submitted in *Fatal Interview* served her well, moreover, disciplining her imagination yet encouraging the emotional scope her poetry instinctively sought.

One may readily take Farr's point that all of Millay's efforts in the Elizabethan mode are not equally successful. More questionable is the assumption here that the poet Millay is a creature of raw emotion or instinct who, when she is good, submits to a form that will tame that rawness, and when she is bad, invades the decorous parlors of poetic form like a spoiled child with her mad manners. The language of power in this passage from Farr's essay is also tellingly confused: the process whereby conventions to which the poet "submits" may then in turn submit to or "serve" her is a complicated one that needs to be explained and argued in specific instances. To assume, as Farr would appear to do, that in choosing "contained forms" Millay either bombards them with mischievous, whimsical "impulses" (are these the same as the "emotional scope her poetry instinctively sought"?) or submissively "composes" within them lest impulse get the better of her, is to imply that Millay worked unwittingly at the mercy of these opposed moods. But the question of whether writing in an established lyric genre is an act of taking command or of being commanded is one upon which Millay's sonnets reflect.

It is, moreover, a reflection to which Millay found the sonnet is supremely suited, in part because it is a subject explored in the English Romantic sonnets Millay knew well. One of the dubious things about Stanbrough's and Farr's accounts of why Millay found the sonnet suited to her poetic needs is that they so strikingly resemble Wordsworth's claim that he turned to the sonnet to find relief from "too much liberty." The sonnet is such a difficult form that from its inception in English it took as one of its topics the paradoxical release and scope to be derived from its intricate formal requirements. (pp. 1-4)

Edna St. Vincent Millay found herself in what was perhaps a unique position in the history of women writing poetry; she was called upon to uphold the tradition of binding lyric forms against the onslaught of what her supporters saw as a dangerously shapeless modernism. In 1917 the prodigious schoolgirl who wrote **"Renascence"** represented "an alternative to the 'new' poetry . . . whose work could serve as a rallying point for the rejection of free verse, imagism, and Prufrockian ennui" [according to Elizabeth P. Perlmutter in "A Doll's Heart: The Girl in the Poetry of Edna St. Vincent Millay and Louise Brogan," *Twentieth Century Literature*, Vol. 23, 1977]. At the same time Millay was identified with the bohemian literary life of Greenwich Village, seen as a kind of poetic flapper who, as Elizabeth Atkins put it in 1936, "represents our time to itself." It was, in short, an interesting time for a woman to be writing sonnets. The issues of poetic and sexual freedom were being explicitly linked; why should free-spirited Millay stick to the sonnet when other women poets were experimenting with free verse? It would be easy to suspect the poet of merely posturing at promiscuity, aping a man's freedom in order to earn the respite of poetic formalism on a man's ground. But for her the sonnet's formal patterns and its brevity both come to figure the price of freedom rather than a welcome retreat from it.

The power of Millay's sonnets, and their usefulness for the study of the relations between gender and genre in twentieth-century poetry, derives from the readiness with which, while working within formal boundaries, they challenge the figurations for which the sonnet has been traditionally a receptive home.

—Debra Fried

To the degree that Millay identifies the working of the sonnet with the poetics of the bohemian life, she rejects the Wordsworthian figuration of the sonnet as controlled respite from freedom. The self-fulfilling prophecies of the sonnet's tight formalities—the set of interlocking rules and obligations any sonnet sets itself early on and its "metrical contract," in Hollander's terms, not to waver from it—Millay found useful as a trope for a poetics of burning one's candle at both ends, of using one's life up completely. The sonnet can embody metrically, sonorously, and syntactically a kind of perfectly efficient hedonism, culminating in a closure with no residue. The sestet of **"Thou famished grave, I will not fill thee yet"** from *Huntsman, What Quarry?* defiantly tells Death how lives and poems are to be ended:

> I cannot starve thee out: I am thy prey
> And thou shalt have me; but I dare defend
> That I can stave thee off; and I dare say,
> What with the life I lead, the force I spend,
> I'll be but bones and jewels on that day,

And leave thee hungry even in the end.

The poet "staves off" death by the achieved design of her stanzas. Here the sonnet's closure—completing its metrical and rhyming requirements, leaving nothing formally unsatisfied, filling its staves—mimes the way the poet vows to use up her force completely and leave nothing behind. Millay allows her life to end with no residue of unlived days, as the completed sonnet, ending "in the end," permits no residue of unpaired rhymes, unbalanced argument, or dangling syntax. Not a matter of wanton wastefulness but of almost methodical, tasking exhaustiveness, the bohemian project is thus aptly figured in the seemingly opposite, straitlacing, vow-keeping, binding contract any sonnet must be. Recalling Farr's charge that Millay "marshall[s] against the lively but serene mathematics of contained forms like the sonnet, quatrain, or couplet a battery of dissheveled impulses," we might rather say that the self-fulfulling equations of poetic forms provide the formula whereby Millay makes sure that those impulses play themselves out to the full.

All this insistence on the scrupulous hard work of being liberated suggests the occupational hazards this job has for women. For them, the weight of too much liberty too often can be translated into a demanding lover's "weight upon my breast" (**"I, being born a woman and distressed"** from *The Harp-Weaver*). Free love itself can be a prison. Dazzled by the sight of her lover, the speaker of **"When I too long have looked upon your face"** (*Second April*) compares her condition, when she "turn[s] away reluctant" from his "light," to a very scanty plot of ground indeed:

> Then is my daily life a narrow room
> In which a little while, uncertainly,
> Surrounded by impenetrable gloom,
> Among familiar things grown strange to me
> Making my way, I pause, and feel, and hark,
> Till I become accustomed to the dark.

The new woman may fret a great deal in her freedom's "narrow room," it seems; and we may take Millay's soft but audible allusion to the opening line of "Nuns Fret Not" as a reflection on the different kinds of narrowness to which their own freedom may condemn men and women. The enclosing solace of the Wordsworthian sonnet becomes here an almost tomblike, if chosen, claustrophobia, a prison into which the woman dooms herself when she turns away, a "silly, dazzled thing deprived of sight," from the overpowering brilliance of her lover's face.

In Millay's posthumous sonnet on the sonnet [included in *Mine the Harvest*], the form appears not as a small plot of ground or a chosen cloister, but as an erotic prison:

> I will put Chaos into fourteen lines
> And keep him there; and let him thence escape
> If he be lucky; let him twist, and ape
> Flood, fire, and demon—his adroit designs
> Will strain to nothing in the strict confines
> Of this sweet Order, where, in pious rape,
> I hold his essence and amorphous shape,
> Till he with Order mingles and combines.
> Past are the hours, the years, of our duress,

His arrogance, our awful servitude:
I have him. He is nothing more or less
Than something simple not yet understood;
I shall not even force him to confess;
Or answer. I will only make him good.

When Millay claims that her sonnets "put Chaos into fourteen lines," she does more than simply repeat the inherited fiction of the sonnet as brief solace or momentary stay against profusion. The stakes seem higher than in Wordsworth's poem, the tasks put upon poetic form more demanding; this sonnet figures poetic form as a cage for a wild creature. Millay may have in mind Donne's dictum that "Grief brought to numbers cannot be so fierce, / For he tames it, that fetters it in verse" ("The Triple Fool"). But the fourteen lines of this sonnet's cage are not rigid iron bars or fetters but tethers whose strength derives from their flexibility. In refusing to make Chaos "confess," Millay refuses to use the machinery of rhyme and meter to force her stubborn, resistant subject into saying something against his will, perhaps with a glance at Ben Johnson's "A Fit of Rhyme against Rhyme," where rhyme is figured as a torture device to extort false words from the poem: "Rime the rack of finest wits / That expresseth but by fits / True conceit." She will not use the sonnet form to urge a confession or reply, to reveal the "something simple" that his complicated "designs" conceal. The simple goodness—virtuosity, well-craftedness—of the poem is sufficient, will "answer" or be adequate to the job of capturing Chaos. That alone will yield the solution, that is the way to make the prisoner speak up—to reform him, not punish him or make him squeal. This is a mildly coercive inquisition, a "pious rape." The curt, determined vows that close the sonnet leave us with a sense that this poetic mastery over an old rival takes its sweetest revenge from its substitution of an inescapable gentleness for the rival's former cruelty and "arrogance."

This late poem gathers up a recurring image in Millay's sonnets of eros as prison. In the fifth poem of the sequence *Fatal Interview,* the speaker counts herself the most abject of prisoners of love since "my chains throughout their iron length / Make such a golden clank upon my ear," and she would not escape even if she had the strength to do so. By sonnet XVIII in the sequence, the speaker questions her voluntary incarceration more closely: "Shall I be prisoner till my pulses stop / To hateful Love and drag his noisy chain?" Chaos is like a fugitive, faithless lover captured at last, his amorphousness like that of the unapproachable man of whom the woman says "I chase your colored phantom on the air. . . . Once more I clasp,—and there is nothing there" ("Once more into my arid days like dew" from *Second April*). **"I Will Put Chaos into Fourteen Lines"** explicitly equates sexual and poetic dominance in its insistence on the control and compression required of the woman poet who seizes upon traditional forms in order to free herself from the forces that would deny her the power to order poetic forms—forces that include traditional male accounts of the need for poetic order.

Like [Wordsworth's] "Nuns Fret Not," Millay's **"I Will Put Chaos"** ends in such a way as to suggest that the controlling process it describes has been enacted in the sonnet as we read it. Wordsworth's closing hope that in the sonnet the liberty-weary "Should find brief solace there, as I have found" fulfills the promise it expresses, as it refers to the solace afforded by this very sonnet as well as by the poet's habitual writing of them. In the same way, Millay's final promise—"I will only make him good"—points to her goal in all her sonnets as well as to the technical excellence of this one she has just finished. A pun gives this closure a double force. Millay makes the sonnet aesthetically good by tempering the behavior of the unruly subject in its artful cage, making him "good" in the sense of training him to be well-mannered, obedient, and orderly. In Millay's figure, the woman poet binds "Chaos"—a kind of male anti-muse, perhaps the divisive forces of sexuality, or whatever the force may be that tears poems apart rather than inspires them—with the "strict confines" of her ordering art [according to Norman A. Britten in his *Edna St. Vincent Millay*]. The entire sonnet is almost an allegory of Judith Farr's somewhat paradoxical formula that the "conventions to which [Millay] submitted . . . served her well."

"I Will Put Chaos into Fourteen Lines" presents the struggle of the syntactic unit to find its completion, and to fit into the metrical and rhyming requirements of the sonnet (here, particularly of the octet), as an erotic tussling. The octet of **"I Will Put Chaos"** entertains the fiction that the single long sentence that comprises it is allowed free rein to flow from line to line, but is gently curbed (by the poet or by Order itself) at each line ending by the bars of rhyme and meter. The sestet, written in short sentences, largely end-stopped, looks back with precarious assurance on the struggles of the octet. The sonnet's trope for its own procedures is a peculiar one: the poet who dooms her subject into the prison of form acts almost like a pander supervising the mating of Chaos and Order. The twisting of the sentence from line to line illustrates Chaos' snaky attempts to wriggle out of the poem's snare, but the "adroit designs" the poem attributes to Chaos are, of course, the poet's designs by whose grace the caged creature may be as lively and various and protean as he wants. Only the sonnet's strict order of meter, rhyme, and syntax allows us to register the twists taken by the long sentence (lines 3-8) describing Chaos' ineffectual attempts to escape. Millay here makes enjambment positively sexy.

Perhaps this is merely to say that Millay makes good use of the resources of the sonnet, combining Miltonic or Romantic use of heavy enjambment with a strict Petrarchan division between octet and sestet. But, as we shall see, in the context of Millay's allusive polemic against the tradition of sexual myths for the sonnet, it is to say rather more. Again the figurative status of poetic closure is at issue. For Wordsworth, when in a sonnet "the sense does not close with the rhyme," the result desired is a "pervading sense of Unity." The way in which that unity is achieved is made invisible in favor of the satisfying fullness of the closure. In Milton's sonnets Wordsworth admires not the unfolding spell of the "sense variously drawn out" in run-on lines, but the achieved plenitude of the completed experience. Once the "brief solace" is found, the poem is over, and the poet can go on to other things, to wander and soar at liberty. For Millay, such run-over lines in the orderly

sonnet figure rather the difficult wrestling of the poet to achieve unity, a wrestling that is inseparable from a rallying of opposed sexual forces. Wordsworth's sonnet ends with a sigh of satisfaction, the remedy having done the trick ("as I have found"), Millay's with the challenge still ahead, a vow the poet makes to herself ("I will only make him good"). She focuses on the syntactic drama itself, rather than the feeling of satisfaction after the curtain is rung down. The tug of line against syntax figures the poet's constant struggle with "Chaos," not the assurance of Miltonic authority, or the comforting sense of respite and accomplishment Wordsworth claims to derive from the sweet order of sonnet constraints. Intricate play with enjambment is a way Millay demonstrates and monitors that she is in charge of the words, not in some "awful servitude" to them. It is a game she knows she is playing, and knows which rules she has invented and which she has inherited. The critical view of Millay that judges her as in need of poetic form to control her emotional impulses merely repeats Millay's own strategic presentation of herself as such, a self-presentation that itself is in need of interpretation and cannot be taken as a straightforward outline of her poetics.

A sonnet from *Second April,* Millay's third volume (1921) brings together the two main figurations for the sonnet which we have been examining. Here a small plot of ground becomes an imprisoning site of too much liberty:

> Not with libations, but with shouts and laughter
> We drenched the altars of love's sacred grove,
> Shaking to earth green fruits, impatient after
> The launching of the colored moths of Love.
> Love's proper myrtle and his mother's zone
> We bound about our irreligious brows,
> And fettered him with garlands of our own,
> And spread a banquet in love's frugal house.
> Not yet the god has spoken; but I fear
> Though we should break our bodies in his flame,
> And pour our blood upon his altar, here
> Henceforward is a grove without a name,
> A pasture to the shaggy goats of Pan,
> Whence flee forever a woman and a man.

Again we see the high price exacted by the bohemian life: the sonnet, and presumably the affair it commemorates, ends with the sickening sense of loss and satiety that follows from banqueting on unripe fruits. No sacrifice to love can make the grove suitable for proper worship again; such overeager illicit lovers can never thereafter become spouses, dutifully bound in marriage. This may be an illicit and transient affair, but as we expect from Shakespearean sonnets, the transient is transformed into something permanent, and the agent of this permanence is the poem itself; Millay's final vision of the goatish couple fleeing "forever" borrows from this expectation while giving it a bohemian twist. But instead of two lovers frozen in the instant before a kiss, as on Keats's urn, this overheated pair is caught in a gesture of self-exile from a hot pastoral they have sullied with their excesses.

As a character in Millay's all-male verse drama *Conversation at Midnight* (1937) argues, with a glance sidelong at Shakespeare's Sonnet 94,

> it seems

> Even to my nostrils that the lilies are beginning
>   to smell;
> And that the time has come to deck our amorous
>   themes
> With the honester stenches.

With its bracing candor about modern love, **"Not with Libations"** lets fresh air into the sonnet, but that air is already tainted with the stench of overindulgence. We might find it a sufficiently revisionary move on Millay's part simply to give the female half of the couple room to admit that she too knows desire and has a sexual will (Millay gives us simply "a woman and a man," no longer poet and disdainful mistress, burning lover and dark lady), and Millay's sonnets often testify that women, too, know the lust that the Renaissance sonnet traditionally allowed only men to feel. But it would be too simple to say that through its act of bestowing on the woman desires as impatient as the man's the poem bestows on the woman poet the capacity to write sonnets as weighted as a man's. The woman's desire cannot resonate in the room of the sonnet with the same force as his desire; it is a room that has been designed to amplify his tones and to silence hers. To bring these issues to the fore, Millay treats the sonnet as an echo chamber, where we can listen to the voices this improperly proper sonnet has appropriated and revised.

"Not with Libations, but with Shouts and Laughter" is burdened with the weight of too much literature. The poem addresses "Nuns Fret Not at Their Convent's Narrow Room" in its marking for erotic indulgence the scanty plot of ground Wordsworth identifies with serene retreat. The narrow room of conventional passion is too restrictive for these lovers, who turn their erotic bonds into a prison in which they doom themselves. Despite the Wordsworthian figures and the Shakespearean design, however, this poem's grove is drenched with Keats, from incidental glances at the hymn to Pan in *Endymion,* the "Ode to Psyche," and the sonnet "On Solitude," to more importantly polemical allusions to Keats's sonnet on the sonnet.

Typically, the Keatsian echoes resound in a coarser tone in Millay's **"Not with Libations."** The lovers crowning themselves with "love's proper myrtle" have plucked some foliage from the "many that are come to pay their vows / With leaves about their brows" (*Endymion*) in the hymn to Pan, but Millay's lovers consign their grove to "the shaggy goats of Pan," not to an uplifted, Keatsian deity who is "the leaven / That spreading in this dull and clotted earth, / Gives it a touch ethereal." The music that drifts over from the "Ode to Psyche" becomes likewise sensualized. The closing prophecy in **"Not with Libations"** that "Henceforward is a grove without a name" alludes audibly enough to the vow in the ode to dress Psyche's sanctuary "With buds, and bells, and stars without a name" ("Ode to Psyche"). Like the speaker of the ode, Millay's lovers consecrate themselves as their own priests to a form of love which does not have its proper cult in poetry, and like him they adapt the available religious emblems to serve their new god and build him an altar that is erected more in the mind than in any special spot. Keats's ode closes with an invitation to "let the warm Love in," while Millay's sonnet ends with the exile of the warm lovers who, once they have celebrated their inven-

tive rites, must abandon the spot. **"Not with Libations"** closes on a note from Keats's early sonnet beginning "O Solitude! if I must with thee dwell." Locating solitude on a natural prospect or " 'mongst boughs pavilioned," the sonnet ends with the anticipation, addressing Solitude, that "it sure must be / Almost the highest bliss of humankind, / When to thy haunts two kindred spirits flee." Whereas Keats's kindred spirits are left fleeing into the grove of solitude, to engage in "sweet converse of an innocent mind," Millay's lovers "flee forever" from the carnal pasture they have desanctified. Keats's gentle sensualism of anticipation becomes in Millay the disheartening aftermath of consummation.

The most resounding echo in Millay's **"Not with Libations"** is to Keats's sonnet on the sonnet, "If by Dull Rhymes Our English Must Be Chained." As in "Nuns Fret Not," in Keats's self-reflexive sonnet the poet effects the cure his poem complains of:

> If by dull rhymes our English must be chained,
> And, like Andromeda, the Sonnet sweet
> Fettered, in spite of pained loveliness,
> Let us find out, if we must be constrained,
> Sandals more interwoven and complete
> To fit the naked foot of Poesy:
> Let us inspect the lyre, and weigh the stress
> Of every chord, and see what may be gained
> By ear industrious and attention meet;
> Misers of sound and syllable, no less
> Than Midas of his coinage, let us be
> Jealous of dead leaves in the bay wreath crown;
> So, if we may not let the Muse be free,
> She will be bound with garlands of her own.

Like the "Ode to Psyche" and **"Not with Libations,"** this sonnet adapts and loosens the instruments of tribute to a deity who is ultimately the muse. In contrast to the trope of the sonnet as a binding place—a scanty plot, writer's colony for one—the sonnet here is explicitly figured as a bound woman, the muse as Andromeda, with the poet as Perseus to the rescue. But rather than free the damsel in distress, this hero simply makes her chains less chafing. It is the fettering, the rules and rhymes and restrictions, that make the sonnet "sweet," for she is sweetest not when she is free but when she is "sweet / Fettered." The intricacies of the sonnet form guarantee that in some measure the poet "must be constrained" in writing it; the poet's task is to make that multiple manacling—of poet to set pattern, of each line handcuffed to its rhyming partner—less constricting, less strictly ornamental and thereby more graceful. The "dull rhymes" of the English sonnet as Keats inherited it are "more interwoven" in this poem's muted, complex rhyme scheme, a double liberation in that it led Keats to develop the pattern of his ode stanzas.

Poetic form itself is the sea-monster that has chained Andromeda to the rock of dull rhyme and stony, unyielding traditions. The poet does not release her, but reweaves her chains, turning them into honoring garlands. The poetic tradition he works in itself has tightened the strands from which Keats is to release her by binding her with new ones, with the assurance that then "She will be bound with garlands of her own." The trick is to make Andromeda her own sea-monster, to craft a chain for her so cleverly natural that she can believe she has woven it herself as an adornment. In this sonnet Keats has woven a very powerful myth of poetic convention as a prison into which poetry willingly dooms itself, and part of its power derives from the identification of a constricting form with a willingly bound woman.

What are we to make of the echoes from Keats's sonnet of gentle shackling that resound in Millay's sonnet of unbridled eros? What in particular are echoes from a man's sonnet about the sonnet as bound woman doing in a woman's sonnet about the (perhaps enslaving) price of throwing off the conventional shackles of love between men and women? Keats promises Andromeda that she will be "bound with garlands of her own," while Millay's improper modern lovers, celebrating Love in their own reckless way, "fettered him with garlands of our own." They impose their own shackles on Love, whereas Keats works to impose no shackles on the sonnet from outside poetry herself. Millay's lovers reject the miserly care marking Keats's project for the sonnet. In their profligacy they "spread a banquet in [Love's] frugal house"; they reinterpret the traditional cestus and myrtle of restrained love as celebratory garlands, binding their brows as a mark of erotic victory with the cinctures designed to bind the waist as a mark of purity in love.

In both sonnets, then, the iconography of celebratory, erotic, and poetic garlanding is playfully unraveled and rewoven into a new pattern. Millay's "grove without a name" should perhaps be named the grove of the Romantic poetics of the sonnet, a lightly constraining enclosure which Millay turns into a bower of irreverent excess. Just as traditionally the woman poet is denied the kind of freedom that may drive the male poet into the retreat of the sonnet's boundaries, so neither can she be given the responsibility of a poetic Perseus to free the muse from her formal strictures, since she is supposed herself to be the muse. Even if a poet wishes to bind her with "garlands of her own" they will be the garlands he has experimentally determined are proper to her, garlands of his own after all. Millay does not take up Keats's call to reshuffle the sonnet's pattern of rhyming, knowing that no rearrangement can make the form more "natural." Poetic forms and genres are not natural but ideological. Andromeda's unfelt, self-willed fetters can figure a perfect marriage (of man and woman, form and subject) or a perfectly crippling ideology. Looking at Keats through the lens of Millay, we can begin to see Andromeda as torn between having to stand for a poetic form herself or for a free spirit that the form holds chained. For a woman writing poetry in the years between the wars, the brittleness of oaths and the shaky fiction of new sexual freedom for women made the sonnet an apt form in which to scrutinize the inherited stances of men toward women and poets toward their muses. By identifying the sonnet's scanty plot of ground with an erotic grove of excess, turning the chastity belt of poetic form into a token of sexual indulgence, Millay invades the sanctuary of male poetic control with her unsettling formalism in the service of freedom, a freedom that can, as the lovers learn in **"Not with Libations,"** turn into another kind of entrapment.

In **"Not with Libations,"** as in **"I Will Put Chaos into Fourteen Lines,"** Millay addresses the Romantic myths of the sonnet as liberating prison and pleasing fetters, the figurations governing Wordsworth's "Nuns Fret Not" and Keats's "If by Dull Rhymes." Her sonnets reshape those myths with the revisionary force of a woman poet who, however rearguard in the phalanx of modernism, recognizes that she has inherited a genre laden with figurations exclusive to a male poetic authority, and who knows that her adaptations of that genre must engage those very myths and figurations that would bar her from the ranks of legitimate practitioners of the sonnet. While more work on Millay along these lines is not likely to result in the elevation of her to the status of a major twentieth-century poet, it should lead to a more searching understanding of why we judge her to be minor, and to our estimate in general of poets in the modernist period who continued to write in traditional forms. Current feminist work on Millay suggests that in her use of poetic forms "the wish for freedom is always qualified by the sense of restriction": such an estimate, I believe, even when intended as evidence of Millay's virtuosity, echoes older dismissals of Millay on the grounds that she moodily concedes to poetic forms or, crippled by emotional turmoil, desperately leans on them, because it tends to see the poet as an unwitting victim of these two desires rather than as working consciously in light of the fact that the tradition itself is constantly troping on just this very debate. I have only suggested how a few of Millay's most effective sonnets engage in and reflect upon the struggle between poet and form as to which shall be master. Such engagement is a sign not only that Millay has mastered these inherited forms, but also that she has taken into account the full implications for the woman poet of the figure of poetic "mastery." (pp. 8-18)

Debra Fried, "Andromeda Unbound: Gender and Genre in Millay's Sonnets," in Twentieth Century Literature, *Vol. 32, No. 1, Spring, 1986, pp. 1-22.*

FURTHER READING

Bibliography

Nierman, Judith. *Edna St. Vincent Millay: A Reference Guide.* Boston: G. K. Hall & Co., 1977, 191 p.

    Lists Millay's works and criticism on her writings, providing annotations, an introduction by Nierman, and an index.

Yost, Karl. *A Bibliography of the Works of Edna St. Vincent Millay.* New York: Harper & Brothers Publishers, 1937, 248 p.

    Provides publishing history of Millay's works through 1937 and contains an introductory essay by Harold Lewis Cook in which he traces the progression of Millay's poetry as an expression of her personal development.

Biography

Hahn, Emily. "Mostly about Vincent." In her *Romantic Rebels: An Informal History of Bohemianism in America,* pp. 231-41. Boston: Houghton Mifflin Co., Riverside Press, 1966.
Discussion of Millay's life in Greenwich Village during the 1920s.

Criticism

Atkins, Elizabeth. *Edna St. Vincent Millay and Her Times.* Chicago: University of Chicago Press, 1936, 266 p.
Critical discussion of Millay's major works through *Wine from These Grapes,* characterizing Millay as the "most popular and representative" poet of her time.

Benét, William Rose. "Round about Parnassus." *The Saturday Review of Literature* XI, No. 17 (10 November 1934): 279.
Positive assessment of *Wine from These Grapes* highlighting several poems.

———. Introduction to *Second April and The Buck in the Snow,* by Edna St. Vincent Millay, pp. v-xii. New York: Harper & Brothers Publishers, 1950.
Discusses Millay's writing style and her themes of nature and childhood.

Burch, Francis F. "Millay's 'Not in a Silver Casket Cool with Pearls'." *The Explicator* 48, No. 4 (Summer 1990): 277-79.
Discusses Sonnet XI of *Fatal Interview,* concluding that "Millay introduces a feminine viewpoint to the English sonnet sequence, but her views are not new."

Clark, Suzanne. "Jouissance and the Sentimental Daughter: Edna St. Vincent Millay." *North Dakota Quarterly* 54, No. 2 (April 1986): 85-108.
Examines issues relating to femininity and motherhood in Millay's poetry, particularly in her poem "Renascence."

Colum, Padraic. "Miss Millay's Poems." *The Freeman* IV, No. 86 (2 November 1921): 189-90.
Asserts that the poems in *A Few Figs from Thistles* and *Second April* are characterized by a childlike tone and often fail to reveal mature experience.

Gould, Jean. "Edna St. Vincent Millay—Saint of the Modern Sonnet." In *Faith of a (Woman) Writer,* edited by Alice Kessler-Harris and William McBrien, pp. 129-42. New York: Greenwood Press, 1988.
Originally presented at a conference on twentieth-century women writers held at Hofstra University in 1982. Gould examines the origins of the sonnet sequences "Fatal Interview" and "Epitaph for the Race of Man" through the events in Millay's life that made her a "a twentieth-century sonneteer of the first rank."

Gregory, Horace, and Zaturenska, Marya. "Edna St. Vincent Millay and the Poetry of Feminine Revolt and Self-Expression." In their *A History of American Poetry, 1900-1940,* pp. 265-81. New York: Harcourt, Brace & Company, 1946.
Discusses the development of Millay's literary personality and the structure and lyricism of her sonnets.

Jones, Phyllis M. "Amatory Sonnet Sequences and the Female Perspective of Elinor Wylie and Edna St. Vincent Millay." *Women's Studies: An Interdisciplinary Journal* 10, No. 1 (1983): 41-61.
Compares Elinor Wylie's sonnet sequence "One Person" with Millay's *Fatal Interview,* asserting that both works represent a Modernist reworking of earlier styles and forms from a female perspective.

Ransom, John Crowe. "The Poet As Woman." *The Southern Review* 2, No. 4 (Spring 1937): 783-806.
Criticizes Millay's poetry in the context of her status as a woman poet and asserts that her fundamental limitation is "her lack of intellectual interest."

Sheean, Vincent. *The Indigo Bunting: A Memoir of Edna St. Vincent Millay.* New York: Harper & Brothers, 1951, 131 p.
Memoir of the critic's acquaintance with Millay during the 1940s. Sheean recounts significant events and relationships in Millay's life in those years and considers her verse in relation to her philosophical and spiritual perspectives.

Tate, Allen. "Edna St. Vincent Millay." In his *Reactionary Essays on Poetry and Ideas,* pp. 221-27. New York: Charles Scribner's Sons, 1936.
Describes Millay as a poet of the second order who is limited by her failure to transcend personal emotions.

Additional coverage of Millay's life and career is contained in the following sources published by Gale Research: *Concise Dictionary of American Literary Biography,* 1917-1929; *Contemporary Authors,* Vols. 104, 130; *Dictionary of Literary Biography,* Vol. 45; *Major 20th-Century Writers;* and *Twentieth-Century Literary Criticism,* Vol. 4.

Eugene O'Neill

Desire under the Elms

(Full name Eugene Gladstone O'Neill) American playwright, poet, and short story writer.

The following entry presents criticism of O'Neill's drama
Desire under the Elms, written and first performed in
1924. For a discussion of O'Neill's complete career, see
TCLC, Volumes 1 and 6. For criticism of O'Neill's drama
Long Day's Journey into Night, see *TCLC,* Volume 27.

INTRODUCTION

Regarded as O'Neill's best early drama, *Desire under the
Elms* established his reputation as one of the foremost
American dramatists of the twentieth century. Set in rural
New England, the play delineates the relationship between
a farmer and his family. Because of its controversial
themes of incest and infanticide, *Desire under the Elms*
was unfavorably reviewed on its debut but has subsequently been recognized as what Travis Bogard terms "the first
important tragedy to be written in America."

O'Neill's early years were profoundly affected by the pressures of his mother's recurring mental illness and drug ad-
diction and by his tumultuous relationship with his father,
aspects of which surface in *Desire under the Elms.* After
a brief, unsuccessful marriage, two years at sea, and a suicide attempt, O'Neill began to write plays while conva-
lescing from a mild case of tuberculosis in 1912. *Desire
under the Elms* was written in 1924, shortly after the death
of his mother and only brother. Its themes of incest and
infanticide outraged most critics at the time, resulting in
calls for censorship and the arrest of members of a Los
Angeles theater company that staged performances of the
play. Subsequently the play was cleared by the authorities
and, benefiting from the controversy, had a successful run
on Broadway.

Desire under the Elms is a drama of complex family relationships. A tyrannical patriarch, Ephraim Cabot is resented by his sons for the control he exerts over their lives
and for the strength of character and physical prowess he
displays in contrast to their weakness. Eben, the youngest
son and only child from Ephraim's second marriage, har-
bors a particularly intense bitterness toward his father. Believing that Ephraim married his mother for her share of
the farm and blaming him for the hard life that subsequently killed her, Eben asserts his right to the land. When
seventy-five-year-old Ephraim marries a young woman,
the two older sons give up hope of inheriting the farm and
set out to prospect for gold in California. Because Ephraim will only allow his property to come into the hands of
a blood relation, his new wife, Abbie, seeks to conceive an
heir to inherit the farm upon Ephraim's death. Attracted
to the youthful Eben, Abbie seduces him and they produce

a son that Ephraim believes is his. Eben reveals the deception to Ephraim, only to be convinced by his father that
he has been duped out of his inheritance by Abbie. In
order to renounce her claim to the farm and prove her love
to Eben, Abbie strangles the infant. Eben acknowledges
his moral complicity in the murder and the two are arrested. In the aftermath of these events, Ephraim considers
joining his two sons out west but ultimately remains on his
farm.

O'Neill claimed that he dreamed the idea for *Desire under
the Elms,* and critical commentary often focuses on
sources for the plot and themes of the play. It is considered
likely that O'Neill read a play by Sidney Howard entitled
They Knew What They Wanted, which features an aged
farmer, his young wife, her lover, and the offspring of their
liaison, a scenario displaying obvious similarities to *Desire
under the Elms.* O'Neill had always acknowledged the influence of dramatist August Strindberg on his life and
work, and Murray Hartman has declared *Desire under the
Elms* the "richest exploitation to date of Strindbergian
sources," particularly for the depiction in the play of the
tragic consequences of a sexual relationship. In addition
to these influences, allusions have been noted in *Desire*

under the Elms to the Phaedra legend contained in Euripedes's play *Hippolytus,* in which a woman is attracted to her handsome stepson and kills herself out of shame. Eben and Ephraim's conflicts over the Cabot farm and Eben's affair with his stepmother have led critics to compare *Desire under the Elms* with Sophocles's Oedipus plays as well as Sigmund Freud's psychological principle of the Oedipus complex. Critics have also commented on Ephraim's concept of the "hard" life of his New England farm and the "soft" life of the West as represented by California, arguing that this dichotomy derives from Friedrich Nietzsche's theory of the Apollonian-Dionysian duality of ancient Greek culture. According to this reading, it is the Apollonian spirit of the American Puritan that dictates Ephraim's remaining on the farm at the conclusion of *Desire under the Elms* rather than embracing the adventurous Dionysian spirit identified with the American West. While the setting of a New England farm in the nineteenth century is important to *Desire under the Elms,* its themes and characters demonstrate that, as Joseph Wood Krutch has asserted, O'Neill's play is "interested less in New England as such than in an aspect of the eternal tragedy of man and his passions."

CRITICISM

Joseph Wood Krutch   (essay date 1924)

[*Krutch is widely regarded as one of America's most respected literary and drama critics. Noteworthy among his works are* The American Drama since 1918 *(1939), in which he analyzed the most important dramas of the 1920s and 1930s, and* "Modernism" in Modern Drama *(1953), in which he stressed the need for twentieth-century playwrights to infuse their works with traditional humanistic values. A conservative and idealistic thinker, he was a consistent proponent for human dignity and the preeminence of literary art. His literary criticism is characterized by such concerns: in* The Modern Temper *(1929) he argued that because scientific thought has denied human worth, tragedy has become obsolete, and in* The Measure of Man *(1954) he attacked modern culture for depriving humanity of the sense of individual responsibility necessary for making important decisions in an increasingly complex age. In the following essay, Krutch reviews the debut of* Desire under the Elms.]

In this age of intellectualized art there is an inevitable but unfortunate tendency to assume of Eugene O'Neill, as of every other arresting artist, that his greatness must lie somehow in the greatness or in the clarity of his thought; to seek in *All God's Chillun* some solution of the problem of race or in the *Hairy Ape* some attitude toward society; and then, not finding them, to fail in the fullest appreciation of the greatness which is his. It was not thought which drove him, as a young man, to seek adventure among the roughest men he could find, and it was not thought which he brought back from this and other experiments in life.

Something tempestuous in his nature made him a brother of tempests, and he has sought wherever he could find them the fiercest passions, less anxious to clarify their causes for the benefit of those who love peace than eager to share them, and happy if he could only be exultantly a part of their destructive fury. It is a strange taste, this, to wish to be perpetually racked and tortured, to proceed from violence to violence, and to make of human torture not so much the occasion of other things as the *raison d'être* of drama; but such is his temperament. The meaning and unity of his work lies not in any controlling intellectual idea and certainly not in a "message," but merely in the fact that each play is an experience of extraordinary intensity.

Young-man-like, O'Neill first assumed that the fiercest passions were to be found where the outward circumstances of life were wildest and most uncontrolled. He sought among men of the sea, ignorant of convention and wholly without inhibitions, powerful appetites and bare tragedies, embodying his observations in the group of little plays now performed for the first time as a whole (and performed well) at the Provincetown Theater under the title of *S. S. Glencairn;* but maturity has taught him the paradox that where there is most smoke there is not necessarily most fire. He has learned that souls confined in a nut-shell may yet be lords of infinite space; that spirits cabined and confined by very virtue of the fact that they have no outlet explode finally with the greatest spiritual violence. As though to signalize the discovery of this truth he has, in his latest play, **Desire Under the Elms** (Greenwich Village Theater), limited the horizon of his characters, physically and spiritually, to the tiny New England farm upon which the action passes, and has made their intensity spring from the limitations of their experience. Whether he or Robert Edmond Jones conceived the idea of setting the stage with a single permanent scene showing one end of the farmhouse, and of removing sections of the wall when it becomes necessary to expose one or more of the rooms inside, I do not know; but this method of staging is admirably calculated to draw attention to the controlling circumstances of the play. It is a story of human relationships become intolerably tense because intolerably close and limited, of the possessive instinct grown inhumanly powerful because the opportunities for its gratification are so small, and of physical passion terribly destructive in the end because so long restrained by the sense of sin. To its young hero the stony farm is all the wealth of the world, the young wife of his father all the lust of the flesh. In that tiny corner each character finds enough to stimulate passions which fill, for him, the universe.

By half a century of unremitting labor Ephraim Cabot has turned a few barren hillsides into a farm, killing two wives in the process but growing himself only harder in body and mind and more fanatical in his possessive passion for the single object which has absorbed his life. Two of his sons, rebelling against the hopelessness of their life, leave him for the gold-fields; the third, who remains with him in dogged determination to inherit the farm, he hates; and so he marries once more in the hope of begetting in his old age a son to whom, as part of himself, he can leave his property without ceasing to own it. But he has reckoned without considering the possessive instinct of the wife herself, and so between the three, and in an atmosphere charged with hate, is fought out the three-cornered battle for what has come to be the symbol of earthly possessions. Love springs up between the wife and her foster son, but in such a battle the directest win, and love, confusing the aims of these two, dooms them to tragedy, while to the old man is left the barrenness of lonely triumph. Unlike the others, he has a god, the hard God who hates the easy gold of California or the easy crops of the West, the God who loves stumps and stones and looks with His stern favor upon such as wring a dour life without softness and without love from a soil barren like their souls. And this God comforts him: "I am hard," he says, when he learns that the baby, murdered by its mother, is not his but his son's: "I am a hard man and I am alone—but so is God."

It may with some show of reason be objected that O'Neill's plays are too crowded with incident, that the imagination of the spectator refuses sometimes to leap with the author so quickly from tense moment to tense moment, or to accept violence piled so unremittingly upon violence, and his latest play is not wholly closed to such objection; but impetuosity is an essential part of his nature and not likely ever to be subdued. To those who, like the present writer, can overlook it, it brings great compensation. *Desire Under the Elms* will be, with one exception, the most moving play seen during the current season. (pp. 578-80)

> Joseph Wood Krutch, "The God of the Stumps," in The Nation, *New York, Vol. CXIX, No. 3099, November 26, 1924, pp. 578-80.*

Conrad Seiler   (essay date 1926)

[*In the following review, Seiler responds to the censorship proceedings following the Los Angeles debut of* Desire under the Elms.]

Lewdness and immorality must not escape punishment in this City of the Angels.

On February 18 at the Orange Grove Theater seventeen actors in the employ of Mr. Thomas Wilkes, theatrical producer, were presenting Eugene O'Neill's somber tragedy, *Desire Under the Elms.* Little did they know of the awful Nemesis of the Law, lurking within the very portals of the theater. Members of the City Vice Squad, acting upon the instructions of Sergeant Sidney Sweetnam, were there to see the performance and to ferret out any possible obscenities. As the curtains closed on the last act all the actors were placed under arrest and taken to the Central Police Station. They were accused of having presented a lewd, obscene, and immoral play.

In the Vice Squad Room of the station, where dipsomaniacs, dope addicts, prostitutes, and perverts are sent before their final consignment either to jail or liberty, as the case may be, these seventeen sons and daughters of Thespis were herded together and their finger-prints taken, like ordinary criminals.

The management of the play made vehement protest. It

was absurd to arrest the actors; they could not be held to account. The management itself assumed all responsibility. But all that did not make the slightest impression on the law. The actors were kept under arrest until 4:30 the following morning, when they were set at liberty under $50 bail each—$850 in all. Later, through the solicitation of Attorney Arthur W. Green, the bail was returned, and the actors were released on their own recognizance.

Sergeant Sweetnam, whom one ungracious reporter called "Key-hole Sweetnam," or "the Chemically Pure Cop," asserted that the Parent Teachers' Association and the Board of Education were behind the arrest, and that it was a serious affair. No member, however, of either the Parent Teachers' Association or the Board of Education ever appeared in the court.

After several words in Mr. O'Neill's work were modified to suit the moral sensibilities of the police, particularly Sergeant Sweetnam—that is, after "whore," which was used twice in the play, was changed to "harlot," and "gone a-whoring" to "gone to get himself a woman"—the performances were permitted to continue, pending the final decision of the court.

A jury trial was demanded. On April 8 the case opened in Judge William Fredrickson's court. Twelve men and women—housewives, salesmen, retired farmers—were asked to pass judgment on the morality of a work of art. Such obviously vulgar aphrodisiacs as "Artists and Models" "Weak Sisters," "Lady be Good," "The Demi-Virgin," "The Gold-Fish," and scores upon scores of cheap burlesque shows had been produced without interference in Los Angeles. Their intrinsic decency or indecency had never even been questioned.

Le Roy Reams—small in body, large in head, pugnacious, irascible, "the fearless boy prosecutor," as one paper described him—called Officer Taylor to the witness stand. Officer Taylor solemnly testified that he "had went" to the play, *Desire Under the Elms,* on the night of February 18; that he had heard such horrible instances of profanity as "damn," "hell," and "whore" used on innumerable occasions during the evening—he couldn't say how many; that, although as a police officer in pursuance of his onerous duties he had gone to the performance "steeled against" anything obscene, he had really been shocked, yes, shocked. When he left the play he felt "like he couldn't look the world in the face again"; he had to walk up dark alleys to hide his shame. Ephraim Cabot (Mr. Frank McGlynn) at the end of the first act had said: "If I catch ye, I'll break your bones!" Officer Taylor swore that on the night of the 18th he had heard: "If I catch ye, I'll bust your —!" The dash indicates a word which even the prosecutor pronounced with reluctance. On cross-examination Officer Taylor said that he had not been able to find any good in the play, but he was certain it was very bad, very bad indeed.

Sergeant Sweetnam, City Mother Gilbert, a salesman, and an elevator operator were the principal witnesses for the prosecution. They testified also that they had heard "damns," "hells," and "certain Biblical words galore." The play was unquestionably immoral—a seducing woman in a nightgown, several beds, and so forth. . . . No, the play had not had an immoral effect on them personally, of course not; they had not left the theater with impure thoughts, or with the intention of committing any abomination, but that was because they had gone "prepared."

The prosecutor stressed the fact that it was not so much the individual lines and expressions—filthy though they were—as the play itself that was in question. Why, the mere idea of a woman seducing her own stepson—think of it, ladies and gentlemen, *her own stepson!*—was lewd and immoral and had no place in any respectable God-fearing community. Would they, the jurors, care to tell that story in their front parlors to their sons and daughters?

Eminent clubwomen, students of the drama, the wife of the dean of the University of Southern California, several producers, all the dramatic critics of the Los Angeles newspapers, and a girl and boy testified in behalf of the defense. To them the play was not immoral—far from it. It was a literary and dramatic *tour de force*. It taught a strong, wholesome, moral lesson: the wages of sin is death. When they came from the theater they felt cleansed, morally elevated. The chairwoman of the drama committee of the Friday Morning Club said that, after seeing the play, she felt as though she wanted to rise from her seat and say with utmost reverence: "Now let us pray." The repetition of hard, perhaps ugly words, did not embarrass or shock any of the defense's witnesses. Such words impressed each of them as being very natural and necessary expressions in the mouths of O'Neill's crude, pathetic characters.

On the afternoon of April 15, at two o'clock, the entire court, including the judge, jury, prosecutor, attorney for the defense, attachés, and witnesses, and also a few reporters, were given a special performance of *Desire Under the Elms* at the Orange Grove Theater. No one else was admitted in the audience. The actors were the seventeen persons under indictment.

Before the play began all the players were summoned before the curtain, and the clerk of the court, B. O. Kersey, asked them: "Do each of you solemnly swear that the performance you will give here today is the play *Desire Under the Elms*, word for word, action for action, identically as it was presented in this theater on the night of February the 18th?" The actors took the oath. And then began the most unusual performance in the annals of the theater. The actors, with a possible jail sentence staring them in the face, and playing before the most critical audience ever assembled in any theater, surpassed themselves. Frank McGlynn as Ephraim Cabot gave a magnificent interpretation; Jessie Arnold as Abbie caused even Bailiff Cummings to say: "She's the greatest actress I've ever seen." Women jurors wept copiously; Sergeant Sweetnam and Judge Fredrickson applauded along with the witnesses and reporters. Four curtain calls were demanded at the conclusion of the play.

On Friday morning, April 16, came the final argument. The court allotted one hour to each side. Frank McGlynn—tall, gaunt, dramatic—attorney in his own right

as well as leading actor in the play, was granted half of the defense's time. McGlynn appealed to the jury as liberal-minded men and women. He hoped they were not prudes. Surely they were not shocked when life was stripped of its veneer. Surely they felt no embarrassment when he told the story of *Desire Under the Elms*. Sex had its place in life; everyone knew that. There was nothing essentially obscene about it. If persons came to see O'Neill's play and smirked and giggled over the poignant lives of Eben Ephraim Cabot and Abbie—as the prosecutor said they had—it was a reflection upon *their* morality, not the actors' or the play's. The jury was not called upon to decide whether *Desire Under the Elms* contained a moral lesson. It didn't have to have one. The question was whether the defendants were guilty of presenting an obscene play.

Attorney Green, of the defense, mentioned the classics of literature, the plays of Sophocles, Euripides, Aeschylus, Racine, Schiller (particularly Schiller's "Don Carlos," Racine's "Phèdre," and Sophocles's "Phaedra," in which women are enamoured of their stepsons) and the tragedies of a certain well-known playwright, William Shakespeare. Most of them are not only read and studied in the classrooms of our high schools and colleges, but are actually performed by thousands of students every year. . . . Eugene O'Neill is one of the few significant figures in the American drama. He is a famous author; his works are read, played, and admired throughout the civilized world. . . . Many of the words which Officer Taylor and Sergeant Sweetnam testified that they had heard on that memorable night of the 18th, were never in the play. The prosecution had not proved its case; there was absolutely nothing obscene in the play and consequently the defendants must be pronounced innocent.

The prosecutor, in his rebuttal, took occasion to castigate "those Greek and French degenerates" who are sullying the minds of our children. *Desire Under the Elms* was mere "smut and filth." There was no justification for such a play. O'Neill a famous author! He was infamous—morbid, lewd, obscene. . . . The play was not true to life. Had any member of the jury ever heard of a mother seducing her own stepson in real life? Of course not. Were the lives of O'Neill's characters similar to the lives of any people in New England or elsewhere that they had ever known or heard about? What a question! But they did know of thousands of clean, patient, hard-working farmer folks, didn't they? O'Neill knew nothing of such people; he only knew about morons, adultresses, infanticides, seducing stepmothers. . . . Suppose it were true to life. So are sewers. But that is no reason for putting them on the stage. . . . *Desire Under the Elms* should be suppressed. The defendants were guilty of presenting a lewd, obscene, and immoral play.

The jury retired at three o'clock that afternoon. It deliberated for almost nine hours. Shortly after midnight the verdict was announced: eight for conviction and four for acquittal.

The jury was dismissed.

At the time of writing Judge Fredrickson has voiced his

intention of proceeding immediately with a new trial. In the meantime the play, which, normally, would have had a run of two, or at the most, three weeks, is doing capacity business the tenth week, and will soon go to San Francisco to commence its sinister demoralizing work there. But—

Los Angeles must be purified.

Lewdness and immorality must not escape punishment in this City of the Angels. (pp. 548-49)

Conrad Seiler, "Los Angeles Must Be Kept Pure," in The Nation, *New York, Vol. CXXII, No. 3176, May 19, 1926, pp. 548-49.*

Edwin A. Engel   (essay date 1953)

[*In the following excerpt, Engel discusses the major themes of* Desire under the Elms.]

Going back to New England days when Thoreau and Emerson saw Paphlagonians in woodchoppers, Greeks in ploughboys, O'Neill perceived pagans in farmers. With a profounder "pantheistic sympathy" than that of the Concord pair, he recorded "the most terrible and most questionable qualities" of New England rural life—greed, lechery, incest, adultery, revenge, murder—declared them good, and sanctified them. *Desire Under the Elms* celebrates the divinity of nature, the triumph of pagan naturalism over indurated religion, the victory of mother and son over the father. All of the principal characters in the play "belong," for their unity with what Macgowan called "the dumb, mysterious processes of nature" is clearly established. Their relationship to the earth is more than reciprocal. Owning it, they are owned by it. Flowing and uniting with all natural objects, they display a process of merging that would have delighted Whitman. Reduced to animals, they possess a harmony with nature that would have been the envy of Yank, the enraged and frustrated anthropoid.

Neither self-conscious nor cosmic-conscious, the Cabots, father and sons, are animal-conscious. Like animals, much of the time they are "placid and self-contained." In the peaceful, final scene of *The Fountain* O'Neill introduced a portly monk whose *eyes* [had] *the opaque calm of a ruminating cow's.* In *Welded* he presented a stolid, bovine Woman who imparted wisdom and peace to the frenzied hero. And in plays subsequent to *Desire Under the Elms* he continued to represent attractive aspects of bovinity. In the present drama Eben Cabot, tormented, has the eyes of a wild animal in captivity. But at other times his behavior is that of a domesticated quadruped. Describing his experience with Min, "the Scarlet Woman," he proudly tells his two brothers how he "begun to beller like a calf." And that pair, as they go off to eat, make their exit by turning, *shouldering each other, their bodies bumping and rubbing together as they hurry clumsily to their food, like two friendly oxen toward their evening meal.* Their eating is as naturally unrestrained as that of *beasts of the field.* This is, perhaps, why "the cows knows us" "an' likes us," "an' the hosses, an' pigs, an' chickens." "They knows us like brothers—an' likes us," and why, after eighteen years, Simeon's memory of his dead wife is of her hair, "long's

a hoss' tail—an yaller like gold." Although the father's relationship with his bovine sons is far from cordial, he is on the best of terms with the other livestock, whom he takes pleasure in visiting because "it's nice smellin' an' warm" with them, because in their company he finds rest and peace and understanding. One of the kindest remarks he makes to Eben is that, like the cows, Eben is queer. Seized by a desire to make love to his new wife, Ephraim, the father, borrows his metaphors from the Song of Solomon: "yer eyes air doves," he tells her, "yer two breasts air like two fawns."

Not only do the Cabots have an affinity and an identity with the animal kingdom, they are part of the earth. Simeon and Peter wear *thick-soled boots caked with earth. Their clothes, their faces, hands, bare arms and throats are earth-stained. They smell of earth.* Simeon *stamps his foot on the earth and addresses it desperately,* "Waal—ye've thirty year o'me buried in ye—spread out over ye—blood an' bone an' sweat—rotted away—fertilizin' ye—richin' yer soul—prime manure, by God, that's what I been t'ye!" Narcissistically they remark that the scene about them is "Purty." Similarly, Ephraim is involved:

> When I came here fifty odd year ago—I was jest twenty an' the strongest an' hardest ye ever seen—ten times as strong an' fifty times as hard as Eben. Waal—this place was nothin' but fields o' stones. Folks laughed when I tuk it. They couldn't know what I knowed. When ye kin make corn sprout out o' stones, God's livin' in yew! They wa'n't strong enuf fur that! They reckoned God was easy. They laughed. They don't laugh no more. Some died here abouts. Some went West an' died. They're all under ground—fur hollerin' arter an easy God. God hain't easy. (*He shakes his head slowly*) An' I growed hard. Folks kept allus sayin' he's a hard man like 'twas sinful t' be hard, so's at last I said back at 'em: Waal then, by thunder, ye'll git me hard an' see how ye like it! . . . God's hard, not easy! God's in the stones! Build my church on a rock—out o' stones! an' I'll be in them! That's what he meant t' Peter! (*He sighs heavily—a pause*) Stones. I picked 'em up an' piled 'em into walls. Ye kin read the years o' my life in them walls, every day a hefted stone, climbin' over the hills up and down, fencin' in the fields that was mine, whar I'd made thin's grow out o' nothin'—like the will o' God, like the servant o' His hand. It wa'n't easy. It was hard an' He made me hard for it.

Contented to be animals and creatures of earth, the sons are nevertheless resentful, because of the way in which their father drives them. He had slaved to death his second wife, Eben's "Maw," and, says Peter, "He's slaved himself t' death. He's slaved Sim 'n' me 'n' yew t' death—" "It's somethin'—drivin' him—t' drive us!" observes Simeon. They resent, moreover, the way in which Ephraim has fenced them in. With *sardonic bitterness* Peter complains: "Here—it's stones atop o' the ground—stones atop o' stones—makin' stone walls—year atop o' year—him 'n' yew 'n' me 'n' then Eben—makin' stone walls fur him to fence us in!" "Stone atop o' stone," adds Eben, "makin' walls till yer heart's a stone ye heft up out o' the way o' growth onto a stone wall in yer heart!" "Something there is that doesn't love a wall." The sons' dislike at being driven, their hostility to walls of stone are aspects of their antagonism to the Old Testament God. The hard God is in the stones and in the father. Both are inimical to a free and peaceful animal existence.

To aggravate matters, the sons have discerned behind Ephraim's religious ardor his essentially animal nature. Simeon, *imitating his father's voice,* says, "I'm ridin' out t' learn God's message t' me in the spring like the prophets done," and then adds, "I'll bet right then an' thar he knew plumb well he was goin' whorin', the stinkin' old hypocrite!" Whatever the outward form of the old man's faith, his lasciviousness betrays him. He is more satyr than saint. Having "hitched up an druv off into the West," Ephraim remains away from the farm for two months. He returns from his sexual quest with his young third wife, Abbie, who, it soon becomes apparent, is the embodiment of a force that is more pervasive and potent than that which Jehovah exerts. Abbie, the incarnation of fertility and love is, like the Cabot men, part of the earth. Whereas Jehovah's symbol is the stones, that of Abbie is the elms—the tree being the primordial symbol of fecundity and maternity. We recognize the potency of her powers when she directs them at Eben:

> ABBIE. Ye look all slicked up like a prize bull.
>
> EBEN. (*with a sneer*) Waal—ye hain't so durned purty yerself, be ye? (*They stare into each other's eyes, his held by hers in spite of himself, hers glowingly possessive. Their physical attraction becomes a palpable force quivering in the hot air.*)
>
> ABBIE. (*softly*) Ye don't mean that, Eben. Ye may think ye mean it, mebbe, but ye don't. Ye can't. It's agin nature, Eben. Ye been fightin' yer nature ever since the day I come—tryin' t' tell yerself I hain't purty t' ye. (*She laughs a low humid laugh without taking her eyes from his. A pause—her body squirms desirously—she murmurs languorously*) Hain't the sun strong an' hot? Ye kin feel it burnin' into the earth—Nature—makin' thin's grow—bigger 'n' bigger—burnin' inside ye—makin' ye want t' grow—into somethin' else—till ye're jined with it—an' it's your'n—but it owns ye, too—an' makes ye grow bigger—like a tree—like them elums—(*She laughs again softly, holding his eyes. He takes a step towards her, compelled against his will*) Nature'll beat ye, Eben. Ye might's well own up t' it fust 's last.

The irresistible Abbie is to be the means of Eben's liberation from a mother complex on the one hand and a tyrannical father on the other.

For if Ephraim is the embodiment of harsh paternity, if the cows talk to Cabot and Cabot talks to God, Eben is the victim of a sinister maternity and therefore talks to his mother although she is dead. He hates his father and prays for him to die. He is possessed by the memory of his mother. Abbie is to displace both parents and to satisfy all of Eben's biological and spiritual needs. Something of an earth spirit herself, she possesses the attributes which Eben admires in Min the prostitute, who is "like t'

night . . . soft 'n' wa'm, her eyes kin wink like a star, her mouth's wa'm, her arms're wa'm, she smells like a wa'm plowed field . . . " Abbie is all this and more. She is not only a whore, she is the tender mother. To Ephraim she is the farm for which he has such deep affection: "Sometimes ye air the farm an' sometimes the farm be yew. That's why I clove t' ye in my lonesomeness . . . Me an' the farm has got t' beget a son!" But the son which she begets is Eben's whose possessiveness includes all of the property. By gaining possession of Abbie, Eben ensures his possession of the farm as well, the rights to the land having been previously asserted by his mother. In Part Two, Scene Three, the convergence of sex, tenderness, and acquisitiveness occurs:

> ABBIE. When I fust come in—in the dark—they seemed somethin' here.
>
> EBEN. (*simply*) Maw.
>
> ABBIE. I kin still feel—somethin'. . . .
>
> EBEN. It's Maw.
>
> ABBIE. At fust I was feered o' it. I wanted t' yell an' run. Now—since yew come—seems like it's growin' soft an' kind t' me. (*Addressing the air—queerly*) Thank yew.
>
> EBEN. Maw allus loved me.
>
> ABBIE. Mebbe it knows I love yew, too. Mebbe that makes it kind t' me.
>
> EBEN. (*dully*) I dunno. I should think she'd hate ye.
>
> ABBIE. (*with certainty*) No. I kin feel it don't—not no more.
>
> EBEN. Hate ye fur stealin' her place—here in her hum—settin' in her parlor whar she was laid—(*He suddenly stops, staring stupidly before him.*)
>
> ABBIE. What is it, Eben?
>
> EBEN. (*in a whisper*) Seems like Maw didn't want me t' remind ye.
>
> ABBIE. (*excitedly*) I knowed, Eben! It's kind t' me! It don't b'ar me no grudges fur what I never knowed an' couldn't help!
>
> EBEN. Maw b'ars him a grudge.
>
> ABBIE. Waal, so does all o' us.
>
> EBEN. Ay-eh. (*With passion*) I does, by God!
>
> ABBIE. (*taking one of his hands in hers and patting it*) Thar! Don't git riled thinkin' o' him. Think o' yer Maw who's kind t' us. Tell me about yer Maw, Eben.
>
> EBEN. They hain't nothin' much. She was kind. She was good.
>
> ABBIE. (*putting one arm over his shoulder. He does not seem to notice—passionately*) I'll be kind an' good t' ye.
>
> EBEN. Sometimes she used t' sing fur me.
>
> ABBIE. I'll sing fur ye!

EBEN. This was her hum. This was her farm.

ABBIE. This is my hum. This is my farm.

EBEN. He married her t' steal 'em. She was soft an' easy. He couldn't 'preciate her.

ABBIE. He can't 'preciate me!

EBEN. He murdered her with his hardness.

ABBIE. He's murderin' me!

EBEN. She died (*A pause*) Sometimes she used to sing fur me. (*He bursts into a fit of sobbing.*)

ABBIE. (*both her arms around him—with wild passion*) I'll sing fur ye! I'll die fur ye! (*In spite of her overwhelming desire for him, there is a sincere maternal love in her manner and voice—a horribly frank mixture of lust and mother love*) Don't cry, Eben! I'll take yer Maw's place! I'll be everythin' she was t' ye—an' ye kin kiss me back 's if yew was my son—my boy—sayin' good-night t' me. Kiss me, Eben.

Then the restrained kissing of mother and son gives way to lustful wild passion, and Abbie pleadingly explains to Eben, who is stricken with terror, that "lovin' like a Maw hain't enuf." To be happy they must love "much more—a hundred times more." Whereupon he dutifully inquires of his mother, whose presence he feels in the room, what he should do about this imminent usurpation of her position. His face suddenly lights up *with a fierce triumphant grin,* and he cries, "I see it! I see why. It's her vengeance on him—so's she kin rest quiet in her grave!" The next morning he announces *with a strange look,* "Maw's gone back t' her grave. She kin sleep now." And Eben, too, should be at peace now, having released his "libidinal desires from his mother." But it is ironical that in freeing himself from his Oedipus complex he should have transferred his love to his stepmother. The father still threatens him.

When Ephraim persuades Eben that Abbie has betrayed him, that she had the child in order to inherit the farm, the son grapples with the father in a *murderous struggle* and is thrown to the earth. *Between sobs and gasps* he accuses Abbie of being "a damn trickin' whore," threatens to go to California and to get his revenge by praying "t' Maw t' come back t' help me—t' put her curse on yew an' him!" But when Abbie vindicates herself by smothering the baby, Eben, moved by this evidence of her love, selflessly insists upon sharing her guilt—a gesture which elicits grudging admiration even from the father. "Purty good—fur yew!" declares Ephraim. Having loved not wisely but too well, the lovers must pay a penalty, their crime being infanticide. As for adultery and incest, these offenses they refuse to recognize. "I don't repent that sin!" cries Abbie, *lifting her head as if defying God.* "I hain't askin' God t' fergive that!" "Nor me—" adds Eben. As they are led off to jail they stop to kiss, to reaffirm their love, to admire the sunrise, and then, as the curtain falls, to look up *raptly in attitudes aloof and devout.* Thus, ecstatic yea-saying has transformed their rapaciousness, cunning, violence into rapturous and unquestioning devotion. *Burning with desire, panting like two animals,* Eben and Abbie, once their passion is consummated, are con-

verted into self-sacrificing lover and tender, forbearing mistress.

On the surface O'Neill's tragedy resembles certain other plays modern and ancient. Sidney Howard's *They Knew What They Wanted,* produced in 1924, dramatized the situation of a younger woman married to an older man, and the consequences: adultery, an illegitimate child, regeneration, forgiveness. In 1920 the Theatre Guild had staged *The Power of Darkness.* Written in 1886, Tolstoy's play contained motifs of adultery, incest, homicide, infanticide—a tragic situation that was resolved by confession and repentance. **Desire Under the Elms,** with its symbolism and its non-Christian ethic, differs radically from both of the foregoing plays. Similar qualities distinguish it from *The Hippolytus* of Euripides wherein the over-powering love of the heroine for her step-son was not only unreciprocated, but was as abhorrent to her as it was to him. And if O'Neill's play has a kinship with *Oedipus,* it is with the complex rather than *Rex.*

Before 1924, familial relationships in the dramas of O'Neill were seldom cordial or affectionate, but the usual variety of family discord was that which obtained between husband and wife. In **Desire Under the Elms** appears for the first time an example of the bitter hatred that exists between father and son, an enmity which persisted until **Ah, Wilderness!** That this relationship had appeared in literature before Freud had called attention to it, is, of course, recognized, but never in pre-Freudian days had the motif appeared with such grim regularity as it had since about 1910, when Freud was beginning to receive the attention of the layman as well as of the psychiatrist. It is impossible to determine whether O'Neill's inhibitions were suddenly removed so that he dared to hold the mirror up to his own inner life; whether he picked up the idea directly from Freud's works; whether it reached him circuitously through such foreign novels as *Sons and Lovers* (1913) or from the German Expressionistic drama which ran its course between 1910 and 1924 and wherein the father-son motif "plays a specially important role"; or whether, like many persons of the 1920's, he simply soaked up such psychological commonplaces.

To anyone who was concerned, as O'Neill surely was, with Greek tragedy and the nature of religion, the theories of both Freud and Jung should have been of inestimable interest. In *Totem and Taboo*—published 1912, translated 1918—Freud speculated on the origins of religion and morality. Reconstructing the conditions of the primal horde, he described a rebellion of the sons against the violent primal father who stood in the way of their sexual demands and of their desire for power. It was evident to Freud that after the idea of god appeared he was "in every case modelled after the father and that our personal relation to god is dependent upon our relation to our physical father, fluctuating and changing with him, and that god at bottom is nothing but an exalted father." The revolt was not Satan's but the son's, that is, Christ's. For he was related to earlier conceptions of gods who had "enjoyed the favours of maternal deities and committed incest with the mother in defiance of the father, finally murdering the latter. But the slaying of the father left its mark, and here is where religion and morality began." Hating their father, the sons also loved and admired him. O'Neill, dramatizing the hostility of sons for fathers, saw no evidence of ambivalent feeling and therefore no cause for remorse, guilt, redemption. Indeed, the Cabot boys never even kill the father; but their resentment, their threats, their overt acts are those of the primal horde. They detest him for his power, for his demonstrable priority in conquest of women, threatening to rape his "new woman." They wish him dead, a desire that for an instant appears to be fulfilled when Abbie informs Eben that she has killed "him." Under a misapprehension, Eben *savagely* cries, "An' serves him right!" But like the stones, the father, as O'Neill saw it, is indestructible. And he is to haunt the heroes and heroines of most of the plays to come.

Eben Cabot's repeated plaintive appeal to his Maw is the earliest indication that O'Neill was to enlist the services of the Mother in the struggle against the Father and against God. In this project Jung, among others, seems to have been especially helpful. If the Swiss psychiatrist incurred the deep displeasure of Freud, he earned the gratitude of such people as assert the coexistence, if not the preeminence, of the spirit. Instinct and spirit he found equally mysterious and expressed their ineffableness in symbol, in allegorical language. For these reasons in general his theories were perhaps attractive to O'Neill; but his assignment of the predominant role in the instinctual and spiritual world to the mother rather than to the father should have been particularly appealing. "The most immediate primordial image," Jung declared, "is the mother,"

> for she is in every way the nearest and most powerful experience; and the one moreover that occurs in the most impressionable period of a man's life. Since the conscious is as yet only weakly developed in childhood, one cannot speak of an individual experience at all. The mother, however, is an archetypal experience; she is known by the more or less unconscious child not as a definite, individual feminine personality, but as the mother, an archetype loaded with significant possibilities. As life proceeds the primordial image fades, and is replaced by a conscious, relatively individual image, which is assumed to be the only mother-image we have. In the unconscious, on the contrary, the mother always remains a powerful primordial image, determining and colouring in the individual conscious life our relation to woman, to society, and to the world of feeling and fact, yet in so subtle a way that, as a rule, there is no conscious perception of the process.

The dementia praecox patient who "seeks to leave the world and to regain the subjectivity of childhood," the universal "secret longing for the maternal depths," the "childish longing for the food-giving mother," the marrying of a woman who resembles the mother, personifications like Mother Germania, mother earth, mother nature, *mater ecclesia*—these are all signs to Jung of the presence of a universal wish to enter the mother's womb a second time and be born again. (pp. 126-34)

Edwin A. Engel, in his The Haunted Heroes *of Eugene O'Neill, Cambridge, Mass.: Harvard University Press, 1953, 310 p.*

Philip Weissman   (essay date 1957)

[*Weissman was an American psychoanalyst and critic. In the following excerpt, he analyzes the play as O'Neill's "unconscious autobiography."*]

Our ambition . . . is to utilize one of O'Neill's significant achievements—*Desire Under the Elms*— as a reciprocal tool to reconstruct specific experiences in his life and to demonstrate how its otherwise obscured or repressed contents were only made available in this aesthetic accomplishment. Our effort is not to be confused with the thoroughgoing work of a psychoanalysis which aims at reconstructing as many infantile, childhood and later experiences as is clinically possible in any given case. It would be wrong to imply that a complete study of all the writings of O'Neill—or for that matter, the total artistic output of any other artist—would lead to a total psychoanalytic reconstruction that would in any way approximate clinical analysis. Studies of applied psychoanalysis frequently assume, explicitly or implicitly that the totality of the artist or the man becomes approachable through the all-inclusive study of his works. It is more likely, however, that many of the individual creations of a given artist utilize the same conflicts repeatedly.

A summary of the plot of *Desire Under the Elms* is indicated. The play is set in the early summer of 1850. Ephraim Cabot, age seventy-five, a New England farmer, a religious man with a concept of a severe God, returns to his home with an attractive, thirty-five-year-old bride, a young widow, as his third wife. Abbie has married Ephraim to have a home for herself. Ephraim has two sons from his first wife—Simeon, age thirty-nine, and Peter, age thirty-seven—and a younger son, Eben, age twenty-five, from his second wife. Both wives have died. The two older sons, upon learning from Eben that their father was en route with his new bride, decided to make their way to California in search of gold. Eben induced the two brothers to assign to him their rights as heirs to the farm for $600.00, which he stole from his father's hiding place. We are informed that the father and the two older sons work the farm, while young Eben keeps house for the family in place of his dead mother. Ephraim regards young Eben as soft and weak, like the boy's mother, whereas the two older brothers see Eben as a tower of strength and determination, not unlike their father.

With the permanent departure of the two older brothers, the play confines itself to the lives of Eben, Ephraim and Abbie. Eben looks upon Abbie as a designing intruder who will rob him of his inheritance. Abbie is attracted to Eben. She wants Ephraim to die and leave her the farm. She seduces the father to believe that she could conceive a child of his. In his enthusiasm, Ephraim promises her that their child will become sole heir to the property. Abbie then deliberately seduces Eben for the purpose of having a child. In this process they fall in love with each other. Eben then feels the power and revenge against his father whom he hates. In the consummating scene, the seduction occurs in Eben's mother's special room. Eben's dead mother sanctions the love act, encourages Eben to love and trust Abbie. Eben's love for Abbie transforms itself from a filial love to a sexual one. The son intensifies his revenge by telling his father that he, Eben, is actually the father of the new-born child. The father counters with a blow, telling Eben that Abbie had only pretended to love the young man, in order to become heir to the property by giving Ephraim, the old man, a son. This revives Eben's original hatred of Abbie and he decides to run away. Then Abbie kills the baby to prove her love for Eben. Momentarily Eben thought that she had killed the father. Eben is reassured by her act that she loves him. Then Eben seeks out the police and confesses voluntarily that he is an accomplice to the murder and is prepared to be punished with Abbie. The final scene shows Abbie and Eben being taken away, happy, united and victorious in their love and crime.

An explanation of the title of the play rounds out the mood and theme of the play. This can best be accounted for by quoting O'Neill's introductory stage directions concerning the house: "Two enormous elms are on each side of the house. They bend their trailing branches down over the roof. They appear to protect and at the same time subdue. There is a sinister maternity in their aspect, a crushing jealous absorption. They have developed from their intimate contact with the life of man in the house an appalling humaneness. They brood oppressively over the house. They are like exhausted women resting their saggy breasts and hands and hair on its roof, and when it rains their tears trickle down monotonously and rot on the shingles."

The intensity of this description has always impressed me as one written by a man who was recently in the midst of the most intense mourning for his mother. Evidence for this was not attainable from direct biographical sources. Subsequent investigation revealed that O'Neill's mother and only brother were dead by the year 1923. His father died in 1920. The play was written in 1924. Thus, the precondition for writing an unconscious family biography and personal autobiography were much the same as they were in 1940, when O'Neill wrote the conscious family biography and personal autobiography, *Long Day's Journey Into Night.* These conditions were that all concerned had died.

The family situation in the two plays is identical. In *Long Day's Journey Into Night* there is first his mother (age fifty-four), who is described as still having "a young graceful figure, a trifle plump, but showing little evidence of middle aged waist and hips, although she is not tightly corseted." The father is sixty-five years, the older brother, age thirty-four and O'Neill himself is age twenty-four. In *Desire Under the Elms,* written in 1924, there is the father, aged seventy-five (in 1923, had he lived, O'Neill's father would have been seventy-six years old). Abbie, the stepmother, attractive and thirty-five years old, is certainly in the image of his mother. The two older brothers, age thirty-nine and thirty-seven, who appear briefly in the play, are portrayed in a twinlike singularity representing unconsciously and biographically O'Neill's older brother and another aspect of his own self. Finally, Eben, age

twenty-five, represents O'Neill (unknown to himself) with his usually unallowable unconscious wishes. The fact that the characters in these two plays are not represented identically does not mean that we are merely juxtaposing matters of slight similarity and overevaluating their identity. The characters in a created play—a product of the unconscious—should be treated like the manifest content of the characters in a dream or fantasy; their latent meaning can be identified only by associations of similarity. To strengthen our contention that, for example, O'Neill's father and Ephraim Cabot are identical, it might be pointed out that in both biographical dramas they are portrayed as older men who are powerful, patriarchal and penurious. Both men have an intense passion for property. In each play, in almost identical dialogues, it is said about each of them that they would buy the sky if it were property. The author's images of the two fathers, real and created, are of a single source.

A similar identity can be demonstrated between O'Neill's mother in the family play and Abbie. Both seek and demand intensely a home from their husbands. Mary complains that they have always lived in second-rate hotels and Abbie tells Eben about her desperate longing for a home. The brothers, Simeon and Peter, chronologically represent O'Neill's older brother who is in his thirties when O'Neill is in his twenties. In their brief appearance, aspects of their histories are more parts of O'Neill's life than his brother's. Thus Simeon, thirty-nine, tells us how at the age of twenty-one he lost his wife Jenn. Jenkins is the maiden name of O'Neill's first wife when he was twenty-one. Simeon and Peter both leave to seek gold in California, as O'Neill did in 1909 when "he set out on his gold-prospecting trys to Honduras." In addition, there is the identity of Eben and O'Neill—they are respectively twenty-five and twenty-four in the biographical plays. However, the matter of being a father to a son is handled very differently in the two plays. Whereas in the conscious autobiography O'Neill's fatherhood is completely obliterated by powerful defense mechanisms, in the unconscious drama he is a father in violation of the most intense taboo known to man. Subsequently he obliterates his fatherhood by accusing himself of an uncommitted crime. This provides us with an opportunity to examine the vicissitudes of an unconscious conflict in the personal life of the artist.

A life situation (marriage, fatherhood and divorce) about which there has been an unconscious conflict is treated in personal life with complete suppression and repression of both its contents and affects, respectively. It reappears in a creation, unknown to the creator, for what it is—a part of his own biography. Under these conditions, it becomes possible for the artistic part of the ego to elaborate the total content of the unconscious conflict with all its painful affects. The creation has the complete content and pain, whereas the life situation is devoid of either content or pain.

The unfolding of Eben's conflicts can be organized into a constellation or a design of an oedipal situation and its fantasies. On the one hand, Eben is his father's rival first with his real mother and then with his stepmother. He had won the love of his mother at the expense of his father. For the fulfillment of this wish he suffers the punishment of surrendering his masculinity by adopting the passive feminine life of his mother: he becomes his father's housekeeper, as his mother had been. When Abbie enters the picture, the old conflict is revived; he wins her sexually and fathers her child. His punishment for this is the loss of his child, the loss of the farm, and imprisonment. He is unable to grow beyond his sexual feelings for his mother and his death wishes toward his father. Thus he is destined to an inability to resolve his oedipal strivings.

Our conclusion would be that O'Neill's life situations are mirrored in the image of his unconscious counterpart, Eben, and that O'Neill's love mates are reflected in the image of Abbie and Eben's mother—a maternal and sexual object rightfully belonging to the father. Further, the role of being father to a real child belonged to the image of Abbie's baby—a child that cannot live and be recognized as long as Ephraim lives—the unconscious image for O'Neill's father. Also, the unconscious identification with his mother's ideal of purity and earthy abstinence contributes to the surrender of parenthood. In the final moment of *Desire Under the Elms,* Eben and Abbie are seen united (identified with each other) in a "child-destroyed" punishable love, reminding us again of Edmund (O'Neill) and Mary (his mother) in the conscious biographical drama.

We can now better understand why O'Neill never saw his first son, Eugene Jr., until the boy was ten years old, in 1920. Not until then—the time of his father's death—could O'Neill recognize his son as his own. Until then O'Neill is denied his paternity, as Eben is denied his child. In 1920, when Eugene Jr. was ten years old, O'Neill went to see him for the first time. He then became interested in his son and began to participate in plans for his education and general care. He was also able to establish some relationship with his son who grew increasingly fond of him.

This is not to be construed to imply that O'Neill was now able to assume the full role of a father. The death of his father was an essential circumstance, momentarily undoing the severest prohibition against having a child. There is much recent evidence that O'Neill had to struggle all his life with the same conflict in connection with his subsequent children from his second wife. Recent newspaper accounts of and interviews with his children clearly establish that O'Neill held himself apart from his children throughout his life, while at the same time he made sporadic though short-lived efforts to recognize and relate to them. At the end of his life he remained unreconciled to them, and they were not recognized as his rightful heirs.

As to O'Neill's relationship with women, it is generally conceded that much unhappiness prevailed in his marriages. It is fairly clear that O'Neill tended to idealize a loved woman to the point of desexualization. In his life and in his dramatic characters unconsciously portraying himself, there is a brief enactment of mature sexuality—that is, love, marriage and children—which then regresses to a desexualized idealization of the loved woman accompanied by a regressive abandonment of the child or children. This regressive path was often followed by establishing relationships with prostitutes who also became desexu-alized and limited to relationships of the mother's nurturing love for a son and the son's love for a comforting mother. As with the regressive abandonment of a child, the regressive surrender of a loved woman is self-directed by the living, punishing father and the identification with a virginal mother.

One wonders whether O'Neill's father in real life was much different from Ephraim, the created prototype. Considerable evidence is available that the father was as morally severe and restrictive to O'Neill and his brother as Ephraim was to Eben and to the other sons. The elder O'Neill made every effort to merge his sons into his own life and into subservience to himself. In *Long Day's Journey Into Night,* James Jr., the elder son, bitterly complains that the father forced him to become an actor which he had never wanted to be. Not until O'Neill developed tuberculosis did his father begrudgingly help him achieve his own ambition—to become a dramatist. Prior to this, his father always encouraged him to work under him as a secretary in his business, an assistant manager, or as a most minor actor in his play. It would seem that he encouraged the passive subservience of his sons. The early sea voyages and endeavors to make his own way had the atmosphere of parental excommunication. Neither in the play nor in biographical material is there evidence that the elder O'Neill encouraged his sons to pursue in their self-directed desires for mature achievements and mature manhood.

In *Desire Under the Elms,* O'Neill chose to set his conflicts in a family of hard-working, primitive, God-fearing people. In this respect too, Ephraim resembles O'Neill's real father, who was an uneducated boy and supported his family from the age of ten. Certainly, O'Neill's choice of a primitive family to mouth the primitive conflicts of the play was also determined by his great talent to construct families appropriate for his dramatic conflict.

In *Desire Under the Elms,* as in *Long Day's Journey Into Night,* the character of the woman (Abbie and his mother) remains an unconscious enigma to the author, in sharp contrast to the realistic portrayals of the father. We cannot fail to recognize that the author intends Abbie to be much more than an attractive stepmother. She is linked with the symbols of long-endured suffering motherhood—the elm trees. She is linked with Eben's mother who loved her son and was more devoted to him and her stepsons than to her husband. This is a composite concept, similar to what O'Neill contended with in his own life in his relationships to women. O'Neill's mother's unconscious ideal of chastity and purity became his own unconscious ideal of womanhood and manhood. The contribution of his mother and father to the formation of his ego ideals and superego gives the personal stamp to many of the unconsciously determined creations of O'Neill.

[In his *The Haunted Heroes of Eugene O'Neill,* E. A. Engel] concluded about O'Neill that "Sequestering himself, he distilled from modern life the futility, the emptiness, the chaos, and left out the particulars of external events. Yet, preoccupied though he was with the universal and the abstract, he continually revealed the thinly disguised particulars and concrete facts of his personal life."

Engel subsequently gives evidence that he evaluates the appearance of the thinly veiled personal life in O'Neill's works as a consciously controlled activity. He is of the opinion that if O'Neill had been born a generation earlier, he would have been a hackneyed dramatist, rewriting a meaningless version of *The Count of Monte Cristo* for his father. We would rather think that if O'Neill rewrote this play, he would—by necessity of overdetermination of unconscious conflicts—write it in the vein of his powerful tragedies, as he transformed the Aeschylean trilogy of The Furies into a more tragic *Mourning Becomes Electra*. . . . O'Neill did not decide to become a dramatist. He was driven to it.

O'Neill's sense of tragedy—referred to as his sixth sense—was a result of psychic conflicts. His personal tragic conflict in which he was unconsciously forbidden to be a real father of his family was utilized by his creative ego—again unconsciously—to recognize that Electra was not correctly conceived in the Greek tragedy where she is permitted to resume her life in a "marriage banality." In the tragedy *Mourning Becomes Electra,* she becomes an eternally haunted character such as he himself was. In this creation it is impossible to separate the contributions derived from the dramatist's personal unconscious conflicts and those from his own creative talents. (pp. 452-59)

> *Philip Weissman, "Conscious and Unconscious Autobiographical Dramas of Eugene O'Neill," in* Journal of the American Twentieth Century, *Vol. 5, No. 3, July, 1957, pp. 432-60.*

Freud's influence on *Desire under the Elms:*

An omnivorous reader, O'Neill happened to be reading Freud (he thought *Group Psychology and the Analysis of the Ego* "very interesting," *Beyond the Pleasure Principle* "interesting but dully written or translated") around the time he heard from several persons who wondered whether he was indebted to Freud for certain aspects of *Desire under the Elms.* O'Neill resented the question, replying to one correspondent: "Playwrights are either intuitively keen analytical psychologists or they aren't good playwrights. I'm trying to be one. To me, Freud only means uncertain conjectures and explanations about truths of the emotional past of mankind that every dramatist has clearly sensed ever since real drama began. Which, I think, covers your question. I respect Freud's work tremendously—but I'm not an addict! Whatever of Freudianism is in *Desire* must have walked in 'through my unconscious.' " To a friend he expressed himself more bluntly: "The Freudian brethren and sisteren seem quite set up about [*Desire*] and, after reading quite astonishing complexes between the lines of my simplicities, claim it for their own. Well, so some of them did with *Emperor Jones.* They are hard to shake!"

> *Louis Sheaffer, in his* O'Neill: Son and Artist, *1973.*

Doris V. Falk   (essay date 1958)

[*Falk is an American critic, educator, and author of* Eugene O'Neill and the Tragic Tension: An Interpretive Study of the Plays. *In the following excerpt from that study, she discusses the themes and characters of* Desire under the Elms.]

[The conflicting opposites in *Desire Under the Elms* (1924)] are not only dream and reality, pride and love, exultation and pain. From *Desire* on, throughout the O'Neill canon, they are Father and Mother. Their overwhelming, unconscious influence upon the characters is expressed in terms roughly equivalent to the Oedipus and Electra complexes. A given character's proud, isolated, expansive self-image now resembles his father's face; the loving, sensitive, submissive self-image wears a mask of the mother. These parental opposites which gave the character birth are at destructive war within him. Both demand expression; if he gives in entirely to his identification with one parent, action—and life—cease for him. The struggle is not limited to the mind of the hero. In fact, sometimes there is no hero. The maternal and paternal forces whose warfare is clearest in one character ultimately sway the destinies of all the characters. The parental images are indifferent gods who plot the action of the drama as they wager and contend for human lives.

Desire Under the Elms is set on a farm in New England. The play is divided into three "parts," the first of which concerns the revolt of the Cabot brothers against their tyrannical father, Ephraim. Although the character of the youngest son, Eben, is the focal point of the play, Part I concentrates on the two elder brothers. They are clumsy, loutish sons of the soil, barely escaping the stock characterizations of stage Yankee and country bumpkin. Their dialogue and action give Part I a crudely comic flavor, suggesting a dramatic pattern which emerges fully in *The Iceman Cometh* and *Moon for the Misbegotten.* The play begins as comedy, but as O'Neill said with reference to *The Iceman Cometh,* it is not long before "the comedy breaks up and the tragedy comes on."

The father against whom the brothers are in rebellion is Ephraim Cabot, a self-centered, loveless man who has projected his own personality into that of his God, a tyrannic, ascetic, restrictive embodiment of Puritanism, "hard and lonesome and old" like Ephraim. He is a God whom Ephraim identifies with the farm itself, from the rocky soil of which he has by sheer doggedness won a living—"God's in the stones!" Ephraim, like the monomaniac "extremists," has dedicated his entire life to this God, who is, of course, only an image of his own ego. Ephraim has already sacrificed his sons by enslaving them to the farm, but the most pathetic sacrificial victim was his second wife (mother of Eben, the youngest son), a gentle, sensitive woman, whom he married not for love, but for land. She died overworked and love-starved, a victim of Ephraim's exploitive egotism.

Opposing the puritanical Ephraim and his God, in whose name love has been desecrated, is the spirit of this woman—her self-sacrifice, her longing for beauty, her need of natural sexual love which demands fulfillment.

This second force is symbolized in the elms that tower over the farmhouse, dominating the entire play:

> There is a sinister maternity in their aspect, a crushing, jealous absorption. . . . They brood oppressively over the house. They are like exhausted women resting their sagging breasts and hands and hair on its roof, and when it rains their tears trickle down monotonously and rot on the shingles.

The violated maternal spirit works its vengeance through Eben, the son of the wronged woman, and through Abbie, the third wife, now Eben's stepmother. Abbie has married Ephraim for the same reason that he married Eben's mother, to acquire property. At first with separate selfish motives—Eben for revenge upon his father, and Abbie to have a son to inherit Ephraim's farm—the two determine to satisfy their desire for each other. Abbie, however, falls in love with Eben. Upon consummation of that love, the maternal ghost is somewhat placated—love has finally had natural sexual expression. After the event the room in which it took place, formerly that of Eben's mother, loses its oppressive, tomb-like atmosphere. As Abbie says,

> We made it our'n last night, didn't we? We give it life—our lovin' did. (*A pause.*)
>
> EBEN. (*with a strange look*) Maw's gone back t'her grave. She kin sleep now.

But they have paid only a part of the ancestral debt. Their physical union has fulfilled the demand of the maternal ghost for normal sexuality, but Eben must still answer for his mother's thwarted spiritual needs. He is drawn to Abbie not by love, but by lust, greed, and the desire for revenge. Eben wears two figurative masks—one ruthless and self-centered like his father, the other sensitive and hungry for beauty and love as his mother was. O'Neill makes this double identity quite clear. While Eben constantly asserts that he is the "heir" of his mother—"I'm Maw—every drop o' blood!"—his brothers keep reminding him that he is the "spittin' image" of his father. His very determination to avenge his mother reflects the personality of his father; in buying out his brothers' share of the farm in order, eventually, to be sole owner, Eben demonstrates his father's greed; in desiring possession of his father's paramours (including a neighboring prostitute, as well as Abbie), he duplicates his father's lust. Eben must break down the mask of egotism, must cast off the prideful father, if he is to become integrated with his other self. The subsequent action of the play makes it possible for him to do so.

After a child is born to him and Abbie, Eben discovers her original motive in having the child, and threatens to leave her. To prove that her love is for Eben, not simply for the infant and his inheritance, Abbie kills the child. Furious at the act, Eben goes to the police to report her. In the process, however, he realizes that he, too, is guilty, that he must give himself up with Abbie, and accept with her the consequences of the crime. In the act of sacrificing himself, his vengeful lust is transformed into love. The two face death or imprisonment together, accepting with exultation the tragic irony that love has not come to fruition until the moment of inevitable loss, just as they accept without

question the justice of their fate. In this acceptance they, like the other "finders," have found their integration. Unlike the couple of *The Straw,* there is no "hopeless hope" for them, nor do they seek it. In the reality of the situation itself they find salvation.

The opposing drives at war within Eben call to mind Horney's description of the strife within the pride system: the expansive and impossibly prideful image of the father is at war with the submissive, giving spirit of the mother. Even stated in terms of sexuality, of desire and its motives, the dichotomy is the same. Old Ephraim's Puritan conception of sex as an ugly, sinful necessity has perverted all sexuality into a brutal lust as egotistical and exploitive as his other greeds; but in the brooding maternal spirit symbolized by the elms sex is a spontaneous, beautiful, unselfish, and amoral life force, perverted into a powerful avenging spirit by suppression. O'Neill views this suppressed maternal aspect as Eben's "real" self, from which he has been alienated in his pursuit of the prideful father in himself. When Eben sacrifices his own life, with Abbie, he has relinquished the chase. The conflict is over, and he becomes capable of spontaneous love. In the young couple's fulfillment of their desire and in the transmutation of sex to love, reality has finally asserted itself, has struck through the illusory mask of pride.

But to "strike through the mask" is not to destroy it. For Pride remains in the person of the old man—although even he has shown some signs of the disunited self. He is locked so fast, however, inside the egotistical one that his only effort to reach beyond it is a failure. When the whole truth has been told about Abbie and Eben, Ephraim decides to escape the loneliness of the farm. He will go to California as his older sons have done, taking with him his hoarded savings. He discovers, however, first with fury, then with secret relief, that the money is gone, Eben having used it to buy out his brothers' shares of the farm. Laying the loss of the money to the will of God, Ephraim recognizes that he can never free himself from that tract of barren land nor does he want to. The farm *is* himself and his prison . . . and only by staying there and working justice on himself can he find self-integration:

> It's a-goin' to be lonesomer now than ever it war afore—an' I'm gittin' old, Lord-ripe on the bough. . . . (*Then stiffening*) Waal—what d'ye want? God's lonesome, hain't he? God's hard and lonesome!

He, too, accepts the tragic fate and its justice.

The lovers find their integration in sacrifice; Ephraim finds his in its opposite, pride. Through the lovers, reality has found its paradoxical destructive-affirmative expression; in their death they have found life. Ephraim lives on, but within the eternal illusion which is living death—the illusion represented by the farm, the mask of his fatal pride. Circles of ironic significance widen around the final curtain speech, an innocuous comment dropped by the sheriff, in the presence of the lovers who "stand for a moment looking up raptly in attitudes strangely aloof and devout."

> SHERIFF. (*looking around at the farm envious-*

ly—to his companion) It's a jim-dandy farm, no denyin'. Wished I owned it!

(pp. 93-9)

Doris V. Falk, in her Eugene O'Neill and the Tragic Tension: An Interpretive Study of the Plays, *second edition, Gordian Press, 1982, 223 p.*

Sophus Keith Winther   (essay date 1960)

[*Winther is a Danish critic and educator. In the following essay, he calls* Desire under the Elms *O'Neill's first "modern tragedy" and a turning point for him as a dramatist.*]

Many critics of O'Neill have commented on **Desire Under the Elms** as marking a turning point in his development as a dramatist. Some have seen it as O'Neill's expression of extreme violence represented in brutal characters who exemplify "greed, lechery, incest, adultery, revenge, murder." O'Neill " . . . declared them good, and sanctified them" [Edward A. Engel, *The Haunted Heroes of Eugene O'Neill*]. This emphasis on all forms of violence and human degradation is the critical counterpart of popular public revulsion which reached its height in Los Angeles where the whole cast of the play was arrested, tried and convicted of giving a public performance of a play that was "mere smut, and filth . . . , morbid, lewd and obscene" [Conrad Seiler, *Nation* (1926)]. From this psychological approach the critic and the public indicate that in this play O'Neill had made a new departure into the lower depths of the psyche. They find it false, revolting, and since it sets its approval on bestiality, it deserves the moral condemnation it receives.

Another critical attack sees the play as centered on overblown pride that balks at no crime to achieve its own ends. In this view Ephraim "has dedicated his entire life to God, who is, of course, only an image of his own ego" [Doris V. Falk, *Eugene O'Neill and the Tragic Tension*]. From this it follows that all the characters who come in contact with Ephraim are sacrificed to his lust for power. His God is in the rocks, hard, uncompromising and pitiless. This judgment of the play is based on the Aristotelian theory of *hamartia,* and so marks a turning point in O'Neill's conception of tragedy. According to this idea, there must be a "flaw" and the "flaw" must account for the hero's "fall."

[In his introduction to **Nine Plays by Eugene O'Neill**] Joseph Wood Krutch also emphasizes **Desire Under the Elms** as a turning point in O'Neill's development as a dramatist. He regards it as the first play "which clearly revealed the kind of artistic problem with which O'Neill's genius was destined to grapple." His conception of the "problem" deals with the manner in which O'Neill succeeded in divorcing the action from the reality of the particular, and thereby concentrating on the interpretation of the abstract, or the idea. By this approach he lifts the play out of the muck of detail to which moralistic criticism is inevitably attached. He considered the play as "interested less in New England as such than in an aspect of the eter-

O'Neill's sketches for the set of Desire under the Elms.

nal tragedy of man and his passions." He holds that "the events really occur out of place and out of time."

This, however, is only a prelude to the real difference between **Desire Under the Elms** and the earlier plays. In this play, for the first time, O'Neill begins to see the problem of tragedy in modern drama as opposed to the classical and traditional interpretation. In this play he departs from the traditional interpretations of Aristotle, a departure that made it possible to develop his later and greater tragedies such as **Mourning Becomes Electra, The Iceman Cometh,** and **Long Day's Journey Into Night.**

O'Neill had, of course, read Aristotle's *Poetics,* but it does not follow that he studied the *Poetics,* analyzed twenty centuries of criticism, and then exemplified his own theory in a conscious dramatic structure. He began in a simpler manner, as no doubt Sophocles did, by seeking an answer to man's relation to the invisible forces that control his destiny. "I am interested only in the relation between man and God," states a point of view that O'Neill expressed many times in many different ways, but always emphasizing the essential and the only problem that is inseparable from any theory of tragedy.

In his notes to **Mourning Becomes Electra** O'Neill states the problem, recognizing that a modern version of the Electra story needs a psychological equivalent which in turn requires a modern conception of tragedy. By the time he wrote this play he had formulated his theory, but it was in **Desire Under the Elms** that he first conceived of tragedy as based on a theory of life and art that rests upon an idea, "a way of life" as Abercrombie states it.

The difference between a modern theory of tragedy as exemplified in drama from Ibsen and Strindberg to O'Neill is that it discards all the superficial requirements of a tragedy as set forth by Aristotle. Of course one should not forget that Aristotle was applying an inductive method to the analysis of Greek practice, and not laying down laws as was assumed by the neo-classics. This is not news, but neither is it an accepted fact that modern tragedy has entirely escaped from the Aristotelian "laws" and the moral implications of *hamartia.*

Such substantial critics of O'Neill as Engel, Falk and Eric Bentley make their judgment within the moral limits of the traditional Aristotelian framework. Even when Bentley can not like O'Neill because he can't do a successful stage production, it is quite obvious that his real difficulty lies in his inability to grasp O'Neill's concept of tragedy. Miss Falk's study of "The Tragic Tension" is penetrating and profound even when it assumes that O'Neill accepted the moral view of *hamartia,* which he certainly did not. On this point he followed Ibsen and Strindberg, and in following them he violated the doctrine so hallowed by tradition that it is very nearly sacred.

No recent critic has developed the contrast between the classical and the modern on this issue better than Whitman in his study of Sophocles. He rejects Aristotle's interpretation of the tragic hero as in some way or other deserving his fall from good fortune to bad because of a flaw in his character, a frailty, or an error in judgment. This as the traditional approach was never better stated than by Butcher in his rejection of Ibsen's plays:

> Some quality of greatness in the situation as well as in the characters appears to be all but indispensable, if we are to be raised above the individual suffering and experience a calming instead of a disquieting feeling at the close. The tragic katharsis requires that suffering shall be exhibited in one of its comprehensive aspects; that the deeds and fortunes of the actors shall attach themselves to larger issues, and the spectator himself be lifted above the special case and brought face to face with universal law and the divine plan of the world. [Samuel H. Butcher, *Aristotle's Theory of Poetry and Fine Art*]

This is the very essence of the traditional approach to tragedy. Butcher has carried the moral interpretation of *hamartia* to its logical conclusion and perhaps the inescapable conclusion implied by Aristotle. It provides a perfect escape from the grim truth that tragedy does not justify a moral order or "a divine plan of the world." This interpretation of the flaw makes the unbelievable assumption that the moral failure or error in judgment justifies the fearful doom that falls upon the tragic hero. It sings a lullaby of dawn after the midnight storm, it offers a pious, little Sunday school moral and actually implies that Sophocles, Shakespeare and O'Neill saw man's tragic conflict in the terms of piety divorced from reason. Whatever Aristotle may have meant by katharsis or for that matter by pity and fear it must have been something greater than this Victorian sense of pious acceptance of a divine order. And it is that something more that lays the foundation for modern tragedy in Strindberg and Ibsen, and this is more fully developed in a conscious conception of tragedy by O'Neill.

In *Desire Under the Elms* the tragic hero is a man apart from other men. He does not accept their manner of living, their morality is beneath his contempt, their ideals are to him the petty dreams of weaklings and cowards. He despises his weak and loutish sons, he scorns the morality so valuable to all those who work in the market place for profit, the church and the dogma it represents is not even worthy of mention, the legal system with its special morality he uses, but only to further his own end. As a man he stems from Ibsen's Brand and the supreme and powerful pride of Strindberg. He is as proud as any man who ever walked onto a stage demanding an answer from the unanswerable. Like Job he wants to know why, with this difference that he knows he must become like the rocks and the hills if he would know God, and then he would be like Him, perhaps even equal to Him.

As a drama every scene in *Desire Under the Elms* is developed with skill to enhance and clarify the nature and meaning of the tragic hero. All other characters are made small in contrast. The two older sons are ignorant and loutish. Eben is a complex of delicate and sentimental love for the memory of his dead mother. Mixed with this emotion is a passion for the farm which is nothing more than a superficial attitude learned from his father. He will steal in the name of his mother to acquire his brother's rights to the land. He will desecrate her love in the company of a whore; he will commit incest and console himself with the thought that the restless spirit of his mother finds peace at last in the approval of his action. Abbie has no fixed value by which she can live. Greed, ambition, power and carnal love are so mixed in her behavior that she never finds a principle by which she can reconcile her practice with a fixed standard of conduct.

Within this network of ignorance and doubtful values that form the outer framework of the plot the character of Ephraim stands hard as the rocks that represent God. He knows that God and the rocks are one, that if he would know God he must know the rocks of the field that are the voice and spirit of God. "God is hard. He ain't easy" is the all-enveloping idea of the play, and the plot is the arrangement of characters in action to emphasize this truth as the all-enveloping idea of man and his world.

This man is a giant in comparison with the human beings who surround him. There is never any suggestion in the play that anyone, either man or woman, understood him. In his presence they can conceal neither their fear nor their awe. He was larger, stronger, older, more daring than other men. He encompassed in his being an understanding of life that embraced all living things. He was a part of the stony hills, the blue sky, the changing seasons; age did not weaken him, and the laws and the morality that are necessary to the essential weakness of most human beings were nonexistent for him. The sense of guilt, sin, and the fear of the law before which other characters of the play cringe, never crossed the threshold of his mind or touched him with either sorrow or regret. He lived in the presence of God as manifested in the stones on his farm. He read the lessons of these stones as the true symbol of God's reality: cold, impersonal, strong, powerful, everlasting; a God untouched and unmoved by the petty, sensuous needs of men. Their pitiful cries for help, their intermittent faith, their identification with the soft and the sentimental was scorned by Ephraim as the God he understood so well also scorned them.

There are four scenes in Part I. Not until near the end of Scene Four does Ephraim appear, yet he dominates the actions and the thoughts of his three sons in the preceding scenes. The older sons are longing to escape from "makin' stone walls fur him to fence us in!" From that reference to "stones atop o' stones" and "Him," Ephraim dominates the action although he is not there in person. He had left the farm two months before. "Hitched up an' druv off into the West." They are puzzled by his queer behavior in leaving the place for the first time in thirty years. Simeon recognized a strange power, an unexplained force which he calls "Somethin'—driving him—t' drive us." He told his son why he was going, but to the younger man's dull mind it had no meaning. As Simeon recalls it his father was "lookin' kinder queer an' sick," and saying "I been hearin' the hens cluckin' an' the roosters crowin' all the durn day. I been lisenin' t' the cows lowin' an' everthin' else kickin' up till I can't stand it no more. It's spring an' I am feelin' damned. . . . An' now I'm ridin' out t' learn God's message t' me in the spring, like the prophets done."

His sons scorn his avowed purpose, but he was speaking a deep conviction of his own. A little less than fifty years before, he had fled from the stones to seek an easy life in the rich lands of the Mississippi valley. Ephraim tells Abbie that as his crops in the rich soil began to flourish he heard the voice of God saying, "This hain't wuth nothin' to Me," and goes on to say, "God's hard, not easy! God's in the stones! Build my church on a rock—out of stones an' I'll be in them! That's what He meant t' Peter! . . . Stones."

In his seeking for identification with the God of Stone, he was set apart from other human beings. He neither shared in their lives nor felt bound by their laws. They in turn could not enter into his (Ibsen) Brand-like conception of man's relations to God. He married and his wife bore him two sons. "She was a good woman. She wuked hard. We was married twenty year. She never knowed me. She helped but she never knowed what she was helpin'. I was allus lonesome. She died." He took a second wife. "She never knowed me for nothin'. It was lonesomer 'n hell with her. After a matter o' sixteen odd years, she died." His sons grew up hating him and coveting the farm not knowing what they coveted; not knowing as Ephraim knew that possession of the farm was equal to the knowledge of God. Then he went forth in the spring to listen to the voice of the Prophets and he found a third wife who for a fleeting instant seemed to grasp the meaning of the farm and then lost it to a calculated carnal desire, because, she like all the others, did not know that this stony stronghold of Ephraim and God could not be possessed by love, illegal or otherwise.

As Part II develops, the battle of love and greed between Abbie and Eben controls the action. It seems to have turned away from Ephraim. He is lost once more in the wilderness of his lonesome world. While Abbie is plotting to deceive him, he makes a last effort to enlist her sympathy and understanding. "Then this spring the call come—the voice o' God cryin' in my wilderness, in my lonesomeness—t' go out an' seek an' find! (Turning to her with strange passion) I sought ye an' I found ye! Yew air my Rose O'Sharon! Yer eyes air like. . . ." He gives up trying to make her understand.

In the blank ignorance of her expression Ephraim realizes that she, like his other wives, like his sons, does not understand his vision of God, his desire to become like God, hard as stone. In disgust he leaves her to join the cows in the barn. They are close to nature. They have accepted God as a stone. They'll give me peace." But in leaving the scene he only emphasizes the fact that he dominates it. The next two scenes bring the lovers together. They believe that in deceiving Ephraim they have avenged Eben's mother. But the closing scene of Part II shows Ephraim contemplating the beauty or the sky and completely scornful of Eben's petty sense of triumph, which he senses without knowing exactly what its source is.

As the play moves to its conclusion in Part III all the action seems to center on the fearful clash between Eben and Abbie. Hate, fear, greed and love dominate their thoughts, feelings and action. It seems for a time as though they had finally taken over the play and the tragedy belonged to them. Then once more the shadow of the rock which is Ephraim looms over them like the ominous shadows of the elms that cover the house of Cabot. The lovers in their attempt to destroy Ephraim destroy themselves. Their end is ignominious defeat. Their actions are ignorant and cowardly. Their cringing acceptance of their fate deserves the towering contempt of Ephraim.

He in turn suffers a moment of weakness. It seems to him that at last the forces against him have won the battle. He has freed the cattle from the barn. "I'll set fire t' house an' barn an' watch 'em burn, an' I'll leave yer Maw t' haunt the ashes, an' I'll will the fields back t' God, so nothin' human kin never touch 'em!"

He finds that Eben had stolen his money, so his easy plan to escape fails. His moment of weakness is over. He turns back to God. "I kin feel I be in the palm of His hand, His fingers guidin' me. It's a-goin' t' be lonesomer now than ever it war afore— . . . Waal—what d'ye want? God's lonesome, hain't He? God's hard an' lonesome!"

The Sheriff comes to take away the sin-sick, contrite lovers. Ephraim is to be left alone with the farm, the stones and God. He is seventy-five years old, he has had three wives and three sons. They have all, each in his own way, betrayed him. Through their weakness, their inability to understand that Nature has no special concern for their well-being, they deserted him.

In the character of Ephraim, O'Neill has developed a modern tragedy. The traditional conception of the tragic hero with his flaw, the idea of purification through suffering, the sense of a divine order based on the punishment of evil and reward for the good—all this is irrelevant to the tragedy of this play. Ephraim has a sense of the ultimate realities, the forces that relate man to the physical world. He senses the need for a living force in the inanimate earth, and he knows that it is hard as stone and as impersonal as the wind. He listens to the voice of nature, he is exalted by her beauty, and he identifies himself with the quality of lonesomeness which must be the character of power divorced from purpose.

His God of stone embodies the spirit of the earth from which mankind has its being. It brings forth the life that flourishes for a moment on the stony hillside under the blue sky in the warmth of the sun. As it brings to life the spirit of man, it likewise invites him to his doom. There is no escape either from birth or death. All this is part of Ephraim's character. In his futile battle to know God's way and be like God he is doomed to defeat; in his determination never to submit or yield, he is heroic. In this struggle that has dominated his life he can never win. At the age of seventy-five, he walks out into the stony fields, in to the beauty of dawn.

His great pride, one of the most hackneyed "flaws" in all criticism of tragedy, is no "frailty" in his character. It is pride that sustains him, it is by pride that he has endured his failures, it has strengthened him in his search for God. Not through humility but by pride does man attain his true humanity as a being that measures the extent of his universe and develops the courage to face his doom. Ephraim's exit is heroic. "Waal—what d'ye want? God's lonesome hain't He? God's hard an' lonesome." (pp. 326-32)

> *Sophus Keith Winther, " 'Desire under the Elms': A Modern Tragedy," in* Modern Drama, *Vol. 3, No. 3, December, 1960, pp. 326-32.*

Murray Hartman   (essay date 1961)

[*In the following essay, Hartman traces the influence of August Strindberg on* Desire under the Elms.]

Desire Under the Elms (1924) constitutes at once Eugene O'Neill's first great tragedy and his richest exploitation to date of Strindbergian sources. It is not sufficiently recognized that August Strindberg was the major influence on O'Neill, biographically as well as dramaturgically. Scholarship and criticism consistently underestimate that influence, but nowhere more clearly than in **Desire.** George Jean Nathan, the critic most likely to mention O'Neill's debt to the Swedish master, states merely that "the Strindberg influence is here again clear," without further elucidation. Edwin A. Engel, author of *The Haunted Heroes of Eugene O'Neill,* while recognizing the general influence of Freud, Jung, and Nietzsche, is at a loss to discover specific plot sources for the play. He makes no mention of Strindberg. "In **Desire Under the Elms,**" he writes, "appears for the first time an example of the bitter hatred that exists between father and son. . . . " What about the father-hatred to be found in such early unpublished plays as *Bread and Butter* (1914), in **The Rope** and **The Straw** (1918), **Gold** and **Anna Christie** (1920), and **The Hairy Ape** (1921)? And if, as Professor Engel suggests, Abbie's mating with Eben is the fruit of Nietzsche's pagan "yea-saying," why does O'Neill surround her with omens of evil? Why does her presence catalyze the tragedy latent in the stone-bound New England farm? The key, which alters the entire complexion of the tragedy, is to be found in Strindberg.

Daughter of the soil, Abbie not only personifies the eternal Earth-Spirit in whom all streams of desire converge; she can also be a sinister force, both nourisher and destroyer. The type came to Strindberg and his American disciple

through both nineteenth-century feminism and particularly its misogynist countercurrent as voiced by Schopenhauer and Nietzsche, heirs of centuries of indurated pagan and monastic woman-hatred. The ambivalence is seen in the words of the Lady, the heroic mother-figure of Strindberg's dramatic trilogy *The Road to Damascus* (1898-1904): "Now I see why I am to be called Eve. She was a mother and brought sin into the world: it was another mother who brought expiation."

O'Neill's central purpose in **Desire** was to show the tragic possibilities in man's involvement with the mother-image, a theme which he encountered regularly in Strindberg, the more profoundly as it was reinforced by his own experience. Upon his discovery of the Swedish poet in 1913, O'Neill found remarkable parallels in their lives and sympathized with Strindberg's tormented sense of man's doom at the hands of woman. As Agnes Boulton, O'Neill's second wife, has written:

> Gene was very impressed by Strindberg's anguished personal life as it was shown in his novels (*The Son of a Servant* and others, all autobiographical); particularly of his tortured relationship with the women who always seemed to be taking advantage of him. . . . These novels Gene kept by him for many years, reading them even more frequently than the plays. . . . I imagine he had the same feeling of identification with the great tortured Swede up to the time of his own death.

Both Strindberg and O'Neill felt, for good reasons, that they were unwanted children. In *The Son of a Servant* Strindberg characterized his boyhood as a period of unrequited mother love in a world dominated by a tyrannical and parsimonious father. "We are dealing," wrote the psychiatrist Uppvall in his biography of Strindberg, "with a real case of psycho-sexual fixation on the mother, with its concomitant feature—hatred of the father."

O'Neill's pursuit of maternal love was similarly blocked by his father, the popular actor James O'Neill. Since the imperious star insisted on his wife's company on tour, his son Eugene knew virtually no home for the first fourteen years of his life. The latter's childhood trauma was the loss of mother love to a domineering and possessive father-rival. But he never renounced the desire; he never gave up the dream of possession: in his later dramatic visions he returned with obsessive iteration to the field of combat. Rivalry between father and son for the mother's love occurs in **The First Man** (1921), **The Great God Brown** (1925), **Dynamo** (1928), **Mourning Becomes Electra** (1931), **The Iceman Cometh** (1939), **Long Day's Journey into Night** (1941), and of course **Desire Under the Elms.**

This was one of the basic frustrations which drove Strindberg and O'Neill through life—through years of withdrawal and wandering culminating in attempts at suicide; each through three agonizing marital ventures in a vain search for the mother. Was their misogyny a defense against being hurt by love? Did they grow to hate their wives because even as substitute mothers the latter could not finally replace the entombed ones? In **Desire,** are these the roots of Eben's ambivalence toward Abbie?

At any rate, there is hardly a plot element in the play that cannot be traced to one or more sources in Strindberg. The basic situation, where the young son has seen his beloved mother worked to death by a hard father and then has had to bear the usurpation of her position by an aggressive stepmother, has its origin in *The Son of a Servant*. In this book Strindberg's new stepmother, like Abbie Putnam, rose in her search for security from an inferior social position (she had been the maid) to head of the household. Young John was embarrassed, for he had been on bad terms with her. The two older sons, like Simeon and Peter, were also chagrined because they had "strongly admired her." The youth (like Eben) criticized his father for remarrying so soon; he conjured up his mother's shade, prophesied misery and ruin, and shut himself up in his room, miserable and hungry. Eventually the father humbled him. Later "A son [was] born to his stepmother. John instinctively hated him as a rival. . . ." The dramatic intensification of this conflict in *Desire* is almost diabolical: Eben believes that he has been betrayed by his stepmother-mistress into begetting that son—his own rival heir.

O'Neill's emendations of the Swede's basic situation are prompted by his own experience. Consequently the miserliness, the arrogance of the father are retained for Ephraim Cabot, but the lust for property and the mask of Puritan piety and respectability are exaggerated. His age, moreover, is advanced to seventy-six, James O'Neill's age had he been living in 1923, when the dramatist began work on the play.

As for the mother, Strindberg pursued her spirit after her death the more avidly as he failed to possess it in her lifetime. Her restless ghost, already noted in *Son of a Servant*, hovers over his other works. The title character of *Swanwhite*, surrounded by the evil magic of her Stepmother, is protected throughout the play by her own dead mother in the form of a Swan. Miss Julie, however, is possessed by the malignant spirit of her dead mother; and other examples of sinister motherhood are to be found in *The Father, Motherlove, The Pelican,* and *On the Seaboard*. In a scene in *The Road To Damascus* which illuminates this ambivalence, the Stranger talks with his wife, who becomes the Earth-Mother incarnate:

> STRANGER. It was my dream to seek redemption through a woman . . . but she wanted to take and not receive: that's why she hated me! When I was helpless and thought the end was near, a desire grew in me to fall asleep on a mother's knee, on a tremendous breast where I could bury my tired head and drink in the tenderness I'd been deprived of. . . . Call me your child, and then I'll love you.
>
> LADY. You shouldn't love me, but your Creator.
>
> STRANGER. He's unfriendly—like my father!
>
> LADY. He is Love itself, and you are Hate.
>
> STRANGER. You're his daughter; but I'm his cast-out son.

When she later accepts him as a son, "a change comes over her: her clothing falls from her and she is seen to have changed into a white-robed woman with a full maternal bosom."

> STRANGER. Mother!
>
> LADY. Yes, my child, your mother! In life I could never caress you—
>
> STRANGER. But my mother's dead?
>
> LADY. She was; but the dead aren't dead, and maternal love can conquer death.

O'Neill's mother died, deeply mourned, in 1922; the following year her wraith was haunting the pages of ***Desire Under the Elms***. But the spectral robes are Strindberg's; and her qualities, like those of the other maternal figures in the play, are often far from admirable. Just as the ghost of Julie's mother rode her to destruction, so O'Neill, haunted by the image of his own drug-ridden, husband-ridden, guilt-ridden mother who virtually denied her own children, often adumbrated his maternal characters in forbidding hues.

And since the elms in the title of the play connote the pervasive influence of the mother, the menacing cosmic note is sounded at once, in the opening description of the setting:

> Two enormous elms are on each side of the house. They bend their trailing branches down over the roof. They appear to protect and at the same time subdue. There is a sinister maternity in their aspect, a crushing, jealous absorption. They have developed from their intimate contact with the life of man in the house an appalling humanness. They brood oppressively over the house. They are like exhausted women resting their sagging breasts and hands and hair on its roof, and when it rains their tears trickle down monotonously and rot on the shingles.

Upon the basic Oedipal relationship, the play develops a fugal pattern of "sinister maternity." Its first voice is the ghost of Eben's mother, of tender and revered memory, but now possessive and vengeful. Having been cheated out of her property and "slaved to death," she now goads her son to wrest the farm from his father, and robs him of the ability to find love with any other woman, except on the animal level. Nor does she give him any respite until she can later pass on to Abbie, the surrogate mother, the role of avenger.

Soon after Maw's wraith is introduced in Part I, scene 2, O'Neill superimposes the second voice of sinister maternity—that of Min the tart. Approaching middle age, she is in many ways another embodiment of Abbie. She is also the prostitute-Earth Mother, and Eben describes his desire for her in the same primal terms of "growin' . . . gettin' stronger" that Abbie later uses toward him. When brother Simeon reveals that "Paw" possessed her first, Eben is again aroused against his father, his old rival and antagonist. As for Min, he will "go smash [his] fist in her face." But soon he succumbs to the call of the summer night. The next day he "proudly" informs his brothers: "She may have been his'n . . . but she's mine now." Later, Abbie recognizes her natural rival in her, and when she attacks her promiscuity in a jealous rage, Eben points out that

Abbie has sold herself, for security, "like any other old whore."

It is Abbie, of course, in whom the outlines of sinister maternity sharpen and culminate but blend with the life-giving force of a nature goddess. In her first appearance she is a vibrant creature, "thirty-five, buxom, full of vitality," with a sensual face expressing strength and determination. Eben at once resents the stepmother and heir-apparent; but Abbie, determined to seduce him, calls his hostility unnatural:

> Ye been fightin' yer nature ever since the day I come—tryin' t' tell yourself I hain't purty t'ye. (*She laughs a low humid laugh . . . ner body squirms desirously*) Hain't the sun strong an' hot? Ye kin feel it burnin' into the earth—Nature . . . makin' ye want t' grow—into somethin' else—till ye're jined with it—an' it's your'n—but it owns ye, too—an' makes ye grow bigger—like a tree—like them elums—(*He takes a step toward her, compelled against his will*) Nature'll beat ye, Eben. Ye might's well own up t' it fust's last.

Abbie and the maternal elms exert their mystic power. For a while Eben resists this cosmic conspiracy—damns her as a "devil," a "witch," and a harlot.

This conflict within as well as between the characters recalls a scene in Strindberg's *Gustavus Vasa*, where Eric has launched some jibes at the fairly young and attractive Queen who is his stepmother:

> QUEEN. Why do you hate me?
>
> ERIC. (*cynically*). Because I am not allowed to love you. . . . You must not be in love with your stepmother, and yet you must love her: that's madness too.
>
> QUEEN. Why do you call me stepmother?
>
> ERIC. Because that's what you are. Is that clear? If it is, then that isn't madness at least.
>
> QUEEN. You have the tongue of a viper. . . . But no heart! . . .
>
> ERIC. My heart lies buried in my mother's coffin. . . .

In Eben's case, however, nature will finally conquer: he must grow and reproduce. But this procreation needs seed as well as soil, and only Eben, not Cabot, can supply the seed. Abbie, for her part, must take his mother's place in order to release his libido. To achieve this substitution in no equivocal way she must do it symbolically as well as actually: hence she leaves her bedroom (which conveniently connects with Eben's) and boldly invites him down to his mother's sacrosanct parlor—only in this shrine can she confront and merge with his mother's spirit. There he is drawn despite himself, and her attack is frontal:

> ABBIE. Tell me about yer Maw, Eben.
>
> EBEN. They hain't nothin' much. She was kind. She was good.
>
> ABBIE. (*putting one arm over his shoulder—passionately*) I'll be kind an' good t' ye!

> EBEN. Sometimes she used t' sing fur me.
>
> ABBIE. I'll sing fur ye!
>
> EBEN. This was her hum. This was her farm.
>
> ABBIE. This is my hum! This is my farm!
>
> EBEN. He married her t' steal 'em. She was soft an' easy. He couldn't 'preciate her.
>
> ABBIE. He can't 'preciate me!
>
> EBEN. He murdered her with his hardness.
>
> ABBIE. He's murderin' me!

"She died," Eben grieves, and Abbie swears she'll die for him. She may be swearing more truly than she knows. "In spite of her overwhelming desire for him, there is a sincere maternal love in her manner and voice—a horribly frank mixture of lust and mother love." Eben wins approval for the deed from his mother's ghost—through a substitute Maw can both possess her son and wreak her vengeance on Cabot. After that night, when the loving of Abbie and Eben "gives life" to the dead parlor, Maw goes back to her grave, and Abbie makes the room hers.

Three times now Eben has symbolically enacted the dispossession of his father, carrying out in a sense his early prayer for old Cabot's death which culminates in Part III with the "murderous struggle" between father and son. The first revolt, however, is as his dead mother's champion against his father; but this love is pure and spiritual, and impossible of consummation. The second attempt is with Min, the paternal tart. This time Eben succeeds in possessing the flesh, but the victory again is elusive, since the carnal alone is a sterile substitute for what Eben is seeking.

In Abbie, however, who combines the mother and the mistress, Eben succeeds in completely deposing his father. He succeeds, in fact, too well. A son is born who must be expunged lest he become a rival for the mother's love. To prove the child is not her trick to cheat Eben out of his inheritance, Abbie smothers it in its cradle. Thus she is doubly the mother sinister, who has at once engulfed Eben and their son. Eben is punished by his guilt and bafflement, the loss of his child, the loss of the farm, and imprisonment. His tongue lashes Abbie: "Ye must 've swapped yer soul t' hell! . . . I want ye took away, locked up from me! I can't stand t' luk at ye! Murderer an' thief 'r not, ye still tempt me!"

This is how desire for, and identification with, the mother can cause evil to spread. "I'm Maw—every drop of blood!" he cries at the beginning of the play. And at the end Cabot affirms it: "A prime chip o' yer Maw ye be!" But if Eben is the blood of his mother, he is just as inescapably the seed of his father. Simeon and Peter agree that Eben is the "dead spit 'n' image of his Paw," and "Let dog eat dog!" The conflict then arises not only from incestuous desire, but incestuous hatred. The curse emanating from the mother, however, dominates, sifting down from the "crushing, jealous" elms and settling into the bones of the house. Cabot, driven from the "oneasy" homestead one night, goes down to sleep with the cows—an ironic maternal symbol. The evil influence continues to permeate the household even as the community "celebrates" the birth of the new heir. As Abbie and Eben are upstairs embracing over their child, Cabot ruminates in the yard: "Even the music can't drive it out—somethin'. Ye kin feel it droppin' off the elums, climbin' up the roof, sneakin' down the chimney, pokin' in the corners!" The household invaded by an evil spirit, a family curse, an overhanging doom, is a Strindbergian staple. It occurs notably in *The Ghost Sonata*, and in *The Father* in connection with the suspected illegitimacy of the Captain's daughter. In *Dance of Death*, Curt, entering the noxious domestic atmosphere, senses the infection: "What is going on in this house? What is happening here? There is a smell as of poisonous wallpaper, and one feels sick the moment one enters."

Two other Strindberg works round out the plot sources for *Desire*. The first is a novel, *The People of Hemsö*, which narrates a similar triangular struggle for possession with strikingly parallel situations. A source which "connects logically" with this novel—according to Björkman's preface to the Scribner translations which O'Neill read—is the play *The Bridal Crown*, wherein Strindberg's rustics have "much in common with the old New England stock"; with "their unmistakably Puritanical outlook" and "quaintly patriarchal" family attitude, "they talk naturally in quotations from the Bible". (This aptly describes old Cabot.) In this play Kersti sacrifices her illegitimate infant by having it smothered so that she may win her lover in the virginal marriage ceremony. The latter is shocked, but love finally triumphs. As in *Desire* there is a celebration scene pervaded by an ironic sense of doom which is only intensified by the animation of the fiddlers and the goading insinuations of the guests. The theme of the murder of an unwanted child recurs in much of Strindberg's work, notably in *There Are Crimes and Crimes, The Confession of a Fool*, and *Inferno*. If, as O'Neill once told Richard Watts, the plot of *Desire* came to him "so easily," the reason was that various Strindbergian seeds planted over a period of time were bursting into hybrid flower.

Abbie the mother-mistress redeems Abbie the ambitious strumpet and murderess; and an anthropoid like Eben can be transfiured into a human being by the terrible power of her love. Yet he was almost destroyed in the maternal web. "We should have imagined life as created in the birth-pain of God the Mother," says Nina in *Strange Interlude*. "Then we would have understood why we, Her Children, have inherited pain, for we would know that our life's rhythm beats from her great heart, torn with the agony of love and birth." With Abbie and Eben the agony of love and birth leads to the agony of death and expiation, but then still greater love. Drama thus returns to its quasi-religious beginnings: the fertility rite mingled with redemption by mortal sacrifice.

In *Desire Under the Elms*, then, with various biographical and literary influences, mainly that of Strindberg, culminating in the death of O'Neill's mother, his mystique of the Madonna, to recur so often in later plays, emerges full-blown for the first time. She "nucleates" the images of mother-god, mother-earth, mother-temptress. She is a figure so fateful that man challenges her, or even submits to

her, at his peril. But from birth he remains in the toils of the umbilical cord, the root of his desires: for growth, for land, for maternal tenderness, for sexual gratification—of even such hidden drives as patricide, the death-wish, and rebirth in the mother free of taint. Here lie the seeds of tragedy. (pp. 360-69)

Murray Hartman, " 'Desire under the Elms': In the Light of Strindberg's Influence," in American Literature, *Vol. 33, No. 3, November, 1961, pp. 360-69.*

Edgar F. Racey   (essay date 1962)

[*In the following essay, Racey proposes Greek tragedy as a model for the structure of O'Neill's tragedy.*]

It is customary to point to the underlying Oedipal theme of Eugene O'Neill's *Desire Under the Elms* and to link this play with *Mourning Becomes Electra* as evidence of his consuming interest in the Oedipus theme, both as myth and complex. The use of myth, or classical source, in *Electra* is obvious, for O'Neill takes great pains to insure that no one misses the elaborate series of correspondences that his trilogy effects. Less elaborate, but equally effective, is his reliance on the *Hippolytus* of Euripides (and perhaps on Racine's treatment of the theme) in *Desire Under the Elms.*

That the play is a tragedy few will dispute (although early critics tended to see it as a mere shoddy domestic tragedy). It combines a traditional tragic theme (the Oedipus legend) with a dramatic reconciliation in the interests of a higher virtue (Justice). Abbie and Eben, as they are reconciled to their fate (which they *will*), assume a dignity which approaches tragic stature. As they acknowledge their guilt and enter into the process of expiation, their characters tend to become generalized, and O'Neill manages to suggest something approaching the idea of universal justice.

On the bare framework of a New England domestic tragedy, O'Neill has grafted a religious symbology, almost an iconography. The Biblical names, while "locally" motivated (a man like Ephraim Cabot could be expected to name his sons after characters in the Bible), seem to dictate at least some of the actions of the characters, and even take on the beginnings of a dialectic. Thus, Peter ("the rock") is associated throughout the play with rocks and stones:

> Here—it's stones atop o' the ground—stones atop o' the stones—makin' stone walls—year atop o' the year. . . .

And it is Peter who first picks up a rock to cast at his father's house. Simeon, on the other hand, reiterates the idea of an eye for an eye (of the Indians which they will presumably meet on the way to California, he retorts that they will repay them "a hair fur a hair") and, in revenge on his tyrannical father, he threatens to rape his new wife. One recalls Jacob's "blessing" of his sons:

> Simeon and Levi are brothers; instruments of cruelty are in their habitations. O my soul, come not thou into their secret; unto their assembly, mine honour, be not thou united; for in their

anger they slew a man, and in their self-will they
digged down a wall.

Cursed be their anger, for it was fierce; and their
wrath, for it was cruel. . . . (*Genesis*, XLIX,5)

In *Desire,* it is Simeon who "digs down a wall," tearing
the gate off the hinges, abolishing "shet gates, an' open
gates, an' all gates, by thunder!"

The predominant features of his two eldest sons are combined in Ephraim: he is hard and stony, and embodies the
ancient law of retaliation in kind. He is Ephraim, progeni-
tor of the Tribes of Israel, the archetypal patriarch (and
for O'Neill, the father-figure). His name ("the fruitful")
may be an underlying source of irony by the end of the
play, and it is significant that his "fruitfulness" is the
greatest source of his *hubris.* He is also identified specifically with God, both in his harshness and solitude. Like
Ezra Mannon, he is the embodiment of that blighting New
England Biblical tradition which represses life.

Eben (Ebenezer? "store of hope") is a typical O'Neill son.
The hope of the line (Simeon and Peter are patently unfit
to carry on the name), he is condemned to be placed in
constant strife with his father, denying his obvious resemblance to the man he hates. The rivalry is characteristically O'Neill: the father has usurped what the son regards as
rightfully his own (the mother and the land). This pattern
of rivalry and usurpation is repeated in the male Cabot's
relationship with Min, the "scarlet woman"; first Ephraim
claimed her, then Simeon, Peter, and finally Eben, who is
enraged on learning that here too, they are "his [the father's] heirs in everythin'." The pattern will continue with
Eben and Abbie.

While these quasi-religious elements serve to generate a
kind of Biblical atmosphere, and perhaps a kind of primitivism, the play says little in the way of definite religious
conclusions, save O'Neill's reiterated statement that the
restrictive ethic (usually Puritanism) tends to kill off life.
Ephraim retires to his stony, solitary existence, submitting
once more to the hard God, whom it is his consolation to
resemble. The young and life-bearing have been destroyed.

As a classical tragedy, however, *Desire* is both successful
and complete. The time is spring, season of awakening and
season of ritual. It is the spring which has sent Ephraim
out "t' learn God's message t' me in the spring, like the
prophets done." It is a spring so compelling in its beauty
and life that even Simeon and Peter are moved to utter,
from their animal existence, "Purty!" The play will end in
late spring a year later.

The situation is the Hippolytus-Phaedra-Theseus plot: the
father has returned, bringing with him a young wife, who
is immediately attracted to her stepson. The stepson too
has responded to the season—his brothers have subjected
him to taunts concerning his affair with Min (a possible
loose parallel to the gentle banter of Theramenes in Racine's *Phaedra*). Traditionally, Hippolytus was chaste, but
the affair with Min affords O'Neill the opportunity to define the usurpation theme.

Like Phaedra, Abbie conceals her growing passion for
Eben with the mask of scorn. Like Phaedra, she asks that

the son be banished—and for the same reason, plus the
fact that Eben is a potential rival for the farm. Like Phaedra, Abbie makes advances, but with more success than
her dramatic ancestor. Like Hippolytus, Eben muses constantly on his mother, who was "foreign."

It is in the murder of Ephraim's supposed child that we
see O'Neill modifying his prototype to suit his dramatic
purposes. The curse on the son, originally uttered by Theseus, is transferred to Eben, who is the rightful father.
Ephraim also utters a curse—the curse of God—on his
sons, but the crucially dramatic curse is Eben's. Eben's
curse is uttered against his son in the throes of error, and
rashly; Abbie proves as implacable an instrument of fate
as Poseidon. Like Theseus, however, it is Ephraim who is
left alone, surveying the wreck of his kingdom.

In the Euripidean version, a sin had been committed
against the gods (or rather, Aphrodite imagined herself
slighted by Hippolytus' devotion to Artemis). While it is
possible to view the "sin" in *Desire* as merely the Freudian
sin of repression (leading to symbolic incest), this view, I
think, underestimates the design of the play. A sin has
been committed, and the sin is Ephraim's. We are reminded of this sin by Eben's continued antagonism, his insistence that the farm is his, and (most strongly) by the
"something" which hangs over the play from the opening
(and gloriously melodramatic!) stage direction to the final
curtain. The "something" is the mother, or rather the
wrong done her by Ephraim. Her fiercely maternal presence broods over the play—even the most imperceptive of
the brothers feels it. She is sensed most strongly at the moment of Eben's sin, the sin which is the beginning of the
retributive process against her oppressor, Ephraim—and
she approves of the sin. It is at this moment, of course, that
Abbie enacts simultaneously the roles of mother and beloved, and this is the second stage (the first being when he
"bought" the farm from his brothers with Ephraim's
hoarded gold) of Eben's revenge on his father.

Of frail disposition, gentle, and unused to Ephraim's ways,
Eben's mother was forced to work intolerably hard; the
work finally killed her. Moreover, there is strong reason
to believe that Ephraim has unlawfully taken the farm
from the mother, and from the son, on whom it should
lawfully devolve. If this is so—that is, if the wrong done
the mother hangs over the play like a curse—then Eben
and Abbie may be seen as agents of the process of justice,
directed against Ephraim. Like Theseus, Ephraim must
atone for his rash injustice; it becomes fitting that Ephraim
is condemned, ironically, to the land he has stolen.

Without this framework of the curse, the reader is faced
with a problem of "dialectical" motivation: Eben and
Abbie become simply the victims of their lust, and fail to
assume the stature of agents of tragic retribution. They
are, of course, "locally" (psychologically, dramatically)
motivated: Eben by the Oedipus complex and the desire
for revenge, Abbie by her desire to provide Ephraim with
an heir, thus assuring her chances of retaining the farm,
and both of them by a strong sexual urge. It is precisely
in the light of these local motivations that Eben and Abbie
are rendered capable of becoming the instruments of a
larger process, directed against Ephraim. In this play, the

spontaneity with which the characters enter their dialectical roles is ample testimony to O'Neill's dramatic integrity. In some of the plays (particularly *The Great God
Brown, All God's Chillun,* and, a times, *Mourning Becomes Electra*), we have the regrettable sense that the
characters are being forced more by their dialectical roles
than by their psychological drives; in *Desire,* however,
this sense is virtually absent.

Tragedy makes its statement in its resolution, and it is here
that O'Neill brings together the various threads of the
play. Eben and Abbie are reunited in their love, even as
they expiate their joint crime of murder. In acknowledging
his responsibility in the crime, Eben submits to the ideals
of love and justice. In so doing, the two insure Ephraim's
complete downfall: his pride in his manhood is destroyed,
and he is condemned (after a final effort to escape) to the
very thing he has coveted. In the quasi-religious terms of
the play, the harsh, puritanical ethic has triumphed—to
its own inevitable defeat: Abbie and Eben are destroyed;
Ephraim has taken an eye for an eye, but in so doing, he
is forced to acknowledge the solitary sterility which has
been in fact his lot. Eben is turned from his dream of revenge, for the sake of a higher ideal, but as he turns, he
insures the completeness of his mother's revenge.
O'Neill's tragic curses do not end with the death of the sinner; they must be expiated in a long and solitary process.
Ephraim Cabot, in the rocky solitude of his farm, and Lavinia Mannon, entering for the last time the "whited sep-
ulchre," confront their fates in the only possible way.

Una Ellis-Fermor has pointed out that the symmetry of
the tragic form may account for the phenomenon of *ca-
tharsis,* that the artistic order of the play may be generalized to a kind of cosmic moral order. With the resolution
of this play, justice has been done, even if O'Neill has not
achieved the artistic symmetry which apparently he feels
is necessary. Eben's and Abbie's last lines (HE: Sun's a-
rizin'. Purty, hain't it? SHE: Ay-eh) echo precisely the
play's opening lines, and the cycle of retribution, hinted
at through use of myth, is artistically completed.

The sheriff, acting as a kind of ironic chorus, underscores
the importance of the ownership of the land, which has
been the basis of the tragic action. His "wish't I owned it!"
is uttered in profound ignorance of the consequences of
coveting the farm: desire for the farm prompted Abbie's
marriage to Ephraim, and her affair with Eben was initially motivated by her desire to secure her position with
Ephraim. Ironically, it is when Eben learns that his father
intends to will the farm to his (Eben's) son that he utters
the curse. It is when Eben is freed of his desire for the
farm, when he returns to Abbie (and the rope), that he assures his salvation. Ephraim, on the other hand, is condemned.

It is perhaps in the tragic aspects of the play that we find
sanction for the Old Testament overlay, as hinted in the
names of the characters. Throughout the play, it is the He-
braic God who is invoked as a God of wrath and retribution. If O'Neill is attempting to enact a classical tragedy
in a modern setting, he needs an ethos which will support
a tragic view of life, and the god of inevitable vengeance
lends sanction to such an ethos.

In *Desire Under the Elms* and *Mourning Becomes Electra,* perhaps the most extensive explorations of O'Neill's
view of the father-son battle/symbolic incest theme, the
author has resorted to the use of myth, adopting the structure of classical tragedies. The use of myth, as Eliot has
pointed out, affords the artist both the necessary artistic
control to explore his subject and the means of generalization. In both plays we see O'Neill creating characters who,
by their very natures, are endowed with the necessary motivation to enact the myth; both plays too, though different in many ways, contribute to a unified dramatic vision
and testify to the fact that this is the way O'Neill found
life. (pp. 57-61)

> *Edgar F. Racey, "Myth as Tragic Structure in
> 'Desire under the Elms',"* in O'Neill: A Col-
> lection of Critical Essays, *edited by John Gass-
> ner, Prentice-Hall, Inc., 1964, pp. 57-61.*

Jay Ronald Meyers   (essay date 1967)

[*In the following essay, Meyers outlines O'Neill's use of
the Phaedra legend in* Desire under the Elms.]

Both critics and scholars long have agreed that classical
tragedy is the underlying conception of *Desire Under the
Elms.* After experimenting with the form of the one act
play, with expressionism and with realism, O'Neil attempted to write tragedy based on Aristotelian precepts.
The unities of place and particularly of time affect the
structural, scheme, and the conception of the tragic hero
who suffers a devastating fall because of *hamartia* provides
the moral focus. A strong case can be made for identifying
the Phédre legend as the direct source of the play.
O'Neill's variant of the story treated dramatically by Euripides and Racine provides us with the clearest explanation of his purposes.

Attempts have been made to establish Ephraim Cabot and
Eben Cabot as the tragic heroes. Sophus Keith Winther
has argued Ephraim's claim:

> In *Desire Under the Elms* the tragic hero is a
> man apart from other men. He does not accept
> their manner of living, their morality is beneath
> his contempt, their ideals are to him the petty
> dreams of weaklings and cowards. He despises
> his weak and loutish sons. . . . He is as proud
> as any man who ever walked onto a stage de-
> manding an answer from the unanswerable.

And then again: "The man is a giant in comparison with
the human beings who surround him."

Most critics are not so sympathetic toward Ephraim. He
has destroyed his two wives and has raised three sons who
despise him. He is set apart from men because he has no
friends. Unfeeling and ruthless, cruel and despotic, his one
defense of his behavior is that "God haint easy." He bears
his heart to Abbie:

> Ye kin read the years o' my life in them walls,
> every day a hefted stone, climbin' over the hills
> up and down, fencin' in the fields that was mine,
> whar I'd made thin's grow out o' nothin'—like
> the will o' God, like the servant o' His hand. It

wa'n't easy. It was hard an' He made me hard
fur it.

His conduct the more common view is that he is a "strict,
miserly, despotic old man "[Camillo Pellizzi, "Irish-
Catholic Anti-Puritan," in *O'Neill and His Plays*]. At best
he is a malcontent who, in his disillusionment with the
world, turns sour. But he is not noble. Moreover, since he
is not really changed by the events in the play, it is difficult
to see him as the tragic hero.

Both Eben and Abbie are more directly affected by the catastrophe. Eben's claim to tragic dimension is based on his
loyalty to the memory of his mother; for her honor he remains on the farm and opposes the Cabots. But his nobility can be called into question. He does not really grow,
suffer, or attain wisdom and compassion. Abbie, on the
other hand, grows during the course of the play and even
attains nobility. Moreover since Abbie is the pursuer not
the pursued, the play is more nearly a variant of the Phèdre rather than of the Oedipus legend.

Euripides and Racine have a different perspective of the
tragedy of Phèdre who falls in love with her stepson and
dies of the shame. For Euripides, man's inability to exercise restraint over his desires reinforces the traditional religious notion of man's impotence before the gods. Aphrodite's stricture in the prologue of *Hippolytus* serves as the
poet's explanation of the events that follow:

> I give honour to those who reverence my power
> And those whose thoughts of me are arrogant I
> crush.

Both Hippolytus and Phaedra are punished for *hubris*—
Phaedra for overweaning passion and Hippolytus for
overweaning confidence. Both characters have outraged
Aphrodite, though in diametrically opposite ways. The
moral of the play would seem to be the necessity for man
to exercise restraint over his passions, though Euripides,
with his characteristic irony, shows the difficulty and even
impossibility of attaining such results.

Racine is not so concerned as Euripides with explaining
and justifying the ways of the gods. For the French Jan-
senist the play studies the effects of guilt on a noble Christian. Here, as in *Hippolytus,* love is *funeste poison,* as Hippolyte exclaims: "Quel funeste poison / L'amour a ré-
pandu sur toute sa maison!" ["What fatal poison / Love
has dispersed throughout this house." My translation.]
The stricken mother declares her madness to her son: "Je
m'égare, / Seigneur, ma folle ardeur malgré moi se dé-
clare." ["Alas, my mad passion cannot be contained."]
After admitting her guilt, Hippolyte's denunciation coupled with her own shame overcome her. When she learns
that Theseus, her husband, has returned, she sees only one
honorable course: "La mort aux malheureux ne cause
point d'effroi. / Je ne crains que le nom que je laisse après
moi." ["Death holds no terror for the unhappy. / I only
fear the name I leave behind."] In death she achieves expiation.

O'Neill's most notable alteration of the Phèdre story in
Desire Under the Elms is the moral viewpoint. Whereas
Euripides and Racine clearly condemn the incestuous na-

ture of Phèdre's love, O'Neil sanctions the immoral relationship. This love, moreover, is good and ennobling.

Though influenced by both treatments of the legend,
O'Neill perhaps owes the greater debt to Racine. Like
Hippolytus, **Desire Under the Elms** sustains the psychological truth of the overwhelming affect of desire or passion on character. But O'Neill perhaps is closer to Racine
in his interest in the study of a woman caught up in such
a situation, though the effects are different in Phèdre and
Abbie Putnam.

Far more immoral, for O'Neill, is love as it exists among
the Cabots. Love, for them, is ownership and possession.
Everything is measured by this standard and is subjected
to this kind of contamination. The principal objects of
their desire—the earth and women—become symbols of
their greed. Though nature is "purty" their lust to own her
destroys their ability to appreciate her beauty. For beauty
is alchemized gold. In the first scene, Simeon recalls his
wife Jenn, who had died eighteen years ago:

> SIMEON. I rec'lect—now an' agin. Makes it lone-
> some. She's hair long's a hoss' tail—and yaller
> like gold!
>
> PETER. Waal-she's gone. (*This with indifferent
> finality—then after a pause*) They's gold in the
> West, Sim.
>
> SIMEON. (*still under the vague influence of sun-
> set—vaguely*) In the sky?
>
> PETER. Wall—in a manner o' speakin'—thar's
> the promise. (*Growing excited*) Gold in the
> sky—in the West—Golden Gate—Californi-
> a!—Golden West! fields o' gold!

Like Jenn, the sky, the west, the fields are identified with
their purchase value. Eben describes, in similar terms, his
possessing Minnas an act of ownership: "Waal—when I
seen her, I didn't hit her—nor I didn't kiss her nuther—I
began t'beller like a calf an' cuss at the same time, I was
so durn mad—an' she got scared—an' I jest grabbed holt
an' tuk her! (*Proudly*) *Yes, sirree! I tuk her. She may've
been his'n—nd your'n, too—but she's mine now!*"

Though Ephraim accuses his sons of "[coveting] the farm
without knowin' what it meant," his attitude is like theirs,
and he too praises the "black [soil] an' rich as gold." He
returns home with his new possession, his wife; for him as
well love means ownership. Abbie's attitude does not differ from that of her husband and stepsons. For her, love
means possessing a home, and she does not attempt to
conceal her love for the land and her desire for security
the first time she sees the farm:

> ABBIE. (*with lust for the word*) Hum! It's purty-
> purty! I can't b'lieve it's r'ally mine.
>
> CABOT. (*sharply*) Yewr'n? Mine! (*He stares at
> her penetratingly. She stares back. He adds re-
> lentingly.*) Our'n-mebbe! It was lonesome too
> long. I was growin' old in the spring. A hum's
> got t'hev a woman.
>
> ABBIE. (*her voice taking possession*) A woman's
> got t'hev a hum!

A dispute soon arises over the possession of the land. Abbie discovers that her security is not so certain as she had expected. Eben claims his right of inheritance to his mother's farm, and he accuses Abbie of preempting his claim: "yew sold yourself for [the farm] like any other old whore—my farm." Moreover, Abbie learns that Ephraim is not willing to relinquish his claim to his possession, even after his death. He explains that he has made no provision for her because she is not his:

> CABOT. But har's the p'int. What son o'mine'll keep on here t' the farm—when the Lord does call me? Simeon an' Peter air gone t'hell—an' Eben's follerin' 'em.
>
> ABBIE. They's me.
>
> CABOT. Ye're on'y a woman.
>
> ABBIE. I'm yewr wife.
>
> CABOT. That hain't me. A son is me—my blood—mine. Mine ought t' git mine. An' then it's still mine—even though I be six foot under. D'ye see?
>
> ABBIE. (giving him a look of hatred) Ay-eh. I see. (She becomes very thoughtful, her face growing shrewd, her eyes studying Cabot craftily.)

Soon afterward she tells him with cold calculation: "Ye'll have a son out o' me, I promise ye" (II, ii). She turns to the son for the same reason that she had married his father: to insure her possession. She offers herself to Eben to protect her "hum" and her fierce determination in seducing Eben sets her apart from Euripides' Phaedra and Racine's Phèdre:

> Hain't the sun strong an' hot? Ye kin feel it burnin' into the earth—Nature—makin' thin's grow—bigger 'n' bigger—burnin' inside ye—makin' ye want t' grow—into somthin' else—till ye're jined with it—an' it's yourn' but it own ye, too—an' makes ye grow bigger—like a tree—like them elums. . . . Nature'll beat ye, Eben. Ye might's well own up t' it fust's last.

Alone with him in his bedroom, she lures him by appealing to his Cabot lust, as she boldly tells him:

> Did ye think I was in love with ye—a weak thin' like yew? Not much! I on'y wanted ye fur purposes o' my own—an' I'll hev ye fur it yet 'cause I'm stronger'n yew be!

Then quite confidently:

> Ye want me, don't ye? Yes, ye do! An' yer Paw's son'll never kill what he wants! Look at yer eyes! They's lust fur me in 'em, burnin' 'em up! Look at yer lips now! Theyre' tremblin' an' longin' t' kiss me, an' yer teeth t' bite! (He is watching her now with a horrible fascination. She laughs a crazy triumphant laugh.) *I'm a-goin' t' make all o' this hum my hum!* They's not one room hain't mine yet, but it's a-goin' t'be tonight. I'm a-goin' down now an' light up! (She makes him a mocking bow.) Won't ye come courtin' me in the best parlor, Mister Cabot?

With justification, audiences and civic leaders have been outraged by this brutal depiction of incest. For O'Neill, however, the incest has symbolic meaning. Abbie's degeneracy underscores the degradation of the Cabot way of life. While Simeon and Peter go off to rape the earth of gold, Abbie secures her future wealth by taking her stepson. Through the juxtaposition of these two symbols, O'Neill shows that these equally repugnant events are the logical consequence of Cabot greed.

The attainment of true love is an effect that Abbie had not expected. She discovers that "nature'll beat ye," and love is its own justification. Through her relationship with Eben, she finds that love is not a means but an end, not merely the desire to own and possess but fulfillment in itself. Therefore her joy at bearing an heir is abrogated by Eben's bitterness. She firmly declares her preference to Eben:

> If that's what his comin's done t'me—killin' yewr love—takin' yew away—my on'y joy—the on'y joy I ever knowed—like heaven t' me—purtier'n heaven—then I hate him, too, even if I be his Maw!

The infanticide for her is the one action that will demonstrate her love. It is an act of selflessness and even an expiation. For by sacrificing her child—her claim to possessing the farm—she severs herself from the Cabot way of life. She redeems her love. The audience is made to sympathize with an action that ordinarily would be repulsive.

To be sure, O'Neill uses an outrageous metaphor with which to make his statement. But since, for him, the greed of the Cabots is baser than incest and even child-murder, it can only be overcome by the act of greatest abnegation. What a pity that the innocent child must suffer! What a pity that in a society in which love is equated with possession, only the sacrifice of one's most cherished possession is an act of true love! We are made to understand and sympathize with Abbie's deed. Abbie, unlike Queen Phèdre, attains tragic nobility in spite of and even through her illicit love.

The play, however, offers a clear moral vision—first and foremost of the evil of the worship of money, and also of the hardness of heart that afflicts those who become infatuated. It is O'Neill's most devastating attack on the lust of acquisition. And yet the play rises above the level of mere propaganda—which limits his achievement in **The Hairy Ape**—to the grandeur of Aristotelian tragedy—its form compact and beautiful, its action pitiful and terrifying. (pp. 120-25)

> *Jay Ronald Meyers, "O'Neill's Use of the Phèdre Legend in 'Desire under the Elms',"* in Revue de littérature comparée, *Vol. XLI, No. 1, January-March, 1967, pp. 120-25.*

Peter L. Hays   (essay date 1969)

[*Hays is a German critic. In the following essay, he addresses the role of religion in* Desire under the Elms.]

While O'Neill's plays are noted primarily for the dramatic force with which they express his tragic view of life, many of them—*The Hairy Ape, All God's Chillun Got Wings, Marco Millions, Iceman Cometh,* and others—contain a great deal of social criticism. So does his early tragedy *Desire Under the Elms,* which has been critically examined for its use of the Hippolytus and Medea myths, its Freudian elements, its relation to O'Neill's early plays (e.g., *The Rope*) and own biography, but there has been little close attention to the way in which religious references inform the play, and the way religion both causes the tragedy and comments upon it.

Eben's first word in the play is "God!" His first line of dialogue is "Honor thy father!"—his sarcastic reply to his brothers' statement that they must wait for their father's death before they can hope to own the farm—which Eben follows with, "I pray he's died." This ironic use of the Biblical commandment and the perverse form of Eben's prayer set the tone of the play and forewarn us to note how almost all expressions of religious origin are similarly twisted. In fact, they help us appreciate the harsh and equally twisted religion practiced on this farm, a loveless religion largely responsible for the play's tragedy.

The reaction of Eben's brothers to his wish that Ephraim Cabot, their father, were dead is typical of the hypocrisy in religious and other matters.

> SIMEON. . . . Looky here! Ye'd oughtn't t' said that, Eben.
>
> PETER. Twa'n't righteous.
>
> EBEN. What?
>
> SIMEON. Ye prayed he'd died.
>
> EBEN. Waal—don't yew pray it?

For it is Simeon himself who says that they must wait for the farm until Ephraim dies. Their denunciation of Eben is perfunctory and conventional rather than an expression either of filial or Christian piety. Later in the play even this sanctimonious facade is dropped, though the dialogue still is couched in canonical terms. Speaking of their new stepmother, Simeon says:

> Waal—I hope she's a she-devil that'll make him wish he was dead an' livin' in the pit o' hell fur comfort.
>
> PETER. (*fervently*) Amen!

Similarly, the townspeople in Part III, Scene 1, suspecting that the baby is Eben's and not Ephraim's, express themselves in terms of ribaldry, concealed envy, or mockery for Ephraim—whose physical strength they respect too much for them to ridicule to his face, but whose cuckoldry makes them feel superior to him. They come to eat, drink, and have fun behind the Cabots' backs:

> MAN. Listen, Abbie—if ye ever git tired o Eben, remember me.
>
> CABOT. . . . [Eben] kin do a day's work a' most up t'what I kin. . . .
>
> FIDDLER. An' he kin do a good night's work, too! (*A roar of laughter.*) (p. 249)

> FIDDLER. . . . Let's celebrate the old skunk gittin' fooled! We kin have some fun now he's went.

No one sympathizes or expresses genuine moral concern. And they too pervert scripture for their own ends. The fiddler says that Eben is in church offering prayers of thanksgiving, " 'Cause unto him a—(*He hesitates just long enough*) brother is born!"

It is Ephraim, though, more than any other character in the play who makes religious statements apply to irreligious acts. He tells Simeon: "I been hearin' the hens cluckin' an' the roosters crowin' all the durn day. I been listenin' t' the cows lowin' an' everythin' else kickin' up till I can't stand it no more. It's spring an' I feel damned. . . . An' now I'm ridin' out t' learn God's message t' me in the spring, like the prophet's done." Then he drives off in the buggy, singing a hymn. In spite of his seventy-five years, what Ephraim feels is need—for a woman, almost any woman. And as Simeon says when he hears that the elder Cabot has remarried for the third time:

> "I'm ridin' out t' learn God's message t' me in the spring like the prophets done," he says. "I'll bet right then an' thar he knew plumb well he was going whorin,' the stinkin' old hypocrite!

But Ephraim is not a hypocrite if we insist that hypocrisy be conscious dissembling. Ephraim is cruel, harsh, and devoid of charity, but knows himself to be so, desires to be so, and feels that he has Divine sanction for his ruthlessness. He practices a harsh and loveless Puritanical religion that worships toil, scorns ease and sentiment or even the expression of honest sentiment. As he says to Abbie in a rare burst of self-expression which she does not hear—like the soliloquys of Chekov's characters, spoken at but rarely to a listener:

> When ye kin make corn sprout out o' stones, God's livin' in yew! . . . God hain't easy. . . . I growed hard. Folks allus sayin' he's a hard man like 'twas sinful t' be hard. . . . God's hard, not easy! God's in the stones! . . . Stones. I picked 'em up an' piled 'em into walls. Ye kin read the years of my life in them walls, every day a hefted stone, . . . fencin' in the fields that was mine, whar I made thin's grow out of nothin'— like the will o' God, like the servant o' His hand. It wa'n't easy. It was hard an' He made me hard fur it.

The whole rambling passage emphasizes possession, hardness, the sinfulness of easy wealth, the equation of virtue with hard work, and Ephraim's loneliness. The "objective correlative" of the passage is *stone*: hard, unyielding, impenetrable. Piled one on top of another, they wall the farm like a prison, as Ephraim's values imprison him, his successive wives, and his sons, creating their mutual lack of contact; for stones piled to make a wall are individual objects, not a unit, without some sort of bond or mortar. And on the Cabot farm there is no such agent until Abbie and Eben realize their love late in the play. Instead there are the worst distortions of the Protestant ethic: greed, vengeance, incessant toil, and individual isolation. Even Ephraim, so insensitive to the real feelings of Eben's mother, Eben, or Abbie, feels this chill sense of loneliness—

"It's cold in this house [though at midsummer]. It's oneasy. They's thin's pokin' about in the dark—in the corners." And so for comfort, Ephraim goes down to the barn where it is warm and peaceful, largely because the animals do not covet one another's possessions, and because their behavior doesn't suffer from the restrictions and inhibitions of Ephraim's Christianity. Edward Arlington Robinson summed up the situation well in his famous sonnet "New England":

> Passion is here a soilure of the wits,
> We're told, and Love a cross for them to bear;
> Joy shivers in the corner where she knits
> And conscience always has the rocking chair. . . .

Thus, though each of the characters has his own desires, each pharisaically condemns the others' as lusts. Abbie, who has married Ephraim for the security of a home, tries to seduce Eben, and when she fails, when Eben goes off to see the town whore instead, screams, "Git out o' my sight! Go on t' yer slut—disgracin' yer Paw 'n' me! Though her motive is jealousy, not piety, she denounces Eben to his father in these terms: "[Eben's gone] t' see that harlot, Min! . . . Disgracin' yew an' me—on the Sabbath, too! As if the day mattered to Abbie. And Cabot replies, "(*rather guiltily*) He's a sinner—natteral-born. It's lust eatin' his heart." Ephraim's guilt is two-fold, for Min was his mistress long before she was Eben's, and he has his own lusts: the one which drove him away from the farm months before to seek a wife, the same one for which he "stares at her [Abbie] desirously" and addresses her in terms of that ancient fertility chant, The Song of Songs; and the lust for a new son, proof of his virility, and worthy heir to the farm. Though Ephraim condemns Eben for lust, he himself calls Abbie his "Rose o' Sharon! Behold, yew air fair; yer eyes air doves; yer lips air like scarlet; yer two breasts air like two fawns. . . . (*He covers her hand with kisses. . . .*)" Though he denounces Simeon and Peter's desire to visit the California goldfields as "Lust fur gold—fur the sinful, easy gold o' Californi-a," he desperately covets a son as an extension of his own right of ownership:

> . . . What son o' mine'll keep on here t' the farm—when the Lord does call me? Simeon an' Peter air gone t'hell—an' Eben's follerin' 'em.

> . . . A son is me—my blood—mine. Mine ought t' git mine. An' then it's still mine—even though I be six foot under.

For good or for bad, Ephraim and even Abbie use prayer. When Abbie sees that her only real security lies in providing Cabot a son, she suggests to him that "mebbe the Lord'll give *us* a son" she emphasizes "us" because a new son will disinherit Eben, even though Eben is his father—which is what we, at this point in the play, suspect, and what Abbie plans. She says to Ephraim, " . . . I been prayin' it'd happen . . . ," and he responds:

> It'd be the blessin' o' God, Abbie—the blessin' o' God A'mighty on me—in my old age—in my lonesomeness! . . .

> Pray t' the Lord agen, Abbie. It's the Sabbath!

I'll jine ye! Two prayers air better nor one. "An' God hearkened unto Rachel"! An' God harkened unto Abbie! Pray fur him to hearken' (*He bows his head, mumbling. She pretends to do likewise but gives him a side glance of scorn and triumph.*)

God does not hear the prayer, for the son Abbie bears is Eben's, even though Ephraim thinks it is his, and when Abbie suffocates the infant and is jailed for the crime with Eben, Cabot is even more alone—without any wife or son. And so this "good" prayer, for a son, is frustrated. But Ephraim prays for evil, too. When Simeon and Peter desert the farm, *his* farm, he prays to God to curse them:

> CABOT. . . . Lord God o' Hosts, smite the undutiful sons with Thy wust cuss!

> EBEN. . . . Yew 'n' yewr God! Allus cussin' folks—allus naggin' 'em!

> CABOT. (*oblivious to him—summoningly*) God o' the old! God o' the lonesome!

> EBEN. (*mockingly*) Naggin' His sheep t' sin! T' hell with yewr God.

Cabot's God is indeed the God of the old—He is the harsh, avenging God of the Old Testament, as popularly conceived of, distinct from the more loving, more forgiving and charitable God of the New Testament. But of course, this is not so—the God of the Old Testament, the same God, is merciful, forgiving, and loving; but Ephraim's perverse belief in Him as a hard and lonesome God has caused Cabot to value hardness and isolation, to work his first two wives to death, to drive off his two elder sons, to instill as values in his sons craftiness, vengeance, and suspicion instead of love, and to wall himself up and prevent any warm, personal, truly communicative relationship with any of his wives or sons. And so Eben seeks vengeance for himself and his mother's death through Abbie; Ephraim seeks to dispossess Eben and hand the farm on to a still younger son; and Abbie—at first—seeks to cheat them both, loving neither. Whatever tendencies of character Ephraim may have inherited that caused him to be as he is, undoubtedly his harsh religion—the same religion as Hawthorne's John Endicott and O'Neill's own Mannons—has developed and confirmed these traits. And by purposeful use of Biblical language or quotations in debased contexts, O'Neill has underscored this perversion of religion for us. He has also provided, by allusion, an analogue for comment and contrast.

For if one believes that Ephraim Cabot does ride from the farm to learn God's message as the prophets did, then one must assume that the message was to marry. And, indeed, God did instruct the first of the so-called Minor Prophets, Hosea, to marry—to marry, in fact, a harlot, which is what Eben calls Abbie for marrying Cabot in order to have a home. Hosea is commanded to wed a prostitute, and, even though she is unfaithful to him and deserts him, he is told to buy her back and to reaffirm his devotion—all as an allegory of the Lord's relation to Israel, which had broken its covenant with God and was prostituting itself both figuratively, with false gods, and literally: "the prophet's personal life is an incarnation of God's redeeming love." And significantly, Hosea addresses Israel, the nation's eponymous name after Jacob, by the name of Joseph's younger son, eponymous founder of one of the twelve tribes (Gen. 48), Ephraim. And like Ephraim Cabot,

> E'phraim is oppressed, cursed in judgment,
>   because he was determined to go after vanity.
>   (Hos. 5:11)

> . . . E'phraim has hired lovers. (8:9)

> E'phraim has said, "Ah, but I am rich,
>   I have gained wealth for myself:"
> but all his riches can never offset
>   the guilt he has incurred. (12:8)

By denying Hosea's message of love and forgiveness, by perverting the message of the Bible, Ephraim Cabot has taught "Bloody instructions, which, being taught, returns to plague the inventor." He has freed his animals before he learns that Eben has taken his savings and all his relations are gone—"It's a-goin' t' be lonesomer now than ever it war afore—an' I'm gittin' old, Lord—ripe on the bough." In the words of Hosea, he has sown the wind and reaped the whirlwind. (8:7)

In his review of *Desire Under the Elms*, Joseph Wood Krutch said that "the meaning and unity of his work lies not in any controlling intellectual idea and certainly not in a 'message,' but merely in the fact that each play is an experience of extraordinary intensity." Certainly this is as true for *Desire* as it is for O'Neill's other plays, but it is no less true that *Desire* is, if not controlled, then at least shaped, by an intellectual idea and a message: that the harsh, loveless, and covetous Puritanical religion practiced by Ephraim Cabot is a perversion of religion that cripples love and destroys men. (pp. 423-28)

> *Peter L. Hays, "Biblical Perversions in 'Desire under the Elms'," in* Modern Drama, *Vol. 11, No. 4, February, 1969, pp. 423-28.*

Hollis L. Cate   (essay date 1971)

[*In the following essay, Cate argues that the poetic language of Ephraim Cabot provides insight into his character.*]

My contention . . . is not only that Eugene O'Neill's character Ephraim Cabot is a spontaneous poet but also that the old man's total character cannot possibly be understood if his poetic nature is not taken into account. With all his faults old Cabot does have at least one inherently redeeming side.

O'Neill once wrote Professor A. H. Quinn: "But where I feel myself most neglected is just where I set most store by myself—as a bit of a poet, who has labored with the spoken word to evolve original rhythms of beauty, where beauty apparently isn't." In making the statement O'Neill mentions *Desire under the Elms* among other of his plays, and well he should have, for old Ephraim Cabot, now generally considered the protagonist of the play, is one of O'Neill's most forceful poets. Professor Quinn in 1926, two years after the appearance of *Desire,* published an ar-

---

The controversy over *Desire under the Elms*:

Toward the end of February O'Neill heard from [Kenneth] Macgowan in New York that *Desire under the Elms* had become something of a cause célèbre. District Attorney Joab H. Banton, a Southerner who was hell-bent on cleaning up the Broadway stage, had demanded that the play be closed.

Banton had not suggested that *Desire under the Elms* be rewritten. It was, he said (not having seen the play), "too thoroughly bad to be purified by a blue pencil," and if it was not closed by the following Wednesday, he threatened to put the matter before a grand jury.

The play jury did, at length, go to see *Desire* and voted that it should neither be suppressed nor corrected, and Macgowan promptly cabled O'Neill the news. O'Neill professed to have been sure of the outcome all along—although earlier he had remarked to a friend that it had been a surprise to him that the play had "fought its way to the top in New York."

While *Desire* profited from the publicity, O'Neill came to feel eventually that it had suffered artistically.

"We got a large audience, but of the wrong kind of people," O'Neill later told an interviewer. "They came for dirt and found it in everything. It ruined the actors because they never knew how a line was going to be taken."

The play was subsequently banned in Boston by the mayor and in England by the Lord Chamberlain, in spite of O'Neill's willingness to make some minor revisions in the dialogue, such as the substitution of the word "harlot" for "whore" and "sluttin' " for "whorin'." And when the road company opened in Los Angeles the following year the entire cast was arrested on the charge of giving an obscene play and tried in Municipal Court, awaking memories for O'Neill of the West Coast arrest and trial, nearly half a century earlier, of James O'Neill's company of *The Passion*.

> *Arthur and Barbara Gelb, in their* O'Neill, *1962.*

---

ticle in *Scribner's Magazine* dealing with O'Neill as poet and mystic. Though the article seems to be gathering a little dust these days, anyone making an approach to *Desire under the Elms* in particular should give it his attention; O'Neill certainly shows his poetic side in creating the speeches of Ephraim Cabot. The old man comes to mind as one reads Mr. Quinn's observation: "Even in the most degraded man, O'Neill recognizes the saving grace that comes from his divine origin." If Cabot is given to degradation on the one hand, his poetry is a "saving grace" on the other. Further, Professor Quinn was speaking boldly, at the time, to several critics in saying "it is a pitiful stupidity of criticism that sees only the repellent . . . in *Desire Under the Elms*." O'Neill himself had a tender feeling for Cabot. He said in a letter: "I have always loved Ephraim so much! He's so autobiographical!" Although O'Neill was, no doubt, referring to his sleeping in the barn as Cabot does, there is no denying that Ephraim, like his creator, is "a bit of a poet." Clearly, one redeeming feature of *Desire* and of Cabot himself is his role as spontaneous poet, a "maker" who turns again and again for his images to the mysterious world of Nature about him.

The role of Nature itself in the play is highly significant. [In his *Eugene O'Neill*] Frederick Carpenter says that in the final analysis the spirit of Nature is the hero of the play. Cabot certainly seems to agree. Nature is for the old man the one true abiding force, God's revelation of Himself to man; and, further, in the Romantic tradition it is a solace, an escape from the encroachments of the everyday world. Ephraim, in his closeness to its presence, habitually looks to Nature for his metaphors and similes. In part he is an Emersonian man who senses that "every natural fact is a symbol of some spiritual fact" and who uses spontaneous images in his speech. No other character in the play even approaches him in his use of poetic diction because no other character longs as he does to have at least a glimpse through Nature of that mysterious sphere beyond temporality. With all his shortcomings Cabot at least recognizes the beauty and harmony of Nature. It is a mistake to assume that Ephraim thinks that God is *only* in the stones, contrary to S. K. Winther's observation that Cabot reads the lessons of the stones as the true symbol of God's reality. Mr. Winther's statement that Cabot "listens to the voice of nature" and is "exalted by her beauty" is to be stressed as much as, if not more than, the point that the old man is preoccupied with identifying the stones with the Deity.

There has been a great deal of critical comment on Cabot's attitude toward God, the crux of it being that Ephraim has created God in his own image, that is, God is hard, isolated, lonesome, and unsympathetic. But there is more to Cabot's nature than what these adjectives describe, despite the fact that he always refers to himself as "tough" and "hard." O'Neill on one occasion describes Cabot's eyes as taking "on a strange, incongruous dreamy quality." Here we get a glimpse of the introspective Cabot whom the other characters fail to see and whom Cabot himself is not fully cognizant of, a man whose vision, from time to time, transcends the external, material world. When he says, "The sky. Feels like a wa'm field up thar", he reveals a sensitivity which is congruous with eyes of "dreamy quality." Later he refers to the sky again in a conversation with Eben:

CABOT. Purty, hain't it?

EBEN. (*looking around him possessively*) It's a durned purty farm.

CABOT. I mean the sky.

EBEN. (*grinning*) How d' ye know? Them eyes o' your'n can't see that fur.

Again Cabot looks upward, comments on the sky, and is typically misunderstood. Eben's remark about the old man's eyesight is, of course, ironic. Cabot "sees" in a spiritual way far more effectively than any other character in the play. Ephraim, like Oedipus and Gloucester in *King Lear,* doesn't see and yet he does. [In his *A Poet's Quest*] Richard Dana Skinner describes him as "the nearsighted one, of narrow vision and narrow pride, imperious, yet in

many ways completely identifying himself with a lonesome and hard God." [In her *Eugene O'Neill and the Tragic Tension*] Doris Falk similarly points out that God to Cabot is an image of his own ego. His poetic diction, however, indicates that he carries on an intuitive search for the Deity's true revelation through Nature; and we must remember that he has a poetic side that one can easily identify with a God not hard and lonesome. Neither of the observations above takes into account the old man's recognition of an aesthetic in Nature. Indeed, there was more of God to be found by Cabot's staying on the farm than by going to the West in search of gold. Another view is that "the harsh, loveless, and covetous Puritanical religion practiced by Ephraim Cabot is a perversion of religion that cripples love and destroys man" [Peter L. Hays, "Biblical Perversion in *Desire Under the Elms*"]. But the spirit of beauty and harmony is within him, as his poetry shows; unfortunately, however, he fails to grasp its full essence or develop its potential and therein lies the heart of the old man's tragedy.

Cabot's reliance on poetic diction is evident in almost every scene in which he appears. At one point he says, "When ye kin make corn sprout out o' stones, God's livin' in ye!" In a sense Cabot's corn is his poetry, which is prompted by a muse at least partially divine, for he draws spiritual strength through his recognition of man's dependence on Nature and, thus, on God for a language which expresses the harmony of existence itself, a language made up of forceful figures of speech: metaphors, similes, personification, and synecdoche.

Cabot's metaphors and similes include references to familiar objects as well as to animals. In the first place he describes himself as he, in part, sees himself and as *he knows* the other characters see him, but his total being, as stated earlier, goes far beyond his own descriptive terms. He says that he is as "sound 'n tough as hickory!", "a hard nut t' crack", "hard as iron yet!", and "like a stone—a rock o' jedgment". Several times he says he is getting old, "ripe on the bough." Revealing a side of his nature seldom seen, Ephraim recalls the Song of Solomon and is very much carried away in a well-known poetic speech addressed to Abbie: "Yew air my Rose o' Sharon! . . . yer eyes air doves; yer lips air like scarlet; yer two breasts air like two fawns; yer navel be like . . ." and so on. Later he says to those who have come to the dance: "What're ye all bleatin' about—like a flock o' goats? . . . thar ye set cacklin' like a lot o' wet hens with the pip! Ye've swilled my likker an' guzzled my vittles like hogs, hain't ye?" His hearers dictate his imagery, and "doves" and "fawns" used in his speech to Abbie are replaced with "goats," "hens," and "hogs," with the appropriately descriptive words "bleatin'," "cacklin'," "swilled," and "guzzled." Cabot, forever the poet, even spontaneously uses onomatopoeia. He later, in typical fashion, tells the others that they are "all hoofs!" and their "veins is full o' mud and water." Quite often in heated moments he reaches for his figurative language. Such is the case when he berates Eben: "It's ye that's blind—blind as a mole underground . . . They's nothin' in that thick skull o' your'n but noise—like a empty keg it be!" Rarely is there a simple statement without the figurative analogy for driving home the point. Speaking to

Eben again the old man says, "A prime chip o' yer ye be!" In addition to the metaphor itself there is internal rhyme, as well as an emphasis on labial formations which Cabot bites off in grim, tight-lipped fashion. His final figure comes late in the play after the death of Abbie and Eben's child and after he has learned of their affair: "Ye make a slick pair o' murderin' turtle doves!" He is the unrelenting poet to the end.

Cabot, as a spontaneous image-maker, uses both personification and synecdoche. When he describes the mysterious "somethin' " that pervades the house, he says: "Ye kin feel it droppin' off the elums, climbin' up the roof, sneakin' down the chimney, pokin' in the corners!" Cabot conveys the personified movement he wishes to convey with well-balanced participial phrases. In speaking to Abbie and Eben at the end of the play, he tells them that young fools like them should "hobble their lust," which, in the image, become an animal of vice that should be restrained. Finally, in saying to Eben, "An' the farm's her'n Abbie's! An' the dust o' the road—that's your'n!", Ephraim makes his point by using a part for the whole, significantly, an unpleasant part.

This . . . is not an attempt to vindicate Ephraim Cabot; several critics have enumerated his faults and shortcomings, making telling points against him. But if he is a man of tragic stature as several critics have said or implied, then one must consider carefully, in reaching such a conclusion, the old man's speech as an integral part of his nature. O'Neill once said in a letter: " . . . I'm always, always, trying to interpret Life in terms of lives, never just lives in terms of character. I'm always actually conscious of the Force behind—(Fate, God, our biological past creating our present, whatever one calls it—Mystery certainly)—and of the eternal tragedy of Man in his glorious, self-destructive struggle to make the Force express him instead of being as an animal is, an infinitesimal incident in its expression." Cabot, in his effort to catch a glimpse of the true Force, seems determined not to be an "infinitesimal incident in its expression." O'Neill leaves us with the impression that Cabot, with all his vitality, robustness, and strength, is living yet somewhere on that rocky New England land because we see him as a part of Nature, the partial essence of which he spontaneously expresses out of his poetic consciousness and because we are secure in the truth that Nature *is* still there, as both O'Neill and Cabot knew it would be. (pp. 115-17)

> *Hollis L. Cate, "Ephraim Cabot: O'Neill's Spontaneous Poet," in* The Markham Review, *Vol. 2, No. 5, February, 1971, pp. 115-17.*

Travis Bogard   (essay date 1972)

[*Bogard is an American educator and critic. In the following excerpt from his study* Contour in Time: The Plays of Eugene O'Neill, *he explores technical, stylistic, and thematic aspects of* Desire under the Elms.]

In 1918, efforts to move the American theatre toward the province of art were spasmodic attempts, lacking as visible proof plays that would attest to the truth of theory. In cooperation, first, with the Provincetown Players, then with an experimental theatre [the Triumvirate] in association with Kenneth Macgowan and Robert Edmond Jones and finally with the Theatre Guild, O'Neill demonstrated decisively that drama could be an art. In very literal terms, his work between 1920 and 1928 proved the theories of "Theatre Art" to be valid. (p. xiv)

O'Neill said he wrote [*Desire Under the Elms*] at Ridgefield, Connecticut, "in the winter and spring of 1924" and finished in June. Like *Welded* and *All God's Chillun Got Wings,* the new play accepted the recommendations of the prophets of the Art Theatre movement that a realistic play, to have value, must move toward a more profound realism, revealing the psychological essences and primitive mythic forces working in modern lives and attempting to reach a state of "spiritual abstraction." O'Neill's earliest plays in this vein were, on the whole, tortured, ambiguous and forced. In *Welded* and *All God's Chillun Got Wings,* as in the earlier *Diff'rent,* the requirements of a scrupulous imitation of the appearances of life often obscured what O'Neill felt to be the spiritual essence behind life. Each of the earlier works is as much a case history of persons with vivid reuroses as it is the super-natural revelation of profound human and spiritual truth. In *All God's Chillun Got Wings,* O'Neill manages to suggest not only that the characters of Jim and Ella are convincing human beings, realistically apprehended, but also that they epitomize general marital and racial problems. Yet their story is hurried in statement, and its resolution is as much melodrama as it is an action eliciting the "religious exultation over the truth" that O'Neill valued. The tension between the demands of the surface narrative and the symbolic underpinnings is dangerously strong.

In *Desire Under the Elms,* however, all strains are eased; surface and interior actions are brought into perfect conjunction. Technical experimentation is no longer self-assertively symbolic as were the shrinking rooms and follow-spots of the earlier plays. Now experiment serves realism and also, unobtrusively, opens the play to fuller perspectives. The characteristic *dramatis personae*—poetic hero, Strindbergian woman, materialistic brother, aloof and difficult father—are present, but they are drawn without the self-consciousness that derives from excessive autobiographical concern. The typical themes—the yearning for a lost mother, for a home, for identification with a life force to be found in nature, and for the discovery of a god in marriage—are rooted, at last, in a credible fiction and characterizations. In all respects, *Desire Under the Elms* fulfills the promise of O'Neill's early career and is the first important tragedy to be written in America.

O'Neill's own response to the play was guarded. He wrote it rapidly and talked little about it while it was being written. After it opened, O'Neill told Walter Huston, who played Ephraim Cabot, that he had dreamed the play in its entirety, a claim he also made for *Ah, Wilderness!* A note in his Work Diary indicates a more conscious process, saying that the "idea" for the play occurred to him in the fall of 1923. It is not possible to trace the elements of the dream, if dream there was, as scholars have traced the antecedents of Coleridge's dream of Xanadu. O'Neill's own play, *The Rope,* anticipated his use of the New England locale and the character of Ephraim. T. C. Murray's *Birthright,* with its monologue describing the hardness of the farmer's life, was centrally formative. The legends of Oedipus, Phaedra and Medea, along with Nietzsche's *The Birth of Tragedy,* are nearly co-equal in importance. But there also exists the possibility of another, closer "source" than any of these—one whose proximity is so close as to raise a question of plagiarism. That work is Sidney Howard's *They Knew What They Wanted,* produced by the Theatre Guild with Pauline Lord on November 24, 1924, twelve days after O'Neill's play opened.

Although the plays differ sharply in texture and tone, the structure of their narratives is close. Each situation centers on the coming of a woman with dubious antecedents to a farm where she becomes the wife of an aging farmer. In each, she is seduced by a young, restless farm worker and becomes pregnant. In O'Neill's play, the relationship is explicitly incestuous; in Howard's, where such a theme would have wiped out the comedy, incest is remotely suggested in Joe's remorse at having betrayed old Tony's affection, which is like that of a father for a son. Finally, although each playwright seeks a different direction in resolving his situation both dispose of their characters in accordance with forces that appear to emanate from the land. To an extent, of course, the similarities can be explained by the fact that in selecting their subjects, both authors were influenced by the generic elements of the American folk play. Such a reason accounts for the similarity between **Anna Christie** and *They Knew What They Wanted.* Nevertheless the close approximation of the central stories, coupled with O'Neill's demonstrable habit of building his plays on the works of others, makes it a possibility to investigate that he created **Desire Under the Elms** after having seen the manuscript of Sidney Howard's comedy.

Interestingly, in 1925, Howard and the Theatre Guild were involved in a plagiarism suit by an author who claimed that Howard had stolen from him the central situation of a husband's being incapacitated on his wedding night, leaving his bride to be seduced by another. In defense, searching for analogues to his comedy, Howard pointed out that *They Knew What They Wanted* was similar to the narratives of *Candida, Pelléas and Mélisande* and *Paolo and Francesca,* and he made much of the fact that it was intentionally patterned after the legend of Tristan and Isolde. So far as Howard was concerned, the incapacitation of the husband was the point at issue and he made no use of the parallels O'Neill's play offered.

Howard's attitude toward O'Neill's work was warm and his praise unstinting. In December, 1924, he wrote to Barrett Clark expressing outrage for both himself and O'Neill after Robert Benchley had reviewed their plays as "French triangles." He added that he was delighted with Clark's review of **Desire Under the Elms,** and commented *"There's* a fine play!" In an article in the *New York Times,* he was lavish with commendation, and in the preface to the original publication of his play he commented on the similarity between the two works, saying that he and O'Neill could agree "that no two plays could possibly bear less resemblance to each other than this simple comedy of mine and his glorious tragedy. . . . "

At the plagiarism trial, which Howard easily won, the judge accepted his testimony that the plot had been noted down in the summer of 1922 and that two acts of the scenario were in type by March, 1923. Howard's correspondence bears this out: in June, 1923, he wrote to his sister that he had in hand two scenarios, a California comedy and a fantastic comedy about pirates. He wrote part of the California comedy in Europe in August, and, with the play unfinished, started his return trip in September, going directly to Hollywood, where his wife, Clare Eames, was to make a film with Mary Pickford. The play was finished in Hollywood by November 21, 1923, when he wrote to his agent, Harold Freedman, "I have today finished *They Knew What They Wanted* which is the comedy I summarized to you last summer and which I wrote out in Venice. It is a good play, very human and funny and simple and clear—I think. It is my contribution to the Macgowan, O'Neill, Jones venture. I hope they will consider it a contribution." There follows a letter of 1923, dated simply "Sunday," discussing with Macgowan the casting of his play and suggesting that his wife, Clare Eames, who had played the lead in the Experimental Theatre production of *Fashion,* be considered as the heroine.

The evidence, therefore, places the script of *They Knew What They Wanted* in the hands of the Triumvirate several months before O'Neill began work on his scenario, at about the time he stated he got the "idea" for the tragedy. Curiously, at this point, the correspondence between Howard and the Triumvirate breaks off. No reply from Macgowan has been preserved in the Howard papers, and there is no further mention that the play was a contribution to the Triumvirate's venture, except that in a deposition made at the time of the trial, Howard stated that the Theatre Guild was not the organization for whom the play was written.

In the end, proof fails, yet the possibility remains suggestive, and the dubious story of the dream, together with O'Neill's uncharacteristic silence about the play as he wrote it, breeds the suspicion that O'Neill was aware that his planet and Howard's were momentarily in uncomfortable close conjunction. If so, it was not a matter of which either playwright expressed cognizance, for neither work was diminished. Perhaps all that needs to be said of the possibility is this: that if O'Neill took anything of real importance from Howard, it was the humanity, simplicity and clarity that Howard rightly found his comedy to contain upon its completion. Howard's major service was to make the way smooth for O'Neill as Conrad's *The Nigger of the Narcissus,* Murray's *Birthright* and Ibsen's *Peer Gynt* had earlier done.

For whatever reason, O'Neill worked with unusual freedom in writing his tragedy. The lack of tension is revealed in many ways, perhaps chiefly in the play's economy of means and its avoidance of startling stage effects and grotesque characterization. In **All God's Chillun Got Wings,** the Congo mask is introduced into the play somewhat arbitrarily, accompanied by a lecture from Hattie as to its meaning and merits. The action associated with it, particularly Ella's "murder" of the mask, forces a symbolic interpretation on the play that may well result in an effect of contrivance and unintegrated artifice. The symbolism arising from the setting of *Desire Under the Elms,* however, is of another order of merit. To be sure, as O'Neill describes the scene in a preliminary note, the meaning of his setting is explicit and forced. The elm trees brood over the house with "a sinister maternity . . . a crushing, jealous absorption . . . They are like exhausted women resting their sagging breasts and hands and hair on its roof, and when it rains their tears trickle down monotonously and rot on the shingles." Fortunately the novelistic rhetoric that links the elms with Eben's dead mother and with an exhausted life force holds no meaning beyond the printed page. In the context of the play's realistic action, the elms are not symbols in any discrete or absolute sense. Their meaning is reached only as the characters become aware of their presence, and as the elms in consequence become part of the action. When, for example, Ephraim Cabot associates the evil he feels in the house with something dropping from the trees, their significance is made clear and psychologically plausible, their symbolism an element of the play's core. They do not, as the Congo mask did, warp the drama's action in order to justify their presence.

The design of the setting was O'Neill's own, as the crude sketches he made to guide Robert Edmond Jones attest. The plan which permitted the simultaneous revelation of the interior and exterior of the house was created to solve the problems of the lengthy scene shifts that had destroyed the rhythm of *Beyond the Horizon.* O'Neill, who aimed again at the effect he had sought in the earlier play—a contrast of cramped and dark interior with radiant exterior—developed a simultaneous setting whose exterior walls were removed to reveal the rooms within. Settings using such devices are routine on today's stages, but they were not in 1924. Whether the technique was O'Neill's invention or not, the setting of *Desire Under the Elms* makes the first important use of the device on the modern stage and must rank as one of O'Neill's most influential innovations.

Within the setting, O'Neill moves the action easily, establishing in the swing from interior to exterior a loosely defined rhythm that is amplified by the cyclic pattern of time. The story is concentrated into three days, one in summer, one in fall and one in spring. Each act follows the course of its day from late afternoon or early evening until the following dawn. The fluid unity of the setting and the cyclic control on the action that his time-scheme exerts cause the play to approximate classical unities of action, place and time and enable O'Neill to avoid the picaresque narrative style of such a work as *Chris Christopherson.*

The use of time and place are successful in part because O'Neill has set the play firmly in a historical context. *Desire Under the Elms* was not his first venture into historical drama. *The Fountain* of 1921 marked his debut as a historian, but its romanticized view of history is unlike the realistic imagery he created of New England in 1850. O'Neill is entirely convincing that the Cabots sprang from that world. Unlike much that passes for history in theatre, the Cabots are not moderns in costume. To envision them

as contemporary beings is not really possible, despite the Freudian overtones in their portraiture; neither can they be conceived of as coming from an earlier period in American history. They are only of their time and place. Notably the play contains no elaborate devices to suggest the period. A few specific references, such as those to the Gold Rush or the songs that are sung, establish the calendar time, but the reality of historical period like the symbolism emerges from the characters themselves. They could not exist in a time different from their own because their problems and their way of reacting to them arise from the world that O'Neill, now emerging as a major historical dramatist, has created for them. The setting, as it is in all great plays, is finally the creation not of the designer, but of the playwright, who evolves its reality through his action.

Such mastery of technical and stylistic means marks the work of a great dramatist of any period. The manifest technical ease eradicates the absurd distinction between the "commercial" and the "art" theatres. Certainly, when O'Neill's tragedy was first produced it was a product of the avant-garde activities of the Triumvirate, staged in what was to become known as an off-Broadway theatre. Yet its standards were professional in the actors it employed, the critics it courted and the publicity on which it capitalized. Significant too is the fact that it was created within the limits set by an acknowledged and essentially commercial theatrical genre, the genre indeed of *"Anna Christie"* which O'Neill had mistrusted as too easy, too like routine Broadway fare.

Desire Under the Elms follows in its general pattern that of the American folk drama as it was developed in the

The set of Desire under the Elms, *Greenwich Village Theatre, 1924.*

1920's for popular commercial consumption. In these works, produced both on Broadway and in the regional theatres springing up throughout the country after the war, there evolved conventionalized patterns of action, character and belief that became for O'Neill among many others one form of theatrical language. The folk play centered thematically on the response of the characters to the land on which they lived. Close to the soil, their identities and destinies were shaped by a force they sensed moving in the earth. The influence of the land was shown in many ways, in the depiction of the hardship that comes when the land turns sterile or in the joy that the land in springtime brings to its people. Most frequently, the significance of the land was made clear by means of a character whose responsiveness to the earth served to bring into the range of consciousness the nature of the environmental forces that shape men's destinies. Old Chris, responding to the sea rather than to the land, is such an interpreter, and, in the work of other dramatists, there are, for example, Tony in *They Knew What They Wanted,* Jeeter Lester in *Tobacco Road* and, to a lesser extent, Aunt Eller in *Green Grow the Lilacs.* This character, forming as he does an important link with the earth, is rooted where he belongs. In contrast, there is introduced into the action a nomad, usually a young man, who moves restlessly from place to place because he has not yet learned where he belongs. Joe in *They Knew What They Wanted* is a migrant worker, only dimly responsive to the beneficent influence from Tony's grapevines. Matt Burke, although he is aware of the sea's power within him, reveals something of the restlessness of the type, and Curly in *Green Grow the Lilacs* is another such character. The woman with whom these men come into contact is frequently an alien, often a city-dweller who comes to the land by accident, as Amy in *They Knew What They Wanted* came, or as Anna came to the sea—suspicious and a little afraid but discovering ultimately that she has come home.

Dialect and rural coloration necessarily form a feature of the style of these plays, and the narratives dramatize the lives of people whose horizons are limited and whose emotions are to a degree repressed, but who normally should be able to obtain a kind of blessing through the simplicity of the routines of their lives. It is of course possible for the dramatist to deny the possibility of blessing from the land. *Tobacco Road,* for instance, depicts rural existence as intolerable, ingrown, incestuous, damned. Yet even in this play, Jeeter's only desire is to die as he lived on the land, and there is a moment at the end when he runs the soil through his fingers that suggests at least the possibility of benison in the earth.

Into this conventionalized pattern of dramatic narrative, *Desire Under the Elms* fits precisely. Ephraim's sense of the earth as the source of his salvation, Eben's feeling of dislocation on the farm, Abbie's alien strangeness and her desire to come home are entirely in the tradition. The elements of incest and adultery, the violence, the crudity are all potentials of the pattern, and, in its thematic exploration of the nature of a "hard" and an "easy" God, the play sees the land both as fertile and as sterile, as giving blessing and as demanding cruel service.

When a dramatist works within a tried theatrical convention, he has two ways to proceed. He may either vary the essential pattern, as Somerset Maugham varies the late-Victorian triangle story in *The Circle* for the sake of a trick and a surprise ending, or he may fulfill it completely as Shaw uses the same pattern in *Candida.* The latter is the more difficult, but more rewarding course, and it is the one O'Neill followed in his folk tragedy. In doing so, he achieved a freedom and a security by the very fact that, through its knowledge of the conventions, his audiences could anticipate the movement of the narrative and understand it without the interference of surprise. Surprise blinds perception; suspense is movement toward the known; tension emerges from foreknowledge and expectation of consequence; satisfaction comes in the fulfillment of prediction. In *Desire Under the Elms,* there is conveyed a sense of operative destiny. The characters are fated men and women moving in predictable courses to known ends, an impression that is achieved partly by the dramatist's acceptance of the elements of the genre. The result, for O'Neill, is that within the pattern he is released from the necessity of devising fictions to embody his meaning. The fiction is there, and he can explore to the full the philosophical and theological implications of his action. The freedom he achieves is complete and the results are profound.

The multiplicity of views it is possible to take of the action of *Desire Under the Elms* is a result of O'Neill's freedom. His plays immediately preceding the tragedy are not complex. Their ambiguities appear to arise more from unwitting ambiguity of statement than from subtlety of thought. In this play, however, interpretation is free to move complexly on several levels that merge, finally, in a single action.

At its least complex, seen as a realistic narrative of life on a mid-nineteenth-century farm, the play presents a convincing account of its characters moving in time. It is a work written in the best tradition of American realism. It is full, but not cluttered with detail; it is credible; and it produces that sense of local and particular inevitability that, in realistic drama and fiction, detailed psychological portraiture can sometimes evolve. In this primary, frontal view of the play, each individual is responsible for his fate. Despite the play's grounding in psychological theory, O'Neill has not contrived destinies for his characters by forcing them into patterns prefabricated by Freud. Oedipal patterns of incest emerge both in Eben's love for Abbie, and in his seeking out the prostitute Min, with whom his father and his brothers have slept. Yet such patterns in the action do not need a Freudian gloss to be understood. By contrast, the sociological and political theories which governed Arthur Miller's determination of a fate for his Willy Loman, suggest that Willy's fate is less a truth of his character than a demonstration of a thesis. The Freudian patterns of *Desire Under the Elms,* however, appear to be characteristic modes of behavior for the individuals under such circumstances as the play defines. Freud is used less for his theories than for his truth, a truth that had preceded Freud by millennia.

Again, viewed as a realistic narrative, the play contains elements characteristic of the naturalistic tragedy of Zola and Hauptmann—those grim, depressing narratives of small men and women defeated by societal and evolutionary forces they cannot control. Yet, as with his use of Freud, O'Neill convinces his audiences that this story is in no way contrived to demonstrate a sociological point. Focusing less on the pressure of external circumstance, more on the response to circumstance by the central characters, he strikes a just balance between an exploration of the harshness of their rural world and the people themselves. Ephraim, Eben and Abbie command sympathy not because they are victims of forces they cannot control, but because they are capable of choice and responsibility. The choices they make are not forced upon them, but O'Neill, aware of the pressures of the farm on its people, is careful to show how the choices evolved, and permit audiences to draw conclusions about that world from the perspective of his characters' choices.

Although the play as a psychological and sociological work maintains an unforced and convincing quality of human truth, more impressive is the way in which it transcends naturalism and becomes a poetic tragedy, capable not only of presenting temporal, local and specific truths, but of achieving the more general perspective that important tragic drama holds on the human condition. Such perspective, after all, was what the drama of heightened realism was supposed to achieve.

The play's narrative and its characters are entirely typical of O'Neill's work. Eben is the hero touched with poetry, but unlike Robert Mayo, he is not a sentimental creation, taking out his frustration in moody longing for beauty. He has in him a "repressed vitality," an animal quality that gives him maturity and manliness foreign to the earlier dreamer. Yet, like Mayo, he reveals the same need to belong. He seeks the same identification with nature and moves listlessly in alien places, in the kitchen, the world of women where he can sink no roots. His desire brings him into inevitable conflict with more hardened souls whose needs are less because they are aware of less.

Eben's sensitivity is the core of the play's poetic extension beyond simple realism. His sensibility creates a perspective within the action that permits a view of all the characters *sub species aeternitatis,* as images of more than particular, external truths. Eben's need, which generates his habits of thought, enlarges the meaning of the life on the farm, giving the events the qualities of a symbolic action, and providing a context wherein may be understood general and universal meanings. Through Eben, for instance, the beauty of the farm is made real, and through his awareness, Abbie is linked with that beauty. He causes Ephraim to become aware of the natural forces that shape his life and enables him to define the nature of the hard and easy Gods, and to clarify the influences that are concentrated in the sinister elms. Through Eben's touch of poetry, the farm is transformed, and what transpires there is heightened as is the action of great poetic drama.

To reinforce the generalized poetic perspective, O'Neill has given his dialogue special properties that lift it above merely realistic speech. No doubt the dialect spoken on the farm is real in that it can be heard in the mouths of

New Englanders even yet. Furthermore, at no point is the rhetoric aggrandized beyond the level appropriate to the station of the characters. The decorum of the realistic theatre is rigidly observed. Yet as the dialogue is spoken, semi-literate and monosyllabic though it is, it emerges under the pressures of the emotions generated in the action as a special and rich language supportive of the play's widest conceptions. It extends its meanings by overtone and implication to present both the multi-levels of the characters' consciousness and, at the same time, their symbolic significance, welding both particular and general into a tonal pattern that has appropriateness, broad meaning and beauty.

Like all poetic dialogue, O'Neill's is rhythmic, but in this play there is none of the overly crafted, highly conscious rhythmic effect found in other of his works. Where rhythmic repetition occurs, it does so naturally, as in Eben's quasi-illiterate use of the word "warm" and the ironic changes rung on the word "pretty" in his final soliloquy in the play's second scene:

> Waal—thar's a star, an' somewhar's they's him, an' here's me, an' thar's Min up the road—in the same night. What if I does kiss her? She's like t'night, she's soft 'n' wa'm, her eyes kin wink like a star, her mouth's wa'm, her arms're wa'm, she smells like a wa'm plowed field, she's purty . . . Ay-eh! By God A'mighty she's purty, an' I don't give a damn how many sins she's sinned afore mine or who she's sinned 'em with, my sin's as purty as any one on 'em!

The rhythm is achieved through the repetition of words and broken phrases—in the continual, choric repetition of "Ay-eh," for example, or in such passages as the "stichomythic" duet between Eben's brothers, Simeon and Peter:

> EBEN. . . . . Why didn't ye never stand between him 'n' my Maw when he was slavin' her to her grave—t'pay her back fur the kindness she done t'yew?
>
> (*There is a long pause. They stare at him in surprise.*)
>
> SIMEON. Waal—the stock'd got t' be watered.
>
> PETER. 'R they was woodin' to do.
>
> SIMEON. 'R plowin'.
>
> PETER. 'R hayin'.
>
> SIMEON. 'R spreadin' manure.
>
> PETER. 'R weedin'.
>
> SIMEON. 'R prunin'.
>
> PETER. 'R milkin'.
>
> EBEN. (*breaking in harshly*) An' makin' walls— stone atop o' stone—makin' walls till yer heart's a stone ye heft up out o' the way o' growth onto a stone wall t' wall in yer heart!

To form imagery and rhythms that evolve naturally from character and setting, but which yet elicit from rural speech rhythms something of the strangeness, the uniqueness of poetry is a device O'Neill may have learned from the work of Synge and other dramatists of the Abbey Theatre. Whatever the source, the technique as displayed in the inarticulate self-justification of Simeon and Peter creates a vivid impression of the way in which diurnal realities obscure moral perception. At the same time, the words that suggest the simple rhythms of farm life provide a foil and balance to Eben's fuller perception of the heart as a stone.

Eben's imagery is drawn from the reality of the farm, indeed helps to create that reality. It is neither decorative nor inappropriately philosophical. Like all else in this play, verbal imagery comes from character and action, as Ephraim's biblical cadences do, for instance, or as Abbie's desire for Eben is expressed in terms of her response to the land itself:

> Hain't the sun strong an' hot? Ye kin feel t burnin' into the earth—Nature—makin' thin's grow—bigger 'n' bigger—burnin' inside ye—makin' ye want t' grow—into somethin' else—till ye're jined with it—an' it's your'n—but it owns ye too—an' makes ye grow bigger—like a tree—like them elums.

The partly ironic phallic imagery expresses Abbie's langorous response to the sun's heat. Beyond the moment, however, her words are to be heard as are the images of other more formal dramatic poems, within the context of a chain of images. Imagery of the sun forms a poetic motif threaded through the play. In the opening dialogue, for example, Eben, Simeon and Peter all respond to the setting sun:

> EBEN. (*gazing up at the sky*) Sun's downin' purty
>
> SIMEON *and* PETER. (*together*) Ay-eh. They's gold in the West.
>
> EBEN. Ay-eh (*Pointing*) Yonder atop o' the hill pasture, ye mean?
>
> SIMEON *and* PETER. (*together*) In Californi-a!

For Simeon and Peter, the sunset holds a vague promise of riches to be found in the golden west, and, a little earlier, it has called to Simeon's mind the memory of his dead wife, Jenn, who had hair "long's a hoss' tail—an' yaller like gold." It conveys a sense both of loss and promise and emblemizes the source of his restlessness and the end of his quest. For Eben, the sun is less and more: a manifestation of the beauty of the farm. It is the agent of the farm's fertility, but when it disappears he has no need to follow it beyond the hill pasture that borders the universe. Although Eben hates the walls of stones that bind in his heart, his desire is not to break out of bondage but to find in the house and in the earth the life he needs. The imagery of the sun thus arises in many contexts and develops meanings crucial to the play. It is, in fact, the last image, where all meanings that have accrued around it, those of nature, of love, of covetousness, are synthesized and restated:

> EBEN. I love ye, Abbie. . . . Sun's a-rizin'. Purty, hain't it!
>
> ABBIE. Ay-eh. (*They both stand for a moment*

looking up raptly in attitudes strangely aloof and devout.)

> SHERIFF. (*looking around at the farm enviously* . . .) It's a jim-dandy farm, no denyin'. Wished I owned it!

Through such skeins of imagery, O'Neill suggests the nature of the desires and destinies of his character on a broad, even symbolic, scale. Yet the imagery remains "natural," its poetic structure concealed by the tight speech rhythms and the dialect that applies a styptic to its overly fecund flow.

Desire Under the Elms, bearing all the characteristics of O'Neill's individual style and predilections, moving comfortably within the frame of popular dramatic tradition, extends its reach toward poetic tragedy in other ways than its dialogue. The narrative's stress on murder and incest is potentially lurid and melodramatic, yet it also moves the work toward the special concerns of all tragic drama. However one may finally judge the play, its subject matter is neither trivial nor arbitrary. In this play, O'Neill was first attempting what he later undertook more explicitly in ***Mourning Becomes Electra:*** to construct a tragedy-by-analogy, using ancient Greek tragedy in an American setting in order that something of the power of the earlier dramatic literature would emerge and strengthen his own concepts.

The play is reminiscent of the circumstances of the story of Phaedra and Hippolytus, and in Abbie's murder of the child, the dim outline of Euripides' *Medea* appears. Neither *Medea* nor *Hippolytus* is a precise source for O'Neill's story. He has used his "source material" much more freely than he did in ***Bound East for Cardiff*** or ***The Emperor Jones*** or than he was to do in ***Mourning Becomes Electra.*** The reminiscence is evoked by tone and texture more than by detailed imitation. What is important is the release of emotion the subject matter permits. One speaks hesitantly of a subject matter "proper" to tragedy. There can be no absolute prescriptions, yet the emotional range of this work is not readily paralleled in other plays of the period, even in O'Neill's own, and this manifestation is in part attributable to the classical analogues. Further, the subject matter justifies in part the lyric eloquence with which the characters speak of their destiny. With such passions as theirs, they speak with convincing propriety in a heightened manner, and in the stark, seemingly elemental confrontations, they appear to be responding to a force of destiny that is at once real and mythic.

If tragedy is in any way ritualistic or if its enactments are to be purgative in any sense, the narrative must be a matter of important public concern. Sociological or political theories wrought into tragic stories are insufficient to provide more than the show of ritual. Great tragedy bespeaks the most profound psychological needs of the culture which produces it. The mythic qualities of the *Oresteia* or of *Oedipus* reflect qualities of Greek life which analysis more profound than that of history must reveal. These dramas are responses to myth, assuming its qualities and its relation to the central needs of the culture which cherished them. In their characters, language and action they give articulate form to the submerged communal desires of a people, and thus bring it to a level of popular awareness, provocative of passion and purgation. In search of such awareness, O'Neill reached back in time to mythic circumstances derived from an earlier culture and reshaped them to the basic story of human desire and its aftermath he narrated for modern America. In this way, he formed a story in a typical tragic pattern: his characters follow a course of sin and find redemption in recognition of error and the assumption of responsibility. Yet he did not do so in an attempt to be "Greek." The pattern is reformed and domesticated, ultimately assumed as O'Neill's own, and told for the sake of his own time.

That America between the two great wars was a mother-oriented society has been the subject of extensive recent comment. In the 1920's and 1930's, however, the truth was chiefly to be remarked in the drama which functioned as a reflector of a scarcely apprehended truth. Since it relies on mass responses, and is irrevocably public, as opposed to novel and poem which evoke private responses from individual readers, it necessarily speaks to and takes its life from those beliefs which many men hold in common. In a sense the drama tells everybody what everybody knows or at least chooses to believe. The stereotype and the cliché are elements of its life blood. The greatest dramatists see the human roots in these elements, and thereby speak to the truth that has evoked them, too easily, from popular belief.

In the films of the time, the mother's boy was occasionally the subject for comedy and the basis of the comedic personality of such actors as Harold Lloyd and Harry Langdon. For the most part, however, the films created the sense of the American hero as vigorous, competent, individualistic and self-reliant. This image, however, was denied in the drama, where the competence and inner strength of the American male was continually questioned. There, under many guises and with many changes of tone, he was shown to be a child questing through a hostile world in search of a lost mother. Sidney Howard's *The Silver Cord* is perhaps the most obvious and painful example of the phenomenon, yet it is surprising in how many other plays a version of the quest appears, and how often the heroine fulfills in some measure the role of mother to the lost hero. Mention may be made of Sidney Kingsley's *Dead End,* with its motherless slum children and its gangster-villain, Baby-Face Martin, who returns to the tenements of his boyhood to seek out a mother who rejects him. S. N. Behrman's typical heroine is sought partly as a mother by the heroes loosed in her sophisticated salons, notably in the scene which ends the second act of *Biography,* between Marion Froude and Richard, the left-wing journalist. The quest is apparent in the comedies of Philip Barry, in, for instance, *Holiday,* where the nursery is seen as a place of special value because it is reminiscent of the dead mother, and it can be found in such works as Odets's *Awake and Sing,* where Bessie Berger's attempt to hold her family together during the Depression has forced her to withdraw from her family those necessary qualities of tenderness and love which alone will redeem them.

The theme of the lost mother and the weak and questing son was important to O'Neill for many personal reasons.

Yet as the work of other dramatists amply demonstrates, it was not only his private concern. It was a theme important to his society, as that society was represented in microcosm in his audiences and in the public that read his works with sufficient eagerness to make them best-selling books. His assumption of a position of leadership in his theatre may well be attributed in part to his sensitive treatment of what was an American "universal," a social truth, a cultural need.

Desire Under the Elms differs from other plays exploring this theme in that it does more than present a simplified, somewhat stereotypical response to the Oedipal drives in American society. Rather, centering on the theme as a basic pattern of American mores, it frames an action that attempts to understand the need by defining it in terms of large philosophical concepts that may be able to explain and thus partly to resolve the tensions the hopeless quest creates. Unlike most of his contemporaries who remained content with the observation of a social phenomenon, O'Neill provided a philosophical scheme that permitted a broad interpretation of his central concern. The scheme was Nietzsche's.

In the writing of Friedrich Nietzsche, O'Neill found a congenial philosophy. He had read *Thus Spake Zarathustra* as early as 1907, and no doubt the quasi-mystical experiences involving the loss of consciousness in visions and dreams which he described in the *persona* of Edmund Tyrone made him responsive to Nietzsche's description of the truth that could be revealed in Dionysian ecstasy. He was slow to find a use for Nietsche in his drama, preferring the distillations to be found in Jack London, George Bernard Shaw or in George Cram Cook's conception of the theatre as a Dionysian dance. Yet the identification with the sea of which he wrote in *"Anna Christie"* and *Beyond the Horizon,* the quest for a God that forms the thematic core of *The Emperor Jones, The Fountain* and *The Hairy Ape,* the ecstatic loss of self in marriage extolled in *Welded,* all point to his ultimate acceptance of Nietzsche's doctrine as the theological matrix of his drama.

In using Nietzsche's doctrine, O'Neill was necessarily highly selective. *Desire Under the Elms* does not dramatize the work of the philosopher but takes from his books, especially *The Birth of Tragedy,* the elements O'Neill felt to be compatible with his own sense of truth. With Nietzsche's conception of the Dionysian way of life, O'Neill felt entirely in accord. He understood well that consciousness can be subdued by a kind of rapturous apprehension, analogous to drunkenness and to dreaming, and that through such intoxication, truths can be reached that are only dimly to be known through cognitive, structured perception.

Nietzsche equates the Dionysian apprehension with intoxication, a rapture that demolishes the defenses of the *principium individuationis.* He speaks of "the powerful approach of spring penetrating all nature with joy," and describes how, when Dionysian emotions awake, man, as if he were under the influence of a narcotic, relinquishes self-awareness: "the subjective vanishes to complete self-forgetfulness." Under the spell, "all the stubborn, hostile barriers, which necessity, caprice or 'shameless fashion' has set up between man and man are broken down. Now, at the evangel of cosmic harmony, each one feels himself not only united, reconciled, blended with his neighbor, but as one with him, as if the veil of Mâyâ had been torn and were now merely fluttering in tatters before the mysterious Primal Unity." By the mystic rapture of Dionysus, "the spell of individuation is broken, and the way lies open to the Mothers of Being, to the innermost heart of things."

Although he was later to make Nietzsche's vision of the "Universal Oneness" a subject of more explicit concern, in its broadest meanings his action implies the centrality of that concept to his play. Abbie takes Eben's mother's place; she is his lover and mother; she becomes pregnant. In her presence the farm becomes warm and fertile, and she and the farm become as one. Through her, Eben achieves an intoxicant rapture, born of a desire that transcends the walls of stones and the confines of the narrow rooms of the house. Together, in love, they come into a profoundly right relationship with the energy that vitalizes the earth, a force that is in effect the power of nature itself. The love story of Abbie and Eben is in effect a dramatization of the condition Nietzsche called "Dionysian."

In opposition to the Dionysian forces, Nietzsche placed powers he called "Apollonian." Apollo's art Nietzsche described as incessantly hostile to the Dionysian state:

> For I can only explain to myself the *Doric* state and Doric art as a permanent war-camp of the Apollonian: Only by incessant opposition to the titanic-barbaric nature of the Dionysian was it possible for an art so defiantly-prim, so encompassed with bulwarks, a training so warlike and rigorous, a constitution so cruel and relentless, to last for any length of time.

As he develops the conception. Nietzsche maintains that the Dionysian could lead humanity by satisfying men's need for beauty, and that he could create a hierarchy of joy that would free the world from the Apollonian hierarchy of terror.

O'Neill had little interest in the joy of Apollonianism. He understood, however, the concept of the constant hostility between the two powers and agreed that "Wherever the Dionysian prevailed, the Apollonian was routed and annihilated." In *Desire Under the Elms,* O'Neill made the anti-Dionysian force approximate to Puritan Christianity, and he tied it in with a fundamentalist, Old-Testament deity, and with the rigorous repression of the flesh and the subjugation of impulse to rock-hard will. Nietzsche spoke of the Dionysian's taking down Apollonian culture stone by stone, as if it had been built in the same way Ephraim erected the stone walls on his farm. Nietzsche's imagery was perhaps as important as his thought, and from it O'Neill framed actions fundamental to his play—especially the conflict between a man who sought to achieve a Dionysian rapture and another who was dedicated to a life of unflinching self-denial and hardship, to whom the service of Dionysus seemed immorally easy and was in effect anathema.

The suggestion of the tragedy's central conflict had been dormant in much of O'Neill's earlier drama. The poet-heroes of whom he had written were to a man "Diony-

sian" in essence, if not detail. The great change in the new tragedy lay in the antagonist, who in his earlier versions had been only a materialist who sought to control the elements of his world. As Andrew Mayo gambled in wheat, as Jones made himself a materialistic Emperor, so all of O'Neill's anti-Dionysians sought power in what they could clutch, enslave and manipulate. Ephraim Cabot marks a change in O'Neill's view of the enemy. With Nietzsche's help, O'Neill was able to see this opponent of the Dionysian as being in his turn a God-driven man, one who, despite his materialism and his stubborn individualism, also "belonged" to a power greater than himself. As O'Neill gained this perspective, what followed in the play was almost inevitable: the warfare of Eben and Ephraim became the embodiment of a theological conflict based broadly on the antagonism of the Dionysian and the Apollonian forces Nietzsche had described, a conflict fought in the "universe" of the farm, in the particular arena its center, the house, created.

The theological conflict is presented explicitly in Ephraim Cabot's monologue in Part II, scene ii, when, moved by his desire for Abbie, he attempts to reach her by confessing something of his nature and telling her of the hardships in his past. The essence of his statement is that he has grown hard in the service of a hard God. "God," he says, "hain't easy"; His presence is in the stones that must be piled up in a cruel life of sacrificial service so that the farm may be fertile. The service is justified by God's commandment to Peter to build his church on a rock. Ephraim says, "When ye kin make corn sprout out o' stones, God's livin' in yew!" He tells Abbie of a time when in despair at so many stones, he gave up the farm and journeyed west and farmed a broad meadow where there were no stones, where "Ye'd on'y to plow an' sow an' then set an' smoke yer pipe an' watch thin's grow." But the easy way had no salvation in it, and he returned to the stony farm and re-entered the service of the hard God.

The loneliness of the life on the farm was part of Ephraim's devotion, but at times, when hefting the stones became overbearingly difficult, when solitude made him "despairful," he sought out a woman, the whore, Min, or he took a wife, the mother of Simeon and Peter, and later, when she died, the mother of Eben. His first wife stood beside him, working hard, but "she never knowed what she was helpin'." With her, Ephraim was always lonesome. After her death, it was not so lonesome: "The farm growed. It was all mine! When I thought o' that I didn't feel lonesome." His second wife, whom he married because her people contested his deeds to the land, was pretty and soft. Ephraim acknowledges that she tried to be hard but failed because "She never knowed me nor nothin'. It was lonesomer 'n hell with her."

Then, for a third time, he hears a call in the Spring, "the voice o' God cryin' in my wilderness, in my lonesomeness—t' go an' seek an' find!" The voice in the wilderness has led him to Abbie, but in her presence as in the presence of the other women, he feels divided from his God, more lonesome, for this reason, than before he had found her. It is as if he had been driven by an alien force, not his hard

God, but by another, one that stimulates desire and breeds weariness with the stones.

At the end of his monologue, he realizes that Abbie has not understood him, perhaps has not even heard him as she yearns for Eben in the adjoining bedroom. He leaves her and stumbles through the night to the barn, "whar it's restful—whar it's warm," and as he rounds the corner of the house, he stretches up his arms into the night and cries out to a God he understands, "God A'-mighty, call from the dark!" The hard God he has served is no longer there to hear him, and, as always when women come to the farm, he is wretched in his loneliness. The women—certainly Eben's mother and Abbie—serve a different God, one who is soft, if not easy, fecund, closely allied with the generative powers of nature, and capable of desire. Later, in *Strange Interlude;* O'Neill will write of the two principles as God the Father and God the Mother. In *Desire Under the Elms,* the conflict between the hard and—in Ephraim's term—easy Gods, the former associated with Ephraim's ascetic Puritanism and essentially masculine strength, the latter associated with Abbie and the fertility of the farm, is the thematic center of the play.

The setting is larger than the stage can show. Conveyed in the dialogue is a picture of the farm, fertile but without the luxuriance associated with natural fertility, settled in a bowl of hills, a pale sky contrasting with the isolated, monumental elms in the farmyard. Rows of stone walls wander across it, marking its boundaries, and through them passes a road which leads vaguely "away." At the center stand the house and barn, in good condition, but still suggesting buildings on the edge of ruin. The exterior walls are "a sickly grayish, the green of the shutters faded." The shingles of the house are rotting from the water that drips off the elms. It is as if the house were deserted and had no life.

While ordinary enough, the house still contains a mystery, for its central room, Eben's mother's parlor, is dark and sealed away. It is not the ordinary closed parlor, reserved for company use only. It is a haunted room, inhabited by his mother's ghost. Eben thinks of it as a room devoted to her memory. Caring for the house, cooking and doing the woman's service, he moves as if he were an acolyte, tending a shrine from which the saint has gone.

The image of the house as a shrine or church is not entirely fanciful. The action of the play begins with the ringing of a bell from the porch as Eben calls his brothers to supper, much as a congregation is called to prayer by the tolling of a bell. His first word, spoken as he looks up to the sunset-colored sky, is "God!" followed by a word spoken with *"puzzled awe,"* the devotional "Purty!" The congregation that comes, the oxen-like brothers from the field, are in Eben's view aliens who do not know the proper forms of devotion, for the service he has undertaken is the service of a priestess, not a priest, and the absent deity is female. Perhaps for this reason, as they approach the house, the men remember dead women. Simeon is reminded of his lost wife, Jenn, and Eben speaks fiercely of his mother.

Such memory has no sustenance. Jenn's name evokes in Simeon and Peter a vague restlessness and is linked with the promise of California gold. Eben's memory of his mother causes him to attack the life around him, blaming his brothers for their failure to help her or take moral responsibility for what happened to her. By turning continually to thoughts of his mother, he finds a way to rebel against the life he is forced to live, retreating from the farm's hardness toward a warmer and more gratifying commitment.

Isolated on the land, the lonely men walk hopelessly through the tired routines of their lives, dreaming only of possessing something that might satisfy them. Simeon and Peter hold to their vision of the riches in the West; Eben dreams of possessing the farm. Both desires are loosely associated with women—Jenn, Eben's mother—but for none of the brothers does the desire to possess material wealth betoken a real need. Simeon's restlessness is merely a reaction to the loss of Jenn. His aim in going west is dimly comprehended, and, although it is clothed in the imagery of bright promise, its ill-success is suggested when he and Peter sell their rights to inherit the farm for the thirty pieces of gold Eben steals from Ephraim. Having sold their birthrights, they leave, quasi-biblical prodigals who will not return to their home.

Eben's need, more articulated by his awareness, is manifested first as a lust for the land that if gratified will dispossess his father from the farm, leaving him in sole charge. Like his brothers, he at first seeks satisfaction in a dream of material possession, yet as the play proceeds it becomes clear that his hatred of his father and his legalistic claims of ownership are only signals of a truer desire, to rediscover through an identification with the land the security love of his dead mother brought him. He has filled the void her death created with vicious hatred, but for all that, his quest is positive and at heart selfless. He desires not to possess, but to be possessed by the force he knew in her love and which he associates with the "purty" land. What this implies is a total renunciation of the self.

His quest for the source of the feminine power in the land sets him apart from his brothers and brings him into fatal opposition with Ephraim and his hard God. To Eben, the prostitute, Min, whom he visits in a kind of incestuous revenge on his father, is warm and soft like the summer night, "like a wa'm plowed field," and he acknowledges the birth of a force in him that is like the fertile power of nature itself, "growin' an' growin'—til it'll bust out—!" Simeon, mocking him, says "Lust—that's what's growin' in ye," but lust is only the manifestation of frustrated desire. For Eben, the true, the consummate condition of being is to belong to the land as an unborn child belongs to the womb. Curiously, moved by this desire, his view of the land changes, and it is no longer stony and unyielding, but warm and filled with life.

Dominant at the heart of the play are, then, the two powerful forces moving through the land and giving it its character: a power that lies in the stones and a power that resides in the soil. The former demands the self-denial and the control Ephraim gives it; the latter promises peace and fulfillment in return for complete surrender. The characters are aware of them. Simeon acknowledges the presence of such powers when, speaking of the death of Eben's mother, he says, "No one ever kills anybody. It's allus somethin'. That's the murderer." Others in the play respond in varying degrees of awareness to the forces that control their lives, as Ephraim calls to the God of the Lonesome, as Eben pays devotion to his mother's ghost, and as Abbie speaks of the force of nature, saying that nature "owns ye . . . an' makes ye grow bigger—like a tree—like them elums."

Essentially, it appears that the two forces are to be equated with the Gods Dionysus and Apollo. Yet while Nietzsche's *The Birth of Tragedy* provided the philosophical underpinning the drama evolved from O'Neill's perception that men who are forced to serve alien Gods are doomed to loneliness. This had been Eben's case until Abbie came, but when they have loved, the feminine principle asserts itself, and Abbie, in the service of the Mother God, finds contentment for herself and brings it to Eben. At the same time, however, Ephraim suffers a sense of alienation and loss—and specifically of the power to serve the hard God who appears to have been driven from the farm by the service Abbie and Eben pay to God the Mother.

Ephraim's dispossession has been signaled by the desire that drove him out to "learn God's message" in the spring. His language is that of an Old Testament prophet, but the desire that moves in him and that drives him to find Abbie is strange to him. He is made aware that he is withered and dry, a branch fit only for the burning, and to reassert his former devotion, he invokes the God of the Old and Lonesome. Simeon has said his father's search for a wife was "whoring," but it was more than this. In succumbing to the desire for life and in deserting the God of the Stones, he has whored not after a woman but a false God, God the Mother. Yet he cannot live in the alien God's service. He says to Abbie, "It's cold in this house. It's oneasy. They's thin's pokin' about in the dark—in the corners." In the end, he is driven from the house, an apostate cast into darkness.

The Dionysian God demands surrender and the suppression of any act of conscious will. Good lies in loss of consciousness, sexual rapture, drunkenness, and in an unthinking response to the life-giving forces of the earth. When he is possessed by it, even Ephraim pays halting tribute to its power by quoting Biblical images of sex and fertility ("yer belly be like a heap o' wheat") and when he is moved by desire, he tacitly acknowledges the presence of the Mother God, saying to Abbie that "Sometimes ye air the farm an' sometimes the farm be yew." Such admission, however, is temporary and in Ephraim a madness that indicates how much he has deserted the limits of his proper devotion, limits that were defined by the stone walls he built as he sought to possess and subdue the farm. Ephraim's is a God served by an unrelenting pressure of will, so single-minded as to amount almost to mania. Or so it seems to Ephraim's neighbors who ridicule his servitude.

The Dionysian power is released when Eben takes Abbie in the night on the sofa in his mother's parlor. Then the mother's ghost disappears, and despite their adultery and their incest, they love free from guilt. The victory of the force they honor comes to a climactic celebration in the

dance that opens Part III, the revel celebrating the birth of Abbie's child by Eben. At the party, Ephraim, the supposed father, acts the role of the satyr, capering in the dance, drinking and bragging of his sexual prowess, while his neighbors mock him to his face. The revels mount in tempo and die at their height. Abbie leaves and joins Eben by their child's cradle, and Ephraim drunkenly staggers outside to stand beneath the elms. The music dies, and a noise *"as of dead leaves"*—the gossiping whispers of the guests—comes from the kitchen. Then, Ephraim feels most strongly the maternal power concentrated in the trees:

> Even the music can't drive it out—somethin'. Ye kin feel it droppin' off the elums, climbin' up the roof, sneakin' down the chimney, pokin' in the corners! They's no peace in houses, they's no rest livin' with folks. Somethin's always livin' with ye. . . . I'll go t' the barn an' rest a spell.

At the Dionysian climacteric, Ephraim is alone.

Later, the guests gone, Ephraim convinces Eben that Abbie has tricked him into fathering the son who will finally possess the farm. Eben's failure to believe in Abbie's love marks the end of the Dionysian reign. He leaves her, crying that he is going to get drunk and dance, but after the betrayal, he is incapable of plunging into forgetful surrender to the God. Abbie clings to him and passionately asks whether he would forgive her if she could prove that she had not schemed against him: "If I could do it—ye'd love me agen, wouldn't ye? Ye'd kiss me agen? Ye wouldn't never leave me, would ye?" Eben replies sardonically, "I calc'late not. But ye hain't God, be ye."

Abbie's murder of her child is her attempt to be God, but the act of self-denying will, the sin against love and the life of the Dionysians, is more proper to the service of Ephraim's God than to hers. Hearing of her action, Eben cries out, "Oh, God A'mighty! A'mighty God! Maw, whar was ye, why didn't ye stop her?" To this, Abbie replies, "She went back t' her grave that night we fust done it, remember? I hain't felt her about since." Her words suggest that perhaps now the ghost will return and wander restlessly, since the God has left. Ephraim in his desolation threatens to set fire to the house and barn: "I'll leave yer Maw t' haunt the ashes." His words are akin to recognition of the force that has haunted him:

> If he was Eben's [baby], I be glad he air gone! An' mebbe I suspicioned it all along. I felt they was somethin' onnateral—somewhars—the house got so lonesome—an' cold—drivin' me down t' the barn—t' the beasts o' the field. . . . Ay-eh. I must've suspicioned—somethin'. Ye didn't fool me—not altogether, leastways—I'm too old a bird—growin' ripe on the bough.

Momentarily, he considers going west, but at the last, he realizes he cannot leave.

> I kin hear His voice warnin' me agen t' be hard an' stay on my farm. I kin see His hand usin' Eben t' steal t' keep me from weakness. I kin feel I be in the palm o' His hand, His fingers guidin' me. . . . It's a-goin' t' be lonesomer now than it ever war afore—an' I'm gittin' old, Lord—ripe

on the bough. . . . Waal—what d'ye want?
God's lonesome, hain't He? God's hard an' lonesome!

At the end Ephraim's God has returned to the farm van-
quishing the maternal force that Eben and Abbie had
served and betrayed.

Yet what is left for them, displays a final, perhaps unexpected, turn, and with the conclusion to his tragedy,
O'Neill introduces a new motif in his writing, centering on
a concept of the power of will. When it is no longer possible for them to belong to their God, the lovers have one
recourse—to belong to one another. Earlier, their love
generated the rapture that permitted them to achieve the
Dionysian immersion into the life force. It brought them
in tune with the fertility of the land and its divinity. Now,
however, the God has left the land, and they are ejected
from the Garden. As Adam accepted Eve's sin, Eben must
accept Abbie's, for what is left to them cannot lie beyond
themselves. In turning back to Abbie, after his violent rejection of her strange act of faith, Eben reestablishes their
love so that they need to rely on nothing outward. Earlier,
in *Welded,* O'Neill had written of two who attempted to
find God in marriage, but in the final moments of *Desire
Under the Elms,* there is only an assertion of responsibility
and an acceptance of the destiny their love has brought.
Without God, man has only himself to provide surcease
from loneliness.

The play's ending awakens echoes of older tragic patterns
that conclude with the protagonist's acknowledgement of
his responsibility for a general guilt. Making such admission Eben becomes nearly heroic in the eyes of his father
who speaks grudgingly of his admiration. Eben's act is
perhaps one which Ephraim's God would exact from one
of his servants, based as it is on a consciousness of guilt
and a need for expiation. Yet in the reunion of the lovers,
O'Neill is announcing strongly what will be a solution for
those who cannot "belong." It was a concept which he
touched crudely in so early a play as *The Web,* and which
in his final plays he will develop into a major statement:
that when all is lost, the only good is in finding another
being, equally lonely and alienated, in whose presence
comfort can be gained and loneliness forgotten for a time.

At the end, O'Neill's God-oriented tragedy comes to focus
on man. The shift is made without a jar, and the play
achieves a fullness of statement and form which no earlier
work of his had attained. It is a major work of art prepared
by a playwright who in mastering his craft and completely
understanding the implications of his theme had finally
come of age. (pp. 199-225)

> *Travis Bogard, in his* Contour in Time: The
> Plays of Eugene O'Neill, *Oxford University
> Press, Inc., 1972, 491 p.*

Alan Ehrlich   (essay date 1977)

[*In the following essay, Ehrlich compares the use of
"dramatic space" in Tennessee Williams's* A Streetcar
Named Desire *and* Desire under the Elms.]

A Streetcar Named Desire and *Desire Under the Elms*

have a much tighter bond than the word "desire." The
plays have identical subjects: the threat of the destruction
of a family unit by the presence of "desire." The destruction of a family is not a new theme; it has been used in the
drama since the Greeks. The house of Atreus, the house
of Laius, the house of Lear—the house of Kowalski, the
house of Cabot. The disintegration of a family is serious
stuff, the stuff of which tragedy is often made. There is no
simple answer for a 2500 year popularity of the dramatist's concern for the family unit; but as Gaston Bachelard
asserts, the house does assume universal significance. For
Bachelard, the house is the center of stability and intimacy—the corner of the world. Everyone yearns for the concentrated, intimate space of a home—the embodiment of
his dreams (*Poetics of Space,* I-II). To be without a home
can be traumatic. Both Blanche in *A Streetcar Named Desire* and Abbie in *Desire Under the Elms* are homeless;
both are unstable, zealous of inhabiting an intimate space.

In this desire to inhabit an intimate space nests the conflict
for both plays. Using a traditional literary technique, each
playwright sets up an established environment or family
unit into which a potentially destructive agent, the catalyst, enters to disrupt the norm. The conflict of the heroine
with her environment is the heart of both dramas. O'Neill
creates a stronger destructive agent to combat a weaker established environment than Williams does, resulting in
Abbie's more successful alteration of her environment.

Both plays adhere to unity of place: they are compact,
with the entire action taking place within the confines of
one setting. To grasp the potential conflict, an audience
must first apprehend the environment established prior to
the arrival of the destructive agent. It is crucial that the
audience register the set at the initial curtain.

O'Neill's set is distinctive. As the curtain rises we see a
New England farmhouse surrounded by stone walls "with
a wooden gate at center opening on a country road." In
addition to this lateral restriction, the two enormous elms
on each side of the house "bend their trailing branches
down over the roof." The vertical restriction complements
the lateral restriction. But of course to the audience this
limitation might not at first appear threatening. To insure
that it does, O'Neill begins scene one with carefully placed
dialogue. Eben, Simeon, and Peter all comment on the
stone walls built by their father to fence them in. The walls
function like a prison to entrap their victims; the restriction becomes a confinement. This prison-house is the established environment for the remaining action of the
play. As with any prison, the inmates want out. Near the
end of part one, when Simeon and Peter finally gain
enough courage and finances to escape, they carry the
front gate with them, symbolically opening the door for
the possibility of the future escape of their younger brother. Although represented by stone walls, the established
environment is initially weakened through Simeon's and
Peter's escape.

In *A Streetcar Named Desire,* the confinement inherent in
the set is more subtle. With no drooping elms or stones to
wall the characters in, the entrapment is less evident.
Rather than blatant imprisonment, the play's confinement
is the claustrophobia resulting from the loss of privacy,

once Blanche arrives. Jo Mielziner, the designer for Elia Kazan's original 1947 New York production, devised a perfect set to depict this loss of privacy: a transparent back wall looking into the courtyard. This transparent wall can function in a manner similar to O'Neill's stone wall and elms. To Cabot, happy on the farm, the wall and the elms remain merely a wall and elms; to his sons, unhappy on the farm, wall and elms are a visual sign of their psychological imprisonment. To Stanley and Stella, happy in their home prior to Blanche's arrival, the transparent wall remains a normal wall; to Stanley, Stella, and Blanche, unhappy in their overcrowded home after Blanche's arrival, the transparent wall becomes a visual sign of their lack of privacy. In *Desire Under the Elms,* the characters are confined to a space that permits escape only after constant effort. In *A Streetcar Named Desire,* the characters are confined to a cramped space that prevents escape altogether.

Both playwrights take great pains to establish their respective environments prior to the arrival of the destructive agent. In addition to their physical settings, both O'Neill and Williams establish a tone for their established environments. A status quo is set up early in both plays as an obstacle against which each destructive agent must combat. In *Desire Under the Elms,* a totally masculine environment has been established. In his stage directions, O'Neill states, "Everything is neat and in order but the atmosphere is of a men's camp kitchen rather than that of a home." Every family unit is governed by its own principles. For the Cabots, with no woman present for years, home is a particular, masculine, established environment. In *A Streetcar Named Desire,* the established environment is simply a happy marriage—the couple lives in "Elysian Fields." Williams establishes this status quo economically in the initial action. Stanley bellows hello to Stella and tosses her a package of meat which she catches, breathelessly laughing—an action that can be interpreted as a symbol of the sex on which their relationship is based. One gives, the other receives; their alliance is established. Stella's whole life is Stanley. She later tells her sister she cannot bear being away from her husband for even one night; in the opening sequence it is only for a few hours, but she must follow him to the bowling alley to watch him bowl.

The order is firmly entrenched; the action impatiently awaits the arrival of the destructive agent. Perhaps, if either Abbie Putnam or Blanche DuBois had entered passively into her respective established environment, there would have been no ensuing tragedy. However, both Abbie and Blanche are powerful individuals accustomed to dominating their surroundings and getting things on their own terms.

The intrusion of any female into a "men's camp kitchen" should be conflict enough, but O'Neill takes no chances. Abbie Putnam, Cabot's new wife, covers all the female archetypes. She is voluptuous and maternal, seductive and matronly, a Helen and a Demeter combined. As soon as she arrives at the farm, she infringes on Eben's territory—the kitchen. When she first sees Eben, "Her eyes take him in penetratingly with a calculating appraisal of his strength as against hers." At first she begins the scene in a playful, seductive manner. "Be you—Eben? I'm

Abbie—(she laughs) I mean, I'm yer new Maw." However, the playful seduction turns more and more bitter. After she realizes Eben will be a difficult conquest, she hardens her attack. "This be my farm—this be my hum—this be my kitchen! . . . An' upstairs—that be my bedroom—an' my bed! . . . I hain't bad nor mean—'ceptin' fur an enemy—but I got t' fight fur what's due me out o' life, if I ever 'spect t' git it." Within five minutes Abbie has taken over; she has altered the established order previously weakened by the escape of Simeon and Peter. Eben furiously flings off her arm, calls her a witch, and yells out that he hates her. But the damage is done: Abbie's foot is more than in the door. Part one ends with Abbie washing *her* dishes.

Blanche takes a streetcar named Desire, transfers to one called Cemeteries, and arrives at Elysian Fields—the heart of the New Orleans French Quarter. Like Abbie, she is at first completely out of place. Williams' stage directions read: "Her appearance is incongruous to this setting. She is daintily dressed . . . as if she were arriving at a summer tea or cocktail party. . . ." Like Abbie, Blanche immediately tries to alter her surroundings. She covers a naked light bulb with a paper lantern; she re-covers a bedroom chair. Blanche's arrival mostly affects Stella, who feels compelled to wait on her older sister. In part, Blanche too alters the established environment. She tells Mitch, "I've done so much with this place since I've been here."

Both Abbie and Blanche attempt to revamp the old order and establish a new one. But the situation gets increasingly more difficult for both, as Eben and Stanley wish to maintain the status quo. Both at first resent the women, but strong love / hate attractions and repulsions later occur. The incest incipient in each plot is eventually consummated. Between the action and the setting is a cyclical pattern. The claustrophobic setting limits all alternatives and invites sin, which in turn is a product of the cramped quarters crowding its occupants to the point of desperation. Constraint converges from all sides sealing off all possible modes of escape. The confining environment creates tension for any character who is out of step with it. In *Desire Under the Elms,* Eben feels entrapped. He is the vulnerable character and he gets seduced by the stronger. In *A Streetcar Named Desire,* Blanche feels entrapped. She is the vulnerable character and she gets raped by the stronger. When a character feels entrapped within his environment, extreme desperation and confusion await him.

In *Desire Under the Elms,* Eben feels imprisoned from the beginning. "His defiant, dark eyes remind one of a wild animal's in captivity. Each day is a cage in which he finds himself trapped but inwardly unsubdued. There is a fierce repressed vitality about him." Later, when the brothers talk of their father's strength in comparison to theirs, only Eben is optimistic. "I'm gittin' stronger. I kin feel it growin' in me—growin' an' growin'—till it'll bust out—!" And "bust out" it does, but only after it is indirectly displaced toward Abbie. Abbie too feels the restraint; and as the hot New England sun bakes the suppressed desire, the audience waits impatiently for the explosion. It comes in scene three of part two—the climax of the play as well as

of their relationship. Abbie: " 'I'll kiss ye pure, Eben—
same 's if I was a Maw t' ye—an' ye kin kiss me back's if
yew was my son—my boy—sayin' good-night t' me! Kiss
me, Eben.' (They kiss in restrained fashion. Then suddenly wild passion overcomes her. She kisses him lustfully
again and again"). He backs off here and can overcome the
presence of Maw's spirit he feels in the room only after he
thinks of her vengeance on his father. He kisses Abbie,
"releasing all his pent-up passion" and confesses his suppressed love for her. With this kiss comes a total release
of the thing he felt "growin' an' growin' " within him that
was seen earlier in the play and felt since his mother's
death.

The location of this climactic scene is crucial. Abbie intends to control the entire house, and her final conquest
must happen "in the one room hain't [hers] yet." She waits
for Eben in the parlor where his mother died and was laid
out. This "repressed room like a tomb" with all its "preserved ugliness" has been sealed off to the family for years.
The claustrophobic room in which time has been frozen
with its stagnant air is about to be given new life. Abbie's
attempt at seduction eventually succeeds. With it, Maw's
mysterious spiritual presence leaves the farm for good.
Abbie: "She went back t' her grave that night we fust done
it, remember? I hain't felt her about since." Maw leaves;
the old environment is completely altered. Abbie has established a new environment, and her original opponent,
Eben, is now a crucial component of the new order.

In *A Streetcar Named Desire,* the weaker character, the
one who feels most out of place in the established environment, is Blanche. Like Abbie, she tries to revamp the environment; but unlike Abbie, she is unable to conquer her
antagonist. Stella is willing to wait on Blanche, but Stanley
is not. Blanche tries to adjust the established environment,
but Stanley is not taken in by his sister-in-law's airs. "You
come in here and sprinkle the place with powder and spray
perfume and cover the light bulb with a paper lantern, and
lo and behold the place has turned into Egypt and you are
the Queen of the Nile! Sitting on your throne and swilling
down my liquor!" Blanche tries to alter the environment
but it is too firm. Because her arrival shrinks the two-room
apartment in half and prevents privacy, Stanley must defend his home against the enemy. All he wants is to return
to the lifestyle he enjoyed before Blanche arrived. "It's
gonna be all right again betwcen you [Stella] and me the
way that it was. . . . God, honey, it's gonna be sweet
when we can make noise in the night the way we used to
and get the colored lights going with nobody's sister behind the curtains to hear us! . . . And wasn't we happy
together, wasn't it all okay till she showed here?" Stanley
evaluates the problem and pursues the solution. Three into
two won't go; Blanche must leave.

After Stanley reveals Blanche's sordid history and gives
her the bus ticket back to Laurel, the heroine is clearly
awaiting her fate. Scene nine opens with Blanche's tragic
theme, the "Varsouviana," playing in the background.
"The music is in her mind; she is drinking to escape it and
the sense of disaster closing in on her. . . ." The air in
her small cubicle is hot and stagnant. She artificially attempts refreshening it with her electric fan "turning back

and forth across her," but it can only recirculate the stale
air, not replenish it. Mitch enters, turns off the fan, turns
on the lights, tears the paper lantern off the light bulb, and
seals her inevitable doom. In scene ten the fall is continued. This time the agent is Stanley, the "executioner" she
had recognized from the beginning. She sits in the claustrophobic room, and confusion, desperation, and destruction await her.

At first the confusion is seen by the workings of her imagination, telling Stanley about Shep Huntleigh's nonexistent
phone call. Stanley believes her for a while, but when she
is momentarily dazed by his demands for details about the
telegram, he finally realizcs thc truth. "There isn't a god-
dam thing but imagination!" He follows her into the bedroom. She begins to feel cramped in the congested space.
Stanley and the enviornment close in around her. "Lurid
reflections appear on the walls around Blanche. The shadows are of a grotesque and menacing form." Stanley goes
into the bathroom and she tries to phone Shep for help.
No time. She hangs up and desperately runs to the kitchen
for escape, but the house is too small and menacing. "The
night is filled with inhuman voices like cries in a jungle.
The shadows and lurid reflections move sinuously as
flames along the wall spaces." There is no privacy, no escape. The transparent wall now performs its theatrical
function and allows the street scenes outside (prostitution,
alcohol, looting) to become a part of the calamitous scene
inside. All avenues of escape are blocked—her last hope,
a desperation telegram to Shep. "In desperate, desperate
circumstances! Help me! Caught in a trap." Stanley enters
in his "brilliant silk pajamas," deliberately sets the phone
back on the hook, as the "blue piano" turns into "the roar
of an approaching locomotive," and settles his account
once and for all: "We've had this date with each other
from the beginning!" And all this while Stella is at the hospital in labor.

Confinement pervades both plays. The claustrophobic environment entraps its victims and eventually leads to their
respective tragedies. In ***Desire Under the Elms,*** the environment is not as escape-proof. Simeon and Peter escape
the farm at the play's beginning. Because the environment
is weakened at the outset and because Abbie Putnam is extremely strong, the established order can be altered. Because Eben wants no part of the old order and every part
of the new, he is assimilated by it, and a new established
order is constructed. In *A Streetcar Named Desire,* the established environment (the happy marriage) is indestructible. Blanche is more delicate than Abbie, Stanley more inflexible than Eben. As a result, unlike Abbie, Blanche cannot alter the environment. Left with no alternative, she
must find ways to escape it.

Williams utilizes two devices to demonstrate Blanche's
need for escape—her drinking and her baths. Blanche is
a heavy drinker and Williams makes her drink to escape
her problems. Besides drinking, her only escape is into the
bathroom for a "hot tub." As the tension heats, so does
the water. Finally, in the tense birthday party scene when
Blanche has been stood up, forty-five minutes after her
bath, Stanley remarks, "it's hot in here with the steam
from the bathroom." But her "hot tubs" are inadequate

escape. She remains entrapped and is ultimately crushed by her environment.

In addition to Williams' use of alcohol and baths, both playwrights utilize yet another device of attempted escape for the characters who feel threatened by their environment. These characters are often described as caged animals who long for their freedom. This longing is subdued in every outward direction—the only alternative is upward. In both *Desire Under the Elms* and *A Streetcar Named Desire,* the captive characters constantly cry out to the sky.

Simeon and Peter despise their captivity by their father and his farm and want to escape to California at the play's very opening. They discuss their prospects excitedly. Simeon: " 'Fortunes layin' just atop o' the ground waitin' t' be picked! Solomon's mines, they says!' (For a moment they continue looking up at the sky . . .)." But their longing for freedom (symbolically shown by their gazing to the sky) is ironically juxtaposed with the cruel reality of their situation. Their eyes drop immediately back down to the earth. Peter: "Here—it's stones atop o' the ground—stones atop o' stones—makin' stone walls—. . . to fence us in!" Eben, too, feels his captivity and begins the play with a defiant apostrophe to the sky, "God! Purty!" After being teased by his two older brothers about going to Min's, Eben escapes the unpleasant situation by running out and standing by the gate, "staring up at the sky." A moment later, "Eben stretches his arms up to the sky—rebelliously." These acts of defiance can only be directed upward. The boundless sky is a perfect device to mock the characters' frustration.

A Streetcar Named Desire has no equivalent to the blatant stone walls. The claustrophobia is the result of an overcrowded house. Blanche's arrival shrinks the house in half. She looks to the sky for her salvation. In scene three when she chats with Mitch, "she looks up at the sky" and says, "There's so much—so much confusion in the world. . . . " There's "confusion" in the cramped apartment, but there is plenty of room above her head. Later in scene six, Mitch fumbles around for her key. When he finally finds it, Blanche exclaims, "Eureka! Honey, you open the door while I take a last look at the sky." Already the ensuing desperation is sensed. Her "last look" recalls that of a prisoner just prior to his return to the cell.

Rather than for her freedom, Blanche longs for her privacy: "When I think of how divine it is going to be to have such a thing as privacy once more—I could weep with joy!" In fact, freedom is one of the last things Blanche wants; to the contrary, she needs security. Whether it comes in the form of Stanley's best friend, Mitch, or the strange doctor from the state institution who escorts her out, Blanche remains in need of support, always depending "on the kindness of strangers." It is peculiar that Williams chooses such a dependent woman to overcrowd the household. One would suppose such a claustrophobic environment would be ideal for an insecure person. But Williams loves irony, and it is for that he chooses such an heroine. It is the same irony that names the streetcar that carried her to her downfall *Desire*—a "rattle-trap streetcar that bangs through the Quarter, up one old narrow street

and down another . . . " until it finally arrives at its destination—"Elysian Fields." The streetcar took her there, and more importantly it can take her away. Just as Williams ironically has the streetcar as a possible vehicle of escape clanging in the background to punctuate the frustration, O'Neill has a big poster of "a ship in full sail and the word 'California' in big letters" right in the middle of the rear wall of the kitchen. Both playwrights effectively mock their characters' tragic situations.

If my theory holds true—that the claustrophobic environment is a crucial determinant of the tragedies—then it is reasonable to assume that the more crowded with people, the more confusing the situation. Conveniently, both plays contain group-party scenes.

Stanley has his friends over to the house to play poker. There being no room, the sisters wisely choose to go out for the evening. When they return, the two-room apartment is at its most crowded point in the play, and the result is utter chaos. Stanley is drunk and uncontrollable. When Blanche and Mitch dance to the music of his radio, Stanley vehemently tosses it out the window. The fiasco ends with Stanley's cold shower and warm, tender reconciliation with Stella. This reconciliation occurs, significantly, outside the apartment. It is the one time since Blanche arrived that Stanley and Stella are close to each other. Blanche is inside, still trying to alter the environment, while outside, the happy couple briefly reestablish their old ways.

In *Desire Under the Elms,* Cabot invites the townspeople over to celebrate the birth of his alleged son (part three, scene one). Everyone guesses the true father except Cabot, and a strong element of vicious ridicule prevails. While Cabot dances merrily inside, the young lovers exchange vows outside. Next, Cabot goes outside and informs his son of Abbie's old plan of calculated seduction, which Eben misinterprets. O'Neill's result, like Williams', is also chaotic, with all the simultaneous action going on. Eben "chokes with rage" and threatens to kill his stepmother. Cabot stops him and they grapple for a brief moment. The total misunderstanding directly leads to Abbie's murdering her child—the major problem with the play.

O'Neill's ending is melodramatic. The heroine is forced to kill her son as the only means left her to prove her love for Eben. The manner in which Abbie murders her son is revealing. In a play perfused with stone walls, dead rooms, and frustrated desires, Abbie symbolically chooses to murder her son in a most appropriate manner—suffocation. However consistent the manner of murder may be, the action itself borders on the incredible. In *Desire Under the Elms,* the outside agent, Abbie Putnam, entered an already established environment and completely altered it to her own standards. The result is a totally new, stronger, established environment comprised primarily of her and Eben. The old environment is initially weakened by the escape of Simeon and Peter. Next, Abbie enters to change it even more. Her arrival shakes the household: Cabot is driven from the house to sleep with the animals in the barn; Maw's mysterious spirit finally abandons the farm for good; a new, illegitimate child briefly appears on the scene. Abbie Putnam obviously leaves her mark.

O'Neill's final stage direction for the couple reads: "They both stand for a moment looking up raptly in attitudes strangely aloof and devout." Their gazing to the sky has run full circle. Eben utters an identical "Purty" as he did at the play's opening; but because he no longer feels entrapped by his environment, the tone of the line is *devout* rather than *defiant.* Eben and Abbie form a new bond to rise above Cabot and his farm. For Eben to believe his father at the end of the party scene about Abbie's old plan of calculated seduction rather than Abbie seems unlikely, and that Abbie would find it necessary for such a melodramatic murder to convince Eben is highly improbable. Because Abbie takes over, she is the dominating character in the newly established environment that supplanted the old. Actions should conform to the new order, and she should not, therefore, have to resort to such theatrics. The murder is unbelievable because the action is not consistent with the newly established dramatic space that O'Neill created. The inconsistency is a major obstacle for a successful production.

In comparison, *A Streetcar Named Desire* also has a newborn baby appearing at the end. For the finale, Blanche is escorted out by the doctor. Precisely *after* this action is completed, the child appears. The household was too crowded for a sister-in-law, as she is an outsider to the established order, the marriage; but for a son there is plenty of room. Blanche has overstayed her welcome but Baby Kowalski is accepted with open arms. "Eunice descends to Stella and places the child in her arms. . . . Stella accepts the child. . . . " The displacement is successful; the family is unified once more. In contrast to O'Neill's final action, Williams has found the perfect gesture to reinforce the dramatic space and environment he created. The established environment, the happy marriage, could not be shaken by a sister-in-law; only a child could be incorporated into it. (pp. 126-36)

> *Alan Ehrlich, "A Streetcar Named Desire under the Elms: A Study of Dramatic Space in 'A Streetcar Named Desire' and 'Desire under the Elms'," in* Tennessee Williams: A Tribute, *edited by Jac Tharpe, University Press of Mississippi, 1977, pp. 126-36.*

Mara Lemanis   (essay date 1978)

[*In the following essay, Lemanis disputes the common assumption among critics that* Desire under the Elms *fulfills the criteria of tragic drama.*]

In his essay, "Tragedy and Melodrama," Robert B. Heilman has made a distinction between disastrous and horrific events occurring in daily life that provide the modus operandi for many dramatic works, and the ordering of perception that comprises tragedy. The disaster drama, dealing with the crisis of man victimized either by other men or by an indifferent or hostile universe, has often gained easy access to tragic rank, but according to Heilman, the validity of tragic experience can be drawn only from a situation in which

> . . . the crucial actions of heroes, though they are exacted by a powerful sense of moral obliga-

tion, nevertheless become infused with guilt. For these heroes the two counterimperatives have so much authority that no observer can say with assurance, "It would be better if [they] had done so and so." . . . Such heroes . . . incorporate the dividedness of a humanity whose values . . . create an apparently insoluble situation . . . [they] can never force out of consciousness the imperatives that [they] run against.

All the commonly recognized hallmarks of tragedy pervade the schema of Eugene O'Neill's *Desire Under the Elms:* the establishment of internal conflict within the central characters; circumstances that require a seemingly inexorable resolution; a heroine who forces that resolution, accepts its nemesis, and consequently arrives at a deeper understanding of her fate.

But since a rubrication of tragic construction alone cannot disclose its experiential values, we do not assent to any work of art that does little more than keep the faith of formula alive. An examination of the confirmation process, the language and behavior that demonstrate the formula's meaning in a vital and coherent pattern, is necessary. Out of tradition, critics still place *Desire* within the tragic genre; could this mark a reflex observance of little more than the tragic formula, without regard for the distinctions between tragedy and disaster? In reevaluating *Desire,* I will focus upon the dialogue and actions surrounding the heroine's (Abbie's) murder of her child, since this is the pivotal act identifying her supposed tragic impetus, and leading to the resolution by which Abbie and Eben's transfiguration occurs.

Abbie, like the tragic heroine, is split between different forces or motives—her materialistic values, her security needs as opposed to her love for Eben—but the split is not compellingly drawn as an intrinsic part of her character; it does not co-exist in her nature in that definitive way we have come to associate with tragic stature as evinced by an Orestes, an Antigone, down through Macbeth and Hamlet. In all of these figures, irreconcilable imperatives cause great psychic and moral schisms which they reveal in forceful dialectic tension, through language that delivers the force of equally demanding alternatives.

Abbie's language and actions leading up to and culminating in the killing of her baby are invested with a singleness of purpose so compressed, it has no room for anguish or struggle over choice. Abbie does assert her love for Eben over her possessive impulse; but her sacrificial act entails no immediate pangs of conscience or moral awe. She does not struggle with counter impulses so much as superimposes one impulse over another (her desire to prove her love to Eben taking precedence over her desire to possess the farm). In her earlier history, the baby has not been meaningful to her except as a vehicle by which to obtain the farm; and the baby's value to her remains that of a vehicle, this time one by which she can prove her love to Eben and thereby regain her life-joy and self-protection. Abbie acts out of expediency, not necessity. Her "tragic recognition" consists of expressing remorse for the act after its execution, and acquiescing to the justice of punishment, but we are presented with an awareness so confined in its conception of the dignity and value of life, that it easily falls within the range of a mechanism or reflex posited in her conscience from outside:

> I didn't want t' do it.—I hated myself for doin' it. I loved him. He was so purty—dead spit 'n' image o' yew. But I loved yew more—an' yew was goin' away—far off whar I'd never see ye agen, never kiss ye, never feel ye pressed agin me agen—ye said ye hated him an' wished he was dead—ye said if it hadn't been for him comin' it'd be the same's afore between us.

This self-reproach conveys what a maudlin desperation has quickened her misguided act toward its disastrous outcome, and the juxtaposition of " . . . I loved him." with "He was so purty . . . " exemplifies a life trivialized to the point of a *tragoedia ad absurdum*. More evidence of Abbie's reductive sensibility comes through her words about Ephraim when Eben thinks it is his father whom she has killed, not the baby: " . . . But that's what I ought t' done, hain't it? I oughter killed him instead! Why didn't ye tell me?" Though she may have gained some conceptual facility here in noting the interchangeability of one life for another, she has not lost the petty perspective that facile slayings deliver one from obstacles.

A killing or murder creates horror regardless of circumstances, but there is a crucial difference between a murder of tragic import and one that is generally deplorable because it wastes life. A tragic perspective derives in part from a depiction of the substantive dignity of human life. This dignity may be assessed unfolding in dramatic exposition, or it may inhere in the contending imperatives that beset them (as in *Antigone,* where the injunction to obey the dignity of a sacred rite contends with the injunction to obey the dignity of a civil law, or communal order).

Learning to love Eben is an important act of self-development for Abbie, but it does not take her into the larger area of tragic awareness and ontological concern. The decision to take a life is an ultimate recourse in this expanded area where stringent moral demands war with equally stringent personal demands. It is their irreconcilability that leads the tragic heroine indomitably to uphold her value, a choice that does not lend to compromise, and is burdened by the admonition of its inevitability.

Before committing her crime, Abbie tries to explain to Eben how distorted and out of context is Ephraim's disclosure of her intentions to have the child in order to inherit the farm and cut Eben off:

> EBEN. Hain't it true? It hain't no good in yew lyin'.
>
> ABBIE. *pleadingly.* Eben, listen—ye must listen—it was long ago—afore we done nothin'—yew was scornin' me—goin' t' see Min—when I was lovin' ye—an' I said it t' git vengeance on ye!

But her attempts are unsuccessful. Eben is too enraged to listen, and his accusations escalate to operatic crescendo replete with invocations of ghosts and curses as he shouts about getting his " . . . Maw t' come back t' help him—t' put her cuss on Abbie . . . with Maw comin' out o' her grave at nights . . . " Abbie protests Eben's calumny as

if his words were a decree sealing her doom, delivered ex cathedra, ultimate and non-negotiable. Traditional heroines ruminate at length before succumbing to ultimate deeds, taking great pains to illustrate the and unmistakable reasons impelling them. Even Medea, most decadent of heroines, meditates a considered exposition before undertaking the murder of her children. Abbie, an unconventional tragic figure, heir to the swift temper of a more laconic age, exchews the slow, old character exhumations; she fights radical words with radical acts. Thus when Eben confuses the identity of her current feelings with past reasons for bearing the child, she does not have the patience to correct him, but hastens to do away as expeditiously as possible with any vestige of that past identity. Streaking through her prologue to exigency is this rapid-transit logic:

> If I could prove t' ye I wa'n't schemin' t' steal from ye—so's everythin' could be jest the same with us, lovin' each other jest the same, kissin' an' happy the same's we've been happy afore he come—if I could do it—ye'd love me agen, wouldn't ye? Ye'd kiss me agen? Ye wouldn't never leave me, would ye?

We feel here the urgency of desperation, yes, inevitability, no. The plaintive " . . . Ye wouldn't never leave me, would ye?" carries the tone of a yearning need to recapture the secure joy of living in Eben's love. Security-seeking is a very human predicament evoking pathos, but it is far from the maturity of a stout crisis worth tragic delineation.

Edgar F. Racey, Jr., in "Myth as Tragic Structure in *Desire Under the Elms,*" says that " . . . if the wrong done to Eben's mother by Ephraim hangs over the play like a curse—then Eben and Abbie may be seen as the agents of the process of justice, directed against Ephraim." Then, referring to the Hyppolytus of either Euripides or Seneca, he states, "like Theseus, Ephraim must atone for his rash injustice." But in both Euripides and Seneca, Theseus is the real agent of the purportedly tragic deed, whereas in *Desire,* his alleged counterpart, Ephraim, is not. Abbie is the agent of the ostensibly tragic deed and the agent of justice against herself and Eben, primarily, and against Ephraim, in but a subordinate way. Ephraim is condemned to loneliness as he always has been, by his own deeds and standards. His predicament is no more nor less than it ever has been, really, since he has never found anyone with whom to share his hard ethic.

To look upon Abbie and Eben as agents of Eben's mother operating against Ephraim is to make Abbie's actions even more automated than they are under the pressure of Eben's false construction. A curse or fateful symbol has significance in tragic drama when the central actor consciously incorporates it as the mainspring for his own ethic, as Oedipus, Macbeth, or Hamlet do, but not when it is thrust upon characters who cannot engage it because they do not vitally acknowledge it. In such a case they become mere ploys or tools of fate.

When Eben submits to Abbie's love, he acknowledges or interprets the fateful symbol of his mother's intent to bring them together for retribution against Ephraim. Eben: "I see it—I see why. It's her vengeance on him—so's she can rest quiet in her grave!" So divine intervention blesses Abbie and Eben's "fierce, bruising kiss," but then, vanishes from the remaining pivotal action. For by the time Eben accuses Abbie of treachery, he has forgotten his mother's endorsement of her. It is both logically and organically unlikely that a man who has spent his life brooding over the wrong done his mother and how to rectify it, can truly believe his own accusations about the very woman who nine months before had received his mother's ghost seal of approval to collaborate against their mutual enemy. Presumably the endorsement came at a moment of sufficiently heightened recognition for it to have borne a durable enough imprint to last nine months. How is it that he can remember his mother's ghost when he needs a threat with which to curse Abbie, but cannot remember the critical role it played in blessing their union? Eben has incorporated the symbol that has driven his life only to shunt it aside at the moment of truth. This is not tragic irony used to expose an indelible character flaw, but a dramatization of how a man under the influence of rash, muddled emotions can jump to conclusions.

Still the greatest fallacy results when Abbie takes these same muddled emotions seriously, as if they had been uttered with weighty conviction. She acts with grim determination to put to rest intermediate feelings. How chaotic—and how out of tragic character. When O'Neill's ghost machina deserts, his stage manager takes over, and the climatic action toward which all speech and sense would have been irrevocably mounted had they effected the process of tragic denouement, simply crumbles under a specious, convulsive staginess. The effect is melodramatic surprise and horror.

John Masefield, in his preface to the *Tragedy of Nan,* has noted that "Tragedy at its best is a vision of the heart of life that can only be laid bare in the agony and exultation of dreadful acts . . . " the power of which comes " . . . from a delighted brooding on excessive, terrible things." This may not conform to the view of tragedy enunciated within this thesis, but it is certainly a compliment that could be paid, without excess, to **Desire Under the Elms.**

Although the criteria I have enlisted here derive from a rather strictured tragic format, one using a predominantly historical focus, they are not meant to preclude an overview that places the whole of the human condition within a more generic tragic perspective. In "Tragedy and the Tragic Spirit," an introduction to *The Forms of Drama,* Robert W. Corrigan reaches toward an existential comprehension of the tragic sense of life when he recognizes tragic stature in the " . . . human will which dares to stand up against the universe and struggle with necessity." He speaks of tragedy as " . . . that quality in man which defies the status quo of being human; and . . . is the protest against the limitations of being a man."

This conflict between the assertive self and the indifferent universe is what provides the absurd ratio that equates life with a seemingly meaningless game of chance. Only recognition of this absurdity and an insistence upon preserving one's own value despite it, fills individual choice with the necessary dignity to turn the meaningless conflict of a game into a meaningful conflict in the sphere of the tragic-absurd.

Existential defiance of fate is not in Abbie and Eben's arsenal. If we construe victimization as their fate, then scheming against Ephraim is their arsenal, though Abbie schemes to possess the farm out of self-protective instincts, and Eben out of the more ennobling dictum of avenging another's (his mother's) victimization. Their defiance never shapes and forces their being into that greater existential quotient which comes from plumbing the division between the assertive self and the indifferent universe with an act that challenges one's fate, and societal and universal laws in such a way that one's own life, having purposefully invaded that realm of life-at-large in the world, becomes many times magnified, made resonant with a profounder sense of the power of its being. Abbie and Eben's love is not challenge enough for their fate. Their love closes them in upon their own small world; it does not extend them outward in confrontation with a large universe.

According to many critics, lack of exalted language is the criterion by which O'Neill is judged an inadequate tragedian. But simplicity of expression is often an index to epic strength, and the character of Ephraim's language illustrates this well. In a long soliloquy in Scene Two of Part Two in the play, Ephraim talks of how he has come to choose a hard life to worship a hard God, how he has had to become hard himself to be worthy of God's dictum, and lonely in his endurance of it. The simple rhetoric Ephraim uses carries the intonation of a prophet's verse, and the monolithic power of a juggernaut forging intractable paths. The very rhythms of his speech convey intense concentration of power. It could be asked how big a stone is necessary to hurl against this builder of stones in order to fell him. Certainly Eben and Abbie, even drawing upon spiritual help and throwing a baby into the bargain, are not big enough for such a feat. Only Ephraim's own hardness, weighing him down like a mammoth stone that he has hewn for himself, is equal to the task. Having chosen his stony fate so many times before Abbie and Eben leave him to yet again, he is undaunted by their life-in-death affirmation, which though joyous, rings a weak echo to his own perverse affirmation of life-as-death.

For Ephraim has created a kind of mute life out of his stones: he has made corn grow out of them and has gleaned sustenance from them; his instincts are with the animals who offer him mute sympathy when he seeks them as comfort from his loneliness. Talking about his sons Simeon and Peter, he notes, " . . . They hated me 'cause I was hard. I hated them 'cause they was soft. They coveted the farm without knowin' what it meant. It made me bitter'n wormwood . . . " To Ephraim the farm has meant a holy mission in life, wherefrom stems his superhuman attachment to it, making him seem inhuman to those (Abbie, Simeon, and Peter) who want just to possess it for self-enrichment. Yet everything the farm yields has been sown with the seeds of death, for Ephraim envisions burning the farm in immolation on the day when his life ends.

Abbie and Eben don't know what it means to be hard like Ephraim, whereas Ephraim doesn't know what it means to be soft. Periodically, he has tried to seek out that softness, journeying out West to easy land, wedding a woman from time to time, always to return to his self-imposed hardships. Ephraim, twisting nature into conformance with his own dour image, has created a life denying love, while Abbie and Eben, imitating nature, have succeeded in creating love. Abbie persuades Eben—" . . . Ye been fightin' yer nature ever since the day I come— . . . Nature'll beat ye, Eben . . . "—until he does the natural thing and yields to her. Yet the dialogue and poetry of their love, for all its affirmative feeling, cannot match Ephraim's stoic obstinacy, which dominates the play like a stern mastiff of death.

A brief portrait of each one's sensibility to life clarifies the contrast between the two lovers and the old man:

> Eben's poesy of love: " . . . She's like t' night, she's soft 'n' wa'm, her eyes kin wink like a star, her mouth's wa'm, her arms 're wa'me, she smells like a wa'm plowed field, she's purty . . . "
>
> Abbie's song to nature: "Hain't the sun strong an' hot? Ye kin feel it burnin' into the earth—Nature—makin' thin's grow—bigger 'n' bigger—burnin' inside ye—makin' ye want t' grow—into somethin' else—"
>
> Ephraim's ode to God and self: "God's hard, not easy! God's in the stones! Build my church on a rock . . . Stones. I picked 'em up an' piled 'em into walls. Ye kin read the years o' my life in them walls, every day a hefted stone, climbin' over the hills up and down, fencin' in the fields that was mine, whar I'd made thin's grow out o' nothin'—like the will o' God, like the servant o' his hand. It wa'n't easy. It was hard an' He made me hard fur it . . . "

Abbie and Eben have both connived to own the farm, have lied to Ephraim, and have very nearly miscarried their crime into a horror farce before reaching a state of atonement and nobility that reads out of sequence, so unconvincingly grafted on to their characters it seems. Yet toward the end of the play, when judgment is imminent, Ephraim says, " . . . He'd ought t' been my son, Abbie. Ye'd ought t' loved me. I'm a man. If ye'd loved me, I'd never told no sheriff on ye no matter what ye did if they was t' brile me alive!" This ringing covenant of distorted superhuman loyalty can only come from a man who has consecrated his life to nothing less than a monomaniacal aspiration to union with the infinite.

The philosophic question to be asked about a man whose death / God worship dominates his human capacities, is whether an Ephraim is not of the same species that generated a Hitler or a Stalin. It could be said of both dictators that they pursued monomaniacal goals to union with infinite power, but it would stretch the imagination greatly to construe deliberate acts of barbarism in terms of tragic stature. For Ephraim, pushing past ordinary human endurance has little to do with capturing wordly power, and everything to do with the intangible reward of a monk receiving grace for and from his labors. Neither does Ephraim's monk-dictator shackle his co-workers to his ideology: when Simeon and Peter leave, he does not try to stop them; he is not a concentration-camp boss militating

against anyone's right to leave the farm. One never senses that it is futile to rebel against Ephraim's authority, but no one ever does, directly, because everyone secretes an ambition to inherit the farm. This then, is a slavery that has been chosen as much as imposed.

After a glib charity has interceded to ennoble Eben's vengeance and Abbie's possessiveness and lust, transforming them into a self-sacrificing love, Ephraim emerges larger than they through his characteristic rigor. He has been constant throughout victimizing himself and others for his queer puritanical creed, neither changing nor growing, nevertheless challenging the limits of man's being with his harsh exactitude. It is as if two crows had been given an eagle's plumes, and the eagle had never been given wings: the nimbus of communion projected on the lovers does not rise to the force of Ephraim's one-dimensional, relentless pursuit of God. Abbie and Eben experience the metamorphosis and rebirth of a tragic hero and heroine, but Ephraim is the man with tragic stature, truncated and "growin' ripe on the bough" though it is. Such misalliance between stature and deed has produced the dramatic hybrid, a miscegenated tragedy. (pp. 46-55)

> Mara Lemanis, " 'Desire under the Elms' and Tragic Form: A Study of Misalliance," in The South Dakota Review, *Vol. 16, No. 3, Autumn, 1978, pp. 46-55.*

Jean Chothia   (essay date 1979)

[*Chothia is an English educator and critic. In the following excerpt, she demonstrates that O'Neill's use of language in* Desire under the Elms *is essential to the themes of the play.*]

[Verbal] patterning is . . . imperative to the structure of **Desire Under the Elms.** This is the opening sequence of the play:

> (*It is sunset . . . The sky above the roof is suffused with deep colours . . . Eben Cabot . . . stares up at the sky. He sighs with a puzzled awe and blurts out with halting appreciation.*)
>
> EBEN. God! Purty!
>
> (*. . . Simeon and Peter come in from their work in the fields . . . Their shoulders stoop a bit from years of farm work. They clump heavily along in their clumsy thick-soled boots caked with earth. Their clothes, their faces, hands, bare arms and throats are earth-stained. They stand together for a moment in front of the house and, as if with one impulse, stare dumbly up at the sky, leaning on their hoes. Their faces have a compressed, unresigned expression. As they look upward, this softens.*)
>
> SIMEON. (*grudgingly*) Purty.
>
> PETER. Ay-eh.
>
> SIMEON. (*suddenly*) Eighteen year ago.
>
> PETER. What?
>
> SIMEON. Jenn. My woman. She died.

PETER. I'd fergot.

SIMEON. I rec'lect—now an' agin. Makes it lonesome. She'd hair long's a hoss's tail—an' yaller like gold!

PETER. Waal—she's gone. (. . .) They's gold in the West, Sim.

SIMEON. (. . .) In the sky?

PETER. Waal—in a manner o' speakin'—thar's the promise. (*Growing excited.*) Gold in the sky—in the west—Golden Gate—Californi-a!—Golden West!—fields o' gold!

SIMEON. (*excited in his turn*) Fortunes layin' just atop o' the ground waitin' t' be picked! Solomon's mines, they says! (. . .)

PETER. (*with sardonic bitterness*) Here—it's stones atop o' the ground—stones atop o' stones—makin' stone walls—year atop o' year—him 'n' yew 'n' me 'n' then Eben—makin' stone walls fur him to fence us in!

SIMEON. We've wuked. Give our strength. Give our years. Ploughed 'em under in the ground (. . .)—rottin'—makin' soil for his crops! (*A pause.*) Waal—the farm pays good for hereabouts.

PETER. If we ploughed in Californi-a, they'd be lumps o' gold in the furrow—!

SIMEON. Californi-a's t'other side o' earth, a'most. We got t' calc'late—

PETER. (*after a pause*) 'Twould be hard fur me, too, to give up what we've 'arned here by our sweat.

O'Neill makes use of the stage picture, filling the stage with golden light to suggest sunset and emphasizing, by their earthiness and their clumsy gait, the incongruity of the farm-hands with the stage-pastoral Romantic light. But O'Neill is no Belasco. (A point he makes himself when he uses the same device more explicitly in *A Moon For The Misbegotten.* Here he teases the audience into recognition of the play as play when Jamie gestures towards the sunrise saying 'rise of curtain, Act-Four stuff'.) His interest is not with stage effects but with creating an impression of verbal poverty. Through lighting and gesture, the upturned face and the softened expression, O'Neill reminds his audience of what must be a virtually universal experience—that of wonder before a magnificent sunset. He then has two characters in succession utter the single weak adjective 'purty', as an expression of that wonder. The silent contemplation and the halting statement about personal loss, 'Jenn. My woman. She died.', draw out the moment, emphasizing how tongue-tied the men are. The adjective is used again several times and always in a similar context of significant human experience so that tension between word and feeling is, again, made painfully apparent. The word 'somethin'' is used in much the same way, and three 'stalling words'—words behind which the characters habitually retreat when the world becomes too complex—'waal', 'mebbe' and 'ayeh', are used repeatedly by all the characters. O'Neill thus epitomizes the extreme inar-

George C. Scott as Ephraim and Colleen Dewhurst as Abbie in a production of Desire under the Elms.

ticulacy of his characters in these few words. As he does also in *Anna Christie,* where the inarticulacy is more directly stated by Chris: 'Anna lilla! Ay—(*He fights for words to express himself, but finds none—miserably—with a sob.*)—Ay can't say it. Good night, Anna'. And so he is free to make other parts of his dialogue resonant, without forfeiting the impression that the speech is realistic. It is in fact, as we can already see, highly contrived.

Even in the brief extract quoted here, we find a shift in the expressive quality of the utterance. There is a quickening of rhythm with the introduction of the word 'gold' which creates an effect of excited thought forcing its way into speech, when a series of thought associations is generated. The substitution of a second word, 'stones', cuts the excitement short. The creative thought association is replaced by that method of circling about a single meaning that O'Neill developed in *The Hairy Ape.* The words 'gold in the West—fields o' gold' and 'stones atop o' stones—year atop o' year' reverberate through the play, usually balanced against each other in any given sequence, and they become identified, increasingly surely, the one with dream and the other with reality. To those pitted against Nature in the fight for the New England soil, Californi-a is El Dorado. The brothers' recurrent song, 'For I'm off to Californi-a', which by virtue of its rhythm, introduces yet another way of saying into the dialogue of the play, becomes a ritualistic chant. They use it to convert their defiance into a spell which will shut out the realities of their harsh life. As the action of the play proceeds, we gradually realize that they are re-enacting the dream which Ephraim had found empty when he, before them, had tried to escape. Already here in the first moments of the play, through the references to 'gold' and 'stones', O'Neill is preparing his audience, is setting before them the first elements of the conundrum of repetition and reduplication between generations of a family. All the sons will be seen to reiterate their father's greed for the farm and his lust for Min, whilst Eben who has taken his father's wife will, when deserted, attempt to escape to the gold fields like father and brothers before him. The stones come to signify the obstinacy of the man who has brought fruit to the barren land making it 'pay good', and to signify the harshness of the servitude his sons have endured and the grinding life on the farm. They have symbolic meaning for the characters: 'God's hard, not easy! God's in the stones', says Ephraim, and, 'I made thin's grow out o' nothin'—like the will o'God, like the servant o' his hand . . . an' he made me hard fur it.' Peter's words, ' 'Twould be hard fur me, too', interjected into the silence, in the opening passage, rouse no surprise in Simeon who is supposedly calculating the journey to Californi-a. Each man is revealed as knowing the other's ways of thought so that no explanation is necessary between them of the leap in thought from gold to stones. A number of such moments in the play make it apparent to the audience that reality will always break through fantasy and that, despite the toll it has demanded of them, the farm is where the reality of these men is rooted. We, therefore, have a strong sense of the inevitable when we witness Ephraim, his world collapsed about him at the end of the play, turn finally to the stones for solace:

> Mebbe they's easy gold in the West, but it hain't God's gold. It hain't fur me. I kin hear his voice warnin' me agen t' be hard an' stay on my farm . . . Waal—what d'ye want? God's lonesome hain't He? God's hard an' lonesome.

The need to pare down the verbiage which the use of low-colloquial imposes on O'Neill, obliges him to image such deep concerns as the interaction between individual identity and rootedness in family and place, in a few single words. (pp. 78-81)

> *Jean Chothia, in her* Forging a Language: A Study of the Plays of Eugene O'Neill, *Cambridge University Press, 1979, 243 p.*

Roger Asselineau   (essay date 1980)

[*Asselineau is a French poet who has written extensively on American literature. In the following essay, he explores the religious and philosophical aspects of* Desire under the Elms.]

Though to all appearances O'Neill was primarily a playwright and an experimenter with dramatic forms who never considered himself a thinker, he was in fact desperately trying to express "something" in all his plays. He chose drama as a medium, but, for all his interest in technique, he never considered it an end in itself, but rather a means to live by proxy a certain number of problems which obsessed him. In *Lazarus Laughed,* he speaks of men as "those haunted heroes." Actually this is less a definition of mankind than a description of himself. He composed plays because he had to write in order to liberate himself and exorcise ghosts. It was a compulsion. The result was plays because of his environment, because his father was an actor and he was an "enfant de la balle," but it might have been novels just as well, and he would probably have written better novels than plays, for he was constantly hampered by the limitations of the stage. In his case literary creation was not a gratuitious activity, but an intense imaginative experience, an *Erlebnis.* He lived it. It was a passionate answer to the problems which tormented him with excruciating strength. This is no mere figure of speech. He roamed the world for years in search of a solution, trying to find a remedy for his fundamental despair, giving up the comfort and security of family life and nearly losing his health and life in the process.

After his wandering years, his *Wanderjahre,* when his health broke down and he was obliged to bring his restless comings-and-goings to a close, he went on exploring the world in imagination, not as a dilettante or a tourist in the realms of thought, but as a passionate pilgrim in quest of a shrine at which to worship. Though brought up a Roman Catholic, he lost his faith as an adolescent. Yet his nature abhorred this spiritual vacuum and he ardently looked for a substitute ever after. His religious faith was killed by rationalism and scientific materialism, but the restlessness and violence of his quest for a personal religion sprang from no coldly rational intellect.

Each of his plays is thus not only an experiment in craftsmanship, but also an attempt to find God or at least some justification for the flagrant inconsistencies of the human condition. His interest was less in psychology than in metaphysics. He said so himself in a letter to Joseph Wood Krutch: "Most modern plays are concerned with the relation between man and man, but that does not interest me at all. I am interested only in the relation between man and God."

In spite of its apparent dramatic directness, therefore, *Desire Under the Elms* is essentially, like his other plays, a philosophical tragedy about man and God rather than a naturalistic chunk of life depicting the mores of a bunch of clumsy New England rustics.

Reduced to essentials in this very primitive setting, man appears primarily as an animal. The first specimens whom we have a chance to observe when the curtain rises, Eben and especially Simeon and Peter, look like oxen, eat, work, and behave like a team of oxen, and feel tied up to the other animals of the farm by bonds of brotherhood: ". . . the cows knows us. . . . An' the hosses, an' pigs, an' chickens. . . . They knows us like brothers—and likes us" (Part I, scene 4). They obey their instincts blindly and think only of drinking, eating, and fornicating. Their lust is quite literally bestial, as shown by Eben's account of his visit to Min: "I begun t'beller like a calf an' cuss at the same time . . . an' she got scared, an' I just grabbed holt an' tuk her" (Part I, scene 3). When Abbie courts Eben, the scene is not much different. She kisses him greedily and at first he submits dumbly, but soon, after returning her kisses, he hurls her away from him and, O'Neill tells us, "they stand speechless and breathless, panting like two animals" (Part II, scene 2).

These inarticulate, animal-like creatures differ from their dumb brothers in only one respect (but it is hardly an improvement): they are possessed with the mania for owning things, whether gold or land. They all crave money or title deeds. In short, they bear a strong family likeness to Swift's Yahoos. They have only one redeeming feature: an embryonic sense of beauty which makes them exclaim "purty" in a rather monotonous manner whenever they notice the beauty of their surroundings. The only exception is the sheriff, who at the very end of the play passes very matter-of-fact and anticlimactic comments on the salable value of the farm while Eben and Abbie admire the beauty of the sunrise.

Far from being a free agent, man is thus by and large the slave of his instincts, and O'Neill here revives the old Calvinistic dogma of predestination. As early as his very first play, **The Web,** of the transparent title, he attempted to show that man is caught in a web of circumstances, a web that is not of his own weaving. At the end of **The Web,** O'Neill tells us that Rose, the prostitute, "seems to be aware of something in the room which none of the others can see—perhaps the personification of the ironic life force that has crushed her." In **Desire Under the Elms,** Eben feels trapped in exactly the same way: "Each day," the stage directions inform us, "is a cage in which he finds himself trapped." He is indeed trapped by circumstances—tied up to that bleak New England farm which he somehow considers part of his mother, and he is also psychologically trapped by an all-powerful mother complex which unknown to him determines his whole behavior toward his father as well as toward women in general. His temperament is wholly determined by his heredity: it is a combination of his mother's softness and lack of will, as his father again and again points out, and of his father's aggressiveness and obstinacy, as his two elder brothers repeatedly tell us: "he is a chip of the old block, the spitting image of his father. . . . "

As for Abbie, she is just as trapped as he is. When she enters the stage, we are warned that she has "the same unsettled, untamed, desperate quality which is so apparent in Eben." And shortly afterward we learn that she "was a orphan early an' had t'wuk fur others in other folks' hums," and her first husband "turned out a drunken spreer" and got sick and died. She then felt free again only to discover that all she was free for was to work again "in other folks' hums, doin' other folks' wuk" till she had almost given up hope of ever doing her own work in her own home (Part I, scene 4).

Ephraim Cabot himself, for all his will power and vigor, is caught in the same web as the others. His whole behavior is conditioned by his Puritan upbringing. He cannot think of anything but work, hard work on a barren New England farm. *Laborare est orare,* Carlyle claimed, "work

is worship." Ephraim Cabot is a degenerate Puritan. Work has ceased to be a form of worship for him, yet he believes in its virtue and absolute value because he has been brought up that way. He once tried to escape his self-imposed serfdom. Like many other New Englanders, he went West and in the broad meadows of the central plains found black soil as rich as gold, without a stone. He had only to plough and sow and then sit and smoke his pipe and watch things grow. He could have become a rich man and led an easy and idle life, but he preferred to give it up and return to his New England farm and to hard work on a stony soil, which proves the extraordinary strength of his Puritan compulsions. They practically deprived him of his freedom of choice.

So, at the start at least, the three major characters of **Desire Under the Elms** are not free. They bear psychological or moral chains. Consequently, they cannot be held responsible for their actions, and Simeon with his pleasant shrewdness is perfectly aware of it. When Eben accuses his father of killing his "Maw," Simeon retorts: "No one never kills nobody. It's allus somethin' that's the murderer" (Part I, scene 2). "Somethin'," that is to say one of those mysterious things which impel men to act this way or that, whether they like it or not, whether they are aware of it or not. This is a modified form of Puritan pessimism: all men are sinners in the clutches of Satan—or of God who is always "nagging his sheep to sin" (Part I, scene 4), the better to punish them afterward, always ready to smite His undutiful sons with His worst curse.

How can a man save his soul under such circumstances? Though, theoretically, O'Neill's approach is strictly non-theological and he is not concerned with the problem of salvation, he is constantly obsessed with it all the same, and in this play, he gives it a Nietzschean answer: passion. Passion alone, he suggests, can enable man to transcend his animal nature. He repeatedly exalts the purity and transfiguring power of love. Eben's passion for Abbie, which at first is mere lust, soon becomes love—and there is a difference in kind between the two. The passage from lust to love is similar to the transmutation of lead into gold. Whereas lust, which is tied to the body, is finite and eternal. Abbie kills her infant son to prove her love to Eben, and at the end of scene 3 of Part III proclaims that her love for Eben will never change, whatever he does to her. The play ends on an apotheosis of love. The two lovers stand "looking up raptly in attitudes strangely aloof and devout" at the "purty" rising sun, which contrasts with the pallid setting sun that lit up the opening of the play, at a time when everything took place on the plane of coarse material things and lust.

Man can thus be redeemed by a great passion and save his soul and attain grandeur. The farm under the elms, which looked so sordid when the curtain rose, witnesses a sublime *dénouement* and at the end almost becomes one of those places where the spirit bloweth.

The reason for this extraordinary change is that, in Hamlet's words:

> There are more things in heaven and earth . . .
> Than are dreamt of in all [our] philosophy,

as Cabot again feels, for all his hardness and insensitivity: "They's thin's pokin' about in the dark—in the corners" (Part II, scene 2). "Even the music can't drive it out—somethin'. Ye kin feel it droppin' off the elums, climbin' up the roof, sneakin' down the chimney, pokin' in the corners. They's no peace in houses, they's no rest livin' with folks. Somethin's always livin' with ye" . . . (Part III, scene 2).

What is that "somethin'" whose presence disturbs him? It is the "Desire" of the title—an irresistible life-force (somewhat similar to G. B. Shaw's), which flows through the elms and through old Cabot himself sometimes, as when it makes him leave his farm in spring and go in search of a new wife. But it is especially powerful in Eben and Abbie. It is that thing which makes Eben look like a wild animal in captivity when he enters the stage, and feel "inwardly unsubdued." It is quite impersonal, and Eben refers to it in the neuter: "I kin feel it growin' in me—growin' an' growin'—till it'll bust out" (Part I, scene 2). It is the magnetic force which draws Eben to Abbie through walls and partitions (Part II, scene 2). It is Nature—and Abbie intones a hymn to her—or it—in her own inarticulate way when she presses Eben to yield to his passion: "Hain't the sun strong an' hot? Ye kin feel it burnin' into the earth—Nature—makin' thin's grow—bigger 'n' bigger—burnin' inside ye—makin' ye want t'grow—into somethin' else—till ye are jined with it—an' it's your 'n—but it owns ye—too—an' makes ye grow bigger—like a tree—like them elums" (Part II, scene 1).

In short, the "Desire" which flows through the elms and drips from them and pervades everything under them is God—though the word is never used. It is not, however, the God of the Christians, but rather a dynamic, impersonal, pantheistic, or panpsychistic deity present in all things, whether animate or inanimate, breaking barriers between individuals as in the case of Eben and Abbie, dissolving their lonesomeness and making them feel one. In a way it is a pagan God, a Dionysian deity, for it partly manifests itself in the form of carnal desire. Under its influence, Eben and Cabot become inspired poets (in prose) and sing woman, the lovely incarnation of the soft and warm goddess of fertility and life: "She's like t'night, she's soft 'n' warm, her eyes kin wink like a star, her mouth's wa'm, her arms 're wa'm, she smells like a wa'm plowed field, she's purty" (Part I, scene 2). "Yew air my Rose o' Sharon! Behold! yew air fair; yer eyes air doves; yer lips air like scarlet; yer two breasts air like two fawns; yer navel be like a round goblet; yer belly be like a heap o' wheat,' exclaims old Cabot, echoing chapters 4 and 7 of the Song of Solomon.

The omnipresent God is fundamentally a cosmic sexual urge, spontaneous, beautiful, unselfish, and amoral. In this perspective the notion of sin becomes meaningless. "He was the child of our sin," says Eben of the baby, but Abbie proudly answers "as if defying God" (the God of the Christians): "I don't repent that sin. I ain't askin' God t'fergive that" (Part III, scene 4). The two lovers have gone back to the Garden of Eden from which Adam and Eve were expelled. They have become "Children of Adam," to take up Walt Whitman's phrase.

The life-force, the desire which circulates through the elms as well as through the *dramatis personae,* is the very reverse of the God worshipped by Ephraim Cabot, which has the hardness and immobility of a stone—and the sterility of one (Part II, scene 2). His God is the God of repression and lonesomeness and hard work—the God humorously called up by Robert Frost in "Of the Stones of the Place," and to some extent a duplicate of Robinson Jeffers's antihuman God.

Abbie, on the contrary, recommends yielding to the life impulse, letting Nature speak at every hazard "without check with original energy." It is against nature, it is impious, she claims, to resist its will: "It's agin nature, Eben. Ye been fightin' yer nature ever since the day I come" . . . (Part II, scenc 1). With her, Emerson's Nature has acquired sex.

This is a combination of Nietzsche's Dionysian philosophy and Freudianism, and in *Desire Under the Elms* it leads—in spite of the Dostoevskian quality of the *Crime and Punishment* situation at the end of the play—to an optimistic conclusion: the couple Eben-Abbie is not crushed by adverse circumstances. They have fulfilled themselves, they have fully lived and, far from being driven to despair by their trials, they are full of a strange "hopeless hope" when the curtain falls.

In this play we thus witness the dramatic clash of two opposite philosophies: Old Cabot's Puritanism and Abbie's worship of Dionysius—a conflict between the stones of the former and the elms of the latter, which O'Neill himself seems to have experienced throughout his life. He obviously sympathized with warm uninhibited characters like Eben and Abbie in *Desire under the Elms* and with Marie Brantome and Christine in *Mourning Becomes Electra,* though he never was warm and uninhibited himself. In everyday life, except when he was under the influence of alcohol, he was to some extent closer to Cabot than to Eben. Other things being equal, he suffered from the same dichotomy as Dr. Jekyll. Two men were at war within him. He was both Billy Brown and Dion Anthony. But the twain never fused. He was probably thinking of his own predicament when he made Dion, "life's lover," complain in *The Great God Brown* "with a suffering bewilderment": "Why am I afraid to dance, I who love music and rhythm and grace and song and laughter? Why am I afraid to live, I who love life and the beauty of flesh and the living colors of the earth and sky and sea? Why am I afraid of love, I who love love? . . . Why must I be so ashamed of my strength, so proud of my weakness"? (Prologue). He would have liked freely to worship "the Great God Pan," as Dion calls him; instead of that he had to bear "the intolerable cilice of life." He would have liked to laugh with Lazarus and shout like Lazarus's followers:

> There is only life
> There is only laughter (Act II, scene 1),

but his ingrained masochistic catholicism made laughter die on his lips. *Desire Under the Elms* is the secret expression of his poignant nostalgia for a joy of life he was unable to experience.

However, his personal failure and his acute awareness of

the cruelty of the human condition did not prevent him from concluding that life is a vivid and exciting experience well worth the trouble to the very end. And that is why Abbie and Eben do not commit suicide in the last act, and even Lavinia refuses to kill herself in **Mourning Becomes Electra,** thus breaking one of the most imperative laws of tragedy. O'Neill's ultimate attitude to life during this nostalgic period (1923 to 1926) is best expressed by the hero of **The Great God Brown:** "I've loved, lusted, won and lost, sung and wept". And anyway, as O'Neill proclaimed in **Lazarus Laughed** in conformity with Nietzsche's teachings: "Men are . . . unimportant . . . Man remains . . . For Man death is not." The same life-force flows through all men, and whatever their personal limitations may be, whether they are bums, drunken sailors, or New England farmers, it endows them all with tragic grandeur. All individuals are potentially as worthy of interest as the mighty kings and queens of Greek tragedies. **Desire Under the Elms** is thus the quiet affirmation of the fundamental dignity of all men in a godless (?) universe—or at least in a universe deprived of the help and support of the personal God posited by Christianity. (pp. 115-23)

> Roger Asselineau, "Eugene O'Neill's Transcendental Phase," in his The Transcendentalist Constant in American Literature, *New York University Press, 1980, pp. 115-23.*

Most modern plays are concerned with the relation between man and man, but that does not interest me at all. I am interested only in the relation between man and God.

—Eugene O'Neill, cited in Joseph Wood Krutch's introduction to Nine Plays of Eugene O'Neill, 1941.

Patrick J. Nolan (essay date 1981)

[In the following essay, Nolan analyzes Desire under the Elms from a Jungian perspective.]

Polarities lie at the heart of Eugene O'Neill's dramas. For a dramatist whose primary concern was the quest to establish a unity, emotionally and psychically, in his characters, a concentration upon polarities focussed attention on whether the polarities could or could not be harmonized. A brief review of O'Neill's plays brings a whole catalog of polar opposites to mind, defining in each case a set of particular spiritual or psychic tensions that, for O'Neill, had to be balanced before twentieth century man could "belong." O'Neill deals with belonging, in ancient terms, that cannot be implemented, spiritually, in the modern context. Like Yank, Brutus Jones seeks consciously to find faithful expression of those yearnings after transpersonal meaning which are unconscious. Jim Harris and Ella Downey record the racial rift between black and white. Dion Anthony represents the personality split between

Dionysiac and Apollonian man. In **Mourning Becomes Electra,** the Freudian Pleasure Principle is set against the repressive Puritan ethic. Con Melody is faced with the double images of himself. And the Tyrones are torn between the symbolic contents of day and night. Yet, the most important polarity of all may be that of the Anima-Animus archetypes, particularly the Anima, as they work themselves out in **Desire Under the Elms.**

Contrary to Oscar Cargill's note dealing with Carl Jung's influence in **The Emperor Jones,** where he holds that, "From the artistic point of view, how far O'Neill subscribed to the Jungian thesis is immaterial," the fact remains that one sees more of the artistic process in operation as one sees O'Neill's dramatic art conform itself to the depth psychology of Jung. How far O'Neill follows Jung's paradigms may shed light on how thoroughly the Jungian psychological model may have set the direction for the playwright's artistic and, even, spiritual vision. Ann Belford Ulanov is quite suggestive for any consideration of O'Neill's general practice with Jungian polarities when she holds that, "The psyche is composed of various opposites, such as: conscious-unconscious, reason-instinct, active-passive, etc.; the symbolism of the masculine-feminine represents all of these polar opposites." Remembering that O'Neill made continuous reference, pejoratively, to God the father, and longingly, to God the mother, one can at least suspect that the Jungian archetypes of Anima-Animus, of soft and hard, may also supply clues toward a pattern in O'Neill's use of polarities.

To begin with, O'Neill was probably very aware of Jung's view of the Collective Unconscious. His constant interest in the Behind Life force would almost assure that he was sensitive to the psychologist's distinction between a personal unconscious, the residue of personal experience that has drifted out of the authority of conscious exercise, and a collective unconscious, a legacy of needs, responses, and instincts so common to man through the millennia that they constitute a body of archetypal experiences implanted in all mankind independent of any individual experience. This body of unconscious life would constitute the Behind Life energy drawing man on to his destiny. It does not derive from subjective experience; it is purely objective to each individual—a body of psychic luggage having everything to do with the formation of men while man, as he receives it, has nothing to do with the formation of it. Access must be had into this objective dimension of the psyche so that the release of its energy at the conscious level of experience be a positive one. As archetypes of the collective unconscious, the anima and animus mediate to the ego this deeper, collective, objective dimension of the psyche. Access to this objective body is given to the conscious, masculine ego through the anima and to the feminine ego through the animus.

The archetypal opposites dictate how, at the level of image, O'Neill structured the play's setting. The elms and the rock walls establish, at the subliminal level, the polar contents of the anima and animus. The rocks which enclose the farm within its boundaries symbolize the masculine elements contained in the animus. The spirit that makes for hardness is the spirit that embraces and controls the farm and the Cabots. It serves to wall in the militant, aggressive animus instincts, while walling out, as best it can, any presence that would temper the harsh obsession with masculinity. But, at the same time, the elms brood over the entire setting, trying to descend and envelop the house with the affects and emotional contents of the anima. The spirit of Woman hangs over the house. At the level of image alone, we are aware that the conflicting energies of these archetypes, by the end of the play, will either be harmonized or be mutually destructive. The issue is, will the spirit of the elms descend to fuse with the spirit of the rocks?

Given their universality and their absolute need to be reconciled, the archetypes constitute the tragic tension between opposites that drives on all individuals to their own form of resolution. In his employment of them, O'Neill found a tragic force that propelled his characters to action, a secular equivalent to the force of the Gods in Sophoclean tragedy. The anima-animus opposition constitutes the Behind Life force which, independent of conscious will, drives the Cabots and Abbie on to tragic consequences with a pressure nearly as absolute as that of the Gods on Oedipus. Finding such an equivalent in modern drama is quite difficult because of the age's aversion to absolutes. But what is wanting by way of viable Gods, O'Neill substituted for from the realm of psychology. Acceptable because sublunary and secular, these forces of the archetypal instincts, as well as the Freudian Pleasure Principle, were seen to operate as universally throughout mankind as once the Gods prevailed. Psychological forces, at the secular level, approximated as closely as possible to the absolute presence that spiritual forces once exercised on man at the religious level. O'Neill was ready to tap Freud and Jung for these equivalents as set pieces in his Behind Life force; and these forces, be they Freudian or Jungian, constitute imperatives upon all being. Man "must" belong, consciously, in the same sense that he once belonged, unconsciously, as animal. Man, consciously, "must" possess transpersonal meaning in the exercise of surviving religious instincts, be the God crocodile or money. Man, merely by being mortal, "must" experience the claims of the pleasure principle which, however, has to accommodate itself to Puritanism. Melody "must" love self before he caters to being loved by others. An imperative set by Nature must be harmonized to another imperative, generally determined by conscious choice. To yield to the anima is the natural imperative in *Desire Under the Elms;* to regulate the animus is the struggle imposed by the anima on Eben's conscious will.

While parallels between drama and its influences are important, the parallels alone would mean little if they were to do nothing more than slavishly incorporate recent psychological theories. What is germane is to show how O'Neill incorporated these theories, and pressed them to their limits within the play, while simultaneously preserving the integrity of his own artistic viewpoint. Contrary to Jung, O'Neill never saw his polarities working to resolution. The original stamp, however, that O'Neill imposes on the polarities is his equating of the feminine archetype to the quality of love, and of the masculine archetype to man's greed for possessions. Even as Jung insists that the

archetypes must be harmonized, O'Neill insists that the unregulated passion for possession must be brought under control by other human needs—in this case, love. Everyone "must" love; yet, everyone must possess some goods. Both must be fulfilled if human needs are to be happily satisfied. The elimination of one (love) by the other (possessiveness) marks the failure of man to attain psychic wholeness as well as, for O'Neill, spiritual unity.

Desire Under the Elms opens with the animus—hardness and possessiveness—exerting the dominant energy in the Cabot household. As the rocks encompass, contain, and gird the property, so the consciousness of the men is held in bondage by the hard, loveless ethic of possessiveness. Eben, Sim and Peter, in thrall to their father's hard nature and greed, make a virtue out of hardness and ownership— and yet they reveal the emptiness of that "virtue" in their dreams of tomorrow and retreats into nostalgia. Visions of possession and dispossession alternately preoccupy them, and from the opening line of "God! Purty!" (a curious juxtaposition of the anima to the divine), through Sim's wistful recollection of his dead wife, Jenn, through the brothers' crude debate over Min, to Eben's lamentation about his Ma, the anima's feminine energy challenges the monolithic authority of masculine hardness. The energy of love seeks expression equal to the energy the Cabots pledge to owning land, money and women. Because the feminine spirit has never been integrated into the Cabot home as an object of dignity and equality, the anima broods as an atmosphere about the house. Though hardly endorsing Jung's views, Dr. Phillip Weissman's psychoanalytic reading of *Desire Under the Elms* does seem to underline the fact that it is the enigmatic feminine presence which insists on a balanced polarity with the masculine spirit: "In *Desire Under the Elms,* as in *Long Day's Journey Into Night,* the character of the woman (Abbie and his mother) remains an unconscious enigma to the author, in sharp contrast to the realistic portrayals of the father."

The Jungian particulars proceed in this fashion. The anima archetype lies quietly suppressed until the entry of Abbie, when sex agitates the anima contents of Eben's psyche and brings them into more violent antagonism with the animus. With Abbie's entrance, springing Sim and Peter loose to California and serving also to intensify more exclusively the opposition of Eben to Ephraim, Sex, prefiguring love, is about to challenge the possessive compulsions of the Cabots. Eben becomes the character in whom the anima energies will be most violently in contest with the animus archetype.

With the death of his mother, Eben had lost, at too early a stage, that object that mediates between the unconscious and the ego. The anima force, love, did not get fully liberated, and Eben's energies came under the aegis of Ephraim's masculine drive to own the farm. Like every individual, Eben must structure a harmony between the feminine and masculine components of his own nature. In O'Neill's terms, Eben's Unity of Being—his belonging—was denied him at his mother's death; and in the ensuing years, his anima, his need for love, has never been able to establish a psychic equality with his need to possess the farm. The whole environment of masculine hardness has forbidden him the means to relate to his feminine archetypal energy as energy that stands in relation to masculine energy as an equal "other." Psychically, for all the sons the patriarchal values of greed cannot be modified, complemented or disciplined by the anima energies of love. Thus it is that while Eben is emotionally bound to his mother and love, he is intellectually bound to his father's possessive greed.

Jung perceives Eben's paradox as the result of his ego being identified to the anima, making no conscious separation between the ego and the compulsive, automatic energy of the anima. The feminine energies in Eben, never maturing, hold on to him, controlling him emotionally until such time as he can create a mature communication with his anima. Eben suffers from the psychic split of wanting love but never admitting that need to a status equal to wanting the farm. Needing to be soft, he cannot be such because his family ethic opposes it. In his environment, softness has been a term of disdain. But until he admits, consciously, the "other," the need to love, to an equality with the need for property, he will never possess an ego in control of the anima, nor will his psyche be a smooth, self-regulating system of balanced polarities. In short, his unity of being will be forfeited. Jung's description of the emotional patterns that identify such an anima immaturity could have served O'Neill as apt descriptive terms for his characterization of Eben. Speaking of the emotional affects of the troubled anima on man, Jung holds that the anima "intensifies, exaggerates, falsifies, and mythologizes all emotional relations with his work and with other people of both sexes. . . . When the anima is strongly constellated, she softens a man's character and makes him touchy, irritable, moody, jealous, vain, and unadjusted. He is in a state of discontent and spreads discontent all around him. Sometimes the man's relationship to the woman who has caught his anima [in this case, Abbie] accounts for the existence of this syndrome."

Given Eben's incomplete and agitated anima energies, Abbie's appearance on the farm establishes the conditions for another Jungian phase of anima experience, projection. With his anima image initially established by his mother, Eben's anima is now caught by Abbie, who almost immediately fulfills several of the archetypal images of the anima, the spiritual guide in the role of mother, the beloved one, and the harlot. The confusion of Eben about the anima's balance with the animus is reflected in his inability to separate his nostalgic love of his mother from the hard desire to revenge himself on Ephraim in her name. But the confusion, slowly, will be resolved. O'Neill accepts Jung's lead when he allows the mother's presence to recede from her room after Eben and Abbie's first sexual ceremony, giving evidence thereby that Eben's psyche is moving toward maturity and wholeness. For Eben, love very quickly becomes an imperative nearly equal to possession. Unfortunately, the imperatives exercise themselves by turns. The desire for love is not yet integrated with but, rather, is *followed by* the desire to own the farm. But the anima-animus polarities cannot be resolved by taking turns at dominance; they cannot both be equal but separate, operating at detached moments in time. They must be made to coexist, to operate as mutual complements, one enhancing the other, not cancelling the other out. So, too, with

love and possessiveness; they must be mutual assets to each other. But as long as Abbie and Eben try to have the farm and each other, at the same time, without letting love qualify their greed, the psychic split of the anima-animus energies, pretending to be psychically merged, creates a self-destructive contradiction. Unqualified materialism pretending to coexist with love—which "must" qualify materialism—is mere illusion preceding the breakdown of relationships both individual and societal. (The self-destructive split, more pronounced in Ephraim than anyone else, must lead to his wild, chaotic, dervish dance that symbolizes, visually, the inability of hard, masculine, possessive energies to maintain, any longer, control over the Cabot fate. The dance, in short, represents the inability of the psyche to maintain the lies any longer.)

In the infant child, the mutual but separate claims of the anima-animus, of love and possession, find incarnation. It is the child of cross purposes, and because the illusion cannot continue, the child must die. But it will die in the name of the anima, in the name of love as a repudiation of unqualified materialism. The patriarchal values, which to now Eben and Abbie support, must be diminished, consciously, so that the claim of love, of the anima, can be given complete respect and be allowed to become as complete and powerful a force as its psychic energy demands. As woman, as love, the anima must be conceived as equal to man, to possessiveness, to the animus. Abbie, making this correction first, attains to the spiritual totality when she kills the child, disavowing herself from greed in her love for Eben. Eben, then, parallels this disavowal, freeing the anima from the control of the unconscious. He now controls the anima; it does not control him. (This Jungian implication contradicts Dr. Weissman's contention that Eben "is unable to grow beyond his sexual feelings for his mother and his death wishes for his father. Thus he is destined to an inability to resolve his Oedipal striving.") The patriarchal values, now modified by the feminine spirit, come under the discipline of love. This sets a great precedent for American society, but one that O'Neill could not accept.

Eben and Abbie have their tragic victory, but O'Neill does not permit the play to end on that note. To do so would contradict his view of history as cyclical. Even as Yank starts in the caged atmosphere of the berthing compartment and ends in the gorilla's cage; even as Jones's flight proceeds in one great circle to return to where he started; even as Jim Harris and Ella start as children playing Painty Face and end in the psychic retreat to the same game; so, too, in *Desire Under the Elms,* possessiveness must return to dominate the closing of the play. Eben and Abbie's tragic wisdom must be undercut. The sheriff's wish to own the farm negates the possibilty that Eben's and Abbie's spiritual maturity will become precedent for any larger section of society. Herein, O'Neill once again denies the view of history as linear process in an indictment of American society's similar denial of the humanizing force of love.

What remains to contemporary, materialist societies is the alternate solution to the archetypal polarities revealed by Ephraim. As the animus-dominated man who fails to detach his ego from the unconscious, Ephraim is nevertheless driven to satisfy the anima's demands with Abbie, who is chosen, not in love but, rather, in lust. And for Ephraim, she cannot be seen for herself but is seen, also, as the farm. "Sometimes ye air the farm an' sometimes the farm be yew," he says. Unable to separate the two drives, Ephraim cannot see love and possessiveness as separate entities to be dealt with, consciously, as equals. Forbidding the equal inclusion of the anima, Ephraim remands his being to an incompleteness, psychically and spiritually. For Ephraim, the anima has been suppressed and attached to the ego for so long that it causes love to be transmuted into mere sex. When this identification of the anima to the ego continues past middle age, as it obviously has for Ephraim, the consequences for that individual are delineated in a personality profile of Jung's which, but for one exception, could stand as a point for point description of Ephraim's character. "After the middle of life, . . . a permanent loss of the Anima means a diminution of vitality, of flexibility, and of human kindness. The result, as a rule, is premature rigidity, crustiness, fanatical onesidedness, obstinacy, pedantry." Rendered incapable, therefore, of learning from Eben's experience, Ephraim has no alternative within the parameters of his psyche but to seek a furtive solution to his anima needs in his pathetic decision to collect the freed cows and continue his prospects of sleeping with them.

The overview to be drawn from this application of Jung's theory derives from the emphasis which Jung and O'Neill gave to the successful resolution of the anima-animus polarity. Jung implied that it was a decisive step in the reconciliation of all opposites, such as consciousness-unconsciousness, spirit-nature, fate-free will. As they depart for jail, Abbie and Eben have harmonized the polarity; each has earned that unity of being which, for Eben, had been lost since his mother's death. With the integration of the anima, they come out of their struggle truly possessed of tragic wisdom and victory. Their strength now is superior to masculine hardness. Each has discovered that quality of self worthy of being perpetuated eternally. And since O'Neill, so often, was willing to have his characters posit the existence of God when they possessed the object of their ideal longing, the spiritual portent of Eben's union with Abbie is somewhat obvious. A God made possible through the incarnation of the feminine spirit—a God in the form of God the mother—comes into being, taking the measure of the incompleteness latent in any devotion to a hardgod, God the father, Ephraim's deity. Ann Belford Ulanov reveals this religious dimension of the Jungian feminine: "The feminine . . . is a factor which must be recognized as essential for the full exercise of the religious function. Thus, if the feminine is neglected, undervalued, or misconstrued, the result, psychologically, is a diminishing of one's growth to wholeness, and the result, theologically, is that the Imago Dei does not achieve its full stature." Unique among O'Neill's plays, **Desire Under the Elms** dramatizes two characters coming into possession of this real unity and spirituality—a tragic victory made possible by O'Neill's steady application of Jung's vision of the anima.

The play's resolution, however, turning as it does upon the

sheriff's concluding remark which dismisses the lesson made available by Abbie and Eben's fate, is exclusively O'Neill's construction. Unlike Jung, there will be no resolution of the polarities for him. O'Neill projects, then, an American society devoted to the hard Gods of masculine greed and possession plunging again and again into the competition for ownership. The Imago Dei will exist only in infantile terms. Americans will never find the spirituality they need, but they will never stop trying to find it in and through the possession of things. (pp. 5-10)

Patrick J. Nolan, " 'Desire under the Elms': Characters by Jung," in The Eugene O'Neill Newsletter, *Vol. V, No. 2, Summer-Fall, 1981, pp. 5-10.*

June Schlueter and Arthur Lewis   (essay date 1984)

[*In the following essay, Schlueter and Lewis explore the moral conflicts within the character of Ephraim Cabot as symbolized by the stones and cows in* Desire under the Elms.]

In his essay on "The Pressure of Puritanism in Eugene O'Neill's New England Plays," Frederick Wilkins quotes the playwright's comment that "the battle of moral forces in the New England scene" is "what I feel closest to as an artist." Wilkins, as well as others, has discussed this battle in terms of opposing characters in **Desire Under the Elms,** looking at Abbie and Eben, who are able to "free themselves from their sordid surroundings and from the Puritan conception of 'sin,' " in opposition to Ephraim Cabot, who, alone and sterile, remains "unaware to the end of the great guilt that is his." Similarly, Roger Asselineau speaks of the life impulse to which Abbie yields and which is the "reverse of the God worshipped by Ephraim Cabot, which has the hardness and immobility of a stone." Clearly Cabot is the "Bible-quoting, tyrannical father" that John H. Raleigh calls him, a man so dedicated to back-breaking labor that he would appear to have become one of the stones with which he and his farm are identified. Yet Cabot is also attracted to cows, sleeping with them when he feels the need for warmth and setting them free when he plans to burn the farm. The stony Cabot may well serve as one polarity in the battle of moral forces that O'Neill mounts between and among his characters. But Cabot's own mind is also a battlefield for the same conflict, which O'Neill expresses symbolically through the old man's relationship to stones and to cows.

Like many of O'Neill's earlier characters, Cabot is not fully in control of his own behavior. As a young man, in a moment of weakness, Cabot left the stony farm after two years of hard work and headed west, where the soil was "black and rich as gold," and stoneless. Farming was easy there, and the promise of prosperity was inviting. But an internal voice, the voice of Cabot's Old Testament God, commanded Cabot to return: "Git ye back t' hum!" Unable to resist the suffering and labor demanded by the Puritan ethic, which was clearly the mainstay of his moral code, Cabot abandoned his crops and rejoined the rocky New England farm, endorsing his action by characterizing God as "hard, not easy! God's in the stones!"

Once he got back to the rocks, Cabot was compelled to construct walls—"Stones. I picked 'em up an' piled 'em into walls"—and began to identify with the stones: "Ye kin read the years o' my life in them walls, every day a hefted stone, climbin' over the hills up and down, fencin' in the fields that was mine, whar I'd made thin's grow out o' nothing'—like the will o'God, like the servant o' His hand." Cabot continues building his "church on a rock—out o' stones an' I'll be in them! That's what He meant 't Peter."

When Cabot married and his wife bore him two sons, he named them Simeon and Peter, clearly suggestive of Simon Peter, the rock upon whom Christ built his church, and, in the case of Peter, derivative of the Greek word "petra," meaning rock. Now, some fifty years after Cabot's own escape to the West, history relives itself through his two sons, who themselves head west, to California. Here again the stones become the symbolic contrast to the freedom and ease of life in the West and the explicit object of rejection. To Simeon and Peter, the "stones atop o' the ground—stones atop o' stones" represent the repression that pervades the farm and perpetuates itself. The two frustrated men are no longer willing to be "slaves t' stone walls" and it takes only a slug of "likker" for them to garner the courage to break away from the "rock-pile of a farm." As they leave the restrictive, valueless stones of New England for the promising, shining gold of the West, they jubilantly declare: "We harby 'bolishes . . . all gates," celebrating their decision in song.

Cabot's third son, Eben, shares Simeon and Peter's nominal identification with stones: "Ebenezer," the fuller version of "Eben," is the name given by the prophet Samuel to the stone he set up in memory of divine assistance. Similarly, Eben shares his half-brothers' bitterness toward stones, seeing them not only as physical walls of restraint but as internal ones that have hardened his brothers' hearts: "makin' walls till yer heart's a stone ye heft up out o' the way of growth onto a stone wall t' wall in yer heart!" (p. 7). To Eben, who himself rejects the stone philosophy not by leaving, as his brothers do, but by loving, the heart and stones are incompatible.

Indeed, Cabot's life since his return to New England has been a loveless one, in which hard work has been his only value. But in his dotage he has surprised his sons by marrying the youthful, vital Abbie, not for the lechery they see in this action but because the conflict of his youth has once again surfaced. Cabot claims he heard "the voice o' God cryin' in my wilderness, in my lonesomeness—t' go out an' seek an' find!", and, in response, he found and married Abbie. But the voice he follows hardly echoes the voice that recalled him to New England five decades earlier; this voice is the one that had summoned him westward and has continued to lure him to the barn, where "it's wa'm . . . nice smellin' an' warm—with the cows."

Despite Cabot's condemnation of his sons' lust "fur the sinful, easy gold o' Californi-a" and his repeated commitment to the hard life, Cabot himself still feels attracted to the warmth of the barn and the softness of the cows. Interestingly, almost every time Cabot speaks of cows, he either calls them queer or speaks of them with "queer affection."

When Abbie is cold to Cabot's advances, he retreats to "whar it's restful—whar it's warm—down t' the barn." With some indignation, he points out to his wife that the cows are more responsive than she is: "I kin talk t' the cows . . . They'll give me peace." The morning after Cabot spends the night in the barn, he announces the success of his self-prescribed therapy: "I rested. I slept good—down with the cows. They know how t' sleep. They're teachin' me."

In marked contrast to the hard, cold stones, the cows offer Cabot softness and warmth, perhaps even the satisfaction of a latent sexuality his Puritan ethic has denied. Indeed, on at least two occasions Cabot calls his son Eben a calf, and in both situations the association with sex is manifest. When Abbie defends Eben against Cabot's rage over his son's sexual advances, the old man concedes, "I oughtn't t' git riled so—at that 'ere fool calf" and, less knowingly, calls him a calf on the morning after the sexual encounter between Eben and Abbie. Similarly, when Abbie suggests the two might have a son, Cabot softens to the point of sentimentality, touchingly revealing his life story to the woman concerned only with what is happening in Eben's bedroom next door. At the end of his monologue, Cabot retreats to the barn to be with the cows. ‑

Some months later, after Abbie has given birth to the child that everyone but Cabot suspects is Eben's, the old man celebrates his sexuality in a display of raw energy that astonishes the neighborhood gossips. Outdancing the fiddler, Cabot becomes seemingly superhuman in vitality. The cold self-denial that characterized Cabot earlier has been transformed into the fecund life force identified not with the stones but with the cows.

In the play's final scene, Cabot identifies himself explicitly with the cows. Having endured the humiliation of discovering the child that Abbie bore and killed was not his, but Eben's, Cabot tells himself, "I got t' be—like a stone—a rock o' jedgment!" But at this point he is unable to restore his commitment and resolves instead to burn the farm, free the cows, and head for California: "T' hell with the farm! I'm leavin' it! I've turned the cows an' other stock loose! I've druv 'em into the woods whar they kin be free! *By freein' 'em, I'm freein'* myself!" (emphasis added). In his plan to "set fire t' house an' barn an' watch 'em burn . . . ", Cabot is renouncing the ethic of work and self-denial to which he has devoted his life; in freeing the cows he is releasing the suppressed desires of those decades, seemingly resolving the moral conflict that he had not consciously acknowledged until now.

But O'Neill, finally, does not allow Cabot to be set free with the cows. Moments after his jubilant declaration that California is "the land fur me," Cabot learns that Eben's entrepreneuring has left him without the financial means to go west. His reaction is severe: "*He stares—feels* [under the floor board for the money]*—stares again. A pause of dead silence. He slowly turns, slumping into a sitting position on the floor, his eyes like those of a dead fish, his face the sickly green of an attack of nausea. He swallows painfully several times—forces a weak smile at last*" (stage direction). And then, sardonically, he reaffirms the philosophy by which he has lived the seventy-plus years of his life:

"God's hard, not easy! Mebbe they's easy gold in the West, but it hain't God's gold. It hain't fur me."

Once again, the hard New England God is in control: "I kin hear His voice warnin' me agen t' be hard an' stay on my farm. I kin see his hand usin' Eben t' steal t' keep me from weakness. I kin feel I be in the palm o' His hand, His finger guiden' me" (pp. 57-8). The God who called the young Cabot back from the West has recalled him again, this time to a life without sons, wife, and cows: "It's a -goin' t' be lonesomer now than ever it war afore." At play's end, the old New Englander is alone, surrounded by stone walls that permanently separate him from the cows, his private "battle of moral forces" resolved. (pp. 111-14)

> *June Schlueter and Arthur Lewis, "Cabot's Conflict: The Stones and Cows in O'Neill's 'Desire under the Elms',"* in Critical Essays on Eugene O'Neill, *edited by James J. Martine, G. K. Hall & Co., 1984, pp. 111-14.*

Margaret Loftus Ranald (essay date 1984)

[*In the following excerpt, Ranald summarizes the major themes and techniques of* Desire under the Elms.]

With [*Desire Under the Elms*] Eugene O'Neill established himself as a playwright of genius. Here everything seems to have fallen into place to create a major work of tragic art. It is sometimes said that tragedy is impossible of achievement by modern playwrights, but with *Desire Under the Elms,* I believe that O'Neill has given that statement the lie. He has developed a play with an American setting and a recognizable locale with its historial and emotional connotations of Puritanism, Protestant ethic, and hardness, but he has superimposed that mythic structure on the ancient myths of Greek drama. One can easily recognize the three basic myths included in this tragedy, Oedipus, Phaedra, and Medea. But the important thing about this play is the freedom with which O'Neill melds these elements into something different by the addition of other psychological-philosophical sources—Friedrich Nietzsche and Sigmund Freud. And out of this collection of materials he managed to create a modern approximation of the Aristotelian pity and fear. His characters seem indeed to be the prisoners of their own destiny, and a hostile first principle broods over their acts, forever forbidding happiness in this life. Only at the end, in a spiritual union, a renunciation of life through love that is unselfish, do the central characters gain a glimmer of something better as they look up at the sunrise.

The Oedipal struggle between father and son is clear from the beginning in the way that Eben's close relationship with his mother is conveyed and also his rage that he has been cheated of Ephraim's farm. It is, then, but a short step to Freud and Eben's acting out of the Oedipal aspect of man's existence by having sexual intercourse first with Min and then with Abbie. Abbie is, of course, a combination of Phaedra and Medea, a statement which also gives Eben some of the qualities of Hippolytus, and certainly he is at first reluctant to recognize his physical longing for Abbie. But the intrusion of the Medea myth is unexpected

in the play, and Abbie realizes that she should have murdered Ephraim, but it nonetheless strengthens her characterization as a woman who gives up everything for love. In her case, she has married in hope of possessing the farm, and she feels herself to be part of nature and even of the farm. As a result, in killing the baby she is cutting herself off from her place, her dreams, her love, and her true identity. She is a creature of Nature and physicality, yet she murders the product of that part of her in order to regain the love of Eben. Here, certainly, the myth gives added resonance.

From Nietzsche, O'Neill has taken the concept of the Apollonian and Dionysian duality which he later used more specifically in *The Great God Brown.* Here he transposes the situation to Ephraim and his vision of God, who is "hard an' lonesome." The whole metaphor of the stones and the hardness of life imposed by the Apollonian-Puritan God upon Cabot is contrasted with his occasional longing for the "easy" God which he had found in the Middle West where one had merely to plant a field and watch the crops grow. Even at the end of the play, Ephraim has a sneaking desire to follow that "easy" God when he speaks of leaving for the West and the goldfields. The stern God does not always remain in total control of Ephraim, as is evidenced by his two momentary lapses in the spring but even more particularly in the Dionysian revel celebrating the birth of Abbie's son. There he turns into a satyr-figure—laughing, capering, drinking, celebrating—reaching a momentary intoxication of joy that blinds and deafens him to what is being said and done around him. His Dionysian side is also in tune with nature because he is in tune with the seasons when he leaves his farm to seek God's will. Here, he also follows the voice of his commanding Apollonian-Puritan God, but in marrying Abbie, he follows the instincts of Dionysus. The great key to the theology of the play (and I do not think this word is too strong) is Ephraim's long monologue to Abbie in Part II, Scene ii, where he tells of his attempt to quit the farm, of his time in the Middle West, and then his return to the rock-strewn farm which had made him as hard as the stone walls he has built. He sees them as a testament to God, but his sons Simeon and Peter perceive them as prison walls. Eben, on the other hand, considers them more as a protective device for his own world—the farm, from which he fears displacement. Both Eben and his father feel themselves part of the farm, and their kinship with nature and the seasons makes their basic conflict credible. The two men are more alike than they realize, but Eben has the ability to love, while Ephraim has not. For this reason Ephraim is always lonesome, always private, revealing himself only to his wrathful, judgmental God, and also to the cows, the only living things with whom he really feels comfortable because, as animals, they do not threaten him into giving too much rein to his physical, Dionysian nature.

In two other aspects O'Neill succeeded brilliantly in this play—in the use of language and sets. The language is spare, laconic, and dialectal, yet through it O'Neill is able to convey an extraordinary emotional power and also communicate theological and philosophical concepts without resort to the lyricism which sounds so strained in plays such as *The Fountain.* For instance, the almost monosyllabic speeches of the brothers in the first two scenes indicate, through their differing reactions to the sunset, quite separate people. Eben thinks of the farm as his own, Simeon remembers his dead wife, and Peter thinks of the gold in California. Even Ephraim's long monologue is pure dialect, yet at the same time it achieves a kind of poetry which O'Neill in his more self-conscious moments was unable to manage.

In terms of the set, O'Neill was himself largely responsible for its design, and he specified his requirements in drawings. It is a permanent set, with the scenes shifting among the various rooms which are emphasized by means of light. One possible defect in this set would seem to be the elms themselves. The stage directions speak of their "sinister maternity" and the way their branches rest on the roof like "hands and hair"; but the trees are never exploited, and certainly it never rains in the course of the play so that "their tears trickle down monotonously and rot the shingles." Perhaps they are meant to give some sense of the fatal destiny of the house of Cabot, but the stone walls of the farm are a better symbol. Nevertheless, throughout the play O'Neill shows himself completely cognizant of the action as it develops on this particular set, and his contrapuntal use of words and images is excellent. The celebration scene in Part III, Scene i, for instance, is brilliant in its contrasts, while the bedroom scene in Part II, Scene i, with Eben on one side and Abbie and Ephraim on the other, is superb in showing the almost telephatic communication between the lovers. The farmhouse and the farm are really central characters in the play, and hence the Sheriff's ironic closing lines seem most à propos. Those lines are an epitaph for Ephraim and for the farm itself, and an act of devout respect to the God who made it possible—but at a cost the Sheriff can neither know nor understand. Only the three Cabots understand as they go off into their sunrise. In their imprisonment, they all find freedom under the aegis of a mighty and cruel God. (pp. 174-76)

> *Margaret Loftus Ranald, in her* The Eugene O'Neill Companion, *Greenwood Press, 1984, 827 p.*

Jean Anne Waterstradt   (essay date 1985)

[*In the following essay, Waterstradt offers an analysis of the character of Ephraim Cabot.*]

Desire Under the Elms, written and first produced in 1924, is Eugene O'Neill's first great tragedy. In fact, Travis Bogard calls it the "first important tragedy to be written in America." Inevitably the play has been much interpreted. In addition to Louis Sheaffer's discussion in his superb critical biography of O'Neill, three basic analyses need acknowledgment here: Philip Weissman, a Freudian psychiatrist, has analyzed the autobiographical structure; Edgar F. Racey, Jr., the mythic structure; and Bogard, the Nietzschean pattern. These are useful, illuminating works and, taken together, appear to constitute a complete probing of the drama, a totality of interpretive criticism. Indeed, little does remain to be said, and the

possibility of suggesting anything new seems remote. There is, however, one unnoted implication for the character of Ephraim Cabot that may help enrich both appreciation and understanding of the density of the play.

Cabot remains one of O'Neill's most remarkable creations. Of this dour, tyrannical old Puritan protagonist, his maker has surprisingly remarked, "I have always loved Ephraim so much! He's so autobiographical." O'Neill's "love" of the old farmer, however, is not shared by commentators on the drama, although Cabot does evoke appreciative comment and analysis as well as damnation. Doris Falk calls Ephraim "a self-centered, loveless man who has projected his own personality into that of his God, a tyrannic, ascetic, restrictive embodiment of Puritanism." She identifies Ephraim's God as "only an image of his own ego." Falk also condemns Cabot's "exploitive egotism," his pride, his "brutal lust."

John Henry Raleigh is somewhat less harsh in his view of Ephraim, calling him first "a great grotesque, a powerful buffoon . . . an almost endearing old miser and lecher." Then Raleigh observes, "But the essence of his character is not dryness and narrowness; on the contrary, he is complex and expansive." Raleigh finds that Ephraim "has an ego of monumental proportions and is, in fact, that very God he keeps referring to and calling upon. For what he really represents is pure power, physically and emotionally."

Racey points out Cabot's "rash injustice" against his second wife and the "solitary sterility which has been his lot." He suggests that Ephraim must atone for his sin by being confined, in the end, to the "rocky solitude of his farm".

All of these observations are, in their way, both persuasive and at least partially correct. Yet each has missed something vital. Even when Frederic Carpenter acknwledges Ephraim's "towering stature" and his "inward reality" as the "embodiment of the highest heroism of modern man," or when Sheaffer asserts that Cabot "takes on epic dimensions," or when Bogard characterizes him as a "God-driven man," there remains unsaid and untouched a central truth of the character. That truth rests on the meaning of the omnipresent stones with which Ephraim has struggled all his life.

The symbolism of stone is analyzed by J. E. Cirlot as follows:

> Stone is a symbol of being, of cohesion and harmonious reconciliation with self. The hardness and durability of stone have always impressed men, suggesting to them the antithesis to biological things subject to the laws of change, decay and death, as well as the antithesis to dust, sand and stone splinters, as aspects of disintegration. The stone when whole symbolized unity and strength; when shattered it signified dismemberment, psychic disintegration, infirmity, death and annihilation. Stones fallen from heaven served to explain the origin of life.

Cirlot also discusses mythic and religious meanings of stone, recalling that many stones have been worshipped and also quoting Genesis 28.22: "And this stone which I have set for a pillar, shall be God's house."

M. L. von Franz reinforces what Cirlot says: "Self is symbolized with special frequency in the form of a stone, precious or otherwise." She also associates the crystal with stone as symbolic of the self, explaining that "The mathematically precise arrangement of a crystal evokes in us the intuitive feeling that even in so-called 'dead' matter, there is a spiritual ordering principle at work." Von Franz continues:

> Perhaps crystals and stones are especially apt symbols of the self because of the "just-so-ness" of their nature. . . . For while the human being is as different as possible from a stone, yet man's innermost center is in a strange and special way akin to it (perhaps because the stone symbolizes mere existence at the farthest remove from the emotions, feelings, fantasies, and discursive thinking of ego-consciousness). In this sense the stone symbolizes what is perhaps the simplest and deepest experience—the experience of something eternal that man can have in those moments when he feels immortal and unalterable.

Von Franz further points out that "The alchemical stone . . . symbolizes something that can never be lost or dissolved, something eternal that some alchemists compared to the mystical experience of God within one's own soul."

If, then, in "dead" matter there is a "spiritual ordering principle at work," the stones on the Cabot farm, the stones from which Ephraim has created walls, have an honorific significance and point to qualities in him not previously acknowledged.

A re-evaluation of the old farmer might begin with the concession that he is rightly named. "Ephraim," from the Hebrew, means "fruitful," and for Cabot the name does not always work ironically. Apart from the fact that he has not fathered the child to whom his third wife gives birth, he has lived a fruitful life, although not a balanced one. Not only has Ephraim made a stony land productive, but the stones with which he is identified do not suggest just sterility, waste, or death—meanings commonly associated with stones. Rather, those stones are the cause of Ephraim's fruitfulness and, as Cirlot and von Franz make clear, also symbols of man's concept of self and thus of life. Additionally, Ephraim's preference for the barn and the company of the cows over his house and association with his wife and son reinforces the symbolism of the stones in his life.

The stoniness of the Cabot farm is first indicated in the stage directions when O'Neill notes that "The south end of the house faces front to a stone wall. . . ." Then, early in Part One, Scene One, Ephraim's son Peter, ironically named, complains, "Here—it's stones atop o' the ground—stones atop o' stones—makin' stone walls—year atop o' year—him 'n' me 'n' me 'n' then Eben—makin' stone walls fur him to fence us in!" He views the farm bitterly as a prison. Eben, the youngest son, accuses his half-brothers of building stone walls in their hearts as they

labor to build the actual walls on the farm because they did nothing to make life more bearable for his mother, their step-mother.

When old Cabot finally appears, O'Neill says that his face "is as hard as if it were hewn out of a boulder . . . " Near the end of the play, after Abbie has confessed the murder of her infant son and has told Ephraim, "An' he was Eben's son—mine an' Eben's—not your'n!," her husband asserts, hardening "his face into a stony mask," that "I got t' be—like a stone—a rock o' jedgment!" Then, as Ephraim tells his son and wife goodbye when they leave with the sheriff, O'Neill once more—and for the last time—describes Cabot's face as stony.

As earlier indicated, however, the pejorative meanings of stone may not be the essence of Ephraim's character. One of the most memorable scenes in all of O'Neill occurs when Cabot tries to convey to the uncomprehending Abbie his feelings about and knowledge of God and of the earth that is his farm. As this oddly mated couple sit side by side on their bed, with Abbie concentrating her attention on the wall that separates their bedroom from Eben's, Ephraim speaks of the fields of stones that used to constitute his farm and of thee consequent "hardness" of his life and of his god. The old man, who is at times almost inarticulate, grows lyrical as he reviews the struggles of his life and his accomplishments while he has followed the admonitions of his "hard God." He remembers succumbing to temptation once when he traveled "t' broad medders, plains whar the soil was black an' rich as gold. Nary a stone. Easy. Ye'd on'y to plow an' sow an' then set an' smoke yer pipe an' watch thin's grow." But he heard "the voice of God sayin': 'This hain't wuth nothin' t' Me. Git ye back t' hum!' I got afeerd o' that voice an' I lit out back t' hum here. . . . " Ephraim obeyed the command of his "hard God" and returned to his stony New England land. The stones he piled into walls. "Ye kin read the years o' my life in them walls, every day a hefted stone, climbin' over the hills up and down, fencin' in the fields that was mine, whar I'd made thin's grow out o' nothin' like the will o' God, like the servant o' His hand. It wa'n't easy. It was hard an' He made me hard fur it."

Significantly, Ephraim acknowledges that the women who had been his wives had made him feel "lonesome." But, "The farm growed. It was all mine! When I thought o' that I didn't feel lonesome." His relationship with his sons has been a tormented one, characterized by mutual loathing. "They hated me 'cause I was hard. I hated them 'cause they was soft. They coveted the farm without knowin' what it meant."

When, at the end of this monologue, Abbie turns "a blank face, resentful eyes to his," Ephraim asks her, "Air ye any the wiser fur all I've told ye?" Then he adds, "Ye don't know nothin'—nor never will." He complains that the house is cold and "oneasy" and departs for the barn, "whar it's warm." He will talk to the cows because "They know. They know the farm an' me. They'll give me peace." Abbie, like her predecessors, has made the old man "lonesome."

Ephraim's belief in an Old Testament deity and his identification with stones associate him with the Apollonian polarity in Nietzsche's *The Birth of Tragedy,* as Bogard has pointed out, while the son who becomes his rival and supplanter and the wife who betrays him with her stepson represent Nietzsche's Dionysian power. Abbie and Eben seek after the "easy God"; Ephraim remains faithful to the "hard God."

As one comes to understand the stones Ephraim has wrested from the earth and the walls he has created from those stones, one sees Ephraim less and less as a hard, life-denying old despot, Peter and Simeon less as deprived offspring, Abbie and Eben less as life-affirming lovers. The truth emerges that Ephraim is the most creative, the most ful-filled member of the Cabot family; that he is the only one who knows who he is; that he has a sense of his own identity and realizes how and where he belongs. Only Ephraim has the strength to make the earth produce; only Ephraim has the will to toil to the end of his days to preserve that productivity; only Ephraim loves the land; only Ephraim is "fruitful"; and ultimately only Ephraim values life.

It is not, of course, just the stones on the Cabot farm that are symbols; the walls that Ephraim has created from the stones also bear symbolic significance. These walls probably mark the boundaries of the farm in addition to identifying individual fields. A pattern of enclosure emerges that identifies those walls with such ancient structures as Stonehenge. Cirlot mentions the sun-symbolism of that "stone-circle" and adds, "It also partakes of circle-symbolism (that is, of the cyclic process, Oneness and perfection) . . . ".

To O'Neill himself the stone walls stood as proof of Ephraim Cabot's faithfulness to his inheritance, of his integrity. The Gelbs have described the playwright's farm in Ridgefield, Connecticut (Brook Farm), as partial inspiration for the Cabot farm. They record that O'Neill told a young man from the Provincetown Players that the kind of stone wall that abounded on Brook Farm was what he was writing about in **Desire Under the Elms.** One wall that O'Neill pointed out, "Though it now ran through a weedy, uncultivated area, . . . had once marked a boundary of tilled soil. These walls, he said, were symbols of the old New England farmer's roots—reproachful monuments to the farmers who left their field to go out west, where there were no stone and where farming was easier. [O'Neill then] quoted some of Ephraim Cabot's lines. . . . "

Ephraim's identification with stones does not ultimately represent the hardness of his heart or of his way of life. The stones suggest more than spirit-numbing, soul-killing labor. They speak of the unity and strength which Cirlot mentions, of Ephraim's "reconciliation with self." Von Franz's comments take the affirmative meaning of stone a step beyond Cirlot's. In following the dictates of his "hard God," Ephraim has obeyed the "spiritual ordering principle"; he has experienced "something eternal"; he may indeed have "God within [his] own soul." (pp. 27-30)

Jean Anne Waterstradt, "Another View of Ephraim Cabot: A Footnote to 'Desire under the Elms'," in The Eugene O'Neill Newsletter, *Vol. IX, No. 2, Summer-Fall, 1985, pp. 27-31.*

Preston Fambrough   (essay date 1986)

[*In the following essay, Fambrough examines the function of mystery and the supernatural in* Desire under the Elms.]

A notion which recurs continually in modern attempts to define tragedy is that of "mystery." According to Richard Sewell, tragedy "sees man as a questioner, naked, unaccommodated, alone, facing mysterious, demonic forces in his own nature and outside." George Steiner locates the uniqueness of the form in the "inexplicable" nature of the forces that destroy the protagonist, forces "which can neither be fully understood nor overcome by rational prudence;" while Richmond Y. Hathorn defines tragedy as "a work of literature which has as its chief emphasis the revelation of a mystery."

The admission of an irreducible core of mystery at the center of the human experience runs counter to the prevailing intellectual current of the past two centuries—the rationalism of the Enlightenment followed by the reductive positivism of its successors. And just as Nietzsche traced the decline of Attic tragedy to the advent of Socratic rationalism, so George Steiner attributes the eclipse of the form after the French classical period to modern faith in reason and science to reveal all truth and resolve every human dilemma. Joseph Mandel is wide of the mark in asserting that nineteenth-century naturalistic determinism is "tragic": fate ceases to be tragic the moment it can be reduced to knowable forces amenable to scientific analysis and control. As Steiner explains, the antithesis of tragedy lies not necessarily in comedy but in didacticism, naturalism and the literature of social criticism, a literature which reduces man's nature and experience to knowable quantities and hence views all his ills, individual and social, as remediable.

In his deliberate and sustained effort to revive Tragedy on the modern stage, Eugene O'Neill, while paying lip service to the modern science of psychology, repeatedly insisted on mystery as the essence of his vision of human destiny. In 1919 he wrote to Barrett Clark, "Perhaps I can explain the nature of my feeling for the impelling, inscrutable forces behind life which it is my ambition to at least faintly shadow at their work in my plays." Elsewhere he asserted that his interest lay in the relationship between man and God, rather than between man and man. In interpreting the latter remark, Törnqvist explains that O'Neill thought of himself as a religious playwright, not "in the strict sense that such a designation can be bestowed on Eliot or Claudel . . . but in the wide sense, that what chiefly concerns him are ultimate, transcendental phenomena."

There are a number of oft-quoted remarks of O'Neill's which might seem, in isolation, to indicate a conventional positivist scepticism toward the transcendental or supernatural, a rejection of mystery in favor of the science of psychology. In the manuscript version of his foreword to **The Great God Brown,** the playwright affirms that "if we have no Gods, [sic] or heroes to portray we have the subconscious, the mother of all gods and heroes." Repeatedly, in his working diary notes for *Mourning Becomes Electra,* he speaks of the necessity for finding a "modern psychological approximation of the Greek conception of fate from without, from the supernatural" and he explicitly denies the existence of any supernatural element in *Electra.*

But thoughtful critics have always discerned an element of intrasigent mysticism beneath this surface allegiance to positivism. Asselineau cautions that, the playwright's disclaimers notwithstanding, the psychological view of fate at work in *Electra* does not "entirely supersede the traditional belief in an external fate." Törnqvist explains that while O'Neill shares the naturalist's preoccupation with heredity and environment as determinants of human destiny, "positivism was foreign to O'Neill's antirationalistic, mystical mind." And he points to the curious mingling of scientific and metaphysical language in such expressions as the following: "I'm always acutely conscious of the Force behind—(Fate, God, our biological past creating our present, whatever one calls it—Mystery certainly)." Chabrowe sees in *Desire, Strange Interlude, Electra,* and *Long Day's Journey Into Night* "attempts to reveal man's struggle against the mysterious force that shapes his existence and limits him." And Krutch contends that "at a time when naturalism was the literary norm, he wrote plays that were symbolic in method and mystical in intention."

Desire Under the Elms, "the first of O'Neill's works in which the influence of Greek tragedy is clearly manifest" (Gelb), is charged with an uncompromisingly mystical view of the forces at work in and through human beings, forces which may *manifest* themselves in forms recognizable by the science of psychoanalysis—e.g. Eben's Oedipus complex—but which ultimately transcend scientific or rational explanation. And whether or not O'Neill's emphasis shifts in the course of his career from an "external" to an "internal" concept of fate, as Chabrowe suggests, in this play the two coincide and fuse much as they do in O'Neill's ancient models. In Greek tragedy, action appears to proceed naturally from a given quantity called "character," a complex of distinguishable human traits usually seen in part as having been shaped by past experience and perhaps even by heredity (e.g. Antigone, Hippolytus) in ways that reflect universal "laws" of the human experience. At the same time, the action appears as the product of supernatural forces, a reaction against some breach of the cosmic order. As Kitto explains, "the gods are not directing events as if from outside; they work *in* the events"; "the action is seen on two planes at once, human and divine." Similarly, in *Desire,* we are made cognizant simultaneously of the dark, only partly knowable forces of the individual subconscious and of a superhuman cosmic principle working itself out through the action of the tragedy.

In *Desire* the leitmotif "thin' " functions to reveal at every turn of the action the transcendent, inscrutable force working through the multiplicity of indentifiable human motives in the play. The motif is established in scene two where it recurs several times in quick succession. When Eben bitterly accuses Ephraim of having killed his mother, Simeon replies, "No one never kills nobody. It's allus some thin'. That's the murderer." When Eben inquires "What's somethin'?" his brother replies "dunno." In this exchange, the basic significance of the motif is already revealed. Simeon contends not merely that people are the pawns of a force beyond their control, but that this force can only be identified as a "thin'." This recourse to the indefinite pronoun establishes from the outset the essential inscrutability of the fate at work in the play. Of course we are tempted to supply an explanation—Ephraim's grimly irrational Puritan work ethic, perhaps a function of sexual guilt or repression. But it is not his inarticulateness that makes Simeon hesitate to oversimplify the old man's motivation by naming it. And this cryptic generalization echoes throughout the play in characters' attempts to account for their own or each other's actions and to articulate the mysterious influences they sense at work around them.

Still in the second scene Simeon, in asking Eben to explain his long-standing grudge against the elder brothers, remarks that "Year after year it's skulked in yer eye—somethin'." Later in the play Ephraim, recounting to Abbie how he once left his stony New England farm for a rich and easy life in Ohio, only to abandon his crop and return home, explains, "I could 'o been a rich man—but somethin' in me fit me and fit me—the voice of God sayin': 'This hain't wuth nothin' t'Me. Get ye back t'hum!' " The tone of wonder in which he exclaims "I actoly give up what was rightful mine!" underscores the profoundly incalculable nature of a force that could drive the intensely covetous Ephraim to such an uncongenial act.

The old man, throughout the play, is conscious of a hostile presence in the house: "They's thin's pokin' about in the dark, in the corners." "Even the music can't drive it out," he exclaims during the festivities in honor of the baby, "somethin'." And finally, after he learns the truth about Eben and Abbie's relationship and the child's paternity: "That was it—what I felt—pokin' around the corners—while ye lied—holdin' yerself from me—sayin' ye'd a'ready conceived. . . . I felt they was somethin' onnateral—somewhars—the house got so lonesome—an' cold—drivin' me down to the barn—t'the beasts o' the field."

The mysterious influence at work on Eben and his father can be identified, at one level, with the avenging spirit of Eben's mother. Having driven Ephraim out of the house, the same "onnateral" force seems to impel Eben toward Abbie in spite of the young man's fierce resistance and to preside over their union in the parlor that is sacred to the dead woman's memory:

> ABBIE. When I first come in—in the dark—they seemed somethin' here.
>
> EBEN. (*simply*) Maw.
>
> ABBIE. I kin still feel—somethin'. . . .
>
> EBEN. It's Maw.

Yet to equate the supernatural element of the play absolutely with the mother's ghost, as Racey does, oversimplifies O'Neill's tragic cosmology. Eben himself, baffled at first that his mother's ghost should seem to favor a union between him and Abbie, her rival for the land, at last thinks he discerns the spirit's purpose: "I see it! I see why. It's her vengeance on him—so's she can rest quiet in her grave!" But we know that in fact this love, while punishing Ephraim, will also destroy the dead woman's beloved son as well as his child. The tragic catastrophe clearly transcends what could conceivably be the will of Eben's mother's ghost. I believe Abbie's frantic rejoinder here, "Vengeance o' God on the hull o' us!", provides a clue to the underlying cosmology of the play. As often seems the case in Greek and Elizabethan tragedy, there appear to be at least two levels of superhuman forces at work here. First there are the immediate and circumscribed influences impinging directly on the characters—Cabot's Old Testament god, the ghost, the darkly irrational "Desire" of the title. But apparently these fragmentary forces partake of a larger, more remote, more inhuman and inscrutable will. This is what Abbie intimates in emending Eben's explanation of their passion as retribution on Cabot for his cruelty to the dead woman. The deity she evokes here is something much vaster than the petty tyrant Ephraim serves: it is Moira, the ultimate will of the universe itself.

When Eben learns that Abbie has murdered their child, he cries "Maw, where was ye, why didn't ye stop her?" Again, it is Abbie who senses the truth: "She went back t' her grave that night we first done it, remember? I hain't felt her about since." This observation not only reveals the limited scope of the ghost's influence within the larger cosmic design; it adumbrates something of the relationship between this cosmic design and human justice or morality. Kitto has explained, in analyzing Greek tragedy, that while the logos of the tragic universe includes principles we recognize as "just"—the wicked seldom if ever go unpunished—there are uncharted realms of the cosmic law which transcend human justice. In *Desire Under the Elms,* as in most tragedies, the innocent suffer with the guilty.

In the *Iliad,* the anthropomorphic gods, even the mightiest of them, are usually seen to be clearly subordinate to Moira. Zeus himself bows to this inexorable force at least twice in relinquishing his determination first to save the life of his son Sarpendon and later the life of Hector. Steiner maintains that the Greek Pantheon, representing the partly intelligible elements of man's destiny, serves as a "reassuring mask" between us and Fate. O'Neill's tragedy reveals a similar cosmology. The principal characters are motivated directly by demonic elements—the ghost, Ephraim's god, the "desire" of the title—which, though beyond the ken of science and reason, are in some way apprehensible and identifiable. The ubiquitous leitmotif "thin'" emerges as the common denominator linking these half-knowable forces and pointing to the ineffable mystery beyond. (pp. 25-8)

Preston Fambrough, "The Tragic Cosmology of O'Neill's 'Desire under the Elms'," in The Eugene O'Neill Newsletter, *Vol. X, No. 2, Summer-Fall, 1986, pp. 25-9.*

Bette Mandl   (essay date 1987)

[In the following essay, Mandl argues that O'Neill

equates the natural setting of Desire under the Elms *with the female gender.]*

In the famous stage directions for the first act of *Desire Under the Elms,* O'Neill describes the trees of the title:

> Two enormous elms are on each side of the house. They bend their trailing branches down over the roof. They appear to protect and at the same time subdue. There is a sinister maternity in their aspect, a crushing, jealous absorption. They have developed from their intimate contact with the life of man in the house an appalling humaneness. They brood oppressively over the house. They are like exhausted women resting their sagging breasts and hands and hair on its roof, and when it rains their tears trickle down monotonously and rot on the shingles.

Travis Bogard praises O'Neill's restraint in imposing these elms as symbols on an essentially realitic play: "the novelistic rhetoric that links the elms with Eben's dead mother and with an exhausted life force holds no meaning beyond the printed page." While this prelude may have its theatrical limitations, however, it does, as Normand Berlin suggests, have its resonance in the play. The description of the elms, which O'Neill referred to as "characters, almost," initiates a metaphoric pattern that O'Neill works with throughout. In linking the maternal—here "a sinister maternity" compounded of opposites—to the natural world, to the landscape, he prepares us for the projection of the intensities of the Freudian "family romance" onto the terrain of the Cabot farm.

O'Neill claimed to have dreamed *Desire Under the Elms* in its entirety. As Louis Sheaffer has pointed out, O'Neill did some borrowing—particularly from Sidney Howard's *They Knew What They Wanted*—as well as dreaming. However, O'Neill certainly drew on *collective* dream, on an enduring tradition of mythic and psychological fantasy, when he identified woman, and particularly the mother, with the land. Theorists who have recently focused on such imagery provide us with a context in which to consider its centrality to the play. In a celebrated essay entitled "Is Female to Male as Nature Is to Culture?" Sherry Ortner suggests that for a variety of reasons, biological, social, and psychological, "women are . . . identified or symbolically associated with nature, . . . [while] men . . . are identified with culture." Women, that is, are seen as coextensive with, or at least much closer to, the natural world. Men, on the other hand, have traditionally felt compelled to master and transcend nature in order to create and maintain culture. This division, Ortner argues, gives rise to a seemingly universal hierarchical structure that places culture and man *over* nature and woman. Ortner is concerned with the ways in which this analogy derives from and influences our experience. As Annette Kolodny points out in her study of the imagery that links woman and the land in American writing about the new world, "language . . . contains verbal cues to underlying psychological patterns" and can therefore "be examined as a repository of internal experience and external expression." Kolodny discusses the tension, fraught with suggestions of oedipal ambivalence, "between the intial urge to . . . join passively with . . . a maternal landscape and the consequent impulse to master and act upon that same femininity." The conceptual fusion of woman and nature tends to put both in jeopardy. Kolodny's work, like that of Ortner, is a vivid reminder of the risk of metaphor.

The power of **Desire Under the Elms** is, in large measure, contingent on such imagery as these theorists hold up to scrutiny. O'Neill could be said to have collaborated in the imaginative tradition whose problematic implications they identify. However, while **Desire** tends to illustrate the conjunction of landscape and gender that Ortner and Kolodny describe, the play also has a distinct affinity with their critique. In 1925, O'Neill called **Desire** "a tragedy of the possessive—the pitiful longing of man to build his own heaven here on earth by glutting his sense of power with ownership of land, people, money." While O'Neill maps out his dramatic territory using the quintessential equation "woman equals nature," he also illuminates the overweening desire to possess and to dominate that is its corollary.

Striking congruities emerge in the play as it becomes apparent that land and woman are at the heart of the struggle between Eben Cabot and his father. Blaming Ephraim for having exhausted, and thereby killed, his mother, Eben is determined to wrest from him the farm she claimed as her own. He believes that only then will her soul finally be at peace. Eben resents his father for the hardness Cabot is so proud of, and insists, "I'm Maw—every drop o' blood." He claims to have learned from doing the arduous domestic tasks she used to do, to "know her, suffer he sufferin'." He is in revolt against the way of life on the Cabot farm, "makin' walls—stone atop o' stone—makin' walls till yer heart's a stone. . . . "

Eben's brothers, Simeon and Peter, the older sons of Cabot's first marriage, are somewhat removed from the primary intensities of the play. They had felt kindly toward Eben's mother, but refuse to blame their father for her death. "No one never kills nobody," Simeon says. "It's allus somethin'. That's the murderer. . . . " Peter agrees: "He's slaved himself t' death. He's slaved Sim 'n' me 'n' yew t' death—on'y none o' us hain't died—yit." They decide to leave rather than fight over the farm when they learn that their father has married and they are likely to lose their inheritance. Likened in O'Neill's description to "friendly oxen" and "beasts of the field," Simeon and Peter say of the farm animals that they "know us like brothers—an' like us" (218). Eben's brothers are not linked with the mother; nor do they aspire to the drive for mastery of the father. It seems appropriate, then, that they do not figure significantly in the highly polarized world of **Desire.**

It is Eben, seeing himself as his mother's heir, who engages most fully in the struggle with the father for power and possession. He has his first sexual experience with Min after he learns that both his father and his brothers had been with her. In a simile characteristic of the drama, Eben says that Min "smells like a wa'm plowed field, she's purty" and later declares to his brothers: "Yes, siree! I tuk her. She may've been his'n—an' your'n, too—but she's mine now!" He uses the money his mother told him Cabot had hidden, to buy their shares of the farm from his broth-

ers. After the transaction is completed, Eben talks with "queer excitement": "It's my farm! Them's my cows!" Simeon and Peter see their father in him: "Dead spit 'n' image!" O'Neill tells us that Eben "stares around him with glowing, possessive eyes. He takes in the whole farm with his embracing glance of desire" and says, "It's purty! It's damned purty! It's mine!" The restricted vocabulary, appropriate to the "inexpressiveness" (O'Neill quoted in Shaeffer) that was a focus for O'Neill in this work, reveals all the more transparently the overlap of landscape and gender that is crucial to its realization.

That there will be a contest between Eben and his father over Abbie, Cabot's new wife, is anticipated even by Simeon, who is slow and plodding. Before we meet Abbie or know what her own intentions are, we sense that her principal role will be to mediate the relationship between father and son. Shortly after Abbie arrives at the farm, Simeon and Peter take off for California to search for gold, choosing, in Cabot's terms, an easy life, which at times tempts even the harsh, scripture-quoting patriarch himself. They leave Cabot, Abbie and Eben on the farm, which itself figures so significantly in the intensely oedipal configuration.

Abbie is a compelling character. O'Neill describes her as thirty-five, and "full of vitality." She has "about her whole personality the same unsettled, untamed, desperate quality which is so apparent in Eben." Like Eben, she wants the farm. An orphan who has already endured a difficult marriage, and whose child and first husband have died, she married the 75-year old Ephraim Cabot in order to have a home. Without exonerating her, O'Neill represents her desire for the farm as different in kind from that of the men. As she says to Eben defiantly, "Waal—what if I did need a hum?" Her relation to nature as a generative force is also different from theirs. She speaks of "Nature—makin' thin's grow—bigger 'n' bigger—burnin' inside ye—makin' ye want t' grow—into somethin' else—till ye're jined with it—and it's your'n but it owns ye, too—and makes ye grow bigger—like a tree—like them elums—". She envisions mutuality of possession which is conspicuously absent on the Cabot farm. And she taunts Cabot when he talks of the sky as "purty" and like a "wa'm field up thar," asking him, "Air yew aimin' t' buy up over the farm too?"

Jealous when Eben goes off to see Min, Abbie tells Cabot that her stepson tried to make love to her. Here she becomes linked with Phaedra, as she has been with Iocasta. In spite of the dramatic stature the mythic dimension adds to her role, however, she remains, like the land, essentially an object of contention between father and son. Ephraim wouldn't consider letting her inherit the farm even though all his sons have disappointed him. "Ye're on'y a woman." When she reminds him that she is his wife, he says, "That hain't me. A son is me—my blood—mine. Mine ought t' get mine. An' then it's still—mine—even though I be six foot under" 234).

Abbie decides to conceive a child who could inherit the farm for her. Cabot, not knowing that she has Eben in mind as the father, is ecstatic at the possibility of a new son. His reflections at this point provide the clearest indication of the kind of symbol system that O'Neill employs with consistency throughout *Desire Under the Elms.* Cabot says to Abbie, "Sometimes ye air the farm an' sometimes the farm be yew. That's why I clove t' ye in my lonesomeness. . . . Me an' the farm has got t' beget a son!" Abbie, hearing what appears to be a barely conscious admission, tells him he's "gittin' thin's all mixed." Cabot insists, "No, I hain't. My mind's clear's a well. Ye don't know me, that's it." Cabot envisions having Abbie *as* the farm produce a son who would guarantee him an eternity of ownership. As Abbie says, he is getting things "all mixed." The confusion he articulates, however, is a primal one.

As Cabot goes on to explain himself to his wife, whose thoughts are actually with Eben, he reveals more fully what Simeon had referred to as the "somethin'—drivin' him—t' drive us!" Cabot describes himself in his youth as having been 'the strongest an' hardest ye ever seen—ten times as strong an' fifty times as hard as Eben." Boasting of his achievement in making "corn sprout out o' stones," he speaks of the God he worships, insisting: "God's hard, not easy! God's in the stones!" He projects, as Frederick Wilkins has said, "his own hardness onto his conception of the deity."

Ephraim's battle with the stony soil and his disdain for the softness of the mother of Simeon and Peter, and the mother of Eben, suggest the hierarchy that Sherry Ortner discerns. His pride derives from his mastery of the land and his sense of superiority over the women. However, his satisfaction with his way of being in the world is flawed. He suffers from a persistent unease and loneliness.

In the book, *Woman and Nature: The Roaring Inside Her,* Susan Griffin suggests that man's efforts to distance himself from the feminine and from the natural world contribute to his sense of exile and homelessness. Her prologue is a meditation on man: "He says that woman speaks with nature. . . . But for him this dialogue is over. He says he is not part of this world, that he was set on this world as a stranger. He sets himself apart from woman and nature." This passage seems to echo the revelation of Cabot's "lonesomeness," which is prefaced by his conflation of Abbie and the farm. The sequence of his reflections seems to suggest, as the theorists do, a profound connection between man's conception of landscape and gender, and the experience of alienation.

Cabot is uncomfortable in the house, the sphere of the feminine: "It's oneasy. They's thin's pokin' about in the dark—in the corners." At home, he is troubled by "somethin'," which he feels "droppin' off the elums"—the symbols of a "sinister," but violated maternity. His grueling work on the land, bound up as it is with assertion and control, affords him no comfort either. He would try to console himself by remembering what he possessed: "It was all mine! When I thought of that I didn't feel lonesome." But neither his periodic efforts to conjure up the exaltation of ownership, nor his attempts to seek temporary refuge in the barn with the cows, alleviate his essential isolation.

The attraction of Abbie and Eben thwarts Cabot's hope for a new heir. With thoughts of a child, and with increasing love for Eben, Abbie re-opens the parlor of Eben's mother and insists that he court her there. When with trepidation they sit together in the parlor, both Eben and Abbie sense the approval of the maternal spirit, and the easing of her cares. Eben decides that his mother accepts his union with Abbie, who insists on her similarity to the mother, because it would serve as revenge against Cabot.

After Abbie bears the child he believes is his own, Cabot arranges a celebration. His neighbors easily guess who the child's father really is. But Cabot outdoes everyone there with his age-defying dance, performing one of what John Henry Raleigh calls his "legendary feats." O'Neill once said, "I have always loved Ephraim so much! He is so autobiographical." But while Ephraim Cabot is permitted a dazzling display of endurance, it is Eben who is granted a release from what O'Neill, in another reference to the play, called "old man Cabotism."

Eben, finding it difficult to respond to his newborn son, tells Abbie, "I don't like this. I don't like lettin' on what's mine's his'n. I been doin' that all my life. I'm gittin' t' the end of b'arin' it!" He is ready for the ultimate confrontation with the father, which is precipitated by Cabot's disclosure that Abbie wanted a son in order to get the farm for herself. When Abbie fears that she will lose Eben, she makes a desperate effort to prove her love for him above all else, by murdering their baby. It is through the appalling act of infanticide that O'Neill resolves the violent tensions of the Cabot household. The death of the baby interrupts a bitter cycle of succession that threatens to stretch into a future where the sins of the fathers—and brother— are visited upon the children. It also shocks Eben into a transformation.

After he reports Abbie to the sheriff, Eben acknowledges his own unwitting complicity in her crime. He says, "I want t' share with ye, Abbie—prison 'r death 'r hell 'r anythin'! . . . If I'm sharin' with ye, I won't feel lonesome, leastways." Eben's lines suggest that he is no longer in the throes of an oedipal obsession with Abbie, or with the farm. Newly able to love Abbie, he has moved beyond his father's relation to woman and the land, and the loneliness it engendered. By having the son break free from its influence, O'Neill seems to subvert the imagery that has informed the play. The son is rewarded for his renunciation of the paradigm his father had glorified. Having made it possible for his mother's spirit to rest. Eben now manages, through his determination to stand by Abbie, to earn the father's "grudging admiration," a reconciliation of sorts. When the sheriff looks around the farm "enviously," and says, "It's a jim-dandy farm, no denyin'. Wished I owned it!", we are able to gauge the distance Eben has travelled from the imperatives that shape the "tragedy of the possessive." (pp. 19-22)

Bette Mandl, "Family Ties: Landscape and Gender in 'Desire under the Elms'," in The Eugene O'Neill Newsletter, *Vol. XI, No. 2, Summer-Fall, 1987, pp. 19-23.*

FURTHER READING

Biography

Gelb, Arthur and Barbara. *O'Neill.* New York: Harper & Row, 1962, 990 p.

    Comprehensive biography of O'Neill, including a discussion of *Desire under the Elms* and the controversy surrounding its debut.

Sheaffer, Louis. *O'Neill: Son and Artist.* Boston: Little, Brown & Co., 1973, 750 p.

    Biography of O'Neill from 1920 to his death in 1953, including discussion of autobiographical elements in *Desire under the Elms.*

Criticism

Cargill, Oscar; Fagin, N. Bryllion; and Fisher, William, eds. *O'Neill and His Plays: Four Decades of Criticism.* New York: New York University Press, 1961, 528 p.

    Contains some of O'Neill's letters, a review of *Desire under the Elms,* and an article chronicling the arrest of the Los Angeles theater company that performed the play in 1926.

Clark, Barrett H. "A New Note in Tragedy— *Desire under the Elms.*" In his *Eugene O'Neill: The Man and His Plays,* pp. 146-53. New York: Robert McBride & Co., 1936.

    Summary of the plot and early production history of the play.

Conlin, Matthew T., O.F.M. "The Tragic Effect in *Autumn Fire* and *Desire under the Elms.*" *Modern Drama* 1, No. 4 (February 1959): 228-35.

    Compares the protagonists and dramatic themes of T. C. Murray's *Autumn Fire* and O'Neill's *Desire under the Elms.*

Floyd, Virginia, ed. *Eugene O'Neill: A World View.* New York: Frederick Ungar, 1979, 309 p.

    Furnishes information on foreign productions of *Desire under the Elms.*

Frenz, Horst. *Eugene O'Neill.* New York: Frederick Ungar, 1971, 121p.

    Compares *Desire under the Elms* with Henrik Ibsen's *Rosmersholm* and claims it "is the construction of plot and characters (especially of Ephraim) and the stylistic sureness" that make the play compelling.

Mikos, Michael, and Mulroy, David. "Reymont's *The Peasants:* A Probable Influence on *Desire under the Elms.*" *The Eugene O'Neill Newsletter* X, No. 1 (Spring 1986): 4-15.

    Outlines the similarities between the two works in setting, characterization, and plot.

Ranald, Margaret Loftus. *"Desire under the Elms."* In her *The Eugene O'Neill Companion,* pp. 164-77. Westport, Conn.: Greenwood Press, 1984.

    Plot summary and critical commentary.

Additional coverage of O'Neill's life and career is contained in the following sources published by Gale Research: *Authors in the News,* **Vol. 1;** *Concise Dictionary of American Literary Biography,* **1929-1941;** *Contemporary Authors,* **Vol. 132;** *Dictionary of Literary Biography,* **Vol. 7;** *Major 20th-Century Writers; Twentieth-Century Literary Criticism,* **Vols. 1, 6, 27; and** *World Literature Criticism.*

Ferdinand de Saussure

1857-1913

Swiss linguist and educator.

INTRODUCTION

Saussure is best known for *Cours de linguistique générale* (*Course in General Linguistics*), which details his theory of language. Departing from nineteenth-century philological scholarship, Saussure analyzed language as a set of rules shared by a community rather than a system of nomenclature unrelated to a social and cultural context. Saussure's theories, which focus on a series of linguistic oppositions, have revolutionized literary and cultural studies and are frequently recognized as having influenced the theories and methodologies of structuralism and semiotics.

Saussure was born in Geneva, Switzerland, into a family of scientists. As a student he proved adept at languages—learning French, German, English, Latin, Greek, and Sanskrit—and was often encouraged in his studies by his mentor, linguist Adolphe Pictet. Planning a career in the physical sciences, Saussure attended the University of Geneva and later transferred to the University of Leipzig, where he began studying Indo-European languages and comparative grammar. In 1878 he published his first full-length work, the critically acclaimed *Mémoire sur le système primitif des voyelles dans les langues indo-européennes,* which examined the use of vowels in Indo-European languages. After completing his dissertation, *De l'emploi du génitif absolu en sanscrit,* Saussure moved to Paris, becoming active in the Linguistic Society of Paris and obtaining employment at the Ecole Practique des Hautes Etudes, where he taught German, Sanskrit, Latin, Persian, and Lithuanian. In 1891 he joined the teaching staff of the University of Geneva as professor of comparative grammar and Indo-European languages, and between 1906 and 1911 he taught three courses in general linguistics; these became the basis for his *Course in General Linguistics.* Saussure died in 1913.

The innovative concepts outlined in the *Course* and the events surrounding its publication have been the subject of much discussion. Because Saussure refused to publish his theories until they were completely refined and proven accurate, the *Course* was never actually written by Saussure but was compiled from his students' notes after his death. The editors, Charles Bally and Albert Sechehaye, have been praised for capturing the essence of Saussure's ideas, but their revisions and deletions have been questioned. Scholars lament that Bally and Sechehaye fail to show how Saussure's ideas evolved as he taught general linguistics and that his theories were, particularly in his opinion, still subject to revision. The controversy surrounding the *Course* has been exacerbated by scholars

who question the originality of Saussurean thought; many critics now recognize that Saussure was deeply influenced by the works of his contemporaries Michel Bréal and W. D. Whitney.

Central to the *Course* is Saussure's concept of language as a constantly evolving system of signs. According to Saussure, words themselves have no meaning; meaning occurs only when individuals agree that a particular combination of sounds designate a certain object or idea, thus creating a "sign" for that particular object or idea. Saussure asserts that signs are composed of two parts: the signifier, or vocal or graphic form, and the thing it represents, the signified. Although the signifier and signified are different entities, the distinctions between the two are blurred, and it is difficult, if not impossible, to separate one from the other. Furthermore, the relationship between signified and signifier is arbitrary—the vocal representation of the thing in no way defines it—and the relationship between signs is differential. As Saussure argues, "linguistic signs are unrelated to what they designate, and that therefore *a* cannot designate anything without the aid of *b* and vice versa, or, in other words, that both have value only by the differences between them, or that neither has value, in any of its constituents, except through this same network of forever negative differences." Saussure believed that this agreement of meaning and creation of value, frequently implicit, takes place on all levels of language, including phonology, morphology, syntax, and semantics, and the successful communication of ideas depends on each speaker's ability to distinguish between signs as well as nuances of meaning.

In addition to the signifer-signified distinction, the *Course* examines several other binary oppositions: *langue* versus *parole,* the diachronic versus the synchronic, and the paradigmatic (associative) versus the syntagmatic. The *langue-parole* dichotomy reemphasizes that language is not merely a system of nomenclature lacking social significance. The concept of *langue* asserts that language is an internalized set of rules and codes shared by members of a community, while *parole* is merely the manifestation, whether graphic or vocal, of an utterance. Saussure's emphasis on a synchronic study of language is also related to *langue.* Before Saussure, linguists viewed language from a diachronic, or historical, perspective. As a comparative grammarian, Saussure recognized the validity of studying language development chronologically, but he additionally stressed the necessity of analyzing language at a given moment and not only as a series of descriptive changes. Saussure's focus on the synchronic anticipated his emphasis on the paradigmatic and syntagmatic axes of combination, which dictate the rules of syntax and the nuances of meaning. The paradigmatic, or associative, is that axis along which one word may be substituted for another; the syntagmatic axis governs the combination of words into coherent and grammatically correct units of speech.

While generally recognized as the father of modern linguistics, Saussure has been criticized for focusing solely on the social aspects of language and ignoring the individual's ability to create and manipulate meaning. Nevertheless, his attempts to scientifically examine the nature of language have had a marked impact outside the field of linguistics. His synchronic and social view of language and signification has revolutionized contemporary literary theory and influenced the evolution of structuralism, New Criticism, deconstructionism, and semiotics. Recognizing the numerous applications of Saussurean thought, Roy Harris observed that Saussure provided "an approach later to be exploited by theorists in such diverse fields as art, architecture, philosophy, literary criticism and social anthropology. The implications of Saussure's technique for dealing with linguistic analysis extend far beyond the boundaries of language, in ways which make the *Cours de linguistique générale* without doubt one of the most far-reaching works concerning the study of cultural activities to have been published at any time since the Renaissance."

PRINCIPAL WORKS

Mémoire sur le système primitif des voyelles dans les langues indo-européennes (nonfiction) 1878

De l'emploi du génitif absolu en sanscrit (nonfiction) 1881
*Cours de linguistique générale (nonfiction) 1916
  [*Course in General Linguistics,* 1959]
Recueil des publications scientifiques de Ferdinand de Saussure (nonfiction) 1922

*This work has been revised and translated several times since its initial publication. Tullio de Mauro's edition (1973) and Rudolf Engler's critical edition (1967-74) are now considered the definitive original language versions, while Wade Baskin and Roy Harris have been responsible for translating the work into English.

CRITICISM

Charles Bally and Albert Sechehaye (essay date 1915)

[*In the following excerpt, which was included in the first edition of Saussure's* Course in General Linguistics, *editors Bally and Sechehaye describe the difficulties they encountered in compiling Saussure's notes and identify the potential weaknesses of their work.*]

We have often heard Ferdinand de Saussure lament the dearth of principles and methods that marked linguistics during his developmental period. Throughout his lifetime, he stubbornly continued to search out the laws that would give direction to his thought amid the chaos. Not until 1906, when he took the place of Joseph Wertheimer at the University of Geneva, was he able to make known the ideas that he had nurtured through so many years. Although he taught three courses in general linguistics—in 1906-1907, 1908-1909, and 1910-1911—his schedule forced him to devote half of each course to the history and description of the Indo-European languages, with the result that the basic part of his subject received considerably less attention than it merited.

All those who had the privilege of participating in his richly rewarding instruction regretted that no book had resulted from it. After his death, we hoped to find in his manuscripts, obligingly made available to us by Mme. de Saussure, a faithful or at least an adequate outline of his inspiring lectures. At first we thought that we might simply collate F. de Saussure's personal notes and the notes of his students. We were grossly misled. We found nothing—or almost nothing—that resembled his students' notebooks. As soon as they had served their purpose, F. de Saussure destroyed the rough drafts of the outlines used for his lectures. In the drawers of his secretary we found only older outlines which, although certainly not worthless, could not be integrated into the material of the three courses.

Our discovery was all the more disappointing since professorial duties had made it impossible for us to attend F. de Saussure's last lectures—and these mark just as brilliant a step in his career as the much earlier one that had witnessed the appearance of his treatise on the vocalic system of Proto-Indo-European.

We had to fall back on the notes collected by students during the course of his three series of lectures. Very complete notebooks were placed at our disposal: for the first two courses, by Messrs. Louis Caille, Léopold Gautier, Paul Regard, and Albert Riedlinger; for the third—the most important—by Mme. Albert Sechehaye and by Messrs. George Dégallier and Francis Joseph. We are indebted to M. Louis Brütsch for notes on one special point. (pp. xvii-xviii)

What were we to do with our materials? First, the task of criticism. For each course and for each detail of the course, we had to compare all versions and reconstruct F. de Saussure's thought from faint, sometimes conflicting, hints. For the first two courses we were able to enlist the services of M. Riedlinger, one of the students who have followed the thought of the master with the greatest interest; his work was most valuable. For the third course one of us, A. Sechehaye, performed the same detailed task of collating and synthesizing the material.

But after that? Oral delivery, which is often contradictory in form to written exposition, posed the greatest difficulties. Besides, F. de Saussure was one of those men who never stand still; his thought evolved in all directions without ever contradicting itself as a result. To publish everything in the original form was impossible; the repetitions—inevitable in free oral presentation—overlappings, and variant formulations would lend a motley appearance to such a publication. To limit the book to a single course—and which one?—was to deprive the reader of the rich and varied content of the other two courses; by itself the third, the most definitive of the three courses, would not give a complete accounting of the theories and methods of F. de Saussure.

One suggestion was that we publish certain particularly original passages without change. This idea was appealing at first, but soon it became obvious that we would be distorting the thought of our master if we presented but fragments of a plan whose value stands out only in its totality.

We reached a bolder but also, we think, a more rational solution: to attempt a reconstruction, a synthesis, by using the third course as a starting point and by using all other materials at our disposal, including the personal notes of F. de Saussure, as supplementary sources. The problem of re-creating F. de Saussure's thought was all the more difficult because the re-creation had to be wholly objective. At each point we had to get to the crux of each particular thought by trying to see its definitive form in the light of the whole system. We had first to weed out variations and irregularities characteristic of oral delivery, then to fit the thought into its natural framework and present each part of it in the order intended by the author even when his intention, not always apparent, had to be surmised.

From this work of assimilation and reconstruction was born the book that we offer, not without apprehension, to the enlightened public and to all friends of linguistics.

Our aim was to draw together an organic whole by omitting nothing that might contribute to the overall impression. But for that very reason, we shall probably be criticized on two counts.

First, critics will say that this "whole" is incomplete. In his teaching the master never pretended to examine all parts of linguistics or to devote the same attention to each of those examined; materially, he could not. Besides, his main concern was not that. Guided by some fundamental and personal principles which are found everywhere in his work—and which form the woof of this fabric which is as solid as it is varied—he tried to penetrate; only where these principles find particularly striking applications or where they apparently conflict with some theory did he try to encompass.

That is why certain disciplines, such as semantics, are hardly touched upon. We do not feel that these lacunae detract from the overall architecture. The absence of a "linguistics of speaking" is regrettable. This study, which had been promised to the students of the third course, would doubtlessly have had a place of honor; why his promise could not be kept is too well known. All we could do was to collect the fleeting impressions from the rough outlines of this project and put them into their natural place.

Conversely, critics may say that we have reproduced facts bearing on points developed by F. de Saussure's predecessors. Not everything in such an extensive treatise can be new. But if known principles are necessary for the understanding of a whole, shall we be condemned for not having omitted them? The chapter on phonetic changes, for example, includes things that have been said before, and perhaps more definitively; but, aside from the fact that this part contains many valuable and original details, even a superficial reading will show to what extent its omission would detract from an understanding of the principles upon which F. de Saussure erects his system of static linguistics.

We are aware of our responsibility to our critics. We are also aware of our responsibility to the author, who probably would not have authorized the publication of these pages.

This responsibility we accept wholly, and we would willingly bear it alone. Will the critics be able to distinguish between the teacher and his interpreters? We would be grateful to them if they would direct toward us the blows which it would be unjust to heap upon one whose memory is dear to us. (pp. xviii-xx)

> *Charles Bally and Albert Sechehaye, in a preface to* Course in General Linguistics *by Ferdinand de Saussure, Charles Bally, Albert Sechehaye, Albert Riedlinger, eds., translated by Wade Baskin, McGraw-Hill Book Company, 1959, pp. xvii-xx.*

Leonard Bloomfield (essay date 1924)

[*In the essay below, Bloomfield provides a positive assessment of the second edition of the* Course in General Linguistics, *praising in particular Saussure's systematic and methodical approach to language study.*]

It is gratifying to see a second edition of de Saussure's post-humous work on language [*Cours de linguistique générale*]; the popularity of the book betokens not only an interest in language, but also a willingness of the scientific public to face linguistic theory, which at almost every step shocks our preconception of human affairs.

In de Saussure's lifetime the history of the Indo-European languages was widely studied; he himself had made at least one great contribution to it, his *Mémoire sur le système primitif des voyelles dans les langues indo-européennes* (1878). But in lecturing on "general linguistics" he stood very nearly alone, for, strange as it may seem, the nineteenth century, which studied intensively the history of one family of languages, took little or no interest in the general aspects of human speech. After de Saussure's death the present book was put together, largely from lecture-notes.

The value of the *Cours* lies in its clear and rigorous demonstration of fundamental principles. Most of what the author says has long been "in the air" and has been here and there fragmentarily expressed; the systematization is his own. It is known that the historical change in language goes on in a surprisingly mechanical way, independent of any needs, desires, or fears of the speakers; we do not know, for instance, in what direction we, in our time, are changing the English language. Outside of the field of historical grammar, linguistics has worked only in the way of a desperate attempt to give a psychologic interpretation to the facts of language, and in the way of phonetics, an endless and aimless listing of the various sound-articulations of speech. Now, de Saussure seems to have had no psychology beyond the crudest popular notions, and his phonetics are an abstraction from French and Swiss-German which will not stand even the test of an application to English. Thus he exemplifies, in his own person and perhaps unintentionally, what he proves intentionally and in all due form: that psychology and phonetics do not matter at all and are, in principle, irrelevant to the study of language. Needless to say, a person who goes out to write down an unknown language or one who undertakes to teach people a foreign language, must have a knowledge of phonetics, just as he must possess tact, patience, and many other virtues; in principle, however, these things are all on a par, and do not form part of linguistic theory.

De Saussure distinguishes sharply between "synchronic" and "diachronic" linguistics. At any given time ("synchronously"), the language of a community is to be viewed as a system of signals. Each signal is made up of one or more units; these units are the "sounds" of the language. Not only has each signal a definite meaning (e. g. *hat, put*), but the combination of these signals proceeds by definite rules and itself adds definite elements of meaning; for instance, the signal *s* in English is not used alone; added to certain other signals it gives plural meaning (*hats*), added to certain others, it gives the third-person present-tense verb form (*puts*). All this is a complex and arbitrary system of social habit, imposed upon the individual, and not directly subject to psychologic interpretation: all psychology will ever be able to do is to provide the general background which makes the thing possible. Similarly, the physiology of the thing (phonetics) does not matter: instead of the thirty-five or so sounds of English, any thirty-five distinct symbols, of whatever nature, would suffice to reproduce the system of the English language.

This rigid system, the subject-matter of "descriptive linguistics," as we should say, is *la langue,* the language. But *le langage,* human speech, includes something more, for the individuals who make up the community do not succeed in following the system with perfect uniformity. Actual speech-utterance, *la parole,* varies not only as to matters not fixed by the system (e.g., the exact phonetic character of each sound), but also as to the system itself: different speakers at times will violate almost any feature of the system. This brings us to "historical linguistics," *linguistique diachronique;* when such personal and temporary features of *la parole* become general and habitual in the community, they constitute a change in the system of *la langue,*—a sound-change or an analogic change, such as are recorded in our historical grammars.

In detail, I should differ from de Saussure chiefly in basing my analysis on the sentence rather than on the word; by following the latter custom de Saussure gets a rather complicated result in certain matters of word-composition and syntax. The essential point, however, is this, that de Saussure has here first mapped out the world in which historical Indo-European grammar (the great achievement of the past century) is merely a single province; he has given us the theoretical basis for a science of human speech. (pp. 317-19)

Leonard Bloomfield, in a review of "Cours de Linguistique Générale," in The Modern Language Journal, *Vol. VIII, No. 5, February, 1924, pp. 317-19.*

Emile Benveniste   (essay date 1963)

[*Benveniste was a world-renowned linguist, educator, and critic who specialized in comparative grammar and Indo-European languages. In the following essay, which was originally delivered as a lecture commemorating the fiftieth anniversary of Saussure's death, Benveniste examines Saussure's aims as a linguist and the influence the* Course in General Linguistics *has had on contemporary theorists.*]

Ferdinand de Saussure died February 22, 1913. Here we are gathered together fifty years later, on the same date, the twenty-second of February in 1963, for a special commemoration in his city and in his university. His figure now takes on its authentic character and appears to us in its true grandeur. There is not a linguist today who does not owe him something. There is not a general theory which does not mention his name. Some mystery surrounded his actual life since he so early retired into silence. It is his work we shall deal with. The only fitting eulogy for such a work is that which explains its origins and causes its influence to be understood.

Today we see Saussure completely differently from the way his contemporaries could see him. A whole part of him, undoubtedly the most important, was not known until after his death. The science of human speech was gradually changed by him. What is it that Saussure brought to the linguistics of his day, and how has he influenced ours?

In order to answer that question, one could go from one of his works to the other, analyzing, comparing, and discussing them. A critical inventory like that is undoubtedly necessary. The admirable and important work of Robert Godel has contributed greatly to this. But this is not our purpose. Leaving to others the detailed description of that work, we shall try to recapture its basic principles in the drive which animated and even formed it.

There is in every creative person a certain drive, hidden and permanent, which sustains him and devours him, guides his thoughts, directs him to his task, spurs him on when he lapses, and shows him no quarter when he attempts to evade it. It is not always to be recognized in the different stages, sometimes tentative, in which Saussure's thought was engaged. But once it has been discerned, it illuminates the meaning of his effort and situates him with regard to his predecessors as well as with respect to us.

Saussure was first and always a man of fundamentals. He went instinctively to the most basic characteristics which govern the diversity of the empirical datum. In the sphere of language, he suspected the existence of certain qualities which were not met with anywhere else. No matter what it was compared to, language always appeared as something different. But how was it different? Considering that activity, human speech, in which so many factors are brought together—biological, physical and psychic, individual and social, historical, aesthetic, and pragmatic—he asked himself, where does language properly belong?

A more precise form could be given to this question by connecting it to the two following problems, which we see as being at the center of Saussure's teaching:

> 1. What are the basic data on which linguistics is to be grounded and how can we grasp them?
>
> 2. What is the nature of the notions of human speech and by what mode of relationship are they articulated?

This preoccupation can be discerned in Saussure from the moment of his entrance into the science, in his *Mémoire sur le système primitif des voyelles dans les langues indo-européennes,* published when he was twenty-one years old and still one of his titles to fame. The brilliant novice attacked one of the most difficult problems of comparative grammar, a question which, as a matter of fact, did not yet exist and which he was the first to formulate in the appropriate terms. Why did he choose, in a field so vast and promising, such a demanding subject? Let us reread his preface. There he shows that his intention had been to study the Indo-European *a* but that he had been led to consider "the system of vowels as a whole." This led him to treat "a series of problems of phonetics and morphology, some of which still await their solution and several of which have not even been posed." And as if to excuse himself for having "to cross the most unexplored regions of Indo-European linguistics," he adds this illuminating justification:

> If we have nevertheless ventured to go there,

convinced in advance that our inexperience will go astray many times in the labyrinth, it is because, for anyone engaged in these studies, attacking such questions is not temerity, as has often been said, but a necessity. It is the first school through which one must pass, for it is not a matter of transcendental speculations but of the quest for elementary data, without which everything wavers, everything is arbitrariness and incertitude.

These last lines could serve as an epigraph to his entire work. They contain the program for his future research, they are portents of his orientation and his goal. Until the end of his life, and more and more insistently—painfully, one might say—the farther he advanced in his thinking, the more he sought for those "elementary data" which constitute language, turning away gradually from the science of his time in which he saw only "arbitrariness and incertitude," and this at a period when Indo-European linguistics, confident of its methods, was following the comparative approach with increasing success.

It is indeed the elementary data which must be discovered, even (one would like to write, especially) if the purpose is to go back from a historical state of the language to a prehistoric one. Otherwise, the historical development will not have a rational basis, for if there is history, what is it a history of? What changes and what remains the same? How can we say of a linguistic phenomenon considered at two different moments of evolution that it is the *same* phenomenon? In what does that sameness reside, and, since it links for linguists two different objects, how shall we define it? A body of definitions is necessary. We must state the logical connections established within the data, their features, the points of view from which they can be apprehended. To go thus to the fundamentals is the only way—but the sure way—to explain a concrete and contingent fact. In order to reach what is historically concrete, to see the very inevitability of the contingent, we must locate each element in the network of correlations which determines it and admit explicitly that the fact does not exist except by virtue of the definition which we give it. Such was the conviction that forced itself upon Saussure's mind from the beginning and which his whole life was not enough to introduce into linguistic theory.

But even if he had formulated then what he was to teach later, he would only have deepened the lack of comprehension or hostility with which his first attempts were met. The chief scholars then, confident of their own truth, refused to listen to this rigorous summons, and the very difficulty of the *Mémoire* was enough to discourage most of them. Perhaps Saussure would have lost heart. It required another generation for his ideas slowly to make their way. It was a fortunate destiny which took him then to Paris. He recovered some confidence in himself, thanks to that remarkable chance which caused him to meet at the same time a sympathetic tutor, [Michel] Bréal, and a group of young linguists like [Antoine] Meillet and M. Grammont, who were to be profoundly influenced by his teaching. A new phase of comparative grammar dates from these years in which Saussure inculcated his doctrine, at the same time that he was maturing it, among those who were to develop it. That is why we recall, not only to gauge the personal influence of Saussure but also to assess the progress of the ideas they reveal, the terms of the dedication which Meillet made to his master, Saussure, in 1903, in his *Introduction à l'étude comparative des langues indo-européennes,* "on the occasion of the twenty-fifth year since the publication of the *Mémoire* . . . (1878-1903)." The event would have been more clearly marked if it had been up to Meillet alone; an unpublished letter from Saussure tells us that Meillet had first intended to write "for the anniversary of the publication," from which he was dissuaded by Saussure.

But even in 1903, that is to say, twenty-five years after the publication of the *Mémoire* of 1878, it still was not possible to know all the prophetic intuitions it contained. Here is a striking example. Saussure had discerned in the Indo-European vowel system several types of *a*. In point of pure knowledge, the different Indo-European *a*'s are as important as the fundamental particles in nuclear physics. Now one of these *a*'s had the singular quality of behaving differently from the other two. Many discoveries have begun with a similar observation—a disagreement within a system, a disturbance in a field, an abnormal movement in an orbit. Saussure characterized this *a* by two specific traits. On the one hand, it was related to neither *e* nor *o*; on the other, it was a sonantic coefficient, i.e., it was capable of playing the same double role, vocalic and consonantal, as the nasals and the liquids, and it combined with vowels. Let us note that Saussure spoke of it as a phoneme and not as a sound or an articulation. He did not tell us how this phoneme was pronounced, what sound it approximated in any observable system, or even if it was a vowel or a consonant. The phonic substance was not considered. We are confronted with an algebraic unit, a term of the system, what he would later call a distinguishing and opposing entity. We could not say that this remark attracted much interest even twenty-five years after it had been published. It required another twenty-five years for it to compel recognition, under circumstances which the most audacious imagination could not have conceived. In 1927, the phoneme that had been defined fifty years before by Saussure as the Indo-European sonantic phoneme was rediscovered by J. Kurylowicz in a historical language, Hittite, which had just then been deciphered, under the guise of the sound written as *h*. This admirable observation made a reality of the theoretical entity postulated by the argument of 1878.

Naturally, the phonetic realization of this entity as *h* in Hittite brought a new element into the debate, but it was of a different nature. From then on, two directions in research appeared. Some endeavored to push further the theoretical investigation and to bring to light, especially in Indo-European, the effects and combinations of this "sonantic coefficient." Today one feels that this phoneme is not unique, that it represents a whole class of phonemes, called "laryngeals," which are unevenly distributed among the historical languages. Other linguists emphasize, on the contrary, the descriptive analysis of these sounds. By this they seek to define their phonetic features, and since the number of laryngeals is still a matter for discussion, from one year to another interpretations can be

seen multiplying and giving rise to new controversies. This problem is today at the center of the theory of Indo-European; it is a matter of passionate interest to the diachronists as well as the descriptivists. All this bears witness to the fruitfulness of Saussure's views, which have been fulfilled only in these last decades, half a century after they were published. Even those modern linguists who have not read the *Mémoire* are still indebted to it.

Here, then, was Saussure, advancing quite young in his career, with the mark of greatness on him. Welcomed with favor at the École des Hautes Études, where he immediately found disciples whom his thought enchanted and inspired, and at the Société de Linguistique where Bréal soon made him assistant secretary, a comfortable career opened before him, and everything seemed to herald a long train of discoveries. This expectation was not deceived. Let us recall only the fundamental articles on Baltic intonation, which show the depth of his analysis and remain models for whoever tackles the same research. It is a fact, however, which has been stressed—and deplored—by those who have had to speak of the Saussure of these years, that soon his productivity slowed down. He confined himself to some more and more infrequent articles, and then only to meet the requests of his friends. When he went back to Geneva to take up a chair at the university, he gradually ceased completely to write. Nevertheless, he never ceased to work. What was it that deterred him from publishing? We are beginning to find out. This silence hid a drama which must have been painful; it was aggravated with the years and never had an outcome. It was partly the result of personal circumstances, on which the testimony of his family and friends could shed some light. It was above all a drama of the mind. Saussure alienated himself from his period in the same proportion as he made himself more and more master of his own truth, for that truth made him reject everything that was then taught on the subject of language. But, while he was hesitating to undertake that radical revision which he felt was necessary, he could not bring himself to publish the slightest note if he was not assured first of the fundamental bases of the theory. The depths to which this trouble reached and how many times he was close to becoming discouraged is revealed in a remarkable document, a passage from a letter to Meillet (January 4, 1894) in which he confides, apropos of his studies on Baltic intonation:

> But I am very disgusted with all that and with the difficulty there is in general to write ten lines concerning the facts of language which have any common sense. I have for a long time been especially concerned with the logical classification of these facts, with the classification of the points of view from which we treat them, and I see more and more both the immensity of the work which is necessary to show the linguist *what he is doing,* by reducing each operation to its previously specified category; and at the same time the very great vanity of everything which can ultimately be done in linguistics.

> It is ultimately only the picturesque aspect of a language, that which makes it different from all others in that it belongs to a certain people having certain origins—it is this almost ethnograph-

ic aspect which still holds an interest for me, and as it happens, I no longer can take any pleasure in devoting myself up to this study without remorse and in enjoying a particular fact which depends on a particular environment.

The absolute ineptness of current terminology, the necessity to reform it, and, in order to do that, to show what sort of subject language in general is, come incessantly to spoil my pleasure in history, although I have no dearer wish than not to have to concern myself with language in general.

In spite of myself, this will result in a book, in which I shall, without enthusiasm or passion, explain why there is not a single term used in linguistics to which I grant any meaning whatsoever. And I confess that it is not until after that that I shall be able to take up my work at the point at which I left it.

That is a perhaps stupid state of mind, which should explain to Duvau why I have, for example, delayed for more than a year over the publication of an article which does not present any material difficulty—and still I have not succeeded in avoiding expressions which are logically odious because a decidedly radical reform would be necessary for this.

One can see in what sort of argument Saussure was entangled. The more he probed into the nature of human speech, the less he could be satisfied with the accepted ideas. And so he sought a diversion in studies of ethnolinguistic typology, but he was always brought back to his first obsession. Perhaps it was to keep on escaping from it that he threw himself into that ceaseless quest for anagrams. . . . But we see today what was at stake: Saussure's drama was going to transform linguistics. The obstacles his thinking encountered were to force him to forge the new dimensions which would reorder the facts of language.

From this moment, indeed, Saussure saw that to study a particular language led inevitably to the study of language in general. We believe we can reach a linguistic phenomenon as an objective reality. Actually we can grasp it only from a certain point of view, which it is first necessary to define. Let us cease to believe that in language we have to do with a simple object, existing by itself and capable of being grasped in its totality. The first task is to show the linguist "what he is doing," what preliminary operations he performs unconsciously when he approaches linguistic data.

Nothing could be more alien to his period than this concern with logic. Linguists were then absorbed in a huge effort of historical investigation, in organizing the comparative materials, and in building up stocks of etymologies. These great undertakings, although quite useful, did not leave room for theoretical concerns. Thus Saussure was alone with his problems. The immensity of the task to be accomplished and the radical character of the necessary reform were enough to make him hesitate and sometimes become discouraged. Nevertheless he did not give it up. He contemplated a book in which he would say these

things, in which he would present his views and undertake the complete overhauling of the theory.

The book was never written, but it survives in rough sketches, in the form of preparatory notes, remarks tossed out rapidly, and drafts; and when he had to give a course in general linguistics in order to fulfill his obligations to the university, he would take up the same themes and bring them to the point at which we know them.

In the linguist of 1910 we find again, in effect, the same purpose which guided the novice of 1880: to establish the bases of linguistics. He rejected the categories and notions which he saw in use everywhere because they seemed to him to be foreign to the proper nature of language. What was that nature? He explained his position briefly in certain of his notes, fragments of a reflection which could neither be abandoned nor completely settled:

> Elsewhere there are things, certain objects, which one is free to consider afterwards from different points of view. In our case there are, primarily, points of view, right or wrong, but simply points of view, with the aid of which, secondarily, one *creates* things. These creations happen to correspond to realities when the point of departure is right, or not to correspond to them in the opposite case, but in both cases, no thing, no object, is given for a single instant in itself. Not even when the most material fact is dealt with, one which would seem most obviously defined in itself, as would be a series of vocal sounds.
>
> . . . . .
>
> Here is our profession of faith regarding linguistic matter: in other fields one can speak of things *from such or such point of view,* certain that one will find oneself again on firm ground in the object itself. In linguistics, we deny in principle that there are given objects, that there are things which continue to exist when one passes from one order of ideas to another, and that one can, as a result, allow oneself to consider "things" in several orders, as if they were given by themselves.

These reflections explain why Saussure considered it so important to show the linguist "what he is doing." He wished to make people understand the error in which linguistics had been engaged from the time it began the study of human speech as a thing, or as a living organism or as a matter to be analyzed by an instrumental technique, or again, as a free and incessant creation of the human imagination. One must get back to the fundamentals and discover that object which is language, to which nothing can be compared.

What then was this object which Saussure set up after having made a clean sweep of all accepted notions? Here we touch upon that which is of prime importance in the Saussurian doctrine, upon a principle which assumes a total intuition of language, total both because it contains the whole of his theory and because it embraces the totality of his subject. This principle is that *human speech,* no matter from what point of view it is studied, *is always a double entity,* formed of two parts of which the one has no value without the other.

There, it seems to me, is the center of the doctrine, the principle from which proceeds all the array of notions and distinctions that constitute the published course. Everything in language is to be defined in double terms; everything bears the imprint and seal of an opposing duality:

—the articulatory/acoustical duality;
—the duality of sound and sense;
—the duality of the individual and society;
—the duality of *langue* and *parole*;
—the duality of the material and the immaterial;
—the duality of the "memorial" (paradigmatic) and the syntagmatic;
—the duality of sameness and opposition;
—the duality of the synchronic and the dia chronic, etc.

And, once again, none of these terms thus placed in opposition has value by itself or refers to a substantial reality; each of them takes its value from the fact that it is in opposition to the other:

> The absolutely final law of language is, we dare say, that there is nothing which can ever reside in *one* term, as a direct consequence of the fact that linguistic symbols are unrelated to what they should designate, so that *a* is powerless to designate anything without the aid of *b,* and the same thing is true of *b* without the aid of *a,* or that both have no value except through their reciprocal difference, or that neither has any value, even through a certain part of itself (I suppose, "the root," etc.) other than through this same plexus of eternally negative differences.

. . . . .

> Since human speech does not present a substance in any of its manifestations but only combined or isolated *actions* of physiological, psychological, or mental forces; and since, nevertheless, all our distinctions, all our terminology, all our ways of speaking are molded according to that involuntary supposition that there is a substance, one cannot refuse, above all, to recognize that the theory of language will have as its most essential task the disentangling of the real nature of our primary distinctions. It is impossible for us to agree that one has the right to construct a theory without performing this essential labor of definition, although this convenient way seems up to now to have satisfied the linguistic public.

Certainly a material phenomenon can be taken as the object of a linguistic analysis, for instance, some meaningless segment of an utterance, considered as a simple production of the vocal apparatus, or even an isolated vowel. It is an illusion to believe that here we have hold of a substance; as a matter of fact, it is only by an operation of abstraction and generalization that we can delimit such a topic of study. Saussure insisted upon this, that only the point of view creates this substance. All the aspects of language which we take as given are the result of logical operations which we employ unconsciously. Let us then become conscious of this. Let us open our eyes to the truth that there is not one single aspect of language which is given without the others and which one can place above the others as anterior and primordial. Whence this observation:

> The more one delves into the material proposed for linguistic study, the more one becomes convinced of this truth, which most particularly—it would be useless to conceal it—makes one pause: that the bond established among things is preexistent, in this area, to *the things themselves,* and serves to determine them.

This thesis appears paradoxical and can cause surprise even today. Some linguists reproach Saussure for a propensity to emphasize paradoxes in the functioning of language. But language is actually the most paradoxical thing in the world, and unfortunate are those who do not see this. The further one goes, the more one feels this contrast between oneness as a category of our perception of objects and the pattern of duality which language imposes upon our thought. The more one penetrates into the mechanism of signification, the better one sees that things do not signify by reason of their substantially being so, but by virtue of the formal features which distinguish them from other things of the same class and which it is incumbent upon us to extract.

From these views proceeds the doctrine which the disciples of Saussure put into shape and published. Today scrupulous exegetes devote themselves to the necessary task of restoring the lessons of Saussure in their exact terms, with the help of all the materials they can recover. Thanks to their pains we shall have a critical edition of the ***Cours de linguistique générale*** which will not only present us with a faithful image of that teaching as it was transmitted in its oral form, but which will allow the Saussurian terminology to be settled with strict accuracy.

This doctrine actually informs in one way or another all of the theoretical linguistics of our time. The influence it has had has been enhanced by the effect of the convergence of Saussurian ideas with those of other theorists. Thus in Russia, Baudouin de Courtenay and his disciple Kruszewski proposed at the same time, but independently, a new concept of the phoneme. They distinguished the linguistic function of the phoneme from its articulatory realization. This teaching approached, on a smaller scale, the Saussurian distinction between *langue* and *parole* and assigned a differentiating value to the phoneme. This was the first germ of what has developed into a new branch of linguistics, phonology, the theory of the distinctive functions of phonemes and of the structures of their relationships. When they founded it, N. Trubetskoy and [Roman] Jakobson expressly recognized Saussure as well as Baudouin de Courtenay as their precursors.

The structuralist trend which emerged in 1928, and which was soon to assume major importance, thus had its origins in Saussure. Although he never used the term "structure" in a doctrinal sense (and it is a term, moreover, which having had to serve as a banner for very different movements has finally lost any precise meaning), the dependence on Saussure is unquestionable among all those who seek the pattern of the general structure of linguistic systems in the relationship of phonemes among themselves.

It might be useful to stress this point relative to one of these structuralist schools, the one which is most characteristically national, the American school, insofar as it derives from [Leonard] Bloomfield. It is not widely enough known that Bloomfield wrote a very laudatory review of the *Cours de linguistique générale* in which he gave credit to Saussure for the distinction between *langue* and *parole* and concluded: "He has given us the theoretical basis for a science of human speech." Different as American linguistics has become, it still keeps a link with Saussure.

Like all productive thought, the Saussurian concept of language had consequences that were not immediately perceived. There is even a part of his teaching which remained unproductive and inactive for a long time. It is the part which relates to language as a system of signs, and the analysis of the sign into the signifier and the signified. That was a new principle, the one of the two-sided unit. In recent years, linguists have debated the notion of sign: to what extent do the two aspects correspond, how does the unit hold or split through diachrony, etc. Many points of the theory are still to be discussed. Among others, it must be asked if the notion of the sign could be retained as a principle of analysis at all levels. We have stated elsewhere that the sentence as such does not admit of segmentation into units of the type of the sign.

But what we wish to emphasize here is the scope of the principle of the sign when set up as a unit of language. From that it results that language becomes a semiotic system: "The task of the linguist," said Saussure, "is to find out what makes language a special system within the mass of semiological data. . . . But to me the language problem is mainly semiological." We see that this principle is now gaining ground outside linguistics and penetrating into the sciences of man, which are becoming aware of their own semiotics. Far from language being swallowed up in society, it is society which is beginning to recognize itself as "a language." Analysts of society ask themselves if certain social structures, or, in another context, those complex discourses which myths are, should not be considered as signifiers for which one has to search out the signified. These innovating investigations suggest that the basic characteristic of language, that it is composed of signs, could be common to all those social phenomena which constitute *culture*.

It seems to us that one should draw a fundamental distinction between two orders of phenomena: on the one side the physiological and biological data, which present a "simple" nature (no matter what their complexity may be) because they hold entirely within the field in which they appear and because their structures form and diversify themselves on successive levels in the order of the same relationships; on the other side, the phenomena belonging to the interhuman milieu, which have the characteristic that they can never be taken as simple data or defined in the order of their own nature but must always be understood as double from the fact that they are connected to something else, whatever their "referent" may be. A fact of culture is such only insofar as it refers to something else. The

day when a science of culture takes shape, it will probably be founded upon that chief feature, and it will develop its own dualities on the model Saussure gave for language, without necessarily conforming to it. No science of man will be spared this reflection on its subject and its place within a general science of culture, for man is not born in nature but in culture.

What a strange destiny ideas have, sometimes seeming to lead lives of their own, revealing or contradicting or recreating the figure of their creator. One could pause a long time over this contrast: the actual life of Saussure compared with the fortunes of his ideas. A man alone in his thought for almost his whole life, unable to bring himself to teach what he deemed wrong or fanciful, feeling that it was necessary to recast everything but less and less tempted to do it, and finally, after many diversions that could not rescue him from the torment of his personal truth, imparting to a few students some ideas on the nature of language which never seemed to him to be matured enough to be published. He died in 1913, little known outside the narrow circle of his pupils and a few friends, even then almost forgotten by his contemporaries. Meillet, in the moving obituary he then devoted to him, deplored the fact that Saussure's life ended on an unfinished work: "After more than thirty years, the ideas expressed by Ferdinand de Saussure in his early work have not exhausted their vitality. And nevertheless his disciples have the feeling that he has not held anything like the place in the linguistics of his time which his brilliant gifts deserved." And he ended with this poignant regret: "[Saussure] had produced the finest book of comparative grammar that has ever been written, he had sown ideas and laid down firm theories; he had left his mark on numerous pupils, and still he had not completely fulfilled his destiny."

Three years after the death of Saussure, the *Cours de linguistique générale* appeared, edited from the notes of students by [Charles] Bally and [Albert] Séchehaye. In 1916, amidst the clash of arms, who could have been concerned with a book on linguistics? Nietzsche's saying, that great events arrive on dove's feet, was never truer.

Today, fifty years have passed since the death of Saussure, two generations separate us from him, and what do we see? Linguistics now holds an important place among the sciences dealing with man and society and is among the most active of them in theoretical research as well as in technical developments. And this new linguistics has its origins in Saussure, and it is in Saussure that it finds its bearings and takes shape. Among all the currents that cross it, among all the schools into which it is divided, the innovating role of Saussure is proclaimed. That seed of brightness, culled by a few disciples, has become a great light which reveals a landscape filled with his presence.

What we are here asserting is that Saussure belongs henceforth to the history of European thought. A forerunner in doctrines which in the past fifty years have transformed the theory of language, he has opened up unforgettable vistas on the highest and most mysterious faculty of man. At the same time, in placing on the horizon of science and philosophy the notion of "sign" as a bilateral unit, he has contributed to the advent of formal thought in the sciences of society and culture, and to the founding of a general semiology.

Taking in at a glance the half-century that has just elapsed, we can say that Saussure really did accomplish his destiny. Beyond his earthly life, his ideas spread further than he could have imagined, and his posthumous destiny has become, so to speak, a second life which henceforth mingles with ours. (pp. 29-40)

> *Emile Benveniste, "Saussure after Half a Century," in his* Problems in General Linguistics, *translated by Mary Elizabeth Meek, University of Miami Press, 1971, pp. 29-40.*

Saussure on writing:

I suffer from a morbid horror of the pen. . . .

In the case of linguistics, the torture is increased for me by the fact that the more simple and obvious a theory may be, the more difficult it is to express it simply, because I state as a fact that there is not one single term in this particular science which has ever been based on a simple idea, and that this being so, one is tempted five or six times between the beginning and end of a sentence to rewrite.

Ferdinand de Saussure, in an undated letter reprinted in Jean Starobinski's Words upon Words: The Anagrams of Ferdinand de Saussure, *translated by Olivia Emmet, Yale University Press, 1979.*

Samuel Weber   (essay date 1976)

[*In the following essay, Weber discusses how perspective is manifested in Saussure's view of language as an intermediary of values and differences.*]

[In "Deconstructing the Deconstructers," *Diacritics,* Summer 1975] J. Hillis Miller discusses a problem that seems destined to play an increasingly important role in contemporary American literary theory and criticism:

> The assimilation of new work in one language by readers of other languages tends to be delayed by the time it takes for the work to become well enough established to make the labor of translation seem desirable and economically feasible. [Alexandre] Kojève's book on [Friedrich] Hegel, for example, was a good many years ago assimilated into the development of 20th-century thought. It has just now been published in English and will have a new life in the context of current American revival of interest in Hegel.

The temporal delay to which Miller refers, becomes all the more crucial when it no longer simply separates "work in one language" from its "assimilation" into another, but rather marks the radical separation of that original work from itself. And yet, this is precisely the case of that movement of thought conveniently, if imprecisely, labelled "Structuralism." Its reception in English, beginning in the mid-sixties, has coincided with its decline and even de-

mise, at least in the French-speaking world, where it developed its most sweeping claim to be a coherent and comprehensive system of description and analysis. Today it would be easier to find "structuralists" in Copenhagen, Tartu or Providence than in Paris, where the term is liable to be taken as an insult rather than an honor. This state of affairs, while important in situating our own reception of Structuralism as being, in some sense, a posthumous one, should not be misconstrued as providing a judgment of the movement itself. What it does suggest, however, is that the significance of Structuralism may reside more in the effects and disruptions it has produced than in its attempts to impose itself as a positive system of thought. If the brief life of Structuralism, at least in France, will prove to have been as necessary as the transformations which it has undergone, then this cannot but influence the manner in which we approach it today, after the fact. We will have to pose the question of the structural instability of Structuralism, thus envisaging at least the possibility that its rapid transformation has been the result not of extraneous events but of its innermost impulses.

In the aftermath of Structuralism, then, and on the eve of its assimilation—a certain assimilation—into the American universe of discourse, let us attempt to reopen the question of the structure of Structuralism by returning to the one text which by common consent forms the seminal work of the movement: Saussure's *Cours de linguistique générale,* first published in 1916, three years after Saussure's death, and translated into English in 1959. Already in its very form, Saussure's *Cours* posed what was to be one of the chief concerns and problems of Structuralism: the status of systematic theory. For the editors could not simply rely on the relatively scanty lecture notes left by Saussure in reconstructing what they hoped would comprise "an organic whole"; they also consulted the notes of his students in producing "this work of assimilation and reconstruction." No doubt that their labor of assimilation, whatever its deficiencies of detail, was faithful to the intention of the Geneva linguist. And yet it is no less doubtful that the difficulty of "assimilating and reconstructing" the thought of Saussure derived not simply from the actual absence of a coherent manuscript but from the texture of that thought itself. Let us attempt to unravel some of its strands.

What vitiates much discussion of Saussure is the tendency to reduce the *Cours* to a body of propositions concerning the nature and function of language while disregarding the context within which that thought defines itself. This context is unmistakably indicated in the very first words of the *Cours*:

> The science that has been developed around the facts of language passed through three stages before finding its true and unique object.

If Saussure begins—in the simulated diachrony of the *Cours*—in this manner, by describing the history of the science of language, it is no accident. For his founding and unwavering concern will be to establish linguistics as an authentic and rigorous *science.* And if this seems so self-evident as to be trivial, it nonetheless determines the entire movement of thought articulated in the *Cours.* More immediately, it defines the central problem to be dealt with: the delineation of the "true and unique object" of linguistics, something hitherto neglected by his predecessors. "Without this elementary operation, no science can develop a method." But if scientific method depends upon the prior identification of its object, what does this identification depend upon? It is in his response to this question that Saussure begins to delineate the specific problematics of linguistics, as opposed to sciences based on observation. For if an autonomous science requires an "integral and concrete" object, then the first thing to be recognized in dealing with language is that it does not offer such an object to mere perception. The phenomena of language do not present a unified aspect to the observer. The object of language is not accessible to empirical perception. If "other sciences work with objects that are given in advance," this is not the case of linguistics. Where the science of language is concerned, "far from the object preceding the point-of-view, it would seem that it is the point-of-view which creates the object."

This assertion marks out the epistemological space of Saussure's theoretical effort, and to neglect its far-reaching implications has inevitably meant to misconstrue the status of his arguments. Thus, the celebrated distinctions of language (*le langage*), the language-system (*la langue*) and speech (*parole*), are not to be taken as descriptions of observable aspects of language: they are products of a point-of-view seeking to construct its object in a manner which will enable linguistics to establish itself as an autonomous science; that is, as a self-contained and coherent system of analysis and classification. [The critic adds in a footnote: "I prefer to translate *la langue* by *language-system* rather than, as Baskin does, simply by *language*—although neither term is entirely correct—for reasons which will become apparent in the course of this essay."] If neither language in general—"*le langage*"—nor speech are considered by Saussure to be the privileged objects of linguistics, this is the result of a point of view which includes a notion of what science ought to be no less than a desire, an intention, to limit language to those aspects which are accessible to scientific study.

This applies neither to the totality of language nor to speech: both are hybrid phenomena and lack the unique and unified essence that an authentic science requires from its object. Language as a whole is "many-sided and heterogeneous," involving the physical, physiological and psychical domains, pertaining at once to the individual and the social; it eludes definitive classification, "for we cannot discover its unity." Speech, on the other hand, involves equally a variety of factors—including the psychical-physical aspects of phonation no less than the individual volition of the speaker—all of which "have no place in linguistics except through their relation to the language-system." By contrast, only *la langue*, the language-system, can be construed as being "a self-contained whole," and, hence, as endowing language as such with "unity."

The attributes of the language-system include, first of all, its homogeneity, as opposed to the hybrid character of language and speech. Secondly, it is "the social side of speech, outside the individual," ratified by collective consent or

convention. Thirdly, both its homogeneous and social aspects are concretized in its character as a system of signs, "in which the only essential thing is the union of meanings and sound-images," which Saussure will go on to term the signified (*signifié*) and the signifier (*significant*). And finally, although it is a theoretical construct, the language-system, as a system of signs, has a tangible reality.

Thus, the semiotic aspect of language, while constituting only part of the larger whole of linguistic phenomena in general, is what endows language with its essential properties. This essence of language, however, is not limited to language, for it is part of a more general realm of semiotics; hence, from this determination of the semiotic essence of language it follows that "the linguistic problem is above all a semiological one." And yet, if language, or rather "linguistics, is only a part of the general science of semiology," it is nonetheless a *privileged* part, for "nothing is more suited (*plus propre*) than the language-system to render intelligible the nature of the semiological problem." To escape the vicious aspects of this "circle," Saussure proposes to study "the language-system itself," uncontaminated by "other things, other points of view."

If this brief recapitulation of Saussure's opening remarks, in which his overall theoretical project is delimited and his notion of language adumbrated, is useful, it is so for at least two reasons. First of all, it displays with clarity certain aspects of what, some fifty years later, will become fundamental tenets of Structuralism, and which include: i) the rejection of mere empirical observation or data as inadequate in establishing the object and method of science; ii) the tendency to construe science as a mode of description and of classification, as a taxonomy involving a semiotic system conceived as a closed, homogeneous and discrete medium; iii) the conviction that the laws which govern the functioning of the sign-system are independent both of the individual subjects participating in it and of the specific material embodiment of the sign; and finally, iv) the assertion that the object of semiotics is dependent upon a prior point-of-view, involving a certain conception of the structure of science and of its object. If this last aspect defines the possibility and necessity of structural linguistics, at least for Saussure, it also—and this brings us to our second point—opens the question of the status of this inaugural and constitutive point-of-view. It is this question, or rather the manner in which Saussure appeared to ignore its implications, that aroused the ire of [C. K.] Ogden and [I. A.] Richards in *The Meaning of Meaning:*

> This author (Saussure) begins by inquiring, "What is the object at once integral and concrete of linguistic?" He does not ask whether it has one, he obeys blindly the primitive impulse to infer from a word some object for which it stands, and sets out determined to find it.

Yet, even if one had never read a word of Saussure, who perhaps more than any of his contemporaries had a profound distrust both of traditional linguistic discourse, and of the *word* as a linguistic form, the very strictures of his nominalist critics should have raised certain doubts as to the imputed "blindness" of the Geneva linguist. After condemning him as a naive realist, Ogden and Richards conclude that he was not realist enough:

> Unfortunately, this theory of signs, by neglecting entirely the things for which signs stand, was from the beginning cut off from any contact with scientific methods of verification.

We will have occasion to return to the "blindness" of Saussure's point-of-view.

. . . . .

It is, of course, his elaboration of the semiotic system of language which remains the distinctive feature of Saussure's linguistic theory. Yet to get at the specific originality of his conception it is first necessary to clear away some dead wood, which, despite its being dead—or perhaps because of it—has proved to be a persistent obstacle in obscuring the nature of that originality. One of the best known and most quoted features of Saussure's semiotic theory is doubtless the one in which he is also the least innovative: that of the *"arbitraire du signe."* For inasmuch as this notion is simply held to state that the signifying material of the sign bears no intrinsic or natural resemblance to what it signifies, it subscribes to the most venerable traditions of Western thought concerning the nature of the sign. Already implicit in the writings of Plato, the notion of the arbitrary relation between sign and signified becomes quite explicit in Aristotle. In his tractatus, "On Interpretation," for instance, he writes:

> Spoken words are the symbols of psychic states and written words the symbols of spoken ones. Just as all men do not have the same written language, so they do not have the same spoken one, whereas the psychic states that these expressions directly designate are identical for all men just as are the things reflected in those states.

Although he does not mention it explicitly, Aristotle clearly implies the arbitrariness of linguistic signs by distinguishing two kinds of relationship of representation or symbolization: on the one hand, that of *resemblance,* obtaining between things and psychic states, which is natural and universal; on the other hand, a relation of *signification or designation,* the arbitrariness of which is demonstrated by the multiplicity and nonuniversality of the different spoken and written languages. As opposed to the mental image of the things themselves, the linguistic sign, whether spoken or written, is thus non-natural and "arbitrary," and it is Aristotle who can thus be regarded as the first theoretician of the *"arbitraire du signe."* Moreover, as though to make matters worse, the Aristotelian model seems already to anticipate the Saussurian division of the sign into signifier (i.e. the spoken or written sign) and signified (the mental image). Saussure's terminology, as [Roman] Jakobson has pointed out, goes back to that of the Stoics, but the conception itself is virtually as old as Western philosophy. If there is something distinctively innovative in Saussurian semiotics, it will have to be sought elsewhere than in the notion of the arbitrariness of the sign, at least interpreted in a conventional manner. Let us return, therefore, to Saussure's discussion of the "Nature of the Linguistic Sign."

The chapter so entitled begins with a critique of the traditional conception of language as a nomenclature, a notion that Saussure finds entirely inadequate. The linguistic sign, he asserts, does not unite "a thing and a name, but a concept and an acoustic image," or, as he will go on to call them, a signified and a signifier. The discussion which follows, concerning the arbitrariness of the sign, its linear character, its mutability and immutability, is curious, because it does not indicate in what sense Saussure is challenging the notion of language as nomenclature. For if he is only concerned with replacing the extralinguistic referent by a mental representation—the "concept" or "signified"—this would by no means radically call into question the underlying category of denomination as the basic structure of the linguistic sign, no more than had the mainstream of Western philosophy from Aristotle to Hegel. For the fundamental category of that tradition has always been that of *representation,* with its logical and ontological implication of the priority of the thing named, as extralinguistic referent, over the process of naming itself. In this view, what is named is held to be present to itself before all representation, as self-identical and constituted anterior to and independently of its designation by signs. The very notion of the arbitrariness of the sign, its nonnaturalness, is only conceivable in contrast to a nonarbitrary relation of resemblance, such as that linking the thing represented to its mental image. The conception of language as denomination thus does not depend upon whether or not the sign designates the object directly, as in proper names, or mediately, via a mental image, the signified, but rather whether the *designatum* is construed as being constituted and self-identical prior to its representation through the sign.

In the chapters which follow Saussure's initial rejection of the conception of language as nomenclature, the traditional model of language as representation remains unshaken. Saussure's use of the notion of arbitrariness remains conventional and limited, designating only the fact that in each individual sign the specific composition of the signifier bears no intrinsic resemblance to the signified. Yet as a form or function, every signifier is by definition the signifier of a signified, whose identity is prior to the process of signification. Thus, despite or even by virtue of the theory of the *"arbitraire du signe,"* the formal conception of language as representation remains intact for the first 150 pages of the *Cours,* in which Saussure repeatedly defines the "concrete linguistic entity" as "the signifier of a certain concept," of a meaning (*un sens*), which in turn "authorizes the delimitation" and determination of signifiers. Confronted by language we can only establish what a signifier is, its limits, because *we know the meaning expressed;* the signified, which is represented, enables us to delimit the signifier, which represents it—and not inversely. And since the concrete linguistic entity is thus dependent upon the meaning it represents, the latter is ontologically and linguistically prior to the former, which it "authorizes."

Indeed, it is only when Saussure proceeds from his description of what the sign *is*—a concrete linguistic *entity*—to how it *works,* that this representational-denominational conception of language is put into question. And this step coincides with his introduction of the notion of "linguistic value." As always, the significance of a theoretical innovation is inseparable from the context, problems and even conflicts which lead to it. The difficulty with which Saussure sees himself confronted will already be familiar to us, for it is nothing other than the problem, where language is concerned, of *sight* itself: that of discerning just what comprises the "real objects" and "concrete entities" of a system, such as that of language, which eludes simple perception and yet which is, in some sense, the product of a point-of-*view*.

Nor is it entirely fortuitous that this problem of perception, or observation, of linguistic data is linked by Saussure to the verbal form itself, to the *word*. For if language is to be a transparent object of theory, the word will have to be—explicitly or implicitly—its privileged element. If language is to be transparent as the representation of meaning, its concrete reality will have to be situated in the word. And yet, when Saussure confronts this question, he finds the verbal form entirely incapable of providing the object he is seeking. The semantic unity of the word, he argues, conceals a variety of elements. The French word, "mois," can be pronounced in different fashions—as in "*le mois de décembre*" and "*un mois après*"—so that *mwa* and *mwas,* although the same word, can hardly be considered as being a single concrete or identical unit. Thus, Saussure concludes, the semantic unity of the word is too abstract to account for the concrete elements of language.

If there are, nevertheless, such elements in the language-system, which, however, are not directly perceptible, they emerge only when the linguistic entity is determined not with reference to a fixed meaning, but within another kind of system, that Saussure compares to a chess game, in which the identity of a particular piece is only intelligible in terms of its function within the whole. Identity thereby appears as a function of the position of the sign with regard to other signs, and Saussure names it "value." The notion of *value* thus comes to replace that of *identity* or *entity* for Saussure:

> We see, then, that in semiological systems like language, where elements hold each other in equilibrium in accordance with fixed rules, the notion of identity blends with that of value and vice versa.

Thus, without pretending to have disposed of the word as a linguistic problem—"for in spite of the difficulty of defining it, the word is a unit that imposes itself upon the mind (as) something central in the mechanism of language"—Saussure finds himself compelled to move beyond it in his search to disengage the essential and effective reality of language. And it is only in his elaboration of the notion of linguistic value that the elusive and imperceptible phenomenon of language begins slowly to emerge. Out of the deceptive clarity of false appearances, language looms up as what Saussure calls "a system of pure values," as distinct from meanings as from sound. If Saussure has hitherto seemed to regard meaning as the arbiter of linguistic reality, his discussion of value begins to cast doubts upon the authority of this arbiter:

> Psychologically our thought—apart from its expression in words—is only an amorphous and

indistinct mass. Philosophers and linguists have always agreed in recognizing that without the help of signs we would be unable to distinguish two ideas in a clear and consistent fashion. Taken in itself, thought is like a nebula in which nothing is necessarily delimited. There are no preestablished ideas and nothing is distinct before the apparition of the language-system (*l'apparition de la langue*).

It is worth remarking that here, precisely at the point where he seems to move decisively beyond the philosophical and linguistic tradition, Saussure feels obliged to invoke the authority of that very tradition to justify his move. That invocation should not, however, obscure the radicality of his conception. For if it is doubtless true, as he asserts, that "philosophers and linguists" have almost always concurred in attributing to language an indispensable function "in distinguishing two ideas in a clear and constant fashion," they have still distinguished between the process by which ideas are *distinguished* from one another, involving language, and the process by which they are *constituted* in themselves, which has been construed as transcending language, *de jure* if not *de facto*. What Saussure is asserting here, by contrast, is not simply that language is indispensable for the distinction of ideas, but for their very constitution. For if "thought is like a nebula," apart from its articulation in language, and if there are no "preestablished ideas" antedating such articulation, then the traditional conception of language as the representation or expression of thought is undermined, at least implicitly. Far from meaning authorizing the delimitations of language, as Saussure had previously asserted, it would seem that language, on the contrary, makes possible the delimitation of meaning, since without language and "in itself, thought is like a nebula in which nothing is necessarily delimited." Meaning is therefore not constituted by the reference to extralinguistic entities, Aristotle's *prágmata,* but rather in and through the semiotic process itself. Yet if this process can consequently no longer be conceived according to the traditional model of representation, how can it be conceived?

Before he attempts to respond to this question, Saussure complicates it by rejecting what might seem to be the most likely answer. For if the linguistic process is not grounded in its referential function, and if verbal discourse is regarded as in some sense the privileged part of the semiotic process, then it would seem plausible to situate that process within the material medium of that discourse, namely that of sound:

> Confronted with this floating realm (of thought), can sounds in themselves be held to offer entities which are circumscribed in advance? No more so than ideas. Phonic substance is neither more fixed nor more rigid (than that of thought); it is not a mold into which thought must of necessity fit its forms, but rather a plastic material which in turn divides itself into distinct parts in order to furnish thought the signifiers it requires.

Thus, if the phonic medium or material conforms to the needs of thought, this is not primarily by virtue of any intrinsic quality it possesses, but only as the material of the semiotic process of language. And this perhaps explains what has been one of the most controversial of Saussure's distinctions: that of the language-system and speech. For inasmuch as speech involves not simply the actualization of the language-process as such, but its determination or rather localization within the medium of sound, Saussure's distinction of *langue* and *parole* responds to his conviction that the process of linguistic articulation is not structurally related to the phonic medium. This is why any discussion of Saussure which equates "signifier" with acoustic or phonic image makes the mistake of identifying what for Saussure is a formal quality with a particular material embodiment.

How, then, are we to describe or situate language? In any case, the model of representation—or, as Saussure writes, "expression"—will no longer do:

> The characteristic role of the language-system with respect to thought is not to create a phonic and material means for the expression of ideas but to serve as an intermediary between thought and sound. . . .

Language is not a representation or expression of thought by sound, but rather an *intermediary*. And yet this first attempt at a positive description of his object immediately involves Saussure in new difficulties. As opposed to the notions of representation or expression, in which one constituted sphere: sound, takes the place or stands for another: thought, the term "intermediary" suggests that the relation of the two is much more complex. However, if an intermediary is necessarily situated *between* two distinct spheres, it is evident that this can hardly be reconciled with Saussure's description of those spheres as being entirely amorphous before and apart from . . . their "intermediary," the semiotic process. Yet this is only an extension of a more radical problem: for if sound and thought lack all definition in themselves, are entirely inarticulate and unarticulated before the process of articulation, can they be held to "exist" *as* sound and thought? Inasmuch as Saussure asserts that language is indispensable not merely to the *distinction,* from without as it were, of thought and sound, but more radically to their *constitution* from within, his postulation of an independent sphere of sound and of thought, existing apart from language, becomes untenable. If "thought (is) chaotic by nature," if it is forced "to determine itself by decomposing itself " through language, and if the same holds true for sound, then the attempt to define language as an intermediary, situated *between* these two chaotic elements becomes highly questionable. The "intermediary" of language must therefore be situated not *between* thought and sound, but *among* them. In conformity with the meaning of the word, "inter-", language as intermediary, or as *intermedium* marks the intrusion of a certain exteriority within the interiority of the medium, be it sound or thought.

Saussure is well aware that his description of language as intermediary involves something rather mysterious:

> There is, therefore, neither materialization of thoughts nor spiritualization of sounds, but instead something rather mysterious, in that the "thought-sound" implies divisions and in that language elaborates its unities by constituting it-

self between (*entre:* also *among*) two amorphous masses.

It is only at this point, vis-à-vis a certain mystery, that Saussure begins to disengage that "true and unique" object of linguistics: the language-system. By excluding the "extraneous" spheres of sound and sense, he appears to have paved the way for a rigorously autonomous science of language, delineating a space which will be uniquely linguistic. By not referring to anything outside of itself, the object that Saussure has isolated might appear to be self-identical. And, indeed, Saussure begins his discussion of this "object" in terms which would suggest its closed, self-contained and comprehensive quality. The name which he gives to this object is: *value.*

> The idea of value . . . shows us that it is an illusion to consider a term as simply the union of a certain sound with a certain concept. To define it thus would be to isolate it from the system of which it is a part; it would mean assuming that one can begin with the (individual) terms and construct the system as the sum (of its parts), whereas, on the contrary, one must begin with the whole in order to obtain, through analysis, the elements it comprises.

Saussure thus introduces the notion of value in a context which would suggest that it involves a closed and autonomous *system,* a self-referential *whole.* And indeed this has been one of the aspects that has been used to identify Structuralism as a mode of holistic thought. However, the category of totality, as such, is entirely inadequate to characterize Structuralist thought—Hegel's celebrated dictum, *Das Wahre ist das Ganze,* does not make him a Structuralist. It is imperative to study *the manner* in which Saussure elaborates the "system of value," the crux of his conception of *la langue.* Can a *system* which is an *intermedium* involve a (w)hole?

. . . . .

Saussure begins his discussion of linguistic value by distinguishing it from "signification":

> When one speaks of the value of a word, one thinks in general and above all of the property it has of representing an idea, and indeed, this is one of the aspects of linguistic value. But if this is the case, how does this value differ from what is called *signification?* Are these two words synonyms? We do not think so, although it is easy enough to confuse the two, not so much because of the analogy of the terms as of the delicacy of the distinctions that they mark. Value, taken in its conceptual aspect, is doubtless an element of signification . . . and yet, it is necessary to elucidate the question of (their difference) if one is to avoid reducing language to a simple nomenclature.

If "signification," despite a certain vagueness, appears to designate the representational, denominational, referential and semantic aspect of language, it is in elaborating his notion of "value" that Saussure will call that aspect into question. Not by rejecting it outright, but by reinscribing it in a process of articulation which it no longer dominates. For it is not signification, according to Saussure, which produces value, but value which enables language to signify. In order for signs to function as representations, they must delineate themselves with regard to other signs: "Its content is only truly determined in concurrence with what exists outside of it." If the French word, "mouton," can be considered as having the same "signification" as the English, "sheep," their value is nonetheless distinct inasmuch as the usage of "sheep" is limited in English by the existence of the word, "mutton," which is lacking in French. We are thus confronted not "with ideas given in advance but with values emanating from the system." The ideational or "conceptual" aspect of signs is thus determined not as the representation of an extralinguistic meaning or of a referent, but as a quality which is

> purely differential, defined not positively by its content, but negatively by its relations with the other terms of the system. Its most exact characteristic is to be what the others are not.

Without the interplay of differences, which constitutes the system of value, "signification would not exist." And if this is true of the significative function of language, it is no less applicable to the signifier than to the signified: "What is crucial in the word is not the sound itself," nor its meaning, but the "phonic (and semantic) differences that permit this word to be distinguished from all others, because these differences support its signification."

It is only when this has been established that the full import and uniqueness of Saussure's notion of the *"arbitraire du signe"* begins to emerge. For "arbitrary and differential are two correlative qualities," according to Saussure, and this entirely transforms the traditional notion. Arbitrariness is no longer a notion governed by that of representation: it no longer designates the fact that the sign is composed of two dissimilar, heterogeneous elements—the signifier and the signified—but instead, points to something far more radical. If the sign is arbitrary, it is because the moment of identity in language, be it signifier or signified, is only conceivable as an after-effect of a play of differences in the "system" of value. The moment of difference is no longer localisable *between* two fixed elements, the signifier which represents, and the signified which is represented, for the simple reason that all determination, all fixation of identical elements, depends upon the differential relations of the system of value.

But what sort of a *system* does value, as difference, constitute? For Saussure, there is no doubt that the differential system of value is the only true object of linguistics, because it is the only one that is sufficiently homogeneous and uncontaminated by impure and extraneous elements to found the study of language as an autonomous and rigorous science.

And yet, if "in language there are only differences, *without positive terms,*" how are those differences to be determined, localised or delineated. As "pure" difference, value cannot be identified with any particular embodiment, either ideational or semiotic. The phonic medium of verbal discourse, which alone enables us to distinguish "language" from other systems of signification, can no longer be regarded as an essential aspect of semiotic value.

When I simply affirm that a word signifies something, and when I mean by that the association of an acoustic image with a concept, I am performing an operation that is, to a certain degree, exact and gives us an idea of the reality involved, but I am by no means expressing the linguistic fact in its essence and its scope.

But where, then, are we to find the "essence" of the linguistic fact? And if it is determined as involving "differences without positive terms," can we justifiably limit its "scope" to the positive phenomenon of "language"? In other words, can we invoke the ideational and phonic *material* of a "system" of *pure* difference to limit that system? If "la langue" is "a form and not a substance," can substantial elements be used to distinguish it from other "systems"?

In using the category of difference to determine what is most proper to the innermost essence of language, Saussure has inadvertently but decisively called that "essence" into question. The appearance of the language-system begins to resemble its *apparition,* not as intermediary but as *intermedium.* And this elaboration of the arbitrary quality of the sign in terms of the differential relations of value confronts Saussure once again with the crucial problem of delimiting the language-object, without which a science of language cannot hope to constitute itself.

. . . . .

The manner in which Saussure responds to this dilemma will prove decisive, not only for his own theory and for structural linguistics, but for Structuralism *tout court.* Repeating a gesture as ancient and as persistent as Western metaphysics itself, he endeavors *to determine difference as opposition,* but with an abruptness that testifies not so much to a solution of the problem as to its acuity. The theory of the intermedium becomes the intermedium, the interval of theory:

> Everything that has been said previously indicates that *within the language-system there is nothing but differences.* Even more important: a difference generally supposes positive terms between which it is situated; but in language (*la langue*) there are only differences without positive terms. . . . But to say that everything in *la langue* is negative only holds if the signified and the signifier are taken separately; once we consider the sign in its totality, we find ourselves in the presence of something positive in its kind. . . . Although the signified and the signifier are, each taken separately, purely differential and negative, their combination is a positive fact; indeed, it is the only type of fact involved in language . . . Two signs, each comprising a signified and a signifier, are not different, they are only distinct. Between them there is only *opposition.* The entire mechanism of language, with which we shall be concerned, is based on oppositions of this kind and on the phonic and conceptual differences that they imply.

Beginning with as radical and uncompromising a determination of the priority of difference over all positive categories in language—and at this point our translation of "la langue" by "language-system" becomes as problematic as

Saussure's systematic intent itself—he suddenly invokes the complex "totality" of the sign in order to reintroduce a "positive" entity into *la langue,* involving not the indeterminable play of differences but *determinate oppositions,* which will now be considered as antedating ("implying") phonic and conceptual difference and, hence, as the basis of the "entire mechanism of language."

That this move is necessary, if there is to a science of language, at least considered as a description and classification of determinate differences, is undeniable. And the progress of Structuralist linguistics, above all in the field of phonology (or phonemics), attests to the fecundity of Saussure's *move.* However, what should be evident by now is that this move by no means ends the game, even if it was to prove decisive for many aspects of orthodox Structuralism, in which taxonomic description in terms of binary opposition becomes a privileged method of analysis. And yet, if the game has continued, it is because the limitation of difference to opposition is as *arbitrary* as the sign itself, which, according to Saussure, acquires value through the multiplicity of the differential relations it entertains with everything "outside and around" it. And if the relation of signification, the positive combination of signified and signifier in the "totality" of the sign, does, as we have read, involve an "assertion" which is not simply *wrong,* since it gives us "an idea of a reality," nothing in Saussure's previous analysis of value justifies elevating the positive "totality" of the sign to the basic element of the mechanism of language. Indeed, the sign taken as a whole—ultimately, the *word*—"in no way . . . expresses the linguistic fact in its essence and its scope." The play of differences, in and through which the signifier and the signified are determined, cannot be restricted to the interaction of individual, already constituted signs. Except, perhaps, by a certain "point-of-view."

. . . . .

"Far from the object preceding the point-of-view, one should say that the point-of-view creates the object." At the beginning of the *Cours,* the point-of-view which guides its course seems simple enough: in order to establish linguistics upon a strictly scientific basis, it is imperative to delineate its veritable object. For a science to be autonomous, its object must be integral, homogeneous and self-contained, purified of all extraneous factors. However, this leads Saussure to identify the essence of language with the "system of pure values," constituted by exclusively differential relations, "without positive terms." Yet this very purity of language, as differential articulation, tends to dislocate its identity and to delimit its scope. For if the value of a linguistic sign, both as a whole and in its elements (signified and signifier), is determined by the network of relations and of differences with all that is "outside and around" it, how is it possible to circumscribe the interplay of differences or to confine it to a determinate space? The question of delineating the object of linguistics converges with that of the point-of-view of the linguist. What, then, is this point-of-view?

Saussure's response is not simple: for there are *two* points-of-view, which, although not mutually exclusive, are nonetheless not simply *different* but *opposed:* "The opposi-

tion between the two points-of-view—synchronic and diachronic—is absolute and suffers no compromise." After his distinction of language from speech, Saussure now elaborates the "second bifurcation" of linguistics: synchrony and diachrony. These terms, which do not simply characterize an object in itself but the perspective and approach of a science in organizing its materials, are defined by Saussure thus:

> Synchronic linguistics will be concerned with the logical and psychological relations linking coexistent terms and forming a system, such as they are perceived by an identical collective consciousness. Diachronic linguistics, on the contrary, will study the relations linking successive terms not perceived by an identical collective consciousness and which replace each other without forming a system among themselves.

It is synchronic linguistics alone which will be able to describe the "laws" that govern the operation of language qua system. That is, only synchronic linguistics will study the *langue as langue,* as "a system of pure values determined by nothing outside of the momentary state of its terms." Synchronic linguistics, by organizing its material according to the simultaneity of its differential relations, *creates* the theoretical boundaries of the closed system of value, of the *langue* as the totality of oppositions between its integral elements, the positive signs. The "laws" it describes are as *necessary* as they are *precarious.* They are necessary because they derive from the internal structure of the language-system; but they are precarious because they have no power to defend themselves against change, against diachronic "events" considered to be *extraneous* to the structure. These events are caused by speech, they are entirely "accidental and particular"—one would be tempted to call them "arbitrary," which Saussure does not—reflecting no law or significance outside of themselves, and yet they can have "imperative" force, altering first individual elements of the system, and thereby transforming the system as a whole. Diachronic events can force a system to change into another, but can never impose one of its own.

In order to elucidate this crucial distinction, Saussure employs the now celebrated comparison between "the play of language (*le jeu de la langue*) and a game of chess." Saussure's chess-game may not have found a place in the annals of chess, but it has certainly entered those of linguistics, and of Structuralism. And since he asserts that a chess-game is "like an artificial realization of what language presents to us in a natural form," let us follow his discussion of it:

> First of all, a state of the game corresponds closely to a state of language. The respective value of the pieces depends upon their position on the chessboard, just as in language (*dans la langue*) each term derives its value from its opposition with all the other terms.

And yet, already this first point of comparison raises the same question we have met in discussing Saussure's reduction of linguistic difference to opposition: Is it permissible to describe the "position" of the respective chess pieces in terms of *opposition?* It might be, were it not for a problem which begins to emerge as Saussure proceeds in elaborating the comparison:

> In the second place, the system is always momentary; it varies from one position to another. It is true that the values depend also and above all on an immutable convention, the rules of the game, which exist before the beginning of the game and persist after each move. This rule, accepted once and for all, also exists in language: it consists of the constant principles of semiology.

Here, despite Saussure's intention, it is the difference rather than the similarity which is striking: for the laws of the language-game, those "constant principles of semiology," obtain only in regard to its discrete, synchronic states; the rules of chess, on the contrary, which are no less constant, to be sure, organize not the functioning of an isolated position but the transformation of one into another, which corresponds rather to diachronic events than to synchronic states. Let us see how Saussure attempts to resolve, or rather to avoid the problem:

> The move of a piece is a fact which is absolutely distinct from the preceding and the succeeding equilibrium. The change effected pertains to neither of these two states; only these states are important. In a game of chess any particular position has the unique characteristic of being entirely detached (*affranchie*) from its antecedents; how one has arrived at it is a matter of total indifference. . . . In order to describe this position it is entirely irrelevant to recall what has happened ten seconds before.

All this might be true if the state or position in a chess-game were, in fact, a single, self-contained entity, a purely synchronic state. That is, if chess were not what it is: a game, *un jeu*. Yet it is precisely its quality as game which tends to disappear in the Saussurean comparison. For, if the game of chess involves not merely the learning of its simplest rules, governing the movement of pieces, or even the characteristics of individual positions, but the study of entire *strategies*, it is first of all because what appears in Saussure's discussion to be a self-identical "state" or position is structurally divided, split off from itself. For the significance of any particular position on the chess-board is inseparable from the fact that there are two positions involved, and that there is always the question of who has the next move? This small fact, involving nothing less than chess *as game*, disrupts the entire comparison of Saussure (and perhaps more as well). For it introduces the diachronic dimension of difference and alterity into what appears to be the closed system of the synchronic state; as part of a game, the position in chess is inherently both a response and an anticipation, involving the calculation of strategies which are neither entirely necessary nor entirely arbitrary.

Saussure is by no means blind to this diachronic aspect of the chess-game, and indeed, it is the sole point in which he admits that his comparison is deficient:

> The chess player has the *intention* of operating a shift and effecting an action on the system; whereas language (*la langue*) premeditates noth-

ing. The pieces of language are displaced, or rather modified, spontaneously and fortuitously. . . . In order for the chess game to resemble the play of language in all points we would have to imagine an unconscious or unintelligent player.

And yet even here, in his own evaluation, Saussure is not entirely in conformity with his "comparison": in order for it to be similar, we would have to imagine not simply "an unconscious or unintelligent player," but moreover *one who was playing the game with himself.* For what separates the game of chess, as game, most profoundly from Saussure's synchronic system of language, is not the presence or absence of a conscious intention, but the *unity* and *singularity* of that consciousness. In order to be true to itself, and at the same time to be the true and proper object of linguistics, Saussure's language-game would have to be one that plays with itself.

Which, strangely enough, is precisely what Saussure implies that it does, or at least tries to do. For in his comment on this final aspect of the comparison, in which he contrasts the conscious chess player with the unconscious participant in the language-game, Saussure concludes by emphasizing the autonomy of the synchronic state with regard to the linguistic subject:

> If the diachronic facts are irreducible to the synchronic system that they condition when the change is intentional (that is, in the game of chess—S.W.), they will be even more so when they pit a blind force against the organisation of a system of signs.

In a gesture which will become one of the hallmarks of Structuralism, the status of the conscious subject appears to be entirely subordinated to the operation of the semiotic system. And yet the ambiguities of this reduction of the subject, which persist in much of Structuralism—albeit unawares—are strikingly legible in Saussure, and nowhere more than in his discussion of the synchronic state. For, if we recall the passage already cited, in which Saussure distinguishes and defines the synchronic as opposed to the diachronic in linguistics, we must recognize that the opposition of coexistence and successivity is not sufficient to describe their difference. The simultaneous system of values must also be "*perceived by an identical collective consciousness,*" whereas the diachronic series of terms is "*not perceived by an identical collective consciousness.*" On this point Saussure never wavers. If the essence of language, the synchronic state of the language-system, *la langue,* is inaccessible to direct perception, it is, nonetheless, not merely the phantasm of the linguist, but a "reality" in its own right. And if one pursues the question of the status of this "reality," Saussure's response, although perhaps surprising, is unequivocal:

> Synchrony knows only one perspective, that of the speaking subjects, and its entire method consists in gathering their testimony; in order to know to what extent a thing is a reality, it will be necessary and sufficient to discover to what extent it exists for the consciousness of subjects.

This response is surprising, because the consciousness of

the speaking subject has hitherto been identified not with the synchronic aspect of language but with its diachronic dimension, in which "everything derives from speech (*la parole*)." And yet here Saussure asserts the contrary, since it is precisely the diachronic factor which acts as a "blind force," devoid of all consciousness.

Moreover, Saussure's description of the nature of this consciousness complicates matters even more. For the consciousness, which defines not only the structure of the synchronic state, but its priority over the diachronic, is none other than that of the "speaking subjects" or "masses," which Saussure has hitherto assigned to the hybrid and subordinate sphere of the *parole.* Now, however, these speaking subjects return in order to establish the priority of the synchronic aspect of the language-system:

> On this point it is evident that the synchronic aspect takes precedence over the other, since for the mass of speakers it is the true and only reality.

Thus, a remark that Saussure made at the very beginning of the **Cours,** and which his commentators have often interpreted as being superseded by his distinction of *langue* and *parole,* returns to resist efforts to explain it away; namely that "language (*la langue*) is not an entity and only exists in speaking subjects."

The question is crucial, because in determining the essential reality of language with reference to the consciousness of speaking subjects, Saussure also establishes the priority of the synchronic perspective for linguistics itself. If it is "the true and only reality" for the "mass of speakers," "the same is true for the linguist." Indeed, the one follows from the other:

> The first thing that strikes us when we study the facts of language (*langue*) is that for the speaking subject their succession in time is nonexistent: he is confronted with a state. That is why the linguist who wishes to understand this state must disregard everything that has produced it and ignore diachrony. He can enter the mind of speakers only by completely suppressing the past. The intervention of history can only falsify his judgment.

We thus find ourselves confronted with a paradox in Saussure's argument: on the one hand, the language-system, as opposed to speech, is said to function independently of the consciousness and volition of the speaking subject; but on the other hand, the synchronic essence of that system, as opposed to its diachronic aspect, is defined precisely by its presence to the consciousness of the mass of speakers, to the identity of the collective consciousness of the linguistic community. It is only this reality for the speakers' consciousness that makes it accessible to that of the linguist as the true and proper object of the science of language. And indeed, it is only in linguistics that the identical collective consciousness of the language-community actualizes itself as *self-consciousness,* since in the individual speakers that consciousness is only present in a state of virtuality.

Yet if this actualization, if linguistics is possible, as a science, it is only by virtue of the fact that the linguist and

the ordinary speaker both participate in the same *reality* of language. What, then, is the nature of this reality?

As we have seen, Saussure vacillates on this point. After determining value as a play of pure difference, one which becomes increasingly difficult to limit or to localize as specifically linguistic in nature, he redetermines linguistic value as opposition, obtaining in the relations not of individual signifieds and signifiers, but of whole signs. In thus redefining the basic and concrete linguistic entity as the totality of the sign, Saussure implicitly makes a judgment as to the fundamental "reality" of language. Historically, this supposition has been so widely held that it might appear to be entirely self-evident if Saussure's own discussion of the nature of linguistic articulation had not put it into question. It involves nothing less than the conviction which is at the basis of the conception of language as representation, a conception that Saussure's notion of difference strongly undermines: namely, that language is a means of *understanding* and of *communication.* Although he nowhere discusses this conception as such, it is clear that wherever Saussure affirms the point-of-view that regards language as a positive phenomenon—as a system of oppositions—he assumes it. In his discussion of syntax, for instance, which he holds to have no reality apart from the "sum of concrete terms," he concludes that "the very fact that we *understand* (*comprend*) a linguistic complex . . . shows that this sequence of terms is the adequate expression of the thought."

And yet, if Saussure's determination of the semiotic process, by which both thought and sound, or whatever the material of the signifier may be, become articulated, implies anything, it is that the play of differences, of language as intermedium, can only be limited by a point-of-view that is necessarily arbitrary, because it is itself ineluctably situated within the sphere of that play. Like every other articulated identity, the "point" of the synchronic point-of-view—whether that of the speaker engaged in communication or of the linguist—is an arbitrary after-effect of an interplay of differences that would seem to be intrinsically illimitable. And this, in turn, places the problem of diachrony, and Saussure's critique of it, in a modified perspective; namely, in the modification of *perspective* itself. For if Saussure is critical of the historical bias of the school of comparative grammar founded by Bopp, it is because its lack of discrimination between synchronic and diachronic caused it to project a continuity onto linguistic transformations that ignored that nature of *what* was being transformed. Against this, Saussure argues for the necessity of defining the point-of-view of the observer and its role in delineating its object. His delineation of that object, however, dislocates and displaces the pertinence of *every* point-of-view, including his own. What he describes and seeks to dismiss as the absurdity of the diachronic perspective, begins to emerge as the ultimate consequence of his theory of difference:

> It would be absurd to attempt to sketch a panorama of the Alps by viewing them simultaneously from various peaks of the Jura; a panorama must be taken from a single point. The same applies to language: one can neither describe it nor fix norms of usage except by placing

oneself in a single state. When the linguist follows the evolution of language, he resembles the moving observer who goes from one peak of the Jura to another in order to record the shifts in perspective.

If Structuralism, and above all, Saussure, will have demonstrated anything in their course (**Cours**), it is that "one can neither describe" anything "nor fix norms of usage" except by assuming a single, fixed point-of-view, which, however, is in a constant "state" of motion that we can never entirely arrest. Saussure's **Cours** describes the necessity of those "shifts in perspective" and thereby places Structuralism, long before its inception, already "beyond" itself, moving towards the heady air of *other* Alpine peaks [described in Friedrich Nietzsche's *Human, All-Too-Human*]:

> "Thou shalt learn to comprehend the perspectival in every value-judgment; also the element of stupidity in regard to opposing values and the entire intellectual sacrifice with which every pro and con is bought. . . . Thou shall see the problem of *hierarchy* with your eyes, and how the power and right and scope of perspective grow together to reach new heights. Thou shalt"—but enough, the free spirit now *knows*, which "thou shalt" he has heard and heeded, and also, what he now *can do*, what only now he—*dare*. . . .

If Saussure begins and ends with the affirmation of the point-of-view, the "blind force" of his descriptions, very different from the simple blindness for which he was dismissed by Ogden and Richards, *points* towards the affirmation of perspective, towards that ineluctable necessity of seeing simultaneously from different points-of-view, which is most fully articulated in the texts of Nietzsche.

And yet if it is Nietzsche, who increasingly dominates that movement of thought in which Saussure, and perhaps Structuralism in general, will have survived, albeit transformed, its own demise, the rereading of the **Cours de linguistique générale** can help to guard against an "assimilation" which only reproduces what it pretends to discard. If "the intervention of history" is not to "falsify" our judgment, as Saussure feared it would, it will not be by excluding if from our "point-of-view," but rather only by patiently retracing the manner by which it has shaped, and [as Nietzsche writes,] continues to determine and to limit "our" perspectives:

> Would it not be possible, that the origin of our apparent "knowledge" (*Erkenntnisse*) is to be sought solely in *older value-judgments*, which have been so firmly incorporated that they have become part of our basic constitution? So that actually only *recent* needs now go hand-in-hand with the *result of the oldest needs?* . . . Our "dissatisfaction," our "ideal" etc. is perhaps the *consequence* of this incorporated piece of interpretation, of our perspectival point-of-view. . . .

If this were so, then the affirmation of the ineluctability of perspective and of interpretation would converge with the manner in which our very "own" point(s)-of-view have been shaped by a "blind force" of which we are perhaps only now becoming aware. "We cannot see around our corner," but perhaps we can glimpse the corner from which we see. . . . (pp. 913-38)

> *Samuel Weber, "Saussure and the Apparition of Language: the Critical Perspective," in* MLN, *Vol. 91, No. 5, October, 1976, pp. 913-38.*

Samuel Kinser (essay date 1979)

[*In the following excerpt, Kinser discusses Saussure's studies of anagrams.*]

Language signifies, and by the same token ideologizes. The tokens of language, tactile or sonorous, written or spoken, are structured, arbitrarily from a materially referential point of view, coherently from a socially referential point of view. Language's tokens make sense because they cor-respond; they systemically, collectively answer to the system of things useful, desirable, needful in a given social milieu.

Language ideologizes because it inculcates a socio-historically definable, circularly interacting system of needs, uses, and desires. The inculcation has often been noticed, but its linguistic mechanisms have rarely been described. One such description occurs in the notebooks of Ferdinand de Saussure on the anagrammatical character of early Indo-European poems, songs, prophecies and hymns.

Consider, for example, Saussure's detection of the Greek name of Venus in a passage from Book I of Vergil's *Aeneid*. "Aphrodite," Saussure explains, is phonically mimed in two ways in the passage where the goddess, previously in disguise, reveals herself to her son Aeneas:

> Ambrosiaeque comae divinum vertice odorem Spiravere; pedes vestis defluxit ad imos. . . .
>
> (and her ambrosial locks sent forth a heavenly fragrance from the crown [of her head], while her robes streamed down to her very feet. . . .)

The simpler of the two mimes offers the listener/reader an outline of "Aphrodite" which Saussure calls a *mannequin* or "little box." One word or one phrase in the anagrammatical passage begins and ends with the same sounds as the latent "word-theme." The *mannequin* "A [phrodit] E" is given here in two ways, either by "A [mbrosiaequ] E" or by "A [mbrosiaeque coma] E."

The more complicated form of miming consists in the "diphonic" reproduction of the sounds of the imitated name. Accepting the Latin *f-* as the equivalent of the Greek *ph-*, Saussure explains that after the initial *A-*, "marked by the mannequin," *Af-* or *fr-* would be "necessary." The anagram, he admits, is defective in this respect because "we find only *fl-* in 'defluxit.'" The rest of the diphonic imitation is more perceptible:

-RO- in "am-b-*ro*-siae."
-OD-: *od*-orem.
-DI-: given twice: *di*-vinum; a*di*-mos.
-IT-: deflux-*it*.
-E: "given by the end of the mannequin, but," admits

Saussure, with the wrong "quantity"; that is, with a short rather than long -*e*.

In this way, [as Saussure recounted in Jean Starobinski's *Les mots sous les mots*], "polyphones visibly reproduce . . . the syllables of a work or a name of importance in the text and thereby become anagrammatical polyphones."

In the small group of Saussure's anagrammatical exercises so far published in full or in part, divine or semi-divine names (such as those of Aphrodite or the Hindu god Agni) account for about a third of the total. The names of political and military heroes, real or imagined to be real (Hector, Caesar, Hadubrand) make up another third. The names which Saussure finds half hidden in the passages are of central importance to the myths which sustain the social structures in which these discourses circulated. What Saussure found—or thought he had found—was a way in which discourse was centered on these central names. "God was, in a manner of speaking, rivetted to the text." In a *manner* of speaking: precisely.

This discussion of Saussure's enterprise in his largely unpublished notebooks on anagrams moves in a different direction from those developed in recent years by [Julia] Kristeva, Starobinski, [Roman] Jakobson, and others. It seeks to develop the initiative of the editors of *Semiotext(e)* in sponsoring a conference on "two Saussures," ostensibly to compare the famed Saussure of the **Course in General Linguistics** with the now emerging Saussure of the notebooks. The proceedings of this conference, held at Columbia University in 1974, have recently been published in two issues of *Semiotext(e)*, and among these studies the essay of Sylvère Lotringer pursues the question of the relation between the two Saussures in the most extended and perceptive way. Lotringer's study attempts to specify the general linguistic implications of Saussure's theory of anagrams. Previous interpretations have been limited largely to the theory's implications for poetics.

In Lotringer's opinion the discoveries recorded in the notebooks cast doubt on the principles of language set forth in the **Course.** Indeed, if there are two Saussures, it is because one was "repressed" by the other. The working of "the historical, the declarative, [and] the real" in and on language was acknowledged and pursued in the notebooks, Lotringer believes. But the specification of how social situations influence discursive activity led Saussure in directions which conflicted with his logocentric theory of signification. Consequently, Saussure abandoned his inquiry, refused to publish his notebooks, and left unresolved ("repressed") the differences between anagrammatical practices and linguistic theory.

Saussure's indecision about the anagrams cannot be resolved retrospectively. Thus, while it is important to affirm with Lotringer that anagrams call in question a logocentric theory of signs, it is also necessary to admit that in Saussure's case their discovery was made possible by the assumptions of logocentric theory. Again, if the anagrams reveal the opening, disseminative character of linguistic meaning, that revelation occurs despite rather than because of Saussure's efforts, which were devoted to specify-

ing how names enclose and control rather than stray from the path of discourse. Saussure both reaffirmed and in reaffirming drew into question the traditional Western metaphysics of language. But unlike [Georges] Bataille, [Jacques] Derrida, and other recent strayers from the path, Saussure stopped at the point of this duplicity rather than pushing forward. He does not seem to have been interested in the uses of excess, nor in the "polyphonic, polysemic nature of poetic language" which Jakobson believes Saussure discovered in his anagrammatical work.

Saussure's indecision cannot be resolved, but it must be probed. The question of *whether* anagrams can be found in the texts of Vergil, of Homer, of the *Rig-Veda*, of the *Hildebrandslied*, of the early Latin verse fragments controversially designated "Saturnian," is inextricably linked with *how* one tries to find them, for no text is readable without a model of reading. If Saussure cannot decide so apparently simple a matter as the number and location of phonemes in a few lines of verse, that is because the entirety of his philosophy of language is at stake in each determination: a 'literal' interpretation of texts is the most, not the least metaphysical.

Saussure's theory of language does not easily fit the texts which he has chosen for investigation. Do the texts then disprove Saussure's theory? or have they rather falsified the model—Saussure's anagrammatical "laws"—constructed in accord with theory and texts? Or has the interworking of text and model displaced the problematic itself, dislocating and forcing a shift in the questions—the verbal energies roused by reading; the needs, uses, desires, of a complex personal and historical situation prompting this enterprise—to which the theory and the model propose an answer? Has the dislocation of theory and the tinkering with models revealed *another textuality*—neither a redoubling of meter nor a redoubling of theme, neither crytographeme nor ana-gram written under or over other *grammata*, but another system of writing interwoven with the poetic one?

Without denying the interest and importance of the first alternatives posed here, it is the last possibility, the possibility of a shift in the field of Saussure's investigation, which will be pursued. Theory, model, and "anagrammatical" texts seem to have forced such changes upon each other that there was a shift in the field itself in which and by means of which Saussure observed anagrams. Instead of a field definable in quantifiable, objective terms—a field of *verses*, of measured and measurable indentations upon the page and upon the ear—Saussure discovered a field where phonemic configurations indent, measure, and channel a range of non-quantifiable, traditionally "subjective" psychic entities which, Saussure insisted, are socially programmed and derived.

This field, emergent in the anagrammatical notebooks, was given a name in the **Course:** semiology. Like the name "ideology" given to it by Destutt de Tracy and Marx, the circumscription of this field with a name both stimulates and misleads investigation. Saussure referred to semiology as the "science which studies the life of signs within social life." Like other, lengthier references which he made to it, this description points toward a vastness rather than artic-

Saussure as a student at the University of Leipzig.

ulates it. It presupposes and encourages the search for a "logic" of signification, a logic which can be reduced to "science," knowledge, rational codification, just as the name ideology presupposes and encourages the search for a logic of ideation.

But the field whose furrows interweave with the writing systems known as 'poetry' and 'art' in the pages of Saussure's notebooks is not circumscribable as sign-logic, any more than the normally chosen 'subject-matter' of ideological analysis—political theory, theology, or, more recently, the images patterning everyday life, such as those of television and other mass media—is circumscribable as idea-logic. The anagrammatical notebooks discover a signifying mechanism which cannot yet and cannot perhaps ever be scientized either as sign-logic or as idea-logic. The discovery itself is sufficient to draw these two "sciences," semiology and ideology, into connection and thus to collapse their frontiers as well as the frontiers of the sciences to which they seem adjacent. By dislodging the study of measured language from its encapsulation as part of an esthetic reserve with little or no relation to ideas, signification, or society; by indicating the psychic means and social functioning of such measured language, Saussure forces upon those following his inquiry a rethinking of the terms in which art, science, ideas, signs, and social life 'work.'

Work in the sense of social, material, and historical efficacy is the primary feature of Marx's theory of ideology, and this feature is emphasized in our consideration of Saussure's enterprise. Saussure described—partly in the notebooks, partly in the *Course*—the elements of a linguistic mechanism which *works* by centering, abstracting, and repeating signs. This centering, abstraction, and repetition reinforce the political, economic, and social ordering of the group in which and on which the linguistic mechanism is used. Because of this power of reinforcement, the linguistic mechanism can be said to perform work which is provisionally called here ideological work—provisionally because the logicality, ideality, and scientificity of knowledge of this work, implied by the term 'ideological,' remain questionable.

The anagrammatical investigations, then, discover a mechanism which performs ideological work. Yet the components of this mechanism are incompletely assembled; its parts are developed in scattered sections of Saussure's writings. To weave these sections together and to indicate their coherence can only be done by conjecture. It can only be done by assuming, as Saussure did about the texts he was analyzing, that Saussure's writing must be supplemented at certain points where it is blocked by unwritten assumptions, and that it must be pulled apart at other points where it is pieced together by incompatible assumptions. Using these procedures, the following main conjectures will be made: Saussure developed the centering and abstracting element of the linguistic mechanism performing ideological work in relation to a theory of naming processes in language. He developed the repetitive element in relation to a theory of mnemonic ritual and in relation to a theory of the organization of memory.

The theories which Saussure developed were closely related to his professional concern with comparative grammar, Sanskrit, and French versification. As a professor of these subjects in Geneva from 1891 to 1913 he was led both by linguistic and poetic analyses to the investigation of phonic rhythms. Similarly, the conjunction of theological, political, and poetic concerns in early Indo-European poetry made the perception of anagrams in these artifacts always a question of more than esthetic interest.

It is helpful, too, to consider Saussure's social and historical position as part of the pre-World War I elite of European professors whose pretensions and social status, although not usually political power, has been frequently called that of a mandarinate. As the purveyor of a culture comprising lower and higher, less and more pure forms, as the fine fruit of a historical process of acculturation thought to have advanced through millenia from the primitive to the civilized, it is not surprising that the word 'ideology,' tarred by Napoleon and feathered by Marx, does not appear in Saussure's writings. Nor is it surprising that his outwardly sociological definition of linguistics as part of the science which studies the life of signs within society is given mainly psychological rather than social or historical meaning in his anagrammatical analysis. Saussure traced the connections between naming, mnemonic repetition, and the making of discourse not to a relation between signifying activity and differential shares in social power but to a "superstitious idea" perpetuating itself through time with (to Saussure) stupefying and stupid inertia.

It will be maintained, then, that Saussure did not develop an explicit theory nor assemble a model of how language is woven in relation to a pattern of social power because of his assumptions about history and the psyche. These assumptions are not personal; they are temporally, spatially, socially commonplace, working ideologically on and through his writing in a way identified by Marx in *The German Ideology.*

In both the notebooks and the *Course* Saussure separates what he calls "pure" psychology from the mixed psycho-social sphere which he calls "language" (*langue*). He separates both these fields in turn from the sphere of "historical" or contingent, material change. As we will see, this double separation produces in his work an inversion of the relation between mental and non-mental reality similar to that which Marx called the characteristic mark of ideological work: the material conditions of human existence are polarized as something 'outside' which is photographed and projected 'inward' by the *camera obscura* of the mind. Given a reserved space of psychic activity, 'inside' and separate from the material world, it was as difficult for Saussure as for most Western thinkers since Plato to avoid the concept of a pure spiritual force emanating 'outward' from that space, incarnating itself in language, and thence directing the affairs of the 'world.' (pp. 1105-11)

Saussure's theory of anagrams is implicitly a theory of ideological work because of the links which the theory establishes between three activities: psycho-linguistic processes which 'center' the human signifying apparatus, sensory and neural, are connected with names as language and with naming as a social process; naming is connected with reiteration of the phonic elements of names as a mode of constructing discourse; and constructing discourse is connected with verbal associations held in memory. To observe this linkage requires shifting away from the topics which have attracted previous students of Saussure's unpublished notebooks. What has most concerned these scholars is a kind of anagram not even mentioned by Saussure in his work on Aphrodite in Vergil's *Aeneid.*

In addition to *mannequins* and diphonic anagrams, there was a "monophonic" type of anagram, Saussure believed, which consisted of finding in every line of poetry an even number of each of the vowels and consonants used in it. Saussure thought that he had discovered a verse form written in accordance with a "law" pairing off each acoustic element in this way. This verse form was called the "Saturnian" and was found in documents preserving early Latin verse, anonymously written and of a mixed religious, legal, and political character.

Saussure abandoned pursuit of the monophonic anagram after a brief period. "As soon as one does not push analysis to the systematic limit of the monophone, which requires a strict arithmetic, . . . one is confronted with a more immediately apprehensible phenomenon. . . . " "Starting with the Saturnian, I investigated or thought of investigating whether in the Greek epic[s of Homer] there was anything as bizarre at first sight as the phonic imitation by

means of verse of the names which have importance for each passage." Thus, the pursuit of the monophonic anagram led Saussure to uncover something quite different: a technique of naming.

Not only Latin but Greek, Sanscrit, and Old German verse seemed to be ordered in accordance with a naming system so insistent and omnipresent that it appeared to be an inescapable part of the tradition of early Indo-European writing. Saussure's problematic in the notebooks on anagrams thus moved away from trying to understand the generalized phonic patterning of poetry exhibited in the "monophonic" form of anagram. Not this "general phonism," but what he later called "anagrammatical phonism" (phonism "directed toward a name") came to fascinate Saussure, just as, he believed, it had fascinated Latin writers from the earliest period of their literature to the "last limits of Latinity."

How does Saussure know which name will be anagrammatized in a particular text? One "could not doubt," he tells us, that a verse like "Áasen argaléōn anémōn amégartos autmé" was "related in its syllables" to Agamemnon. But how does Saussure know that this verse, which occurs in the *Odyssey* as part of Odysseus' tale to King Alcinous of his encounter with the shade of Agamemnon in Hades, is "on Agamemnon" rather than on Alcinous, Odysseus, or Poseidon? (Odysseus is addressing the shade: "Did Poseidon smite you, . . . *when he roused a furious blast of racking winds?*") Presumably in a case like this Saussure checked whether the phonemic ordering allowed a mannequin or diphone rendering of such alternatives as Odysseus, Alcinous, or Poseidon. This was easy enough, since the mannequin aspect of the anagram allowed one to quickly eliminate names whose first and last phonemes did not occur in the passage in question.

The more important question to ask is this: how does Saussure know that a passage is about a name at all? Is it perhaps that Saussure "knows" that *every* literary passage is 'on' a signified expressed by a signifier in the form of a noun or name, a 'word-theme' name which captures and encloses, like a mannequin, the verbal energy of the linguistic movement? If this is so, then the thematic reading of literary passages upon which Saussure's anagrammatical exercises partly depend is entailed by the logocentric theory of signs developed in the *Course.*

Saussure's logocentric or concept-centered understanding of signification associates "concept" (signified) with a corresponding "sound-image" (signifier). These two make up the indissoluble oneness of verbal signs. The examples of verbal signs which Saussure uses to explain the theory in the *Course* are nouns ("horse," "tree"), and this is not an accident. Concepts can be summed up in nouns, offered in unified, delimited words rather than in phrases or in fragments, as would be the case with other parts of speech ("up," "run," "to"). To make the paradigm of verbal sign be a noun, a substantive, a naming segment of language, thus parallels and reinforces Saussure's tendency to favor synchrony over diachrony, his tendency to try and discover "language-states" which can be fixed, defined, and summed up rather than to investigate language dynamically, as a set of reciprocal movements which flow into and out of each other and their contexts.

The effect of these doctrines of language on Saussure's analysis of the texts considered in the notebooks is double. On one hand, the coherence of the text is understood to consist of a set of sound-images which unfolds in parallel with a set of concepts. This coherence builds, increment by increment, sign by sign, the text's meaning. On the other hand, such a building could not take place if the signs were not capable of being considered as increments. Thus the signs have to be self-centered; each one must approximate to the "state" of being a substantive or noun so that it can incrementally combine with others. Since approximation to the nominative state is not clear in the case of conjunctions, prepositions, and some other words taken singly, it becomes easier to posit such approximation if one considers them not one by one but as parts of sentences, as parts of signifying chains which present, taken as a whole, a statement. Given a logocentric theory of signification, a text's meaning emerges ultimately from the conjuncture of its parallel movement with its centering movement.

To discover the phonemic repetition of names in texts powerfully reinforces these assumptions. For the name thus hidden is the center of the passage, the meaning toward which it moves (sound-image by sound-image, phoneme by phoneme) and around which it moves. (The anagram repeats the meaning which the chain of signs is unfolding.) An anagrammatical text, then, does not simply offer sound-images cohering to concepts one by one. It reinforces and offers a kind of guarantee for this incremental movement by providing the sound-image of the passage's central concept, spaced out over the passage as a whole: A-ph-ro-od-di-it-e.

Saussure's project, insofar as it is given impetus by a logocentric theory of sign, is to prove that the phonic movement of texts is in agreement with their centering concepts. The central concepts/sound-images will nearly always be nouns because nouns best sum up the text. As nouns they name the text, pulling it together—like the mannequins—into little boxes.

It is not surprising, then, that Saussure discovered a noun, and usually a name, in all but two of the some ninety exercises thus far published which are concerned with anagrammatical phonism. Nor should it be surprising to discover among Saussure's other unpublished manuscripts, as Lévi-Strauss has recently done, a text which describes the process of naming as if it were a movement which, by centering and abstracting a concept, purifies and even deifies the concept's sound-image.

The Saussurean text published by Lévi-Strauss [in *Méthodologie de l'histoire et des sciences humaines*], untitled and full of erasures, announces its subject as "the deification of a thing." It is a remarkable fragment because of the extraordinary lengths to which Saussure here pushes his characteristic dichotomy between the chaos of material contingencies and the logic internal to *langue.*

The deification of a thing, Saussure says, is a naming process which comes about by historical accident. The process consists of two steps. First there is a stage in which the name of an everyday "object" is the same as the name of the power of that object, a power somewhat mysterious and thus somehow divine. The household fire, for example, is at one time called "agni" in Sanskrit. A "community of name" "subsists" in this case between the sensible object fire and the abstract power of fieriness. At a second stage some other name is given to the everyday object and the old name is reserved for the abstraction. Thus Agni becomes "a figure of the same order as Varuna or Apollo, whose names have the particularity of not referring to anything [in particular] on earth at the same moment." Such abstract beings fill the "purely mythological" realm of "Olympus," Saussure declares.

The linguistic cause of this evolution of names is a historical "accident." The accident which "brings the rupture *of the name* from the sensible object" is "at the mercy of the first linguistic fact which happens along and has no necessary relation to the sphere of mythological ideas. Just as one may call a cauldron first   and then   [Saussure left blanks for these names], so one may call fire first agni and then something else." "Nothing," then, determines such a "capital" change in "mythology" except a *"purely linguistic* fact without any visible importance in the flow of linguistic events which take place every day." Thus, the evolution of religious thought toward more abstract and general notions of divine power is given the form of a familiar scene—something like a kitchen scene in which Goodwife Brown calls the cauldron *y* instead of *x* and the fire a *thingamajig* instead of *agni.*

Of course such *paroles* must be adopted by others, must become socially general, in order to become part of the associative series which are integral to *langue.* But whether or not the definition of the relation of language-states to language flows, of synchrony to diachrony, had already been achieved by Saussure by 1894 (the date of this fragment), his theory of the fortuitousness of language-states, of the dependency of linguistic features upon accidents of historical context, remained the same. As Saussure put it in the ***Course,*** "No [linguistic] characteristic has a right to permanent existence; it persists only through sheer luck."

Implicit in this depiction of the fortuitous cause of the linguistic rise of Agni from earth to heaven are two other assumptions which both aided and hindered Saussure in his attempts to find and explain anagrammatized names. One is the assumption of a one-way movement from "mixed" toward "pure" names. The naming process moves away from physically existing *mixtures* of sensibles and intelligibles, away from a referential orientation to the physical world, and toward *pure* forms, "purely mythological beings."

Is this naming perhaps a kind of historicized projection of Saussure's doctrine of the arbitrary relation between signs and their referents? Could this theory of the movement of religious thought be considered a fictitious representation of one of the structural assumptions of his linguistics—in this case, the raising of the semiological bar between words and things? Certainly the usefulness of the fragment for anthropological study of the naming process is rather slight. In addition to the exiguity of the references to particular gods and to particular tribal usages, Lévi-Strauss shows in his commentary that Saussure's theory is false with respect to a number of known tribal naming processes. Naming seems to be a circulatory rather than one-way process in "savage thought," with words passing from secular to sacred usage and back again in a complex way regulated by and explicable in relation to a particular tribe's social structure.

As long as there was any logic in the adhesion of word to thing, any rationally specifiable relations 'outside' or 'beyond' the associative and syntagmatic relations 'in' the mind, it did not seem possible to Saussure for there to be a purely mythological thought, a clear analysis of the relations among the gods in heaven, a clarity about a *science of names.* (Manuscript note, undated, concerning the state of linguistics as Saussure found it: " . . . I assert as a fact that there is not a single term whatsoever in that science [linguistics] which has ever rested on a clear idea . . . Any clear theory, in the measure in which it is clear, is inexpressible in linguistics.") Only with the 'rupture' of name from sensed object, only with the dissolution of all 'sensible' ties, could the chimera of some 'natural relation' between signs and referents be exposed as illusion. Just as clarity about the logic relating different mythic beings requires thinking about their relations on Olympus rather than about their relations to particular things on earth, so linguistic rules can be specified only by isolating signs from referents.

The first of the three assumptions which Saussure makes in this fragment on Agni is thus paradoxically connected with the second. Linguistic rules can be specified because of the *logical* independence of signs from things. But this very independence from the rationality governing entities 'outside' language only makes linguistic signs the more vulnerable to *temporally* definable as opposed to logically definable influence: " . . . Language changes, or rather evolves, under the influence of all the forces which can affect either sounds or meanings. The evolution is inevitable; there is no example of a single language that resists it" [*Course*]. The peculiarity and interest of the fragment on Agni is that no contrast is made in it between logical and temporal influences, the one 'inside' and the other 'outside' language. Instead, the attempt to formulate the separation of logical from temporal influence is given in the historicizing form of a movement from mixed toward pure names.

In Saussure's *Course* the logical implications of language are consistently set forth in terms suggesting stasis rather than dynamism. The study of *langue* is a study of *simultaneities,* of language-states. Saussure's 'project' in the largest sense is to change linguistics from a primarily dynamic, diachronic science to a primarily static, synchronic science of logical implications. There is a metaphorical bias in Saussure's work toward representing logical implications as stasis, while representing temporal implications as movement. This bias expresses itself on the grammatical level, and thence on the mytho-religious and anagrammatical levels, as a concentration on the linguistic logic of

nouns. Saussure's third assumption in the fragment on Agni derives from this. The process of deification is seen as a process of *nomination,* a movement from verbal paraphrase—that - over - there - which - sparkles - and - leaps - high—toward nominative substance—that fire—and finally to static, categorical universality: the spirit of fire, the idea anywhere and everywhere of fire, Agni.

Saussure's conclusion in the fragment on Agni, based upon the three assumptions just considered, is as contradictory to the symbolist *Naturmythologie* of his day as his later linguistic theory was to historical linguistics: " . . . upon the fate of the *name* depends, . . . so to speak, from second to second, that of the *god.* . . . [There is a] fundamental influence of names and language on the creation of [mythic] figures. . . . The word here is simply *determining.*"

Those who control names, then, control the "gods," or, as Francis Bacon put it in perhaps the most remarkable analysis of ideological work before that of Marx, the "idols of the tribe." One need not move very far from such a conclusion to decide that those who control names control the ideas of the tribe. Saussure never made that move. His exploration of the question of who weaves names into poetry as anagrams seems to force him toward this conclusion, and yet he avoids it completely.

Two-thirds of the some ninety names which Saussure finds anagrammatized in the exercises thus far published are those of gods or heroes. They are, then, relatively "pure" names, names liberated from material contingencies, names with universal social power. Their circulation would be useful in obfuscating particular material conditions and in reinforcing general understanding of the world in terms of a *status quo* which poses itself as universal and eternal.

The other third of the anagrammatized names are less pure. They are names of authors, patrons, authors' writings, and persons or places figuring in the writings which Saussure studied (Pindar, Maecenas, the *Eclogues,* Falernus, etc.), and thus they seem to be declarations of personal rather than of social power relationships (power of the author over his or her work; power of a patron, a mistress, or a cherished locale over the author's ability to write, etc.). But this third of the names does share with the other two-thirds the property of consisting nearly entirely of proper names. It is as if Saussure's attempt to discover the centering movement of anagrammatized texts could not stop until the text became the property, the appropriated appendage of a real or imagined, but always particularized, living being.

Saussure's tendency to see proper names holding together or centering this or that passage is a repetition on another level of his tendency to explain the origin of the text by referring to the psychology of the author. The signs which center these texts on names were, Saussure seems to have assumed, woven by particular persons, by the authors to whom the texts belonged. By thus turning his investigation toward a problematic of personal motivation, of conscious intentions, Saussure moved—as indeed a logocentric theory of signification ultimately *must* move, since the concepts which are matched with sound-images are always something some *one* has 'in mind'—Saussure moved from a theory of text to one of context. He elaborated this theory in a double way, corresponding to his idea that linguistic activity (*langue*) is psychological and yet in important respects beyond the individual will. Thus, he tried to work out theories both of inward psychic arrangements which would motivate the making of anagrams and also of outward social and historical circumstances which would shape and regularize psychic work.

Saussure believed that the first persons to choose names and anagrammatize them were members of an Indo-European priestly elite like the *vates* of early Roman times:

> Ever since Indo-European times a person composing a *carmen* thus had to occupy himself in a *conscious* manner with the syllables entering into the *carmen* and with the rhymes they formed among themselves or with a given name. Every *vates* was above all a specialist in phonemes.

The *vates* were Roman soothsayers and interpreters of oracles who delivered their discourses in versified form. They were in early times not only religious leaders but law-givers, and it is important to note that the *carmina* which they composed were versified formulas of religion and law in the "Saturnian" prosodic form which first attracted Saussure's attention to the possibility that Latin and other early poetry was anagrammatized. *Vates* was the earliest Latin word for poet, and after falling into disuse, was revived and cultivated by Vergil and by those admiring Vergilian poetry as the proper term for poets. Whatever Vergil's motivations were—and this was a problem which eventually caused much perplexity to Saussure—the early *vates*, Saussure thought, wove names into their poetry out of superstition:

> One understands the superstitious idea which suggested that, in order for a prayer to be effective, it was necessary for the very syllables of the divine name to be indissolubly mixed in it: the god was, in a manner of speaking, rivetted to the text.

In reducing the *vates'* motives to false belief, to a "superstitious idea," Saussure moves his psychological projection of the problem of anagrams in an individuating direction, obscuring thereby the social functioning of the *vates'* work. The repetitive exchange and distribution of certain names chosen by the priestly elite appears less as a social practice directing psychic activity and more as the superstition of individuals, the pre-scientific failure of the *vates* to comprehend the difference between words and things, names and divine beings. Consideration of the *vates'* beliefs makes it less easy to see the manipulation of names by the *vates* as ideological practice, as collectively developing control over what names, nouns, and significations receive privileged circulation in a society.

Saussure's turning of the question of the *vates'* expertise toward a problematic of motivation did not, however, preclude an ingenious reconstruction of the means by which the *vates* might have developed their technique of rivetting concept to sound-image. Saussure believed that the ancient Latin, Greek, and Hindu peoples all used anagrammatical techniques in their *carmina*, and that each of them possessed a priestly caste similar to the *vates*. The old Germans too, he thought, had cultivated this technique, and in musing upon how they could have done so, even before the invention of writing, he conjures up a strange and emblemmatic scene. A group of Germanic *vates*, he imagines, sits in a clearing in a forest, chanting a prayer. Before each priest lie two heaps of twigs carved in ways resembling the runic characters found in early German inscriptions. From the pile to his left a priest-poet regularly picks up certain of these twigs and transfers them to the pile to his right as he chants. In this way, Saussure says, by allowing a given twig to represent a given phoneme (the German word *Stab*, 'stick' or 'wand,' is used in the compound, *Buchstabe*, to mean 'letter' or 'written character'), the exact number of times which each verbal sound had been used in the spell could be remembered, and thus the "poetic homophony," the balanced repetition of sounds, the anagrammatical repetition of names and themes, could be achieved "in the absence of writing."

> For in asking myself how without writing, an individual with even an exceptional memory could count the exact number of T's, R's, etc., in a hymn, vedic or not, which he was composing, I said to myself that there was only one natural means, that of making an exterior sign for each phonic element, as for example blue, black, and white pebbles . . . But since pebbles with the desired differences would be difficult to find, . . . the simplest thing was to take some shapable material, some wood, some twigs, cut in a certain fashion or chosen in accordance with [differences of] thickness, form, angles, and so on.

The action of the *vates* reconstructed here is not simply one of weaving in the name of a god or hero. It is also, as Saussure emphasizes, a mnemonic ritual, a method of impressing certain phonemic series on the memory. In thus depicting the means by which a priestly elite insured the preservation of ideologically central names, Saussure exemplified the specifically semiological manipulations of an ideological apparatus, in this case a religio-legal apparatus which eventually became an educational-cultural apparatus through the inertial power of Indo-European myth. But for Saussure the *vates* were not part of an ideological apparatus. The priests were proto-scientists, not proto-ideologists, and it was their knowledge, not their political power, which elevated them above others: "from the earliest Indo-European times this science of the vocal form of words . . . was probably the reason for the superiority, the particular [social] quality of the Hindu *kavis*, the Latin *vates*, etc."

Before assessing the significance of this reference to the *kavis* and the *vates* as the founding fathers of an important part of that semiological science which Saussure saw himself as developing, we must consider the last element of the unnamed ideological mechanism which Saussure constructed. This element is developed in the *Course* rather than in the notebooks. It explains how the mnemonic rituals of the *vates* may be seen as a way not just of preserving names but of generating discourse.

Differences between linguistic terms fall into two groups, syntagmatic and associational, according to Saussure's *Course in General Linguistics.* Saussure depicts the relation between the two groups as a linearly horizontal movement from left to right in the case of syntagmatic relations among terms, and as a star-like spraying-out of terms below the line of discourse in the case of associative relations among terms. . . .

In associative space linguistic terms move in mnemonic rather than in grammatical ways. 'Outside discourse' and 'in the memory,' this space is nonetheless indispensable to *langue,* to the linguistic behavior which displays itself as syntagmatic. It is field-like and open-ended, in contrast to the linearly coded space of syntagms. It is not, of course, unstructured; it contains paradigmatic series of various sorts, declensions of nouns, conjugations of verbs. But it contains such series in "indefinite order" and "indefinite number," unlike the perfectly ordered space of syntagmatic series.

The indefiniteness with which associated linguistic terms are arranged is itself variable. The pull of syntagmatic relations 'in discourse' upon the associated terms 'outside discourse' constantly moves the latter toward definite, constellar form, like that which Saussure portrays in his diagram of *enseignement.* But the associated terms never achieve perfect constellation because they float freely in memory, and are thus subject to every linguistically provoking wind which sweeps through the psyche. "A word can always evoke everything that can be associated with it in one way or another." What, then, orders these associative terms? " . . . The order in which terms are called depends on circumstances," that is, on diachrony, on history. Since historical circumstances are themselves multiple and changing, their effect on associative relations is to threaten constant flux. Take the discourses called legends, for example. If one offers "five or six material elements" (words, phrases) to "five or six persons working separately," their "sense" (their associated order) "will change in the space of several minutes."

With such an atomized conception of "circumstances" (five or six atom-individuals set to work in an anonymous time-space of several atom-minutes), Saussure could only think about the psyche as a place of little order and always threatening chaos. "Psychologically our thought—apart from its expression in words—is only a shapeless and indistinct mass. . . . " Between the potential chaos of associative relations "in memory" and the helter-skelter of "circumstances" surrounding the signifying individual stood only the rules and order of syntagmatic relations, calm and unalterable, the work of the community rather than of the individual; of the community as a "whole" rather than of any identifiable, socially structured groups within it.

The shapelessness of Saussure's theory of society (mass and individual: nothing in between) complements the shapelessness of his theory of mind (concepts pulled into order by *langue,* dropping into disorder with the end of discourse: nothing in between). What Saussure regards as true of the moving, changing world outside is converted into what is true of the individual's world inside by means

of his concept of associative relations. But the two spaces remain separate, held apart from each other by the iron laws of *langue.* Why was Saussure unable to connect the mnemonic series of associative space with the space of social relations, the space where the *vates* weave phonemes into memorable strands? If the idea of associative relations is so parallel to the idea of the *vates'* ritual, why are the two ideas disjoined, so that Saussure never explicitly considered the priestly-poetic guardians of words as a group whose job it was to save ideologically central names from the accidents to which language's regularities are exposed every "several minutes"? Why did Saussure never consider associational space as the area of ideological work, where the memory, the "seat" of association "in the brain," is filled with ideologically charged phonemes, arranging them not only according to their "radical," (*enseignement, enseigner,* etc.), according to the analogy of the concepts signified (*enseignement, apprentissage,* etc.), according to the "suffix" (*enseignement, changement,* etc.), according to the "sound-image" (*enseignement, justement,* etc.), but also according to the *mannequin* form of the sound-image, the diphonic form of the sound-image?

Like the systems elaborated by the ideological apparatuses of present-day mass culture, the arrangements of society are kept apart by relating them in a theatrical way. On a stage, on a screen before our mind's eye we glimpse the phonic hovering of discourse around key signs, projected forward into this theater of our space and time from its dim beginnings in pre-history. Seated thus safely apart from the space-time depicted on stage, we the students of language can view with equanimity this astonishing chronicle of primitive superstition, this ancient vatic ritual "of another age." Behind us, out of sight, is situated the camera or the director projecting the spectacle. Behind us, in the opposite direction from what we analyze as *paroles* or discursive activity, is situated the mechanism governing this phonic play, with its mnemonic hovering around series of associated terms, terms inscribed more or less deeply in the nervous system by their repeated use in contiguity.

In Saussure's opinion we can describe this camera, located diametrically opposite the place where phenomena appear, only by observing the camera's effects and not by looking at it directly. The psyche is a black box, a *camera obscura* where "language works out its units while taking shape between two shapeless masses. . . . " Linguists, then, are not camera-makers, they are only projectors: "Linguistics . . . works in the border-land where the elements of sound and thought combine."

The consequence of this polarization of inner from outer and of this barring of penetration into the inner, is that a continuously interweaving idea of signifying activity is not possible within the terms of Saussure's system. As in most information theory today, signs for Saussure boomerang back and forth between two psyches, two poles which are mysterious amalgams of rule-bound *langue* and rule-less individual acts of volition and intellect. Verbal activity is classifiable only in the "borderland," where the effects of "pure" psychic activity can be arranged into associative and syntagmatic categories. The associative area, mediating as it does between inside and outside, is the theater of ideological work, but that theater is one of mystification because access to the projecting room of the psyche is barred. Saussure offers no entrance to that inside via the work of mediating groups of persons working together out of habit, tradition, or institutional coercion. He allows no *contingent,* temporally-spatially definable, diachronic interweaving of society and psyche.

The memory stores things at the internal end of the linguistic apparatus, offering them to the outside world in accordance with the laws of *langue,* which, however "social," are not and can not be sociohistorical. History is 'outside,' a question of events. The 'properly' historical—the diachronic—and the 'properly' linguistic—the synchronic—occupy different places. Signs sent from one person's inside to another's may be pushed and pulled, damaged or even cancelled by events en route, but they are not 'made' there in that outside area. Such modifications as take place are 'accidents' which are not controllable by and not describable as properly linguistic forces. Linguistic decisions are made only 'inside,' by the brain—not only the rules of *langue* but the rules of *littérature.*

Anagrammatical practice, too, therefore, begins 'inside'; and if "every Latin who took up the pen found it the habitual accompaniment of his thought, almost at the moment when it sprang from his brain and he thought of putting it into prose or verse," Saussure must explain why this habit was so coercive in every instance where he discovers the practice. That is, Saussure was required by his logocentrically linear model of the making of signs (thought→intention of putting into prose or verse→writing) to provide not only an explanation of the practice of anagrams in the other space of history, the prehistory of Europe where anagrammatical practitioners could be lumped together as primitive, superstitious, and in any case anonymous. He had also to explain Vergil "with his original poetry," Lucretius "with his intense preoccupation with ideas," Horace "with his solid good sense about everything": how could these great individuals subject themselves to "that incredible relic of another age?" "I recognize," Saussure says in another place, "that the question is related very closely to a *poetic intention,* which I denied or presented under other aspects in the case of the centuries before that personal poetry."

How did Saussure explain the necessarily intentional origin of anagrams in self-conscious poets? In the long run he did not, and it is amusing to observe how Saussure's inability to give up the principle of elite self-consciousness, of individual control of literary signification, gradually undermined his scientism, his sense of the experimental impeccability and objective existence of anagrammatized names. Finally, when he wrote directly to a practicing neo-Latin poet whose works also revealed the presence of anagrams, a fellow academician—who would have to know the anagrammatical rules in a conscious way—when Giovanni Pascoli refused to acknowledge the rules, Saussure's project apparently collapsed not because the anagrams were disproved, but because the theory on the basis of which Saussure was able to see them had no place

for collective unconscious ideological activity. Saussure could not wedge the anagram in between a polarized and undifferentiated "individual" and "society."

Saussure's impasse can be articulated in the form of three antinomies concerning the clarity of truth, the inwardness of impulse, and the individuation of development.

1. The clarity of truth: "there is not a single term in that science which has ever rested on a clear idea. . . . " Saussure's theory of synchronic linguistics in the *Course* is "clear" to just the degree that it is general. Similarly, the problem of the origin of anagrams becomes clear to just the degree that it is remote. The practice of the *vates* is clear and that of Vergil is comprehensible when one gives enough weight to "tradition," but the practice of Giovanni Pascoli, so close at hand, is impossible to understand. As the phenomena retreat from the scientist in time, space, and social involvement, they become indistinct historically, socially, and psychologically, but how wonderfully clear they become in their general linguistic contours! As long as anagrammatical exercises take place thousands of years ago, their reality is incontestable. This "relic," this "curiosity," this "superstitious idea" becomes a reality to just the degree to which it has nothing to do with the investigator—with Saussure's own French language, for example (Starobinski points out that Saussure offered a course on French versification nearly every year and yet he never ventured an anagrammatical analysis of anything written in French), or with his own ideological status as a 'self-conscious' individual, choosing what he wishes to write about with 'freedom.' When the phenomena occur nearer home, when the question of intention becomes unavoidable, when the problem of anagrams presents itself in socio-historical and personally involving clarity—in the form of a letter to Pascoli, for example—then science becomes troubled, murky, unsafe, insecure.

2. The inwardness of impulse: If 'in' is eternally in and 'out' is absolutely out, then what stimulates an 'in' to go 'out'? or what prompts people to make signs? Of course, 'in' speaks to 'in': one psyche stimulates another, but what stimulated the first psyche? and how did psyches become so marvellously, theatrically separate from the socio-material conditions of stimulation? A 'speech-circuit' which only boomerangs between two inwardly enclosed poles can only be explained by moving down a double tunnel of intentional and historical regress, both tunnels infinitely long and dark. Each speech-act has to be verified, individual volition by individual volition, and its inspiration carried back individual moment by individual moment all the way to the forests where perhaps, on the basis of a "superstitious idea," one could suppose a linguistic shaping which is neither the work of individuals nor that of an undifferentiated collectivity, but is rather the work of a specific group which in competition and consonance with other social groups has achieved control over the inculcation of words. But can one think out the interfiliation of that prehistoric breakdown of privacy in mental action with the historic polarity of out from in? One cannot, because

3. History is a process of individuation, of development toward the freedom of individuals, not of development to-

ward a multiplying variability of social interaction. "The question becomes *more personal* the more one *advances in time.* . . ." Time is progress; time is the progressive individuation of the person, and so of necessity everything *traditional,* as it hangs on, becomes oppressive and banal, even to the ruling minority and the cultural elites. In the future, some day, a poet will be free of all traditions, free to choose to anagrammatize or not—unlike Vergil— unlike Mallarmé?

> I don't say that Vergil took up the anagram because of the esthetic advantages which he saw in it, but I do want to make this point: first, that one can never measure the force of a tradition of that kind. There are many French nineteenth-century poets who would not have written their verses in the form prescribed by Malherbe if they had been free.

With such a concept of history, one cannot think the continued existence, let alone the indispensability, of ideologized linguistic action, of an inevitable associative inertia and at the same time a positive will to exert power over associativeness on the part of conflicting social groups— on the part of all social groups, not in order to communicate 'what they have inside,' but simply in order to orient themselves to their daily realities.

Ritualization is remembering. A ritual is a sociophysically describable way of performing a psychophysical action. And vice-versa. In temporal-spatial terms, then, a socially signifying form of action like ritual behavior should be understood as interfiliated with a psychically signifying form of action like remembering. Understood in this way, the problem of penetrating to intentions 'behind' signifying actions dissolves. What Saussure projected outside and behind 'our' history in a pre-history of European literature—a collective work ritually enforcing the remembering of names—can be admitted as a mode of ideological work going on at any time irrespective of intentions. Ritual action is repetition, so as to secure fixation of the kind of response behaviorally demanded in certain situations. Thus it is an ideological procedure. Remembering is a matter of repetition, so as to secure fixation of response, an availability of the signs demanded in certain situations. Thus, it is an ideological procedure. Syllabic repetitions and phonic outlines of ideologically important words will occur in any writing, Latin or French, old or new, insofar as the words have been ritually— collectively, unconsciously—fixed as memorable.

But fixity of signification is only relatively possible in a temporal and spatial world. We measure lack of fixity by temporal and spatial coordinates. The coordinates, since they cannot start 'from the beginning,' begin from a norm: Greenwich mean time; the rigid rod, metrically subdivided, on deposit at the Bureau of Standards; Jesus' birth; the zero meridian. The function of ideology in relation to the working of social systems could be described generally as that of obscuring the lack of fixity in reality-as-humanly-experienced by means of establishing norms.

The establishment of norms: a centering process. Just as time and space cannot be used as measures of fixity and its lack except by reference to norms which are themselves

arbitrary centerings of changeability as humanly experienced, so the particulars of social life cannot be measured in terms of their fixity and its lack except by reference to arbitrary centerings of social structure: the patriarchal family, the capitalist factory, the kingship, the presidency. In the first section of this paper I suggested replacing the Marxian concept of *illusion* with the Saussurean concept of *arbitrariness* in order to avoid the dualism of reflection theories of ideology. Ensuing sections indicated how Saussure both in the *Course* and in the notebooks used the idea of the arbitrariness of signs with respect to referents and the idea of the centering work of signs with respect to discourse. In this concluding section let us consider the implications of this concept of ideology as arbitrary centering for a concept of nonideologized signification. What space and time is left for the nonideological in such a problematic?

Ideology, by its centering, works to make life meaningless except in terms of its norms, which are nevertheless merely arbitrary rather than reflective of reality. But the more successful an ideology is in making significance depend upon its arbitrarily fixed norms, the less meaningful the norms become. The oppressiveness of ideology lies in its emptying effect rather than in its falsehoods, but this oppressive zeal undoes itself. The more that signifying practices appear not simply normative but normal, the more that abnormal signifying practices appear not simply deviant but *without any significance,* the less the center can remain the center because it has fewer and fewer signifying items to integrate in its arbitrary way. Ideological work consists in showing how apparently diverse things signify the same thing, but if it were possible to show not only that all things signify the same thing but that insofar as they do not so signify, they are entirely without significance, then the center would disappear due to its reiterative sameness. Repetition, the ideological dinning of "sound images" into the memory, is impossible without differences.

Ideological work, then, thrives on differences, and in this it distinguishes itself from the work of repression, which consists in censoring rather than in centering deviance from norms. A 'repressive' state system does not try to eliminate its subjects, which remain resources for its accumulation of value; its aim is merely to eliminate resistant and deviant behaviors. The same is true of the individual who tries to repress thoughts or emotions; the effort is to prohibit certain appearances, not to annihilate the means of their appearance, thinking or feeling itself. Ideologization is less a prohibiting than an integrating process. Eagerly accepting as grist for their mill the variability of significations which occur due to differences in class position, historical traditions, or physical location, ideologists direct attention to those signs which promise social inclusion by their imitation. These signs can only be such as stabilize and perpetuate society as it is; they are signs which center attention on behavior which serves the interests of existing class hierarchies, rather than directing attention to their questionability. They identify the place where a member of a community will be at the center of things, where there is least chance of exclusion and most chance of being included in an intrinsically variable world.

Whether the center thus identified is aristocratic (to be at the center is to be a person admired, a person of prowess, of ideal moral and physical powers), bourgeois (to be at the center is to be the average one, the normal one, the person who is like everyone else, who fits in), communal (to be at the center is to be adequate; it is to be a person whose functions are economically, morally, physically necessary, who cooperates with social goals), or other, the function of ideological work in this respect is to center signifying behavior around activities which support the social system.

Any centering is already a polarizing of significations. If ideological work aims at equipping people to fulfill their daily tasks by portraying a centered system of social roles, it always implies a system of polarities: center/margin, inclusion/exclusion, group/individual. To use the term which plays the centering role in both Saussure's linguistic theory and in the "concrete description" of the theory in his manuscripts, ideological work polarizes by offering a set of denominations, of central, less central, and marginal names. There is no "place" in the work of ideologists for words which fall between the lines, for signs which direct attention to process, or to ambivalences, or to incoherences. To center linguistic efforts on the arrangement of nouns checks every dispersal of meaning, affirming the ideological project of ruling out what cannot be arranged with respect to given social names. Deviance and resistance is not prohibited, for to prohibit such behavior would make it significant by acknowledging it. Ideology controls meaning positively by integrating deviance and negatively by neglecting it. It achieves its goal insofar as all meaning is arrayed in due degree around its centering norms, while all resistance to it is not crushed but on its way either to insertion or oblivion.

The purpose of ideological work, then, is to naturalize the arbitrary: "The anagrammatical writer was first attentive to the equilibrium of sounds, because it seemed natural, since one had to repeat the same sounds, to choose especially those which alluded at the same time to a name that everyone had in mind." "Aphrodite," "Agamemnon": remember these names, listen to the *vates* recalling you to remembrance of these names. If you remember them, then they have placed you in relation to them, and not vice-versa. You have a place near or far from, but in any case located, integrated in relation to several central themes of our society. The themes of love, the themes of war: the socio-psycho-semio-structures which parse love as an ambrosial fragrance, a flowing of robes; which rouse the warrior to smite like a storm-blast, to resist death like a king.

The memory, which in Saussure's synchronic theory serves up associative items to be inserted into syntagmetic slots, can only "store," as Saussure says, what is packed into it. If it is filled up with some phonemes more than others, in certain orders rather than others, then the associative series which are selected by the linguistic "machine" for insertion in a syntagmatic series will tend to select the more frequently stored phonemes and phonemic orders rather than the less frequently stored ones. This machine works equally in and on the ideologized and the ideolo-

gizers: its semio-logic is universal and inexorable within the confines of the social group using a given language.

If, then, the characteristic work of ideological institutions—above all the representatives of religion in Vergil's or Homer's time, and above all the representatives of science in Saussure's—is to center and polarize (categorize, denominate), and if this is characteristically achieved through the ritualization of sign behavior (not only or always verbal sign behavior), such that certain signs tend to be forgotten while others are ones which 'everyone has in mind,' then the linguistic function of priest-poets is simply that of centering associative series on social norms: on divine names, on the writer's patron, on one's 'self,' one's *legitimate,* which is to say one's ideologically definable existence as a writer. Saussure's anagrams, observed at a safe distance from his own culture (born in the pre-linguistic sphere of psychic intentions, carried on in an Indo-European pre-history before poets achieved full freedom from "apparatuses" for their poetry), could only bring to phonic clarity the presence of names known by the investigator to be already there. This field of ideological practices is only the first level of ideological work. Saussure never moved to a second level of ideological presences in language, a level often referred to as that of "belief-systems." It is this level to which we have referred in showing how Saussure's logocentric theory of sign works together with his polarization of 'in' from 'out' to stop his investigation of anagrams. Without a method capable of analyzing ideological work in discourse on this level, the larger ideologies at work in Homer, Seneca, Vergil, Lucretius, and the rest remained undiscovered by Saussure. There is no sense of aristocratic social system, no analysis of patron-client relations, no awareness of the ideological usefulness of love and war. Finally, Saussure did not move from the sense of systems at work to the concept of apparatuses insuring the material production of the elements of those systems. The embeddedness of "belief-systems" such as elite/mass, in/out, and center/periphery in religious, educational, and artistic—let alone scientific—institutions remains outside Saussure's discourse.

Saussure's system can be simply summarized. Anagrams repeat names, in order to induce memorization of names. The memorization of names produces an association of sounds inside the brain so that they achieve a regularized relation to each other. This regularized relation or associative series fixes words in relation to each other, though not in relation to the world, so that anagrammatical practices tend to perpetuate themselves. But there is always the chance that the series will be undone by "linguistic accidents" caused by the chaotic forces of diachrony.

Underpinning this system is the set of unspoken metaphysical equations to which, following Jacques Derrida, we have referred as logocentrism. Saussure's emphasis on naming in anagrammatical practice is equivalent to his emphasis on nouns and on the grammatical and semantic functions of the nominative in his general linguistic theory. Emphasis on the nominative and on naming are in turn equivalent to his emphasis on myth-making as a purifying of sensory impressions. The rising of fire/Agni from earth to heaven is a centering and abstracting process which separates the word from its source in a sensory impression, and allows it to float freely in the brain where it can be associated—arbitrarily—with other words. Thus Saussure mythologized his doctrine of the arbitrary 'nature' of the sign.

In translating this theory into the terms of a possible problematic of ideology which moves beyond and against logocentric assumptions, only one intervention is necessary. Instead of locating the place of the dislocation of signs from their referents in the never-never land of the psyche ("heaven"), one may suggest that sensory impressions on the human neural system are integrated with the already signified needs, uses, and desires of a determinate social structure. In the case of the Indo-European peoples whose discourses Saussure studied, that social structure has at most epochs and in most places been a hierarchically oppressive one. As a result the naming has been neither purifying nor logical in its abstracting movement but a mystification of the diverse relations existing among materially existing things. Nomination of these relations has operated to pull together, to center and classify the world's diversity in such a way as to achieve the kind of stasis which would solidify the status quo.

The value of Saussure's work on anagrams remains that he suggested how this mystification is processed as a ritually mnemonic method of creating associations among linguistic forms. He thus offers in incipient form some of the semiological links missing from Marx's, Gramsci's and Althusser's theories of ideology. These links make it possible to avoid bipolar organizations of the ideological problematic. They encourage elaboration of a timing, spacing, gapped, intermittently 'feedback' model of signifying activity. Such a linguistic mechanism works as often to dislocate and transform as to complete the circuits moving between the material, social, and signifying elements which affect and compose human activity. In developing this kind of model the concept of associative relations of language remains extremely useful both because of and in spite of Saussure's explicit aims, because they show how language characteristically operates in a gaping, dislocative way, even as it pursues centralizing goals.

Saussure, we remember, emphasized that most associative series are indefinite both in number and in the order in which they "occur" to the "memory." But that occurrence to memory is always ideologically offered: the order and the number of items in an associative series—that is, the items which may be substituted for each other, which are 'alternatives' in a given discourse—are progressively, continuously, although never definitively organized by the socially, naturally, historically conditioned process of signification. If Saussure, therefore, places at the *center* of his diagram of associative relations the French noun *enseignement* ('teaching'), that is an ideological question: Saussure is a French professor teaching a course in linguistics to a group of students. Of course, he could have chosen some other word equally well. But he didn't choose another word, and his choice of this word, *enseignement,* is not ideologically 'free' either in its occurrence or in its implications.

But it is not 'determined' ideologically, either. The advan-

tage of Saussure's associative space is its avoidance of determinism, linguistic or otherwise. Far from conceiving the associative space as a determined realm of specific levels and formal classes, Saussure says that "the mind"—let us substitute the phrase, 'the ideological process'—"creates as many associative series as there are diverse relations." Thus in his diagram each series ends with the word "etc.," not from lack of diagrammatic space but because the ideological process is simultaneously centering and open-ended.

> If we associate *painful, delightful, frightful,* etc., we are unable to predict the number of words that the memory will suggest or the order in which they will appear. A particular word is like the center of a constellation; it is the point of convergence of an indefinite number of coordinated terms. [*Course*]

An ideological process is centering and coordinating only in its connection to the work of specifiable social groups; it is not intrinsically centered, coordinated, and closed. It cannot be because the rituals which help and enforce remembering cannot be eternally fixed in the midst of changing spaces and times. Rather it is the interaction of associative series with the syntagmatic series of discourses—the contexts of an unfolding communication—which center and link items in an ideological process in a provisional way. Since associative series are thus openended, they can be recentered and linked together in "as many associative series as there are diverse relations." They can be systematically *de*centered and *un*linked, although this process, the more it is systematically pursued, the more it too becomes an ideological undertaking.

The removal of mystery from the non-place of the psyche, its relocation as a route rather than a place, its exposure as a process of linkage and centering and of unlinking and decentering, destroys at the same time the occult power of the priestly, scientific, or other coteries who ritualize its forms. The structure of the psyche behind or below the line of discourse may be understood more easily, less secretly, as the set of provisional ideologies, obsessing—that is, with attention to that verb's Latin root, besieging, attempting to fix in his or her proper social place—a 'reader.'

In the measure in which readers fail to recognize that every signifying text, verbal or non-verbal, which they choose to read (never freely; never deterministically) was guided in its composition by ideologically organized parameters; in the measure in which readers fail to recognize that their reading is also guided in its understanding by ideologically organized canons of interpretation—in these measures they capitulate to the Guardians of Truth, to the Makers of Right Names, to the *vates,* savant shapers of language, modern manipulators of mystic names.

The associative space of an ideologically ineluctable winding and rewinding of significations is not simply a physically controlled space, whose paths are effaced automatically by a hypostasized time. It is not simply a psychologically controlled space, where paths are traced by structures of desires and needs peculiar to the psychic development of the human infant in the triangulated structure of the family. It is not simply a socio-logically con-trolled space, where paths become deep ruts due to the tired repetitions of sovereign interests, institutionalized in ideological apparatuses. It is not simply a materially con-tingent space, where effects of nearness and distance, of this letter next to that, of attraction and repulsion, dissoci-ation and hiatus, repetition and avoidance, dance along the way. It is *at least* the congeries of combinations sug-gested by these perspectives, these categories, these names. And it is also the deficit of objects blocked off by the trac-ing of these paths, objects which reappear when the paths are traced in other ways.

The psyche, then, is not a black box, a receptacle of thoughts and motives where the things of this world are arranged in locked, categorical drawers. It is rather like the spacing out of associative relations along materially traceable physico-chemical neural trails, such that the dif-ferent aspects of words—or more generally, of significa-tions—have relative but not definite order and number. These signifying streams are not structures, but rather structures-to-be, structurings called out by the syntagma-tic exigencies of a given language, and thereby given—but again provisionally—a name as part of a specific dis-course. Naming, then, is definite, inevitable, useful, from the point of view of the specific discourse, but it is indefi-nite, avoidable, and sooner or later useless from the point of view of the associative nets from which and to which particular terms pass.

Associative work is not clarifying, moving fire to the heav-en of pure names, but distributive, like the *vates* moving their twigs. It moves things around, defeating at the same time as it tends to capitulate to the pressure, the rhythm, the comforting repetition of anagrammatic rituals of un-derstanding. (pp. #1112-35)

Samuel Kinser, "Saussure's Anagrams: Ideo-logical Work," in MLN, *Vol. 94, No. 5, De-cember, 1979, pp. 1105-38.*

Saussure on the aims of the linguist:

[I am very disgusted] with the difficulty there is in general to write ten lines concerning the facts of language which have any common sense. I have for a long time been espe-cially concerned with the logical classification of these facts, with the classification of the points of view from which we treat them, and I see more and more both the immensity of the work which is necessary to show the linguist *what he is doing,* by reducing each operation to its previously specified category; and at the same time the very great vanity of ev-erything which can ultimately be done in linguistics.

Ferdinand de Saussure, in an 1894 letter to Antoine Meillet, later reprinted in Emile Benveniste's Problems in General Linguistics, *translated by Mary Elizabeth Meek, University of Miami Press, 1971.*

Roy Harris   (essay date 1983)

[*An English linguist and educator, Harris has been praised for his English translations of Saussure's work. In the following excerpt, taken from the introduction to the 1983 edition of the* Course in General Linguistics, *he assesses Saussure's achievements and contributions.*]

Saussure's *Cours de linguistique générale* occupies a place of unique importance in the history of Western thinking about man in society. It is a key text not only within the development of linguistics but also in the formation of that broader intellectual movement of the twentieth century known as 'structuralism'. With the sole exception of Witt-genstein, no thinker has had as profound an influence on the modern view of *homo loquens* as Saussure.

The revolution Saussure ushered in has rightly been de-scribed as 'Copernican'. For instead of men's words being seen as peripheral to men's understanding of reality, men's understanding of reality came to be seen as revolving about their social use of verbal signs. In the *Cours de linguistique générale* we see this new approach clearly ar-ticulated for the first time. Words are not vocal labels which have come to be attached to things and qualities al-ready given in advance by Nature, or to ideas already grasped independently by the human mind. On the con-trary languages themselves, collective products of social interaction, supply the essential conceptual frameworks for men's analysis of reality and, simultaneously, the ver-bal equipment for their description of it. The concepts we use are creations of the language we speak.

Saussure's standing as the founder of modern linguistics remains unchallenged more than half a century after his death. It is based on two facts. One fact is that Saussure, although only one among many distinguished linguists of his day, was the first to recognise the particular range of theoretical questions which had to be answered if linguis-tics was ever to take its place among the sciences. The other fact is that Saussure himself proposed answers to those questions which have remained either the basis or the point of departure for all subsequent linguistic theory within the academic discipline which thereafter claimed the designation 'linguistics'.

This dual achievement suffices to explain Saussure's pivot-al place in the evolution of language studies. But he plays a no less crucial role when his work is seen in a wider cul-tural context. For the founder of modern linguistics at the same time founded semiology, the general science of signs, within which linguistics was to be one special branch. In so doing, Saussure opened up a new approach to the study of many other human patterns of behaviour. It was an ap-proach later to be exploited by theorists in such diverse fields as art, architecture, philosophy, literary criticism and social anthropology. The implications of Saussure's technique for dealing with linguistic analysis extend far beyond the boundaries of language, in ways which make the *Cours de linguistique générale* without doubt one of the most far-reaching works concerning the study of human cultural activities to have been published at any time since the Renaissance.

Saussure's proposals for the establishment of linguistics as an independent science may—at the risk of making them sound rather unexciting—be summarised as follows. He rejected the possibility of an all-embracing science of language, which would deal simultaneously with physiological, sociological, philosophical and psychological aspects of the subject. Instead, he proposed to cut through the perplexing maze of existing approaches to the study of linguistic phenomena by setting up a unified discipline, based upon a single, clearly defined concept: that of the *linguistic sign*. The essential feature of Saussure's linguistic sign is that, being intrinsically arbitrary, it can be identified only by contrast with coexisting signs of the same nature, which together constitute a structured system. By taking this position, Saussure placed modern linguistics in the vanguard of twentieth-century structuralism.

It was a position which committed Saussure to drawing a radical distinction between *diachronic* (or evolutionary) linguistics and *synchronic* (or static) linguistics, and giving priority to the latter. For words, sounds and constructions connected solely by processes of historical development over the centuries cannot possibly, according to Saussure's analysis, enter into structural relations with one another, any more than Napoleon's France and Caesar's Rome can be structurally united under one and the same political system.

Truism though this may now seem, there is no doubt that in arguing along these lines Saussure was swimming against the prevailing tide in language studies throughout his lifetime. For the great philological achievements of the nineteenth century had all been founded upon a historical and comparativist approach to language. Late-nineteenth-century philology was as uncompromisingly 'evolutionary' in outlook as Darwinian biology. Saussure was the first to question whether the historical study of languages could possibly provide a satisfactory foundation for a science of linguistics. The question was as profound as it was startling: for the assumption most of Saussure's contemporaries made was that historical philology already *had* provided the only possible scientific foundation. They believed, as Max Müller optimistically put it in the 1860s, that linguists were already dealing with the facts of language just as scientifically as 'the astronomer treats the stars of heaven, or the botanist the flowers of the field'. In Saussure's view, nothing could have been more profoundly mistaken.

Where historical philology had failed, in Saussure's opinion, was in simply not recognising the structural nature of the linguistic sign. As a result, it had concentrated upon features which were merely superficially and adventitiously describable in mankind's recorded linguistic history. The explanations philological historians provided were in the final analysis simply appeals to the past. They did not—and could not—offer any analysis of what a language is from the viewpoint of its current speakers. Whereas for Saussure it was *only* by adopting the users' point of view that a language could be seen to be a coherently organised structure, amenable to scientific study. For linguistic signs, Saussure insisted, do not exist independently of the complex system of contrasts implicitly recognised in the day-to-day vocal interactions of a given community of speakers.

Similarly, in all other fields of human activity where signs are arbitrary, it is the system of structural contrasts implemented in human interaction which must become the focus of attention for any scientific semiological investigation. For signs are not physical objects. We cannot study them as we can plants, or animals, or chemical substances. Signs are not to be equated with sounds uttered, or marks on paper, or gestures, or visual configurations of various kinds. These are merely the vehicles by which signs are expressed. To confuse the two would make it impossible to establish a science of signs at all, in Saussure's estimation, whether in the domain of language or any other.

Nor, although the terminology of the **Cours** itself falls short of ideal consistency on this point, are signs to be equated simply with the signals (*signifiants*) by which they are identified. Each sign is a dual entity, uniting signal with signification (*signifié*). Neither facet of this duality exists independently of the other, just as no sign exists independently of the other signs united in the same system of structural contrasts. A language (*langue*) is for Saussure this whole system which alone makes it possible to identify and describe constituent parts: it is not a whole fortuitously built up out of parts already existing in their own right. Linguistic signs are therefore not like individual bricks, put together in a certain way to form an architectural structure. Unlike bricks, they are not separate self-contained units. Except as parts of the total structure, they do not even exist, any more than the circumference or the radii of a circle exist without the circle.

Thus to treat words as linguistic units somehow capable of surviving through time from Latin down to modern Italian is, for Saussure, no more than a historian's metaphor. It is a metaphor which does no harm provided we recognise it as a projection based on our own acquaintance, as language-users, with the reality of the linguistic sign. But it is not a metaphor which can provide us with any genuine understanding of the reality, nor any foundation for a scientific account of it either.

This is not the place to discuss how far Saussure succeeded in answering his own searching questions about language and human signs in general, or in providing modern linguistics with the satisfactory theoretical basis he thought it lacked. These are issues which have been and still are controversial. There is no doubt, however, that it was Saussure who was responsible not merely for sparking the controversy, but also for giving that controversy the particular intellectual shape which it has taken ever since. Whether or not it is the right shape is another matter. But anyone who wishes to understand modern linguistics needs to be able to recognise that shape. In just the same way, although we may not agree with the terms in which the controversy between anomalists and analogists was formulated in Classical antiquity, we need to be able to recognise the shape that controversy took in order to appreciate both the achievements and the limitations of the linguistic theorising of that age. (pp. ix-xii)

Roy Harris, in an introduction to Course in

General Linguistics *by Ferdinand de Saus-sure, Charles Bally, Albert Sechehaye, Albert Riedlinger, eds., translated by Roy Harris, Duckworth, 1983, pp. ix-xvi.*

E. F. Konrad Koerner   (essay date 1983)

[*Koerner is the author of several critical studies on Saus-sure. In the following excerpt taken from an essay pres-ented at the 6th International Conference on Historical Linguistics in 1983, he discusses the critical reception of Saussure's* Mémoire sur le système primitif des voyelles dans les langues indo-européennes.]

Recent translations into Russian (1977) and Italian (1978) of Ferdinand de Saussure's *Mémoire sur le système primi-tif des voyelles dans les langues indoeuropéennes,* which had first appeared in Leipzig in December 1878, may be taken as an indication of the continuing interest in an ap-preciation of Saussure's contribution to comparative-historical Indo-European linguistics. I do not know of any other book in linguistics of the last quarter of the 19th cen-tury that has been translated in recent years, with the ex-ception of Hermann Paul's *Prinzipien der Sprachge-schichte* of 1880 (5th revised edition, 1920), which had translations into Russian and Japanese in 1960 and 1965, respectively. But Paul's book was a contribution to gener-al linguistics rather than historical linguistics as the title of his book may suggest, and as such it was much less quickly outdated as is common in a field in which new dis-coveries and advances make yesterday's findings obsolete tomorrow. The fact that Saussure's *Mémoire* did not share the fate of most other studies of the period calls for special reasons. . . . (p. 323)

There are indications that Saussure's 300-page study on the sound system of Proto-Indo-European made a notable impact on linguistic circles of the time, though perhaps not the impact that the young author might have hoped for. We may recall that when the book was published, Saussure was just 21 years old, and a student of linguistics at the University of Leipzig for barely four semesters; in-deed, when he defended his thesis on the absolute genitive in Sanskrit in February 1880, it is said that one of his ex-aminers assumed that he was a young relative of the well-known author of the *Mémoire*! But apart from Saussure's precocity, there were other factors that hampered the im-mediate success and the acceptance of the ideas he pro-posed in the *Mémoire.* Despite the fact that he was a stu-dent of the *Junggrammatiker,* notably Karl Brugmann (1849-1919), the prime mover of this group of young 'rev-olutionaries' in historical-comparative linguistics at the time, Brugmann did not concur with the main tenets of Saussure's argument, although he was impressed by his breadth of coverage, circumspection, and "nicht gewöhn-liche Combinationsgabe". Indeed, Brugmann felt that Saussure had proposed a purely aprioristic scheme (rein aprioristische Construction), which did not hold water, and he was not convinced that Saussure's proposals would have to lead him to a substantial revision of his own views.

Hermann Osthoff (1847-1909), Brugmann's close collabo-rator during the 1870s and 1880s, expressed himself in a much more hostile manner to Saussure's theories in sever-al articles published in volumes 2 and 4 of *Morphologische Untersuchungen* in 1879 and 1881, qualifying them as a 'total failure', 'radical error', and the like. Gustav Meyer (1850-1900), another member of the group, incorporated part of Saussure's findings in his *Griechische Grammatik* of 1880, without ever mentioning the source of the series of the Indo-European ablaut he was basing his work on. In short, it can be said that, at least in its initial phase, Saussure's *Mémoire* did not find the reception within the immediate circle of the Leipzig linguists one might per-haps have expected. However, other reviewers of the book who were either opposed to the Young Turks at Leipzig or abroad and thus far removed from the scientific quar-rels among German scholars, seem to have agreed on at least one trait of Saussure's *Mémoire,* namely, that it was theoretically very demanding, that the author had a pen-chant for algebraic formulae, and that the argument was difficult to follow because of a predilection for abstraction. Thus August Fick (1833-1916), the head of the Göttingen linguistic circle which included, inter alios, Hermann Col-litz (1855-1935), reviewing Saussure's book at consider-able length, noted Saussure's fondness of 'mathematische Formulierungen', but concluded, after having criticized a number of points of detail in Saussure's argument:

> Die etwas künstliche Anordnung des Stoffs und eine eigentümliche Vorliebe des Verf[assers] für mathematische Formulierungen erschweren das Studium des sonst klar geschriebenen Werkes, wer aber die Mühe nicht scheut, wird sich durch mannigfache Belehrung und Anregung reichlich entschädigt finden.

The Celtologist, (Sir) John Rhys (1840-1915), writing for a more general audience in a British monthly, likewise noted, in his very positive review:

> The work is so technical and the reasoning so complicated that it is very difficult to give any idea of it excepting to those who have had a thor-ough training in Aryan glottology [i.e., Indo-European linguistics]; but it may at once be said that it is the most important and epoch-making work that has appeared since [Johannes] Schmidt's [(1843-1901)] [*Zur Geschichte des in-dogermanischen*] *Vocalismus* was published.

We may also cite a similar opinion by the French Latinist and comparative linguist Louis Havet (1849-1925), who in fact wrote the most extensive review of Saussure's *Mémoire,* but had similar misgivings, arguing that it had "un defaut grave: il est extraordinairement dur à lire". Havet found that Saussure was abusing abstract designa-tions and was engaging in an excessive use of (at times newly coined) technical terms, concluding his complaints by stating that "Ainsi, M. de Saussure fait suer sang et eau à ceux qui le lisent". However, apart from these criticisms, Havet's review of Saussure's book was very favourable in-deed, leading to a life-long friendship and correspondence between the two scholars.

There is still at least another review of the *Mémoire* that deserves being mentioned, namely, the one by the young Polish linguist Mikołaj Kruszewski (1851-87), which ap-peared in Russian in 1880. It also included an account of

Brugmann's "Nasalis sonans" article of 1876, but it is obvious that Saussure's *Mémoire* was far more attractive to the theoretically inclined Kruszewski, who regarded Saussure's book as an important contribution to the method of phonology, and in fact as marking a new phase in the study of Indo-European phonology. (I may also mention in parenthesis that the *Mémoire* inspired Kruszewski's work in various ways; apart from leading him to study questions of ablaut in Indo-European, especially in Slavic, Kruszewski—and his mentor and collaborator Baudouin de Courtenay—took from the *Mémoire* a number of concepts and terms, such as 'phoneme', 'alternation', and 'zero'. Indeed, Kruszewski translated 'phoneme' into Russian as 'fonema' and proposed to use it as a phonological term in contradistinction to 'zvuk' "sound", a distinction which made history in linguistics.)

In sum, we may say that outside the narrow circle of the Leipzigers Saussure's work was well received when it was first published. It is true that in France Saussure's proposal found a untiring critic in Paul Regnaud (1838-1910), a professor of Classics and comparative grammar at the University of Lyon, but it seems that Regnaud's attacks on Saussure's system of the proto-Indo-European vowels were ignored by most of his contemporaries, probably for the simple reason that the younger generation of Indo-Europeanists had long since rejected the basic assumptions of August Schleicher (1821-1868) in matters of PIE phonology, to which Regnaud still subscribed.

Ignoring for the moment the peculiar reception Saussure's theories received from scholars such as Hermann Möller (1850-1923) and Albert Cuny (1869-1947) . . . we may note that members of the next generation of Indo-Europeanists, notably Saussure's former student at the Ecole Pratique des Hautes Etudes in Paris, Antoine Meillet (1866-1936), and two German scholars, Wilhelm Streitberg (1864-1925) and Herman Hirt (1865-1936), had a particularly high opinion of the *Mémoire.* Hirt can be said to have been the first scholar to fully incorporate Saussure's findings in his monograph of 1900, *Der indogermanische Ablaut;* already in 1885, the brilliant comparative linguist Heinrich Hübschmann (1848-1908), one of Saussure's former teachers at Leipzig, was close to accepting Saussure's theory part and parcel had it not been for an error on Saussure's part in taking Lat. *agō* and the like as an aorist present of **Ag̍-*. Hirt, for his part, regarded Saussure's *Mémoire* as "ein bahnbrechendes Werk, noch heute von grösster Bedeutung", some two generations after its publication, thus echoing Streitberg's opinion expressed in his obituary of Saussure of 1914:

> Das Buch ist de Saussures Meisterwerk: noch heute, nach einem Menschenalter, wirken Inhalt und Form mit derselben bezwingenden Macht wie am Tage des Erscheinens—von wieviel sprachwissenschaftlichen Werken, auch solchen höchsten Ranges, kann man das Gleiche sagen?

Last but not least, reference should be made to Meillet, in particular to his influential *Introduction à l'étude comparative des langues indo-européennes,* which first appeared in 1903, and which bears the inscription "A mon maître Ferdinand de Saussure à l'occasion des vingt-cinq ans écoulés depuis la publication du *Mémoire* . . . (1878-1903)", and inscription that was retained in the many subsequent editions of the text. As a matter of fact, this book remained for Meillet Saussure's major achievement, and not the posthumus *Cours de linguistique générale,* with the result that even after the latter's appearance, Meillet associated the well-known phrase (wrongly ascribed to Saussure, though undoubtedly in his spirit) that language is a system 'où tout se tient' with the *Mémoire.*

In 1887, Saussure's *Mémoire* was republished in Paris; at this time, Saussure contemplated accompanying the new edition with an attack on his detractors. One may speculate who or what circumstances persuaded Saussure to suppress his ill feelings toward those who did neither understand nor appreciate his accomplishments. It could have been the recognition he received from scholars outside the narrow circle of the *Junggrammatiker,* notably Havet, Fick, and Hübschmann, all between 9 and 24 years his seniors, and perhaps by the opinion expressed by the doyen of Indo-European linguistics at Leipzig, Georg Curtius (1820-85), in a personal letter of 1884: "Lange habe ich nichts der Art gelesen, was mich so entschieden überzeugt hat."

The phase following Saussure's death in 1913 may well be regarded as the most important period in the development of the discussion of the PIE phonological system, a phase which has not yet come to a close. Saussure's *Mémoire* may be said to have played an important role in this discussion, which in fact began as early as in 1879, though more as a fairly weak undercurrent as we may see later on. There were a number of reasons for the slow posthumous recognition of Saussure's work in Indo-European linguistics. For example the *Cours* of 1916, owing to its seeming anti-historical bias, tended to detract from the fact that Saussure's life-time contribution lay almost exclusively within diachronic linguistics. Also the hostile feelings toward anything German of the period during and following the First World War made the work of a French Swiss scholar rather attractive as it appeared to oppose the traditional kind of linguistics widely associated with Germany. As a result, among many of the new generation of linguists Historical Linguistics became a side-issue and the preoccupation of a comparatively small number of experts. This development is clearly reflected in most histories of linguistics. If they mention Saussure's *Mémoire* at all, they present it as something of marginal interest, focussing instead almost their entire attention on the work that in fact did not have his imprimatur and, as we have come to understand in recent years, does not reflect his true intentions. In short, it has become customary to refer to a Saussure who wrote the *Mémoire* in his youth, and another who is the author of the *Cours,* which brought about a revolution in modern linguistics, with the result that even the large portions devoted to diachronic linguistics it contains are patently passed over in silence.

It would exceed the frame of the present paper to show, as Cristina Vallini (1969) has already done to some extent, that in fact there is no justification for the traditional conception of the existence of 'deux Saussure', but that the early work is consistent with his later, largely unpublished theories. Perhaps it should be stated in the present context that the critical edition of the *Cours,* carefully compiled by Rudolf Engler, contradicts affirmations in the text as edited by Bally and Sechehaye, including those frequently attacked ones according to which synchrony and diachrony are supposed to be regarded as two subjects apart: Nothing could have been more contrary to Saussure's view on the proper relationship between these two 'points de vue'.

We know from the *Cours* the central role that the concept of 'system' has played in Saussure's linguistic theory. But if we analyse his *Mémoire* carefully, we will notice that the same notion is basic to Saussure's argument therein as well. Indeed, we may say that in the *Mémoire* 'system' is the 'clé de voûte', the key stone holding the entire edifice together. Interestingly enough, while others referred to Saussure's book as the *Mémoire* for short, he himself preferred to refer to it as his *Système des voyelles,* with a capital 'S'. Moreover, Saussure justified the title of his book in the following terms, at the same time indicating his approach to the subject matter:

> Etudier les formes multiples sous lesquelles se manifeste ce qu'on appelle l'a indo-européen, tel est l'objet immédiat de cet opuscule: le reste des voyelles ne sera pris en considération qu'autant que les phénomènes relatifs à l'*a* en fourniront l'occasion. Mais si, arrivé au bout du champ ainsi circonscrit, le tableau du vocalisme indo-européen s'est modifié peu à peu sous nos yeux et que nous le voyions se grouper tout entier autour de l'*a,* prendre vis-à-vis de lui une attitude nouvelle, il est clair qu'en fait c'est le *système des voyelles dans son ensemble* qui sera entré dans le rayon de notre observation et dont le nom doit être inscrit à la première page. (emphasis added)
>
> (pp. 323-28)

[In the *Mémoire*] Saussure presented his theory of the PIE vowel system in a highly organized fashion, proceding with a step-by-step interpretation of the material together with his reasoning about the data. Most importantly, he put forward a theory arrived at not merely in a wholly deductive fashion deriving from the premise that the vowel system of any language must be a complete system of relationships, but at the same time by adducing inductively, as much as was possible at the time, anything that could lead to substantiating the veracity of his general assumption. That he produced a hypothesis of consequence was therefore not simply the strike of genius—which is nevertheless true of course, but the result of a considerable familiarity with the available data, the tools of the craft, and a particularly lucid mind. This last-mentioned criterion may be the key to Saussure's success, distinguishing himself from the great majority of his contemporaries and, we may add, followers. Saussure was very conscious about this, and critical especially of the linguists of his day who evidently lacked the capacity which he regarded as vital to the advancement of the field. In an unpublished draft of a letter probably dating from the 1890s, when he was planning on writing a book on the principles of linguistic science, Saussure stated:

> Je veux malgré cela résumer quel est pour moi

l'exact état des preuves, car ce que je déteste chez tous les Germains comme [aussi Holger] Pedersen, c'est la manière subreptice d'amener la preuve, et de ne jamais la formuler, comme si la preuve de leurs réflexions les dispensait de mettre à nu leur opération logique.

What we may learn from Saussure's example for Historical Linguistics as well as for the study of language in general is the following:

> (a) The analyst must lay bare, to himself and others, the entire *procedere* of his argument; his approach must be clearly presented and well reasoned.
>
> (b) Historical-comparative linguistics is not a field of mere data gathering and ordering, a barren positivistic enterprise as has been common at least since the 1870s, but a subject which can only advance significantly if it admits the setting-up of hypotheses which must be substantiated by subsequent research.
>
> (c) Language in general is an ordered whole; as a result, the tools of analysis must be used on the assumption of the basic systematicity of the data.

These and other ideas have become familiar to us through the *Cours de linguistique générale,* although the manner in which it was compiled has left the impression on three generations of linguists that Saussure was holding Historical Linguistics in low esteem. However, a close reading of Saussure's *Mémoire sur le système primitif des voyelles* makes these points very clear, indeed offering us in hindsight a proof for the desirability of a sound combination of theory and empirical evidence, of deduction and induction, in historical linguistic research. (pp. 340-41)

> *E. F. Konrad Koerner, "The Place of Saussure's 'Mémoire' in the Development of Historical Linguistics," in* Papers from the 6th International Conference on Historical Linguistics, *edited by Jacek Fisiak, John Benjamins Publishing Company and Adam Mickiewicz University Press, 1985, pp. 323-45.*

John Holloway   (essay date 1983)

[*In the following excerpt, Holloway examines the relationships between meaning, value, and self-definition in Saussurean linguistics.*]

Saussure's thinking (as reproduced for us, one must remember, merely from the notes of some who were in his lecture audiences) was indeed intricate and specialist, as well as highly original in certain respects. But the record we have of it is in a terse, dry style, a style that indeed seems to seek the kind of exactitude and lucidity possible for such thinking, and for which the introduction of technical terms is of course perfectly acceptable. All the more interest attaches therefore to one crucial area of Saussure's thought, the area which has meant so much to those who see him as having veritably transformed the totality of human self-understanding.

This crucial area concerns Saussure's account of how

words have meaning. I shall discuss it in some detail, but perhaps it will be helpful if as a preliminary to that, I try to show why it is worth while to do so. Let me state first of all, and in Saussure's own words, the conclusion he comes to. 'A word' (or linguistic sign), he begins, 'unites . . . a concept and a sound-image'. The key question for him then becomes, how does the meaning of the concept get determined?' In brief, his final answer is expressed in his words, 'it is quite clear that initially the concept is nothing, that is only a value determined by its relation to other similar values, and that without them the signification would not exist'. That, at least, is the English translation, which is all that our popularizers refer to. The French in the original edition reads, 'il est bien entendu que ce concept n'a *rien d'initial . . .* '; and in another version, 'le schéma idee: image auditive *n'est donc pas initial* dans la langue' (italics mine).

One could barely assert that those words in the English edition, as they stand by themselves, are perfectly self-explanatory. But before discussing them more closely, it is to the point to see how much has been made to hang upon them, and upon the general Saussurian position which they express. In brief, Saussure's remarks there have led to a strong tradition in language-theory that—to put the matter loosely—thought consists in using language, and language is a self-defining system. The words in a language, that is, derive their meaning from each other, not through any relation to objects in the world. Thus Roland Barthes, in 1964 [in his *Elements of Semiology*]: 'this "something" which is meant by the person who uses the sign . . . being neither an act of consciousness nor a real thing . . . can be defined only within the signifying process, in a quasi-tautological way'. Fredric Jameson, eight years later [in his *The Prison House of Language*], was more emphatic: 'the traditional concept of truth itself becomes outmoded, because the process of thought bears rather on the adjustment of the signi*fied* to the signi*fier*'—not, notice, the other way round. Barthes, Jameson adds, has replaced truth by 'internal coherence'. Terence Hawkes writes [in *Structuralism and Semiotics*]: 'We thus invent the world we inhabit'; though he seems immediately to retract that in part, by adding 'we *modify and reconstruct* what is *given*' (italics mine). 'Language gives not given entities, but socially constructed signifieds', writes Catherine Belsey [in *Critical Practice*]; later she adds, 'if the world is constructed by language, then to say that language reflects reality is a tautology'. I take that to mean that what it reflects is the 'invented' world that it constitutes. Given the likeness between these views, and the 'coherence theory of truth' in writers like Bradley and Bosanquet, it is remarkable that for Belsey the term 'idealist' (in the expression 'empiricist-idealist', in fact) is a term of condemnation.

The second stage in what has been drawn from Saussure's position extends into certain central matters in the study of literature; and Roland Barthes, in 1970, enunciated something like the principle upon which this extension rests. 'The structure of the sentence, the object of linguistics, is found again, homologically, in the structure of works' [in 'To Write: Intransitive Verb' in R. Macksey's and Eugene Donato's *The Structuralist Controversy*]. We

may compare Tzvetan Todorov, [also included in *The Structuralist Controversy*]: 'The concept we have of language today . . . if this perspective is followed, it is obvious that all knowledge of literature will follow a path parallel to that of the knowledge of language: moreover these two paths will tend to merge'. Structuralist criticism, wrote Jameson, is 'a kind of transformation of form into content . . . literary works are about language'; and he quotes from an article of 1967 in which Todorov said that every work tells the story of its own creation: 'the meaning of a work lies in its speaking of its own existence'.

It is not difficult to see how all these observations hang together. No one thinks that the structure of a *sentence* is a matter of its content. We refer to its structure by the categories of traditional grammar, the 'tree' diagrams of linguistics, or whatever it may be. Also by tradition, however, the structure of the literary work is seen in other terms; and those terms do make reference to content, at least in large part. If the analogy between work and sentence (see particularly the quotations from Barthes and Todorov above: again, assertions not proofs, be it noted) holds good, that would be a fundamental error. The structure of literary works would be constituted entirely by their language-features, without reference to what, conventionally, they are taken to be 'about'. Perhaps some of those concerned would wish to go further, indeed, and deny that it was a matter of analogy at all. Perhaps they would claim that it was a matter of literal truth: a novel could be studied profitably simply because, and in so far as, it was an extended sentence (in some sense) with the grammar of a sentence. (pp. 63-5)

But I do not now have in mind to embark upon a critical examination of this ambitious and far-reaching body of work. I have hitherto simply been expounding its conclusions briefly, because the point of interest here is to see how this vast edifice of thought has been erected, by the writers from whom I have quoted (and also by others) upon that central and decisive line of discussion in Saussure. It is Saussure's own argument at which I propose to look closely, and I select him because his work is the key to all the rest. I shall not attempt to prove, and there is no need to prove, that any of Saussure's conclusions were false; but if he did not succeed in establishing them beyond question, two things follow: first that the views of those who have simply based their work on his are (whether false or true) unproved; and second, that if they relied confidently and unquestioningly on Saussure when his argument was in fact an inconclusive one, that speaks ill of their capacity to argue at all.

I should like to begin by saying that Saussure's work also deserves such close examination because it is worthy of, and from myself it certainly enjoys, deep respect. Saussure tries to argue and elucidate his position as fully as the difficulty of its subject-matter will allow. If it transpires that he did not quite clinch his case, that is not the same as saying that his conclusions are false. But it reflects adversely upon his followers in the two ways I have just mentioned. First, their own vastly more sweeping conclusions (for Saussure had nothing to say in the **Cours** about literary works, realism, capitalism, ideology and so forth) remain dubious. Secondly, since in most cases Saussure's followers have simply accepted his conclusions and been content to paraphrase them and to insist on them as preliminary to their own wider opinions, but have done nothing to seek out the weak points in Saussure's work and to remedy them, it does not speak well of their own powers of logic or scruples about carrying readers along with them unjustifiably. One conspicuous exception to that should however be noted: Culler's short introduction to the 1974 English edition of the *Cours,* in which certain very fundamental difficulties in Saussure are touched on briefly but effectively.

I suggested earlier that the crucial area in Saussure's thought was his account of how words have meaning. There is no need to emphasize that that has been found an area of difficulty, perhaps supreme difficulty, since Plato. Saussure does not consider the Nominalist tradition of thought about this problem, save very briefly and generally in a discussion which alternates the words 'thing' and 'idea' ('choses', 'idées toutes faites') with a somewhat disquieting ease. But that matter aside, Saussure goes on to say, as I mentioned, that the right way to think about a linguistic sign is to see it as uniting a sound-image (the word, that is, in spoken language) and a concept. Saussure is perhaps not perfectly explicit and consistent at this point, but on the whole his position is clear enough: the sign 'carries the concept', 'I mean by sign the whole ['le total'] that results from the association of the signifier with the signified'. He goes on to say that linguistic signs are arbitrary in that an 'idea' is not 'linked by any inner relationship ['rapport intérieur'] to the succession of sounds . . . which serves as its signifier' in any particular language; and that 'no one disputes the principle of the arbitrary nature of the sign'.

The term 'inner relationship' is perhaps not clear to us today, and it may be that in using it, Saussure was consciously or unconsciously recalling the use of the term 'internal relation' in certain Idealist philosophers of the late nineteenth century. Be that as it may, Saussure is surely right if what he means is that no word for a certain something in English, or French let us say, will be intrinsically better than the word for it any other language; and right also to say that no one would dispute that opinion. By way of elucidation he adds, 'the signifier . . . is arbitrary in that it actually has no natural connection with the signified'. It is fair to add that in the vast majority of cases—words like 'hiccough' might be different—it is not easy even to see what a 'natural connection' would be; and self-evident that there is no actual need to have a 'natural connection' in any particular case, 'hiccough' or anything else.

As part of his explanation of the difference between diachronic and synchronic language studies, Saussure likens 'a state of language' at a given point in its history to a 'state of a set of chessmen' at a given point in a game of chess. In some respects this is a helpful comparison, but in one respect it is not self-evidently so. This is the way in which the comparison seems to introduce the term 'values' ['valeurs'] as something to some extent analagous to 'meanings' in the field of language. These new terms play key roles in Saussure's argument as a whole, yet I cannot avoid the conclusion that Saussure uses the term 'value' ambiguously in regard to the game of chess. 'The respective value of the pieces depends on their position on the chessboard', he says, referring to the state of a game at a given point in it: and this is what is compared to the state of a language as studied, at a given point in time, by synchronic study. Yet almost immediately he adds: 'values depend above all else ['surtout'] on an unchangeable convention ['une convention immuable'] the set of rules that exists before a game begins and persists after each move'. But in this sense, the value of this or that chesspiece, so far as I can see, in no way 'depends on [its] position on the chessboard'; nor is there any analogy between values depending on rules that 'exist before a game begins', and linguistic values (however that expression is to be explained) which can and do change steadily over the history of a language, and cannot possibly be formulated before that history begins, because they do not exist. Saussure said that a given state of the chess-game 'corresponds closely' ['corréspond bien'] to a given state of the language at a certain point in history; but in the course of his remarks he has in effect gone beyond the limits of that 'close correspondence'.

Perhaps it was a pity that Saussure ever introduced the comparison with chess: it provided him with a title for Part II, Chapter IV of the *Cours,* 'Linguistic Value'; and this is both a key chapter, and in some ways an especially disquieting one. Here, Saussure begins by asserting that 'psychologically our thought—apart from its expression in words—is only a shapeless and indistinct mass' ['une masse amorphe et indistincte']. I hesitate to comment upon this, because I am unsure of what wordless mental activities would generally be allowed as 'thought'. Does someone steering a bicycle, or an observer at sea, watching two distant ships, and estimating their relative speeds and courses—or indeed, mentally rehearsing such an activity—engage in thought which is 'only a shapeless and indistinct mass?' I am much disposed to doubt that. What about cases such as those where we realize that we have expressed ourselves ambiguously and rephrase our remarks, or recognize that an argument, as we follow it in reading a book, contains an as yet unidentified logical fallacy? My own experience is that such reactions or intuitions do not take the form of verbal thinking. They are preliminary, of course, to fresh verbal thinking; but the 'something has gone wrong' intuition (though not, I believe, in those words, nor any others) precedes that. On the other hand, it is barely satisfactory to say that the first stage in identifying an inadequacy in verbal thought, and so correcting it, is not thought at all; as also, to say that the first step towards making verbal thought more exact is itself wholly without exactitude, because, in Saussure's words, part of 'a shapeless and amorphous mass'. If on the other hand I am told that these and all other such activities are 'really' performed in words, then I have to admit that I have no knowledge of wordless thought; but then, I can neither agree nor disagree with Saussure's assertion about it.

Saussure goes on, at this point, to raise a most important question. Let us concede that it is language which, in many cases, or no doubt easily most, makes it possible for us to think in a 'distinct' way. How do the units of language acquire their distinctness? Earlier, he has rightly pointed out that words as units of significance are made up of individual sounds—let us briefly say, vowels, consonants—and that these individual sounds are not vehicles of meaning by virtue of their absolute and exact quality, as some phonetician might record them for some given speaker at a given time. They are adequate vehicles of meaning, in that speakers consistently maintain certain recognizable differences within the whole system of sounds that they employ in speech. If one lisps all one's Rs, from this point of view it hardly matters. If one lisps some of them, however, and trills the others, hearers may think that the lisped Rs were intended for Ws and confusion will result. The sounds one makes in speech, then, have their meaning-values (that is, the ways in which they can contribute to the meanings of the words they enter) from the whole system of sounds that meaning depends on, in a given language, not from their intrinsic phonetic quality. Just as Saussure said, 'no one disputes the principle of the arbitrary nature of the sign'—though from how his disciples labour the point, you might think they had forgotten that—so he could have said, 'no one disputes' his assertion that individual sounds gain their meaning-values in language from the system of differences in which they occur.

There then comes a crucial step in Saussure's discussion. In examining the relation between signs as wholes (not simply the individual sounds which are joined together to make signs) and their own distinctive kind of meaning, Saussure extends the principle that he enunciated for individual sounds. In doing so, he may seem to contradict what he had said earlier:

> . . . to consider a term as simply the union of a certain sound with a certain concept is grossly misleading ['une grande illusion'] . . . it would mean assuming that one can start from the terms and construct the system by adding them together when, on the contrary, it is from the interdependent whole that one must start and through analysis obtain its elements.

Saussure seems inclined to say that 'significance' is the counterpart of a sound-image, while 'value' is what a term has 'solely from the simultaneous presence of the other [terms]'. That is an interesting distinction, and he illustrates it with, for example, the English words 'sheep' and 'mutton'. 'Sheep' can have the same significance as the French word 'mouton' ['Le français *mouton* peut avoir la même signification que l'anglais *sheep* . . .']; and so, I suppose, what you may have on your plate for dinner is indeed, in a certain sense, 'sheep stew'. It is impossible to say that the meat in it is not sheep, with the implication that it is some other animal. But the word 'sheep', in English, does not have the same *value* as 'mouton' in French. We cannot, in our language, combine it like that with 'stew'. Saussure adds that the same thing is true about 'grammatical entities', like for example tenses.

I cannot but ask myself whether Saussure's discussion, at this point, is altogether self-consistent. To begin with, he distinguishes very clearly between the 'signification' of a word and the 'value' that attaches to that word: 'this is something quite different' ['c'est tout autre chose']. Then he draws attention to several quite distinct features of language, apparently in amplification of that distinction. First he observes that in a given language, groups of words with related meanings 'limit each other reciprocally'. An example in English, possibly, would be 'beautiful, handsome, pretty, attractive'. Learning fully how to use each of those four words is in part anyhow a matter of learning when not to use the other three. That is certainly a reasonable suggestion. Saussure also mentions how words in two languages which are loosely called 'synonyms' are often not entirely so. 'Louer une maison' in French will be the equivalent in English of both 'to let a house' and 'to rent a house'. 'There is obviously no exact correspondence of values', he writes; and he claims that this shows how words do not stand for 'pre-existing concepts' ['concepts données d'avance']—a claim which on that evidence, by the way, is valid only on the additional premiss that the relation between word and concept should in all cases be a one-one relation. Third, Saussure draws attention to how 'grammatical entities' are not constant as between languages. 'The value of a French plural does not coincide with that of a Sanskrit plural, even though their signification is usually identical'. What he means there, I believe, is that a French plural usually 'means the same' as the corresponding Sanskrit plural, but that Sanskrit plurals cannot be used to translate French ones in the particular case where the French plural is for two items only; in Sanskrit the dual must then be used. He also offers further examples, about tenses of verbs or about verbal 'aspects' as in Russian. Finally he says 'We find in all the foregoing examples *values* emanating from the system' ['au lieu d'idées données d'avance, des valeurs émanant du système']. The concepts to which these values may be said to correspond are defined 'by their relation with other terms in the system. Their most precise characteristic is in being what the others are not'. It might have been better to say 'relation with other concepts', but that is a detail.

But now comes the most crucial state in Saussure's argument. He produces once again the diagram that he initially made use of to illustrate the signified/signifier or concept/auditory-image basis of the 'sign'; and it is now that he says, 'it is quite clear that initially the concept is nothing ['n'a rien d'initial', remember], that is only a value determined by its relations with other similar values, and that without them the signification would not exist' ['sans elles la signification n'existerait pas'].

At this point, one wonders whether Saussure should not have written 'without them the *value* would not exist', instead of 'the signification'. That, after all, is what he has proved; and he has already told us that 'value' and 'signification' are quite different. If so, how can he simply replace the word 'value' by the word 'signification' in that passage, as if the two were not 'quite different' but just the same?

We may concede that there are certain cases where the 'value' of a term, in Saussure's sense, is determined, even exclusively so, by its relations with other terms in a group of terms. 'Certain cases': Saussure actually specified these cases, speaking of 'all words used to express related ideas', of 'words enriched through contact with others', and thirdly, of words which do not have exact equivalents in meaning 'from one language to another'. It is no good, of course, to claim at this stage that *all* words in every language belong to these classes. If that were so, the whole enterprise of opening a further stage in the discussion, distinguishing the three classes, and offering examples of each, would have been otiose and indeed profoundly misleading. One must therefore ask whether Saussure shifted, in his conclusion as above, from 'some' to 'all'; and whether he was perhaps led into doing so, by his momentary identification of 'signification' and 'value'. I admit freely that I do not know quite for sure whether this stage in Saussure's argument is definitely defective, or whether it could be salvaged. I know of no follower of Saussure who has tried to resolve the difficulty. If one turns, for example, to Section II.5 of Roland Barthes' *Elements of Semiology,* all one finds is a statement that value and signification are not the same, and that Saussure 'increasingly concentrated' on value. That is to rehearse what may be a weak link in the train of thought in a style that identifies weakness with strength.

In this connection, there seems to be a fundamental problem which Saussure fails to discuss. Suppose we concede that the 'value' of, say, the term 'mutton' is that it is the proper term to use when 'sheep' would not be so, but 'mouton' would. Is it possible to go further, to the extent of saying that *all* terms are of this kind, and may be 'defined negatively by their relations with the other terms in the system'? Can that process of 'negative definition' be maintained indefinitely, round and round as it were, so as to cover, in the end, the language as a whole? It is easy to see how certain terms may be defined, even must be so, in this manner. The term 'miscellaneous' in budgets of income and expenditure is an obvious example. In the Cambridge University Library there is a small group of relatively unimportant nineteenth-century books with the class-mark 'LO': so far as I recollect, I once found a cataloguer's note in one of them, which indicated that 'LO' in fact stood for 'left over'. But could *all* the items in a budget, or a catalogue, or any other such system, be so defined? If 'mutton' is defined negatively, merely through its relation to 'sheep' and to 'mouton' (let us say), can we then go on to define 'sheep' negatively in relation to 'mutton'? If so, how would we distinguish that pair of words from 'pig/pork' or 'cattle/beef'? Or should we say that 'sheep' means something like 'not pig, not cattle . . . ' and so on indefinitely, which is exactly how we define a word like 'miscellaneous'? Such questions call for answers from those who insist on this kind of account; and in the absence of such answers, I remain inclined to wonder (this is putting it mildly) whether there is not some absolutely basic distinction between the system of language-*sounds,* and the system of language-*words* or terms. I am too much numbed by my reading of Saussure's followers, and their self-emancipation from the 'tyranny of lucidity' to say quite what that distinction is; and it does not fall to someone in my position to say what it is, because it falls to them to prove that it does not exist. In this context, moreover, I begin to imagine how, given leisure, one might as a kind of enormously elaborated 'consequences' game build up something like an imaginary language (not, though, for communication in the ordinary sense) where all the terms one invented had 'values' deter-

---

An excerpt from *Course in General Linguistics*

The subject matter of linguistics comprises all manifestations of human speech, whether that of savages or civilized nations, or of archaic, classical or decadent periods. In each period the linguist must consider not only correct speech and flowery language, but all other forms of expression as well. And that is not all: since he is often unable to observe speech directly, he must consider written texts, for only through them can he reach idioms that are remote in time or space.

The scope of linguistics should be:

a) to describe and trace the history of all observable languages, which amounts to tracing the history of families of languages and reconstructing as far as possible the mother language of each family;

b) to determine the forces that are permanently and universally at work in all languages, and to deduce the general laws to which all specific historical phenomena can be reduced; and

c) to delimit and define itself.

Linguistics is very closely related to other sciences that sometimes borrow from its data, sometimes supply it with data. The lines of demarcation do not always show up clearly. For instance, linguistics must be carefully distinguished from ethnography and prehistory, where language is used merely to document. It must also be set apart from anthropology, which studies man solely from the viewpoint of his species, for language is a social fact. But must linguistics then be combined with sociology? What are the relationships between linguistics and social psychology? Everything in language is basically psychological, including its material and mechanical manifestations, such as sound changes; and since linguistics provides social psychology with such valuable data, is it not part and parcel of this discipline? . . .

Finally, of what use is linguistics? Very few people have clear ideas on this point, and this is not the place to specify them. But it is evident, for instance, that linguistic questions interest all who work with texts—historians, philologists, etc. Still more obvious is the importance of linguistics to general culture: in the lives of individuals and societies, speech is more important than anything else. That linguistics should continue to be the prerogative of a few specialists would be unthinkable—everyone is concerned with it in one way or another. But—and this is a paradoxical consequence of the interest that is fixed on linguistics—there is no other field in which so many absurd notions, prejudices, mirages, and fictions have sprung up. From the psychological viewpoint these errors are of interest, but the task of the linguist is, above all else, to condemn them and to dispel them as best he can.

Ferdinand de Saussure, in his Course in General Linguistics, *translated by Wade Baskin, McGraw-Hill, 1959.*

mined negatively, in reference to their fellow-terms. In such a language, it could be as much against the rules to say things like 'mutton is cooked pig', or 'sheep moo' as it is in English to say things like 'mutton is cooked neither' or 'sheep whenever'. The question remains, though, whether such an invented system would not be something fundamentally different in kind from English or French, and so on. One reason for that is that given more leisure and nothing much to do with it, one could invent not one but fifty such 'languages', using the same 'dictionary' of terms in each case; and the 'values' of the terms could be totally different in each case, because there would be total liberty in setting up the rules of the system every time. But there is something, something which does not enter into activities of that kind, which prevents us from playing, as we might put it, variations in our own language in this way; and that something is not merely the social group that speaks it. Something else prevents us from saying 'cows moo' and also 'sheep moo', something which brings it about that, while of course language in the abstract is collectively manipulable to any extent, this is like saying that if we want we can turn our real language into a game-language. Language is not so manipulable, if what it enables us to do is to be preserved. (pp. 68-76)

> *John Holloway, "Language, Realism, Subjectivity, Objectivity," in* Reconstructing Literature, *edited by Laurence Lerner, Barnes & Noble Books, 1983, pp. 60-80.*

Robert Godel   (essay date 1984)

[*Godel is the author of* Les sources manuscrites du "Cours de linguistique générale" de Ferdinand de Saussure *(1957), a full-length study of the notebooks from which the* Course in General Linguistics *was compiled. In the following essay, he analyzes Saussure's theories of language and communication.*]

In 1875 a book came out in New York as the sixteenth volume of a scientific series. It was entitled *The life and growth of language: an outline of linguistic science.* The author, W. D. Whitney, Professor of Sanskrit and Comparative Grammar at Yale College, was an outstanding philologist, with a mind open to every kind of linguistic question. Although chiefly absorbed in Vedic studies, he devoted a great part of his labor to modern languages—English, German, French—for which he prepared grammars and reading books. *The life and growth of language,* which he translated into French himself, was the second exposition of his views about language. He was induced to write these books by a sense of disgust at the inconsistency of the prevalent doctrine which was then preached in England with unquestioned authority by the German scholar, Max Müller. Later on, Whitney expressed his feeling more openly in a booklet, *Max Müller and the science of language* (New York, 1892), which is still worth reading as an example of acute criticism and good American humor.

Among the European readers of Whitney's book, there was a young man from Geneva, F. de Saussure. We do not know when he happened to read it. As a student, he had gone to Leipzig, which was at that time the most lively center of comparative philology in Europe. In the short

memoirs he later jotted down about his student years, de Saussure speaks of his teachers, Brugmann and Hübschmann, with kindly reverence. He seems to have liked their personalities, but their approach to language certainly disappointed him. His personal theory of language originated as a criticism of the conceptions that prevailed among the German philologists in the 1870s (the *Junggrammatiker*) and of their terminology. Yet I do not believe that in those busy years he had much leisure to reflect on the fundamentals of language: he wrote, first, at the age of twenty-one, his ***Mémoire sur le système primitif des voyelles dans les langues indo-européennes,*** published in 1878; and, two years later, his doctoral thesis, ***De l'emploi du génitif absolu en Sanscrit.*** These are the only books he ever published. Subsequently, and for many years, while teaching courses in comparative philology in Paris and later in Geneva, he was engrossed by the problem of the nature of speech and searched for a correct approach. Whitney's ideas undoubtedly stimulated de Saussure. He never ceased to feel indebted to the American scholar and many years later, when he offered courses in general linguistics at the University of Geneva, he did not fail to mention Whitney's name with praise and to discuss his ideas.

I purposely emphasize Whitney's influence on de Saussure, because the latter is commonly considered as the man who opened a new era in European linguistics. And this is true. The most prominent French philologists of the early 20th century—[Antoine] Meillet, Grammont and others—had attended his courses in Paris and been impressed by the rigor and clarity of his lectures. He had, indeed, much of the Cartesian insight; it is no wonder that his teaching should have been particularly attractive to French disciples. He was also acquainted with the works of the Russian philologists, Baudouin de Courtenay and [Mikołaj] Kruszewski. With the former, he had personal intercourse: he had met him in Paris; later, he wrote to him, and two letters of his were discovered last year in the Leningrad Library.

However, American linguists should not regard de Saussure as a stranger. There is, on the one hand, his indebtedness to Whitney; and, on the other, [Leonard] Bloomfield's appraisal of his ideas. Bloomfield's review of the *Cours de linguistique générale,* in spite of a roguish allusion to some weak points in psychology and phonetics, is very positive. Let me quote some lines from its conclusion: "In detail, I should differ from de Saussure chiefly in basing my analysis on the sentence rather than on the word . . . The essential point, however, is this, that de Saussure has here first mapped out the world in which historical Indo-European grammar (the great achievement of the past century) is merely a single province; he has given us the theoretical basis for a science of human speech". Thus there is no reason to contrast 'Saussurean linguistics' with 'American linguistics': they are linked together, inasmuch as de Saussure valued Whitney's view of language as an institution, and Bloomfield, in 1924 at least, valued the *Cours* for 'its clear and rigorous demonstration of fundamental principles'.

Linguists have to be conscious of "what they are doing". These last words are underlined in a letter of Jan. 4, 1894, to Meillet; they recur in a note-book in November of the same year. De Saussure meant that those who speak about language and explain linguistic facts have no adequate idea of the very object they are studying. We saw that he probably felt this defect as early as his student years in Leipzig and Berlin. He was thus induced to face the problem by himself, and it is no wonder that what he achieved is not an elaborated method for analyzing speech, but, rather, as Bloomfield rightly states, a 'demonstration of fundamental principles'.

He first rejected as inconsistent everything he had learned or been taught: conceptions, methods and terminology. Like Descartes, he started from a radical doubt. In human speech, he perceived, there is no given definite object which lends itself to observation and analysis. There is only a most complex phenomenon, involving physical and psychological processes, individual freedom and social constraint, change and stability. Such a phenomenon is not liable to classification or description. The first scientific approach, therefore, is to make distinctions: what is essential in human speech? What is primary? What is real? These questions can be answered, and the distinctions made, only on the basis of valid criteria. Thus, before applying any experimental method, one must formulate a theory of human speech. Reason must act and work out the principles: it would be useless to try to study and explain facts as long as the very nature of the facts is at issue.

De Saussure's approach to language is therefore a philosophical one. This may well surprise present-day linguists, who are used to relying on methodical observation, statistics, or even mathematical devices, to describe, or to account for, linguistic reality. Yet de Saussure was right. Modern linguistics would hardly have developed as it has, had he not previously outlined the universal framework in which each particular fact would assume its proper place. His philosophical attitude toward the fundamental problems, needless to say, does not involve any defect in scientific capacity: it is enough to mention his studies on Phrygian inscriptions and on word stress in Lithuanian. He was able to carry out the most precise study on such minute philological items as a peculiar use of the genitive in Sanskrit, as well as to discover, under apparently unrelated facts, the hidden connections that make them appear as parts of a coherent system. He certainly had as much respect for the bare facts as any scientist and his dearest concern was to cast the theory of language into the rigid mold of a mathematical treatise. But as he found himself confronted with the problem of human speech, he felt he had to appeal, first, to his own powers of abstraction, to separate the various aspects of the phenomenon and reach its deepest level.

So much for his beginnings. Now, besides the philosophical character of his approach, I would also point out that, like every philologist in those days, de Saussure was an Indo-Europeanist. All through his career, he had to teach courses in Sanskrit and comparative grammar. This professional incumbency may well have had a bearing on his doctrine, especially on his analysis which, as Bloomfield points out, is based on the word, rather than on the sentence. In archaic IE languages, there is a clear-cut bound-

ary between morphology and syntax, whereas in modern languages the boundary is often blurred. In the course of the last thirty or forty years, much progress has been made in the analysis of speech with the help of such new methods as phonemics and structural analysis. The common characteristic of these methods lies in their more accurate observation and study of modern languages such as, English and Russian. Let us not forget that de Saussure's teaching belongs to an earlier period: toward the end of 1906, he was entrusted with a yearly course in general linguistics at the University of Geneva. This course was offered only three times, the last one in 1910-1911. De Saussure used to give examples from the classical languages, Latin and Greek; French, German or English occur less frequently. This will escape the notice of readers of the *Cours,* because the editors have here and there substituted modern examples for classical ones.

Since I allude to the editors, I would remind you that de Saussure never published a book or monograph on general linguistics. Thus it would be unfair to appraise the *Cours* as we judge and evaluate Bloomfield's *Language,* Trubetzkoy's *Grundzüge,* Hjelmslev's *Omkrings,* and such works of modern scholars who have taken pains, and had the leisure, to present their own theories in the most accurate and systematic form. The book published in 1916 by his disciples and friends, [Charles] Bally and [Albert] Sechehaye, is a mixture of the various contents of three courses, as they had been preserved in a few students' note-books. It is planned along the general line of the last one (1910-1911), although fragments from de Saussure's earlier sketches have been integrated here and there. Bally and Sechehaye deserve unqualified approval for their accuracy and insight: one can only admire their skill in assembling a variety of material into a clear and consistent exposition. Yet they may have been too careful in 'weeding out' every discrepancy and unevenness, and setting out the absolute coherence of the theory, its—so to speak—monolithic unity. The consequence was that every criticism directed against one particular item apparently entailed the rejection of the whole theory. On the other hand, many linguists hesitated to acknowledge the truth of any part of it, lest they be supposed to subscribe to every article of the 'Saussurean creed'.

The main lines of the theory had been worked out in the early 1890s. In May 1911, de Saussure told one of his former students that he did not believe he had added anything new since then. In his last course, however, there is evidence of a new start. Not that he would have upset his theory and changed the views he had entertained for so many years, but he would have corrected them. The 'principle of arbitrariness had been previously presented without qualification; in 1911, de Saussure explained that it actually applies to linguistic signs which cannot be analyzed into smaller constituents; in compound signs, arbitrariness is balanced by 'motivation'. Death prevented him from developing these new ideas.

Contemporary linguists are familiar with de Saussure's theory. So I need not sum it up once again—although this might be done in a somewhat different way from that which the editors of the *Cours* thought appropriate. I would rather take advantage of this paper to make some new comments, in addition to my previous statements. On writing a book, some years ago, on the manuscript sources of the **Cours,** I chiefly paid attention to the variations in de Saussure's ideas and expressions. I had to do this precisely because Bally and Sechehaye had taken pains to blot out these variations, as simply "characteristic of oral delivery", as they put it in the Preface. I do not want to repeat here what I have written in my book. I would rather make some remarks on the 'fundamental principles' which Bloomfield seemed to approve.

The primary distinctions to be made hold, on the one hand, between 'language' (*la langue*) and 'speaking' (*la parole*); on the other hand, between synchrony and diachrony. The latter seems to have occurred to de Saussure much earlier than the former: in 1894, he alluded to it as to a conviction he had acquired many years ago. He may have felt the contrast between language as a system and linguistic change ever since his student years. He was then engaged in comparative studies. But it is a significant fact that the word 'system' occurs in the title of the first book he published, the **Mémoire** on the IE vowels. What he aimed at, and actually achieved, was the integration of the partial and somewhat confused results of comparative philology into a systematic outline of IE word structure and morphology. This he could not have done without a sense of the contrast between synchronic facts (vowel alternation, root structure, inflection) and diachronic events (sound change, analogical innovations). The necessity of keeping them apart seemed to him unquestionable, and he maintained his distinction to the end; it is still dealt with in his last course, with new arguments, in a most extensive chapter.

As to the former distinction (*langue* vs. *parole*), it is not mentioned in the earliest records. It does not appear as an explicit statement before 1907 (first course). From a theoretical viewpoint, this distinction is the primary one, supporting and justifying the division of linguistics into synchrony and diachrony, as de Saussure seems to have thought afterwards. One may wonder why he did not start by contrasting language with actual speech: the definition of language as a system entails, but does not presuppose, the distinction between the system as it is and the changes by which it is altered. In fact, both distinctions do not pertain to the same object. Language and speaking (*langue* and *parole*) are divisions in linguistic reality, that is, in human speech; synchrony and diachrony are necessary divisions in the science of language. De Saussure was first concerned with the latter because he was searching for a methodical principle. In the above quoted letter to Meillet, he complains about the difficulty of writing on any philological topic for want of a consistent terminology. He very soon discovered that all the errors and inconsistencies in traditional linguistics originate in a confusion of two sets of connections or relationships: those which hold between contemporary forms belonging to the same system (e.g. Eng. *father, fathers, fatherly; mother, son; he,* etc.) and those which hold between forms that succeed each other in time (e.g. IE **pǝtér-* and Eng. *father*). In order to set up this principle and the consequent distinction of synchronic and diachronic linguistics, he must

have had a clear conception of 'language'; he cannot have hesitated as to what language is and what it is not. But he did not need an accurate definition of 'speaking' (*la parole*). He simply discarded phonology, that is, the description and classification of speech sounds as external and irrelevant to the study of language.

His reflections had focused on a genuine philosophical problem, identity, with justification; for identity, as psychologists usually admit, is the proper criterion of reality. Knowing something is being able to acknowledge it as *the same thing,* whenever it occurs. In the universal phenomenon of human speech de Saussure perceived three kinds, or levels, of identity.

In such words as Eng. *book* and Fr. *bouc,* or in homonyms, like Eng. *due, dew,* there is a bare phonic sameness, which is irrelevant for the linguist, since linguistic reality does not lie in sounds alone. If we have to understand actually uttered sounds, this negative statement will not be questioned. But what about phonemes? The identity of /buk/ in *books, booking, bookstore, note-book,* etc., is not irrelevant for English speakers; consequently, the identity of each phoneme, /b/, /u/, /k/, in its turn, cannot be neglected by the linguist as a trivial fact not worth discussing in an accurate description of modern English. De Saussure would have answered that linguistic reality can never be described in terms of bare sounds, even of phonemes; because the formal identity of the segment /buk/ in the above quoted English words would not deserve any more attention than the fortuitous likeness of Eng. *book* and Fr. *bouc* except for the fact that in the former case the phonemic sequence is united with the same idea. In other words, what is identical is not the sequence as such, but the *signifiant* of a certain English word. De Saussure, it is true, never did justice to the phonemic level of language. Since oral speech has been preferred to any other means of communication, and since vowels and consonants are natural productions of our speech organs, we expect to find in any language a finite number of such sounds used as material for coining words; and in describing a language, we might be satisfied with designating each sound by a bare figure, regardless of its articulatory and acoustic features.

The section of the **Cours** which is entitled "Principles of Phonology" has nothing to do with modern phonemics. De Saussure repeatedly asserted that what he termed 'phonology', that is, the study of speech sounds, is nothing more than an auxiliary science; and what he taught about it was meant only as an appendix to a chapter on writing.

Yet the problem of phonemics did not escape him altogether. According to his general view of linguistic reality, he clearly perceived that in a given language the 'minimal units' (we would say the *phonemes,* but he precisely avoided the word in this case) are merely differential: the value of *t* in modern French, for example, consists solely in the acoustical features which prevent it from merging or being confused with *k* or *d* or *n,* etc. This statement is the very basis of phonemics. It occurs, unexpectedly enough, in a chapter of the first course on the reconstruction of IE words. But de Saussure did not draw further conclusions from this principle. He was more concerned with avoiding any confusion of 'language' and speech sounds. Indeed, this is the first sketch of the distinction between *langue* and *parole.*

As to the other cases of identity, they can be easily exemplified. On the one hand, Eng. *father* is identical with IE **pətér-,* in spite of all the changes in form and meaning brought about by time. De Saussure's comment on this case is somewhat enigmatic. He seems to mean that we have a right to say that it is the same word because it is, and has always been, a word, that is, neither a bare sequence of sounds nor an abstract idea, but an entity of a quite peculiar kind. It is the same word, as opposed to IE **mātér-* > Eng. *mother,* and to all the English words inherited from IE.

On the other hand, *father* is of course identical with *father:* whenever it recurs in a talk or a tale, it is similarly understood by the partners or the reader, regardless of the fact that its pronunciation may vary from one utterance to another, and the person referred to as a *father* may be Mr. Jones as well as Mr. Smith or anybody else. The identity of a word does not lie in the actually uttered and perceived sounds, nor in the individual or the object alluded to: it is immaterial, quite different from the identity of any material thing or being.

I would stress here, parenthetically the originality of de Saussure's approach. The question he raised, though a very important one, has never been thoroughly discussed. Only two pages are devoted to it in the middle part of the **Cours,** so that no reader will perceive that he is here confronted with a capital issue on which de Saussure's thoughts concentrated for a long time. Diachronic identity, involving the preservation of a sign through centuries, is a linguistic datum: whatever alterations this sign has undergone it still preserves its peculiar nature; it has never ceased to be a linguistic entity. But linguistic signs are primarily members of a system; and the system cannot function as a means of communication unless each sign preserves its identity throughout the innumerable utterances in which it occurs. Therefore, synchronic identity is the primary issue in the science of language. Indeed, any description of a language involves statements about identity. But how can the identity of a linguistic sign be checked? What criteria are available? The issue cannot be discussed at length within the limits of this paper. Allow me to make it clear through one particular instance. On reading Bloomfield's *Language,* I was struck by the fact that he does not make a distinction between the infinitive and the imperative of English verbs. He seems to regard the latter as a peculiar use of the infinitive—just as he does not separate calls (vocatives) from the other occurrences of a noun. Thus there is one identical sign *go* (as infinitive) in: *Go to your room; You had better go; I want you to go,* etc., and another one in: *I go, you go, the people go,* etc. (*go* as present tense, opposed to *went*). I had reason to wonder, for in French, as in most modern languages, the imperative is not formally identical with the infinitive, and a formal difference points to different functions. Bloomfield's view, however, is in agreement with the English verb system: it is based upon the paradigm of the verb *to be.* This is clear evidence to the fact that functions, like *signifiés,* do not exist outside particular systems or languages; in de Saus-

sure's terms, they simply proceed from the system. Synchronic identity is therefore less obvious or trifling than it may appear at first sight, and the problem actually deserves more attention than has been paid to it so far.

But let us return to de Saussure's views about the identity of linguistic signs. Here we have the logical ground for a distinction between diachronic and synchronic relationship. We also have the core of the Saussurean conception of 'language' (*la langue*) as a system of immaterial signs. Language is not only a social institution, as Whitney rightly stated; it is a *semiological* institution, that is, a code.

I need not dwell on the implications of such a definition. The nature of the linguistic sign, the psychic character of both the *signifié* and the *signifiant,* the principle of arbitrariness, entailing the existence of only differential features, have been too often discussed to call for any new comment.

Yet it is perhaps worthwhile to consider, once more, the definition of the sign, together with the sign diagram. This diagram, as appears from the examples, is meant for such signs as *words.* If derivative and compound words, as it seems, fit into its framework as well as simple ones, it is equally applicable to more extensive segments, such as phrases or sentences; for any significant sequence of syllables can be viewed as one sign, since no extensional limitation is suggested by the definition. Let us now consider a morpheme (or, in de Saussure's terms, a 'sub-unit'), e.g. the plural ending *-s* in modern English. Undoubtedly, it is a sign; and yet, such a diagram as:

$$\frac{\text{plurality}}{\text{/-s/}}$$

would not make sense, because the *signifiant* cannot be described barely as 'final *-s*'. And if we correct the description by saying: "*-s* added to a noun" then we take into account a feature of the *signifié:* for nouns are a class of signs definable only by a common feature of the 'concepts', not of the phonemic forms. Even by using distributional criteria, we cannot abstract from the 'conceptual' side of the sign: distribution pertains to signs, not to bare *signifiants.* The sign diagram, therefore, does not fit morphemes; and consequently, it does not fully illustrate de Saussure's original conception of the sign. Nay, it is somewhat misleading: even the editors of the **Cours** went astray in adding to the genuine diagram a second one with the design of a tree for the *signifié* of Lat. *arbor,* thus suggesting to the readers the very erroneous conception against which de Saussure warned his students, that is, the idea of the *signifié* being the image of an object. But in most cases (e.g. in finite verb forms) it is not any more a 'concept'.

Is then *signifié* merely a new word for what we usually call 'meaning'? Indeed, the sign diagram seems to express the fact that a meaning is attached to a given sequence of phonemes. The consequence would be that every significant sequence that can serve as an utterance must be regarded as a sign, whether it consists of one word, a phrase, or a sentence; for meaning, in speech at least, is readily definable as what is conveyed by an utterance. On the other hand, the sign would be defined as a possible utterance. But not all signs are fit to be used alone in this way; morphemes and auxiliary words are not. And yet no one will deny that they are signs. The meaning of an actual utterance is therefore something very different from the *signifié* of an isolated word, considered as a single item in the lexicon of a language, or of a morpheme. A *signifié* is not merely the meaning of the segment under examination, but the product of various connections, by which words and morphemes of one language are mutually related: a *signifié* is not primarily a concept but a value (*une valeur*). As to meaning in its usual accepted sense, it is inseparable from actual speech. The problem of meaning properly belongs in the study of *la parole,* that is, that part of linguistics which de Saussure never approached in his courses.

This interpretation seems to agree with de Saussure's statement about the linear nature of the *signifiant*. Visual (optic) signs, as he remarks, can be arranged in various ways, so as to effect different shapes or figures. Vocal signs, on the contrary, combine into sequences, following each other as segments of the spoken chain. In emphasizing the linear nature of the *signifiant,* de Saussure had not in mind the successive phonemes: he thought of the significant units or sub-units, that is, of the word components (or morphemes), as shown by the examples. Undoubtedly, he considered words as the linguistic signs *par excellence*. But phrases and sentences are, likewise, linear combinations, sequences; and de Saussure did not regard the latter as something basically different from compound words or

MÉMOIRE

SUR LE

SYSTÈME PRIMITIF DES VOYELLES

DANS LES

LANGUES INDO-EUROPÉENNES

PAR

FERDINAND DE SAUSSURE.

LEIPSICK
EN VENTE CHEZ B. G. TEUBNER.
1879.

Title page of Saussure's Mémoire.

derivates: he even provided an over-all denomination for every kind of complex sign: he termed them "syntagms". The word does not occur before the second course (1908-1909); it applies to sentences and phrases as well as to analyzable words: *John's father died suddenly last night* is a syntagm; but *John's father* is also one, and likewise *John's* or *suddenly*. De Saussure was well aware of the fact that syntagms are not all alike, except for the linear character of the combinations. Pointing out this common feature is only the first step: the next one would be to classify the syntagmatic patterns on the basis of formal and semantic criteria. Obviously, this should be done within each language, since the greatest differences between languages lie precisely in the variety of the syntagm patterns, ranging from primary derivates to full sentences. In the third course, there is an allusion to various 'grades of combination' in French syntagms. But de Saussure did not go further. The problem he was concerned with was a morphological problem; to syntax, he paid little attention. This is no surprise since he was, as I pointed out, an Indo-Europeanist. In his opinion, the rules for building sentences would not raise so many questions as those of word formation, and he probably thought the latter more relevant to the system of a language than the former.

Anyway, his conception of grammar as a description of paradigms, on the one hand, and of syntagms (or, better, syntagmatic patterns) on the other, still remains a theoretical prospect. No serious attempt has been made, as yet, to set up the hierarchy of syntagms in a given language. One may believe that morphemic analysis, as it is currently carried on, is a satisfactory approach to syntagmatics: *junctures* are a valuable criterion to check the 'grade of combination' in various kinds of syntagms. But syntagmatics, as defined by de Saussure, would be confronted with more difficult problems. Formal analysis is certainly not easy. Yet in whatever syntagm, the *signifiant,* as a result of its linear nature, is divisible into segments; and though controversial cases are not wanting, a correct analysis can be achieved by a careful study of all possible substitutions. But what about the *signifié*? Is it linear? Linguists usually proceed as if this were the case: a sentence is split up into as many 'morphs' as seems required by the system, and each of these is supposed to bear a part of the total meaning. This is perhaps nothing more than a practical device. Actually, the *signifié* of a complex word (e.g. of an inflected noun form) is not made up of successive segments: it is a bundle of significant features, liable to analysis insofar as it can be compared and contrasted with the *signifiés* of other noun forms in the same language. But the number of these features is not predictable from the number of morphs: in Lat. *dominus,* there are only two morphs (*domin-,-us*), but at least three significant features; and if we choose to split the ending *-us* into two morphs (a declension marker *-u-* and a case ending *-s*), the disagreement of the formal analysis and the analysis of the *signifié* will appear all the more striking.

Let us now consider a phrase or a sentence. It may be surmised that in this case the linear nature of the *significant* is shared to a certain extent by the *signifié*. The succession of the words, at least, is not irrelevant to the latter; and the terms of a sentence could hardly be viewed as 'features' of the total *signifié*. There is a difference between such syntagms and those which consist of 'sub-units', that is, of segments that never occur alone. But there are probably intermediate cases. In view of these difficulties, it is apparently safer to cling to the traditional division of grammar into morphology and syntax. However, I cannot help believing that de Saussure's division is more in agreement with the structure of language. Furthermore, it would afford a basis for linguistic typology.

I started, necessarily, with the fundamental distinctions: diachrony vs. synchrony; 'language' (*langue*) vs. 'speaking' (*parole*). We noticed that de Saussure was able to set up the former without reference to the latter. Or rather, he was able to ground it on his definition of 'language' as the essential part of human speech. As soon as we abstract from the actually uttered sounds, we are confronted with a system of immaterial signs, a code. And we have to perceive that the description of such a system must not be biased by a regard to its previous evolution. This definition of language, together with the distinction of diachrony and synchrony, was prompted, as we saw, by an inquiry on the problem of identity in human speech, not by an analysis of the speech act. Such an analysis was actually presented by de Saussure in his third course. But it was meant to bring additional support to his conception of *la langue*. To speaking (*la parole*), he paid less attention.

Only in his last years, from 1907 onward, had he begun to contrast language, as a code, with speaking, as the individual application of the code; and he eventually came to offer a new definition of the latter, the implications of which he had no time to discuss. Let us examine his successive statements.

According to the above mentioned rough distinction of language and speech sounds, he conceived speaking as the 'performance' (*exécution*) of linguistic signs. A quite peculiar view of the production of sentences is here involved. Since utterances usually, though not always, consist of more than one word, here again we have to understand 'sign' in a wider sense. In fact, de Saussure had in mind sentences, as he explicitly states in his third course. Now, the individual speech act is viewed as a mere performance: the uttering of a complex sign, a sentence. How is this complex sign created? If the code of a language is present in each individual's brain as a collection of simple signs, it is up to the speaker to select the appropriate ones, according to his purpose, and to arrange them into a coherent sentence. But then speaking is no more a performance, but a creative act. And this seems hardly questionable, in view of the fact that every speaker is apt to utter and to understand new sentences, which he has never uttered or heard before. De Saussure certainly did not overlook such an obvious truth: how then could he regard speaking as a bare performance, as if the speaker's activity were nothing more than uttering sounds and exerting his speech organs? Actually, de Saussure never pictured language as a collection of signs, a *nomenclature*. Language, as an institution, is a system, and in each individual's brain it is deposited in the form of a system. What the speaker disposes of is not only a collection of linguistic units (words and morphemes); each of these units is connected with the oth-

ers in many ways, allowing various combinations and substitutions so that the building of a sentence appears to be, to a certain extent, a mechanical process. What is left to the speaker's own activity is, on the one hand, thinking, that is, conceiving what he wants to say; and, on the other hand, uttering sentences. Now, de Saussure never considered thinking as part of 'language'; he did not even raise the question. But he repeatedly emphasized that actually uttered sounds, too, are something outside language (*la langue*), and he was prompted to urge this by the fact that philologists as well as phonologists were not quite conscious of the true nature of language.

The definition of 'speaking' (*la parole*) as a performance is therefore more than a paradox or a careless statement. It may well surprise the readers of the *Cours;* yet it is quite in agreement with de Saussure's conception: the system of a language is not solely a set of items, a lexicon; it is also a network of connections, a grammar. So it cannot be handled at random or at will. Every speaker, in building his sentences, unconsciously applies the rules of the language; and the same rules enable him to understand and correctly interpret the utterances of other speakers. This amounts to saying that sentences belong in 'language' insofar as the sentence patterns are comprehended in the code. If we remember that sentences are syntagms, and syntagmatics a part of grammar, we must acknowledge the consistency of de Saussure's theory. We can also notice that there is but one step from his syntagmatics to [Noam] Chomsky's transformational grammar: for transformation rules rely upon syntagmatic connections, in de Saussure's terms, or upon what he called, in his second course, the 'mechanism of language'.

However, besides the definition of 'speaking' (*la parole*) as a performance, another one occurs in the second course: speaking is viewed as 'discourse'. De Saussure starts with observing that words, and linguistic signs in general, are connected with each other in two ways. There are connections, on the one hand, between all the forms of an inflected word, or between words of the same inflectional pattern, or between derivative and basic words, etc.; and, on the other hand, between morphemes within a word, or between words within a phrase or a sentence. The former lie in memory. We may term these paradigmatic connections (de Saussure said: *rapports associatifs*). The latter are, as we know, syntagmatic; they occur in the discourse. Paradigmatic connections surely belong in the system, since the system, as de Saussure pointed out in a previous chapter, is stored in the memory of each individual. As to the syntagmatic connections, they require a creative act on the speaker's part—an actual combination of two or more members. This can hardly be true of such syntagms as compound words, derivates, or usual phrases; de Saussure meant sentences.

This reasoning leads to amazing conclusions. First, syntagmatics turns out not to be an homogeneous object: only one part of it is included in the system, namely, such syntagms as consist of morphemes or 'sub-units'. Furthermore, sentences are no longer automatically brought forth by the rules of the language; they are produced by individual creative acts, and consequently belong in 'speaking' (*la parole*), not in 'language' (*la langue*).

Here, and only here, I cannot help feeling a positive contradiction in the theory. De Saussure, too, must have felt it, for he expresses himself with such caution, in his third course, that I do not venture to record his conclusion as a well-considered and definitive opinion.

He is certainly right in contrasting paradigmatic and syntagmatic connections. He also rightly points out that the latter are supported by the former, as he demonstrates in the peculiar case of analogical innovations. But here, again, he appears to have been more concerned with morphology than with syntax. Otherwise, he would have applied his demonstration to phrases and sentences, and it would have proved right. Practically, the contrast lies in the fact that speaking individuals never utter paradigms (except in a classroom) or enumerate prepositions or derivates of the same pattern; but every day and at every time they produce sentences. In producing them, they operate paradigms and syntagmatic rules. Since all the members of a linguistic community produce similar sentences, we have to conclude that they conform to the same rules. In other words, their memory supplies them with similar material: paradigms and syntagm patterns.

But de Saussure's uneasiness in approaching the sentence problem simply proves that he perceived a real difficulty. Linguists are still far from agreeing on the answer to be given to this capital question: is a sentence the production of an individual's free creative act, or is it previously outlined by the rules of the language? Or, in de Saussure's terms, does it belong in 'speaking' or in 'language'?

Let us start, as many linguists do, with considering the function of speech. Speech is the normal form of social intercourse. Communication is the aim, and usually the result, of every speech act. In fact, communication does not always succeed: misunderstandings occur in everyday talk as in diplomatic conversations. Such accidental failures, however, do not prevent men from communicating by speech, rather than by some other device. If communication is the function of speech, speech, in its turn, is the proper means for human beings to communicate with each other. Casual misunderstandings, therefore, though not negligible, are not primarily relevant to the science of language.

It is a quite different case when communication is hindered by the bare fact that two individuals do not or cannot use the same language. Partner B does not catch the message uttered by partner A, not for lack of attention, or of understanding, or of general knowledge, but simply because he does not know the code. This is what de Saussure insisted upon: the primary fact to observe and account for, in linguistics, does not lie in the behavior of individuals communicating, or trying to communicate, with each other, but in the existence and peculiar structure of the common code they are using to formulate their messages. This code is what we call a language: English, or Russian, or some Arabic dialect, etc. What must individuals do in order to communicate? Or what is involved in the individual application of a speech code? On the one hand, select-

ing signs in connection with actual objects and environments, that is, in Bally's terms, 'actualizing' the *signifiés;* on the other hand, delivering the message by articulating the appropriate speech sounds, that is, in the phonemicist's terms, 'realizing' the phonemic sequence of the *signifiant.* The conception of the message, the formless idea by which it is prompted, is beyond language; similarly, according to de Saussure, the actual utterance. The selection of signs with regard to a particular situation requires a variable amount of creative activity: new thoughts call up new sentences, and even commonplace ideas or feelings can be expressed in a new manner. At any rate, the application of a speech code in given circumstances is never predictable, as Bloomfield rightly emphasized. At any moment, a choice has to be made, either of words or of syntagmatic patterns. Thus, it cannot be denied that the linguistic elaboration of a message is a creative act, unless the message is a readymade sentence such as frequently occurs in everyday conversation.

Conversely, the most unusual message—say, a modernistic poem—is made up of units supplied by the common speech code, according to rules of combination which are equally part of the same code. Thus, a sentence is, at the same time, but not to the same extent, the result of a creative act and of mechanical operations. Which is more important? De Saussure's personal bent was probably to understate the creative act and to emphasize the mechanical process, just because the former, at first sight, seems to be the very essence of speech. This is the reason why his definition of 'speaking' as a performance seems to me more in agreement with his general line of thinking. But the other definition ('speaking' as discourse) cannot be simply discarded. He would have discussed its implications had he had time to get through his third course as he had planned it: 1) *Les langues;* 2) *La langue;* 3) *La faculté et l'exercice du langage chez les individus.* He had started with the primary fact: the existence of various speech codes, or languages; he then brought to light the general characteristics of any language; he would have examined, at last, the processes involved in the individual application of a speech code. He was prevented from doing it, and none will ever presume to complete his exposition as he would have himself.

De Saussure's fate is a strange one. As a youth, before getting his doctorate, he asserted himself as an outstanding scholar, even as a master in comparative philology. In the following years, in addition to his particular researches (especially on Lithuanian) and his activity as professor in the Ecole des Hautes Etudes and as secretary of the Linguistic Society of Paris, he reflected more than any linguist of that time on the fundamentals of language. Scattered material for a book he intended to write have been preserved among his papers. But he did not carry out this purpose, and from 1893 onward, he scarcely published any paper. The letter he sent to Meillet in the beginning of 1894 throws a dismal light on his state of mind: he was dispirited, and the problems he had been engrossed with had become to him a kind of nightmare. At any rate, he was then engaged in quite different, somewhat strange researches.

Toward the end of 1906, he was appointed to offer a course in general linguistics at the University of Geneva, where he had been teaching Sanskrit and comparative philology for fifteen years. A friend of his told me that this new appointment simply terrified him: he did not feel up to the task, and had no desire to wrestle with the problems once more. However, he undertook what he believed to be his duty.

We must keep this in mind in view of what he achieved in such unfavorable circumstances. He laid the foundations of a theory of language; he built the framework of modern linguistics; he set up the problems in the most enlightening manner. His teaching is not dogmatic, but suggestive and stimulating. To everyone who correctly understands it, it is an inducement to personal reflection and research. (pp. 83-97)

> Robert Godel, "F. de Saussure's Theory of Language," in Cahiers Ferdinand de Saussure, *Vol. 38, 1984, pp. 83-97.*

Allen Thiher   (essay date 1984)

[*Thiher is an American critic and educator. In the following excerpt, he examines Saussure's presentation of the scientific and social paradigms of language in* Course in General Linguistics.]

In returning to that period at the end of the nineteenth century when Saussure was an academic philologist, working within the paradigms of the "New Grammarians," we should recall that he was also the contemporary of the philologist Friedrich Nietzsche, who understood well how systems of thought must work as a necessary consensus. There are historical limits that condition the possibility for thought in terms of the reigning systems of concepts, and Nietzsche saw this correlation of concepts to function as a historical law:

> That the separate philosophical ideas are not anything optional or autonomously evolving, but grow up in connection and relationship with each other; that, however suddenly and arbitrarily they seem to appear in the history of thought, they nevertheless belong just as much to a system as the collective members of the fauna of a Continent—is betrayed in the end by the circumstance: how unfailingly the most diverse philosophers always fill in again a definite fundamental scheme of *possible* philosophies.

The Nietzsche of *Beyond Good and Evil* saw the necessity of the systemic interrelation of thought at any time (of what [Michel] Foucault would later call the possibilities of the *epistemē*); and if we accept Nietzsche's reading of the systemic nature of thought, it was perhaps no accident that his contemporary Saussure made the notion of *system* the cornerstone of his thought about language. Moreover, Saussure was the kind of demystifier who would have quickly understood the kind of philology Nietzsche was undertaking.

For, among other things, Nietzsche was putting an end to the Lockean belief that ideas—the basis for language—

arise passively from the reception of sense data. Ideas are bound up in language as systems existing in history.

To place Saussure in this context, with Nietzsche, is to suggest similarities that account for Saussure's belated appeal to our minds, well after the "Copernican revolution" he effected in linguistics seems to have been displaced by another "Copernican turn" by [Noam] Chomsky and his generative theory. Saussure belongs to the era of demystifiers that begins with Nietzsche and includes Wittgenstein, the logical positivists, and the early Heidegger. This era finds its final thinkers, it might appear, in the varieties of structuralist thought that have proliferated in France and Italy—and of which Jacques Derrida would be the latest product. Saussure, the philologist and inventor of modern linguistics, inaugurates a way of thinking that finds its full resonance when read as a response to nineteenth-century thought about language and, ultimately, to the way modernism attempted to revive the Western Platonic tradition.

Saussure's work in linguistic methodology was elaborated at the beginning of this century, during a teaching career that unfolded first in Paris, then in Geneva, where he taught until his death in 1913. Like Aristotle's work and much of Hegel's, Saussure's major work, the *Course of General Linguistics*, published in 1916, is based on collocations of notes taken by students. In its present form this work is based on three different courses on general linguistics that he gave at the end of his life. As such, the *Course* does not represent any final formulation. In its present state the book seems at times to be animated by two discordant impulses: to make language an isolated object of scientific inquiry and to show that language is a form of social practice. It has also been subject to criticism for supposedly utilizing elements taken from earlier thought on language. To be sure, Saussure was influenced by Enlightenment theories, but to point out this influence in no way diminishes the originality of his thought. His *Course* proposes an analytic methodology—in effect an all-encompassing scientific paradigm—that may well incorporate earlier views on language but that in its totality represents an entirely new means for explaining language. This methodology makes Saussure the father, or rather grandfather, of the modern study of linguistics; for the *Course* has opened a field of inquiry emblematic of the twentieth century's scrutiny of language as an object of scientific investigation.

Before Saussure, language had, of course, been the object of categorizing and of various types of grammatical inquiries (usually inherited from the Greeks, as far as Western thought is concerned). In the nineteenth century it had been the object of historical inquiries that, using models adapted from philosophy, history, and biology, had made great achievements in classifying various languages and in developing various taxonomies. But for modern purposes linguistics—taking language as a separate object of scientific investigation, using its own procedural model—begins with Saussure. Reacting against the models of organicity used by comparative grammar in the nineteenth century, Saussure stressed that the very nature of what philologists were investigating had not yet been defined by historical linguistics:

This school, which had the incontestable merit of opening a new and fertile field, did not succeed in constituting a true linguistic science. It was never concerned with bringing to light the object of its study. Without this elementary operation, a science is incapable of becoming a method.

Saussure criticizes those nineteenth-century comparatists who saw in language "an organism that develops by itself" and failed to recognize that language is the "product of the collective spirit of linguistic groups." This criticism might seem incompatible with the final words that the editors added to conclude the course, to the effect that linguistics has for its unique and true object language envisaged in itself and for itself. The editors have, to be sure, given us a *Course* that seems to reflect their preoccupation with isolating the study of language from its social matrix. But Saussure's thought also includes the procedural necessity of a methodological separation of linguistics from other sciences. Even in placing words in Saussure's mouth, the editors have not been unfaithful to the basic orientation of the course. Only after this separation is made can language be seen, in a Saussurean perspective, as a social product or a collection of social practices. Saussure's critique of nineteenth-century metaphors of organicity takes one step toward identifying the social locus of language, while his stress on the need for identifying precisely what language is shows that language is a unique phenomenon. Needless to say, this dual thrust to Saussure's thought has given rise to various interpretations as to how the *Course* should have been edited in order better to reflect whatever might have been Saussure's real thought.

In the following discussion I propose to discuss the *Course* as it exists. Had Saussure lived longer, he undoubtedly would have given us a different book. What concerns us here is the *Course* as it has existed for a number of decades. The following exposition of its basic principles is perforce an interpretation, but one that many of Saussure's critical readers agree upon. Scientific paradigms must, after all, be transmissible. As my point of departure for characterizing Saussure's model for understanding what language is (and let us bear in mind the passage from Nietzsche), I take the premise that language is a system. Though some of Saussure's later critics have claimed that his conception of language as an autonomous system is either invalid or not consonant with his own premises about language being a sum of social practices, the description of language as a system is at the center of Saussure's thought. This characterization (or premise) makes language amenable to rational description. As such, the notion of system commands all the other perspectives in the *Course.* Certainly Saussure's formulations of system have, in various guises, found constant application in later linguistic thought, ranging from the models proposed by such European structuralists as [Lovis] Hjelmslev or Martinet to the transformational grammars of Chomsky and his followers. For example, Hjelmslev's *Prolegomena to a Theory of Language* sets forth a clear definition of system that has become the operational hypothesis for all linguistics after Saussure:

A priori it would seem to be a generally valid thesis that for every *process* there is a corresponding *system,* by which the process can be analyzed and described by means of a limited number of premises. It must be assumed that any process can be analyzed into a limited number of elements recurring in various combinations. Then, on the basis of this analysis, it should be possible to order these elements into classes according to their possibilities of combination.

The description of the system will then, according to this structuralist credo, give rise to "a generalizing science, in the theory of which all events (possible combination of elements) are foreseen and the conditions for their realization established."

"Process" and "system" are new formulations for Saussure's distinction between *parole,* or individual speech acts, and *langue,* or language as a hypothesized system. This separation of the individual speech act and the system of which it is a realization is the first operative step in describing the system. One danger in such a structuralist approach to language is that the linguist invents a hypothesized model that he then projects onto the process of speech acts that supposedly embody the system. The hypothesized systemic model is taken to be the system studied. Such a shift hypostatizes the model and makes of the linguist's fiction a substantial reality. ([Claude] Lévi-Strauss's application of Saussure's models has, for instance, been subject to such a criticism.) Saussure himself noted this problem when he remarked that it might appear that it is the observer's point of view that creates the object of his study. This problem raises a basic problem of scientific epistemology. A model's giving rise to the object studied represents, it seems to me, a circularity that underlies much scientific method; one must look to other criteria to decide if an operational hypothesis is satisfactory or not. As Wittgenstein remarked about Newtonian mechanics, nothing is said about the world when it allows itself to be described by such a model—except that the world does allow itself to be so described. The question is how well.

The system that underlies the language we speak is not apparent to ordinary speakers of that language. As Saussure describes it, this system is a "complex mechanism" that cannot be understood except by "reflexive activity": "those who use it every day are profoundly ignorant of it." In stressing the unconscious nature of the system as mechanism, Saussure has replaced the organic metaphor, with its biological and historical connotations, that the nineteenth century had used to describe language. To be sure, he has replaced it with another metaphor, for however much the idea of system may motivate the choice of "mechanism," this descriptive term is equally metaphorical. This metaphor stresses at once the self-contained nature of language and the structuralist view of the language-machine as a system in which all parts are hooked to all other parts. As we shall see, this is a favored postmodern metaphor, offering the writer possibilities for affirming both his creativeness and his alienation.

This mechanism lies beyond our conscious mind. It can only be laid bare by the model that might illuminate it. As might be expected from a thinker who did not live to put his thoughts in final form, Saussure is not always consistent in his thought with this metaphor that presents language as a mechanism lying beyond consciousness. He also states that the system of language, though invisible to the speaker who makes use of it, is completely psychological in its ultimate reality: "At bottom everything in language is psychological in nature, including its material and mechanical manifestations, such as the changes of sounds." I take Saussure to mean by this statement that the material embodiment of language—graphic signs or oral performance—is a matter of indifference with regard to the system itself. However, such a formulation tends to suggest that the individual subject is the locus for the study of language. But this psychological particularization would make the notion of system ultimately untenable or inapplicable. The primary orientation of Saussure's thought argues clearly against a view of language as a series of psychological determinations. As the mechanism metaphor implies, his views also give support to the idea, comparable to Heidegger's later thought, that the subject is spoken by language. Or, as Jacques Derrida later formulated it in a thought that joins together Saussure and Heidegger, the subject only exists thanks to language.

Saussure's view of system is not harmed by the psychologizing vocabulary, the "mentalism," that today seems to inhabit the *Course* as a reminder that Saussure lived most of his life in the nineteenth century. The twentieth-century linguist, as prepared by Saussure, need take note of individual speech acts only as manifestations of the underlying system. This system's locus is disclosed by the self-reflexive act that brings it to light. It exists in the public space of what we can call the space of description. In the *Course of General Linguistics* the system is described by a series of binary oppositions or pairings that are as powerful in their scope as they are exhaustive in their intent. Though Saussure did not explicitly set forth a binary creed as the ordering operation for linguistic description, binary ordering does constitute the heart of his methodology and has remained the major model for structuralist thought. In this discussion of Saussure, I propose to examine these binary oppositions and some of the problems they present for a description of the system that makes up every language. With this description of language as a system of oppositions, it would appear that Saussure believed he had laid bare for the first time what language is when considered in itself.

The first binary pairing in the system in operational terms is found in Saussure's principle that linguistics must be divided into diachronic and synchronic domains. In describing language one must distinguish between the study of the change of the system through time—the diachronic—and the description of the hypothesized static state of the linguistic system at any given moment in time—the synchronic. At every moment language is, as Saussure says, a current institution (*institution actuelle*) and a product of evolution through time. As a product of the past, language can be described diachronically. This was the principal preoccupation of nineteenth-century philology. For Saussure, however, linguistics as a science must give priority to the synchronic description of language as a fixed sys-

tem. The primacy given to synchrony effects a break with those nineteenth-century studies of language that used biologically oriented models of evolution and taxonomy. It also marks a break with the historicism of the linguistic work that had developed from the time of [Jacob] Grimm, [Rasmus] Rask, [Friedrich] Schlegel, and [Franz] Bopp and which, during Saussure's lifetime, had culminated in the studies of the Neo-grammarians at the end of the nineteenth century.

To speak of this break is not to say that Saussure intended to disparage the historical study of language. Historical work interested him personally more than any other aspect of the study of language. The distinction between diachronic and synchronic linguistics, however, imposed itself upon him as a methodological necessity, as a way of introducing some rationality into the study of language. For, as Saussure saw, no reason, no cause, can be given for the diachronic nature of language. No satisfactory answer can be given as to why every aspect of language changes in time. Confronted with this fundamentally irrational side of language, Saussure felt, perhaps, that he must find a way of ordering the description of language that would be as rational as possible: hence, language as a fixed mechanism. The primacy of the sychronous language machine portended one of the most significant shifts in our contemporary intellectual economy. To generalize the primacy of this ordering entails the exclusion of history from our intellectual concerns. Such an exclusion is not the least of the dilemmas facing postmodern thinkers.

Working with the first premise, that language is a system, and having excluded the diachronic dimension from the space of his description, the linguist uses another set of oppositions to order the object of his inquiry: each instance of *parole* is an individual manifestation of the *langue* or the system of the natural language in question. Difficulties of translation arise from the existence in French of a third term, *language,* that, like *langue,* can be translated as "language." *Langage,* as distinguished from *langue,* is the faculty of speech as opposed to a given natural "tongue" or *langue. Langage* can also mean a repository of signs or techniques for communication (in the sense of, say, *langage cinématographique*). *Langue* is, for Saussure, the system of the individual language such as French or English, whereas *parole* is the individualized utterance of that *langue* or language system. The same kind of distinction lies behind Chomsky's separation of competence and performance, in that transformational grammar also hypothesizes an internalized linguistic system in the individual that allows him to "generate" individual speech utterances in conformity with the rules of the system. Semioticians have also used Saussure's distinction to specify that the *langue* is a code (an expression used only once in the *Course*), whereas the *parole* is the individual message expressed. In all these formulations language is considered an autonomous entity, a virtual code or system, that transcends any individual use of the system, and yet can be said to exist only as the totality of the individual language-users' possession of the code. Such a totality exists as a definition of what constitutes a language community.

If we say that the language system transcends any individual speaker's comprehension of it, we might well give the impression that Saussure's *langue* exists in some metaphysical heaven of ideal French or English. That the *langue* exists seemingly as an abstraction has certainly given rise to suspicions that it is a metaphysical construct, perhaps a Durkheimian creation, existing in some ideal realm apart from social reality. Such a suspicion strikes me as having little validity, for Saussure's description of *la langue* allows a reading that emphasizes its concrete social nature:

> If we were able to embrace the sum of verbal images stored in all individuals, we would touch the social bond [*lien*] that constitutes language. It is a store [*trésor*] placed, through the practice of speech [*parole*], in all subjects belonging to the same community, a grammatical system existing in virtual terms in every brain.

The abstraction *langue* exists as the foundation of a culture, as a collective realization, but one that can only be revealed in the space of inquiry.

There are other ways of describing the nature of *langue*. In Roland Barthes' semiotic perspective, it is not only a code but also a social contract. The contractual metaphor is sanctioned by Saussure's use of it in the ***Course.*** Saussure may well have remembered this metaphor's success during the Enlightenment, especially in the work of a fellow citizen of Geneva, Jean-Jacques Rousseau. The metaphor likening the language system to a contract is felicitous in that it stresses the reciprocal bond linking language and culture and the type of access to communal membership that is essentially defined by language. This metaphor points, moreover, to affinities with Wittgenstein's view of language as the ethnological bond that creates a people's world view. Tullio de Mauro, for example, interprets the thought of the "later" Saussure—the Saussure of the third course—to be quite compatible with Wittgenstein's notion that language derives from a series of social practices that can be identified in a public space of social recognition. Mauro is correct, though one scarcely need examine the manuscript sources to see Saussure's emphasis on social usage as the locus of the language system.

The distinction between a virtual system and individual instances of real speech brings up the question of the individual subject's capacity to deal, in some autonomous manner, with the system that lies beyond his consciousness. In purely methodological terms this was not a problem for Saussure, since the only object of linguistic inquiry is *la langue,* the sum of all individual cases of *parole.* And for Saussure it is only the operational hypothesis about *langue* that matters. Yet, Saussure did briefly address himself to the question of the relation between the subject and his language. These comments seem to anticipate Chomsky's view of the rule-bound freedom of the individual speaker: bound by a finite series of transformational rules, the speaker has the capacity for the genesis of an indefinite number of utterances. Saussure also sees in language a space in which freedom and necessity are conjoined:

> Language is not a function of the speaking subject; it is a product that the individual registers passively. Speech is on the other hand an indi-
>
> vidual act of will and intelligence, in which one should distinguish (1) the combinations through which the speaking subject uses the language code in order to express his personal thoughts and (2) the psycho-physical mechanism that allows him to exteriorize these combinations.

These remarks also seem to have a dual thrust. On the one hand Saussure does appear to vouchsafe the autonomy of the subject and the possibility of individual creativity—within the limits of the "psycho-physical" mechanism that underlies language. On the other hand, with a shift in perspective, these limits might appear to circumscribe severely the individual's autonomy. Moreover, the mechanism metaphor might appear to undermine the very act of will that Saussure here ascribes to the subject's use of language. As a passive receptor who acquires a language system in the same way he acquires the destiny prepared for him by biology and culture, the individual subject can be construed to be a mere topographical point in a space formed by forces that determine his entire being. Such an interpretation resembles, say, that of Lévi-Strauss, for whom Saussure, along with Freud and Marx, taught that "true reality" is never what is most manifest to consciousness.

Meaning within the linguistic system is first to be defined in terms of the linguistic sign. Saussure uses another set of binary oppositions to define the sign: it is composed of a concept and an "acoustical image" or, as he prefers to say, a signified and a signifier. In common with the Wittgenstein of the *Philosophical Investigations* Saussure begins his definition of the sign by denying that linguistic signs constitute a nomenclature. Rejecting the common sense Occidental view that the sign is a noun referring to an idea or, more naively, to an object, Saussure rejected the Augustinian and the Lockean views of language in quick succession:

> There is first of all the superficial concept that most people hold: they see in language only a nomenclature, an idea which does away with any research into the true nature of language. Then there is the psychologist's point of view who studies the mechanism of the sign in the individual. This is the easiest approach, but it does not lead beyond the individual performances [*exécution*] and does not reach the sign, which is social by nature.

Saussure shares with Wittgenstein and Heidegger the repudiation of the Aristotelian view of language as a representation of ideas in the soul or mind; and, as suggested before, he agrees with Wittgenstein that the social space of shared culture is the locus of the sign's functioning. The sign is transsubjective by its very nature. There are no private languages for Saussure any more than for Wittgenstein.

This rejection of the naive or traditional metaphysics of representation is the first step in defining the sign as the union of the signified and the signifier. If the sign cannot be defined in terms of representation—or if it cannot simply be identified with a word—then the linguist must locate it in terms of its place in the linguistic system. Representation and reference are therefore excluded as criteria for identifying a sign, a procedure that recalls Wittgenstein's demonstration of the difficulty of using ostensive definitions for knowing what a word means: one must already have an understanding of the linguistic space a word occupies before one can know how to use it. For Saussure, the autonomy of the linguistic system demands that signs be identified, both phonologically and semantically, in terms of their opposition to other signs. Signs derive their identity and meaning from their position in the space of the linguistic system: this position can be defined only by their opposition to and difference from other signs.

The notion that language is a differential sign system represents Saussure's greatest break with traditional views of language. As Tullio de Mauro has pointed out, from Plato to early Wittgenstein Western philosophy has agreed to the common premise that the signified—the concept or that to which the sign refers—could be defined in itself. This autonomy of the signified meant that the external form of the sign—material language—is only a negligible support for what is signified. Nineteenth-century historical linguistics had propagated this view in that it took as its object of study the transformations of the mere exterior or material forms of language. Saussure chastised this approach at the outset of the *Course* by declaring that the essential aspect of language has nothing to do with the phonic nature of the sign. The functioning of the sign cannot be grasped through its material forms, but only through its opposition to other signs, whatever be the morphological embodiment of the sign.

In defining the sign in itself as the union of a signifier and a signified, Saussure uses a vocabulary that, as [Roman] Jakobson has noted, seems to go back to the Stoics. In anticipation of Jacques Derrida's charge that at this point metaphysics makes an entry into Saussure's thought, one must point out that Saussure's use of such classical terminology takes place in an entirely new context. A more problematic issue is that, in defining the sign, Saussure's language suggests that he reverts to a kind of Lockean mentalism that is not consonant with his own view of language as a social practice: "The linguistic sign unites, not a thing and a word, but a concept and an acoustical image. The latter is not the material sound, a purely physical thing, but the psychic imprint of the sound; it is the representation for which our senses offer evidence." Clearly the concept is not the same as a Platonic idea, since it exists only in opposition to other concepts within the semantic space of a given language. Yet more problematic is the recourse to the "psyche" to define the signifier. This recourse does not square with Saussure's claim that the signifier is neither a material sound nor a purely physical thing. Derrida is right to point this out, especially with regard to writing, for if the signifier is in principle not tied to any material form—be it phonic, graphic, or whatever—then no form can be privileged over another. Yet, one should not be too quick to make Saussure a footnote to Plato. As Giulio Lepschy has noted, "psychic elements" in Saussure's language means essentially immaterial elements, and one can translate this notion into the modern sense of "abstract models." Seen in this light, signified and signifier are both relational entities, to be defined in terms of their relative position to other signifieds and signifiers within the space of the linguistic system. They need no psyche for their existence, nor a Platonic heaven.

The definition of the linguistic sign is based in turn upon two axioms: the arbitrary nature of the linguistic sign and the linear nature of the language chain of signifiers. Saussure so highly valued the first axiom that in one lesson he called it the "first law" of linguistics. The principle of the arbitrary, as opposed to some motivated, nature of the linguistic sign is hardly new in itself. Before Plato this principle is to be found in Democritus and later in such thinkers as [John] Locke—who found a lively opponent on the subject in [Gottfried] Leibniz. Within the context of Saussure's system, the principle of the arbitrary nature of the relationship between the signifier and the signified, between what, in one example, Saussure calls the acoustical image *boy* and the concept "boy," can account for a number of different features of language. Perhaps the most important is the way that the arbitrary relation between signifier and signified allows the diachronic change of language to occur unimpeded, without the linguistic system necessarily undergoing fundamental change. The irrationality of historical change corresponds to the arbitrary character of the sign.

In this respect Saussure makes a sharp distinction between the sign and the symbol. The symbol is not arbitrary, since it always has a degree of motivation to justify its symbolizing relationship. In this sense language is never symbolic. By radicalizing the principle of the arbitrary nature of the linguistic sign, Saussure demolished the underpinnings of aesthetic modernism. The *Course* can be read as something of an antimodernist manifesto, for it leaves no justification for a belief in the imagistic power of poetic revelation in language. To put this in a different light, Saussure brings a linguistic corrective to what Frank Lentricchia in a recent book calls the "naturalistic error" of those modernists who sought a motivated language:

> The mainstream of aesthetic modernism (even the structuralist Todorov draws from it when he tells us that linguistic structure is a mirror of the structure of the universe) has primarily characterized itself not by its misleading propaganda against science and philistinism that the aesthetic world is a thing wholly apart, but by its claim that the aesthetic world plumbs the nature of things; and the pivot of this claim is the prior ontological claim for a natural bond between signifier and signified, and between sign and thing.

Virtually every aspect of the *Course* is directed against this belief in a natural bond: the rejection of nomenclature, the dismissal of the naive metaphysics of representation, the reduction of the signified and the signified to relational entities. But it is the clear distinction between symbol and sign that is perhaps most telling as a critique of modernist views or, should I say, hopes about language.

Saussure's second axiom for defining the linguistic sign has equally antimodernist implications in the way it would undermine belief in the possibility of iconic or simultaneous representation. The second axiom is that the signifier has a linear and thus measurable character:

> The signifier, being auditory in nature, unfolds

in time alone and has those characteristics that it borrows from time: (a) it represents an extension [*étendue*], and (b) this extension is measurable in only one dimension: for it is a line.

Noting that this principle seems so obvious that it is often overlooked, Saussure goes on to state:

> The entire mechanism of language depends upon it. By opposition to visual signifiers (maritime signals, etc.), which can offer simultaneous, intricate developments in several dimensions, acoustical signifiers have at their disposition only the line of time. Their elements present themselves one after another. They form a chain. This characteristic appears immediately as soon as they are represented by writing, and the spatial line of graphic signs is substituted for their succession in time.

In this view time seems to be an integral part of the ontology of language, or at least of spoken language. For the linearity Saussure speaks of can only be understood as a geometrical model drawn from our usual conception of the flow of time. To place time at the heart of the ontology of language creates significant problems. For the writer, the temporalizing of language means, in a rather perverse way, that all he says is condemned to the evanescence of the moving line. Modernism had reacted against this self-destruction inherent in language with its search for the icon. And postmodern writers find in this description of their language the conditions for their alienation from their own voice.

The model of language as a linear continuum, derived from the model of a linear temporal flow, obliges one to ask how discrete units of meaning are identified. This is a question of import primarily for linguists, since our daily meta-linguistic needs are met by using such approximate terms as "word." But the linguist himself occupies no privileged position when it comes to language. In order to identify the sign, he must already know its signified—its meaning—which means that he must make an intuitive appeal to knowledge of a language's semantic segmentation of the linear flow. As Wittgenstein said, the way into language is through language, which finds an echo in Heidegger's belief that the way into language is the circular path of already being there. We begin and end in language. All three views here seem to be variants of a single demonstration of the autonomy of language and the primacy of the word.

When looking at the linguistic system strictly in terms of *la langue,* however, the **Course** does propose a conceptual way to consider the sign, and that is by separating the signifier and the signified in terms of their position on two axes. Signifiers can be isolated from other signifiers in terms of their opposition along a horizontal axis that corresponds to the linear chain of language flow. In turn, the signifier and the signified maintain a relationship along a vertical axis. Signification is characterized as a vertical relationship between the two faces of the sign, whereas the horizontal relationship of opposition is what Saussure calls value. Value is not one of the clearest notions in the **Course,** and at times it is difficult to see how it differs from meaning, signification, or what we would today call connotation. Whatever be the economic metaphor that stands behind the term, value is the horizontally differential organization of signs. Value presumably applies to both signifiers and signifieds. For practical purposes, however, it would seem that only by isolating the value of the signified can one then identify the signifier—so that a knowledge of meaning is still the way into language.

Value, difference, and opposition are three central notions in Saussure's view of how the linguistic system of functions both phonologically and semantically. These concepts are central, in particular, to his view that language is not a substance. Rather than as a substance, the linguistic system can be defined only as a set of formal relations: "Let one consider the signified or the signifier: language includes neither ideas or sounds that preexist the linguistic system, but only conceptual and phonemic differences which result from the system." All entities within the system function in terms of their differences from other comparable entities within the system. Signifieds or meanings can be identified through their difference from other signifieds; and signifiers, or the material forms of signs, through their difference from other signifiers (or, as a phonologist would say today of phonemes, through their correlative opposition of pertinent features).

A number of conceptual problems inhere in this view that signs can be identified only through their difference from other signs. Such a view presupposes that the linguistic system imposes conceptual differences and phonemic differences on the same kind of undifferentiated, linear continuum. The symmetry has an aesthetic appeal, but one can wonder how the signifier and the signified can impose the same kind of differential ordering, one on a sound spectrum, the other on a conceptual field. The notion of difference is without question a fundamental axiom in Saussure's thought and can, as an operational procedure, do without the notion of linearity. Difference functions as a negative notion that allows one to identify the signified or signifier in purely relational terms. Once differences have been established, it would appear that one can speak of the sign in some positive sense, much as we do of "words." The *opposition* between signs, as Saussure puts it in one passage, is like a positive relation between discrete entities.

From Plato on, the metaphysical view of signs has been that each recurrence of the same sign can be identified as a recurrence because a universal is embodied in the sign. The next logical step says that this universal that confers identity must be somewhere other than in the sign. How could a sign be used to identify itself? The universal then becomes an essence, at once in the sign and elsewhere, allowing the identification of all different instances of the sign as the same sign. With this doctrine in mind, one can understand that the differential relation of signifieds is of the greatest significance. For this relation allows one to see, without recourse to a metaphysical doctrine of universals, how signs can have identity. Saussure offers an ingenious comparison to make clear his thought as to how signs have only a relational identity. He asks in what sense can we speak of the identity of such objects as express trains or streets, for which it would be most uneconomical to posit an essence. How does one define identity?

> The linguistic mechanism runs entirely on identities and differences, the latter being the counterpart of the former. The problem of identity is found everywhere; but, on the other hand, it overlaps in part the problem of entities and units, of which, moreover, it is a fecund ramification. The nature of this problem can be made clear when compared with a few matters taken from extra-linguistic domains.

And how can we speak of the identity of an entity such as an express train or a sign, entities that are always different instances of the same?

> Thus we speak of identity concerning the 8:45 P.M. Paris-Geneva express which leaves at intervals of 24 hours. In our eyes it is the same express train, and yet, locomotive, cars, personnel, everything about it is probably different. Or take the case of a street that is demolished and rebuilt. We say it is the same street even though in material terms nothing subsists of the former street. Why can one completely rebuild a street without its ceasing to be the same? Because the entity that it constitutes is not purely material. It is founded on certain conditions for which chance materials are a matter of indifference: for example, on its position relative to other streets. In the same way what makes up the express train is the hour of its departure, its itinerary, and in general all the circumstances that differentiate it from other express trains. Every time the same conditions are obtained, the same entities are obtained.

And, as if in anticipation of Derrida's charge that metaphysics hides within the system, Saussure goes on to say: "And yet, these entities are not abstract, since a street or an express train cannot be conceived outside of a material representation." With this formulation of difference, Saussure has struck a blow, as Jonathan Culler would have it, against "the metaphysics of presence" by defining identity in terms of common absences.

Or has he? Certainly Saussure intends to do away with our recourse to a universal essence, defined as a positive idea, that allows us to identify each occurrence of a sign. In this respect Saussure's fundamental project can be compared with that of Wittgenstein and Heidegger in rendering essence problematic as the foundation of metaphysical thought. The difficulty that arises at this point in Saussure's thought is, as the above passage makes clear, the indifference of the material form of the signifier to the presence of the signified. The signified can be united to a phonic, graphic, or other type of signifier. One immediately wants to ask, What is the common X that can be united to all these material signifiers that gives them the same meaning? At this point the analogy with the train may well be inadequate since a train can only be identified as a train and not in a multiplicity of material forms. I shall return to the point in a moment; suffice it to say here that Saussure wants to propose a non-metaphysical way of identifying signs through their recurrence in a system of differences.

The play of these differential relations along the horizontal axis gives rise to value. Within the context of the autonomous linguistic system whose signs accrue meaning differentially, value would appear to be the way each sign system organizes these differences in various semantic fields. To make the difference between meaning and value clear, Saussure offers a comparative example drawing on French and English. *Mouton* has the same meaning as *sheep,* but it does not have the same value, since *sheep* has a differential value when contrasted with *mutton* in English. A problem of consistency again arises here, for strictly speaking, in Saussure's own terms, *mouton* cannot have exactly the same signified as *sheep.* No signified is defined except in terms of differences within the system of differences to which it belongs, in this case, the French language. Saussure frequently uses translation examples to which, strictly speaking, he is not entitled.

In illustrating value with such French synonyms as *redouter, avoir peur,* and *craindre* (all of which can be translated "to fear"), Saussure shows that part of value is connotation. Yet, how value differs from meaning is not made clear. With regard to these synonyms Saussure notes that, if one of them were to disappear, its contents would be divided among the remaining terms. It is difficult to see what "contents" might be, if it is not meaning. Value undoubtedly attempts to define what we would today call polysemy and connotation. For our purposes, the essential here is that, in defining value, Saussure is searching for a way to define the multiple relationships that signs maintain with other signs; that signs have meaning only in function of their relation to other signs; and that signifieds have conceptual value only in terms of their differential relationship to other signifieds. As part of the autonomous system of differences that make up the semantic dimension of language, the notion of value suggests that there is no intrinsic bond between reality and language. There is no necessary relationship between the so-called continuum of experience and those conceptual fields that organize what we take to be reality.

These comments do not intend to place Saussure in the same camp with those thinkers, such as Whorf and Sapir, who claim that language conditions the way we perceive reality. Rather, it seems to me that the social emphasis in Saussure's thought would better lead one to conclude that value represents the multiple ways a given culture, through its language, organizes its experience of the world. In this sense language articulates a societally shared world and, in terms not unlike Wittgenstein's, a culturally determined sense of reality. This interpretation finds support in Saussure's declaration that "the community is necessary if values that owe their existence solely to usage and general acceptance are to be established." The view that society articulates its world through language means that values are far more than a passive taxonomy reflecting whatever is exterior to language. In an active sense values are a priori articulations, or as Saussure put it in a letter: "As one progressively gets deeper into the material that is offered to linguistic study, one is increasingly convinced that the links that are established among things pre-exist, in this area, things themselves and that they serve to determine them." Parallels one can establish with both Wittgenstein and Heidegger reveal in this regard a larger consensus about language, a consensus that defines how we think about language today. To speak of the play of differences articulating a world points to analogies with Heidegger; whereas to comment on the a priori articulation by a language of a culture's reality is to offer a summary of Wittgenstein's thought.

In his discussion of system, difference, and value Saussure also uses the metaphor of play that Wittgenstein and Heidegger, in their comparable ways, used to explain the nature of language. When a future historian undertakes the project of explaining our contemporary fascination with chess, he will have to add Saussure to that list of thinkers and writers who have placed the square board in the limelight of our intellectual and creative concerns. Play, and especially chess, has become an almost obsessive leitmotif of the postmodern mind. For his part Saussure sees chess as the most elucidating metaphor he can offer to explain the linguistic system. With regard to the basic notion of system, for example, he insists that one must distinguish between that order of facts that is intrinsic (*interne*) to the linguistic system and that order of facts that is extrinsic (*externe*) to it. This distinction can be explained by comparison with the intrinsic system that makes up the game of chess:

> The fact that it [chess] came from Persia to Europe is an extrinsic matter; everything that concerns its system and rules is, on the other hand, intrinsic. If I replace wooden chessmen with ivory chessmen, the change is a matter of indifference for the system; but if I reduce or increase the number of pieces, this change profoundly affects the "grammar" of the game.

In proposing the comparison of language with a finite game-set, the chess metaphor also stresses that an analogy is to be drawn between grammar and a rule-bound type of behavior such as play. The metaphor elucidates, moreover, the structural view of language according to which all entities or minimal pertinent units are to be identified strictly on the basis of their position within the system. And it again shows that the various material realizations of language are secondary to its structure as a *langue*.

Saussure uses the chess metaphor to throw light on practically every other aspect of language; he is quite as enthusiastic about the game as Wittgenstein. Consider the distinction between the diachronic and synchronic realms. In likening historical change and fixed states to the moves in a chess match, Saussure claims that any given move in the game brings about a new fixed state that corresponds to the synchronic system at any given moment. After each diachronic change, after each move, the respective value of each piece in the game, or linguistic system, depends on the position of the piece on the board, much as in language each entity has value through its differential relation opposing it to all other terms in the system. And as in language, each fixed moment is only temporary; subsequent moves are inevitable.

Saussure recognizes that chess moves are intentional and that diachrony is unintentional; for diachronic change is irrational. Perhaps he should have also recognized anoth-

er limitation. For Saussure, in using the chess metaphor to explain the nature of value, asserts that value in the system depends on an unchanging convention, that is, the rules of the game. These rules are unchanged by any given move and are the same before and after the game. It is misleading, however, to say that value can depend on immutable rules, since values, surely, can change as semantic shifts occur diachronically. To use the admittedly weak sheep-*mouton* example, there is no reason why we should not someday eat "sheep chops" as signs come to divide up semantic fields in a different manner. The history of any language is in part a history of the way words or signs have given up or acquired new values.

The chess analogy works well to elaborate the problem of identifying the entities that make up the system. In another comparison, which also throws light on the nature of value, Saussure asks us to consider the example of a chess knight. Can its material aspect—say, a plastic representation of a medieval knight—be considered an element in the game's system:

> Assuredly not, since in its pure materiality, taken outside its square and the other conditions of the game, the piece represents nothing for the player and can only become a real and concrete element once it has taken on its value and embodied it. Let us suppose that in the course of a game this piece happened to be lost or destroyed; can one replace it with another, equivalent one? Certainly, not only with another knight, but even a figure having no resemblance with it at all can be declared identical, provided it is given the same value. One can thus see that in semiological systems, such as language, in which the elements are held reciprocally in equilibrium according to determined rules, the notion of identity overlaps that of value and vice versa.

This comparison could support the contention that, in a Wittgensteinian perspective, the identity of a sign is given by its use. Value would then be the sign's grammar—or the rules of the language game. I should not wish to push this analogy too far, since Saussure's comparison with a chess knight is designed to clarify the nature of the linguistic system, the *langue,* and not the *parole.* The analogy points, nonetheless, to important convergences between these two thinkers, which in turn point to how thought about play organizes much of what we think we can do with language today. Perhaps most important with regard to play is that, for both Saussure and Wittgenstein, meaning or value is determined by a relation within the game space of language itself, not by some relation to an exterior realm.

Saussure buttresses his analysis with other analogies between chess and the linguistic system. Just as chess moves involve only single chessmen, so language changes involve only isolated elements, not the entire system. Each move, or diachronic shift, can have a different effect on the entire system, ranging from no effect to an enormous influence. Each moving of a piece, like each change in the linguistic system, creates a new state that is entirely distinct from any preceding static equilibrium that existed or that will subsequently exist. These comparisons underscore the fact that for Saussure, as for Wittgenstein and Heidegger, the game analogy is far more than a mere rhetorical comparison. To paraphrase Johan Huizinga, viewing language *sub specie ludi* is the beginning of a way of integrating language into a different, perhaps more complete way of viewing the relation between language and culture. At the same time, this metaphor assures the autonomy of language by making it—like a chessboard—a self-enclosed space within which an indefinite number of rule-bound permutations can take place.

The chess metaphor is also motivated in Saussure by a recurrent desire to translate the notion of system into a geometric or algebraic set of operations. We have already seen this desire at work in the geometric spatialization underlying the distinction of meaning and value. The same attempt to offer a geometric model is found in the final pair of binary oppositions that describe the linguistic system. This pair is of particular relevance for throwing light on later attitudes toward voice in fiction, and I shall therefore give a fairly detailed discussion of their function. Saussure calls this binary pair the associative and the syntagmatic relations of language, though today the term "paradigmatic" has replaced "associative." These relations are again to be conceived of in terms of the relations of a vertical and a horizontal axis (on the model of a Cartesian coordinate system). The syntagmatic axis is the horizontal axis, or the linear flow of elements that combine as speech takes place:

> In discourse . . . words acquire relations, in virtue of their being chained together, based on the linear nature of language, which excludes the possibility of two elements being said at the same time. These elements are arranged one after the other along the chain of speech. These combinations which use linear extension for their support are called syntagms. The syntagm is always composed of two or more consecutive units (for example: re-read; against everyone; human life; God is good; if the weather is nice, we'll go out; etc.).

The syntagmatic axis defines the unfolding linear flow of differences in which every term, at every level of analysis, acquires value through its opposition "to whatever precedes or what follows, or both." Phonemes, morphemes (the smallest units of signification), and what Saussure calls larger "organized masses" (such as the phrases above) are defined by their opposition to comparable units along the horizontal axis.

The system's geometry includes a vertical axis, or a vertical order of relations constituted outside of speech or actualized discourse. Consisting in all the possible elements that could appear on the horizontal axis, this vertical relation, existing *in absentia* as Saussure says, makes up the paradigmatic axis. This axis stands in a vertical relationship to each point of the horizontal chain. At each point of the syntagmatic axis an opposition occurs between what is actually said and all the elements that could have been said at the point. The vertical axis forms a virtual opposition between what is actualized and what could have been actualized. According to Saussure the meaning of any element derives from this virtual opposition. For example,

when I say the syntagm "I see," the pronoun "I" derives its meaning from its opposition to all the units—nouns and pronouns, in traditional terms—that might replace the first person singular "I," such as "we," "you," "it," "Howard," etc. Syntagmatic relations actualize themselves in speech; they are nonetheless composed mainly of codified elements that make up the *langue* or linguistic system. The locus of paradigmatic relations would also appear to be the *langue,* for they are found in "the inner storehouse that makes up the language of each speaker."

There are a good many problems involved in this kind of axial geometry, especially with the notion that paradigmatic oppositions exist, like syntagmatic combinations, at all levels of linguistic analysis. Phonology is a closed system, which allows one to identify and describe the codification of permissible combinations and the virtual oppositions that exist when a combination is actualized. The "p" of "pet" stands in virtual opposition of the "m" of "met" as a possible actualization in English. "Mwz" stands in opposition to nothing, since this actualization is not part of the system of possible phonemic combinations in English. In morphemic analysis the "re" of "redo" stands in opposition to the "un" of "undo," while it bears an associative relation to the "re" of "remake." Its meaning depends on both an oppositional and an associative relation. But in the case of the "I" of "I write," it is difficult to see how the indefinite number of possible oppositions, with no associative relations, enters into the genesis of meaning. The problem redoubles when one considers entire syntagms such as those given by Saussure in the quotation above. Such problems notwithstanding, this kind of analysis has brought about an extraordinary self-consciousness with regard to the limits of expressing original meaning in language. (pp. 63-81)

Allen Thiher, "Ferdinand de Saussure and Jacques Derrida," in his Words in Reflection: Modern Language Theory and Postmodern Fiction, *The University of Chicago Press, 1984, pp. 63-90.*

John T. Waterman on Saussure's contributions to language studies:

Saussure stands at the beginning of the twentieth century as one of the greatest theoretical linguists of our era. There are, of course, many who do not accept his mechanistic explanation of linguistic change, nor is it possible in practice to adhere to a complete separation of his diachronic and synchronic phases of investigation. His great service to linguistics, though, is that he laid the theoretical basis for an objective, controllable method of analyzing language. His *Cours de Linguistique Générale* is still an indispensable text to the student who is interested not only in the techniques of language investigation, but also in the origin and evolvement of modern linguistic theory.

John T. Waterman, in his "Ferdinand de Saussure— Forerunner of Modern Structuralism," in The Modern Language Journal, *April 1956.*

Jonathan Culler (essay date 1986)

[*An American critic and educator, Culler has written
extensively on structuralism, deconstructionism, and
postmodernism. In the following excerpt, taken from the
revised edition of his critically acclaimed monograph*
Ferdinand de Saussure, *which was originally published
in 1976, Culler examines the basic tenets of Saussurean
linguistics.*]

Ferdinand de Saussure is the founder of modern linguistics, the man who reorganized the systematic study of language and languages so as to make possible the achievements of twentieth-century linguistics. This alone makes
him worth studying, but he has other claims to our attention as well.

First, together with his two great contemporaries, Emile
Durkheim in sociology and Sigmund Freud in psychology, he helped to set the study of human behavior on a new
footing. These three thinkers realized that one could not
approach an adequate understanding of human practices
and institutions if one treated human behavior as a series
of events similar to events in the physical world. A scientist can study the behavior of objects under certain conditions, such as the trajectories of projectiles fired at different angles and velocities, or the reactions of a chemical
substance to a variety of temperatures. She can describe
what happens and try to explain why without paying any
attention to ordinary people's impressions or ideas about
these matters. But human behavior is different. When
studying human behavior the investigator cannot simply
dismiss as subjective impressions the meaning behavior
has for members of a society. If people see an action as im-
polite, that is a crucial fact, a social fact. To ignore the
meanings actions and objects have in a society would be
to study mere physical events. Anyone analyzing human
behavior is concerned not with events themselves but with
events that have meaning.

Saussure, Freud, and Durkheim also saw that the study
of human behavior misses its best opportunities if it tries
to trace the historical causes of individual events. Instead,
it must focus on the functions events have within a general
social framework. It must treat social facts as part of a system of conventions and values. What are the values and
conventions which enable people to live in society, to communicate with one another, and generally to behave as
they do? If one tries to answer these questions, the result
is a discipline very different from one which replies to
questions about the historical causes of various events.
Saussure and his two contemporaries established the su-
premacy of this type of investigation, which looks for an
underlying system rather than individual causes, and they
thus made possible a fuller and more apposite study of
human experience.

Second, by his methodological example and various prophetic suggestions, Saussure helped to promote semiotics,
the general science of signs and systems of signs, and
structuralism, an important trend in contemporary anthropology and literary criticism as well as in linguistics.
The revival of interest in Saussure in the past few years is
largely due to the fact that he has been the inspiration for
semiotics and structuralism as well as for structural linguistics.

Third, in his methodological remarks and general approach to language Saussure gives us a clear expression of
what we might call the formal strategies of Modernist
thought: the ways in which scientists, philosophers, artists, and writers working in the early part of this century
tried to come to terms with a complex and chaotic universe. How does one cope, systematically, with the apparent chaos of the modern world? This question was being
asked in a variety of fields, and the replies which Saussure
gives—that you cannot hope to attain an absolute or God-
like view of things but must choose a perspective, and that
within this perspective objects are defined by their relations with one another, rather than by essences of some
kind—are exemplary. Saussure enables us to grasp with
unusual clarity the strategies of Modernist thought.

Finally, Saussure's treatment of language focuses on problems which are central to new ways of thinking about the
human subject, and especially about the intimate relation
between language and mind. If "man" is indeed the "language animal," a creature whose dealings with the world
are characterized by the structuring and differentiating
operations that are most clearly manifested in human language, then it is Saussure who set us on his track. When
we speak of the human tendency to organize things into
systems by which meaning can be transmitted, we place
ourselves in what is very much a Saussurian line of
thought.

These contributions—to linguistics, to the social sciences
generally, to semiotics and structuralism, to Modernist
thought, and to our conception of human beings—make
Saussure a seminal figure in modern intellectual history,
and this book must range widely over linguistics, semiotics, philosophy, and the social sciences if it is to define
Saussure's importance. But paradoxically, Saussure himself wrote nothing of general significance. A book on the
vowel system of early Indo-European language, a doctoral
thesis on the use of the genitive case in Sanskrit, and a
handful of technical papers are all that he ever published.
Nor did he leave behind a rich hoard of unpublished writings. His influence, both within and beyond linguistics, is
based on something he never wrote. Between 1907 and
1911, as professor at the University of Geneva, he gave
three courses of lectures on general linguistics. After his
death, in 1913, his students and colleagues decided that
his teachings should not be lost and constructed out of
various sets of lecture notes a volume entitled ***Cours de
linguistique générale***—a course in general linguistics. (pp.
15-18)

[Whatever] Saussure's general significance for modern
thought—and it is considerable—he himself was first and
foremost, perhaps even exclusively, a linguist, a student of
language. Someone who knows Saussure only by reputation, as the founder of modern linguistics, promoter of a
new conception of language, and inspiration for anthropologists and literary critics, might expect to find the
Course in General Linguistics a book full of broad gener-
alizations, portentous observations about the nature of
language and mind, elaborate and eloquent theories about

social and communicative behavior. In fact, nothing could be further from the truth. What strikes one most forcibly in the *Course* is Saussure's active and scrupulous concern for the foundations of his subject.

His concern with the nature of language and the foundations of linguistics takes the form of a questioning of the assumptions we make when we talk about language. For example, if you make a noise and at some other time I make a noise, under what conditions would we be justified in saying that we had uttered the same words? Such questions may seem trivial. One might be tempted to reject them as pointless quibbling, arguing that we simply *know* whether two people have uttered the same words or not. But the point is, how do we know? What is involved in knowing this? For whatever is involved is part of our knowledge of language, our knowledge of the units of that language. Such questions are far from trivial. If we are to analyze a language we must be able to form a clear and coherent idea of the units or elements of that language. If, for example, we are to think of the "word" as a unit of language, then we must know how we determine that two people have uttered the same word, though the actual physical sounds they made were different.

Saussure asks fundamental and probing questions that linguists before him had failed to ask, and he provides answers that have revolutionized the way language is studied. Though the solutions and definitions he offers might initially seem of interest only to students of linguistics, they have direct bearing on the fundamental problems of what the French call the "human sciences": the disciplines that deal with the world of meaningful objects and actions (as opposed to physical objects and events themselves). Saussure's reflections on the sign and on sign-systems pave the way for a general study of the ways in which human experience is organized.

This wider significance is doubtless of greater interest to readers of this book than debates about the precise nature of Saussure's distinctions and linguistic categories, and therefore discussion in the following chapters will always aim toward larger issues. But if we are to grasp the radical implications of Saussure's ideas we must follow the logic of his argument in some detail. We must go back, with Saussure, to first principles and ask elementary questions about human language, about the nature of the sign, about the identity of units of a language. We must begin by exploring Saussure's theory of language. (pp. 18-19)

Saussure was unhappy with linguistics as he knew it because he thought that his predecessors had failed to think seriously or perceptively about what they were doing. Linguistics, he wrote, "never attempted to determine the nature of the object it was studying, and without this elementary operation a science cannot develop an appropriate method."

This operation is all the more necessary because human language is an extremely complex and heterogeneous phenomenon. Even a single speech act involves an extraordinary range of factors and could be considered from many different, even conflicting points of view. One could study the way sounds are produced by the mouth, vocal chords,

and tongue; one could investigate the sound waves that are emitted and the way they affect the hearing mechanism. One could consider the signifying intention of the speaker, the aspects of the world to which his utterance refers, the immediate circumstances of the communicative context that might have led him to produce a particular series of noises. One might try to analyze the conventions that enable speaker and listeners to understand one another, working out the grammatical and semantic rules that they must have assimilated if they are to communicate in this way. Or again, one could trace the history of the language that makes available these particular forms at this time.

Confronted with all these phenomena and these different perspectives from which one might approach them, the linguist must ask what one is trying to describe. What in particular is one looking at or looking for? What, in short, is language?

Saussure's answer to this question is unexceptionable but extremely important, since it serves to direct attention to essentials. Language is a system of signs. Noises count as language only when they serve to express or communicate ideas; otherwise they are just noise. And for noises to express or communicate ideas they must be part of a system of conventions that relate noises to ideas. They must, in other words, be part of a system of signs. The sign is the union of a form which signifies, which Saussure calls the *signifiant* (signifier), and an idea signified, the *signifié* (signified). Though we may speak of signifier and signified as if they were separate entities, they exist only as components of the sign. The sign is the central fact of language, and therefore in trying to separate what is essential from what is secondary or incidental we must start from the nature of the sign itself, its primary characteristics.

The first principle of Saussure's theory of language concerns the essential quality of the sign. The linguistic sign is arbitrary. A particular combination of signifier and signified is an arbitrary entity. This enigmatic principle, if properly understood, is central to one's conception of language and linguistic method.

> No one contests the principle of the arbitrary nature of the sign, but it is often easier to discover a truth than to assign it its rightful place. The above principle dominates the whole of linguistic analysis of a language. Its consequences are innumerable, though they are not all, it is true, equally evident right away. It is after many detours that one discovers them, and with them the fundamental importance of this principle. (*Course*)

What does Saussure mean by the arbitrary nature of the sign? In one sense the answer is quite simple. There is no natural or inevitable link between the signifier and the signified. Since I speak English I may use the signifier represented by *dog* to talk about an animal of a particular species, but this sequence of sounds is no better suited to that purpose than another sequence. *Lod, tet,* or *bloop* would serve equally well if it were accepted by members of my speech community. There is no intrinsic reason why one of these signifiers rather than another should be linked with the concept of a "dog." (Note that here, as throughout, I use italics to cite linguistic forms [e.g., *dog, lod*] and quotation marks to designate meanings [e.g., "dog"].)

Are there no exceptions to this basic principle? Certainly. There are two ways in which linguistic signs may be motivated, that is to say, made less arbitrary. First, there are cases of onomatopoeia, where the sound of the signifier seems in some way mimetic or imitative, as in the English *bow-wow* or *arf-arf.* But there are few such cases, and the fact that we identify them as a separate class and special case only emphasizes more strongly that ordinary signs are arbitrary.

However, within a particular language, signs may be partially motivated in a different way. The machine on which I am writing is called a *typewriter.* There is no intrinsic reason why it should not be called a *grue* or a *blimmel,* but, within English, *typewriter* is motivated because the meanings of the two sound sequences which compose its signifier, *type* and *writer,* are related to its signified, to the notion of a "typewriter." We might call this "secondary motivation." Notice, for example, that only in English is the relation between this sound sequence and the concept motivated. If the French were to use the same form to speak of this machine, that would be a wholly arbitrary sign, since the primary constituent, *writer* is not a sign in the French language. Moreover, for Saussure, as we shall see, the process of combining *type* and *writer* to create a new motivated sign is fundamentally similar to the way in which we combine words to form a phrase (whose meaning is related to the combined meanings of individual words). We can say, therefore, that languages have as their basic elements arbitrary signs. They then have various processes for combining these signs, but that does not alter the essential nature of language and its elementary constituents.

The sign is arbitrary in that there is no intrinsic link between signifier and signified. This is how Saussure's principle is usually interpreted, but in this form it is a wholly traditional notion, a rather obvious fact about language. Interpreted in this limited way, it does not have the momentous consequences which, according to the students' notes, Saussure repeatedly claimed for it: "the hierarchical place of this truth is at the very summit. It is only little by little that one recognizes how many different facts are but ramifications, hidden consequences of this truth." There is more to the arbitrary nature of the sign than the arbitrary relation between signifier and signified. We must push further.

From what I have said so far about signifier and signified, one might be tempted to think of language as a nomenclature: a series of names arbitrarily selected and attached to a set of objects or concepts. It is, Saussure says, all too easy to think of language as a set of names and to make the biblical story of Adam naming the beasts an account of the very nature of language. If one says that the concept "dog" is rendered or expressed by *dog* in English, *chien* in French, and *Hund* in German, one implies that each language has an arbitrary name for a concept that exists prior to and independently of any language.

If language were simply a nomenclature for a set of univer-

sal concepts, it would be easy to translate from one language to another. One would simply replace the French name for a concept with the English name. If language were like this, the task of learning a new language would also be much easier than it is. But anyone who has attempted either of these tasks has acquired, alas, a vast amount of direct proof that languages are not nomenclatures, that the concepts or signifieds of one language may differ radically from those of another. The French "aimer" does not go directly into English; one must choose between "to like" and "to love." . . . Or again, what English calls "light blue" and "dark blue" and treats as two shades of a single color are in Russian two distinct primary colors. Each language articulates or organizes the world differently. Languages do not simply name existing categories; they articulate their own.

Moreover, if language were a set of names applied to independently existing concepts, then in the historical evolution of a language the concepts should remain stable. Signifiers could evolve; the particular sequence of sounds associated with a given concept might be modified; and a given sequence of sounds could be attached to a different concept. Occasionally, of course, a new sign would have to be introduced for a new concept which had been produced by changes in the world. But the concepts themselves, as language-independent entities, would not be subject to linguistic evolution. In fact, though, the history of languages is full of examples of concepts shifting, changing their boundaries. The English word *cattle,* for example, at one point meant property in general, then gradually came to be restricted to four-footed property (a new category), and finally attained its modern sense of domesticated bovines. Or again, a "silly" person was once happy, blessed, and pious. Gradually this particular concept altered; the old concept of "silliness" transformed itself, and by the beginning of the sixteenth century a silly person was innocent, helpless, even deserving of pity. The alteration of the concept continued until, eventually, a silly person was simple, foolish, perhaps even stupid.

If language were a nomenclature we should be obliged to say that there exist a number of distinct concepts and that the signifier *silly* was attached first to one and then to another. But clearly this is not what happened: the concept attached to the signifier *silly* was continually shifting its boundaries, gradually changing its semantic shape, articulating the world in different ways from one period to the next. And, incidentally, the signifier also evolved, undergoing a modification of its central vowel.

What is the significance of this? What does it have to do with the arbitrary nature of the sign? Language is not a nomenclature and therefore its signifieds are not pre-existing concepts but changeable and contingent concepts which vary from one state of a language to another. And since the relation between signifier and signified is arbitrary, since there is no necessary reason for one concept rather than another to be attached to a given signifier, there is therefore no defining property which the concept must retain in order to count as the signified of that signifier. The signified associated with a signifier can take any form; there is no essential core of meaning that it must retain in order to count as the proper signified for that signifier. The fact that the relation between signifier and signified is arbitrary means, then, that since there are no fixed universal concepts or fixed universal signifiers, the signified itself is arbitrary, and so is the signifier. We then must ask, as Saussure does, what defines a signifier or a signified, and the answer leads us to a very important principle: both signifier and signified are purely relational or differential entities. Because they are arbitrary they are relational. This is a principle that requires explanation.

Saussure attaches great importance—more so than it would appear from the published *Course*—to the fact that language is not a nomenclature, for unless we grasp this we cannot understand the full ramifications of the arbitrary nature of the sign. A language does not simply assign arbitrary names to a set of independently existing concepts. It sets up an arbitrary relation between signifiers of its own choosing on the one hand, and signifieds of its own choosing on the other. Not only does each language produce a different set of signifiers, articulating and dividing the continuum of sound in a distinctive way, but each language produces a different set of signifieds; it has a distinctive and thus "arbitrary" way of organizing the world into concepts or categories.

It is obvious that the sound sequences of *fleuve* and *rivière* are signifiers of French but not of English, whereas *river* and *stream* are English but not French. Less obviously, but more significantly, the organization of the conceptual plane is also different in English and French. The signified "river" is opposed to "stream" solely in terms of size, whereas a "fleuve" differs from a "rivière" not because it is necessarily larger but because it flows into the sea, while a "rivière" does not. In short, "fleuve" and "rivière" are not signifieds or concepts of English. They represent a different articulation of the conceptual plane.

The fact that these two languages operate perfectly well with different conceptual articulations or distinctions indicates that these divisions are not natural, inevitable, or necessary, but, in an important sense, arbitrary. Obviously it is important that a language have ways of talking about flowing bodies of water, but it can make its conceptual distinctions in this area in any of a wide variety of ways (size, swiftness of flow, straightness or sinuosity, direction of flow, depth, navigability, etc.). Not only can a language arbitrarily choose its signifiers; it can divide up a spectrum of conceptual possibilities in any way it likes.

Moreover, and here we come to an important point, the fact that these concepts, or signifieds, are arbitrary divisions of a continuum means that they are not autonomous entities, each of which is defined by some kind of essence. They are members of a system and are defined by their relations to the other members of that system. If I am to explain to someone the meaning of *stream* I must discuss the difference between a stream and a river, a stream and a rivulet, and so on. And, similarly, I cannot explain the French concept of a "rivière" without describing the distinction between "rivière" and "fleuve" on the one hand, and "rivière" and "ruisseau" on the other. (pp. 27-34)

In other words, it is the distinctions which are important,

and it is for this reason that linguistic units have a purely relational identity. The principle is not easy to grasp, but Saussure offers a concrete analogy. We are willing to grant that in an important sense the 8:25 Geneva-to-Paris Express is the same train each day, even though the coaches, locomotive, and personnel change from one day to the next. What gives the train its identity is its place in the system of trains, as indicated by the timetable. And note that this relational identity is indeed the determining factor: the train remains the same train even if it leaves a half-hour late. In fact, it might always leave late without ceasing to be the 8:25 Geneva-to-Paris Express. What is important is that it be distinguished from, say, the 10:25 Geneva-to-Paris Express, the 8:40 Geneva-to-Dijon Local, and so on.

Another analogy Saussure uses to illustrate the notion of relational identity is the comparison between language and chess. The basic units of chess are obviously king, queen, rook, knight, bishop, and pawn. The actual physical shape of the pieces and the material from which they are made is of no importance. The king may be of any size and shape, as long as there are ways of distinguishing it from other pieces. The two rooks need not be of identical size and shape, so long as they can be distinguished from other pieces. Thus, as Saussure points out, if a piece is lost from a chess set we can replace it with any other sort of object, provided always that this object will not be confused with the objects representing pieces of a different value. The actual physical properties of pieces are of no importance, so long as there are differences of some kind—any kind will do—between pieces which have a different value.

Thus one can say that the units of the game of chess have no material identity: there are no physical properties necessary to a king or pawn. Identity is wholly a function of differences within a system. If we now apply the analogy to language we shall be in a position to understand Saussure's paradoxical claim that in the system of a language "there are only differences, with no positive terms." Normally, when we think of differences we presuppose two things that differ, but Saussure's point is that signifier and signified are not things in this sense. Just as we cannot say anything about what a pawn must look like, except that it will be different from knight, rook, and so on, so the signifier which we represent as *bed* is not defined by any particular noises used in uttering it. Not only do the actual noises differ from one case to another, but English could be arranged so that noises now used to express the signifier *pet* were used for the signifier *bed,* and vice versa. If these changes were made, the units of the language would be expressed differently; but they would still be fundamentally the same units (the same differences remain, both on the level of the signifier and on the level of the signified), and the language would still be English. Indeed, English would remain, in an important sense, the same language if the units of the signifier were never expressed in sound but only in visual symbols of some kind.

In saying this I am obviously making a distinction between units of the linguistic system and their actual physical manifestations or realizations. Before discussing this very important distinction in greater detail, it may be useful to recapitulate the line of reasoning that led to it. We began by noting that there was no natural link between signifier and signified, and then, trying to explain the arbitrary nature of the linguistic sign, we saw that both signifier and signified were arbitrary divisions or delimitations of a continuum (a sound spectrum on the one hand and a conceptual field on the other). This led us to infer that both signifier and signified must be defined in terms of their relations with other signifiers and signifieds, and thus we reached the conclusion that if we are to define the units of a language, we must distinguish between these purely relational and abstract units and their physical realizations. The actual sounds we produce in speaking are not in themselves units of the linguistic system, nor is the physical color which we designate in calling a book "brown" the same thing as the linguistic unit (the signified, or concept) "brown." In both cases, and this is a point on which Saussure rightly insists, the linguistic unit is form rather than substance, defined by the relations that set it off from other units.

Here, in the distinction between the linguistic system and its actual manifestations, we have reached the crucial opposition between *langue* and *parole*. *La langue* is the system of a language, the language as a system of forms, whereas *parole* is actual speech, the speech acts that are made possible by the language. *La langue* is what individuals assimilate when they learn a language, a set of forms or "hoard deposited by the practice of speech in speakers who belong to the same community, a grammatical system which, to all intents and purposes, exists in the mind of each speaker." "It is the social product whose existence permits the individual to exercise his linguistic faculty." *Parole,* on the other hand, is the "executive side of language," and for Saussure involves both "the combinations by which the speaker uses the code of the linguistic system in order to express his own thoughts" and "the psychophysical mechanisms which permit him to externalize these combinations." In the act of *parole* the speaker selects and combines elements of the linguistic system and gives these forms a concrete phonic and psychological manifestation, as sounds and meanings.

If these remarks on *parole* seem somewhat confusing it is because they contain a problem, to which we shall return. If the combination of linguistic elements belongs to *parole,* then syntactic rules have an ambiguous status. To make *la langue* a system of forms and *parole* the combination and externalization of these forms is not quite the same as making *langue* the linguistic faculty and *parole* the exercise of that faculty, for the linguistic faculty includes knowledge of how to combine elements, rules of combination. This latter distinction, between *langue* as system and *parole* as realization, is the more fundamental, both in Saussure and in the Saussurian tradition. However, it is not essential to define here the specific characteristics of *parole,* since, as Saussure makes clear, the principal and strategic function of the distinction between *langue* and *parole* is to isolate the object of linguistic investigation. *La langue,* Saussure argued, must be the linguist's primary concern. What one is trying to do in analyzing a language is not to describe speech acts but to determine the units

and rules of combination which make up the linguistic system. *La langue,* or the linguistic system, is a coherent, analyzable object; "it is a system of signs in which the only essential thing is the union of meanings and acoustic images." In studying language as a system of signs, one is trying to identify its essential features: those elements which are crucial to the signifying function of language or, in other words, the elements which are functional within the system in that they create signs by distinguishing them one from another.

The distinction between *langue* and *parole* thus provides a principle of relevance for linguistics. "In separating *langue* from *parole,*" Saussure writes, "we are separating what is social from what is individual and what is essential from what is ancillary or accidental." If we tried to study everything related to the phenomenon of speech we would enter a realm of confusion where relevance and irrelevance were extremely difficult to determine; but if we concentrate on *la langue,* then various aspects of language and speech fall into place within or around it. Once we put forward this notion of the linguistic system, then we can ask of every phenomenon whether it belongs to the system itself or is simply a feature of the performance or realization of linguistic units, and we thus succeed in classifying speech facts into groups in which they can profitably be studied.

For example, the distinction between *langue* and *parole* leads to the creation of two distinct disciplines that study sound and its linguistic functions: phonetics, which studies sound in speech acts from a physical point of view, and phonology, which is not interested in physical events themselves but in the distinctions between the abstract units of the signifier which are functional within the linguistic system. (It is important to note here that although Saussure states unequivocally that physical sounds themselves are not part of *la langue* and thus paves the way for the distinction between phonetics and phonology as defined above, he himself uses the terms *phonetics* and *phonology* in a very different sense. I shall continue to use them in the modern sense defined here.)

The distinction between phonetics and phonology takes us back to points made earlier about the linguistic identity of the form *bed.* Phonetics would describe the actual sounds produced when one utters the form, but, as we argued above, the identity of *bed* as a unit of English does not depend on the nature of these actual sounds but on the distinctions which separate *bed* from *bet, bad, head,* etc. Phonology is the study of these functional distinctions, and "functional" is what should be stressed here. For example, in English utterances there is a perceptible and measurable difference between the "l-sound" that occurs before vowels (as in *lend* or *alive*) and that which occurs before consonants or at the end of words (as in *melt or peel*). This is a real phonetic difference, but it is not a difference ever used to distinguish between two signs. It is not a functional difference and therefore is not a part of the phonological system of English. On the other hand, the difference between the vowels of *feel* and *fill* is used in English to distinguish signs (compare *keel* and *kill, keen* and *kin, seat* and *sit, heat* and *hit,* and the like). This opposition plays a very important role in the phonological system of English in that it creates a large number of distinct signs.

The same distinction between what belongs to particular linguistic acts and what belongs to the linguistic system itself is important at other levels too, not just that of sound. We can distinguish, for example, between utterance, as a unit of *parole,* and sentence, a unit of *la langue.* Two different utterances may be manifestations of the same sentence; so once again we encounter this central notion of identity in linguistics. The actual sounds and the contextual meanings of the two utterances will be different; what makes the two utterances instances of a single linguistic unit will be the distinctions which give that unit a relational identity. (pp. 37-42)

Pronouns are obvious illustrations of the difference between meanings which pertain to utterances only, and meanings which pertain to elements of the linguistic system. To characterize this distinction Saussure uses the terms *signification* and *valeur* ("value"). Linguistic units have a value within the system, a meaning which is the result of the oppositions that define them; but when these units are used in an utterance, they have a signification, a contextual realization or manifestation of meaning. For example, if a French speaker says "J'ai vu un mouton" and an English speaker says "I saw a sheep" their utterances are likely to have the same signification; they are making the same claim about a state of affairs (namely, that at a time in the past the speaker saw a sheep). However, as units of their respective linguistic systems, *mouton* and *sheep* do not have the same meaning or value, for "sheep" is defined by an opposition with "mutton," whereas *"mouton"* is bounded by no such distinction but is used both for the animal and for the meat. There are certain philosophical problems here that Saussure did not tackle; in particular, philosophers would want to say that what Saussure calls the signification of an utterance involves both meaning and reference. But Saussure's point is that there is one kind of meaning, a relational meaning or value, which is based on the linguistic system, and another kind of meaning or signification which involves the use of linguistic elements in actual situations of utterance.

The distinction between *langue* and *parole* has important consequences for other disciplines besides linguistics, for it is essentially a distinction between institution and event, between the underlying system that makes possible various types of behavior and actual instances of such behavior. Study of the system leads to the construction of models that represent forms, their relations to one another, and their possibilities of combination, whereas study of actual behavior or events would lead to the construction of statistical models that represent the probabilities of particular combinations under various circumstances. (pp. 43-4)

Within linguistics itself, though, study of *la langue* involves an inventory of the distinctions that create signs and of rules of combination, whereas study of *parole* would lead to an account of language use, including the relative frequencies with which particular forms or combinations of forms were used in actual speech. By separating *langue* from *parole* Saussure gave linguistics a suitable object of study and thus a much clearer sense of what it was

doing: if one focused on language as a system, then one knew what one was trying to reconstruct and could, within this perspective, determine what evidence was relevant and how it should be organized.

We shall consider in more detail the structure of the linguistic system, but there is one point about the concept of *la langue* which should be stressed here. Saussure's editors organized the **Course** so that it began with the distinction between *langue* and *parole.* Saussure was thus portrayed as saying that language is a confused mass of heterogeneous facts, and the only way to make sense of it is to postulate the existence of something called the linguistic system and to set aside everything else. The distinction has thus seemed extremely questionable to many people: a postulate that had to be accepted on faith if one were to proceed. But in fact, as Saussure's notes suggest and as the sequence of argument which we have adopted here should have demonstrated, the distinction between *langue* and *parole* is a logical and necessary consequence of the arbitrary nature of the sign and the problem of identity in linguistics. In brief: if the sign is arbitrary then, as we have seen, it is a purely relational entity, and if we wish to define and identify signs we must look to the system of relations and distinctions which create them. We must therefore distinguish between the various substances in which signs are manifested and the actual forms which constitute signs; and when we do this what we have isolated is a system of forms which underlies actual linguistic behavior or manifestation. This system of forms is *la langue;* the attempt to study signs leads us, inexorably, to take this as the proper object of linguistic investigation. The isolation of *la langue* is not, as the published **Course** may suggest, an arbitrary point of departure but a consequence of the nature of signs themselves.

There is another important consequence of the arbitrary nature of the sign which has also been treated by Saussure's critics as a questionable and unnecessary imposition. This is the distinction between the *synchronic* study of language (study of the linguistic system in a particular state, without reference to time) and the *diachronic* study of language (study of its evolution in time). It has been suggested that in distinguishing rigorously between these two perspectives and in granting priority to the synchronic study of language, Saussure was ignoring, or at least setting aside, the fact that a language is fundamentally historical and contingent, an entity in constant evolution. But, on the contrary, it was precisely because he recognized, more profoundly than his critics, the radical historicity of language that he asserted the importance of distinguishing between facts about the linguistic system and facts about linguistic evolution, even in cases where the two kinds of facts seem extraordinarily intertwined. There is an apparent paradox here and it requires elucidation.

What is the connection between the arbitrary nature of the sign and the profoundly historical nature of language? We can put it in this way: if there were some essential or natural connection between signifier and signified, then the sign would have an essential core which would be unaffected by time or which at least would resist change. This unchanging essence could be opposed to those "accidental" features which did alter from one period to another. But, in fact, as we have seen, there is no aspect of the sign which is a necessary property and which therefore lies outside time. Any aspect of sound or meaning can alter; the history of languages is full of radical evolutionary alterations of both sound and meaning. . . . In short, neither signifier nor signified contains any essential core that time cannot touch. Because it is arbitrary, the sign is totally subject to history, and the combination at a particular moment of a given signifier and signified is a contingent result of the historical process.

The fact that the sign is arbitrary or wholly contingent makes it subject to history but also means that signs require an ahistorical analysis. This is not as paradoxical as it might seem. Since the sign has no necessary core that must persist, it must be defined as a relational entity, in its relations to other signs. And the relevant relations are those which obtain at a particular time. A language, Saussure says, "is a system of pure values which are determined by nothing except the momentary arrangement of its terms." Because the language is a wholly historical entity, always open to change, one must focus on the relations that exist in a particular synchronic state if one is to define its elements.

In asserting the priority of synchronic description, Saussure is pointing out the irrelevance of historical or diachronic facts to the analysis of *la langue*. Some examples will show why diachronic information is irrelevant. In modern English the second-person pronoun *you* is used to refer both to one person and to many and can be either the subject or object in a sentence. In an earlier state of the language, however, *you* was defined by its opposition to *ye* on the one hand (*ye* a subject pronoun and *you* an object pronoun) and to *thee* and *thou* on the other (*thee* and *thou* singular forms and *you* a plural form). At a later stage *you* came to serve also as a respectful way of addressing one person, like the modern French *vous*. Now in modern English *you* is no longer defined by its opposition to *ye, thee,* and *thou.* One can know and speak modern English perfectly without knowing that *you* was once a plural and objective form, and indeed, if one knows this, there is no way in which this knowledge can serve as part of one's knowledge of modern English. The description of modern English *you* would remain exactly the same if its historical evolution had been wholly different, for *you* in modern English is defined by its role in the synchronic state of the language. (pp. 44-7)

Saussure's insistence on the difference between synchronic and diachronic perspectives and on the priority of synchronic description does not mean, however, that he had deceived himself into thinking that language exists as a series of totally homogeneous synchronic states: English of 1920, English of 1940, English of 1960. In a sense, the notion of a synchronic state is a methodological fiction. When we talk about the linguistic system of French at a given time we are abstracting from a reality which consists of a very large number of native speakers, whose linguistic systems may differ in various ways. Nevertheless, the linguistic system of French is a definite reality, in that all these speakers understand one another, whereas someone

who speaks only English cannot understand them. Since we want to represent this fact and speak of the system which these native speakers have in common, we produce statements about the linguistic system in a particular synchronic state. (p. 48)

Saussure argues that despite their different status, diachronic statements are derived from synchronic statements. What allows us, he asks, to state the fact that Latin *mare* became French *mer* ("sea")? The historical linguist might argue that we know *mare* became *mer* because here, as elsewhere, the final *e* was dropped and *a* became *e*. But, Saussure argues, to suggest that these regular sound changes are what create the link between the two forms is to get things backward, because what enables us to identify this sound change is our initial notion that one form became the other. "We are using the correspondence between *mare* and *mer* to decide that *a* became *e* and that final *e* fell."

In fact, what we are supposing in connecting *mare* and *mer* is this: that *mare, mer,* and the intermediate forms constitute an unbroken chain of synchronic identities. At each period where, retrospectively, we can say that a change occurred, there was an old form and a new form which were phonetically different but phonologically or functionally identical. They may of course have had different associations (e.g., one form might have seemed a bit old-fashioned) but they could be used interchangeably by speakers. No doubt some would stick to the old form and others prefer the new, but since the move from one to the other would not produce a difference in actual meaning, from the point of view of the linguistic system there would be a synchronic identity between the two forms. It is in this sense that diachronic identity depends on a series of synchronic identities. (pp. 49-50)

[One] cannot argue that diachronic linguistics is in some way closer to the reality of language, while synchronic analysis is a fiction. Historical filiations are derived from synchronic identities. Not only that: they are facts of a different order. Synchronically speaking, diachronic identities are a distortion, for the earlier and later signs which they relate have no common properties. Each sign has no properties other than the specific relational properties which define it within its own synchronic system. From the point of view of systems of signs, which after all is the point of view that matters when dealing with signs, the earlier and later signs are wholly disparate.

Whence the importance of separating the synchronic and diachronic perspectives, even when the facts they are treating seem inextricably intertwined. This is a point one must stress, because linguists who oppose Saussure's radical distinction between synchronic and diachronic approaches and wish to envisage a synthetic, panchronic perspective, often point to the entanglement of synchronic and diachronic facts as if it supported their case. Saussure is all too aware of the intertwining of synchronic and diachronic facts; indeed, for him the whole difficulty is one of separating these elements when they are mixed, because only in this way can linguistic analysis attain coherence. Linguistic forms have synchronic and diachronic aspects which must be separated because they are facts of a different order, with different conditions of existence.

A panchronic synthesis is impossible, Saussure argues, because of the arbitrary nature of linguistic signs. In other sorts of systems, one might hold together the synchronic and diachronic perspectives: "insofar as a value is rooted in things themselves and in their natural relations, one can, to a certain extent, follow this value through time, bearing in mind that it depends at each moment on a system of values that coexist with it." Thus, the value of a piece of land at a given moment will depend on a great many other factors in the economic system, but the value is somewhat rooted in the nature of the land itself and variations will not involve simply the replacement of one arbitrary value by another. But in the case of language, where the value of a sign has no natural basis or inherent limits, historical change has a different character. Elements of a language, Saussure says, "are abandoned to their own historical evolution in a way that is wholly unknown in areas where forms have the smallest degree of natural connection with meaning." Since no signifier is naturally more suited to a signified than any other, sound change takes place independently of the system of values: "a diachronic fact is an event with its own rationale; the particular synchronic consequences which may follow from it are completely foreign to it."

Saussure's argument here is a complicated one. The claim is that diachronic facts are of a different order from synchronic facts in that historical change originates outside the linguistic system. Change originates in linguistic performance, in *parole,* not in *la langue,* and what is modified are individual elements of the system of realization. Historical changes affect the system in the end, in that the system will adjust to them, make use of the results of historical change, but it is not the linguistic system which produces them.

One thing Saussure is opposing here is the notion of teleology in linguistics: the idea that there is some end toward which linguistic changes are working and that they take place in order to achieve that end. Changes do not occur *in order to* produce a new state of the system. What happens is that "certain elements are altered without regard to their solidarity within the system as a whole." These isolated changes have general consequences for the system, in that its network of relations will be altered. However, "it is not that one system has produced another but that an element of the first has been changed, and that has sufficed to bring into existence another system." Changes are part of an independent evolutionary process to which the system adjusts.

A diachronic fact involves the displacement of one form by another. This displacement does not in itself have any significance; from the point of view of the linguistic system, it is nonfunctional. A synchronic fact is a relationship or opposition between two forms existing simultaneously: a relationship which is significant in that it carries meaning within the language. Whenever linguistic change has repercussions for the system, one will have a situation where both sorts of facts are mixed together and are easy to confuse. But they are very different and must be separated. (pp. 50-3)

Saussure urges the necessity of distinguishing the synchronic and diachronic perspectives in all cases, but his discussion treats only sound changes. Of course, the examples he discusses do have morphological and grammatical consequences within the system, and such readjustments may eventually have semantic consequences, but he never deals with the problem of semantic change itself, the diachronic alterations of signifieds. He admits, in passing, that once one leaves the plane of sound it becomes more difficult to maintain the absolute distinction between the synchronic and the diachronic; but the theory certainly enjoins one to do so, and one can make out a plausible though unfashionable case for the extension of the distinction to semantics. (p. 55)

The two major consequences of the arbitrary nature of the sign, which we have now explored, both point to a single fact, which may be considered the center of Saussure's theory of language: language is form, not substance. A language is a system of mutually related values, and to analyze the language is to set out the system of values which constitute a state of the language. As opposed to the positive phonic and signifying elements of speech acts, or *parole, la langue* is a system of oppositions or differences, and the task of the analyst is to discover what are these functional differences.

The basic problem, as we have followed Saussure in insisting, is that of linguistic identity. Nothing is given in linguistics. There are no positive, self-defined elements with which to start. In order to identify two instances of the same unit, we must construct a formal and relational entity by distinguishing between differences which are nonfunctional (and hence, for Saussure, nonlinguistic) and differences which are functional. Once we have identified the relations and oppositions which delimit signifiers on the one hand, and signifieds on the other, we have things we may speak of as positive entities, linguistic signs, though we must remember that they are entities which emerge from and depend on the network of differences that constitutes the linguistic system at a given time.

But, so far, in speaking of signs or linguistic units, it may sound as though we were speaking of words only, as if language consisted of nothing more than a vocabulary, organized according to phonological and semantic oppositions. Naturally language consists also of many grammatical relations and distinctions, but Saussure insists, in a passage that is worth quoting at length, that there is no fundamental difference between a linguistic unit and a grammatical fact. Their common nature is a result of the fact that signs are entirely differential objects and that what constitutes a linguistic sign (of whatever kind) is nothing but differences between signs.

"A rather paradoxical consequence of this principle is that, in the final analysis, what is commonly referred to as a 'grammatical fact' fits our definition of a linguistic unit." It is always expressed by an opposition between terms. Thus, in the case of the German opposition between *Nacht* ("night") and *Nächte* ("nights") it is the difference which carries grammatical meaning.

> Each of the terms present in the grammatical fact (the singular without umlaut and final *e,* as opposed to the plural with umlaut and final *e*) is itself the result of the interplay of oppositions within the system. Taken by itself, neither *Nacht* nor *Nächte* is anything; thus everything lies in the opposition. In other words, one could express the relationship between *Nacht* and *Nächte* by an algebraic formula *a/b,* where *a* and *b* are not simple terms but are themselves each the result of a set of oppositions. The linguistic system is, as it were, an algebra which contains only complex terms. Among its oppositions some are more significant than others, but "linguistic unit" and "grammatical fact" are only different names for designating aspects of the same general phenomenon: the play of linguistic oppositions. So true is this that we could approach the problem of linguistic units by starting with grammatical facts. Taking an opposition like *Nacht: Nächte,* we could ask what are the units involved in this opposition? Are they these two words only, or the whole series of similar words? or *a* and *ä,* or all singulars and plurals, and so forth?

Linguistic unit and grammatical fact would not be similar to one another if linguistic signs were made up of something besides differences. But the linguistic system being what it is, wherever one begins one will find nothing simple, but always and everywhere this same complex equilibrium of reciprocally defined or conditioned terms. In other words, language is a form and not a substance. One cannot steep oneself too deeply in this truth, for all the mistakes in our terminology, all our incorrect ways of designating aspects of language, come from this involuntary assumption that linguistic phenomena must have substance.

(pp. 57-9)

In studying a language, then, the linguist is concerned with relationships: identities and differences. One discovers, Saussure argues, two major types of relationship. On the one hand, there are those which we have so far been discussing: oppositions which produce distinct and alternative terms (*b* as opposed to *p; foot* as opposed to *feet*). On the other hand, there are the relations between units which combine to form sequences. In a linguistic sequence, a term's value depends not only on the contrast between it and the others that might have been chosen in its stead but also on its relations with the terms that precede and follow it in sequence. The former, which Saussure calls *associative* relations, are now generally called *paradigmatic* relations. The latter are called *syntagmatic* relations. Syntagmatic relations define combinatory possibilities: the relations between elements that might combine in a sequence. Paradigmatic relations are the oppositions between elements that can replace one another.

These relations hold at various levels of linguistic analysis. Thus, the phoneme /p/ in English is defined both by its opposition to other phonemes that could replace it in contexts such as /_et/ (cf. *bet, let, met, net, set*), and by its combinatory relations with other phonemes (it can pre-

cede or follow any vowel; within a syllable the liquids /l/ and /r/ are the only consonants that can follow it and /s/ the only one that can precede it).

At the level of morphology or word structure we also find both syntagmatic and paradigmatic relationships. A noun is partly defined by the combinations into which it can enter with prefixes and suffixes. Thus we have *friendless, friendly, friendliness, unfriendly, befriend, unbefriended, friendship, unfriendliness,* but not **disfriend, *friender, *friendation, *subfriend, *overfriend, *defriendize.* The combinatory possibilities represent syntagmatic relationships, and the paradigmatic relationships are to be found in the contrast between a given morpheme and those that could replace it in a given environment. Thus, there is paradigmatic contrast between *-ly, -less,* and *-ship* in that they can all occur after *friend,* and replacement of one by another brings a change in meaning. Similarly, *friend* has paradigmatic relations with *lecture, member, dictator, partner, professor,* and so on, in that they all contrast with one another in the environment ____ *ship.*

If we move up to the level of syntax proper, we can continue to identify the same types of relationship. The syntagmatic relations that define the constituent *he frightened* permit it to be followed by certain types of constituent only: *George, the man standing on the corner, thirty-one fieldmice,* etc.; but not *the stone, sincerity, purple, in,* etc. Our knowledge of syntagmatic relations enables us to define for *he frightened* a paradigmatic class of items that can follow it. These items are in paradigmatic contrast with one another, and to choose one is to produce meaning by excluding others.

Saussure claims that the entire linguistic system can be reduced to and explained in terms of a theory of syntagmatic and paradigmatic relations, and that in this sense all synchronic facts are fundamentally identical. This is perhaps the clearest assertion of what may be called the structuralist view of language: not simply that a language is a system of elements that are wholly defined by their relations to one another within the system, though it is that, but that the linguistic system consists of different levels of structure; at each level one can identify elements that contrast with one another and combine with other elements to form higher-level units, and the principles of structure at each level are fundamentally the same.

We can summarize and illustrate this view by saying that since language is form and not substance, its elements have only contrastive and combinatorial properties, and that at each level of structure one identifies the units or elements of a language by their capacity to differentiate units of the level immediately above them. We identify phonological distinctive features as the relational features that differentiate phonemes: /b/ is to /p/ and /d/ is to /t/ as voiced is to voiceless; thus voiced versus voiceless is a minimal distinctive feature. These phonemes in turn are identifiable because the contrasts between them have the capacity to differentiate morphemes: we know that /b/ and /p/ must be linguistic units because they contrast to distinguish *bet* from *pet.* And we must treat *bet* and *pet* as morphological units because the contrast between them is what differentiates, for example, *betting* from *petting* or

bets from *pets*. Finally, these items, which we can infor-
mally call words, are defined by the fact that they play different roles in the higher-level units of phrases and sentences.

In thus asserting the mutual dependence of the various
levels of language we are once again showing how it is that
in linguistics nothing is given in advance. Not only that:
we are arguing that one cannot first identify the elements
or units of one level and then work out the way they combine to form units of the next level, because the elements
with which one tries to start are defined by both syntagmatic and paradigmatic relations. The only way we can identify the prefix *re-* as a morphemic unit of English is by asking not just whether it contrasts with other elements but
whether, when it combines with other elements to form a
higher-level unit, it enters into contrasts which distinguish
and define this higher-level combination. We know that
re- contrasts paradigmatically with *un-, out-,* and *over-*
because *redo* contrasts with *undo, outdo,* and *overdo;* and
we know that *do* is a separable morphemic element because *redo* contrasts with *rebuild, reuse, reconnect.* It is,
shall we say, only contrasts between words which enable
us to define the lower-level constituents of words, morphemes. One must simultaneously work out syntagmatic
and paradigmatic relations. This basic structural principle, that items are defined by their contrasts with other
items and their ability to combine to form higher-level
items, operates at every level of language.

In explaining these technical aspects of Saussure's theory
of language I have not emphasized sufficiently one principle to which he gave great weight: that in analyzing a language we are analyzing social facts, dealing with the social
use of material objects. As I have said, a language could
be realized in various substances without alteration to its
basic nature as a system of relations. What is important,
indeed all that is relevant, are the distinctions and relations that have been endowed with meaning by a society.
The question the analyst constantly asks is what are the
differences that have meaning for members of the speech
community. It may often be difficult to assign a precise
form to those things that function as signs, but if a difference bears meaning for members of a culture, then there
is a sign, however abstract, which must be analyzed. For
speakers of English, *John loves Mary* is different in meaning from *Mary loves John;* therefore the word-order constitutes a sign, a social fact, whereas some physical differences between the way two speakers utter the sentence
John loves Mary may bear no meaning and therefore be
purely material facts, not social facts.

We can see then that linguistics studies not large collections of sound sequences but a system of social conventions. One is trying to determine the units and rules of
combination which make up that system and which make
possible linguistic communication between members of a
society. It is one of the virtues of Saussure's theory of language to have placed social conventions and social facts
at the center of linguistic investigation by stressing the
problem of the sign. What are the signs of this linguistic
system? On what does their identity as signs depend? Asking these simple questions, demonstrating that nothing

can be taken for granted as a unit of language, Saussure
continually stressed the importance of adopting the right
methodological perspective and seeing language as a system of socially determined values, not as a collection of
substantially defined elements. One might, to conclude
this discussion, quote two relevant passages which he actually wrote:

> The ultimate law of language is, dare we say,
> that nothing can ever reside in a single term.
> This is a direct consequence of the fact that lin-
> guistic signs are unrelated to what they desig-
> nate, and that therefore *a* cannot designate any-
> thing without the aid of *b* and vice versa, or, in
> other words, that both have value only by the
> differences between them, or that neither has
> value, in any of its constituents, except through
> this same network of forever negative differ-
> ences.

> Since language consists of no substance but only
> of the isolated or combined action of physiologi-
> cal, psychological, and mental forces; and since
> nevertheless of all our distinctions, our whole
> terminology, all our ways of speaking about it
> are molded by the involuntary assumption that
> there is substance, one cannot avoid recognizing,
> before all else, that the most essential task of lin-
> guistic theory will be to disentangle the state of
> our basic distinctions. I cannot grant anyone the
> right to construct a theory while avoiding the
> work of definition, although this convenient pro-
> cedure seems so far to have satisfied students of
> language.

To promote dissatisfaction and stimulate thought about
fundamentals, to insist on the relational nature of linguistic phenomena: these are the vectors of Saussure's theory.
(pp. 59-64)

Jonathan Culler, in his Ferdinand de Saussure, *revised edition, Cornell, 1986, 157 p.*

Nigel Fabb   (essay date 1988)

[*In the following essay, Fabb maintains that while modern linguistics is often "anti-Saussurean," Saussure's
theories are accurate and helpful when applied to literary and cultural scholarship.*]

Ferdinand de Saussure's **Course in General Linguistics**
(1916) has had a very substantial influence on literary and
cultural studies, particularly in the fields of structuralism
and poststructuralism, something which is often a surprise
to currently practising linguists, for many of whom Saussure's ideas are of historical interest but of little current
relevance. This article is about why the state of affairs exists where Saussure has become a 'prophet without honour' in linguistics but a father-figure in literary and cultural studies. My argument is basically that Saussure's linguistics is not appropriate to the study of language, though
as a methodology it might be adopted in other areas. I aim
to show how thinking about Saussure from the different
contemporary perspectives of literary study and linguistics shows up basic differences between these disciplines.
It is in this light that an exploration of Saussure is of inter-

est in the context of an interdisciplinary journal like *Critical Quarterly*. Arguments against Saussure's ideas of language are potentially arguments against the many theoretical movements which base themselves on Saussure, and so they become arguments against large parts of structuralism and some parts of poststructuralism; [Jacques] Lacan's claim that 'the Unconscious is structured like a language' assumes Saussure's account of language, and various influential literary—theoretical books such as [Anthony] Easthope's *Poetry as Discourse* and Coward and Ellis's *Language and Materialism* develop the linguistics of Saussure. An argument about a linguistic theory (Saussure's) from a linguistic rather than literary point of view can thus have some fairly severe consequences for literary studies by undermining the support that linguistics offers to forms of structuralism and poststructuralism, now widely institutionalised in literary and cultural studies departments throughout the world.

A discipline might be formulated in terms of a set of investigative and descriptive procedures, axioms, etc., or it might be formulated to correspond to a coherent division already there in nature/reality. An example of the first kind of disciplinary formation would be New Criticism or social work, an example of the second would be botany. For Saussure, psychology, physiology and acoustics are clearly all the second kind of discipline; the status of linguistics as he formulates it, however, is rather uncertain. Saussure's linguistics is the study of signs in language, but for Saussure signs come into being when they are identified as such by the discipline of linguistics—the discipline gives rise to the data rather than vice versa: 'Other sciences work with objects that are given in advance and that can then be considered from different viewpoints; but not linguistics . . . Far from it being the object that antedates the viewpoint, it would seem that it is the viewpoint that creates the object'; 'language does not offer itself as a set of predelimited signs that need only be studied according to their meaning and arrangement; it is a confused mass and only attentiveness and familiarization will reveal its particular elements'. Saussure can be read—and often in structuralism/poststructuralism has been read—to say that linguistics is an *a priori* discipline, existing in advance of (and creating) its object rather than being derived from its object. This may be another source of attraction for literary studies, whose post-Leavis shift as regards its adopted relation to cultural value is a shift from thinking of itself as a discipline of the second kind, studying a pre-given object 'literature', to thinking of itself as a discipline of the first kind—as a set of procedures, or perhaps even a set of political or cultural acts, with no particular range of subject-matter delimited in advance (other than saying that the subject matter is 'discourse' or 'texts'; all-encompassing terms).

The relationship between the discipline of literary studies and literature, its object, may well be such that the discipline creates (delimits) the objects of analysis (i.e. texts are not pre-given as literary or non-literary). However, much work in linguistics since Saussure, particularly the work of [Noam] Chomsky (and other generativists), suggests that facts about the structure of language are objective facts, to be discovered by linguistics rather than created

Title page from the first edition of Saussure's Course in General Linguistics.

by linguistics, that language *does* pre-exist the act of analysis. What this line of research suggests is that explanation in linguistics is going to be different in kind from explanation in literary studies, because the relations between the disciplines and their objects are different. Fundamental differences of this kind go some way towards explaining why the nature and applicability of linguistic theory tend to be seen differently from inside and outside the discipline of linguistics.

We might distinguish two kinds of argumentation about language in the *Course.* There is the argumentation that relates to specific data, such as the material on phonology, and there is the argumentation which is in some sense independent of any specific facts about language, and which is correspondingly not supported by a range of data. It is the argumentation of the second kind, the more speculative part of the *Course,* about *langue* and *parole,* signs, static linguistics and so on, which has been the most influential in literary and cultural theory. The speculativeness and non-data-specific nature of Saussure's ideas about language may be the properties most important for understanding why they survive in literary studies much more strongly than in linguistics. The introduction by Harris to his 1983 translation of the *Course* is very revealing in this respect. He says: 'Fortunately, most of Saussure's examples are merely illustrative: few are actually essential to the points he makes.' This is fortunate, Harris thinks, because it enables a modern reader not familiar with the context of the book (nineteenth-century linguistics, and French) to nevertheless read the book fruitfully. The implication that we might extract is that Saussure's linguistics as it survives is 'a-disciplinary', the ideas existing outside a particular context of issues and data. Harris then says that he makes 'the assumption that a reader who will find this translation useful is not likely to be interested in a critical examination of Saussure's exemplificatory material', an assumption that suggests that it is as speculation rather than as proof that Saussure's ideas survive. There is something *a priori* about them, ideas that one might have about language even if one knew very few facts about language, and which are necessarily true about language: how else could language be imagined other than in terms of signs, signifiers, signifieds, etc? 'It is quite clear . . .', says Saussure, in stating that a concept (signified) is not a positive term, only a value determined by its relations with other similar values: the appeal is to the common sense of the reader, not to the facts of language. In a few pages, Saussure dismisses an issue which is currently of considerable and controversial interest: whether syntax and morphology are distinct. His dismissal appears again to be on vaguely commonsensical grounds, whereas the current controversy relies crucially on the facts of a wide variety of languages, many of which had been little studied at the time that Saussure was working; the difference points up the fundamental disagreement in approach between Saussure, for whom linguistics tells one about language, and modern linguists, for whom language tells one about linguistics.

One of the ways in which linguistics as a discipline develops is that new facts about language are discovered. One consequence of this is that linguistic theories need updating, changing, perhaps abandoning. A corollary is that one way for a theory to be a good theory is to be extensively predictive: facts are often discovered by following up and confirming or disconfirming the predictions made by a theory. The more predictive a theory, the more chance it has of being wrong, of course, and much work in modern linguistics (particularly in generative grammar) consists of adjusting theoretical formulations in the light of the facts that these formulations throw up; this might be called a dialectical process. One of the problems with Saussure's linguistics, which is linked to its *a priori*stic relation with its object of analysis, is that it is not clearly predictive. Instead this kind of linguistics is oriented towards taxonomy—collection and classification of data. This may be one reason for its later neglect by linguists who were interested more in explanation than in description according to arbitrary and pre-given classificatory categories. However, it may be this *a priori*-ness of Saussure's argument—the fact that it is mainly 'armchair' philosophising rather than proof supported by extensive data—that ensures Saussure's survival outside linguistics while making his book little used within linguistics.

Saussure's ideas about language seem initially very convincing. His framework of binary distinctions between *langue* and *parole,* diachronic and synchronic, are elegant and methodologically satisfying, while his notion that the basic element of language is the word (strictly, the sign) seems commonsensical, as does his signifier/signified distinction which can be interpreted as a theorising of the form/content distinction familiar to literary scholars. The problem, then, is to imagine how language could be otherwise than Saussure presents it. Even when new linguistic issues arise, such as the importance of syntax, it may seem that they can coexist with a Saussurean linguistics, which is assumed somehow to provide the theoretical underpinnings for subsequent and current work. My aim in this article, though, is to show how linguistics can be anti-Saussurean, how language might be other than as Saussure describes it.

In the *Course,* Saussure is concerned to distinguish his theoretical approach from that of traditional grammar and traditional grammatical modes of argument. This intention appears to lie behind his marginalisation of syntax, which includes the regular groupings of words in a language (parsing) and the identification of parts of speech. Saussure discusses modes of argumentation relating to these which he considers inappropriate because non-linguistic; for example, the identification of parts of speech according to the demands of logic. His account of syntactic regularities is in terms of the non-explicit notion of 'latent syntactical patterns': apparently this means model sign-groupings which can be altered to produce new sign-groupings. In retrospect, it is probably this marginalisation of syntax which most later linguists would identify as Saussure's weakest area. 'To think that there is an incorporeal syntax outside material units distributed in space would be a mistake' is a claim which a very large body of twentieth-century linguistics (particularly generativist) and psycholinguistics has been concerned to refute. Some examples of the kinds of counter-evidence that have been produced are the following: words seem to have parts of speech as linguistic properties (i.e. as part of the system); otherwise it is impossible to explain why stress-patterns for English nouns, verbs, and adjectives are systematically related to part of speech (compare, for example, the way that the two alternative stressings of 'permit' reflect its two alternative parts of speech). And the reality of syntactic representations (i.e. cognitive 'images' of sentences which incorporate information about the grouping of words into phrases) is evidenced by, for example, the two systematically alternative meanings of sentences like 'flying planes can be dangerous', or the systematic differences between active and passive sentences, or the complex determinants on when names and pronouns and reflexives can co-refer. Moreover, it is not only the neglect of syntax which now seems an error in the *Course,* but the failure to take into account the possibility that linguistic representations could consist of other than linearly-ordered strings of elements. One of the central arguments in Chomsky's *Syntactic Structures* is that words are grouped not just into strings but into hierarchical (tree) structures. Moreover, Firthian prosodic phonology and current 'three-dimensional' phonology and morphology suggest that sound-structures are themselves more than just linearly patterned; that there may be simultaneity of structural elements, which are not ordered one after the other (e.g. tonal patterns in tone languages, vowel versus consonant patterns in Semitic, etc.).

Saussure's historical importance comes from his orientation of linguistics away from the history of languages and towards the workings of a language at any given time. He distinguishes the former as the diachronic study of language from the latter as the synchronic study of language, and his influence has lain primarily in what he said about synchronic linguistics, and his claim that in studying language it is possible to study a static system whose formations are independent of historical change. Though the distinction between diachronic and synchronic makes perfect sense as an idea, however, it now seems that Saussure was wrong to formulate it as he did. Crucially, for Saussure, there is a separation of the diachronic and the synchronic; diachronic facts are not directly related to changes in the synchronic system: 'It is obvious that the diachronic facts are not related to the static facts which they produced. They belong to a different class'. Saussure's belief that this was obvious may stem from the impoverished nature of the synchronic system as he formulates it. Working with more detailed and explanatory synchronic systems, however, work in historical linguistics since Jakobson has shown that linguistic change is understandable as simplification of the system (*langue*) in such a way that the altered system governs only minor changes in the observed data (*parole*) so that there is an interaction of the diachronic and the synchronic. [Valentin Kiparsky says in *Explanation in Phonology*]: 'Recent linguistics has moved from the structuralist segregation of synchronic and diachronic study towards a reintegration of the two, based on the idea that structure can determine change, with the corollary that change can therefore be diagnostic of structure'.

When Saussure distinguishes *langue* from *parole,* his claim is that the time and place-specific instances of linguistic behaviour—an act of speaking, of reading, etc.—are regulated by their relation to some ordered system: utterances are not randomly structured. The distinction between system (*langue*) and behaviour (*parole*) is plausible, but it enables an explanation of why linguistic behaviour (*parole*) shows regularities only if there is a realistic and plausible account of how *langue* and *parole* connect, how system governs behaviour. In order to construct such an account, we need to be able to trace back the causal chain from behaviour to system. The *langue/parole* distinction does not in itself imply any particular solution to this problem, and some adaptations of it, for example those by Chomsky and [Claude] Lévi-Strauss, account for the government of behaviour by system by putting the system in the mind or brain; since behaviour is (at least partly) mind/brain-driven, the regulation of behaviour by the system is understandable along these lines. In part this appears to fit with Saussure's own views: he speaks of *langue* as 'a grammatical system that has a potential existence in each brain, or more specifically in the brains of a group of individuals'.

In this approach the system is instantiated in the physical/material world. However, this approach, though characteristic of certain forms of structuralism (e.g. Lévi-Strauss), is probably not characteristic of much current work in literary theory/cultural studies. Though systems underlying behaviour are still assumed, they are not instantiated in any specific material objects (like brains) in the world; Barthes, for example, tries to redescribe Saus-

sure's notion of the signified in order to get rid of its 'stamp of psychologism'. However, here, as before, it may be crucial to distinguish between language and other kinds of cultural or communicative phenomena. The general problem is that there is some regularity to be found in behavioural, historical or social facts; this regularity is explained by claiming some relation between the facts and some regular system. Consider, for example, causation in historical change; we might identify a causal chain: 'poor harvest→dearth→rising mortality→the consumption of next year's seed→a second poor harvest→extreme dearth→a peak in mortality, accompanied by epidemic→a sharply rising conception rate[1] [E. P. Thompson, *The Poverty of Theory, and Other Essays*]. This chain would be a hypothesis as to causation; we could call it the system, which governs (in some sense) the actual historical facts. But it is not instantiated as a system; as E. P. Thompson puts it: 'It does not of course actually exist, like some plasma adhering to the facts, or as some invisible kernel within the shell of appearances': the system is not a set of rules which causes history, but instead a true generalisation about history. One reason for saying that it is a generalisation rather than a set of instantiated rules is that actual historical events will not always follow this pattern. By a particular turn of phrase Thompson in fact indicates the difference between historical explanation and linguistic explanation: 'History knows no regular verbs'—but, we might add, language does know regular verbs. In fact, natural languages show very complex regularities; modern linguistic works like Chomsky and Halle's *The Sound Pattern of English* are devoted to uncovering the complex rule systems which underlie linguistic facts, and *post-hoc* generalisations turn out to be too weak to account for the consistent systematicity of human languages. Linguistic rules, unlike 'rules' about historical change, actually are predictive. The claim that the linguistic system has a some determining relation with linguistic behaviour disagrees with Saussure, who said that the synchronic law 'reports a state of affairs'. This claim fits with his notion that linguistics creates its object and appeared correct to him when he formulated it because he knew little of the enormous synchronic regularities which would be discovered in languages after his death (and which modern linguistics continues to discover). Because we now know a lot more about language than Saussure did, we can now see that regularities in language are qualitatively different from the regularities in historical change; that in fact an adequate explanation of the regularities in language must posit a system consisting of rules which *is* materially instantiated—in the brain. The position that most linguists would now take, that language is not like other kinds of communication, runs contrary to Saussure's own beliefs. 'Language', he said, is 'the most characteristic of all systems of expression'. Structuralists proceeded on this assumption; the indications are now that it is incorrect.

Cognitivist claims that *langue* is instantiated not in a community mind but in an individual's mind/brain appear to run into the problem of explaining 'the social nature of *langue*'—the fact that languages are shared. Presumably we understand this in the way that we understand any kind of common knowledge: people know the same things because they acquired their knowledge from data in the world *which, as people living in a similar environment, they have in common,* by means of data-acquiring, processing, and storing devices *which, as humans, they have in common.* This is roughly speaking Lévi-Strauss's interpretation of how Saussure's insights can be made to work for cultural knowledge (a cognitively instantiated cultural system underlies cultural behaviour in a social context). Though Lévi-Strauss may be reading Saussure partly via Jakobson's ideas, he suggests that Saussure's insight, which takes linguistics from the pre-modern to the modern, is this: that the reason that many human or social facts in the world are regular is because they are processed by human minds (in human brains) which are themselves regular.

Linguistics for Saussure is independent of psychology, and the basic unit of linguistic analysis, the sign, is neither psychological nor physiological; the units of analysis are created by analysis rather than pre-existing it. In this section I want to present a different account of linguistic behaviour which is incompatible with Saussure's. The approach that I will outline (basically generative grammar, supplemented with psycholinguistics and cognitive science) takes its task to be that of finding cognitively real linguistic units, which pre-exist the act of analysis. The comparison between Saussure's linguistics and a cognitive linguistics shows how Saussure's conception of the sign, signified, and signifier do not correspond to the realities of language.

Saussure's position is this. The basic linguistic unit is the sign; it 'exists only through the associating of the signifier with the signified'. The signifier and the signified, independent of each other, are not in the domain of linguistics and are delimited only mutually. Independent of delimitation by being associated with a signified, signifiers are indistinguishable as part of a continuous stretch of sound. Independent of delimitation by being associated with a signifier, signifieds form a confused mass of thought. The sign is two-sided; language is thus like a piece of paper (signifiers one side, signifieds the other) which, when cut, is cut alike on both sides. Both signifier and signified are identifiable not by any inherent ('positive') properties, but instead are identifiable ('negatively') by their difference from other signifiers and signifieds respectively.

Consider now a cognitivist model. There is little agreement in this area, and I will describe a simplified version which at least is plausible, if not necessarily a fully correct account. It will serve to show up some of the problems which Saussure's account faces when confronted with the problem of explaining linguistic behaviour. For the sake of explanation, we will focus on a situation where someone hears sound (an utterance) and thoughts result in the hearer's head as a consequence. Thus there is an input (utterance) which is ultimately translated into an output (thoughts) by the linguistic system. The first difference from Saussure is that instead of a single unified system we will have a number of subsystems, each of which does specific things to an input or output. For example, in order of operation there is a subsystem which decodes the utterance; the output of that decoding is then the input to a different subsystem, inferencing, which produces, as *its* out-

put, thoughts. Within the decoding subsystem there are further subsystems; one subsystem takes the 'raw' sound input and changes it into a structured sequence of phonemes, working out syllabic structure, word boundaries, and so on; another subsystem matches the sound-patterns of perceived words with the sound-patterns of words stored in memory; another subsystem works out the grouping of words into phrases, and the relationship between the phrases (e.g. deciding in a sentence like 'the man ate the fish' which phrase represents the actor and which the acted-upon), building a sentence-structure; another subsystem determines what scope words like 'not' and 'every' have in the sentence structure that has been built. These subsystems are alike in that they are all decoding processes (alternatively, in a speaker, encoding processes), as determinate as the translation of a Morse Code sequence of letters. What they end up with is what we might call an *annotated representation* of the input data. This annotated representation is not yet sound translated into thought, but it is as much as can be derived automatically from what was heard. A different kind of process is now needed to make sense of this representation; making sense will include taking into account supplementary visual information, knowledge which the hearer assumes to be shared with the speaker, memory of various facts about the world, etc. This second stage is the stage of inferencing; it is possible that here an account of evocation, of pleasure in language, of how metaphors work, and why people misunderstand each other, can be found. In inferencing, the process is no longer determinate; the annotated representation is transformed into thought by bringing it into the context of other thoughts and, via bridging inferences, moving from one thought to another. There may be no sub-components of inferencing (unlike the many subcomponents of the decoding process).

There are clear differences between the two approaches. Saussure's model is unitary, and has one basic element of analysis (the sign); the cognitive model has a number of components, none of which has any priority and which involve different basic elements: thus sentences are the basic units of analysis for the syntax, morphemes for the morphology, etc. One line of thought is that the various distinct processes are 'encapsulated' and interact only by passing the representations from one component to another; this means, for example, that (*contra* Saussure) information about meaning will not be available for the process of 'cutting words out of the flow'. Another fundamental difference is that the cognitivist account consists basically of an input being translated into a sequence of different kinds of representations—phonetic, several different phonological representations, several different syntactic representations (one showing surface order, another showing quantifier scope, another showing predicate—argument relations), etc. This multi-representational approach is very different from Saussure's two-representation (signifier + signified) approach. Both Saussurean and cognitivist approaches take linguistics to be a form of explanation which can not be reduced to psychology and physiology; they differ in how they relate the explanations in linguistics to the explanations of language behaviour which can be found in physiology and psychology. Saussure appears to do so in two ways: (a) by distinguishing linguistics from the other sciences in terms of its relation with its object (linguistics constitutes its object; the others have objects existing in advance of enquiry), and (b) by locating language in something non-material—the speech community; language 'exists only by virtue of a sort of contract signed by the members of a community'. The cognitivist approach, on the other hand, works from the basic position that linguistics is the study of aspects of the mind, and that a mind is materially instantiated in a brain. Cognitive science, of which linguistics is a sub-part, is the study of mental representations; mental representations (including linguistic representations) will be instantiated in our heads as networked organisations and electrochemical behaviour-patterns of neurones. Thus the distinction between linguistics and physiology/neurophysiology will be a distinction of level of description, where the two levels of description are linked together.

Having now summarised a few basic differences, I want to move on to make some detailed comparisons between the two approaches, with the aim of showing that the cognitivist approach fits best with what we now know about language.

The Saussurean sign is two-faced, involving a word having just two representations (signifier and signified); the cognitivist approach, on the other hand, involves the linguistic input forming a large number of representations. It might be said that this is a question of level of detail—that the two-representation Saussurean system is a way of summarising the multi-representation cognitivist system—but the reason for thinking that this is not the case is that not all representations clearly belong to the signifier or the signified side of the two-way division, and that there would be no unity between the set of representations forming the signifier and between the set forming the signified: the sets would not be well-formed and coherent. A cognitivist hypothesis about the constitution of words, for example (based in part on experimentation), is that words are stored in different components as follows: there is an ordered list of sound-structures, an ordered list of spelling-structures (for a literate language-user only), a range of potential syntactic and semantic properties. For a given word, information is drawn together from these distinct lists and domains by linking an item from each of the distinct lists and a selection of syntactic/semantic properties together to a position in the system, which has no inherent content other than tying these kinds of information together. This position is then linked up by semantic networks with other kinds of information about the world, connotations of the word, and so on. The range of potential semantic and syntactic properties which are associated with a word are formal properties of the word and its meaning which are syntactically relevant, and implicated in rules of some kind. For example, in some languages (e.g. Navajo), the syntactic location of a referring expression in a sentence is related to how 'animate' it is (according to an animacy hierarchy which makes a human more animate than a mule and a mule more animate than a stone). Supplementing this kind of semantic information, however, it is probable that many aspects of the meaning of a word are not coded via some direct link with the word-slot (or the sound-structure) but instead are derived by applying inferential processes to the word in a context, or by pursuing networked connections between words in the brain.

Notice that one implication of this is that the signified is not delimited; there is no limit in principle to the accessing of ever weaker or more distant information connected with a word. Moreover, 'meaning' as it is conventionally imagined is split between a limited componential part (involving components of meaning like causation, state, animacy, plurality, etc.) and an implicational part which is in principle infinite. Thus it is not clear that the notion of 'signified' has any unified content. The same might be said of the signifier. For Saussure the signifier is relational, its identity being a matter of its difference from other signifiers in the language. However, sound-structural regularities raise something of a problem for this account. For example, every word in English that begins with three consonants in a row has as the first of those the consonant 's'; there is a language-specific (i.e. it applies to English) generalisation to this effect. This means that any signifier beginning with three consonants will not need to have 's' specified as the first consonant; so the word 'split' could be stored as 'Consonant + plit'—this information is enough to differentiate it from any other signifier (there are also explanatory linguistic reasons to think that the remembered sound-structure of the word might be constituted along these lines). However, such a signifier is identified not only by its difference from the other signifiers, but more specifically is identified as such *in the context of* the generalisation about the three-consonant cluster. The generalisation (= a rule about initial consonant sequences in English) in some sense forms part of the signifer. Here—as in the case of the signified—the signifier seems to be split between different kinds of thing, a representation and the rules which operate over that representation.

Consider now the crucial issue of the mutual delimitation of the signifier and signified. Saussure claims, for example, that the signifier can be identified as such only when it is paired with a signified. This claim is incompatible with one cognitivist position, which is that different parts of the linguistic faculty work independently of each other; moreover, it appears to be untrue. Words (the typical case of signifiers) in English can be 'cut out' of a sound-sequence because word-boundaries are identifiable on the basis of acoustic cues, such as stress patterns; moreover, certain phonological processes take place at word-boundaries (e.g. final devoicing of consonant classes in many languages, or the loss of 'b' in word-final 'mb' clusters, as in 'bomb'; compare the pronunciation of nonfinal 'mb' in 'bombard'), which again helps to delimit the word without reference to any semantic information. Saussure similarly claims that the signified has no existence prior to association with a signifier; that thought is shapeless outside expression. One argument against this is that thought may sometimes be in the form of non-linguistic images; another is that thought may itself be like a language—Fodor, for example, suggests that thoughts are sentences in a language of thought (independent of any actual spoken human language).

Saussure emphasises the social nature of language, the fact

that as a shared system it enables communication between individuals. However, communication also sometimes fails; implications, connotations, and intended meanings may be lost—particularly when the producer and consumer of a text are separated by history or geography. Some post-Saussureans in literary studies ascribe this to properties of the signifier—signified system; Easthope, for example, argues that failures of communication may arise because the signifier and signified are 'of an entirely different order'—materially (perhaps ontologically?) different, hence disrupting the direct translation of meaning into sound and back into meaning. An alternative approach is available in a cognitivist framework. Recall that we distinguished between decoding/encoding linguistic materials and inferencing over them. The processes are different in kind, in that decoding/encoding are determinate and reliable (and in practice efficient in recovering information out of noise) in decoding exactly the information that was encoded into some instance of speech or writing, while the results of inferencing depend on highly variable factors. A difference in knowledge, beliefs, assumptions, relevant visual information, attentiveness, etc., between speaker/writer and hearer/reader will be enough to allow different inferential paths in the two, with the result that intended meanings, connotations, etc., may not be conveyed. A theoretical innovation in this area which promises interesting rewards for literary studies is Relevance Theory.

Saussurean linguistics and modern linguistic theories such as generative linguistics differ in how linguistics is conceived, specifically in what the relation between theory and data should be. The basically taxonomic methodology proposed by Saussure, and the closure of his theoretical base (little theoretical modification to the Saussurean system is possible because the system is so monolithic and has so few parts) have resulted in Saussurean linguistics being left behind as the study of language has developed. However, Saussureanism has survived and has had considerable importance in the study of cultural artefacts—particularly literary texts. It may be that the success of Saussure's ideas in this area complements the failure of his ideas in linguistics; the pre-existence of the theory and its classificatory tendencies seem appropriate to the study of texts, perhaps the most interesting properties of which are cultural and produced by 'reading', rather than—as in the case of many linguistic structures—natural and pre-given. Saussure may have been right in thinking that his linguistics would form the basis for a study of all kinds of communicative process; where he seems to have been wrong was his belief that language was exemplary in this respect. For many contemporary linguists, language is interesting not because it is the central example of 'the life of signs within society', but because in many of its structural properties it is distinct from the life of signs; language is characterised not by its exemplariness but by its difference from other forms of communication. (pp. 58-71)

Nigel Fabb, "Saussure and Literary Theory: From the Perspective of Linguistics," in Critical Quarterly, Vol. 30, No. 2, Summer, 1988, pp. 58-72.

Saussure on the role of the linguist:

Since language consists of no substance but only of the isolated or combined action of physiological, psychological, and mental forces; and since nevertheless of all our distinctions, our whole terminology, all our ways of speaking about it are molded by the involuntary assumption that there is substance, one cannot avoid recognizing, before all else, that the most essential task of linguistic theory will be to disentangle the state of our basic distinctions. I cannot grant anyone the right to construct a theory while avoiding the work of definition, although this convenient procedure seems so far to have satisfied students of language.

Ferdinand de Saussure, quoted in Jonathan Culler's monograph Ferdinand de Saussure, *Cornell University Press, 1986.*

Ora Avni   (essay date 1990)

[*In the following excerpt, Avni examines the ways in which Saussure refined his theories while teaching linguistics at the University of Geneva between 1906 and 1911 and claims that the editors of* Course in General Linguistics *neglected to demonstrate the evolution of Saussure's theories during this period.*]

Saussure's name is associated with innovative concepts in the theories of signs, language, and linguistics. Structuralism, for example, originates in an adaptation of the basic tenets of Saussure's philosophy of language to other disciplines. [Claude] Lévi-Strauss' "L'Analyse structurale en linguistique et en anthropologie," which is generally regarded as the founding structuralist text, acknowledges its debt to Saussure. It suffices to leaf rapidly through the pages of the influential *Qu'est-ce que le structuralisme?* to realize the impact of Saussurean concepts like signifier/signified, value, system, linearity of discourse, *langue,* synchronic investigation, and so on. It is interesting to note that as long as Saussure remained known to linguists only, his most innovative and productive insights were often overlooked: his fellow linguists, trained as linguists only—that is, in the historical comparative philology that prevailed at that time—did not always realize the full epistemological implications of his teaching; instead they adopted and discussed his more technical, purely linguistic insights and overlooked the more theoretical aspects of this thinking—his philosophy of language, as he called it while teaching his famous three courses. Only after his discovery by Lévi-Strauss and [Maurice] Merleau-Ponty was Saussure's revolutionary emphasis on nonhistorical (synchronic) systems, the parts of which do not preexist the whole, fully understood. What was adopted by and integrated into other disciplines is not so much the content or message of his teaching (the linguistics proper) as the underlying epistemic principles on which he built his theory of linguistics, and the methodology he developed to suit these principles. Poststructuralism, an ill-defined intellectual movement inaugurated principally by [Jacques] Derrida and [Michel] Foucault, still relies heavily on the same tenets. Even today, after Poststructuralism and Postmodernism, the framework of the most vigorous investigations remains unchanged: current approaches that rely on the interplay between culture (or literature) and social and historical contexts (Marxism, new historicism, feminism, black studies, etc.) nonetheless rest their views on the unquestioned premise of cultural constructs akin to *langue* and on the relativity of the ideological systems of thought and signs that they command.

Of particular interest to us is the influence of Saussurean concepts on literary theory and its impact on French literary modernity and post-modernity. Lévi-Strauss, [Roland] Barthes, [Jacques] Lacan, Derrida, and Foucault, to name just a few of the most seminal figures of modernity, have all admitted their debt to Saussure. Deriving all semantics from a construct (*langue* for Saussure, and text, ideology, or language for literary critics) along with a professed disregard for any interaction this construct may have with other factors—of which reference to objects is the most obvious—can be traced directly to the influence of the *Cours de linguistique générale.* Combined with the French discovery of Russian Formalism, the adaptation of Saussure's methodological and epistemological principles to literature is responsible for Postmodernism's emphasis on the notions of text, intertextuality, literarity, formal and semantic constructs, closure, function, slippage of values, etcetera—in short, for the major concepts associated today with literary criticism. (pp.17-18)

The impact of Saussure's teaching was such that, after his death, [Charles] Bally and [Albert] Sechehaye collected the notes his students had taken during his three courses on general linguistics (Geneva, 1906-7, 1908-9, and 1910-11) and attempted "a reconstruction, a synthesis, by using the third course as a starting point and by using all other materials at [their] disposal, including the personal notes of F. de Saussure, as supplementary sources." This endeavor led to the publication of the *Cours de linguistique générale* (1916), which in turn stirred up an intellectual revolution.

The editors were faced with formidable difficulties: Saussure had not kept the (very partial) notes that he had used for his course. The material found in his drawers consisted for the most part of different drafts and versions of unfinished papers often written long before the three courses. To make matters worse, Saussure himself had raised two major objections to the publication of his courses.

First, the pedagogical concern inherent in a course had dictated certain simplifications and compromises incompatible with the scientific objectivity required for a publication. For example, since complexity was intrinsic to his subject matter, how could he simplify its presentation to his students without betraying it and defeating his teaching? On the other hand, how could he share his doubts and hesitations—however fruitful or revealing they might be—when these doubts and hesitations constituted the very stuff on which his students would be examined at the end of the school year?

Second, Saussure considered his course more a tentative inquiry, a work in progress, than a coherent theory. Therefore, he judged it unpublishable in this early stage

("As for a book on this subject, one could not imagine it: it must, says M. de Saussure, give the *definitive* thought of its author" [interview with [Albert] Riedlinger, 19 January 1909, reprinted in Robert Godel's *Les sources manuscrites du cours linguistique générale de F. de Saussure*]). It seems that he found it disheartening to bring just about everything to what he saw as completion: "(*I had asked him if he had written up his ideas on this subject.*)—'Yes, I have some notes buried in piles [of paper], and I wouldn't know how to find them again.' (*I had hinted that he ought to have something published on these subjects.*)—'It would be absurd to begin again the long research for the publication, when I have there [he gestures] piles and piles of unpublished work'" (interview with Gautier, Godel's emphasis).

Fortunately, Bally and Sechehaye, colleagues and admirers of Saussure, paid no heed to his scruples. With the help of Dégallier, who had attended the last two courses and taken detailed notes, they rounded up all the students' notes and proceeded to collate them in order to represent Saussure's teaching as faithfully as possible. At all times, they say [in the preface to the *Course*], they did their best to respect the intention of the master, "even when his intention, not always apparent, had to be *surmised.*" Surmising the intentions of the master would have been very risky if the notes had not been so complete. Despite the editors' claim to the contrary, these notes were remarkably coherent, and the variations from student to student rarely exceeded minimal changes in formulation. Very little was therefore left to surmise. The comparison of notes with the *Course* generally yields few differences, with the exception of one category that, incidentally, is not mentioned in the editors' Preface: when Saussure added restrictive clauses to an otherwise dogmatic assertion, or when he left his own question unanswered, they generally "cleaned it up" so as not to weaken his case.

But the editors had to grapple with an insoluble problem, one that accounted for Saussure's acknowledged reluctance ever to write his course.

> What makes this subject difficult is that one can take it, like certain geometric theorems, from many sides: *everything is corollary* from everything else in static linguistics [*tout est corollaire l'un de l'autre* en linguistique *statique*]: whether one speaks of units, of differences, of oppositions, it comes back to the same [*cela revient au même*]. *Langue* is a tight system and the theory must be a system just as tight as *langue. There is the difficult point,* for it is nothing to present assertions and views one after the other about *langue;* the whole thing is to coordinate them in a system. (Interview with Riedlinger, 1909, [*Les sources manuscrites du cours linguistique générale de F. de Saussure.*]

Hence the real problem was not, as the editors claimed in their Preface, the ever changing nature of Saussure's thinking and the "conflicting" views he expressed from one course to another. (Besides, at another point in the same Preface, they also recognized that the courses complemented rather than contradicted one another; see, for example, "To limit the book to a single course—and which one?—was to deprive the reader of the rich and varied content of the other two courses; by itself the third, the most definitive of the three courses, would not give a complete accounting of the theories of F. de Saussure". Even so, if indeed Saussure had revised or renewed his theory from one course to another, to be consistent with their declared method Bally and Sechehaye should have reproduced and even stressed the increasing doubts, hesitations, and half-restrictions that abound in the last course and should have construed them as a telltale sign of the evolution of Saussure's thinking. They did not, however, but borrowed instead the most theoretical passages on *langue* from the second course—a practice that contradicts their professed method.

One thing is indisputable: if we consider only the actual content of each course, we find no major discoveries in the later courses. Except for a few taxonomic refinements, the first course already presented all of the major concepts of the later two. More importantly, the Introduction to the second course offers the most comprehensive and systematic account of Saussure's general linguistics, one in which the multiple elements are best coordinated into a wide-ranging "system." Saussure ended his Introduction in January 1909, at about the same time that he complained about the circular "difficulty of the subject" in his interview with Riedlinger. We may therefore safely assume that, despite its definitive tone, the Introduction had not satisfied his exigency to present the part and the whole simultaneously. On the contrary, we may also assume that it is *because* the second course was the most comprehensive, the most emphatically and dogmatically "theoretical" of the three, that Saussure came to realize the number of arbitrary choices he had been compelled to make in order to align his thoughts in the proper "theoretical" form. His discouraged comments to Riedlinger underscore the difference—or even the tension—between individual notations or observations and their coordination into a system ("it is nothing to present assertions and views one after another about *langue;* the whole thing is to coordinate them into a system"). They constitute a critique of the "theoretical" system that he elaborated for his students' sake in the second course, and they hint at the reasons behind the pedagogical changes he would introduce in the third course.

A brief comparison of the three courses is all we need to ascertain that the changes in focus and emphasis from one course to another do not reflect Saussure's so-called new or evolving perception or conception. His revisions do not affect so much the factual content of his teaching as its form, as the order of introduction of concepts. What changes is the narrative he uses to present to his students the logical relations that build a system out of a series of random notations and observations; in short, his pedagogical and rhetorical strategies.

In the first course [1906-7], Saussure adopted an inferring strategy: throughout most of the year, he accumulated numerous divergent linguistic phenomena and raised hosts of questions. His aim was clearly to frustrate his students and arouse their curiosity by confronting them with a considerable number of problems that comparative philology

and neogrammar—the main linguistic trends of his time—could not solve. The partial solutions he offered to each new problem he raised implied, again and again, the existence of *langue* as an underlying system responsible for the otherwise unexplainable linguistic phenomena. At that time he was also toying with the idea that a more philosophical conception of *langue* might be suitable material for a different course, thus separating the pragmatics of linguistics from its philosophical overview (an idea he would try to realize in the second course but abandon in the third): "Linguistics: One can hesitate a lot as to the best procedure [*le meilleur plan*]. *It is more profitable to place certain general ideas at the end of the course rather than at the beginning.* This is why we do not want to define the nature of language [*la nature du langage*]. *This will in fact make up the object of a course:* one will have to notice that language is not an immediately classifiable object." The first course (1906-7) abounded in details. In a typical neogrammarian vein, its major part dealt with diachronic linguistics: it attempted to track down and to comprehend various aspects and patterns of the evolution of languages. Forever consistent with his opposition to historical linguistics, however, Saussure also cleverly brought each and every discussion of morphological changes to a dead end. Only toward the end of the course did Saussure introduce a clearly stated solution providing a unifying pattern for the various irritating questions and partial answers he had furnished all along. While comparative philology explained each and every morphological derivation diachronically, the end of the first course suggested that a derivation not be taken in isolation: each instance is determined by the state of the general system in which it is taking place at any given time, or in short, by *langue*. Not surprisingly, however, before the grand solution of the end, each time Saussure sketched a partial or tentative answer to a specific linguistic phenomenon, he had to rely heavily on the still unpresented (yet ever implied) importance of *langue* for the study of linguistics as well as on the twofold and unmotivated nature of the linguistic sign. This methodological difficulty gave his course a rocky pace and caused numerous repetitions. It was also probably frustrating for his students, who must have sensed that their teacher was holding back something crucial that would have dissipated their difficulties. And yet, from this line of questioning and the partial solutions with which he punctuated his course, it is clear that he himself was not discovering *langue* as he proceeded but rather waiting for the right moment to introduce it as a key concept. There can be no doubt that he already had a firm grasp on the findings and the conclusions to which his inquiry seemed to be leading him. In short, the first course is a fake "inquiry" into language, a heuristic play staged for the benefit of his students.

In the second course (1908-9), Saussure reversed this strategy: "In order to assign a place to linguistics, one must not take *langue* from all its sides. It is evident that in this way many sciences (psychology, physiology, anthropology, [grammar, philology], etc.) will be able to claim *langue* as their object. This analytic route has never amounted to anything [cette voie analytique n'a donc jamais abouti à rien]: We will pursue a synthetic route." Abandoning the analytical method that he used in the first course, Saussure drew a broad synthesis for the second course—in fact, the broadest he was ever to sketch.

> It is now evident that before all else *langue is a system of signs* and that it is necessary to go back to the science of signs, which introduces us to what signs are made of, their laws, etc? This discipline does not exist within the known disciplines. This would be a *semiology*. . . .
>
> It is also evident that *langue* does not encompass every kind of system formed by signs. There must exist therefore a science of signs more vast than linguistics (system of maritime signs, systems of signs for the blind and deaf, and finally [the most important]: writing itself!)
>
> But right off it must be said that *langue* will occupy the principal place of this science; it will be its master model [patron].

This time, Saussure widens his scope of interest to a panoramic perspective: whereas the first course culminates in *langue,* the second opens onto a system larger than *langue,* of which linguistics is simultaneously a branch and a model (a *patron*). The umbrella term is *semiology,* the yet inexistent general science of signs indispensable for a full comprehension of the isolated facts of language.

This highly theoretical, dense, and even at times aphoristic Introduction took up about half of the year-long course. It is undoubtedly the clearest account we have today of the wide scope of Saussure's intellectual enterprise and the originality of his thinking. This is due not so much to the novelty of the material as to its strikingly coherent organization. The concepts themselves did not differ significantly from what he had presented two years before in the first course, but their compact organization and their forceful systematic presentation succeeded in creating a "theory," whereas the dispersion of the notations in the first attempt did not give the same impression of conceptual power and cogency. The only important change was the extension of the study of *langue* to a new science: semiology. Even this was hardly an innovation, however, since Saussure had already alluded to this science as early as 1894: in his notes on Whitney, for example, he wrote that "the faculty of speech" (*la faculté du langage*) and the faculty by which we perceive "conventional relations" are one and the same. As early as thirteen years before the first course and fifteen before the second, he was already convinced that there had to be a connection between a theory of language and a general theory of signs. The only possible innovation we may therefore attribute to the period of the second course is the name he coined for the science he had envisaged in 1894 and the emphasis and force with which he mentioned the new discipline. Godel, who sees in the omission of semiology from the first course a case of didactic restraint, comments, "In his first course he did not dare speak, straightaway, about semiology."

I am not convinced that this was a case of simply "daring." The meticulously detailed inferring strategy of the first course did not lend itself to the large vistas Saussure intended to open with semiology. By the end of the first course he must have realized that his inferring pedagogy was not totally suitable for the project at hand: the system

he had in mind (even if we limit it to *langue*) exceeded by far the sum of the linguistic puzzles he had presented to his students. It was larger than anything that had been done before him in linguistics. In addition, his pedagogical strategy consisted of well-chosen cases in diachronic linguistics whose narrow specificity may have proven disproportionate to the generality and complexity of *langue.* The "connect the dots" method of the first course simply did not do justice to the scope of his vision; enlarging this vision even more into semiology would have been downright forced.

We may also think of the reception of the first course. Couldn't the accumulation of details and questions have blurred the consistency of the answers and their underlying principles? Didn't his baffled students perhaps fail to see the forest for the trees? It would explain why, in the second course, Saussure chose to reverse the order of presentation, spelling out at length his theoretical principles and presenting his students with a panoramic, conceptual introduction.

The second course avoided the mistakes of the first one, but it went to the opposite extreme. Saussure's theoretical Introduction seems harsh, dogmatic, and not always convincing (mostly for lack of examples or real demonstration). Considering the level of abstraction of the Introduction, I doubt that this course made his students happier than the first one did. While correcting *devoirs* and exams (which he did often and very thoroughly), Saussure must have realized for the second time that his method had not done justice to his subject.

In the third course, Saussure struck the golden mean. He borrowed the best of each from the previous courses: while the first part (from October to April) was mostly analytical (inferring) again and dealt with LES *langues* (languages) in the tradition of comparative linguistics, the second part (25 April to the end of June) returned to the panoramic synthesis, reiterating the importance of the distinction between *langue, langage,* and *parole,* the election of *langue* as a "platform" for linguistics, and the nature of the linguistic sign. It is in fact a return to the strategy of the first course, with two noticeable differences: 1) the first part of the third course replaced diachronic evolutions within one language with synchronic oppositions between languages, thus opening a larger picture and opposing one system to the other (rather than working within the same system); and 2) unlike the hurried synthesis he whipped up at the end of the first course, Saussure gave himself enough time to develop fully a larger theoretical perspective.

In the introduction to the third course, he explained this new strategy (note in particular the insistence on the linear presentation of the linguistic facts and on the pedagogical motivation of the chosen sequence): "Let us return to the outline of the course [*plan*]. Let us take up again this term: languages [*les langues*]. Linguistics has to study the social product, *langue.* But this social product manifests itself through a large diversity of languages. . . . One must first study languages, a diversity of languages. Through observation of these languages, one will extract that which is universal. He [the linguist] will then have before him a set of abstractions: this will be *langue* (*la langue*), where we will study that which is observable in the different languages." In this quotation, Saussure's main objective is clearly pedagogical. In the best French academic tradition, he justifies his outline or order of presentation (*plan*) so as to make his students' task more manageable. The theory itself remains essentially identical to that of the earlier courses, while the problems with which he grapples concern the method, that is, the transition from the specific to the universal and vice versa. The new organization of the material was undoubtedly more successful than the previous ones (hence its definitive character in the eyes of the editors): it allowed him to illustrate and motivate the most difficult and crucial points of the second course.

I did not delve into the three courses for the sheer pleasure of displaying an erudite historical account of Saussure's pedagogical dilemma. For the *Cours de linguistique générale,* the stakes were high: if indeed in synchronic linguistics "everything is corollary, from everything else," any point of entry would and should lead the teacher and his students (or the editors and the readers) to the system as a whole as well as to the other points. Hence the "difficulty of the subject" deplored by Saussure: if each point implies the whole, and if the whole presupposes the points, then *the subject matter can no longer logically dictate the order of presentation; logically, we are in a circle. Only a rhetorical or pedagogical preoccupation can affect the sequence in which these points will be presented in the classroom.* Long before his three courses, in 1894 (in a draft for a book about general linguistics that he never wrote), Saussure recognized this circular aspect: "There is (therefore) a real (necessary) absence of any starting point [*point de départ*], and if some reader wants to follow attentively our thought from one end to the other of this volume he will recognize, we are convinced of it, that it was as it were impossible to follow a very rigorous order. We will permit ourselves to submit, up to three and four times, the same idea to the eyes of the reader, because *there exists really no starting point more valid than another upon which to ground the demonstration.*" The lack of a starting point derived naturally from Saussure's distinction between diachronic and synchronic linguistics and his privileging of the latter over the former: once a linguist decides not to address the temporal aspect of language, the very idea of firstness clearly becomes irrelevant. If all the functions and the units in a given synchronic system are corollary, causal and temporal firstness vanishes. The starting point can no longer be either the state of affairs that preceded the one examined or some logical axiom. It becomes merely a heuristic device. This was a revolutionary concept in an age imbued with Darwinism, in which historical linguistics was the rule. It is with regard to this concept that Saussure is often associated with sociology and particularly with Durkheim. As we shall see, Frege, too, insisted on the irrelevance of a historical approach to epistemological problems. Despite the marked differences between them, these thinkers were engaged in the same critique of the philosophy of knowledge that prevailed at the time, and of the scientific method of investigation it entailed. It is highly ironic that this essential point of Saussure's thinking has been so badly misunderstood by later critics who have found fault with his starting point.

Faced with the change of organization from one course to another, Bally and Sechehaye came to the same impasse: the nature of their project required the existence of a starting point in order for them to ground their demonstration on some simple principle—in a typical Cartesian manner. We can even look at their problem from a simpler and more pragmatic viewpoint: they *had* to start somewhere. They realized that the point with which they chose to start would necessarily be arbitrary (since there is no real starting point) but would nonetheless acquire a logical priority over the rest in the eyes of the readers. Since the third course was more recent, more diverse in nature, and better constructed pedagogically than the first two, the editors resolved to use it as the basis for their reconstruction. The first course was used mostly for the chapters "Analogy," "Analogy and Evolution," and "Phonetic Changes," while numerous inserts from the second course complemented and expanded the third. It is important to stress that while they did indeed use the content of the third course as the basis of the *Cours,* they did not follow its sequence, its line of reasoning (the principle of organization is in fact closer to that of the second course—although it does not espouse it either).

This decision entails a series of editorial paradoxes. As his comments to Riedlinger toward the end of the second course indicate, Saussure's difficulty—and consequently his revisions—lay not in the actual content of any of the courses but in the organization of the content's parts into a system. It is in this respect that he had experimented the most and also expressed reservations about the results of such experiments. Unfortunately, because of the differences that resulted from these experiments, it is also in this respect that the editors were compelled to make the most editorial decisions. Since they had intended to base their collation on the third course, it would have been logical to adopt its outline as well as its content, all the more so since, pedagogically, it was the most satisfying of the three. They opted instead for a combination of the three courses. As a result, *the principle of organization of the Cours is not to be found in any of the courses given by Saussure:* in search of a "starting point" that would allow them to derive the other elements with maximum coherence, the editors wrote yet a fourth course, electing a fourth pedagogical strategy that Saussure himself had not tried.

The *Cours* opens rather traditionally with a brief glance (*coup d'oeil*) at the history of linguistics and moves on to a vague definition of its project (totaling nine pages). It then presents forcefully its foundation: *langue.* In choosing *langue* as the foundation stone of the theory, the editors relied on the second course, in which Saussure had expressed his preference for such a synthesis. They did not follow the outline of the second course either, however. This is one of the rare instances in which the editors knowingly and assertively "corrected" Saussure. (On other occasions, even when they had to write sections to fill in gaps, they made a laudable effort to respect the spirit if not the letter of Saussure's teaching.)

The editors were aware of the tentative aspect of the *Cours,* but they were also aware that to ensure the wide acceptance of Saussure's teaching, they had to make it hold together as coherently and cogently as the material allowed, even at the price of some editorial sanctions. Therefore, when they write, "We are aware of our responsibility to our critics. We are also aware of our responsibility to the author, who probably would not have authorized the publication of these pages," I suggest that we take them literally: their warning is not the conventional final bow of the editors to the "author," but the candid admission of crucial, albeit inevitable, editorial choices that risk opening the door to various textual distortions, repetitions, or omissions. (pp.18-28)

> *Ora Avni, "Saussure," in* The Resistance of Reference: Linguistics, Philosophy, and the Literary Text, *The Johns Hopkins University Press, 1990, pp. 17-77.*

FURTHER READING

Bibliography

Koerner, E. F. K[onrad]. *Bibliographia Saussureana 1870-1970.* Metuchen, N. J.: Scarecrow Press, 1972, 406 p.

> Complete listing of works by and about Saussure through 1970.

Criticism

Aarsleff, Hans. "Taine and Saussure" and "Bréal, 'la sémantique,' and Saussure." In his *From Locke to Saussure: Essays on the Study of Language and Intellectual History,* pp. 356-71, pp. 382-98. Minneapolis: University of Minnesota Press, 1982.

> Details the contributions of Saussure, Hippolyte Taine, and Michel Bréal to modern linguistics.

Angenot, Marc. "Structuralism as Syncretism: Institutional Distortions of Saussure." In *The Structural Allegory: Reconstructive Encounters with the New French Thought,* edited by John Fekete, pp. 150-63. Minneapolis: University of Minnesota Press, 1984.

> Examines Saussure's influence on French critics and scholars during the 1960s and 1970s, a period generally known as the structuralist age.

Antal, László. "Some Comments on the Relationship between Paul and Saussure." *Cahiers Ferdinand de Saussure* 39 (1985): 121-30.

> Challenges E. F. Koerner's belief that many of Saussure's ideas are found in the work of Hermann Paul and that subsequently Paul—and not Saussure—was one of the first proponents of structuralism.

Attridge, Derek. "Language as History/History as Language: Saussure and the Romance of Etymology." In *Post-Structuralism and the Question of History,* edited by Derek Attridge, Geoff Bennington, and Robert Young, pp. 183-211. Cambridge: Cambridge University Press, 1987.

> Asserts that Saussure's theories of synchronic and diachronic linguistics are built on and perpetuate two contradictory views of language: "history as the complex of social and material forces which modify the individual and the community in a succession of experienced presents, and history as a supra-individual, supra-communal, transtemporal continuum, genetically or teleologically oriented."

Barnouw, Jeffrey. "Signification and Meaning: A Critique of the Saussurean Conception of the Sign." *Comparative Literature Studies* XVIII, No. 3 (September 1981): 260-71.

> Discusses the need to replace Saussure's theory of the sign with one that incorporates the issue of referentiality.

Bredin, Hugh. "Sign and Value in Saussure." *Philosophy* 59, No. 227 (January 1984): 67-77.

> Analyzes Saussure's concepts of sign, value, and difference.

Davis, Philip W. "Ferdinand de Saussure." In his *Modern Theories of Language,* pp. 14-38. Englewood Cliffs, N. J.: Prentice-Hall, 1973.

> Explains how Saussure's theories distinguish between speech and language as well as the universal and culture-specific aspects of language.

Harris, Roy. "Saussure and the Dynamic Paradigm." In *Developmental Mechanisms of Language,* edited by Charles-James N. Bailey and Roy Harris, pp. 167-83. Oxford, England: Pergamon Press, 1985.

> Attempts to reconcile Saussure's synchronic and static study of language with models that emphasize language's dynamic aspects.

Harris, Wendell V. "On Being Sure of Saussure." *The Journal of Aesthetics and Art Criticism* XLI, No. 4 (Summer 1983): 387-97.

> Argues for a reexamination of Saussure's theories, particularly how context and extra-linguistic reality determine the arbitrary nature of the sign.

Hodge, Robert, and Kress, Gunther. "Rereading as Exorcism: Semiotics and the Ghost of Saussure." *Southern Review* 19, No. 1 (March 1986): 38-51.

> Examines how Saussurean thought reflects and has influenced semiotics.

Hurford, James R. "Biological Evolution of the Saussurean Sign as a Component of the Language Acquisition Device." *Lingua* 77, No. 2 (February 1989): 187-222.

> Compares Saussure's views of language to Charles Darwin's theory of evolution and Noam Chomsky's concept of language acquisition, arguing that "over an evolutionary timespan, the Saussurean strategy displaces all rivals, and ends up being *the* strategy by which communication systems are naturally acquired."

Jay, Gregroy S. "Values and Deconstructions: Derrida, Saussure, Marx." *Cultural Critique,* No. 8 (Winter 1987-1988): 153-96.

> Explores Saussure's definition of linguistic value and its impact on the writings of Jacques Derrida.

Koerner, E. F. K[onrad]. *Ferdinand de Saussure: Origin and Development of His Linguistic Thought in Western Studies of Language, A Contribution to the History and Theory of Linguistics.* Braunschweig, Germany: Vieweg, 1973, 428 p.

> In-depth overview of Saussure's life, career, and theories in which Koerner discusses the linguist's predecessors and influences.

Koerner, [E. F.] Konrad. "French Influences on Saussure." *The Canadian Journal of Linguistics* 29, No. 1 (Spring 1984): 20-41.

    Examines the influence that such French scholars as Michel Bréal, Gaston Paris, and Antoine Meillet had on Saussure. This article is also known as "Saussure's French Connection."

————. *Saussurean Studies/Etudes Saussuriennes.* Geneva: Editions Slatkine, 1988, 207 p.

    Reprints essays which "deal in a broad way with linguistic ideas frequently associated with the name of Ferdinand de Saussure, and which were written between 1971 and 1986."

Lehmann, W. P. "Saussure's Dichotomy between Descriptive and Historical Linguistics." In *Directions for Historical Linguistics: A Symposium,* edited by W. P. Lehmann and Yakov Malkiel, pp. 3-20. Austin: University of Texas, 1968.

    Examines the Saussurean oppositions of diachronics and synchronics, *langue* and *parole,* and signifier and signified.

Leška, O.; Nekvapil, O.; and Šoltys, O. "Ferdinand de Saussure and the Prague Linguistic Circle." *Philologica Pragensia* 30, No. 2 (1987): 77-109.

    Examines the similarities between Saussurean linguistics and the theories of the Prague Linguistic Circle, noting that the latter's emphasis on "functional stylistics, although not directly stemming from Saussure's *Cours,* unfolds its principles to the full."

Lévi-Strauss, Claude. "Religion, Language, and History: Concerning an Unpublished Text by Ferdinand de Saussure." In his *The View from Afar,* translated by Joachim Neugroschel and Phoebe Hoss, pp. 148-56. New York: Basic Books, 1985.

    Briefly discusses an unpublished essay in which Saussure speculates on the relationships between history, language, and religion.

Levin, Jules F. "Saussure and the *Arbre* 'Tree': A Fundamental Misunderstanding." In *The Semiotic Bridge: Trends from California,* edited by Irmengard Rauch and Gerald F. Carr, pp. 355-62. Berlin: Mouton de Gruyter, 1989.

    Argues that Saussure did not originate the concept of the arbitrary nature of the sign, nor did he view language as completely motivated or wholly arbitrary.

Nerlich, Brigitte. "Saussurean Linguistics and the Problem of Meaning—From Dynamic Statics to Static Dynamics." *Language and Communication* 6, No. 4 (1986): 267-76.

    Argues for a reevaluation of the problematic aspects of Saussure's theories, stating that "some clarification might be achieved by a more dynamic interpretation of the Saussurean study of language."

Percival, W. Keith. "Ferdinand de Saussure and the History of Semiotics." In *Semiotic Themes,* edited by Richard T. De George, pp. 1-32. Lawrence: University of Kansas Publications, 1981.

    Assesses the strengths and weaknesses of Saussure's science of signs by providing an historical overview of semiology.

Porter, James I. "Saussure and Derrida on the Figure of the Voice." *Modern Language Notes* 101, No. 4 (September 1986): 871-94.

Reevaluates Saussure's focus on the relationship between *langue, parole,* voice, and the spoken and written word, noting that these concerns are "the object of Saussurian linguistics and the linguistic object par excellence."

Rauch, Irmengard. "Peirce, Saussure, and Uexküll." In *Papers in the History of Linguistics: Proceedings of the Third International Conference on the History of the Language Sciences (ICHoLS III), Princeton, 19-23 August 1984,* edited by Hans Aarsleff, Louis G. Kelly, and Hans-Josef Niederehe, pp. 575-83. Amsterdam: John Benjamins Publishing Company, 1987.

    Examines how the sign theories of Saussure, Charles Sanders Peirce, and Jakob von Uexküll are interrelated and have contributed to linguistic theory.

Robey, David. "Modern Linguistics and the Language of Literature." In *Modern Literary Theory: A Comparative Introduction,* edited by Ann Jefferson and David Robey, pp. 38-64. London: Batsford Academic and Educational Ltd., 1982.

    Discusses the impact Saussure, the Russian Formalist Roman Jakobson, and the Prague Linguistic Circle have had on literary scholarship.

Shepheard, David. "Saussure's Vedic Anagrams." *The Modern Language Review* 77, No. 3 (July 1982): 513-23.

    Technical analysis of Saussure's study of Vedic literature and anagrams. Shepheard concludes by relating Saussure's interest in anagrams to the *Course in General Linguistics* and recent scholarship on " 'literality' and the nature of the poetic function of language."

Silverman, Kaja. "From Sign to Subject: A Short History." In her *The Subject of Semiotics,* pp. 3-53. New York: Oxford University Press, 1983.

    Discusses the basic tenets of Saussurean linguistics and their relation to semiotics.

Starobinski, Jean. *Words upon Words: The Anagrams of Ferdinand de Saussure.* Translated by Olivia Emmet. New Haven: Yale University Press, 1979, 129 p.

    Reprints and explicates some of Saussure's notes on anagrams.

Tallis, Raymond. "Not Saussure." *PN Review* 14, No. 2 (1987): 24-8.

    Argues that it was Saussure's followers and not Saussure who concluded that "realistic fiction is illusory."

"Signs and Relations." *Times Literary Supplement,* No. 3770 (7 June 1974): 617.

    Favorable review of the second edition of Wade Baskin's English translation of the *Cours de linguistique générale.*

Watson, Stephen H. "Merleau-Ponty's Involvement with Saussure." In *Continental Philosophy in America,* edited by Hugh J. Silverman, John Sallis, and Thomas M. Seebohm, pp. 208-26. Pittsburgh: Duquesne University Press, 1983.

    Uses Saussurean concepts to examine Maurice Merleau-Ponty's phenomenological approach to philosophy.

Wells, Rulon S. "De Saussure's System of Linguistics." In *Introduction to Structuralism,* edited by Michael Lane, pp. 85-123. New York: Basic Books, 1970.

    Analyzes Saussurean linguistics by approaching the *Course in General Linguistics* "as a synchronic self-contained system" of language.

Wittman, Henri. "Two Models of the Linguistic Mechanism." *Canadian Journal of Linguistics* 11, No. 2 (Spring 1966): 83-93.

    Compares Saussure's theories of language by comparing it to Noam Chomsky's transformational view of language.

Twentieth-Century
Literary Criticism

Cumulative Indexes
Volumes 1-49

How to Use This Index

The main references

list all author entries in the following Gale Literary Criticism series:

CLC = *Contemporary Literary Criticism*
CLR = *Children's Literature Review*
CMLC = *Classical and Medieval Literature Criticism*
DC = *Drama Criticism*
LC = *Literature Criticism from 1400 to 1800*
NCLC = *Nineteenth-Century Literature Criticism*
PC = *Poetry Criticism*
SSC = *Short Story Criticism*
TCLC = *Twentieth-Century Literary Criticism*

The cross-references

list all author entries in the following Gale biographical and literary sources:

AAYA = *Authors & Artists for Young Adults*
AITN = *Authors in the News*
BLC = *Black Literature Criticism*
BW = *Black Writers*
CA = *Contemporary Authors*
CAAS = *Contemporary Authors Autobiography Series*
CABS = *Contemporary Authors Bibliographical Series*
CANR = *Contemporary Authors New Revision Series*
CAP = *Contemporary Authors Permanent Series*
CDALB = *Concise Dictionary of American Literary Biography*
CDBLB = *Concise Dictionary of British Literary Biography*
DLB = *Dictionary of Literary Biography*
DLBD = *Dictionary of Literary Biography Documentary Series*
DLBY = *Dictionary of Literary Biography Yearbook*
HW = *Hispanic Writers*
MAICYA = *Major Authors and Illustrators for Children and Young Adults*
MTCW = *Major 20th-Century Writers*
SAAS = *Something about the Author Autobiography Series*
SATA = *Something about the Author*
WLC = *World Literature Criticism, 1500 to the Present*
YABC = *Yesterday's Authors of Books for Children*

Literary Criticism Series
Cumulative Author Index

A. E......................... TCLC 3, 10
See also Russell, George William
See also DLB 19

A. M.
See Megged, Aharon

Abasiyanik, Sait Faik 1906-1954
See Sait Faik
See also CA 123

Abbey, Edward 1927-1989...... CLC 36, 59
See also CA 45-48; 128; CANR 2

Abbott, Lee K(ittredge) 1947-...... CLC 48
See also CA 124

Abe Kobo 1924- .... CLC 8, 22, 53
See also CA 65-68; CANR 24; MTCW

Abell, Kjeld 1901-1961............ CLC 15
See also CA 111

Abish, Walter 1931-.............. CLC 22
See also CA 101; CANR 37

Abrahams, Peter (Henry) 1919- ..... CLC 4
See also BW; CA 57-60; CANR 26;
DLB 117; MTCW

Abrams, M(eyer) H(oward) 1912-... CLC 24
See also CA 57-60; CANR 13, 33; DLB 67

Abse, Dannie 1923-............. CLC 7, 29
See also CA 53-56; CAAS 1; CANR 4;
DLB 27

Achebe, (Albert) Chinua(lumogu)
1930- ..... CLC 1, 3, 5, 7, 11, 26, 51, 75
See also BLC 1; BW; CA 1-4R; CANR 6,
26; CLR 20; DLB 117; MAICYA;
MTCW; SATA 38, 40; WLC

Acker, Kathy 1948- .... CLC 45
See also CA 117; 122

Ackroyd, Peter 1949-.......... CLC 34, 52
See also CA 123; 127

Acorn, Milton 1923-.............. CLC 15
See also CA 103; DLB 53

Adamov, Arthur 1908-1970 ...... CLC 4, 25
See also CA 17-18; 25-28R; CAP 2; MTCW

Adams, Alice (Boyd) 1926- ... CLC 6, 13, 46
See also CA 81-84; CANR 26; DLBY 86;
MTCW

Adams, Douglas (Noel) 1952- ... CLC 27, 60
See also AAYA 4; BEST 89:3; CA 106;
CANR 34; DLBY 83

Adams, Francis 1862-1893....... NCLC 33

Adams, Henry (Brooks)
1838-1918 .... TCLC 4
See also CA 104; 133; DLB 12, 47

Adams, Richard (George)
1920- .... CLC 4, 5, 18
See also AITN 1, 2; CA 49-52; CANR 3,
35; CLR 20; MAICYA; MTCW;
SATA 7, 69

Adamson, Joy(-Friederike Victoria)
1910-1980 .... CLC 17
See also CA 69-72; 93-96; CANR 22;
MTCW; SATA 11, 22

Adcock, Fleur 1934-.............. CLC 41
See also CA 25-28R; CANR 11, 34;
DLB 40

Addams, Charles (Samuel)
1912-1988 .... CLC 30
See also CA 61-64; 126; CANR 12

Addison, Joseph 1672-1719 .... LC 18
See also CDBLB 1660-1789; DLB 101

Adler, C(arole) S(chwerdtfeger)
1932- .... CLC 35
See also AAYA 4; CA 89-92; CANR 19,
40; MAICYA; SAAS 15; SATA 26, 63

Adler, Renata 1938-............ CLC 8, 31
See also CA 49-52; CANR 5, 22; MTCW

Ady, Endre 1877-1919 .... TCLC 11
See also CA 107

Afton, Effie
See Harper, Frances Ellen Watkins

Agapida, Fray Antonio
See Irving, Washington

Agee, James (Rufus)
1909-1955 .... TCLC 1, 19
See also AITN 1; CA 108;
CDALB 1941-1968; DLB 2, 26

Aghill, Gordon
See Silverberg, Robert

Agnon, S(hmuel) Y(osef Halevi)
1888-1970 .... CLC 4, 8, 14
See also CA 17-18; 25-28R; CAP 2; MTCW

Aherne, Owen
See Cassill, R(onald) V(erlin)

Ai 1947-.................... CLC 4, 14, 69
See also CA 85-88; CAAS 13; DLB 120

Aickman, Robert (Fordyce)
1914-1981 .... CLC 57
See also CA 5-8R; CANR 3

Aiken, Conrad (Potter)
1889-1973 ... CLC 1, 3, 5, 10, 52; SSC 9
See also CA 5-8R; 45-48; CANR 4;
CDALB 1929-1941; DLB 9, 45, 102;
MTCW; SATA 3, 30

Aiken, Joan (Delano) 1924-........ CLC 35
See also AAYA 1; CA 9-12R; CANR 4, 23,
34; CLR 1, 19; MAICYA; MTCW;
SAAS 1; SATA 2, 30, 73

Ainsworth, William Harrison
1805-1882 .... NCLC 13
See also DLB 21; SATA 24

Aitmatov, Chingiz (Torekulovich)
1928- .... CLC 71
See also CA 103; CANR 38; MTCW;
SATA 56

Akers, Floyd
See Baum, L(yman) Frank

Akhmadulina, Bella Akhatovna
1937- .... CLC 53
See also CA 65-68

Akhmatova, Anna
1888-1966 .... CLC 11, 25, 64; PC 2
See also CA 19-20; 25-28R; CANR 35;
CAP 1; MTCW

Aksakov, Sergei Timofeyvich
1791-1859 .... NCLC 2

Aksenov, Vassily................. CLC 22
See also Aksyonov, Vassily (Pavlovich)

Aksyonov, Vassily (Pavlovich)
1932- .... CLC 37
See also Aksenov, Vassily
See also CA 53-56; CANR 12

Akutagawa Ryunosuke
1892-1927 .... TCLC 16
See also CA 117

Alain 1868-1951 .... TCLC 41

Alain-Fournier.................. TCLC 6
See also Fournier, Henri Alban
See also DLB 65

Alarcon, Pedro Antonio de
1833-1891 .... NCLC 1

Alas (y Urena), Leopoldo (Enrique Garcia)
1852-1901 .... TCLC 29
See also CA 113; 131; HW

Albee, Edward (Franklin III)
1928- ... CLC 1, 2, 3, 5, 9, 11, 13, 25, 53
See also AITN 1; CA 5-8R; CABS 3;
CANR 8; CDALB 1941-1968; DLB 7;
MTCW; WLC

Alberti, Rafael 1902- .... CLC 7
See also CA 85-88; DLB 108

Alcala-Galiano, Juan Valera y
See Valera y Alcala-Galiano, Juan

Alcott, Amos Bronson 1799-1888 .. NCLC 1
See also DLB 1

Alcott, Louisa May 1832-1888 .... NCLC 6
See also CDALB 1865-1917; CLR 1;
DLB 1, 42, 79; MAICYA; WLC;
YABC 1

Aldanov, M. A.
See Aldanov, Mark (Alexandrovich)

Aldanov, Mark (Alexandrovich)
1886(?)-1957 .... TCLC 23
See also CA 118

Aldington, Richard 1892-1962...... CLC 49
See also CA 85-88; DLB 20, 36, 100

Aldiss, Brian W(ilson)
1925- .... CLC 5, 14, 40
See also CA 5-8R; CAAS 2; CANR 5, 28;
DLB 14; MTCW; SATA 34

Alegria, Claribel 1924-............ CLC 75
See also CA 131; CAAS 15; HW

Alegria, Fernando 1918-.......... CLC 57
See also CA 9-12R; CANR 5, 32; HW

Appleton, Lawrence
See Lovecraft, H(oward) P(hillips)

Apuleius, (Lucius Madaurensis)
125(?)-175(?) . . . . **CMLC 1**

Aquin, Hubert 1929-1977. . . . . **CLC 15**
See also CA 105; DLB 53

Aragon, Louis 1897-1982. . . . . **CLC 3, 22**
See also CA 69-72; 108; CANR 28;
DLB 72; MTCW

Arany, Janos 1817-1882. . . . . **NCLC 34**

Arbuthnot, John 1667-1735 . . . . **LC 1**
See also DLB 101

Archer, Herbert Winslow
See Mencken, H(enry) L(ouis)

Archer, Jeffrey (Howard) 1940- . . . . **CLC 28**
See also BEST 89:3; CA 77-80; CANR 22

Archer, Jules 1915- . . . . **CLC 12**
See also CA 9-12R; CANR 6; SAAS 5;
SATA 4

Archer, Lee
See Ellison, Harlan

Arden, John 1930- . . . . **CLC 6, 13, 15**
See also CA 13-16R; CAAS 4; CANR 31;
DLB 13; MTCW

Arenas, Reinaldo 1943-1990 . . . . **CLC 41**
See also CA 124; 128; 133; HW

Arendt, Hannah 1906-1975 . . . . **CLC 66**
See also CA 17-20R; 61-64; CANR 26;
MTCW

Aretino, Pietro 1492-1556 . . . . **LC 12**

Arguedas, Jose Maria
1911-1969 . . . . **CLC 10, 18**
See also CA 89-92; DLB 113; HW

Argueta, Manlio 1936- . . . . **CLC 31**
See also CA 131; HW

Ariosto, Ludovico 1474-1533 . . . . **LC 6**

Aristides
See Epstein, Joseph

Aristophanes
450B.C.-385B.C. . . . . **CMLC 4; DC 2**

Arlt, Roberto (Godofredo Christophersen)
1900-1942 . . . . **TCLC 29**
See also CA 123; 131; HW

Armah, Ayi Kwei 1939- . . . . **CLC 5, 33**
See also BLC 1; BW; CA 61-64; CANR 21;
DLB 117; MTCW

Armatrading, Joan 1950- . . . . **CLC 17**
See also CA 114

Arnette, Robert
See Silverberg, Robert

Arnim, Achim von (Ludwig Joachim von
Arnim) 1781-1831 . . . . **NCLC 5**
See also DLB 90

Arnim, Bettina von 1785-1859. . . . **NCLC 38**
See also DLB 90

Arnold, Matthew
1822-1888 . . . . **NCLC 6, 29; PC 5**
See also CDBLB 1832-1890; DLB 32, 57;
WLC

Arnold, Thomas 1795-1842 . . . . . . **NCLC 18**
See also DLB 55

Arnow, Harriette (Louisa) Simpson
1908-1986 . . . . **CLC 2, 7, 18**
See also CA 9-12R; 118; CANR 14; DLB 6;
MTCW; SATA 42, 47

Arp, Hans
See Arp, Jean

Arp, Jean 1887-1966. . . . . **CLC 5**
See also CA 81-84; 25-28R

Arrabal
See Arrabal, Fernando

Arrabal, Fernando
1932- . . . . **CLC 2, 9, 18, 58, 73**
See also CA 9-12R; CANR 15

Arrick, Fran. **CLC 30**

Artaud, Antonin 1896-1948 . . . . . **TCLC 3, 36**
See also CA 104

Arthur, Ruth M(abel) 1905-1979. . . . **CLC 12**
See also CA 9-12R; 85-88; CANR 4;
SATA 7, 26

Artsybashev, Mikhail (Petrovich)
1878-1927 . . . . **TCLC 31**

Arundel, Honor (Morfydd)
1919-1973 . . . . **CLC 17**
See also CA 21-22; 41-44R; CAP 2;
SATA 4, 24

Asch, Sholem 1880-1957 . . . . **TCLC 3**
See also CA 105

Ash, Shalom
See Asch, Sholem

Ashbery, John (Lawrence)
1927- . . . **CLC 2, 3, 4, 6, 9, 13, 15, 25, 41**
See also CA 5-8R; CANR 9, 37; DLB 5;
DLBY 81; MTCW

Ashdown, Clifford
See Freeman, R(ichard) Austin

Ashe, Gordon
See Creasey, John

Ashton-Warner, Sylvia (Constance)
1908-1984 . . . . **CLC 19**
See also CA 69-72; 112; CANR 29; MTCW

Asimov, Isaac
1920-1992 . . . . **CLC 1, 3, 9, 19, 26**
See also BEST 90:2; CA 1-4R; 137;
CANR 2, 19, 36; CLR 12; DLB 8;
MAICYA; MTCW; SATA 1, 26

Astley, Thea (Beatrice May)
1925- . . . . **CLC 41**
See also CA 65-68; CANR 11

Aston, James
See White, T(erence) H(anbury)

Asturias, Miguel Angel
1899-1974 . . . . **CLC 3, 8, 13**
See also CA 25-28; 49-52; CANR 32;
CAP 2; DLB 113; HW; MTCW

Atares, Carlos Saura
See Saura (Atares), Carlos

Atheling, William
See Pound, Ezra (Weston Loomis)

Atheling, William Jr.
See Blish, James (Benjamin)

Atherton, Gertrude (Franklin Horn)
1857-1948 . . . . **TCLC 2**
See also CA 104; DLB 9, 78

Atherton, Lucius
See Masters, Edgar Lee

Atkins, Jack
See Harris, Mark

Atticus
See Fleming, Ian (Lancaster)

Atwood, Margaret (Eleanor)
1939- . . . . **CLC 2, 3, 4, 8, 13, 15, 25, 44;**
SSC 2
See also BEST 89:2; CA 49-52; CANR 3,
24, 33; DLB 53; MTCW; SATA 50; WLC

Aubigny, Pierre d'
See Mencken, H(enry) L(ouis)

Aubin, Penelope 1685-1731(?) . . . . **LC 9**
See also DLB 39

Auchincloss, Louis (Stanton)
1917- . . . . **CLC 4, 6, 9, 18, 45**
See also CA 1-4R; CANR 6, 29; DLB 2;
DLBY 80; MTCW

Auden, W(ystan) H(ugh)
1907-1973 . . . . . **CLC 1, 2, 3, 4, 6, 9, 11,**
14, 43; PC 1
See also CA 9-12R; 45-48; CANR 5;
CDBLB 1914-1945; DLB 10, 20; MTCW;
WLC

Audiberti, Jacques 1900-1965 . . . . . . **CLC 38**
See also CA 25-28R

Auel, Jean M(arie) 1936- . . . . **CLC 31**
See also AAYA 7; BEST 90:4; CA 103;
CANR 21

Auerbach, Erich 1892-1957 . . . . **TCLC 43**
See also CA 118

Augier, Emile 1820-1889 . . . . **NCLC 31**

August, John
See De Voto, Bernard (Augustine)

Augustine, St. 354-430 . . . . **CMLC 6**

Aurelius
See Bourne, Randolph S(illiman)

Austen, Jane
1775-1817 . . . . **NCLC 1, 13, 19, 33**
See also CDBLB 1789-1832; DLB 116;
WLC

Auster, Paul 1947- . . . . **CLC 47**
See also CA 69-72; CANR 23

Austin, Frank
See Faust, Frederick (Schiller)

Austin, Mary (Hunter)
1868-1934 . . . . **TCLC 25**
See also CA 109; DLB 9, 78

Autran Dourado, Waldomiro
See Dourado, (Waldomiro Freitas) Autran

Averroes 1126-1198 . . . . **CMLC 7**
See also DLB 115

Avison, Margaret 1918- . . . . **CLC 2, 4**
See also CA 17-20R; DLB 53; MTCW

Ayckbourn, Alan
1939- . . . . **CLC 5, 8, 18, 33, 74**
See also CA 21-24R; CANR 31; DLB 13;
MTCW

Aydy, Catherine
See Tennant, Emma (Christina)

Ayme, Marcel (Andre) 1902-1967 . . . **CLC 11**
See also CA 89-92; CLR 25; DLB 72

Barry, Philip 1896-1949......... **TCLC 11**
See also CA 109; DLB 7

Bart, Andre Schwarz
See Schwarz-Bart, Andre

Barth, John (Simmons)
1930- ...... **CLC 1, 2, 3, 5, 7, 9, 10, 14,**
27, 51; SSC 10
See also AITN 1, 2; CA 1-4R; CABS 1;
CANR 5, 23; DLB 2; MTCW

Barthelme, Donald
1931-1989 ..... **CLC 1, 2, 3, 5, 6, 8, 13,**
23, 46, 59; SSC 2
See also CA 21-24R; 129; CANR 20;
DLB 2; DLBY 80, 89; MTCW; SATA 7,
62

Barthelme, Frederick 1943-........ **CLC 36**
See also CA 114; 122; DLBY 85

Barthes, Roland (Gerard)
1915-1980 .... **CLC 24**
See also CA 130; 97-100; MTCW

Barzun, Jacques (Martin) 1907- .... **CLC 51**
See also CA 61-64; CANR 22

Bashevis, Isaac
See Singer, Isaac Bashevis

Bashkirtseff, Marie 1859-1884 ... **NCLC 27**

Basho
See Matsuo Basho

Bass, Kingsley B. Jr.
See Bullins, Ed

Bassani, Giorgio 1916-............. **CLC 9**
See also CA 65-68; CANR 33; MTCW

Bastos, Augusto (Antonio) Roa
See Roa Bastos, Augusto (Antonio)

Bataille, Georges 1897-1962 .... **CLC 29**
See also CA 101; 89-92

Bates, H(erbert) E(rnest)
1905-1974 .... **CLC 46; SSC 10**
See also CA 93-96; 45-48; CANR 34;
MTCW

Bauchart
See Camus, Albert

Baudelaire, Charles
1821-1867 .... **NCLC 6, 29; PC 1**
See also WLC

Baudrillard, Jean 1929-........... **CLC 60**

Baum, L(yman) Frank 1856-1919 ... **TCLC 7**
See also CA 108; 133; CLR 15; DLB 22;
MAICYA; MTCW; SATA 18

Baum, Louis F.
See Baum, L(yman) Frank

Baumbach, Jonathan 1933- ...... **CLC 6, 23**
See also CA 13-16R; CAAS 5; CANR 12;
DLBY 80; MTCW

Bausch, Richard (Carl) 1945- ...... **CLC 51**
See also CA 101; CAAS 14

Baxter, Charles 1947-............. **CLC 45**
See also CA 57-60; CANR 40

Baxter, George Owen
See Faust, Frederick (Schiller)

Baxter, James K(eir) 1926-1972 .... **CLC 14**
See also CA 77-80

Baxter, John
See Hunt, E(verette) Howard Jr.

Bayer, Sylvia
See Glassco, John

Beagle, Peter S(oyer) 1939-......... **CLC 7**
See also CA 9-12R; CANR 4; DLBY 80;
SATA 60

Bean, Normal
See Burroughs, Edgar Rice

Beard, Charles A(ustin)
1874-1948 .... **TCLC 15**
See also CA 115; DLB 17; SATA 18

Beardsley, Aubrey 1872-1898 ..... **NCLC 6**

Beattie, Ann
1947- .... **CLC 8, 13, 18, 40, 63; SSC 11**
See also BEST 90:2; CA 81-84; DLBY 82;
MTCW

Beattie, James 1735-1803 .... **NCLC 25**
See also DLB 109

Beauchamp, Kathleen Mansfield 1888-1923
See Mansfield, Katherine
See also CA 104; 134

Beauvoir, Simone (Lucie Ernestine Marie
Bertrand) de
1908-1986 ... **CLC 1, 2, 4, 8, 14, 31, 44,**
50, 71
See also CA 9-12R; 118; CANR 28;
DLB 72; DLBY 86; MTCW; WLC

Becker, Jurek 1937-............. **CLC 7, 19**
See also CA 85-88; DLB 75

Becker, Walter 1950-............. **CLC 26**

Beckett, Samuel (Barclay)
1906-1989 ..... **CLC 1, 2, 3, 4, 6, 9, 10,**
11, 14, 18, 29, 57, 59
See also CA 5-8R; 130; CANR 33;
CDBLB 1945-1960; DLB 13, 15;
DLBY 90; MTCW; WLC

Beckford, William 1760-1844 .... **NCLC 16**
See also DLB 39

Beckman, Gunnel 1910-........... **CLC 26**
See also CA 33-36R; CANR 15; CLR 25;
MAICYA; SAAS 9; SATA 6

Becque, Henri 1837-1899........ **NCLC 3**

Beddoes, Thomas Lovell
1803-1849 .... **NCLC 3**
See also DLB 96

Bedford, Donald F.
See Fearing, Kenneth (Flexner)

Beecher, Catharine Esther
1800-1878 .... **NCLC 30**
See also DLB 1

Beecher, John 1904-1980........... **CLC 6**
See also AITN 1; CA 5-8R; 105; CANR 8

Beer, Johann 1655-1700............. **LC 5**

Beer, Patricia 1924-............. **CLC 58**
See also CA 61-64; CANR 13; DLB 40

Beerbohm, Henry Maximilian
1872-1956 ....**TCLC 1, 24**
See also CA 104; DLB 34, 100

Begiebing, Robert J(ohn) 1946-..... **CLC 70**
See also CA 122; CANR 40

Behan, Brendan
1923-1964 .... **CLC 1, 8, 11, 15**
See also CA 73-76; CANR 33;
CDBLB 1945-1960; DLB 13; MTCW

Behn, Aphra 1640(?)-1689 .... **LC 1**
See also DLB 39, 80; WLC

Behrman, S(amuel) N(athaniel)
1893-1973 .... **CLC 40**
See also CA 13-16; 45-48; CAP 1; DLB 7,
44

Belasco, David 1853-1931 .... **TCLC 3**
See also CA 104; DLB 7

Belcheva, Elisaveta 1893- .... **CLC 10**

Beldone, Phil "Cheech"
See Ellison, Harlan

Beleno
See Azuela, Mariano

Belinski, Vissarion Grigoryevich
1811-1848 .... **NCLC 5**

Belitt, Ben 1911-................. **CLC 22**
See also CA 13-16R; CAAS 4; CANR 7;
DLB 5

Bell, James Madison 1826-1902 ... **TCLC 43**
See also BLC 1; BW; CA 122; 124; DLB 50

Bell, Madison (Smartt) 1957- ...... **CLC 41**
See also CA 111; CANR 28

Bell, Marvin (Hartley) 1937-..... **CLC 8, 31**
See also CA 21-24R; CAAS 14; DLB 5;
MTCW

Bell, W. L. D.
See Mencken, H(enry) L(ouis)

Bellamy, Atwood C.
See Mencken, H(enry) L(ouis)

Bellamy, Edward 1850-1898 ...... **NCLC 4**
See also DLB 12

Bellin, Edward J.
See Kuttner, Henry

Belloc, (Joseph) Hilaire (Pierre)
1870-1953 .... **TCLC 7, 18**
See also CA 106; DLB 19, 100; YABC 1

Belloc, Joseph Peter Rene Hilaire
See Belloc, (Joseph) Hilaire (Pierre)

Belloc, Joseph Pierre Hilaire
See Belloc, (Joseph) Hilaire (Pierre)

Belloc, M. A.
See Lowndes, Marie Adelaide (Belloc)

Bellow, Saul
1915- ..... **CLC 1, 2, 3, 6, 8, 10, 13, 15,**
25, 33, 34, 63
See also AITN 2; BEST 89:3; CA 5-8R;
CABS 1; CANR 29; CDALB 1941-1968;
DLB 2, 28; DLBD 3; DLBY 82; MTCW;
WLC

Belser, Reimond Karel Maria de
1929- .... **CLC 14**

Bely, Andrey .... **TCLC 7**
See also Bugayev, Boris Nikolayevich

Benary, Margot
See Benary-Isbert, Margot

Benary-Isbert, Margot 1889-1979... **CLC 12**
See also CA 5-8R; 89-92; CANR 4;
CLR 12; MAICYA; SATA 2, 21

Benavente (y Martinez), Jacinto
1866-1954 .... **TCLC 3**
See also CA 106; 131; HW; MTCW

Benchley, Peter (Bradford)
1940- .... CLC 4, 8
See also AITN 2; CA 17-20R; CANR 12,
35; MTCW; SATA 3

Benchley, Robert (Charles)
1889-1945 .... TCLC 1
See also CA 105; DLB 11

Benedikt, Michael 1935- .... CLC 4, 14
See also CA 13-16R; CANR 7; DLB 5

Benet, Juan 1927- .... CLC 28

Benet, Stephen Vincent
1898-1943 .... TCLC 7; SSC 10
See also CA 104; DLB 4, 48, 102; YABC 1

Benet, William Rose 1886-1950 ... TCLC 28
See also CA 118; DLB 45

Benford, Gregory (Albert) 1941-.... CLC 52
See also CA 69-72; CANR 12, 24;
DLBY 82

Bengtsson, Frans (Gunnar)
1894-1954 .... TCLC 48

Benjamin, Lois
See Gould, Lois

Benjamin, Walter 1892-1940 ..... TCLC 39

Benn, Gottfried 1886-1956......... TCLC 3
See also CA 106; DLB 56

Bennett, Alan 1934- .... CLC 45
See also CA 103; CANR 35; MTCW

Bennett, (Enoch) Arnold
1867-1931 .... TCLC 5, 20
See also CA 106; CDBLB 1890-1914;
DLB 10, 34, 98

Bennett, Elizabeth
See Mitchell, Margaret (Munnerlyn)

Bennett, George Harold 1930-
See Bennett, Hal
See also BW; CA 97-100

Bennett, Hal .... CLC 5
See also Bennett, George Harold
See also DLB 33

Bennett, Jay 1912- .... CLC 35
See also AAYA 10; CA 69-72; CANR 11;
SAAS 4; SATA 27, 41

Bennett, Louise (Simone) 1919-..... CLC 28
See also BLC 1; DLB 117

Benson, E(dward) F(rederic)
1867-1940 .... TCLC 27
See also CA 114

Benson, Jackson J. 1930-.......... CLC 34
See also CA 25-28R; DLB 111

Benson, Sally 1900-1972 .... CLC 17
See also CA 19-20; 37-40R; CAP 1;
SATA 1, 27, 35

Benson, Stella 1892-1933......... TCLC 17
See also CA 117; DLB 36

Bentham, Jeremy 1748-1832 ..... NCLC 38
See also DLB 107

Bentley, E(dmund) C(lerihew)
1875-1956 .... TCLC 12
See also CA 108; DLB 70

Bentley, Eric (Russell) 1916-....... CLC 24
See also CA 5-8R; CANR 6

Beranger, Pierre Jean de
1780-1857 .... NCLC 34

Berger, Colonel
See Malraux, (Georges-)Andre

Berger, John (Peter) 1926- ...... CLC 2, 19
See also CA 81-84; DLB 14

Berger, Melvin H. 1927-.......... CLC 12
See also CA 5-8R; CANR 4; SAAS 2;
SATA 5

Berger, Thomas (Louis)
1924- .... CLC 3, 5, 8, 11, 18, 38
See also CA 1-4R; CANR 5, 28; DLB 2;
DLBY 80; MTCW

Bergman, (Ernst) Ingmar
1918- .... CLC 16, 72
See also CA 81-84; CANR 33

Bergson, Henri 1859-1941 .... TCLC 32

Bergstein, Eleanor 1938-.......... CLC 4
See also CA 53-56; CANR 5

Berkoff, Steven 1937-............. CLC 56
See also CA 104

Bermant, Chaim (Icyk) 1929- ...... CLC 40
See also CA 57-60; CANR 6, 31

Bernanos, (Paul Louis) Georges
1888-1948 .... TCLC 3
See also CA 104; 130; DLB 72

Bernard, April 1956- .... CLC 59
See also CA 131

Bernhard, Thomas
1931-1989 .... CLC 3, 32, 61
See also CA 85-88; 127; CANR 32;
DLB 85, 124; MTCW

Berrigan, Daniel 1921-............. CLC 4
See also CA 33-36R; CAAS 1; CANR 11;
DLB 5

Berrigan, Edmund Joseph Michael Jr.
1934-1983
See Berrigan, Ted
See also CA 61-64; 110; CANR 14

Berrigan, Ted..................... CLC 37
See also Berrigan, Edmund Joseph Michael
Jr.
See also DLB 5

Berry, Charles Edward Anderson 1931-
See Berry, Chuck
See also CA 115

Berry, Chuck..................... CLC 17
See also Berry, Charles Edward Anderson

Berry, Jonas
See Ashbery, John (Lawrence)

Berry, Wendell (Erdman)
1934- .... CLC 4, 6, 8, 27, 46
See also AITN 1; CA 73-76; DLB 5, 6

Berryman, John
1914-1972 ..... CLC 1, 2, 3, 4, 6, 8, 10,
13, 25, 62
See also CA 13-16; 33-36R; CABS 2;
CANR 35; CAP 1; CDALB 1941-1968;
DLB 48; MTCW

Bertolucci, Bernardo 1940- .... CLC 16
See also CA 106

Bertrand, Aloysius 1807-1841 .... NCLC 31

Bertran de Born c. 1140-1215 ..... CMLC 5

Besant, Annie (Wood) 1847-1933 ... TCLC 9
See also CA 105

Bessie, Alvah 1904-1985.......... CLC 23
See also CA 5-8R; 116; CANR 2; DLB 26

Bethlen, T. D.
See Silverberg, Robert

Beti, Mongo..................... CLC 27
See also Biyidi, Alexandre
See also BLC 1

Betjeman, John
1906-1984 .... CLC 2, 6, 10, 34, 43
See also CA 9-12R; 112; CANR 33;
CDBLB 1945-1960; DLB 20; DLBY 84;
MTCW

Betti, Ugo 1892-1953 .... TCLC 5
See also CA 104

Betts, Doris (Waugh) 1932-.... CLC 3, 6, 28
See also CA 13-16R; CANR 9; DLBY 82

Bevan, Alistair
See Roberts, Keith (John Kingston)

Beynon, John
See Harris, John (Wyndham Parkes Lucas)
Beynon

Bialik, Chaim Nachman
1873-1934 .... TCLC 25

Bickerstaff, Isaac
See Swift, Jonathan

Bidart, Frank 19(?)-.............. CLC 33

Bienek, Horst 1930-............ CLC 7, 11
See also CA 73-76; DLB 75

Bierce, Ambrose (Gwinett)
1842-1914(?) ..... TCLC 1, 7, 44; SSC 9
See also CA 104; 139; CDALB 1865-1917;
DLB 11, 12, 23, 71, 74; WLC

Billings, Josh
See Shaw, Henry Wheeler

Billington, Rachel 1942-........... CLC 43
See also AITN 2; CA 33-36R

Binyon, T(imothy) J(ohn) 1936- .... CLC 34
See also CA 111; CANR 28

Bioy Casares, Adolfo 1914-.... CLC 4, 8, 13
See also CA 29-32R; CANR 19; DLB 113;
HW; MTCW

Bird, C.
See Ellison, Harlan

Bird, Cordwainer
See Ellison, Harlan

Bird, Robert Montgomery
1806-1854 .... NCLC 1

Birney, (Alfred) Earle
1904- ....CLC 1, 4, 6, 11
See also CA 1-4R; CANR 5, 20; DLB 88;
MTCW

Bishop, Elizabeth
1911-1979 ..... CLC 1, 4, 9, 13, 15, 32;
PC 3
See also CA 5-8R; 89-92; CABS 2;
CANR 26; CDALB 1968-1988; DLB 5;
MTCW; SATA 24

Bishop, John 1935-............... CLC 10
See also CA 105

Bissett, Bill 1939-................ CLC 18
See also CA 69-72; CANR 15; DLB 53;
MTCW

Bitov, Andrei (Georgievich) 1937-... CLC 57

Biyidi, Alexandre 1932-
See Beti, Mongo
See also BW; CA 114; 124; MTCW

Bjarme, Brynjolf
See Ibsen, Henrik (Johan)

Bjornson, Bjornstjerne (Martinius)
1832-1910 .... TCLC **7, 37**
See also CA 104

Black, Robert
See Holdstock, Robert P.

Blackburn, Paul 1926-1971 ...... CLC **9, 43**
See also CA 81-84; 33-36R; CANR 34;
DLB 16; DLBY 81

Black Elk 1863-1950 .... TCLC **33**

Black Hobart
See Sanders, (James) Ed(ward)

Blacklin, Malcolm
See Chambers, Aidan

Blackmore, R(ichard) D(oddridge)
1825-1900 .... TCLC **27**
See also CA 120; DLB 18

Blackmur, R(ichard) P(almer)
1904-1965 .... CLC **2, 24**
See also CA 11-12; 25-28R; CAP 1; DLB 63

Black Tarantula, The
See Acker, Kathy

Blackwood, Algernon (Henry)
1869-1951 .... TCLC **5**
See also CA 105

Blackwood, Caroline 1931- .... CLC **6, 9**
See also CA 85-88; CANR 32; DLB 14;
MTCW

Blade, Alexander
See Hamilton, Edmond; Silverberg, Robert

Blaga, Lucian 1895-1961 .... CLC **75**

Blair, Eric (Arthur) 1903-1950
See Orwell, George
See also CA 104; 132; MTCW; SATA 29

Blais, Marie-Claire
1939- .... CLC **2, 4, 6, 13, 22**
See also CA 21-24R; CAAS 4; CANR 38;
DLB 53; MTCW

Blaise, Clark 1940-............... CLC **29**
See also AITN 2; CA 53-56; CAAS 3;
CANR 5; DLB 53

Blake, Nicholas
See Day Lewis, C(ecil)
See also DLB 77

Blake, William 1757-1827 .... NCLC **13**
See also CDBLB 1789-1832; DLB 93;
MAICYA; SATA 30; WLC

Blasco Ibanez, Vicente
1867-1928 .... TCLC **12**
See also CA 110; 131; HW; MTCW

Blatty, William Peter 1928-......... CLC **2**
See also CA 5-8R; CANR 9

Bleeck, Oliver
See Thomas, Ross (Elmore)

Blessing, Lee 1949-............... CLC **54**

Blish, James (Benjamin)
1921-1975 .... CLC **14**
See also CA 1-4R; 57-60; CANR 3; DLB 8;
MTCW; SATA 66

Bliss, Reginald
See Wells, H(erbert) G(eorge)

Blixen, Karen (Christentze Dinesen)
1885-1962
See Dinesen, Isak
See also CA 25-28; CANR 22; CAP 2;
MTCW; SATA 44

Bloch, Robert (Albert) 1917-....... CLC **33**
See also CA 5-8R; CANR 5; DLB 44;
SATA 12

Blok, Alexander (Alexandrovich)
1880-1921 .... TCLC **5**
See also CA 104

Blom, Jan
See Breytenbach, Breyten

Bloom, Harold 1930- .... CLC **24**
See also CA 13-16R; CANR 39; DLB 67

Bloomfield, Aurelius
See Bourne, Randolph S(illiman)

Blount, Roy (Alton) Jr. 1941-...... CLC **38**
See also CA 53-56; CANR 10, 28; MTCW

Bloy, Leon 1846-1917............ TCLC **22**
See also CA 121; DLB 123

Blume, Judy (Sussman) 1938-... CLC **12, 30**
See also AAYA 3; CA 29-32R; CANR 13,
37; CLR 2, 15; DLB 52; MAICYA;
MTCW; SATA 2, 31

Blunden, Edmund (Charles)
1896-1974 .... CLC **2, 56**
See also CA 17-18; 45-48; CAP 2; DLB 20,
100; MTCW

Bly, Robert (Elwood)
1926- .... CLC **1, 2, 5, 10, 15, 38**
See also CA 5-8R; DLB 5; MTCW

Bobette
See Simenon, Georges (Jacques Christian)

Boccaccio, Giovanni 1313-1375
See also SSC 10

Bochco, Steven 1943-............. CLC **35**
See also CA 124; 138

Bodenheim, Maxwell 1892-1954 ... TCLC **44**
See also CA 110; DLB 9, 45

Bodker, Cecil 1927- .... CLC **21**
See also CA 73-76; CANR 13; CLR 23;
MAICYA; SATA 14

Boell, Heinrich (Theodor) 1917-1985
See Boll, Heinrich (Theodor)
See also CA 21-24R; 116; CANR 24;
DLB 69; DLBY 85; MTCW

Bogan, Louise 1897-1970..... CLC **4, 39, 46**
See also CA 73-76; 25-28R; CANR 33;
DLB 45; MTCW

Bogarde, Dirk .... CLC **19**
See also Van Den Bogarde, Derek Jules
Gaspard Ulric Niven
See also DLB 14

Bogosian, Eric 1953- .... CLC **45**
See also CA 138

Bograd, Larry 1953-.............. CLC **35**
See also CA 93-96; SATA 33

Boiardo, Matteo Maria 1441-1494 .... LC **6**

Boileau-Despreaux, Nicolas
1636-1711 .... LC **3**

Boland, Eavan 1944-.......... CLC **40, 67**
See also DLB 40

Boll, Heinrich (Theodor)
1917-1985 ... CLC **2, 3, 6, 9, 11, 15, 27,
39, 72**
See also Boell, Heinrich (Theodor)
See also DLB 69; DLBY 85; WLC

Bolt, Lee
See Faust, Frederick (Schiller)

Bolt, Robert (Oxton) 1924- .... CLC **14**
See also CA 17-20R; CANR 35; DLB 13;
MTCW

Bomkauf
See Kaufman, Bob (Garnell)

Bonaventura.................... NCLC **35**
See also DLB 90

Bond, Edward 1934-....... CLC **4, 6, 13, 23**
See also CA 25-28R; CANR 38; DLB 13;
MTCW

Bonham, Frank 1914-1989......... CLC **12**
See also AAYA 1; CA 9-12R; CANR 4, 36;
MAICYA; SAAS 3; SATA 1, 49, 62

Bonnefoy, Yves 1923-........ CLC **9, 15, 58**
See also CA 85-88; CANR 33; MTCW

Bontemps, Arna(ud Wendell)
1902-1973 .... CLC **1, 18**
See also BLC 1; BW; CA 1-4R; 41-44R;
CANR 4, 35; CLR 6; DLB 48, 51;
MAICYA; MTCW; SATA 2, 24, 44

Booth, Martin 1944-.............. CLC **13**
See also CA 93-96; CAAS 2

Booth, Philip 1925-................ CLC **23**
See also CA 5-8R; CANR 5; DLBY 82

Booth, Wayne C(layson) 1921- ..... CLC **24**
See also CA 1-4R; CAAS 5; CANR 3;
DLB 67

Borchert, Wolfgang 1921-1947 ..... TCLC **5**
See also CA 104; DLB 69, 124

Borges, Jorge Luis
1899-1986 ... CLC **1, 2, 3, 4, 6, 8, 9, 10,
13, 19, 44, 48; SSC 4**
See also CA 21-24R; CANR 19, 33;
DLB 113; DLBY 86; HW; MTCW; WLC

Borowski, Tadeusz 1922-1951...... TCLC **9**
See also CA 106

Borrow, George (Henry)
1803-1881 .... NCLC **9**
See also DLB 21, 55

Bosman, Herman Charles
1905-1951 .... TCLC **49**

Bosschere, Jean de 1878(?)-1953... TCLC **19**
See also CA 115

Boswell, James 1740-1795........... LC **4**
See also CDBLB 1660-1789; DLB 104;
WLC

Bottoms, David 1949-............. CLC **53**
See also CA 105; CANR 22; DLB 120;
DLBY 83

Boucolon, Maryse 1937-
See Conde, Maryse
See also CA 110; CANR 30

Bourget, Paul (Charles Joseph)
1852-1935 .... TCLC **12**
See also CA 107; DLB 123

Bronte, Anne 1820-1849......... **NCLC 4**
See also DLB 21

Bronte, Charlotte
1816-1855 .... **NCLC 3, 8, 33**
See also CDBLB 1832-1890; DLB 21; WLC

Bronte, (Jane) Emily
1818-1848 .... **NCLC 16, 35**
See also CDBLB 1832-1890; DLB 21, 32;
WLC

Brooke, Frances 1724-1789 .... **LC 6**
See also DLB 39, 99

Brooke, Henry 1703(?)-1783 .... **LC 1**
See also DLB 39

Brooke, Rupert (Chawner)
1887-1915 .... **TCLC 2, 7**
See also CA 104; 132; CDBLB 1914-1945;
DLB 19; MTCW; WLC

Brooke-Haven, P.
See Wodehouse, P(elham) G(renville)

Brooke-Rose, Christine 1926-...... **CLC 40**
See also CA 13-16R; DLB 14

Brookner, Anita 1928-...... **CLC 32, 34, 51**
See also CA 114; 120; CANR 37; DLBY 87;
MTCW

Brooks, Cleanth 1906-............ **CLC 24**
See also CA 17-20R; CANR 33, 35;
DLB 63; MTCW

Brooks, George
See Baum, L(yman) Frank

Brooks, Gwendolyn
1917-.......... **CLC 1, 2, 4, 5, 15, 49**
See also AITN 1; BLC 1; BW; CA 1-4R;
CANR 1, 27; CDALB 1941-1968;
CLR 27; DLB 5, 76; MTCW; SATA 6;
WLC

Brooks, Mel..................... **CLC 12**
See also Kaminsky, Melvin
See also DLB 26

Brooks, Peter 1938-.............. **CLC 34**
See also CA 45-48; CANR 1

Brooks, Van Wyck 1886-1963...... **CLC 29**
See also CA 1-4R; CANR 6; DLB 45, 63,
103

Brophy, Brigid (Antonia)
1929-................. **CLC 6, 11, 29**
See also CA 5-8R; CAAS 4; CANR 25;
DLB 14; MTCW

Brosman, Catharine Savage 1934-.... **CLC 9**
See also CA 61-64; CANR 21

Brother Antoninus
See Everson, William (Oliver)

Broughton, T(homas) Alan 1936- ... **CLC 19**
See also CA 45-48; CANR 2, 23

Broumas, Olga 1949-.......... **CLC 10, 73**
See also CA 85-88; CANR 20

Brown, Charles Brockden
1771-1810 .... **NCLC 22**
See also CDALB 1640-1865; DLB 37, 59,
73

Brown, Christy 1932-1981........ **CLC 63**
See also CA 105; 104; DLB 14

Brown, Claude 1937-............ **CLC 30**
See also AAYA 7; BLC 1; BW; CA 73-76

Brown, Dee (Alexander) 1908- .. **CLC 18, 47**
See also CA 13-16R; CAAS 6; CANR 11;
DLBY 80; MTCW; SATA 5

Brown, George
See Wertmueller, Lina

Brown, George Douglas
1869-1902 .... **TCLC 28**

Brown, George Mackay 1921-.... **CLC 5, 48**
See also CA 21-24R; CAAS 6; CANR 12,
37; DLB 14, 27; MTCW; SATA 35

Brown, (William) Larry 1951-...... **CLC 73**
See also CA 130; 134

Brown, Moses
See Barrett, William (Christopher)

Brown, Rita Mae 1944-........ **CLC 18, 43**
See also CA 45-48; CANR 2, 11, 35;
MTCW

Brown, Roderick (Langmere) Haig-
See Haig-Brown, Roderick (Langmere)

Brown, Rosellen 1939-........... **CLC 32**
See also CA 77-80; CAAS 10; CANR 14

Brown, Sterling Allen
1901-1989 .... **CLC 1, 23, 59**
See also BLC 1; BW; CA 85-88; 127;
CANR 26; DLB 48, 51, 63; MTCW

Brown, Will
See Ainsworth, William Harrison

Brown, William Wells
1813-1884 .... **NCLC 2; DC 1**
See also BLC 1; DLB 3, 50

Browne, (Clyde) Jackson 1948(?)-... **CLC 21**
See also CA 120

Browning, Elizabeth Barrett
1806-1861 .... **NCLC 1, 16; PC 6**
See also CDBLB 1832-1890; DLB 32; WLC

Browning, Robert
1812-1889 .... **NCLC 19; PC 2**
See also CDBLB 1832-1890; DLB 32;
YABC 1

Browning, Tod 1882-1962 .... **CLC 16**
See also CA 117

Bruccoli, Matthew J(oseph) 1931- .. **CLC 34**
See also CA 9-12R; CANR 7; DLB 103

Bruce, Lenny..................... **CLC 21**
See also Schneider, Leonard Alfred

Bruin, John
See Brutus, Dennis

Brulls, Christian
See Simenon, Georges (Jacques Christian)

Brunner, John (Kilian Houston)
1934-..................... **CLC 8, 10**
See also CA 1-4R; CAAS 8; CANR 2, 37;
MTCW

Brutus, Dennis 1924-............. **CLC 43**
See also BLC 1; BW; CA 49-52; CAAS 14;
CANR 2, 27; DLB 117

Bryan, C(ourtlandt) D(ixon) B(arnes)
1936-..................... **CLC 29**
See also CA 73-76; CANR 13

Bryan, Michael
See Moore, Brian

Bryant, William Cullen
1794-1878 .... **NCLC 6**
See also CDALB 1640-1865; DLB 3, 43, 59

Bryusov, Valery Yakovlevich
1873-1924 .... **TCLC 10**
See also CA 107

Buchan, John 1875-1940 .... **TCLC 41**
See also CA 108; DLB 34, 70; YABC 2

Buchanan, George 1506-1582 .... **LC 4**

Buchheim, Lothar-Guenther 1918- ... **CLC 6**
See also CA 85-88

Buchner, (Karl) Georg
1813-1837 .... **NCLC 26**

Buchwald, Art(hur) 1925-.......... **CLC 33**
See also AITN 1; CA 5-8R; CANR 21;
MTCW; SATA 10

Buck, Pearl S(ydenstricker)
1892-1973 .... **CLC 7, 11, 18**
See also AITN 1; CA 1-4R; 41-44R;
CANR 1, 34; DLB 9, 102; MTCW;
SATA 1, 25

Buckler, Ernest 1908-1984......... **CLC 13**
See also CA 11-12; 114; CAP 1; DLB 68;
SATA 47

Buckley, Vincent (Thomas)
1925-1988 .... **CLC 57**
See also CA 101

Buckley, William F(rank) Jr.
1925-.................. **CLC 7, 18, 37**
See also AITN 1; CA 1-4R; CANR 1, 24;
DLBY 80; MTCW

Buechner, (Carl) Frederick
1926-............... **CLC 2, 4, 6, 9**
See also CA 13-16R; CANR 11, 39;
DLBY 80; MTCW

Buell, John (Edward) 1927-........ **CLC 10**
See also CA 1-4R; DLB 53

Buero Vallejo, Antonio 1916- ... **CLC 15, 46**
See also CA 106; CANR 24; HW; MTCW

Bufalino, Gesualdo 1920(?)-........ **CLC 74**

Bugayev, Boris Nikolayevich 1880-1934
See Bely, Andrey
See also CA 104

Bukowski, Charles 1920-.... **CLC 2, 5, 9, 41**
See also CA 17-20R; CANR 40; DLB 5;
MTCW

Bulgakov, Mikhail (Afanas'evich)
1891-1940 .... **TCLC 2, 16**
See also CA 105

Bullins, Ed 1935- .... **CLC 1, 5, 7**
See also BLC 1; BW; CA 49-52; CAAS 16;
CANR 24; DLB 7, 38; MTCW

Bulwer-Lytton, Edward (George Earle Lytton)
1803-1873 .... **NCLC 1**
See also DLB 21

Bunin, Ivan Alexeyevich
1870-1953 .... **TCLC 6; SSC 5**
See also CA 104

Bunting, Basil 1900-1985.... **CLC 10, 39, 47**
See also CA 53-56; 115; CANR 7; DLB 20

Bunuel, Luis 1900-1983 .... **CLC 16**
See also CA 101; 110; CANR 32; HW

Bunyan, John 1628-1688 .... **LC 4**
See also CDBLB 1660-1789; DLB 39; WLC

Burford, Eleanor
See Hibbert, Eleanor Burford

Burgess, Anthony
    1917- ..... **CLC 1, 2, 4, 5, 8, 10, 13, 15,
                    22, 40, 62**
    See also Wilson, John (Anthony) Burgess
    See also AITN 1; CDBLB 1960 to Present;
    DLB 14

Burke, Edmund 1729(?)-1797........ **LC 7**
    See also DLB 104; WLC

Burke, Kenneth (Duva) 1897- .... **CLC 2, 24**
    See also CA 5-8R; CANR 39; DLB 45, 63;
    MTCW

Burke, Leda
    See Garnett, David

Burke, Ralph
    See Silverberg, Robert

Burney, Fanny 1752-1840 .... **NCLC 12**
    See also DLB 39

Burns, Robert 1759-1796....... **LC 3; PC 6**
    See also CDBLB 1789-1832; DLB 109;
    WLC

Burns, Tex
    See L'Amour, Louis (Dearborn)

Burnshaw, Stanley 1906- ..... **CLC 3, 13, 44**
    See also CA 9-12R; DLB 48

Burr, Anne 1937- .... **CLC 6**
    See also CA 25-28R

Burroughs, Edgar Rice
    1875-1950 .... **TCLC 2, 32**
    See also CA 104; 132; DLB 8; MTCW;
    SATA 41

Burroughs, William S(eward)
    1914- ...... **CLC 1, 2, 5, 15, 22, 42, 75**
    See also AITN 2; CA 9-12R; CANR 20;
    DLB 2, 8, 16; DLBY 81; MTCW; WLC

Busch, Frederick 1941- ... **CLC 7, 10, 18, 47**
    See also CA 33-36R; CAAS 1; DLB 6

Bush, Ronald 1946- .... **CLC 34**
    See also CA 136

Bustos, F(rancisco)
    See Borges, Jorge Luis

Bustos Domecq, H(onorio)
    See Bioy Casares, Adolfo; Borges, Jorge
    Luis

Butler, Octavia E(stelle) 1947- ..... **CLC 38**
    See also BW; CA 73-76; CANR 12, 24, 38;
    DLB 33; MTCW

Butler, Samuel 1612-1680 .... **LC 16**
    See also DLB 101

Butler, Samuel 1835-1902 ...... **TCLC 1, 33**
    See also CA 104; CDBLB 1890-1914;
    DLB 18, 57; WLC

Butler, Walter C.
    See Faust, Frederick (Schiller)

Butor, Michel (Marie Francois)
    1926- .... **CLC 1, 3, 8, 11, 15**
    See also CA 9-12R; CANR 33; DLB 83;
    MTCW

Buzo, Alexander (John) 1944- ...... **CLC 61**
    See also CA 97-100; CANR 17, 39

Buzzati, Dino 1906-1972 .... **CLC 36**
    See also CA 33-36R

Byars, Betsy (Cromer) 1928-....... **CLC 35**
    See also CA 33-36R; CANR 18, 36; CLR 1,
    16; DLB 52; MAICYA; MTCW; SAAS 1;
    SATA 4, 46

Byatt, A(ntonia) S(usan Drabble)
    1936- .... **CLC 19, 65**
    See also CA 13-16R; CANR 13, 33;
    DLB 14; MTCW

Byrne, David 1952-............... **CLC 26**
    See also CA 127

Byrne, John Keyes 1926-......... **CLC 19**
    See also Leonard, Hugh
    See also CA 102

Byron, George Gordon (Noel)
    1788-1824 .... **NCLC 2, 12**
    See also CDBLB 1789-1832; DLB 96, 110;
    WLC

C.3.3.
    See Wilde, Oscar (Fingal O'Flahertie Wills)

Caballero, Fernan 1796-1877..... **NCLC 10**

Cabell, James Branch 1879-1958 ... **TCLC 6**
    See also CA 105; DLB 9, 78

Cable, George Washington
    1844-1925 .... **TCLC 4; SSC 4**
    See also CA 104; DLB 12, 74

Cabrera Infante, G(uillermo)
    1929- .... **CLC 5, 25, 45**
    See also CA 85-88; CANR 29; DLB 113;
    HW; MTCW

Cade, Toni
    See Bambara, Toni Cade

Cadmus
    See Buchan, John

Caedmon fl. 658-680............. **CMLC 7**

Caeiro, Alberto
    See Pessoa, Fernando (Antonio Nogueira)

Cage, John (Milton Jr.) 1912-...... **CLC 41**
    See also CA 13-16R; CANR 9

Cain, G.
    See Cabrera Infante, G(uillermo)

Cain, Guillermo
    See Cabrera Infante, G(uillermo)

Cain, James M(allahan)
    1892-1977 .... **CLC 3, 11, 28**
    See also AITN 1; CA 17-20R; 73-76;
    CANR 8, 34; MTCW

Caine, Mark
    See Raphael, Frederic (Michael)

Calderon de la Barca, Pedro
    1600-1681 .... **DC 3**

Caldwell, Erskine (Preston)
    1903-1987 .... **CLC 1, 8, 14, 50, 60**
    See also AITN 1; CA 1-4R; 121; CAAS 1;
    CANR 2, 33; DLB 9, 86; MTCW

Caldwell, (Janet Miriam) Taylor (Holland)
    1900-1985 .... **CLC 2, 28, 39**
    See also CA 5-8R; 116; CANR 5

Calhoun, John Caldwell
    1782-1850 .... **NCLC 15**
    See also DLB 3

Calisher, Hortense 1911-.... **CLC 2, 4, 8, 38**
    See also CA 1-4R; CANR 1, 22; DLB 2;
    MTCW

Callaghan, Morley Edward
    1903-1990 .... **CLC 3, 14, 41, 65**
    See also CA 9-12R; 132; CANR 33;
    DLB 68; MTCW

Calvino, Italo
    1923-1985 .... **CLC 5, 8, 11, 22, 33, 39,
                     73; SSC 3**
    See also CA 85-88; 116; CANR 23; MTCW

Cameron, Carey 1952-............ **CLC 59**
    See also CA 135

Cameron, Peter 1959-............. **CLC 44**
    See also CA 125

Campana, Dino 1885-1932........ **TCLC 20**
    See also CA 117; DLB 114

Campbell, John W(ood Jr.)
    1910-1971 .... **CLC 32**
    See also CA 21-22; 29-32R; CANR 34;
    CAP 2; DLB 8; MTCW

Campbell, Joseph 1904-1987 .... **CLC 69**
    See also AAYA 3; BEST 89:2; CA 1-4R;
    124; CANR 3, 28; MTCW

Campbell, (John) Ramsey 1946- .... **CLC 42**
    See also CA 57-60; CANR 7

Campbell, (Ignatius) Roy (Dunnachie)
    1901-1957 .... **TCLC 5**
    See also CA 104; DLB 20

Campbell, Thomas 1777-1844 .... **NCLC 19**
    See also DLB 93

Campbell, Wilfred................. TCLC 9
    See also Campbell, William

Campbell, William 1858(?)-1918
    See Campbell, Wilfred
    See also CA 106; DLB 92

Campos, Alvaro de
    See Pessoa, Fernando (Antonio Nogueira)

Camus, Albert
    1913-1960 ... **CLC 1, 2, 4, 9, 11, 14, 32,
                     63, 69; DC 2; SSC 9**
    See also CA 89-92; DLB 72; MTCW; WLC

Canby, Vincent 1924-............. **CLC 13**
    See also CA 81-84

Cancale
    See Desnos, Robert

Canetti, Elias 1905- ...... **CLC 3, 14, 25, 75**
    See also CA 21-24R; CANR 23; DLB 85,
    124; MTCW

Canin, Ethan 1960-............... **CLC 55**
    See also CA 131; 135

Cannon, Curt
    See Hunter, Evan

Cape, Judith
    See Page, P(atricia) K(athleen)

Capek, Karel
    1890-1938 .... **TCLC 6, 37; DC 1**
    See also CA 104; WLC

Capote, Truman
    1924-1984 ..... **CLC 1, 3, 8, 13, 19, 34,
                     38, 58; SSC 2**
    See also CA 5-8R; 113; CANR 18;
    CDALB 1941-1968; DLB 2; DLBY 80,
    84; MTCW; WLC

Capra, Frank 1897-1991.......... **CLC 16**
    See also CA 61-64; 135

Caputo, Philip 1941-.............. **CLC 32**
    See also CA 73-76; CANR 40

Card, Orson Scott 1951- .... **CLC 44, 47, 50**
    See also CA 102; CANR 27; MTCW

Chaplin, Charles Spencer
  1889-1977 .... CLC 16
  See also Chaplin, Charlie
  See also CA 81-84; 73-76

Chaplin, Charlie
  See Chaplin, Charles Spencer
  See also DLB 44

Chapman, Graham 1941-1989 ..... CLC 21
  See also Monty Python
  See also CA 116; 129; CANR 35

Chapman, John Jay 1862-1933 ..... TCLC 7
  See also CA 104

Chapman, Walker
  See Silverberg, Robert

Chappell, Fred (Davis) 1936-....... CLC 40
  See also CA 5-8R; CAAS 4; CANR 8, 33;
  DLB 6, 105

Char, Rene(-Emile)
  1907-1988 .... CLC 9, 11, 14, 55
  See also CA 13-16R; 124; CANR 32;
  MTCW

Charby, Jay
  See Ellison, Harlan

Chardin, Pierre Teilhard de
  See Teilhard de Chardin, (Marie Joseph)
  Pierre

Charles I 1600-1649 .... LC 13

Charyn, Jerome 1937- .... CLC 5, 8, 18
  See also CA 5-8R; CAAS 1; CANR 7;
  DLBY 83; MTCW

Chase, Mary (Coyle) 1907-1981 ...... DC 1
  See also CA 77-80; 105; SATA 17, 29

Chase, Mary Ellen 1887-1973 .... CLC 2
  See also CA 13-16; 41-44R; CAP 1;
  SATA 10

Chase, Nicholas
  See Hyde, Anthony

Chateaubriand, Francois Rene de
  1768-1848 .... NCLC 3
  See also DLB 119

Chatterje, Sarat Chandra 1876-1936(?)
  See Chatterji, Saratchandra
  See also CA 109

Chatterji, Bankim Chandra
  1838-1894 .... NCLC 19

Chatterji, Saratchandra .... TCLC 13
  See also Chatterje, Sarat Chandra

Chatterton, Thomas 1752-1770 .... LC 3
  See also DLB 109

Chatwin, (Charles) Bruce
  1940-1989 .... CLC 28, 57, 59
  See also AAYA 4; BEST 90:1; CA 85-88;
  127

Chaucer, Daniel
  See Ford, Ford Madox

Chaucer, Geoffrey 1340(?)-1400 ..... LC 17
  See also CDBLB Before 1660

Chaviaras, Strates 1935-
  See Haviaras, Stratis
  See also CA 105

Chayefsky, Paddy .... CLC 23
  See also Chayefsky, Sidney
  See also DLB 7, 44; DLBY 81

Chayefsky, Sidney 1923-1981
  See Chayefsky, Paddy
  See also CA 9-12R; 104; CANR 18

Chedid, Andree 1920-............ CLC 47

Cheever, John
  1912-1982 ..... CLC 3, 7, 8, 11, 15, 25,
                            64; SSC 1
  See also CA 5-8R; 106; CABS 1; CANR 5,
  27; CDALB 1941-1968; DLB 2, 102;
  DLBY 80, 82; MTCW; WLC

Cheever, Susan 1943-........... CLC 18, 48
  See also CA 103; CANR 27; DLBY 82

Chekhonte, Antosha
  See Chekhov, Anton (Pavlovich)

Chekhov, Anton (Pavlovich)
  1860-1904 ...... TCLC 3, 10, 31; SSC 2
  See also CA 104; 124; WLC

Chernyshevsky, Nikolay Gavrilovich
  1828-1889 .... NCLC 1

Cherry, Carolyn Janice 1942-
  See Cherryh, C. J.
  See also CA 65-68; CANR 10

Cherryh, C. J. .... CLC 35
  See also Cherry, Carolyn Janice
  See also DLBY 80

Chesnutt, Charles W(addell)
  1858-1932 .... TCLC 5, 39; SSC 7
  See also BLC 1; BW; CA 106; 125; DLB 12,
  50, 78; MTCW

Chester, Alfred 1929(?)-1971....... CLC 49
  See also CA 33-36R

Chesterton, G(ilbert) K(eith)
  1874-1936 .... TCLC 1, 6; SSC 1
  See also CA 104; 132; CDBLB 1914-1945;
  DLB 10, 19, 34, 70, 98; MTCW;
  SATA 27

Chiang Pin-chin 1904-1986
  See Ding Ling
  See also CA 118

Ch'ien Chung-shu 1910-........... CLC 22
  See also CA 130; MTCW

Child, L. Maria
  See Child, Lydia Maria

Child, Lydia Maria 1802-1880 .... NCLC 6
  See also DLB 1, 74; SATA 67

Child, Mrs.
  See Child, Lydia Maria

Child, Philip 1898-1978 .... CLC 19, 68
  See also CA 13-14; CAP 1; SATA 47

Childress, Alice 1920-........... CLC 12, 15
  See also AAYA 8; BLC 1; BW; CA 45-48;
  CANR 3, 27; CLR 14; DLB 7, 38;
  MAICYA; MTCW; SATA 7, 48

Chislett, (Margaret) Anne 1943-.... CLC 34

Chitty, Thomas Willes 1926-....... CLC 11
  See also Hinde, Thomas
  See also CA 5-8R

Chomette, Rene Lucien 1898-1981 .. CLC 20
  See also Clair, Rene
  See also CA 103

Chopin, Kate .... TCLC 5, 14; SSC 8
  See also Chopin, Katherine
  See also CDALB 1865-1917; DLB 12, 78

Chopin, Katherine 1851-1904
  See Chopin, Kate
  See also CA 104; 122

Chretien de Troyes
  c. 12th cent. - .... CMLC 10

Christie
  See Ichikawa, Kon

Christie, Agatha (Mary Clarissa)
  1890-1976 ...... CLC 1, 6, 8, 12, 39, 48
  See also AAYA 9; AITN 1, 2; CA 17-20R;
  61-64; CANR 10, 37; CDBLB 1914-1945;
  DLB 13, 77; MTCW; SATA 36

Christie, (Ann) Philippa
  See Pearce, Philippa
  See also CA 5-8R; CANR 4

Christine de Pizan 1365(?)-1431(?) .... LC 9

Chubb, Elmer
  See Masters, Edgar Lee

Chulkov, Mikhail Dmitrievich
  1743-1792 .... LC 2

Churchill, Caryl 1938- .... CLC 31, 55
  See also CA 102; CANR 22; DLB 13;
  MTCW

Churchill, Charles 1731-1764........ LC 3
  See also DLB 109

Chute, Carolyn 1947-............. CLC 39
  See also CA 123

Ciardi, John (Anthony)
  1916-1986 .... CLC 10, 40, 44
  See also CA 5-8R; 118; CAAS 2; CANR 5,
  33; CLR 19; DLB 5; DLBY 86;
  MAICYA; MTCW; SATA 1, 46, 65

Cicero, Marcus Tullius
  106B.C.-43B.C. .... CMLC 3

Cimino, Michael 1943-............ CLC 16
  See also CA 105

Cioran, E(mil) M. 1911-........... CLC 64
  See also CA 25-28R

Cisneros, Sandra 1954-............ CLC 69
  See also AAYA 9; CA 131; DLB 122; HW

Clair, Rene....................... CLC 20
  See also Chomette, Rene Lucien

Clampitt, Amy 1920- .... CLC 32
  See also CA 110; CANR 29; DLB 105

Clancy, Thomas L. Jr. 1947-
  See Clancy, Tom
  See also CA 125; 131; MTCW

Clancy, Tom...................... CLC 45
  See also Clancy, Thomas L. Jr.
  See also AAYA 9; BEST 89:1, 90:1

Clare, John 1793-1864 .... NCLC 9
  See also DLB 55, 96

Clarin
  See Alas (y Urena), Leopoldo (Enrique
  Garcia)

Clark, (Robert) Brian 1932-........ CLC 29
  See also CA 41-44R

Clark, Eleanor 1913- .... CLC 5, 19
  See also CA 9-12R; DLB 6

Clark, J. P.
  See Clark, John Pepper
  See also DLB 117

Clark, John Pepper 1935- .... **CLC 38**
See also Clark, J. P.
See also BLC 1; BW; CA 65-68; CANR 16

Clark, M. R.
See Clark, Mavis Thorpe

Clark, Mavis Thorpe 1909- .... **CLC 12**
See also CA 57-60; CANR 8, 37; MAICYA;
SAAS 5; SATA 8

Clark, Walter Van Tilburg
1909-1971 .... **CLC 28**
See also CA 9-12R; 33-36R; DLB 9;
SATA 8

Clarke, Arthur C(harles)
1917- ...... **CLC 1, 4, 13, 18, 35; SSC 3**
See also AAYA 4; CA 1-4R; CANR 2, 28;
MAICYA; MTCW; SATA 13, 70

Clarke, Austin C(hesterfield)
1934- .... **CLC 8, 53**
See also BLC 1; BW; CA 25-28R;
CAAS 16; CANR 14, 32; DLB 53, 125

Clarke, Austin 1896-1974........ **CLC 6, 9**
See also CA 29-32; 49-52; CAP 2; DLB 10,
20

Clarke, Gillian 1937- .... **CLC 61**
See also CA 106; DLB 40

Clarke, Marcus (Andrew Hislop)
1846-1881 .... **NCLC 19**

Clarke, Shirley 1925- .... **CLC 16**

.... **CLC 30**
See also Headon, (Nicky) Topper; Jones,
Mick; Simonon, Paul; Strummer, Joe

Claudel, Paul (Louis Charles Marie)
1868-1955 .... **TCLC 2, 10**
See also CA 104

Clavell, James (duMaresq)
1925- .... **CLC 6, 25**
See also CA 25-28R; CANR 26; MTCW

Cleaver, (Leroy) Eldridge 1935- .... **CLC 30**
See also BLC 1; BW; CA 21-24R;
CANR 16

Cleese, John (Marwood) 1939- ..... **CLC 21**
See also Monty Python
See also CA 112; 116; CANR 35; MTCW

Cleishbotham, Jebediah
See Scott, Walter

Cleland, John 1710-1789 .... **LC 2**
See also DLB 39

Clemens, Samuel Langhorne 1835-1910
See Twain, Mark
See also CA 104; 135; CDALB 1865-1917;
DLB 11, 12, 23, 64, 74; MAICYA;
YABC 2

Clerihew, E.
See Bentley, E(dmund) C(lerihew)

Clerk, N. W.
See Lewis, C(live) S(taples)

Cliff, Jimmy...................... **CLC 21**
See also Chambers, James

Clifton, (Thelma) Lucille
1936- .... **CLC 19, 66**
See also BLC 1; BW; CA 49-52; CANR 2,
24; CLR 5; DLB 5, 41; MAICYA;
MTCW; SATA 20, 69

Clinton, Dirk
See Silverberg, Robert

Clough, Arthur Hugh 1819-1861.. **NCLC 27**
See also DLB 32

Clutha, Janet Paterson Frame 1924-
See Frame, Janet
See also CA 1-4R; CANR 2, 36; MTCW

Clyne, Terence
See Blatty, William Peter

Cobalt, Martin
See Mayne, William (James Carter)

Coburn, D(onald) L(ee) 1938- ...... **CLC 10**
See also CA 89-92

Cocteau, Jean (Maurice Eugene Clement)
1889-1963 .... **CLC 1, 8, 15, 16, 43**
See also CA 25-28; CANR 40; CAP 2;
DLB 65; MTCW; WLC

Codrescu, Andrei 1946- .... **CLC 46**
See also CA 33-36R; CANR 13, 34

Coe, Max
See Bourne, Randolph S(illiman)

Coe, Tucker
See Westlake, Donald E(dwin)

Coetzee, J(ohn) M(ichael)
1940- .... **CLC 23, 33, 66**
See also CA 77-80; MTCW

Cohen, Arthur A(llen)
1928-1986 .... **CLC 7, 31**
See also CA 1-4R; 120; CANR 1, 17;
DLB 28

Cohen, Leonard (Norman)
1934- .... **CLC 3, 38**
See also CA 21-24R; CANR 14; DLB 53;
MTCW

Cohen, Matt 1942- .... **CLC 19**
See also CA 61-64; CANR 40; DLB 53

Cohen-Solal, Annie 19(?)- .... **CLC 50**

Colegate, Isabel 1931- .... **CLC 36**
See also CA 17-20R; CANR 8, 22; DLB 14;
MTCW

Coleman, Emmett
See Reed, Ishmael

Coleridge, Samuel Taylor
1772-1834 .... **NCLC 9**
See also CDBLB 1789-1832; DLB 93, 107;
WLC

Coleridge, Sara 1802-1852....... **NCLC 31**

Coles, Don 1928- .... **CLC 46**
See also CA 115; CANR 38

Colette, (Sidonie-Gabrielle)
1873-1954 ...... **TCLC 1, 5, 16; SSC 10**
See also CA 104; 131; DLB 65; MTCW

Collett, (Jacobine) Camilla (Wergeland)
1813-1895 .... **NCLC 22**

Collier, Christopher 1930- .... **CLC 30**
See also CA 33-36R; CANR 13, 33;
MAICYA; SATA 16, 70

Collier, James L(incoln) 1928- ..... **CLC 30**
See also CA 9-12R; CANR 4, 33;
MAICYA; SATA 8, 70

Collier, Jeremy 1650-1726.......... **LC 6**

Collins, Hunt
See Hunter, Evan

Collins, Linda 1931-.............. **CLC 44**
See also CA 125

Collins, (William) Wilkie
1824-1889 .... **NCLC 1, 18**
See also CDBLB 1832-1890; DLB 18, 70

Collins, William 1721-1759 .... **LC 4**
See also DLB 109

Colman, George
See Glassco, John

Colt, Winchester Remington
See Hubbard, L(afayette) Ron(ald)

Colter, Cyrus 1910- .... **CLC 58**
See also BW; CA 65-68; CANR 10; DLB 33

Colton, James
See Hansen, Joseph

Colum, Padraic 1881-1972........ **CLC 28**
See also CA 73-76; 33-36R; CANR 35;
MAICYA; MTCW; SATA 15

Colvin, James
See Moorcock, Michael (John)

Colwin, Laurie (E.)
1944-1992 .... **CLC 5, 13, 23**
See also CA 89-92; 139; CANR 20;
DLBY 80; MTCW

Comfort, Alex(ander) 1920-........ **CLC 7**
See also CA 1-4R; CANR 1

Comfort, Montgomery
See Campbell, (John) Ramsey

Compton-Burnett, I(vy)
1884(?)-1969 .... **CLC 1, 3, 10, 15, 34**
See also CA 1-4R; 25-28R; CANR 4;
DLB 36; MTCW

Comstock, Anthony 1844-1915 .... **TCLC 13**
See also CA 110

Conan Doyle, Arthur
See Doyle, Arthur Conan

Conde, Maryse .... **CLC 52**
See also Boucolon, Maryse

Condon, Richard (Thomas)
1915- .... **CLC 4, 6, 8, 10, 45**
See also BEST 90:3; CA 1-4R; CAAS 1;
CANR 2, 23; MTCW

Congreve, William
1670-1729 .... **LC 5, 21; DC 2**
See also CDBLB 1660-1789; DLB 39, 84;
WLC

Connell, Evan S(helby) Jr.
1924- .... **CLC 4, 6, 45**
See also AAYA 7; CA 1-4R; CAAS 2;
CANR 2, 39; DLB 2; DLBY 81; MTCW

Connelly, Marc(us Cook)
1890-1980 .... **CLC 7**
See also CA 85-88; 102; CANR 30; DLB 7;
DLBY 80; SATA 25

Connor, Ralph.................... **TCLC 31**
See also Gordon, Charles William
See also DLB 92

Conrad, Joseph
1857-1924 ...... **TCLC 1, 6, 13, 25, 43;**
                                        SSC 9
See also CA 104; 131; CDBLB 1890-1914;
DLB 10, 34, 98; MTCW; SATA 27; WLC

Conrad, Robert Arnold
See Hart, Moss

Conroy, Pat 1945-............. **CLC 30, 74**
See also AAYA 8; AITN 1; CA 85-88;
CANR 24; DLB 6; MTCW

Dick, Philip K(indred)
1928-1982 . . . . CLC **10, 30, 72**
See also CA 49-52; 106; CANR 2, 16;
DLB 8; MTCW

Dickens, Charles (John Huffam)
1812-1870 . . . . NCLC **3, 8, 18, 26**
See also CDBLB 1832-1890; DLB 21, 55,
70; MAICYA; SATA 15

Dickey, James (Lafayette)
1923- . . . . CLC **1, 2, 4, 7, 10, 15, 47**
See also AITN 1, 2; CA 9-12R; CABS 2;
CANR 10; CDALB 1968-1988; DLB 5;
DLBD 7; DLBY 82; MTCW

Dickey, William 1928- . . . . CLC **3, 28**
See also CA 9-12R; CANR 24; DLB 5

Dickinson, Charles 1951- . . . . CLC **49**
See also CA 128

Dickinson, Emily (Elizabeth)
1830-1886 . . . . NCLC **21**; PC **1**
See also CDALB 1865-1917; DLB 1;
SATA 29; WLC

Dickinson, Peter (Malcolm)
1927- . . . . CLC **12, 35**
See also AAYA 9; CA 41-44R; CANR 31;
DLB 87; MAICYA; SATA 5, 62

Dickson, Carr
See Carr, John Dickson

Dickson, Carter
See Carr, John Dickson

Didion, Joan 1934- . . . . . CLC **1, 3, 8, 14, 32**
See also AITN 1; CA 5-8R; CANR 14;
CDALB 1968-1988; DLB 2; DLBY 81,
86; MTCW

Dietrich, Robert
See Hunt, E(verette) Howard Jr.

Dillard, Annie 1945- . . . . CLC **9, 60**
See also AAYA 6; CA 49-52; CANR 3;
DLBY 80; MTCW; SATA 10

Dillard, R(ichard) H(enry) W(ilde)
1937- . . . . CLC **5**
See also CA 21-24R; CAAS 7; CANR 10;
DLB 5

Dillon, Eilis 1920- . . . . CLC **17**
See also CA 9-12R; CAAS 3; CANR 4, 38;
CLR 26; MAICYA; SATA 2

Dimont, Penelope
See Mortimer, Penelope (Ruth)

Dinesen, Isak . . . . CLC **10, 29**; SSC **7**
See also Blixen, Karen (Christentze
Dinesen)

Ding Ling . . . . CLC **68**
See also Chiang Pin-chin

Disch, Thomas M(ichael) 1940- . . . CLC **7, 36**
See also CA 21-24R; CAAS 4; CANR 17,
36; CLR 18; DLB 8; MAICYA; MTCW;
SAAS 15; SATA 54

Disch, Tom
See Disch, Thomas M(ichael)

d'Isly, Georges
See Simenon, Georges (Jacques Christian)

Disraeli, Benjamin 1804-1881 . . NCLC **2, 39**
See also DLB 21, 55

Ditcum, Steve
See Crumb, R(obert)

Dixon, Paige
See Corcoran, Barbara

Dixon, Stephen 1936- . . . . CLC **52**
See also CA 89-92; CANR 17, 40

Doblin, Alfred . . . . TCLC **13**
See also Doeblin, Alfred

Dobrolyubov, Nikolai Alexandrovich
1836-1861 . . . . NCLC **5**

Dobyns, Stephen 1941- . . . . CLC **37**
See also CA 45-48; CANR 2, 18

Doctorow, E(dgar) L(aurence)
1931- . . . . . CLC **6, 11, 15, 18, 37, 44, 65**
See also AITN 2; BEST 89:3; CA 45-48;
CANR 2, 33; CDALB 1968-1988; DLB 2,
28; DLBY 80; MTCW

Dodgson, Charles Lutwidge 1832-1898
See Carroll, Lewis
See also CLR 2; MAICYA; YABC 2

Doeblin, Alfred 1878-1957 . . . . TCLC **13**
See also Doblin, Alfred
See also CA 110; DLB 66

Doerr, Harriet 1910- . . . . CLC **34**
See also CA 117; 122

Domecq, H(onorio) Bustos
See Bioy Casares, Adolfo; Borges, Jorge
Luis

Domini, Rey
See Lorde, Audre (Geraldine)

Dominique
See Proust,
(Valentin-Louis-George-Eugene-)Marcel

Don, A
See Stephen, Leslie

Donaldson, Stephen R. 1947- . . . . . . CLC **46**
See also CA 89-92; CANR 13

Donleavy, J(ames) P(atrick)
1926- . . . . CLC **1, 4, 6, 10, 45**
See also AITN 2; CA 9-12R; CANR 24;
DLB 6; MTCW

Donne, John 1572-1631 . . . . LC **10**; PC **1**
See also CDBLB Before 1660; DLB 121;
WLC

Donnell, David 1939(?)- . . . . CLC **34**

Donoso (Yanez), Jose
1924- . . . . CLC **4, 8, 11, 32**
See also CA 81-84; CANR 32; DLB 113;
HW; MTCW

Donovan, John 1928-1992 . . . . CLC **35**
See also CA 97-100; 137; CLR 3;
MAICYA; SATA 29

Don Roberto
See Cunninghame Graham, R(obert)
B(ontine)

Doolittle, Hilda
1886-1961 . . . . CLC **3, 8, 14, 31, 34, 73**;
PC **5**
See also H. D.
See also CA 97-100; CANR 35; DLB 4, 45;
MTCW; WLC

Dorfman, Ariel 1942- . . . . CLC **48**
See also CA 124; 130; HW

Dorn, Edward (Merton) 1929- . . . CLC **10, 18**
See also CA 93-96; DLB 5

Dorsan, Luc
See Simenon, Georges (Jacques Christian)

Dorsange, Jean
See Simenon, Georges (Jacques Christian)

Dos Passos, John (Roderigo)
1896-1970 . . . CLC **1, 4, 8, 11, 15, 25, 34**
See also CA 1-4R; 29-32R; CANR 3;
CDALB 1929-1941; DLB 4, 9; DLBD 1;
MTCW; WLC

Dossage, Jean
See Simenon, Georges (Jacques Christian)

Dostoevsky, Fedor Mikhailovich
1821-1881 . . . . NCLC **2, 7, 21, 33**; SSC **2**
See also WLC

Doughty, Charles M(ontagu)
1843-1926 . . . . TCLC **27**
See also CA 115; DLB 19, 57

Douglas, Ellen
See Haxton, Josephine Ayres

Douglas, Gavin 1475(?)-1522 . . . . LC **20**

Douglas, Keith 1920-1944 . . . . TCLC **40**
See also DLB 27

Douglas, Leonard
See Bradbury, Ray (Douglas)

Douglas, Michael
See Crichton, (John) Michael

Douglass, Frederick 1817(?)-1895 . . NCLC **7**
See also BLC 1; CDALB 1640-1865;
DLB 1, 43, 50, 79; SATA 29; WLC

Dourado, (Waldomiro Freitas) Autran
1926- . . . . CLC **23, 60**
See also CA 25-28R; CANR 34

Dourado, Waldomiro Autran
See Dourado, (Waldomiro Freitas) Autran

Dove, Rita (Frances) 1952- . . . CLC **50**; PC **6**
See also BW; CA 109; CANR 27; DLB 120

Dowell, Coleman 1925-1985 . . . . CLC **60**
See also CA 25-28R; 117; CANR 10

Dowson, Ernest Christopher
1867-1900 . . . . TCLC **4**
See also CA 105; DLB 19

Doyle, A. Conan
See Doyle, Arthur Conan

Doyle, Arthur Conan 1859-1930 . . . . TCLC **7**
See also CA 104; 122; CDBLB 1890-1914;
DLB 18, 70; MTCW; SATA 24; WLC

Doyle, Conan
See Doyle, Arthur Conan

Doyle, John
See Graves, Robert (von Ranke)

Doyle, Sir A. Conan
See Doyle, Arthur Conan

Doyle, Sir Arthur Conan
See Doyle, Arthur Conan

Dr. A
See Asimov, Isaac; Silverstein, Alvin

Drabble, Margaret
1939- . . . . CLC **2, 3, 5, 8, 10, 22, 53**
See also CA 13-16R; CANR 18, 35;
CDBLB 1960 to Present; DLB 14;
MTCW; SATA 48

Drapier, M. B.
See Swift, Jonathan

Drayham, James
See Mencken, H(enry) L(ouis)

Drayton, Michael 1563-1631 . . . . LC **8**

Dreadstone, Carl
See Campbell, (John) Ramsey

Dreiser, Theodore (Herman Albert)
1871-1945 . . . . TCLC 10, 18, 35
See also CA 106; 132; CDALB 1865-1917;
DLB 9, 12, 102; DLBD 1; MTCW; WLC

Drexler, Rosalyn 1926- . . . . CLC 2, 6
See also CA 81-84

Dreyer, Carl Theodor 1889-1968. . . . CLC 16
See also CA 116

Drieu la Rochelle, Pierre(-Eugene)
1893-1945 . . . . TCLC 21
See also CA 117; DLB 72

Drop Shot
See Cable, George Washington

Droste-Hulshoff, Annette Freiin von
1797-1848 . . . . NCLC 3

Drummond, Walter
See Silverberg, Robert

Drummond, William Henry
1854-1907 . . . . TCLC 25
See also DLB 92

Drummond de Andrade, Carlos
1902-1987 . . . . CLC 18
See also Andrade, Carlos Drummond de
See also CA 132; 123

Drury, Allen (Stuart) 1918- . . . . CLC 37
See also CA 57-60; CANR 18

Dryden, John 1631-1700 . . . . LC 3, 21; DC 3
See also CDBLB 1660-1789; DLB 80, 101;
WLC

Duberman, Martin 1930- . . . . CLC 8
See also CA 1-4R; CANR 2

Dubie, Norman (Evans) 1945- . . . . . . CLC 36
See also CA 69-72; CANR 12; DLB 120

Du Bois, W(illiam) E(dward) B(urghardt)
1868-1963 . . . . CLC 1, 2, 13, 64
See also BLC 1; BW; CA 85-88; CANR 34;
CDALB 1865-1917; DLB 47, 50, 91;
MTCW; SATA 42; WLC

Dubus, Andre 1936- . . . . CLC 13, 36
See also CA 21-24R; CANR 17

Duca Minimo
See D'Annunzio, Gabriele

Ducharme, Rejean 1941- . . . . CLC 74
See also DLB 60

Duclos, Charles Pinot 1704-1772 . . . . . LC 1

Dudek, Louis 1918- . . . . CLC 11, 19
See also CA 45-48; CAAS 14; CANR 1;
DLB 88

Duerrenmatt, Friedrich
1921-1990 . . . . . CLC 1, 4, 8, 11, 15, 43
See also Durrenmatt, Friedrich
See also CA 17-20R; CANR 33; DLB 69,
124; MTCW

Duffy, Bruce (?)- . . . . CLC 50

Duffy, Maureen 1933- . . . . CLC 37
See also CA 25-28R; CANR 33; DLB 14;
MTCW

Dugan, Alan 1923- . . . . CLC 2, 6
See also CA 81-84; DLB 5

du Gard, Roger Martin
See Martin du Gard, Roger

Duhamel, Georges 1884-1966 . . . . CLC 8
See also CA 81-84; 25-28R; CANR 35;
DLB 65; MTCW

Dujardin, Edouard (Emile Louis)
1861-1949 . . . . TCLC 13
See also CA 109; DLB 123

Dumas, Alexandre (Davy de la Pailleterie)
1802-1870 . . . . NCLC 11
See also DLB 119; SATA 18; WLC

Dumas, Alexandre
1824-1895 . . . . NCLC 9; DC 1

Dumas, Claudine
See Malzberg, Barry N(athaniel)

Dumas, Henry L. 1934-1968 . . . . . CLC 6, 62
See also BW; CA 85-88; DLB 41

du Maurier, Daphne
1907-1989 . . . . CLC 6, 11, 59
See also CA 5-8R; 128; CANR 6; MTCW;
SATA 27, 60

Dunbar, Paul Laurence
1872-1906 . . . . TCLC 2, 12; PC 5; SSC 8
See also BLC 1; BW; CA 104; 124;
CDALB 1865-1917; DLB 50, 54, 78;
SATA 34; WLC

Dunbar, William 1460(?)-1530(?) . . . . LC 20

Duncan, Lois 1934- . . . . CLC 26
See also AAYA 4; CA 1-4R; CANR 2, 23,
36; MAICYA; SAAS 2; SATA 1, 36

Duncan, Robert (Edward)
1919-1988 . . . CLC 1, 2, 4, 7, 15, 41, 55;
PC 2
See also CA 9-12R; 124; CANR 28; DLB 5,
16; MTCW

Dunlap, William 1766-1839 . . . . NCLC 2
See also DLB 30, 37, 59

Dunn, Douglas (Eaglesham)
1942- . . . . CLC 6, 40
See also CA 45-48; CANR 2, 33; DLB 40;
MTCW

Dunn, Katherine (Karen) 1945- . . . . . CLC 71
See also CA 33-36R

Dunn, Stephen 1939- . . . . CLC 36
See also CA 33-36R; CANR 12; DLB 105

Dunne, Finley Peter 1867-1936. . . . TCLC 28
See also CA 108; DLB 11, 23

Dunne, John Gregory 1932- . . . . CLC 28
See also CA 25-28R; CANR 14; DLBY 80

Dunsany, Edward John Moreton Drax
Plunkett 1878-1957
See Dunsany, Lord; Lord Dunsany
See also CA 104; DLB 10

Dunsany, Lord . . . . TCLC 2
See also Dunsany, Edward John Moreton
Drax Plunkett
See also DLB 77

du Perry, Jean
See Simenon, Georges (Jacques Christian)

Durang, Christopher (Ferdinand)
1949- . . . . CLC 27, 38
See also CA 105

Duras, Marguerite
1914- . . . . . . CLC 3, 6, 11, 20, 34, 40, 68
See also CA 25-28R; DLB 83; MTCW

Durban, (Rosa) Pam 1947- . . . . CLC 39
See also CA 123

Durcan, Paul 1944- . . . . CLC 43, 70
See also CA 134

Durrell, Lawrence (George)
1912-1990 . . . . CLC 1, 4, 6, 8, 13, 27, 41
See also CA 9-12R; 132; CANR 40;
CDBLB 1945-1960; DLB 15, 27;
DLBY 90; MTCW

Durrenmatt, Friedrich
. . . . CLC 1, 4, 8, 11, 15, 43
See also Duerrenmatt, Friedrich
See also DLB 69, 124

Dutt, Toru 1856-1877 . . . . NCLC 29

Dwight, Timothy 1752-1817 . . . . . . NCLC 13
See also DLB 37

Dworkin, Andrea 1946- . . . . CLC 43
See also CA 77-80; CANR 16, 39; MTCW

Dylan, Bob 1941- . . . . CLC 3, 4, 6, 12
See also CA 41-44R; DLB 16

Eagleton, Terence (Francis) 1943-
See Eagleton, Terry
See also CA 57-60; CANR 7, 23; MTCW

Eagleton, Terry . . . . CLC 63
See also Eagleton, Terence (Francis)

East, Michael
See West, Morris L(anglo)

Eastaway, Edward
See Thomas, (Philip) Edward

Eastlake, William (Derry) 1917- . . . . . CLC 8
See also CA 5-8R; CAAS 1; CANR 5;
DLB 6

Eberhart, Richard (Ghormley)
1904- . . . . CLC 3, 11, 19, 56
See also CA 1-4R; CANR 2;
CDALB 1941-1968; DLB 48; MTCW

Eberstadt, Fernanda 1960- . . . . CLC 39
See also CA 136

Echegaray (y Eizaguirre), Jose (Maria Waldo)
1832-1916 . . . . TCLC 4
See also CA 104; CANR 32; HW; MTCW

Echeverria, (Jose) Esteban (Antonino)
1805-1851 . . . . NCLC 18

Echo
See Proust,
(Valentin-Louis-George-Eugene-)Marcel

Eckert, Allan W. 1931- . . . . CLC 17
See also CA 13-16R; CANR 14; SATA 27,
29

Eckhart, Meister 1260(?)-1328(?) . . CMLC 9
See also DLB 115

Eckmar, F. R.
See de Hartog, Jan

Eco, Umberto 1932- . . . . CLC 28, 60
See also BEST 90:1; CA 77-80; CANR 12,
33; MTCW

Eddison, E(ric) R(ucker)
1882-1945 . . . . TCLC 15
See also CA 109

Edel, (Joseph) Leon 1907- . . . . . . CLC 29, 34
See also CA 1-4R; CANR 1, 22; DLB 103

Eden, Emily 1797-1869 . . . . NCLC 10

Edgar, David 1948- . . . . CLC 42
See also CA 57-60; CANR 12; DLB 13;
MTCW

Edgerton, Clyde (Carlyle) 1944- .... **CLC 39**
See also CA 118; 134

Edgeworth, Maria 1767-1849..... **NCLC 1**
See also DLB 116; SATA 21

Edmonds, Paul
See Kuttner, Henry

Edmonds, Walter D(umaux) 1903- .. **CLC 35**
See also CA 5-8R; CANR 2; DLB 9;
MAICYA; SAAS 4; SATA 1, 27

Edmondson, Wallace
See Ellison, Harlan

Edson, Russell .... **CLC 13**
See also CA 33-36R

Edwards, G(erald) B(asil)
1899-1976 .... **CLC 25**
See also CA 110

Edwards, Gus 1939- .... **CLC 43**
See also CA 108

Edwards, Jonathan 1703-1758 .... **LC 7**
See also DLB 24

Efron, Marina Ivanovna Tsvetaeva
See Tsvetaeva (Efron), Marina (Ivanovna)

Ehle, John (Marsden Jr.) 1925- .... **CLC 27**
See also CA 9-12R

Ehrenbourg, Ilya (Grigoryevich)
See Ehrenburg, Ilya (Grigoryevich)

Ehrenburg, Ilya (Grigoryevich)
1891-1967 .... **CLC 18, 34, 62**
See also CA 102; 25-28R

Ehrenburg, Ilyo (Grigoryevich)
See Ehrenburg, Ilya (Grigoryevich)

Eich, Guenter 1907-1972 .... **CLC 15**
See also CA 111; 93-96; DLB 69, 124

Eichendorff, Joseph Freiherr von
1788-1857 .... **NCLC 8**
See also DLB 90

Eigner, Larry .... **CLC 9**
See also Eigner, Laurence (Joel)
See also DLB 5

Eigner, Laurence (Joel) 1927-
See Eigner, Larry
See also CA 9-12R; CANR 6

Eiseley, Loren Corey 1907-1977 ..... **CLC 7**
See also AAYA 5; CA 1-4R; 73-76;
CANR 6

Eisenstadt, Jill 1963- .... **CLC 50**

Eisner, Simon
See Kornbluth, C(yril) M.

Ekeloef, (Bengt) Gunnar
1907-1968 .... **CLC 27**
See also Ekelof, (Bengt) Gunnar
See also CA 123; 25-28R

Ekelof, (Bengt) Gunnar .... **CLC 27**
See also Ekeloef, (Bengt) Gunnar

Ekwensi, C. O. D.
See Ekwensi, Cyprian (Odiatu Duaka)

Ekwensi, Cyprian (Odiatu Duaka)
1921- .... **CLC 4**
See also BLC 1; BW; CA 29-32R;
CANR 18; DLB 117; MTCW; SATA 66

Elaine .... **TCLC 18**
See also Leverson, Ada

El Crummo
See Crumb, R(obert)

Elia
See Lamb, Charles

Eliade, Mircea 1907-1986 .... **CLC 19**
See also CA 65-68; 119; CANR 30; MTCW

Eliot, A. D.
See Jewett, (Theodora) Sarah Orne

Eliot, Alice
See Jewett, (Theodora) Sarah Orne

Eliot, Dan
See Silverberg, Robert

Eliot, George 1819-1880.... **NCLC 4, 13, 23**
See also CDBLB 1832-1890; DLB 21, 35,
55; WLC

Eliot, John 1604-1690 .... **LC 5**
See also DLB 24

Eliot, T(homas) S(tearns)
1888-1965 .... **CLC 1, 2, 3, 6, 9, 10, 13,
15, 24, 34, 41, 55, 57; PC 5**
See also CA 5-8R; 25-28R;
CDALB 1929-1941; DLB 7, 10, 45, 63;
DLBY 88; MTCW; WLC 2

Elizabeth 1866-1941 .... **TCLC 41**

Elkin, Stanley L(awrence)
1930- .... **CLC 4, 6, 9, 14, 27, 51**
See also CA 9-12R; CANR 8; DLB 2, 28;
DLBY 80; MTCW

Elledge, Scott .... **CLC 34**

Elliott, Don
See Silverberg, Robert

Elliott, George P(aul) 1918-1980..... **CLC 2**
See also CA 1-4R; 97-100; CANR 2

Elliott, Janice 1931- .... **CLC 47**
See also CA 13-16R; CANR 8, 29; DLB 14

Elliott, Sumner Locke 1917-1991 ... **CLC 38**
See also CA 5-8R; 134; CANR 2, 21

Elliott, William
See Bradbury, Ray (Douglas)

Ellis, A. E. .... **CLC 7**

Ellis, Alice Thomas .... **CLC 40**
See also Haycraft, Anna

Ellis, Bret Easton 1964-........ **CLC 39, 71**
See also AAYA 2; CA 118; 123

Ellis, (Henry) Havelock
1859-1939 .... **TCLC 14**
See also CA 109

Ellis, Landon
See Ellison, Harlan

Ellis, Trey 1962-................. **CLC 55**

Ellison, Harlan 1934-........ **CLC 1, 13, 42**
See also CA 5-8R; CANR 5; DLB 8;
MTCW

Ellison, Ralph (Waldo)
1914- .... **CLC 1, 3, 11, 54**
See also BLC 1; BW; CA 9-12R; CANR 24;
CDALB 1941-1968; DLB 2, 76; MTCW;
WLC

Ellmann, Lucy (Elizabeth) 1956-.... **CLC 61**
See also CA 128

Ellmann, Richard (David)
1918-1987 .... **CLC 50**
See also BEST 89:2; CA 1-4R; 122;
CANR 2, 28; DLB 103; DLBY 87;
MTCW

Elman, Richard 1934-............. **CLC 19**
See also CA 17-20R; CAAS 3

Elron
See Hubbard, L(afayette) Ron(ald)

Eluard, Paul .... **TCLC 7, 41**
See also Grindel, Eugene

Elyot, Sir Thomas 1490(?)-1546 ..... **LC 11**

Elytis, Odysseus 1911-......... **CLC 15, 49**
See also CA 102; MTCW

Emecheta, (Florence Onye) Buchi
1944- .... **CLC 14, 48**
See also BLC 2; BW; CA 81-84; CANR 27;
DLB 117; MTCW; SATA 66

Emerson, Ralph Waldo
1803-1882 .... **NCLC 1, 38**
See also CDALB 1640-1865; DLB 1, 59, 73;
WLC

Eminescu, Mihail 1850-1889..... **NCLC 33**

Empson, William
1906-1984 .... **CLC 3, 8, 19, 33, 34**
See also CA 17-20R; 112; CANR 31;
DLB 20; MTCW

Enchi Fumiko (Ueda) 1905-1986.... **CLC 31**
See also CA 129; 121

Ende, Michael (Andreas Helmuth)
1929- .... **CLC 31**
See also CA 118; 124; CANR 36; CLR 14;
DLB 75; MAICYA; SATA 42, 61

Endo, Shusaku 1923- ..... **CLC 7, 14, 19, 54**
See also CA 29-32R; CANR 21; MTCW

Engel, Marian 1933-1985......... **CLC 36**
See also CA 25-28R; CANR 12; DLB 53

Engelhardt, Frederick
See Hubbard, L(afayette) Ron(ald)

Enright, D(ennis) J(oseph)
1920- .... **CLC 4, 8, 31**
See also CA 1-4R; CANR 1; DLB 27;
SATA 25

Enzensberger, Hans Magnus
1929- .... **CLC 43**
See also CA 116; 119

Ephron, Nora 1941-........... **CLC 17, 31**
See also AITN 2; CA 65-68; CANR 12, 39

Epsilon
See Betjeman, John

Epstein, Daniel Mark 1948- .... **CLC 7**
See also CA 49-52; CANR 2

Epstein, Jacob 1956- .... **CLC 19**
See also CA 114

Epstein, Joseph 1937-............. **CLC 39**
See also CA 112; 119

Epstein, Leslie 1938- .... **CLC 27**
See also CA 73-76; CAAS 12; CANR 23

Equiano, Olaudah 1745(?)-1797...... **LC 16**
See also BLC 2; DLB 37, 50

Erasmus, Desiderius 1469(?)-1536.... **LC 16**

Erdman, Paul E(mil) 1932- .... **CLC 25**
See also AITN 1; CA 61-64; CANR 13

Erdrich, Louise 1954-.......... **CLC 39, 54**
See also AAYA 10; BEST 89:1; CA 114;
MTCW

Erenburg, Ilya (Grigoryevich)
See Ehrenburg, Ilya (Grigoryevich)

Ferlinghetti, Lawrence (Monsanto)
　1919(?)- . . . . **CLC 2, 6, 10, 27; PC 1**
　See also CA 5-8R; CANR 3;
　　CDALB 1941-1968; DLB 5, 16; MTCW

Fernandez, Vicente Garcia Huidobro
　See Huidobro Fernandez, Vicente Garcia

Ferrer, Gabriel (Francisco Victor) Miro
　See Miro (Ferrer), Gabriel (Francisco
　　Victor)

Ferrier, Susan (Edmonstone)
　1782-1854 . . . . **NCLC 8**
　See also DLB 116

Ferrigno, Robert . . . . **CLC 65**

Feuchtwanger, Lion 1884-1958 . . . . . **TCLC 3**
　See also CA 104; DLB 66

Feydeau, Georges (Leon Jules Marie)
　1862-1921 . . . . **TCLC 22**
　See also CA 113

Ficino, Marsilio 1433-1499 . . . . **LC 12**

Fiedler, Leslie A(aron)
　1917- . . . . **CLC 4, 13, 24**
　See also CA 9-12R; CANR 7; DLB 28, 67;
　　MTCW

Field, Andrew 1938- . . . . **CLC 44**
　See also CA 97-100; CANR 25

Field, Eugene 1850-1895 . . . . **NCLC 3**
　See also DLB 23, 42; MAICYA; SATA 16

Field, Gans T.
　See Wellman, Manly Wade

Field, Michael . . . . **TCLC 43**

Field, Peter
　See Hobson, Laura Z(ametkin)

Fielding, Henry 1707-1754 . . . . **LC 1**
　See also CDBLB 1660-1789; DLB 39, 84,
　　101; WLC

Fielding, Sarah 1710-1768 . . . . **LC 1**
　See also DLB 39

Fierstein, Harvey (Forbes) 1954- . . . **CLC 33**
　See also CA 123; 129

Figes, Eva 1932- . . . . **CLC 31**
　See also CA 53-56; CANR 4; DLB 14

Finch, Robert (Duer Claydon)
　1900- . . . . **CLC 18**
　See also CA 57-60; CANR 9, 24; DLB 88

Findley, Timothy 1930- . . . . **CLC 27**
　See also CA 25-28R; CANR 12; DLB 53

Fink, William
　See Mencken, H(enry) L(ouis)

Firbank, Louis 1942-
　See Reed, Lou
　See also CA 117

Firbank, (Arthur Annesley) Ronald
　1886-1926 . . . . **TCLC 1**
　See also CA 104; DLB 36

Fisher, Roy 1930- . . . . **CLC 25**
　See also CA 81-84; CAAS 10; CANR 16;
　　DLB 40

Fisher, Rudolph 1897-1934 . . . . **TCLC 11**
　See also BLC 2; BW; CA 107; 124; DLB 51,
　　102

Fisher, Vardis (Alvero) 1895-1968 . . . . **CLC 7**
　See also CA 5-8R; 25-28R; DLB 9

Fiske, Tarleton
　See Bloch, Robert (Albert)

Fitch, Clarke
　See Sinclair, Upton (Beall)

Fitch, John IV
　See Cormier, Robert (Edmund)

Fitgerald, Penelope 1916- . . . . **CLC 61**

Fitzgerald, Captain Hugh
　See Baum, L(yman) Frank

FitzGerald, Edward 1809-1883 . . . . **NCLC 9**
　See also DLB 32

Fitzgerald, F(rancis) Scott (Key)
　1896-1940 . . . . **TCLC 1, 6, 14, 28; SSC 6**
　See also AITN 1; CA 110; 123;
　　CDALB 1917-1929; DLB 4, 9, 86;
　　DLBD 1; DLBY 81; MTCW; WLC

Fitzgerald, Penelope 1916- . . . . . . **CLC 19, 51**
　See also CA 85-88; CAAS 10; DLB 14

FitzGerald, Robert D(avid)
　1902-1987 . . . . **CLC 19**
　See also CA 17-20R

Fitzgerald, Robert (Stuart)
　1910-1985 . . . . **CLC 39**
　See also CA 1-4R; 114; CANR 1; DLBY 80

Flanagan, Thomas (James Bonner)
　1923- . . . . **CLC 25, 52**
　See also CA 108; DLBY 80; MTCW

Flaubert, Gustave
　1821-1880 . . . . . **NCLC 2, 10, 19; SSC 11**
　See also DLB 119; WLC

Flecker, (Herman) James Elroy
　1884-1915 . . . . **TCLC 43**
　See also CA 109; DLB 10, 19

Fleming, Ian (Lancaster)
　1908-1964 . . . . **CLC 3, 30**
　See also CA 5-8R; CDBLB 1945-1960;
　　DLB 87; MTCW; SATA 9

Fleming, Thomas (James) 1927- . . . . **CLC 37**
　See also CA 5-8R; CANR 10; SATA 8

Fletcher, John Gould 1886-1950 . . . **TCLC 35**
　See also CA 107; DLB 4, 45

Fleur, Paul
　See Pohl, Frederik

Flying Officer X
　See Bates, H(erbert) E(rnest)

Fo, Dario 1926- . . . . **CLC 32**
　See also CA 116; 128; MTCW

Fogarty, Jonathan Titulescu Esq.
　See Farrell, James T(homas)

Folke, Will
　See Bloch, Robert (Albert)

Follett, Ken(neth Martin) 1949- . . . . **CLC 18**
　See also AAYA 6; BEST 89:4; CA 81-84;
　　CANR 13, 33; DLB 87; DLBY 81;
　　MTCW

Fontane, Theodor 1819-1898 . . . . . **NCLC 26**

Foote, Horton 1916- . . . . **CLC 51**
　See also CA 73-76; CANR 34; DLB 26

Foote, Shelby 1916- . . . . **CLC 75**
　See also CA 5-8R; CANR 3; DLB 2, 17

Forbes, Esther 1891-1967 . . . . **CLC 12**
　See also CA 13-14; 25-28R; CAP 1;
　　CLR 27; DLB 22; MAICYA; SATA 2

Forche, Carolyn (Louise) 1950- . . . . . **CLC 25**
　See also CA 109; 117; DLB 5

Ford, Elbur
　See Hibbert, Eleanor Burford

Ford, Ford Madox
　1873-1939 . . . . **TCLC 1, 15, 39**
　See also CA 104; 132; CDBLB 1914-1945;
　　DLB 34, 98; MTCW

Ford, John 1895-1973 . . . . **CLC 16**
　See also CA 45-48

Ford, Richard 1944- . . . . **CLC 46**
　See also CA 69-72; CANR 11

Ford, Webster
　See Masters, Edgar Lee

Foreman, Richard 1937- . . . . **CLC 50**
　See also CA 65-68; CANR 32

Forester, C(ecil) S(cott)
　1899-1966 . . . . **CLC 35**
　See also CA 73-76; 25-28R; SATA 13

Forez
　See Mauriac, Francois (Charles)

Forman, James Douglas 1932- . . . . . . **CLC 21**
　See also CA 9-12R; CANR 4, 19;
　　MAICYA; SATA 8, 70

Fornes, Maria Irene 1930- . . . . . . **CLC 39, 61**
　See also CA 25-28R; CANR 28; DLB 7;
　　HW; MTCW

Forrest, Leon 1937- . . . . **CLC 4**
　See also BW; CA 89-92; CAAS 7;
　　CANR 25; DLB 33

Forster, E(dward) M(organ)
　1879-1970 . . . . **CLC 1, 2, 3, 4, 9, 10, 13,
　　　　　　　　　　　　　　　　15, 22, 45**
　See also AAYA 2; CA 13-14; 25-28R;
　　CAP 1; CDBLB 1914-1945; DLB 34, 98;
　　DLBD 10; MTCW; SATA 57; WLC

Forster, John 1812-1876 . . . . **NCLC 11**

Forsyth, Frederick 1938- . . . . . . **CLC 2, 5, 36**
　See also BEST 89:4; CA 85-88; CANR 38;
　　DLB 87; MTCW

Forten, Charlotte L. . . . . **TCLC 16**
　See also Grimke, Charlotte L(ottie) Forten
　See also BLC 2; DLB 50

Foscolo, Ugo 1778-1827 . . . . **NCLC 8**

Fosse, Bob . . . . **CLC 20**
　See also Fosse, Robert Louis

Fosse, Robert Louis 1927-1987
　See Fosse, Bob
　See also CA 110; 123

Foster, Stephen Collins
　1826-1864 . . . . **NCLC 26**

Foucault, Michel
　1926-1984 . . . . **CLC 31, 34, 69**
　See also CA 105; 113; CANR 34; MTCW

Fouque, Friedrich (Heinrich Karl) de la Motte
　1777-1843 . . . . **NCLC 2**
　See also DLB 90

Fournier, Henri Alban 1886-1914
　See Alain-Fournier
　See also CA 104

Fournier, Pierre 1916- . . . . **CLC 11**
　See also Gascar, Pierre
　See also CA 89-92; CANR 16, 40

Fowles, John
　1926- . . . . **CLC 1, 2, 3, 4, 6, 9, 10, 15, 33**
　See also CA 5-8R; CANR 25; CDBLB 1960
　　to Present; DLB 14; MTCW; SATA 22

Gallup, Ralph
See Whitemore, Hugh (John)

Galsworthy, John 1867-1933 .... **TCLC 1, 45**
See also CA 104; CDBLB 1890-1914;
DLB 10, 34, 98; WLC 2

Galt, John 1779-1839 .... **NCLC 1**
See also DLB 99, 116

Galvin, James 1951- .... **CLC 38**
See also CA 108; CANR 26

Gamboa, Federico 1864-1939 ..... **TCLC 36**

Gann, Ernest Kellogg 1910-1991 .... **CLC 23**
See also AITN 1; CA 1-4R; 136; CANR 1

Garcia Lorca, Federico
1898-1936 .. **TCLC 1, 7, 49; DC 2; PC 3**
See also CA 104; 131; DLB 108; HW;
MTCW; WLC

Garcia Marquez, Gabriel (Jose)
1928- ... **CLC 2, 3, 8, 10, 15, 27, 47, 55;
SSC 8**
See also Marquez, Gabriel (Jose) Garcia
See also AAYA 3; BEST 89:1, 90:4;
CA 33-36R; CANR 10, 28; DLB 113;
HW; MTCW; WLC

Gard, Janice
See Latham, Jean Lee

Gard, Roger Martin du
See Martin du Gard, Roger

Gardam, Jane 1928- .... **CLC 43**
See also CA 49-52; CANR 2, 18, 33;
CLR 12; DLB 14; MAICYA; MTCW;
SAAS 9; SATA 28, 39

Gardner, Herb .... **CLC 44**

Gardner, John (Champlin) Jr.
1933-1982 .... **CLC 2, 3, 5, 7, 8, 10, 18,
28, 34; SSC 7**
See also AITN 1; CA 65-68; 107;
CANR 33; DLB 2; DLBY 82; MTCW;
SATA 31, 40

Gardner, John (Edmund) 1926- ..... **CLC 30**
See also CA 103; CANR 15; MTCW

Gardner, Noel
See Kuttner, Henry

Gardons, S. S.
See Snodgrass, William D(e Witt)

Garfield, Leon 1921- .... **CLC 12**
See also AAYA 8; CA 17-20R; CANR 38;
CLR 21; MAICYA; SATA 1, 32

Garland, (Hannibal) Hamlin
1860-1940 .... **TCLC 3**
See also CA 104; DLB 12, 71, 78

Garneau, (Hector de) Saint-Denys
1912-1943 .... **TCLC 13**
See also CA 111; DLB 88

Garner, Alan 1934- .... **CLC 17**
See also CA 73-76; CANR 15; CLR 20;
MAICYA; MTCW; SATA 18, 69

Garner, Hugh 1913-1979 .... **CLC 13**
See also CA 69-72; CANR 31; DLB 68

Garnett, David 1892-1981 .... **CLC 3**
See also CA 5-8R; 103; CANR 17; DLB 34

Garos, Stephanie
See Katz, Steve

Garrett, George (Palmer)
1929- .... **CLC 3, 11, 51**
See also CA 1-4R; CAAS 5; CANR 1;
DLB 2, 5; DLBY 83

Garrick, David 1717-1779 .... **LC 15**
See also DLB 84

Garrigue, Jean 1914-1972 .... **CLC 2, 8**
See also CA 5-8R; 37-40R; CANR 20

Garrison, Frederick
See Sinclair, Upton (Beall)

Garth, Will
See Hamilton, Edmond; Kuttner, Henry

Garvey, Marcus (Moziah Jr.)
1887-1940 .... **TCLC 41**
See also BLC 2; BW; CA 120; 124

Gary, Romain .... **CLC 25**
See also Kacew, Romain
See also DLB 83

Gascar, Pierre .... **CLC 11**
See also Fournier, Pierre

Gascoyne, David (Emery) 1916- .... **CLC 45**
See also CA 65-68; CANR 10, 28; DLB 20;
MTCW

Gaskell, Elizabeth Cleghorn
1810-1865 .... **NCLC 5**
See also CDBLB 1832-1890; DLB 21

Gass, William H(oward)
1924- .... **CLC 1, 2, 8, 11, 15, 39**
See also CA 17-20R; CANR 30; DLB 2;
MTCW

Gasset, Jose Ortega y
See Ortega y Gasset, Jose

Gautier, Theophile 1811-1872 ..... **NCLC 1**
See also DLB 119

Gawsworth, John
See Bates, H(erbert) E(rnest)

Gaye, Marvin (Penze) 1939-1984 ... **CLC 26**
See also CA 112

Gebler, Carlo (Ernest) 1954- .... **CLC 39**
See also CA 119; 133

Gee, Maggie (Mary) 1948- .... **CLC 57**
See also CA 130

Gee, Maurice (Gough) 1931- .... **CLC 29**
See also CA 97-100; SATA 46

Gelbart, Larry (Simon) 1923- ... **CLC 21, 61**
See also CA 73-76

Gelber, Jack 1932- .... **CLC 1, 6, 14**
See also CA 1-4R; CANR 2; DLB 7

Gellhorn, Martha Ellis 1908- ... **CLC 14, 60**
See also CA 77-80; DLBY 82

Genet, Jean
1910-1986 ... **CLC 1, 2, 5, 10, 14, 44, 46**
See also CA 13-16R; CANR 18; DLB 72;
DLBY 86; MTCW

Gent, Peter 1942- .... **CLC 29**
See also AITN 1; CA 89-92; DLBY 82

George, Jean Craighead 1919- ...... **CLC 35**
See also AAYA 8; CA 5-8R; CANR 25;
CLR 1; DLB 52; MAICYA; SATA 2, 68

George, Stefan (Anton)
1868-1933 .... **TCLC 2, 14**
See also CA 104

Georges, Georges Martin
See Simenon, Georges (Jacques Christian)

Gerhardi, William Alexander
See Gerhardie, William Alexander

Gerhardie, William Alexander
1895-1977 .... **CLC 5**
See also CA 25-28R; 73-76; CANR 18;
DLB 36

Gerstler, Amy 1956- .... **CLC 70**

Gertler, T. .... **CLC 34**
See also CA 116; 121

Ghalib 1797-1869 .... **NCLC 39**

Ghelderode, Michel de
1898-1962 .... **CLC 6, 11**
See also CA 85-88; CANR 40

Ghiselin, Brewster 1903- .... **CLC 23**
See also CA 13-16R; CAAS 10; CANR 13

Ghose, Zulfikar 1935- .... **CLC 42**
See also CA 65-68

Ghosh, Amitav 1956- .... **CLC 44**

Giacosa, Giuseppe 1847-1906 ...... **TCLC 7**
See also CA 104

Gibb, Lee
See Waterhouse, Keith (Spencer)

Gibbon, Lewis Grassic .... **TCLC 4**
See also Mitchell, James Leslie

Gibbons, Kaye 1960- .... **CLC 50**

Gibran, Kahlil 1883-1931 .... **TCLC 1, 9**
See also CA 104

Gibson, William (Ford) 1948- ... **CLC 39, 63**
See also CA 126; 133

Gibson, William 1914- .... **CLC 23**
See also CA 9-12R; CANR 9; DLB 7;
SATA 66

Gide, Andre (Paul Guillaume)
1869-1951 .... **TCLC 5, 12, 36**
See also CA 104; 124; DLB 65; MTCW;
WLC

Gifford, Barry (Colby) 1946- .... **CLC 34**
See also CA 65-68; CANR 9, 30, 40

Gilbert, W(illiam) S(chwenck)
1836-1911 .... **TCLC 3**
See also CA 104; SATA 36

Gilbreth, Frank B. Jr. 1911- .... **CLC 17**
See also CA 9-12R; SATA 2

Gilchrist, Ellen 1935- .... **CLC 34, 48**
See also CA 113; 116; MTCW

Giles, Molly 1942- .... **CLC 39**
See also CA 126

Gill, Patrick
See Creasey, John

Gilliam, Terry (Vance) 1940- .... **CLC 21**
See also Monty Python
See also CA 108; 113; CANR 35

Gillian, Jerry
See Gilliam, Terry (Vance)

Gilliatt, Penelope (Ann Douglass)
1932- .... **CLC 2, 10, 13, 53**
See also AITN 2; CA 13-16R; DLB 14

Gilman, Charlotte (Anna) Perkins (Stetson)
1860-1935 .... **TCLC 9, 37**
See also CA 106

Gilmour, David 1944- .... **CLC 35**
See also Pink Floyd
See also CA 138

Grabbe, Christian Dietrich
1801-1836 .... NCLC 2

Grace, Patricia 1937- .... CLC 56

Gracian y Morales, Baltasar
1601-1658 .... LC 15

Gracq, Julien .... CLC 11, 48
See also Poirier, Louis
See also DLB 83

Grade, Chaim 1910-1982 .... CLC 10
See also CA 93-96; 107

Graduate of Oxford, A
See Ruskin, John

Graham, John
See Phillips, David Graham

Graham, Jorie 1951- .... CLC 48
See also CA 111; DLB 120

Graham, R(obert) B(ontine) Cunninghame
See Cunninghame Graham, R(obert)
B(ontine)
See also DLB 98

Graham, Robert
See Haldeman, Joe (William)

Graham, Tom
See Lewis, (Harry) Sinclair

Graham, W(illiam) S(ydney)
1918-1986 .... CLC 29
See also CA 73-76; 118; DLB 20

Graham, Winston (Mawdsley)
1910- .... CLC 23
See also CA 49-52; CANR 2, 22; DLB 77

Granville-Barker, Harley
1877-1946 .... TCLC 2
See also Barker, Harley Granville
See also CA 104

Grass, Guenter (Wilhelm)
1927- .. CLC 1, 2, 4, 6, 11, 15, 22, 32, 49
See also CA 13-16R; CANR 20; DLB 75,
124; MTCW; WLC

Gratton, Thomas
See Hulme, T(homas) E(rnest)

Grau, Shirley Ann 1929- .... CLC 4, 9
See also CA 89-92; CANR 22; DLB 2;
MTCW

Gravel, Fern
See Hall, James Norman

Graver, Elizabeth 1964- .... CLC 70
See also CA 135

Graves, Richard Perceval 1945- .... CLC 44
See also CA 65-68; CANR 9, 26

Graves, Robert (von Ranke)
1895-1985 ..... CLC 1, 2, 6, 11, 39, 44,
45; PC 6
See also CA 5-8R; 117; CANR 5, 36;
CDBLB 1914-1945; DLB 20, 100;
DLBY 85; MTCW; SATA 45

Gray, Alasdair (James) 1934- ...... CLC 41
See also CA 126; MTCW

Gray, Amlin 1946- .... CLC 29
See also CA 138

Gray, Francine du Plessix 1930-.... CLC 22
See also BEST 90:3; CA 61-64; CAAS 2;
CANR 11, 33; MTCW

Gray, John (Henry) 1866-1934 .... TCLC 19
See also CA 119

Gray, Simon (James Holliday)
1936- .... CLC 9, 14, 36
See also AITN 1; CA 21-24R; CAAS 3;
CANR 32; DLB 13; MTCW

Gray, Spalding 1941- .... CLC 49
See also CA 128

Gray, Thomas 1716-1771 ...... LC 4; PC 2
See also CDBLB 1660-1789; DLB 109;
WLC

Grayson, David
See Baker, Ray Stannard

Grayson, Richard (A.) 1951- .... CLC 38
See also CA 85-88; CANR 14, 31

Greeley, Andrew M(oran) 1928-.... CLC 28
See also CA 5-8R; CAAS 7; CANR 7;
MTCW

Green, Brian
See Card, Orson Scott

Green, Hannah
See Greenberg, Joanne (Goldenberg)

Green, Hannah .... CLC 3
See also CA 73-76

Green, Henry .... CLC 2, 13
See also Yorke, Henry Vincent
See also DLB 15

Green, Julian (Hartridge)
1900- .... CLC 3, 11
See also CA 21-24R; CANR 33; DLB 4, 72;
MTCW

Green, Julien 1900-
See Green, Julian (Hartridge)

Green, Paul (Eliot) 1894-1981 ...... CLC 25
See also AITN 1; CA 5-8R; 103; CANR 3;
DLB 7, 9; DLBY 81

Greenberg, Ivan 1908-1973
See Rahv, Philip
See also CA 85-88

Greenberg, Joanne (Goldenberg)
1932- .... CLC 7, 30
See also CA 5-8R; CANR 14, 32; SATA 25

Greenberg, Richard 1959(?)- .... CLC 57
See also CA 138

Greene, Bette 1934- .... CLC 30
See also AAYA 7; CA 53-56; CANR 4;
CLR 2; MAICYA; SATA 8

Greene, Gael .... CLC 8
See also CA 13-16R; CANR 10

Greene, Graham (Henry)
1904-1991 ... CLC 1, 3, 6, 9, 14, 18, 27,
37, 70, 72
See also AITN 2; CA 13-16R; 133;
CANR 35; CDBLB 1945-1960; DLB 13,
15, 77, 100; DLBY 91; MTCW;
SATA 20; WLC

Greer, Richard
See Silverberg, Robert

Greer, Richard
See Silverberg, Robert

Gregor, Arthur 1923- .... CLC 9
See also CA 25-28R; CAAS 10; CANR 11;
SATA 36

Gregor, Lee
See Pohl, Frederik

Gregory, Isabella Augusta (Persse)
1852-1932 .... TCLC 1
See also CA 104; DLB 10

Gregory, J. Dennis
See Williams, John A(lfred)

Grendon, Stephen
See Derleth, August (William)

Grenville, Kate 1950- .... CLC 61
See also CA 118

Grenville, Pelham
See Wodehouse, P(elham) G(renville)

Greve, Felix Paul (Berthold Friedrich)
1879-1948
See Grove, Frederick Philip
See also CA 104

Grey, Zane 1872-1939 .... TCLC 6
See also CA 104; 132; DLB 9; MTCW

Grieg, (Johan) Nordahl (Brun)
1902-1943 .... TCLC 10
See also CA 107

Grieve, C(hristopher) M(urray)
1892-1978 .... CLC 11, 19
See also MacDiarmid, Hugh
See also CA 5-8R; 85-88; CANR 33;
MTCW

Griffin, Gerald 1803-1840 .... NCLC 7

Griffin, John Howard 1920-1980.... CLC 68
See also AITN 1; CA 1-4R; 101; CANR 2

Griffin, Peter .... CLC 39

Griffiths, Trevor 1935-......... CLC 13, 52
See also CA 97-100; DLB 13

Grigson, Geoffrey (Edward Harvey)
1905-1985 .... CLC 7, 39
See also CA 25-28R; 118; CANR 20, 33;
DLB 27; MTCW

Grillparzer, Franz 1791-1872...... NCLC 1

Grimble, Reverend Charles James
See Eliot, T(homas) S(tearns)

Grimke, Charlotte L(ottie) Forten
1837(?)-1914
See Forten, Charlotte L.
See also BW; CA 117; 124

Grimm, Jacob Ludwig Karl
1785-1863 .... NCLC 3
See also DLB 90; MAICYA; SATA 22

Grimm, Wilhelm Karl 1786-1859 .. NCLC 3
See also DLB 90; MAICYA; SATA 22

Grimmelshausen, Johann Jakob Christoffel
von 1621-1676 .... LC 6

Grindel, Eugene 1895-1952
See Eluard, Paul
See also CA 104

Grossman, David .... CLC 67
See also CA 138

Grossman, Vasily (Semenovich)
1905-1964 .... CLC 41
See also CA 124; 130; MTCW

Grove, Frederick Philip .... TCLC 4
See also Greve, Felix Paul (Berthold
Friedrich)
See also DLB 92

Grubb
See Crumb, R(obert)

Grumbach, Doris (Isaac)
1918- .... CLC **13, 22, 64**
See also CA 5-8R; CAAS 2; CANR 9

Grundtvig, Nicolai Frederik Severin
1783-1872 .... NCLC **1**

Grunge
See Crumb, R(obert)

Grunwald, Lisa 1959- .... CLC **44**
See also CA 120

Guare, John 1938- .... CLC **8, 14, 29, 67**
See also CA 73-76; CANR 21; DLB 7;
MTCW

Gudjonsson, Halldor Kiljan 1902-
See Laxness, Halldor
See also CA 103

Guenter, Erich
See Eich, Guenter

Guest, Barbara 1920- .... CLC **34**
See also CA 25-28R; CANR 11; DLB 5

Guest, Judith (Ann) 1936- .... CLC **8, 30**
See also AAYA 7; CA 77-80; CANR 15;
MTCW

Guild, Nicholas M. 1944- .... CLC **33**
See also CA 93-96

Guillemin, Jacques
See Sartre, Jean-Paul

Guillen, Jorge 1893-1984 .... CLC **11**
See also CA 89-92; 112; DLB 108; HW

Guillen (y Batista), Nicolas (Cristobal)
1902-1989 .... CLC **48**
See also BLC 2; BW; CA 116; 125; 129;
HW

Guillevic, (Eugene) 1907- .... CLC **33**
See also CA 93-96

Guillois
See Desnos, Robert

Guiney, Louise Imogen
1861-1920 .... TCLC **41**
See also DLB 54

Guiraldes, Ricardo (Guillermo)
1886-1927 .... TCLC **39**
See also CA 131; HW; MTCW

Gunn, Bill .... CLC **5**
See also Gunn, William Harrison
See also DLB 38

Gunn, Thom(son William)
1929- .... CLC **3, 6, 18, 32**
See also CA 17-20R; CANR 9, 33;
CDBLB 1960 to Present; DLB 27;
MTCW

Gunn, William Harrison 1934(?)-1989
See Gunn, Bill
See also AITN 1; BW; CA 13-16R; 128;
CANR 12, 25

Gunnars, Kristjana 1948- .... CLC **69**
See also CA 113; DLB 60

Gurganus, Allan 1947- .... CLC **70**
See also BEST 90:1; CA 135

Gurney, A(lbert) R(amsdell) Jr.
1930- .... CLC **32, 50, 54**
See also CA 77-80; CANR 32

Gurney, Ivor (Bertie) 1890-1937 ... TCLC **33**

Gurney, Peter
See Gurney, A(lbert) R(amsdell) Jr.

Gustafson, Ralph (Barker) 1909- .... CLC **36**
See also CA 21-24R; CANR 8; DLB 88

Gut, Gom
See Simenon, Georges (Jacques Christian)

Guthrie, A(lfred) B(ertram) Jr.
1901-1991 .... CLC **23**
See also CA 57-60; 134; CANR 24; DLB 6;
SATA 62; SATO 67

Guthrie, Isobel
See Grieve, C(hristopher) M(urray)

Guthrie, Woodrow Wilson 1912-1967
See Guthrie, Woody
See also CA 113; 93-96

Guthrie, Woody .... CLC **35**
See also Guthrie, Woodrow Wilson

Guy, Rosa (Cuthbert) 1928- .... CLC **26**
See also AAYA 4; BW; CA 17-20R;
CANR 14, 34; CLR 13; DLB 33;
MAICYA; SATA 14, 62

Gwendolyn
See Bennett, (Enoch) Arnold

H. D. .... CLC **3, 8, 14, 31, 34, 73; PC 5**
See also Doolittle, Hilda

Haavikko, Paavo Juhani
1931- .... CLC **18, 34**
See also CA 106

Habbema, Koos
See Heijermans, Herman

Hacker, Marilyn 1942- .... CLC **5, 9, 23, 72**
See also CA 77-80; DLB 120

Haggard, H(enry) Rider
1856-1925 .... TCLC **11**
See also CA 108; DLB 70; SATA 16

Haig, Fenil
See Ford, Ford Madox

Haig-Brown, Roderick (Langmere)
1908-1976 .... CLC **21**
See also CA 5-8R; 69-72; CANR 4, 38;
DLB 88; MAICYA; SATA 12

Hailey, Arthur 1920- .... CLC **5**
See also AITN 2; BEST 90:3; CA 1-4R;
CANR 2, 36; DLB 88; DLBY 82; MTCW

Hailey, Elizabeth Forsythe 1938- ... CLC **40**
See also CA 93-96; CAAS 1; CANR 15

Haines, John (Meade) 1924- .... CLC **58**
See also CA 17-20R; CANR 13, 34; DLB 5

Haldeman, Joe (William) 1943- ..... CLC **61**
See also CA 53-56; CANR 6; DLB 8

Haley, Alex(ander Murray Palmer)
1921-1992 .... CLC **8, 12**
See also BLC 2; BW; CA 77-80; 136;
DLB 38; MTCW

Haliburton, Thomas Chandler
1796-1865 .... NCLC **15**
See also DLB 11, 99

Hall, Donald (Andrew Jr.)
1928- .... CLC **1, 13, 37, 59**
See also CA 5-8R; CAAS 7; CANR 2;
DLB 5; SATA 23

Hall, Frederic Sauser
See Sauser-Hall, Frederic

Hall, James
See Kuttner, Henry

Hall, James Norman 1887-1951 ... TCLC **23**
See also CA 123; SATA 21

Hall, (Marguerite) Radclyffe
1886(?)-1943 .... TCLC **12**
See also CA 110

Hall, Rodney 1935- .... CLC **51**
See also CA 109

Halliday, Michael
See Creasey, John

Halpern, Daniel 1945- .... CLC **14**
See also CA 33-36R

Hamburger, Michael (Peter Leopold)
1924- .... CLC **5, 14**
See also CA 5-8R; CAAS 4; CANR 2;
DLB 27

Hamill, Pete 1935- .... CLC **10**
See also CA 25-28R; CANR 18

Hamilton, Clive
See Lewis, C(live) S(taples)

Hamilton, Edmond 1904-1977 .... CLC **1**
See also CA 1-4R; CANR 3; DLB 8

Hamilton, Eugene (Jacob) Lee
See Lee-Hamilton, Eugene (Jacob)

Hamilton, Franklin
See Silverberg, Robert

Hamilton, Gail
See Corcoran, Barbara

Hamilton, Mollie
See Kaye, M(ary) M(argaret)

Hamilton, (Anthony Walter) Patrick
1904-1962 .... CLC **51**
See also CA 113; DLB 10

Hamilton, Virginia 1936- .... CLC **26**
See also AAYA 2; BW; CA 25-28R;
CANR 20, 37; CLR 1, 11; DLB 33, 52;
MAICYA; MTCW; SATA 4, 56

Hammett, (Samuel) Dashiell
1894-1961 .... CLC **3, 5, 10, 19, 47**
See also AITN 1; CA 81-84;
CDALB 1929-1941; DLBD 6; MTCW

Hammon, Jupiter 1711(?)-1800(?).. NCLC **5**
See also BLC 2; DLB 31, 50

Hammond, Keith
See Kuttner, Henry

Hamner, Earl (Henry) Jr. 1923- .... CLC **12**
See also AITN 2; CA 73-76; DLB 6

Hampton, Christopher (James)
1946- .... CLC **4**
See also CA 25-28R; DLB 13; MTCW

Hamsun, Knut 1859-1952... TCLC **2, 14, 49**
See also Pedersen, Knut

Handke, Peter 1942- .. CLC **5, 8, 10, 15, 38**
See also CA 77-80; CANR 33; DLB 85,
124; MTCW

Hanley, James 1901-1985 ...CLC **3, 5, 8, 13**
See also CA 73-76; 117; CANR 36; MTCW

Hannah, Barry 1942- .... CLC **23, 38**
See also CA 108; 110; DLB 6; MTCW

Hannon, Ezra
See Hunter, Evan

Hillis, Rick 1956- .... **CLC 66**
See also CA 134

Hilton, James 1900-1954 .... **TCLC 21**
See also CA 108; DLB 34, 77; SATA 34

Himes, Chester (Bomar)
1909-1984 .... **CLC 2, 4, 7, 18, 58**
See also BLC 2; BW; CA 25-28R; 114;
CANR 22; DLB 2, 76; MTCW

Hinde, Thomas .... **CLC 6, 11**
See also Chitty, Thomas Willes

Hindin, Nathan
See Bloch, Robert (Albert)

Hine, (William) Daryl 1936- .... **CLC 15**
See also CA 1-4R; CAAS 15; CANR 1, 20;
DLB 60

Hinkson, Katharine Tynan
See Tynan, Katharine

Hinton, S(usan) E(loise) 1950- ..... **CLC 30**
See also AAYA 2; CA 81-84; CANR 32;
CLR 3, 23; MAICYA; MTCW;
SATA 19, 58

Hippius, Zinaida .... **TCLC 9**
See also Gippius, Zinaida (Nikolayevna)

Hiraoka, Kimitake 1925-1970
See Mishima, Yukio
See also CA 97-100; 29-32R; MTCW

Hirsch, Edward 1950- .... **CLC 31, 50**
See also CA 104; CANR 20; DLB 120

Hitchcock, Alfred (Joseph)
1899-1980 .... **CLC 16**
See also CA 97-100; SATA 24, 27

Hoagland, Edward 1932- .... **CLC 28**
See also CA 1-4R; CANR 2, 31; DLB 6;
SATA 51

Hoban, Russell (Conwell) 1925- .. **CLC 7, 25**
See also CA 5-8R; CANR 23, 37; CLR 3;
DLB 52; MAICYA; MTCW; SATA 1, 40

Hobbs, Perry
See Blackmur, R(ichard) P(almer)

Hobson, Laura Z(ametkin)
1900-1986 .... **CLC 7, 25**
See also CA 17-20R; 118; DLB 28;
SATA 52

Hochhuth, Rolf 1931- .... **CLC 4, 11, 18**
See also CA 5-8R; CANR 33; DLB 124;
MTCW

Hochman, Sandra 1936- .... **CLC 3, 8**
See also CA 5-8R; DLB 5

Hochwaelder, Fritz 1911-1986 ...... **CLC 36**
See also Hochwalder, Fritz
See also CA 29-32R; 120; MTCW

Hochwalder, Fritz .... **CLC 36**
See also Hochwaelder, Fritz

Hocking, Mary (Eunice) 1921- ..... **CLC 13**
See also CA 101; CANR 18, 40

Hodgins, Jack 1938- .... **CLC 23**
See also CA 93-96; DLB 60

Hodgson, William Hope
1877(?)-1918 .... **TCLC 13**
See also CA 111; DLB 70

Hoffman, Alice 1952- .... **CLC 51**
See also CA 77-80; CANR 34; MTCW

Hoffman, Daniel (Gerard)
1923- .... **CLC 6, 13, 23**
See also CA 1-4R; CANR 4; DLB 5

Hoffman, Stanley 1944- .... **CLC 5**
See also CA 77-80

Hoffman, William M(oses) 1939- ... **CLC 40**
See also CA 57-60; CANR 11

Hoffmann, E(rnst) T(heodor) A(madeus)
1776-1822 .... **NCLC 2**
See also DLB 90; SATA 27

Hofmann, Gert 1931- .... **CLC 54**
See also CA 128

Hofmannsthal, Hugo von
1874-1929 .... **TCLC 11**
See also CA 106; DLB 81, 118

Hogan, Linda 1947- .... **CLC 73**
See also CA 120

Hogarth, Charles
See Creasey, John

Hogg, James 1770-1835 .... **NCLC 4**
See also DLB 93, 116

Holbach, Paul Henri Thiry Baron
1723-1789 .... **LC 14**

Holberg, Ludvig 1684-1754 .... **LC 6**

Holden, Ursula 1921- .... **CLC 18**
See also CA 101; CAAS 8; CANR 22

Holderlin, (Johann Christian) Friedrich
1770-1843 .... **NCLC 16; PC 4**

Holdstock, Robert
See Holdstock, Robert P.

Holdstock, Robert P. 1948- .... **CLC 39**
See also CA 131

Holland, Isabelle 1920- .... **CLC 21**
See also CA 21-24R; CANR 10, 25;
MAICYA; SATA 8, 70

Holland, Marcus
See Caldwell, (Janet Miriam) Taylor
(Holland)

Hollander, John 1929- ...... **CLC 2, 5, 8, 14**
See also CA 1-4R; CANR 1; DLB 5;
SATA 13

Hollander, Paul
See Silverberg, Robert

Holleran, Andrew 1943(?)- .... **CLC 38**

Hollinghurst, Alan 1954- .... **CLC 55**
See also CA 114

Hollis, Jim
See Summers, Hollis (Spurgeon Jr.)

Holmes, John
See Souster, (Holmes) Raymond

Holmes, John Clellon 1926-1988.... **CLC 56**
See also CA 9-12R; 125; CANR 4; DLB 16

Holmes, Oliver Wendell
1809-1894 .... **NCLC 14**
See also CDALB 1640-1865; DLB 1;
SATA 34

Holmes, Raymond
See Souster, (Holmes) Raymond

Holt, Victoria
See Hibbert, Eleanor Burford

Holub, Miroslav 1923- .... **CLC 4**
See also CA 21-24R; CANR 10

Homer c. 8th cent. B.C.- .... **CMLC 1**

Honig, Edwin 1919- .... **CLC 33**
See also CA 5-8R; CAAS 8; CANR 4;
DLB 5

Hood, Hugh (John Blagdon)
1928- .... **CLC 15, 28**
See also CA 49-52; CANR 1, 33; DLB 53

Hood, Thomas 1799-1845 .... **NCLC 16**
See also DLB 96

Hooker, (Peter) Jeremy 1941- ...... **CLC 43**
See also CA 77-80; CANR 22; DLB 40

Hope, A(lec) D(erwent) 1907- .... **CLC 3, 51**
See also CA 21-24R; CANR 33; MTCW

Hope, Brian
See Creasey, John

Hope, Christopher (David Tully)
1944- .... **CLC 52**
See also CA 106; SATA 62

Hopkins, Gerard Manley
1844-1889 .... **NCLC 17**
See also CDBLB 1890-1914; DLB 35, 57;
WLC

Hopkins, John (Richard) 1931- ...... **CLC 4**
See also CA 85-88

Hopkins, Pauline Elizabeth
1859-1930 .... **TCLC 28**
See also BLC 2; DLB 50

Horatio
See Proust,
(Valentin-Louis-George-Eugene-)Marcel

Horgan, Paul 1903- .... **CLC 9, 53**
See also CA 13-16R; CANR 9, 35;
DLB 102; DLBY 85; MTCW; SATA 13

Horn, Peter
See Kuttner, Henry

Horovitz, Israel 1939- .... **CLC 56**
See also CA 33-36R; DLB 7

Horvath, Odon von
See Horvath, Oedoen von
See also DLB 85, 124

Horvath, Oedoen von 1901-1938... **TCLC 45**
See also Horvath, Odon von
See also CA 118

Horwitz, Julius 1920-1986........ **CLC 14**
See also CA 9-12R; 119; CANR 12

Hospital, Janette Turner 1942-..... **CLC 42**
See also CA 108

Hostos, E. M. de
See Hostos (y Bonilla), Eugenio Maria de

Hostos, Eugenio M. de
See Hostos (y Bonilla), Eugenio Maria de

Hostos, Eugenio Maria
See Hostos (y Bonilla), Eugenio Maria de

Hostos (y Bonilla), Eugenio Maria de
1839-1903 .... **TCLC 24**
See also CA 123; 131; HW

Houdini
See Lovecraft, H(oward) P(hillips)

Hougan, Carolyn 19(?)- .... **CLC 34**
See also CA 139

Household, Geoffrey (Edward West)
1900-1988 .... **CLC 11**
See also CA 77-80; 126; DLB 87; SATA 14,
59

Johnson, B(ryan) S(tanley William)
1933-1973 . . . . **CLC 6, 9**
See also CA 9-12R; 53-56; CANR 9;
DLB 14, 40

Johnson, Charles (Richard)
1948- . . . . **CLC 7, 51, 65**
See also BLC 2; BW; CA 116; DLB 33

Johnson, Denis 1949- . . . . **CLC 52**
See also CA 117; 121; DLB 120

Johnson, Diane (Lain)
1934- . . . . **CLC 5, 13, 48**
See also CA 41-44R; CANR 17, 40;
DLBY 80; MTCW

Johnson, Eyvind (Olof Verner)
1900-1976 . . . . **CLC 14**
See also CA 73-76; 69-72; CANR 34

Johnson, J. R.
See James, C(yril) L(ionel) R(obert)

Johnson, James Weldon
1871-1938 . . . . **TCLC 3, 19**
See also BLC 2; BW; CA 104; 125;
CDALB 1917-1929; DLB 51; MTCW;
SATA 31

Johnson, Joyce 1935- . . . . **CLC 58**
See also CA 125; 129

Johnson, Lionel (Pigot)
1867-1902 . . . . **TCLC 19**
See also CA 117; DLB 19

Johnson, Mel
See Malzberg, Barry N(athaniel)

Johnson, Pamela Hansford
1912-1981 . . . . **CLC 1, 7, 27**
See also CA 1-4R; 104; CANR 2, 28;
DLB 15; MTCW

Johnson, Samuel 1709-1784 . . . . **LC 15**
See also CDBLB 1660-1789; DLB 39, 95,
104; WLC

Johnson, Uwe
1934-1984 . . . . **CLC 5, 10, 15, 40**
See also CA 1-4R; 112; CANR 1, 39;
DLB 75; MTCW

Johnston, George (Benson) 1913- . . . **CLC 51**
See also CA 1-4R; CANR 5, 20; DLB 88

Johnston, Jennifer 1930- . . . . **CLC 7**
See also CA 85-88; DLB 14

Jolley, (Monica) Elizabeth 1923- . . . **CLC 46**
See also CA 127; CAAS 13

Jones, Arthur Llewellyn 1863-1947
See Machen, Arthur
See also CA 104

Jones, D(ouglas) G(ordon) 1929- . . . . **CLC 10**
See also CA 29-32R; CANR 13; DLB 53

Jones, David (Michael)
1895-1974 . . . . **CLC 2, 4, 7, 13, 42**
See also CA 9-12R; 53-56; CANR 28;
CDBLB 1945-1960; DLB 20, 100; MTCW

Jones, David Robert 1947-
See Bowie, David
See also CA 103

Jones, Diana Wynne 1934- . . . . **CLC 26**
See also CA 49-52; CANR 4, 26; CLR 23;
MAICYA; SAAS 7; SATA 9, 70

Jones, Gayl 1949- . . . . **CLC 6, 9**
See also BLC 2; BW; CA 77-80; CANR 27;
DLB 33; MTCW

Jones, James 1921-1977 . . . . **CLC 1, 3, 10, 39**
See also AITN 1, 2; CA 1-4R; 69-72;
CANR 6; DLB 2; MTCW

Jones, John J.
See Lovecraft, H(oward) P(hillips)

Jones, LeRoi . . . . **CLC 1, 2, 3, 5, 10, 14**
See also Baraka, Amiri

Jones, Louis B. . . . . **CLC 65**

Jones, Madison (Percy Jr.) 1925- . . . . **CLC 4**
See also CA 13-16R; CAAS 11; CANR 7

Jones, Mervyn 1922- . . . . **CLC 10, 52**
See also CA 45-48; CAAS 5; CANR 1;
MTCW

Jones, Mick 1956(?)- . . . . **CLC 30**
See also The Clash

Jones, Nettie (Pearl) 1941- . . . . **CLC 34**
See also CA 137

Jones, Preston 1936-1979 . . . . **CLC 10**
See also CA 73-76; 89-92; DLB 7

Jones, Robert F(rancis) 1934- . . . . **CLC 7**
See also CA 49-52; CANR 2

Jones, Rod 1953- . . . . **CLC 50**
See also CA 128

Jones, Terence Graham Parry
1942- . . . . **CLC 21**
See also Jones, Terry; Monty Python
See also CA 112; 116; CANR 35; SATA 51

Jones, Terry
See Jones, Terence Graham Parry
See also SATA 67

Jong, Erica 1942- . . . . **CLC 4, 6, 8, 18**
See also AITN 1; BEST 90:2; CA 73-76;
CANR 26; DLB 2, 5, 28; MTCW

Jonson, Ben(jamin) 1572(?)-1637 . . . . . . **LC 6**
See also CDBLB Before 1660; DLB 62, 121;
WLC

Jordan, June 1936- . . . . **CLC 5, 11, 23**
See also AAYA 2; BW; CA 33-36R;
CANR 25; CLR 10; DLB 38; MAICYA;
MTCW; SATA 4

Jordan, Pat(rick M.) 1941- . . . . **CLC 37**
See also CA 33-36R

Jorgensen, Ivar
See Ellison, Harlan

Jorgenson, Ivar
See Silverberg, Robert

Josipovici, Gabriel 1940- . . . . **CLC 6, 43**
See also CA 37-40R; CAAS 8; DLB 14

Joubert, Joseph 1754-1824 . . . . **NCLC 9**

Jouve, Pierre Jean 1887-1976 . . . . . . **CLC 47**
See also CA 65-68

Joyce, James (Augustine Aloysius)
1882-1941 . . . . **TCLC 3, 8, 16, 35; SSC 3**
See also CA 104; 126; CDBLB 1914-1945;
DLB 10, 19, 36; MTCW; WLC

Jozsef, Attila 1905-1937 . . . . **TCLC 22**
See also CA 116

Juana Ines de la Cruz 1651(?)-1695 . . . **LC 5**

Judd, Cyril
See Kornbluth, C(yril) M.; Pohl, Frederik

Julian of Norwich 1342(?)-1416(?) . . . . **LC 6**

Just, Ward (Swift) 1935- . . . . **CLC 4, 27**
See also CA 25-28R; CANR 32

Justice, Donald (Rodney) 1925- . . **CLC 6, 19**
See also CA 5-8R; CANR 26; DLBY 83

Juvenal c. 55-c. 127 . . . . **CMLC 8**

Juvenis
See Bourne, Randolph S(illiman)

Kacew, Romain 1914-1980
See Gary, Romain
See also CA 108; 102

Kadare, Ismail 1936- . . . . **CLC 52**

Kadohata, Cynthia . . . . **CLC 59**

Kafka, Franz
1883-1924 . . . . . . **TCLC 2, 6, 13, 29, 47;
SSC 5**
See also CA 105; 126; DLB 81; MTCW;
WLC

Kahn, Roger 1927- . . . . **CLC 30**
See also CA 25-28R; SATA 37

Kain, Saul
See Sassoon, Siegfried (Lorraine)

Kaiser, Georg 1878-1945 . . . . **TCLC 9**
See also CA 106; DLB 124

Kaletski, Alexander 1946- . . . . **CLC 39**
See also CA 118

Kalidasa fl. c. 400- . . . . **CMLC 9**

Kallman, Chester (Simon)
1921-1975 . . . . **CLC 2**
See also CA 45-48; 53-56; CANR 3

Kaminsky, Melvin 1926-
See Brooks, Mel
See also CA 65-68; CANR 16

Kaminsky, Stuart M(elvin) 1934- . . . **CLC 59**
See also CA 73-76; CANR 29

Kane, Paul
See Simon, Paul

Kane, Wilson
See Bloch, Robert (Albert)

Kanin, Garson 1912- . . . . **CLC 22**
See also AITN 1; CA 5-8R; CANR 7;
DLB 7

Kaniuk, Yoram 1930- . . . . **CLC 19**
See also CA 134

Kant, Immanuel 1724-1804 . . . . . . **NCLC 27**
See also DLB 94

Kantor, MacKinlay 1904-1977 . . . . . . **CLC 7**
See also CA 61-64; 73-76; DLB 9, 102

Kaplan, David Michael 1946- . . . . . . **CLC 50**

Kaplan, James 1951- . . . . **CLC 59**
See also CA 135

Karageorge, Michael
See Anderson, Poul (William)

Karamzin, Nikolai Mikhailovich
1766-1826 . . . . **NCLC 3**

Karapanou, Margarita 1946- . . . . **CLC 13**
See also CA 101

Karinthy, Frigyes 1887-1938 . . . . . . **TCLC 47**

Karl, Frederick R(obert) 1927- . . . . . **CLC 34**
See also CA 5-8R; CANR 3

Kastel, Warren
See Silverberg, Robert

Kataev, Evgeny Petrovich 1903-1942
See Petrov, Evgeny
See also CA 120

Kingman, Lee. . . . . CLC 17
See also Natti, (Mary) Lee
See also SAAS 3; SATA 1, 67

Kingsley, Charles 1819-1875 . . . . . NCLC 35
See also DLB 21, 32; YABC 2

Kingsley, Sidney 1906- . . . . CLC 44
See also CA 85-88; DLB 7

Kingsolver, Barbara 1955- . . . . CLC 55
See also CA 129; 134

Kingston, Maxine (Ting Ting) Hong
1940- . . . . CLC 12, 19, 58
See also AAYA 8; CA 69-72; CANR 13,
38; DLBY 80; MTCW; SATA 53

Kinnell, Galway
1927- . . . . CLC 1, 2, 3, 5, 13, 29
See also CA 9-12R; CANR 10, 34; DLB 5;
DLBY 87; MTCW

Kinsella, Thomas 1928- . . . . CLC 4, 19
See also CA 17-20R; CANR 15; DLB 27;
MTCW

Kinsella, W(illiam) P(atrick)
1935- . . . . CLC 27, 43
See also AAYA 7; CA 97-100; CAAS 7;
CANR 21, 35; MTCW

Kipling, (Joseph) Rudyard
1865-1936 . . . . TCLC 8, 17; PC 3; SSC 5
See also CA 105; 120; CANR 33;
CDBLB 1890-1914; DLB 19, 34;
MAICYA; MTCW; WLC; YABC 2

Kirkup, James 1918- . . . . CLC 1
See also CA 1-4R; CAAS 4; CANR 2;
DLB 27; SATA 12

Kirkwood, James 1930(?)-1989 . . . . . . CLC 9
See also AITN 2; CA 1-4R; 128; CANR 6,
40

Kis, Danilo 1935-1989 . . . . CLC 57
See also CA 109; 118; 129; MTCW

Kivi, Aleksis 1834-1872 . . . . NCLC 30

Kizer, Carolyn (Ashley) 1925- . . . CLC 15, 39
See also CA 65-68; CAAS 5; CANR 24;
DLB 5

Klabund 1890-1928 . . . . TCLC 44
See also DLB 66

Klappert, Peter 1942- . . . . CLC 57
See also CA 33-36R; DLB 5

Klein, A(braham) M(oses)
1909-1972 . . . . CLC 19
See also CA 101; 37-40R; DLB 68

Klein, Norma 1938-1989 . . . . CLC 30
See also AAYA 2; CA 41-44R; 128;
CANR 15, 37; CLR 2, 19; MAICYA;
SAAS 1; SATA 7, 57

Klein, T(heodore) E(ibon) D(onald)
1947- . . . . CLC 34
See also CA 119

Kleist, Heinrich von 1777-1811 . . . . NCLC 2
See also DLB 90

Klima, Ivan 1931- . . . . CLC 56
See also CA 25-28R; CANR 17

Klimentov, Andrei Platonovich 1899-1951
See Platonov, Andrei
See also CA 108

Klinger, Friedrich Maximilian von
1752-1831 . . . . NCLC 1
See also DLB 94

Klopstock, Friedrich Gottlieb
1724-1803 . . . . NCLC 11
See also DLB 97

Knebel, Fletcher 1911- . . . . CLC 14
See also AITN 1; CA 1-4R; CAAS 3;
CANR 1, 36; SATA 36

Knickerbocker, Diedrich
See Irving, Washington

Knight, Etheridge 1931-1991 . . . . CLC 40
See also BLC 2; BW; CA 21-24R; 133;
CANR 23; DLB 41

Knight, Sarah Kemble 1666-1727 . . . . . LC 7
See also DLB 24

Knowles, John 1926- . . . . . . CLC 1, 4, 10, 26
See also AAYA 10; CA 17-20R; CANR 40;
CDALB 1968-1988; DLB 6; MTCW;
SATA 8

Knox, Calvin M.
See Silverberg, Robert

Knye, Cassandra
See Disch, Thomas M(ichael)

Koch, C(hristopher) J(ohn) 1932- . . . CLC 42
See also CA 127

Koch, Christopher
See Koch, C(hristopher) J(ohn)

Koch, Kenneth 1925- . . . . CLC 5, 8, 44
See also CA 1-4R; CANR 6, 36; DLB 5;
SATA 65

Kochanowski, Jan 1530-1584 . . . . LC 10

Kock, Charles Paul de
1794-1871 . . . . NCLC 16

Koda Shigeyuki 1867-1947
See Rohan, Koda
See also CA 121

Koestler, Arthur
1905-1983 . . . . CLC 1, 3, 6, 8, 15, 33
See also CA 1-4R; 109; CANR 1, 33;
CDBLB 1945-1960; DLBY 83; MTCW

Kohout, Pavel 1928- . . . . CLC 13
See also CA 45-48; CANR 3

Koizumi, Yakumo
See Hearn, (Patricio) Lafcadio (Tessima
Carlos)

Kolmar, Gertrud 1894-1943 . . . . TCLC 40

Konrad, George
See Konrad, Gyoergy

Konrad, Gyoergy 1933- . . . . . . CLC 4, 10, 73
See also CA 85-88

Konwicki, Tadeusz 1926- . . . . . CLC 8, 28, 54
See also CA 101; CAAS 9; CANR 39;
MTCW

Kopit, Arthur (Lee) 1937- . . . . CLC 1, 18, 33
See also AITN 1; CA 81-84; CABS 3;
DLB 7; MTCW

Kops, Bernard 1926- . . . . CLC 4
See also CA 5-8R; DLB 13

Kornbluth, C(yril) M. 1923-1958 . . . . TCLC 8
See also CA 105; DLB 8

Korolenko, V. G.
See Korolenko, Vladimir Galaktionovich

Korolenko, Vladimir
See Korolenko, Vladimir Galaktionovich

Korolenko, Vladimir G.
See Korolenko, Vladimir Galaktionovich

Korolenko, Vladimir Galaktionovich
1853-1921 . . . . TCLC 22
See also CA 121

Kosinski, Jerzy (Nikodem)
1933-1991 . . . CLC 1, 2, 3, 6, 10, 15, 53,
70
See also CA 17-20R; 134; CANR 9; DLB 2;
DLBY 82; MTCW

Kostelanetz, Richard (Cory) 1940- . . CLC 28
See also CA 13-16R; CAAS 8; CANR 38

Kostrowitzki, Wilhelm Apollinaris de
1880-1918
See Apollinaire, Guillaume
See also CA 104

Kotlowitz, Robert 1924- . . . . CLC 4
See also CA 33-36R; CANR 36

Kotzebue, August (Friedrich Ferdinand) von
1761-1819 . . . . NCLC 25
See also DLB 94

Kotzwinkle, William 1938- . . . CLC 5, 14, 35
See also CA 45-48; CANR 3; CLR 6;
MAICYA; SATA 24, 70

Kozol, Jonathan 1936- . . . . CLC 17
See also CA 61-64; CANR 16

Kozoll, Michael 1940(?)- . . . . CLC 35

Kramer, Kathryn 19(?)- . . . . CLC 34

Kramer, Larry 1935- . . . . CLC 42
See also CA 124; 126

Krasicki, Ignacy 1735-1801 . . . . NCLC 8

Krasinski, Zygmunt 1812-1859 . . . . NCLC 4

Kraus, Karl 1874-1936 . . . . TCLC 5
See also CA 104; DLB 118

Kreve (Mickevicius), Vincas
1882-1954 . . . . TCLC 27

Kristofferson, Kris 1936- . . . . CLC 26
See also CA 104

Krizanc, John 1956- . . . . CLC 57

Krleza, Miroslav 1893-1981 . . . . CLC 8
See also CA 97-100; 105

Kroetsch, Robert 1927- . . . . . . CLC 5, 23, 57
See also CA 17-20R; CANR 8, 38; DLB 53;
MTCW

Kroetz, Franz
See Kroetz, Franz Xaver

Kroetz, Franz Xaver 1946- . . . . CLC 41
See also CA 130

Kropotkin, Peter (Aleksieevich)
1842-1921 . . . . TCLC 36
See also CA 119

Krotkov, Yuri 1917- . . . . CLC 19
See also CA 102

Krumb
See Crumb, R(obert)

Krumgold, Joseph (Quincy)
1908-1980 . . . . CLC 12
See also CA 9-12R; 101; CANR 7;
MAICYA; SATA 1, 23, 48

Krumwitz
See Crumb, R(obert)

Krutch, Joseph Wood 1893-1970 . . . . CLC 24
See also CA 1-4R; 25-28R; CANR 4;
DLB 63

Krutzch, Gus
See Eliot, T(homas) S(tearns)

Krylov, Ivan Andreevich
1768(?)-1844 . . . . NCLC 1

Kubin, Alfred 1877-1959 . . . . TCLC 23
See also CA 112; DLB 81

Kubrick, Stanley 1928- . . . . CLC 16
See also CA 81-84; CANR 33; DLB 26

Kumin, Maxine (Winokur)
1925- . . . . CLC 5, 13, 28
See also AITN 2; CA 1-4R; CAAS 8;
CANR 1, 21; DLB 5; MTCW; SATA 12

Kundera, Milan
1929- . . . . CLC 4, 9, 19, 32, 68
See also AAYA 2; CA 85-88; CANR 19;
MTCW

Kunitz, Stanley (Jasspon)
1905- . . . . CLC 6, 11, 14
See also CA 41-44R; CANR 26; DLB 48;
MTCW

Kunze, Reiner 1933- . . . . CLC 10
See also CA 93-96; DLB 75

Kuprin, Aleksandr Ivanovich
1870-1938 . . . . TCLC 5
See also CA 104

Kureishi, Hanif 1954(?)- . . . . CLC 64
See also CA 139

Kurosawa, Akira 1910- . . . . CLC 16
See also CA 101

Kuttner, Henry 1915-1958 . . . . TCLC 10
See also CA 107; DLB 8

Kuzma, Greg 1944- . . . . CLC 7
See also CA 33-36R

Kuzmin, Mikhail 1872(?)-1936 . . . . TCLC 40

Kyd, Thomas 1558-1594 . . . . DC 3
See also DLB 62

Kyprianos, Iossif
See Samarakis, Antonis

La Bruyere, Jean de 1645-1696 . . . . . . LC 17

Lacan, Jacques (Marie Emile)
1901-1981 . . . . CLC 75
See also CA 121; 104

**Laclos, Pierre Ambroise Francois Choderlos
de** 1741-1803 . . . . NCLC 4

Lacolere, Francois
See Aragon, Louis

La Colere, Francois
See Aragon, Louis

La Deshabilleuse
See Simenon, Georges (Jacques Christian)

Lady Gregory
See Gregory, Isabella Augusta (Persse)

Lady of Quality, A
See Bagnold, Enid

**La Fayette, Marie (Madelaine Pioche de la
Vergne Comtes** 1634-1693 . . . . LC 2

Lafayette, Rene
See Hubbard, L(afayette) Ron(ald)

Laforgue, Jules 1860-1887 . . . . NCLC 5

Lagerkvist, Paer (Fabian)
1891-1974 . . . . CLC 7, 10, 13, 54
See also CA 85-88; 49-52; MTCW

Lagerkvist, Par
See Lagerkvist, Paer (Fabian)

Lagerloef, Selma (Ottiliana Lovisa)
1858-1940 . . . . TCLC 4, 36
See also Lagerlof, Selma (Ottiliana Lovisa)
See also CA 108; CLR 7; SATA 15

Lagerlof, Selma (Ottiliana Lovisa)
See Lagerloef, Selma (Ottiliana Lovisa)
See also CLR 7; SATA 15

La Guma, (Justin) Alex(ander)
1925-1985 . . . . CLC 19
See also BW; CA 49-52; 118; CANR 25;
DLB 117; MTCW

Laidlaw, A. K.
See Grieve, C(hristopher) M(urray)

Lainez, Manuel Mujica
See Mujica Lainez, Manuel
See also HW

Lamartine, Alphonse (Marie Louis Prat) de
1790-1869 . . . . NCLC 11

Lamb, Charles 1775-1834 . . . . NCLC 10
See also CDBLB 1789-1832; DLB 93, 107;
SATA 17; WLC

Lamb, Lady Caroline 1785-1828 . . NCLC 38
See also DLB 116

Lamming, George (William)
1927- . . . . CLC 2, 4, 66
See also BLC 2; BW; CA 85-88; CANR 26;
DLB 125; MTCW

L'Amour, Louis (Dearborn)
1908-1988 . . . . CLC 25, 55
See also AITN 2; BEST 89:2; CA 1-4R;
125; CANR 3, 25, 40; DLBY 80; MTCW

Lampedusa, Giuseppe (Tomasi) di . . . TCLC 13
See also Tomasi di Lampedusa, Giuseppe

Lampman, Archibald 1861-1899 . . NCLC 25
See also DLB 92

Lancaster, Bruce 1896-1963 . . . . CLC 36
See also CA 9-10; CAP 1; SATA 9

Landau, Mark Alexandrovich
See Aldanov, Mark (Alexandrovich)

Landau-Aldanov, Mark Alexandrovich
See Aldanov, Mark (Alexandrovich)

Landis, John 1950- . . . . CLC 26
See also CA 112; 122

Landolfi, Tommaso 1908-1979 . . . CLC 11, 49
See also CA 127; 117

Landon, Letitia Elizabeth
1802-1838 . . . . NCLC 15
See also DLB 96

Landor, Walter Savage
1775-1864 . . . . NCLC 14
See also DLB 93, 107

Landwirth, Heinz 1927-
See Lind, Jakov
See also CA 9-12R; CANR 7

Lane, Patrick 1939- . . . . CLC 25
See also CA 97-100; DLB 53

Lang, Andrew 1844-1912 . . . . TCLC 16
See also CA 114; 137; DLB 98; MAICYA;
SATA 16

Lang, Fritz 1890-1976 . . . . CLC 20
See also CA 77-80; 69-72; CANR 30

Lange, John
See Crichton, (John) Michael

Langer, Elinor 1939- . . . . CLC 34
See also CA 121

Langland, William 1330(?)-1400(?) . . . LC 19

Langstaff, Launcelot
See Irving, Washington

Lanier, Sidney 1842-1881 . . . . NCLC 6
See also DLB 64; MAICYA; SATA 18

Lanyer, Aemilia 1569-1645 . . . . LC 10

Lao Tzu . . . . CMLC 7

Lapine, James (Elliot) 1949- . . . . CLC 39
See also CA 123; 130

Larbaud, Valery (Nicolas)
1881-1957 . . . . TCLC 9
See also CA 106

Lardner, Ring
See Lardner, Ring(gold) W(ilmer)

Lardner, Ring W. Jr.
See Lardner, Ring(gold) W(ilmer)

Lardner, Ring(gold) W(ilmer)
1885-1933 . . . . TCLC 2, 14
See also CA 104; 131; CDALB 1917-1929;
DLB 11, 25, 86; MTCW

Laredo, Betty
See Codrescu, Andrei

Larkin, Maia
See Wojciechowska, Maia (Teresa)

Larkin, Philip (Arthur)
1922-1985 . . . CLC 3, 5, 8, 9, 13, 18, 33,
39, 64
See also CA 5-8R; 117; CANR 24;
CDBLB 1960 to Present; DLB 27;
MTCW

Larra (y Sanchez de Castro), Mariano Jose de
1809-1837 . . . . NCLC 17

Larsen, Eric 1941- . . . . CLC 55
See also CA 132

Larsen, Nella 1891-1964 . . . . CLC 37
See also BLC 2; BW; CA 125; DLB 51

Larson, Charles R(aymond) 1938- . . . CLC 31
See also CA 53-56; CANR 4

Latham, Jean Lee 1902- . . . . CLC 12
See also AITN 1; CA 5-8R; CANR 7;
MAICYA; SATA 2, 68

Latham, Mavis
See Clark, Mavis Thorpe

Lathen, Emma . . . . CLC 2
See also Hennissart, Martha; Latsis, Mary
J(ane)

Lathrop, Francis
See Leiber, Fritz (Reuter Jr.)

Latsis, Mary J(ane)
See Lathen, Emma
See also CA 85-88

Lattimore, Richmond (Alexander)
1906-1984 . . . . CLC 3
See also CA 1-4R; 112; CANR 1

Laughlin, James 1914- . . . . CLC 49
See also CA 21-24R; CANR 9; DLB 48

Laurence, (Jean) Margaret (Wemyss)
1926-1987 . . CLC 3, 6, 13, 50, 62; SSC 7
See also CA 5-8R; 121; CANR 33; DLB 53;
MTCW; SATA 50

Lerman, Eleanor 1952-............ **CLC 9**
See also CA 85-88

Lerman, Rhoda 1936-............ **CLC 56**
See also CA 49-52

Lermontov, Mikhail Yuryevich
1814-1841 .... **NCLC 5**

Leroux, Gaston 1868-1927....... **TCLC 25**
See also CA 108; 136; SATA 65

Lesage, Alain-Rene 1668-1747....... **LC 2**

Leskov, Nikolai (Semyonovich)
1831-1895 .... **NCLC 25**

Lessing, Doris (May)
1919- .... **CLC 1, 2, 3, 6, 10, 15, 22, 40;**
SSC 6
See also CA 9-12R; CAAS 14; CANR 33;
CDBLB 1960 to Present; DLB 15;
DLBY 85; MTCW

Lessing, Gotthold Ephraim
1729-1781 .... **LC 8**
See also DLB 97

Lester, Richard 1932-............ **CLC 20**

Lever, Charles (James)
1806-1872 .... **NCLC 23**
See also DLB 21

Leverson, Ada 1865(?)-1936(?) .... **TCLC 18**
See also Elaine
See also CA 117

Levertov, Denise
1923- ...... **CLC 1, 2, 3, 5, 8, 15, 28, 66**
See also CA 1-4R; CANR 3, 29; DLB 5;
MTCW

Levi, Peter (Chad Tigar) 1931-..... **CLC 41**
See also CA 5-8R; CANR 34; DLB 40

Levi, Primo 1919-1987........ **CLC 37, 50**
See also CA 13-16R; 122; CANR 12, 33;
MTCW

Levin, Ira 1929- .... **CLC 3, 6**
See also CA 21-24R; CANR 17; MTCW;
SATA 66

Levin, Meyer 1905-1981 .... **CLC 7**
See also AITN 1; CA 9-12R; 104;
CANR 15; DLB 9, 28; DLBY 81;
SATA 21, 27

Levine, Norman 1924- .... **CLC 54**
See also CA 73-76; CANR 14; DLB 88

Levine, Philip 1928-.. **CLC 2, 4, 5, 9, 14, 33**
See also CA 9-12R; CANR 9, 37; DLB 5

Levinson, Deirdre 1931-........... **CLC 49**
See also CA 73-76

Levi-Strauss, Claude 1908- .... **CLC 38**
See also CA 1-4R; CANR 6, 32; MTCW

Levitin, Sonia (Wolff) 1934- .... **CLC 17**
See also CA 29-32R; CANR 14, 32;
MAICYA; SAAS 2; SATA 4, 68

Levon, O. U.
See Kesey, Ken (Elton)

Lewes, George Henry
1817-1878 .... **NCLC 25**
See also DLB 55

Lewis, Alun 1915-1944............ **TCLC 3**
See also CA 104; DLB 20

Lewis, C. Day
See Day Lewis, C(ecil)

Lewis, C(live) S(taples)
1898-1963 .... **CLC 1, 3, 6, 14, 27**
See also AAYA 3; CA 81-84; CANR 33;
CDBLB 1945-1960; CLR 3, 27; DLB 15,
100; MAICYA; MTCW; SATA 13; WLC

Lewis, Janet 1899-............... **CLC 41**
See also Winters, Janet Lewis
See also CA 9-12R; CANR 29; CAP 1;
DLBY 87

Lewis, Matthew Gregory
1775-1818 .... **NCLC 11**
See also DLB 39

Lewis, (Harry) Sinclair
1885-1951 .... **TCLC 4, 13, 23, 39**
See also CA 104; 133; CDALB 1917-1929;
DLB 9, 102; DLBD 1; MTCW; WLC

Lewis, (Percy) Wyndham
1884(?)-1957 .... **TCLC 2, 9**
See also CA 104; DLB 15

Lewisohn, Ludwig 1883-1955...... **TCLC 19**
See also CA 107; DLB 4, 9, 28, 102

Lezama Lima, Jose 1910-1976 ... **CLC 4, 10**
See also CA 77-80; DLB 113; HW

L'Heureux, John (Clarke) 1934-.... **CLC 52**
See also CA 13-16R; CANR 23

Liddell, C. H.
See Kuttner, Henry

Lie, Jonas (Lauritz Idemil)
1833-1908(?) .... **TCLC 5**
See also CA 115

Lieber, Joel 1937-1971............. **CLC 6**
See also CA 73-76; 29-32R

Lieber, Stanley Martin
See Lee, Stan

Lieberman, Laurence (James)
1935- .... **CLC 4, 36**
See also CA 17-20R; CANR 8, 36

Lieksman, Anders
See Haavikko, Paavo Juhani

Li Fei-kan 1904-................. **CLC 18**
See also CA 105

Lifton, Robert Jay 1926-.......... **CLC 67**
See also CA 17-20R; CANR 27; SATA 66

Lightfoot, Gordon 1938-........... **CLC 26**
See also CA 109

Ligotti, Thomas 1953- .... **CLC 44**
See also CA 123

Liliencron, (Friedrich Adolf Axel) Detlev von
1844-1909 .... **TCLC 18**
See also CA 117

Lima, Jose Lezama
See Lezama Lima, Jose

Lima Barreto, Afonso Henrique de
1881-1922 .... **TCLC 23**
See also CA 117

Limonov, Eduard.................. **CLC 67**

Lin, Frank
See Atherton, Gertrude (Franklin Horn)

Lincoln, Abraham 1809-1865..... **NCLC 18**

Lind, Jakov .... **CLC 1, 2, 4, 27**
See also Landwirth, Heinz
See also CAAS 4

Lindsay, David 1878-1945 .... **TCLC 15**
See also CA 113

Lindsay, (Nicholas) Vachel
1879-1931 .... **TCLC 17**
See also CA 114; 135; CDALB 1865-1917;
DLB 54; SATA 40; WLC

Linke-Poot
See Doeblin, Alfred

Linney, Romulus 1930- .... **CLC 51**
See also CA 1-4R; CANR 40

Li Po 701-763 .... **CMLC 2**

Lipsius, Justus 1547-1606 .... **LC 16**

Lipsyte, Robert (Michael) 1938-.... **CLC 21**
See also AAYA 7; CA 17-20R; CANR 8;
CLR 23; MAICYA; SATA 5, 68

Lish, Gordon (Jay) 1934-......... **CLC 45**
See also CA 113; 117

Lispector, Clarice 1925-1977....... **CLC 43**
See also CA 139; 116; DLB 113

Littell, Robert 1935(?)- .... **CLC 42**
See also CA 109; 112

Littlewit, Humphrey Gent.
See Lovecraft, H(oward) P(hillips)

Litwos
See Sienkiewicz, Henryk (Adam Alexander
Pius)

Liu E 1857-1909................ **TCLC 15**
See also CA 115

Lively, Penelope (Margaret)
1933- .... **CLC 32, 50**
See also CA 41-44R; CANR 29; CLR 7;
DLB 14; MAICYA; MTCW; SATA 7, 60

Livesay, Dorothy (Kathleen)
1909- .... **CLC 4, 15**
See also AITN 2; CA 25-28R; CAAS 8;
CANR 36; DLB 68; MTCW

Lizardi, Jose Joaquin Fernandez de
1776-1827 .... **NCLC 30**

Llewellyn, Richard .... **CLC 7**
See also Llewellyn Lloyd, Richard Dafydd
Vivian
See also DLB 15

Llewellyn Lloyd, Richard Dafydd Vivian
1906-1983
See Llewellyn, Richard
See also CA 53-56; 111; CANR 7;
SATA 11, 37

Llosa, (Jorge) Mario (Pedro) Vargas
See Vargas Llosa, (Jorge) Mario (Pedro)

Lloyd Webber, Andrew 1948-
See Webber, Andrew Lloyd
See also AAYA 1; CA 116; SATA 56

Locke, Alain (Le Roy)
1886-1954 .... **TCLC 43**
See also BW; CA 106; 124; DLB 51

Locke, John 1632-1704 .... **LC 7**
See also DLB 101

Locke-Elliott, Sumner
See Elliott, Sumner Locke

Lockhart, John Gibson
1794-1854 .... **NCLC 6**
See also DLB 110, 116

Lodge, David (John) 1935-........ **CLC 36**
See also BEST 90:1; CA 17-20R; CANR 19;
DLB 14; MTCW

Loennbohm, Armas Eino Leopold 1878-1926
See Leino, Eino
See also CA 123

Loewinsohn, Ron(ald William)
1937- . . . . CLC 52
See also CA 25-28R

Logan, Jake
See Smith, Martin Cruz

Logan, John (Burton) 1923-1987. . . . . CLC 5
See also CA 77-80; 124; DLB 5

Lo Kuan-chung 1330(?)-1400(?). . . . . . LC 12

Lombard, Nap
See Johnson, Pamela Hansford

London, Jack. . . . . . . TCLC 9, 15, 39; SSC 4
See also London, John Griffith
See also AITN 2; CDALB 1865-1917;
DLB 8, 12, 78; SATA 18; WLC

London, John Griffith 1876-1916
See London, Jack
See also CA 110; 119; MAICYA; MTCW

Long, Emmett
See Leonard, Elmore (John Jr.)

Longbaugh, Harry
See Goldman, William (W.)

Longfellow, Henry Wadsworth
1807-1882 . . . . NCLC 2
See also CDALB 1640-1865; DLB 1, 59;
SATA 19

Longley, Michael 1939-. . . . . CLC 29
See also CA 102; DLB 40

Longus fl. c. 2nd cent. - . . . . CMLC 7

Longway, A. Hugh
See Lang, Andrew

Lopate, Phillip 1943- . . . . CLC 29
See also CA 97-100; DLBY 80

Lopez Portillo (y Pacheco), Jose
1920- . . . . CLC 46
See also CA 129; HW

Lopez y Fuentes, Gregorio
1897(?)-1966 . . . . CLC 32
See also CA 131; HW

Lorca, Federico Garcia
See Garcia Lorca, Federico

Lord, Bette Bao 1938- . . . . CLC 23
See also BEST 90:3; CA 107; SATA 58

Lord Auch
See Bataille, Georges

Lord Byron
See Byron, George Gordon (Noel)

Lord Dunsany . . . . TCLC 2
See also Dunsany, Edward John Moreton
Drax Plunkett

Lorde, Audre (Geraldine)
1934- . . . . CLC 18, 71
See also BLC 2; BW; CA 25-28R;
CANR 16, 26; DLB 41; MTCW

Lord Jeffrey
See Jeffrey, Francis

Lorenzo, Heberto Padilla
See Padilla (Lorenzo), Heberto

Loris
See Hofmannsthal, Hugo von

Loti, Pierre . . . . TCLC 11
See also Viaud, (Louis Marie) Julien
See also DLB 123

Louie, David Wong 1954- . . . . CLC 70
See also CA 139

Louis, Father M.
See Merton, Thomas

Lovecraft, H(oward) P(hillips)
1890-1937 . . . . TCLC 4, 22; SSC 3
See also CA 104; 133; MTCW

Lovelace, Earl 1935-. . . . . CLC 51
See also CA 77-80; DLB 125; MTCW

Lowell, Amy 1874-1925 . . . . TCLC 1, 8
See also CA 104; DLB 54

Lowell, James Russell 1819-1891 . . NCLC 2
See also CDALB 1640-1865; DLB 1, 11, 64,
79

Lowell, Robert (Traill Spence Jr.)
1917-1977 . . . CLC 1, 2, 3, 4, 5, 8, 9, 11,
15, 37; PC 3
See also CA 9-12R; 73-76; CABS 2;
CANR 26; DLB 5; MTCW; WLC

Lowndes, Marie Adelaide (Belloc)
1868-1947 . . . . TCLC 12
See also CA 107; DLB 70

Lowry, (Clarence) Malcolm
1909-1957 . . . . TCLC 6, 40
See also CA 105; 131; CDBLB 1945-1960;
DLB 15; MTCW

Lowry, Mina Gertrude 1882-1966
See Loy, Mina
See also CA 113

Loxsmith, John
See Brunner, John (Kilian Houston)

Loy, Mina . . . . CLC 28
See also Lowry, Mina Gertrude
See also DLB 4, 54

Loyson-Bridet
See Schwob, (Mayer Andre) Marcel

Lucas, Craig 1951- . . . . CLC 64
See also CA 137

Lucas, George 1944-. . . . . CLC 16
See also AAYA 1; CA 77-80; CANR 30;
SATA 56

Lucas, Hans
See Godard, Jean-Luc

Lucas, Victoria
See Plath, Sylvia

Ludlam, Charles 1943-1987 . . . . . CLC 46, 50
See also CA 85-88; 122

Ludlum, Robert 1927- . . . . CLC 22, 43
See also AAYA 10; BEST 89:1, 90:3;
CA 33-36R; CANR 25; DLBY 82;
MTCW

Ludwig, Ken. . . . . CLC 60

Ludwig, Otto 1813-1865. . . . . NCLC 4

Lugones, Leopoldo 1874-1938 . . . . . TCLC 15
See also CA 116; 131; HW

Lu Hsun 1881-1936 . . . . TCLC 3

Lukacs, George . . . . CLC 24
See also Lukacs, Gyorgy (Szegeny von)

Lukacs, Gyorgy (Szegeny von) 1885-1971
See Lukacs, George
See also CA 101; 29-32R

Luke, Peter (Ambrose Cyprian)
1919- . . . . CLC 38
See also CA 81-84; DLB 13

Lunar, Dennis
See Mungo, Raymond

Lurie, Alison 1926-. . . . . CLC 4, 5, 18, 39
See also CA 1-4R; CANR 2, 17; DLB 2;
MTCW; SATA 46

Lustig, Arnost 1926-. . . . . CLC 56
See also AAYA 3; CA 69-72; SATA 56

Luther, Martin 1483-1546. . . . . LC 9

Luzi, Mario 1914-. . . . . CLC 13
See also CA 61-64; CANR 9

Lynch, B. Suarez
See Bioy Casares, Adolfo; Borges, Jorge
Luis

Lynch, David (K.) 1946-. . . . . CLC 66
See also CA 124; 129

Lynch, James
See Andreyev, Leonid (Nikolaevich)

Lynch Davis, B.
See Bioy Casares, Adolfo; Borges, Jorge
Luis

Lyndsay, Sir David 1490-1555 . . . . LC 20

Lynn, Kenneth S(chuyler) 1923- . . . . CLC 50
See also CA 1-4R; CANR 3, 27

Lynx
See West, Rebecca

Lyons, Marcus
See Blish, James (Benjamin)

Lyre, Pinchbeck
See Sassoon, Siegfried (Lorraine)

Lytle, Andrew (Nelson) 1902-. . . . . . CLC 22
See also CA 9-12R; DLB 6

Lyttelton, George 1709-1773. . . . . LC 10

Maas, Peter 1929- . . . . CLC 29
See also CA 93-96

Macaulay, Rose 1881-1958 . . . . . TCLC 7, 44
See also CA 104; DLB 36

MacBeth, George (Mann)
1932-1992 . . . . CLC 2, 5, 9
See also CA 25-28R; 136; DLB 40; MTCW;
SATA 4; SATO 70

MacCaig, Norman (Alexander)
1910- . . . . CLC 36
See also CA 9-12R; CANR 3, 34; DLB 27

MacCarthy, (Sir Charles Otto) Desmond
1877-1952 . . . . TCLC 36

MacDiarmid, Hugh. . . . . CLC 2, 4, 11, 19, 63
See also Grieve, C(hristopher) M(urray)
See also CDBLB 1945-1960; DLB 20

MacDonald, Anson
See Heinlein, Robert A(nson)

Macdonald, Cynthia 1928-. . . . . . CLC 13, 19
See also CA 49-52; CANR 4; DLB 105

MacDonald, George 1824-1905 . . . . . TCLC 9
See also CA 106; 137; DLB 18; MAICYA;
SATA 33

Macdonald, John
See Millar, Kenneth

MacDonald, John D(ann)
1916-1986 . . . . **CLC 3, 27, 44**
See also CA 1-4R; 121; CANR 1, 19;
DLB 8; DLBY 86; MTCW

Macdonald, John Ross
See Millar, Kenneth

Macdonald, Ross . . . . . **CLC 1, 2, 3, 14, 34, 41**
See also Millar, Kenneth
See also DLBD 6

MacDougal, John
See Blish, James (Benjamin)

MacEwen, Gwendolyn (Margaret)
1941-1987 . . . . **CLC 13, 55**
See also CA 9-12R; 124; CANR 7, 22;
DLB 53; SATA 50, 55

Machado (y Ruiz), Antonio
1875-1939 . . . . **TCLC 3**
See also CA 104; DLB 108

Machado de Assis, Joaquim Maria
1839-1908 . . . . **TCLC 10**
See also BLC 2; CA 107

Machen, Arthur . . . . **TCLC 4**
See also Jones, Arthur Llewellyn
See also DLB 36

Machiavelli, Niccolo 1469-1527 . . . . . . **LC 8**

MacInnes, Colin 1914-1976 . . . . . . **CLC 4, 23**
See also CA 69-72; 65-68; CANR 21;
DLB 14; MTCW

MacInnes, Helen (Clark)
1907-1985 . . . . **CLC 27, 39**
See also CA 1-4R; 117; CANR 1, 28;
DLB 87; MTCW; SATA 22, 44

Mackenzie, Compton (Edward Montague)
1883-1972 . . . . **CLC 18**
See also CA 21-22; 37-40R; CAP 2;
DLB 34, 100

Mackintosh, Elizabeth 1896(?)-1952
See Tey, Josephine
See also CA 110

MacLaren, James
See Grieve, C(hristopher) M(urray)

Mac Laverty, Bernard 1942- . . . . **CLC 31**
See also CA 116; 118

MacLean, Alistair (Stuart)
1922-1987 . . . . **CLC 3, 13, 50, 63**
See also CA 57-60; 121; CANR 28; MTCW;
SATA 23, 50

MacLeish, Archibald
1892-1982 . . . . **CLC 3, 8, 14, 68**
See also CA 9-12R; 106; CANR 33; DLB 4,
7, 45; DLBY 82; MTCW

MacLennan, (John) Hugh
1907- . . . . **CLC 2, 14**
See also CA 5-8R; CANR 33; DLB 68;
MTCW

MacLeod, Alistair 1936- . . . . **CLC 56**
See also CA 123; DLB 60

MacNeice, (Frederick) Louis
1907-1963 . . . . **CLC 1, 4, 10, 53**
See also CA 85-88; DLB 10, 20; MTCW

MacNeill, Dand
See Fraser, George MacDonald

Macpherson, (Jean) Jay 1931- . . . . . . **CLC 14**
See also CA 5-8R; DLB 53

MacShane, Frank 1927- . . . . **CLC 39**
See also CA 9-12R; CANR 3, 33; DLB 111

Macumber, Mari
See Sandoz, Mari(e Susette)

Madach, Imre 1823-1864 . . . . **NCLC 19**

Madden, (Jerry) David 1933- . . . . **CLC 5, 15**
See also CA 1-4R; CAAS 3; CANR 4;
DLB 6; MTCW

Maddern, Al(an)
See Ellison, Harlan

Madhubuti, Haki R.
1942- . . . . **CLC 6, 73; PC 5**
See also Lee, Don L.
See also BLC 2; BW; CA 73-76; CANR 24;
DLB 5, 41; DLBD 8

Madow, Pauline (Reichberg) . . . . **CLC 1**
See also CA 9-12R

Maepenn, Hugh
See Kuttner, Henry

Maepenn, K. H.
See Kuttner, Henry

Maeterlinck, Maurice 1862-1949 . . . **TCLC 3**
See also CA 104; 136; SATA 66

Maginn, William 1794-1842 . . . . . . **NCLC 8**
See also DLB 110

Mahapatra, Jayanta 1928- . . . . **CLC 33**
See also CA 73-76; CAAS 9; CANR 15, 33

Mahfouz, Naguib (Abdel Aziz Al-Sabilgi)
1911(?)-
See Mahfuz, Najib
See also BEST 89:2; CA 128; MTCW

Mahfuz, Najib . . . . **CLC 52, 55**
See also Mahfouz, Naguib (Abdel Aziz
Al-Sabilgi)
See also DLBY 88

Mahon, Derek 1941- . . . . **CLC 27**
See also CA 113; 128; DLB 40

Mailer, Norman
1923- . . . . . . **CLC 1, 2, 3, 4, 5, 8, 11, 14,
28, 39, 74**
See also AITN 2; CA 9-12R; CABS 1;
CANR 28; CDALB 1968-1988; DLB 2,
16, 28; DLBD 3; DLBY 80, 83; MTCW

Maillet, Antonine 1929- . . . . **CLC 54**
See also CA 115; 120; DLB 60

Mais, Roger 1905-1955 . . . . **TCLC 8**
See also BW; CA 105; 124; DLB 125;
MTCW

Maitland, Sara (Louise) 1950- . . . . . . **CLC 49**
See also CA 69-72; CANR 13

Major, Clarence 1936- . . . . **CLC 3, 19, 48**
See also BLC 2; BW; CA 21-24R; CAAS 6;
CANR 13, 25; DLB 33

Major, Kevin (Gerald) 1949- . . . . **CLC 26**
See also CA 97-100; CANR 21, 38;
CLR 11; DLB 60; MAICYA; SATA 32

Maki, James
See Ozu, Yasujiro

Malabaila, Damiano
See Levi, Primo

Malamud, Bernard
1914-1986 . . . . . **CLC 1, 2, 3, 5, 8, 9, 11,
18, 27, 44**
See also CA 5-8R; 118; CABS 1; CANR 28;
CDALB 1941-1968; DLB 2, 28;
DLBY 80, 86; MTCW; WLC

Malcolm, Dan
See Silverberg, Robert

Malherbe, Francois de 1555-1628 . . . . . **LC 5**

Mallarme, Stephane
1842-1898 . . . . **NCLC 4; PC 4**

Mallet-Joris, Francoise 1930- . . . . . . **CLC 11**
See also CA 65-68; CANR 17; DLB 83

Malley, Ern
See McAuley, James Phillip

Mallowan, Agatha Christie
See Christie, Agatha (Mary Clarissa)

Maloff, Saul 1922- . . . . **CLC 5**
See also CA 33-36R

Malone, Louis
See MacNeice, (Frederick) Louis

Malone, Michael (Christopher)
1942- . . . . **CLC 43**
See also CA 77-80; CANR 14, 32

Malory, (Sir) Thomas
1410(?)-1471(?) . . . . **LC 11**
See also CDBLB Before 1660; SATA 33, 59

Malouf, (George Joseph) David
1934- . . . . **CLC 28**
See also CA 124

Malraux, (Georges-)Andre
1901-1976 . . . . . . **CLC 1, 4, 9, 13, 15, 57**
See also CA 21-22; 69-72; CANR 34;
CAP 2; DLB 72; MTCW

Malzberg, Barry N(athaniel) 1939- . . . **CLC 7**
See also CA 61-64; CAAS 4; CANR 16;
DLB 8

Mamet, David (Alan)
1947- . . . . **CLC 9, 15, 34, 46**
See also AAYA 3; CA 81-84; CABS 3;
CANR 15; DLB 7; MTCW

Mamoulian, Rouben (Zachary)
1897-1987 . . . . **CLC 16**
See also CA 25-28R; 124

Mandelstam, Osip (Emilievich)
1891(?)-1938(?) . . . . **TCLC 2, 6**
See also CA 104

Mander, (Mary) Jane 1877-1949 . . . **TCLC 31**

Mandiargues, Andre Pieyre de . . . . **CLC 41**
See also Pieyre de Mandiargues, Andre
See also DLB 83

Mandrake, Ethel Belle
See Thurman, Wallace (Henry)

Mangan, James Clarence
1803-1849 . . . . **NCLC 27**

Maniere, J.-E.
See Giraudoux, (Hippolyte) Jean

Manley, (Mary) Delariviere
1672(?)-1724 . . . . **LC 1**
See also DLB 39, 80

Mann, Abel
See Creasey, John

Mann, (Luiz) Heinrich 1871-1950 . . . **TCLC 9**
See also CA 106; DLB 66

Mann, (Paul) Thomas
1875-1955 . . . **TCLC 2, 8, 14, 21, 35, 44;
SSC 5**
See also CA 104; 128; DLB 66; MTCW;
WLC

Manning, David
See Faust, Frederick (Schiller)

Manning, Frederic 1887(?)-1935 . . . **TCLC 25**
See also CA 124

Manning, Olivia 1915-1980 . . . . . . **CLC 5, 19**
See also CA 5-8R; 101; CANR 29; MTCW

Mano, D. Keith 1942- . . . . **CLC 2, 10**
See also CA 25-28R; CAAS 6; CANR 26;
DLB 6

Mansfield, Katherine. . . **TCLC 2, 8, 39; SSC 9**
See also Beauchamp, Kathleen Mansfield
See also WLC

Manso, Peter 1940- . . . . **CLC 39**
See also CA 29-32R

Mantecon, Juan Jimenez
See Jimenez (Mantecon), Juan Ramon

Manton, Peter
See Creasey, John

Man Without a Spleen, A
See Chekhov, Anton (Pavlovich)

Manzoni, Alessandro 1785-1873 . . **NCLC 29**

Mapu, Abraham (ben Jekutiel)
1808-1867 . . . . **NCLC 18**

Mara, Sally
See Queneau, Raymond

Marat, Jean Paul 1743-1793 . . . . **LC 10**

Marcel, Gabriel Honore
1889-1973 . . . . **CLC 15**
See also CA 102; 45-48; MTCW

Marchbanks, Samuel
See Davies, (William) Robertson

Marchi, Giacomo
See Bassani, Giorgio

Marie de France c. 12th cent. -. . . . **CMLC 8**

Marie de l'Incarnation 1599-1672. . . . **LC 10**

Mariner, Scott
See Pohl, Frederik

Marinetti, Filippo Tommaso
1876-1944 . . . . **TCLC 10**
See also CA 107; DLB 114

Marivaux, Pierre Carlet de Chamblain de
1688-1763 . . . . **LC 4**

Markandaya, Kamala . . . . **CLC 8, 38**
See also Taylor, Kamala (Purnaiya)

Markfield, Wallace 1926-. . . . . **CLC 8**
See also CA 69-72; CAAS 3; DLB 2, 28

Markham, Edwin 1852-1940 . . . . . . **TCLC 47**
See also DLB 54

Markham, Robert
See Amis, Kingsley (William)

Marks, J
See Highwater, Jamake (Mamake)

Marks-Highwater, J
See Highwater, Jamake (Mamake)

Markson, David M(errill) 1927- . . . . **CLC 67**
See also CA 49-52; CANR 1

Marley, Bob . . . . **CLC 17**
See also Marley, Robert Nesta

Marley, Robert Nesta 1945-1981
See Marley, Bob
See also CA 107; 103

Marlowe, Christopher 1564-1593 . . . . . **DC 1**
See also CDBLB Before 1660; DLB 62;
WLC

Marmontel, Jean-Francois
1723-1799 . . . . **LC 2**

Marquand, John P(hillips)
1893-1960 . . . . **CLC 2, 10**
See also CA 85-88; DLB 9, 102

Marquez, Gabriel (Jose) Garcia. . . . . **CLC 68**
See also Garcia Marquez, Gabriel (Jose)

Marquis, Don(ald Robert Perry)
1878-1937 . . . . **TCLC 7**
See also CA 104; DLB 11, 25

Marric, J. J.
See Creasey, John

Marrow, Bernard
See Moore, Brian

Marryat, Frederick 1792-1848 . . . . **NCLC 3**
See also DLB 21

Marsden, James
See Creasey, John

Marsh, (Edith) Ngaio
1899-1982 . . . . **CLC 7, 53**
See also CA 9-12R; CANR 6; DLB 77;
MTCW

Marshall, Garry 1934- . . . . **CLC 17**
See also AAYA 3; CA 111; SATA 60

Marshall, Paule 1929- . . **CLC 27, 72; SSC 3**
See also BLC 3; BW; CA 77-80; CANR 25;
DLB 33; MTCW

Marsten, Richard
See Hunter, Evan

Martha, Henry
See Harris, Mark

Martin, Ken
See Hubbard, L(afayette) Ron(ald)

Martin, Richard
See Creasey, John

Martin, Steve 1945- . . . . **CLC 30**
See also CA 97-100; CANR 30; MTCW

Martin, Webber
See Silverberg, Robert

Martin du Gard, Roger
1881-1958 . . . . **TCLC 24**
See also CA 118; DLB 65

Martineau, Harriet 1802-1876. . . . **NCLC 26**
See also DLB 21, 55; YABC 2

Martines, Julia
See O'Faolain, Julia

Martinez, Jacinto Benavente y
See Benavente (y Martinez), Jacinto

Martinez Ruiz, Jose 1873-1967
See Azorin; Ruiz, Jose Martinez
See also CA 93-96; HW

Martinez Sierra, Gregorio
1881-1947 . . . . **TCLC 6**
See also CA 115

Martinez Sierra, Maria (de la O'LeJarraga)
1874-1974 . . . . **TCLC 6**
See also CA 115

Martinsen, Martin
See Follett, Ken(neth Martin)

Martinson, Harry (Edmund)
1904-1978 . . . . **CLC 14**
See also CA 77-80; CANR 34

Marut, Ret
See Traven, B.

Marut, Robert
See Traven, B.

Marvell, Andrew 1621-1678. . . . . **LC 4**
See also CDBLB 1660-1789; WLC

Marx, Karl (Heinrich)
1818-1883 . . . . **NCLC 17**

Masaoka Shiki. . . . . **TCLC 18**
See also Masaoka Tsunenori

Masaoka Tsunenori 1867-1902
See Masaoka Shiki
See also CA 117

Masefield, John (Edward)
1878-1967 . . . . **CLC 11, 47**
See also CA 19-20; 25-28R; CANR 33;
CAP 2; CDBLB 1890-1914; DLB 10;
MTCW; SATA 19

Maso, Carole 19(?)- . . . . **CLC 44**

Mason, Bobbie Ann
1940- . . . . **CLC 28, 43; SSC 4**
See also AAYA 5; CA 53-56; CANR 11,
31; DLBY 87; MTCW

Mason, Ernst
See Pohl, Frederik

Mason, Lee W.
See Malzberg, Barry N(athaniel)

Mason, Nick 1945-. . . . . **CLC 35**
See also Pink Floyd

Mason, Tally
See Derleth, August (William)

Mass, William
See Gibson, William

Masters, Edgar Lee
1868-1950 . . . . **TCLC 2, 25; PC 1**
See also CA 104; 133; CDALB 1865-1917;
DLB 54; MTCW

Masters, Hilary 1928- . . . . **CLC 48**
See also CA 25-28R; CANR 13

Mastrosimone, William 19(?)-. . . . . . **CLC 36**

Mathe, Albert
See Camus, Albert

Matheson, Richard Burton 1926- . . . **CLC 37**
See also CA 97-100; DLB 8, 44

Mathews, Harry 1930-. . . . . **CLC 6, 52**
See also CA 21-24R; CAAS 6; CANR 18,
40

Mathias, Roland (Glyn) 1915-. . . . . . **CLC 45**
See also CA 97-100; CANR 19; DLB 27

Matsuo Basho 1644-1694. . . . . **PC 3**

Mattheson, Rodney
See Creasey, John

Matthews, Greg 1949- . . . . **CLC 45**
See also CA 135

Matthews, William 1942-. . . . . **CLC 40**
See also CA 29-32R; CANR 12; DLB 5

Matthias, John (Edward) 1941-. . . . . . **CLC 9**
See also CA 33-36R

Matthiessen, Peter
1927- .... **CLC 5, 7, 11, 32, 64**
See also AAYA 6; BEST 90:4; CA 9-12R;
CANR 21; DLB 6; MTCW; SATA 27

Maturin, Charles Robert
1780(?)-1824 .... **NCLC 6**

Matute (Ausejo), Ana Maria
1925- .... **CLC 11**
See also CA 89-92; MTCW

Maugham, W. S.
See Maugham, W(illiam) Somerset

Maugham, W(illiam) Somerset
1874-1965 .... **CLC 1, 11, 15, 67; SSC 8**
See also CA 5-8R; 25-28R; CANR 40;
CDBLB 1914-1945; DLB 10, 36, 77, 100;
MTCW; SATA 54; WLC

Maugham, William Somerset
See Maugham, W(illiam) Somerset

Maupassant, (Henri Rene Albert) Guy de
1850-1893 .... **NCLC 1; SSC 1**
See also DLB 123; WLC

Maurhut, Richard
See Traven, B.

Mauriac, Claude 1914-............ **CLC 9**
See also CA 89-92; DLB 83

Mauriac, Francois (Charles)
1885-1970 .... **CLC 4, 9, 56**
See also CA 25-28; CAP 2; DLB 65;
MTCW

Mavor, Osborne Henry 1888-1951
See Bridie, James
See also CA 104

Maxwell, William (Keepers Jr.)
1908- .... **CLC 19**
See also CA 93-96; DLBY 80

May, Elaine 1932- .... **CLC 16**
See also CA 124; DLB 44

Mayakovski, Vladimir (Vladimirovich)
1893-1930 .... **TCLC 4, 18**
See also CA 104

Mayhew, Henry 1812-1887 ...... **NCLC 31**
See also DLB 18, 55

Maynard, Joyce 1953-............ **CLC 23**
See also CA 111; 129

Mayne, William (James Carter)
1928- .... **CLC 12**
See also CA 9-12R; CANR 37; CLR 25;
MAICYA; SAAS 11; SATA 6, 68

Mayo, Jim
See L'Amour, Louis (Dearborn)

Maysles, Albert 1926- .... **CLC 16**
See also CA 29-32R

Maysles, David 1932-............ **CLC 16**

Mazer, Norma Fox 1931- .... **CLC 26**
See also AAYA 5; CA 69-72; CANR 12,
32; CLR 23; MAICYA; SAAS 1;
SATA 24, 67

Mazzini, Guiseppe 1805-1872 .... **NCLC 34**

McAuley, James Phillip
1917-1976 .... **CLC 45**
See also CA 97-100

McBain, Ed
See Hunter, Evan

McBrien, William Augustine
1930- .... **CLC 44**
See also CA 107

McCaffrey, Anne (Inez) 1926-...... **CLC 17**
See also AAYA 6; AITN 2; BEST 89:2;
CA 25-28R; CANR 15, 35; DLB 8;
MAICYA; MTCW; SAAS 11; SATA 8,
70

McCann, Arthur
See Campbell, John W(ood Jr.)

McCann, Edson
See Pohl, Frederik

McCarthy, Cormac 1933-........ **CLC 4, 57**
See also CA 13-16R; CANR 10; DLB 6

McCarthy, Mary (Therese)
1912-1989 ... **CLC 1, 3, 5, 14, 24, 39, 59**
See also CA 5-8R; 129; CANR 16; DLB 2;
DLBY 81; MTCW

McCartney, (James) Paul
1942- .... **CLC 12, 35**

McCauley, Stephen 19(?)- .... **CLC 50**

McClure, Michael (Thomas)
1932- .... **CLC 6, 10**
See also CA 21-24R; CANR 17; DLB 16

McCorkle, Jill (Collins) 1958-...... **CLC 51**
See also CA 121; DLBY 87

McCourt, James 1941-............ **CLC 5**
See also CA 57-60

McCoy, Horace (Stanley)
1897-1955 .... **TCLC 28**
See also CA 108; DLB 9

McCrae, John 1872-1918........ **TCLC 12**
See also CA 109; DLB 92

McCreigh, James
See Pohl, Frederik

McCullers, (Lula) Carson (Smith)
1917-1967 .. **CLC 1, 4, 10, 12, 48; SSC 9**
See also CA 5-8R; 25-28R; CABS 1, 3;
CANR 18; CDALB 1941-1968; DLB 2, 7;
MTCW; SATA 27; WLC

McCulloch, John Tyler
See Burroughs, Edgar Rice

McCullough, Colleen 1938(?)-...... **CLC 27**
See also CA 81-84; CANR 17; MTCW

McElroy, Joseph 1930- .... **CLC 5, 47**
See also CA 17-20R

McEwan, Ian (Russell) 1948- ... **CLC 13, 66**
See also BEST 90:4; CA 61-64; CANR 14;
DLB 14; MTCW

McFadden, David 1940-........... **CLC 48**
See also CA 104; DLB 60

McFarland, Dennis 1950- .... **CLC 65**

McGahern, John 1934-........ **CLC 5, 9, 48**
See also CA 17-20R; CANR 29; DLB 14;
MTCW

McGinley, Patrick (Anthony)
1937- .... **CLC 41**
See also CA 120; 127

McGinley, Phyllis 1905-1978 ...... **CLC 14**
See also CA 9-12R; 77-80; CANR 19;
DLB 11, 48; SATA 2, 24, 44

McGinniss, Joe 1942-............ **CLC 32**
See also AITN 2; BEST 89:2; CA 25-28R;
CANR 26

McGivern, Maureen Daly
See Daly, Maureen

McGrath, Patrick 1950-........... **CLC 55**
See also CA 136

McGrath, Thomas (Matthew)
1916-1990 .... **CLC 28, 59**
See also CA 9-12R; 132; CANR 6, 33;
MTCW; SATA 41; SATO 66

McGuane, Thomas (Francis III)
1939- .... **CLC 3, 7, 18, 45**
See also AITN 2; CA 49-52; CANR 5, 24;
DLB 2; DLBY 80; MTCW

McGuckian, Medbh 1950-...... **CLC 48**
See also DLB 40

McHale, Tom 1942(?)-1982....... **CLC 3, 5**
See also AITN 1; CA 77-80; 106

McIlvanney, William 1936-........ **CLC 42**
See also CA 25-28R; DLB 14

McIlwraith, Maureen Mollie Hunter
See Hunter, Mollie
See also SATA 2

McInerney, Jay 1955- .... **CLC 34**
See also CA 116; 123

McIntyre, Vonda N(eel) 1948- ..... **CLC 18**
See also CA 81-84; CANR 17, 34; MTCW

McKay, Claude .... **TCLC 7, 41; PC 2**
See also McKay, Festus Claudius
See also BLC 3; DLB 4, 45, 51, 117

McKay, Festus Claudius 1889-1948
See McKay, Claude
See also BW; CA 104; 124; MTCW; WLC

McKuen, Rod 1933-............. **CLC 1, 3**
See also AITN 1; CA 41-44R; CANR 40

McLoughlin, R. B.
See Mencken, H(enry) L(ouis)

McLuhan, (Herbert) Marshall
1911-1980 .... **CLC 37**
See also CA 9-12R; 102; CANR 12, 34;
DLB 88; MTCW

McMillan, Terry 1951- .... **CLC 50, 61**

McMurtry, Larry (Jeff)
1936- .... **CLC 2, 3, 7, 11, 27, 44**
See also AITN 2; BEST 89:2; CA 5-8R;
CANR 19; CDALB 1968-1988; DLB 2;
DLBY 80, 87; MTCW

McNally, Terrence 1939-...... **CLC 4, 7, 41**
See also CA 45-48; CANR 2; DLB 7

McNamer, Deirdre 1950-.......... **CLC 70**

McNeile, Herman Cyril 1888-1937
See Sapper
See also DLB 77

McPhee, John (Angus) 1931- ...... **CLC 36**
See also BEST 90:1; CA 65-68; CANR 20;
MTCW

McPherson, James Alan 1943- ..... **CLC 19**
See also BW; CA 25-28R; CANR 24;
DLB 38; MTCW

McPherson, William (Alexander)
1933- .... **CLC 34**
See also CA 69-72; CANR 28

McSweeney, Kerry .... **CLC 34**

Mead, Margaret 1901-1978........ **CLC 37**
See also AITN 1; CA 1-4R; 81-84;
CANR 4; MTCW; SATA 20

Meaker, Marijane (Agnes) 1927-
See Kerr, M. E.
See also CA 107; CANR 37; MAICYA;
MTCW; SATA 20, 61

Medoff, Mark (Howard) 1940- . . . CLC 6, 23
See also AITN 1; CA 53-56; CANR 5;
DLB 7

Meged, Aharon
See Megged, Aharon

Meged, Aron
See Megged, Aharon

Megged, Aharon 1920- . . . . CLC 9
See also CA 49-52; CAAS 13; CANR 1

Mehta, Ved (Parkash) 1934- . . . . CLC 37
See also CA 1-4R; CANR 2, 23; MTCW

Melanter
See Blackmore, R(ichard) D(oddridge)

Melikow, Loris
See Hofmannsthal, Hugo von

Melmoth, Sebastian
See Wilde, Oscar (Fingal O'Flahertie Wills)

Meltzer, Milton 1915- . . . . CLC 26
See also AAYA 8; CA 13-16R; CANR 38;
CLR 13; DLB 61; MAICYA; SAAS 1;
SATA 1, 50

Melville, Herman
1819-1891 . . . . . . NCLC 3, 12, 29; SSC 1
See also CDALB 1640-1865; DLB 3, 74;
SATA 59; WLC

Menander
c. 342B.C.-c. 292B.C. . . . CMLC 9; DC 3

Mencken, H(enry) L(ouis)
1880-1956 . . . . TCLC 13
See also CA 105; 125; CDALB 1917-1929;
DLB 11, 29, 63; MTCW

Mercer, David 1928-1980. . . . . CLC 5
See also CA 9-12R; 102; CANR 23;
DLB 13; MTCW

Merchant, Paul
See Ellison, Harlan

Meredith, George 1828-1909 . . . TCLC 17, 43
See also CA 117; CDBLB 1832-1890;
DLB 18, 35, 57

Meredith, William (Morris)
1919- . . . . CLC 4, 13, 22, 55
See also CA 9-12R; CAAS 14; CANR 6, 40;
DLB 5

Merezhkovsky, Dmitry Sergeyevich
1865-1941 . . . . TCLC 29

Merimee, Prosper
1803-1870 . . . . NCLC 6; SSC 7
See also DLB 119

Merkin, Daphne 1954- . . . . CLC 44
See also CA 123

Merlin, Arthur
See Blish, James (Benjamin)

Merrill, James (Ingram)
1926- . . . . CLC 2, 3, 6, 8, 13, 18, 34
See also CA 13-16R; CANR 10; DLB 5;
DLBY 85; MTCW

Merriman, Alex
See Silverberg, Robert

Merritt, E. B.
See Waddington, Miriam

Merton, Thomas
1915-1968 . . . . CLC 1, 3, 11, 34
See also CA 5-8R; 25-28R; CANR 22;
DLB 48; DLBY 81; MTCW

Merwin, W(illiam) S(tanley)
1927- . . . . . . CLC 1, 2, 3, 5, 8, 13, 18, 45
See also CA 13-16R; CANR 15; DLB 5;
MTCW

Metcalf, John 1938- . . . . CLC 37
See also CA 113; DLB 60

Metcalf, Suzanne
See Baum, L(yman) Frank

Mew, Charlotte (Mary)
1870-1928 . . . . TCLC 8
See also CA 105; DLB 19

Mewshaw, Michael 1943-. . . . . CLC 9
See also CA 53-56; CANR 7; DLBY 80

Meyer, June
See Jordan, June

Meyer-Meyrink, Gustav 1868-1932
See Meyrink, Gustav
See also CA 117

Meyers, Jeffrey 1939- . . . . CLC 39
See also CA 73-76; DLB 111

Meynell, Alice (Christina Gertrude Thompson)
1847-1922 . . . . TCLC 6
See also CA 104; DLB 19, 98

Meyrink, Gustav . . . . TCLC 21
See also Meyer-Meyrink, Gustav
See also DLB 81

Michaels, Leonard 1933- . . . . CLC 6, 25
See also CA 61-64; CANR 21; MTCW

Michaux, Henri 1899-1984 . . . . . . CLC 8, 19
See also CA 85-88; 114

Michelangelo 1475-1564. . . . . LC 12

Michelet, Jules 1798-1874 . . . . . . NCLC 31

Michener, James A(lbert)
1907(?)- . . . . CLC 1, 5, 11, 29, 60
See also AITN 1; BEST 90:1; CA 5-8R;
CANR 21; DLB 6; MTCW

Mickiewicz, Adam 1798-1855 . . . . . NCLC 3

Middleton, Christopher 1926- . . . . . . CLC 13
See also CA 13-16R; CANR 29; DLB 40

Middleton, Stanley 1919-. . . . . CLC 7, 38
See also CA 25-28R; CANR 21; DLB 14

Migueis, Jose Rodrigues 1901- . . . . . CLC 10

Mikszath, Kalman 1847-1910 . . . . . TCLC 31

Miles, Josephine
1911-1985 . . . . CLC 1, 2, 14, 34, 39
See also CA 1-4R; 116; CANR 2; DLB 48

Militant
See Sandburg, Carl (August)

Mill, John Stuart 1806-1873 . . . . . NCLC 11
See also CDBLB 1832-1890; DLB 55

Millar, Kenneth 1915-1983 . . . . CLC 14
See also Macdonald, Ross
See also CA 9-12R; 110; CANR 16; DLB 2;
DLBD 6; DLBY 83; MTCW

Millay, E. Vincent
See Millay, Edna St. Vincent

Millay, Edna St. Vincent
1892-1950 . . . . TCLC 4, 49; PC 6
See also CA 104; 130; CDALB 1917-1929;
DLB 45; MTCW

Miller, Arthur
1915- . . . . . . CLC 1, 2, 6, 10, 15, 26, 47;
DC 1
See also AITN 1; CA 1-4R; CABS 3;
CANR 2, 30; CDALB 1941-1968; DLB 7;
MTCW; WLC

Miller, Henry (Valentine)
1891-1980 . . . . . . CLC 1, 2, 4, 9, 14, 43
See also CA 9-12R; 97-100; CANR 33;
CDALB 1929-1941; DLB 4, 9; DLBY 80;
MTCW; WLC

Miller, Jason 1939(?)- . . . . CLC 2
See also AITN 1; CA 73-76; DLB 7

Miller, Sue 19(?)-. . . . . CLC 44
See also BEST 90:3; CA 139

Miller, Walter M(ichael Jr.)
1923- . . . . CLC 4, 30
See also CA 85-88; DLB 8

Millett, Kate 1934-. . . . . CLC 67
See also AITN 1; CA 73-76; CANR 32;
MTCW

Millhauser, Steven 1943-. . . . . . . CLC 21, 54
See also CA 110; 111; DLB 2

Millin, Sarah Gertrude 1889-1968 . . CLC 49
See also CA 102; 93-96

Milne, A(lan) A(lexander)
1882-1956 . . . . TCLC 6
See also CA 104; 133; CLR 1, 26; DLB 10,
77, 100; MAICYA; MTCW; YABC 1

Milner, Ron(ald) 1938-. . . . . CLC 56
See also AITN 1; BLC 3; BW; CA 73-76;
CANR 24; DLB 38; MTCW

Milosz, Czeslaw
1911- . . . . CLC 5, 11, 22, 31, 56
See also CA 81-84; CANR 23; MTCW

Milton, John 1608-1674. . . . . LC 9
See also CDBLB 1660-1789; WLC

Minehaha, Cornelius
See Wedekind, (Benjamin) Frank(lin)

Miner, Valerie 1947- . . . . CLC 40
See also CA 97-100

Minimo, Duca
See D'Annunzio, Gabriele

Minot, Susan 1956- . . . . CLC 44
See also CA 134

Minus, Ed 1938-. . . . . CLC 39

Miranda, Javier
See Bioy Casares, Adolfo

Miro (Ferrer), Gabriel (Francisco Victor)
1879-1930 . . . . TCLC 5
See also CA 104

Mishima, Yukio
. . . . CLC 2, 4, 6, 9, 27; DC 1; SSC 4
See also Hiraoka, Kimitake

Mistral, Gabriela. . . . . TCLC 2
See also Godoy Alcayaga, Lucila

Mistry, Rohinton 1952-. . . . . CLC 71

Mitchell, Clyde
See Ellison, Harlan; Silverberg, Robert

Mitchell, James Leslie 1901-1935
See Gibbon, Lewis Grassic
See also CA 104; DLB 15

Mitchell, Joni 1943-. . . . . CLC 12
See also CA 112

Mitchell, Margaret (Munnerlyn)
1900-1949 . . . . **TCLC 11**
See also CA 109; 125; DLB 9; MTCW

Mitchell, Peggy
See Mitchell, Margaret (Munnerlyn)

Mitchell, S(ilas) Weir 1829-1914 . . **TCLC 36**

Mitchell, W(illiam) O(rmond)
1914- . . . . **CLC 25**
See also CA 77-80; CANR 15; DLB 88

Mitford, Mary Russell 1787-1855. . **NCLC 4**
See also DLB 110, 116

Mitford, Nancy 1904-1973. . . . . **CLC 44**
See also CA 9-12R

Miyamoto, Yuriko 1899-1951 . . . . . **TCLC 37**

Mo, Timothy (Peter) 1950(?)- . . . . . . **CLC 46**
See also CA 117; MTCW

Modarressi, Taghi (M.) 1931- . . . . . . **CLC 44**
See also CA 121; 134

Modiano, Patrick (Jean) 1945- . . . . . **CLC 18**
See also CA 85-88; CANR 17, 40; DLB 83

Moerck, Paal
See Roelvaag, O(le) E(dvart)

Mofolo, Thomas (Mokopu)
1875(?)-1948 . . . . **TCLC 22**
See also BLC 3; CA 121

Mohr, Nicholasa 1935-. . . . . **CLC 12**
See also AAYA 8; CA 49-52; CANR 1, 32;
CLR 22; HW; SAAS 8; SATA 8

Mojtabai, A(nn) G(race)
1938- . . . . **CLC 5, 9, 15, 29**
See also CA 85-88

Moliere 1622-1673 . . . . **LC 10**
See also WLC

Molin, Charles
See Mayne, William (James Carter)

Molnar, Ferenc 1878-1952. . . . . . . **TCLC 20**
See also CA 109

Momaday, N(avarre) Scott
1934- . . . . **CLC 2, 19**
See also CA 25-28R; CANR 14, 34;
MTCW; SATA 30, 48

Monroe, Harriet 1860-1936. . . . . . **TCLC 12**
See also CA 109; DLB 54, 91

Monroe, Lyle
See Heinlein, Robert A(nson)

Montagu, Elizabeth 1917- . . . . **NCLC 7**
See also CA 9-12R

Montagu, Mary (Pierrepont) Wortley
1689-1762 . . . . **LC 9**
See also DLB 95, 101

Montague, John (Patrick)
1929- . . . . **CLC 13, 46**
See also CA 9-12R; CANR 9; DLB 40;
MTCW

Montaigne, Michel (Eyquem) de
1533-1592 . . . . **LC 8**
See also WLC

Montale, Eugenio 1896-1981. . . **CLC 7, 9, 18**
See also CA 17-20R; 104; CANR 30;
DLB 114; MTCW

Montesquieu, Charles-Louis de Secondat
1689-1755 . . . . **LC 7**

Montgomery, (Robert) Bruce 1921-1978
See Crispin, Edmund
See also CA 104

Montgomery, Marion H. Jr. 1925-. . . **CLC 7**
See also AITN 1; CA 1-4R; CANR 3;
DLB 6

Montgomery, Max
See Davenport, Guy (Mattison Jr.)

Montherlant, Henry (Milon) de
1896-1972 . . . . **CLC 8, 19**
See also CA 85-88; 37-40R; DLB 72;
MTCW

Python . . . . **CLC 21**
See also Chapman, Graham; Cleese, John
(Marwood); Gilliam, Terry (Vance); Idle,
Eric; Jones, Terence Graham Parry; Palin,
Michael (Edward)
See also AAYA 7

Moodie, Susanna (Strickland)
1803-1885 . . . . **NCLC 14**
See also DLB 99

Mooney, Edward 1951- . . . . **CLC 25**
See also CA 130

Mooney, Ted
See Mooney, Edward

Moorcock, Michael (John)
1939- . . . . **CLC 5, 27, 58**
See also CA 45-48; CAAS 5; CANR 2, 17,
38; DLB 14; MTCW

Moore, Brian
1921- . . . . **CLC 1, 3, 5, 7, 8, 19, 32**
See also CA 1-4R; CANR 1, 25; MTCW

Moore, Edward
See Muir, Edwin

Moore, George Augustus
1852-1933 . . . . **TCLC 7**
See also CA 104; DLB 10, 18, 57

Moore, Lorrie . . . . **CLC 39, 45, 68**
See also Moore, Marie Lorena

Moore, Marianne (Craig)
1887-1972 . . . **CLC 1, 2, 4, 8, 10, 13, 19,
47; PC 4**
See also CA 1-4R; 33-36R; CANR 3;
CDALB 1929-1941; DLB 45; DLBD 7;
MTCW; SATA 20

Moore, Marie Lorena 1957-
See Moore, Lorrie
See also CA 116; CANR 39

Moore, Thomas 1779-1852. . . . . **NCLC 6**
See also DLB 96

Morand, Paul 1888-1976 . . . . **CLC 41**
See also CA 69-72; DLB 65

Morante, Elsa 1918-1985. . . . . **CLC 8, 47**
See also CA 85-88; 117; CANR 35; MTCW

Moravia, Alberto. . . . . . **CLC 2, 7, 11, 27, 46**
See also Pincherle, Alberto

More, Hannah 1745-1833 . . . . **NCLC 27**
See also DLB 107, 109, 116

More, Henry 1614-1687. . . . . **LC 9**

More, Sir Thomas 1478-1535 . . . . **LC 10**

Moreas, Jean . . . . **TCLC 18**
See also Papadiamantopoulos, Johannes

Morgan, Berry 1919- . . . . **CLC 6**
See also CA 49-52; DLB 6

Morgan, Claire
See Highsmith, (Mary) Patricia

Morgan, Edwin (George) 1920-. . . . . **CLC 31**
See also CA 5-8R; CANR 3; DLB 27

Morgan, (George) Frederick
1922- . . . . **CLC 23**
See also CA 17-20R; CANR 21

Morgan, Harriet
See Mencken, H(enry) L(ouis)

Morgan, Jane
See Cooper, James Fenimore

Morgan, Janet 1945- . . . . **CLC 39**
See also CA 65-68

Morgan, Lady 1776(?)-1859. . . . . . . **NCLC 29**
See also DLB 116

Morgan, Robin 1941-. . . . . **CLC 2**
See also CA 69-72; CANR 29; MTCW

Morgan, Scott
See Kuttner, Henry

Morgan, Seth 1949(?)-1990 . . . . **CLC 65**
See also CA 132

Morgenstern, Christian
1871-1914 . . . . **TCLC 8**
See also CA 105

Morgenstern, S.
See Goldman, William (W.)

Moricz, Zsigmond 1879-1942 . . . . . **TCLC 33**

Morike, Eduard (Friedrich)
1804-1875 . . . . **NCLC 10**

Mori Ogai . . . . **TCLC 14**
See also Mori Rintaro

Mori Rintaro 1862-1922
See Mori Ogai
See also CA 110

Moritz, Karl Philipp 1756-1793 . . . . . . **LC 2**
See also DLB 94

Morland, Peter Henry
See Faust, Frederick (Schiller)

Morren, Theophil
See Hofmannsthal, Hugo von

Morris, Julian
See West, Morris L(anglo)

Morris, Steveland Judkins 1950(?)-
See Wonder, Stevie
See also CA 111

Morris, William 1834-1896 . . . . **NCLC 4**
See also CDBLB 1832-1890; DLB 18, 35, 57

Morris, Wright 1910-. . . **CLC 1, 3, 7, 18, 37**
See also CA 9-12R; CANR 21; DLB 2;
DLBY 81; MTCW

Morrison, Chloe Anthony Wofford
See Morrison, Toni

Morrison, James Douglas 1943-1971
See Morrison, Jim
See also CA 73-76; CANR 40

Morrison, Jim . . . . **CLC 17**
See also Morrison, James Douglas

Morrison, Toni 1931-. . . . . **CLC 4, 10, 22, 55**
See also AAYA 1; BLC 3; BW; CA 29-32R;
CANR 27; CDALB 1968-1988; DLB 6,
33; DLBY 81; MTCW; SATA 57

Morrison, Van 1945- . . . . **CLC 21**
See also CA 116

Mortimer, John (Clifford)
1923- . . . . **CLC 28, 43**
See also CA 13-16R; CANR 21;
CDBLB 1960 to Present; DLB 13;
MTCW

Mortimer, Penelope (Ruth) 1918- . . . . **CLC 5**
See also CA 57-60

Morton, Anthony
See Creasey, John

Mosher, Howard Frank . . . . **CLC 62**
See also CA 139

Mosley, Nicholas 1923- . . . . **CLC 43, 70**
See also CA 69-72; DLB 14

Moss, Howard
1922-1987 . . . . **CLC 7, 14, 45, 50**
See also CA 1-4R; 123; CANR 1; DLB 5

Motion, Andrew 1952- . . . . **CLC 47**
See also DLB 40

Motley, Willard (Francis)
1912-1965 . . . . **CLC 18**
See also BW; CA 117; 106; DLB 76

Mott, Michael (Charles Alston)
1930- . . . . **CLC 15, 34**
See also CA 5-8R; CAAS 7; CANR 7, 29

Mowat, Farley (McGill) 1921- . . . . . **CLC 26**
See also AAYA 1; CA 1-4R; CANR 4, 24;
CLR 20; DLB 68; MAICYA; MTCW;
SATA 3, 55

Moyers, Bill 1934- . . . . **CLC 74**
See also AITN 2; CA 61-64; CANR 31

Mphahlele, Es'kia
See Mphahlele, Ezekiel
See also DLB 125

Mphahlele, Ezekiel 1919- . . . . **CLC 25**
See also Mphahlele, Es'kia
See also BLC 3; BW; CA 81-84; CANR 26

Mqhayi, S(amuel) E(dward) K(rune Loliwe)
1875-1945 . . . . **TCLC 25**
See also BLC 3

Mr. Martin
See Burroughs, William S(eward)

Mrozek, Slawomir 1930- . . . . **CLC 3, 13**
See also CA 13-16R; CAAS 10; CANR 29;
MTCW

Mrs. Belloc-Lowndes
See Lowndes, Marie Adelaide (Belloc)

Mtwa, Percy (?)- . . . . **CLC 47**

Mueller, Lisel 1924- . . . . **CLC 13, 51**
See also CA 93-96; DLB 105

Muir, Edwin 1887-1959 . . . . **TCLC 2**
See also CA 104; DLB 20, 100

Muir, John 1838-1914 . . . . **TCLC 28**

Mujica Lainez, Manuel
1910-1984 . . . . **CLC 31**
See also Lainez, Manuel Mujica
See also CA 81-84; 112; CANR 32; HW

Mukherjee, Bharati 1940- . . . . **CLC 53**
See also BEST 89:2; CA 107; DLB 60;
MTCW

Muldoon, Paul 1951- . . . . **CLC 32, 72**
See also CA 113; 129; DLB 40

Mulisch, Harry 1927- . . . . **CLC 42**
See also CA 9-12R; CANR 6, 26

Mull, Martin 1943- . . . . **CLC 17**
See also CA 105

Mulock, Dinah Maria
See Craik, Dinah Maria (Mulock)

Munford, Robert 1737(?)-1783 . . . . **LC 5**
See also DLB 31

Mungo, Raymond 1946- . . . . **CLC 72**
See also CA 49-52; CANR 2

Munro, Alice
1931- . . . . **CLC 6, 10, 19, 50; SSC 3**
See also AITN 2; CA 33-36R; CANR 33;
DLB 53; MTCW; SATA 29

Munro, H(ector) H(ugh) 1870-1916
See Saki
See also CA 104; 130; CDBLB 1890-1914;
DLB 34; MTCW; WLC

Murasaki, Lady . . . . **CMLC 1**

Murdoch, (Jean) Iris
1919- . . . . . . **CLC 1, 2, 3, 4, 6, 8, 11, 15,**
22, 31, 51
See also CA 13-16R; CANR 8;
CDBLB 1960 to Present; DLB 14;
MTCW

Murphy, Richard 1927- . . . . **CLC 41**
See also CA 29-32R; DLB 40

Murphy, Sylvia 1937- . . . . **CLC 34**
See also CA 121

Murphy, Thomas (Bernard) 1935- . . . **CLC 51**
See also CA 101

Murray, Albert L. 1916- . . . . **CLC 73**
See also BW; CA 49-52; CANR 26; DLB 38

Murray, Les(lie) A(llan) 1938- . . . . . **CLC 40**
See also CA 21-24R; CANR 11, 27

Murry, J. Middleton
See Murry, John Middleton

Murry, John Middleton
1889-1957 . . . . **TCLC 16**
See also CA 118

Musgrave, Susan 1951- . . . . **CLC 13, 54**
See also CA 69-72

Musil, Robert (Edler von)
1880-1942 . . . . **TCLC 12**
See also CA 109; DLB 81, 124

Musset, (Louis Charles) Alfred de
1810-1857 . . . . **NCLC 7**

My Brother's Brother
See Chekhov, Anton (Pavlovich)

Myers, Walter Dean 1937- . . . . **CLC 35**
See also AAYA 4; BLC 3; BW; CA 33-36R;
CANR 20; CLR 4, 16; DLB 33;
MAICYA; SAAS 2; SATA 27, 41, 70, 71

Myers, Walter M.
See Myers, Walter Dean

Myles, Symon
See Follett, Ken(neth Martin)

Nabokov, Vladimir (Vladimirovich)
1899-1977 . . . . **CLC 1, 2, 3, 6, 8, 11, 15,**
23, 44, 46, 64; SSC 11
See also CA 5-8R; 69-72; CANR 20;
CDALB 1941-1968; DLB 2; DLBD 3;
DLBY 80, 91; MTCW; WLC

Nagy, Laszlo 1925-1978 . . . . **CLC 7**
See also CA 129; 112

Naipaul, Shiva(dhar Srinivasa)
1945-1985 . . . . **CLC 32, 39**
See also CA 110; 112; 116; CANR 33;
DLBY 85; MTCW

Naipaul, V(idiadhar) S(urajprasad)
1932- . . . . **CLC 4, 7, 9, 13, 18, 37**
See also CA 1-4R; CANR 1, 33;
CDBLB 1960 to Present; DLB 125;
DLBY 85; MTCW

Nakos, Lilika 1899(?)- . . . . **CLC 29**

Narayan, R(asipuram) K(rishnaswami)
1906- . . . . **CLC 7, 28, 47**
See also CA 81-84; CANR 33; MTCW;
SATA 62

Nash, (Frediric) Ogden 1902-1971 . . **CLC 23**
See also CA 13-14; 29-32R; CANR 34;
CAP 1; DLB 11; MAICYA; MTCW;
SATA 2, 46

Nathan, Daniel
See Dannay, Frederic

Nathan, George Jean 1882-1958 . . . **TCLC 18**
See also Hatteras, Owen
See also CA 114

Natsume, Kinnosuke 1867-1916
See Natsume, Soseki
See also CA 104

Natsume, Soseki . . . . **TCLC 2, 10**
See also Natsume, Kinnosuke

Natti, (Mary) Lee 1919-
See Kingman, Lee
See also CA 5-8R; CANR 2

Naylor, Gloria 1950- . . . . **CLC 28, 52**
See also AAYA 6; BLC 3; BW; CA 107;
CANR 27; MTCW

Neihardt, John Gneisenau
1881-1973 . . . . **CLC 32**
See also CA 13-14; CAP 1; DLB 9, 54

Nekrasov, Nikolai Alekseevich
1821-1878 . . . . **NCLC 11**

Nelligan, Emile 1879-1941 . . . . **TCLC 14**
See also CA 114; DLB 92

Nelson, Willie 1933- . . . . **CLC 17**
See also CA 107

Nemerov, Howard (Stanley)
1920-1991 . . . . **CLC 2, 6, 9, 36**
See also CA 1-4R; 134; CABS 2; CANR 1,
27; DLB 6; DLBY 83; MTCW

Neruda, Pablo
1904-1973 . . . . **CLC 1, 2, 5, 7, 9, 28, 62;**
PC 4
See also CA 19-20; 45-48; CAP 2; HW;
MTCW; WLC

Nerval, Gerard de 1808-1855 . . . . . . **NCLC 1**

Nervo, (Jose) Amado (Ruiz de)
1870-1919 . . . . **TCLC 11**
See also CA 109; 131; HW

Nessi, Pio Baroja y
See Baroja (y Nessi), Pio

Neufeld, John (Arthur) 1938- . . . . . . **CLC 17**
See also CA 25-28R; CANR 11, 37;
MAICYA; SAAS 3; SATA 6

Neville, Emily Cheney 1919- . . . . **CLC 12**
See also CA 5-8R; CANR 3, 37; MAICYA;
SAAS 2; SATA 1

O'Donovan, Michael John
    1903-1966 . . . . CLC 14
    See also O'Connor, Frank
    See also CA 93-96

Oe, Kenzaburo 1935- . . . . CLC 10, 36
    See also CA 97-100; CANR 36; MTCW

O'Faolain, Julia 1932- . . . . CLC 6, 19, 47
    See also CA 81-84; CAAS 2; CANR 12;
    DLB 14; MTCW

O'Faolain, Sean
    1900-1991 . . . . CLC 1, 7, 14, 32, 70
    See also CA 61-64; 134; CANR 12;
    DLB 15; MTCW

O'Flaherty, Liam
    1896-1984 . . . . CLC 5, 34; SSC 6
    See also CA 101; 113; CANR 35; DLB 36;
    DLBY 84; MTCW

Ogilvy, Gavin
    See Barrie, J(ames) M(atthew)

O'Grady, Standish James
    1846-1928 . . . . TCLC 5
    See also CA 104

O'Grady, Timothy 1951- . . . . CLC 59
    See also CA 138

O'Hara, Frank 1926-1966 . . . . . CLC 2, 5, 13
    See also CA 9-12R; 25-28R; CANR 33;
    DLB 5, 16; MTCW

O'Hara, John (Henry)
    1905-1970 . . . . CLC 1, 2, 3, 6, 11, 42
    See also CA 5-8R; 25-28R; CANR 31;
    CDALB 1929-1941; DLB 9, 86; DLBD 2;
    MTCW

O Hehir, Diana 1922- . . . . CLC 41
    See also CA 93-96

Okigbo, Christopher (Ifenayichukwu)
    1932-1967 . . . . CLC 25
    See also BLC 3; BW; CA 77-80; DLB 125;
    MTCW

Olds, Sharon 1942- . . . . CLC 32, 39
    See also CA 101; CANR 18; DLB 120

Oldstyle, Jonathan
    See Irving, Washington

Olesha, Yuri (Karlovich)
    1899-1960 . . . . CLC 8
    See also CA 85-88

Oliphant, Margaret (Oliphant Wilson)
    1828-1897 . . . . NCLC 11
    See also DLB 18

Oliver, Mary 1935- . . . . CLC 19, 34
    See also CA 21-24R; CANR 9; DLB 5

Olivier, Laurence (Kerr)
    1907-1989 . . . . CLC 20
    See also CA 111; 129

Olsen, Tillie 1913- . . . . . CLC 4, 13; SSC 11
    See also CA 1-4R; CANR 1; DLB 28;
    DLBY 80; MTCW

Olson, Charles (John)
    1910-1970 . . . . . CLC 1, 2, 5, 6, 9, 11, 29
    See also CA 13-16; 25-28R; CABS 2;
    CANR 35; CAP 1; DLB 5, 16; MTCW

Olson, Toby 1937- . . . . CLC 28
    See also CA 65-68; CANR 9, 31

Olyesha, Yuri
    See Olesha, Yuri (Karlovich)

Ondaatje, Michael 1943- . . . . CLC 14, 29, 51
    See also CA 77-80; DLB 60

Oneal, Elizabeth 1934-
    See Oneal, Zibby
    See also CA 106; CANR 28; MAICYA;
    SATA 30

Oneal, Zibby . . . . CLC 30
    See also Oneal, Elizabeth
    See also AAYA 5; CLR 13

O'Neill, Eugene (Gladstone)
    1888-1953 . . . . TCLC 1, 6, 27, 49
    See also AITN 1; CA 110; 132;
    CDALB 1929-1941; DLB 7; MTCW;
    WLC

Onetti, Juan Carlos 1909- . . . . CLC 7, 10
    See also CA 85-88; CANR 32; DLB 113;
    HW; MTCW

O Nuallain, Brian 1911-1966
    See O'Brien, Flann
    See also CA 21-22; 25-28R; CAP 2

Oppen, George 1908-1984 . . . . CLC 7, 13, 34
    See also CA 13-16R; 113; CANR 8; DLB 5

Oppenheim, E(dward) Phillips
    1866-1946 . . . . TCLC 45
    See also CA 111; DLB 70

Orlovitz, Gil 1918-1973 . . . . CLC 22
    See also CA 77-80; 45-48; DLB 2, 5

Orris
    See Ingelow, Jean

Ortega y Gasset, Jose 1883-1955 . . . TCLC 9
    See also CA 106; 130; HW; MTCW

Ortiz, Simon J(oseph) 1941- . . . . CLC 45
    See also CA 134; DLB 120

Orton, Joe . . . . CLC 4, 13, 43; DC 3
    See also Orton, John Kingsley
    See also CDBLB 1960 to Present; DLB 13

Orton, John Kingsley 1933-1967
    See Orton, Joe
    See also CA 85-88; CANR 35; MTCW

Orwell, George . . . . TCLC 2, 6, 15, 31
    See also Blair, Eric (Arthur)
    See also CDBLB 1945-1960; DLB 15, 98;
    WLC

Osborne, David
    See Silverberg, Robert

Osborne, George
    See Silverberg, Robert

Osborne, John (James)
    1929- . . . . CLC 1, 2, 5, 11, 45
    See also CA 13-16R; CANR 21;
    CDBLB 1945-1960; DLB 13; MTCW;
    WLC

Osborne, Lawrence 1958- . . . . CLC 50

Oshima, Nagisa 1932- . . . . CLC 20
    See also CA 116; 121

Oskison, John M(ilton)
    1874-1947 . . . . TCLC 35

Ossoli, Sarah Margaret (Fuller marchesa d')
    1810-1850
    See Fuller, Margaret
    See also SATA 25

Ostrovsky, Alexander
    1823-1886 . . . . NCLC 30

Otero, Blas de 1916- . . . . CLC 11
    See also CA 89-92

Otto, Whitney 1955- . . . . CLC 70

Ouida . . . . TCLC 43
    See also De La Ramee, (Marie) Louise
    See also DLB 18

Ousmane, Sembene 1923- . . . . CLC 66
    See also BLC 3; BW; CA 117; 125; MTCW

Ovid 43B.C.-18th cent. (?) . . . CMLC 7; PC 2

Owen, Hugh
    See Faust, Frederick (Schiller)

Owen, Wilfred 1893-1918 . . . . . . TCLC 5, 27
    See also CA 104; CDBLB 1914-1945;
    DLB 20; WLC

Owens, Rochelle 1936- . . . . CLC 8
    See also CA 17-20R; CAAS 2; CANR 39

Oz, Amos 1939- . . . CLC 5, 8, 11, 27, 33, 54
    See also CA 53-56; CANR 27; MTCW

Ozick, Cynthia 1928- . . . . . . CLC 3, 7, 28, 62
    See also BEST 90:1; CA 17-20R; CANR 23;
    DLB 28; DLBY 82; MTCW

Ozu, Yasujiro 1903-1963 . . . . CLC 16
    See also CA 112

Pacheco, C.
    See Pessoa, Fernando (Antonio Nogueira)

Pa Chin
    See Li Fei-kan

Pack, Robert 1929- . . . . CLC 13
    See also CA 1-4R; CANR 3; DLB 5

Padgett, Lewis
    See Kuttner, Henry

Padilla (Lorenzo), Heberto 1932- . . . CLC 38
    See also AITN 1; CA 123; 131; HW

Page, Jimmy 1944- . . . . CLC 12

Page, Louise 1955- . . . . CLC 40

Page, P(atricia) K(athleen)
    1916- . . . . CLC 7, 18
    See also CA 53-56; CANR 4, 22; DLB 68;
    MTCW

Paget, Violet 1856-1935
    See Lee, Vernon
    See also CA 104

Paget-Lowe, Henry
    See Lovecraft, H(oward) P(hillips)

Paglia, Camille 1947- . . . . CLC 68

Pakenham, Antonia
    See Fraser, Antonia (Pakenham)

Palamas, Kostes 1859-1943 . . . . TCLC 5
    See also CA 105

Palazzeschi, Aldo 1885-1974 . . . . CLC 11
    See also CA 89-92; 53-56; DLB 114

Paley, Grace 1922- . . . . CLC 4, 6, 37; SSC 8
    See also CA 25-28R; CANR 13; DLB 28;
    MTCW

Palin, Michael (Edward) 1943- . . . . . CLC 21
    See also Monty Python
    See also CA 107; CANR 35; SATA 67

Palliser, Charles 1947- . . . . CLC 65
    See also CA 136

Palma, Ricardo 1833-1919 . . . . TCLC 29

Pancake, Breece Dexter 1952-1979
    See Pancake, Breece D'J
    See also CA 123; 109

Pancake, Breece D'J . . . . CLC 29
    See also Pancake, Breece Dexter

Papadiamantis, Alexandros
   1851-1911 .... TCLC 29

Papadiamantopoulos, Johannes 1856-1910
   See Moreas, Jean
   See also CA 117

Papini, Giovanni 1881-1956...... TCLC 22
   See also CA 121

Paracelsus 1493-1541.............. LC 14

Parasol, Peter
   See Stevens, Wallace

Parfenie, Maria
   See Codrescu, Andrei

Parini, Jay (Lee) 1948- .... CLC 54
   See also CA 97-100; CAAS 16; CANR 32

Park, Jordan
   See Kornbluth, C(yril) M.; Pohl, Frederik

Parker, Bert
   See Ellison, Harlan

Parker, Dorothy (Rothschild)
   1893-1967 .... CLC 15, 68; SSC 2
   See also CA 19-20; 25-28R; CAP 2;
   DLB 11, 45, 86; MTCW

Parker, Robert B(rown) 1932-..... CLC 27
   See also BEST 89:4; CA 49-52; CANR 1,
   26; MTCW

Parkes, Lucas
   See Harris, John (Wyndham Parkes Lucas)
   Beynon

Parkin, Frank 1940-............. CLC 43

Parkman, Francis Jr. 1823-1893.. NCLC 12
   See also DLB 1, 30

Parks, Gordon (Alexander Buchanan)
   1912- .... CLC 1, 16
   See also AITN 2; BLC 3; BW; CA 41-44R;
   CANR 26; DLB 33; SATA 8

Parnell, Thomas 1679-1718 .... LC 3
   See also DLB 94

Parra, Nicanor 1914-.............. CLC 2
   See also CA 85-88; CANR 32; HW; MTCW

Parson Lot
   See Kingsley, Charles

Partridge, Anthony
   See Oppenheim, E(dward) Phillips

Pascoli, Giovanni 1855-1912 ...... TCLC 45

Pasolini, Pier Paolo
   1922-1975 .... CLC 20, 37
   See also CA 93-96; 61-64; MTCW

Pasquini
   See Silone, Ignazio

Pastan, Linda (Olenik) 1932- ...... CLC 27
   See also CA 61-64; CANR 18, 40; DLB 5

Pasternak, Boris (Leonidovich)
   1890-1960 ..... CLC 7, 10, 18, 63; PC 6
   See also CA 127; 116; MTCW; WLC

Patchen, Kenneth 1911-1972... CLC 1, 2, 18
   See also CA 1-4R; 33-36R; CANR 3, 35;
   DLB 16, 48; MTCW

Pater, Walter (Horatio)
   1839-1894 .... NCLC 7
   See also CDBLB 1832-1890; DLB 57

Paterson, A(ndrew) B(arton)
   1864-1941 .... TCLC 32

Paterson, Katherine (Womeldorf)
   1932- .... CLC 12, 30
   See also AAYA 1; CA 21-24R; CANR 28;
   CLR 7; DLB 52; MAICYA; MTCW;
   SATA 13, 53

Patmore, Coventry Kersey Dighton
   1823-1896 .... NCLC 9
   See also DLB 35, 98

Paton, Alan (Stewart)
   1903-1988 .... CLC 4, 10, 25, 55
   See also CA 13-16; 125; CANR 22; CAP 1;
   MTCW; SATA 11, 56; WLC

Paton Walsh, Gillian 1939-
   See Walsh, Jill Paton
   See also CANR 38; MAICYA; SAAS 3;
   SATA 4, 72

Paulding, James Kirke 1778-1860.. NCLC 2
   See also DLB 3, 59, 74

Paulin, Thomas Neilson 1949-
   See Paulin, Tom
   See also CA 123; 128

**Paulin, Tom...................... CLC 37
   See also Paulin, Thomas Neilson
   See also DLB 40

Paustovsky, Konstantin (Georgievich)
   1892-1968 .... CLC 40
   See also CA 93-96; 25-28R

Pavese, Cesare 1908-1950 .... TCLC 3
   See also CA 104

Pavic, Milorad 1929-............. CLC 60
   See also CA 136

Payne, Alan
   See Jakes, John (William)

Paz, Gil
   See Lugones, Leopoldo

Paz, Octavio
   1914- ...... CLC 3, 4, 6, 10, 19, 51, 65;
                                              PC 1
   See also CA 73-76; CANR 32; DLBY 90;
   HW; MTCW; WLC

Peacock, Molly 1947-............. CLC 60
   See also CA 103; DLB 120

Peacock, Thomas Love
   1785-1866 .... NCLC 22
   See also DLB 96, 116

Peake, Mervyn 1911-1968....... CLC 7, 54
   See also CA 5-8R; 25-28R; CANR 3;
   DLB 15; MTCW; SATA 23

**Pearce, Philippa .... CLC 21
   See also Christie, (Ann) Philippa
   See also CLR 9; MAICYA; SATA 1, 67

Pearl, Eric
   See Elman, Richard

Pearson, T(homas) R(eid) 1956- .... CLC 39
   See also CA 120; 130

Peck, John 1941- .... CLC 3
   See also CA 49-52; CANR 3

Peck, Richard (Wayne) 1934-...... CLC 21
   See also AAYA 1; CA 85-88; CANR 19,
   38; MAICYA; SAAS 2; SATA 18, 55

Peck, Robert Newton 1928-........ CLC 17
   See also AAYA 3; CA 81-84; CANR 31;
   MAICYA; SAAS 1; SATA 21, 62

Peckinpah, (David) Sam(uel)
   1925-1984 .... CLC 20
   See also CA 109; 114

Pedersen, Knut 1859-1952
   See Hamsun, Knut
   See also CA 104; 119; MTCW

Peeslake, Gaffer
   See Durrell, Lawrence (George)

Peguy, Charles Pierre
   1873-1914 .... TCLC 10
   See also CA 107

Pena, Ramon del Valle y
   See Valle-Inclan, Ramon (Maria) del

Pendennis, Arthur Esquir
   See Thackeray, William Makepeace

Pepys, Samuel 1633-1703........... LC 11
   See also CDBLB 1660-1789; DLB 101;
   WLC

Percy, Walker
   1916-1990 ... CLC 2, 3, 6, 8, 14, 18, 47,
                                              65
   See also CA 1-4R; 131; CANR 1, 23;
   DLB 2; DLBY 80, 90; MTCW

Perec, Georges 1936-1982 .... CLC 56
   See also DLB 83

Pereda (y Sanchez de Porrua), Jose Maria de
   1833-1906 .... TCLC 16
   See also CA 117

Pereda y Porrua, Jose Maria de
   See Pereda (y Sanchez de Porrua), Jose
   Maria de

Peregoy, George Weems
   See Mencken, H(enry) L(ouis)

Perelman, S(idney) J(oseph)
   1904-1979 ... CLC 3, 5, 9, 15, 23, 44, 49
   See also AITN 1, 2; CA 73-76; 89-92;
   CANR 18; DLB 11, 44; MTCW

Peret, Benjamin 1899-1959 .... TCLC 20
   See also CA 117

Peretz, Isaac Loeb 1851(?)-1915... TCLC 16
   See also CA 109

Peretz, Yitzkhok Leibush
   See Peretz, Isaac Loeb

Perez Galdos, Benito 1843-1920... TCLC 27
   See also CA 125; HW

Perrault, Charles 1628-1703 .... LC 2
   See also MAICYA; SATA 25

Perry, Brighton
   See Sherwood, Robert E(mmet)

Perse, Saint-John
   See Leger, (Marie-Rene) Alexis Saint-Leger

Perse, St.-John .... CLC 4, 11, 46
   See also Leger, (Marie-Rene) Alexis
   Saint-Leger

Peseenz, Tulio F.
   See Lopez y Fuentes, Gregorio

Pesetsky, Bette 1932-............. CLC 28
   See also CA 133

Peshkov, Alexei Maximovich 1868-1936
   See Gorky, Maxim
   See also CA 105

Pessoa, Fernando (Antonio Nogueira)
   1888-1935 .... TCLC 27
   See also CA 125

Potter, Beatrice
See Webb, (Martha) Beatrice (Potter)
See also MAICYA

Potter, Dennis (Christopher George)
1935- . . . . **CLC 58**
See also CA 107; CANR 33; MTCW

Pound, Ezra (Weston Loomis)
1885-1972 . . . . . **CLC 1, 2, 3, 4, 5, 7, 10,**
13, 18, 34, 48, 50; PC 4
See also CA 5-8R; 37-40R; CANR 40;
CDALB 1917-1929; DLB 4, 45, 63;
MTCW; WLC

Povod, Reinaldo 1959- . . . . **CLC 44**
See also CA 136

Powell, Anthony (Dymoke)
1905- . . . . **CLC 1, 3, 7, 9, 10, 31**
See also CA 1-4R; CANR 1, 32;
CDBLB 1945-1960; DLB 15; MTCW

Powell, Dawn 1897-1965 . . . . **CLC 66**
See also CA 5-8R

Powell, Padgett 1952- . . . . **CLC 34**
See also CA 126

Powers, J(ames) F(arl)
1917- . . . . **CLC 1, 4, 8, 57; SSC 4**
See also CA 1-4R; CANR 2; MTCW

Powers, John J(ames) 1945-
See Powers, John R.
See also CA 69-72

Powers, John R. . . . . **CLC 66**
See also Powers, John J(ames)

Pownall, David 1938- . . . . **CLC 10**
See also CA 89-92; DLB 14

Powys, John Cowper
1872-1963 . . . . **CLC 7, 9, 15, 46**
See also CA 85-88; DLB 15; MTCW

Powys, T(heodore) F(rancis)
1875-1953 . . . . **TCLC 9**
See also CA 106; DLB 36

Prager, Emily 1952- . . . . **CLC 56**

Pratt, Edwin John 1883-1964 . . . . . . **CLC 19**
See also CA 93-96; DLB 92

Premchand . . . . **TCLC 21**
See also Srivastava, Dhanpat Rai

Preussler, Otfried 1923- . . . . **CLC 17**
See also CA 77-80; SATA 24

Prevert, Jacques (Henri Marie)
1900-1977 . . . . **CLC 15**
See also CA 77-80; 69-72; CANR 29;
MTCW; SATA 30

Prevost, Abbe (Antoine Francois)
1697-1763 . . . . **LC 1**

Price, (Edward) Reynolds
1933- . . . . **CLC 3, 6, 13, 43, 50, 63**
See also CA 1-4R; CANR 1, 37; DLB 2

Price, Richard 1949- . . . . **CLC 6, 12**
See also CA 49-52; CANR 3; DLBY 81

Prichard, Katharine Susannah
1883-1969 . . . . **CLC 46**
See also CA 11-12; CANR 33; CAP 1;
MTCW; SATA 66

Priestley, J(ohn) B(oynton)
1894-1984 . . . . **CLC 2, 5, 9, 34**
See also CA 9-12R; 113; CANR 33;
CDBLB 1914-1945; DLB 10, 34, 77, 100;
DLBY 84; MTCW

Prince, F(rank) T(empleton) 1912- . . **CLC 22**
See also CA 101; DLB 20

Prince 1958(?)- . . . . **CLC 35**

Prince Kropotkin
See Kropotkin, Peter (Aleksieevich)

Prior, Matthew 1664-1721 . . . . **LC 4**
See also DLB 95

Pritchard, William H(arrison)
1932- . . . . **CLC 34**
See also CA 65-68; CANR 23; DLB 111

Pritchett, V(ictor) S(awdon)
1900- . . . . **CLC 5, 13, 15, 41**
See also CA 61-64; CANR 31; DLB 15;
MTCW

Private 19022
See Manning, Frederic

Probst, Mark 1925- . . . . **CLC 59**
See also CA 130

Prokosch, Frederic 1908-1989 . . . . **CLC 4, 48**
See also CA 73-76; 128; DLB 48

Prophet, The
See Dreiser, Theodore (Herman Albert)

Prose, Francine 1947- . . . . **CLC 45**
See also CA 109; 112

Proudhon
See Cunha, Euclides (Rodrigues Pimenta) da

Proust,
(Valentin-Louis-George-Eugenc-)Marcel
1871-1922 . . . . **TCLC 7, 13, 33**
See also CA 104; 120; DLB 65; MTCW;
WLC

Prowler, Harley
See Masters, Edgar Lee

Prus, Boleslaw . . . . **TCLC 48**
See also Glowacki, Aleksander

Pryor, Richard (Franklin Lenox Thomas)
1940- . . . . **CLC 26**
See also CA 122

Przybyszewski, Stanislaw
1868-1927 . . . . **TCLC 36**
See also DLB 66

Pteleon
See Grieve, C(hristopher) M(urray)

Puckett, Lute
See Masters, Edgar Lee

Puig, Manuel
1932-1990 . . . . **CLC 3, 5, 10, 28, 65**
See also CA 45-48; CANR 2, 32; DLB 113;
HW; MTCW

Purdy, A(lfred) W(ellington)
1918- . . . . **CLC 3, 6, 14, 50**
See also Purdy, Al
See also CA 81-84

Purdy, Al
See Purdy, A(lfred) W(ellington)
See also DLB 88

Purdy, James (Amos)
1923- . . . . **CLC 2, 4, 10, 28, 52**
See also CA 33-36R; CAAS 1; CANR 19;
DLB 2; MTCW

Pure, Simon
See Swinnerton, Frank Arthur

Pushkin, Alexander (Sergeyevich)
1799-1837 . . . . **NCLC 3, 27**
See also SATA 61; WLC

P'u Sung-ling 1640-1715 . . . . **LC 3**

Putnam, Arthur Lee
See Alger, Horatio Jr.

Puzo, Mario 1920- . . . . **CLC 1, 2, 6, 36**
See also CA 65-68; CANR 4; DLB 6;
MTCW

Pym, Barbara (Mary Crampton)
1913-1980 . . . . **CLC 13, 19, 37**
See also CA 13-14; 97-100; CANR 13, 34;
CAP 1; DLB 14; DLBY 87; MTCW

Pynchon, Thomas (Ruggles Jr.)
1937- . . **CLC 2, 3, 6, 9, 11, 18, 33, 62, 72**
See also BEST 90:2; CA 17-20R; CANR 22;
DLB 2; MTCW; WLC

Qian Zhongshu
See Ch'ien Chung-shu

Qroll
See Dagerman, Stig (Halvard)

Quarrington, Paul (Lewis) 1953- . . . . **CLC 65**
See also CA 129

Quasimodo, Salvatore 1901-1968 . . . **CLC 10**
See also CA 13-16; 25-28R; CAP 1;
DLB 114; MTCW

Queen, Ellery . . . . **CLC 3, 11**
See also Dannay, Frederic; Davidson,
Avram; Lee, Manfred B(ennington);
Sturgeon, Theodore (Hamilton); Vance,
John Holbrook

Queen, Ellery Jr.
See Dannay, Frederic; Lee, Manfred
B(ennington)

Queneau, Raymond
1903-1976 . . . . **CLC 2, 5, 10, 42**
See also CA 77-80; 69-72; CANR 32;
DLB 72; MTCW

Quin, Ann (Marie) 1936-1973 . . . . **CLC 6**
See also CA 9-12R; 45-48; DLB 14

Quinn, Martin
See Smith, Martin Cruz

Quinn, Simon
See Smith, Martin Cruz

Quiroga, Horacio (Sylvestre)
1878-1937 . . . . **TCLC 20**
See also CA 117; 131; HW; MTCW

Quoirez, Francoise 1935- . . . . **CLC 9**
See also Sagan, Francoise
See also CA 49-52; CANR 6, 39; MTCW

Raabe, Wilhelm 1831-1910 . . . . **TCLC 45**

Rabe, David (William) 1940- . . . **CLC 4, 8, 33**
See also CA 85-88; CABS 3; DLB 7

Rabelais, Francois 1483-1553 . . . . **LC 5**
See also WLC

Rabinovitch, Sholem 1859-1916
See Aleichem, Sholom
See also CA 104

Radcliffe, Ann (Ward) 1764-1823 . . **NCLC 6**
See also DLB 39

Radiguet, Raymond 1903-1923 . . . . **TCLC 29**
See also DLB 65

Radnoti, Miklos 1909-1944 . . . . **TCLC 16**
See also CA 118

Rado, James 1939-.............. CLC 17
See also CA 105

Radvanyi, Netty 1900-1983
See Seghers, Anna
See also CA 85-88; 110

Raeburn, John (Hay) 1941-........ CLC 34
See also CA 57-60

Ragni, Gerome 1942-1991 .... CLC 17
See also CA 105; 134

Rahv, Philip..................... CLC 24
See also Greenberg, Ivan

Raine, Craig 1944-.............. CLC 32
See also CA 108; CANR 29; DLB 40

Raine, Kathleen (Jessie) 1908- ... CLC 7, 45
See also CA 85-88; DLB 20; MTCW

Rainis, Janis 1865-1929......... TCLC 29

Rakosi, Carl..................... CLC 47
See also Rawley, Callman
See also CAAS 5

Raleigh, Richard
See Lovecraft, H(oward) P(hillips)

Rallentando, H. P.
See Sayers, Dorothy L(eigh)

Ramal, Walter
See de la Mare, Walter (John)

Ramon, Juan
See Jimenez (Mantecon), Juan Ramon

Ramos, Graciliano 1892-1953 ..... TCLC 32

Rampersad, Arnold 1941-......... CLC 44
See also CA 127; 133; DLB 111

Rampling, Anne
See Rice, Anne

Ramuz, Charles-Ferdinand
1878-1947 .... TCLC 33

Rand, Ayn 1905-1982....... CLC 3, 30, 44
See also AAYA 10; CA 13-16R; 105;
CANR 27; MTCW; WLC

Randall, Dudley (Felker) 1914-...... CLC 1
See also BLC 3; BW; CA 25-28R;
CANR 23; DLB 41

Randall, Robert
See Silverberg, Robert

Ranger, Ken
See Creasey, John

Ransom, John Crowe
1888-1974 .... CLC 2, 4, 5, 11, 24
See also CA 5-8R; 49-52; CANR 6, 34;
DLB 45, 63; MTCW

Rao, Raja 1909-.............. CLC 25, 56
See also CA 73-76; MTCW

Raphael, Frederic (Michael)
1931-....................... CLC 2, 14
See also CA 1-4R; CANR 1; DLB 14

Ratcliffe, James P.
See Mencken, H(enry) L(ouis)

Rathbone, Julian 1935- .... CLC 41
See also CA 101; CANR 34

Rattigan, Terence (Mervyn)
1911-1977 .... CLC 7
See also CA 85-88; 73-76;
CDBLB 1945-1960; DLB 13; MTCW

Ratushinskaya, Irina 1954- .... CLC 54
See also CA 129

Raven, Simon (Arthur Noel)
1927-...................... CLC 14
See also CA 81-84

Rawley, Callman 1903-
See Rakosi, Carl
See also CA 21-24R; CANR 12, 32

Rawlings, Marjorie Kinnan
1896-1953 .... TCLC 4
See also CA 104; 137; DLB 9, 22, 102;
MAICYA; YABC 1

Ray, Satyajit 1921-.............. CLC 16
See also CA 114; 137

Read, Herbert Edward 1893-1968.... CLC 4
See also CA 85-88; 25-28R; DLB 20

Read, Piers Paul 1941- ...... CLC 4, 10, 25
See also CA 21-24R; CANR 38; DLB 14;
SATA 21

Reade, Charles 1814-1884 .... NCLC 2
See also DLB 21

Reade, Hamish
See Gray, Simon (James Holliday)

Reading, Peter 1946-............. CLC 47
See also CA 103; DLB 40

Reaney, James 1926-............. CLC 13
See also CA 41-44R; CAAS 15; DLB 68;
SATA 43

Rebreanu, Liviu 1885-1944 .... TCLC 28

Rechy, John (Francisco)
1934-................. CLC 1, 7, 14, 18
See also CA 5-8R; CAAS 4; CANR 6, 32;
DLB 122; DLBY 82; HW

Redcam, Tom 1870-1933 .... TCLC 25

Reddin, Keith..................... CLC 67

Redgrove, Peter (William)
1932-...................... CLC 6, 41
See also CA 1-4R; CANR 3, 39; DLB 40

Redmon, Anne.................... CLC 22
See also Nightingale, Anne Redmon
See also DLBY 86

Reed, Eliot
See Ambler, Eric

Reed, Ishmael
1938-........ CLC 2, 3, 5, 6, 13, 32, 60
See also BLC 3; BW; CA 21-24R;
CANR 25; DLB 2, 5, 33; DLBD 8;
MTCW

Reed, John (Silas) 1887-1920 ...... TCLC 9
See also CA 106

Reed, Lou........................ CLC 21
See also Firbank, Louis

Reeve, Clara 1729-1807 .... NCLC 19
See also DLB 39

Reid, Christopher 1949-........... CLC 33
See also DLB 40

Reid, Desmond
See Moorcock, Michael (John)

Reid Banks, Lynne 1929-
See Banks, Lynne Reid
See also CA 1-4R; CANR 6, 22, 38;
CLR 24; MAICYA; SATA 22

Reilly, William K.
See Creasey, John

Reiner, Max
See Caldwell, (Janet Miriam) Taylor
(Holland)

Reis, Ricardo
See Pessoa, Fernando (Antonio Nogueira)

Remarque, Erich Maria
1898-1970 .... CLC 21
See also CA 77-80; 29-32R; DLB 56;
MTCW

Remizov, A.
See Remizov, Aleksei (Mikhailovich)

Remizov, A. M.
See Remizov, Aleksei (Mikhailovich)

Remizov, Aleksei (Mikhailovich)
1877-1957 .... TCLC 27
See also CA 125; 133

Renan, Joseph Ernest
1823-1892 .... NCLC 26

Renard, Jules 1864-1910 .... TCLC 17
See also CA 117

Renault, Mary............... CLC 3, 11, 17
See also Challans, Mary
See also DLBY 83

Rendell, Ruth (Barbara) 1930- .. CLC 28, 48
See also Vine, Barbara
See also CA 109; CANR 32; DLB 87;
MTCW

Renoir, Jean 1894-1979.......... CLC 20
See also CA 129; 85-88

Resnais, Alain 1922-............. CLC 16

Reverdy, Pierre 1889-1960 .... CLC 53
See also CA 97-100; 89-92

Rexroth, Kenneth
1905-1982 ...... CLC 1, 2, 6, 11, 22, 49
See also CA 5-8R; 107; CANR 14, 34;
CDALB 1941-1968; DLB 16, 48;
DLBY 82; MTCW

Reyes, Alfonso 1889-1959 .... TCLC 33
See also CA 131; HW

Reyes y Basoalto, Ricardo Eliecer Neftali
See Neruda, Pablo

Reymont, Wladyslaw (Stanislaw)
1868(?)-1925 .... TCLC 5
See also CA 104

Reynolds, Jonathan 1942-........ CLC 6, 38
See also CA 65-68; CANR 28

Reynolds, Joshua 1723-1792 .... LC 15
See also DLB 104

Reynolds, Michael Shane 1937- .... CLC 44
See also CA 65-68; CANR 9

Reznikoff, Charles 1894-1976 .... CLC 9
See also CA 33-36; 61-64; CAP 2; DLB 28,
45

Rezzori (d'Arezzo), Gregor von
1914-...................... CLC 25
See also CA 122; 136

Rhine, Richard
See Silverstein, Alvin

Rhys, Jean
1890(?)-1979 .... CLC 2, 4, 6, 14, 19, 51
See also CA 25-28R; 85-88; CANR 35;
CDBLB 1945-1960; DLB 36, 117; MTCW

Ribeiro, Darcy 1922-............. CLC 34
See also CA 33-36R

Ribeiro, Joao Ubaldo (Osorio Pimentel)
1941- . . . . CLC **10, 67**
See also CA 81-84

Ribman, Ronald (Burt) 1932- . . . . CLC **7**
See also CA 21-24R

Ricci, Nino 1959- . . . . CLC **70**
See also CA 137

Rice, Anne 1941- . . . . CLC **41**
See also AAYA 9; BEST 89:2; CA 65-68;
CANR 12, 36

Rice, Elmer (Leopold)
1892-1967 . . . . CLC **7, 49**
See also CA 21-22; 25-28R; CAP 2; DLB 4,
7; MTCW

Rice, Tim 1944- . . . . CLC **21**
See also CA 103

Rich, Adrienne (Cecile)
1929- . . . . . . CLC **3, 6, 7, 11, 18, 36, 73;**
PC **5**
See also CA 9-12R; CANR 20; DLB 5, 67;
MTCW

Rich, Barbara
See Graves, Robert (von Ranke)

Rich, Robert
See Trumbo, Dalton

Richards, David Adams 1950- . . . . . . CLC **59**
See also CA 93-96; DLB 53

Richards, I(vor) A(rmstrong)
1893-1979 . . . . CLC **14, 24**
See also CA 41-44R; 89-92; CANR 34;
DLB 27

Richardson, Anne
See Roiphe, Anne Richardson

Richardson, Dorothy Miller
1873-1957 . . . . TCLC **3**
See also CA 104; DLB 36

Richardson, Ethel Florence (Lindesay)
1870-1946
See Richardson, Henry Handel
See also CA 105

Richardson, Henry Handel . . . . TCLC **4**
See also Richardson, Ethel Florence
(Lindesay)

Richardson, Samuel 1689-1761 . . . . LC **1**
See also CDBLB 1660-1789; DLB 39; WLC

Richler, Mordecai
1931- . . . . CLC **3, 5, 9, 13, 18, 46, 70**
See also AITN 1; CA 65-68; CANR 31;
CLR 17; DLB 53; MAICYA; MTCW;
SATA 27, 44

Richter, Conrad (Michael)
1890-1968 . . . . CLC **30**
See also CA 5-8R; 25-28R; CANR 23;
DLB 9; MTCW; SATA 3

Riddell, J. H. 1832-1906 . . . . TCLC **40**

Riding, Laura . . . . CLC **3, 7**
See also Jackson, Laura (Riding)

Riefenstahl, Berta Helene Amalia 1902-
See Riefenstahl, Leni
See also CA 108

Riefenstahl, Leni . . . . CLC **16**
See also Riefenstahl, Berta Helene Amalia

Riffe, Ernest
See Bergman, (Ernst) Ingmar

Riley, Tex
See Creasey, John

Rilke, Rainer Maria
1875-1926 . . . . TCLC **1, 6, 19;** PC **2**
See also CA 104; 132; DLB 81; MTCW

Rimbaud, (Jean Nicolas) Arthur
1854-1891 . . . . NCLC **4, 35;** PC **3**
See also WLC

Ringmaster, The
See Mencken, H(enry) L(ouis)

Ringwood, Gwen(dolyn Margaret) Pharis
1910-1984 . . . . CLC **48**
See also CA 112; DLB 88

Rio, Michel 19(?)- . . . . CLC **43**

Ritsos, Glannes
See Ritsos, Yannis

Ritsos, Yannis 1909-1990 . . . . . CLC **6, 13, 31**
See also CA 77-80; 133; CANR 39; MTCW

Ritter, Erika 1948(?)- . . . . CLC **52**

Rivera, Jose Eustasio 1889-1928 . . . TCLC **35**
See also HW

Rivers, Conrad Kent 1933-1968 . . . . . . CLC **1**
See also BW; CA 85-88; DLB 41

Rivers, Elfrida
See Bradley, Marion Zimmer

Riverside, John
See Heinlein, Robert A(nson)

Rizal, Jose 1861-1896 . . . . NCLC **27**

Roa Bastos, Augusto (Antonio)
1917- . . . . CLC **45**
See also CA 131; DLB 113; HW

Robbe-Grillet, Alain
1922- . . . . . . CLC **1, 2, 4, 6, 8, 10, 14, 43**
See also CA 9-12R; CANR 33; DLB 83;
MTCW

Robbins, Harold 1916- . . . . CLC **5**
See also CA 73-76; CANR 26; MTCW

Robbins, Thomas Eugene 1936-
See Robbins, Tom
See also CA 81-84; CANR 29; MTCW

Robbins, Tom . . . . CLC **9, 32, 64**
See also Robbins, Thomas Eugene
See also BEST 90:3; DLBY 80

Robbins, Trina 1938- . . . . CLC **21**
See also CA 128

Roberts, Charles G(eorge) D(ouglas)
1860-1943 . . . . TCLC **8**
See also CA 105; DLB 92; SATA 29

Roberts, Kate 1891-1985 . . . . CLC **15**
See also CA 107; 116

Roberts, Keith (John Kingston)
1935- . . . . CLC **14**
See also CA 25-28R

Roberts, Kenneth (Lewis)
1885-1957 . . . . TCLC **23**
See also CA 109; DLB 9

Roberts, Michele (B.) 1949- . . . . CLC **48**
See also CA 115

Robertson, Ellis
See Ellison, Harlan; Silverberg, Robert

Robertson, Thomas William
1829-1871 . . . . NCLC **35**

Robinson, Edwin Arlington
1869-1935 . . . . TCLC **5;** PC **1**
See also CA 104; 133; CDALB 1865-1917;
DLB 54; MTCW

Robinson, Henry Crabb
1775-1867 . . . . NCLC **15**
See also DLB 107

Robinson, Jill 1936- . . . . CLC **10**
See also CA 102

Robinson, Kim Stanley 1952- . . . . CLC **34**
See also CA 126

Robinson, Lloyd
See Silverberg, Robert

Robinson, Marilynne 1944- . . . . CLC **25**
See also CA 116

Robinson, Smokey . . . . CLC **21**
See also Robinson, William Jr.

Robinson, William Jr. 1940-
See Robinson, Smokey
See also CA 116

Robison, Mary 1949- . . . . CLC **42**
See also CA 113; 116

Roddenberry, Eugene Wesley 1921-1991
See Roddenberry, Gene
See also CA 110; 135; CANR 37; SATA 45

Roddenberry, Gene . . . . CLC **17**
See also Roddenberry, Eugene Wesley
See also AAYA 5; SATO 69

Rodgers, Mary 1931- . . . . CLC **12**
See also CA 49-52; CANR 8; CLR 20;
MAICYA; SATA 8

Rodgers, W(illiam) R(obert)
1909-1969 . . . . CLC **7**
See also CA 85-88; DLB 20

Rodman, Eric
See Silverberg, Robert

Rodman, Howard 1920(?)-1985 . . . . . CLC **65**
See also CA 118

Rodman, Maia
See Wojciechowska, Maia (Teresa)

Rodriguez, Claudio 1934- . . . . CLC **10**

Roelvaag, O(le) E(dvart)
1876-1931 . . . . TCLC **17**
See also CA 117; DLB 9

Roethke, Theodore (Huebner)
1908-1963 . . . . . . CLC **1, 3, 8, 11, 19, 46**
See also CA 81-84; CABS 2;
CDALB 1941-1968; DLB 5; MTCW

Rogers, Thomas Hunter 1927- . . . . . CLC **57**
See also CA 89-92

Rogers, Will(iam Penn Adair)
1879-1935 . . . . TCLC **8**
See also CA 105; DLB 11

Rogin, Gilbert 1929- . . . . CLC **18**
See also CA 65-68; CANR 15

Rohan, Koda . . . . TCLC **22**
See also Koda Shigeyuki

Rohmer, Eric . . . . CLC **16**
See also Scherer, Jean-Marie Maurice

Rohmer, Sax . . . . TCLC **28**
See also Ward, Arthur Henry Sarsfield
See also DLB 70

Roiphe, Anne Richardson 1935- . . . CLC **3, 9**
See also CA 89-92; DLBY 80

Rolfe, Frederick (William Serafino Austin Lewis Mary) 1860-1913...... TCLC 12
See also CA 107; DLB 34

Rolland, Romain 1866-1944....... TCLC 23
See also CA 118; DLB 65

Rolvaag, O(le) E(dvart)
See Roelvaag, O(le) E(dvart)

Romain Arnaud, Saint
See Aragon, Louis

Romains, Jules 1885-1972.......... CLC 7
See also CA 85-88; CANR 34; DLB 65;
MTCW

Romero, Jose Ruben 1890-1952 ... TCLC 14
See also CA 114; 131; HW

Ronsard, Pierre de 1524-1585........ LC 6

Rooke, Leon 1934-............ CLC 25, 34
See also CA 25-28R; CANR 23

Roper, William 1498-1578.......... LC 10

Roquelaure, A. N.
See Rice, Anne

Rosa, Joao Guimaraes 1908-1967 ... CLC 23
See also CA 89-92; DLB 113

Rosen, Richard (Dean) 1949-....... CLC 39
See also CA 77-80

Rosenberg, Isaac 1890-1918....... TCLC 12
See also CA 107; DLB 20

Rosenblatt, Joe .... CLC 15
See also Rosenblatt, Joseph

Rosenblatt, Joseph 1933-
See Rosenblatt, Joe
See also CA 89-92

Rosenfeld, Samuel 1896-1963
See Tzara, Tristan
See also CA 89-92

Rosenthal, M(acha) L(ouis) 1917-... CLC 28
See also CA 1-4R; CAAS 6; CANR 4;
DLB 5; SATA 59

Ross, Barnaby
See Dannay, Frederic

Ross, Bernard L.
See Follett, Ken(neth Martin)

Ross, J. H.
See Lawrence, T(homas) E(dward)

Ross, (James) Sinclair 1908-....... CLC 13
See also CA 73-76; DLB 88

Rossetti, Christina (Georgina)
1830-1894 .... NCLC 2
See also DLB 35; MAICYA; SATA 20;
WLC

Rossetti, Dante Gabriel
1828-1882 .... NCLC 4
See also CDBLB 1832-1890; DLB 35; WLC

Rossner, Judith (Perelman)
1935- .... CLC 6, 9, 29
See also AITN 2; BEST 90:3; CA 17-20R;
CANR 18; DLB 6; MTCW

Rostand, Edmond (Eugene Alexis)
1868-1918 .... TCLC 6, 37
See also CA 104; 126; MTCW

Roth, Henry 1906-........... CLC 2, 6, 11
See also CA 11-12; CANR 38; CAP 1;
DLB 28; MTCW

Roth, Joseph 1894-1939......... TCLC 33
See also DLB 85

Roth, Philip (Milton)
1933- ...... CLC 1, 2, 3, 4, 6, 9, 15, 22,
31, 47, 66
See also BEST 90:3; CA 1-4R; CANR 1, 22,
36; CDALB 1968-1988; DLB 2, 28;
DLBY 82; MTCW; WLC

Rothenberg, Jerome 1931-....... CLC 6, 57
See also CA 45-48; CANR 1; DLB 5

Roumain, Jacques (Jean Baptiste)
1907-1944 .... TCLC 19
See also BLC 3; BW; CA 117; 125

Rourke, Constance (Mayfield)
1885-1941 .... TCLC 12
See also CA 107; YABC 1

Rousseau, Jean-Baptiste 1671-1741 ... LC 9

Rousseau, Jean-Jacques 1712-1778... LC 14
See also WLC

Roussel, Raymond 1877-1933 ..... TCLC 20
See also CA 117

Rovit, Earl (Herbert) 1927-......... CLC 7
See also CA 5-8R; CANR 12

Rowe, Nicholas 1674-1718.......... LC 8
See also DLB 84

Rowley, Ames Dorrance
See Lovecraft, H(oward) P(hillips)

Rowson, Susanna Haswell
1762(?)-1824 .... NCLC 5
See also DLB 37

Roy, Gabrielle 1909-1983....... CLC 10, 14
See also CA 53-56; 110; CANR 5; DLB 68;
MTCW

Rozewicz, Tadeusz 1921-........ CLC 9, 23
See also CA 108; CANR 36; MTCW

Ruark, Gibbons 1941- .... CLC 3
See also CA 33-36R; CANR 14, 31;
DLB 120

Rubens, Bernice (Ruth) 1923-... CLC 19, 31
See also CA 25-28R; CANR 33; DLB 14;
MTCW

Rudkin, (James) David 1936- ...... CLC 14
See also CA 89-92; DLB 13

Rudnik, Raphael 1933-............. CLC 7
See also CA 29-32R

Ruffian, M.
See Hasek, Jaroslav (Matej Frantisek)

Ruiz, Jose Martinez .... CLC 11
See also Martinez Ruiz, Jose

Rukeyser, Muriel
1913-1980 .... CLC 6, 10, 15, 27
See also CA 5-8R; 93-96; CANR 26;
DLB 48; MTCW; SATA 22

Rule, Jane (Vance) 1931-........ CLC 27
See also CA 25-28R; CANR 12; DLB 60

Rulfo, Juan 1918-1986............ CLC 8
See also CA 85-88; 118; CANR 26;
DLB 113; HW; MTCW

Runyon, (Alfred) Damon
1884(?)-1946 .... TCLC 10
See also CA 107; DLB 11, 86

Rush, Norman 1933-............. CLC 44
See also CA 121; 126

Rushdie, (Ahmed) Salman
1947- .... CLC 23, 31, 55
See also BEST 89:3; CA 108; 111;
CANR 33; MTCW

Rushforth, Peter (Scott) 1945- ..... CLC 19
See also CA 101

Ruskin, John 1819-1900.......... TCLC 20
See also CA 114; 129; CDBLB 1832-1890;
DLB 55; SATA 24

Russ, Joanna 1937-............... CLC 15
See also CA 25-28R; CANR 11, 31; DLB 8;
MTCW

Russell, George William 1867-1935
See A. E.
See also CA 104; CDBLB 1890-1914

Russell, (Henry) Ken(neth Alfred)
1927- .... CLC 16
See also CA 105

Russell, Willy 1947-............... CLC 60

Rutherford, Mark .... TCLC 25
See also White, William Hale
See also DLB 18

Ruyslinck, Ward
See Belser, Reimond Karel Maria de

Ryan, Cornelius (John) 1920-1974 ... CLC 7
See also CA 69-72; 53-56; CANR 38

Ryan, Michael 1946- .... CLC 65
See also CA 49-52; DLBY 82

Rybakov, Anatoli (Naumovich)
1911- .... CLC 23, 53
See also CA 126; 135

Ryder, Jonathan
See Ludlum, Robert

Ryga, George 1932-1987 .... CLC 14
See also CA 101; 124; DLB 60

S. S.
See Sassoon, Siegfried (Lorraine)

Saba, Umberto 1883-1957 .... TCLC 33
See also DLB 114

Sabatini, Rafael 1875-1950 .... TCLC 47

Sabato, Ernesto (R.) 1911-...... CLC 10, 23
See also CA 97-100; CANR 32; HW;
MTCW

Sacastru, Martin
See Bioy Casares, Adolfo

Sacher-Masoch, Leopold von
1836(?)-1895 .... NCLC 31

Sachs, Marilyn (Stickle) 1927- ..... CLC 35
See also AAYA 2; CA 17-20R; CANR 13;
CLR 2; MAICYA; SAAS 2; SATA 3, 68

Sachs, Nelly 1891-1970 .... CLC 14
See also CA 17-18; 25-28R; CAP 2

Sackler, Howard (Oliver)
1929-1982 .... CLC 14
See also CA 61-64; 108; CANR 30; DLB 7

Sacks, Oliver (Wolf) 1933- .... CLC 67
See also CA 53-56; CANR 28; MTCW

Sade, Donatien Alphonse Francois Comte
1740-1814 .... NCLC 3

Sadoff, Ira 1945-................. CLC 9
See also CA 53-56; CANR 5, 21; DLB 120

Saetone
See Camus, Albert

Safire, William 1929-............. **CLC 10**
See also CA 17-20R; CANR 31

Sagan, Carl (Edward) 1934-....... **CLC 30**
See also AAYA 2; CA 25-28R; CANR 11,
36; MTCW; SATA 58

Sagan, Francoise .... **CLC 3, 6, 9, 17, 36**
See also Quoirez, Francoise
See also DLB 83

Sahgal, Nayantara (Pandit) 1927-... **CLC 41**
See also CA 9-12R; CANR 11

Saint, H(arry) F. 1941- .... **CLC 50**
See also CA 127

St. Aubin de Teran, Lisa 1953-
See Teran, Lisa St. Aubin de
See also CA 118; 126

Sainte-Beuve, Charles Augustin
1804-1869 .... **NCLC 5**

Saint-Exupery, Antoine (Jean Baptiste Marie
Roger) de 1900-1944 .... **TCLC 2**
See also CA 108; 132; CLR 10; DLB 72;
MAICYA; MTCW; SATA 20; WLC

St. John, David
See Hunt, E(verette) Howard Jr.

Saint-John Perse
See Leger, (Marie-Rene) Alexis Saint-Leger

Saintsbury, George (Edward Bateman)
1845-1933 .... **TCLC 31**
See also DLB 57

Sait Faik .... **TCLC 23**
See also Abasiyanik, Sait Faik

Saki .... **TCLC 3**
See also Munro, H(ector) H(ugh)

Salama, Hannu 1936-............ **CLC 18**

Salamanca, J(ack) R(ichard)
1922- .... **CLC 4, 15**
See also CA 25-28R

Sale, J. Kirkpatrick
See Sale, Kirkpatrick

Sale, Kirkpatrick 1937- .... **CLC 68**
See also CA 13-16R; CANR 10

Salinas (y Serrano), Pedro
1891(?)-1951 .... **TCLC 17**
See also CA 117

Salinger, J(erome) D(avid)
1919- .... **CLC 1, 3, 8, 12, 55, 56; SSC 2**
See also AAYA 2; CA 5-8R; CANR 39;
CDALB 1941-1968; CLR 18; DLB 2, 102;
MAICYA; MTCW; SATA 67; WLC

Salisbury, John
See Caute, David

Salter, James 1925- .... **CLC 7, 52, 59**
See also CA 73-76

Saltus, Edgar (Everton)
1855-1921 .... **TCLC 8**
See also CA 105

Saltykov, Mikhail Evgrafovich
1826-1889 .... **NCLC 16**

Samarakis, Antonis 1919- .... **CLC 5**
See also CA 25-28R; CAAS 16; CANR 36

Sanchez, Florencio 1875-1910 ..... **TCLC 37**
See also HW

Sanchez, Luis Rafael 1936-........ **CLC 23**
See also CA 128; HW

Sanchez, Sonia 1934-.............. **CLC 5**
See also BLC 3; BW; CA 33-36R;
CANR 24; CLR 18; DLB 41; DLBD 8;
MAICYA; MTCW; SATA 22

Sand, George 1804-1876......... **NCLC 2**
See also DLB 119; WLC

Sandburg, Carl (August)
1878-1967 ... **CLC 1, 4, 10, 15, 35; PC 2**
See also CA 5-8R; 25-28R; CANR 35;
CDALB 1865-1917; DLB 17, 54;
MAICYA; MTCW; SATA 8; WLC

Sandburg, Charles
See Sandburg, Carl (August)

Sandburg, Charles A.
See Sandburg, Carl (August)

Sanders, (James) Ed(ward) 1939-... **CLC 53**
See also CA 13-16R; CANR 13; DLB 16

Sanders, Lawrence 1920-......... **CLC 41**
See also BEST 89:4; CA 81-84; CANR 33;
MTCW

Sanders, Noah
See Blount, Roy (Alton) Jr.

Sanders, Winston P.
See Anderson, Poul (William)

Sandoz, Mari(e Susette)
1896-1966 .... **CLC 28**
See also CA 1-4R; 25-28R; CANR 17;
DLB 9; MTCW; SATA 5

Saner, Reg(inald Anthony) 1931- .... **CLC 9**
See also CA 65-68

Sannazaro, Jacopo 1456(?)-1530...... **LC 8**

Sansom, William 1912-1976....... **CLC 2, 6**
See also CA 5-8R; 65-68; MTCW

Santayana, George 1863-1952 ..... **TCLC 40**
See also CA 115; DLB 54, 71

Santiago, Danny .... **CLC 33**
See also James, Daniel (Lewis); James,
Daniel (Lewis)
See also DLB 122

Santmyer, Helen Hooven
1895-1986 .... **CLC 33**
See also CA 1-4R; 118; CANR 15, 33;
DLBY 84; MTCW

Santos, Bienvenido N(uqui) 1911-... **CLC 22**
See also CA 101; CANR 19

Sapper .... **TCLC 44**
See also McNeile, Herman Cyril

Sappho fl. 6th cent. B.C.-.... **CMLC 3; PC 5**

Sarduy, Severo 1937-.............. **CLC 6**
See also CA 89-92; DLB 113; HW

Sargeson, Frank 1903-1982........ **CLC 31**
See also CA 25-28R; 106; CANR 38

Sarmiento, Felix Ruben Garcia 1867-1916
See Dario, Ruben
See also CA 104

Saroyan, William
1908-1981 ..... **CLC 1, 8, 10, 29, 34, 56**
See also CA 5-8R; 103; CANR 30; DLB 7,
9, 86; DLBY 81; MTCW; SATA 23, 24;
WLC

Sarraute, Nathalie
1900- .... **CLC 1, 2, 4, 8, 10, 31**
See also CA 9-12R; CANR 23; DLB 83;
MTCW

Sarton, (Eleanor) May
1912- .... **CLC 4, 14, 49**
See also CA 1-4R; CANR 1, 34; DLB 48;
DLBY 81; MTCW; SATA 36

Sartre, Jean-Paul
1905-1980 ... **CLC 1, 4, 7, 9, 13, 18, 24,
44, 50, 52; DC 3**
See also CA 9-12R; 97-100; CANR 21;
DLB 72; MTCW; WLC

Sassoon, Siegfried (Lorraine)
1886-1967 .... **CLC 36**
See also CA 104; 25-28R; CANR 36;
DLB 20; MTCW

Satterfield, Charles
See Pohl, Frederik

Saul, John (W. III) 1942- .... **CLC 46**
See also AAYA 10; BEST 90:4; CA 81-84;
CANR 16, 40

Saunders, Caleb
See Heinlein, Robert A(nson)

Saura (Atares), Carlos 1932-....... **CLC 20**
See also CA 114; 131; HW

Sauser-Hall, Frederic 1887-1961.... **CLC 18**
See also CA 102; 93-96; CANR 36; MTCW

Saussure, Ferdinand de
1857-1913 .... **TCLC 49**

Savage, Catharine
See Brosman, Catharine Savage

Savage, Thomas 1915- .... **CLC 40**
See also CA 126; 132; CAAS 15

Savan, Glenn .... **CLC 50**

Saven, Glenn 19(?)- .... **CLC 50**

Sayers, Dorothy L(eigh)
1893-1957 .... **TCLC 2, 15**
See also CA 104; 119; CDBLB 1914-1945;
DLB 10, 36, 77, 100; MTCW

Sayers, Valerie 1952-.............. **CLC 50**
See also CA 134

Sayles, John Thomas 1950-... **CLC 7, 10, 14**
See also CA 57-60; DLB 44

Scammell, Michael .... **CLC 34**

Scannell, Vernon 1922- .... **CLC 49**
See also CA 5-8R; CANR 8, 24; DLB 27;
SATA 59

Scarlett, Susan
See Streatfeild, (Mary) Noel

Schaeffer, Susan Fromberg
1941- .... **CLC 6, 11, 22**
See also CA 49-52; CANR 18; DLB 28;
MTCW; SATA 22

Schary, Jill
See Robinson, Jill

Schell, Jonathan 1943-............ **CLC 35**
See also CA 73-76; CANR 12

Schelling, Friedrich Wilhelm Joseph von
1775-1854 .... **NCLC 30**
See also DLB 90

Scherer, Jean-Marie Maurice 1920-
See Rohmer, Eric
See also CA 110

Schevill, James (Erwin) 1920-....... **CLC 7**
See also CA 5-8R; CAAS 12

Schiller, Friedrich 1759-1805 .... **NCLC 39**
See also DLB 94

Shackleton, C. C.
See Aldiss, Brian W(ilson)

Shacochis, Bob .... CLC **39**
See also Shacochis, Robert G.

Shacochis, Robert G. 1951-
See Shacochis, Bob
See also CA 119; 124

Shaffer, Anthony (Joshua) 1926-.... CLC **19**
See also CA 110; 116; DLB 13

Shaffer, Peter (Levin)
1926- .... CLC **5, 14, 18, 37, 60**
See also CA 25-28R; CANR 25;
CDBLB 1960 to Present; DLB 13;
MTCW

Shakey, Bernard
See Young, Neil

Shalamov, Varlam (Tikhonovich)
1907(?)-1982 .... CLC **18**
See also CA 129; 105

Shamlu, Ahmad 1925- .... CLC **10**

Shammas, Anton 1951-............ CLC **55**

Shange, Ntozake
1948- .... CLC **8, 25, 38, 74; DC 3**
See also AAYA 9; BLC 3; BW; CA 85-88;
CABS 3; CANR 27; DLB 38; MTCW

Shanley, John Patrick 1950-....... CLC **75**
See also CA 128; 133

Shapcott, Thomas William 1935- ... CLC **38**
See also CA 69-72

Shapiro, Karl (Jay) 1913- .. CLC **4, 8, 15, 53**
See also CA 1-4R; CAAS 6; CANR 1, 36;
DLB 48; MTCW

Sharp, William 1855-1905 .... TCLC **39**

Sharpe, Thomas Ridley 1928-
See Sharpe, Tom
See also CA 114; 122

Sharpe, Tom...................... CLC **36**
See also Sharpe, Thomas Ridley
See also DLB 14

Shaw, Bernard................... TCLC **45**
See also Shaw, George Bernard

Shaw, G. Bernard
See Shaw, George Bernard

Shaw, George Bernard
1856-1950 .... TCLC **3, 9, 21**
See also Shaw, Bernard
See also CA 104; 128; CDBLB 1914-1945;
DLB 10, 57; MTCW; WLC

Shaw, Henry Wheeler
1818-1885 .... NCLC **15**
See also DLB 11

Shaw, Irwin 1913-1984....... CLC **7, 23, 34**
See also AITN 1; CA 13-16R; 112;
CANR 21; CDALB 1941-1968; DLB 6,
102; DLBY 84; MTCW

Shaw, Robert 1927-1978 .... CLC **5**
See also AITN 1; CA 1-4R; 81-84;
CANR 4; DLB 13, 14

Shaw, T. E.
See Lawrence, T(homas) E(dward)

Shawn, Wallace 1943- .... CLC **41**
See also CA 112

Sheed, Wilfrid (John Joseph)
1930- .... CLC **2, 4, 10, 53**
See also CA 65-68; CANR 30; DLB 6;
MTCW

Sheldon, Alice Hastings Bradley
1915(?)-1987
See Tiptree, James Jr.
See also CA 108; 122; CANR 34; MTCW

Sheldon, John
See Bloch, Robert (Albert)

Shelley, Mary Wollstonecraft (Godwin)
1797-1851 .... NCLC **14**
See also CDBLB 1789-1832; DLB 110, 116;
SATA 29; WLC

Shelley, Percy Bysshe
1792-1822 .... NCLC **18**
See also CDBLB 1789-1832; DLB 96, 110;
WLC

Shepard, Jim 1956-................ CLC **36**
See also CA 137

Shepard, Lucius 19(?)-............. CLC **34**
See also CA 128

Shepard, Sam
1943- .... CLC **4, 6, 17, 34, 41, 44**
See also AAYA 1; CA 69-72; CABS 3;
CANR 22; DLB 7; MTCW

Shepherd, Michael
See Ludlum, Robert

Sherburne, Zoa (Morin) 1912-...... CLC **30**
See also CA 1-4R; CANR 3, 37; MAICYA;
SATA 3

Sheridan, Frances 1724-1766........ LC **7**
See also DLB 39, 84

Sheridan, Richard Brinsley
1751-1816 .... NCLC **5; DC 1**
See also CDBLB 1660-1789; DLB 89; WLC

Sherman, Jonathan Marc.......... CLC **55**

Sherman, Martin 1941(?)-......... CLC **19**
See also CA 116; 123

Sherwin, Judith Johnson 1936-... CLC **7, 15**
See also CA 25-28R; CANR 34

Sherwood, Robert E(mmet)
1896-1955 .... TCLC **3**
See also CA 104; DLB 7, 26

Shiel, M(atthew) P(hipps)
1865-1947 .... TCLC **8**
See also CA 106

Shiga, Naoya 1883-1971.......... CLC **33**
See also CA 101; 33-36R

Shimazaki Haruki 1872-1943
See Shimazaki Toson
See also CA 105; 134

Shimazaki Toson................ TCLC **5**
See also Shimazaki Haruki

Sholokhov, Mikhail (Aleksandrovich)
1905-1984 .... CLC **7, 15**
See also CA 101; 112; MTCW; SATA 36

Shone, Patric
See Hanley, James

Shreve, Susan Richards 1939-...... CLC **23**
See also CA 49-52; CAAS 5; CANR 5, 38;
MAICYA; SATA 41, 46

Shue, Larry 1946-1985............ CLC **52**
See also CA 117

Shu-Jen, Chou 1881-1936
See Hsun, Lu
See also CA 104

Shulman, Alix Kates 1932- ...... CLC **2, 10**
See also CA 29-32R; SATA 7

Shuster, Joe 1914- .... CLC **21**

Shute, Nevil...................... CLC **30**
See also Norway, Nevil Shute

Shuttle, Penelope (Diane) 1947- ..... CLC **7**
See also CA 93-96; CANR 39; DLB 14, 40

Sidney, Mary 1561-1621 .... LC **19**

Sidney, Sir Philip 1554-1586....... LC **19**
See also CDBLB Before 1660

Siegel, Jerome 1914- .... CLC **21**
See also CA 116

Siegel, Jerry
See Siegel, Jerome

Sienkiewicz, Henryk (Adam Alexander Pius)
1846-1916 .... TCLC **3**
See also CA 104; 134

Sierra, Gregorio Martinez
See Martinez Sierra, Gregorio

Sierra, Maria (de la O'LeJarraga) Martinez
See Martinez Sierra, Maria (de la
O'LeJarraga)

Sigal, Clancy 1926-................ CLC **7**
See also CA 1-4R

Sigourney, Lydia Howard (Huntley)
1791-1865 .... NCLC **21**
See also DLB 1, 42, 73

Siguenza y Gongora, Carlos de
1645-1700 .... LC **8**

Sigurjonsson, Johann 1880-1919... TCLC **27**

Sikelianos, Angelos 1884-1951 .... TCLC **39**

Silkin, Jon 1930- .... CLC **2, 6, 43**
See also CA 5-8R; CAAS 5; DLB 27

Silko, Leslie Marmon 1948- .... CLC **23, 74**
See also CA 115; 122

Sillanpaa, Frans Eemil 1888-1964... CLC **19**
See also CA 129; 93-96; MTCW

Sillitoe, Alan
1928- .... CLC **1, 3, 6, 10, 19, 57**
See also AITN 1; CA 9-12R; CAAS 2;
CANR 8, 26; CDBLB 1960 to Present;
DLB 14; MTCW; SATA 61

Silone, Ignazio 1900-1978 .... CLC **4**
See also CA 25-28; 81-84; CANR 34;
CAP 2; MTCW

Silver, Joan Micklin 1935- .... CLC **20**
See also CA 114; 121

Silver, Nicholas
See Faust, Frederick (Schiller)

Silverberg, Robert 1935- .... CLC **7**
See also CA 1-4R; CAAS 3; CANR 1, 20,
36; DLB 8; MAICYA; MTCW; SATA 13

Silverstein, Alvin 1933-............ CLC **17**
See also CA 49-52; CANR 2; CLR 25;
MAICYA; SATA 8, 69

Silverstein, Virginia B(arbara Opshelor)
1937-........................ CLC **17**
See also CA 49-52; CANR 2; CLR 25;
MAICYA; SATA 8, 69

Snow, C(harles) P(ercy)
1905-1980 .... CLC 1, 4, 6, 9, 13, 19
See also CA 5-8R; 101; CANR 28;
CDBLB 1945-1960; DLB 15, 77; MTCW

Snow, Frances Compton
See Adams, Henry (Brooks)

Snyder, Gary (Sherman)
1930- .... CLC 1, 2, 5, 9, 32
See also CA 17-20R; CANR 30; DLB 5, 16

Snyder, Zilpha Keatley 1927- ...... CLC 17
See also CA 9-12R; CANR 38; MAICYA;
SAAS 2; SATA 1, 28

Soares, Bernardo
See Pessoa, Fernando (Antonio Nogueira)

Sobh, A.
See Shamlu, Ahmad

Sobol, Joshua.................... CLC 60

Soderberg, Hjalmar 1869-1941 .... TCLC 39

Sodergran, Edith (Irene)
See Soedergran, Edith (Irene)

Soedergran, Edith (Irene)
1892-1923 .... TCLC 31

Softly, Edgar
See Lovecraft, H(oward) P(hillips)

Softly, Edward
See Lovecraft, H(oward) P(hillips)

Sokolov, Raymond 1941- .... CLC 7
See also CA 85-88

Solo, Jay
See Ellison, Harlan

Sologub, Fyodor .... TCLC 9
See also Teternikov, Fyodor Kuzmich

Solomons, Ikey Esquir
See Thackeray, William Makepeace

Solomos, Dionysios 1798-1857 ... NCLC 15

Solwoska, Mara
See French, Marilyn

Solzhenitsyn, Aleksandr I(sayevich)
1918- ... CLC 1, 2, 4, 7, 9, 10, 18, 26, 34
See also AITN 1; CA 69-72; CANR 40;
MTCW; WLC

Somers, Jane
See Lessing, Doris (May)

Sommer, Scott 1951- .... CLC 25
See also CA 106

Sondheim, Stephen (Joshua)
1930- .... CLC 30, 39
See also CA 103

Sontag, Susan 1933-... CLC 1, 2, 10, 13, 31
See also CA 17-20R; CANR 25; DLB 2, 67;
MTCW

Sophocles
496(?)B.C.-406(?)B.C.... CMLC 2; DC 1

Sorel, Julia
See Drexler, Rosalyn

Sorrentino, Gilbert
1929- .... CLC 3, 7, 14, 22, 40
See also CA 77-80; CANR 14, 33; DLB 5;
DLBY 80

Soto, Gary 1952-................. CLC 32
See also AAYA 10; CA 119; 125; DLB 82;
HW

Soupault, Philippe 1897-1990 ...... CLC 68
See also CA 116; 131

Souster, (Holmes) Raymond
1921-......................... CLC 5, 14
See also CA 13-16R; CAAS 14; CANR 13,
29; DLB 88; SATA 63

Southern, Terry 1926- .... CLC 7
See also CA 1-4R; CANR 1; DLB 2

Southey, Robert 1774-1843 ...... NCLC 8
See also DLB 93, 107; SATA 54

Southworth, Emma Dorothy Eliza Nevitte
1819-1899 .... NCLC 26

Souza, Ernest
See Scott, Evelyn

Soyinka, Wole
1934- .... CLC 3, 5, 14, 36, 44; DC 2
See also BLC 3; BW; CA 13-16R;
CANR 27, 39; DLB 125; MTCW; WLC

Spackman, W(illiam) M(ode)
1905-1990 .... CLC 46
See also CA 81-84; 132

Spacks, Barry 1931-................ CLC 14
See also CA 29-32R; CANR 33; DLB 105

Spanidou, Irini 1946-.............. CLC 44

Spark, Muriel (Sarah)
1918- .... CLC 2, 3, 5, 8, 13, 18, 40;
SSC 10
See also CA 5-8R; CANR 12, 36;
CDBLB 1945-1960; DLB 15; MTCW

Spaulding, Douglas
See Bradbury, Ray (Douglas)

Spaulding, Leonard
See Bradbury, Ray (Douglas)

Spence, J. A. D.
See Eliot, T(homas) S(tearns)

Spencer, Elizabeth 1921-.......... CLC 22
See also CA 13-16R; CANR 32; DLB 6;
MTCW; SATA 14

Spencer, Leonard G.
See Silverberg, Robert

Spencer, Scott 1945-.............. CLC 30
See also CA 113; DLBY 86

Spender, Stephen (Harold)
1909- .... CLC 1, 2, 5, 10, 41
See also CA 9-12R; CANR 31;
CDBLB 1945-1960; DLB 20; MTCW

Spengler, Oswald (Arnold Gottfried)
1880-1936 .... TCLC 25
See also CA 118

Spenser, Edmund 1552(?)-1599 .... LC 5
See also CDBLB Before 1660; WLC

Spicer, Jack 1925-1965 ...... CLC 8, 18, 72
See also CA 85-88; DLB 5, 16

Spielberg, Peter 1929- .... CLC 6
See also CA 5-8R; CANR 4; DLBY 81

Spielberg, Steven 1947- .... CLC 20
See also AAYA 8; CA 77-80; CANR 32;
SATA 32

Spillane, Frank Morrison 1918-
See Spillane, Mickey
See also CA 25-28R; CANR 28; MTCW;
SATA 66

Spillane, Mickey .... CLC 3, 13
See also Spillane, Frank Morrison

Spinoza, Benedictus de 1632-1677 .... LC 9

Spinrad, Norman (Richard) 1940-... CLC 46
See also CA 37-40R; CANR 20; DLB 8

Spitteler, Carl (Friedrich Georg)
1845-1924 .... TCLC 12
See also CA 109

Spivack, Kathleen (Romola Drucker)
1938-........................ CLC 6
See also CA 49-52

Spoto, Donald 1941-.............. CLC 39
See also CA 65-68; CANR 11

Springsteen, Bruce (F.) 1949- ...... CLC 17
See also CA 111

Spurling, Hilary 1940-............ CLC 34
See also CA 104; CANR 25

Squires, Radcliffe 1917-.......... CLC 51
See also CA 1-4R; CANR 6, 21

Srivastava, Dhanpat Rai 1880(?)-1936
See Premchand
See also CA 118

Stacy, Donald
See Pohl, Frederik

Stael, Germaine de
See Stael-Holstein, Anne Louise Germaine
Necker Baronn
See also DLB 119

Stael-Holstein, Anne Louise Germaine Necker
Baronn 1766-1817 .... NCLC 3
See also Stael, Germaine de

Stafford, Jean 1915-1979... CLC 4, 7, 19, 68
See also CA 1-4R; 85-88; CANR 3; DLB 2;
MTCW; SATA 22

Stafford, William (Edgar)
1914- .... CLC 4, 7, 29
See also CA 5-8R; CAAS 3; CANR 5, 22;
DLB 5

Staines, Trevor
See Brunner, John (Kilian Houston)

Stairs, Gordon
See Austin, Mary (Hunter)

Stannard, Martin.................. CLC 44

Stanton, Maura 1946- .... CLC 9
See also CA 89-92; CANR 15; DLB 120

Stanton, Schuyler
See Baum, L(yman) Frank

Stapledon, (William) Olaf
1886-1950 .... TCLC 22
See also CA 111; DLB 15

Starbuck, George (Edwin) 1931-.... CLC 53
See also CA 21-24R; CANR 23

Stark, Richard
See Westlake, Donald E(dwin)

Staunton, Schuyler
See Baum, L(yman) Frank

Stead, Christina (Ellen)
1902-1983 ....CLC 2, 5, 8, 32
See also CA 13-16R; 109; CANR 33, 40;
MTCW

Stead, William Thomas
1849-1912 .... TCLC 48

Steele, Richard 1672-1729.......... LC 18
See also CDBLB 1660-1789; DLB 84, 101

Steele, Timothy (Reid) 1948-....... CLC 45
See also CA 93-96; CANR 16; DLB 120

Steffens, (Joseph) Lincoln
  1866-1936 .... TCLC 20
  See also CA 117

Stegner, Wallace (Earle) 1909- .. CLC 9, 49
  See also AITN 1; BEST 90:3; CA 1-4R;
  CAAS 9; CANR 1, 21; DLB 9; MTCW

Stein, Gertrude
  1874-1946 .... TCLC 1, 6, 28, 48
  See also CA 104; 132; CDALB 1917-1929;
  DLB 4, 54, 86; MTCW; WLC

Steinbeck, John (Ernst)
  1902-1968 ..... CLC 1, 5, 9, 13, 21, 34,
                    45, 75; SSC 11
  See also CA 1-4R; 25-28R; CANR 1, 35;
  CDALB 1929-1941; DLB 7, 9; DLBD 2;
  MTCW; SATA 9; WLC

Steinem, Gloria 1934-............. CLC 63
  See also CA 53-56; CANR 28; MTCW

Steiner, George 1929-............. CLC 24
  See also CA 73-76; CANR 31; DLB 67;
  MTCW; SATA 62

Steiner, Rudolf 1861-1925....... TCLC 13
  See also CA 107

Stendhal 1783-1842............. NCLC 23
  See also DLB 119; WLC

Stephen, Leslie 1832-1904....... TCLC 23
  See also CA 123; DLB 57

Stephen, Sir Leslie
  See Stephen, Leslie

Stephen, Virginia
  See Woolf, (Adeline) Virginia

Stephens, James 1882(?)-1950...... TCLC 4
  See also CA 104; DLB 19

Stephens, Reed
  See Donaldson, Stephen R.

Steptoe, Lydia
  See Barnes, Djuna

Sterchi, Beat 1949-............. CLC 65

Sterling, Brett
  See Bradbury, Ray (Douglas); Hamilton,
  Edmond

Sterling, Bruce 1954-............. CLC 72
  See also CA 119

Sterling, George 1869-1926....... TCLC 20
  See also CA 117; DLB 54

Stern, Gerald 1925- .... CLC 40
  See also CA 81-84; CANR 28; DLB 105

Stern, Richard (Gustave) 1928-... CLC 4, 39
  See also CA 1-4R; CANR 1, 25; DLBY 87

Sternberg, Josef von 1894-1969..... CLC 20
  See also CA 81-84

Sterne, Laurence 1713-1768......... LC 2
  See also CDBLB 1660-1789; DLB 39; WLC

Sternheim, (William Adolf) Carl
  1878-1942 .... TCLC 8
  See also CA 105; DLB 56, 118

Stevens, Mark 1951- .... CLC 34
  See also CA 122

Stevens, Wallace
  1879-1955 .... TCLC 3, 12, 45; PC 6
  See also CA 104; 124; CDALB 1929-1941;
  DLB 54; MTCW; WLC

Stevenson, Anne (Katharine)
  1933- .... CLC 7, 33
  See also CA 17-20R; CAAS 9; CANR 9, 33;
  DLB 40; MTCW

Stevenson, Robert Louis (Balfour)
  1850-1894 .... NCLC 5, 14; SSC 11
  See also CDBLB 1890-1914; CLR 10, 11;
  DLB 18, 57; MAICYA; WLC; YABC 2

Stewart, J(ohn) I(nnes) M(ackintosh)
  1906- .... CLC 7, 14, 32
  See also CA 85-88; CAAS 3; MTCW

Stewart, Mary (Florence Elinor)
  1916- .... CLC 7, 35
  See also CA 1-4R; CANR 1; SATA 12

Stewart, Mary Rainbow
  See Stewart, Mary (Florence Elinor)

Still, James 1906-................ CLC 49
  See also CA 65-68; CANR 10, 26; DLB 9;
  SATA 29

Sting
  See Sumner, Gordon Matthew

Stirling, Arthur
  See Sinclair, Upton (Beall)

Stitt, Milan 1941-................ CLC 29
  See also CA 69-72

Stockton, Francis Richard 1834-1902
  See Stockton, Frank R.
  See also CA 108; 137; MAICYA; SATA 44

Stockton, Frank R................ TCLC 47
  See also Stockton, Francis Richard
  See also DLB 42, 74; SATA 32

Stoddard, Charles
  See Kuttner, Henry

Stoker, Abraham 1847-1912
  See Stoker, Bram
  See also CA 105; SATA 29

Stoker, Bram .... TCLC 8
  See also Stoker, Abraham
  See also CDBLB 1890-1914; DLB 36, 70;
  WLC

Stolz, Mary (Slattery) 1920-....... CLC 12
  See also AAYA 8; AITN 1; CA 5-8R;
  CANR 13; MAICYA; SAAS 3;
  SATA 10, 70, 71

Stone, Irving 1903-1989............ CLC 7
  See also AITN 1; CA 1-4R; 129; CAAS 3;
  CANR 1, 23; MTCW; SATA 3; SATO 64

Stone, Oliver 1946-................ CLC 73
  See also CA 110

Stone, Robert (Anthony)
  1937- .... CLC 5, 23, 42
  See also CA 85-88; CANR 23; MTCW

Stone, Zachary
  See Follett, Ken(neth Martin)

Stoppard, Tom
  1937- ... CLC 1, 3, 4, 5, 8, 15, 29, 34, 63
  See also CA 81-84; CANR 39;
  CDBLB 1960 to Present; DLB 13;
  DLBY 85; MTCW; WLC

Storey, David (Malcolm)
  1933- .... CLC 2, 4, 5, 8
  See also CA 81-84; CANR 36; DLB 13, 14;
  MTCW

Storm, Hyemeyohsts 1935- .... CLC 3
  See also CA 81-84

Storm, (Hans) Theodor (Woldsen)
  1817-1888 .... NCLC 1

Storni, Alfonsina 1892-1938 ...... TCLC 5
  See also CA 104; 131; HW

Stout, Rex (Todhunter) 1886-1975 ... CLC 3
  See also AITN 2; CA 61-64

Stow, (Julian) Randolph 1935- .. CLC 23, 48
  See also CA 13-16R; CANR 33; MTCW

Stowe, Harriet (Elizabeth) Beecher
  1811-1896 .... NCLC 3
  See also CDALB 1865-1917; DLB 1, 12, 42,
  74; MAICYA; WLC; YABC 1

Strachey, (Giles) Lytton
  1880-1932 .... TCLC 12
  See also CA 110; DLBD 10

Strand, Mark 1934-...... CLC 6, 18, 41, 71
  See also CA 21-24R; CANR 40; DLB 5;
  SATA 41

Straub, Peter (Francis) 1943- ...... CLC 28
  See also BEST 89:1; CA 85-88; CANR 28;
  DLBY 84; MTCW

Strauss, Botho 1944- .... CLC 22
  See also DLB 124

Streatfeild, (Mary) Noel
  1895(?)-1986 .... CLC 21
  See also CA 81-84; 120; CANR 31;
  CLR 17; MAICYA; SATA 20, 48

Stribling, T(homas) S(igismund)
  1881-1965 .... CLC 23
  See also CA 107; DLB 9

Strindberg, (Johan) August
  1849-1912 .... TCLC 1, 8, 21, 47
  See also CA 104; 135; WLC

Stringer, Arthur 1874-1950 ...... TCLC 37
  See also DLB 92

Stringer, David
  See Roberts, Keith (John Kingston)

Strugatskii, Arkadii (Natanovich)
  1925-1991 .... CLC 27
  See also CA 106; 135

Strugatskii, Boris (Natanovich)
  1933- .... CLC 27
  See also CA 106

Strummer, Joe 1953(?)- .... CLC 30
  See also The Clash

Stuart, Don A.
  See Campbell, John W(ood Jr.)

Stuart, Ian
  See MacLean, Alistair (Stuart)

Stuart, Jesse (Hilton)
  1906-1984 .... CLC 1, 8, 11, 14, 34
  See also CA 5-8R; 112; CANR 31; DLB 9,
  48, 102; DLBY 84; SATA 2, 36

Sturgeon, Theodore (Hamilton)
  1918-1985 .... CLC 22, 39
  See also Queen, Ellery
  See also CA 81-84; 116; CANR 32; DLB 8;
  DLBY 85; MTCW

Sturges, Preston 1898-1959....... TCLC 48
  See also CA 114; DLB 26

Styron, William
  1925-.......... CLC 1, 3, 5, 11, 15, 60
  See also BEST 90:4; CA 5-8R; CANR 6, 33;
  CDALB 1968-1988; DLB 2; DLBY 80;
  MTCW

Suarez Lynch, B.
  See Borges, Jorge Luis

Suarez Lynch, B.
  See Bioy Casares, Adolfo; Borges, Jorge
    Luis

Su Chien 1884-1918
  See Su Man-shu
  See also CA 123

Sudermann, Hermann 1857-1928 .. **TCLC 15**
  See also CA 107; DLB 118

Sue, Eugene 1804-1857 .... **NCLC 1**
  See also DLB 119

Sueskind, Patrick 1949- .... **CLC 44**

Sukenick, Ronald 1932- ..... **CLC 3, 4, 6, 48**
  See also CA 25-28R; CAAS 8; CANR 32;
    DLBY 81

Suknaski, Andrew 1942- .... **CLC 19**
  See also CA 101; DLB 53

Sullivan, Vernon
  See Vian, Boris

Sully Prudhomme 1839-1907 ..... **TCLC 31**

Su Man-shu .... **TCLC 24**
  See also Su Chien

Summerforest, Ivy B.
  See Kirkup, James

Summers, Andrew James 1942- ..... **CLC 26**
  See also The Police

Summers, Andy
  See Summers, Andrew James

Summers, Hollis (Spurgeon Jr.)
  1916- .... **CLC 10**
  See also CA 5-8R; CANR 3; DLB 6

Summers, (Alphonsus Joseph-Mary Augustus)
  Montague 1880-1948 .... **TCLC 16**
  See also CA 118

Sumner, Gordon Matthew 1951- .... **CLC 26**
  See also The Police

Surtees, Robert Smith
  1803-1864 .... **NCLC 14**
  See also DLB 21

Susann, Jacqueline 1921-1974 .... **CLC 3**
  See also AITN 1; CA 65-68; 53-56; MTCW

Suskind, Patrick
  See Sueskind, Patrick

Sutcliff, Rosemary 1920-1992 ...... **CLC 26**
  See also AAYA 10; CA 5-8R; 139;
    CANR 37; CLR 1; MAICYA; SATA 6,
    44; SATO 73

Sutro, Alfred 1863-1933 .... **TCLC 6**
  See also CA 105; DLB 10

Sutton, Henry
  See Slavitt, David R.

Svevo, Italo .... **TCLC 2, 35**
  See also Schmitz, Aron Hector

Swados, Elizabeth 1951- .... **CLC 12**
  See also CA 97-100

Swados, Harvey 1920-1972 .... **CLC 5**
  See also CA 5-8R; 37-40R; CANR 6;
    DLB 2

Swan, Gladys 1934- .... **CLC 69**
  See also CA 101; CANR 17, 39

Swarthout, Glendon (Fred)
  1918-1992 .... **CLC 35**
  See also CA 1-4R; 139; CANR 1; SATA 26

Sweet, Sarah C.
  See Jewett, (Theodora) Sarah Orne

Swenson, May 1919-1989 ..... **CLC 4, 14, 61**
  See also CA 5-8R; 130; CANR 36; DLB 5;
    MTCW; SATA 15

Swift, Augustus
  See Lovecraft, H(oward) P(hillips)

Swift, Graham 1949- .... **CLC 41**
  See also CA 117; 122

Swift, Jonathan 1667-1745 .... **LC 1**
  See also CDBLB 1660-1789; DLB 39, 95,
    101; SATA 19; WLC

Swinburne, Algernon Charles
  1837-1909 .... **TCLC 8, 36**
  See also CA 105; CDBLB 1832-1890;
    DLB 35, 57; WLC

Swinfen, Ann .... **CLC 34**

Swinnerton, Frank Arthur
  1884-1982 .... **CLC 31**
  See also CA 108; DLB 34

Swithen, John
  See King, Stephen (Edwin)

Sylvia
  See Ashton-Warner, Sylvia (Constance)

Symmes, Robert Edward
  See Duncan, Robert (Edward)

Symonds, John Addington
  1840-1893 .... **NCLC 34**
  See also DLB 57

Symons, Arthur 1865-1945 .... **TCLC 11**
  See also CA 107; DLB 19, 57

Symons, Julian (Gustave)
  1912- .... **CLC 2, 14, 32**
  See also CA 49-52; CAAS 3; CANR 3, 33;
    DLB 87; MTCW

Synge, (Edmund) J(ohn) M(illington)
  1871-1909 .... **TCLC 6, 37; DC 2**
  See also CA 104; CDBLB 1890-1914;
    DLB 10, 19

Syruc, J.
  See Milosz, Czeslaw

Szirtes, George 1948- .... **CLC 46**
  See also CA 109; CANR 27

Tabori, George 1914- .... **CLC 19**
  See also CA 49-52; CANR 4

Tagore, Rabindranath 1861-1941 .... **TCLC 3**
  See also CA 104; 120; MTCW

Taine, Hippolyte Adolphe
  1828-1893 .... **NCLC 15**

Talese, Gay 1932- .... **CLC 37**
  See also AITN 1; CA 1-4R; CANR 9;
    MTCW

Tallent, Elizabeth (Ann) 1954- ..... **CLC 45**
  See also CA 117

Tally, Ted 1952- .... **CLC 42**
  See also CA 120; 124

Tamayo y Baus, Manuel
  1829-1898 .... **NCLC 1**

Tammsaare, A(nton) H(ansen)
  1878-1940 .... **TCLC 27**

Tan, Amy 1952- .... **CLC 59**
  See also AAYA 9; BEST 89:3; CA 136

Tandem, Felix
  See Spitteler, Carl (Friedrich Georg)

Tanizaki, Jun'ichiro
  1886-1965 .... **CLC 8, 14, 28**
  See also CA 93-96; 25-28R

Tanner, William
  See Amis, Kingsley (William)

Tao Lao
  See Storni, Alfonsina

Tarassoff, Lev
  See Troyat, Henri

Tarbell, Ida M(inerva)
  1857-1944 .... **TCLC 40**
  See also CA 122; DLB 47

Tarkington, (Newton) Booth
  1869-1946 .... **TCLC 9**
  See also CA 110; DLB 9, 102; SATA 17

Tarkovsky, Andrei (Arsenyevich)
  1932-1986 .... **CLC 75**
  See also CA 127

Tasso, Torquato 1544-1595 .... **LC 5**

Tate, (John Orley) Allen
  1899-1979 .... **CLC 2, 4, 6, 9, 11, 14, 24**
  See also CA 5-8R; 85-88; CANR 32;
    DLB 4, 45, 63; MTCW

Tate, Ellalice
  See Hibbert, Eleanor Burford

Tate, James (Vincent) 1943- ... **CLC 2, 6, 25**
  See also CA 21-24R; CANR 29; DLB 5

Tavel, Ronald 1940- .... **CLC 6**
  See also CA 21-24R; CANR 33

Taylor, Cecil Philip 1929-1981 ..... **CLC 27**
  See also CA 25-28R; 105

Taylor, Edward 1642(?)-1729 .... **LC 11**
  See also DLB 24

Taylor, Eleanor Ross 1920- .... **CLC 5**
  See also CA 81-84

Taylor, Elizabeth 1912-1975 ... **CLC 2, 4, 29**
  See also CA 13-16R; CANR 9; MTCW;
    SATA 13

Taylor, Henry (Splawn) 1942- ...... **CLC 44**
  See also CA 33-36R; CAAS 7; CANR 31;
    DLB 5

Taylor, Kamala (Purnaiya) 1924-
  See Markandaya, Kamala
  See also CA 77-80

Taylor, Mildred D. .... **CLC 21**
  See also AAYA 10; BW; CA 85-88;
    CANR 25; CLR 9; DLB 52; MAICYA;
    SAAS 5; SATA 15, 70

Taylor, Peter (Hillsman)
  1917- ..... **CLC 1, 4, 18, 37, 44, 50, 71;**
                                            SSC 10
  See also CA 13-16R; CANR 9; DLBY 81;
    MTCW

Taylor, Robert Lewis 1912- .... **CLC 14**
  See also CA 1-4R; CANR 3; SATA 10

Tchekhov, Anton
  See Chekhov, Anton (Pavlovich)

Teasdale, Sara 1884-1933 .... **TCLC 4**
  See also CA 104; DLB 45; SATA 32

Tegner, Esaias 1782-1846 .... **NCLC 2**

Teilhard de Chardin, (Marie Joseph) Pierre
    1881-1955 .... TCLC 9
    See also CA 105

Temple, Ann
    See Mortimer, Penelope (Ruth)

Tennant, Emma (Christina)
    1937- .... CLC 13, 52
    See also CA 65-68; CAAS 9; CANR 10, 38;
    DLB 14

Tenneshaw, S. M.
    See Silverberg, Robert

Tennyson, Alfred
    1809-1892 .... NCLC 30; PC 6
    See also CDBLB 1832-1890; DLB 32; WLC

Teran, Lisa St. Aubin de .... CLC 36
    See also St. Aubin de Teran, Lisa

Teresa de Jesus, St.   1515-1582 ...... LC 18

Terkel, Louis   1912-
    See Terkel, Studs
    See also CA 57-60; CANR 18; MTCW

Terkel, Studs .... CLC 38
    See also Terkel, Louis
    See also AITN 1

Terry, C. V.
    See Slaughter, Frank G(ill)

Terry, Megan   1932- .... CLC 19
    See also CA 77-80; CABS 3; DLB 7

Tertz, Abram
    See Sinyavsky, Andrei (Donatevich)

Tesich, Steve   1943(?)-......... CLC 40, 69
    See also CA 105; DLBY 83

Teternikov, Fyodor Kuzmich   1863-1927
    See Sologub, Fyodor
    See also CA 104

Tevis, Walter   1928-1984 .... CLC 42
    See also CA 113

Tey, Josephine................... TCLC 14
    See also Mackintosh, Elizabeth
    See also DLB 77

Thackeray, William Makepeace
    1811-1863 .... NCLC 5, 14, 22
    See also CDBLB 1832-1890; DLB 21, 55;
    SATA 23; WLC

Thakura, Ravindranatha
    See Tagore, Rabindranath

Tharoor, Shashi   1956- .... CLC 70

Thelwell, Michael Miles   1939- ..... CLC 22
    See also CA 101

Theobald, Lewis Jr.
    See Lovecraft, H(oward) P(hillips)

The Prophet
    See Dreiser, Theodore (Herman Albert)

Theroux, Alexander (Louis)
    1939- .... CLC 2, 25
    See also CA 85-88; CANR 20

Theroux, Paul (Edward)
    1941- .... CLC 5, 8, 11, 15, 28, 46
    See also BEST 89:4; CA 33-36R; CANR 20;
    DLB 2; MTCW; SATA 44

Thesen, Sharon   1946-............. CLC 56

Thevenin, Denis
    See Duhamel, Georges

Thibault, Jacques Anatole Francois
    1844-1924
    See France, Anatole
    See also CA 106; 127; MTCW

Thiele, Colin (Milton)   1920- .... CLC 17
    See also CA 29-32R; CANR 12, 28;
    CLR 27; MAICYA; SAAS 2; SATA 14,
    72

Thomas, Audrey (Callahan)
    1935- .... CLC 7, 13, 37
    See also AITN 2; CA 21-24R; CANR 36;
    DLB 60; MTCW

Thomas, D(onald) M(ichael)
    1935- .... CLC 13, 22, 31
    See also CA 61-64; CAAS 11; CANR 17;
    CDBLB 1960 to Present; DLB 40;
    MTCW

Thomas, Dylan (Marlais)
    1914-1953 ...... TCLC 1, 8, 45; PC 2;
                                        SSC 3
    See also CA 104; 120; CDBLB 1945-1960;
    DLB 13, 20; MTCW; SATA 60; WLC

Thomas, (Philip) Edward
    1878-1917 .... TCLC 10
    See also CA 106; DLB 19

Thomas, Joyce Carol   1938-........ CLC 35
    See also BW; CA 113; 116; CLR 19;
    DLB 33; MAICYA; MTCW; SAAS 7;
    SATA 40

Thomas, Lewis   1913- .... CLC 35
    See also CA 85-88; CANR 38; MTCW

Thomas, Paul
    See Mann, (Paul) Thomas

Thomas, Piri   1928-.............. CLC 17
    See also CA 73-76; HW

Thomas, R(onald) S(tuart)
    1913- .... CLC 6, 13, 48
    See also CA 89-92; CAAS 4; CANR 30;
    CDBLB 1960 to Present; DLB 27;
    MTCW

Thomas, Ross (Elmore)   1926-...... CLC 39
    See also CA 33-36R; CANR 22

Thompson, Francis Clegg
    See Mencken, H(enry) L(ouis)

Thompson, Francis Joseph
    1859-1907 .... TCLC 4
    See also CA 104; CDBLB 1890-1914;
    DLB 19

Thompson, Hunter S(tockton)
    1939- .... CLC 9, 17, 40
    See also BEST 89:1; CA 17-20R; CANR 23;
    MTCW

Thompson, Jim   1906-1976........ CLC 69

Thompson, Judith .... CLC 39

Thomson, James   1700-1748........ LC 16

Thomson, James   1834-1882...... NCLC 18

Thoreau, Henry David
    1817-1862 .... NCLC 7, 21
    See also CDALB 1640-1865; DLB 1; WLC

Thornton, Hall
    See Silverberg, Robert

Thurber, James (Grover)
    1894-1961 .... CLC 5, 11, 25; SSC 1
    See also CA 73-76; CANR 17, 39;
    CDALB 1929-1941; DLB 4, 11, 22, 102;
    MAICYA; MTCW; SATA 13

Thurman, Wallace (Henry)
    1902-1934 .... TCLC 6
    See also BLC 3; BW; CA 104; 124; DLB 51

Ticheburn, Cheviot
    See Ainsworth, William Harrison

Tieck, (Johann) Ludwig
    1773-1853 .... NCLC 5
    See also DLB 90

Tiger, Derry
    See Ellison, Harlan

Tilghman, Christopher   1948(?)-..... CLC 65

Tillinghast, Richard (Williford)
    1940-....................... CLC 29
    See also CA 29-32R; CANR 26

Timrod, Henry   1828-1867 .... NCLC 25
    See also DLB 3

Tindall, Gillian   1938-.............. CLC 7
    See also CA 21-24R; CANR 11

Tiptree, James Jr............... CLC 48, 50
    See also Sheldon, Alice Hastings Bradley
    See also DLB 8

Titmarsh, Michael Angelo
    See Thackeray, William Makepeace

Tocqueville, Alexis (Charles Henri Maurice
    Clerel Comte)   1805-1859..... NCLC 7

Tolkien, J(ohn) R(onald) R(euel)
    1892-1973 .... CLC 1, 2, 3, 8, 12, 38
    See also AAYA 10; AITN 1; CA 17-18;
    45-48; CANR 36; CAP 2;
    CDBLB 1914-1945; DLB 15; MAICYA;
    MTCW; SATA 2, 24, 32; WLC

Toller, Ernst   1893-1939.......... TCLC 10
    See also CA 107; DLB 124

Tolson, M. B.
    See Tolson, Melvin B(eaunorus)

Tolson, Melvin B(eaunorus)
    1898(?)-1966 .... CLC 36
    See also BLC 3; BW; CA 124; 89-92;
    DLB 48, 76

Tolstoi, Aleksei Nikolaevich
    See Tolstoy, Alexey Nikolaevich

Tolstoy, Alexey Nikolaevich
    1882-1945 .... TCLC 18
    See also CA 107

Tolstoy, Count Leo
    See Tolstoy, Leo (Nikolaevich)

Tolstoy, Leo (Nikolaevich)
    1828-1910 ..... TCLC 4, 11, 17, 28, 44;
                                        SSC 9
    See also CA 104; 123; SATA 26; WLC

Tomasi di Lampedusa, Giuseppe   1896-1957
    See Lampedusa, Giuseppe (Tomasi) di
    See also CA 111

Tomlin, Lily..................... CLC 17
    See also Tomlin, Mary Jean

Tomlin, Mary Jean   1939(?)-
    See Tomlin, Lily
    See also CA 117

Tomlinson, (Alfred) Charles
    1927- . . . . CLC 2, 4, 6, 13, 45
    See also CA 5-8R; CANR 33; DLB 40

Tonson, Jacob
    See Bennett, (Enoch) Arnold

Toole, John Kennedy
    1937-1969 . . . . CLC 19, 64
    See also CA 104; DLBY 81

Toomer, Jean
    1894-1967 . . . . . CLC 1, 4, 13, 22; SSC 1
    See also BLC 3; BW; CA 85-88;
        CDALB 1917-1929; DLB 45, 51; MTCW

Torley, Luke
    See Blish, James (Benjamin)

Tornimparte, Alessandra
    See Ginzburg, Natalia

Torre, Raoul della
    See Mencken, H(enry) L(ouis)

Torrey, E(dwin) Fuller   1937-. . . . . . . CLC 34
    See also CA 119

Torsvan, Ben Traven
    See Traven, B.

Torsvan, Benno Traven
    See Traven, B.

Torsvan, Berick Traven
    See Traven, B.

Torsvan, Berwick Traven
    See Traven, B.

Torsvan, Bruno Traven
    See Traven, B.

Torsvan, Traven
    See Traven, B.

Tournier, Michel (Edouard)
    1924- . . . . CLC 6, 23, 36
    See also CA 49-52; CANR 3, 36; DLB 83;
        MTCW; SATA 23

Tournimparte, Alessandra
    See Ginzburg, Natalia

Towers, Ivar
    See Kornbluth, C(yril) M.

Townsend, Sue   1946- . . . . CLC 61
    See also CA 119; 127; MTCW; SATA 48,
    55

Townshend, Peter (Dennis Blandford)
    1945- . . . . CLC 17, 42
    See also CA 107

Tozzi, Federigo   1883-1920. . . . . . . TCLC 31

Traill, Catharine Parr
    1802-1899 . . . . NCLC 31
    See also DLB 99

Trakl, Georg   1887-1914. . . . . TCLC 5
    See also CA 104

Transtroemer, Tomas (Goesta)
    1931- . . . . CLC 52, 65
    See also CA 117; 129

Transtromer, Tomas Gosta
    See Transtroemer, Tomas (Goesta)

Traven, B.   (?)-1969. . . . . CLC 8, 11
    See also CA 19-20; 25-28R; CAP 2; DLB 9,
    56; MTCW

Treitel, Jonathan   1959- . . . . CLC 70

Tremain, Rose   1943-. . . . . CLC 42
    See also CA 97-100; DLB 14

Tremblay, Michel   1942-. . . . . CLC 29
    See also CA 116; 128; DLB 60; MTCW

Trevanian (a pseudonym)   1930(?)-. . . CLC 29
    See also CA 108

Trevor, Glen
    See Hilton, James

Trevor, William
    1928- . . . . CLC 7, 9, 14, 25, 71
    See also Cox, William Trevor
    See also DLB 14

Trifonov, Yuri (Valentinovich)
    1925-1981 . . . . CLC 45
    See also CA 126; 103; MTCW

Trilling, Lionel   1905-1975. . . . CLC 9, 11, 24
    See also CA 9-12R; 61-64; CANR 10;
        DLB 28, 63; MTCW

Trimball, W. H.
    See Mencken, H(enry) L(ouis)

Tristan
    See Gomez de la Serna, Ramon

Tristram
    See Housman, A(lfred) E(dward)

Trogdon, William (Lewis)   1939-
    See Heat-Moon, William Least
    See also CA 115; 119

Trollope, Anthony   1815-1882 . . NCLC 6, 33
    See also CDBLB 1832-1890; DLB 21, 57;
        SATA 22; WLC

Trollope, Frances   1779-1863 . . . . . NCLC 30
    See also DLB 21

Trotsky, Leon   1879-1940. . . . . TCLC 22
    See also CA 118

Trotter (Cockburn), Catharine
    1679-1749 . . . . LC 8
    See also DLB 84

Trout, Kilgore
    See Farmer, Philip Jose

Trow, George W. S.   1943-. . . . . CLC 52
    See also CA 126

Troyat, Henri   1911-. . . . . CLC 23
    See also CA 45-48; CANR 2, 33; MTCW

Trudeau, G(arretson) B(eekman)   1948-
    See Trudeau, Garry B.
    See also CA 81-84; CANR 31; SATA 35

Trudeau, Garry B.. . . . . CLC 12
    See also Trudeau, G(arretson) B(eekman)
    See also AAYA 10; AITN 2

Truffaut, Francois   1932-1984. . . . . . CLC 20
    See also CA 81-84; 113; CANR 34

Trumbo, Dalton   1905-1976 . . . . CLC 19
    See also CA 21-24R; 69-72; CANR 10;
        DLB 26

Trumbull, John   1750-1831. . . . . . . NCLC 30
    See also DLB 31

Trundlett, Helen B.
    See Eliot, T(homas) S(tearns)

Tryon, Thomas   1926-1991 . . . . . . CLC 3, 11
    See also AITN 1; CA 29-32R; 135;
        CANR 32; MTCW

Tryon, Tom
    See Tryon, Thomas

Ts'ao Hsueh-ch'in   1715(?)-1763. . . . . . LC 1

Tsushima, Shuji   1909-1948
    See Dazai, Osamu
    See also CA 107

Tsvetaeva (Efron), Marina (Ivanovna)
    1892-1941 . . . . TCLC 7, 35
    See also CA 104; 128; MTCW

Tuck, Lily   1938-. . . . . CLC 70
    See also CA 139

Tunis, John R(oberts)   1889-1975 . . . CLC 12
    See also CA 61-64; DLB 22; MAICYA;
        SATA 30, 37

Tuohy, Frank. . . . . CLC 37
    See also Tuohy, John Francis
    See also DLB 14

Tuohy, John Francis   1925-
    See Tuohy, Frank
    See also CA 5-8R; CANR 3

Turco, Lewis (Putnam)   1934- . . . CLC 11, 63
    See also CA 13-16R; CANR 24; DLBY 84

Turgenev, Ivan
    1818-1883 . . . . NCLC 21; SSC 7
    See also WLC

Turner, Frederick   1943-. . . . . CLC 48
    See also CA 73-76; CAAS 10; CANR 12,
        30; DLB 40

Tusan, Stan   1936-. . . . . CLC 22
    See also CA 105

Tutuola, Amos   1920- . . . . CLC 5, 14, 29
    See also BLC 3; BW; CA 9-12R; CANR 27;
        DLB 125; MTCW

Twain, Mark
    . . . . TCLC 6, 12, 19, 36, 48; SSC 6
    See also Clemens, Samuel Langhorne
    See also DLB 11, 12, 23, 64, 74; WLC

Tyler, Anne
    1941- . . . . CLC 7, 11, 18, 28, 44, 59
    See also BEST 89:1; CA 9-12R; CANR 11,
        33; DLB 6; DLBY 82; MTCW; SATA 7

Tyler, Royall   1757-1826. . . . . NCLC 3
    See also DLB 37

Tynan, Katharine   1861-1931. . . . . . . TCLC 3
    See also CA 104

Tytell, John   1939- . . . . CLC 50
    See also CA 29-32R

Tyutchev, Fyodor   1803-1873. . . . . NCLC 34

Tzara, Tristan . . . . CLC 47
    See also Rosenfeld, Samuel

Uhry, Alfred   1936-. . . . . CLC 55
    See also CA 127; 133

Ulf, Haerved
    See Strindberg, (Johan) August

Ulf, Harved
    See Strindberg, (Johan) August

Unamuno (y Jugo), Miguel de
    1864-1936 . . . . TCLC 2, 9; SSC 11
    See also CA 104; 131; DLB 108; HW;
        MTCW

Undercliffe, Errol
    See Campbell, (John) Ramsey

Underwood, Miles
    See Glassco, John

Undset, Sigrid   1882-1949. . . . . TCLC 3
    See also CA 104; 129; MTCW; WLC

Ungaretti, Giuseppe
1888-1970 . . . . CLC 7, 11, 15
See also CA 19-20; 25-28R; CAP 2;
DLB 114

Unger, Douglas 1952- . . . . CLC 34
See also CA 130

Updike, John (Hoyer)
1932- . . . . . . CLC 1, 2, 3, 5, 7, 9, 13, 15,
23, 34, 43, 70
See also CA 1-4R; CABS 1; CANR 4, 33;
CDALB 1968-1988; DLB 2, 5; DLBD 3;
DLBY 80, 82; MTCW; WLC

Upshaw, Margaret Mitchell
See Mitchell, Margaret (Munnerlyn)

Upton, Mark
See Sanders, Lawrence

Urdang, Constance (Henriette)
1922- . . . . CLC 47
See also CA 21-24R; CANR 9, 24

Uriel, Henry
See Faust, Frederick (Schiller)

Uris, Leon (Marcus) 1924- . . . . . . CLC 7, 32
See also AITN 1, 2; BEST 89:2; CA 1-4R;
CANR 1, 40; MTCW; SATA 49

Urmuz
See Codrescu, Andrei

Ustinov, Peter (Alexander) 1921- . . . . CLC 1
See also AITN 1; CA 13-16R; CANR 25;
DLB 13

V
See Chekhov, Anton (Pavlovich)

Vaculik, Ludvik 1926- . . . . CLC 7
See also CA 53-56

Valenzuela, Luisa 1938- . . . . CLC 31
See also CA 101; CANR 32; DLB 113; HW

Valera y Alcala-Galiano, Juan
1824-1905 . . . . TCLC 10
See also CA 106

Valery, (Ambroise) Paul (Toussaint Jules)
1871-1945 . . . . TCLC 4, 15
See also CA 104; 122; MTCW

Valle-Inclan, Ramon (Maria) del
1866-1936 . . . . TCLC 5
See also CA 106

Vallejo, Antonio Buero
See Buero Vallejo, Antonio

Vallejo, Cesar (Abraham)
1892-1938 . . . . TCLC 3
See also CA 105; HW

Valle Y Pena, Ramon del
See Valle-Inclan, Ramon (Maria) del

Van Ash, Cay 1918- . . . . CLC 34

Vanbrugh, Sir John 1664-1726 . . . . . . LC 21
See also DLB 80

Van Campen, Karl
See Campbell, John W(ood Jr.)

Vance, Gerald
See Silverberg, Robert

Vance, Jack . . . . CLC 35
See also Vance, John Holbrook
See also DLB 8

Vance, John Holbrook 1916-
See Queen, Ellery; Vance, Jack
See also CA 29-32R; CANR 17; MTCW

Van Den Bogarde, Derek Jules Gaspard Ulric
Niven 1921-
See Bogarde, Dirk
See also CA 77-80

Vandenburgh, Jane . . . . CLC 59

Vanderhaeghe, Guy 1951- . . . . CLC 41
See also CA 113

van der Post, Laurens (Jan) 1906- . . . CLC 5
See also CA 5-8R; CANR 35

van de Wetering, Janwillem 1931- . . CLC 47
See also CA 49-52; CANR 4

Van Dine, S. S. . . . . TCLC 23
See also Wright, Willard Huntington

Van Doren, Carl (Clinton)
1885-1950 . . . . TCLC 18
See also CA 111

Van Doren, Mark 1894-1972 . . . . . CLC 6, 10
See also CA 1-4R; 37-40R; CANR 3;
DLB 45; MTCW

Van Druten, John (William)
1901-1957 . . . . TCLC 2
See also CA 104; DLB 10

Van Duyn, Mona (Jane)
1921- . . . . CLC 3, 7, 63
See also CA 9-12R; CANR 7, 38; DLB 5

Van Dyne, Edith
See Baum, L(yman) Frank

van Itallie, Jean-Claude 1936- . . . . CLC 3
See also CA 45-48; CAAS 2; CANR 1;
DLB 7

van Ostaijen, Paul 1896-1928 . . . . . TCLC 33

Van Peebles, Melvin 1932- . . . . . . CLC 2, 20
See also BW; CA 85-88; CANR 27

Vansittart, Peter 1920- . . . . CLC 42
See also CA 1-4R; CANR 3

Van Vechten, Carl 1880-1964 . . . . . . CLC 33
See also CA 89-92; DLB 4, 9, 51

Van Vogt, A(lfred) E(lton) 1912- . . . . . CLC 1
See also CA 21-24R; CANR 28; DLB 8;
SATA 14

Vara, Madeleine
See Jackson, Laura (Riding)

Varda, Agnes 1928- . . . . CLC 16
See also CA 116; 122

Vargas Llosa, (Jorge) Mario (Pedro)
1936- . . . . CLC 3, 6, 9, 10, 15, 31, 42
See also CA 73-76; CANR 18, 32; HW;
MTCW

Vasiliu, Gheorghe 1881-1957
See Bacovia, George
See also CA 123

Vassa, Gustavus
See Equiano, Olaudah

Vassilikos, Vassilis 1933- . . . . CLC 4, 8
See also CA 81-84

Vaughn, Stephanie . . . . CLC 62

Vazov, Ivan (Minchov)
1850-1921 . . . . TCLC 25
See also CA 121

Veblen, Thorstein (Bunde)
1857-1929 . . . . TCLC 31
See also CA 115

Venison, Alfred
See Pound, Ezra (Weston Loomis)

Verdi, Marie de
See Mencken, H(enry) L(ouis)

Verdu, Matilde
See Cela, Camilo Jose

Verga, Giovanni (Carmelo)
1840-1922 . . . . TCLC 3
See also CA 104; 123

Vergil 70B.C.-19B.C. . . . . CMLC 9

Verhaeren, Emile (Adolphe Gustave)
1855-1916 . . . . TCLC 12
See also CA 109

Verlaine, Paul (Marie)
1844-1896 . . . . NCLC 2; PC 2

Verne, Jules (Gabriel) 1828-1905 . . . TCLC 6
See also CA 110; 131; DLB 123; MAICYA;
SATA 21

Very, Jones 1813-1880 . . . . NCLC 9
See also DLB 1

Vesaas, Tarjei 1897-1970 . . . . CLC 48
See also CA 29-32R

Vialis, Gaston
See Simenon, Georges (Jacques Christian)

Vian, Boris 1920-1959 . . . . TCLC 9
See also CA 106; DLB 72

Viaud, (Louis Marie) Julien 1850-1923
See Loti, Pierre
See also CA 107

Vicar, Henry
See Felsen, Henry Gregor

Vicker, Angus
See Felsen, Henry Gregor

Vidal, Gore
1925- . . . . . CLC 2, 4, 6, 8, 10, 22, 33, 72
See also AITN 1; BEST 90:2; CA 5-8R;
CANR 13; DLB 6; MTCW

Viereck, Peter (Robert Edwin)
1916- . . . . CLC 4
See also CA 1-4R; CANR 1; DLB 5

Vigny, Alfred (Victor) de
1797-1863 . . . . NCLC 7
See also DLB 119

Vilakazi, Benedict Wallet
1906-1947 . . . . TCLC 37

Villiers de l'Isle Adam, Jean Marie Mathias
Philippe Auguste Comte
1838-1889 . . . . NCLC 3
See also DLB 123

Vincent, Gabrielle . . . . CLC 13
See also CA 126; CLR 13; MAICYA;
SATA 61

Vinci, Leonardo da 1452-1519 . . . . . . LC 12

Vine, Barbara . . . . CLC 50
See also Rendell, Ruth (Barbara)
See also BEST 90:4

Vinge, Joan D(ennison) 1948- . . . . . . CLC 30
See also CA 93-96; SATA 36

Violis, G.
See Simenon, Georges (Jacques Christian)

Visconti, Luchino 1906-1976 . . . . CLC 16
See also CA 81-84; 65-68; CANR 39

Vittorini, Elio 1908-1966 . . . . . CLC 6, 9, 14
See also CA 133; 25-28R

Vizinczey, Stephen 1933- . . . . CLC 40
See also CA 128

Vliet, R(ussell) G(ordon)
　　1929-1984 .... **CLC 22**
　　See also CA 37-40R; 112; CANR 18

Vogau, Boris Andreyevich 1894-1937(?)
　　See Pilnyak, Boris
　　See also CA 123

Voigt, Cynthia 1942- .... **CLC 30**
　　See also AAYA 3; CA 106; CANR 18, 37,
　　40; CLR 13; MAICYA; SATA 33, 48

Voigt, Ellen Bryant 1943- .... **CLC 54**
　　See also CA 69-72; CANR 11, 29; DLB 120

Voinovich, Vladimir (Nikolaevich)
　　1932- .... **CLC 10, 49**
　　See also CA 81-84; CAAS 12; CANR 33;
　　MTCW

Voltaire 1694-1778 .... **LC 14**
　　See also WLC

von Daeniken, Erich 1935- .... **CLC 30**
　　See also von Daniken, Erich
　　See also AITN 1; CA 37-40R; CANR 17

von Daniken, Erich .... **CLC 30**
　　See also von Daeniken, Erich

von Heidenstam, (Carl Gustaf) Verner
　　See Heidenstam, (Carl Gustaf) Verner von

von Heyse, Paul (Johann Ludwig)
　　See Heyse, Paul (Johann Ludwig von)

von Hofmannsthal, Hugo
　　See Hofmannsthal, Hugo von

von Horvath, Odon
　　See Horvath, Oedoen von

von Horvath, Oedoen
　　See Horvath, Oedoen von

von Liliencron, (Friedrich Adolf Axel) Detlev
　　See Liliencron, (Friedrich Adolf Axel)
　　Detlev von

Vonnegut, Kurt Jr.
　　1922- ...... **CLC 1, 2, 3, 4, 5, 8, 12, 22,**
　　　　　　　　　　　　40, 60; SSC 8
　　See also AAYA 6; AITN 1; BEST 90:4;
　　CA 1-4R; CANR 1, 25;
　　CDALB 1968-1988; DLB 2, 8; DLBD 3;
　　DLBY 80; MTCW; WLC

Von Rachen, Kurt
　　See Hubbard, L(afayette) Ron(ald)

von Rezzori (d'Arezzo), Gregor
　　See Rezzori (d'Arezzo), Gregor von

von Sternberg, Josef
　　See Sternberg, Josef von

Vorster, Gordon 1924- .... **CLC 34**
　　See also CA 133

Vosce, Trudie
　　See Ozick, Cynthia

Voznesensky, Andrei (Andreievich)
　　1933- .... **CLC 1, 15, 57**
　　See also CA 89-92; CANR 37; MTCW

Waddington, Miriam 1917- .... **CLC 28**
　　See also CA 21-24R; CANR 12, 30;
　　DLB 68

Wagman, Fredrica 1937- .... **CLC 7**
　　See also CA 97-100

Wagner, Richard 1813-1883 .... **NCLC 9**

Wagner-Martin, Linda 1936- .... **CLC 50**

Wagoner, David (Russell)
　　1926- .... **CLC 3, 5, 15**
　　See also CA 1-4R; CAAS 3; CANR 2;
　　DLB 5; SATA 14

Wah, Fred(erick James) 1939- ...... **CLC 44**
　　See also CA 107; DLB 60

Wahloo, Per 1926-1975 .... **CLC 7**
　　See also CA 61-64

Wahloo, Peter
　　See Wahloo, Per

Wain, John (Barrington)
　　1925- .... **CLC 2, 11, 15, 46**
　　See also CA 5-8R; CAAS 4; CANR 23;
　　CDBLB 1960 to Present; DLB 15, 27;
　　MTCW

Wajda, Andrzej 1926- .... **CLC 16**
　　See also CA 102

Wakefield, Dan 1932- .... **CLC 7**
　　See also CA 21-24R; CAAS 7

Wakoski, Diane
　　1937- .... **CLC 2, 4, 7, 9, 11, 40**
　　See also CA 13-16R; CAAS 1; CANR 9;
　　DLB 5

Wakoski-Sherbell, Diane
　　See Wakoski, Diane

Walcott, Derek (Alton)
　　1930- .... **CLC 2, 4, 9, 14, 25, 42, 67**
　　See also BLC 3; BW; CA 89-92; CANR 26;
　　DLB 117; DLBY 81; MTCW

Waldman, Anne 1945- .... **CLC 7**
　　See also CA 37-40R; CANR 34; DLB 16

Waldo, E. Hunter
　　See Sturgeon, Theodore (Hamilton)

Waldo, Edward Hamilton
　　See Sturgeon, Theodore (Hamilton)

Walker, Alice (Malsenior)
　　1944- ...... **CLC 5, 6, 9, 19, 27, 46, 58;**
　　　　　　　　　　　　　　　　SSC 5
　　See also AAYA 3; BEST 89:4; BLC 3; BW;
　　CA 37-40R; CANR 9, 27;
　　CDALB 1968-1988; DLB 6, 33; MTCW;
　　SATA 31

Walker, David Harry 1911-1992 .... **CLC 14**
　　See also CA 1-4R; 137; CANR 1; SATA 8;
　　SATO 71

Walker, Edward Joseph 1934-
　　See Walker, Ted
　　See also CA 21-24R; CANR 12, 28

Walker, George F. 1947- .... **CLC 44, 61**
　　See also CA 103; CANR 21; DLB 60

Walker, Joseph A. 1935- .... **CLC 19**
　　See also BW; CA 89-92; CANR 26; DLB 38

Walker, Margaret (Abigail)
　　1915- .... **CLC 1, 6**
　　See also BLC 3; BW; CA 73-76; CANR 26;
　　DLB 76; MTCW

Walker, Ted .... **CLC 13**
　　See also Walker, Edward Joseph
　　See also DLB 40

Wallace, David Foster 1962- .... **CLC 50**
　　See also CA 132

Wallace, Dexter
　　See Masters, Edgar Lee

Wallace, Irving 1916-1990 ...... **CLC 7, 13**
　　See also AITN 1; CA 1-4R; 132; CAAS 1;
　　CANR 1, 27; MTCW

Wallant, Edward Lewis
　　1926-1962 .... **CLC 5, 10**
　　See also CA 1-4R; CANR 22; DLB 2, 28;
　　MTCW

Walpole, Horace 1717-1797......... **LC 2**
　　See also DLB 39, 104

Walpole, Hugh (Seymour)
　　1884-1941 .... **TCLC 5**
　　See also CA 104; DLB 34

Walser, Martin 1927- .... **CLC 27**
　　See also CA 57-60; CANR 8; DLB 75, 124

Walser, Robert 1878-1956 .... **TCLC 18**
　　See also CA 118; DLB 66

Walsh, Jill Paton .... **CLC 35**
　　See also Paton Walsh, Gillian
　　See also CLR 2; SAAS 3

Walter, Villiam Christian
　　See Andersen, Hans Christian

Wambaugh, Joseph (Aloysius Jr.)
　　1937- .... **CLC 3, 18**
　　See also AITN 1; BEST 89:3; CA 33-36R;
　　DLB 6; DLBY 83; MTCW

Ward, Arthur Henry Sarsfield 1883-1959
　　See Rohmer, Sax
　　See also CA 108

Ward, Douglas Turner 1930- .... **CLC 19**
　　See also BW; CA 81-84; CANR 27; DLB 7,
　　38

Ward, Peter
　　See Faust, Frederick (Schiller)

Warhol, Andy 1928(?)-1987........ **CLC 20**
　　See also BEST 89:4; CA 89-92; 121;
　　CANR 34

Warner, Francis (Robert le Plastrier)
　　1937- .... **CLC 14**
　　See also CA 53-56; CANR 11

Warner, Marina 1946- .... **CLC 59**
　　See also CA 65-68; CANR 21

Warner, Rex (Ernest) 1905-1986 .... **CLC 45**
　　See also CA 89-92; 119; DLB 15

Warner, Susan (Bogert)
　　1819-1885 .... **NCLC 31**
　　See also DLB 3, 42

Warner, Sylvia (Constance) Ashton
　　See Ashton-Warner, Sylvia (Constance)

Warner, Sylvia Townsend
　　1893-1978 .... **CLC 7, 19**
　　See also CA 61-64; 77-80; CANR 16;
　　DLB 34; MTCW

Warren, Mercy Otis 1728-1814... **NCLC 13**
　　See also DLB 31

Warren, Robert Penn
　　1905-1989 ... **CLC 1, 4, 6, 8, 10, 13, 18,**
　　　　　　　　　　　　39, 53, 59; SSC 4
　　See also AITN 1; CA 13-16R; 129;
　　CANR 10; CDALB 1968-1988; DLB 2,
　　48; DLBY 80, 89; MTCW; SATA 46, 63;
　　WLC

Warshofsky, Isaac
　　See Singer, Isaac Bashevis

Warton, Thomas 1728-1790........ **LC 15**
　　See also DLB 104, 109

Weston, Allen
See Norton, Andre

Wetcheek, J. L.
See Feuchtwanger, Lion

Wetering, Janwillem van de
See van de Wetering, Janwillem

Wetherell, Elizabeth
See Warner, Susan (Bogert)

Whalen, Philip 1923- .... CLC 6, 29
See also CA 9-12R; CANR 5, 39; DLB 16

Wharton, Edith (Newbold Jones)
1862-1937 ...... TCLC 3, 9, 27; SSC 6
See also CA 104; 132; CDALB 1865-1917;
DLB 4, 9, 12, 78; MTCW; WLC

Wharton, James
See Mencken, H(enry) L(ouis)

Wharton, William (a pseudonym)
.... CLC 18, 37
See also CA 93-96; DLBY 80

Wheatley (Peters), Phillis
1754(?)-1784 .... LC 3; PC 3
See also BLC 3; CDALB 1640-1865;
DLB 31, 50; WLC

Wheelock, John Hall 1886-1978 .... CLC 14
See also CA 13-16R; 77-80; CANR 14;
DLB 45

White, E(lwyn) B(rooks)
1899-1985 .... CLC 10, 34, 39
See also AITN 2; CA 13-16R; 116;
CANR 16, 37; CLR 1, 21; DLB 11, 22;
MAICYA; MTCW; SATA 2, 29, 44

White, Edmund (Valentine III)
1940- .... CLC 27
See also AAYA 7; CA 45-48; CANR 3, 19,
36; MTCW

White, Patrick (Victor Martindale)
1912-1990 .. CLC 3, 4, 5, 7, 9, 18, 65, 69
See also CA 81-84; 132; MTCW

White, Phyllis Dorothy James 1920-
See James, P. D.
See also CA 21-24R; CANR 17; MTCW

White, T(erence) H(anbury)
1906-1964 .... CLC 30
See also CA 73-76; CANR 37; MAICYA;
SATA 12

White, Terence de Vere 1912- ...... CLC 49
See also CA 49-52; CANR 3

White, Walter
See White, Walter F(rancis)
See also BLC 3

White, Walter F(rancis)
1893-1955 .... TCLC 15
See also White, Walter
See also CA 115; 124; DLB 51

White, William Hale 1831-1913
See Rutherford, Mark
See also CA 121

Whitehead, E(dward) A(nthony)
1933- .... CLC 5
See also CA 65-68

Whitemore, Hugh (John) 1936- ..... CLC 37
See also CA 132

Whitman, Sarah Helen (Power)
1803-1878 .... NCLC 19
See also DLB 1

Whitman, Walt(er)
1819-1892 .... NCLC 4, 31; PC 3
See also CDALB 1640-1865; DLB 3, 64;
SATA 20; WLC

Whitney, Phyllis A(yame) 1903- .... CLC 42
See also AITN 2; BEST 90:3; CA 1-4R;
CANR 3, 25, 38; MAICYA; SATA 1, 30

Whittemore, (Edward) Reed (Jr.)
1919- .... CLC 4
See also CA 9-12R; CAAS 8; CANR 4;
DLB 5

Whittier, John Greenleaf
1807-1892 .... NCLC 8
See also CDALB 1640-1865; DLB 1

Whittlebot, Hernia
See Coward, Noel (Peirce)

Wicker, Thomas Grey 1926-
See Wicker, Tom
See also CA 65-68; CANR 21

Wicker, Tom .... CLC 7
See also Wicker, Thomas Grey

Wideman, John Edgar
1941- .... CLC 5, 34, 36, 67
See also BLC 3; BW; CA 85-88; CANR 14;
DLB 33

Wiebe, Rudy (H.) 1934- ...... CLC 6, 11, 14
See also CA 37-40R; DLB 60

Wieland, Christoph Martin
1733-1813 .... NCLC 17
See also DLB 97

Wieners, John 1934- .... CLC 7
See also CA 13-16R; DLB 16

Wiesel, Elie(zer) 1928- ..... CLC 3, 5, 11, 37
See also AAYA 7; AITN 1; CA 5-8R;
CAAS 4; CANR 8, 40; DLB 83;
DLBY 87; MTCW; SATA 56

Wiggins, Marianne 1947- .... CLC 57
See also BEST 89:3; CA 130

Wight, James Alfred 1916-
See Herriot, James
See also CA 77-80; SATA 44, 55

Wilbur, Richard (Purdy)
1921- .... CLC 3, 6, 9, 14, 53
See also CA 1-4R; CABS 2; CANR 2, 29;
DLB 5; MTCW; SATA 9

Wild, Peter 1940- .... CLC 14
See also CA 37-40R; DLB 5

Wilde, Oscar (Fingal O'Flahertie Wills)
1854(?)-1900 .... TCLC 1, 8, 23, 41;
SSC 11
See also CA 104; 119; CDBLB 1890-1914;
DLB 10, 19, 34, 57; SATA 24; WLC

Wilder, Billy .... CLC 20
See also Wilder, Samuel
See also DLB 26

Wilder, Samuel 1906-
See Wilder, Billy
See also CA 89-92

Wilder, Thornton (Niven)
1897-1975 ..... CLC 1, 5, 6, 10, 15, 35;
DC 1
See also AITN 2; CA 13-16R; 61-64;
CANR 40; DLB 4, 7, 9; MTCW; WLC

Wilding, Michael 1942- .... CLC 73
See also CA 104; CANR 24

Wiley, Richard 1944- .... CLC 44
See also CA 121; 129

Wilhelm, Kate .... CLC 7
See also Wilhelm, Katie Gertrude
See also CAAS 5; DLB 8

Wilhelm, Katie Gertrude 1928-
See Wilhelm, Kate
See also CA 37-40R; CANR 17, 36; MTCW

Wilkins, Mary
See Freeman, Mary Eleanor Wilkins

Willard, Nancy 1936- .... CLC 7, 37
See also CA 89-92; CANR 10, 39; CLR 5;
DLB 5, 52; MAICYA; MTCW;
SATA 30, 37, 71

Williams, C(harles) K(enneth)
1936- .... CLC 33, 56
See also CA 37-40R; DLB 5

Williams, Charles
See Collier, James L(incoln)

Williams, Charles (Walter Stansby)
1886-1945 .... TCLC 1, 11
See also CA 104; DLB 100

Williams, (George) Emlyn
1905-1987 .... CLC 15
See also CA 104; 123; CANR 36; DLB 10,
77; MTCW

Williams, Hugo 1942- .... CLC 42
See also CA 17-20R; DLB 40

Williams, J. Walker
See Wodehouse, P(elham) G(renville)

Williams, John A(lfred) 1925- .... CLC 5, 13
See also BLC 3; BW; CA 53-56; CAAS 3;
CANR 6, 26; DLB 2, 33

Williams, Jonathan (Chamberlain)
1929- .... CLC 13
See also CA 9-12R; CAAS 12; CANR 8;
DLB 5

Williams, Joy 1944- .... CLC 31
See also CA 41-44R; CANR 22

Williams, Norman 1952- .... CLC 39
See also CA 118

Williams, Tennessee
1911-1983 .... CLC 1, 2, 5, 7, 8, 11, 15,
19, 30, 39, 45, 71
See also AITN 1, 2; CA 5-8R; 108;
CABS 3; CANR 31; CDALB 1941-1968;
DLB 7; DLBD 4; DLBY 83; MTCW;
WLC

Williams, Thomas (Alonzo)
1926-1990 .... CLC 14
See also CA 1-4R; 132; CANR 2

Williams, William C.
See Williams, William Carlos

Williams, William Carlos
1883-1963 ... CLC 1, 2, 5, 9, 13, 22, 42,
67
See also CA 89-92; CANR 34;
CDALB 1917-1929; DLB 4, 16, 54, 86;
MTCW

Williamson, David Keith 1942- ..... CLC 56
See also CA 103

Williamson, Jack .... CLC 29
See also Williamson, John Stewart
See also CAAS 8; DLB 8

Williamson, John Stewart 1908-
See Williamson, Jack
See also CA 17-20R; CANR 23

Willie, Frederick
See Lovecraft, H(oward) P(hillips)

Willingham, Calder (Baynard Jr.)
1922- . . . . CLC 5, 51
See also CA 5-8R; CANR 3; DLB 2, 44;
MTCW

Willis, Charles
See Clarke, Arthur C(harles)

Willy
See Colette, (Sidonie-Gabrielle)

Willy, Colette
See Colette, (Sidonie-Gabrielle)

Wilson, A(ndrew) N(orman) 1950- . . CLC 33
See also CA 112; 122; DLB 14

Wilson, Angus (Frank Johnstone)
1913-1991 . . . . CLC 2, 3, 5, 25, 34
See also CA 5-8R; 134; CANR 21; DLB 15;
MTCW

Wilson, August
1945- . . . . CLC 39, 50, 63; DC 2
See also BLC 3; BW; CA 115; 122; MTCW

Wilson, Brian 1942- . . . . CLC 12

Wilson, Colin 1931- . . . . CLC 3, 14
See also CA 1-4R; CAAS 5; CANR 1, 22,
33; DLB 14; MTCW

Wilson, Dirk
See Pohl, Frederik

Wilson, Edmund
1895-1972 . . . . CLC 1, 2, 3, 8, 24
See also CA 1-4R; 37-40R; CANR 1;
DLB 63; MTCW

Wilson, Ethel Davis (Bryant)
1888(?)-1980 . . . . CLC 13
See also CA 102; DLB 68; MTCW

Wilson, John (Anthony) Burgess
1917- . . . . CLC 8, 10, 13
See also Burgess, Anthony
See also CA 1-4R; CANR 2; MTCW

Wilson, John 1785-1854 . . . . NCLC 5

Wilson, Lanford 1937- . . . . CLC 7, 14, 36
See also CA 17-20R; CABS 3; DLB 7

Wilson, Robert M. 1944- . . . . CLC 7, 9
See also CA 49-52; CANR 2; MTCW

Wilson, Robert McLiam 1964- . . . . . CLC 59
See also CA 132

Wilson, Sloan 1920- . . . . CLC 32
See also CA 1-4R; CANR 1

Wilson, Snoo 1948- . . . . CLC 33
See also CA 69-72

Wilson, William S(mith) 1932- . . . . . CLC 49
See also CA 81-84

Winchilsea, Anne (Kingsmill) Finch Counte
1661-1720 . . . . LC 3

Windham, Basil
See Wodehouse, P(elham) G(renville)

Wingrove, David (John) 1954- . . . . . . CLC 68
See also CA 133

Winters, Janet Lewis . . . . CLC 41
See also Lewis, Janet
See also DLBY 87

Winters, (Arthur) Yvor
1900-1968 . . . . CLC 4, 8, 32
See also CA 11-12; 25-28R; CAP 1;
DLB 48; MTCW

Winterson, Jeanette 1959- . . . . CLC 64
See also CA 136

Wiseman, Frederick 1930- . . . . CLC 20

Wister, Owen 1860-1938 . . . . TCLC 21
See also CA 108; DLB 9, 78; SATA 62

Witkacy
See Witkiewicz, Stanislaw Ignacy

Witkiewicz, Stanislaw Ignacy
1885-1939 . . . . TCLC 8
See also CA 105

Wittig, Monique 1935(?)- . . . . CLC 22
See also CA 116; 135; DLB 83

Wittlin, Jozef 1896-1976 . . . . CLC 25
See also CA 49-52; 65-68; CANR 3

Wodehouse, P(elham) G(renville)
1881-1975 . . . CLC 1, 2, 5, 10, 22; SSC 2
See also AITN 2; CA 45-48; 57-60;
CANR 3, 33; CDBLB 1914-1945;
DLB 34; MTCW; SATA 22

Woiwode, L.
See Woiwode, Larry (Alfred)

Woiwode, Larry (Alfred) 1941- . . . CLC 6, 10
See also CA 73-76; CANR 16; DLB 6

Wojciechowska, Maia (Teresa)
1927- . . . . CLC 26
See also AAYA 8; CA 9-12R; CANR 4;
CLR 1; MAICYA; SAAS 1; SATA 1, 28

Wolf, Christa 1929- . . . . CLC 14, 29, 58
See also CA 85-88; DLB 75; MTCW

Wolfe, Gene (Rodman) 1931- . . . . . . CLC 25
See also CA 57-60; CAAS 9; CANR 6, 32;
DLB 8

Wolfe, George C. 1954- . . . . CLC 49

Wolfe, Thomas (Clayton)
1900-1938 . . . . TCLC 4, 13, 29
See also CA 104; 132; CDALB 1929-1941;
DLB 9, 102; DLBD 2; DLBY 85;
MTCW; WLC

Wolfe, Thomas Kennerly Jr. 1930-
See Wolfe, Tom
See also CA 13-16R; CANR 9, 33; MTCW

Wolfe, Tom . . . . CLC 1, 2, 9, 15, 35, 51
See also Wolfe, Thomas Kennerly Jr.
See also AAYA 8; AITN 2; BEST 89:1

Wolff, Geoffrey (Ansell) 1937- . . . . . CLC 41
See also CA 29-32R; CANR 29

Wolff, Sonia
See Levitin, Sonia (Wolff)

Wolff, Tobias (Jonathan Ansell)
1945- . . . . CLC 39, 64
See also BEST 90:2; CA 114; 117

Wolfram von Eschenbach
c. 1170-c. 1220 . . . . CMLC 5

Wolitzer, Hilma 1930- . . . . CLC 17
See also CA 65-68; CANR 18, 40; SATA 31

Wollstonecraft, Mary 1759-1797 . . . . . LC 5
See also CDBLB 1789-1832; DLB 39, 104

Wonder, Stevie . . . . CLC 12
See also Morris, Steveland Judkins

Wong, Jade Snow 1922- . . . . CLC 17
See also CA 109

Woodcott, Keith
See Brunner, John (Kilian Houston)

Woodruff, Robert W.
See Mencken, H(enry) L(ouis)

Woolf, (Adeline) Virginia
1882-1941 . . . . TCLC 1, 5, 20, 43; SSC 7
See also CA 104; 130; CDBLB 1914-1945;
DLB 36, 100; DLBD 10; MTCW; WLC

Woollcott, Alexander (Humphreys)
1887-1943 . . . . TCLC 5
See also CA 105; DLB 29

Wordsworth, Dorothy
1771-1855 . . . . NCLC 25
See also DLB 107

Wordsworth, William
1770-1850 . . . . NCLC 12, 38; PC 4
See also CDBLB 1789-1832; DLB 93, 107;
WLC

Wouk, Herman 1915- . . . . CLC 1, 9, 38
See also CA 5-8R; CANR 6, 33; DLBY 82;
MTCW

Wright, Charles (Penzel Jr.)
1935- . . . . CLC 6, 13, 28
See also CA 29-32R; CAAS 7; CANR 23,
36; DLBY 82; MTCW

Wright, Charles Stevenson 1932- . . . CLC 49
See also BLC 3; BW; CA 9-12R; CANR 26;
DLB 33

Wright, Jack R.
See Harris, Mark

Wright, James (Arlington)
1927-1980 . . . . CLC 3, 5, 10, 28
See also AITN 2; CA 49-52; 97-100;
CANR 4, 34; DLB 5; MTCW

Wright, Judith (Arandell)
1915- . . . . CLC 11, 53
See also CA 13-16R; CANR 31; MTCW;
SATA 14

Wright, L(aurali) R. . . . . CLC 44
See also CA 138

Wright, Richard B(ruce) 1937- . . . . . . CLC 6
See also CA 85-88; DLB 53

Wright, Richard (Nathaniel)
1908-1960 . . . CLC 1, 3, 4, 9, 14, 21, 48,
74; SSC 2
See also AAYA 5; BLC 3; BW; CA 108;
CDALB 1929-1941; DLB 76, 102;
DLBD 2; MTCW; WLC

Wright, Rick 1945- . . . . CLC 35
See also Pink Floyd

Wright, Rowland
See Wells, Carolyn

Wright, Stephen 1946- . . . . CLC 33

Wright, Willard Huntington 1888-1939
See Van Dine, S. S.
See also CA 115

Wright, William 1930- . . . . CLC 44
See also CA 53-56; CANR 7, 23

Wu Ch'eng-en 1500(?)-1582(?) . . . . . . LC 7

Wu Ching-tzu 1701-1754 . . . . LC 2

Wurlitzer, Rudolph 1938(?)- . . . CLC 2, 4, 15
See also CA 85-88

Wycherley, William 1641-1715 .... **LC 8, 21**
See also CDBLB 1660-1789; DLB 80

Wylie, Elinor (Morton Hoyt)
1885-1928 .... **TCLC 8**
See also CA 105; DLB 9, 45

Wylie, Philip (Gordon) 1902-1971... **CLC 43**
See also CA 21-22; 33-36R; CAP 2; DLB 9

Wyndham, John
See Harris, John (Wyndham Parkes Lucas) Beynon

Wyss, Johann David Von
1743-1818 .... **NCLC 10**
See also MAICYA; SATA 27, 29

Yakumo Koizumi
See Hearn, (Patricio) Lafcadio (Tessima Carlos)

Yanez, Jose Donoso
See Donoso (Yanez), Jose

Yanovsky, Basile S.
See Yanovsky, V(assily) S(emenovich)

Yanovsky, V(assily) S(emenovich)
1906-1989 .... **CLC 2, 18**
See also CA 97-100; 129

Yates, Richard 1926-1992 ..... **CLC 7, 8, 23**
See also CA 5-8R; 139; CANR 10; DLB 2; DLBY 81

Yeats, W. B.
See Yeats, William Butler

Yeats, William Butler
1865-1939 .... **TCLC 1, 11, 18, 31**
See also CA 104; 127; CDBLB 1890-1914; DLB 10, 19, 98; MTCW; WLC

Yehoshua, Abraham B. 1936- ... **CLC 13, 31**
See also CA 33-36R

Yep, Laurence Michael 1948- ...... **CLC 35**
See also AAYA 5; CA 49-52; CANR 1; CLR 3, 17; DLB 52; MAICYA; SATA 7, 69

Yerby, Frank G(arvin)
1916-1991 .... **CLC 1, 7, 22**
See also BLC 3; BW; CA 9-12R; 136; CANR 16; DLB 76; MTCW

Yesenin, Sergei Alexandrovich
See Esenin, Sergei (Alexandrovich)

Yevtushenko, Yevgeny (Alexandrovich)
1933- .... **CLC 1, 3, 13, 26, 51**
See also CA 81-84; CANR 33; MTCW

Yezierska, Anzia 1885(?)-1970 ..... **CLC 46**
See also CA 126; 89-92; DLB 28; MTCW

Yglesias, Helen 1915- .... **CLC 7, 22**
See also CA 37-40R; CANR 15; MTCW

Yokomitsu Riichi 1898-1947 ...... **TCLC 47**

Yonge, Charlotte (Mary)
1823-1901 .... **TCLC 48**
See also CA 109; DLB 18; SATA 17

York, Jeremy
See Creasey, John

York, Simon
See Heinlein, Robert A(nson)

Yorke, Henry Vincent 1905-1974 ... **CLC 13**
See also Green, Henry
See also CA 85-88; 49-52

Young, Al(bert James) 1939- .... **CLC 19**
See also BLC 3; BW; CA 29-32R; CANR 26; DLB 33

Young, Andrew (John) 1885-1971.... **CLC 5**
See also CA 5-8R; CANR 7, 29

Young, Collier
See Bloch, Robert (Albert)

Young, Edward 1683-1765........... **LC 3**
See also DLB 95

Young, Neil 1945- .... **CLC 17**
See also CA 110

Yourcenar, Marguerite
1903-1987 .... **CLC 19, 38, 50**
See also CA 69-72; CANR 23; DLB 72; DLBY 88; MTCW

Yurick, Sol 1925- .... **CLC 6**
See also CA 13-16R; CANR 25

Zamiatin, Yevgenii
See Zamyatin, Evgeny Ivanovich

Zamyatin, Evgeny Ivanovich
1884-1937 .... **TCLC 8, 37**
See also CA 105

Zangwill, Israel 1864-1926....... **TCLC 16**
See also CA 109; DLB 10

Zappa, Francis Vincent Jr. 1940-
See Zappa, Frank
See also CA 108

Zappa, Frank..................... **CLC 17**
See also Zappa, Francis Vincent Jr.

Zaturenska, Marya 1902-1982.... **CLC 6, 11**
See also CA 13-16R; 105; CANR 22

Zelazny, Roger (Joseph) 1937- ..... **CLC 21**
See also AAYA 7; CA 21-24R; CANR 26; DLB 8; MTCW; SATA 39, 57

Zhdanov, Andrei A(lexandrovich)
1896-1948 .... **TCLC 18**
See also CA 117

Zhukovsky, Vasily 1783-1852 .... **NCLC 35**

Ziegenhagen, Eric .... **CLC 55**

Zimmer, Jill Schary
See Robinson, Jill

Zimmerman, Robert
See Dylan, Bob

Zindel, Paul 1936- .... **CLC 6, 26**
See also AAYA 2; CA 73-76; CANR 31; CLR 3; DLB 7, 52; MAICYA; MTCW; SATA 16, 58

Zinov'Ev, A. A.
See Zinoviev, Alexander (Aleksandrovich)

Zinoviev, Alexander (Aleksandrovich)
1922- .... **CLC 19**
See also CA 116; 133; CAAS 10

Zoilus
See Lovecraft, H(oward) P(hillips)

Zola, Emile (Edouard Charles Antoine)
1840-1902 .... **TCLC 1, 6, 21, 41**
See also CA 104; 138; DLB 123; WLC

Zoline, Pamela 1941- .... **CLC 62**

Zorrilla y Moral, Jose 1817-1893.. **NCLC 6**

Zoshchenko, Mikhail (Mikhailovich)
1895-1958 .... **TCLC 15**
See also CA 115

Zuckmayer, Carl 1896-1977....... **CLC 18**
See also CA 69-72; DLB 56, 124

Zuk, Georges
See Skelton, Robin

Zukofsky, Louis
1904-1978 .... **CLC 1, 2, 4, 7, 11, 18**
See also CA 9-12R; 77-80; CANR 39; DLB 5; MTCW

Zweig, Paul 1935-1984........ **CLC 34, 42**
See also CA 85-88; 113

Zweig, Stefan 1881-1942 .... **TCLC 17**
See also CA 112; DLB 81, 118

Literary Criticism Series
Cumulative Topic Index

This index lists all topic entries in the Gale Literary Criticism Series *Contemporary Literary Criticism, Literature Criticism from 1400 to 1800, Nineteenth-Century Literature Criticism,* and *Twentieth-Century Literary Criticism.*

Havel, Václav, Playwright and President CLC 65: 406-63

Holocaust, Literature of the TCLC 42: 355-450
historical overview, 357-61
critical overview, 361-70
diaries and memoirs, 370-95
novels and short stories, 395-425
poetry, 425-41
drama, 441-48

Hungarian Literature of the Twentieth Century TCLC 26: 126-88
surveys of, 126-47
Nyugat and early twentieth-century literature, 147-56
mid-century literature, 156-68
and politics, 168-78
since the 1956 revolt, 178-87

Italian Futurism
See **Futurism, Italian**

Italian Humanism LC 12: 205-77
origins and early development, 206-18
revival of classical letters, 218-23
humanism and other philosophies, 224-39
humanisms and humanists, 239-46
the plastic arts, 246-57
achievement and significance, 258-76

Irish Literary Renaissance TCLC 46: 172-287
overview, 173-83
development and major figures, 184-202
influence of Irish folklore and mythology, 202-22
Irish poetry, 222-34
Irish drama and the Abbey Theatre, 234-56
Irish fiction, 256-86

Muckraking Movement in American Journalism TCLC 34: 161-242
development, principles, and major figures, 162-70
publications, 170-79
social and political ideas, 179-86
targets, 186-208
fiction, 208-19
decline, 219-29
impact and accomplishments, 229-40

Multiculturalism in Literature and Education CLC 70: 361-413

Natural School, Russian NCLC 24: 205-40
history and characteristics, 205-25
contemporary criticism, 225-40

Naturalism NCLC 36: 285-382
definitions and theories, 286-305
critical debates on Naturalism, 305-16
Naturalism in theater, 316-32
European Naturalism, 332-61
American Naturalism, 361-72
the legacy of Naturalism, 372-81

New Criticism TCLC 34: 243-318
development and ideas, 244-70
debate and defense, 270-99
influence and legacy, 299-315

Newgate Novel NCLC 24: 166-204
development of Newgate literature, 166-73
Newgate Calendar, 173-77
Newgate fiction, 177-95
Newgate drama, 195-204

New York Intellectuals and *Partisan Review* TCLC 30: 117-98
development and major figures, 118-28
influence of Judaism, 128-39
Partisan Review, 139-57
literary philosophy and practice, 157-75
political philosophy, 175-87
achievement and significance, 187-97

Nigerian Literature of the Twentieth Century TCLC 30: 199-265
surveys of, 199-227
English language and African life, 227-45
politics and the Nigerian writer, 245-54
Nigerian writers and society, 255-62

Northern Humanism LC 16: 281-356
background, 282-305
precursor of the Reformation, 305-14
the Brethren of the Common Life, the Devotio Moderna, and education, 314-40
the impact of printing, 340-56

Nuclear Literature: Writings and Criticism in the Nuclear Age TCLC 46: 288-390
overviews, 290-301
fiction, 301-35
poetry, 335-38

nuclear war in Russo-Japanese literature, 338-55
nuclear war and women writers, 355-67
the nuclear referent and literary criticism, 367-88

Opium and the Nineteenth-Century Literary Imagination NCLC 20: 250-301
original sources, 250-62
historical background, 262-71
and literary society, 271-79
and literary creativity, 279-300

Periodicals, Nineteenth-Century British NCLC 24: 100-65
overviews, 100-30
in the Romantic Age, 130-41
in the Victorian era, 142-54
and the reviewer, 154-64

Pre-Raphaelite Movement NCLC 20: 302-401
overview, 302-04
genesis, 304-12
Germ and *Oxford and Cambridge Magazine,* 312-20
Robert Buchanan and the "Fleshly School of Poetry," 320-31
satires and parodies, 331-34
surveys, 334-51
aesthetics, 351-75
sister arts of poetry and painting, 375-94
influence, 394-99

Psychoanalysis and Literature TCLC 38: 227-338
overviews, 227-46
Freud on literature, 246-51
psychoanalytic views of the literary process, 251-61
psychoanalytic theories of response to literature, 261-88
psychoanalysis and literary criticism, 288-312
psychoanalysis as literature/literature as psychoanalysis, 313-34

Robin Hood, Legend of LC 19: 205-58
origins and development of the Robin Hood legend, 206-20
representations of Robin Hood, 220-44
Robin Hood as hero, 244-56

Rushdie, Salman, *Satanic Verses* Controversy CLC 55: 214-63; 59: 404-56

TCLC Cumulative Nationality Index

Santayana, George 40
Sherwood, Robert E. 3
Slesinger, Tess 10
Steffens, Lincoln 20
Stein, Gertrude 1, 6, 28, 48
Sterling, George 20
Stevens, Wallace 3, 12, 45
Stockton, Frank R. 47
Sturges, Preston 48
Tarbell, Ida 40
Tarkington, Booth 9
Teasdale, Sara 4
Thurman, Wallace 6
Twain, Mark 6, 12, 19, 36, 48
Van Dine, S. S. 23
Van Doren, Carl 18
Veblen, Thorstein 31
Washington, Booker T. 10
Wells, Carolyn 35
West, Nathanael 1, 14, 44
Wharton, Edith 3, 9, 27
White, Walter 15
Wister, Owen 21
Wolfe, Thomas 4, 13, 29
Woollcott, Alexander 5
Wylie, Elinor 8

ARGENTINE
Arlt, Roberto 29
Güiraldes, Ricardo 39
Lugones, Leopoldo 15
Storni, Alfonsina 5

AUSTRALIAN
Brennan, Christopher John 17
Franklin, Miles 7
Furphy, Joseph 25
Ingamells, Rex 35
Lawson, Henry 27
Paterson, A. B. 32
Richardson, Henry Handel 4
Warung, Price 45

AUSTRIAN
Broch, Hermann 20
Hofmannsthal, Hugo von 11
Kafka, Franz 2, 6, 13, 29, 47
Kraus, Karl 5
Kubin, Alfred 23
Meyrink, Gustav 21
Musil, Robert 12
Roth, Joseph 33
Schnitzler, Arthur 4
Steiner, Rudolf 13
Trakl, Georg 5
Werfel, Franz 8
Zweig, Stefan 17

BELGIAN
Bosschère, Jean de 19
Lemonnier, Camille 22
Maeterlinck, Maurice 3
Van Ostaijen, Paul 33
Verhaeren, Émile 12

BRAZILIAN
Andrade, Mário de 43
Cunha, Euclides da 24
Lima Barreto 23
Machado de Assis, Joaquim Maria 10
Ramos, Graciliano 32

BULGARIAN
Vazov, Ivan 25

CANADIAN
Campbell, Wilfred 9
Carman, Bliss 7
Carr, Emily 32
Connor, Ralph 31
Drummond, William Henry 25
Garneau, Hector Saint-Denys 13
Grove, Frederick Philip 4
Leacock, Stephen 2
McCrae, John 12
Nelligan, Emile 14
Pickthall, Marjorie 21
Roberts, Charles G. D. 8
Scott, Duncan Campbell 6
Service, Robert W. 15
Seton, Ernest Thompson 31
Stringer, Arthur 37

CHILEAN
Huidobro, Vicente 31
Mistral, Gabriela 2

CHINESE
Liu E 15
Lu Hsün 3
Su Man-shu 24
Wen I-to 28

COLOMBIAN
Rivera, Jose Eustasio 35

CZECHOSLOVAKIAN
Čapek, Karel 6, 37
Czechoslovakian Literature of the Twentieth
  Century 42
Hašek, Jaroslav 4
Nezval, Vítězslav 44

DANISH
Brandes, Georg 10
Hansen, Martin A. 32
Jensen, Johannes V. 41
Nexo, Martin Andersen 43
Pontopiddan, Henrik 29

DUTCH
Couperus, Louis 15
Frank, Anne 17
Heijermans, Herman 24
Hillesum, Etty 49

ENGLISH
Barbellion, W. N. P. 24
Baring, Maurice 8
Beerbohm, Max 1, 24
Belloc, Hilaire 7, 18
Bennett, Arnold 5, 20
Benson, E. F. 27
Benson, Stella 17
Bentley, E. C. 12
Besant, Annie 9
Blackmore, R. D. 27
Blackwood, Algernon 5
Bridges, Robert 1
Brooke, Rupert 2, 7
Butler, Samuel 1, 33
Chesterton, G. K. 1, 6
Conrad, Joseph 1, 6, 13, 25, 43
Coppard, A. E. 5

Crowley, Aleister 7
De la Mare, Walter 4
Doughty, Charles 27
Douglas, Keith 40
Dowson, Ernest 4
Doyle, Arthur Conan 7, 26
Eddison, E. R. 15
Elizabeth 41
Ellis, Havelock 14
Field, Michael 43
Firbank, Ronald 1
Ford, Ford Madox 1, 15, 39
Freeman, R. Austin 21
Galsworthy, John 1, 45
Gilbert, W. S. 3
Gissing, George 3, 24, 47
Gosse, Edmund 28
Granville-Barker, Harley 2
Gray, John 19
Gurney, Ivor 33
Haggard, H. Rider 11
Hall, Radclyffe 12
Hardy, Thomas 4, 10, 18, 32, 48
Henley, William Ernest 8
Hilton, James 21
Hodgson, William Hope 13
Housman, A. E. 1, 10
Housman, Laurence 7
Hudson, W. H. 29
Hulme, T. E. 21
Jacobs, W. W. 22
James, M. R. 6
Jerome, Jerome K. 23
Johnson, Lionel 19
Kaye-Smith, Sheila 20
Kipling, Rudyard 8, 17
Lawrence, D. H. 2, 9, 16, 33, 48
Lawrence, T. E. 18
Lee, Vernon 5
Lee-Hamilton, Eugene 22
Leverson, Ada 18
Lewis, Wyndham 2, 9
Lindsay, David 15
Lowndes, Marie Belloc 12
Lowry, Malcolm 6, 40
Macaulay, Rose 7, 44
MacCarthy, Desmond 36
Manning, Frederic 25
Meredith, George 17, 43
Mew, Charlotte 8
Meynell, Alice 6
Milne, A. A. 6
Murry, John Middleton 16
Noyes, Alfred 7
Oppenheim, E. Phillips 45
Orwell, George 2, 6, 15, 31
Ouida 43
Owen, Wilfred 5, 27
Pinero, Arthur Wing 32
Powys, T. F. 9
Richardson, Dorothy 3
Rohmer, Sax 28
Rolfe, Frederick 12
Rosenberg, Isaac 12
Ruskin, John 20
Rutherford, Mark 25
Sabatini, Rafael 47
Saintsbury, George 31
Saki 3
Sapper 44
Sayers, Dorothy L. 2, 15
Shiel, M. P. 8

Nationality Index

TCLC-49 Title Index

Title Index

ISBN 0-8103-7974-0